MOBILE COMPUTING PRINCIPLES

Written to address technical concerns that mobile developers face regardless of the platform (J2ME, WAP, Windows CE, etc.), this book explores the differences between mobile and stationary applications and the architectural and software development concepts needed to build a mobile application. Using UML as a tool, Reza B'Far guides the developer through the development process, showing how to document the design and implementation of the application. He focuses on general concepts while using platforms as examples or as possible tools.

After introducing UML, XML, and the derivative tools necessary for developing mobile software applications, B'Far shows how to build user interfaces for mobile applications. He covers location sensitivity, wireless connectivity, mobile agents, data synchronization, security, and push-based technologies and finally discusses the practical issues of mobile application development including the development cycle for mobile applications, testing mobile applications, and architectural concerns. These are illustrated with a case study.

Reza B'Far (Behravanfar) is an executive consultant currently serving as the CTO of Voice Genesis and Acting CTO of Semantic Messaging Systems Inc. His company, Cienecs Inc., has had a variety of engagements in the mobile arena with startups as well as Fortune 500 companies. Early in his career, he worked for Weyerhaueser Company, Parr & Associates Inc., and the National Oceanic Research Department of NASA. He has spent the past ten years working for Noor Electrical Engineering, Virtual Mortgage Network, AdForce Inc., eBuilt Inc., and Data Trace Corporation. He is currently an independent contractor working with a variety of companies as an architect and/or CTO, including some in the mobile arena.

-6 OCT 2005
28 APR 2006
7-DAY
LOAN
TEL. 0151 231 4022
LIBREX

WITHDRAWN

Mobile Computing Principles

Designing and Developing Mobile Applications with UML and XML

Reza B'Far
Cienecs Inc.

Foreword by Roy T. Fielding

PUBLISHED BY THE PRESS SYNDICATE OF THE UNIVERSITY OF CAMBRIDGE
The Pitt Building, Trumpington Street, Cambridge, United Kingdom

CAMBRIDGE UNIVERSITY PRESS
The Edinburgh Building, Cambridge CB2 2RU, UK
40 West 20th Street, New York, NY 10011-4211, USA
477 Williamstown Road, Port Melbourne, VIC 3207, Australia
Ruiz de Alarcón 13, 28014 Madrid, Spain
Dock House, The Waterfront, Cape Town 8001, South Africa

http://www.cambridge.org

First published 2005

Printed in the United States of America

Typefaces ITC Berkeley Oldstyle 10.75/13 pt. and ITC Franklin Gothic *System* LaTeX 2ε [TB]

A catalog record for this book is available from the British Library.

Library of Congress Cataloging in Publication Data

B'Far, Reza.

Mobile computing principles : designing and developing mobile applications with UML and XML / Reza B'Far ; foreword by Roy T. Fielding.

p. cm.

Includes bibliographical references and index.

ISBN 0-521-81733-1

1. Mobile computing. 2. UML (Computer science) 3. XML (Document markup language) I. Title.

QA76.59.B43 2004
005.268 – dc22 2004045705

ISBN 0 521 81733 1 hardback

Contents

Chapter 7
VUIs and Mobile Applications 399

Chapter 8
Multichannel and Multimodal User Interfaces 497

SECTION 3
ADDITIONAL DIMENSIONS OF MOBILE APPLICATION DEVELOPMENT

Chapter 9
Mobile Agents and Peer-to-Peer Architectures for Mobile Applications 557

Chapter 14
Mobile Security 735

SECTION 4
PUTTING THE PROJECT TOGETHER

Chapter 15
The Mobile Development Process 755

Chapter 16
Architecture, Design, and Technology Selection for Mobile Applications 773

Chapter 17
Mobile Application Development Hurdles 788

Foreword

Back and forth, back and forth . . .

Four years ago, Reza and I were working together at eBuilt when he first stopped by my office to talk about frameworks for wireless application development. We were in the final months of the so-called "dot-com era," when dreams of a new economy allowed just about anyone to get funding for a network-based application, particularly when it also involved some form of mobile computing device. Those people with ideas (and sometimes funding) would come to our company and ask us to implement their vision. Of course, they would also ask for a few miracles, such as a working prototype within a month and deployment across all devices in six months. Oddly enough, we could actually accomplish implementations like that, if it were not for one problem out of our control: mobile devices had a market lifetime of only about four months.

It was the year 2000, just a couple months after Y2K became a non-issue, and there was so much variance in the types of mobile devices, both in terms of their feature sets and in their application development environments, that an application developed for one device environment would be obsolete by the time it was ready to market. Reza had a solution in mind, which is why he was busy pacing in my office. Back and forth, back and forth, all the while explaining to me why eBuilt needed a device-independent application development environment and how we might sell such an environment to other software organizations.

This was prior to the eventual unification of platforms around base operating systems, such as PalmOS, Symbian, and J2ME, and about the same time that device manufacturers realized the impact of design turnover on device sales: innovation had become so frenzied that most of the application developers simply could not keep up. Unfortunately, eBuilt did not have the resources and necessary alliances with device manufacturers to pursue Reza's vision, aside from one project at a time, but he never gave up on the general idea. That is demonstrated by the enormous amount of information and effort he has put into this book.

The funny thing about "mobile computing" is that mobility is the easy part. What is actually of interest to the consumer, and hence to those who need to sell to the consumer, is computing despite mobility. There is a small segment of the population who will buy a new device purely for the sake of its coolness, but mass appeal does not come until there exists an application that is sufficiently compelling to justify purchasing (and carrying around) a new device.

Like most people whose work involves a lot of travel, I think most about mobile computing when I suffer from the lack of it. While I am writing this, my wife and I are on our first real vacation together: a late honeymoon trip to Italy. Our first day of travel involved 27 hours of planes, trains, and automobiles, in which the limitations of current mobile computing have been readily apparent. We are so close to a world in which all of the information needed is available, when and where we need it, and yet I knowingly embarked on this trip without my cellphone (CDMA doesn't work in Europe), laptop (too heavy, expensive, and tempting of work), or even a PDA. In fact, the only technology we have with us are two wristwatches and a new digital camera.

I used the Web to purchase all of our tickets and accommodations in advance, something that was unthinkable just ten years ago. However, even a well-planned trip is susceptible to change. What is traffic like to the airport? Should we go up the coast or take the freeway? Is our flight on time? What terminal? Do we have time to park in the remote lot? Those are just the basic questions that fill my mind while readying the car. The more complex question is this: can we get better seats on the flight? I wouldn't even have considered such a question a few years ago, but today it is possible to store my itinerary on the airline's Web site, access it from any Web browser, and make use of a visual diagram for discovering what seats are available on each leg of the flight. That is great design, even though it assumes a broadband connection to the Internet and a full-color 1024 × 768 display.

I know there are mobile devices on the market that can answer my questions (i.e., perform my application), if only they had the software to do so. I can buy a five-ounce PDA with built-in 802.11b and bluetooth wireless connectivity, a bluetooth GPS device to provide geographical positioning, card-slot memory for gigabytes of data, and a color TFT display that is just as clear as a laptop LCD screen (if not more so). In addition to the airline's Web site, there are real-time traffic maps available on the Internet for the freeways in Southern California.

All I really need is an application that monitors my itinerary, collects data from the appropriate sources whenever it can do so, and notifies me when conditions change (or at least makes the information continuously available so that I can read it at the push of a button).

Unfortunately, the mobility of software is considerably behind that of hardware devices. An 802.11b interface can automatically detect and switch from one hotspot to another, but the device software will invariably ask the user if they wish to do so each time—it seems that folks haven't considered the option of pre-approving a set of wireless carriers for automatic switch-over. Likewise, applications that expect a network interface to exist tend to drop like flies in the presence of intermittent connectivity, and geographic applications don't understand the concept of a device that is only occasionally within range of a GPS. I can't really blame this state of affairs on the device manufacturers—after all, they are building devices that are intended to be generic and thus usable for many different applications.

My travel assistant application isn't a particularly novel vision of mobile computing. Whether it be called ubiquitous computing or mobility-aware applications, the desire for continuous information support has been imagined, if not expressed, by countless technologists as they rush to meet their next travel connection for some far-away conference at which techno-visionaries are sure to speak about their latest advances in shrinking hardware into lighter but less useful forms. The hardware, networking, and network-accessible information is already available to support a mobile travel assistant, and yet I felt no compelling need to buy a new device this past year. That is, other than our new digital camera.

Digital Camera?

I already had one digital camera, but my wife wanted something a little smaller. Something inconspicuous, fitting within her purse. In other words, something a little more mobile. What we bought has a four-megapixel CCD, internal clock, high-density TFT display, AV-output port (supporting both NTSC and PAL formats), USB interface, and a CPU with sufficient computing power to obtain, compress, and store a four-MB image in less than a second (or a small-format movie at 24 frames per second). It weighs five ounces, uses a standard flash card for storage (a 256-MB card at the moment), and costs roughly the same as the PDA described above. Sales of digital cameras are pretty hot right now, judging from the digital print services that have cropped up all over the place. Why? Because they are selling an application (personal photography) on a device that provides all of the traditional affordances (user interface controls) of a film-based camera. It just happens to also be a device capable of mobile computing. In fact, the only reason I do not classify our camera as a mobile computing device is that its firmware has no built-in support for communicating directly on a network, even though its USB interface is more than capable of doing so.

Would it make sense to add networking capabilities to the camera? It would be nice to upload pictures directly to our personal Web site. There are, after all, many other noncamera features within the firmware, such as running a slideshow via the AV interface and the ability to postprocess images for special effects. Camera firmware, though, is just as proprietary as the mobile devices of 2000. Eventually, to keep up with requests for new functionality, camera manufacturers will have to move to more modular designs based on common platforms. I can only hope that, in doing so, they do not succumb to the same mistakes as the cellphone and PDA manufacturers: adding low-tech camera lenses as a feature suitable only for toy use.

A truly modular device would consist of a self-contained camera with almost all of the features of our new camera, a self-contained PDA with almost all the features one would expect to find in a PDA, a self-contained GPS unit that tells everything in range where they are, and a self-contained wireless communication device that services the other devices in much the same way that consumer firewall/gateway devices service computers on a home network. That is, essentially, the way that bluetooth is intended to work. Communication alone, however, is not sufficient: we need platforms that are capable of recognizing such interfaces (even when they are inactive) and flexible enough to select the one that is best used for image capture, the one that is best used for display, the one that can be used for Web-based retrieval, and the several that are available for "storage." A common platform allows application development to mature despite the rapid pace of device evolution, which allows software developers to build interesting applications before their platforms become obsolete, which in turn gives consumers a reason to buy devices that do something useful for them (computing despite their mobility), driving further demand for that platform of devices.

Therefore, while reading this book, I hope that you keep in mind that the above describes not a single technology development, but rather the development of a system that is intended, if successful, to become a self-sustaining feedback loop. Just as the Web has become the preferred platform for successful Internet services, one of the platforms that Reza describes herein will become the basis for future mobile applications. It will be up to you to determine which one, because it is the application developers that drive consumer demand.

Roy T. Fielding
Somewhere between Laguna Beach, California, and Venice, Italy
January 2004

Acknowledgments

There are so many people who I need to thank. And since this may be my one and only opportunity to thank them in a semipublic forum, then I must take the opportunity to do so. I thank Robert Gottesman for his support throughout my professional endeavors and David Armstrong, Dr. Roy Fielding, and Phillip Lindsay for their mentorship. Many thanks are owed to my loyal clients (Charity Funding Services and Barney Mckinley, Voice Genesis, eBuilt Inc., and a few others) that helped me put food on the table while I was authoring this text. Also, thanks are owed to Dr. Dennis H. Parr for having given me an opportunity when few would and to Abe and Najmeh Khadem who helped me with a monumental problem and showed me the road to Southern California, the best place on earth. Many thanks go to Brenda and Roger Eeds, who have become my lifelong friends with their advice and support, and to Nima Oreizy, Jos Bergmans, Mark Scheele, and Mark Mariott, who have become closer friends during the time of authoring this text.

I thank Susan Boettger, who has recently become my wife, for her encouragement in life and her family, Laura, Jane, and John Boettger, for their friendship. I am certain that her achievements musically as a classical composer and a pianist will dwarf mine as an engineer.

I dedicate this book to my wife; to my mother Shahrnaz Karimzadeh, who fostered a notion of excellence and sent me to the greatest country—the United States of America—that I call home; to my uncle and aunt Amir and Shauna Karimzadeh, who stuck with me all the way; to Bill, Deena, Scott, and Cindy Bernhardt, who made their home my home as I grew from a teenager to an adult; to Durrelle Singleton, who I know always has my back covered; to my brothers Abdollah and Atta, whom I miss; and to my little cousins Nikoo and Natasha, who embody innocence and purity to me.

Finally, I want to thank Jim Turner of SIGS, Lothlorien Homet, formerly of Cambridge University Press, and Lauren Cowles and Katherine Hew, currently of Cambridge University Press, who all had something to do with my deciding to write this book and helping me to carry it out. And I thank Albrecht Muller whose input has been invaluable during the reviews.

To no-look passes by Magic, hook shots by Kareem, dunks by Dr. J, and finger-roles by the Ice Man. To Steve Urkel's laugh, Getting' Jiggy with It, *Revenge of the Nerds*, Trekkers, and comebacks by number 7 in Mile High, which inspire me never to give up. To Terri Tower and Elizabeth Elam: Whoop, there it is, I did it my way! To Beethoven, Gorecki, Arvo Part, Lauridson, Red Hot Chili Peppers, Sting, Durufle, Delerium, and Dire Straits for keeping me company late at nights and to the following: It's all about old school, it'll never be as good as it was, and the older I get the better I was. I only wish I could invent phrases like Dicky V., to whom I say "here is a diaper dandy writer for you baby" and John Madden, to whom I say "I stuck to it for two and a half years!" I wish anyways. To slow-mo, Flo-Jo, go Bo, go. To Andre, who looks a ton better bald than with hair, and to Freddy Mercury, who used to be Farookh Mohammad and taught me all about name changes.

SECTION 1

Introductions to the Main Topics

CHAPTER 1

Introduction to Mobile Computing

Where is the life we have lost in living? Where is the knowledge we have lost in information? Where is the wisdom we have lost in knowledge?

T. S. Elliot

1.1 INTRODUCTION

Mobile computing systems are computing systems that may be easily moved physically and whose computing capabilities may be used while they are being moved. Examples are laptops, personal digital assistants (PDAs), and mobile phones. By distinguishing mobile computing systems from other computing systems we can identify the distinctions in the tasks that they are designed to perform, the way that they are designed, and the way in which they are operated. There are many things that a mobile computing system can do that a stationary computing system cannot do; these added functionalities are the reason for separately characterizing mobile computing systems.

Among the distinguishing aspects of mobile computing systems are their prevalent wireless network connectivity, their small size, the mobile nature of their use, their power sources, and their functionalities that are particularly suited to the mobile user. Because of these features, mobile computing applications are inherently different than applications written for use on stationary computing systems. And, this brings me to the central motivation behind authoring this book.

The application development and software engineering disciplines are very young engineering disciplines compared to those such as structural, mechanical, and electrical engineering. Software design and implementation, for the most part,

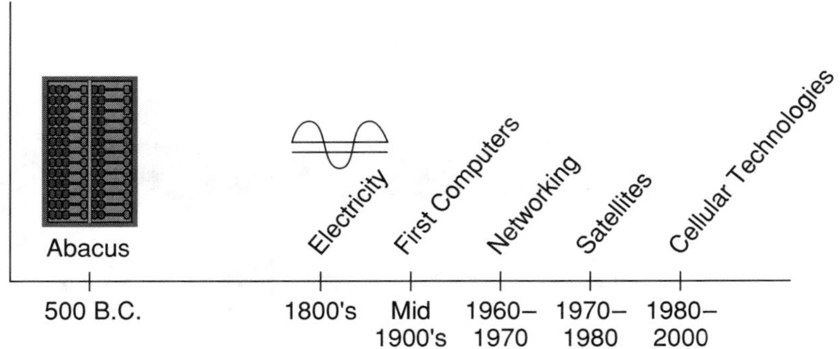

FIGURE 1.1. A Timeline of Mobile Computing.

remain part art and part science. However, there are definite signs of maturation with the development of architectures, metrics, proven tools, and other methodologies that give an engineering discipline its structure. Whereas there are a variety of methodologies, techniques, frameworks, and tools that are used in developing software for stationary systems, there are very few for mobile systems. Although mobile computing systems have existed as long as their stationary counterparts, most of the mature tools, methodologies, and architectures in software engineering today address the needs of stationary systems. One of our goals in this book will be to reflect on the research being done today to help evolve mobile application development and to outline some of the early proven techniques and technologies being tried in the commercial and academic environments.

In this text, we will look at those things that make the functional nature of mobile applications different than their stationary counterparts, take a survey of various development techniques that can be used to address these differences, and look at various basic technologies that allow us, as software developers, to create meaningful mobile applications in an extensible, flexible, and scalable manner.

1.1.1 A Brief History of Mobile Computing

Figure 1.1 shows a timeline of mobile computing development. One of the very first computing machines, the abacus, which was used as far back as 500 B.C., was, in effect, a mobile computing system because of its small size and portability. As technology progressed, the abacus evolved into the modern calculator. Most calculators today are made with an entire slew of mathematical functions while retaining their small size and portability. The abacus and calculators became important parts of technology not only because of their ability to compute but also because of their ease of use and portability. You can calculate the proceeds of a financial transaction anywhere as long as you had an abacus in 500 B.C. or have a calculator today. But, calculating numbers is only one part of computing.

Other aspects of computing, namely storage and interchange of information, do not date as far back as the abacus. Though writing has always been a way of storing information, we can hardly call a notebook a computing storage mechanism. The first mobile storage systems can be traced back only as far as the advent of the age of electronics.

FIGURE 1.2. Wireless Communication Systems.

A mobile computing system, as with any other type of computing system, can be connected to a network. Connectivity to the network, however, is not a prerequisite for being a mobile computing system. Dating from the late 1960s, networking allowed computers to talk to each other. Networking two or more computers together requires some medium that allows the signals to be exchanged among them. This was typically achieved through wired networks. Although wired networks remain the predominant method of connecting computers together, they are somewhat cumbersome for connecting mobile computing devices. Not only would network ports with always-available network connectivity have to be pervasive in a variety of physical locations, it would also not be possible to be connected to the network in real time if the device were moving. Therefore, providing connectivity through a wired system is virtually cost prohibitive. This is where wireless communication systems come to the rescue (Figure 1.2).

By the 1960s, the military had been using various forms of wireless communications for years. Not only were wireless technologies used in a variety of voice communication systems, but the aviation and the space program had created great advances in wireless communication as well. First, the military developed wireless communication through line of sight: If there were no obstacles between point A and point B, you could send and receive electromagnetic waves. Then came techniques that allowed for wireless communication to encompass larger areas, such as using the atmosphere as a reflective mechanism. But, there were limitations on how far a signal could reach and there were many problems with reliability and quality of transmission and reception.

By the 1970s, communication satellites began to be commercialized. With the new communication satellites, the quality of service and reliability improved enormously. Still, satellites are expensive to build, launch, and maintain. So the available bandwidth provided by a series of satellites was limited. In the 1980s cellular telephony technologies became commercially viable and the 1990s were witness to advances in cellular technologies that made wireless data communication financially feasible in a pervasive way.

Today, there are a plethora of wireless technologies that allow reliable communication at relatively high bandwidths. Of course, bandwidth, reliability, and all other qualitative and quantitative aspects of measuring wireless technologies are relative to time and people's expectations (as seems to be with everything else in life!). Though most wireless networks today can transmit data at orders of magnitude faster speeds than just ten years ago, they are sure to seem archaically slow soon. It should, however, be noted that wired communication systems will almost certainly always offer us better reliability and higher data transmission bandwidths as long as electromagnetic communications is the primary means of data communications. The higher frequency sections of the electromagnetic spectrum are difficult to use for wireless communications because of natural noise, difficulty of directing the signal (and therefore high losses), and many other physical limitations. Since, by Nyquist's principle [Lathi 1989], the bandwidth made available by any communication system is bound by the frequencies used in carrying the signal, we can see that lack of availability of higher frequency ranges places a limitation on wireless communication systems that wired communication systems (such as fiber optic–based systems) do not have to contend with.

Because the greatest advances in mobile communications originated in the military, it is no surprise that one of the first applications of wireless communication for mobile computing systems was in displaying terrain maps of the battlefield. From this, the global positioning system (GPS) evolved so that soldiers could know their locations at any given time. Portable military computers were provided to provide calculations, graphics, and other data in the field of battle. In recent years, wireless telephony has become the major provider of a revenue stream that is being invested into improving the infrastructure to support higher bandwidth data communications.

1.1.2 Is Wireless Mobile or Is Mobile Wireless?

In wireless connectivity, mobile computing devices found a great way to connect with other devices on the network. In fact, this has been a great source of confusion between *wireless communications* and *mobile computing*. Mobile computing devices need not be wireless. Laptop computers, calculators, electronic watches, and many other devices are all mobile computing devices. None of them use any sort of wireless communication means to connect to a network. Even some hand-held personal assistants can only be synchronized with personal computers through a docking port and do not have any means of wireless connectivity. So, before we embark on our journey in learning about mobile computing, it should be clear that *wireless communication systems are a type of communication system. What distinguishes a wireless communication system from others is that the communication channel is space itself.* There are a variety of physical waveguide channels such as fiber optics or metallic wires. Wireless communication systems do not use a waveguide to guide along the electromagnetic signal from the sender to the receiver. They rely on the mere fact that electromagnetic waves can travel through space if there are no obstacles that block them. Wireless communication systems are often used in mobile computing systems to facilitate network connectivity, but they are not mobile computing systems.

Recently, computer networks have evolved by leaps and bounds. These networks have begun to fundamentally change the way we live. Today, it is difficult to imagine computing without network connectivity. Networking and distributed computing are two of the largest segments that are the focus of current efforts in computing. Networks and computing devices are becoming increasingly blended together. Most mobile computing systems today, through wired or wireless connections, can connect to the network. Because of the nature of mobile computing systems, network connectivity of mobile systems is increasingly through wireless communication systems rather than wired ones. And this is quickly becoming somewhat of a nonmandatory distinguishing element between mobile and stationary systems. Though it is not a requirement for a mobile system to be wireless, most mobile systems are wireless. Nevertheless, let us emphasize that wireless connectivity and mobility are orthogonal in nature though they may be complementary. For example, we can have a PDA that has no wireless network connectivity; however, most PDAs are evolving into having some sort of wireless connectivity to the network.

Also, though it is important to understand that stationary and mobile computing systems are inherently different, this does not mean that they do not have any commonalities. We will build on existing software technologies and techniques used for stationary systems where these commonalities exist or where there is a logical extension of a stationary technique or technology that will mobilize it.

Because of the constant comparison between mobile systems and other types of systems, we will have to have a way to refer to the "other" types of systems. We will use the terms *nonmobile* and *stationary* interchangeably. Although mobile is an industry-wide accepted terminology to distinguish a group of systems with the characteristics that we have just mentioned, there is no consensus on a system that is not a mobile system. For this reason, we will simply use the terms stationary or nonmobile when speaking of such systems. It is also important to note the there is probably no system that is truly not mobile because just about any system may be moved. We will assume that cranes, trucks, or other large vehicles are not required for moving our mobile systems! A mobile system should be movable very easily by just one person.

There are four pieces to the mobile problem: the mobile user, the mobile device, the mobile application, and the mobile network. We will distinguish the mobile user from the stationary user by what we will call the *mobile condition:*

the set of properties that distinguishes the mobile user from the user of a typical, stationary computing system. We will wrap the differences between typical devices, applications, and networks with mobile devices, applications, and networks into a set of properties that we will call the *dimensions of mobility*: *the set of properties that distinguishes the mobile computing system from the stationary computing system.* Once we have some understanding of the mobile problem, we will look at some established nonproprietary methodologies and tools of the software industry trade such as Unified Modeling Language (UML) as well as some commercial proprietary tools such as Sun Microsystem's Java, Microsoft's Windows CE, Symbian, and Qualcomm's BREW. Once we have looked at these tools, we will set out to solve the problem of architecting, designing, and implementing solutions for mobile computing problems.

Let us start by looking at some of those variables that create a distinction between mobile and stationary computing systems.

1.2 Added Dimensions of Mobile Computing

It should be obvious that any mobile computing system can also be stationary! If we stop moving it, it is stationary. So, we can say that mobile computing systems are a superset of stationary computing systems. Therefore, we need to look at those elements that are outside of the stationary computing subset. These added dimensions will help us pick out variables that in turn allow us to divide and conquer the problems of mobile computing. The *dimensions of mobility*, as we will refer to them in this text, will be the tools that allow us to qualify our problem of building mobile software applications and mobile computing systems. Although these dimensions of mobility are not completely orthogonal with respect to each other, they are separate enough in nature that we can distinguish them and approximate them as orthogonal variables. Also, keep in mind that some of these dimensions are limitations; nevertheless, they are still added dimensions that need not be considered when dealing with the typical stationary application. These dimensions of mobility (Figure 1.3) are as follows:

1. location awareness,
2. network connectivity quality of service (QOS),
3. limited device capabilities (particularly storage and CPU),
4. limited power supply,
5. support for a wide variety of user interfaces,
6. platform proliferation, and
7. active transactions.

It is absolutely crucial that the reader understands these dimensions of mobility and keeps them in mind throughout the process of design and implementation of the mobile application. Too often, engineers begin with attention to design and get bogged down in details of the tools that they use and small focused problems within the bigger picture of the system, its design, and its architecture. The definition of the word "mobile" reveals the first dimension we will consider: location.

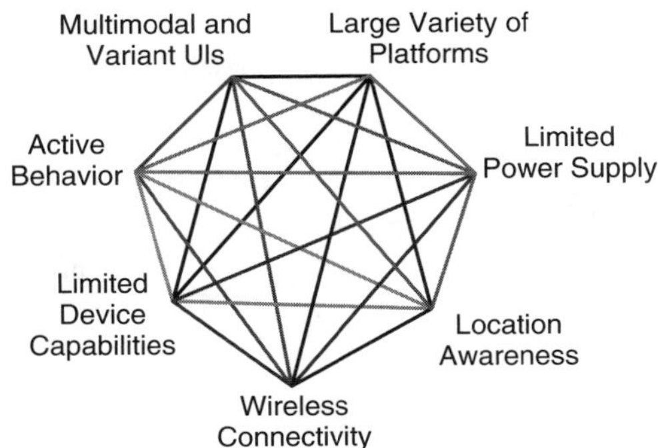

FIGURE 1.3. Dimensions of Mobility.

1.2.1 Location

A mobile device is not always at the same place: Its location is constantly changing. The changing location of the mobile device and the mobile application presents the designers of the device and software applications with great difficulties. However, it also presents us with an opportunity of using the location and the change in location to enhance the application. These challenges and opportunities can be divided into two general categories: *localization* and *location sensitivity*.

Localization is the mere ability of the architecture of the mobile application to accommodate logic that allows the selection of different business logic, level of work flow, and interfaces based on a given set of location information commonly referred to as locales. Localization is not exclusive to mobile applications but takes a much more prominent role in mobile applications. Localization is often required in stationary applications where users at different geographical locations access a centralized system. For example, some point-of-sale (POS) systems and e-commerce Web sites are able to take into account the different taxation rules depending on the locale of the sale and the location of the purchase. Whereas localization is something that stationary applications can have, location sensitivity is something fairly exclusive to mobile applications.

Location sensitivity is the ability of the device and the software application to first obtain location information while being used and then to take advantage of this location information in offering features and functionality. Location sensitivity may include more than just the absolute location of the device (if there is such a thing as absolute location—Einstein must be rolling in his grave now!). It may also include the location of the device relative to some starting point or a fixed point, some history of past locations, and a variety of calculated values that may be found from the location and the time such as speed and acceleration.

There are a variety of methods for collecting and using the location of the user and the device. The user may simply be prompted for his or her location, but this wouldn't make a very user-friendly application. Imagine a system that can only give you directions to where you want to go if you know where you are: It will be useful often, but occasionally, you won't know where you are or it would be too difficult to figure out your location. The device may be reset for a relative location if it has the ability to sense motion and can keep track of the change of location

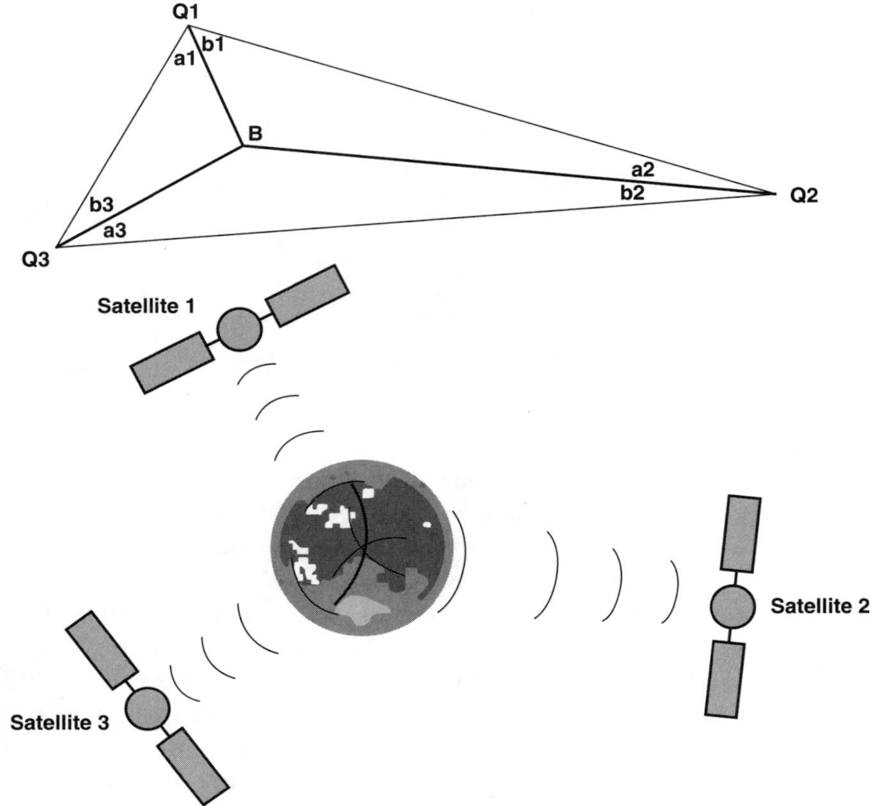

FIGURE 1.4. Determining Position Based on Triangulation.

for some period of time after this reset. Most location-sensing technologies (the particulars of which will be discussed in Chapter 12) use one or more of three categories of techniques: *triangulation*, *proximity*, and *scene analysis* [Hightower and Borriello 2001].

Triangulation (Figure 1.4) relies on age-old geometric methods that allow calculation of the location of a point that lies in the middle of three other points whose exact locations are known. If the distance to each one of the three points is known, we can use geometric techniques to calculate the exact location of the unknown point. *Proximity*-based methods measure the relative position of the unknown point to some known point. *Scene analysis* relies on image processing and topographical techniques to calculate the location of the unknown point based on a view of the unknown point from a known point.

The most well known location sensing system today is GPS. GPS-enabled devices can obtain latitude and longitude with accuracy of about 1–5 m. GPS has its roots in the military; until recently, the military placed restrictions on the accuracy of GPS available for public use. Most of these restrictions have now been lifted. GPS devices use triangulation techniques by triangulating data points from the satellite constellation that covers the entire surface of the earth. If a device does not have GPS capabilities but uses a cellular network for wireless connectivity, signal strength and triangulation or other methods can be used to come up with some approximate location information, depending on the cellular network.

Regardless of how location information is obtained, it is one of the major differences between mobile and stationary systems. Location information can be to mobile applications what depth can be to two-dimensional pictures; it can give us an entirely new tool to automate tasks. An example of a stand-alone mobile software application that uses location information could be one that keeps track of the route that a user drives from home to work every day without the user entering the route manually; this could then be used to tell the user which route is the fastest way to get to work on a particular day or which route may result in the least amount of gas consumed. An example of a wirelessly networked mobile application taking advantage of location could be one that shows a field service worker where to go next, once he or she is finished with a task at one site, based on the requests for work in the queue and the location of the field service worker. It should be noted that acquiring position information requires connectivity to some network-based infrastructure. This infrastructure is typically isolated from the other network-based application infrastructures. Therefore, when we say stand-alone, we mean an application that may use some specific network-based infrastructure, such as GPS, for obtaining location information but is not connected to any other networks as a part of a distributed or network-based application.

Location information promises to be one of the biggest drivers of mobile applications as it allows for the introduction of new business models and fundamentally new methods of adding productivity to business systems.

1.2.2 Quality of Service

Whether wired or wireless connectivity is used, mobility means loss of network connectivity reliability. Moving from one physical location to another creates physical barriers that nearly guarantee some disconnected time from the network. If a mobile application is used on a wired mobile system, the mobile system must be disconnected between the times when it is connected to the wired docking ports to be moved. Of course, it is always a question whether a docking port is available when required let alone the quality and type of the available network connectivity at that docking port. In the case of wireless network connectivity, physical conditions can significantly affect the quality of service (QOS). For example, bad weather, solar flares, and a variety of other climate-related conditions can negatively affect the QOS. This unreliability in network connectivity has given rise to the QOS field and has led to a slew of accompanying products. QOS tools and products are typically used to quantify and qualify the reliability, or unreliability, of the connectivity to the network and are mostly used by network operators. Network operators control the physical layer of the network and provide the facilities, such as Internet Protocol (IP), for software application connectivity.

Usually, the QOS tools, run by the network operators, provide information such as available bandwidth, risk of connectivity loss, and statistical measurements that allow software applications to make smart computing decisions. The key to designing and implementing mobile applications is that network connectivity and QOS need to be taken into account with an expanded scope. Most software applications, mobile or not, take advantage of networking in some way and, therefore, do have network connectivity features. Stationary applications typically need not worry about the quality of network connectivity as this is handled by lower level layers than the application: the operating system, the hardware (such as the network card in a personal computer), the network itself, and all of the other components that make network computing possible. Stationary software applications typically assume some discrete modes of connectivity mostly limited to connected or disconnected. This works for most applications because most wired network connectivity is fairly reliable.

However, the effect of QOS in designing mobile applications is much more profound. Whereas typical nonmobile applications need to know how to stop operating "gracefully" when suddenly disconnected from the network, mobile applications have to know how to continue to operate even after they are disconnected from the network or while they connect and disconnect from the network intermittently and frequently. For example, let us take the case of a user who is traveling on a train, is using an application on his PDA connected wirelessly to some network, and is downloading a work-related report to look over when the train passes through a tunnel and he loses network connectivity. If the application does not have the ability to stop partway through the download process and restart when connectivity is restored, the user may never be able to retrieve the desired file as he passes through one tunnel after the other and the download process starts over and over again. The application, therefore, must know how to deal with lack of reliable connectivity.

When it comes to taking into account the QOS in most applications, certain functionality is expected of most mobile applications. For example, almost all mobile applications should know how to stop working when the application suddenly disconnects from the network and then resume working when it connects again. Other functionality may be desired but not required. For example, often QOS data are measured and provided by the network operator. For example, the real-time bandwidth available may be part of the data provided and refreshed on some time interval. Such data can be utilized to design applications that dynamically adapt their features and functionality to the available bandwidth.

1.2.3 Limited Device Storage and CPU

No one wants to carry around a large device, so most useful mobile devices are small. This physical size limitation imposes boundaries on volatile storage, nonvolatile storage, and CPU on mobile devices. Though solid-state engineers are working on putting more and more processing power and storage into smaller and smaller physical volumes, nevertheless, as most mobile applications today are very rudimentary, there will be more and more that we will want to do with them. Today's mobile applications are resource-starved. So, although the designers of modern applications designed to run on personal computers (PCs) and servers continue to care less and less about system resources such as memory and processing power, it is a sure bet that memory limitations will be around for a long time for mobile applications because *when it comes to mobile systems and devices, smaller is nearly always better.*

Smaller devices are easier to carry and, consequently, may become more pervasive. This pervasiveness also largely depends on the price of the devices. Making electronic devices very small normally increases the cost, as the research and development that go into making devices smaller are very expensive. But, once a technology matures and the manufacturing processes for making it becomes mostly automated, prices begin to decline. At the point when the device is more and more of a commodity, smaller also means less expensive. This is why a PDA is much less expensive than a PC and yet it is much smaller. So, there is not a simple proportional relationship between size of device and cost of device. Our general rule stands that *when it comes to mobile systems and devices, smaller is nearly always better.* The small size serves the mobile purpose of the device the best. And, we all know that there are physical boundaries on the size of transistors on modern microchips. This means that there is some ceiling for storage and processing power of a device with a limited size bound by the heat produced by the transistors, the number of transistors that can possibly fit into each component, and the many other factors that the microprocessor industry has been studying since the birth of microchips.

Limitations of storage and CPU of mobile devices put yet another constraint on how we develop mobile applications. For example, a mobile calendaring application may store some of its data on another node on the network (a PC, server, etc.). The contacts stored on the device may be available at any time. However, the contact information that exists only on the network is not available while the device is disconnected from the network. But, because the amount of data that can be stored on each type of device varies depending on the device type, it is not possible to allocate this storage space statically. Also, some information may be used more frequently than others; for example, the two weeks surrounding the current time may be accessed more frequently in the calendar application or there may be some contacts that are used more frequently. Mobile applications must be designed to optimize the use of data storage and processing power of the device in terms of the application use by the user.

In this example, the calendaring application may or may not be the only application that uses the storage capacity of the device. So, the first step in designing the application would be designing the appropriate functionality for discovery of other applications on the device, the storage space that they use, and the total storage space available, and then computing the amount of storage available to the calendaring application. The operating system of some devices may offer the available storage space, but this is not guaranteed. So, we need to design with the least amount of assumptions about the hardware capabilities of the device or with all those assumptions valid for all of the devices to be supported by the mobile application.

Storage and processing issues are largely addressed by the various operating systems and platforms on the mobile devices. Therefore, a large part of engineering mobile applications requires first a theoretical understanding of the various types of platforms and operating systems available on mobile devices, then an understanding of the available commercial implementations of the varieties of types of operating systems and platforms and the type of applications best suited for each platform–device combination. We will look at these issues closer in Chapter 2.

This dimension of mobile application design, namely the effect of device limitations, is perhaps the most well known of all dimensions in today's mobile application design. This was the first problem that software developers approached as they tried to port frameworks, platforms, and methodologies of application development of the 1980s and 1990s to mobile applications. It soon became obvious to researchers and developers that existing paradigms and platforms did not suffice. For now, many have simply adopted older methodologies and are building mobile applications as pure embedded applications using assembly language native to the device on which they want the application to run. However, we have already seen, in the evolution of application development for PCs and servers, that developing native applications is cost prohibitive. This is the reason that most of today's complex applications are not written in assembly; rather, they are written in C, C++, or a similar language and then compiled for the platform of need. Virtual machines have given us yet another level of indirection to avoid authoring device- and platform-specific code in languages such as Java, thereby, decreasing the cost of application development even more.

The point is that there is typically some cost involved with layers of indirection in software. Though these layers of abstraction and indirection can have many benefits, we need to balance their use with the single fact that mobile devices are limited in their CPU, memory, and other computing capabilities. And, this muddies solutions to some design and implementation problems that would otherwise be very clear.

1.2.4 Limited Power Supply

We have already seen that the size constraints of the devices limit their storage capabilities and that their physical mobility affects network connectivity. For the same set of reasons that wireless is the predominant method of network connectivity for mobile devices, batteries are the primary power source for mobile devices. Batteries are improving every day and it is tough to find environments where suitable AC power is not available. Yet, often the user is constantly moving and devices are consuming more and more power with processors that have more and more transistors packed into them. For example, a user who walks in New York City and lives in the suburbs may leave work, begin using his or her PDA, get on the subway, and continue using it until returning home. When traveling in Asia, Africa, and South America, users are certain to rely on their batteries more frequently as reliable wired power sources are less pervasive than they are in North America and Europe.

The desirability of using batteries instead of an AC power source combined with the size constraints creates yet another constraint, namely a *limited power supply*. This constraint must be balanced with the processing power, storage, and size constraints; the battery is typically the largest single source of weight in the mobile

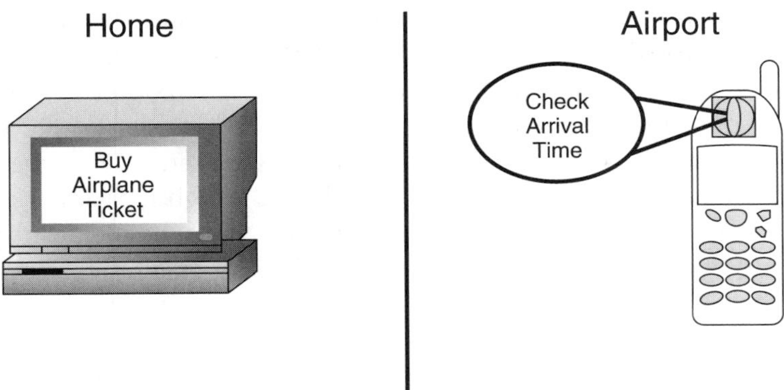

Figure 1.5. An Application That Uses Both Voice and Text User Interfaces.

device [Welch 2000]. The power supply has a direct or an indirect effect on everything in a mobile device. For example, the brighter the display, the more battery power is used, so the user interface is indirectly coupled to the power supply.

Most power management functionality is built into the operating system of the mobile device. Therefore, when it comes to device power management, the design focus is more on making the right choice in selecting the proper platform (device, operating system, etc.) and configuring the platform properly. In a typical stationary application, this would suffice. But, in mobile applications, we need to look everywhere we can to save power. Because the operating systems of mobile devices are typically very lean and have as few functionalities as possible, many times the application must carry some burden of awareness of the power supply.

Some platforms allow monitoring of the remaining power and other related power information. Some platforms allow multiprocessing and multithreading, which have an effect on the control over the variation of the CPU activity, which in turn has an effect on the control over the power consumed by the device. Overall, the design and implementation of the application itself is affected less by this dimension of mobility than by any of the others mentioned in this book. This is merely because operating systems and platforms are largely responsible for handling the power consumption issues. However, we will discuss the effects on choice of platform and other architectural and implementation effects that the power supply has on mobile computing systems in a bit more detail in Chapters 15 and 16.

1.2.5 Varying User Interfaces

Stationary users use nonmobile applications while working on a PC or a similar device. The keyboard, mouse, and monitor have proved to be fairly efficient user interfaces for such applications. This is not at all true for mobile applications. Examples of some alternative interfaces are voice user interfaces, smaller displays, stylus and other pointing devices, touch-screen displays, and miniature keyboards. Using a combination of interface types is not uncommon (see Figure 1.5).

For example, drivers who want to get some directions to their destination may use a data-enabled cellular phone, navigate through a simple graphical user interface (GUI) menu to a driving directions application, and then retrieve the desired directions through a voice user interface by saying the address of the source and destination and listening to the directions. Note that navigating to the application may be done much more efficiently on a GUI: It may be as simple as pushing two or three numbers that activate some choices on the screen. However, entering text on the small display of a cellular phone and through the numeric keys of a phone is very cumbersome. It is much easier to say the source and destination and, subsequently, have a voice recognition system translate them, find the directions, and read them to the user by using a text-to-speech system.

A mobile application, based on its device support, the type of users using it, the conditions under which it is used, and many other factors discussed later in this book offers a variety of user interfaces. Perhaps the biggest paradigm shift that designers and implementers of mobile applications must undergo is to understand the necessity of finding the best user interface(s) for the application, architecting the system to accommodate the suitable user interface(s), implementing them, and keeping in mind that a new user interface may be required at any time. Although these user interface advances promise to be one of the main aspects of the next computing revolution, they add much complexity and confusion to the application design as the current application design and implementation methodologies only take into account keyboards, monitors, pointing devices, and sometimes touchscreens. The developer can no longer make any assumptions about the input and output mechanisms to the system; therefore, the development process becomes altogether different, complicating an already complex design process.

User interfaces are difficult to design and implement for the following reasons [Meyers 1993]:

1. Designers have difficulties learning the user's tasks.
2. The tasks and domains are complex.
3. A balance must be achieved among the many different design aspects, such as standards, graphic design, technical writing, internationalization, performance, multiple levels of detail, social factors, and implementation time.
4. The existing theories and guidelines are not sufficient.
5. Iterative design is difficult.
6. There are real-time requirements for handling input events.
7. It is difficult to test user interface software.
8. Today's languages do not provide support for user interfaces.
9. Programmers report an added difficulty of modularization of user interface software.

Meyers recognizes the problems associated with user interfaces of stationary computing systems. These problems are compounded by the *multichannel* requirement of mobile systems. Multichannel systems are systems that use multiple types of user interfaces for input and output such as text, voice, and video (see Chapter 8).

Since the recognition of the complexity of designing user interfaces by Meyers and others, some headway has been made in providing us some tools to reduce this complexity. First, because many GUI-based applications have been developed for stationary systems, the iterative process of design and implementation and feedback from the users have taught us much about what works and what does not. So, we now know more about how to design user interfaces (item 4 in the preceding list).

But, methodologies, tools, and patterns used in the development of stationary applications do very little to separate concerns of user interface from the rest of the application. Sure, there are several design patterns such as the (often misused, abused, and overused) model-view-controller (MVC), but the use of these patterns alone does not take into account the special concerns of various types of user interfaces. They merely make some attempt at separating some of the concerns of the user interface from the rest of the system. They serve us well when we are dealing with a single set of textual inputs and outputs, but today's popular architectural techniques and design patterns are insufficient for a large variety of user interfaces. And this is why much of the research in the area of mobile computing focuses precisely on this problem: How does one separate the concerns of the user interface from the application regardless of the type of user interface?

Today, we also have proven software design and development methodologies, such as that of object oriented programming (OOP) and use of unified modeling language (UML), and the supporting languages and tools, that allow us to gather the requirements of the system more clearly (item 1 in the list of difficulties), to modularize software design (item 9), and to design software without dependence on the language of choice (item 8). But, we have no such methodologies and tools to take into account the multichannel requirements of mobile systems or any of the other added dimensions of mobile application design. Though there is no consensus today how to use these tools to ease the development of multichannel user interfaces, the reader will be presented with what we see as emerging methodologies and tools that leverage existing proven methodologies and tools such as OOP and UML.

Not only do most software applications designed today have large coupling between the user interface and the application, but also very few are designed to render to any desired user interface with few modifications. Most of today's applications need to be massively retrofitted or rewritten altogether every time a new set of user interfaces must be supported. Of course, there is also the special concerns of each type of user interface, such as voice user interfaces, that must be taken into account.

We dedicate several chapters in this book to discussing various issues surrounding software architecture for rendering to any type of user interface, voice user interfaces, and the ways that users communicate with systems. For now, the important factor is to recognize that the user interface design and implementation process has a much bigger effect on an average mobile application than its counterpart nonmobile application.

1.2.6 Platform Proliferation

Because mobile devices are small and there is much less hardware in them than in a PC, they are typically less costly to assemble for a manufacturer. This means that more manufacturers can compete in producing these devices. These cheaper, and typically smaller, devices are often used for special purposes. The sum of these and other similar reasons gives rise to proliferation of the types of devices in the marketplace that an application must support.

Platform proliferation has very significant implications on the architecture, design, and development of mobile applications. Platform proliferation heightens the importance of designing and developing devices independent of the platform. Writing native code specific to the mobile device, unless absolutely necessary because of performance requirements, is not a recommended practice because of the proliferation of devices. For example, it is not wise to write a voice-driven phone book application that runs only on one type of platform. Of course, the platform makers and manufacturers of devices and operating systems of those devices will always try to create restrictions on the developer to prohibit writing platform-independent applications. They may conversely give the developer features that may only be implemented on their platform to tie the developer to that platform. Regardless of the efforts of commercial platform builders, the software architects and developers should be focused on their primary task of meeting the user's requirements. And if these requirements include support of multiple platforms, which happens more frequently than not for mobile computing systems, platform independence should be on the top of the architects' and developers' list when choosing the tools to build an application.

We will try to address the problem of platform proliferation by using nonproprietary methodologies and tools, such as UML, when possible. Throughout the book, we will show our sample code for multiple platforms, alternating from one to the other, so that the reader is exposed to particulars of implementation on several of the most prevalent commercial platforms.

1.2.7 Active Transactions

Most of today's stationary applications have a restriction that can reduce the benefits of a mobile application system enormously: The user of the system must initiate all interactions with the system. We call such systems *passive* systems because they are in a passive state, waiting for some external signal from the user to tell them to start doing some particular thing. With stationary applications, this typically works well. Most people sit down to use a computer because they intend to perform some task. Whatever actions they may perform could signal one or more other passive systems to perform some computing task such as retrieving information or calculating some numbers.

At the same time, during the past two decades, messaging-based systems have been born and have evolved. With messaging systems, any one participant of the system can send a message to the other participant(s), and, if desired, under a specific topic in an *asynchronous* manner. We will discuss both asynchronous and messaging systems later in this chapter and other sections of this book. But, the key idea to take away is that any one participant in the system could send a *message* to another participant in the system. Later came the idea of *push*. In the push model of communication, an information producer announces the availability of certain types of information, an interested consumer subscribes to this information, and the producer periodically publishes the information (pushes it to the consumer) [Hauswirth and Jazayeri 1999]. There is much in common between the concepts of messaging systems and push systems. The principle difference is that messaging systems are asynchronous by definition. This requirement does not exist for push-based systems.

Push systems, by definition, are *active* systems. For example, a particular user could be browsing the Web and, while purchasing some goods online, be notified of the change in the price of a particular stock. In this example, the system has taken an *active* role in starting communication with the user on a particular topic.

Push–pull systems (a more complete name for push systems as the receiver of the "pushing" is said to be "pulling" on a particular topic) can be implemented in a number of ways, including using event-driven systems, messaging middleware, and poll-based systems. Implementation aside, unfortunately, push systems have mostly been a disappointing failure. One of the reasons for this failure has been that most push pull systems have targeted users who are largely focused on the task at hand.

If a user sits at his or her desk and begins using a PC, the user is constantly reminded, in an indirect manner, that he or she can access some piece of information. Even if the user is not performing some exact task, the simple condition of sitting down and using a keyboard and a mouse puts the user in a state where he or she is more likely to remember information processing related tasks. Educators often call this principle being *on-task*: As long as students are sitting at their desks, with their books open, there is a much higher chance of accomplishing tasks related to studying. Based on the same principle, the user who is sitting behind his or her desk working on a PC is *on-task and focused*. For example, if the user sits down and begins to type a memo to a coworker, the chances of the user remembering to check, say, his or her stock portfolio has increased by the mere fact that there are visual reminders, such as the browser icon on the desk top, that will remind the user to perform the task. Even if the user forgets (which is unlikely, particularly if you are sitting on thousands of shares of stock that are worth a tenth of what they used to be after a market crash), if he or she is merely reminded by an e-mail, the user can very easily begin the transaction that performs whatever tasks are needed to retrieve the necessary information and perform the necessary tasks. A reminder system certainly helps mainly because the user is focused on the task of computing and is available to receive the reminder. (We will talk about the lack of focus of the mobile user more in the next section.)

In this book, we will define *active transactions* as those transactions initiated by the system. Active transactions may be *synchronous* or *asynchronous*. *All active transactions are initiated by the system.* Synchronous transactions are time-dependent transactions. Note that the term *transaction* is used in data storage and other systems to indicate boundaries for roll-back and committing of a series of actions that must be successfully executed, in some predetermined manner, for the completion of the transaction. We use the term in a slightly different manner. We use it to refer to a sequence of interactions between the user and the computing system. Synchronous active transactions can be summarized by a set of properties:

1. The transaction is initiated by the system, and during the same transaction, the user is given an opportunity, for a finite period of time, to respond to the action initiated by the system.
2. Synchronous active transactions require a timely response from the user.
3. The interactions between the system and the user work in a sequential and serial manner during a synchronous transaction.
4. Synchronous active transactions are established between the system and a single user. This may be replicated for many users, but at the most elemental level, there is only one user in each active transaction.

Let us look at an example of a synchronous active transaction. One of the tasks often forgotten by the field work force is logging time for tasks. For example, a cable company repair person who forgets to log his or her hours by noon may be called by the system at noon and asked to log these hours, through a voice user interface. The system asks the employee to start telling it, using the key pad or the voice, the time intervals worked and the tasks accomplished during those hours. If the employee does not answer the call, the system logs him or her as unavailable and may try again at a later time. If the employee does answer the call, but does not respond to any one of the questions within some allotted time, the system may record that the transaction has failed because of user irresponsiveness. If the employee answers all of the questions so that the system can successfully log the accomplished tasks, the transaction completes successfully and is logged accordingly by the central system. Of course, there are many reasons for the transaction to fail, including dropped connections, inaccurate interpretation of voice commands, and others. Regardless, the idea is that the user is called by the system and, if the user answers the phone, he or she is asked some questions and expected to respond within some given time frame. Also, the questions are asked in a sequential and serial manner. The system does not ask all of the questions at once and then wait for the user to respond to them one by one. Neither does the system ask questions while the user is answering any one of the questions.

Most of today's active systems are asynchronous. Asynchronous transactions are not time-dependent. Asynchronous active transactions, like their synchronous counterparts, can be described by a set of properties:

1. Asynchronous active transactions work just like messaging systems. They can be established with either 1–*n* receivers or 1–*n* topics to which 1–*m* receivers are subscribed.
2. Asynchronous active transactions may be a composition of 1–*n* messages sent by the system and may require 1–*m* messages back from the users. If 1–*m* messages required as responses from the users are not received within some time frame specified by the system, the transactions may be deemed as failed. Note that we are not defining the semantics of messaging systems (for if that

is what we were referring to, we would be wrong). Rather, we are defining the semantics of asynchronous active transactions to be such that they encapsulate a number of messages being sent from the system to the user and from the user to the system and that some messages from the user, marked as responses to the messages from the system, can be required for the successful completion of the transaction.

Now, let us look at the asynchronous version of the same time-logging application that we observed for synchronous active transactions. The system could call the user and wait for the user to answer the phone. Once again, if the user does not answer the phone, it logs the transaction as failed and the user's absence as the cause of the failure. If the user answers the phone, the system reminds the user that he or she has not logged his or her time for the day and needs to do so. At this point, the system asks the user to do this as soon as possible. The user can then call the system back at some later time and log his or her hours, upon which the transaction is considered successful. If the user never calls back to complete the transaction, the system may continue to call the user back with periodic reminders 1–*n* times. Once the *n* limit of times is surpassed, the transaction may be considered as failed. Once again, there are a variety of reasons for the failure of the transaction that can be recorded by the system. However, the main thrust of the example is that the system does not require a timely response. The system may have even asked the user to perform several tasks at a later time and the user may have done each one of those tasks out of order. In this example, the time dependence, sequential order, and serial manner of the tasks of the transactions are irrelevant. This gives the system more flexibility but we lose certainty in when and how a response from the user is going to be received. Also, the serial order of the tasks during the transaction may be desired or undesired.

Choosing whether the active behavior of a system is implemented using an asynchronous active transactional model or a synchronous active transactional model is completely dependent on the user requirements and the available tools (which translates to the available budget).

So, we have now defined the basics of what we will need to treat active transactions. Active transactions are an absolute essential part of mobile application development mainly because of the lack of focus on the part of the user while the user is mobile. The semantics of active transactions are defined only for the purpose of this book. One may argue against these transactions in different contexts. But, for the context of mobile application development, they will serve us well in communicating requirements, architecture, design, and implementation. And why are they less important to stationary applications? Because the stationary user is typically focused on the task of computing while the mobile user is not. We will consider the condition of the mobile user more in the next section.

Finally, it is important to note that active transactions differ from push–pull systems and messaging systems not only because they can be both synchronous and asynchronous but also because they can contain 1–*n* interactions between the system and the user. We will discuss active transactions in much greater detail in Chapter 13.

We have now looked at the added dimensions that we need in our thinking paradigm to understand mobile application development. Let us quickly look at the root cause of the existence of these dimensions of mobility, namely the environmental effects on the mobile user's requirements.

1.3 Condition of the Mobile User

Any computing system with end users has at least two participants, the computer and the user. We have looked at the computing system in analyzing the dimensions of mobility, those things that make mobile applications different from stationary applications. Now let us look at how the mobile user differs from the stationary user. We will call this difference between the mobile user and the stationary user the *mobile condition*. The elements of mobile condition distinguished here are not necessarily comprehensive as the user studies done and the industry experience with mobile applications are in an infancy stage. However, together, they contain all of the major differences between mobile and stationary users.

The mobile user is fundamentally different from the stationary user in the following ways:

1. The mobile user is moving, at least occasionally, between known or unknown locations.
2. The mobile user is typically not focused on the computing task.
3. The mobile user frequently requires high degrees of immediacy and responsiveness from the system.
4. The mobile user is changing tasks frequently and/or abruptly.
5. The mobile user may require access to the system anywhere and at any time.

Note that the mobile condition is not just about the physical condition of the mobile user but also about the mental state of the user: his or her expectations and state of mind. Note, also, that the differentiating elements between the mobile user and the stationary user are the root causes of the dimensions of mobility. So the relationship between the mobile condition and the dimensions of mobility is one of cause and effect.

Now, recall that we recognized the dimensions of mobility as the difference between mobile and stationary applications. We have now come full circle; we can see that the dimensions of mobility are a byproduct of the requirements of a mobile user to use a mobile application. To complete the chain of logic for our dimensions of mobility, let us look at the differences between the mobile user and the stationary user that comprise the *mobile condition*.

1.3.1 Changing Location

It may seem trivial to state that a mobile user is always, or at least frequently, moving. But, this motion has a significant implication in that the location information can be used to draw conclusions about the context in which the user is using the application. This is the reason location sensitivity and QOS are dimensions of mobility. The location of the user at a given time is a variable. Other variables may be the speed at which the mobile user may be traveling, what network connectivity modes are available to the user, what the quality of that connectivity may be at any given place and time, or how long he or she may stay connected or disconnected. The mobile user also expects the system to have good connectivity coverage. The mobile users will come to also expect the system to know the device's location with fair accuracy as location services become more commonplace. This aspect of mobile computing presents the developers with the opportunity of giving the users functionality not possible with stationary applications. It is a clear differentiator that presents the mobile user with great value that cannot be obtained through a stationary application. Therefore, building applications that take advantage of the location information and that are localized is often a must with commercial mobile applications.

The changing location of the mobile user also forces restrictions on power, size of device, wireless connectivity of the device, and just about every other aspect of the state of the mobile user. In those respects, it creates restrictions that we have already looked at. In using the location information of the application, we have an opportunity to provide functionality beyond that of stationary applications. The moving nature of the mobile user is a physical aspect that gives way to a mental state of *lack of focus*.

1.3.2 Lack of Focus

The primary focus of the mobile user is seldom on the computing task (although, obviously, there are exceptions to this, but we are talking about the majority of time when the user has a device and is mobile). This is the primary reason for the necessity of active transactions. While a user is driving from work to home, the task of driving takes the primary focus. During this time, if the stock price of one of the user's holdings begins to plummet, he or she cannot sell it before it falls too far. The user either does not know of the plummeting price at all or is not focused on checking on the stock price at regular intervals. Mobile users are typically mobile because they are moving between two points with the primary task of reaching the destination.

Another reason for lack of focus is multitasking. Mobile users often multitask. For example, a user may be driving and talking on the phone. Another example could be a user who is entering some data into a PDA out in the field (collecting information on power lines as a field electrician, measuring environmental effects as an environmental engineer, etc.) while doing the primary field work task at the site (such as climbing a pole and paying attention to power lines, finding the right place to measure, and keeping the environmental conditions stable while measuring, etc.). Because of this multitasking nature of the mobile user, a variety of user interface input types such as voice may be needed to take advantage of the senses that are not preoccupied by another task. Also, the user interface to the system must be very user friendly and require as few of the user's senses focused on communicating with the machine as efficiently as possible. For example, voice user interfaces allow users to focus on driving while still getting whatever information they need from the system.

1.3.3 Immediacy

Mobile users are often in a situation where they need to quickly perform one or more computing tasks, such as retrieving contact information, sending a voice or e-mail message, or triggering some remote process. They don't have the time to go through a long boot sequence or long application setup times. Mobile users normally have higher expectations of performance from their devices than stationary users do. Performance of mobile applications is not an afterthought as it often is in the development of stationary applications. A short delay in application responsiveness can decrease its usefulness enormously. For example, a user who cannot get the necessary contact information from a mobile contact application will eventually become frustrated and use a directory service to find the necessary contact information in urgent situations. It is also important to note that there are different types of immediacy. For example, the user's tolerance, depending on the application, will vary in first connecting to the network compared to the system response time. The types of immediacy depend on the application.

1.3.4 Abrupt Changes in Tasks

As we mentioned before, the mobile user is typically mobile because he or she is focused on something else other than computing. For example, many mobile users will try to use commute time: Whether in a train, in a plane, or in an automobile the user will be distracted by different environmental factors.[†] These factors must be kept in mind in designing and implementing the flow and, once again, the interface of the application. The mobile user needs to be able to stop performing some computing task abruptly, do something that may be completely unrelated, then return to the application after some unknown period of time, and, without much effort to remember what he or she had been doing, continue the computing task. Mobile users expect applications that flow smoothly and do not require complex navigation despite the abrupt nature of their actions.

1.3.5 Anywhere, Anytime

The cliché of "Anywhere, Anytime," along with all of its synonyms or similar clichés ("Everywhere," "Everyplace," or "Anyplace") and other words that refer to this phenomenon such as "Pervasive" and "Ubiquitous" are perhaps the most overused set of words in mobile computing. Nevertheless, this is still one of the most important aspects of mobile computing. The mobile user expects to be able to retrieve data and do computing at any given moment and any given time. And this is precisely why the support for a variety of platforms with a variety of user interfaces is critical for a mobile application: To use an application anywhere and anytime, one may have to use it through whatever device (any device) is available and convenient for that given place and time. Mobile users expect to start a transaction and leave it unfinished on one device at a given place and time

[†] Note that not all of the mobile conditions of the user may coexist at the same time—sometimes users are focused on the task of computing (for example, when they are in a train or a plane); other times, they are not (for example, when a real estate sales person is selling a house and, unbeknownst to that person, another listing comes open that may be a better fit for his or her buyer).

and finish the same transaction later on a different device and at a different place and time.

The *mobile condition* of the mobile user should be the primary guiding tool in architecting, designing, and implementing the mobile application. The various problems presented to us by the mobile condition may require solutions that have inherent conflicts. For example, to increase the number of devices and user interfaces supported, we may want to centralize the business logic and use the devices only as thin clients. (Thin clients are discussed in detail in Chapter 16.) However, to make the user interface as friendly as possible and to make the use of application possible even when the device is not connected to the network, we would want to push a significant portion of the application to the client. Obviously, these two aspects are in direct conflict. In another example, we may see that a particular mobile application requires increased CPU to perform a particular task faster. But the increased CPU may mean a considerably larger device, making it more difficult to carry. As with any other engineering problem, while designing mobile applications, we will find that we often need to balance the solutions to problems presented by each mobility dimension. There is no better balancing guide than the mobile condition of the mobile user. Of course, cost in itself can offset the benefits of any solution. Once again, as with any other engineering problem, the solution needs to fit the problem of the customer, in our case the mobile user, within a given budget. With an unlimited budget, nearly anything can be done. But, of course, we all know that there is not such a thing as an unlimited budget.

Therefore the cost and the mobile condition comprise the variables that describe our customer. Every mobile user will have a specific set of needs, but those two are constants. In added dimensions of mobility, we have the major effects of the mobile condition on the requirements for building mobile applications. Once we have gathered the requirements from the user, the first step in building the mobile application is to decide on the architecture. And this is what we will discuss next.

1.4 Architecture of Mobile Software Applications

The first step in building a software application, after the process of gathering requirements, is to lay down a high-level plan of what the application will be like when it is finished. Mobile applications, like any other software application, require such a high-level plan. We call this high-level plan of the mobile application a "mobile software architecture." Our approach to architecture in this text will be bottom up: we will introduce a variety of design patterns, application architectures, and processes with each addressing some specific problem with mobile applications (Figure 1.6).

If you are not familiar with the basic prevalent application architectures in today's distributed Web applications, we recommend that you read Sections 16.1.1 and 16.1.2 of Chapter 16. You will see the terms *N*-Tier, client–server, mobile agent, and peer-to-peer quite frequently throughout this text and you should have at least a passing familiarity with them. In Chapter 16, we will define

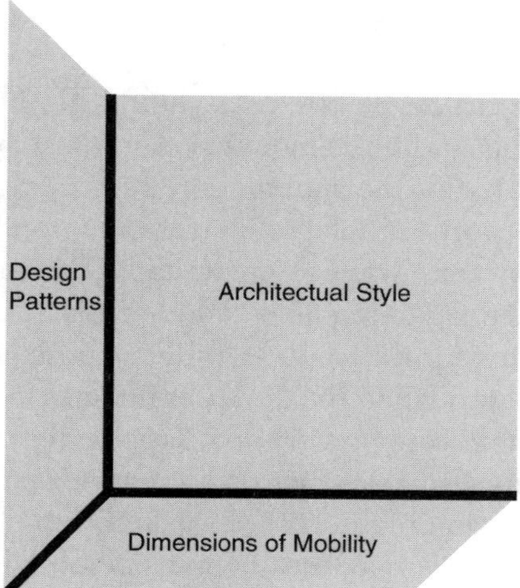

FIGURE 1.6. Mobile Application Development Design Consideration Space.

software architecture to be *a particular high-level abstraction of the system and how its components collaborate*. Then, we will summarize what we will learn in Chapters 1 through 15 to get a feeling for various architectural designs and techniques for mobile applications. For now, let us look at what software architectures will mean to us within the confines of mobile application development.

There are also *architectural patterns*; these are patterns that are recognizable once they are used prevalently in some architectures. Although there are no fully established design patterns, architectural patterns, or even architectures in the field of mobile computing because of its infancy, one of our goals in this text is to outline some techniques that show evidence of such techniques beginning to mature. These patterns exhibit themselves in a variety of families of problems. For example, we will introduce several different architectures for design and implementation of multimodal user interfaces. We will also introduce some lower level design patterns for separating the concerns of building user interfaces from our core application.

Note that the architectural decisions made in a software system are typically the most important during the lifetime of that software system. Architecture is also as much of an art as a skill gained through experience. It is at least partially a stylistic aspect of software. With this said, we will try to lay out the various alternatives made available by commercial vendors and academics. You will need to make the appropriate decisions based on the requirements of the individual project.

1.5 Our Road Map

In this first chapter, we looked at the dimensions of mobility and the mobile condition. These two helped us understand the fundamental differences between designing a mobile application and a stationary application. Next, we surveyed some high level architectures. As we mentioned, much of what architectures do for us is to lay out a high-level plan of how the components of the system interact with each other and what the general properties of the system are. We will spend the rest of this text discussing the components: the nitty-gritty of how to make things work; but, we will come back to architectural issues periodically and examine how the components fit within the architecture.

To create mobile applications, we will need some tools. Section 1 of this text will give an introduction to those tools. In Chapter 2, we will look at some commercial and open-source frameworks and tools that ease the development process and show some different approaches to creating mobile applications. We will use these frameworks and tools to show examples in the later chapters. In Chapter 3, we will look at Extensible Markup Language (XML) and the nature of XML content. XML is an important piece of the puzzle in distribution of content to any device. In Chapter 4, we will look at UML, the tool we will use in modeling the design of our applications. Though not all mobile platforms use OOP technologies, most do. UML gives us an industry-accepted way of documenting requirements, design, and implementation of the system.

In the second section of this text, we will look at the problems of the user interface. Chapter 5 will show the reader how to separate concerns of particular user interfaces, such as graphical user interfaces, from the concerns shared by all types of user interfaces. In Chapter 6, we will see how to complement the generic user interfaces and render graphical user interfaces for a variety of visual text-driven devices such as PDAs and data-enabled cell phones. In Chapter 7, we will look at VUI (voice user interface) technologies such as voice recognition, text-to-speech technologies, voice transcription, and VoiceXML. At the end of Section 2, we will combine what we have learned in Chapters 5–7 and, in Chapter 8, we will see how to design user interfaces that interface with the user through multiple media types and multiple channels. This section will show us how to design the user interface components to fit the needs of the mobile user. It will also show us how to fit them within the mobile architecture of the system.

In the third section, we will look at a disparate set of topics, each relating to a dimension of mobility or an aspect of the mobile condition. We will start with examining mobile agent and mobile code architectures more closely. These architectures are often neglected in other texts. Because of their importance to mobile computing, we will pay special attention to them. We will then look at various wireless technologies as they are the prevalent means of connectivity for mobile applications; we will also look at the effect of wireless connectivity on architecture, protocols, and other aspects of design and implementation of a mobile system. The disconnected user needs data at the device even when disconnected; for this, we will need a discussion of data replication and synchronization design and implementation issues. We will move on to two key dimensions of mobility, location sensitivity and active transactions, how to incorporate such functionality into the design of the system, and how to implement functionality for some of the frameworks and tools talked about in Section 1. We will finish Section 3 by discussing mobile security issues.

In Section 4, we will see how to put all these aspects together to make a successful system. This section should be a great read for those project managers who want to know what to do differently for a mobile application. And there are plenty of differences, from the requirements-gathering process to testing. In this last section, we will also look at some typical "dos and don'ts" and a case study of implementation of some of the concepts introduced in this text.

It is important to keep in mind that this text is not a text on "how to implement the technology de jour." We are focused on issues of design and engineering that apply across tools. Specific implementations come and go. They evolve based on the demands of the market, economic situation, and many other factors. Though we will use examples from a variety of commercial and open-source specific implementations, we are focused on issues that apply to any and all specific implementations of mobile application platforms; we are concerned with design.

Let us now get started by looking at the tools and frameworks that are available today to create a mobile application.

CHAPTER 2

Introduction to Mobile Development Frameworks and Tools

The truth of the fact is easier to bear than the truth of the fantasy.

James Hillman

2.1 INTRODUCTION

At its most primitive level, software is a set of instructions for hardware written in machine language. At a higher level, there are assemblers and higher level programming languages. There are frameworks, tools, and other methods of abstracting various aspects of software design that help us achieve one central goal: to handle complexity of software more reliability and faster. The biggest problem with software design and implementation is complexity and it is this complexity that leads into buggy systems, high cost of development, and long development cycles, and the existence of programming languages, frameworks, and other development tools is primarily to solve this very problem of software complexity. In other words, as one of the most fundamental software design concepts, abstraction reduces complexity (at least theoretically).

Today, there are many programming languages, frameworks, and tools designed to develop server-based and desktop applications. These languages, frameworks, and tools have matured through the years, becoming more efficient and more reliable as they get tested in real environments by real users. Along with the maturation of these tools has come the maturation of the process of software design and implementation. Ideas such as OOP, design patterns, and de facto standard software development processes have been developed and have matured with the tools and frameworks in a symbiotic manner. So the question is whether we can take the same methodologies, frameworks, and tools and use them to develop mobile applications. And the answer, just as the answer to all of the other great questions in life, is "Yes and No!"

These notions of abstraction of various concerns in designing and implementing software have been mostly based on reducing the complexity of those systems with the most financial benefits: business systems being used by users of PCs, main frame systems, and other computing systems that require the user to sit in front of a monitor and type. For example, frameworks such as class libraries to write user interface code for Java (AWT, JFC, etc.) or C++ (MFC, Borland, etc.) are all designed around a user interface that allows for data entry through keyboard and mouse and displays information to the user through a monitor. Even at a more rudimentary level, most software is written for PCs and servers without regard to the power consumed by the system, the amount of storage available, and the variety of user interfaces. So, it is fair to say that most of the development tools and frameworks today are designed to facilitate writing software for stationary and non mobile systems.

With that said, though there are many aspects of mobile software design and implementation that are not addressed in today's frameworks and tools, there is much that mobile and stationary software applications share. For starters, most commercial software, whether it is mobile or not, is intended to be run on microprocessors. Developing for mobile or nonmobile applications includes similar processes of requirements gathering, design, implementation, and testing. But, we repeat the question, "Can we or can we not use the same methodologies, frameworks, and tools for mobile application development?"

The answer is more of a "Yes" as the software gets closer to the hardware and more of a "No" as it gets farther from the hardware. The frameworks that help us when writing software that is "closer" to the hardware such as compilers and assemblers focus on easing the process of programming granular tasks such as moving bits and bytes between memory locations and performing additions, subtractions, and multiplications; these are all very basic operations when looking at software applications from the bird's-eye view. However, high-level frameworks and tools such as user interface development tools (HTML, JFC, Visual Basic, etc.) and other component development tools (COM/DCOM, EJB, etc.) that try to solve high-level business logic problems do not lend themselves well to mobile application development. The layers of abstraction in most of today's frameworks and tools have been done with a strong bias toward developing software for stationary applications.

These tools do not take into account the concerns, mentioned in Chapter 1, that make mobile software development inherently different from software development for stationary systems. With this in mind, an entirely new market is expanding around developing software tools and frameworks for mobile application development. Most of what exists today is in the infancy stage; therefore, we can expect a significant amount of organic evolution in these frameworks and tools: The weak will die and the strong will evolve and improve. Nevertheless, we can start to see families of frameworks and tools as well as the features that create the taxonomy of this space. In this chapter, our focus will be on the feature sets and the taxonomy while using real tools and frameworks in the market today. The reader should focus on the concepts of the frameworks rather than the implementations. Although some will die and others will evolve, the reasons for their formulation, design concepts, and feature sets will remain applicable.

Frameworks and tools for mobile application development are evolving based on the growth of architectural techniques and innovations that accommodate the dimensions of mobility. Although the purpose of any significant tool and framework used in mobile application development should be to reduce the complexity of the mobile application, all tools, regardless of their implementations, attempt to address the same issues. However, depending on the architectures that each may support, their implementation and usage significantly vary. Therefore, it makes sense to create the taxonomy of these tools based on the architectures. Let us begin by looking at the frameworks and tools that address mobile application development in a fully centralized architecture.

2.2 Fully Centralized Frameworks and Tools

Developing fully centralized mobile applications differs from other fully centralized applications by virtue of QOS, limited power supply, active transactions, and location awareness (four of the dimensions of mobility mentioned in Chapter 1). Fully centralized mobile applications typically have custom-designed clients to perform specific tasks. So, the user interface on the devices used to access the centralized system is optimized to the task being performed. The software on such devices is typically embedded in nature and is designed to do only one thing. Also, because of this embedded nature of fully centralized mobile systems, resources of the device are not a concern in software development: The abilities of the client are known beforehand. Platform proliferation, once again for the same reason, is not a concern: Software systems in fully centralized mobile systems are all about the software on the fully centralized host; the client devices are dumb with little or no ability to perform dynamic computing tasks and what little software exists on them is embedded. Therefore, three of the dimensions of mobility—namely platform proliferation, limited device capabilities, and support for a variety of user interfaces—do not apply to fully centralized applications.

Location sensitivity, in most fully centralized systems, is achieved as an integral part of the network system or hardware-based location information on the client device (such as GPS modules). Call centers are a prime example of what *can* be a fully centralized mobile application. A cell phone user may call a call center to access the system. The call center may approximate the location of the user through receiving information from the cellular telephony system, from a GPS module on the cell phone communicating with the system through the same or different channel. (Circuit-switched phone calls carry only voice whereas packet-switched calls can contain multiple channels of data and voice.)

The application at the central host as well as the embedded software on the client must be designed with QOS issues in mind. Because all of the software on the device is embedded, the module handling the communications piece can be considered tightly coupled to the other modules on the client; therefore, taking into account that QOS issues become natural.

In summary, fully centralized mobile applications are about a monolithic layer of software from the client to the server with very little software on the client. What software resides on the client is typically embedded, or at least highly coupled to the device, in nature. Fully centralized mobile applications are the right solutions for applications that require little to no flexibility in changing the requirements of the client over the lifetime of the application and that have large development and deployment budgets allowing for custom-designed hardware and embedded software. Some good examples of such systems are battlefield systems used in determining the location of a target and sending it to a centralized system, which then relays it to another system responsible for launching a missile. Another good example is the kind of system used in grocery stores for inventory tracking as stock personnel track and refill the on-the-shelf inventory. In this case the mobile devices are customized to record information about groceries and relay them to some centralized inventory management system.

This is seldom the case in the world of commercial application development. If mobile applications are to be pervasive, the same agile economic models that surround the stationary applications on the PC and servers must succeed. Precisely for this reason, we will not spend much time dwelling on issues surrounding embedded software. For those interested, there are a variety of resources for embedded software development. Our focus in this text will be mobile applications that can be used on at least a small variety of devices and ones that do not require custom-designed hardware. With this said, let us look at *N*-tier client–server applications and the corresponding tools and frameworks.

2.3 *N*-Tier Client–Server Frameworks and Tools

As we discussed in Chapter 1, client–server architectures allow us to enable communication between two applications with one application acting as the server and the other acting as the client. For mobile applications, the server may have special needs, but it is typically powerful enough to run a wide range of applications. For mobile applications, there may be special logic that treats the dimensions of mobility. Client applications, in the case of mobile development, are typically those being run on mobile devices. Writing large applications for the devices to serve as the client is typically not possible, primarily because of the limited resources on the devices and the large variety of them. So, more often than not, mobile applications are distributed. The state of the art, as of the date of authoring this text, in proven distributed computing systems are the *N*-tier client–server architectures.

One of basic problems of application development that is magnified in mobile environments is code portability and mobility. The varieties of the so-called platforms (combination of hardware and operating systems) have prompted the creation of tools and frameworks such as Sun's Java Virtual Machine and Microsoft's Common Language Run-time. The primary goal of these tools is to give code more portability across platforms. The problem is magnified when considering the added factors that the variety of mobile devices dwarfs the variety among PC and server operating systems, that virtual machines tend to be large and require lots of memory and CPU cycles, and that, once more, they are designed primarily with the primary task of designing applications for stationary computing systems.

Here, there are two factors that are inherently opposite in nature. First, we need a layer of software, be it a virtual machine or otherwise, that abstracts us away from the specificity of hardware. This is the only practical way to write software rapidly for mobile systems. But then, as software layers are added, performance is hampered and system requirements go up. This tension between these diametrically opposed factors has given rise to the creation of numerous frameworks and tools for mobile application design. More than ever, selection of the frameworks and tools depends on the requirements of the application.

We can address this problem in three ways:

1. *Thin-Client Wireless Client–Server*: We can have some homogeneous browser specifications and implement the browsers for each device in a client–server environment. The browser can then load markup code and render it or even load plug-ins. This approach would be similar to the Web-model approach where the browsers are implemented for a variety of operating systems so that Web developers do not have to worry about the environment in which those browsers run. As we saw in Chapter 1, this would require a persistent and stable connection to the network and only allow for the lowest common denominator feature set among the various platforms and devices. So, at least today, this model is implemented by having different families of devices and platforms with one corresponding browser for each. We will look at various techniques for serving the right type of content to each type of browser. Such tools and techniques focus on building a server-side structure that serves up the right type of markup language to the browser that interprets it on the client. The Wireless Access Protocol (WAP) and its user interface markup language of WML give us a framework for building thin-client wireless applications with an *N*-tier client–server architecture.
2. *Thick-Client Wireless Client–Server*: The client application on the mobile device may be a custom application. If so, this thick client may communicate with the server, with the client executing some tasks and the server executing the others. Stationary client–server architectures using thick clients typically use the client as a means of storing a small subset of the data for use of the application when disconnected from the network and performing business logic that does not need to be centralized. Having thick clients for mobile devices is a bit more difficult. For one thing, as we have mentioned time and time again, mobile devices have very restricted resources. There are those who say that Moore's Law will eventually eliminate any practical restrictions that affect the application developer; however, there are other problems. There is the deployment and provisioning problem: How do you distribute software to such a wide range of

devices? How do you even write software for such a large variety of platforms? The platforms that allow thick-client development for mobile devices address this in two ways:

a. Some provide an operating system or a virtual machine that provides the application programmers with a platform that lessens the number of permutations for writing code. J2ME (Java 2 Micro Edition) allows this through a small virtual machine that sits on top of the hardware (or the operating system that is run on the hardware). Microsoft requires an installation of some flavor of Windows on the device (such as Windows CE) that allows the application programmer to write programs for Windows. Symbian also provides an operating system for mobile devices. Both Sun Microsystem's Java and Microsoft technologies, despite their differences, allow developers to create applications on top of an *operating environment*. These tools are typically products of software vendors who want to sell software and do not want to limit themselves to a given hardware platform.
b. Hardware manufacturers, such as Qualcomm and Texas Instruments, provide programming environments directly on top of hardware (ASIC, EEPROM, etc.). We will look at Qualcomm's BREW as an example of this.

Client–server architectures that rely on a thick client require a full-blown development platform for the device. Such platforms, however, may be used in environments other than just thick-client client-server-based systems. For example, we can use J2ME to build stand-alone applications for small mobile phones. Typically, many of the same programming environments that are used for building client applications on the devices for a client–server system are those same environments used to build applications for the devices in a peer-to-peer or mobile agent–based system. In the case of J2ME and Symbian for example, the development tools provided by the platforms can be used for building applications for a variety of architectures.

3. *Stand-alone Applications*: Lastly, we can build stand-alone applications for the devices using those same platforms that we mentioned for the thick-client client-server-based systems. The only difference here is that stand-alone applications do not really need networking components. For example, many of the first applications for the Palm operating system were only downloadable through the cradle that attaches the Palm to the serial port of the device. From there, you can download an application and run it with no network connectivity. Building stand-alone mobile applications is somewhat of a novelty as the mobile user needs to be able to at least synchronize the application with some external system periodically. There are few applications, such as stand-alone games, that just need to be downloaded and executed on the device.

But, in the mobile world, the manufacturer's of devices want to differentiate their hardware from their competitors. One way of doing this is by allowing the developers to write programs very specific to the device platforms in platform-specific languages such as C or C++, as in the case of BREW and BREW-like environments.

Figure 2.1 shows some of the more popular platforms at the date of authoring this text and their ability to provide functionality based on connectivity to the

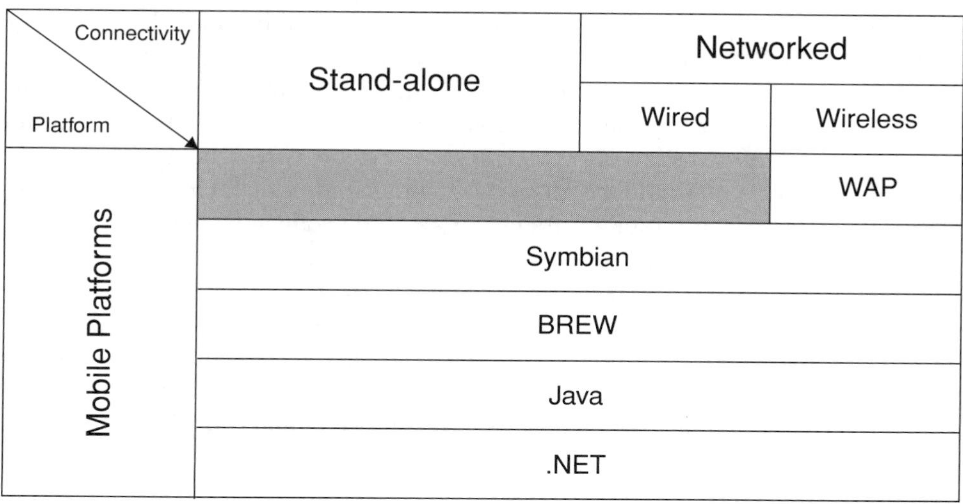

Figure 2.1. Some Products in Various Categories of *N*-Tier Client–Server Frameworks and Solutions.

network. Today's popular operating systems allow applications to be written without a lot of low-level programming to access hardware. They also allow multiple applications to use the same hardware simultaneously and have standard functionality such as accessing permanent storage (such as disk IO), volatile storage (such as RAM), and interface peripherals such as the monitor and the keyboard. But, traditional operating systems are typically large and take up considerable permanent storage. They also typically require quite a bit of volatile storage to get started. For this reason, embedded software development will always be around. Platforms such as Qualcomm's BREW present another alternative in writing applications for the device. Developing in such environments as BREW represents the opposite end of the spectrum to Java: The applications are written specifically for a given hardware platform without the traditional notion of the operating system. Such platforms as BREW allow for developing software that is optimized for a "chip set" or specific hardware. The code is then compiled and then "burned" onto the device. Depending on the type of hardware used, this "burning" process can be repeated *n* times. Because these types of tools and frameworks are specific to the device itself, they focus on solving the problem of writing applications for devices. So, the problem of transporting data back and forth between the network and these devices as well as transforming them to the proper formats used by each type of device remains unsolved.

There is yet another family of tools and frameworks written to handle processing of data on the server and communicating with a wide variety of devices. Typical tasks solved by these tools include support for messaging as a means of asynchronous communication; support for HTTP or a similar protocol as a means of synchronous communication; and the ability to transform different types of XML by accommodating some complex set of rules that include workflow, device-type recognition, and multichannel rendering of content. Apache's Cocoon project and IBM's Wireless Transcoding Publisher are examples of frameworks that try to fulfill some of these goals.

Whereas Java offers an open and relatively mature environment to program in the same language on any platform, Microsoft is trying to take advantage of its large lead in the software development market to extend its technologies to include application development tools with its .NET and Windows CE technologies. Java allows the developer to program in Java and run the code anywhere. In contrast, .NET promises to allow the developer to program in any language and run it on any .NET-based environment (various Microsoft Windows family of products). Of course, this means that any device running the applications written using the CLR (Common Language Runtime) has to run an operating system that supports that CLR. Such operating systems are limited to the Windows family of operating systems. So, although Java is language bound and *cross-platform*, .NET is platform bound and *cross-language*.

2.3.1 Mobile Operating Systems and Virtual Machines

Although Java tries to solve the proliferation problem by making the code portable between different platforms, there are other plausible approaches. One of these approaches is to create tools that make the applications native to one platform. Microsoft's .NET framework deploys such a strategy. The tools provided by the .NET framework allow the programmer to develop the application in a variety of languages supported by the framework. The individual applications are then compiled to code that can be executed on the same platform. Microsoft's creation of the .NET platform is spurred by economic reasons, namely to keep Windows as the dominant computer operating system. However, this does not imply that the tools provided by the .NET framework are either superior or inferior. It is simply a different technical approach whose merit should be judged by the implementing developers and the users of applications that use this platform.

The principal technical difference between the .NET and Java approaches is that .NET generalizes by operating system and Java generalizes by programming language. So, with .NET, every device, be it a PC or any other type of computing device, is required to run some flavor of Microsoft Windows as its operating system.

Something important to remember as we go through various tools is that developing applications for mobile devices typically involves use of an emulator provided by the platform or device manufacturer. In this way, the unit testing and quality control of mobile applications differs from that of stationary applications: Everything is typically finished and tested on the emulator first and, then, tested on the actual device.

2.3.2 Hardware-Specific Tools and Frameworks

One way to deal with device proliferation is to avoid it! Device manufacturers can allow the application programmers to develop code that directly takes advantage of the device features and functionality. The notion of an operating system, in such case, is much different than what we typically think of as an operating system. The services offered by the operating system are few and very low level. The downside here is a tight coupling to a platform that, in turn, can translate to heavy reliance on the manufacturer of that platform. This is the approach that Qualcomm offers in its BREW platform. BREW is a framework designed to allow application developers program applications for devices based on Qualcomm's CDMA technology. We will look at CDMA further in Chapter 9. It is a physical layer communication protocol that offers very efficient use of the bandwidth available in a segment of the spectrum.

In this chapter, we will address the development tools and frameworks in a client-server context. In Chapter 9, we will look at some mobile agent tools as well as seeing how the tools that we look at in this chapter apply to mobile-agent architectures. We will look at the various families of frameworks and tools that may be used to develop mobile software applications and some commercial platforms that fall into each family. We will select the most common environment as opposed to the most elegant environments. There are many reasons for this, the most obvious of which is that the commercial success of products, often, does not have a direct relationship with the elegance of the technical solution. Also, as engineers, we often have to select popular platforms to build systems for economic and other business reasons. Once we have selected our frameworks and tool sets, we will use them, later on in the book, to develop sample applications.

Let us start with Java, as it is today's most popular application development programming environment.

2.4 Java

Today, it is widely accepted that Java as a programming language offers the most portable commercial environment for writing software applications. The success of Java has been mostly in providing standard Application Program Interfaces (APIs), a very thoughtfully designed infrastructure for OOP that prohibits many bad design and implementation habits such as multiple inheritance. Standard and open APIs offer a process of evolving a language that is open to many vendors. Furthermore, there exist implementations of the virtual machine and the native dependencies of the APIs for most popular operating systems. There are three major categories of Java APIs and virtual machines, namely J2ME, J2SE, and J2EE.

Java offers three distinct features as a mobile application platform:

1. Java is an object oriented programming language. As any other programming language, it can be used to write applications.
2. Java offers complete code mobility and weak mobile agent ability. Java allows for platform-independent programming.
3. Java is a platform.

We will assume that the reader has at least an understanding of what Java is as a programming language and will discuss the code mobility aspects of Java further in Chapter 9.

First, Java, as with any other programming language, is just that: a programming language. It allows us to program a set of instructions. Perhaps just as importantly,

Java is somewhat of a *vendor-neutral language-based platform*." Java seems to have solved the problem that has plagued many other programming languages in the past: the lack of standardizing libraries. With C++ and many of the other programming languages, one of the biggest problems has been the lack of industry-wide standards in APIs, components, and tools. Different vendors have offered similar components and frameworks with no uniformity among them in their APIs and interfaces. Vendors have done this to differentiate their products; however, this forces developers to rewrite code when moving from one component set or framework to another or even to completely redo the architecture of the system. Java has solved this problem by enforcing standard API interfaces to the components and frameworks and allowing for vendors to compete on the basis of the implementation of the APIs. For example, Java Database Connectivity (JDBC) APIs present the same interface to the developers regardless of what database is being used

Java, as a platform and programming language, offers mobile code. But, the standard Java Virtual Machine was designed for desktop computers and requires far too many resources for the typical cell phone, PDA, or mobile device. The standard Java Virtual Machine is packaged, along with accompanying tools and class libraries, into Java 2 Standard Edition (J2SE). A smaller version of the virtual machine, along with a subset of classes and tools of J2SE plus a few additional tools, forms J2ME designed for small devices.

2.4.1 J2ME

J2ME is a specification for a virtual machine and some accompanying tools for resource-limited devices. J2ME specifically addresses those devices that have between 32 kB and 10 MB of memory. J2ME addresses the needs of two categories of devices [Sun Micro J2ME Spec 2000]:

1. *Personal, mobile, connected information devices.* This portion of J2ME is called CLDC for Connected, Limited Device Configuration. These types of devices include cell phones, PDAs, and other small consumer devices. CLDC addresses the needs of devices with 32 to 512 kB of memory. The virtual machine for the CLDC is called KVM for K-Virtual Machine.
2. *Shared, fixed, connected information devices.* Internet-enabled appliances, mobile computers installed in cars, and similar systems that have a total memory of 2 to 16 MB and can have a high bandwidth and continuous connection to the network are in this group. CDC, or Connected Device Configuration, is the part of J2ME that addresses such devices. CDC is a superset of CLDC.

Let us look at both CDC and CLDC and how we can use them to develop mobile applications.

CLDC and MIDP

Figure 2.2 shows how J2ME components, and other parts of Java as a platform, stack up. Figure 2.3 shows the breakdown of the J2ME MID Profile stack. As we mentioned previously, CLDC is mainly intended for devices that are

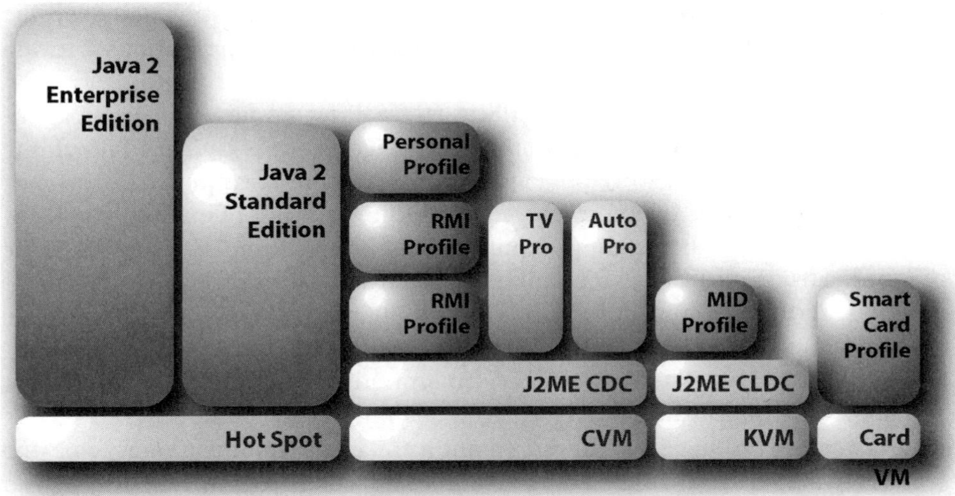

FIGURE 2.2. J2ME Stack (CLDC/CDC and MIDP).

resource-starved such as mobile phones and PDAs. CLDC addresses the following features:

1. *Providing a virtual machine for providing language features.* Perhaps the most important thing to keep in mind for those who have built applications using the Java Virtual Machine on desktops and servers is that the J2ME/CLDC Virtual Machine is not at all like the version that comes with J2SE. To cut down on the required resources for running it, the KVM does not provide many of the advanced features that the J2SE Virtual Machine does. The KVM is based on the Spotless project, which started at Sun Labs. The KVM takes up anywhere from 40 to 80 kB depending on the device. The KVM is written in C (as are most other Java Virtual Machines). Some features not offered on the KVM are the following:
   a. *Floating point arithmetic*: Floating point operations are expensive or require the chipset on the device to have specific implementations for them. Many of

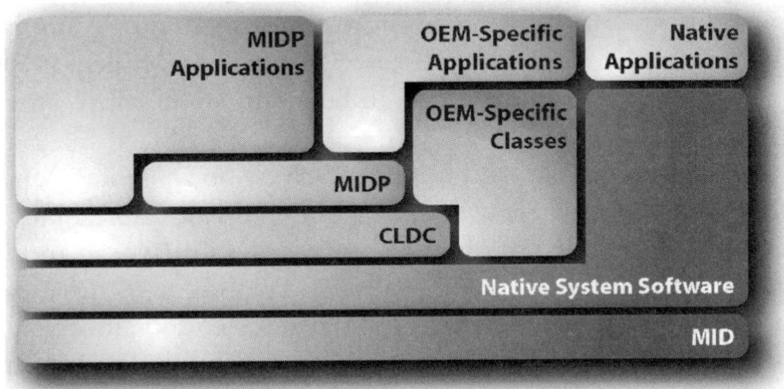

FIGURE 2.3. Layering of Functionality between CLDC and MIDP.

the resource-starved mobile devices either do not have floating point specific features on the chip set or do not expose them for use by applications software running on the device.

b. *Support for JNI*: Java Native Interfaces (JNI) allow developers to write applications that use C/C++ programming languages along with Java in providing Java APIs to modules or applications not written in Java.
c. *Thread grouping*: Advanced threading features are not offered on the KVM and CLDC. Multithreading requires a baseline amount of resources to be dedicated to creating, maintaining, and destroying threads. Each thread takes up a certain amount of resources by simply existing, even if it never does any actual work. Because the KVM is intended for resource-starved devices, it is natural to assume that doing lots of advanced multithreading is not something that makes much sense on such devices.
d. *Full-blown exception handling*: Exception and error handling seems to be one of the first places that platform providers trim when building frameworks and tools for limited devices. Although this makes more work for the application developer, it allows the framework and the applications to be linear.
e. *Automatic garbage collection of unused objects*: Though the KVM does offer some of the memory management features of the J2SE Virtual Machine, it does not offer *finalization* of objects. This means that you have to tell the KVM when you are done with an object. The KVM is not capable of finalizing based on the scope of methods, etc.
f. *Weak references*: An object is said to be weakly referenced if it is necessary to traverse the object that refers to it to reach it. The J2SE Virtual Machine does not allow finalization of an object until all weak and strong references to that object are cleared. The KVM does not provide this functionality for weakly referenced objects. The elimination of weak references and finalization in the KVM make programming for the KVM more like writing C and C++ applications than writing a typical J2SE application. Much of the automatic memory management benefits of Java are in its ability to manage memory based on weak references and to automatically finalize. These features have been eliminated to shrink the virtual machine. Although they allow the applications to be faster, the static size of the applications grow as memory management is more manual and there is a higher probability for typical C/C++ memory management type bugs in the applications. This is not to imply that there is no garbage collection. Indeed, there is a garbage collector in the KVM. However, the garbage collector has to be manually notified when to discard objects.

2. *Providing a security framework for tasks such as downloading MIDlets (J2ME CLDC/MIDP applications)*. Security is one of the most troublesome and complicated features for providers of mobile application frameworks and tools. J2ME builds on the experiences of Java applets in creating a security paradigm for mobile applications. It should be noted that CLDC does not provide the full J2SE security model, though it does provide enough low-level virtual-machine security to guarantee that the application can not harm the device in any way.

It also provides a sandbox model, though it is different than the J2SE sandbox model.

The security sandbox of CLDC is provided by removing the ability to write JNI code to access native functions on the device, providing a very limited set of APIs (which we will look at next), taking away the ability to write custom classloaders (there are no custom classloaders in CLDC), and a class file verification process that assures that the files called to be executed are Java class files. The verification of a class file is also different from its counterpart in J2SE. CLDC class file verification is a two-step process that offloads some of the task of verification from the device. The CLDC verifier needs about 10 kB to execute. But, because of the offloading of some of the verification process from run-time, the size of the class files is slightly larger (about 5%).

3. *Providing a reasonable amount of functionality for input and output.* Most programs need a persistence mechanism. CLDC provides a very limited and yet sufficient set of APIs to read and write to the nonvolatile memory provided by devices. It should be noted that the persistence of data on the device is hardware dependent.
4. *Providing some internationalization capabilities.* CLDC's input/output (I/O) package (see the next section) provides input and output stream readers that can handle different character encoding schemes. This allows internationalization in two ways:
   a. *Dynamic*: The program can determine the required character set dynamically and use the proper character set at run time. Programmatically, this is the more elegant option. However, it requires additional code to implement the rules for discovery of the required character set. This approach works well for small applications where the device resources are not taken to their limit.
   b. *Static*: There can be multiple versions of the J2ME application ready to be loaded onto the device. Provisioning of the application can take care of the version of software that is distributed to the application. Though this approach is less elegant, both the amount of code downloaded by the device and the amount of logic executed at run time can be reduced. The flexibility of having different character sets for the same device is still available as different versions of the application are available for download on the network.
5. *Providing a reasonable amount of networking capabilities.* CLDC provides a connection framework to provide basic networking capabilities. Profiles such as MIDP build on top of this framework and can introduce more advanced networking capabilities.

As we saw, there are some features whose support was eliminated to shrink the CLDC to a manageable size on the device. Some features have been intentionally left out to be handled by "profiles" that are built on top of the CLDC. Profiles address features that can be addressed, in the same manner, for a group of devices but whose implementations vary because of the differences among those devices. The best example of a feature set falling into a profile is the user interface capabilities. Because various devices have different methods of entering data, different screen sizes, etc., the best place for the user interface functionality is in the profile. The areas addressed by profiles are the following:

1. download and installation of applications,
2. life-cycle management of applications,
3. user interface feature,
4. database functionality, and
5. event handling.

The Mobile Information Device Profile (MIDP) is currently the only widely known and accepted CLDC profile. There are other profiles, such as Personal Digital Assistant Profile (PDAP) designed for PDAs (typically assumed to have more memory, processing power, and other resources than MIDs), that extend CLDC. MIDP is designed for devices that are assumed to have the following characteristics:

1. Small displays of approximately 96 × 24 of 1:1 shaped pixels with a depth of 1 bit.
2. A minimum of 128 kB of nonvolatile memory (for storing information that is not lost when the device is shut off and turned back on). This is mainly intended for storing the application itself.
3. Wireless connection to the network (with all of the implications of what wireless connectivity is at the time this text is being written: low-bandwidth, intermittent connectivity, no standard protocol such as TCP/IP, etc.).
4. A minimum of 8 kB of nonvolatile memory for use by the application. This 8 kB refers to information that the application should be allowed to store on the device.
5. An ITU-T phone keypad (this is the standard alphabet mapping to the ten digits on a phone keypad) or a QWERTY keyboard (such as those available on Palm, RIM, or Handspring devices).

Now, let us quickly look at the Java APIs for CLDC and MIDP so that we can write a simple application.

Overview of the CLDC and MIDP Java APIs

There is a core set of APIs that every implementer of CLDC (device manufacturers and hardware integrators) must implement. These APIs fall within two groups:

1. J2SE-like APIs: There are three packages, namely java.lang.*, java.io.*, and java.util.*, that are inherited from the J2SE environment. It is important to note that only a small subset of the classes available with J2SE in each package is available for CLDC. Also, those classes available in these packages are not identical to their J2SE counterparts in interface or implementation (though the designers have done their best to keep the interfaces as similar as possible to ease the task of porting).
2. CLDC-specific APIs: In the current version of CLDC (1.0.2) a small set of classes provides I/O and networking capabilities particularly needed by small and mobile devices. The package holding these classes is javax.microedition.io. The

main class that the J2ME application developers must familiarize themselves with is the *connector* class. J2SE networking facilities assume the availability of a TCP/IP connection. Obviously, this assumption is not a valid one for mobile applications as a variety of communication protocols and schemes may be used to allow the device to communicate with the network. So, CLDC defines a connection framework in its Java API, providing a method for various network providers, device manufacturers, and protocol designers to offer the application developers options other than TCP/IP for communicating with the network. For example, it is possible that a vendor provides WAP-style connections (WDP/UDP) that can be invoked by CLDC connection objects by passing the right parameters to it. An example could be the following:

```
Connection c = Connector.open("http://www.cienecs.com");
```

As we mentioned previously, MIDP builds on the top of CLDC to offer the functionality required to build a real application. Let us review the MIDP APIs quickly.

1. *Timers*: Two classes, java.util.Timer and java.util.TimerTask, allow developers to write MIDlets that are started, one time or at some specified interval, at a given time.
2. *Networking*: Whereas CLDC provides a generic connection framework that can be built upon by the device manufacturers and network providers, MIDP provides HTTP implementation, a high-level application networking protocol, that hides the lower layer implementation of networking between the device and the network (TCP/IP, WAP, etc.). The javax.microedition.io.* package holds the lone class of HttpConnection that allows connecting to network resources through HTTP.
3. *Storage*: javax.microedition.rms.* (where rms stands for record management system) provides a very simple API for storing and retrieving data. The query capabilities provided by this package, though extremely rudimentary, are invaluable as they provide the basics of database-like access to nonvolatile persistence on the device.
4. *User Interface*: javax.microedition.lcdui.* offers a set of rudimentary user interface APIs to build interfaces for MIDlets. Like the storage package, the user interface package is very simple. However, it accomplishes much by offering an interface that is fairly generic, leaving the mapping of the interface to the implementation to the MIDP implementers. This increases the portability by allowing authoring of user interfaces without worrying about a great amount of detail on the implementation of MIDP on a particular device (though it still does not mean perfect portability).

Now, let us look at a simple J2ME/CLDC application.

Hello MIDP

CLDC applications only make sense as an application of a profile. Because the user interface of the J2ME application is reserved for the profiles, writing a CLDC Hello

World application really does not make that much sense. The profile of choice for our example, obviously, will be MIDP. Applications for MIDs (Mobile Information Devices) are appropriately called MIDlets (like their counterparts of server-side applications, which are called servlets, small browser-based applications called applets, etc.).

As in applets and servlets, MIDlets are treated as components controlled by a framework under the inversion of the control principle to which we refer to frequently in this book. For a J2ME class to qualify as a MIDlet, it has to do the following:

1. Extend the MIDlet class.
2. Implement the following methods:
   a. startApp(): This method gets called after the class is instantiated. Think of this like the run() method of a thread in Java.
   b. pauseApp(): This method is called if the application has to be suspended for some reason. Suspension of the application can be required for power saving, an incoming phone call, or a series of other reasons.
   c. destroyApp(boolean b): This is used to do any maintenance necessary before the application is discarded. This method is necessary mainly because finalization and weak references are not available in J2ME. (It can be used for release of other resources as well depending on the type of the application.)

Figure 2.4 shows a simple MIDP application that simply shows a message on the screen and allows the user to exit the application.

A variety of vendors, such as Borland and Sun, offer J2ME development tools. Sun Microsystems has a free tool kit that offers the following components for development of J2ME applications:

1. *KToolbar*: This is the overtool that provides a GUI to manage collecting the classes that are put into the MIDlet, any name-value property sets that are used by the classes, and any resources such as icons used by the MIDlet. It also provides GUI control over build and bundling of the MIDlet into a deliverable package to the device.
2. *Preverifier*: As we mentioned previously, preverification of classes allows J2ME to offload some work from the device.
3. *Compiler*: The J2ME compiler compiles the classes. Remember that J2ME classes need to be preverified before they are ready to be used.
4. *Emulators*: There is a series of emulators that ship with any development kit. Mobile device and mobile software vendors provide other emulators for J2ME.
5. *Emulation of Performance*: The Preferences tool allows the developers to adjust for the virtual machine proficiency, network performance, storage monitoring, and network traffic monitoring. These features have only been available in the latest version of the tool kit. Though they may seem secondary, they actually provide a huge leap over the previous versions of the tool as, for the first time, some of the dimensions of mobility are treated within the tool kit. These are namely limited devices resources and QOS.

```
import javax.microedition.midlet.*;
import javax.midroedition.lcdui.*;

public class HelloMIDP extends MIDlet implements
  CommandListenter {

    public static final String HELLO = "Hello MIDP";

    private Display mDisplay;
    private Command mExit;

    public HelloMIDP() {
        mDisplay = Display.getDisplay(this);
        mExit = new Command("Exit", Command.SCREEN, 1);
    }

    public void startApp() {
        TextBox myMessage = new TextBox(HELLO, HELLO, 256, 0);
        myMessage.addCommand(mExit);
        myMessage.addCommand((CommandListener) this);
        mDisplay.setCurrent(mDisplay);
    }

    public void pauseApp() {
        //Our application is very simple and does not really
        //require any manual finalization or other actions if
        //the application is suspended. The implementation of
        //this method is not trivial for more complicated
        //applications.
    }

    public void commandAction(Command aCommand, Displayable
      aDisplayHandle) {
        if (aCommand == mExit) {
            destroyApp(false);
        }
    }

    public void destroyApp(boolean b) {
        notifyDestroyed();
    }
    }
}
```

FIGURE 2.4. Hello MIDP.

Though the Java community is working on it, unfortunately, J2ME still does not treat multimodal user interfaces and location sensitivity at all. These are two dimensions of mobility that have gone nearly completely neglected in J2ME.

Using the KToolbar to generate an application is fairly intuitive once you have your source code in. Tools such as Borland's JBuilder and Websphere Anywhere Suite offer editors specially customized for J2ME code. Once the code is compiled, you will run a *.jad file in one of the emulators. The *.jad files encapsulate information about MIDlets.

To deploy a J2ME application, everything is bundled into a JAR file. A JAR file can have one or more MIDlets (classes that inherit from the MIDlet class and implement the appropriate methods). The JAR manifest file (a text file that specifies the classes that are in the JAR file along with some attributes for those classes) is used by the MIDP environment (implemented by the J2ME device) to recognize and install the applications. There are a set of required attributes in the manifest file needed for the environment to run an application. The J2ME tool kit provides a GUI to create the attributes. Although the JAR manifest contains a set of attributes for all of the MIDlets in the JAR, there is a JAD file for every MIDlet. The JAD file acts as an application descriptor. The JAD file must have the name, version, vendor, JAR URL, and JAR size of a MIDlet. It may contain other information such as a description and an icon.

Treatment of Dimensions of Mobility by CLDC and Profiles

Because of the way profiles are layered on the top of CLDC, dimensions of mobility are treated in a peculiar way. Let us look at the dimensions individually.

1. *Location Awareness*: To date, there is no treatment of location awareness in J2ME. However, this is being treated. JSR 179, Location API for J2ME is defining an optional package to build on top of CLDC version 1.1 and higher. This JSR is intended to work with various positioning methodologies such as GPS or cell-based triangulation; however, it is explicitly intended to hide the implementation, and complexities thereof, of the positioning system. Therefore, the API will be agnostic to the method of finding the location. Currently, the package name is proposed to be javax.microedition.location.
2. *Network QOS*: During the development, as we mentioned earlier, various development tools offer emulation of QOS conditions for wireless devices. J2ME's connection framework addresses this issue, in an extremely elegant manner, after deployment of the application on the device. Because the connection framework is able to create any type of connection, network providers and device vendors can provide their own APIs on the device. The connection framework also provides the flexibility to use datagrams of various protocols such as WAP. Obviously, standard connections of TCP/IP and HTTP are available as well.
3. *Limited Device Capabilities*: KVM takes away large chunks of functionality, which is helpful but not necessary, for development of applications to shrink the size of the virtual machine. This was obviously done with limited device capabilities in mind. The tools provided with the J2ME tool kit also provide settings to emulate the behavior of the limited device such as a setting that allows one

to account for the performance of the virtual machine (KVM) on the various devices.

4. *Limited Power Supply Management*: This is one of the areas left virtually untreated by J2ME. But, this lack of treatment seems to be common throughout the application development platforms. Next-generation mobile platforms and tools will include intuitive techniques to take into account the power supply levels, at run time, to optimize the use and performance of the application.
5. *Support for a Large Variety of User Interfaces*: Though J2ME takes into account the variations in simple graphical user interfaces in CLDC/MIDP, there are no parts of that to treat multichannel user interfaces (e.g., mixtures of audio, video, text, etc. for input and output to the system). This lack of treatment of voice and other nontextual channels exists in both development and deployment environments.
6. *Platform Proliferation*: By allowing one to select from a different sets of emulators, J2ME provides fair support, at least in CLDC/MIDP stack, for developing applications for various devices. In its architectural design, by breaking down various devices into families of devices supported by CDC, CLDC, etc. and creation of layers such as MIDP, J2ME is perhaps the most well designed application development framework in treating platform proliferation. Furthermore, though we do not address various embedded Java technologies outside of J2ME in any considerable depth, Java, as a platform, offers the most comprehensive treatment of the variation of hosts for software applications.
7. *Active Transactions*: Because CLDC/MIDP applications are components run by a virtual machine and within a tightly controlled sandbox, writing an active application is a difficult task. The components do not control their own life cycles (they are controlled by a state machine that calls predefined methods depending on the events that are sent to it), thereby making J2ME applications inherently passive. It is possible to achieve a limited amount of active behavior by polling. Supporting active transactions (sometimes referred to as *push* if it is between two different hosts on a network) is something that the Java community is actively discussing.

Overall, J2ME offers a very good treatment of dimensions of mobility. Although some aspects are currently neglected, the Java community is continually working on treating them. Though it may take a long time, it is comforting to know that they will eventually treat each dimension and that the treatment will be vendor neutral, creating an environment of competition where new products will flourish and the better products will survive.

XML and J2ME

XML is the document format of choice when it comes to ubiquitous applications; we will look at this and related XML issues in detail in the next chapter. However XML is not only text, but it also requires considerable horse power to parse it. Although XML-based technologies such as XML-based Web services are ideal for providing ubiquitous content for mobile devices, they are tremendously troublesome for a resource-starved platform that has to save every bit of memory and every cycle of CPU.

As you have noticed in our discussion of CLDC and the profiles that accompany it, there is currently no special treatment of XML (though such are being discussed at the time of writing this text in the Java community). There are three types of parsers [Knudsen 2002]:

1. *Model Parsers*: These parsers go through the entire XML document and create some representation of the document in a programmatic model. DOM (Document Object Model) parsers are model parsers. Model parsers use considerable memory and processing power because, regardless of what you need out of the XML document, the entire document is parsed and represented in some other format in memory.
2. *Push Parsers*: These parsers emit events as they parse through the document. Once again, they go through the entire document; however, the advantage they offer over the model parsers is that they do not keep a representation of the document in memory.
3. *Pull Parsers*: Pull parsers do not go through the entire document. Rather, they leave the control on how much of the document is parsed to the client.

Selecting the parser is somewhat of a balancing act that often requires some knowledge of the average and maximum size of documents. The application always knows what information it needs from the document. Putting together what needs to be extracted from the document, the typical size of the document, and the size of the application depending on the parser used tells us what the best fit for our need is. For example, whereas pull parsers are typically larger in size (kXML is a pull parser for CLDC/MIDP), they have a simple interface allowing for a small application to do all the necessary work without taking up a lot of memory to store the entire document. This works well for scenarios involving larger documents and straightforward data extraction from XML. However, if the documents are going to be small, the cost of storing them in memory is less, so a smaller model or push parser does the job effectively.

We will have some samples later in this text that parse XML on the device with J2ME.

Using UML to Model J2ME Applications

As we mentioned in Chapter 1, one of our objectives in this text is to tie the entire development cycle into UML and use it as a tool to facilitate the development process. Java and UML have been married during their evolution. As part of the Java platform, it is natural that we think about modeling J2ME applications with UML.

There are two aspects to modeling J2ME applications with UML. First, J2ME applications have a great deal in common with all other Java applications: They are written in Java, which is an object-oriented language. UML is designed to model object-oriented languages. Second, there are features of desktop and server-side virtual machines (e.g., J2SE Virtual Machine) that are not available in J2ME, such as finalization and weak references. The elimination of these features forces the developer to take care of some tasks manually. Most Java developers are not used to managing memory semimanually or worrying about weak references; therefore, UML gives us a great visual tool to track down weak references, make sure objects are finalized in a proper way, etc.

Let us enumerate the various uses of UML in a J2ME application:

1. *Class Diagrams*: As with any other Java application, we can model the classes and the relationships among them with UML class diagrams. The class diagrams present us with an invaluable tool to see where weak references may be. To do this, however, we need to be very explicit in specifying association types and life-cycle controls within our UML diagrams. When it comes to modeling J2ME classes with UML class diagrams, the more detail, the better. J2ME applications are typically not very large (remember the resource restrictions), so a significant amount of detail added to the class diagram does not create an unmanageable situation.
2. *State Diagrams*: State diagrams can be used in representing the life cycles of the various objects. With J2ME, having numerous state diagrams can be invaluable in giving developers a visual tool to analyze the life cycle of various objects that may need to be finalized and to reveal bugs that are caused by the lack of support for weak references. State diagrams can also be used to represent the effect of various events. Because CLDC applications, and most other J2ME applications, are components used in an environment of inversion of control, the driver component (for example the MIDlet) implements a particular set of methods and/or inherits from some class with some default behavior. State diagrams can help in clarifying the behavior of the components as various events, driven by the user interface or otherwise, change the state of objects.
3. *Component Diagrams*: Though most J2ME applications are fairly small, component diagrams can come in handy too. One of the techniques used in creating multifunction J2ME applications is to divide them into smaller applications, each represented by a component in a component diagram, and to make the user interface hide the disparateness of the small applications, disguising them as one large application.
4. *Sequence Diagrams*: As we will see in later chapters, these diagrams can be extremely useful in representing user interfaces. The profile layer (MIDP) encapsulates the user interface implementation, and the MIDP APIs are designed in such a way that user interface actions are specified generically and the specific functionality is delegated to the MIDP implementation. Because of these features, sequence diagrams help in documenting the exact various interactions on various implementations on MIDP on devices that are all CLDC/MIDP compliant but vary slightly in specifics such as the number of buttons on the keypad, extra buttons, the number of lines on the screen, etc.

We will discuss using UML for various parts of the development process of mobile applications throughout this text. Keep in mind that UML is a general tool and its use can be subjective when applied to specific things like various APIs and platforms.

2.4.2 CDC

We have looked at CLDC, one of the two parts of J2ME intended for devices (Java Card and other embedded technologies being somewhat tangent to our discussions). The other part of J2ME is CDC, which is targeted at environments, where more than 512 kB (usually about 2 MB) of memory is available for the Java environment and the application [Laukkanen 2002]. Whereas CLDC can have a variety of profiles built on top of it, CDC profiles are built on top of the so-called Foundation Profile. Like CLDC's KVM, the CDC has its own virtual machine, the CVM (C Virtual Machine).

Unlike the KVM, the CVM supports all of the features that the J2SE Virtual Machine does. The CDC is smaller than J2SE by the virtue of its lack of many of the class libraries that are shipped with J2SE. The CVM also offers some changes to improve performance on resource-starved devices. These include lower memory usage (about 60% less than the J2SE virtual machine), an extensible CVM architecture (to add functionality), and a design that accommodates real-time operating systems (RTOSs). Because the CVM has been implemented mostly in C, it can be ported to, and between, real-time operating systems easily. (The more assembly-level code exists in the implementation of a software application, the more difficult it becomes to port to, and between, RTOSs because assembly code is specific to platforms—hardware and operating system combinations).

The most significant classes eliminated from the CDC/Foundation Profile are the GUI classes. To date, CDC implementations exist for several handheld operating systems, including Windows CE, Linux, and Symbian.

In his paper [Laukkanen 2002] Laukkanen looks at the performance aspects of CDC versus J2SE under a variety of conditions. For those planning on implementing CDC applications, this paper is a must read. Laukkanen's testing results show that although CDC performs nearly as advertised with smaller applications (fewer objects, threads, etc.), as the application gets larger, it begins to underperform. Keep in mind, though, that in a resource-starved mobile device, we should not have large applications anyway. Although CDC minimizes the use of memory resources, as Laukkanen puts it, "the fact is that without Foundation Profile, the CDC is quite useless." This is because the architecture of CDC simply modularizes the functionality of J2SE into multiple profiles, allowing the vendors and application developers to only use the part of the Java platform that they need while still having the full functionality of a full-blown Java Virtual Machine in CVM.

We will not be using CDC-based examples in this text. Although CDC increases in its relevancy to mobile application development because of the increasing resources on the mobile devices, the programming paradigm of CDC is not much different than that of J2SE. So, writing CDC-based J2ME applications is much the same as writing any J2SE application. Also, there is no special treatment of dimensions of mobility in CDC as, to date, it is mostly used for network appliances (e.g., TVs) that are always connected and fairly stationary (though this does not

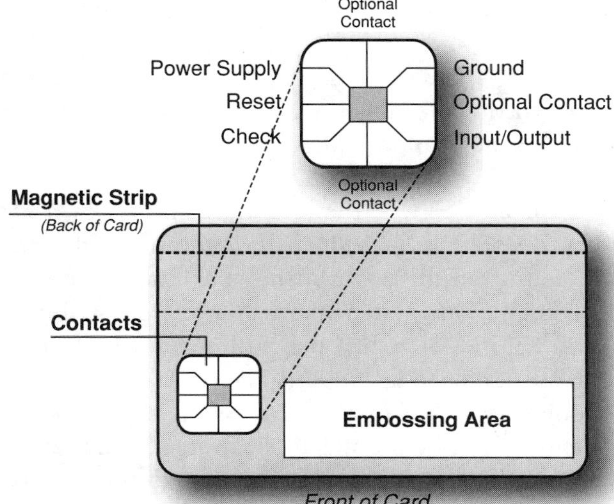

FIGURE 2.5. Java Card.

mean that CDC has any limitations that prohibit it from being used for mobile applications).

2.4.3 Java Card

Smart cards have been around for a long time. A smart card is a card that has an embedded processor or some type of electronic memory device able to store data, interface with some known set of devices, and allow the stored data to be retrieved. Most smart card technology, prior to Java Card, has been based on proprietary technologies. So, interoperability between different cards and card readers/writers has only been possible if the manufacturer of the card or the reader/writer offers an open API and the counterpart implements that open API. Obviously, with every manufacturer having its own API, managing smart cards and their readers/writers has been one of the most technically challenging tasks in creating smart cards. It has also created economic scaling problems in using smart cards across different businesses, locations, languages, etc.

The Java Card (Figure 2.5) specification is designed to solve these two problems. The Java Card API provides an API that, when abided by, allows for interoperability between different card readers/writers and cards regardless of the manufacturer and Java Card API implementer.

Today, there are three types of smart cards [Ruuskanen 2000]:

1. *IC (Integrated Circuit) Memory Cards*: This is the most common type of smart card. These types of cards hold a small amount of data (less than 4 kB) and have no processing power. These cards are used as debit cards, security cards, and others.
2. *IC Microprocessor Cards*: These cards typically have 16 kB or less of read-only memory and half of kilobyte of random-access memory. Java Card falls into this family. These types of cards provide a very small amount of processing power

that can be used for things like encryption and decryption of the user profile information on the card.

3. *Optical Memory Cards*: These cards provide the largest amount of storage of all smart cards. Though they do not provide any processing power, they can be very useful since they hold up to 4 MB of data.

As in the case of CDC and CLDC, the Java Card has its own virtual machine, the Java Card Virtual Machine (JCVM). But, the Java Card Virtual Machine is fundamentally different from the other virtual machines we have discussed. The JCVM never stops! The JCVM's state is permanently persisted into the electronically erasable PROM (EEPROM) when the card is removed from the reader. It is restored when it is inserted back into the reader.

Smart card technologies such as the Java Card offer a very unique and innovative approach to problems solved by mobile applications. Smart cards are one of the smallest devices in the range of mobile devices. Though they do not offer much in the way of input/output or processing power, they introduce a different paradigm of mobile computing where the user depends on card readers to exist everywhere he or she goes. Though this paradigm is not as flexible as a device that is available to the user all of the time, smart cards are smaller and less intrusive. The smart card of the future may even offer things such as a small display for receiving messages and wireless access to the network.

We will not discuss the Java Card much during the remainder of this text. Smart card technologies promise to be a sizable part of the solution set to the mobile computing problem; however, the applications for smart cards are very small, passive, and typically not applicable to anything that is represented by UML.

Now, let us look at another key Java technology that can help us in tying the network of mobile devices together.

2.4.4 JINI

The Java Naming and Directory Interface (JNDI) allows various resources to be identified in a generic manner on the server side; however, it is far too heavy for implementation on mobile devices. But, we already know that one of the necessary pieces of functionality to write mobile applications is discovery of devices and services. In Chapter 3 and the remainder of the book, we will look at platform-independent discovery mechanisms such as RDF, CC/PP, and UAProf. Java, however, gives us Java Intelligence Network Infrastructure (JINI), a base technology for ad-hoc networking. JINI provides lookup services and its own discovery protocol. Let us go through the basic transactions that JINI provides:

1. *Lookup*: This is a JINI service that maps interfaces indicating the functionality offered by a service to sets of objects that implement the service [Hashman and Knudsen 2001]. Lookup functionality of JINI provides the basic foundation for a federated service in which a variety of services cooperate and various processes can offer each other various services.
2. *Discovery*: Before a given process begins using a service found by the lookup process, it must find that service. The act of finding lookup services is called

discovery. This is typically done by the underlying infrastructure that offers the JINI implementation.

3. *Events*: The various JINI participants can register to listen to the various events emitted by the other JINI participants. Any so called JINI device (anything that can become a participant in a JINI network) can register events with any other JINI device. In this way, the architectural communication model is more like peer-to-peer than it is client–server.
4. *Leasing*: JINI devices share resources through a process called leasing. The term leasing is used because the amount of time for which the service is available to the lessee is known in advance, at the time of the lease. This is a distinct requirement of JINI. Although the amount of time for which the service is being used by the lessee has to be known at the time of the lease, this time can be dictated by the leaser (the device whose service is being used) or through a negotiated process between the leaser and the lessee.
5. *Joining*: For a JINI device to offer its services to other devices, it first has to join the JINI federation. This is done through a process called joining.
6. *Transaction Management*: Interactions between the various JINI devices may be compound, being made of several simple atomic interactions. Because of this, transaction management is needed to ensure the proper semantics are provided to avoid partial results and bad data.

JINI specification merely provides us with a set of rules on how JINI devices must behave. Most implementations that exist today are not designed for mobile devices because they take up too many resources; however, there are some that offer "mobilized JINI." PSINaptic, for example, offers an implementation of JINI suitable for mobile devices in its JMatos. A clear advantage the JINI and other ad-hoc networking technologies offer is that they allow mobile devices to roam through a variety of networks. This promise, however, is difficult to fulfill primarily for two reasons. First, the network operators of different networks roamed by a JINI device may be operated by different entities, thereby having closed boundaries to the JINI devices. Second, even if these network operators open up their networks for interoperability, a JINI implementation would have to live on the top of a quilt of different low-level communication protocols implemented by each network.[†]

As Eronen recognizes [Eronen 2000], the biggest downfall of JINI today is its requirement of a virtual machine: "JINI's Java dependency, while enabling most of JINI's best features, is at the same time the most limiting aspect of the technology. A Java Virtual Machine that is required for each JINI service is not a light piece of software." Today, JINI and J2ME on the same device is not widely available. The Java community is working on making JINI a more usable technology for mobile devices with real implementations.

[†] As a side note, a group of JINI devices that are aware of one another are often called a JINI Federation. The word "Federation" is frequently used in cooperative and ad-hoc networking environments to indicate participation in a distributed computing system that requires some level of autonomous behavior on first joining the federation, then allowing others to discover the device and the services on the device, and finally interacting with the other members of the federation.

2.4.5 Java-Based Peer-to-Peer Protocol

JXTA is a peer-to-peer protocol and part of the Java platform. As we discussed in Chapter 1, peer-to-peer architectures allow peers to discover one another and communicate. Whereas the process of discovery of other peers and the services offered by those peers is covered by JINI as well as other protocols, JXTA provides an actual protocol for those peers to send messages back and forth to one another. The JXTA development community is now working on specifications that allow both direct and indirect JXTA implementations for J2ME.

1. *Direct Implementation*: This is the case if the JXTA protocol and the relevant APIs are provided on the J2ME device. The implementation may be done on the top of one of the profiles (such as MIDP) or provided by the manufacturer using native code and exposed as Java APIs on the top of CLDC.
2. *Indirect Implementation*: Because many devices may have some built-in native networking capabilities, and because implementing multiple protocols on such resource-starved devices is fairly expensive, it is possible to implement JXTA through proxies. In this model, some or all of the peers connect to the other peers through a proxy called a relay. This proxy, sometimes also referred to as a surrogate, violates the trueness of a peer-to-peer architecture if it lives outside of the device. However, it still allows us to take advantage of many useful properties of peer-to-peer networks.

JXTA is the recommended APIs for peer-to-peer application layer protocols by Sun Microsystems. However, this is one area of the Java platform where implementations such as Endeavor's MAGI outside of the Java community have gained more commercial success. JXTA has struggled to be adopted and is thin when it comes to implementations and functionality. We will discuss the area of peer-to-peer application architectures in detail in the latter sections of this text.

2.4.6 Where Does Java Fit In?

As subjective as it may be, within the developer community, it is well accepted that Java, as a platform, offers the most open and the most complete solution to application programming. Though it leads all other platforms in the marketplace, whether or not it is the right approach to mobile applications remains under question. Besides all of its strengths as a nonproprietary technology, Java enjoys a unique process that allows it to evolve without bias toward any particular hardware or software vendor: the Java Community Process. This process can roughly be thought of as a negotiation process where various vendors get together and decide on the evolution of the platform and the APIs. Obviously, J2ME and other parts of Java relevant to mobile development evolve under the same process.

Unfortunately, this strength is also a weakness for this process is extremely slow. Although this process has worked well in the evolutionary environment of stationary application development, it remains to be seen whether J2ME and other Java-related technologies can remain agile enough to adapt to mobile application development. Desktop and server application development techniques had matured by the time Java, as a programming language and as a platform, came around. The same is not true of mobile application development techniques. Mobile applications are still very young. The challenge for the Java Community Process, as well as others who are forming Java as a platform, remains one of finding the right balance among the low-level embedded approach to software development, the high-level business application approach to software development, and the incorporation of treatment for the dimensions of mobility.

As we wait to see the evolution of the platform, it is important to note that Java remains the dominant force in mobile development and offers the most vendor neutral and nonproprietary solutions to mobile application developers.

2.5 BREW

Qualcomm's BREW (Binary Run-time Environment for Wireless) gives application developers a new and different approach in producing mobile applications. BREW is built directly into the hardware. It is offered as an API to access the CDMA, GSM/GPRS, or UMTS chip sets that provide the support for it. But, it is primarily intended for the variations of CDMA, a technology owned and licensed by Qualcomm. BREW applications can be written on a PC using the BREW Software Development Kit (SDK). Once the application is developed, it must be tested, and then deployed. Deployment of BREW applications is a process done jointly by Qualcomm and telecommunications carriers and not just the developer.

Though the creators of BREW say that they first came up with the acronym BREW and then found the words to fit the acronym, the platform is somewhat biased toward wireless applications that run on phones. And this may be the only weakness of BREW as a mobile development platform. Although today developing mobile applications means targeting cell phones or PDAs, this is changing rapidly with new devices being introduced to the market.

BREW applications, also referred to as BREW applets, are written in C though some support for C++ is provided (although some fundamental things such as extending the base API through inheritance are not possible) and, using code generation or virtual machine technologies, other languages such as Java can be supported. One of the most impressive things about BREW is its near-full treatment of dimensions of mobility in its architecture, feature implementation, and SDK. Let us look at the various components that allow the developer to build a BREW application.

2.5.1 BREW SDK Overview

To get started programming in BREW, the first thing you need to do is to go to http://www.qualcomm.com/brew and register as a developer. This will allow you to download the BREW SDK. To date, the BREW SDK is offered mainly as an integrated set of components with Microsoft Visual C++ 6.0. Once you have downloaded the BREW SDK and installed it, you can begin developing. At the time of authoring this text, the BREW SDK is at its 2.0 version and its effective use requires installation of Microsoft Visual C++ 6.0. Once you have installed the BREW SDK, you will have the following set of applications available for development:

1. *BREW MIF Editor*: Every BREW module, defined as the classes that make up one or more BREW applications, has an associated Module Information File (MIF). MIFs are *required*. Every BREW module must have a MIF. The MIF Editor provides a GUI tool for editing the MIF file associated with the classes that make up a module. The MIF Editor that comes with BREW SDK version 2.0 can be started as a wizard inside Visual C++ 6.0 or independently as a stand-alone application. We will look at the use of the MIF Editor and building a simple application.
2. *BREW Device Configurator*: This is a stand-alone application that allows developers to make up their own handset by configuring a vanilla mobile phone and specifying the behavior of the keys, the look and feel of the screen, and other specifics of the device. This development tool addresses the large variety of existing devices by allowing developers to create their own device emulator and testing the application. Remember, also, that because BREW is a platform for writing application for the handset, it is possible to use the application to build some adaptive behavior to adapt to each type of device. Still, the Device Configurator is invaluable in that it allows developers to test the application on their own emulated device environment.
3. *BREW Emulator*: For those who have designed and implemented any mobile application, it is obvious that one of the most difficult steps in the development process is the incremental unit testing. Although most platforms provide some sort of a generic emulator, most do not allow for custom configuration of a device (done by the Device Configurator) or using the custom configuration to simulate running an application. This is what the BREW Emulator does. But, the most impressive part is its treatment of location sensitivity, quality of service, and telephony functionality. Not only does the BREW Emulator allow the developer to load and run the application on a custom configuration, but also it allows for the adjustment of various components of the network's connectivity, such as traffic up-delay and down-delay, so that the application may be tested under various QOS conditions. The emulator also allows for emulating location-sensitive applications by configuring a GPS output file manually and using it to simulate the location input to the device. Finally, it allows the developer to simulate various telephony events such as an incoming call or sending a Short Messaging Service (SMS) message. The BREW Emulator, though primitive in its look and feel, is perhaps the most complete emulator for applications that run on mobile devices.
4. *BREW Image Authoring Tool*: There is an image authoring tool that allows creation of images for BREW. This tool can use PNG or BMP files.
5. *BREW ARM Compiler*: Many mobile devices are based on the ARM or Strong-ARM hardware platform (registered trademarks of ARM Corporation). The ARM Compiler enables the BREW developers to compile their code for the mobile devices that carry the ARM-based technologies (16/32 bit RISC-based microprocessors). The ARM Compiler has a licensing fee associated with it.

6. *Image Converter*: The tool set provides an image converter to convert 4-bit bitmaps to 2-bit bitmaps as BREW only supports 2-bit bitmaps because of the limited resources on mobile devices
7. *BREW Resource Editor*: If you have worked with Java or C++ to build GUI client-side applications, then you are familiar with the concept of a resource bundle. Resource files in BREW are a collection of images, strings, and dialog look-and-feel components that allow changing the look and feel of the application for internationalization and similar purposes without changing the code base. The BREW Resource Editor gives the developers a GUI interface to manage the resource files.
8. *BREW Pure Voice Converter*: This command line utility allows the developers to convert wave files (audio) to Pure Voice files or vice versa.
9. *BREW AppLoader*: This tool allows the developer to deploy an application on a handset through a PC connector. This is a testing and not a deployment tool.
10. *BREW Grinder*: The Grinder generates a variety of inputs and tests the application.
11. *BREW TestSig Generator and AppSigner*: The TestSig tool provides the developer a mechanism to generate a test Class ID. The AppSigner uses the Class 3 Certification from Verisign (see Section 2.5.2 for how this plays into the development process) to authenticate and sign an application.

Now, let us proceed by building a real BREW application.

2.5.2 Building and Deploying a Simple BREW Application

Before we start building a BREW application, let us understand the process of deploying a BREW application. This process is quite different from the deployment of most other mobile applications onto mobile devices.

To deploy a BREW application, here are the steps you would take (see Figure 2.6):

1. *Download the SDK and get started*: The first step is easy. Simply download the free BREW SDK and begin developing your application. There are unit testing tools such as the emulator that ship with the SDK so that you can test your application in an emulated environment on your PC.
2. *Obtain a Verisign Class 3 certificate*: All BREW applications are fully authenticated using a Verisign certificate. So, you will have to purchase a Verisign certificate to start the process of getting your application onto a real handset.
3. *Get a BREW phone*: To test your application on a real device, you will have to get a BREW phone. As we mentioned previously, though BREW is designed to target a wide range of mobile devices, today support is only provided for mobile phones. You can find a list of available phones on the BREW Web site. With a data connection to your BREW phone, you can upload your sample application to the phone and start testing it on the phone. However, you will not be able to send it to any other devices or have anyone else download it onto their device. Using the data connection is for simple testing only. To see how the application works in a real environment and to deploy it to phones owned by actual users, read on to the next steps.

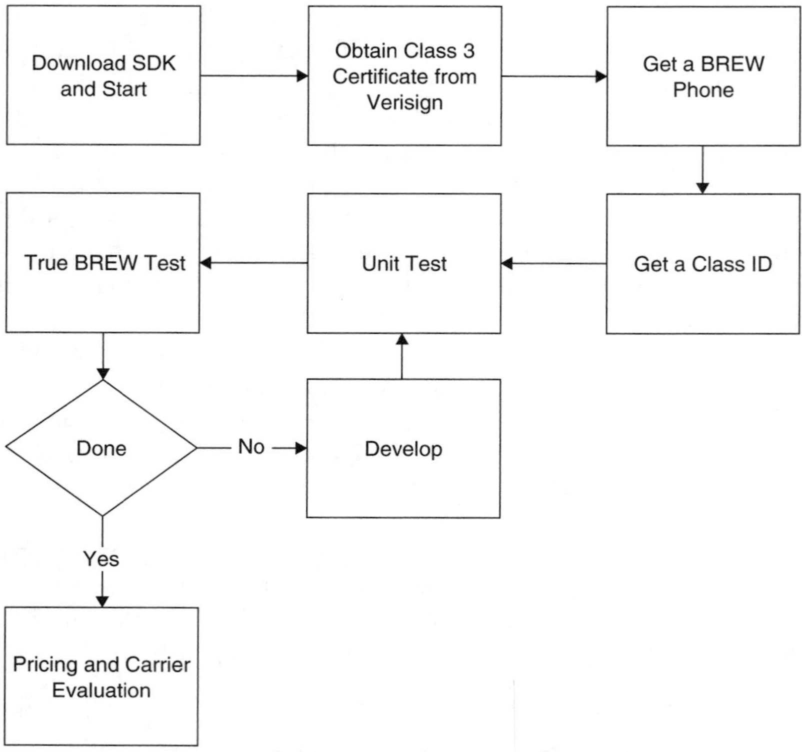

FIGURE 2.6. Steps of Developing a BREW Application.

4. *Register as a BREW developer*: This is not a simple sign up for notifications and other news about BREW. You will have to have the Verisign Class 3 certificate before you can become an "Authenticated Developer." Once you are an authenticated developer, you are ready to work.
5. *Obtain a Class ID for your application*: During the development process, you can use a dummy Class ID. But, to get the application out on a real device, you need to get a Class ID for the application. This Class ID uniquely distinguishes your application from all other BREW applications. Every BREW application has to have a Class ID and the Class IDs are issued and provisioned by Qualcomm centrally to avoid ID collision.
6. *Perform a unit test and send it to a testing lab*: If you are done with steps 1–5, you are ready to submit your application for testing. To get the application onto your phone, a Qualcomm-approved testing center needs to test your application. It should be obvious that you want to bullet-proof the application before submitting it to the testing center. This process is put in place to avoid "crashing" the mobile device. Because the BREW application will be running on a device whose environment is controlled by the device manufacturer and the carrier, the constraints are much stricter than a stationary application running on a PC. A BREW application runs directly on top of the ASIC so the potential for damage or a system crash as opposed to a mere application crash is much higher. The testing lab assures that the application is resilient, written

according to the BREW specifications, and can coexist with other applications on the mobile device.

7. *Perform a pricing and carrier evaluation*: Once the testing lab approves an application, it is ready to be provisioned. Deployment of an application is done by Qualcomm and the carriers supporting BREW. Therefore, the application developer must submit the software to Qualcomm and the carriers for actual deployment. Of course, deployment is done after the carrier and Qualcomm approve of the application. There are a variety of factors such as the stability of the application, how good the application is, the negotiated pricing, and others that are critical in delivering the application to the mobile device. Though these factors have nothing to do with the technical viability of the application, they are business problems that must be solved before the application can be deployed. This is both a strength and weakness in BREW. This model allows the carriers (who are very protective of their domains), Qualcomm, and the device manufacturers to have a say in the deployment process, thereby providing a sound economic foundation on which BREW is built. However, mixing business propositions into the technical details of how an application is deployed seems a little absurd from the developers' perspective. This also means that Qualcomm and the carrier are in complete control of provisioning and distribution of the application.

Unfortunately, deploying a BREW application onto a device is not free. Before you get an application up and working on a device, you need to pay various types of fees for the Verisign certificate and, in practicality, become a Qualcomm developer, requiring a significant membership fee depending on what type of membership you want to sign up for. The positive spin on this, of course, is that the membership fee pays for some marketing and weeds out those developers who do not have a product and are just playing around with the platform. If you want to just learn the platform, the best thing is probably just to download the SDK and the tools after reading this section and then experiment with it.

Now, let us go on to the actual code.

2.5.3 Hello BREW

Once you have downloaded and installed the BREW SDK, you can get started. Remember that BREW development is only practical within the Microsoft Visual Studio 6.0 platform (with support for the .NET version of MS Studio coming soon). Once you have installed the BREW SDK, you will be able to enter Microsoft Visual Studio 6.0 and use the integrated components of the BREW SDK. You should note that everything in the BREW API is in terms of interfaces. Extensibility is possible through building your own BREW libraries, but a developer may not provide implementations for the existing interfaces (and, therefore, may not inherit from the existing APIs). Here is the procedure:

1. Click on File, New, and then Projects. You will see the BREW Application Wizard. Choose it.

2. The wizard will ask you if you want File, Network, Database, TAPI, or Sound functionality. These selections correspond to the organization of the BREW standard libraries:
   a. *Files*: BREW provides an API that allows storage of small amounts of information in structures with which application developers are familiar: files and directories of files.
   b. *Database*: Information is often better stored in a database instead of files if the data must be searched, sorted, or indexed. BREW provides a set of APIs to store, manipulate, and retrieve data that have a small amount of database-like functionality. What BREW offers, it should be noted, is not nearly as complete as a full-blown database system. However, it offers enough for useful functionality.
   c. *TAPI (Telephony API)*: Because BREW is built on a wireless telephony platform (CDMA), it is natural that it provides telephony functionality. At the time of release of BREW SDK 2.0, functionality is limited to sending SMS messages and switching back and forth between incoming and outgoing telephony calls. However, being built on a telephony platform, it is almost certain that BREW will offer functionality that provides control and manipulation of the audio over the telephony channel, integration with voice recognition, and other useful functionality.
   d. *Sound functionality*: Sound functionality is provided through a set of multimedia APIs. Sound can be stored on the device in BREW's own format of QCELP (a Qualcomm technology).
3. Once you have selected which libraries you will be using in your application, you will need to create a MIF file for it. If you do not yet have a true valid Class ID, you have to get the Verisign certificate, become a Qualcomm developer, and go through the steps that we mentioned previously. Once again, every BREW application must have an MIF file. Click on the MIF Editor. You will see these different tabs on the wizard:
   a. *Applets*: This is where you generate a test Class ID (or if you have already become a Qualcomm developer, get a real Class ID from Qualcomm). The other basic properties of the BREW application (as we mentioned before, interchangeably referred to as BREW applet) are set in this pane. Note that if you click on the *Advanced* button on this pane, another window pops up with some features that seem to be programmatic. In BREW, certain behaviors of the application such as its treatment of incoming telephony events (when a call comes in while the application is running) have to be specified. Some behaviors are fundamental to the behavior of the application and, therefore, are required to have a footprint in the MIF file.
   b. *General*: This pane is for entering the security-related information. Every BREW application may provide access to other BREW applications and modules or require a particular access level for certain functionality on the device. It is important for this information to be on the MIF file because other applications must know whether they are usable by other applications or not and so that the application container (the BREW environment

running on the BREW device) knows whether it can load and execute the application.

c. *Extensions and Dependencies*: Because BREW applications can come in several modules or have interdependencies among themselves, the MIF files allow for specifying these dependencies. The Extensions and Dependencies panes provide a graphical way of manipulating these dependencies.

Once you finish navigating through the wizard, the BREW wizard generates the code for your simple application. Figure 2.7 shows the important functional calls in the generated C code.

There are two things that should stand out to you:

1. *AEEClsCreateInstance*: This function, required for every BREW application, is called by the BREW run-time environment. This is the initialization function. AEEApplet_New must be called within this function. AEEApplet_New takes the Class ID as an argument so that it can verify the validity of the application. It also takes a pointer to the main event handler of the application as an argument, giving the BREW run-time environment a call-back mechanism to listen for the event that triggers the actions in the application. The type of this handle is AEEHANDLER.
2. *helloBREW_HandleEvent*: In our application, this is the event handler that is passed into the constructor for the new application, thereby making it the main event handler of the application. You can think of the event handler passed into the AEEApplet_NEW as the main() method of your application. This is similar to the driver method of an object-oriented application. This is where the actual displaying of the "Hello BREW" text is done.

You should note that there are some architectural concerns to understand about BREW applications:

1. Everything in BREW is event driven. This comes from the tight coupling to the hardware platform. So, the application starts by events that come from the user activating it through the device keypad.
2. There are two groups of APIs you can use: those provided by Qualcomm as part of the base BREW platform and those provided by third-party vendors (such as device manufacturers), Qualcomm, and software vendors that provide additional functionality on top of the standard BREW platform or a set of BREW extensions. If you are developing an application in BREW, make sure that you do not reinvent the wheel for every single problem. If you are trying to achieve something that is basic, there is probably already a third-party vendor that provides the functionality. There are various channels through which you can find what is offered out there at the BREW developer site.
3. Though the BREW API itself is an object-oriented API, up to the SDK 2.0 version of the BREW tool set, developing BREW applications really only make sense in C.

```
#include "AEEModGen.h"      //Module interface definitions
#include "AEEAppGen.h"      //Applet interface definitions
#include "AEEShell.h"     //Shell interface definitions
#include "AEEFile.h"        //File interface definitions
#include "AEEDB.h"          //Database interface definitions
#include "AEENet.h"         //Socket interface definitions
#include "AEESound.h"       //Sound Interface definitions
#include "AEETapi.h"        //TAPI Interface definitions

static boolean helloBREW_HandleEvent(IApplet * pi, AEEEvent
  eCode, uint16 wParam, uint32 dwParam);
int AEEClsCreateInstance(AEECLSID ClsId,IShell *
  pIShell,IModule * po,void ** ppObj) {
    *ppObj = NULL;
    if(ClsId == AEECLSID_TESTAGAIN){
        if(AEEApplet_New(sizeof(AEEApplet), ClsId,
          pIShell,po,(IApplet**)ppObj,
            (AEEHANDLER) helloBREW_HandleEvent,NULL)
            == TRUE) {
                //Add your code here...
            return (AEE_SUCCESS);
        }
    }
                return (EFAILED);
}
static boolean helloBREW_HandleEvent(AEEAPPLET *myApplet,
  AEEEvent eCode, uint16 wParam, uint32 dwParam) {
    AECHAR helloBREWString[] = {'H','e','l','l','o','','
      B','R,'E','W','\0'};
    AECHAR goodbyeBREWString[]= {'B','y','e','','B','R,'E',
      'W','\0'};
    switch (eCode) {
        case EVT_APP_START:
                IDISPLAY_DrawText(myApplet->m_pIDisplay,
                  AEE_FONT_BOLD, helloBREWString,-1,0,0,NULL,
                  IDF_ALIGN_CENTER)
                IDISPLAY_Update (pMe->m_pIDisplay);
            return(TRUE);
        case EVT_APP_STOP:
                IDISPLAY_DrawText(myApplet->m_pIDisplay,
                  AEE_FONT_BOLD, goodbyeBREWString,-1,0,0,
                  NULL,IDF_ALIGN_CENTER);
                IDISPLAY_Update (pMe->m_pIDisplay);
            return TRUE;
        default:
            break;
    }
    return FALSE;
}
```

FIGURE 2.7. Simple Application Generated by the Wizard.

BREW SDK 2.0 provides much more functionality than what we have presented here. If you want to develop real BREW applications, the best thing to do is to start at Qualcomm's BREW site and read the documents that are provided. What we have presented here is a bird's-eye view of the development environment and tools: the big picture that is often missing from the documentation provided by the vendor itself. BREW offers a rich API to build wireless mobile applications.

2.5.4 Where Will BREW and BREW-Like Technologies Fit?

A fundamental difference between BREW (and similar frameworks and tools such as Texas Instrument's OMAP) and the other software frameworks and tools is that the designers of BREW have approached the problem of building development platforms for software applications from a more hardware-oriented perspective. Most other platforms create a thick abstraction layer on top of the hardware and hide the behavior of the hardware. BREW and like tools choose to build an application framework based on the hardware platform. This has the following implications:

1. Because mobile devices vary greatly in the features that they offer, it is difficult to build a virtual machine or an operating system that allows full usage of all of the functionality of these devices. In this way, BREW and its cousins OMAP and others are superior in allowing the application developer to take full advantage of device features. Also, on a resource-starved mobile device, this presents the developer with the opportunity of optimizing applications for the platform.
2. Hardware-based platforms are inherently proprietary platforms from an application development perspective. If an enterprise develops a set of applications for BREW, neither porting over to other hardware-based application development platforms such as OMAP nor porting over to software-based platforms such as Windows CE and J2ME is a possibility. The code is specifically written for the ASIC design of Qualcomm's (or third-party licensee's) hardware.
3. Though Qualcomm touts BREW as an "open platform," this openness is only relative. BREW is extensible by hardware manufacturers and software vendors. But, basic APIs are provided by Qualcomm and other vendors are not allowed the opportunity to compete in that market. This, in itself, is not important; however, because the basic API is controlled by Qualcomm, issues such as integrating with other mobile platforms and evolving the toolsets and APIs become very much reliant on what Qualcomm wants to do with the platform. This, in turn, reduces the true openness of the platform.

BREW, like J2ME, provides enough capabilities to be used as a framework for writing mobile agents that implement weak mobility. We will look at mobile agents closely in Chapter 9.

Although BREW uses Microsoft tools to ease development in addition to the SDK that it provides, Microsoft itself is another vendor that provides a set of tools and frameworks for development of mobile applications. Let us look at Microsoft's current offering in the mobile space, Windows CE.

2.6 Windows CE

An operating system is the master control program that enables the hardware by abstracting it to the application via drivers [Development tools for Mobile and Embedded Applications 2002]. Microsoft's various products revolve around different versions of an operating system. The versions that concern us, the mobile application developers, most are Windows CE and Embedded Windows XP. Windows CE has been around since 1997 and Embedded Windows XP is being released at the time of authoring this text. These two operating systems are designed for two different purposes. There are different flavors of the Windows CE operating systems, of course, depending on the hardware platform. Some of these flavors are the Pocket PC, Windows CE .NET, and Pocket PC 2002. These flavors largely depend on the commercial bundling of different feature sets and hardware platforms with which they are shipped (such as Compaq's IPAQ). Embedded Windows XP, in contrast, is a subset of the desktop version of Windows XP components. Development for Embedded Windows XP is a bit more straightforward than developing for Windows CE.

Mobile application frameworks that are based on an operating system treat developing mobile applications in the same way as they treat their stationary counterparts on PCs. As we mentioned previously, the operating system provides basic access to the hardware such as I/O, networking, etc. So, the applications that run on Windows CE and Embedded Windows XP are controlled by them, respectively. Microsoft provides tools to build applications for each environment too. These are as follows:

1. *Embedded Visual C++*: This is a tool set separate from Visual Studio, the typical development environment for PC-based Windows applications. It allows for authoring mobile applications in C++. Emulators and a debugger are provided. The latest version of this tool provides advanced features such as exception handling and run-time debugging, features you will cherish if you are actually developing an application in C++ for mobile devices.
2. *Embedded Visual Basic*: This tool provides the ability to write applications using Visual Basic. Visual Basic applications can be developed faster but do not offer the developer the ability to tune and optimize the application for resource-starved mobile devices. Therefore, Embedded Visual Basic is really not a suitable tool for developing large commercial applications, but it does well for proof-of-concept and prototype applications.
3. *Smart Device Extensions for .NET*: The .NET application programming platform, the newest set of tools for building Microsoft Windows-based applications, can be complemented with a set of extensions that allow developers to author .NET applications for mobile devices.
4. *Microsoft Mobile Internet Toolkit*: This is really a server-side framework. We will discuss it along with the other publishing tools later in this chapter.

As in the other Microsoft Windows platforms, Windows CE allows the use of COM and ActiveX components in addition to the Win32 API. The other significant features are markup language processing (HTML, XML, XSL, etc.), security (e.g., SSL), a subset of the Windows ADO database access framework in ADOCE

(ADO for Windows CE), and limited functionality in coupling with the Microsoft messaging queue in MSMQ.

2.6.1 Hello Visual Basic on Windows CE!

Building Microsoft Visual Basic applications on Windows CE is very similar to building Visual Basic applications for the MS Windows desktop. The development paradigm is based on forms and a series of GUI controls that can be placed on the forms. To start, you will need to download and install the Microsoft eMbedded Visual Tools 3.0 (or higher as new versions become available). Then, do the following:

1. Start the eMbedded Visual Basic tool. You will find the environment different from the Visual Basic IDE for the desktop, but it is very similar.
2. When you create a new project, the IDE automatically creates the base form for your application. You will place the various controls on this form.
3. Drag and drop a label control anywhere on your form and type in "Hello Visual Basic" in the "Caption" property of the control.
4. In the menu bar, you will see a combo box that allows you to select an emulator. One of the emulators should be Pocket PC Emulator. Select it and then click on the "Play" button in the menu bar.

That is all there is to it! Your application is finished. Just like MS Visual Basic for the desktop gives desktop developers one of the fastest ways to develop applications, eMbedded Visual Basic does the same for the Windows CE platform. Now, you have to move the application onto a real device. Because Windows CE is different for the various hardware platforms that it runs on (such as Pocket PC), you need to compile your application for the appropriate platform.

To test your application on the real device, you will need to physically connect the device to your desktop. There are various ways of connecting, the most popular of which is the RS232 connection (the serial port) on your PC. Once you have connected the device to your PC, you need to make the application installable on a Windows CE device. To do this, perform the following steps:

1. From the Tools menu, select Remote Tools, and then Application Install Wizard.
2. The wizard will walk you through a simple installation process; one of the steps is the selection of the hardware platform. You will be asked what processor you want. This is because different devices use different processors (Intel x86 based, ARM, StrongARM, etc.). The compiler for each one of these processors is different.
3. From here installation proceeds as with any other application on Windows CE.

To add more advanced functionality to the application, you will have to bind the even listeners on the forms and controls to MS Visual Basic functions and subroutines.

As in the desktop version of Visual Basic, you can pass variables into subroutines and functions by value or by reference.

Remember that you can only develop applications, using eMbedded Visual Basic, for the higher end hardware platforms for Windows CE. For example, you cannot develop Microsoft Smart Phone applications with eMbedded Visual Basic. When you develop a mobile application with Visual Basic, you should try to find most of your components as COM/ActiveX components provided by third parties.

Now, let us look at developing applications with the Microsoft eMbedded Visual C++ tool.

2.6.2 eMbedded Visual C++ on Windows CE

eMbedded Visual C++ is an environment, very similar to its desktop counterpart of Visual C++ 6.0, designed for developing applications and software components for Windows CE in C++. At the time of authoring this book, compilers are available for varieties of ARM, MIPS, Intel's x86, PowerPC, and Hitachi processors. eMbedded Visual C++ (eVC) provides the following:

1. use of a subset of the Win32 APIs for building Windows CE applications,
2. use of a subset of the MFC (Microsoft Foundation Classes) libraries,
3. use of a subset of ATL libraries, and
4. a set of classes specific to the Windows CE platform.

As in the case of Visual C++ 6.0, eVC is a very advanced development environment compared to its counterparts in the marketplace as a development tool. However, by looking at the libraries supported by eVC, it becomes obvious that the developers are expected to use the tool primarily to build applications that are subsets of some stationary application or to build their own libraries to support advanced functionality specific to mobile application development such as location sensitivity.

eVC allows a significant amount of control over the look and feel of GUI applications designed for the Stylus and the small user interface. For example, most navigation in Windows CE is done by a single press (referred to as Stylus Tap—analogous to a mouse click). One also has the ability to press and hold, similar to a double press (like a mouse double-click).

Just like Windows 2000, Windows CE utilizes a protected memory architecture. When a Windows CE machine first boots, it creates a single 4 GB virtual address space [Introduction to eVC++]. This, however, does not mean that there is 4 GB of random-access memory (RAM) available! In fact, currently most Windows CE devices are limited to under 64 MB. Moreover, although we expect mobile devices to continue to grow in their processing ability and memory, it is unlikely that we will ever want to run memory-intensive applications on mobile devices because physical size is a limiting factor and battery life is not growing as fast as processing power. This virtual address space is then divided into 33 different "slots," each of which is available for use by a process. The maximum size of each slot is 32 MB. This is simply the model with which the memory is managed; it does not mean that the device is required to have 4 GB of memory or that it offers 32 MB of memory per process. Also, keep in mind that Windows CE does not allow paging (file swaps), so you can exceed the available RAM. File swapping is something that is typically not implemented as a strategy for improving the memory limitations of mobile devices as it is cost prohibitive to the battery life and takes considerable processing power.

```
....
Private Sub Form_MouseDown(aMessage As String, aDisplay As
  Boolean)
    If aDisplay = true then
        aMessage = "This Message Is Displayed When You Push
          The Mouse"
    End If
End Sub
....
```

FIGURE 2.8. Creating an eMbedded Visual Basic Application by Filling the Events.

When building eVC applications, keep the following in mind:

1. Graphics are expensive. Whether you decided to use GDI or another method of rendering graphics, delivering them takes more memory, more CPU, more time, and more power from the battery. So, try to avoid graphics when possible.
2. Use events instead of polling when possible. Figure 2.8 shows some sample code that involves events in Windows CE environment. Polling is expensive for the same set of reasons as graphics are. Sleeps and event notifications are both features available to the eVC programmer to produce efficient applications.
3. Be very frugal in the use of RAM in your applications. Remember that persistent and RAM memory are typically handled by one set of hardware on mobile devices. Today, most mobile devices, including Windows CE devices, do not have hard drives (though this is changing).
4. As mentioned in item 3, because RAM and persistent memory often share the same hardware, being frugal in persisting data or handling data in memory pays off in reducing power consumption as well.
5. There is some functionality provided to the application developer to get the status of the power consumption. You can use this functionality in two ways. First, you can use it while designing and testing to see the power consumption during the life cycle of the usage of the application. Alternatively, you may want to use the power status (called up by GetPowerStatusEx function) to change the behavior of the application. For example, if the battery is getting low, you might want to persist the data to the network or locally and shut down the application after warning the user.
6. Make sure that you clean up memory resources whenever you get a WM_HIBERNATE event (which sends the device into hibernation). Failing to do a good memory cleanup there will lead to memory leaks and application instability.

Figure 2.9 shows a simple application using eVC. The eVC wizard is friendly and similar to the other wizards that ship with various Microsoft development tools.

```
#include <windows.h>
#include <windowsx.h>
#include "resource.h"

HWND mMainWindow = NULL;
HINSTANCE mInstance = NULL;
TCHAR mHelloWorldText[] = TEXT("HELLO WORLD");
BOOL InitApp(HINSTANCE anInstance);
LRESULT CALLBAC Show(HWND aWindowHandle, UNIT aMessage,
  WPARAM aParm1, LPARAM aParam2);

int WINAPI WinMain(HINSTANCE cInstance, HINSTANCE pInstance,
  LPWSTR aCmdLine, int aCmdShow) {return init(cInstance);}

BOOL init(HINSTANCE cInstance, int aCommand) {
    WNDCLASS myWindow;
    BOOL b;
    mInstance = cInstance;
    mMainWindow = CreateWindow(mHelloWorldText,
      mHelloWorldText, WS-VISIBLE,
CW_USEDEFUALT,CW_USEDEFAULT,
      CW_USEDEFAULT, NULL, NULL, cInstance,NULL);
    If (! mMainWindow) {return FALSE;}
    myWindow.style = CS_HREDRW | CS_VREDRAW;
    myWindow.lpfnWndProc = (WNDPROC) Show;
    b = (RegisterClass(&myWIndow));
    if (!b) {return FALSE;}
    ShowWindow(mMainWindow, aCommand);
    Return TRUE;
}

LRESULT CALLBACK Show(HWND aWindow, UINT aMessage,) {
        HDC  aHDC = NULL;
        PAINTSTRUCT  aPaintStructure = NULL;
        RECT  aRectangle = NULL;
        LRESULT  aResult = TURE;
        switch (aMessage) {
            case WM_PAINT: {
                aHDC = BeginPaint (aWindow, &aPaintStructure);
                GetClientRect (hwnd, &rect);
                DrawText (aHDC, L"Hello World", -1,
                  &aRectangle, DT_SINGLELINE | DT_CENTER |
                  DT_VCENTER);
                EndPaint (hwnd, &aPaintStructure);
                break;
            }
            default:
                DestroyWindow(aWindow);
                break;
        }
        return (LRESULT);
}
```

Figure 2.9. A Simple Application Written for Windows CE Using eVC++.

Something that we should not overlook before moving on is the ability to use an asynchronous messaging model to communicate with the network. This is possible through the use of Microsoft Messaging Queuing (MSMQ). There are a couple of different scenarios under which the use of MSMQ implementation for Windows CE would make sense:

1. Because the device may or may not be connected to the network at the time a particular application is executing, messages from the application to the network may have to be queued up.
2. To use the connection to the network efficiently, we may want to connect, send a large amount of data to the network, disconnect, accumulate more data, and then start the cycle over again. This can allow for more efficient usage of the network connection.

MSMQ is integrated into all other versions of Microsoft Windows; therefore, it allows for a certain amount of ubiquity as long as the application developer stays within the Microsoft product bundle. As in the case of all of the other tools we have looked at in the Windows CE arena, MSMQ for Windows CE offers a subset of the functionality offered by its older and bigger brother running on the desktop and server versions of Windows. Nevertheless, the ability to use a simple API to communicate with the network asynchronously and without worrying about the intermittent network connectivity is invaluable.

2.6.3 Databases on Windows CE

Data storage is one of the best addressed areas on the Windows CE platform. There are three ways to store data on a Windows CE device:

1. MS SQL Server Windows CE Edition: This is the highest end solution providing the most amount of functionality. However, it is also the one that takes up the most resources on the device. MS SQL Server Windows CE offers a subset of the functionality offered by the desktop/server version of MS SQL Server. Advanced features such as Views and Stored Procedures are not supported. It takes up more than 1 MB of resources on the device (not including the data itself) and allows for replication and synchronization through HTTP.
2. CEDB: This solution allows storage of information in a small and simple database. CEDB is typically a better solution for most applications on most devices because it occupies fewer resources than the MS SQL Server for Windows CE. CEDB offers crucial functionality, such as storage of information as records, that make it more useful than a simple file system. Yet, it is light and does not take up a lot of the resources on the device. It is important to note that CEDB is not a relational database; for example, every record may have a variable number of data members. So, working with CEDB is a bit different from working with the typical relational database.
3. File system: As with most client-side mobile platforms, the application can store data in a file system. This solution takes the fewest resources but may increase the size of the application (to replicate functionality such as querying

the data that may be prebuilt into databases) and increases the development time. Depending on the hardware and version of Windows CE, there is a range of 16 to 256 MB of RAM-based storage available for storage and a range of 16 to 32 MB for the maximum size of a single file. The number of possible files can be anywhere from 2^{16} to 2^{22}. Though it may seem, at first glance, that this is far more files than you could possibly want, because of the intermittent connectivity issues with mobile applications, we often have to store a large number of cached files.

To access these data programmatically, there is ADOCE (ActiveX Database Objects for Windows CE). ADOCE provides a subset of functionality of ADO in storing and manipulating data programmatically in memory and then persisting it. Although persisting to a file system has to be done manually, ADOCE provides a good API for persisting data to CEDB and MS SQL Server for Windows CE.

2.6.4 Windows CE and Web Services

As you will see in the next chapter, XML is the document standard for much of the distributed content that exists today. Mobile applications, in particular, should be designed in a way that they can take advantage of existing and future content and be interoperable with existing systems. XML-based Web services are particularly important as content can be exchanged over the Web and disparate systems may be made interoperable using HTTP and XML. Such interoperability is a particular aim of Web services. Microsoft's .NET is a collection of various Microsoft technologies: ones that had existed prior to .NET, new Web service–based functionality, C# as a programming language, and several other important technologies.

.NET Web services are based on two key technologies: WSDL (Web Services Definition Language) and SOAP (Simple Object Access Protocol). We will discuss both of these in detail in the next chapter. When developing desktop and server-side Microsoft Windows applications, ROPE (Remote Object Proxy Engine), a DLL that provides a simple API to use SOAP, facilitates the job of building Web service–based applications. Currently, ROPE is not available for Windows CE. Figure 2.10 shows a Visual Basic program for the Windows CE platform that builds and submits a SOAP envelope. However, XML parsing, communication through HTTP, and other facilities are still available to build Web service–based applications. In addition, Pocket SOAP, a SOAP client COM component for Windows CE, allows Windows CE applications to directly interact with various Web services.

.NET adds much to the existing capabilities of the Windows CE platform. Microsoft is certain to continue to add features to it to move the Windows CE platform more toward a full-blown mobile development platform from its current form as a subset of the desktop Microsoft Windows platform.

2.6.5 Treatment of Dimensions of Mobility by Windows CE

With the exception of treatment of the possibility of disconnected use of devices from the network, unfortunately, there seems to be an inherent lack of treatment of the dimensions of mobility by the current versions of Windows CE. However,

```
Option Explicit

Private mEnvelope As PocketSOAP.CoEnvelope
Private mTransport As PocketSOAP.HTTPTransport

Public Sub SOAPInit()
    Set mEnvelope = CreateObject("PocketSOAP.Envelope.2")
    Set mHTTP = CreateObject("PocketSOAP.HTTPTransport.2")
End Sub

Public Function Submit(aListener As String, aSOAPMethod As
  String, _aParam_1 As Variant, aParam_2 As Variant, aURI As
  String) As String

    Dim myRequest As String

    mEnvelope.SetMethod aSOAPMethod, aURI
    mEnvelope.Parameters.Clear
    mEnvelope.Parameters.Create aParam_1, aParam_2
    myRequest = mEnvelope.Serialize
    mHTTP.send aListener, myRequest
    mEnvelope.parse mHTTP
    Submit = mEnvelope.Parameters.Item(0).Value

End Function
```

FIGURE 2.10. Using eMbedded Visual Basic to Build and Submit SOAP Envelopes.

future versions are slated to have better support for treating the dimensions of mobility.

As we mentioned before, Windows CE essentially treats mobile applications like their stationary counterpart. Nevertheless, because of Microsoft's market penetration in the personal computing arena, and because of the seamless compatibility with all other Windows-based technologies, Windows CE has a very significant base in the market and will continue to be one of the most widely deployed base platforms for mobile applications. ActiveSync gives developers a well-integrated mechanism for synchronizing data between the device and the network.

Windows CE treats the problem of disconnected use better than all of the other problems of mobility. Because it is based on Windows and offers a practiced data storage subsystem as well as a programmatic interface to do it in ADOCE, storage of data as well as synchronizing/replication operations is well taken care of in Windows CE.

Microsoft Smart Phone is a significant move on Microsoft's part to treat mobile applications in a fundamentally different manner from the typical desktop application.

2.6.6 Microsoft Smart Phone

Microsoft Smart Phone 2002, an attempt by Microsoft to enter the mobile telephony market, can host custom applications written using the Smart Phone SDK. This SDK is provided as a plug-in for eVC and enables the application developers to develop applications for the Smart Phone much the same as they do for the Windows CE platform using eVC.

The Smart Phone SDK provides some interesting controls that are designed based on sophisticated user interfaces but are small for the screen of a mobile phone. An example is the "Roll-over" box. This is similar in appearance to a combo box but allows for flipping through a list of options by rolling.

Developing for the Smart Phone is much like of any other eVC++-based development. The only thing to be aware of is the fact that deployment is different and that the Smart Phone is designed to be more of a phone than a PDA.

2.7 WAP

Wireless Application Protocol (WAP) is the single framework most used in building mobile applications today. Despite all of its initial high promises, its lack of meeting those promises, and being written off for dead, WAP seems to have survived the critics and continues to improve. WAP, which was initially intended to be as pervasive for wireless and mobile applications as HTTP has been for the Web, never achieved the level of success initially expected. However, to date, WAP has the largest install base of all open application development platforms (second to NTT Docomo's closed and proprietary i-mode system) on mobile phones, meaning that WAP is installed on more mobile phones than any other software.

WAP shares some similarities to HTTP. From its inception to now, it has become more and more like HTTP. WAP 1.x and WAP 2.x are significantly different with WAP 1.x being the basis for nearly all the current installations in the market today and WAP 2.x being the target platform for WAP devices during 2003 and 2004. Let us go over some basics about WAP.

1. *WAP is intended for thin clients.* Much like HTTP, the designers of WAP 1.x were thinking about a thin-client technology: a case where nearly all logic is calculated on the server and very simple display instructions are bundled in some markup language to be displayed by the client. In HTTP, this markup language was HTML; in WAP 1.x, it is WML, the Wireless Markup Language. The latest version of HTTP and WAP 2.x both move to deploy XHTML, a markup language designed for graphical user interfaces that can be extended and is well formed with XML standards.
2. *WAP is built on its own lower level communication protocol.* Whereas HTTP assumes the existence of TCP/IP (which in turn provides persistent connections), WAP is built on its own set of communication protocols that wrap around TCP, UDP, or a variety of other possible protocol implementations. This is a topic of considerable discussion. TCP/IP is the way most computers are connected together on the Internet. Yet, TCP is based on the existence of a persistent

connection. There is somewhat of an inherent conflict between a truly persistent connection and wireless connectivity (the typical choice of connectivity for mobile applications). This does not mean that it is impossible to have a TCP/IP-based network that is wireless, but rather that the technical challenge is higher by orders of magnitude when compared to wired networks. Reestablishing a persistent connection in a low-bandwidth environment is slow and takes network and device resources. This and a variety of other reasons are what drove the WAP Forum to design the WAP 1.x connectivity model as they did. In WAP 2.x, the WAP Forum has moved a bit to the TCP side on its position, providing both datagrams and connections (TCP/IP connections) as methods of connectivity. True persistent connections seem more realistic as wireless networks are being upgraded to GPRS, GSM, and other similar high-bandwidth technologies.

3. *Typical deployment of WAP includes a proxy or a gateway*. Wireless carriers (also referred to as *bearer networks*) like to have control of every single incoming and outgoing bit of data that travels on their network. This is understandable as usage time is the typical mechanism for billing. However, it introduces some interesting nuances, such as the prevalence of proxies, into most of the deployable architectural schemes for mobile applications. Proxies play many roles in WAP. They provide a bridge between proprietary functionality implementations of various wireless networks and standard implementations. They also provide well-defined interfaces for various parts of WAP (e.g., WTLS, which treats secure communication in WAP). These well-defined interfaces allow vendors to compete based on implementations. They also allow the networks deploying WAP to select best-of-bread solutions without compromising interoperability or functionality.
4. *WAP is a complete framework for mobile applications*. Whereas most tools created for development of applications treat a part of the mobile application chain, WAP treats, or at least attempts to treat, all parts of the mobile equation. Although this means that WAP treats the entire gamut of problems such as security, content types, application layer protocol, and others, it also means that compromises and idiosyncrasies are created because of the marriage of all of the different parts of the mobile domain. The fact that WAP has various parts, however, does not mean that some of its parts cannot be used individually. For example, J2ME applications can use WAP as a communication protocol while not using the WAP browser (instead using a client-side J2ME application to provide a richer and better user experience).

To better understand WAP, let us briefly go through its major components. Rather than address WAP comprehensively, as the most widely deployed mobile platform, we will survey its various components and their functionality.

2.7.1 WAP Architecture

WAP adheres to a client–server architecture with implementation standards for the client that interpret content, the communication mechanisms between the clients and the servers, and additional required features in the servers, particularly

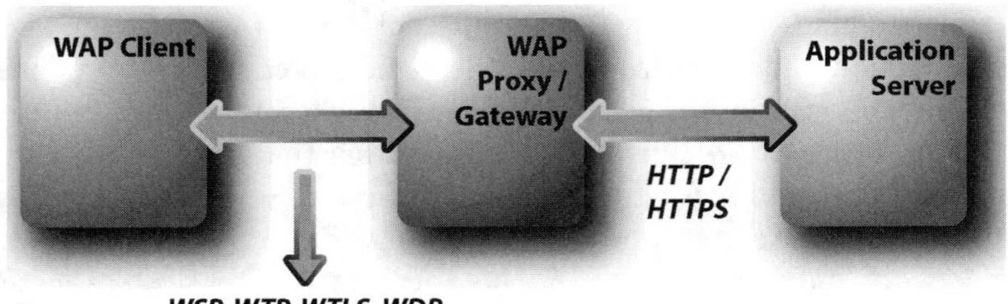

FIGURE 2.11. Basic Communication Architecture in WAP.

proxy servers. WAP attempts to follow the success of HTTP by mimicking some of its properties and providing a standard for a thin client, commonly referred to as a microbrowser. Figure 2.11 shows the basic communication architecture in WAP.

WAP adds a couple of pieces of functionality to the communication between the client and the server (WAP Gateway or WAP Proxy):

1. *Handling of Telephony on the Device*: Currently, devices and networks treat voice and data differently. Most voice is processed, and will continue to be processed for a very long time, through a telephony system that does not provide much in the way of complex operations. WAP specifies that the client must be able to handle simple telephony interactions on the device such as making an outbound call.
2. *Push*: Push offers some degree of treatment for one of the dimensions of mobility, namely support for active behavior.

It needs to be reiterated that the WAP architecture was designed with a subset of the mobile application arena in mind: wireless applications. WAP does not treat the entirety of mobile applications and dimensions of mobility. But, in focusing on wireless applications, it treats QOS and lack of bandwidth or reliability thereof extensively and fully. Furthermore, the WAP architecture lends itself to clients that are very resource-starved such as cellular telephones. It begins to seem useless once one begins to move toward the more powerful end of the device spectrum, starting with PDAs and moving on.

2.7.2 WAP UI

To most software developers, developing WAP 1.x applications has been about developing WML pages. WML was the markup language rendered by the WAP microbrowsers. There are a plethora of good books on WML development (see the references). WML offered some distinct advantages over HTML:

1. The WML tag set is smaller and therefore better suited for resource-starved devices.
2. WML is XML compliant. HTML pages can be rendered in different ways by different browsers partly because HTML is not well formed and there is more than one way to do some things. This non-well-formed behavior of HTML also

causes a problem in that the HTML browsers are fairly complex to be able to render all of the different possible permutations of tag sets. Finally, the well-formed nature of WML allows for faster and less complex validation of WML pages.
3. WML is designed with small monochrome screens in mind. It allows for things like breaking a page into a deck of cards, displaying one card at a time, and allowing client-side navigation between the cards.
4. WML has markup tags that allow interacting with the telephony functionality of wireless devices offered through the WAP WTA agent.

There is a problem with WML though. Most existing content on the wired Internet is in HTML. Because of the quirky properties of HTML, such as its non-well-formed nature, conversion of HTML to WML is not a process that can be easily automated. And when it is automated, it typically renders poor results because context of the various pieces of content is only half the story when it comes to rendering user interface elements. In its 2.x incarnation, WAP is taking an approach to converge with the wired Web in using XHTML. Although XHTML is similar to HTML, it is extensible and well formed, thereby allowing application of various XML techniques such as application of XSLs to convert XHTML to WML and selection of a subset of the XML document.

2.7.3 WAP Proxies and Gateways

There is typically an intermediary server between the wireless network that supports WAP and the supporting Internet protocol of HTTP. This intermediary server can act as a proxy or a gateway. Note that the difference between a proxy and a gateway is that a client determines when it will use a proxy [Fielding 2000]. Some WAP-enabled devices do have the ability to change their proxy settings; however, this feature is typically disabled from access by the user by the network provider or the device manufacturer as it can circumvent billing mechanisms (especially for the United States compared to Europe). Therefore, whether used as a proxy or a true gateway, WAP intermediaries are typically referred to as WAP Gateways.

WAP gateways provide six important features:

1. *Security*: The WAP gateway provides a secure handoff point between WTLS (Wireless Transport Layer Security) to external security mechanisms such as SSL for HTTP in the form of HTTPS. Although the implementation of security mechanisms on WAP deployments can vary, the interface to the WAP gateway must be able to support WTLS and the corresponding hookups to HTTPS.
2. *Network Access*: The WAP gateway is the access point for the WAP client devices. Network providers are able to restrict access to users and connect their usage to billing systems by using the WAP gateways. It is also possible to create so-called walled gardens that disallow access to particular resources on the Internet or provide other Internet-based services not offered to nonsubscribers.
3. *Protocol Conversion*: The gateway is responsible for converting Wireless Session Protocol (WSP) to HTTP. This allows WAP to be based on a non-TCP/IP application layer protocol (WDP) and yet interact with the HTTP-based

Internet. Since WDP and WSP are lightweight and very generic wrappers for the implementation of the communication protocol by the network providers and device manufactures (CDMA, TDMA, GSM, etc.), the gateway's job is to convert the communications received in the form of WDP and WSP and provide HTTP client and server capabilities for communicating with other entities on the Internet. Even though WAP 2.x moves more toward the HTTP model, for backward compatibility reasons, the WSP/WDP layer remains.

4. *Caching*: If you have built an application with WAP using WML and WMLScript, you have invariably ran into a problem with caching issues. The WAP gateways provide a caching mechanism equivalent to (and even surpassing) that provided by HTTP. In fact, most implementations of WAP gateways are configured, out of the box, with extremely aggressive caching, leaving it to the developer of the application to manually expire the cache using standard HTTP headers or custom headers. The value delivered by the implementation of the various caching functionalities on the WAP gateways is of questionable value. HTTP seems to have got it right in the caching functionality it offers, so creating different caching schemes for content is a hotly debated topic. Although bandwidth preservation is something that aggressive caching can treat, it reduces portability and accessibility of content. Therefore, it reduces the pervasiveness of content that needs to be accessed by various mobile applications.
5. *Preparation of Content and Scripts*: WML is textual, and text is not a very efficient format for transfer of data. Therefore, the gateway encodes WML into "Compiled WML" (WMLC) before shipping it to the WAP-enabled device. Also, for security and syntax-checking reasons, WMLScripts must be checked and compiled before being sent to the client. Some WMLScripts use telephony functionality that requires interactions with other servers on the network. Even though the interface to these scripts are standard (such as making an outbound call and dialing extra digits), the implementation varies depending on the network. All of these types of tasks involve some preparation of content or code before it is sent to the WAP-enabled device. The gateway takes care of these tasks in WAP 1.x. Compilation and encoding, though still somewhat relevant, is less relevant in WAP 2.x as the WAP Forum moves to a model that resembles the Web-based user interfaces more with the use of XHTML.
6. *Functionality Offered through WAP 2.x and Higher*: Although WAP 2.x is not yet deployed in the United States and is just beginning to be rolled out in Europe, it offers a variety of changes to the role of the proxy/gateway in WAP deployments. First, as WAP moves more and more toward the Web, and as network QOS improves, WAP is beginning to offer a model of connectivity that puts increasingly less functionality into the proxy. One thing is important to remember though: The QOS issues will always exist because the nature of mobile connectivity is inherently different from wired connectivity and because intermittent connectivity can be caused by the mobile nature of the user and devices. So, although the gateways are taking on less and less, they will always be necessary to bridge the gap between the requirements of two distinct types of network participants: mobile and stationary.

In addition, WAP 2.x offers WAP push, support for UAProf (which we talk about in Chapter 3), additional functionality for WTA (Wireless Telephony Application), an External Functionality Interface (EFI) offering an extensibility mechanism for WAP APIs, data synchronization using SyncML, a persistent storage interface for storing data on the device, a multimedia messaging service, pictograms (small images used in messages), and provisioning. All of this new functionality must be supported by both the gateway and the client-side agent. This is because these functions are not standard parts of the Web today and some server-side mechanism must implement the support for such functionality.

2.7.4 Multimedia Messaging Services

The Multimedia Messaging Service (MMS) is the more mature child of the ever popular Short Messaging Service (SMS). Although sending multimedia messages can be implemented using any proprietary or standard technology, WAP's MMS specification is quickly gaining ground in becoming the industry standard for multimedia messages.

WAP MMS has several different aspects that we will look at in more depth, but let us go through an overview now:

1. *Presentation*: Because WAP is based on a thin-client architecture, the microbrowser must know how to render the multimedia message. MMS presentation is handled through SMIL (Synchronized Multimedia Integration Language). SMIL, which we will look at in great detail later in this text, is an XML-based language that allows one to specify the temporal behavior of various components of a multimedia message (audio, pictures, text, etc.), how they may be layered, how they are to be sequenced, etc.
2. *Addressing*: As in the case of any other type of message, an MMS message must be addressed to a receiver and by a sender. The MMS addressing model contains two addresses: the address of the MMS Proxy-Relay and the address of the recipient user and terminal [WAP MMS Encapsulation 2002]. Basically, this means that the MMS message must have the address of a server that knows how to send it and the address of a receiver. The address of the receiver can be a valid e-mail address [RFC822], a valid phone number, an IPv4, or an IPv6 address.
3. *Delivery*: Delivery of an MMS message is possible through a variety of interfaces. These interfaces include the following:
   a. *MMS proxy-relay*: This proxy server acts as an intermediary between MMS clients and other messaging systems or MMS clients.
   b. *Standard e-mail interface*: This interface would support any protocol supported by various Internet-based e-mail systems such as SMTP, POP, IMAP, and others.
   c. *Legacy wireless messaging systems*: Though there is no specific method or interface for interfacing with legacy wireless messaging systems such as SMS, the MMS specification recommends that such an interface be built by the implementers of an MMSC.

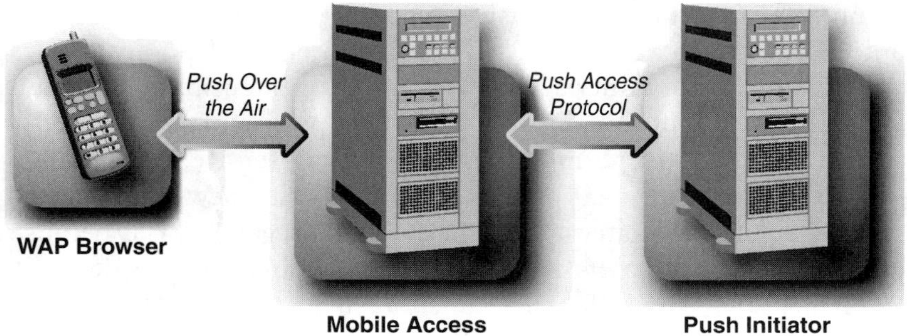

FIGURE 2.12. WAP 2.x Push.

The MMS proxy-relay can be hosted in the same environment or is a part of the Push Proxy Gateway (PPG) to facilitate sending of the message. MMS is perhaps one of the most critical parts of WAP 2.x as asynchronous messaging has been one of the early successful applications of wireless communications. Although asynchronous messaging is only a small subset of mobile applications, it is an important part of mobile applications because it presents the perfect way to deal with the disconnected user in an active manner: Simply send the message to the user's device as soon as it is available.

2.7.5 WAP Push

WAP Push is based on Push Access Protocol (PAP). Because of the thin-client architecture of WAP, it should be noted that "push" refers to sending a piece of content to the mobile device without the user explicitly requesting the particular content. There is no treatment of pushing code modules to the client in WAP Push.

A Push operation (see Figure 2.12) is accomplished by allowing a Push Initiator (PI) to transmit Push content and delivery instructions to a PPG, which then delivers the Push content to the WAP client (henceforth referred to as "device" or "terminal") according to the delivery instructions [Openwave 2002].

A WAP Push event goes through the following:

1. The mobile device (wireless phone in the case of WAP) connects and registers with a so-called Master Pull Proxy. This registration process is similar to registration of an object to become an event listener.
2. An application server, most probably external to the network of the wireless access provider, establishes a connection to a PPG through PAP protocol.
3. The content of the message being pushed can be a multipart document following the MIME format.
4. The user agent profile, through the implementation of UAProf, of the device receiving the push is accessed. This profile specifies the behavior of the push such as whether the user should be interrupted or not.
5. The message is then sent to the PPG. The device (previously registered with the PPG) receives the message.

Addressing of WAP Push is done through the MSISDN, which is typically the phone number of the device.

2.7.6 Security

WAP treats security issues in a comprehensive manner—rightly so, as wireless communications lend themselves to intruders more than their wired counterparts. WTLS allows for a mapping to Internet-based security of TLS (also known as SSL). WAP does not have application authorization. (This makes sense as WAP depends on applications that are running on servers and probably connect through HTTP, on a network running some protocol other than WAP.) It does, however, offer guaranteed authentication of the user devices as well as guaranteed integrity of the transactions that take place between the WAP-enabled devices and the WAP gateways. We will look at the WAP security issues later in this text.

2.7.7 Treatment of Dimensions of Mobility by WAP

As we have already mentioned several times, WAP intends to solve the problem of wireless applications rather than those of mobile applications. Because wireless applications are a subset of mobile applications, it is able to solve only a subset of problems presented to mobile application developers. So, once again, as we did with the other tools that we have looked at, let us see how WAP as a mobile application development platform measures up:

1. *Location awareness*: Though there is talk of supporting various location-based APIs in future versions of WAP, the intended mechanism to support location sensitivity in the 2.x version of WAP is the extensibility mechanism in EFI. So, whereas WAP 1.x does not treat location awareness at all, WAP 2.x offers a generic extensibility mechanism that can be applied to a variety of desired functionalities such as location awareness. However, WAP 2.x fails in proper treatment of location awareness functionality.
2. *QOS*: WSP, WDP, WTLS, and the other components that make WAP were designed with a great deal of attention paid to QOS. This dimension of mobility is perhaps best treated. However, it has been neglected until recently in WAP 2.x, where some attention has been paid to the possibility of using the device in a completely disconnected fashion.
3. *Limited device capabilities*: WAP does a good job of properly treating resource-starved devices. However, WAP is a thin-client environment and does not allow the application developer to optimize, make creative and clever user interfaces, or take advantage of an application that can run on the client. Whereas the thin-client nature of WAP allows it to treat resource-starved devices, the thin-client model is not particularly well suited for *all* mobile applications (which does not mean that some mobile applications can take advantage of it).
4. *Limited power supply*: Though WML and XHTML pages can be optimized, once again, the thin-client treatment of the applications disables the developers from optimizing the applications and/or building applications that behave differently depending on the amount of power available on the device.

5. *Support for a wide variety of user interfaces*: WAP 1.x addressed the interface problem of small screens by introducing the concept of cards and reducing the tag set available to the developers to those only necessary to render a simple user interface. WAP 2.x allows better support yet by moving toward XHTML and mobile cascading style sheets.
6. *Platform proliferation*: With the exception of WML attempting to address the small user interface of most mobile phones, WAP 1.x did not treat platform proliferation in any way. With UAProf (User Agent Profiles) based on CC/PP (both of which will be discussed in Chapter 3 and later on in this text), WAP 2.x offers a discovery mechanism for device properties and services offered. Such a mechanism is a necessity for treating platform proliferation. Because WAP 2.x uses standard mechanisms such as UAProf for this task, it offers a more solid and open solution over the other mobile application development tools to deal with the problem of platform proliferation.
7. *Active transactions*: Though the WAP 1.x architecture is based on a completely passive thin client, WAP 2.x allows for a more active client by adding WAP Push. This is a big improvement over the previous version of WAP in that application servers can invoke active behavior. However, WAP still lacks in this area because of its thin-client architecture.

We will use WAP for our code samples frequently in this text. It is crucial to remember, though, that WAP looks at the mobile application problem as a wireless problem. In some ways, this is good: It allows WAP to achieve very specific goals and treat very specific problems. The reality, however, is that the users of WAP are looking for mobile solutions and not a subset of those mobile solutions (wireless solutions). Therefore, WAP falls seriously short in many respects.

2.8 Symbian EPOC

Symbian, one of the most powerful and popular platforms for mobile development, was created jointly by Ericsson, Nokia, Panasonic, Psion, Samsung Electronics, and Siemens. The effort in creating this new operating system targeted at mobile devices started in 1998 and the first Symbian phones became available in 2001. The majority of the user base of Symbian devices is in Europe with very little user base in the United States; however, the market share in Europe is large and growing, with other markets wide open between the various contenders of mobile operating systems including Symbian. The Symbian OS 7.0 comes with considerable basic functionality for mobile applications: support for MMS, HTTP communication, SyncML synchronization, SMS, support for Mobile IP (through support for IPv6), and short-range wireless networking with IrDA and Bluetooth.

Symbian started as an operating system that supported primarily C^{++}, but it evolved to providing support for Java as well. Like the other tools that we have looked at, you can download the development SDK for free from the Symbian site and there are a variety of commercial IDE (Integrated Development Environment) that support application development for Symbian. The Java Virtual Machine implementation of EPOC is based on the Personal Java standard.

Deploying Java applications to Symbian is much easier than deploying BREW or J2ME and more like deploying them onto a Windows CE device. This is because Symbian is designed more as a PDA operating system than as an ultra-light mobile environment. Symbian's latest operating system (Symbian OS 7.0) supports multithreading.

We will not delve much into the details of programming a Symbian device. Symbian, as an operating system, is in the same class as Palm OS and Windows CE with one principle difference: Symbian has been designed for wirelessly connected devices. If you are interested in this topic, we recommend you look at *Symbian OS C++ for Mobile Phones* by Richard Harrison and published by Symbian Press and *Wireless Java for Symbian Devices* by Jonathan Allin and also published by Symbian Press.

2.9 Publishing Frameworks

Thus far, we have discussed tools and frameworks designed to allow the device to run an application such as J2ME, Windows CE, and BREW. We have also looked at WAP as a thin-client infrastructure for building content-driven applications. An alternative to these thick-client client–server models is a thin-client client–server architecture where a standard browser interprets the markup language sent to it by the server. What we have not looked at yet is work that may need to be done on the server to produce content suitable for devices to render. And this is where publishing frameworks, transcoding engines, and other types of server-side applications can come to the rescue. Some of the major things that we need such applications to accomplish are the following:

1. *Presenting content in several different formats*: Publishing frameworks have been used, in the context of network computing applications such as the Web, to create multiple views of the same document for the users. For example, a publishing framework may allow creation of HTML and PDF from the same data set. It is important to note that this does not mean that a publishing framework is a reporting system. Whereas reporting systems are required to manipulate data, create summaries, and do a series of other tasks, publishing frameworks are only required to push the data out into specific formats supported by the publishing framework.
2. *Matching the type of document requested with the type of document available (or one that may need to be generated at run time)*: For the publishing framework to publish a document readable by the requester, it needs to know what type of a document is required. Although the type of document can be explicitly specified by the requester, this creates requirements in how to communicate the necessary document type between the requester and the publishing framework. To avoid this situation, the publishing framework should be smart enough to use things

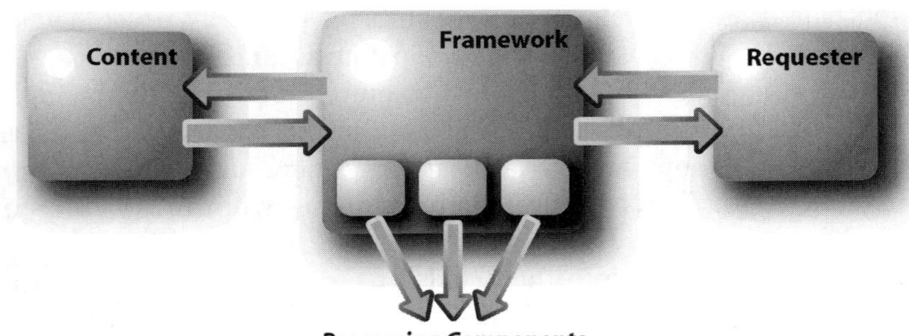

FIGURE 2.13. Publishing Content through a Publishing Framework.

such as HTTP headers, UAProf, or other requester-independent mechanisms to recognize the requester.

3. *Modularized infrastructure that separates the various components of the framework, the processing components, and the content*: As seen in Figure 2.13, publishing frameworks should be designed so that the framework itself does not need to be modified to use it. The processing modules (the modules that actually do the custom work on publishing the raw content to the desired content of the application developer) should be cleanly separated from the publishing framework and specific content (though it is obvious that these processing components do depend on the type of content). This modularization is critical in allowing effective use of the publishing framework because application developers should not be expected to change the framework to make it work and neither should they be expected to generate content. Likewise, content creators typically know nothing about developing software applications.

Apache's Cocoon is perhaps the best-known publishing framework today. Cocoon's framework is written in Java though the processing components can be written in a variety of languages including ASP (Microsoft's Advanced Server Pages), Java, and XSL. We will look at Cocoon in great detail in this text. We will also look at other examples such as IBM's Wireless Transcoding Publisher.

Publishing frameworks address the user interface–related dimensions of mobility. Namely, they allow us to publish the same static or dynamic content to a variety of devices, supporting a variety of user interfaces, by knowing the properties of those devices. They also present us with a great opportunity to cleanly internationalize and localize the content—two aspects of content that can vary based on the location of the user. Publishing frameworks can also publish content of multiple types to multiple channels (for example, publish audio and text content, each directed to the appropriate channel of the client). So, in summary, publishing frameworks treat the user interface problems presented by the following:

1. Proliferation of mobile devices.
2. Localized and internationalized user interfaces and their relationship with location of the user and the device being used.

3. Selection of the segments of multichannel content and directing them to the appropriate communication channels.
4. Selection and composition of content based on device information, such as the amount of available memory or the amount of power left, or based on the QOS and network properties. For example, whereas certain segments of the content may always be required, others, such as banner ads, may be eliminated when the device is running out of power or otherwise if the network latency is high owing to poor QOS.

At first glance then, publishing frameworks seem to be somewhat of a silver bullet for the problems of mobile application development. However, readers must beware of the antipattern, frequently referred to in this text. Publishing frameworks focus on the user interface. They are also very complex applications. Therefore, publishing frameworks are typically not very distributed: They run on servers and not the mobile devices; they are the server end of the thin-client architecture we talked about. So, the user interfaces that they render are usually not very sophisticated (HTML, XHTML, WML, VXML, etc.). They also do not take advantage of the computing power of the device, nor are they aware of the state of the device in a real-time or near-real-time manner. Just like we cannot use browsers to do all of our PC-based computing, we cannot use the content produced by publishing frameworks to solve all of the problems that mobile applications must solve.

Now, let us look at Cocoon, an open-source publishing framework by Apache that demonstrates the qualities we look for in a publishing framework well suited for mobile applications.

2.9.1 Cocoon

Because it is open source, and because it is widely accepted for implementing the main principles of publishing, in this book we will use Apache Software Foundation's Cocoon as one of the tools for our examples of a publishing framework that can publish content, in a centralized manner, to a variety of clients.

Cocoon, the brainchild of Stefano Mazzochi, started in 1999 and has gone through one major revision from its inception. Cocoon 2.0, the revision of the original Cocoon 1.0, will be the version on which we will focus in this text. Cocoon's architecture aims to separate *content* from *style* (the formatting of content), *logic* (how content is generated or chosen), and *management* of content (the process of creating content and everything else that goes with it). In an article Mazzochi wrote later [Cocoon 2002], he says Cocoon came about for the purpose of handling documentation for open-source projects and that its name came about as follows: "This was at the very end of 1998 and Ron Howard's movie *Cocoon* was playing on television, which explains the weird name only partially. I believed at the time that these technologies were a key part of the future of the Web, so a cocoon was just what was needed to allow them to incubate and grow stronger."

Cocoon is typically used as an XML-based publishing framework; however, it is flexible enough to deal with any type of input and to generate any type of output. As you will see in Chapter 3, XML is the preferred format for the content handled

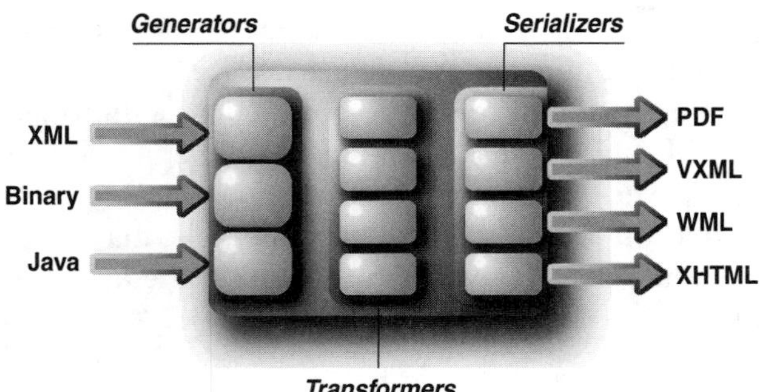

FIGURE 2.14. Cocoon's Basic Architecture.

by mobile applications, so the two are well-fit in that we practically only need to worry about XML-based input and output.

There is a great deal of documentation on Cocoon at Apache's Web site. Mazzochi and his team have produced high-quality documentation. Our purpose here is not to duplicate that work, but rather to look at the functionality of Cocoon from the perspective of mobile application development tasks. To do this, we will start with the Cocoon architecture, its installation, creating content and style for Cocoon, and finally managing application development for Cocoon.

Cocoon's Architecture

Cocoon is a framework that employs the principle of *inversion of control* referred to frequently throughout this book. Even though it is an open-source framework, modifying it is not something for the faint of heart and requires a high level of expertise in Java as well as design patterns not to mention a tremendous amount of time to come up to speed on a fairly complex framework. As a user of Cocoon, though, you will be happily surprised to see that creating components for Cocoon is a fairly easy and straightforward task. Mobile application developers, as users of Cocoon, develop components controlled by Cocoon. So, as far as we are concerned, Cocoon is a "black-box" framework (one whose internal operation does not concern us). As shown in Figure 2.14, there are three types of components in Cocoon:

1. *Generators*: These components provide us with a method to feed data into our black box. Generators give us a hook to pull the raw content into Cocoon.
2. *Transformers*: These components transform the raw content into other content.
3. *Serializers*: These components provide the output for our black box from the transformed content provided to them by the transformers.

The latest version of Cocoon adds a new component called the *aggregator*. An aggregator does just what the name implies: It aggregates various pieces of content. Though this aggregation can be done using a transformer component, there are occasions where it is more elegant. To reduce the complexity of our usage of Cocoon, we will not discuss aggregators much here. Please refer to the Cocoon documentation available at the Apache XML project [Apache XML 2002].

Whereas the generators and the serializers are typically the external hooks to, respectively, the input and output into Cocoon, the transformers are the modules that change the content to what it needs to be. Cocoon's architecture allows feeding the contents of one component into another, making it ideal for a modular transformation of content.

Cocoon, in its current form, is a J2EE Web application archive (WAR file). In this way, it can be deployed on any J2EE application server (or a subset thereof in the form of a servlet engine such as Tomcat). In fact, Cocoon's most prevalent deployment is with Tomcat, another open-source project from Apache for building Web-based applications using Java servlets.

Because Cocoon is a Web-based application, an interaction with Cocoon is initiated through an HTTP request. This HTTP request is then routed through a series of generators, transformers, and serializers to create, transform, and produce the content to be sent back through the HTTP response. The route that the content takes from its origination to being published to the viewing client is analogous to a work flow. Cocoon documentation refers to this work flow–like treatment of components as a "pipeline," driving the name from Unix pipelining where the output of one process is fed into another process. Pipelines are created with a set of XML-based instructions in a configuration file called the *sitemap*. The sitemap maps out the flow of request and response for all possible requests made into the Cocoon Web application.

Installing and Using Cocoon

Before you install Cocoon, you should either have a J2EE 1.2 application server or servlet engine installed and running. If you do not have one, there is a free one available from Apache and you can find it at http://jakarta.apache.org. It is called Tomcat. In fact, Tomcat is currently used as the industry de facto standard for servlet engines.

Once you have an application server or Servlet engine installed, you need to download the Cocoon WAR file from http://xml.apache.org. Simply install the Web application and you are ready to go! Installing a WAR file involves only one step: putting the WAR file in the webapps directory. You are now ready to use Cocoon by simply typing in the URL of the application server plus /cocoon (for example, http://localhost:8081/cocoon).

If you do this, you will get an introductory page on how to use Cocoon. There are plenty of excellent examples that ship with the download of Cocoon. Go through them if you are interested in writing your own components. They serve as a great hands-on tutorial because writing components for Cocoon can be a little complex.

Now, let us look at what these components are and how we write them.

Generators, Transformers, and Serializers

As we mentioned in the previous section, the basic building blocks of a Cocoon-based application are generators, transformers, and serializers. These components must be authored in either Java or XSP, an XML-based language in Cocoon that can be compiled into Java classes. By default, XSP is in JSP (Java Server Pages); however, it is extensible to support other scripting languages based on other languages such as ASP (Microsoft's scripting language for Web-based applications using MS Visual Basic syntax) or whatever language is preferred. The only catch is that if something other than Java is preferred for the XSP pages, you will have to write a compiler that converts your XSP pages to Java classes. Let us go through the components one by one:

1. *Generators*: The basic job of a generator is to take static or dynamic content pointed to by the incoming request or a property of the incoming request (we will discuss how the content is selected more when we discuss sitemaps) and generate XML in the form of SAX events. Although Cocoon 1.x was based on DOM, it was not efficient at handling large documents. So, in the interest of making Cocoon more flexible and scalable, its designers moved to the SAX model (discussed in Chapter 3) in Cocoon 2.x. There are a variety of generators that are available with the standard download of Cocoon. Generators are Java classes (or a collection of Java classes with one class that wraps their functionality). To write a custom generator, the wrapper class must implement the interface org.apache.cocoon.generation.Generator. There are a series of generators that come with Cocoon including the following:
   a. *File generator*: This generator can read an XML file and create SAX events from it
   b. *Server pages generator*: This particularly important generator creates another generator, at compile time, which knows what type of scripting language is used in the XSP page (if one is used for generation) so that it compiles the XSP page properly.
   c. *JSP generator*: The JSP generator allows usage of JSP pages as the source of dynamic data.
   d. *Request generator*: This generator is peculiar in that it creates a series of SAX events with the data encapsulated in the incoming HTTP request.

   There are other generators that come with Cocoon, these are just a few examples. XSP pages can be used very effectively to generate dynamic content through the server page generator. We will look at XSP briefly.
2. *Transformers*: As in the case of generators, there are several transformers that come with the download of Cocoon. The most important of all these is the Xalan transformer, which essentially uses the Xalan (another solid application from Apache) XSL (Extensible Stylesheet Language) transformation engine to transform XML using XSLs. Though there are other transformers that ship with Cocoon, the transformers that allow XSL documents to be the engine for transformation are key to writing Cocoon-based applications. The advantage that XSL offers over other transformation techniques are numerous. XSLs are neither language dependent nor platform dependent, and they allow for mapping any XML document to any other XML document. But, in case you need to author your own transformer, you need to create a class that implements the interface org.apache.cocoon.transformation.Transformer.
3. *Serializer*: Once the content has been generated and transformed, it needs to be published to the client through the HTTP response. The serializer is responsible for this. In most cases, we will want to publish XML because most clients are

moving toward supporting some XML-based format. For this, there is a standard XML serializer that comes with Cocoon. However, there are cases when we need non-XML-based text or nontextual binary data. For these, we have to write our own serializers. Once again, this is done by implementing the interface org.apache.cocoon.serialization.Serializer. Along with Cocoon come several handy serializers, including the FOPSerializer (which uses the Apache FOP libraries to convert HTML to PDF). Although PDF is typically too CPU- and memory-intensive for most mobile application clients, another serializer that comes with Cocoon is the SVG serializer, which supports a new graphics standard for the Internet in SVG. SVG is a promising area for rendering graphics on mobile devices as it has mobile extensions.

A very simple and dynamic Cocoon application may use an XSP page to generate the content, then an XSL document to transform it, and finally an XML serializer to publish the produced document to the client. We will look at a simple example later on.

The Cocoon Sitemap

Once we have written the classes or pages to generate the content, transform it, and serialize it, we need to tell Cocoon: 1. in which sequence the input of one component is fed into another and 2. which requests are diverted to go through a particular set of components. Both of these tasks are accomplished through the sitemap file (Sitemap.xmap). The sitemap is a file where the instructions that form the pipelines (the work flow–like piping of input of one component into another in chains to produce content in response to a request) and the definition of Cocoon components are outlined using an XML-based syntax. So, the two pieces of information we listed lie within the sitemap file.

Let us start with the second item. Assuming that we have a set of content flows, the job becomes selecting which content flow should produce the response for a given request. Because we know that the incoming request is an HTTP request, we can look at the request headers, the request content, or the Universal Resource Identifier (URI) to extract information about the request. In Cocoon 2.x and extensions such as DELI (Cocoon extensions produced by HP Labs to support CC/PP and UAProf), support for more advanced mechanisms of discovery of the client and client capabilities exist. So, the request has some information about the client and the type of content that the client expects encapsulated in it directly in the header, content, or URI or indirectly through mechanisms such as CC/PP and UAProf (which will be discussed in detail in Chapter 3). *Matchers* and *selectors* are the two components designed to do this.

We did not mention Matchers and selectors earlier because they are not components that a user of Cocoon 2.x will typically have to extend or modify. Rather, the reminisces of Matchers and selectors are seen in the sitemap file. Matchers that come with Cocoon allow one to make lexical pattern matches using Regular Expressions (Perl-like syntax for comparing character strings) on the URI, HTTP request parameters, and HTTP session parameters (where the session is supported and applied). The selectors that come with Cocoon allow one to select the pipeline based on browser type, HTTP header parameters in the request, HTTP session parameters, or environment parameters (environment on which Cocoon is running–for example, Linux environment variables).

Example 2.1: Using XML Based Tags in the Sitemap to Drive Components.

```
<map:match pattern="*.wml">
   <map:generate src="helloCocoon_xforms.xml" />
   <map:transform src="xformsTowml.xsl" />
   <map:serialize />
</map:match>
```

Example 2.1 shows a simple code snippet out of the sitemap file that directs Cocoon to use an XForms file as the data source for the generator, apply an XSL transform to it, and then use the default serializer to serialize out the content (the default serializer simply produces XML). The condition for this set of events is any file that has a wml extension.

Matchers are fairly simple. The tags within the matcher tags are processed sequentially. You can have one or more of each component, but the like components have to be bunched together to keep the flow consistent (so that the first transformer gets its input from a generator rather than a serializer). Selectors offer more complex logic. With selectors, you can use logic of the if-then-else type in specifying which component is used under what conditions.

There are other components involved in the sitemap and the rest of Cocoon. For example, action components provide an effort for further separating logic from style and aggregators allow for composition of blocks of content into new blocks of content. We will not look at these components as our intent here is a mere introduction to Cocoon. To get an in-depth understanding of Cocoon refer to the Cocoon documentation at Apache's site. It is well written. But, before we look at writing a simple mobile application with Cocoon, let us look at XSPs.

Introduction to XSP

As we mentioned previously, XSPs are used to feed dynamic content into a generator component. XSPs can use a variety of programming languages such as Java in the form of JSP. In fact, Java Server Pagess are the default implementation. If you want to use another programming language such as ASP (based on Microsoft's Visual Basic), you will have to write your own programming language processor and compiled programming language components.

Internal to Cocoon are *logic sheets*, also referred to as *tag libraries*, which define a set of custom tags usable in an XSP document in addition to the programming language used for scripting. A standard set of logic sheets providing hooks to the syntax for the scripting language supported must be provided. In the case of the de facto scripting language, JSP, these are logic sheets that allow imports of classes, declaring classes, defining methods, etc. There are two other logic sheets that come with Cocoon: the request logic sheet and the session logic sheet. These two give us hooks into the HTTP request and response.

TABLE 2.1. Logic Sheet Tags

Request Logic Sheet	Purpose
<xsp-request:get-parameter name="someURIParameter"/>	Allows retrieval of parameters from the request into the XSP page (and further using it in display or logic of the page).
<xsp-request:get-header name="someHeaderName"/>	Allows retrieval of the value of a header and its subsequent usage.
<xsp-request:get-attribute name="someAttribute"/>	Allows retrieval of the value of an attribute in the servlet context of Cocoon within the servlet container.
<xsp-request:set-attribute name="someAttribute"/>	Allows setting an attribute in the request. This attribute is only useful when another component looks inside the request to pick up an attribute as the life cycle of the attribute is limited to the HTTP request.
Session Logic Sheet	Purpose
<xsp-session:get-attribute name="someAttribute"/>	Allows retrieval of an attribute value (string) stored in the session.
<xsp-session:set-attribute name="someAttribute"/>	Allows putting an attribute value in the session for later retrieval.
<xsp-session:get-attribute-names/>	Returns the name of the attributes currently in the session.

These two logic sheets are the most important in creating dynamic content to be consumed by a generator. Table 2.1 lists the important tags for each tag library.

Remember that this is not a comprehensive list. Such a list is available at Cocoon's Web site. Once again, our purpose for reviewing a subset of functionality and syntax-related issues of Cocoon is to simply get a feel for the framework and provide an intuitive high-level comparative understanding with other available tools.

Code snippets of JSP (or whatever language is supported as we have explained) must be wrapped within <xsp:logic></xsp:logic> tags to mark them for compilation. There are a few other tags that we have to know about to write the most basic XSP page. These include the following:

1. *<xsp:page>*: This tag (and its closing companion) wrap around the entire XSP page.
2. *<xsp:structure>*: This tag wraps around multiple directives.
3. *<xsp:include>*: This tag imports classes to be used on the XSP page.

4. *<xsp:expr>*: This is an XSP expression, similar to a JSP expression, where the value of the expression is evaluated and printed out on the page.

There is much more to XSP and understanding it. For one thing, to write an XSP page, you should be fluent in JSP and XSL. Unless Cocoon is the central framework of your application, you are probably not going to implement the components necessary to support another scripting language (though PHP and others are being worked on by other various open-source development teams). So, count on having to write JSP and XSLs. Actions, a new set of components that allow better separation of logic and style, will let you extract the business logic from your XSP pages better and leave only style-related elements in there. XSPs provide a perfect tool for writing generic user interfaces, which we will discuss in Chapter 5, allowing you to build user interfaces in layers and specializing them to the specific clients when necessary.

Hello Cocoon

Now, let us look at building a very simple mobile application. Perhaps the most popular use of Cocoon for mobile applications today is to generate XHTML, WML, and HTML from the same content based on the requesting browser type. Let us first build a basic XSP page that will create our basic content. This is seen in Example 2.2.

Example 2.2: HelloCocoon.xsp.

```
<xsp:page language="java"
    xmlns:xsp = "http://www.apache.org/xsp"
    xmlns:xsp-request = "http://www.apache.org/xsp/request/2.0">
    <content>
        <para>This would be some text that shows on any
          interface</para>
    </content>
    <xsp:logic>
        String myBrowser = <xsp-request:get-header
          name="user-agent">;
        myBrowser = myBrowser.toUpperCase();
        if (myBrowser.substring("IE")) {
        <xsp:text>Some things, like a DHTML control, that only
          work in IE</xsp:text>
        }
        <ul>
            <li>list item 1</li>
            <li>list item 2</li>
        </ul>
    </xsp:logic>
</xsp:page>
```

Notice that we can recognize the browser and add content using selectors and aggregator components (not discussed here). But, we are shooting for a very simple example.

Next, we need to transform this content. For our example, we will create the transformer using an XSL page. There is an important side note here that we will get to extensively in Chapter 5. The XSP page produces some content that needs to be transformed. This content is XML-based content, but the question is what document type definition (DTD) does this follow? Cocoon has provided a markup language called XMLForm, which is a concoction taken from W3C's XForms and the popular open-source J2EE MVC implementation in Apaches Struts. XForms alone should be the preferred markup language to use in rendering this intermediary user interface format. Whereas XMLForm is not a standard accepted by other application frameworks and vendors and is something very specific to Cocoon, XForms is not specific to Cocoon.

Example 2.3: Section 1 of XSL Document Transforming XMLForms to HTML.

```
<?xml version="1.0" encoding="iso-8859-1" ?>
<!--Basic XMLForm processing stylesheet. Converts XMLForm tags
  to HTML tags.
Syntax is borrowed from the XForms standard:
  http://www.w3.org/TR/2002/WD- xforms-20020118/
This style sheet is usually applied at the end of a
  transformation process after laying out the XMLForm tags on
  the page is complete. At this stage XMLFormtags are rendered
  in device-specific format.
Different widgets are broken into templates to allow
  customization in importing style sheets. Authors are Ivelin
  Ivanov, Andrew Timberlake, Michael Ratliff, Torsten Curdt,
  Simon Price, Konstantin Piroumian, and Robert Ellis Parrott.
  -->

<xsl:stylesheet version="1.0"
    xmlns:xsl="http://www.w3.org/1999/XSL/Transform";
    xmlns:xf="http://xml.apache.org/cocoon/xmlform/2002";>
    <xsl:output method = "xml" omit-xml-declaration = "no"/>
    <xsl:template match="/">
        <xsl:apply-templates/>
    </xsl:template>
    <xsl:template match="xf:form">
        <form>
            <xsl:copy-of select="@*"/>
            <!--the xf:form/@view attributed is sent back to the
              server as a hidden field-->
            <input type="hidden" name="cocoon-xmlform-view"
              value="test@cienecs.com"/>
```

```
            <!--render the child form controls-->
            <xsl:apply-templates />
        </form>
    </xsl:template>
    <xsl:template match="xf:output">
        [<xsl:value-of select="xf:value/text()"/>]
    </xsl:template>
    <xsl:template match="xf:textbox">
        <input name="test@cienecs.com" type="textbox"
          value="{xf:value/text()}">
            <!-- copy all attributes from the original markup,
              except for "ref"-->
            <xsl:copy-of select="@*[not(name()='ref')]"/>
            <xsl:apply-templates select="xf:hint"/>
        </input>
    <xsl:template>
    <xsl:template match="xf:textarea">
        <textarea name="test@cienecs.com">
            <xsl:copy-of select="@*[not(name()='ref')]"/>
            <xsl:value-of select="xf:value/text()"/>
            <xsl:apply-templates select="xf:hint"/>
        </textarea>
    </xsl:template>
```

Example 2.3: Section 2 of XSL Document Transforming XMLForms to HTML.

```
<xsl:template match="xf:password">
    <input name="test@cienecs.com" type="password"
      value="{xf:value/text()}">
        <xsl:copy-of select="@*[not(name()='ref')]"/>
        <xsl:apply-templates select="xf:hint"/>
    </input>
</xsl:template>
<xsl:template match="xf:hidden">
    <input name="test@cienecs.com" type="hidden"
      value="{xf:value/text()}">
        <xsl:copy-of select="@*[not(name()='ref')]"/>
    </input>
</xsl:template>
<xsl:template match="xf:selectBoolean">
    <input name="test@cienecs.com" type="checkbox"
      value="true">
        <xsl:copy-of select="@*[not(name()='ref')]"/>
            <xsl:if test="xf:value/text() = 'true'">
```

```
            <xsl:attribute name="checked"/>
        </xsl:if>
        <xsl:apply-templates select="xf:hint"/>
    </input>
</xsl:template>
<xsl:template match="xf:selectOne |
  xf:test@cienecs.com'listbox']">
    <select name="test@cienecs.com">
    <xsl:copy-of select="@*[not(name()='ref')]"/>
    <!-- all currently selected nodes are listed as value
      elements -->
        <xsl:variable name="selected" select="xf:value"/>
        <xsl:for-each select="xf:item">
            <option value="{xf:value}">
                <!-- If the current item value matches one of
                  the selected values -->
                <!-- mark it as selected in the listbox -->
                <xsl:if test="$selected = xf:value">
                    <xsl:attribute name="selected"/>
                </xsl:if>
                <xsl:value-of select="xf:caption"/>
            </option>
        </xsl:for-each>
    </select>
</xsl:template>
    <xsl:template match="xf:test@cienecs.com'radio']">
        <xsl:variable name="selected" select="xf:value"/>
        <xsl:variable name="ref" select="@ref"/>
        <xsl:for-each select="xf:item">
            <input name="{$ref}" type="radio" value="{xf:value}">
                <xsl:copy-of select="@*[not(name()='ref')]"/>
                <xsl:if test="xf:value = $selected">
                    <xsl:attribute name="checked"/>
                </xsl:if>
            </input>
            <xsl:value-of select="xf:caption"/>
            <br/>
        </xsl:for-each>
    </xsl:template>
    <xsl:template match="xf:selectMany | xf:test@cienecs.com'
      listbox']">
        <xsl:variable name="selected" select="xf:value"/>
            <xsl:copy-of select="@*[not(name()='ref')]"/>
        <xsl:attribute name="multiple"/>
            <select name="test@cienecs.com">
```

Example 2.3: Section 3 of XSL Document Transforming XMLForms to HTML.

```
        <xsl:for-each select="xf:item">
            <option value="{xf:value}">
                <xsl:if test="xf:value = $selected">
                    <xsl:attribute name="selected"/>
                </xsl:if>
                <xsl:value-of select="xf:caption"/>
            </option>
        </xsl:for-each>
    </select>
</xsl:template>
    <xsl:template match="xf:test@cienecs.com'checkbox']">
    <xsl:variable name="selected" select="xf:value"/>
    <xsl:variable name="ref" select="@ref"/>
    <xsl:for-each select="xf:item">
        <input name="{$ref}" type="checkbox"
          value="{xf:value}">
            <xsl:copy-of select="@*[not(name()='ref')]"/>
            <xsl:if test="xf:value = $selected">
                <xsl:attribute name="checked"/>
            </xsl:if>
        </input>
        <xsl:value-of select="xf:caption"/>
        <br/>
    </xsl:for-each>
</xsl:template>
<xsl:template match="xf:submit">
    <!-- the id attribute of the submit control is sent to
      the server -->
    <!-- as a conventional Cocoon Action parameter of the
      form cocoon-action-* -->
    <input name="test@cienecs.com" type="submit"
      value="{xf:caption/text()}">
        <xsl:copy-of select="@*[not(name()='id')]"/>
        <xsl:apply-templates select="xf:hint"/>
    </input>
</xsl:template>
<xsl:template match="xf:hint">
    <xsl:attribute name="title"><xsl:value-of select="."/>
      </xsl:attribute>
</xsl:template>
<!-- copy all the rest of the markup which is not recognized
  above -->
```

```
<xsl:template match="*">
   <xsl:copy><xsl:copy-of select="@*"/><xsl:apply-templates/>
     </xsl:copy>
</xsl:template>
<xsl:template match="text()">
   <xsl:value-of select="." />
</xsl:template>
</xsl:stylesheet>
```

Although XMLForm touches on issues such as persistence that are not related to the user interface, it is very much a thin-client-based markup language. XForms, in contrast, addresses only user interface issues and is more flexible in being used in thick and thin clients. Nevertheless, because the existing Apache documentation uses XMLForm for their examples, we will follow suit. As will be mentioned in later chapters, particularly Chapters 5 and 6, we will cover use of XForms and its integration with publishing frameworks.

Now, we need to transform the content generated by our simple XSP page. We are going to do this using an XSL page. Although there are preexisting XSL pages bundled with Cocoon to transform XMLForm pages into various other markup languages, we will assume that we have to write our own XSL pages. Example 2.3 shows the XSL page that transforms a subset of an XMLForm document used in our Example 2.2 into an HTML document. This code ships with Cocoon and can be found at http://cocoon.apache.org.

Now that we have the basis for our transformers, how do we tell Cocoon to apply them? As we mentioned previously, this is done in the sitemap. First, let us think about what conditions we may need to apply to find out which transformer to apply to the generated content. We could use the headers in the HTTP request, the extension of the file resource requested in the URI, or a combination of those to find out if the request is coming from a WML browser or an HTML browser. If the device is a WAP 2.x-enabled device, we could also use CC/PP and UAProf to recognize the capabilities of the device. Let us consider the simplest case though and use the string pattern in the URI. Often, an extension of .html or .htm is attached to a request that expects an HTML document for its response. In the same manner, an extension of .wml is attached to a request that expects a WML document for its response. Example 2.4 shows the XML snippet needed in the sitemap file to finish our task.

In this way, we put the content generation logic into the generator components and the XSP page, put the style information into the transformer, and put the management of which style is applied to what content and when in the sitemap.

We have now created the basic components needed to publish content. As you go through the documentation in Cocoon's site, you will notice that Stefano Mazzochi and the other authors of Cocoon designed Cocoon with the problem of Web publishing in mind. Though Web services are not addressed, this concept of publishing XML can be extended to provide a Web service framework that competes in flexibility and extensibility with the best of other Web service frameworks. Using Cocoon, we can generate XML documents that are consumed by the requesting entity and then used for other purposes.

Though Cocoon is primarily used for publishing markup languages understood by browsers, to solve the problems with mobile user interfaces in particular, it can be used to publish XML that is further modified and indirectly used to produce a user interface. In other words, we do not have to generate, transform, and serialize content that is eventually consumable by one browser or another. A thick client or other servers can consume the content. In such cases Cocoon provides us with a neatly organized pipelining infrastructure.

We will discuss the use of Cocoon further in Chapters 6 and 7 in creating graphical and voice user interfaces.

Example 2.4: XML Segments to Apply the Appropriate Pipeline for Example 2.3.

```
<map:sitemap xmlns:"http://www.apache.org/cocoon/sitemap/1.0">
...
...
    <map:pipeline>
        <map:match pattern="*.wml">
            <map:generate type="serverpages" src="docs/{1}.xsp">
            <map:transform src="stylesheets/XMLForm2WML.xsl"/>
            <map:serialize type="wap"/>
        </map:match>

        <map:match pattern="*.htm*">
            <map:generate type="serverpages" src="docs/{1}.xsp"/>
            <map:transform src="stylesheets/XMLForm2HTML.xsl"/>
            <map:serialize type="html"/>
        </map:match>
    </map:pipeline>
...
...
</map:sitemap>
```

2.9.2 IBM Wireless Transcoding Publisher

The best places to learn about IBM software are the IBM Red Books and the IBM developer Web site. Meanwhile, the IBM Wireless Transcoding Publisher (WTP) is IBM's commercial product to satisfy the needs of those in need of a publishing framework, plus some complementing utilities, to create mobile applications. The particular document of interest for the suite of products that encompasses the WTP, namely the IBM Wireless Everyplace Suite, can be found in the reference guide [Appleby et al. 2000]. Before we start though, let us understand that the encompassing product, the Wireless Everyplace Suite, is actually intended to do more than publishing. It is an integrated environment with IBM's Websphere

Application Server and supports J2EE applications. However, our focus here will be on the pervasive and mobile aspects of this suite of products and comparing it to the open-source alternative in Cocoon.

As in the case of many products, we would have a tough time comparing the features of the Wireless Transcoding Publisher to Cocoon one-to-one. For proper comparison, we need to first look at the functionality by the umbrella product, the Everyplace Suite.

Overview of IBM Everyplace Suite

The IBM Everyplace Suite covers a variety of topics that address more the overall issues of mobility rather than solely publishing. The Everyplace Suite addresses issues related to wireless connectivity, content management for wireless clients, wireless security, provisioning and device management, and integration with the IBM Websphere application suite of products. It also includes integration with IBM's messaging platforms, allowing for asynchronous communication.

In this way, the Everyplace Suite addresses some of the issues of various dimensions of mobility, namely, QOS, multichannel user interfaces, device proliferation, and active transactions. Of course, as with many other commercial products from their rivals Microsoft, Sun Microsystems, and others, much of what is claimed is marketing rather than true functionality. Nevertheless, the Everyplace Suite does offer valuable functionality in the way of treating the issues of mobile application development. In fact, of all commercial products that intend to address all of the dimensions of mobility on the server, it offers the most amount of functionality.

When it comes to security, the Everyplace Suite offers implementation of WTLS and mapping to SSL, single sign-on, authorization for various components of your application, and integration with LDAP (X.500) for simple lookups such as user names and passwords. The Everyplace Suite also offers some very useful messaging functionality in integrating with MQ Series messaging servers. MQe Application, a component of the Everyplace Suite, runs on higher end mobile devices such as those that can run EPOC or Windows CE that support Java. This feature is particularly useful as it enables asynchronous messaging between any device that can support MQe; this means that messages can be composed while the device is disconnected and sent when it is reconnected, wait in the queue until the recipient is available, and be delivered to the recipient upon its availability. Figure 2.15 shows the layout for asynchronous communication using MQe.

The Everyplace Suite comes with a complete implementation of a WAP gateway, which can be used as either a proxy server or as a true gateway (by the carriers in the United States where gateway access is restricted to carriers and by all in Europe where gateway access is open).

Basic WTP

WTP is a fairly open commercial product with its API in Java and a component-based architecture. But it should be said that WTP, at least at its 1.1 version, is intended to do far less as a publishing framework than Cocoon. The concepts still

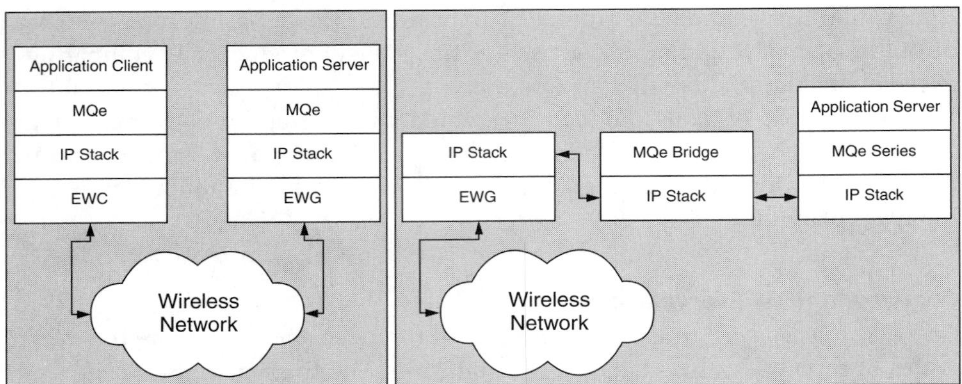

FIGURE 2.15. Using MQe for Asynchronous Communication with Mobile Devices.

remain somewhat the same: Content is generated, then transformed, and finally published. So, let us compare and contrast the WTP and Cocoon:

1. WTP offers a large degree of functionality in converting existing HTML on the Web to other markup languages such as WML that are consumable by mobile devices. HTML is not well-formed XML (see Chapter 3). In fact, the name Wireless "Transcoding" Publisher refers to this conversion of HTML to other markup languages: "Transcoding" is the process of converting this HTML to other markup languages by adding custom tags to the content and using XSL transformation documents. Cocoon offers less out-of-the-box functionality here, but it is more flexible as you can create your own generators and serializers, using your own domain-dependent or independent generators and transformers. Apache's Tidy is the tool to supplement Cocoon to get close to the functionality offered by WTP in converting HTML to other markup languages. WTP allows extension of the transformers through writing Java MEGlet's (a MEGlet being defined as a "content *Monitor, Editor, or Generator*" [Appleby et al. 2000]). Extending WTP through MEGlets is similar to creating Cocoon transformers.
2. WTP also offers custom transformers that convert a variety of image formats. Some examples of such conversions are conversion of JPEG images to WBMP images (the format displayable by WAP devices).
3. WTP offers a set of WAP devices, along with their profiles and suitable HTML to WML transformers, that allow very simple publishing of HTML and XML content to WML-enabled devices. Devices can be selected for how the content is targeted.
4. WTP offers a very rich set of tools for developers. This is a big advantage over all the other publishing frameworks available. These tools include various GUI interfaces that facilitate management of device profiles, WTP components, content-generation flows, and other tasks that the WTP is used for.
5. WTP provides integration with the other components of the Everyplace Suite. Although this integration does not relate to the task of publishing, it facilitates building a system as a whole when using an all-IBM component-based environment.

Overall, WTP is more focused on providing development tools and integration with the other IBM products to deliver a total solution whereas Cocoon provides a more flexible and extensible infrastructure for publishing content for mobile applications. There are also other products on the market by IBM competitors such as Sun Microsystems and Microsoft. We chose WTP because it is open, uses Java, and is widely used compared to the other products. Cocoon provides us with the open-source (and therefore license-free) alternative. Your choice for your project will depend on the requirements of your organization and your project.

2.10 Other Tools

We looked at publishing frameworks on the server side as well as programming tools for creating distributed applications that run on a variety of devices. There are a host of other tools that we will use for our examples in this text. Let us categorize them briefly and introduce some real products and implementations.

2.10.1 Asynchronous Messaging Systems

HTTP represents the most pervasive synchronous messaging in computing today. Though it is often misused and abused, it is flexible, extensible, and scalable. These are properties that make it invaluable as a tool for exchanging synchronous messages between two systems. There are also less pervasive synchronous messaging solutions such as OMG's CORBA, Microsoft's COM/DCOM, and others. Although, to date, there is no equivalent to HTTP in the asynchronous world of messaging, there are various asynchronous messaging solutions that we will need to look at in this text.

The importance of asynchronous messaging in mobile computing is fourfold:

1. Asynchronous messaging systems are highly scalable, lending themselves to networks that have to serve the exchanging of messages among millions of different devices.
2. Active behavior on the part of a mobile device is less costly when implemented using an asynchronous messaging model as opposed to a synchronous messaging model. Synchronous messaging models either require persistent connections through which the active clients register with the active servers or use some sort of a polling technique. Both of these methods have a high overhead.
3. Asynchronous messaging allows us to treat both the connected and the disconnected devices. Asynchronous messages either have no guaranteed time period for delivery or have very long message expiration times. In both cases, the message is delivered to the user when the user's device is available.
4. Depending on the architecture, asynchronous messaging between the devices (without the use of the network servers—in the case of peer-to-peer or mobile agent architectures) can have a variety of performance as well as up-time benefits.

Previously, we mentioned the IBM Everyplace Suite, a product that integrates a variety of IBM's solutions to deliver an integrated mobile application development and deployment environment. The Everyplace Suite includes an adapted version of the IBM MQ Series asynchronous messaging in MQe mobile messaging as well as a Java API usable on the various mobile devices that support Java. Of course, this environment is well integrated with the other versions of the MQ Series that allow asynchronous messaging for medium-size and larger networks.

There are also competing products from various J2EE vendors as well as Microsoft (on the Windows platform) for asynchronous messaging. Categorizing the asynchronous messaging tools is typically done through the type of APIs they expose (Java Messaging Service, Microsoft's Windows Messaging, etc.) or the type of service that they provide (either publish–subscribe or point-to-point). Most messaging products today support both publish–subscribe and point-to-point messaging models.

The key, then, becomes selecting a messaging platform standard before choosing a specific product. Today, there are basically three camps: messaging on the Microsoft platform, Java Messaging Service (JMS) implemented on a variety of platforms, and performance-tuned messaging systems such as ones offered by Tivoli and TIBCO with their own proprietary APIs. These products all address messaging in a manner independent of the application domain. What suits you and your organization depends on your needs; however, JMS-compliant platforms offer the most interoperability—a factor that is extremely important in the world of messaging where messages can be exchanged between disparate systems run by a variety of organizations.

There is also asynchronous messaging specific to mobile applications such as Short Messaging Service (SMS) and Multimedia Messaging Service (MMS). Whereas implementations of such messaging systems used in mobile applications can utilize products such as those compliant with a JMS interface or others such as TIBCO, it is possible that to get the best performance, such broad-reaching systems are written from scratch. There are currently a number of products in the SMS market that allow asynchronous messaging implementations for text messages. Implementations for MMS are being worked on at the time this book is being written.

2.10.2 UML Tools

Because this text aims to use UML and the methodologies surrounding it to bring mobile application development methodologies up to par with typical software development methodologies, it is befitting that we discuss some UML tools. We will have more in-depth discussion of these tools in Chapter 4 (which solely focuses on the topic of UML) and in later chapters. For now, let us take a quick overview of what is out there and how we intend to use these tools.

Several of the founding fathers of UML are currently employed by Rational Software, the company that produces the industry de facto standards for UML-based development. So, the various Rational tools such as Rational Rose are only "rational" to mention when discussing UML! Besides Rational Rose, most modern object-oriented development tools now support designing in UML or integration with a UML tool and there are a wide range of other tools that compete with Rational Software's product in implementing UML.

To date, because there are no established ways of using UML, or extending UML, for mobile application development, there is no tool that supports the specific needs of mobile applications, particularly as we will address them in this text. However, there are tools that are more easily extended than the others. For our purposes, we will be concerned with three such tools:

1. *ArgoUML*: ArgoUML is an open-source project managed by Tigris.org. As in the case of all other open-source projects, the price is right: ArgoUML is free. Despite its bug-ridden inception, it has become much more stable and clean. Today, it is a commercial-grade tool for implementing software solutions with UML-based techniques. ArgoUML is written in Java, so it can basically run on any platform you choose for development.
2. *Rational Rose*: As we have already mentioned, Rational Software is the leading provider of tools for UML-based development. Rational is the most sophisticated of UML tools. By paying top dollar, you get a complete solution. Although Rational adds considerable functionality in implementing various extensions to UML, those extensions tend to be somewhat proprietary and incompatible with other tools in the market. But, because extensions to a given version of UML are fairly loosely defined, compatibility among the different tools is something that is hard to come by anyway. All in all, if you and your organization have the budget to get the Rational set of UML-based tools, it is the right way to go. Rational Software products are typically written in C^{++} and aimed for Windows. So, if you plan to develop on a platform other than Windows, you need to check for the availability of the tool you want on the platform you intend to use for development.
3. *Object Domain*: Like ArgoUML, Object Domain is written in Java so you can develop on any platform that you want (e.g., Windows, Linux, or others). Object Domain is not an open-source piece of software, but it is very extensible by offering scripting in Python, the standard UML extension mechanisms, as well as having an easily modifiable graphical widget set (so that if your organization needs its own set of widgets for a particular domain, you can ask Object Domain to add them without much delay or difficulty). We will use Object Domain frequently for our examples as it is much more affordable than Rational Software's tools.

The main reason for our choosing the aforementioned tools for UML is that they all allow extending the functionality of UML in a pragmatic way. ArgoUML is open source and extensible in any way you want it by its open-source nature. Rational Rose offers a variety of ways to extend UML, including the standard UML extension mechanism; there are also more plug-ins for Rational tool sets than for any other UML tool set. Object Domain offers graphical widgets that are flexible and very extensible in their design; it offers perhaps the most flexible user interface. Object Domain also offers Python-based scripting. These three tools are very distinct, each representing a group of UML tools available in the marketplace. Which you choose depends on the needs of your organization. The important point to keep in mind is that when using a UML tool, you need to learn the extension mechanisms

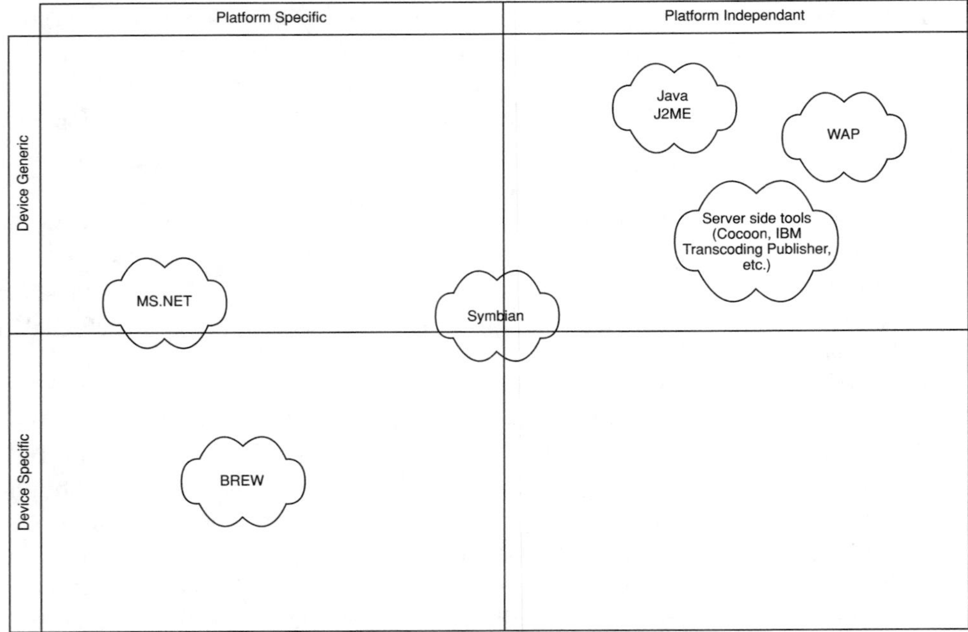

FIGURE 2.17. Mobile Development Tool Landscape.

because there are no formal UML extensions treating the problems or the process of mobile application development, nor are there any implementations of industry de facto extensions. After this book was authored, Borland acquired TogetherJ and is now producing a complete development environment that supports Java and UML development hand-in-hand. This offers some interesting possibilities in providing a mature end-to-end development environment for mobile applications with UML because Borland's JBuilder has support for J2ME, J2SE, and J2EE. However, because of the timing of authoring of this text, we will not be discussing this tool.

2.11 So What Now?: What Do We Do with These Tools?

We dedicated this chapter to the categories of tools needed to develop mobile applications. We also looked at some commercial and open-source implementations of the tools in each category. Let us quickly summarize the approach of each type of platform considered.

First, we looked at running network-aware applications on a mobile device. Virtual machines, such as Java's, are clearly the best choice if we assume that all of the device manufacturers will agree on a common software framework interface (although they can choose their own implementations that abide by the specifications) and that the functionality offered by the devices will not vary greatly. J2ME and CLDC provide a limited set of functionality to be augmented by the manufacturer and by the profiles. However, these profiles are designed to the lowest common denominator of functionality among the devices: Supporting the superset of functionality among devices means that some device will never be able to execute some of the functionality of the application, creating a nightmare for developers to deal with at run time. Also, growing CLDC is counterintuitive as it was shrunk so that it can run on resource-hungry devices. We will call this approach the *single-language with virtual machine* approach.

The second approach is the *single-operating system multiple-language* approach. This is the approach that Microsoft has taken with the .NET platform. The advantage of this approach is that the code is mobile regardless of what language it has been written in. The obvious disadvantage is that the system users are tied to a single operating system. Also, the operating system, much like the virtual machine, must implement the lowest common denominator of functionality on its devices. There is also the fact that a pragmatic manager does not allow the developers to implement a solution in any language that their hearts desire. Today, software development is dominated by C, C^{++}, and Java. Although other languages such as Eiffel and SmallTalk have very advanced features and may be considered more evolved in some respects, they are not widely deployed commercially. We also reviewed BREW as an innovative, though very proprietary, approach to mixing the best of the hardware world with the best of the software world in coming up with a platform for mobile application development. There are other platforms that are very significant. Later on, we will touch upon a couple of additional platforms, such as Symbian, the most popular platform for wireless devices in Europe to date.

Then, we looked at the server-side tools such as Cocoon. Mobile applications, as we continue to stress, are distributed by nature. Therefore, server technologies play a crucial role in executing tasks that are too large and complicated for resource-starved devices. Besides, the Web has shown the way for distributing content in a thin-client environment. And though the thin-client environment does not fit many mobile applications, it is still a useful method of distributing content.

Finally, we looked at some UML tools. In this text, we use UML itself as a base tool for driving the development process and implementation of software in building mobile applications. UML tools facilitate use of UML.

Next, we will look at XML and UML in more detail. Those two languages will give us the basic pieces to get started on building real mobile applications with UML.

CHAPTER 3

XML: The Document and Metadata Format for Mobile Computing

It is God whom every lover loves in every beloved!

Al Arabi

3.1 INTRODUCTION

The Extensible Markup Language—XML—is a subset of the Standard Generalized Markup Language (SGML) specified in ISO standard 8879. SGML was created to create and maintain complex and portable documents to be used in highly scalable systems in a nonproprietary manner to any particular vendor. XML has become a key technology in the development of content for the World Wide Web. Today, with the birth of Web services, it is used for more than its original purpose of representing documents.

There are many excellent writings and books on the topic of XML. If you are not familiar with XML, you should probably stop here, familiarize yourself with the basics of XML, and then come back and continue. In this chapter, our intent is to outline some XML-based or XML-related technologies that are key in developing mobile applications.

To understand how and why XML is used in mobile applications, we should understand a brief history of how it came to be.

3.1.1 Brief History

In the beginning, there was SGML. And then, from SGML, came the less intelligent, but more likable son, XML.

If there were a bible of computer science, it would tell us the history of XML with a bit more flare. But, that essentially sums up where XML came from.

When the Web was first created, XML's sister, HTML, was born first. And you guessed it: It has the same unisex parent, SGML. SGML, which is an international standard for textual data, was conceived in the 1970s primarily by Charles F. Goldfarb. It became a standard in the 1980s. SGML is extremely powerful, but it is also very complex—so complex that not only is it difficult to author SGML documents, but supporting SGML is very CPU and memory intensive. Moreover, many features are not necessary for most documents. Formats that compare to SGML are Postscript, RTF, DCA, and MIF. SGML applications are written in the Document Type Definition format (DTDs). These are the same DTDs that are used to design XML applications today. When you think SGML, think of two main concepts: rules and structures. These form the basis of SGML. An SGML document, much like XML, can be thought of in terms of a data structure of nodes. Each node is an element. Rules, general to SGML, or specific to the document, make up the semantics of SGML.

HTML was written in SGML specifically created for HTTP. HTML is parsed using an HTML browser. HTML's popularity increased much faster than SGML's did. It took SGML nearly a decade to just become a standard. HTML became the most viewed type of user interface language within a few years (largely due to the success of HTTP as a protocol). Though HTML was not extensible, it was designed with some forgiving behavior. Eventually, this behavior proved to be one of the disadvantages of HTML. In fact, one could create several HTML pages that look identical but have significant differences in their source. Also, HTML was never designed to handle data, just to render a simple user interface.

The complexity of SGML and downfalls of HTML made it clear that something else was needed. And this is when Tim Bray and C. M. Sperberg-McQueen came up with XML. XML evolved and became a W3C (World Wide Web Consortium) Standard. XML's primary purpose is to give us a markup language for documents and features to encapsulate metadata about those documents.

Today, XML is used for much more than what it was originally intended for. Web services, for example, use XML for not just encapsulating data and metadata but also for representing behavior and providing an integration platform for disparate systems. Although such uses of XML are questionable and have not been proven to scale yet, one thing is certain: XML is the most universal vehicle today for creating documents and for storing data. In this arena, it has been designed, deployed, utilized, and proven.

XML is easy to read and understand. It is textual in nature, though references to nontextual context can be made and binary information can be serialized into an XML document.

Example 3.1: Representing an Address in XML.

```
<Address>
    <StreetAddress>2652 McGaw Avenue</StreetAddress>
    <City>Costa Mesa</City>
    <State>California</State>
    <Locale>
        <Country_Code mId="1">US</Country_Code>
        <Language mId="1">English</Language>
    </Locale>
</Address>
```

A look at a simple example of representing an address shows us this. See Example 3.1. Throughout this text, we will use an address example as a straightforward method of writing some sample code. Let us see how we may represent a given address in XML. XML is extensible, thereby allowing developers to create their own applications of XML serving particular problem domains.

Now, let us look at how XML is used to facilitate development of mobile applications.

3.1.2 XML and Mobile Applications

Mobile applications relate to XML in the following two ways:

1. Mobile applications should understand and be able to manipulate XML content. As content on the Internet, and other networks, moves into an XML format, it is very desirable that a given mobile application can handle XML. How the XML is handled is of particular interest. Although the task of parsing and interpreting the XML can be done on the mobile device itself, or some proxy such as an application server that processes all content for the device, issues such as performance become of paramount concern. We will look at various ways of dealing with XML content in this chapter.
2. Mobile applications use XML to facilitate their implementations. For example, XML documents can be used by mobile applications to exchange data; configuration of a device or a server may be encapsulated in an XML file; some protocols such as WAP use XML as the means for presentation. There are countless places where mobile applications and related frameworks can use XML internally. We will look at some nonproprietary examples of such use in this chapter.

Whether the mobile application is handling XML content or using XML internally, it must be able to construct XML documents, to parse them, and to take actions based on the contents of the XML documents. When it comes to parsing XML, there are two widespread methods: DOM and SAX.

3.1.3 DOM Parsing

The Document Object Model (DOM) is the tree representation of all of the XML elements. Every element becomes a node and nodes. Nodes can have children to

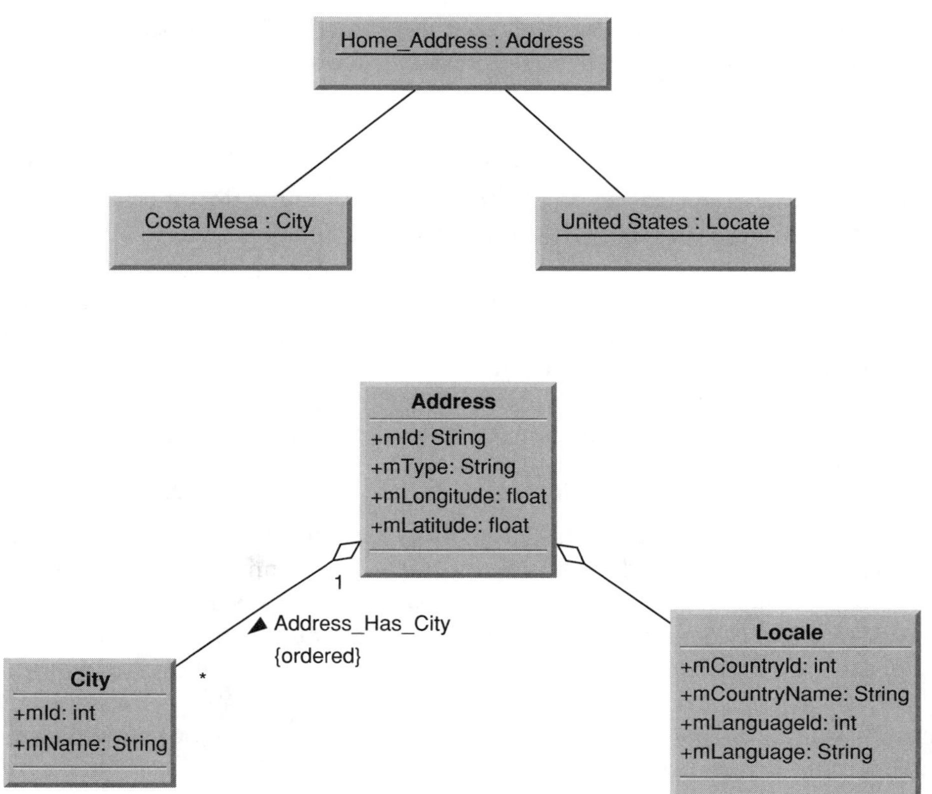

FIGURE 3.1. Representing the Address Document with Class and Object Diagrams.

support nesting of nodes in the same way as an XML element can have other elements. The mapping of DOM to UML is very simple. Every node is an object, an instance of a class. The XML attributes are the object attributes and the children nodes are encapsulated data members. A DOM parser written in an object-oriented language such as Java, C++, or C# goes through the entire XML document and creates a tree of nodes, with the nodes being objects. DOM parsers are also required to preserve the order of elements. There may be meaning in the order of elements. The same is not required of attributes. Figure 3.1 shows how a UML Object Diagram can be used to represent a DOM. We will discuss Object Diagrams further in Chapter 4.

DOM parsers allow a convenient method for accessing any piece of data in the document. For the DOM parser to make the data available, it has to parse the entire document; therefore, once the parsing is done, all of the data are available. Also, as we just mentioned, because of the nature of what DOM is, it is very easy and intuitive to implement DOM parsers in object-oriented languages or to use object-oriented languages for an application that, in turn, uses a DOM parser. Although DOM parsers are a good solution for parsing of most XML, they run into performance problems when dealing with numerous documents or unusually large documents. DOM is best when there is a one-to-one relationship between the objects that we need from the document and the elements in the document.

Often, this is not the case and we can improve performance with custom code. SAX parsers, in most cases, allow better optimization of performance.

3.1.4 SAX Parsing

SAX (Simple API for XML) creates a series of events as it parses through the XML document instead of creating an object model of the entire document in memory. There are two key advantages that SAX offers over DOM:

1. Most of the time, we do not need all of the information in the document. So, the object model desired does not have to have every element and attribute of the document. A custom object model in this case is more efficient. We can write a custom object model and a driver that catches the SAX events as the SAX parser reads through the document and emits them and fills up the custom object model.
2. We do not have to wait for the entire document to be processed before using the contents of the document. For very large documents, DOM becomes problematic as it has to load the entire document into memory before it makes its contents available. In contrast, as a SAX parser progresses through processing a document, it emits events; therefore, by nature, it allows immediate processing of the information.

Undoubtedly, it is more work to write an application with a SAX parser than it is with a DOM parser. Let us go back to our address example.

Example 3.2: Why Use SAX for Parsing an Address?

```
<Address>
    <StreetAddress>2520 College Avenue</StreetAddress>
    <Locale>
        <Country>US</Country>
        <PostalCode>92626</PostalCode>
        <Language>English</Language>
    </Locale>
    <City>Costa Mesa</City>
    <State>California</State>
</Address>
```

Let us say that we have a list of addresses in XML and need to categorize them by the postage fee that needs to be paid for shipping materials to each. We could use the DOM parser to load every address, formatted as the one in Example 3.2, into an object model in memory. This would mean that we have read hundreds, perhaps thousands, of addresses into memory. This could take a while. However, for our particular application, we may only need the postal code. We could use the SAX parser to emit an event that encapsulates the value of the postal code as it parses through the document. This would give us considerable improvement in performance not just because we would be looking only for one piece of data, but also because we have decreased the amount of memory usage.

SAX parsing can prove quite useful for mobile applications. Although many documents are comprehensive and hold large amounts of information, only parts of them are useful for certain devices. Considerable performance gain can be achieved by using the SAX parser in such cases.

To create an XML document, we typically need the entire document. Therefore, when persisting or streaming XML, the DOM parser is typically a better fit.

SAX and DOM parsers are available for most PC platforms (such as Java and .NET) on a variety of operating systems. Apache's Xerces is perhaps the most popular parser for Java developers, offering both DOM and SAX parsing. Microsoft supports SAX and DOM through an MSXML component for the .NET or other Windows-based applications.

Parsing XML in mobile applications can be tricky. Most mobile devices are typically resource-starved: short in memory, unreliably connected to the network, and not having a lot of excess CPU to spend on parsing XML. Both Java and Microsoft offer XML parsers for their mobile platforms. There are a variety of XML parsing techniques for the J2ME with the KVM and CLDC. Profiles can add additional XML parsing features to a given J2ME stack. kXML, for example, offers an implementation of an XML parser with a Java API for the J2ME platform. kXML is an API built on top of a SAX-based API and implementation. MIDP-NG (MIDP Next Generation) is slated to have a built-in XML parser. Another alternative is available through an open-source project at Source Forge called NanoXML.

Microsoft offers XML parsing on the Windows CE platform. Microsoft has a trimmed-down version of the .NET XML parser for the .NET platform in its Smart Device Extensions for Pocket PC, Windows CE 3.0.

WAP 1.x offers XML parsing in being able to process WML, an application of XML. However, it does not offer an ability to process any other applications or types of XML. WAP 2.x is a bit more friendly in allowing processing of XHTML, but there is still no flexible XML processor slated for WAP 2.x.

Besides parsing, another core operation in dealing with XML is transforming it. Because XML is well-formed, it has a well-defined data structure that can be transformed to other well-formed data structures. The Extensible Stylesheet Language (XSL) provides a simple mechanism for different applications of XML, addressing the same problem domain, to exchange document instances. The primary standard for transforming one type of XML to another is XSL.

3.1.5 Transforming XML with XSLT

XSL is an application of XML. It is a language for designing Extensible Stylesheet Language Transformations (XSLT). The XSL specification also includes XML Path Language (XPath), the expression language that enables navigation to particular parts of an XML document, and XML Formatting Objects (XSL-FO), an application of XSL that is designed specifically for specifying formatting of viewable documents. Since the inception of XSL, XPath has become its own standard at

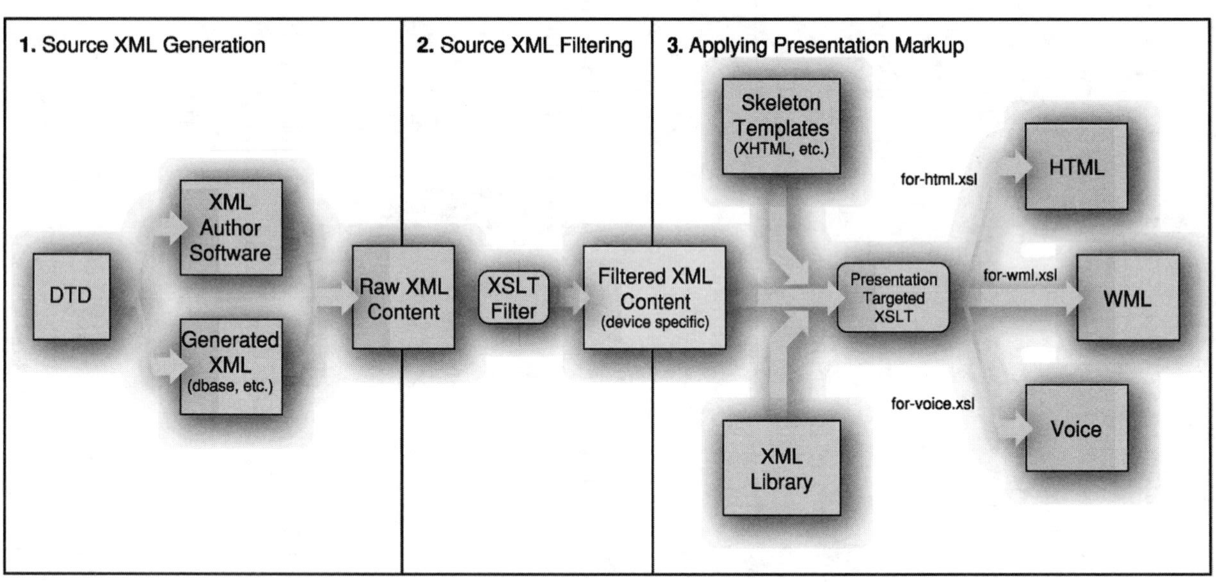

FIGURE 3.2. Using XSL and XSLTs to Produce the Right Content for the Right Device.

W3C as it proves useful in navigating documents whether or not a transformation is performed; still, it is a core part of what is needed to use XSL successfully.

On the Web, XSLTs are used much the same way as Cascading Style Sheets (CSS) to format HTML pages. The first-generation applications using XSLT and CSS used them to layer look-and-feel attributes on top of some vanilla HTML. Today, as much of the content on the Internet is moving from HTML to XML, it is more customary to use XSLTs to produce HTML.

An important thing to know is that XSL templates operate on the DOM. Therefore, the entire document must be available before we start transforming it. XSLT pages are documents full of instructions for the XSLT processor. The XSLT processor may be an interpreter or a compiler. The latter performs better while requiring a compilation action that may prevent real-time changes to the code base and enforce more rigorous restrictions on the template.

When it comes to mobile applications, the most popular use of XSLTs is to transform raw content designed for multiple types of user interfaces to a specific type of content. The input must be XML and the output is most probably XML. A typical content generation and transformation chain is shown in Figure 3.2. We discuss frameworks and tools that support such transformations in other chapters throughout this text.

Because XSL is a scripting language, it has control structures such as if–then statements and loops. These control structures are meant to operate on XML document elements, their values, and their attribute values. XSL takes one DOM in and spits out another DOM. Mathematically, it nearly works as a mathematical transformation.

Most of the tools that use XSL and its facilities to generate content for mobile devices today perform the transformation process on the server side. Today's mobile devices do not have the ability to perform XSL transformations because they are resource-starved. However, as devices are becoming more and more capable and it is becoming more obvious that content is exchanged primarily in the XML format, device vendors are moving to support XSLs as a part of the platform offered.

When running XSL processors on the device, one prefers to use an XSLT compiler to reduce overhead. Code is then generated, native to the platform (this could be the operating system, such as Windows CE, or the language, such as Java), and executed to process the input XML. Sun's XSLT compiler, for example, enables the developers to compile XSLT for J2ME CLDC for the MIDP on the Palm platform.

We will discuss XSL and related XSL technologies several times throughout this text. Now, let us quickly look at XML-based Web services.

3.2 XML Web Services

Web Services are a prime example of an organic, as opposed to a synthetic, evolution in technology. They exist because the HTTP protocol is ubiquitous: Just about everyone today has access to the Web. Web services build on the HTTP protocol methods, mostly GET and POST, to build an RPC (Remote Procedure Call) that allows two systems to exchange messages over HTTP. But, why not use

CORBA, COM, JINI, or other distributed computing protocols? XML based Web services are not efficient: They convert binary to text to convert it back to binary again. This is a weak point of XML based Web services when it comes to dealing with mobile applications. However, there are work-arounds. Web services are a text-based MMI (Machine-to-Machine Interface). However, they are simple to build and they take advantage of the ubiquity of the Web. Protocols such as CORBA have failed in becoming ubiquitous. Other protocols such as COM are proprietary to a platform. The platform of Web services is the Web. Regardless of level of efficiency, those two aspects alone create an economic reason for Web services to exist. Another consideration that accompanies the use of Web services (typically HTTP based though they can be based on other protocols such as SMTP) is security. Because many people use Web services as a method to circumvent security (since most firewalls are open for HTTP traffic on port 80), this also presents a security problem.

Although Web services do not have to use XML, most do. Web services use XML to represent both behavior and data. Even though the majority of Web services have custom behavior defined as a part of their defining schema or DTD, it is possible to build Web services that use only HTTP's methods with messages containing only data.

There are different types of Web services. Some Web services are designed to allow for an RPC mechanism; XML-RPC and SOAP are examples. UDDI (Universal Description, Discovery and Integration Service) is an example of a Web service that is a registry. WSDL (Web Services Definition Language) is sort of a meta-Web service and focuses on what Web services can do and how they communicate—the semantics of Web services—as opposed to defining a domain-dependent schema.

As in any other technology, there are proprietary and nonproprietary Web services. Though some vendors claim that completely proprietary services are not possible, indeed this is a big misconception. For example, Microsoft's Passport is a proprietary Web service. Proprietary Web services may have an open schema with definitions understood by all possible entities, but they may require software or infrastructure specific to one or more vendors, and be closed to being implemented by other vendors, for generating messages that use the given Web service to interact with other systems or system components.

The ubiquity of Web services is what makes them interesting to use for mobile applications. Device proliferation should not cause protocol proliferation. For this reason, using Web services, in the absence of any other more efficient communication protocol, makes much sense for distributed mobile applications.

Let us go through a few different Web services. Keep in mind that Web services are increasing in number and variation by day.

3.2.1 SOAP

SOAP is probably the best known of all Web services. SOAP started in 1998 and is a behavioral application of XML. SOAP is a W3C standard and is implemented by a variety of vendors such as Sun Microsystems, IBM, and Microsoft. SOAP is not designed to work with any specific transport protocols; it simply specifies the format of the message to be transported. However, the publicly available commercial implementations of SOAP to date only support binding to HTTP.

SOAP services are accessed through URLs. In this way, every service offered has a unique identifier. Example 3.3 shows the code for an address response in SOAP.

Example 3.3: Address Response in SOAP.

```
HTTP/1.1 200 OK
Content-Type: text/xml; charset="utf-8"
Content-Length: 434

<env:Envelope xmlns:env=http://www.w3.org/2001/06/soap-
  envelope>
  <env:Body>
     <myAddressDefinition:GetAddressResponse
       env:encodingStyle=http://www.w3.org/2001/06/soap-encoding
        xmlns:myAddressDefinition=http://www.cienecs.com/
          examples/SOAP/myAddress>
           <Address>
              <Street>2652 McGaw Avenue</Street>
              <City>Irvine</City>
              <State>California</State>
              <Country>United States</Country>
           </Addrss>
     </myAddressDefinition:GetAddressResponse>
  </env:Body>
</env:Envelope>
```

Let us briefly summarize the key concepts of SOAP:

1. *Binding*: As we already mentioned, SOAP is not a transport protocol. It only defines the format of the messages to be exchanged by senders and receivers in a messaging system. But, an application using SOAP must use a transport protocol. The process of tying the XML message to the protocol so that it can be shipped from one endpoint to another is called binding.
2. *Node*: Anything that produces or consumes a SOAP message is a node. Nodes are the clients, servers, or peers in the system. Nodes can be SOAP receivers, SOAP senders, or both. As the names imply, SOAP receivers are listening for SOAP messages and can process them upon receiving them. SOAP senders produce SOAP messages and find a receiving node to send them to.
3. *Envelope*: The SOAP envelope merely puts the tag boundaries around the SOAP message in the XML document. The SOAP envelope is there to preserve the extensibility of XML and keep it well formed without creating multiple documents (which would obviously add much complexity).

4. *Body, header, block, and fault*: These are the SOAP syntactical constructs specific to the SOAP envelope structure.

The SOAP message format is an application of XML. The nodes must have XML parsing capabilities so that they may bind to the transport protocol on one side and to some computing system that actually does the computing task on the other side. Although SOAP, and similar XML-based RPC mechanisms such as XML-RPC, can simplify distributed computing, we need to keep in mind the following inefficiencies:

1. There is a great price to be paid in performance. Parsing XML is expensive. And building an application layer protocol such as SOAP on top of another application layer protocol brings us very near to the dangers of overabstraction.
2. One significant source of inefficiency in SOAP is the use of multiple system calls to send one logical message [Davis and Prashar 2002]. A given transaction defined within the confines of one system may mean several calls to another system. In other words, there may not be a one-to-one mapping between the interface exposed and the implementation that uses the API. This can lead to many different calls being made to complete one transaction, which otherwise may be completed with one transaction. This factor acts as a multiplier to the other performance problems of SOAP.
3. Encoding data instances (per the requirements of Section 8 of the SOAP Specification) basically defines an object serialization method into an XML-based text format. This has inherent inefficiency: Machines deal with binary information and not text. So, the sender node must serialize to text-based XML and the receiver node must first parse the XML and then map the text into the object model that it requires to perform its internal functions.

Although these inefficiencies pose problems, SOAP can justify itself as a means of connecting systems that use different networking technologies and do not require high performance levels.

SOAP is a great example of a Web service that defines a domain-independent protocol for sending remote procedure calls from one node on the network to another. There are many other types of Web services. Let us look next at WSDL, a Web service designed for discovery of other Web services.

3.2.2 WSDL

WSDL is an XML-based language used to describe other Web services and how to interact with those Web services. WSDL provides a mechanism to define interfaces that can be used to generate code, thereby making Web services language independent. WSDL is implemented as an XML document that holds a series of definitions of various Web services. WSDL is to Web services described in various XML formats what the Resource Description Framework (RDF) is to various resources. The only difference is that WSDL is not part of the Semantic Web (to be discussed later in this chapter). WSDL is not a W3C recommendation; rather, it is a proposal by IBM, Microsoft, and Ariba to W3C for future recommendation. A WSDL document defines the following:

1. *Type*: A Web service may define its own data types in this section of the WSDL document. WSDL types must be based on XSD (XML Schema, the W3C standard) data types. This capability can be used to define custom data types that make sense within the domain being served by the particular Web services.
2. *Message*: This section of a WSDL document defines the format of the messages being passed around among the different nodes. For example, in the case of SOAP, this would be the definition of the SOAP Envelope.
3. *Operation*: This section of the document defines the various services offered by the Web service. Think of this as the metadata for the remote procedure calls that each Web service exposes.
4. *Binding*: WSDL does not force binding to a particular transport protocol. Moreover, most (well-designed) Web services do not force binding to a particular protocol. In the binding section of the WSDL document, we can define what protocol bindings are possible for a given Web service and how those bindings are supported. It is also important to note that binding does not have to be to a particular type of protocol. For example, WSDL could be used to describe a Web service that is built on top of SOAP, which in turn could be using HTTP for its transport protocol. Or, alternatively, it could be used to describe a Web service built on top of HTTP itself (with messages that are in the XML format to preserve the definition of a Web service).
5. *Port*: Whereas operations allow us to describe the metadata about each "procedure call," ports are what we get after the operation is bound to a transport protocol. The port is the mechanism used by the nodes to send messages back and forth.
6. *Port Type*: Sometimes, a given operation may be supported by one or more ports. If this is the case, we still need a way to group the ports that support that operation so that a selection of which port offers what operation can be made. Port type is a way to group ports, for this purpose, by the operations that they support
7. *Service*: Service is the high-level abstraction that allows grouping of end points and operations to create a Web service.

Example 3.4 shows a WSDL document for an address directory Web service.

Example 3.4: A WSDL Document for an Address Directory Web Service.

```
<wsdl:definitions name="myAddressService" xmlns="http://www.
  cienecs.com/examples/wsdl/">
    <wsdl:service name="myAddressService">
        <wsdl:documentation name="myAddressDocumentation"/>
```

```
        <wsdl:port name="myAddressPortName" binding=
          "mySOAPAddressBinding">
            <soap:address location=http://www.cienecs.com/
              examples/wsdl/myAddress.xsp/>
        </wsdl:port>
    </wsdl:service>

    <wsdl:message name="AddressQuery">
        <wsdl:part name="mFirstName" type="xsd:string" />
        <wsdl:part name="mLastName" type="xsd:string" />
        <wsdl:part name="mSSN" type="xsd:integer" />
    </wsdl:message>
    <wsdl:message name="Address">
        <wsdl:part name="StreetAddress" type="xsd:string" />
        < wsdl:part name="City" type="xsd:string" />
        < wsdl:part name="State" type="xsd:string" />
        < wsdl:part name="Country" type="xsd:string" />
        < wsdl:part name="PostalCode" type="xsd:string" />
    </ wsdl:message>

    < wsdl:operation name="FindAddress" parameterOrder=
      "mFirstName, mLastName, mSSN">
        < wsdl:input message="AddressQuery" />
        < wsdl:output message="Address" />
    </ wsdl:operation>

    < wsdl:portType name="addressFinder" >
        < wsdl:operation name="FindAddress" parameterOrder=
          "mFirstName, mLastName, mSSN">
            < wsdl:input message="AddressQuery" />
            <wsdl:output message="Address" />
        </wsdl:operation>
    </wsdl:portType>

    <wsdl:binding name="mySOAPAddressBinding" type=
      "myAddressSOAPPort">
        <soap:binding stype="rpc" transport=http://schemas.
          xmlsoap.org/soap/http" />
        <operation name="FindAddress">
        <soap:operation soapAction=http://www.cienecs.com/
          cocoon/examples/myAddressService />
        </operation>
    </wsdl:binding>

</wsdl:definitions>
```

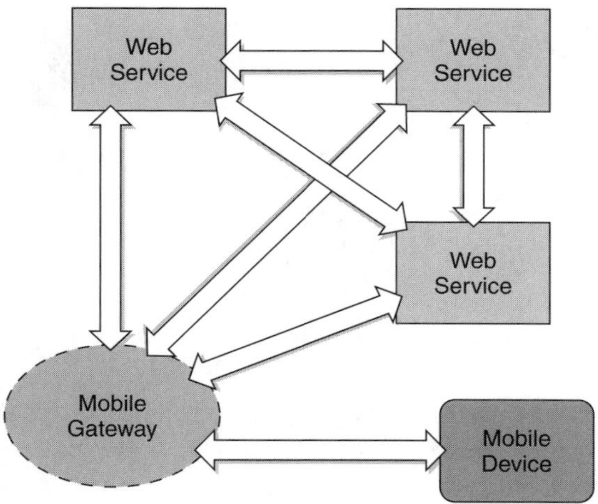

FIGURE 3.3. Web Services for the Mobile Infrastructure Using Gateways.

Once again, it is important to understand that WSDL is not a Web service; rather, it is a facility to build introductory descriptions for other Web services. One example of a Web service that uses WSDL is UDDI, which is designed for discovering and introducing business services on the Internet. UDDI allows binding to both HTTP and SOAP. UDDI is not a standard but is an industry effort driven by several large entities such as Dell, HP, and IBM.

We have now looked at two different key Web service technologies. Let us see how Web services are related to mobile application development.

3.2.3 Web Services and Mobile Applications

Web services and mobile applications can be related in two ways:

1. *Web Service Proxy*: The infrastructure of mobile applications can use Web services for messaging. For example, a given system may allow mobile users to find someone's phone number through a directory service and subsequently get the driving directions to that person's place of residence. These two functions, finding the phone number and the driving directions, may be fulfilled by two different systems, each implemented in a different environment. So, the back end for our mobile system may use Web services to connect to each one of these systems and retrieve the information we need to return it to us. The interface between the back-end system and the device remains consistent and can be implemented through whatever communication protocol may be necessary. This is the more likely scenario for most systems. Figure 3.3 shows a mobile device using services offered by several Web Services through a gateway.
2. *Direct Connection to Web Services*: Mobile devices with more resources can directly access the network through the use of Web services (see Figure 3.4). Of course, this requires a considerably advanced mobile device as we have to have very efficient XML parsing as well as the ability to write substantial applications that implement the application of XML that supports the particular Web service to which the mobile device must connect to. The clear advantage of such

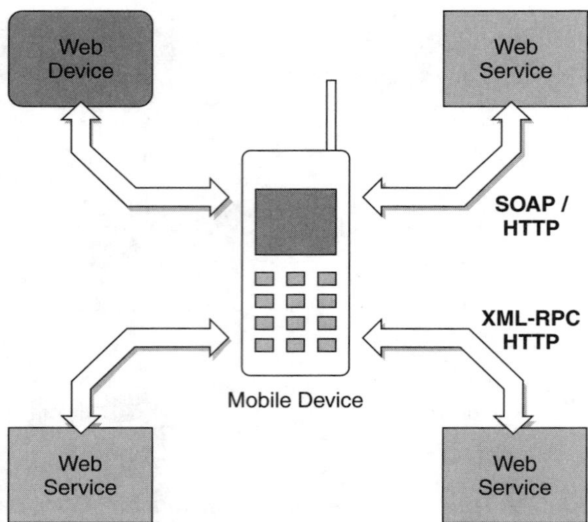

FIGURE 3.4. Mobile Devices Using Web Services Directly.

an implementation is the elimination of the proxy and the direct usage of the service by the device. An example of a technology that allows us to do this is XForms. We will discuss XForms in detail in Chapter 5. It provides a generic user interface markup language that can be specialized for a particular user interface. Specialization may be done at the receiving node (in our case the mobile device) or at a sending node (server, peer, etc.). The beauty of XForms is that it allows for binding to any transport protocol. Therefore, we can bind XForms to use a Web service, thereby allowing the mobile device to communicate directly with various available Web services.

We have now seen some basic ways in which XML is used for documents, for metadata, and for behavioral systems. Note that our focus here has been on the various types of XML applications rather than products or technologies that implement them. Different vendors apply these technologies in a variety of ways, each with their own proprietary flavor and twist.

Now, let us look at some applications of XML that have been specifically designed for use by mobile devices and the other XML applications that they, in turn, take advantage of.

3.3 KEY XML TECHNOLOGIES FOR MOBILE COMPUTING

Some standard applications of XML have been specifically designed with mobile applications in mind. Standardization of such applications of XML is required to provide interoperability between disparate systems.

As we mentioned previously, mobile applications should be able to handle XML content. This may mean parsing the content to take some actions based on the content, transforming the content for various user interfaces, or using XML as the metadata for handling various types of content. There are a set of standards by W3C and proprietary recommendations by various vendors that apply for these cases. We will focus on standards recommended by W3C as they are typically more encompassing than proprietary recommendations. These standards apply across various vendors that either base their interface to their products on W3C standards or provide interoperability with them. Before we begin a survey of these technologies, we must look at one key XML standard that is used by most other applications of XML, XML Schema. XML Schema defines the data types and structure language for validating an XML document much the same way as DTDs used to. Whereas DTDs are an SGML application and written in SGML, XML Schema is an application of XML. Therefore, instances of XML Schema are XML documents that can be parsed and treated as any other XML document.

3.3.1 XML Schema

XML Schema is an application of XML to define the type of elements and attributes, the structure of the elements, and any constraints on the elements and attributes of a given XML document. The XML Schema namespaces begin with xs; if you have developed a sizable application in XML, you have probably seen or used some XML Schema instance data as XSI or data types as XSD within XML documents.

Example 3.5: DTD of an Address.

```
<!ELEMENT address (streetAddress, city, state, zip) >
<!ELEMENT streetAddress (#PCDATA) >
<!ELEMENT city (#PCDATA)>
<!ELEMENT state (#PCDATA)>
<!ELEMENT zip (#PCDATA)>
```

Let us compare a simple DTD with its equivalent XML Schema. The DTD in Example 3.5 defines an address. The XML Schema in Figure 3.5 does the same thing.

XML Schema allows us to build new data types and to reuse those data types across multiple documents. In our case, we have defined a data type called Address that can be used across other documents. A document using XML Schema for defining itself may look like the XML code shown in Figure 3.6.

Many XML applications use XML Schema to define new data types that can be reused within the namespace of the given XML application, to define the structure of the various elements within an instance document of the particular XML application, and for allowing the developers to place constraints on the data defined within the XML application. XForms is such a sample application that uses XML Schema. The XForms definition is written in XML Schema: Its data types and structure are defined by the XML Schema–based document that defines XForms.

Although the reader is expected to be familiar with various XML technologies, let us quickly review the list of data types in XML Schema as they are referred to frequently within this text.

```
<?xml version="1.0">
<xs:schema xmlns:xs="http://www.w3.org/2001/XMLSchema/"
  targetNamespace="http://www.cienecs.com/examples/schema">
    <xs:Address>
        <xs:sequence>
            <xs:element name="streetAddress" type="xs:string"/>
            <xs:element name="city" type="xs:string" />
            <xs:element name="state" type="xs:string" />
            <xs:element name="postalCode" type="xs:string" />
            <xs:element name="country" type="xs:string" />
        </xs:sequence>
    </xs:Address>
</xs:schema>
```

FIGURE 3.5. Using XML Schema to Define a Data Type for Address.

1. *Basic XML Schema Data Types*: There are several data types defined by XSD on which all other data types are built. Here are some of the built-in types:
   a. *String* (*<xsd:string>*): You may easily guess that this is a sequence of any valid characters with the exception of those reserved for XML (the brackets, comment sign, etc.). Several other built-in data types are driven from the String.
   b. *Date* (*<xsd:date>*): This element is used to specify dates. It allows for specifying a format for the data and using character data as the text of the element. The character data must comply with the format specified if one is specified.
   c. *Numeric* (*xs:decimal*): There are several different numeric types allowed in XML Schema. They are all derived from the decimal data type. The decimal data type allows for specifying any decimal number, with no more than 18!

```
<?xml version="1.0">
<Address xmlns="http://www.cienecs.com/examples/XSD/Location"
         xmlns:xsi="http://www.w3.org/2001/XMLSSchema-
           instance"
   xsi:schemaLocation="http://www.cienecs.com/examples/XSD/
     Address.XSD">
   <streetAddress>2652 McGaw Avenue</streetAddress>
   <city>Irvine</city>
   <state>California</state>
   <postalCode>92626</postalCode>
   <country>US</country>
</Address>
```

FIGURE 3.6. Using XML Schema to Define a Data Type for Address.

(= 18 × 17 × 16 × ... × 3 × 2 × 1) digits. See the XML Schema specification for all of the other numeric types that inherit from the decimal type.

d. *Boolean (<xs:Boolean>)*: This type allows specifying a Boolean. Values can be "true" or "false."

e. *Base-64 Encoded Binary Data (<xs:base64Binary>)*: The text specified by this data type is treated as base 64 encoded binary data.

f. *Hexadecimal Encoded Binary Data (xs:hexBinary)*: This is the same as base 64 except the encoding is based on hexadecimal encoding.

g. *URI (<xs:anyURI>)*: One of the most important concepts in various Web related activities is the concept of a Universal Resource Identifier (URI). This tag allows for specifying an element that refers to a URI. In this way, large documents can be broken up into multiple documents and the XML Schema definitions can be modularized.

2. *Simple Data Types*: These are data types that can only contain text. Simple data types cannot have any attributes nor have elements nested within them. Simple data can refer to the data types that are built into XML Schema or are custom data types that are built on top of the built-in data types. The important point is that they do not have children elements and that they do not have custom attributes.
3. *Complex Data Types*: These are the data types that contain other elements and/or attributes. Complex data types are typically used to define custom data types.

XML Schema data types and structures are crucial to understanding the XML applications specifically designed for mobile applications or ones that have put a great amount of emphasis into accommodating mobile applications.

XHTML, Extensible Hypertext Markup Language, was one of the first such applications of XML addressing many of the issues involved with mobile user interfaces. Let us look at XHTML and other applications of XML that address the problems of the mobile user interface.

3.3.2 XML-Based User Interface Technologies for Mobile Applications

As we previously mentioned, one of the first markup languages to be pervasively used was HTML. Most of the Web documents today exist in HTML. HTML is an application of SGML, but it is not very clean. XHTML is an attempt at cleaning up the HTML syntax and providing a version of HTML that is an application of XML. XHTML will replace HTML past version 4.01 and it is an approved W3C standard.

One of the biggest problems that HTML presented was that it was not designed to be used by a wide variety of user interface types. HTML was designed with minimum requirements of a color screen of 640 × 480 pixels and the PC in mind. Though some considerations were made for screens that did not display graphics, not much else was available to the developer. Also, HTML was not strict enough in enforcing syntax. So, programmatic changes to HTML to make it fit various devices was not possible without making assumptions (which in turn create bugs). During the first year or two of WAP applications, many companies based their sole products on tools that converted HTML to XML. XHTML eliminates the need for such techniques. XHTML allows for development of GUIs using a thin-client model where the XHTML browser renders a GUI. We will look at XHTML in depth in Chapter 6 where we look at GUIs for mobile applications.

Voice Extensible Markup Language (VXML) is another application of XML specifically designed for voice user interfaces. VXML allows specification of a command-based voice dialog through a markup language. We will discuss VXML as a tool for creating voice user interfaces.

WML is the markup language of WAP version 1.x. It is designed for WAP browsers to display a GUI that is mostly comprised of text with support for small black-and-white pictures. WAP 2.x will use XHTML as its markup language because current devices have more capabilities and XHTML is a more flexible markup language, allowing dynamic adaptation to various types of user interfaces.

Finally, and perhaps most importantly, XForms is an application of XML that we discuss in great depth in Chapter 5. XForms allows us to build user interfaces with a focus on the interactions and data exchanges between the user and the user interface as opposed to specific types of user interface. XForms allows us to separate concerns among presentation logic specific to the application, the presentation logic specific to the device, the data exchanged between the user and the system, and the interaction flow.

It is natural for XML to be the core of a user interface system infrastructure, mobile or not. XML is textual, structured, and document based. Those three elements are of utmost importance in building a human–computer interface (HCI).

There are other applications of XML for mobile application infrastructures as well. We will now briefly introduce some applications of XML that control flow of interactions. Let us start with CCXML, an application of XML designed to flow the control of interactions with a telephony system.

3.3.3 CCXML

Call Control Extensible Markup Language (CCXML) is an application of XML for managing voice calls. Whereas VXML defines user interfaces for the interactions between a user and a voice-recognition system or a text-to-speech engine, CCXML focuses on routing the calls and connecting calls. CCXML is specific to the telephony part of voice user interfaces.

Because CCXML does not specify a binding to a particular voice system, it can be used to implement call control in voice-over-IP or conventional PSTN telephony systems, thereby assuring that the call control mechanism is independent of the underlying implementation. CCXML was based on Java Telephony APIs (JTAPI). We will look at both JTAPI and CCXML more closely in Chapter 7.

Next, let us take a brief look at an application of XML that allows us to specify processing flows for various XML documents.

3.3.4 XML Pipeline

XML Pipeline is a W3C recommendation that specifies how to process various XML resources. This standard takes many of its ideas from software building tools such as GNU's MAKE and frameworks such as Cocoon that use the concept of inversion of control prevalently.

XML Pipeline can be thought of in two different contexts:

1. It specifies the flow of processing instructions that are applied to one or more given documents residing on one host. Take, for example, the process of applying a set of XSLs to a given document. Applying XSLs is not communicative: Given document A, applying first XSL B, then XSL C, and finally XSL D may result in a different output document than applying first XSL B, then XSL C, and finally XSL D.
2. It specifies the flow of processing instructions that are applied to a variety of XML documents, residing at a variety of hosts. Such processing is a superset of processing documents residing on the same host as problems such as versioning and timing can make processing the documents problematic.

Example 3.6: Sample XML Pipeline Document.

```
<?xml version="1.0">
<pipeline xmlns="http://www.w3.org/2002/02/xml-pipeline"
    xml:base="http://www.cienecs.com/Examples/XMLPipeline">

    <param name="target" select="'result'" />

    <!-- This section defines the processes and links them
      to their definitions (typically some hint to the
      controller on where and how to start off the processes).
      We chose Java for our examples, so the definition is in
      terms of Java classes. -->
    <processdef name="selector" definition="com.cienecs.mobile.
      device_selector"/>
    <processdef name="selected_content" definition="com.cienecs.
      mobile.http.get_content_generator"/>
    <processdef name="authenticator" definition="com.cienecs.
      mobile.security.authenticator ($username) ($password)"/>
    <processdef name="transformer" definition="com.cienecs.
      mobile.transformer.xslt"/>

    <!-- For our example, we chose a set of processes that
      select some content based on the user's request. So, the
      first thing to do is to find the content that the user
      requested. -->
    <process id="3" type="selected_content" >
        <input name="uri_param_1" label="content_finder_param_1"/>
        <input name="uri_param_2" label="content_finder_param_2"/>
        <output name="cresult" label="generic_content_URI"/>
    </process>
```

```
    <!-- For our example, we want to transform the content based
     on the device that the user is using. So, we need to fire
     off a process that finds out the user's device type..-->
    <process id="1" type="selector" >
       <input name="deviceId" label="unique_device_id"/>
       <input name="ccpp_header_string" label="ccpp_header_
         string"/>
       <output name="result" label="device_type"/>
    </Process>

    <process id="4" type="authenticator">
       <input name="username" label="username" select=
         "($username)"/>
       <input name="password" label="password" select=
         "($password)"/>
       <output name="authenticated" label="authenticated"/>
    </process>

    <!-- Now, based on the user's device type and the selected
     content, we can find the right type of transformer and
     transform the content properly. -->
    <process id="2" type="transformer" >
       <input name="device_type" label="device_type"/>
       <input name="generic_content_URI" label="generic_content_
         URI"/>
       <input name="authenticated" label="authenticated"/>
       <output name="device_specific_content" label="device_
         specific_content"/>
    </process>

 </pipeline>
```

Example 3.6 show a sample XML Pipeline document.

There are currently several efforts at designing standards that specify interfaces for such processing. Examples are XPipe, DSDL, and XML Pipeline. We chose XML Pipeline as it is a W3C standard. At the time this book is being authored, XML Pipeline is only a recommendation.

XML Pipeline recognized five different types of processes [W3C XML Pipeline]:

1. *Constructive* processes produce new information, such as a new XML document, as a result of the process. XSL processing is an example of a constructive process.
2. *Augmenting* processes add new types (definitions) of information. For example, we can introduce new types in an XML Schema.
3. *Inspection* processes look at the content of a document and indicate whether the inspection processes succeeded or failed based on whether the document

conformed to a given set of rules. Validation of a document using an XML Schema or a DTD is an inspection process.

4. *Extraction* processes copy a part of the document that they look into. The copied section may then be removed from the document being inspected or left in.
5. *Packaging* processes are distributed processes that address the processing of distributed resources. The scope of such an initiative is simply huge. So, even the XML Pipeline specification clarifies that the XML Pipeline addresses only a subset of those issues involved in providing a standard for specifying distributed processing of distributed resources.

In XML Pipeline, resources, as in the case of RDF, are identified by URIs: Anything that can be represented by a URI can be a resource. The controller is the entity that processes the XML Pipeline document. It first validates the document, then determines what the first process is, points the first process to its input, tells it to run, and redirects the output where it should go.

The controller processes the instructions on the document based on the availability of the input. An obvious implementation may require multiple passes through the document. Other implementations may use SAX to map the events to language-specific event models. Regardless of the implementation, the controller figures out which processes depend on which, then produces the results of ones with appropriate available input in the order of availability of input.

Although XML Pipeline and similar pipelining languages are not likely to be used on most mobile clients, they can prove invaluable in building distributed mobile applications that are not tightly coupled to commercial implementations, thereby allowing more flexibility in implementing the initial solution and in changing the implementation during the lifetime of the mobile application system. Cocoon, for example, uses a pipelining system. Though Cocoon's Sitemap, which essentially accomplishes the same purpose as an XML Pipeline document for content generation, is written with a different vocabulary set, structurally and functionally it is very similar to an XML Pipeline document. Cocoon is one of the most popular frameworks for generating the right type of content for the right type of device/user interface (and, as we will see later in this book, it can be used for much more than just that).

XML Pipeline has become a recommendation very recently, and even more recent is the release of the first (currently only) reference implementation for it by Sun Microsystems. It is very likely that many frameworks, such as Cocoon, will eventually migrate from proprietary pipelining languages to XML Pipeline. XML Pipeline may need to be extended to accommodate features special for some mobile application frameworks, but then, that is one of the beauties of XML: It is extensible!

3.3.5 WBXML

The WAP Binary Extensible Markup Language (WBXML) format defines a way to represent XML in 0's and 1's instead of text. The primary purpose of WBXML is to reduce bandwidth requirements on transporting XML documents.

The interest in WBXML has gone far beyond WAP. The argument for binary XML is that it reduces bandwidth and the time required for transport. Arguments also have been made that parsing binary XML may be more efficient because machines are better at dealing with numbers than text. However, this is in doubt. Namely, without knowing the contextual usage of XML, it is questionable whether it is possible to come up with an encoding scheme that applies with consistent efficiency across one set of domains although not causing loss of efficiency across another set of domains. So, although WBXML is a binary representation of XML, it has been designed with a bias toward WAP; it does not necessarily work well for other mobile application frameworks and protocols.

There are several open-source tools that provide parsing of WBXML. KXML, an open-source application that we previously referred to as an XML parser in the J2ME environment, has the ability to parse WBXML for the J2ME environment. KXML is a DOM-based parser for WBXML. If you are looking for a SAX WBXML parser, check out Trantor [Trantor 2002], a collection of various open-source applications for mobile devices.

Making XML parsing, transport, and translation more and more efficient is one of the hot topics of current discussions. Resource-starved mobile applications can certainly use faster ways of dealing with XML and requiring less bandwidth to transport it. There is currently no prevailing standard, nor implementation, nor even consensus in the industry on how to do this.

We will not look at WBXML in any depth here. If you are interested in finding out more about WBXML, check out W3C's Web site.

3.3.6 SSML

The Synthetic Speech Markup Language (SSML) is an example of an application of XML that addresses a specific functionality API. SSML and other markup languages that address syntax serve mostly to get rid of proprietary APIs.

SSML is designed so that speech may be synthesized without use of proprietary APIs. By using SSML, the speech synthesizer (typically a TTS—Text-To-Speech—engine) can be changed without having to make programmatic changes in the application that uses the engine.

We will discuss SSML in Chapter 7 when we reach voice user interfaces; the point of discussing it now is that it is a good example for various markup languages that are used for the infrastructure. In the case of SSML, it is used for the infrastructure of the voice user interface. Although VXML remains the primary mechanism for creating voice user interfaces, SSML allows nonplatform-specific programming for a variety of features specific to a system that utilizes text-to-speech technologies. VXML allows simple TTS directives whereas SSML lets us customize TTS operations and build a rich voice user interface.

A great deal of mobile application development focuses on developing for multiple user interfaces. Various types of user interfaces require special functionality and the appropriate syntax and instruction set to accommodate such custom functionality. Applications of XML such as SSML prove to be invaluable in keeping the custom portion of the mobile application infrastructure as platform-neutral as possible. Such technologies are also exemplified by the natural language grammars defined in XML. Although such grammars are not a direct part of any specific user interface, they can be used to specify constraints as well as voice user interface (VUI) voice-recognition grammars.

3.3.7 RDF

One of the biggest problems in development of mobile applications is that of discovery and identification: How do all the various devices introduce what they are and what they can do? The Resource Description Framework has been the dark horse in the standards race for the mobile development discovery mechanism.

Though RDF was not designed to treat the problem of mobile application development in particular, it has been talked about as the key enabling standard for tying together the different resources in ad-hoc and steady-state mobile application networks for several years now. Unfortunately, the standard has been slow in evolving, implementations have been rare and slow in being developed, and the promise remains far from being fulfilled. Nevertheless, RDF is a key technology that we need to discuss.

RDF was created specifically to allow discovery of various resources (such as documents on the Internet), the indexing of them, and even the creation of resources that are made up of other RDF resources by simply nesting the RDF descriptions.

The most popular example of RDF in introductory documents is its use to encapsulate information about a Web document, such as author, subject, date of publication, and copyright information. In this sense, RDF is used to encapsulate metadata. The logical question following this is "Why not just use XML?" Well, RDF can actually use XML, but it tries to accomplish a set of tasks that XML does not address.

Any time we have a resource, not only do we need to identify the resource by some metadata, but we also need to specify a relationship between the metadata and the resource. Let us take, for example, a company named eBuilt, Inc. A piece of metadata about this company could be its phone number. But, without specifying the fact that the metadata item is the phone number, the item is meaningless. So, RDF defines a mechanism for two things: It first structures the metadata and then it relates the metadata to anything that can be represented by a URI.

RDF is part of the so-called Semantic Web. Tim Berners-Lee (the father of the World Wide Web), James Hendler, and Ora Lassila define the Semantic Web as follows:

> The Semantic Web is an extension of the current Web in which information is given well-defined meaning, better enabling computers and people to work in cooperation. [W3C Semantic Web]

The Semantic Web is essentially an attempt to set forth standards and tools that will allow organization of the information on the World Wide Web as we know it today. RDF sits at the core of the Semantic Web and is designed primarily to describe resources. Of course, what better way to describe something than a linguistic semantic approach such as "The phone number for Cienecs is 714-555-5555." Following linguistic models, RDF uses such an approach to identifying resources. There are three parts:

1. *Resource*: This is the thing that we are trying to describe with RDF: the data. It can be of any format as long as we can represent it with a URI.
2. *Property*: This is the attribute of the resource that is to be described by the statement (next). The property can be simple text or another resource.
3. *Statement*: This is the "sentence" that relates the property and the resource. And, as a sentence, it has a "noun" or "subject," an "object," and a "predicate" that describes the relationship between the subject and the object. For example, consider the following statement about a mobile device: "The screen-size of http://www.x.y.com/AMobilePhone.xml is 24 x 58." The screen-size, in this case, is the subject, in this case the property. The resource is described by the URL (a subset of URI) http://www.x.y.com/AMobilePhone.xml. The value of the property is "24 x 58" and the predicate defines the relationships among the resource, the property, and the value of the property.

Example 3.7: Simple RDF Describing a Device.

```
<rdf:Description about='http://www.voicegenesis.com/RDF/
  TestPhone.xml'>
    <ScreenSize>24x48</ScreenSize>
    <Wap=Support rdf:resource='http://www.voicegenesis.com/RDF/
      wap/>
</rdf:Description>
```

Let us look at some sample code showing how we might use RDF to describe a device (without taking advantage of any other standards for we will see later that some mobile standards use RDF in a particular way). Example 3.7 shows an example of how a test phone could be described using RDF in a nonstandard manner.

As you can see, RDF uses XML. In our example, the resource being described is represented by an HTTP URL. This URL could be the URL that represents all the devices of the "TestPhone" family because these devices may not be connected or have an available Web server on them at all times. There are a couple of properties that are used to describe the device (RDF resource), namely, the screen size and the type of WAP support that the device may have. Note also that the first property is simple text whereas the second property (the version of WAP support) is another RDF resource.

When a TestPhone device is contacted by another device or the TestPhone device contacts another device or the network, it needs to introduce itself (the other device may be a mobile device, a server, a PC, etc.). Because TestPhone has RDF support, it introduces itself by sending its RDF description, or a pointer to its URI description such as a URI, to the receiver (the network or another device). This is the RDF in Figure 3.7. Once the receiver of the description has the RDF, if it supports RDF, it parses through RDF and interprets the description of the described resource.

This might seem quite simple. One might think that the same exact thing could be done using just XML. But, if you look closer, you will note some key differences between RDF and simple XML:

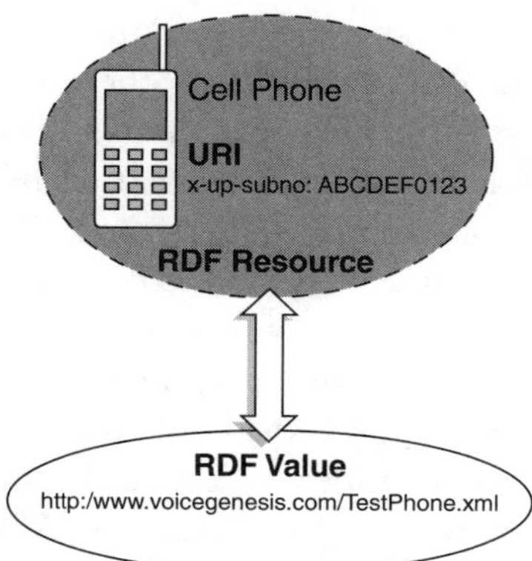

FIGURE 3.7. Using RDF for Describing Mobile Devices and Their Capabilities.

1. If we wanted to implement the same mechanism using simple XML, we would have to build a schema that would define a canonical way of describing devices. Unfortunately, not all manufacturers of devices and software want to define devices the same way. Principally, the creators of resources have different ideas about how their resources should be described. The same is true for the users of different types of resources. There are a couple of ways that we can get around this in XML: agree on a method to share definitions per domain area in XML (which has given rise to the $n \times m$ different XML standards that attempt to come up with canonical XML schemas or DTDs for n domains interpreted by m vendor groups) or define a semantic way of doing the same thing using XML such as what WSDL does. Obviously, the first becomes meaningless after a while. Every vendor pushes its own biases for its own set of products in defining what the schema or the DTD should be. WSDL and similar technologies define a format for describing various services. There are a separate set of problems with this: The vendors tend to implement standards such as WSDL differently to create product differentiation. Even without these differences, a domain layer implementation has to reside that defines the network services offered by the WSDL-compliant components of the network for a particular domain. RDF is able to address these issues better than XML because it handles everything as a resource. And resources can be described by other resources. RDF is simple, yet it allows modeling of a sophisticated description of behavior by using existing resource descriptions of existing resources. It also lets the resource creators and users define the resources however they want to as opposed to depending on vendor-specific implementations.
2. On the Semantic Web, the target audience comprises machines rather than humans [Melnik and Decker 2000]. Web services as they exist today, using XML-based protocols such as SOAP on top of HTTP, have been questioned in their ability to scale (though the term "Web service" does not really imply the use of any particular technology—this is just the case for the implementations that exist and are currently becoming popular). Remember that machines are not designed to understand text. Computing machines do much better with 1's and 0's. Whereas Web services essentially force the exchange of all information through well-formed XML, there is no such restriction with RDF. All that is

necessary is that the resource can be described by a URI. Even though nontextual data such as audio, video, MMIs, and many other resources on the network can be described by XML, the implementation often seems unnatural. The metadata describing some information may not be textual in nature or may be better represented in a format other than well-formed XML. RDF allows this. The biggest benefit of the Semantic Web, and RDF as a part of the Semantic Web, is that it provides for a much more highly scalable environment than the XML-only world of having to parse documents and reconstruct them repeatedly and do complex, resource-consuming lexical operations.

3. The order in which elements appear in an XML document is significant and often very meaningful [Bray and Brickley 2001]. When it comes to describing resources, it does not matter which attribute of the resource we describe first or even how we describe it, provided it is something that can be a URI. Hence, RDF is more flexible in creating descriptions for various resources.

Note that RDF uses XML and that XML is still needed to build much of metadata; nevertheless, RDF offers some interesting features not offered by XML alone. In short, RDF gives us a simple, scalable, and flexible way of introducing and discovering resources. Obviously, this addresses a wide range of problems with distributed computing on the Web. But, particular to our interest, RDF addresses one of the fundamental problems of mobile computing: "How do I know what resource is receiving my message, what resource a given message comes from, and how I can handle the message coming from this resource?" RDF allows us to treat all of these as resources and provide descriptions for these resources, thereby providing a mechanism for discovery and introduction.

For the mobile developer, the particular interest will be the applications of RDF that let mobile devices and applications exchange information about each other with each other. Two such applications of RDF are Composite Capabilities/Preferences Profiles (CC/PP) and User Agent Profiles, both of W3C. We will look at both in detail. First, let us look at RDF Schema.

3.3.8 RDF Schema

The RDF Schema defines an XML-based syntax for RDF. RDF Schema does not define RDF. Rather, it is an implementation of RDF that uses XML Schema and its relevant data types. As already mentioned, RDF is not, in itself, dependent on XML. However, XML gives us the perfect tool to serialize it. To serialize RDF and then unserialize it to and from XML, we have to establish a consistent XML vocabulary with which disparate implementations supporting RDF can maintain consistent semantics. This is why RDF Schema exists. Now, there are several XML Schema vocabularies for RDF, one of which is RDF Schema. Another is DAML, or DARPA Agent Markup Language.

As you may guess, RDF Schema is very simple and nonrestrictive. This is almost a requirement of anything on the Semantic Web. RDF Schema is important to mobile applications because the serialization of many RDF-dependent mobile standards is done in XML with a baseline vocabulary of RDF Schema. Examples include CC/PP and UAProf, which we will see later on in this chapter.

Much like the UML metamodel where classifiers and relationships between them are defined, RDF Schema vocabulary has <rdfs:Resource>, <rdfs:Class>, <rdfs:Property>, and <rdf:Statement> to explain resources, classes, and properties at a metalevel. A particular instance of RDF Schema, then, could be equivalent to a class diagram. Another group of RDF classes (<rdfs:Literal>, <rdfs:Container>, <rdf:Bag>, <rdf:Seq>, and <rdf:Alt>) provides data constructs such as containers and literals.

RDF Schema then uses the mathematical concepts of a domain and a range to define data types that fall within a domain and a range of the metadata-level classes and data constructs. For example, a comment is an RDF resource and is literal; therefore its domain is rdfs:Resource and its range is rdfs:Literal.

Data types that you will see in standards using RDF will typically be those defined by RDF Schema. To understand these data types better, refer to the RDF Schema specification at W3C's Web site. If you need additional data types, you can do this by extending RDF Schema (which works for both simple and complex data types).

We will use RDF and its applications throughout this text and see how it is used to build real mobile applications.

3.3.9 UML and RDF

At their core, UML and RDF have much in common. Both define a meta-metadata model. In UML, this is the layer that defines what classifiers are and the relationships among the classifiers. RDF defines entities as resources, properties, and statements in a semantic model. So, you can think of the RDF Schema much the same way as you think of the metadata model in UML: These are the templates for instances of things. Finally, there are the instances themselves; they are the RDF documents or the UML objects.

UML class diagrams provide a static modeling capability that is well suited for representing ontologies [Cranefield et al. 1999]. This can be done by deriving a semantic statement (as defined in RDF) from the classes and the relationships among the classes (association, inheritance, aggregation, etc.). We can use the UML Object Constraints Language (OCL) to complement the typical class diagrams to give us full flexibility for modeling UML with RDF.

Figure 3.8 shows the RDF entity relationship (graph) for the address example we have been using throughout the book. Figure 3.9 shows the equivalent as represented by a UML class diagram (with no OCL used in our example).

Cranefield [Cranefield et al. 1999, Cranefield 2001] outlines a comprehensive methodology for mapping RDF entities to class diagrams. It is noteworthy to understand that though UML allows us to model RDF, RDF can describe more things than UML can. So, in a sense, the things that can be represented by UML are a subset of those that can be represented by RDF. Therefore, there may be scenarios in which UML becomes very difficult to use (although probably never impossible because you can use OCL almost like a programming language—a practice that is not recommended).

There has also been a great deal of work done on representing UML in RDF. This is probably less relevant to our goal: We are using UML as a tool to simplify

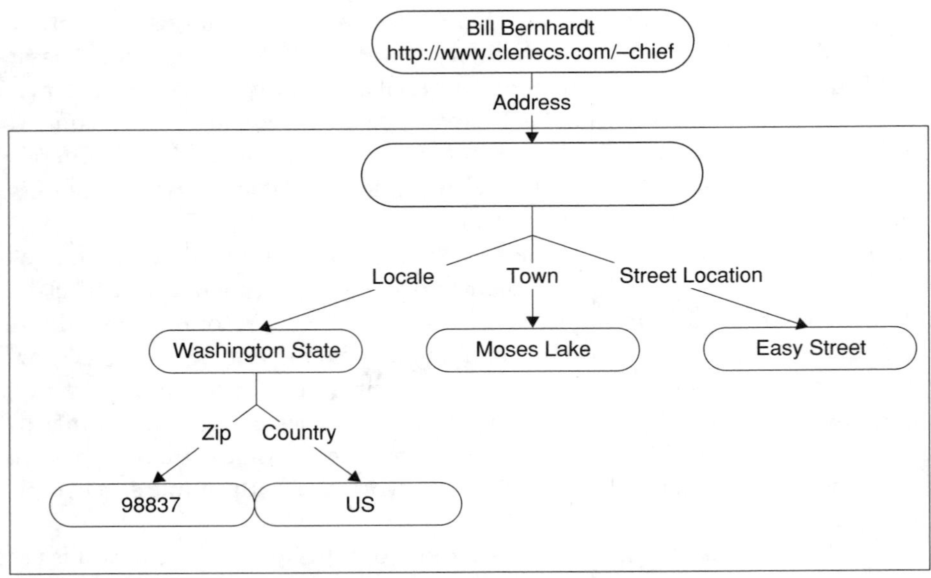

FIGURE 3.8. Partial RDF Graph of an Address.

the development process, and RDF, with all of its great capabilities, is undoubtedly more abstract and more difficult to understand than the simple shapes that UML provides to represent programs.

Finally, when we map RDF to UML, we probably want to use RDF Schema to specify data types (see Figure 3.9). Because UML accommodates a larger range of data types and constructs than those introduced in RDF Schema, extensions may be required to allow a full round trip between a UML model and an RDF graph (actually, probably its serialization to XML).

We now return to our original reason to do all of this: RDF can be verbose and complicated whether as an XML document or as a graph. UML gives us a way to model RDF visually to reduce complexity. An example of when we may want to do this is CC/PP, an application of RDF for recognizing the capabilities of various mobile devices.

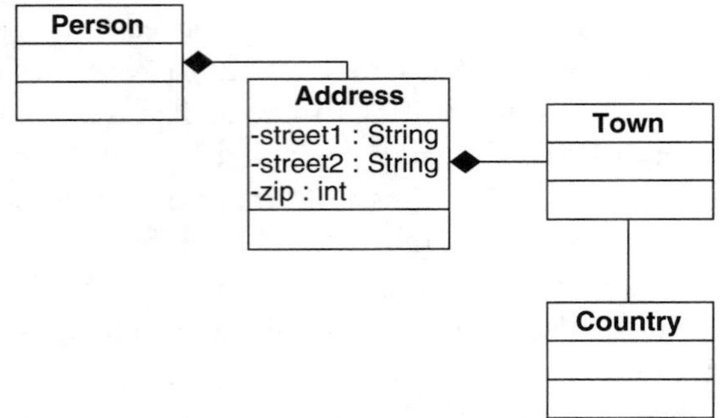

FIGURE 3.9. UML Representation of the Address in Figure 3.8.

3.3.10 CC/PP

CC/PP is an extension of the HTTP protocol that uses RDF to describe the capabilities of various devices and the user settings for each device. CC/PP was specifically designed for various network resources to be able to recognize devices that try to use them. CC/PP is implemented by adding an RDF statement, in XML format, to the header of the request and modifying and adding to some other request headers. Before we delve into the details of CC/PP, we should note that there are very few devices today with actual implementations of CC/PP. However, device manufacturers are moving toward implementing this capability. In particular, WAP 2.x is closely married to CC/PP and its sister standard UAProf (which we will look at next).

Within this text, we will assume that the transport protocol for CC/PP is HTTP and that CC/PP is implemented as an HTTP extension. However, it must be noted that CC/PP does not require any particular transport protocol; binding with other protocols may be provided.

A CC/PP implementation requires two pieces: implementation at the HTTP server side and implementation at the HTTP client side. Because CC/PP is implemented through an HTTP extension, it is important to remember that the basic architecture is built on the HTTP model: stateless and client–server.

Let us start by looking at what needs to be implemented on the client side, in our case, the mobile device:

1. The mobile device may be able to directly use HTTP. In this case, the implementation of the header extensions must be done on the device (most likely a browser or some piece of software that uses an HTTP connection framework).
2. The mobile device may not be able to use HTTP directly. This is the case with many mobile devices such as WAP phones. A proxy that creates the HTTP request must somehow implement the header extensions. The proxy may receive the information in some other format from the device, may have the device information in a registry referenced by some unique ID, or may simply guess the capabilities of the device (which is not a good idea because CC/PP is designed to remove the guess work). Because introducing a proxy to the system adds another resource to be described, a reasonable question is whether CC/PP requires description of the proxy as well as the device when a proxy is used to augment or provide some of the information. The answer is that although a description of the proxy is recommended, it is not required.

Example 3.8: Example of a CC/PP Profile.

```
<rdf:RDF xmlns:rdf="http://www.w3.org/1999/02/22-rdf-syntax-ns#"
         xmlns:ccpp="http://www.w3.org/2000/07/04-ccpp#">
   <rdf:Description rdf:about="http://www.cienecs.com/examples/
     RDF/SampleDevice">
      <ccpp:component>
         <rdf:Description rdf:about="TerminalHardware">
```

```
            <rdf:type rdf:resource="http://www.cienecs.com/
              examples/RDF/PDA"/>
            <display>34x50</display>
            <memory>4Mb</memory>
          </rdf:Description>
       </ccpp:component>
   </rdf:Description>
</rdf:RDF>
```

Let us look at a sample CC/PP profile (for an imaginary device) in Example 3.8. In this example, the RDF statement describes some of the capabilities of the device pointed to by the URI http://www.cienecs.com/examples/RDF/SampleDevice. Remember, in RDF, the subject can be a URI (because the implementation is in XML and an Xpath-compliant expression would qualify for the URI). In this example, we have only described the amount of memory and the display size available on the particular device, but much more can be described using RDF.

This is made possible by the CC/PP RDF vocabulary and the accompanying UAProf standard. The RDF vocabulary for CC/PP is a set of attribute names and valid values for the RDF document instances to describe devices through CC/PP. Obviously, CC/PP also defines the meaning of the vocabulary set so that it is used, by various implementers, consistently. It is important to note that the vocabulary set is extensible through the extensibility of XML and use of namespaces. However, to provide interoperability among various devices and nodes that interact with those devices, a small set of attributes and values have been predefined in the form of CC/PP vocabulary. Keep in mind that any UAProf document is a valid CC/PP document as CC/PP was designed after UAProf (which we will look at next) and is meant to be backward compatible with it. Let us go through the CC/PP RDF vocabulary.

CC/PP is made of a profile that has one or more components. Each component has one or more attributes. If a device has multiple profiles, they must be encapsulated in multiple XML documents.

1. *Components*: These are logical groupings of the attributes that describe the device. In CC/PP examples, you will often see three popular groupings of TerminalHardware, TerminalSoftware, and TerminalBrowser. These three are definitely good ways to group some of the attributes of the device. However, additional components can be added as long as they may be represented by URIs (which would most likely be a publicly available URL if we are talking about a real device being used across many different networks). Components in turn have attributes. Every CC/PP component is enclosed in opening and closing tags of <ccpp:component> and </ccpp:component>.
2. *Attributes*: Every component has many other elements called "attributes." Do not mistake these with the XML attributes. These are component attributes represented by XML elements in an XML representation of the RDF. It is recommended that one confine these attributes to a single level. In other words,

try not to nest attributes unless absolutely necessary. The attributes of a component are wrapped within the opening and closing tags of <rdf:Description> and </rdf:Description>. The opening tag must have an XML attribute of rdf:about to specify the subject of the component (the logical grouping of the attributes, which we have determined to make up the component). The client profile attributes have some important characteristics as follows:

a. Two frequently used attributes for every component are *type and name*. We recommend that you always use these two. The type attribute is roughly equivalent to the HTTP "accept" header: It tells us what types of content are understandable by a given device. The values are the valid Multipurpose Internet Mail Extension (MIME) content types.
b. Along with type and name, there is a recommended list based on the work done by IETF. These attributes are specified in the CC/PP specification, but we will list them here as they have special importance:
   i. *charWidth* (ccpp:Integer): This attribute applies to devices with the capability to render text. It is the maximum number of characters that can be represented horizontally across one line of the display.
   ii. *charWidth* (ccpp:Integer): This is the maximum number of lines of text that a textual display can show at one time.
   iii. *charset* (ccpp:Text): This is the character set supported by the device. This is a particularly important parameter as many devices are designed to work with a variety of parameter sets and are configured by the vendors prior to sale. This attribute can be set to all valid MIME character sets such as UTF-8.
   iv. *deviceIdentifier* (ccpp:URI): This attribute allows you to specify the device through a URI. In addition to the flexibility advantages that URIs offer us, this attribute offers us the ability to abstract the versioning away from the device so that backward compatibility can be done more elegantly.
   v. *color* (ccpp:Text): This attribute can be set to "gray," "full," or similar values but can be somewhat useless because of its qualitative nature. Unfortunately, this attribute was not designed to specify an RGB (or similar numeric) range of colors. If you need to specify a range of colors supported by a device, the chances are that you will need to specify custom attributes to do this.
   vi. *pix-x* (ccpp:Integer): For GUIs, this attribute describes the number of pixels across the screen (horizontally).
   vii. *pix-y* (ccpp:Integer): For GUIs, this attribute describes the number of pixels vertically on the screen.
   viii. *schema* (ccpp:URI): This attribute can be a URI pointing to a DTD, an XML Schema, or an RDF Schema. Whichever document the schema attribute points to is used to specify what type of documents are understandable by a given device. For example, this could be the WML DTD for WAP 1.x phones and browsers.
c. If there is more than one value for a given attribute, the "set" of values is implemented using <rdf:Bag> as the container of the set and <rdf:li> for

representing the elements of the set. CC/PP specification refers to "sets" of attributes as the only type of complex data types. Amazingly, the other type is the simple data type!

d. Simple data types are the atomic data types of CC/PP. (They cannot be broken down into finer pieces without losing their meaning.) As you may have noticed, CC/PP defines its own data types. These data types are based on the RDF literal objects. These data types are *URI*, *Text*, *Token*, *Integer*, and *Rational Number*. Refer to the CC/PP specification document [CC/PP W3C Specification] for the details on these data types.

Once again, these attributes are specified based on the IETF media feature registration, which has defined a wide range of sets of tags used for describing various media features. Try your best not to extend outside of the recommended attributes of the CC/PP specification, although, because of the fast evolution of user interfaces and device capabilities, it is fully expected that extending is unavoidable.

One prime example of extensions that you might want to implement are attributes that tell the other nodes which input and output channels are supported (voice, text, graphics, etc.) and what the means of their support is (screen, speaker, handset, phone keypad, etc.).

Let us now go back and look at profiles. There are four types of profiles predefined by the CC/PP specification:

1. *Profile*: This is the top-level profile. All other profiles can be considered a subclass of *Profile*.
2. *Client-Profile*: This profile describes the capabilities of a client (the mobile device). This is the most frequently used profile as CC/PP is most used to introduce the capabilities of a device. An example is a profile that describes a WAP phone. The client-profile typically includes those attributes of the device that do not change often, so this is typically a static file or may be cached.
3. *Proxy-Profile*: This profile describes the capabilities of a proxy, if one is used. An example is a profile that describes a WAP proxy. As in the case of the client-profile, the settings on the proxy do not change frequently, so this is typically a static file or may be cached.
4. *Request-Profile*: This profile is typically generated dynamically at run time. A request-profile proxy is a combination of the proxy-profile and another profile showing the features on the device supported by the proxy. This is an important profile because the capabilities of the proxies and devices are often different. For example, a WAP 2.x phone connected to a WAP 1.x proxy can only support WAP 1.x-like features.

In addition to these profiles, there is a proxyProfile and a nextProfile, both of which are used by the request-profile for referring to other profiles from within the request-profile.

Figure 3.10 shows the relationships among the different profile types in UML. (Note that this is an approximate mapping as there is more than one way of

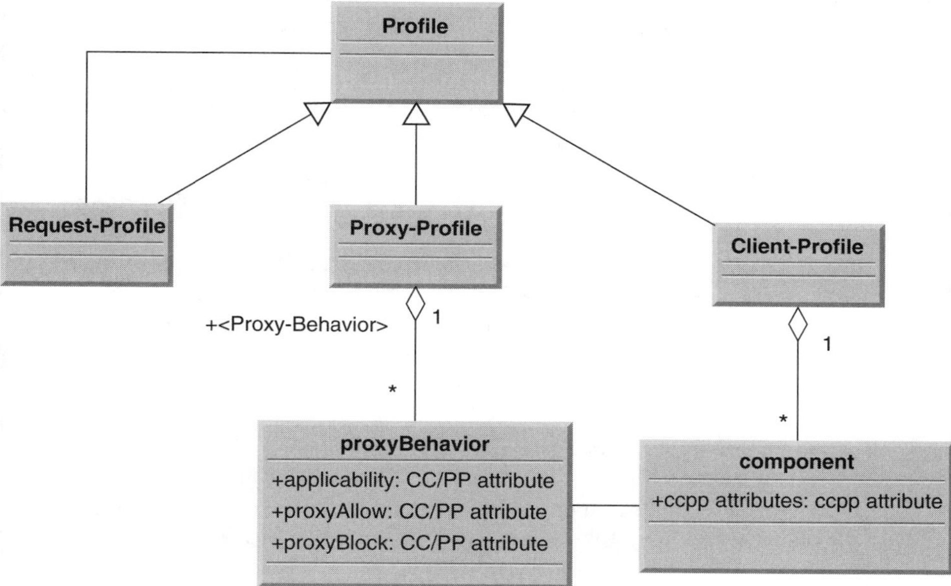

FIGURE 3.10. UML Representation of a Subset of the CC/PP RDF Model.

mapping RDF to UML, as we will discuss later.) The association between request request-profile and profile represents the use of a proxy-profile instance and client-proxy instance, respectively, through the proxyProfile and nextProfile attributes.

An example of a CC/PP document for a proxy is shown in Figure 3.11. Note that we have introduced our own custom attributes for a custom proxy and a custom device. This is not recommended. Try to use only those attributes recommended by the CC/PP specification [CC/PP W3C].

One important feature of CC/PP that we have not discussed yet is the ability to create default values for the client-profile values. Every component in an instance of the client-profile can have default values. These default values are represented, in the XML serialization of the CC/PP RDF, by using the <ccpp:defaults> tag. The values within the components follow the same convention as any other CC/PP attribute(s) for a given component. Default values are particularly important as they prevent wasted network traffic and processing power in values that are repeated for the majority of devices.

As a side note, remember that CC/PP is an RDF application. The XML representation on which we have focused is simply an XML serialization of the given RDF.

We have now reviewed the basics of CC/PP. There is one more piece, though. Because CC/PP is designed to describe the capabilities of a device and the profile preferences, some of the information, particularly in the profile preferences, may be private. So, it is important to keep such information secure. Let us quickly look at how we can achieve this.

```
<?xml version="1.0"?>

<!-- This section of the document defines the namespaces
  external to the document.-->
<!DOCTYPE rdf:RDF [
    <ENTITY ns-rdf 'http://www.w3.org/1999/02/22-rdf-syntax-
      ns#'>
    <ENTITY ns-rdfs 'http://www.w3.org/2000/01/rdf-schema#'>
    <ENTITY ns-ccpp 'http://www.w3.org/2000/07/04-ccpp#'>
    <ENTITY ns-ccpp-proxy 'http://www.w3.org/2000/07/04-ccpp-
      proxy#'>
    <ENTITY ns-ccpp-client 'http://www.w3.org/2000/07/04-
      ccpp-client#>
    <ENTITY ns-custom-client 'http://www.cienecs.com/
      Examples/RDF/custom-device#>
    <ENTITY ns-custom-proxy 'http://www.cienecs.com/Examples/
      RDF/custom-proxy#]>

<!---This section of the document defines the actual
  profile,in this case, a profile about MyProxy. -->
<rdf:RDF  xmlns:rdf = '&ns-rdf;'
          xmlns:rdfs = '&ns-rdfs;'
          xmlns:ccpp = '&ns-ccpp;'
          xmlns:ccpp-proxy= '&ns-ccpp-proxy;'
          xmlns:ccpp-client= '&ns-ccpp-client;'
          xmlns:custom-client ='&ns-custom-client;'
          xmlns:custom-proxy='&ns-custom-proxy;'>

    <ccpp-proxy:Proxy-profile rdf:about='http://www.cienecs.
      com/Examples/RDF/MyProxy'>
        <ccpp-proxy:proxyBehavior>
            <ccpp-proxy:applicability>
                <ccpp:Component>
                    <custom-proxy:Channel>
                        <rdf:Bag>
                            <rdf:li>play-only-audio</rdf:li>
                            <rdf:li>record-audio</rdf:li>
                            <rdf:li>play-only-video</rdf:li>
                            <rdf:li>text-entry</rdf:li>
                            <rdf:li>text-output</rdf:li>
                        </rdf:Bag>
                    </custom-proxy:Channel>
                </ccpp:Component>
            </ccpp-proxy:applicability>
```

FIGURE 3.11. Example of a Proxy Profile.

```
            <ccpp-proxy:proxyAllow>
                <ccpp:Component>
                    <custom-proxy:Channel>
                        <rdf:Bag>
                            <rdf:li>text-entry</rdf:li>
                            <rdf:li>text-output</rdf:li>
                        </rdf:Bag>
                    </custom-proxy:Channel>
                </ccpp:Component>
            </ccpp-proxy:proxyAllow>
        </ccpp-proxy:proxyBehavior>
    </ccpp-proxy:Proxy-profile>
</rdf:RDF>
```

FIGURE 3.11 *(continued)*

Delivering Private Information with CC/PP

Because profiles and device description may have some information that is private, we need a mechanism to maintain the privacy although allowing authenticated users proper access level to the information.

As we mentioned previously, there are two ways to implement CC/PP: directly through the client (the mobile device) or through a proxy (such as a WAP gateway). To date, there is no approved standard for CC/PP privacy implementation through W3C; however, there is a recommendation draft that is very likely to eventually become a standard. This recommendation is iterated in the document *CC/PP Implementer's Guide: Privacy and Protocols* [CC/PP P3P W3C 2001]. This recommendation specifies the Platform for Privacy Preferences (P3P) of W3C be used as the security measure. We will look at P3P in Chapter 14 when we discuss security in depth. For now, you should know that P3P is a standard for expressing privacy information regarding a resource.

There is also the variable of the transport protocol, which for security is extremely important. The aforementioned document [CC/PP P3P W3C 2001] outlines suggested standard interfaces for P3P with W-HTTP (Wireless Profiled HTTP) and HTTP Exchange Protocol (this is the HTTP extension we already talked about that allows transport of an XML serialized version of the CC/PP RDF).

CCPP-ex uses two headers, one for the defaults and one for the updates (profile-diff:s), which are separated using MD5 hashes; A third header carries warning information [CC/PP P3P W3C 2001]. For the details on P3P implementation on CCPP-ex refer to the aforementioned document. In the next section, we will look at how the UAProf standard treats security with P3P on top of W-HTTP transport.

These two methods, P3P with W-HTTP and P3P with CCPP-ex, address both devices and intermediaries such as gateways and proxies. However, other techniques could be used to provide security and privacy if an intermediary is used. If the device goes through the intermediary for all network access, and vice

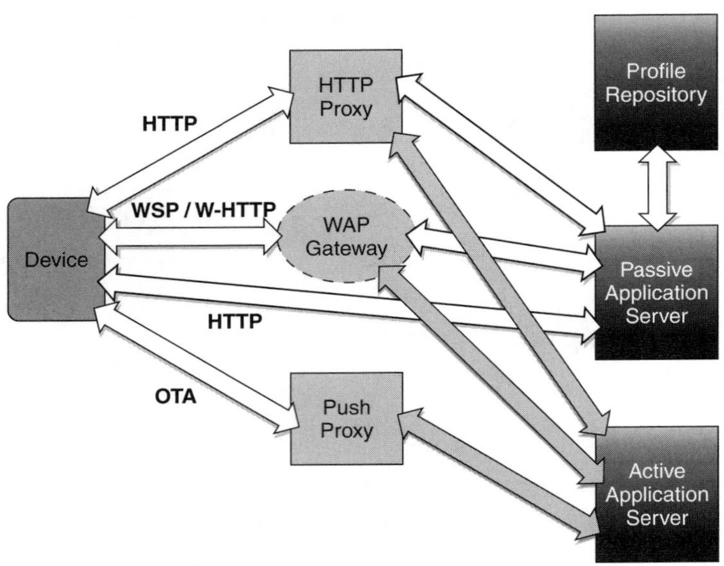

FIGURE 3.12. Overview of WAP 2.x Architecture with CCPP-ex and W-HTTP.

versa, then the implementation of the device to intermediary security and privacy becomes secondary and could be left specific to the implementation (though use of standards are still recommended for extensibility and flexibility reasons).

Although there are other techniques for recognizing devices, such as using custom headers in HTTP, CC/PP outlines a comprehensive method for describing both capabilities of a device and the profiles including the user preferences on the device using RDF. It is truly extensible and scalable. CC/PP is a very well-thought-out standard. What we saw here is a quick summary of CC/PP with a focus on the XML serialization and its usage for describing mobile devices. Now, let us look at UAProf, a predecessor of CC/PP.

3.3.11 User Agent Profile Specification

Figure 3.12 shows an overview of WAP 2.x Architecture with CCPP-ex and W-HTTP. User Agent Profile Specification, better known as UAProf, intends to solve a subset of the problems addressed by CC/PP: to create an RDF-based mechanism for describing the capabilities of a device and the profile preferences on that device. In a way, UAProf is an application of CC/PP within the WAP specifications. CC/PP is fairly general and designed to be used with a very wide range of devices. UAProf is a specific application of CC/PP and related technologies (RDF, XML, etc.) to WAP 2.x.

UAProf introduces a predefined vocabulary with well-defined meanings that apply particularly well to the domain of WAP. Specifically, the following components are recognized [WAP UAProf]:

1. *HardwarePlatform*: This CC/PP component bundles the attributes that relate to the hardware properties of the device (WAP phone). Attributes include model, display size, and type of device.

2. *SoftwarePlatform*: This CC/PP component describes the properties of the various software programs running on the device including the operation system and any other applications (but browser attributes are typically put into BrowserUA).
3. *BrowserUA*: This CC/PP component describes the characteristics of the HTML browser.
4. *NetworkCharacteristics*: This CC/PP component describes the capabilities of the network to which the device is connected. Attributes may include those related to bandwidth and quality of service.
5. *WapCharacteristics*: Because the implementation of various WAP features is not consistent throughout various devices, this component bundles the features included, the versions supported, etc. regarding the various WAP components such as the Wireless Telephony Application Interface (WTAI) functionality.
6. *PushCharacteristics*: WAP 2.x provides push functionality through a push proxy. For the proxy and the remainder of the infrastructure to recognize the level of support on the device for push, this component outlines push-related attributes of the device such as MIME types supported for push.

To help you visualize the components of UAProf, you'll find a partial representation of the UAProf components using a UML Class Diagram in Figure 3.13. Because UAProf is closely related to CC/PP, most of the rules that have to be applied to an instance XML serialization of a device profile are the same as the rules for CC/PP. There are a few additional rules as follows:

1. *UAProf Namespace (prf)*: UAProf specifically requires use of namespaces for all elements in the document. Particularly, all RDF elements must use the namespace of "rdf:" and "prf" for UAPRof elements. RDF and UAProf namespaces must not be referred to as anything else.
2. *Single Instance of Each Specified Component Type*: This is not a requirement of RDF or CC/PP, but to make a practical implementation, it is reasonable to require that there is only one instance of every component type. This avoids name collision.
3. *rdf:ID and rdf:type*: Every component must have an rdf:type and an rdf:ID attribute. The rdf:ID must be unique in the document. If multiple component parts are used to create a component, then all the subcomponents must have the same rdf:ID. As an analogy to programming languages, think of rdf:type as the variable declaration and the rdf:ID as the variable name or the pointer to the variable instance. So, if you are operating on an element with the same rdf:ID, you are in essence pointing to a component to work on. This allows the UAProf parser to be able to merge multiple RDF subcomponents.
4. *Merging*: The notion of merging exists primarily to enable the system to combine multiple parts of the same component. Merging rules (the rules that specify how document A and document B are combined to produced document C) may be specified or default rules will be used. If no merging rules are specified, then a default set of rules for merging are used. Refer to the UAProf specification if you need to understand the merging rules as the implementer of a UAProf parser or a system that handles its own UAProf parsing.

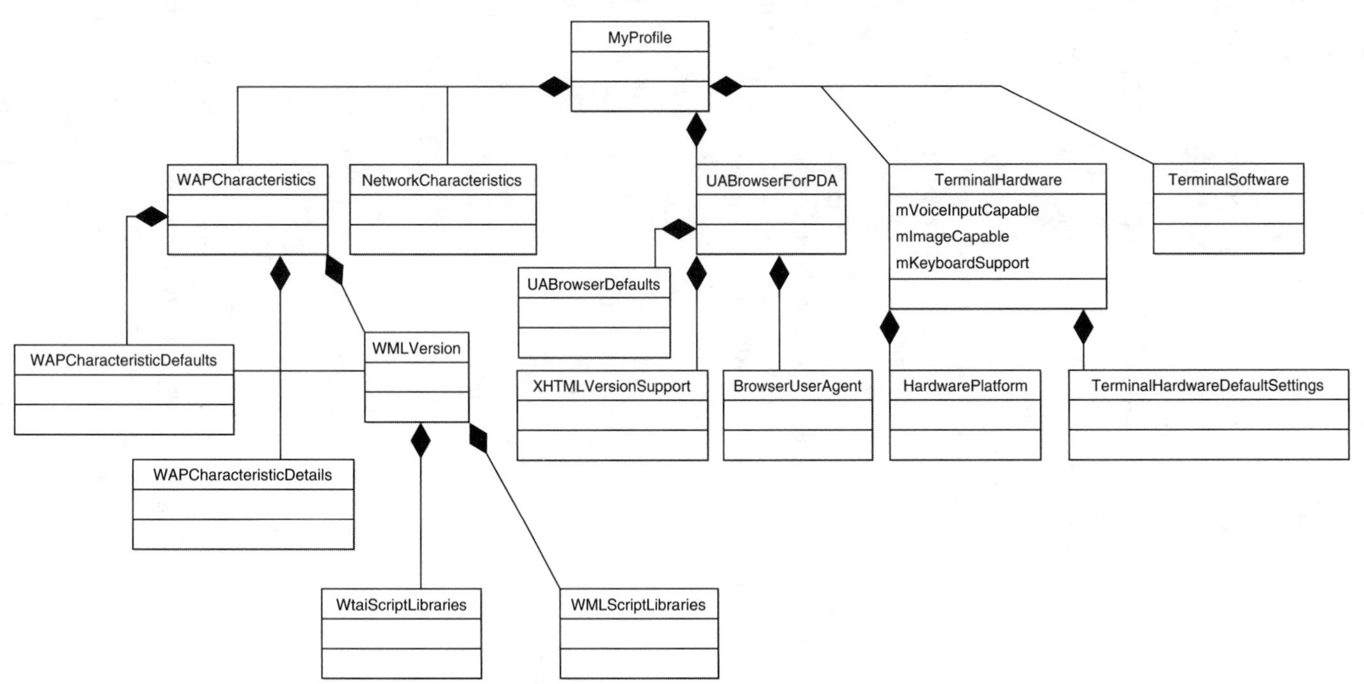

FIGURE 3.13. Partial Representation of UAProf Components in the UML Class Diagram.

There is much more to UAProf; our goal here was to briefly review it in an introductory manner. UAProf allows extension of the vocabulary through well-defined semantics for adding components as well as a mechanism to specify how to merge such extensions with the existing required components. The important thing to remember is that UAProf is specific to WAP. If you need a more generic mechanism, you need to think about using CC/PP. However, "don't rebuild Rome!" If your requirements are same as that laid out by the designers of UAProf, then use UAProf! Remember that using existing standards gives you two clear advantages: First, the problem has been thoroughly thought out by experts and second, interoperability issues are simpler (not simple!) if you use standards.

Example 3.9 shows a sample UAProf document. (Note that this sample does not include all the required components.)

Example 3.9: A Sample UAProf Document.

```
<?xml version="1.0"?>
<RDF xmlns="http://www.w3.org/1999/02/22-rdf-syntax-ns#"
     xmlns="http://www.w3.org/1999/02/22-rdf-syntax-ns#"
     xmlns="http://www.wapforum.org/profiles/UAPROF/ccppschema-
       20010430#">
     <rdf:Description ID="MyVerySimpleDeviceProfile">
       <prf:component>
           <rdf:Description ID="HardwarePlaform">
               <rdf:type resource="http://www.wapforum.org/
                 profiles/UAPROF/ccppschema-20010430#
                 HardwarePlatform">
                   <prf:SampleLocationSensitivityFunctionality>
                       <rdf:Bag>
                           <rdf:li>GPS</rdf:li>
                           <rdf:li>Proximity</rdf:li>
                           <rdf:li>Cell-site Triagulation</rdf:li>
                       </rdf:Bag>
                   </prf:SampleLocationSensitivityFunctionality>
                   <prf:InputCharSet>
                       <rdf:Bag>
                           <rdf:li>UTF-8</rdf:li>
                           <rdf:li>US-ASCII</rdf:li>
                       </rdf:Bag>
                   </prf:InputCharSet>
               </rdf:type>
           </rdf:Description>
       </prf:component>
       <prf:component>
           <rdf:Description ID="SoftwarePlaform">
```

```
                <rdf:type resource="http://www.wapforum.org/
                  profiles/UAPROF/ccppschema-20010430#
                  SoftwarePlatform">
                    <prf:AcceptDownloadableSoftware>Yes</prf:
                      AcceptDownloadableSoftware>
                </rdf:type>
            </rdf:Description>
        </prf:component>
      </rdf:Description>
</RDF>
```

3.4 XML AND UML

UML and XML relate in two ways:

1. UML's standard serialization mechanism is XMI, an application of XML.
2. UML can be used to model various applications of XML.

XMI (XML Metadata Interchange) is briefly covered in Chapter 4. XMI is simply an application of XML to serialize UML diagrams and accompanying information added to the diagram in OCL and other textual information. The main purpose of XMI is to specify a standard serialization format for all UML tools and facilitate interoperability among them. As a side benefit, XMI presents us with possibilities to use XML technologies to transform UML models into XML documents of other formats such as XHTML. We will discuss XMI itself briefly in Chapter 4 and its possible use in generating rudimentary user interfaces from UML models in Chapter 6. For now, all you need to know is that any set of UML diagrams can be persisted into an XMI file.

Our focus will be in discussing how to use UML to model XML applications. There are advantages to modeling XML with UML, such as discovering the difference in two different schemas representing the same business domain, that fall outside of the mobile realm. When it comes to mobile development, the primary reasons for using UML to model XML applications are the following:

1. *Using UML allows you to create one model for several code bases*: As we have seen, proliferation of code bases is a byproduct of device proliferation.
2. *Using UML enables you to create a visual aid to design mobile applications*: XML applications can be quite verbose and long. For this reason, it is often difficult to fathom various design complications by looking at XML documents. UML diagrams are visual. They ease the process of designing and analyzing.
3. *Using UML enables you to communicate the design and implementation throughout the development process of an application that relies on XML*: This has been a recurring theme for us. Because mobile applications, more so than their stationary

XML	UML
XML Schema	MetaModel
DTDs and Schemas	Model (Class Diagram, etc.)
XML Documents	Instance (Sequence Diagram, Object Diagram, etc.)

FIGURE 3.14. Mapping XML to/from UML.

counterparts, use myriad technologies, it is crucial to have one consistent tool for communicating design and implementation. UML provides such a tool. Because various XML technologies are used prevalently throughout the way we prescribe for building mobile applications, we need to know how to model XML with UML.

We have already discussed RDF to UML mappings. As we mentioned, we are not much interested in mapping UML to RDF for our purposes. RDF is widely accepted to be more complex (though more flexible) than UML. With this said, let us look at the types of mapping from XML to UML.

We can map XML to UML at three different levels (see Figure 3.14):

1. *Metamodel (also known as meta-metadata)*: XML schemas, DTDs, and even some applications of XML such as WSDL help us define an infrastructure for defining vocabularies. We can map this layer to either the model or the metamodel layer of UML. We can do this by extending mapping XML to existing features of UML and, when necessary, extending UML. One of the authors of UML, Grady Booch, along with others, has devised a mapping between XML and UML using stereotypes and tagged values to extend UML to represent artifacts specific to XML [Booch et al. 1999]. We will use this document along with others as a guide in our mapping.
2. *Model (also known as metadata)*: Various applications of XML provide us with structures and definitions for a particular domain of problems. This is the model layer. For example, VXML provides us with a model layer for building voice user interfaces. Such domains are often referred to as "vertical" for those domains focused on solving a business problem (i.e., MathML, CXML, eBXML, etc.) or "horizontal" for those domains focused on solving a technical problem across businesses (i.e., VXML, CCXML, etc.). Regardless of the type of problem domain that the application of XML is designed to address, we can map the domain represented in the XML application's XML Schema or DTD to a model in UML using class diagrams, collaboration diagrams, and the other model-level diagrams.
3. *Instance (also known as Data)*: This is an actual instance of an XML document. XML documents can be represented using a mixture of model and instance

diagrams in UML. If there is behavior encapsulated in the document, the behavior can be represented using sequence diagrams or state diagrams. OCL may be needed to augment these for full and proper mapping. For the data, we can use object diagrams; however, instance data is probably best kept in XML itself. Graphical modeling of pure instance data seldom provides us with an easier and more effective way of dealing with the data.

It should also be noted that UML involves more than just mapping of syntax and modeling elements. UML includes features such as support for requirements gathering in use-case diagrams and analysis in various development methodologies that have evolved around UML. Today, there is really no industry-wide accepted methodology for requirements gathering and analysis of XML schemas or DTDs. Therefore, we will focus on the mapping of the elements of the two standards.

Although generating the code for an entire application is something that we shun, UML offers us all the tools that we need to generate metamodel and model-level XML (DTDs, schemas, etc.). There is not much use in modeling instance data and generating XML based on it as the verbosity of the UML diagrams often make such an endeavor cost-prohibitive. Most of the time the mapping between UML and DTDs or schemas is straightforward. But, there are times when there are multiple ways to represent one UML feature in DTDs or schemas. In such cases, it is typically not important which mapping we choose, as long as we are consistent in applying the mapping throughout the generation of a given DTD or schema.

Let us start with the metamodel-level mapping of XML to UML.

3.4.1 XML Schema and UML

As we outlined in the previous section, XML Schema defines data types and provides facilities for defining new data types. (Although SGML provides for the same functionality in DTDs and is much more powerful, it lies beyond the scope of this text to provide a detailed mapping of SGML to UML.) Such functionality can be mapped to UML. XML Schema provides many other applications of XML with the data typing system. Let us start by mapping the XML Schema constructs to the UML constructs.

Table 3.1 gives us a starting point to do this. We use primarily two documents for our guide to construct this mapping: *tML Guidelines for Mapping UML Notation to XML Schemas and Vice Versa* by Oasis [OASIS tML 2001] and *UML for XML Schema Mapping Specification* [Booch et al. 1999].

The specific data types such as xsd:string can be mapped to language-dependent class libraries such as java.lang.String in Java. Table 3.1 gives the most important basic rules you need for mapping XML applications to UML and is not meant to be exhaustive. The references used here outline further mapping of features and constructs between XML and UML, but we will focus on mapping specific applications of XML to UML, for example XForms to UML. Every application of XML may use XML Schema data types and have its own data types.

Table 3.1. Mapping XML Schema Constructs to UML Constructs

XML and XML Schema Construct	UML Construct	Tips on Mapping
Namespace	package	Namespaces and packages both allow logical groupings of entities. Both UML packages and XML namespaces are used for referencing names that may be repeated within two different groupings of elements or classes. The primary purpose of both is to provide the developer and the framework with some organizational grouping of components and to avoid name collisions. Example 3.10 shows how a namespace can be used to represent a package in Java called com.cienecs.devices. Note that we could have called the namespace something else, such as http://www.cienecs.com/test_devices. The important thing to remember is the cardinality of the mapping. There is one namespace for every attribute. In our particular case, we have chosen the OASIS recommendation in the subject particulars of the mapping: 1. targetNamespace: This is the name of the namespace. 2. xmlns: This should be assigned whatever schema is used for the data types of the schema. Although you can create your own data type system, it is strongly recommended that you use XML Schema or some other W3C standard. 3. The "id" and "version" attributes have to be explicitly defined in the UML to be generated.
Attribute	class data member	We can model attributes as data members of classes.
Element	class data member	We can model elements as data members too.
Element	stereotyped class	Although we can model elements as data members, we may choose to model them as stereotyped classes and use aggregation (possibly composition if enough information is specified in the DTD and XML Schema) to model an element's nesting structure.
Structural sequence	stereotype and tagged value (<<sequence>> per [Booch et al. 1999])	Because the order of appearance and nesting of elements in XML is significant, we need to model this order in UML. We can specify the need for order through the stereotype and the specifics of the order through the tagged value.

(continued)

Table 3.1 (continued)

XML and XML Schema Construct	UML Construct	Tips on Mapping
Default value	stereotype and tagged value (<<default>> per [Booch et al. 1999])	The default value for a given data item (attribute or element data) in XML can be specified. Because this does not exist in UML, we have to extend UML using stereotype and tagged value to allow for default value for instances of classes.
Abstract types	abstract stereotype (such as abstract classes) [OASIS tML 2001]	There are data types that are to be extended but never instantiated in and of themselves. Such data types are said to be “abstract” (a notion in OOP discussed in Chapter 4). UML allows specifying such data types by specifying the *abstract* stereotype.
Enumerated types	<<enumeration>> stereotype (both [OASIS tML 2001] and [Booch et al. 1999])	Enumerated types (enumerations) are data types that have “list-like” structure and treatment. Enumerations in XML Schema allow only simple types (literals). So, regardless of implementation of the list in the specific programming language used to code the UML model, we can distinguish a class that is an enumerated type by a stereotype.
Choice	<<choice>> stereotype (both [OASIS tML 2001] and [Booch et al. 1999])	The choice classes allow us to specify a grouping of data in XML Schema. Although groupings can be modeled using classes, the choice specifies a particular type of a group that allows choosing one of many elements. This is specified through a stereotype in UML.
Derivation by extension	inheritance (generalization) or realization (implementing an interface) [OASIS tML 2001]	We can extend data types specified in XML Schema. This extension can be modeled using inheritance and realization.

Example 3.10: Mapping UML Namespaces to XML.

```
<schema targetNamespace="http://www.cienecs.com/devices"
    xmlns="http://www.w3.org/2001/XMLSchema"
    version="2002/04/01"
    id="devices.xsd" >
<!-- The Schema Rules should go here -->
</schema>
```

There are also some additional rules that we can think of as "rules of thumb" when mapping XML to UML:

1. If you are using XML Schema data types, make sure that there is a mapping between the data types offered in the language of your choice (Java, C++, etc.) and the XML Schema data types. Most tools will let you bring the core class libraries of the popular programming languages (or may already have those core classes). You will have to have the XML Schema data types in the model so that you can use them to represent attributes of elements. If there is a data type in the schema that is not part of the standard language libraries, you should create the proper data type in the form of a class (metadata layer) so that it may be referenced when creating the UML (and subsequently the schema or DTD based on the UML).
2. If you are using DTDs, your job is a bit simpler in modeling the data types but more difficult because DTDs are not well-formed XML. Also, because data types are a bit more loose in DTDs, every data type has to become its own element in the DTD (though you can reuse these data types once you have created a namespace and a DTD for them). Fortunately, once again, most UML tools can generate DTDs despite their format being not well formed.
3. Other data constraints can be represented using constraints or stereotypes. It is largely up to the developer which to use and when to use them. The key is to stay consistent.
4. Class diagrams are ideal for representing the structure of the XML document. If XML is being used for messaging, you can use sequence diagrams to represent the messaging interactions among the various systems or system components.
5. To represent dependencies in UML, we use the dashed association line with an arrow. Stereotypes can be used to specify the particular type of the association unless there is a particular iconic version of the association (such as aggregation). See Example 3.10 and corresponding Figure 3.15.

Figures 3.16 and 3.17 show a mapping of XML to UML for the address example we use throughout this text. Figure 3.16 is an XML Schema that defines the grid as a part of the GML standard (which we will look at in Chapter 12). Figure 3.17 is one possible class diagram that can be used as a UML representation of the XML Schema. The XML Schema can be found at http://schemas.opengis.net/gml/3.0.1/base/grids.xsd.

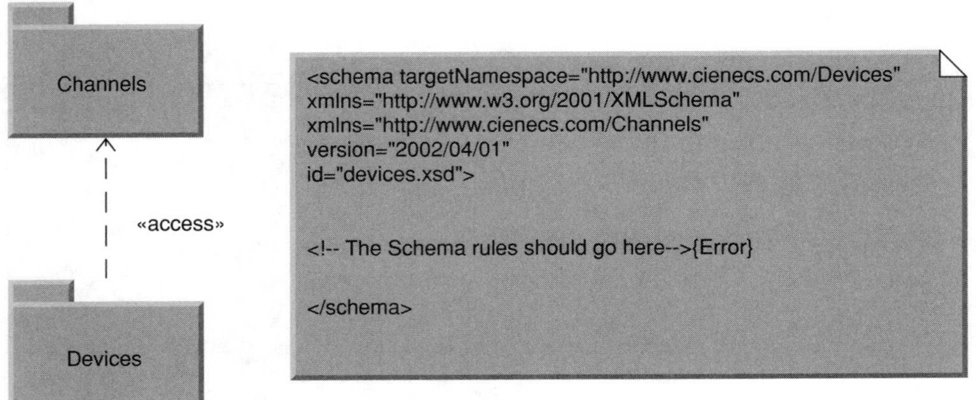

FIGURE 3.15. Mapping Package Dependencies from UML to XML Namespaces.

```
<?xml version="1.0" encoding="UTF-8"?>
<schema targetNamespace="http://www.opengis.net/gml"
xmlns:gml="http://www.opengis.net/gml"
xmlns="http://www.w3.org/2001/XMLSchema"
xmlns:xlink="http://www.w3.org/1999/xlink"
  elementFormDefault="qualified" version="3.0.1">
    <annotation>
        <appinfo source="urn:opengis:specification:gml:schema-
          xsd:grids:v3.0.1">grids.xsd</appinfo>
        <documentation xml:lang="en">Grid geometries A subset
          of implicit geometries designed for use with GML.
            Coverage schema, but maybe useful elsewhere as
              well.
        Copyright (c) 2002 OGC, All Rights Reserved.
        </documentation>
    </annotation>
    <include schemaLocation="geometryBasic0d1d.xsd"/>
    <element name="_ImplicitGeometry" type="gml:
      AbstractGeometryType" abstract="true"
      substitutionGroup="gml:_Geometry"/>
    <element name="Grid" type="gml:GridType"
      substitutionGroup="gml:_ImplicitGeometry"/>
    <complexType name="GridType">
        <annotation>
            <documentation>Implicitly defines an unrectified
              grid, which is a network composed of two or more
              sets of equally spaced parallel lines in which
              the members of each set intersect the members of
              the other sets at right angles.</documentation>
        </annotation>
        <complexContent>
            <extension base="gml:AbstractGeometryType">
                <sequence>
```

FIGURE 3.16. Sample XML Schema Representing the Opengis GML Grid.

```
                <element name="limits" type="gml:
                  GridLimitsType"/>
                <element name="axisName" type="string"
                  maxOccurs="unbounded"/>
            </sequence>
            <attribute name="dimension" type=
              "positiveInteger" use="required"/>
        </extension>
    </complexContent>
</complexType>
<complexType name="GridLimitsType">
    <sequence>
        <element name="GridEnvelope" type="gml:
          GridEnvelopeType"/>
    </sequence>
</complexType>
<complexType name="GridEnvelopeType">
    <annotation>
        <documentation>Provides grid coordinate values for
          the diametrically opposed corners of an envelope
          that bounds a section of grid. The value of a
          single coordinate is the number of offsets from
          the origin of the grid in the direction of a
          specific axis.</documentation>
    </annotation>
    <sequence>
        <element name="low" type="gml:integerList"/>
        <element name="high" type="gml:integerList"/>
    </sequence>
</complexType>
<element name="RectifiedGrid" type="gml:
  RectifiedGridType" substitutionGroup="gml:Grid"/>
<complexType name="RectifiedGridType">
    <annotation>
        <documentation>A rectified grid has an origin and
          vectors that define its post locations.
        </documentation>
    </annotation>
    <complexContent>
        <extension base="gml:GridType">
            <sequence>
                <element name="origin" type="gml:
                  PointPropertyType"/>
                <element name="offsetVector" type="gml:
                  VectorType" maxOccurs="unbounded"/>
            </sequence>
        </extension>
    </complexContent>
</complexType>
</schema>
```

Figure 3.16 *(continued)*

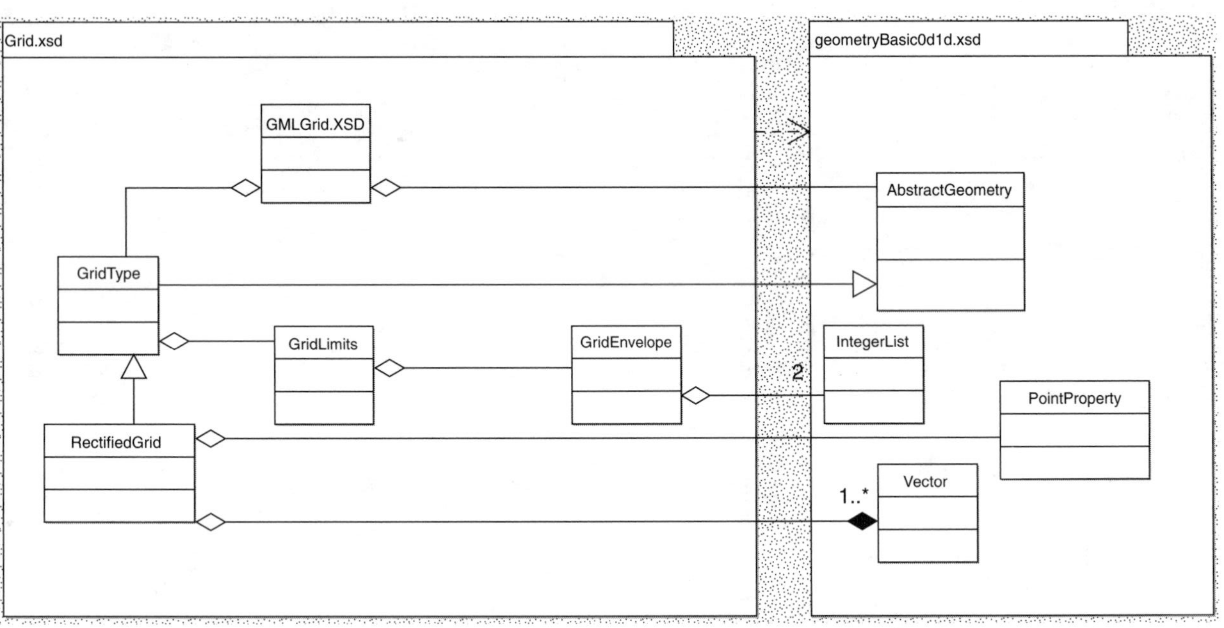

FIGURE 3.17. Possible UML Representation of the Schema of Figure 3.16.

It is important to note that there is more than one way of mapping XML to UML whereas there is only one way of mapping UML to XML (XMI). Therefore, two UML diagrams used to model a particular application of XML may both be correct despite their differences.

In fact, this is somewhat of a problem in mapping XML to UML. The recommended strategy is to use the method of Booch et al. for basic mapping and defer to what makes sense for a particular application of XML. For example, state diagrams and sequence diagrams can be very useful in representing interaction sequences outlined in VXML (which we will look at in Chapter 7). However, without understanding the semantics of VXML, it is not possible to intelligently and fully use UML to model an instance VXML document. Mapping application-specific features of XML to UML has another hidden benefit in encapsulating the semantics of the application of XML and making it easier to understand those semantics through the graphical tools that UML offers.

This ends our introductory look at the mapping between UML and XML. Let us take a step back and review. There are two occasions when we want to model XML schemas or DTDs with UML:

1. When we are designing schemas and DTDs: UML gives us all the tools we need to actually design DTDs and schemas. Most of the UML tools such as Object Domain and Rational Rose offer such capabilities. Typically, you can construct a metamodel with class diagrams and, with a simple click, get a DTD or XML Schema. Currently, DTD support is more widespread, but most tools are moving to support both DTDs and XML schemas.
2. When we are reverse engineering: Sometimes we need to model an existing schema or DTD with UML. The benefits range from understanding the schema or DTD better to building custom parsing code using an object-oriented language faster. Until, and if, UML becomes the standard way to model XML schemas and DTDs, most of the time we will be reverse engineering existing schemas and DTDs if we want to model them with UML.

As we previously mentioned, we will look at mapping of specific XML applications to UML during the remainder of this text.

3.5 Putting XML to Work

XML has already become the de facto document standard for exchange of human-readable data. Whether such will be the case for machine-to-machine communication is questionable; nevertheless, such applications exist and their popularity is increasing.

In this chapter, we looked at a variety of XML-based technologies and took an an introductory glimpse at their use in mobile applications. Then, we looked at RDF, a part of the Semantic Web that is becoming pervasively more crucial to mobile applications. We followed this by discussions of CC/PP and UAProf as applications of RDF and XML for mobile applications and finished off the chapter by talking about XML to UML mapping.

The significance of XML to mobile applications is twofold: First, it offers a well-formed and deterministically modifiable format for human-readable data, and second, it offers interoperability. Throughout the remainder of this book, we will focus on building mobile applications that use XML as one of the core pieces in their infrastructure and apply the principles that we learned here in this chapter.

CHAPTER 4

Introduction to UML

David Brady

If one has to jump a stream and knows how wide it is, he will not jump. If he does not know how wide it is, he will jump, and six times out of ten he will make it.

Persian Proverb

4.1 INTRODUCTION

The unified modeling language (UML) is a standardized language for modeling software systems. Although small systems are easy for a single person or a small group to comprehend and develop, large systems are more difficult to design successfully, because there are often many people and entities controlling different aspects of the system and defining how they should work from their own professional specialty or prerogative. For example, a large company requesting a new piece of software might assign the job to a project manager who has a thorough understanding of the overall system requirements, whereas a software developer assigned to work on the system is likely to care more about the ways that individual portions of a system work on a detailed level and less about the practical requirements of users and management. Similarly, an end user of the system is likely to care about how the user interface is organized and that the software is built to facilitate ease of use for everyday users, rather than that a particular software component was designed exquisitely or that the project fulfills the stated requirements that its originator decided on. The process of building software can be very complex, and, moreover, there are few cases where a single person has full comprehension of how a system should be designed to fulfill all of its requirements.

Designing a system that takes into consideration all of the different requirements for the system, from the viewpoint of its stakeholders, developers, users, domain experts, and others, and which still can adapt to change readily and without causing unforeseen problems is next to impossible without defining the system in a manner that illustrates the various facets of a system, but still recognizing a common set of entities between those facets. If you have used UML in your projects as a developer and have a fair understanding of the underlying concepts of UML, you can skip this chapter and move on to the next. This chapter will serve as a very basic introduction to UML. Many details of UML are missing here, but we have gathered a basic introduction that should suffice for our purposes.

Let us first take the case of stationary applications and then we will extend it to mobile applications. The problem for typical software applications is twofold: First, systems are difficult to manage conceptually. By providing different diagrams that illuminate differing views of a system, UML allows a system to be seen piece by piece in consistent pieces, which, together, give a complete view of the system.

Second, with multiple people working with a microcosmic view of a system, one person's change can have an impact on aspects of the system that are unknown to the others. Because the UML uses common elements in the different diagrams, it becomes much easier to see the ramifications of a change throughout a system. During the development process, team members often let their individual goals take priority over the project at the expense of the business goals for which it was designed. Their misguided targets are often caused by an adherence to outdated requirements and their inaccurate interpretation of them. So keeping a model synchronized with the requirements that are being defined while maintaining accuracy becomes of the utmost importance.

The solution to the problem leads us to modeling. Because modeling helps the design phase so significantly, a byproduct is often reduced costs of the system. Furthermore, it is an effective way to ensure at the outset that a system can be built, that the costs of doing so are not unreasonable, and that the system will fulfill the business requirements and meet the needs of its users.

Modeling is not unique to software. It is used in a variety of disciplines to think through a system or product, describe it, and discover design flaws before it is built. Modeling is used in architecture, in mathematics, in the sciences (seismology is a good example), in civil engineering, in auto manufacturing, and in an almost infinite number of things that are conceptually complex and benefit from a modeling illustration of the problem at hand, its ability to encourage understanding of its parts, and the facilitation of communication among the people involved. You can think of the model as a blueprint of the software system to be built. A model should include different perspectives of the system from the viewpoints of the various team members, such as developers, end users, and the entity that determined the need for the system and instigated its development. The UML provides different views based on who is interpreting the model and in what way.

What the UML provides in a nutshell, then, is a manner of modeling software that provides a full range of views, from very general overviews of how the system works as a whole, to detailed interactions and descriptions of how each object functions and communicates.

Modeling a software system has many benefits and goals. First, modeling helps people to visualize a system as they want it to be. It provides a template for constructing the system, which specifies details of system implementation in a specific enough way that software developers can implement it rapidly and with fewer work stoppages to clarify requirements. By separating system development by architecture, UML allows architects to focus on building systems, whereas developers are able to implement them more rapidly because the system's various components are already defined for them. Architects can specify how something should be built without implementing it themselves, yet this can be done in a specific manner that essentially gives the developer a blueprint for the software.

Another benefit of UML is that is helps us to document the decisions that are made throughout the design process. In complex systems, it is difficult for a single person to understand both a specific component of a system and its context in the system as a whole. One way of dealing with this limitation is to narrow our focus to one aspect at a time. UML facilitates this by allowing us to model individual parts of a system while also providing a broad overview.

Most developers use some sort of modeling technique inherently. From diagrams sketched on napkins to complex models of their own design, to textual descriptions or logic tables, developers almost always draw out a system or components of a system in some manner to help them think through the problem before the implementation. The problem, however, is that many developers have their own methodologies for modeling, which, though they help to illuminate the system's structure for that particular person, may fail to take into consideration needs of the system beyond the developer. Furthermore, that particular developer's method of modeling a system may be largely incomprehensible to others. Although no particular modeling technique works perfectly for everyone, UML provides diagrams that are applicable to many different roles. More importantly, however, UML, because it is a standardized language that is well documented by a detailed specification, can be understood by anyone with sufficient training. By providing a standard, UML encourages application designers to use a consistent vocabulary and methodology.

The more complex the project, the higher the likelihood that you will fail to complete it successfully or that it will not be completed as intended. Worse, many systems start out simply and then become more complex; thus the initial simple design fails to encompass the complexity that the system grows into. When this happens without an adequate modeling system, things rapidly spiral out of control and result in heaping piles of "spaghetti code" (code so unwieldy that it looks like spaghetti in a visual sense).

When object-oriented languages began to appear in the mid-1970s, they were conceptually new for software developers and architects accustomed to using procedural languages. Because procedural languages have a well-defined flow, they are easy to model with simple flow charts. That model was only able to express a small part of how object-oriented systems interoperate. Something else was needed to illustrate the way that object-oriented systems interacted.

There was no shortage of ideas about how object-oriented software should be modeled, as a variety of different methodologies quickly emerged. The late 1980s saw a plethora of competing methodologies and plenty of experimenting within those. By 1994 there were close to fifty of them competing to become the de facto standard. As we mentioned earlier, the result of not standardizing on a single methodology is a fragmented vocabulary and the inability to communicate. By providing a standard, UML encourages a consistent methodology.

The creators of the early methodologies, including Grady Booch, Ivar Jacobson, and James Rumbaugh, began collaborating and their work eventually developed into UML. Also involved in the effort were Fusion, Shlar-Mellor, Coad-Yourdan, and David Harel. In 1994, Grady Booch and James Rumbaugh decided to unify their own personal methodologies. They had both recognized the strengths of the other's techniques as well as the benefits of the State Machine as a behavioral component, so they combined the three and created the Object Modeling Technique (OMT) with input from Eran Gery on object-oriented state chart diagrams.

In 1996 they expanded their modeling language into UML and established the UML Consortium, enlisting the support and design assistance from major computing and software-related companies, including DEC, Hewlett-Packard, IBM, MCI, Microsoft, Oracle, Rational, and Texas Instruments. The UML 1.0 Standard was completed in January 1997. At this point the UML Consortium was expanded again to include a wider variety of companies. They released UML version 1.1 in July of that same year. In November 1997 the Object Management Group (OMG) adopted UML 1.1.

At the time of authoring this text, the UML 2.0 specification is months away from being released in its final form. This represents the first version to be developed by committee instead of primarily Booch, Jacobson, and Rumbaugh. UML 2.0 has been improved in many ways. It aims to be more consistent and adds many new features. Sequence diagrams have been enhanced to support data-flow modeling. Interface and architecture elements have added support for elaborated interfaces, ports, interaction fragments, and operators. It also supports multiplicities and conditions for the extends relationship and is now explicit between use case and state diagrams. Timing diagrams have been added and show a timeline across the horizontal axis. Most importantly, as far as we are concerned, there are two formal methods of adding large-grained functionality to UML 2.0 to treat specific domains such as mobile applications. First, the metamodel can be modified to create an extension; alternatively, profiles can be created to extend UML 2.0. Those things that we add to UML in this text can be represented by either a profile or a metamodel change. Because this book is written with UML 1.4 in mind, we do not address this issue; however, a profile may be preferred for practical purposes.

The current version of UML is 1.4. The full UML Specification and supporting documentation are located at the Object Management Group's Web site: http://www.omg.org.

4.1.1 Why Was It Created?

UML was created as a language to model an object-oriented system from many different views. We can get a top-down view of the system's basic purpose, we can focus on its detailed structure, or we may choose to look at our system from the perspective of a conceptual user. Additionally, the UML creators strove to address the problem of conceptualizing a system. Because object-oriented systems of any complexity tend to be difficult to comprehend by a single person, UML attempts to simplify the complexity by breaking down the model into various view points of the same components of a system, thus making it easier to see how various parts of the system work in context, and hopefully eliminating the need for all participants to fully comprehend the entire system as a whole. More ambitiously, the creators of UML strove to create a modern language usable by both humans and machines.[Booch, Rumbaugh, and Jacobsen 1999] In other words, UML was created not only with the intention of helping humans understand and create a system, but also with the intention of allowing for machine-generated code based on models and the reverse, models based on an existing code base.

Forward engineering combined with a standards-based modeling language is currently emerging through widespread availability in software development packages offered by IBM, Microsoft, Borland, and others. Good template-based open-source tools are emerging as well (e.g., the AndroMDA project, which can be found at www.andromda.org).

These fourth-generation tools have enabled highly complex systems to be changed with relative ease and can save costs by reducing the staff hours required to develop and maintain a system. Their benefits are only beginning to be exploited and as they increase, so will its adoption, which will enable more complex and more capable systems. Surely this century will be recorded as the birth of the industrial age of software, that is, software creating software.

4.1.2 Understanding UML

Many guides to UML mix methodology with modeling. Although both are obviously important in the software development process, you should be very clear on one point: UML is a language, and, like any language, it is a flexible tool that can be used in a variety of ways. Its purpose is to explain and illustrate ideas in a meaningful way, and, although opinions abound on which way is the correct way to express an idea, those ideas are simply opinions. It is important to understand that UML has a detailed specification that details the syntax and regulations for each diagram and their various elements. In this text, however, we will mix methodology with modeling because our primary concern is in the application of UML to mobile software.

UML is modeled on human languages, like English, and was designed to take advantage of the strengths of human languages: flexibility and extensibility. Like any language UML has a set of rules that ought to be followed, like the grammar of a human language. Just like the rules of the English language dictate that you should capitalize a proper name, the rules of UML dictate that the name of a class should be in the top section of the class rectangle. These are the rules of language, and following them ensures that your sentences—or diagrams—are clear to your audience. Often, though, you will find the rules of UML interspersed with opinions about how UML should be used. To go back to the English analogy, there are plenty of people that say formal writing should be done in the third person. That is their particular preference for how formal writing should be done, but it is not a rule of the English language. When reading about UML it is important to keep that distinction in mind. In the following sections, we will describe the basic purpose of the major diagrams in UML, their common uses, and the rules of their use. We intend this to be a guide to the rules of UML, rather than a stylistic modeling guide.

Rarely is a single model sufficient to model a system; modeling a system usually requires several different models to illustrate a system as well as its subsystems. For an example of this, think about modeling your car, which can be modeled in terms of its architecture, and also in terms of the different systems it contains, such as the transmission and braking system. How we model a system depends on the perspective, application, and use of the system by the observer and this is something that has been taken into account in UML. As we discussed earlier, one of the benefits to using UML is that it provides different views on the same elements of a system and therefore can help to show how a change in one aspect of a system can have an impact on other parts and their interacting behaviors. Viewing a system through its diagrams can help you understand how your decisions have an impact on the other parts of the system. UML is composed of a variety of different diagrams, each of which provides a different view of the system, while maintaining the relationships among the contained components. Each diagram represents a different view of the same entities.

Because of this, a modeling tool greatly enhances the usefulness of the models because relationships among its parts are carried over between diagrams by the software, rather than relying on a human to understand and enforce the changes between them. When software, rather than a human, enforces consistency and rules that are established in other diagrams, change management for a system becomes comparatively easy, with the added bonus that it also is easier for a system's documentation and code to remain synchronized. This, as you may imagine, helps to solve one of software's age-old problems.

UML specifies nine major types of diagrams, divided into five different views of the system. These five system views correspond to the major phases of a software development project. These views are, respectively, per order defined in the specification, as follows:

1. *System Requirements View*: This view is defined by the end users' interaction with the system and other systems and is manifest in the form of a use case diagram.
2. *Design View*: This view is used where the system vocabulary is defined. Diagrams included in the design view include class, object, interaction, state, and activity diagrams.
3. *Process View*: This view models the processes and procedures of a system. Diagrams related to the process view are the same as for the design view, but with an emphasis on the active classes.
4. *Implementation View*: This view includes diagrams that are useful to software developers as they create the system and includes the sequence and collaboration diagrams.
5. *Deployment View*: This view describes the system from the viewpoint of a system engineer.

Together, all of these views provide a fairly complete picture of a software system that can be used as a blueprint for its development. In this text, we will be focused on all of these different views according to the application to mobile software development, so you will see the appropriate extensions in the place of the appropriate discussion.

UML distinguishes between static and dynamic types of diagrams. *Static diagrams*, which are also called structural diagrams, are used to represent the structure of a system, and things within the system that do not change. The static diagrams include class diagrams, object diagrams, component diagrams, and deployment diagrams. *Dynamic diagrams*, in contrast, illustrate the dynamic aspects of a system, which are also known as its behavioral aspects. The dynamic diagrams in UML are use case diagrams, sequence diagrams, state chart diagrams, collaboration diagrams, and activity diagrams.

In the proposed UML 2.0 draft, the relationship between use cases and state diagrams is now explicit.

4.1.3 Building Blocks of UML

We will start with some basic terminology needed to understand UML:

1. *System*: A collection of subsystems organized for a purpose, described by a set of models, possibly from different viewpoints.
2. *Subsystem*: A grouping of elements that constitute a specific behavior offered by the containing elements.
3. *Model*: An abstraction representing a complete and self-consistent simplification of reality created to better understand the system.
4. *View*: A projection into the organization and structure of a system, focused on one aspect of that system.
5. *Diagram*: Semantically, in the UML specification, a graphical presentation of a set of elements.

Let us get started with some of the basic defining elements of UML. *Classifiers* are the fundamental building units of UML. Classifiers refer to the parts of UML that may have instances. Classifiers may have both *structural features*, such as *attributes*, as well as *behavioral attributes*, such as *operations*. A classifier acts as a template for the instances from which they are derived, and each instance of a classifier shares the behavioral and structural features that are specified by the classifier. The following elements are all classifiers:

1. *Class*[D2]: UML classes are perhaps the single most frequently used artifact in UML. UML classes encapsulate the attributes and behaviors shared by a certain group of entities. UML classes closely follow the definition of classes in object oriented programming.
2. *Interface*: A named set of operations that characterize the behavior of an element.
3. *Data Type*: A type with values that have no individual identity. These can include primitive data types, built-in data types, and enumerated types.
4. *Signal*: An asynchronous message sent from one instance to another to communicate things such as state, status, and events.

5. *Component*: A physical element of a system that provides the realization of a set of interfaces. Components can include source code, executable code, libraries, and data files.
6. *Node*: A physical element of a system that is able to do computations. Nodes exist at run time and typically have memory and processing capabilities.
7. *Use Case*: A set of action sequences whose result is of value to a particular actor, as well as variant cases of those sequences. In the proposed UML version 2.0 draft, the relationship between use cases and state diagrams are explicit.
8. *Subsystem*: A group of elements that specify the behavior of its containing elements.

The heart of UML's usefulness lies in its diagrams. The nine major types are as follows:

1. *Class diagrams* show classes, interfaces, and collaborations and the relationships among them. Class diagrams are used to represent the static design of a system.
2. *Object diagrams* show a group of objects and their relationships. Object diagrams show static views of objects, which are snapshots of a system at a given point in time. Object diagrams, like class diagrams, show the static view of a system, but from the perspective of a specific scenario, rather than a general case.
3. *Collaboration diagrams* are a type of interaction diagram and are semantically equivalent to sequence diagrams. They emphasize the organization of and relationships among objects that send and receive messages. Collaboration diagrams show a set of objects involved in an interaction, the relationships among them, and the messages they send and receive. Collaboration diagrams are used to illustrate the dynamic view of the system.
4. *Sequence diagrams*, like collaboration diagrams, are interaction diagrams. They are semantically equivalent to collaboration diagrams. When designing a system, in fact, you often start with a sequence diagram and then turn it into a collaboration diagram to determine the structure. Sequence diagrams emphasize the order of messages at a moment in time. They show a group of objects and the messages that are sent and received arranged sequentially according to their temporal progression. Sequence diagrams are used to illustrate the dynamic view of the system.
5. *Activity diagrams* show the dynamic view of the system by capturing the flow from one activity to the next within a system and are semantically equivalent to state diagrams. Activity diagrams model a group of activities and the flow of activity, sequential or branching, from one to the next, as well as the objects that participate in that flow, either as users of the system or recipients of the action. Activity diagrams typically emphasize the flow of control among objects but can be used for more generic purposes as well.
6. *State chart diagrams* show a State Machine, which includes states, transitions, activities, and events, and are semantically equivalent to activity diagrams. Like activity diagrams, they show a dynamic view of the system. State chart diagrams, or state diagrams, are particularly important in modeling how a particular class,

interface, or collaboration behaves and are used to illustrate behaviors that are ordered by events.

7. *Component diagrams* model physical software components, such as source code, libraries, and executables, and the relationships among them, particularly as they relate to realized interfaces. They are used to model a static view of the system's implementation and typically map to classes, interfaces, or collaborations.
8. *Deployment diagrams* model a set of nodes—that is, computational resources—and the relationships among them. As such, deployment diagrams model a static view of a system's deployment. Deployment diagrams are related to component diagrams, because a node typically contains one or more components.
9. *Use case diagrams* show a set of scenarios depicting interactions with the system and the resulting behavior. They show the relationships between the system and its users and together represent snapshots of the system in action or its static views. They are analogous to the film industry's storyboards used for a movie production.

Activity and state chart diagrams, as well as sequence and collaboration diagrams, are listed as being semantically equivalent. In other words, these diagrams display the same information. Why, then, you may wonder, do we need two separate diagrams for each case? The answer is that, because the material contained in both can be difficult to conceptualize, providing two separate viewpoints helps to illuminate that facet of the system. In addition to being semantically equivalent, interaction diagrams (i.e., sequence and collaboration diagrams) are isomorphic, which means that they carry an additional requirement: You should be able to display the information in a sequence diagram in a collaboration diagram without loss of information and vice versa.

Another set of similar diagrams are class, component, and deployment diagrams. They are all drawn similarly and have as their distinguishing feature only the major diagram element that is shown. Class diagrams show classes, whereas component diagrams and deployment diagrams show components and nodes, respectively.

4.2 The User View

The user view is going to be of particular importance within the context of our discussions. The user view encapsulates how the user looks at the system and his or her interactions with the system. This view is particularly important to mobile computing, because, as we will see in Chapters 5–8, the view of the user may depend on the device, the network, and the dimensions of mobility. Let us start with *use cases* and *use case diagrams*: those building blocks that let us start to put together requirements for a project.

4.2.1 Use Case Diagrams

A use case diagram is a high level requirements overview that shows one path of activity or scenario from start to finish. A use case diagram depicts a system in terms of user interaction and shows scenarios of system use as well as a sequence of events initiated by a user, another system, hardware, or the passage of time. A use case can be drawn as a diagram, or it can simply be a list of steps that are performed in a given interaction. To produce effective use cases, you should be sure that each use case represents only a specific interaction with the system.

Use cases are designed to model a system's behavior without delving into its inner-workings. For example, a use case for a mobile user receiving a traffic report might detail the step-by-step process of communication between a mobile user and the traffic service used to retrieve current traffic reports without describing how the interaction works in a detailed manner. Every use case diagram should illustrate a complete flow of events including what event triggers the use case and when it ends. Remember, however, that use case diagrams are not concerned with the system's implementation details. Rather, they should illustrate the high-level scenarios possible within a system.

Because use case diagrams show system events on a high level, they should describe the flow of events in a manner that is clear and concise enough to be comprehensible to people unfamiliar with the system. To that end, it is important to provide only the information necessary to understand a particular behavior in its context in a use case, while ensuring that you have provided sufficient information to explain the scenario in its context.

Use cases are classifiers and have attributes and operations (just like classes, as you will see later in the chapter). These may be used in interaction diagrams to specify the behavior of a use case. Because use cases are classifiers, you can also attach State Machines to them. State Machines are covered in more detail later on in this chapter.

There are three general types of use case flow of events: the *main case, variations to the main case*, and the *exceptional case*. The main case is the flow of events assuming that everything goes according to plan. The main case is the best and most common scenario. Variations to the main case include flows of events that vary from the main case. An exceptional case illustrates the path through the system in a single error case. Use cases defer the detail of their implementation process to other diagrams specified by UML. The sequence of specific events that a use case represents generically are specified in a use case diagram. A collaboration diagram shows the objects necessary to complete the process along with their relationships and interactions.

4.2.2 Using Use Cases

Use cases are helpful in designing aspects of the system with which users will interact, including things like GUIs, voice interfaces, and a variety of other potential ways that a user might interact with the system. When users are involved in creating use cases, that generally means that the system will likely be more useful to them and that it will respond in a way in which they expect. Use scenarios should be from the viewpoint of the different types of users, forming a representative collection of use cases. The users' role depends on the stated purpose of the interaction.

Use case diagrams can benefit system development in many ways. They can help with user interface design, aid developers in gaining a high-level understanding of the system requirements, and can be used as a basis for developing testing plans.

Use case diagrams are useful in the process of defining how a product or system will be used and what requirements it will have to meet. Most software projects begin by management defining the specific requirements. This initial phase typically produces a system design document or specification that will detail the system to be built. These design specifications also serve as a reference for the software developers during the implementation of the system.

Once the design document is created, however, it becomes a significant challenge to prevent the ideas captured in this document from becoming out of date as the system requirements change. This frequently occurs when the requirements change verbally or by some other means, but the design document is not updated to reflect the changes. The result is that developers become less confident in the accuracy of the design document and they tend to use it less frequently, growing more dependent on their individual memory and interpretation of how the system should be built.

This is a problem that consistently plagues software development teams and has proven to be difficult to solve. One reason most solutions fail is that they require an awkward maintenance step that would not be needed at all except to keep the requirements synchronized. Therefore, a successful solution is one that can be maintained while defining and modifying requirements and one that is naturally integrated into the developers' implementation process.

Use cases are one such solution. When used successfully, use cases drive discussions with the software's founders and are fully integrated with the developer's design documents. As we will see throughout the rest of this chapter, use cases are the underlying design concept that weaves together all the other UML diagrams and helps us to ensure that the software that is built is the software the founders designed. Use cases are also valuable in the testing phase of an application. Because quality assurance teams responsible for the testing of an application may be unfamiliar with its scenarios of use, use cases can show them how the application was designed to be used and can help them in developing test plans.

An actor typically initiates a use case and derives some benefit from its use. This benefit may be realized by the actor who initiated the use case, but it could also be a different actor. An actor may be an actual person, another system, or even a hardware device, but it always represents a set of roles that will be interacting with the system from the outside. Table 4.1 shows an overview of the elements used in creating use case diagrams.

Figure 4.1 shows three actors: a mobile user, a 911 emergency system, and a service administrator. You will notice that each actor is represented as a stick figure, although they may be actual humans or computer systems, such as the 911 emergency system. The one thing that all three of these actors have in common is that they represent interactions with entities that reside outside of the system we are modeling.

Table 4.1. Overview of the Elements in Use Cases Diagrams

Element Name	Iconic Representation	Description
Use Cases	UseCaseName	A use case is represented by an oval that is labeled with the name of the use case. A use case element represents a system behavior, generally enough to not clutter the diagram and specifically enough to illustrate the purpose and context of the behavior.
Actors	ActorName	Actors are either a role or an entity that participates in a system. Actors can be, among other things, human users or other systems. Systems can have a variety of users, such as customers, employees, and other computer systems. They each represent a role or set of roles that interacts with the system from the outside. Identifying all the actors is an important step in defining the context of the system. Each one can interact with the system in a number of different ways.
Association		Associations are shown as solid lines between diagram elements. An association between an actor and a use case indicates that they communicate with one another. This association can also indicate that they are sending and receiving messages to and from one another.
Notes	Textual Notes Go In Here	Notes, which contain comments, or human-readable descriptions, can be included in use case diagrams. The detail of a use case diagram can be either in a design document or in notes attached to the diagram. Beware, though, that notes can quickly clutter up a diagram. Usually each use case diagram will have a page in a design document with information about the initiation of the use case by an actor, preconditions of the use case, the steps in its scenario, its post conditions, and the actor to benefit from it.

Generalization		Generalization provides both a complex version and a generic version of a scenario and is applicable to both actors and use cases in a use case diagram. Use case generalization specifies a relationship where a use case inherits its parents' context and behavior. Generalization allows the child use case to override behavior of its parent and to be substituted in place of its parent. Generalization is used to model object-oriented inheritance. The use case generalization relationship is rendered with the standard notation for generalization: a solid line with an open arrowhead.
Package	PackageName	Grouping use cases together by related interactions is a way to simplify a set of behaviors. For example, in a system with many subsystems, it may be difficult to define all the requirements. Categorizing a system's many requirements into related behaviors is a way of managing the complexity and may also be useful for grouping design discussions with the appropriate users.
Include	<<Include>>	The *include* relationship describes an action that is repeated with the purpose of saving you from having to describe the same behavior repeatedly. Say that you have several use cases, each with a similar series of steps, and you want to avoid repeating those same steps in each use case. What you do in this case is include a use case containing those steps into each use case that required them. To include a use case, you would first make a use case that represented the common steps shared by the other use cases. Then you would include that use case in the more detailed use cases that required them. The include relationship, a stereotype notated by <<include>>, differs from the other use case relationships in that the included use case never stands alone and is always included. Essentially, this is an example of delegation. The include relationship is modeled as a dependency stereotype and is sometimes stereotyped with the use's keyword.

(*continued*)

Table 4.1 (continued)

Element Name	Iconic Representation	Description
Extends	<<extends>>	A use case can also be reused with the extends relationship, in which you add steps to an existing use case. This is known as extending a use case. In this relationship, the base use case incorporates the behavior of another use case inherently. Unlike with the include relationship, the base use case can stand alone. Additionally, it can be extended using specified extension points. The extends relationship is denoted by generalization arrows (closed arrowhead). The extends relationship is useful in modeling optional system behavior and for separating optional from required behavior. An example of the extends relationship is the J2ME, which contains both required packages (a minimum configuration) and optional packages for resource-plentiful devices. The extends relationship, a stereotype notated by <<extends>>, relates an extension use case to a base use case, specifying how the behavior defined for the extension use case augments the behavior defined for the base use case. The base use case does not depend on performing the behavior of the extension use case. The extends relationship is also useful in modeling potential flows of events that could occur at a given point based on an interaction with an actor, and it can be used to capture exceptional behavior and variations from the norm. For example, you may want to offer some optional behaviors, in addition to the required ones. This may be modeled by specifying a number of extension points. This relationship may also be used to model different scenarios based on an actor's interaction. The proposed UML 2.0 draft now supports multiplicities and conditions for the extends relationship.

Constraints	{Constraint definition in OCL}	Use case constraints allow new rules to be added and existing rules to be modified. For example, you might add a constraint to a use case that requires a particular permission or valid password. Constraints allow the UML to adapt to new languages by limiting a model to specific semantic rules. This allows the UML to adapt to new technologies as they become available. Because of this, constraints are a valuable extension mechanism to the UML.
Communicates Relationship	* -ActorEnd * -UseCaseEnd	This is a relationship between an actor and a use case. It indicates that the actor communicates with the system (through some user interface) and gives input and receives output that relate to that use case. Like the simple association, it is indicted by a straight line, but one end must be attached to an actor and the other to a use case.
Uses Relationship	<<uses>>	A use case may "use" another use case: It does not have to "include" or "extend" the other use case to use it. This relationship is indicated by a specialized association with a stereotype of <<uses>>. This relationship indicates that two use cases share common behavior. The relationship can then be constrained to more specifically describe the relationship.

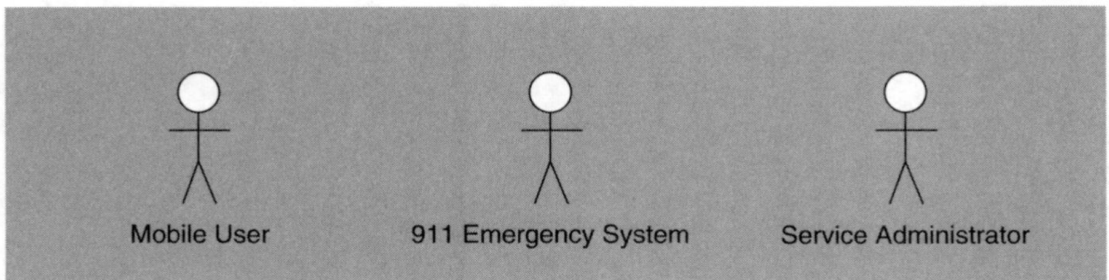

FIGURE 4.1 Example of a Use Case Where Multiple Actors Interact with the System.

If we were to list all the ways each actor could interact with our system, we would be well on our way to defining all the behaviors our system is capable of. Conversely, if we neglected to include a key actor, our system would be missing some major functionality.

With the actors defined, we list all the interactions each one can have. Each interaction represents a specific behavior of the system. Each one of these behaviors is called a use case. A use case diagram typically includes an actor, a use case, and their relationship. Figure 4.2 show an example.

Figure 4.3 is a use case diagram that shows a generalization relationship between a cell phone user, a PDA user, and the user of an advanced hybrid device such as the Handspring Treo (which has both PDA and phone capabilities). This diagram implies that a mobile phone user might operate under one set of circumstances, whereas a PDA user has a different set, and the cell phone user has the attributes of a mobile phone user as well as those of a PDA user. Keep in mind that the attributes of each are not defined here and that the exact manners in which the generalization relationship is defined remains ambiguous. That is because such details are beyond the scope of this diagram.

Figure 4.4 is a use case diagram that shows an actor (our mobile user) interacting with a request dispatcher, which presumably accepts a request from the user and dispatches it to the appropriate service to handle the user request. The request dispatcher communicates with the traffic service, to fulfill the user's request. The traffic service interacts with the map service. Note here, again, that the diagram does not actually tell us how the request dispatcher routes requests, or how the traffic service uses the map service. All the use case diagram does is establishes

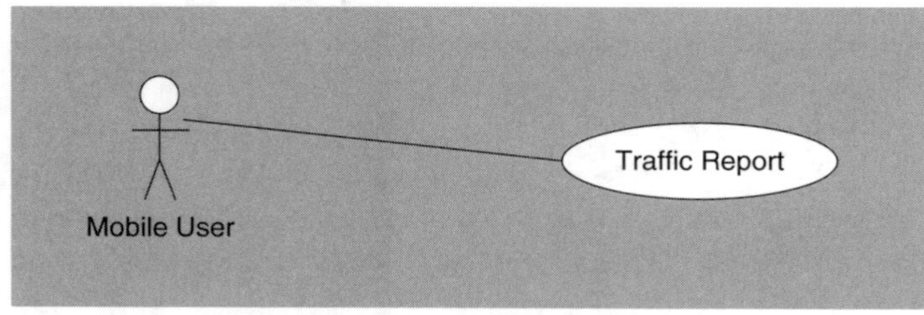

FIGURE 4.2 Use Case of a User Receiving Traffic Information.

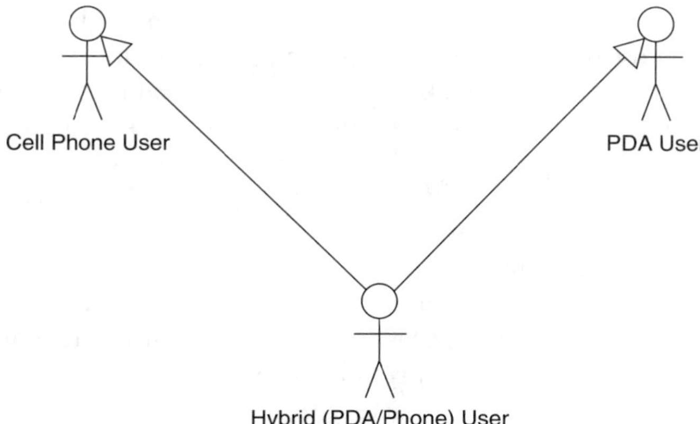

Figure 4.3 Using Generalization to Build Inheritance of Properties among Actors.

that the relationship exists. Other diagrams will help to define how the specific relationships and interactions among users actually work.

4.3 The Structural View

Class diagrams are used to model classes, interfaces, collaborations, and the associations among them. They are the most common diagram type in UML and are used to model a static design view of a system. Class diagrams are used to model the basic building blocks of a system, its collaborations, and schema. They are the foundation of component and deployment diagrams, which we will talk about later in this chapter. They are sometimes referred to as static (as opposed to behavioral) structural diagrams.

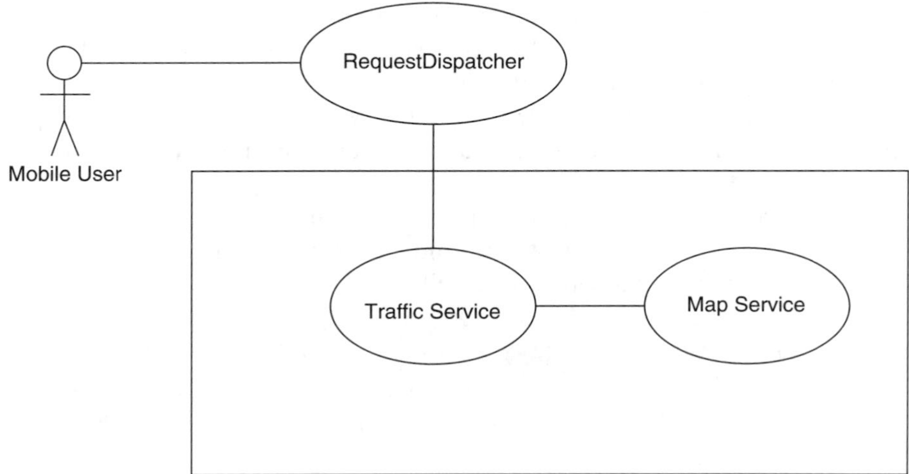

Figure 4.4 An Actor (Mobile User) Interacting with the System in a Use Case Diagram.

Class diagrams can contain a variety of classifiers to further delineate their structural and behavioral features. Classes can have associations, which illustrate relationships between classes, and have a variety of applicable stereotypes that may be used to further define more detail to relationships. Class diagrams can contain objects to show state as well as conditions for which an expression applies to a state. Class diagrams are one of the core diagrams in UML. A class diagram is a foundation diagram for both deployment and component diagrams and models the structural view of a system.

Classes can be named with a simple name or a pathname, which includes package information for the class. Classes may also have attributes and operations. Packages are a way of organizing a set of classes into logical units. Typically all of the classes in a package work together to form some common functionality. Many object-oriented languages support this concept directly and enforce access permissions based on packages. The attributes of a class represent the state of an object of that class. As the attributes change, so does the state of the object. The operations of a class represent its behavior. Class diagrams can show signals, which are primarily used in state chart and activity diagrams. Signals are stereotyped with the <<signal>> keyword. Signals are not permitted to contain operations.

Classes can be either active or passive. Active classes are modeled as a regular class with a heavy border. They are responsible for initiating the flow of control in an interaction. Passive classes have regular borders and participate in an interaction by being invoked by an active class and always return control back to the calling class before the interaction ends. When creating a class diagram, the primary elements that you will be dealing with are *classes* and *interfaces*. These can be thought of as the core elements of a class diagram, whereas the other elements show relationships between classes and interfaces. Table 4.2 shows the basic elements of the structural view.

4.3.1 Defining Classes

As previously mentioned, class diagrams are perhaps the most frequently used diagrams in UML. Their semantics are particularly important to understand because they are the staple of UML diagramming.

Class attributes are optionally defined in the second compartment. Class variables take the form of variableName:dataType and may optionally define an initial value. See Table 4.3.

You specify an attribute's visibility by preceding its name with a visibility symbol: + for public access, – for private access, and # for protected access. See Table 4.4.

Formal notation for an attribute is as follows:

[visibility] name [multiplicity] [: type] [= initial-value] [(property)]

We will discuss multiplicity and the optional property stereotypes later in this section.

Class methods are optionally defined in the third compartment of a class. For example, the methods may be an additional behavior for an existing interface or internal utility methods used by the class itself. Like attributes, you may specify as

TABLE 4.2. The Structural View

Element	Representation	Description
Classes	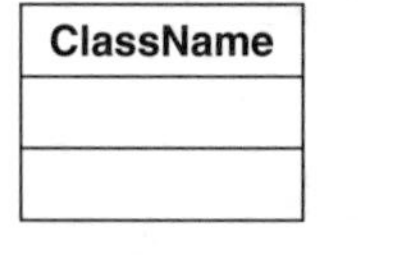	The basic element of the class diagram is the class. More than any other diagram, class diagrams can usually be translated directly to code—sometimes referred to as forward engineering. The class is drawn as a rectangle and may be split into multiple compartments. Each of these compartments provides distinct information about the class being modeled. With the exception of anonymous classes, a diagram of a class indicates the class's name at the top of the rectangle for which it represents. The name is typically a noun that describes the nature of the class. You may optionally show a class's nested package structure by indicating the pathname, which includes the fully qualified path of the class with each of the subpackage names separated by double colons: Simple name: Volunteer Pathname: org::kindpeople::Volunteer Its name can be any number of letters, numbers, and punctuation marks except the colon (since it is used to separate package names), and names are typically capitalized. Noun phrases may be useful to indicate more complex classes. In such cases, cap-notation is useful for making the name more readable. Cap-notation is the practice of capitalizing each word in the phrase, without using spaces to separate each word. Depending on the detail level you wish to model, a class may include multiple compartments; these are most commonly used to show the names of the class's attributes and operations. The top compartment lists the name of the class. The second compartment lists the class's attributes, and the third lists the operations of the class. More compartments may be added as well.

(*continued*)

Table 4.2 (continued)

Element	Representation	Description
		A class's attributes are used to store its state information. For your initial designs, your main objective may be to identify all of a class's attributes by showing only its attribute names. As you move closer to the implementation stage of development, you may add more details to include the attribute's visibility and data types. Data types are shown after the attribute name with a colon separating the name and type. Showing data types is especially useful for modeling tools that can use the types to verify method calls, or for automatically (based on a given rule set) making suggestions for appropriate uses. Setting an attribute's visibility is akin to granting permissions to other classes to access them. Indeed, they are sometimes referred to as access modifiers.
Interfaces	<<interface>> **Name**	Interfaces are modeled like classes but are stereotyped with the <<Interface>> stereotype. Like classes, all interfaces must have a name. That name can be a simple name, or a pathname, like java::util::List. Although interfaces are similar to both classes and types, they are dissimilar in that they cannot specify any attributes, and they cannot provide implementations to operations, which are known as methods. As with classes, the operation of an interface can include information about their concurrency, visibility, constraints, stereotypes, and tagged values. Interfaces may participate in a variety of relationships as well, including generalization, association, and dependency relationships. The relationship of a class to an interface is called realization. The realization implies that the interface is a contract that the class agrees to fulfill. Realization relationships may also exist between components and interfaces, where the component provides a source code or executable implementation of the interface. The interface is responsible for defining the operations that the implementing class or component will provide, without dictating actual implementation of those operations.

(continued)

Table 4.2 (continued)

Element	Representation	Description
Package	PackageName	Grouping use cases together by related interactions is a way to simplify a set of behaviors. For example, in a system with many subsystems it may be difficult to define all the requirements. Categorizing a system's many requirements into related behaviors is a way of managing the complexity and may also be useful for grouping design discussions with the appropriate users.
Association	———	An association specifies a relationship between multiple classifiers, providing a template for a set of links between instances of those classifiers. It is modeled as a line between two elements and is labeled with a name. The name of an association should always be capitalized. Associations have an open arrowhead at one end, indicating the direction in which you read the association. These are known as navigation arrows. Many times when you are at the beginning stages of modeling a system, your design is not yet refined enough to determine the type of association that various classes will have. In situations like this, it is better to model the associations between classes generically, rather than to not capture them at all. A good rule of thumb is that you should start simply, then elaborate as your details emerge. Additionally, when modeling use cases, if you see that classes interact with one another during the course of a use case, then that is usually a good indication that there is an association between them. Associations can also be labeled with a *role name*, which shows additional information about the association and how the related classes participate in that association. Role names are placed at the end of an association nearest the class that they correspond to. Role names are always specified as lowercase names to distinguish them from the association name. The number of instances of a given class that can participate in a given interaction is shown with a multiplicity indicator. A multiplicity indicator can be a single number, such as 1, a range of numbers, like 0, . . .,4, or an unlimited number,

(continued)

Table 4.2 (continued)

Element	Representation	Description
		represented by an asterisk (*). An asterisk on its own indicates 0 or more instances.
Generalization		A generalization relationship specifies that a set of classes all share a general subset of behaviors, which is defined in a parent class. The parent class is the most general case, and attributes and operations specified in it will also be provided by its child classes. Instances of child classes may be used anywhere the parent is used. The child will typically add new attributes and operations. A class that has no parent class, but has at least one child class, is known as a base class. A class that has no child classes is called a leaf class. Classes that have a single parent follow what is known as the single inheritance model, whereas child classes with multiple parents follow the multiple inheritance model. Generalization is modeled by a solid line with a closed arrowhead pointing toward the parent class.
Collaboration		A collaboration is a group of classifiers and associations that work together in a specific way to provide some cooperative behavior. For example, a database connection and an encryption algorithm might collaborate in a system to provide user authentication. A diagram of a class by itself is not very useful for visualizing an operational system. Rather, the manner in which classes work together is more useful for illustrating the means by which a system behavior is carried out.
Realization		Realization is a contract between two entities in which the implementing entity guarantees the behavior specified in a given interface. Realization specifies a behavioral contract where one classifier, usually an interface, specifies a contract that the other guarantees to carry out. Realization is shown by a dashed line with a closed arrowhead. In Figure 4.5 a CallRequestHandler realizes both the voice and keypad interfaces.

(continued)

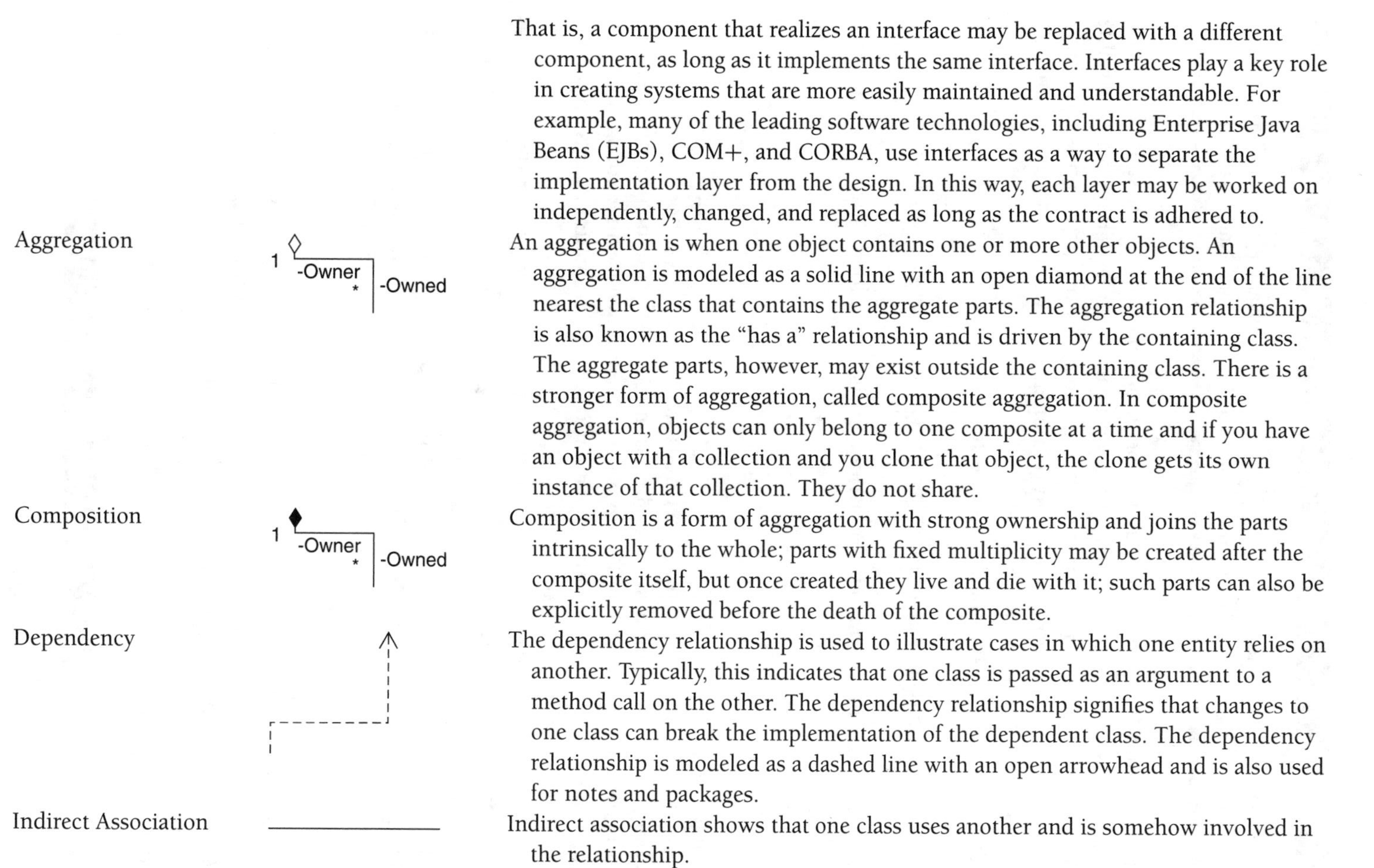

	That is, a component that realizes an interface may be replaced with a different component, as long as it implements the same interface. Interfaces play a key role in creating systems that are more easily maintained and understandable. For example, many of the leading software technologies, including Enterprise Java Beans (EJBs), COM+, and CORBA, use interfaces as a way to separate the implementation layer from the design. In this way, each layer may be worked on independently, changed, and replaced as long as the contract is adhered to.
Aggregation	An aggregation is when one object contains one or more other objects. An aggregation is modeled as a solid line with an open diamond at the end of the line nearest the class that contains the aggregate parts. The aggregation relationship is also known as the "has a" relationship and is driven by the containing class. The aggregate parts, however, may exist outside the containing class. There is a stronger form of aggregation, called composite aggregation. In composite aggregation, objects can only belong to one composite at a time and if you have an object with a collection and you clone that object, the clone gets its own instance of that collection. They do not share.
Composition	Composition is a form of aggregation with strong ownership and joins the parts intrinsically to the whole; parts with fixed multiplicity may be created after the composite itself, but once created they live and die with it; such parts can also be explicitly removed before the death of the composite.
Dependency	The dependency relationship is used to illustrate cases in which one entity relies on another. Typically, this indicates that one class is passed as an argument to a method call on the other. The dependency relationship signifies that changes to one class can break the implementation of the dependent class. The dependency relationship is modeled as a dashed line with an open arrowhead and is also used for notes and packages.
Indirect Association	Indirect association shows that one class uses another and is somehow involved in the relationship.

TABLE 4.3. Declare Variables

Declaring Variables	variableName:dataType
Declaring Variables with an Initial Value	variableName:dataType = value

little or as much detail as required. An operation's name typically starts lowercase and then uses cap-notation. You may specify a parameter list similarly to a variable definition. An operation's name, parameters, and return type comprise its signature. A method is an implementation of a operation, whereas an operation only specifies a service that a class provides.

The formal syntax for operations is as follows:

[visibility] name [(parameter list)] [: returnType][{property string}]

Each parameter in the operation's parameter list has a formal syntax of its own, which is

[direction] name : type [= defaultValue]

There are three possible values for the direction element in a parameter's syntax: in, out, and inout. A parameter with a direction of in cannot be modified. A parameter whose direction is out can be modified with the intent of communicating information to the caller of the operation. A parameter whose direction is inout may be modified. As with the definition of an attribute, a parameter list can optionally specify default values for parameters.

An operation's property string can be used to specify greater detail such as its concurrent behaviors or its influence on the object's state. Its possible values include leaf, isQuery, sequential, guarded, concurrent.

The leaf property string, which is distinct from the leaf class, indicates that an operation cannot be overridden. UML refers to such an operation as a concrete operation. The isQuery property string indicates that the execution of the operation does not alter the state of the system.

The sequential property string is used in situations where the operation's callers must coordinate among themselves to ensure that only one flow is in the object at a given time, indicating that the object's integrity cannot be guaranteed when faced with multiple concurrent flows of control.

The guarded property string indicates that all calls to the object are sequentialized for that particular operation, and thus the integrity of the object is guaranteed

TABLE 4.4. Visibility Identifiers in UML

−	private
+	public
#	protected

TABLE 4.5. Method Types

Void Method	visibility methodname(variableName:dataType, variableName:dataType):
Method with Return Type	visibility methodname(variableName:dataType, variableName:dataType): returnType
Simplified Method	Methodname

in the face of multiple concurrent flows of control. This means, essentially, that the operation ensures that only a single call is executed simultaneously. The concurrent property string indicates that the operation is treated like an atomic operation and that the operation is thus capable of handling multiple concurrent calls without compromising the integrity of the object. Consider the following:

visibility methodname(variableName:dataType, variableName:dataType): returnType

Visibility shows the access level of that particular method. The methodname defines the name of the actual method to be used. The parameter list is a listing of variables that are passed into the method. These take the form of class variables, as is covered in the previous section.

The final element of a method is the returnType, which, when omitted, indicates that the method is void. Stereotypes can also be used for method definitions to indicate special circumstances for methods. For example, use of the constructor stereotype indicates that all subsequent methods are object constructors. The misc stereotype indicates that subsequent elements are regular methods.

The method definition section can be simplified in many ways (see Table 4.5). First, the parameter listing can be simplified by omitting names for the elements passed to the method. Second, ellipses (. . .) can be used to indicate that the class contains additional methods not specified in the diagram. Finally, a method listing can use the simple notation that lists only function names, omitting additional detail like the parameter list.

Additionally, class rectangles can be used to model the responsibilities. A class's responsibilities can be modeled in a fourth box. Responsibilities are often used in early stages of development before a class's operations and attributes are well defined. Responsibilities are useful to describe what, generally, a class will do.

You may use the stereotype <<type>> to indicate a class of objects that all share a general subset of operations and that all may be treated in a similar manner. Types are typically seen in generalization relationships.

Abstract Classes

Abstract classes can also be illustrated within a class diagram. An abstract class is modeled like a regular class, except that its name is placed in italics. As the diagram in Figure 4.5 depicts, Voice and Keyboard are both interfaces that are realized by the *CallRequestHandler* class.

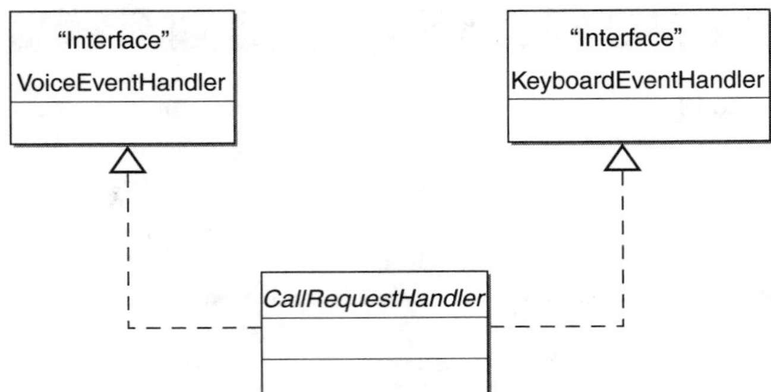

FIGURE 4.5. Representing an Abstract Class.

Roles

Roles are general behaviors of entities, describing how they perform in a given context. Roles are tied to interfaces, so a class that implements a given interface plays a particular role. Individual interfaces can each represent a role, and a class can implement many interfaces and thus have many roles. A role can be thought of as an abstraction that represents generally the way that an object reacts in a certain situation. Roles can be labeled on associations and can be formally declared using the <<type>> stereotype.

Classes and components may realize multiple interfaces. Interfaces are similar to abstract classes: Both specify a set of operations that, respectively, an implementing or extending class will manifest and neither can be directly instantiated. They are different, however, in that abstract classes may have attributes, whereas interfaces may not.

Using interfaces helps to delineate the responsibilities of people who are building the various aspects of a system. Additional detail can be provided about an interface by specifying pre- and postconditions to its interfaces, or by using the OCL (Object Constraint Language) to formally specify its semantics. Interfaces specify a service that a class or component provides to others by specifying the operations they are guaranteed to provide. A well-structured interface has a clear purpose that can be easily understood without delving into the details of its implementation. Interfaces are represented in a class diagram in a manner similar to classes. Like classes, they are drawn as a rectangle and typically contain two or three compartments, representing the interface name, methods, and additional information. As with classes, they can have additional compartments. An additional requirement of interfaces is that they have an interface stereotype on top.

Stereotypes

Stereotypes are ways of extending the UML to more specifically suit your needs. They allow you to expand upon and customize existing elements for your purposes. There are several common stereotypes defined by UML for classifiers, components, relationships, and others. Stereotypes ensure that UML can adapt to new technologies and languages.

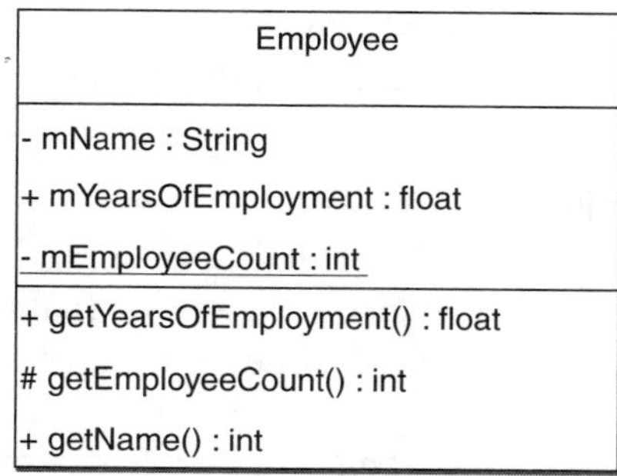

FIGURE 4.6. Employee Class.

Tagged values are an extension of an element's properties that enable specific extensions that may be meaningful when implementing the system. Tagged values are represented by a string containing name/value pairs, enclosed in curly braces ({}). In cases where the context of a value is clear, the corresponding name can be omitted.

Tagged values can be useful in forward engineering to provide additional details about how code should be produced. Additionally, tagged values can be used to specify author and versioning information, the programming language, auto-documentation information, and other details. Tagged values must be specified below the name of the element they correspond to.

Constraints specify conditions that are required for the model to be "well formed." For example, you could use a constraint to specify that a user must be logged in to the system to use a particular operation. Constraints also allow you to add new rules or alter existing ones. They can be used to list the applicable values of a property. They can be written as plain text or may also be specified using the OCL. Like tagged values, constraints are placed within curly braces. Unlike tagged values, a constraint is placed near the associated element. Constraints can apply to a variety of elements, including properties, associations, or operations.

The leaf stereotype can be applied to classes, meaning that they cannot be extended (or play the parent role in a generalization relationship).

Figure 4.6 shows a class representing an employee. Its purpose is to illustrate the structure of the Employee class and to provide us with basic information about it, such as its fields and its operations, as well as some detail about each. The representation of a single class constitutes the simplest of class diagrams—it shows only a single class. The top section of the class rectangle contains the name of the class, in this case Employee. The middle section of the class rectangle shows the field of the class. Note that here we have three fields, name, years of employment, and count of employees. Name and employee count have private access whereas years of employment has public access. Note also that the variable for employee count is static.

In the third section of the class rectangle are the operations that the Employee class defines. In this case, getYearsOfEmployment is public and returns a floating point number whereas getEmployeeCount is a protected static method that returns an integer. Finally, getName is also a public method that returns a string. (Note that this class is not exactly practical; we probably would not have a field that is public and a method that simply returns that field that is also public.)

4.3.2 Object Diagrams

Object diagrams represent the structural view in UML, and, although they are technically separate diagrams, they can also be seen as variations of class diagrams—they are actually just class diagrams that contain objects and links, rather than classes and associations. Because objects are instances of classes and links are instances of associations, object diagrams can be seen as different scenarios based on the template of a class diagram. Object diagrams represent a snapshot of a system at a given time and are often used with class diagrams to show various object configurations. Multiple object diagrams can be distilled into a single class diagram that allows for them all. Object diagrams, which are also commonly called instance diagrams, can also be compared to collaboration diagrams, which we will discuss later on in this chapter. Object diagrams model instances of the elements illustrated in class diagrams. An object diagram shows the state of objects within a system at a single moment in time. It expresses the static part of an interaction, but without any of the messages passed among the objects it contains.

Why Use Object Diagrams?

Because many objects have precise relationships to one another, failures of a system are more often due to inappropriate object states or failures of communication between objects, rather than flawed logic. Object diagrams thus play an important role in system design, as they can help to illuminate the relationships among various objects and identify situations in which system failure may occur. Object diagrams can be used to model the static design or static process view of a system; that is, they show how a system's objects are related to one another and the associations among them, without showing the actual interactions among the objects. Interactions among objects are shown by interaction diagrams, which include both sequence and collaboration diagrams. In addition to sequence and collaboration diagrams, component and deployment diagrams, which are used to model physical components of a system, can also show objects. When these diagrams contain only instances, and do not show messages, they can be seen as special cases of object diagrams. Object diagrams let you model static data structures. Object diagrams, are, in their appearance, very similar to class diagrams. Whereas class diagrams are composed primarily of objects and associations, object diagrams are composed of objects and links, which are instances of classes and associations, respectively.

An object is an instance of a class and may represent a concrete implementation of an interface. Objects have state, which may change the manner in which the object behaves. Object rectangles look very similar to class rectangles, except that the names of objects are underlined to differentiate them from classes. Anonymous objects, however, do not require that their names be underlined. Objects are unique; that is, each object has its own identity. You will sometimes hear objects referred to as instances. The terms instance and object are synonymous and can be used interchangeably with few exceptions. Object and instance are used interchangeably because objects are instances of classes, the most common instances in object-oriented systems are objects.

The term object tends to be more clear than instance, however, because you can have instances of associations, which are links, as well as instances of components, nodes, or use cases. You can specify active objects by putting a thick border around them. Active objects represent the root of a flow of control, which means that they initiate the flow of control in an interaction. Objects can also be added to class diagrams to show state. Multiple objects are shown as a stack of two object rectangles.

Some of the important object attributes are the following:

1. *Object Names*: The names of objects, with the exception of anonymous objects, are underlined to differentiate them from classes. Object names are located in the top compartment of the object rectangle and take the form instanceName: ClassName, where both the instance name and the class name are optional. So, in David:Person, David and :Person are all legal object names. Note that the class name is preceded by a colon to distinguish it from the instance name. As with class diagrams, the instance and class names are typically shown using cap-notation, although this is a stylistic preference and not a requirement of UML. Objects that do not have a specified type are known as orphan objects. Orphan objects must specify at least a name. Object names, like class names, can also be specified as a pathname. Naming objects clarifies their purpose and makes them easier for people to talk about.
2. *Object Operations*: Objects, like classes, can specify operations. To show that an operation is being called on a particular object, you can use the dot notation, which specifies the object name, followed by a period, followed by the name of the operation. Depending on the object's relationships, it, like any other object, may be polymorphic.
3. *Object State*: Objects have state, which is a changeable condition derived from the current values of each of its properties. These properties include the object's attributes as well as its aggregate parts; therefore, an object's state is dynamic. Changes in an object's state can be modeled on an object diagram by providing multiple instances of the same object, each with a different state. Furthermore, State Machines can be associated with objects for a period of time. An object's state is specified below its name, in square brackets. Because objects can have multiple states simultaneously, you can also provide a list of states in that location.

Relationships among Objects

Like classes, objects can be related to one another as well as to some other artifacts in UML such as classes. In this section, we will go through these various relationships.

Relationships are defined by *links* and *stereotypes*. Links are instances of associations and specify a relationship between two objects. Links can be named, in which case their names should be capitalized. Links can also have roles, which

e1:Employee
mName = "John Doe" mYearsOfEmployment = 2.4 mEmploymentCount = 185

FIGURE 4.7. An Employee Object: An Instance of the Employee Class.

are typically lowercase and next to the object they describe. A link between two objects indicates that one object can send a message to the other.

There are five stereotypes that can be applies to the objects in an object diagram:

- *instanceOf*: The instanceOf stereotype shows that the recipient object is an instance of the classifier that supplies it. Although the class that an object is an instance of can be shown as a part of the object's name, the instanceOf stereotype could be used, for example, to illustrate that the object is an instance of a class from which the object's class inherits.
- *instantiate*: The instantiate stereotype specifies that the recipient object creates instances of the supplier class.
- *becomes*: The becomes stereotype specifies that the recipient object and the supplier object are the same object, but that each represents that object at a different point in time, and possibly with different states, values, or roles. The becomes stereotype applies to messages and transitions.
- *copy*: The copy stereotype is used to show that one object is an exact but wholly independent copy of another.
- *transient*: The transient stereotype is used to mark objects that are created during an interaction's execution but are destroyed before the completion of that interaction.

This object diagram in Figure 4.7 shows an instance of the Employee class that we defined in the last section. You will notice that the representation for an object is very similar to the class rectangle that we saw in the last section. The name on an object, however, is underlined; this is a clear mark that distinguishes classes from objects in a UML diagram. Additionally, you will notice that the fields that we defined in the class diagram are provided in the second section of the object diagram and that they have values associated with them. These values apply to the single instance (e1) that this object diagram defines. An object diagram illustrates an object as it appears at a given moment in time. It is neither necessary nor desirable to capture every aspect of an object in an object diagram.

4.4 THE BEHAVIORAL VIEW

The diagrams in the behavioral view are designed to do just what the name "behavioral view" suggests: to represent the behavior of the components within the system and how those components interact with one another. The behavior view can also be used to model the behavior of the entire system as a whole.

4.4.1 Interaction Diagrams

Interaction diagrams are a category of diagrams in UML, rather than a specific diagram in their own right. Interaction diagrams include sequence diagrams and collaboration diagrams and describe how a particular behavior is accomplished through object interactions. Interactions are composed of messages sent between objects to accomplish a purpose. Interaction diagrams are modeled as flows of control that can include sequential execution as well as branches, forks, loops, concurrency, and recursion. You can think of interaction diagrams as special cases of object diagrams, showing the messages passed between objects.

Sequence diagrams model interactions by focusing on the ordering of messages as they occur over time. Collaboration diagrams, in contrast, place greater focus on the relationships between objects. Although they still show the sequence of the messages passed between objects, the ordering of those messages is of secondary importance to the relationships between the objects passing those messages. In spite of their differences, sequence and collaboration diagrams are isomorphic, meaning they have similar structures and appearance but differing ancestry: They display identical information in different manners, so that you should be able to create a sequence diagram from a collaboration diagram, and vice versa, with no additional information.

Messages specify a name, optional parameters for the message, and the message's sequence in the interaction. Messages are modeled by a directed line with a closed arrowhead. At a minimum, messages are labeled with the name of the operation that they represent. Messages represent a communication between objects, which includes the passage of information from one object to another, and results in an action being carried out as a result of the message. Messages can also be used to illustrate the creation or destruction of objects. The receipt of a message can also be considered an instance of an event. It triggers an executable statement to be called, which may result in a change of state. There are five typical actions used in UML that can be specified in interaction diagrams: call, return, send, create, and destroy. These are specified as stereotypes. The call action specifies that an operation on an object should be invoked. The return action indicates that a value will be returned to the object that invokes the operation. The send action describes one object sending a signal to another. If an object does not exist at the start of the interaction, the create action can be used to specify the object's creation during that interaction. Similarly, if an object is destroyed during an interaction, this is indicated with the destroy action. To model additional behavior not specified by the five basic actions, you may specify a string containing complex expressions, although UML does not specify the syntax of such strings. The objects in an interaction diagram generally represent object prototypes playing a particular role in the interaction, rather than concrete, real-world entities.

Relationships between objects are modeled as links. As we saw in the last section, links are instances of associations, just as objects are instances of classes. A link between objects indicates that they are able to exchange messages, and it specifies the path along which those messages can be dispatched. Links can also specify common stereotypes that indicate the scope of the object they are attached to.

The association stereotype indicates that the object is in scope by means of association. The *self* stereotype indicates that the object is in scope because it dispatched the operation. The *global* stereotype indicates that the object is in an enclosing scope. The *local* stereotype indicates that the object is in the local scope. The *parameter* stereotype indicates that the object is in scope because it is a parameter. Most attributes of an association are applicable to a link as well, with the exception of the multiplicity indicator, which cannot be applied to links. When an object passes a message to another object, it is delegating an action to the receiving object. A sequence of messages always has a beginning and continues for the duration of the process or thread that owns it. Each process or thread contains a unique flow of control that contains messages ordered sequentially by time. These sequences are most commonly modeled as nested flows of control with solid, filled arrowheads. Alternatively, they can be represented by flat flows of control, which are modeled as solid lines with stick arrowheads. The name of the controlling process or thread can be placed at the root of the sequence, and, if specified, should take the form

threadOrProcessName:methodCall

You may also specify its return values. More specificity can be given to a sequence with timing marks and constraints, guarded conditions, branching, and iteration.

There are several stereotypes that can be applied to links to illustrate the creation and destruction of objects. The new stereotype specifies that the instance is created at that point in the interaction; the destroyed stereotype signifies that the object is destroyed before the termination of that interaction. The transient stereotype indicates that the object is created during the interaction and destroyed before the interaction completes. Changes to the state of an object during the course of an interaction are illustrated by multiple copies of an object, each showing different states. In a sequence diagram, these two objects would be placed on the same lifeline to show that they are different states of the same object, whereas on a collaboration diagram they would be connected and marked with the become stereotype.

Sequence and collaboration diagrams vary greatly in their manner of displaying messages, and, as such, each is better suited for displaying certain kinds of information. Sequence diagrams, for example, are easily able to illustrate separate paths extending from a branch, where each has separate messages extending from it, as well as message returns and both synchronous and asynchronous messages. Collaboration diagrams, by contrast, are not terribly well suited for displaying detailed information about messages and are better able to illustrate simple messages in the context of the overall relationship of objects in a diagram, because a complex arrangement of messages or various message types easily clutters up a collaboration diagram.

4.4.2 Sequence Diagrams

Sequence diagrams typically contain objects, links, and messages. Like all diagrams, they can also contain notes and constraints. The two features that distinguish sequence diagrams from their semantic equivalents, collaboration diagrams, are *lifelines* and *focus of control*. You can think of a sequence diagram as a table that shows objects on its *X* axis and messages progressing through time along its *Y* axis. Although there is no particular meaning to the order of objects in a sequence diagram from left to right, by convention the object that initiates the action specified in the diagram will be listed at the left of the diagram and increasingly subordinate objects will be listed to the right.

The order of messages does have a special significance, which is their temporal ordering. Messages occurring first should be placed at the top of a sequence diagram; subsequent actions should follow, in sequential order. A sequence diagram represents the detail of how a behavior gets completed by showing classes exchanging messages sequentially over time. It displays messages in order of occurrence, which build on one another to accomplish a desired behavior. Sequence diagrams portray a behavior, which can consist of either a single message exchange or a set of them. Sequence diagrams illustrate the states of an object and its communications over time.

Sequence diagrams can take either a *generic form* or an *instance form*. The generic form describes a message exchange sequence within a set of classes. The instance form of the sequence diagram describes a single message exchange that follows the generic form. The generic form includes neither loops nor branches. Sequence diagrams are especially good at specifying scenarios where the sequence of events or the timing of a message exchange is critical, or where concurrency needs to be modeled, or for a synchronous message exchange. Sequence diagrams illustrate the passage of time in the vertical dimension of the diagram. Typically time begins at the top of the page and proceeds toward the bottom. This can, however, be reversed. Although the passage of time illustrated in a sequence diagram may be quantified in the diagram, the sequence of events is more important than the amount of time that passes during the illustrated sequence. The horizontal plane of a sequence diagram shows the class roles that participate in the specified sequence. The ordering of these roles is insignificant.

Because many other diagrams do not show time, it can be difficult to tell how a system operates in time. Sequence diagrams clarify this as well as concurrent processes. A simple sequence diagram shows only a single scenario (or one instance) and shows simple messages, each moving the flow of control from one object to another. A simple diagram does not show concurrency. There are some simple things that you can do while building a sequence diagram that will make it more useful and effective. First, giving the diagram a clear name helps communicate its purpose to others. Next, you only need to include the elements that are essential to the understanding of the interaction that the diagram models. Adding too much information can obscure the interaction rather than clarifying it. However, you should use caution and avoid making the diagram so minimalist that it misinforms the diagram viewer. Finally, use branching sparingly as it can make a sequence diagram that is difficult to follow. Complex branching sequences are better illustrated in activity diagrams.

The elements of sequence diagrams are listed in Table 4.6.

In Figure 4.8 we see a high-level interaction among a mobile user, a traffic service, and a map service. The diagram is laid out vertically with the actions presented progressing in order from top to bottom. The diagram is divided by

Table 4.6. The Elements of Sequence Diagrams

Element	Description
Lifeline	A lifeline is a dashed line arranged vertically down a sequence diagram that represents an objects existence through the passage of time. Lifelines represent the life of an object during an interaction. If the object that the lifeline represents exists when the interaction starts, the lifeline must begin at the top of the diagram. If the lifeline's object exists at the end of the interaction, then the lifeline must end at the bottom of the diagram. Otherwise, the lifeline must start at the point in the diagram where the object is created. The message that creates it should have an arrowhead pointing to it. If the lifeline's object is destroyed during the interaction, the lifeline must be terminated with an X at the point that the object is destroyed. Because most objects exist for the entirety of an interaction, most lifelines extend from the top of the diagram to the bottom, with all of an interaction's objects aligned at the top. However, when an object is created during the interaction, the object's lifeline will start at the message that creates it. This message will be marked with the create stereotype to show that the object is being created at that point. Similarly, if an object is destroyed during an interaction, its lifeline will stop at the point that it is destroyed, and the message that causes the object's destruction will be marked with the <<destroy>> stereotype. The end of the lifeline on a destroyed object will be marked with a large X to identify the object's destruction.
Activation	Activations represent a focus of control and are represented as a thin rectangular box shown over the lifeline during a method call. An activation must have an initiation time, which should be aligned with the top of the rectangle that represents it. The completion time of an activation should be aligned with the bottom of the rectangle. Activations may have a label that states their operation and have the ability to call or pass control to other objects. They may be recursive (i.e., they may be self-invoking) and may be used in conjunction with a variety of different objects, including concurrent or nonconcurrent objects and multiple active objects. They extend along the lifeline for the period of time that an object is performing an action, whether it performs the action directly or via a subordinate procedure. Additionally, the completion of an action may be marked explicitly with a return.Recursion, which is either a self-call or a callback

Element	Description
	from another object, can be modeled with an additional activation rectangle stacked just to the right of its parent.
Class Roles	The class role is an element that defines the behavior or the class in a given context. Class roles illustrate general ways that a group of entities participates in interactions and collaborations. A class role is denoted by a class rectangle and shows only the information relevant to the definition of that role. A class role may have a multiplicity expression that indicates that a set of objects—rather than a single object—participates in a role. Additionally, class roles may use other notations applicable to classes and objects to further clarify their properties and behavior. In the name compartment of the class rectangle representing the role, the class role must have its role name, which should be underlined. The role name is followed by a colon and then the name of the class that represents the role. This name is also underlined. The role name can be omitted, in which case the colon separating the role from the class name remains and the role is played by an anonymous object. The class role may also provide information in compartments other than the name compartment to further delineate other properties of the role; however, this information is typically omitted.
Interaction	Interactions are classes that define sequences of message exchanges among classes working together to accomplish a purpose. The purpose of an interaction is to illustrate the communications between these entities. They may have associations to use cases and operations. In this case, the role of the sequence diagram is to specify the behavior provided.
Object	Objects are drawn in the standard way, as a rectangle, with an underlined name.
Returns	Returns indicate a return from a message rather than a new message. Unlike regular messages, returns are indicated with a dashed line. You can draw them for each message, or only when you think that they add clarity to the diagram.
Object Creation	If a system creates a new object as it executes, that can be shown on a sequence diagram as well. The new object will be represented as a rectangle with an underlined name, as for any other object. The difference between a newly created object and preexisting objects, however, is the positioning of that object on the diagram. Although preexisting objects will appear at the top of a sequence diagram, newly created objects should appear vertically in the diagram, in a place

(continued)

Table 4.6 (continued)

Element	Description
	that corresponds to its point of creation. The message that creates the new object should be labeled Create(). This implies two things. On a general level, it implies an operation, whereas on a more specific level, it implies an object constructor. Alternatively, you can use the <<Create>> stereotype to show object creation.
Time	Time is shown on a sequence diagram as a vertical progression, which begins at the top of the diagram and ends at the bottom.
Message	Messages indicate communication among the various objects in a sequence diagram. They are represented as solid lines with varying arrows to represent their message type, which can be one of three types: simple, synchronous, or asynchronous. The message arrow is drawn between the lifelines of two objects to indicate their communication. Messages are named by a label on their message arrow. This may include a return list of comma-separated values, arguments to a message, and additional control information. The order of messages in a diagram is shown from top to bottom.
	Simple messages have an open arrowhead and indicate the transfer of flow of control from one object to another.
	Synchronous messages have a solid arrowhead. With a synchronous message, the object sends a message and then awaits a response from the recipient. Asynchronous messages have a half-open arrowhead. With an asynchronous message, the object sends a message but does not wait for a response from the receiving object. Because an asynchronous message, unlike a synchronous one, does not block the caller, the caller can carry on with its own processing. Useful tasks for asynchronous messages include the creation of new threads of control and new objects and communications with existing running threads.
	The difference between synchronous and asynchronous communication can be seen in the difference between the TCP and UDP protocols. Additional detail specified on a message can also help to clarify its functionality. A multiplicity marker can be used to show a message that is sent multiple times. The multiplicity marker should be followed by an indication of the number of times that the message is sent. Messages can also contain *control* information, which generally comes in the form of a *condition* or an iteration marker. A condition shows the case when a message is sent [isOverdue]. A message marked with a condition will be sent only if that condition is true.

Element	Description
	Although this is useful for illustrating simple conditions, you should keep in mind that more complex cases lend themselves to separate sequence diagrams for each case. To represent an "if" condition, you place the condition that you want to test for in square brackets above the message arrows. Each condition creates a fork, which separates a message into different paths; that is, it causes a branch of control in the lifeline of the recipient object and separates its lifeline into separate paths. Branches and forks eventually merge. An *iteration marker* shows that a message is sent many times to multiple recipient objects, as would happen in an iteration. The basis of the iteration is shown in square brackets, which are preceded by the multiplicity marker (*). A "while" condition can also be shown on a sequence diagram and is represented by a set of square brackets, preceded by the multiplicity marker (*). Recursion is an operation that involves an object invoking itself. This is shown by a message arrow that originates from and returns to the same object. To lend clarity to the document, message sequence numbers and sending and receiving times of messages may also be displayed. Asynchronous messages are modeled with a solid line and a half arrowhead. Simultaneous messages are shown by two messages extending from a lifeline at the same point.
Labels	Labels are elements that clarify a document. Their placement is arbitrary: They can be placed in either margin of the diagram or near the element to which they refer.

lifelines, which help to show which object has responsibility for each step along the horizontal plane. This is a generic sequence diagram, and, as such, it uses simple messages, that is, messages that do not indicate whether they are synchronous or asynchronous but simply show a communication from one object to another. At the top of the diagram, the mobile user requests the fastest route from the traffic service, and passes it two parameters: its current location and its target location. The traffic service then contacts the map service asking for a list of frequent routes from one point to the other. Again, it is important to keep in mind that this is a general case designed to illustrate the communication among these objects on a high level and that steps may be—and should be—omitted from this diagram. It is possible, for example, that the traffic service may choose two better-known points near the user's origin and destination that will be more applicable to the map service's listing of frequent routes. The map service responds to the traffic service with a collection of frequent routes based on the input it was given. The traffic service then takes the routes provided by the map service, derives the shortest route

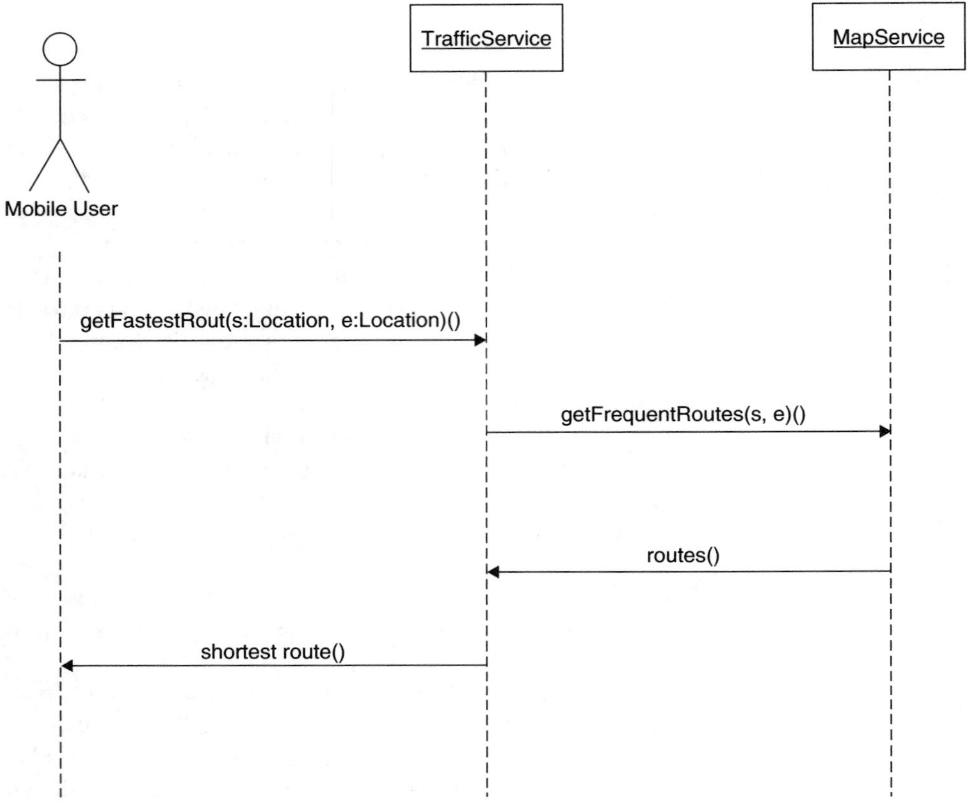

FIGURE 4.8 Using Sequence Diagrams to Show the Temporal Nature of Interactions.

(we assume that it does this based on traffic conditions, but, again, the diagram does not specify how the action is completed), and returns it to the mobile user.

This sequence diagram elaborates on some of the details left out of our generic diagram in the last example. You will recall from our last example that the way in which the traffic service determined the shortest route from the list that the map service provided was not specified. This diagram elaborates further on that sequence. Because, even with our added detail, this is still a high-level and not very detailed diagram, we have just added this detail to the diagram from our last example. Typically, however, when you are creating sequences that add further detail to a preexisting sequence diagram, that detail will be shown in a separate sequence diagram. Another difference between this sequence diagram and the last is that it uses synchronous messages rather than simple messages. The synchronous messages indicate that the message sender waits for a response from the recipient before sending additional messages. Also, the section from getTravelSegments through storeJobResults is labeled with the word routes preceded by the multiplicity marker. This indicates that the listed actions will be executed once for each route returned to the traffic service from the map service. Finally, you will notice that the final three messages in that section go from the traffic service directly back to the traffic service. That indicates that the traffic service completes the operation itself.

4.4.3 Collaboration Diagrams

A collaboration diagram is an interaction diagram that emphasizes the organization of and relationships among objects, rather than the sequential progression of the messages passed among them, as sequence diagrams do. The primary elements of the collaboration diagram are objects, links, and messages. The diagram elements that distinguish collaboration diagrams from their isomorphic equivalent—the sequence diagram—are paths and sequence numbers.

When creating a collaboration diagram, it is useful to begin by modeling the objects that are going to participate in the interaction, as you would to build an object diagram. With the objects established, you can then model the relationships among them and finally the messages that they send among themselves to complete the interaction.

A collaboration diagram shows the interaction among objects. At their core, collaboration diagrams and sequence diagrams are equivalent. That is, they show the same information. The way they show that information, however, allows for different and useful perspectives from each diagram. Whereas a sequence diagram emphasizes the temporal ordering of a series of events, a collaboration diagram illustrates the interactions of various objects. Collaboration diagrams are useful for exploring the manner in which one object affects another, as well as to detail its behavior. Both diagrams illustrate an interaction between classes that defines a behavior. Sequence diagrams have the passage of time as their focal point; collaboration diagrams focus on the interactions playing a smaller role. Collaboration diagrams are excellent at illustrating the links between objects.

Collaboration diagrams can be thought of as an extension to the class diagram, showing not only the associations among objects but also the messages that the objects send to one another. "Multiplicities" are usually left out of a collaboration diagram to prevent it from getting too cluttered. Collaboration diagrams can also appear in an instance or generic formats. The order of messages is shown by sequence numbers on a collaboration diagram. As with a sequence diagram, a collaboration diagram can show conditions, iterations, and loops.

Some interaction diagrams focus on grouping of classes and associations that are involved in realizing and implementing a specific behavior. Such a diagram will illustrate class and association formats and their interactions.

Collaboration diagrams can take either a generic or instance form. The generic form shows a general case of interactions among classes and associations, whereas the instance form shows objects and links and an actual message exchange that is consistent with the generic form of the diagram. You can think of the difference between the generic form of a collaboration diagram and the instance form as being similar to the difference between a class diagram and an object diagram. The generic form shows the interaction in general terms and can be extrapolated into different instance cases.

Collaboration diagrams must illustrate the class roles and association roles among them that are relevant to realizing the behavior that they depict. They may include message flows, attached to the association roles. A diagram that does not include messages can be used to show the context in which interactions occur without explicitly defining those interactions.

Table 4.7 shows some interaction diagram characteristics.

Table 4.7. Some Interaction Diagram Characteristics

Element	Representation	Description
Objects	Instance	One of the primary elements on a collaboration diagram is the object. An object is depicted in its usual format, which is the class rectangle with an underlined name in the form of objectName:className, where either can be omitted. The class name is preceded by a colon to avoid ambiguity should only the object name or class name be shown.
Time Expression	N/A	Time expressions can be used with operations to indicate the expected time requirements for a given operation. A timing mark is an identifier that precedes the name of the message it applies to. From a timing mark, you can derive the start time, stop time, and execution time, which can subsequently be used in an expression, contained within a timing constraint.
Link	———	As in an object diagram, a link is an instance of an association and shows a relationship between objects. A link between two objects indicates that one object can send messages to another.
Active Object	Instance	There are some interactions in which a particular object controls the flow. Such an object typically sends messages to passive objects and interacts with other active objects. A situation in which two or more active objects do work simultaneously is known as concurrency. An active object is modeled like any other object except that its border is drawn thicker and bolder than that of a regular object.
Synchronization	MessageName() ——> Synchronous Message MessageName() ——⇀ Asynchronous Message	In a synchronized interaction, one entity sends a message but does not wait for a response from the receiving object. Because an asynchronous message, unlike a synchronous message, does not block the caller, the caller can carry on with its own processing. Useful tasks for asynchronous messages include the creation of new threads of control and new objects and communications with existing running threads. Synchronized messages are indicated by a line ending in a full arrow whereas asynchronous messages are indicated with a line ending in a half arrow.

Multi-Roles	Multi-Role Objects	Multi-roles are represented as a stack of two rectangles. They are class associations that represent a set of objects that participate in an interaction or collaboration. Multi-roles are used to illustrate the roles of a set of entities. Multi-roles can be class roles, in which case they may receive messages. When a multi-role receives a message, the indication is that the message is received by the set of instances, rather than each instance in the set. In other words, they describe a set of objects as a single entity, rather than delving into their individual behaviors. To perform an operation on each object in a set of instances, a multi-role requires two messages. The first message extracts links from the set and the second message goes directly to each object referenced by an extracted ink. These separate messages can be combined into a single message that includes an iteration and an operation to perform on each object. Multi-roles can also be attached to a multiclass role using a composition link. As association roles, multi-roles must use the multiplicity indicator (*) to imply that there are many individual links. As association roles, multi-roles may also propagate messages.
Messages	SomeMessage() →	In a collaboration diagram, a message is shown by an arrow that appears near the association line between objects. Multiple message can be attached to the arrow, which points to the object that receives the message. The label near a message describes its contents. A message usually tells the recipient to execute an operation. A pair of parentheses end the message and contain any parameters that need to be passed to it. Messages in collaboration diagrams correspond to the message between class roles in a sequence diagram. Messages are indicated by arrows, as in a sequence diagram. An object can also send a message to multiple objects of the same class. Multiple objects of a single class type are represented as a stack of rectangles with the class name. Labeling the message with *[all] indicates that the message goes to all recipients in an unspecified order. Order of receipt can, however, be specified, using a while condition with an implied order (e.g., line positoin = 1.n).

(*continued*)

TABLE 4.7 (continued)

Element	Representation	Description
		A message can represent a request for an object to return a value, in which case it is written as an expression with the name of the returned value, followed by :=, then the name of the operation and quantities to operate on, as, for example, totalPrice: = compute(itemPrice, salesTax) The position following the := is referred to as the message signature. Messages may also have a return list, which specifies values returned by that message. A return list is a list of comma-separated names that designate the message's return values. It is a requirement of UML that the names in the return list match the number, types, and order of the operation's formal return list. The names from the return list are not included; the assignment operator (:=) is likewise omitted.
Condition	[condition]	Conditions can also be represented on a collaboration diagram, just as they are on a sequence diagram. They are placed in square brackets before the message label. Nesting is shown on a collaboration diagram using subdecimal points. When a transaction is over, you should add the <<transaction over>> stereotype to the message.
Object State Change	<<become>> ——→	A collaboration diagram can also show changes in the state of an object. To show state changes, the first step is to model the original state of an object by providing an object with its state in square brackets after its name. Next you provide an additional object rectangle to show the state to which the object transitions in square brackets just as the first did. With both states shown, you illustrate the transition from one to the other by connecting them with a dashed line and an open arrowhead, labeled with the <<become>> stereotype.
Path Stereotype		A path, which is a stereotype attached at the end of a link, indicates the manner in which one object is linked to another. The most common paths found in a collaboration diagram are local, global, parameter, and self.

Because sequence diagrams and collaboration diagrams show the same things, it should be easy to convert well-designed diagrams from one type to the other. In sequence diagrams, the ordering of messages is important, and although this is of less importance to a collaboration diagram, it is still important, then, that the sequence be shown. That is done with a number, followed by a colon, preceding each message, which shows its sequence in the overall flow of behavior.

The sequence of messages is shown by their being numbered. There are two ways this numbering is commonly done, although UML specifies the decimal notation. Simple numbers are common too [Fowler and Scott 1999]. Decimal notation makes it clearer which operation is calling another.

Each message may specify a comma-separated list of sequence numbers that correspond to other messages that must have executed and completed prior to its execution. Sequence numbers that precede the sequence number of the current message are implicitly considered to be predecessors and do not need to be specified. This can be extremely useful when illustrating the synchronization of threads. Messages can have a guard condition, which is a Boolean condition that must return true for the message to execute. Additionally, messages may specify branching concurrency and iteration.

A message may have parentheses that contain either an argument list or a comma-separated list of parameters passed into a method. These must match the order type and number specified in the parameter list of the operation. A message may use data tokens to represent its argument and return lists. Data tokens are small circles drawn near messages that are labeled with the names of parameter return values. Data tokens have a small arrow to indicate the flow of data. For argument names, that arrow points toward the message; returns point away from the message.

As in sequence diagrams, the messages in a collaboration diagram can take one of three forms: simple messages, synchronous messages, and asynchronous messages. Simple messages have an open arrowhead and indicate the transfer of flow of control from one object to another. Synchronous messages have a solid arrowhead.

Sequence numbers are used to specify the order in which messages occur. They begin with message number one, and increase by one for each ensuing message. To show the ordering of nested messages, you use Dewey Decimal notation. A single link can illustrate multiple messages being sent in multiple directions. Each of these messages should have a unique sequence number.

You can model iterations in a collaboration diagram by prefixing the message with an iteration expression. An iteration expression is specified by an asterisk (*), followed by an operational expression that is enclosed in square brackets. An asterisk without the subsequent expression indicates that there is an iteration but does not specify any details of how that iteration occurs. The iteration marker indicates that not only the current message, but also all nested messages, will be repeated as specified by the expression in square brackets.

You can also specify a condition to a message that represents a Boolean condition that dictates whether or not the message should be executed based on

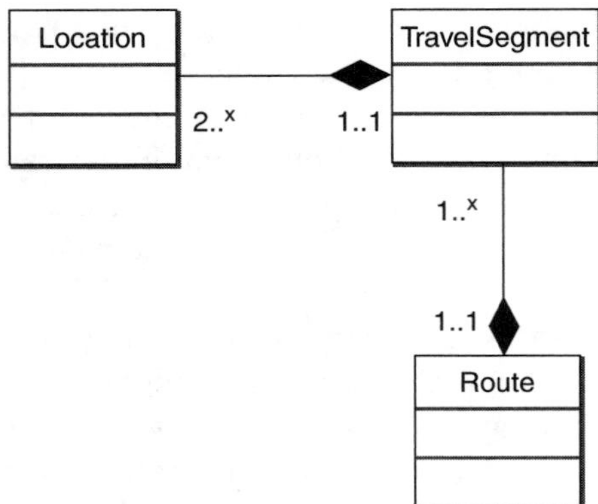

FIGURE 4.9. A Simple Class Diagram Representing the Relationship Between Locations, Routes, and Travel Segments.

the evaluation of that expression. To model a condition, you prefix the message's sequence number with an expression representing the condition, in square brackets.

Usually collaboration diagrams will illustrate a sequential flow of events, although they can show branching. The separate paths of a branch will each have the same sequence number, although each path must specify a mutually exclusive condition. For both iteration and branching, UML does not specify how to build the expression, so you can use pseudo code or another language.

Collaboration

A collaboration is a named group of static and dynamic elements that work together to perform a behavior. Collaborations realize operations and use cases. They are indicated, at a high level, by a dashed oval, containing its name. A more detailed view of a collaboration can be seen in class diagrams, which illustrate their structural aspects, and in interaction diagrams, which show their behavioral aspects.

So, let us start with a class diagram, seen in Figure 4.9, and then use a collaboration diagram to expound upon the interactions among the different classes. The first element defined in our diagram is a Route class, which has an aggregation relationship with the TravelSegment class. Notice the multiplicity marker along the association line between the two classes near TravelSegment. It indicates that one or more travel segments will make up our route. Each travel segment has a starting location and an ending location. These locations are specified by an additional aggregation relationship between the TravelSegment and Location objects. This relationship specifies that each travel segment will have exactly two locations: a starting location and an ending location. The location object stores its coordinates in minutes, seconds, and degrees from the nearest longitudinal and latitudinal coordinates.

The TravelSegment, then, is a collection of location objects, where two locations exist for each travel segment. Routes are similar collections of one or more routes.

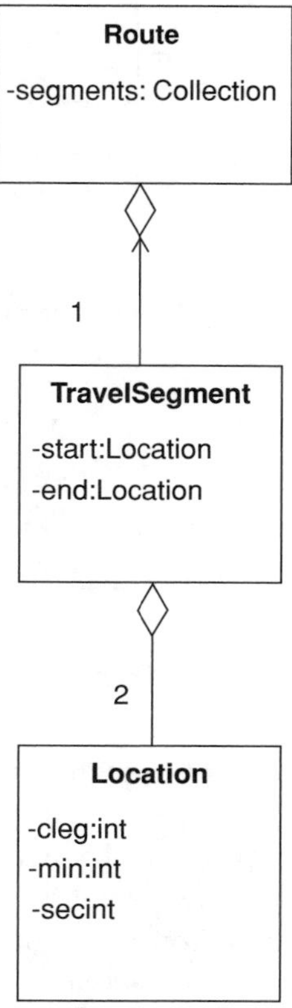

FIGURE 4.10

The diamond symbol on the association line between the objects on this diagram signifies that they have an aggregation relationship. The fact that the aggregation diamond is not filled in means that the objects they contain may exist outside of this collection. For example, you might have a collection of locations that represented the various locations of a particular restaurant. We can use an object diagram, such as the one in Figure 4.10, to illustrate roughly the same thing, except this time we are representing instances and not the structures that created those instances.

The collaboration diagram in Figure 4.11 expands on our last example, adding in the traffic service and the map service. You may want to refer back to the diagrams that we looked at in the sequence diagram section to compare the diagrams at this point. You will recall that the sequence diagram and the collaboration diagram show the same information from different perspectives, so looking back to that last example should shed some light on this diagram. Since our last example, we have added map service and traffic service objects to the diagram. The route object, you will recall, is composed of travel segments, which are in turn composed of locations. The route object has an association relationship with the traffic service and the map service. The relationship simply specifies that the objects involved are

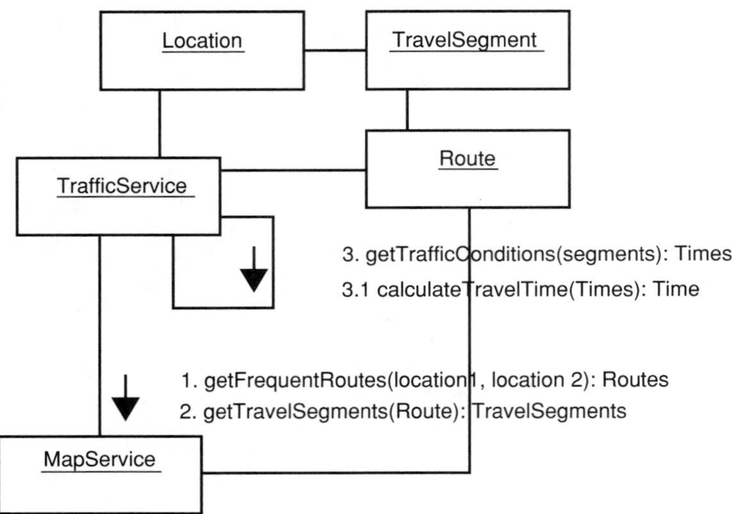

FIGURE 4.11 A Collaboration Diagram for a Mapping Service.

aware of each other, but the details of how they actually interact are not specified in this diagram.

The traffic service and the map service have a similar association relationship. In addition to that, they have an arrow between them that indicates that messages are being passed between the two. You may notice that the traffic service sends messages to itself. These are the self-calls that we saw illustrated in the sequence diagram. The sequence that the messages are called in is not as important to a collaboration diagram. The sequence is shown less prominently as a numerical sequence that precedes the message name. Here these are shown using the decimal notation specified by UML. Simple sequence notation can be used, but decimal notation is preferred for its clarity.

Events and Signals

Events and signals are applicable to activity and state diagrams. Things that happen within a system are known as events. Events are occurrences that are significant to the system and can be located in both time and space. Because events can be either asynchronous or synchronous, their modeling is highly dependent on the modeling of threads and processes. A signal is a special case of an event, which is an asynchronous stimulus sent from one object to another.

Events come in two varieties: internal and external. Internal events are events that occur within the system, among the objects it is composed of, and do not require an external stimulus. Events that are external to the system are communicated between the system's actors and the system itself. External events include, for example, a user of the system pressing buttons on its user interface. UML specifies four primary types of events: signals, calls, time passage, and state change.

Signals are objects that are sent by one object and received by another. Like classes, signals can have instances, generalization relationships, operations, and attributes. The attributes of a signal are the parameters passed to it. Signals are typically noted on the models of objects and interfaces that send them. This relationship can also be specified by a dependency relationship marked with the send stereotype.

Calls, Time Passage, Events, Exceptions, and States

A call represents the inception of an operation and is similar to the sending of a signal. Calls may cause a change of state within a state machine and can be either synchronous or asynchronous, though asynchronous calls are more common. In terms of how they are modeled, calls and signals are not distinguishable, as they both are shown as a simple transition labeled with their name and any parameters passed to them. Call events, however, can be differentiated because their receivers will specify them in their operation list. Additionally, whereas signals are typically handled by state machines, calls are usually handled by methods.

Time events are used in UML to indicate the passage of time. They are modeled with the after keyword followed by an expression evaluating to a period of time, which can either be simple (in 7 seconds) or complex (1.5 milliseconds after XYZ occurs). The starting time of the expression need not be explicitly mentioned. If it is omitted, its default value is the time elapsed since the current state was entered. State change is represented by a change event that is also used to specify the satisfaction of a certain condition. Change events are shown with the when keyword, followed by a conditional expression. These expressions can mark either a set time, such as 1:24 A.M., or an ongoing test, such as when humidity is greater than 50%.

Signal and call events both involve at least two objects, a sending object and one or more recipients. Multicasting is when a single object sends a signal to multiple objects, or to a given set of listener objects. Broadcasting is when an object sends a signal to a general messaging bus, to any object that may be listening.

Exceptions, indicating aberrant conditions, are a special type of signal. They are modeled, like interfaces, as stereotyped classes. The <<Exception>> stereotype is used to mark an exception. Exceptions may be associated with the operations that may cause them.

An event is an occurrence with a temporal and spatial context. There are two types of events: external and internal. External events are interactions between the system and its actors, whereas internal events are internal to the system. UML specifies four event types: signals, calls, time passage, and state change. Signal events are defined like classes, stereotyped with the signal keyword with the name of the event specified below the signal stereotype. To indicate that a particular class sends a signal, use the dependency relationship between the class and the signal, labeled with the send stereotype. A call event is a method invocation and is modeled by showing the event name along with its parameters. You can distinguish a call event from a signal by their handlers: A signal is handled by its State Machine, whereas a call event is handled by a method.

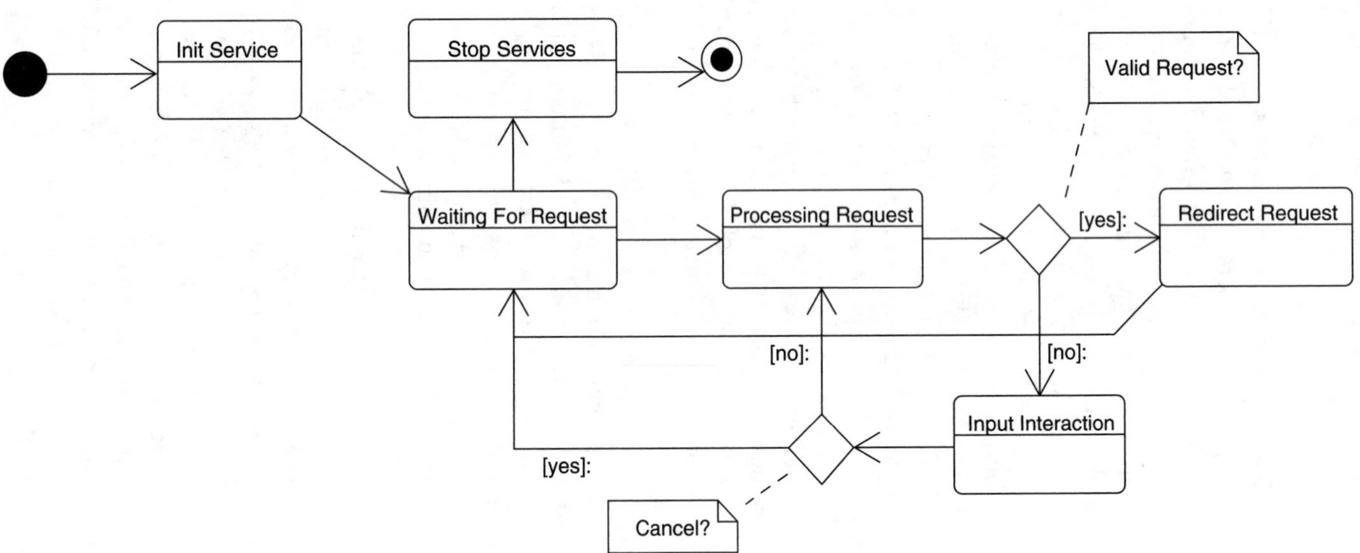

FIGURE 4.12 Sample UML State Chart Diagram.

State Machines and State Chart Diagrams

State chart diagrams show change over time. Objects in any given system will change over time to accommodate interactions with users and other systems. This is known as an object changing state. A state chart diagram represents a State Machine, which shows the states and transitions describing the response of an object of a given class to external stimuli. States are used to convey the condition that an object is in at a given point; transitions show the manner in which these conditions are related. It shows the possible states of an object, the transitions between states, and the starting and end points in a series of state changes. State diagrams are used to illustrate the lifecycle of an object by rendering its potential states and responses. They describe all possible states of an object. State diagrams are usually drawn for a single class, to show the possible states for an instance of that class throughout its entire lifetime. A State Machine thus models the behavior of a single object.

A State Machine defines a behavior that encompasses the various states an object goes through during its lifetime. State Machines show the events that an object can receive during its lifetime and the manner in which the object responds to these various events. State Machines model dynamic aspects of a system by specifying the detail of an object's lifetime. When an event occurs in a system, an activity will take place in response to that event. The response varies based on the object's state. A State Machine illustrates the possible responses based on the objects potential states.

Activities, which are nonatomic executions occurring within a State Machine over a period of time, result in an action composed of atomic executions resulting in either a return value or a state change. State Machines can be modeled from two different perspectives, emphasizing either flow of control between activities or transitions between an object's potential states.

Objects react to a variety of things, including signals and events, the invocation of operations, the passage of time, change in a guard condition, and their own creation and destruction. A State Machine chronicles an object's reactions to these occurrences. Table 4.8 shows the basic components of state diagrams.

Figure 4.12 shows a simple state chart diagram. History states, which are modeled as with an H enclosed in a circle, are useful in cases where states need to recall a past state of one or more of their substates. When a state is not modeled as a history state, that indicates that the state, when it is entered, begins with the substate in its initial state. There are cases where this is not desirable, and where a state may prefer that its substate instead begin in the last state that it was in. To model this, a state should be marked as a history state, which indicates that the substate should resume at its last known state. Cases where a transition should activate the last entered state can be indicated by an outside transition attached directly to the history state.

A composite state has no history when it is first entered; however, the history state is available subsequently. When a nested State Machine reaches its final state it reverts back to its initial state for the purposes of the history state.

State Machines have an initial and a final state. The initial state is represented by a solid circle; the final state is modeled as a solid circle enclosed in another

Table 4.8. State Diagram Elements

Element	Representation	Description
States	StateName	States are points in an object's life where it fulfills a particular set of conditions, and during which it is able to perform a particular activity or where it waits for certain events. Objects that respond to an asynchronous stimulus or that determine their current behavior from their past conditions are well suited to be modeled as State Machines. States are rendered as rectangles with rounded corners. Transitions are solid directed lines with open arrowheads between states. States specify a name, which distinguishes them from other states. States that do not have a specified name are anonymous. States can specify entry and exit actions, which are actions that are triggered when a state is entered or exited, respectively. States may have internal transitions, which are transitions that the state handles internally. Internal transitions, unlike other transitions, do not trigger the state's entry and exit actions. States may have State Machines nested within them, which have two varieties. Nested states that are entered simultaneously are called concurrent states; nested states that may only be entered one at a time are sequential states. States can also specify deferred events, which are events which that particular state cannot handle, but which it will pass on to subsequent states that the object enters, until one of those states handles the events. States that do not have State Machines nested within them are known as simple states, whereas states that do have nested states are called composite states. Composite states may themselves be composite states, and there is no limit to the level of nesting that a state can contain. States are named with nouns that describe them and are typically drawn from the vocabulary of the system. These names are typically specified using cap-notation, and, by convention, begin with a capital letter.

Transition		Transitions model the relationships between a source state and a target state. They are denoted as a solid arrow between states and are labeled with a descriptive string. An entity in one state performs actions that may cause it to move into another state, either when an event occurs, or, if it operated conditionally, when its condition is satisfied. The movement from one state to another is known as a transition "firing." The transition line is the line connecting two states.
Events	EventName 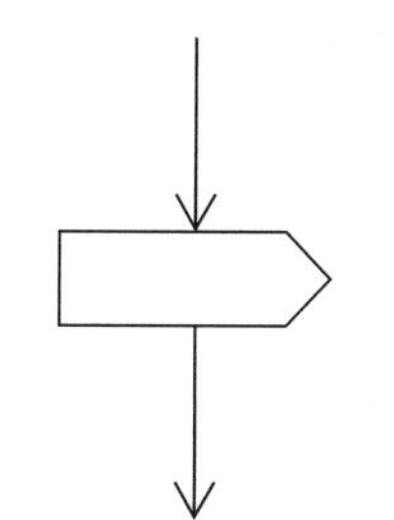 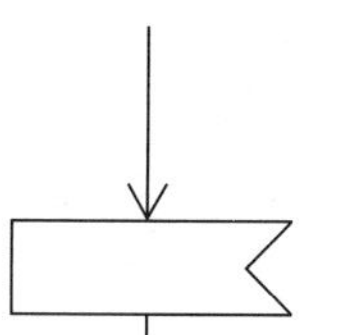 	Events are occurrences that trigger an object to change states. They are used to model the occurrences and stimuli that effect an entity. Events are shown as a string that contains the name of the event. The event's name will reference the operation it represents in the class that receives it. The event name may be followed by a set of parentheses containing a list of the parameters passed to the event. An event must appear no more than once in any given state. Events can take a variety of forms, including signal events, call events, change events, and time events. Although events typically trigger transitions, they are not required to do so. An event that does not trigger a transition is lost or ignored. Events may also trigger multiple transitions. Only one of these transitions will fire, based on the priorities of the specified transitions. An event that is marked with the "after" keyword will generate an event after a specified period of time. Additionally, an event can be marked with the "when" keyword indicates that an event can be generated as that condition becomes true. A signal is a message that triggers a transition in the receiving object's state chart diagram. Events, in the context of State Machines, are occurrences that can trigger a transition from one state to another.

(continued)

Table 4.8 (continued)

Element	Representation	Description
Deferred Event		Deferred events are events that a particular state may choose to postpone until a state that is more appropriate for handling those events is entered. Deferred events are indicated with the keyword "defer" ("/defer") and require the presence of an internal event queue. These events are removed from the queue when an object that does not defer them is entered.
Action	ActionStateName	Actions are classes that define an atomic executable procedure or series of statements. An action, unlike an activity, cannot be interrupted. They are associated with transitions and are assumed to execute quickly (although, of course, speed is relative). Using the defer keyword, actions can be used to show a deferred event. Normally an event is either handled immediately or ignored by a system. Sometimes, however, you will want to be able to model a system with the ability to save events and defer their handling until the object enters another state. Actions that create an instance of a class are called create actions, whereas actions that destroy an instance of a class are called destroy actions. Neither create nor destroy actions can have a target object. Return actions return either a single value or a set of values to the caller. Terminate actions cause objects to self-destruct. Terminate actions cannot take arguments. Local invocation actions are actions that occur within a state and that do not generate a call or signal event. Exception actions indicate that an error occurred during execution. In the case of an exception action, the sender stops execution and transfers control to the exception's receiver. The receiver is determined by the sequence of interactions during execution, rather than by an explicit specification.

		Actions may specify a comma-separated list of action clauses to be executed sequentially, but not atomically. Actions are computations with two major requirements. First, they are atomic, meaning that they cannot be interrupted. Second, they are expected to be executed in a short amount of time. Actions result in either a change of state or a return value. There are special actions that are specified for states, called entry and exit actions. These are executed when a state is entered or exited, respectively, and are specified within the state box with the prefix entry/ for an entry action and exit/ for an exit action. Following the slash of each is the name of the action to be executed in those cases. These are useful for cases in which you always want to execute the same action upon entering or leaving a state without regard to the transition that took you to the state. There is an alternative approach to this, as well, which is that, using a flat State Machine, you can specify these actions on each transition that enters or exits a state depending on the type of action that you are trying to specify. Although this approach is equivalent semantically, it is not recommended as it is comparatively error prone, requiring you to change the action to multiple transitions, as well as to change multiple transitions should the requirement for or the specification of the action change. Unless the entry or exit action creates an object, they may not have arguments, nor may they have guard conditions. Actions are atomic executions that are considered to occur more or less instantaneously.
Activity	ActivityName	Unlike actions, which are short-lived atomic sequences associated with transitions, activities are associated with state and are expected to take longer than an action. Additionally, activities are nonatomic; that is, they can be interrupted. Activities consist of a sequence of operations and actions. Activities may also be expressed using nested state chart diagrams.

(continued)

TABLE 4.8 (continued)

Element	Representation	Description
		Objects in a particular state will generally remain idle, waiting until an event occurs that triggers them to do otherwise. There are cases, however, where you may wish to model a state during which an object performs a particular activity while it remains in that state. This is modeled with a do/ transition, which specifies an activity that the object performs until after the state's entry action is performed, and until an event triggers the object to change states. The activity specified by a do/ transition may be the name of another State Machine, or it may be a semicolon-delimited list of actions to perform. Although the actions themselves are not interruptible, if the state with an ongoing activity is a substate, its superstate may handle events that cause its state to change.
Guard Condition	[condition] ⟶	Guard conditions are conditions that are specified by a Boolean expression enclosed in square brackets. This condition may include conditions related to the object's state. Guard conditions indicate a condition that must be satisfied for a transition to be fired; they are not evaluated until the transition's trigger event has occurred. It is possible that a single source state can have multiple transitions with the same trigger event as long as these transitions have mutually exclusive guard conditions.
Objects	SomeClassInstance : ClassName [SomeState]	Objects only remain in a particular state for a certain period of time and can be in many different states throughout the course of their lifetimes. Objects are modeled in a state chart diagram using their standard form. An object can only have one current state, although multiple states of a single object can be illustrated by modeling the object once for each state it enters. A composite state, that is, one with multiple concurrent substates, determines its state as the states of all its parts. In a state chart diagram, objects can be said to model the way in which an object responds to a stimulus from the outside. An object

can change states as a result of an event and may perform both actions and activities either within or while changing states. Before an object is destroyed it also has a final state.

Pseudo-States

Additionally, a state may also be what is known as a pseudo-state. Pseudo-states have no state variables and no activities, and therefore they are not considered "full" states. There are three varieties of pseudo-state: initial, final, and history. The initial pseudo-state is represented by a small solid circle. The final pseudo-state is represented by a circle surrounding a small solid circle. There are two types of history: deep and shallow. Shallow history is indicated by an H enclosed in a circle and deep history in indicated in the same way, except it has a multiplicity sign following the H.

Event Labels

The transition label has three parts, all of which are optional. The transition label takes the following form:

Event[Guard]/Action

You can add details to it, like a trigger event (an event that causes a transition to occur). This should be written near the transition line, using a forward slash (/) to separate a triggering event from an action.

The event portion of the label indicates which event causes the transition to fire. Parameters from that event are available to both the action on the transition and the actions in the subsequent state. An event can cause a transition without an associated action. A transition can also be caused by a state completing an activity rather than an event. This is known as a "triggerless transition."

(continued)

Table 4.8 (continued)

Element	Representation	Description
Transition Label		The transition label may additionally specify a guard condition in square brackets. A guard condition is a condition that will return either true or false. Only if the guard condition resolves to true will the transition fire. You should ensure that your guard conditions are mutually exclusive, since only a single transition can be taken out of a state. The transition label may also have as its third part a forward slash, which is followed by an action expression or sequence that will show the actions resultant from the transition's firing. When a transition has no event within its label, that means that the transition occurs as soon as any activity associated with the given state is completed. An internal state transition is a transition that occurs in response to events but does not trigger a state change. As you might assume, internal state transitions do not invoke the entry or exit actions of the state.

circle. States are drawn as rectangles that have rounded corners. States can be either active or inactive. A state is entered when a transition fires. It is at this point that the state is considered to be active. When a transition fires to exit a state, the state becomes inactive. A state may be the source of an outgoing transition or the target of an incoming transition.

A state may have provided an optional name compartment, which contains the name of that state. States that do not provide a name compartment are anonymous. A state may provide an additional internal compartment where it specifies its internal transitions. If a state provides this compartment it should be labeled as such. Internal transitions specify actions and activities that are performed while an object is in that state and that do not trigger a state change. Internal transitions do not trigger the entry and exit actions of the state.

A state may specify nested State Machines of any number. Nested State Machines are state chart diagrams that are nested within a particular state, each one corresponding to an action. These can be modeled by tiling the nested state diagrams within the state. A state that contains one or more nested State Machines is known as a composite state. In relation to the nested states, or substates, the composite state is known as the superstate. Nested states may be referred to using pathnames, which follow the syntax of the class pathname, except that instead of specifying a package structure, they specify the states in which they are nested, to the composite state, delimited by pairs of colons (::). A state may have additional compartments to describe additional information pertaining to that state, although they do not typically.

The state element can be subdivided into three sections to show details of the state. The top third of the state element contains its name. This must be included, but the other two sections are optional. The middle third of the state element contains state variables. This can include things like timers and counters, which show state-related information. The lower third of the state box contains the activities of a particular state. These are the events and actions that occur during this state. Typically, activities are divided into three types. First, there are entry activities that are executed upon entering the state. Next, there are do activities that occur while in the state. Finally, there are exit activities that are executed upon leaving the state.

An activity can be specified within a state using the form do/activity, where activity specifies the name of the particular activity being represented. An action that does not cause a transition from one state to another is known as an internal transition. These can be specified within a state with text in the form of eventName/actionName, where eventName is the event that caused the action to be executed and where actionName specifies the action that is executed in response to the event. States can also contain nested State Machines. Substates are changes of state within a state. There are two distinct varieties: sequential and concurrent. Sequential substates occur one after the other. Concurrent substates proceed simultaneously.

A dotted line is used to separate concurrent substates. A state with concurrent substates is known as a composite state. The nested state chart diagrams in a state illustrate the activities of the state. States may be simple, with no nesting, they may be top-level, not nested themselves, but containing nested states, or they may be substates. History pseudo-states are represented by the history symbol, which is a letter H enclosed by a circle. The history state signifies that a composite state remembers the state of its substate when the object transitions out of that composite state. A history state that remembers states through multiple levels of nesting is called deep and is represented by an H followed by an *, enclosed in a circle. The standard history marker is shallow; that is, it only remembers the highest nested substate.

A self-transition is a transition in which the source state and the target state are the same state. Unlike with an internal state transition, however, the entry and exit actions of the state are executed with a self-transition. Completion, or automatic, transitions are transitions that can occur without an event trigger. The completion transition fires automatically upon the completion of the actions within a state.

When transitions are not mutually exclusive, they may conflict with one another. In the case of a conflict, it is necessary for priorities to be established to resolve the conflict, with one exception. The transitions of substates always have a higher priority than those of their containing states. Otherwise, however, it is necessary to specify the priority of transitions when ambiguity exists. A transition may specify its sending time as well as its receiving time. The sending and receiving times are formal names that can be in expressions used to specify constraints. Compound transitions are transitions that contain several simple transitions, which are grouped using branching, forks, and joins. Transitions may also be a part of a branch or a decision. A decision uses guard conditions to indicate the basis for choosing potential transitions.

Transitions may point toward composite states, which indicates that the state's initial state, as well as the initial state of all of its substates, should be entered. Transitions may also come out of composite states. In this case, the transition applies not only to the top-level state but also to its nested states. In other words, transitions are inherited by nested states. Inherited transitions may be overridden by a nested transition with an identical trigger event. When a composite state is exited, its nested states exit actions are triggered and, when they complete, the object transitions into another state. Transitions may be drawn directly to a nested state at any level. The entry actions for all states that are entered as a result of this transition are fired when the transition occurs. A transition is a relationship between two different states that indicates that when an event triggers the first state to change states, the object to which these states apply will enter the subsequent state.

The state of the object before a particular transition fires is the source state of that transition, and the subsequent state is called its target state. The event that causes the transition to occur is known as a trigger event, but the transition only fires assuming that its guard conditions are met. Guard conditions are preconditions of a transition and indicate that the transition may only fire when those conditions are met. In a case where a trigger event occurs but the transition's guard condition is false and no other transitions are applicable to that event, the event is simply lost.

There can be many sources for a given transition, as well as multiple targets. Actions that are handled within a state and that do not cause a state change are known as internal transitions. Although they are conceptually similar to self-transitions, that is, transitions where the source and target states are the same state, they are distinct. The major difference between self-transitions and internal transitions is that self-transitions cause a state change, and thus fire the state's entry and exit actions. Internal transitions, in contrast, do not cause a state change and thus do not invoke the state's entry and exit actions. Internal transitions may have events that specify parameters and guard conditions. They can be considered to be interrupts.

Transitions between states can also be triggerless, which means that there is no event required to change from one state to the next. Triggerless transitions, which are also known as completion transitions, generally belong to states that perform some activity and are triggered implicitly when that activity completes. Event triggers can be polymorphic.

Activity Diagrams

An activity diagram illustrates the steps involved in an operation or process. Activity diagrams model the focus of control in an interaction and the specification of a behavior. Activity diagrams are similar to flowcharts, where the steps of a flowchart are roughly equivalent to the activities represented in an activity diagram. Activity diagrams can also be seen as a simplified view of what occurs during a process. Activity diagrams describe the activities that a set of objects engage in and can be associated with classes, methods, and use cases. They illustrate the activities and actions that an object engages in to complete a behavior. In contrast to state diagrams, which show behavior in response to external events, activity diagrams describe behavior that is the result of internal processing.

Activity diagrams are an extension of state chart diagrams, where most if not all of the states are activity states. They are triggerless; that is, they happen unconditionally. Activity diagrams have both an initial state and a final state. Activity diagrams borrow much of their terminology from state chart diagrams. Activity diagrams are typically used for business modeling and to validate use cases. Activity diagrams show the dynamic aspects of a system, showing a system's flow of control from activity to activity, or the flow of an object as it moves from state to state. Whereas interaction diagrams emphasize the flow of control from one object to the next, activity diagrams illustrate an object's flow of control from activity to activity and the activities that take place between objects.

Whereas interaction diagram illustrates objects and the messages that they pass to one another, activity diagrams focus on the operations that are passed among objects. In this regard, they are similar to Pert charts. Activity diagrams are particularly useful for constructing executable systems via forward information because the flow of control is so similar to a program's flow of execution. Activity diagrams help to model a process in numerous ways. First, they help with the initial visualization of the process, and the specification of its parts and their flow from one to the next. Activity diagrams also assist in creating and documenting the process. Activity diagrams are essentially flow charts, illustrating an activity that progresses over time.

The most common elements in an activity diagram are activity states, action states, objects, and transitions. Additionally, they may contain forks and joins, branches, and states, both simple and composite. As is true for UML's other diagrams, activity diagrams may also contain notes and constraints.

Activity diagrams are primarily used to model workflow and to model the details of an operation. They can be attached to use cases to model a scenario of that use case or they can be attached to collaborations to expand upon the dynamic aspects of a group of objects. They can additionally be used to elucidate the behaviors of classes, interfaces, nodes, and components. When modeling workflow, it is useful to consider object flow, or the manner in which objects will participate. To determine the boundaries of the workflow, it is helpful to identify both the preconditions and postconditions of the workflow's initial and final states. Activity diagrams are useful for their flowchart-like functionality in modeling operations and provide additional capabilities that are not found in flow charts, like the ability to model forks, joins, and branches. Activity diagrams focusing on operations typically focus on the details of the computation. The context of such a diagram typically includes any parameters passed into the operation, as well as objects local to it.

Activity diagrams, in addition to being useful for modeling workflow and operations, can be used to model any sequence of activity, including procedures for a given scenario, the software development process, or any other scenario. Although there are many other ways of modeling a flow of activities outside of UML, including flow charts, activity diagrams are particularly useful in that they are tied semantically to the various elements, other diagrams, and specifications of UML. This allows the activity diagram to exist in a context of other models, allowing, for example, an operation referenced by an action to be type checked against its target classes or object.

When deciding what to model in an activity diagram, it is useful to start with operations that are difficult to understand just by examining the code that defines them. In other words, operations that are complex or have detailed algorithms that are not apparent on first glance are good candidates for activity diagrams. You will typically use several activity diagrams to model a single operation or workflow. As such, you should avoid the temptation to encompass all facets of an operation or workflow into a single diagram. Rather, you should focus only on those elements that require illumination and leave out those that are easily understood without assistance from a diagram.

Activity diagram elements are listed in Table 4.9.

An activity diagram can illustrate object flows or an object's participation in the flow of control. To illustrate an object flow in an activity diagram, you add the object to the diagram with a dependency relationship with the activity or transition that creates, destroys, or modifies the object. When showing an object's participation in an activity, you can provide additional information about that object, such as its state, changes to the values of its attributes, and its role. As in an object diagram, you specify the object's state in square brackets directly under its name and the values of its attributes are specified in the compartment below the object's name.

Table 4.9. Activity Diagram Elements

Element	Representation	Description
Activity	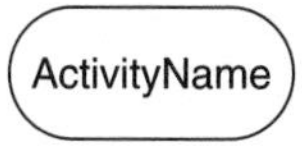 ActivityName	An activity is a state during which something occurs. This could be an actual activity, like buying a book, or the execution of a "software routine." Just as a state chart diagram can be broken into superstates and substates, an activity diagram can be broken into subactivities. Activities are nonatomic, meaning they can be interrupted, with ongoing executions occurring within a State Machine. Activities result in an action, which is an atomic, or noninterruptible, executable computation resulting in a change of state or return value.
Start Point		The starting point of an activity diagram is represented by a solid circle. It indicates the point at which the activity represented in the diagram begins.
End Point		The end point of an activity diagram is represented by a solid circle enclosed in another circle. It indicates the point at which the activity represented in the diagram terminates.
Decision	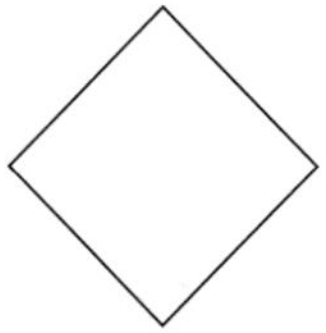	A decision is when there is a point to be made that determines the flow of activity. It is represented explicitly by a diamond from which two separate paths proceed, or more simply as two separate paths coming out of an activity.
Signals	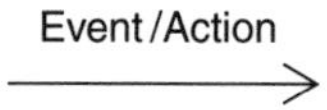 Event/Action	Signals are objects that are sent by one object and received by another. Like classes, signals can have instances, generalization relationships, operations, and attributes. The attributes of a signal are the parameters passed to it.
Concurrent Paths, Forks, and Joins	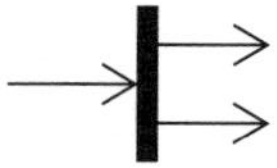	Concurrent paths occur when a transition forks into separate paths that run concurrently. This is modeled by a bold line that is positioned perpendicular to the transition, with the multiple paths extending from it. A merge is represented by multiple paths terminating at another perpendicular line. Further execution occurs beyond that point until each of the concurrent paths have reached the merging point.
	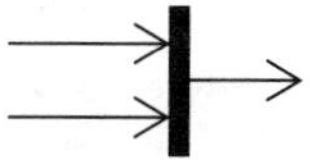	An activity diagram shows the order in which things are done. Unlike a flow chart, however, it can handle parallel processes. These parallel processes are shown by forks and joins. A fork

(continued)

Table 4.9 (continued)

Element	Representation	Description
		has one incoming transition and several outgoing transitions. When the incoming transition is triggered, the outgoing transitions are taken in parallel. The sequence of executions among the parallel transitions is unimportant. They may be completed in any order, or in subparts, with mixed order. A join provides synchronization for parallel processes; therefore there should be a join for each fork. Forks can themselves fork, but they must join before the root fork joins. However, if a first join proceeds directly to a second join, the first join in that sequence can be omitted to simplify the diagram. The same concept applies to forks. There is an advanced construct called the sync state that allows for synchronization where the 1:1 fork:join ratio would prevent it otherwise. All incoming states on a join must have finished before a join can be taken, with the exception being that you can add a condition to a thread coming out of a fork. If that condition is false, then the thread is considered to be complete in terms of the join. Forks and joins can be used within an activity diagram to model concurrent flows of activity. A synchronization bar, which is modeled as a thick horizontal line, is used to specify both forks and joins. A fork—when a single flow of control splits into two or more concurrent flows of control—is specified by a synchronization bar with a single incoming transition and multiple outgoing transitions. Each outgoing transition represents a single flow of control. A join, which represents the synchronization of two or more concurrent flows of control into a single flow of control, is specified by a synchronization bar with two or more incoming transitions and a single outgoing transition. Because a join is the synchronization point for multiple concurrent flows of control, execution subsequent to the join does not proceed until all incoming flows of control reach the join. Every fork requires a corresponding join, where the number of incoming transitions on the join matches the number of outgoing transitions on the fork.

		Activities within concurrent flows of control are permitted to communicate with activities in other simultaneous flows. They do this by sending signals to one another. You can alternatively model the process of sending and receiving these signals in submachines.
Branch and Merge	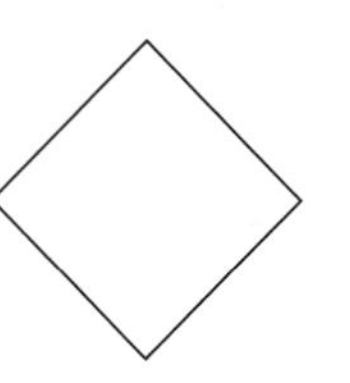	A branch is a single incoming transition with several guarded outgoing transitions. Because only one outgoing transition can be taken, it is important that the guards are mutually exclusive. The default transition, which is taken if the others are false, is labeled ELSE. A merge has multiple input transitions and a single output. A diamond shows a merge and marks the end of conditional behavior started by a branch. Although the diamond symbol is optional, it helps clarify the diagram. Branching is the means of representing an if statement in an activity diagram. A branch is specified by a diamond and is used to specify separate paths that can be taken, depending on the value of a Boolean condition specified on each transition coming out of the branch. Because only one transition can be taken out of a branch, the Boolean conditions for each transition proceeding from the branch must be mutually exclusive. Branches may have only one incoming transition, and they must have at least two outgoing transitions. The keyword else can be used to specify the default transition out of a branch when none of the other conditions are true. To create an iteration from a branch, you would begin with an action state specifying a value for an iterator, followed by another responsible for incrementing that iterator, and finally, a branch to evaluate when that process is completed.
Swimlane	(Represented by two vertical lines that run up and down on the diagram and enclose a set of activities)	Swimlanes can be used to expand an activity diagram to show responsibility for the various activities in a process. The name of the role diagrammed in each swimlane is at the top of the swimlane and within the swimlane itself are the activities of each role. Swimlanes are solid vertical lines that separate an activity diagram by groups of responsibility. Each swimlane has a responsible group, which can be either an object or a group of objects that share responsibility for its completion. A swimlane must be labeled with the group responsible for it. The actions that a group is responsible for completing will be placed within that group's swimlane. The ordering of swimlanes from right to left is unimportant. Swimlanes may

(*continued*)

Table 4.9 (continued)

Element	Representation	Description
		include either activities or action states and occasionally have transitions that cross lanes to get to actions or target action states. Swimlanes are useful when you need to partition activity states into groups by the entity responsible for their completion. They are represented by solid vertical lines that are uniquely named according to their responsible entity. The responsible entity for each swimlane may eventually be implemented by one or more classes. When an activity diagram is partitioned into multiple swimlanes, each activity must belong to one swimlane only, although transitions are permitted to cross swimlanes. Swimlanes may indicate concurrent flows of control, although this is not always the case. Because different entities are responsible for them, the activities in one swimlane are considered separate from the activities in other swimlanes.
Transition	——————>	A transition specifies the transfer of control from one action or activity state to another. Transitions are modeled as directed, solid lines with open arrowheads.
Triggerless Transition		Transitions as they appear in activity diagrams are often called triggerless or completion transitions, because they do not require an event to fire for control to transfer. Rather, control passes from one action or activity to the next as each completes. When an action or activity completes, its exit action, of present, fires and control is transferred. At that point, and without pause, control is transferred to the subsequent state. If that state has an entry action, that is executed, followed by the action or activity itself. This continues until the final state is reached. The initial state is indicated on an activity diagram by a solid ball; the final state is modeled as a solid ball inside of a circle.
Object Flow	------>	An object flow is the association between objects and action states. Object flows model how action states use objects as well as the effects of action states on objects. Object flows are written as dashed lines between action states and objects. When an object flow is output as a result of an action, that relationship is modeled with a dashed arrow proceeding from the action to the object symbol. Alternatively, when an object flow serves as input to an action, that relationship is depicted by a dashed arrow from the object to the action.

		Object flows may be controlled by multiple activities. An action state's output action may serve as an input action to any number of other action states. Object flows may appear multiple times on the same diagram. Each appearance denotes a different point in the life of the object. The object's state may be specified and placed in square brackets appended to the name of the object.
Action Flows		The association between action states is called an action flow. Action flows are the activities that one object performs on another and are modeled as solid lines. The purpose of an action flow is to specify the flow of control between states. A guard condition can be specified on an action flow to indicate a Boolean condition to evaluate to determine whether or not that transition should execute. The guard condition will be specified in square brackets. An entity begins in one action state, performs the action specified, and then enters another action state when the action is completed. Action flows are really just state chart diagram transitions with additional constraints. As such, they can use additional notation specific to state chart transitions. Action flows can be specified by a forward slash followed by an action expression that shows the actions that result when the action fires. These are the same as actions in a state chart diagram. An action state can be implied when an object flow exists between states. This indicates that the action produces some output and that the output is used in turn as the input to an action. In this case the object flow relationship implies the action flow.
Action State	ActionStateName	Action states are states that represent the execution of an atomic set of actions or operations. Action states have a flat top and bottom with curved sides. Action states are actually just regular states as on a state chart diagram, with added constraints. Because of this, they may use additional notation applicable to a state. Action states are states with an internal action and one or more outgoing transitions indicating that their internal action has completed. Action states specify an internal action expression that describes the action of the state. Action states must belong to a single swimlane. The group responsible for the swimlane will execute the action state.

(continued)

Table 4.9 (continued)

Element	Representation	Description
		Action states are not allowed to have entry actions, exit actions, internal transitions, or incoming transitions. An action state can appear multiple times within a diagram, each representing a distinct state in the same action. An action state can have both relevant and nonrelevant events. Relevant events are those that appear on the state's outgoing transitions; those that do not appear on the state's outgoing transitions are nonrelevant. All events that are nonrelevant in an action state must be deferred until they become relevant. Examples of action states include sending a signal to an object, calling an operation on an object, and creating or destroying an object, all of which are noninterruptible operations that take a minuscule amount of time. An action state is drawn as a rounded rectangle, the inside of which is labeled with the name of the action state. An action state cannot be broken into smaller segments.
Activity State	Action State	Activity states, unlike action states, are composite and thus can be broken into action states and other activity states, which may be represented by other activity diagrams as necessary. Activity states are not atomic and, as such, can be interrupted. They are considered to require an amount of time to complete, unlike action states. Although there is no notational distinction between action states and activity states, activity states may have additional parts such as entry and exit actions and submachine specifications, which are not applicable to action states.

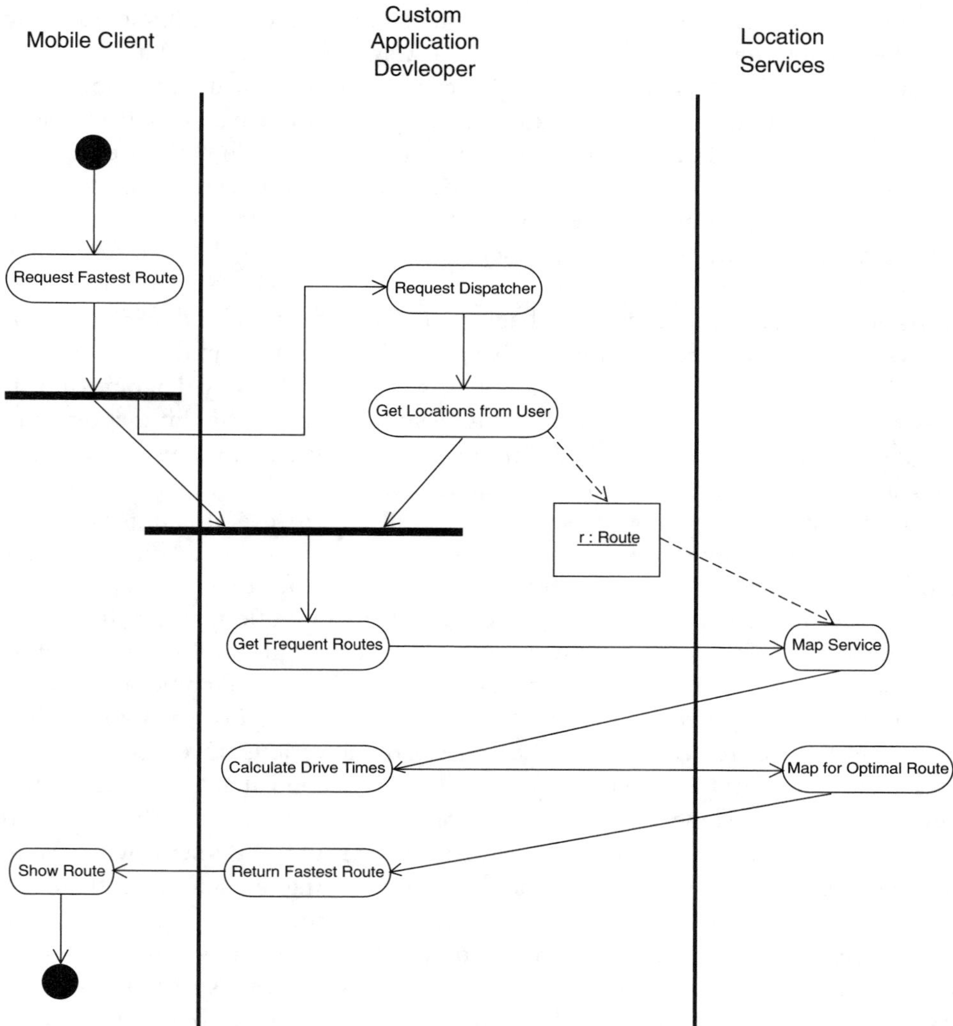

FIGURE 4.13 Activity Diagram Divided into Swimlanes.

Figure 4.13 shows an activity diagram that is divided into swimlanes, showing role responsibilities for implementing the functionality listed in the diagram. The flow of our activity diagram begins in its top left corner, with the solid circle with the arrow protruding from it. The diagram ends at the bottom of the diagram, also on the left-hand side, with the solid circle in a larger circle, with a line connecting it to the diagram element prior to it. The diagram proceeds to its first activity, which is that the mobile user requests the fastest route between his or her current and target destinations. From there, the diagram moves to a synchronization bar indicating the point of flow of control at which the control will be split into several separate processes or threads, which will execute simultaneously.

The mobile user continues on at that point, transmitting information about his or her current location (in a manner not specified by this diagram) and the target destination. Simultaneously, the Request Dispatcher will take the request from the mobile user and integrate that with the location information that it subsequently supplies to determine the best path for the user to follow. The point at which the Request Dispatcher has acquired all of the information that it needs about the user's location is represented by another synchronization bar, which indicates the point at which simultaneous execution ends and a single path of execution begins again. At this point the diagram shows the creation of route and location objects related to the mobile user's path. From that point, the interactions begin with the map and traffic services, which finally terminate with the fastest route being returned to the mobile user.

As you may have noted, activity diagrams begin with the solid dot. Figure 4.14 shows a higher level of detail, for acquiring the fastest route from the map service, than Figure 4.13. It's important to note that we can use Activity diagrams in this way to break down many states and activities into several different diagrams. In Figure 4.14, for there is a precondition the current route that the user is on. The diagram shows that we start out with acquiring the frequent routes for the current location from the map service. Map service will return several common routes. Then, our application creates a new variable called shortest route and assigns the current route to that. It continues by checking all routes for their length/ time and returns the shortest one. Finally, it proceeds to its first iteration, where the system will check to see if there are additional routes to process. This process will continue until all of the routes available are processed. For each route, a temporary variable v1 will be set to the value of that route object. Another temporary variable, called segments, will be created and its value set to all of the various travel segments that make up that route. The diagram then enters its second iteration as it iterates through all of the elements of that collection set by the segment's value in a temporary variable called s1. For each segment of the route, the time it will take to travel that segment is calculated and added to any existing segment times that have already been calculated, creating an elapsed time for the entire journey from the various segments. If the elapsed time to complete the segment is shorter than the current value for shortest Route (which could either be the user's current route or a previously calculated new route) then it becomes the new value for shortest Route. At this point, the system determines again whether or not there are additional routes remaining, and, while there are, this process is repeated. When all of the routes have been processed the final value for shortestRoute variable is returned.

4.5 Implementation View: Component Diagrams

Component diagrams illustrate software components, such as source code, object code, executable code, and libraries, and the dependencies among components. Components can be distributed across nodes, which are computational resources. Component diagrams model physical software components that compose a system and represent its actual software implementation. Component diagrams are useful in a number of ways. They assist software developers by clarifying the goals and structure of the system and help technical writers understand how the system is assembled so that they can better document it. Component diagrams are great

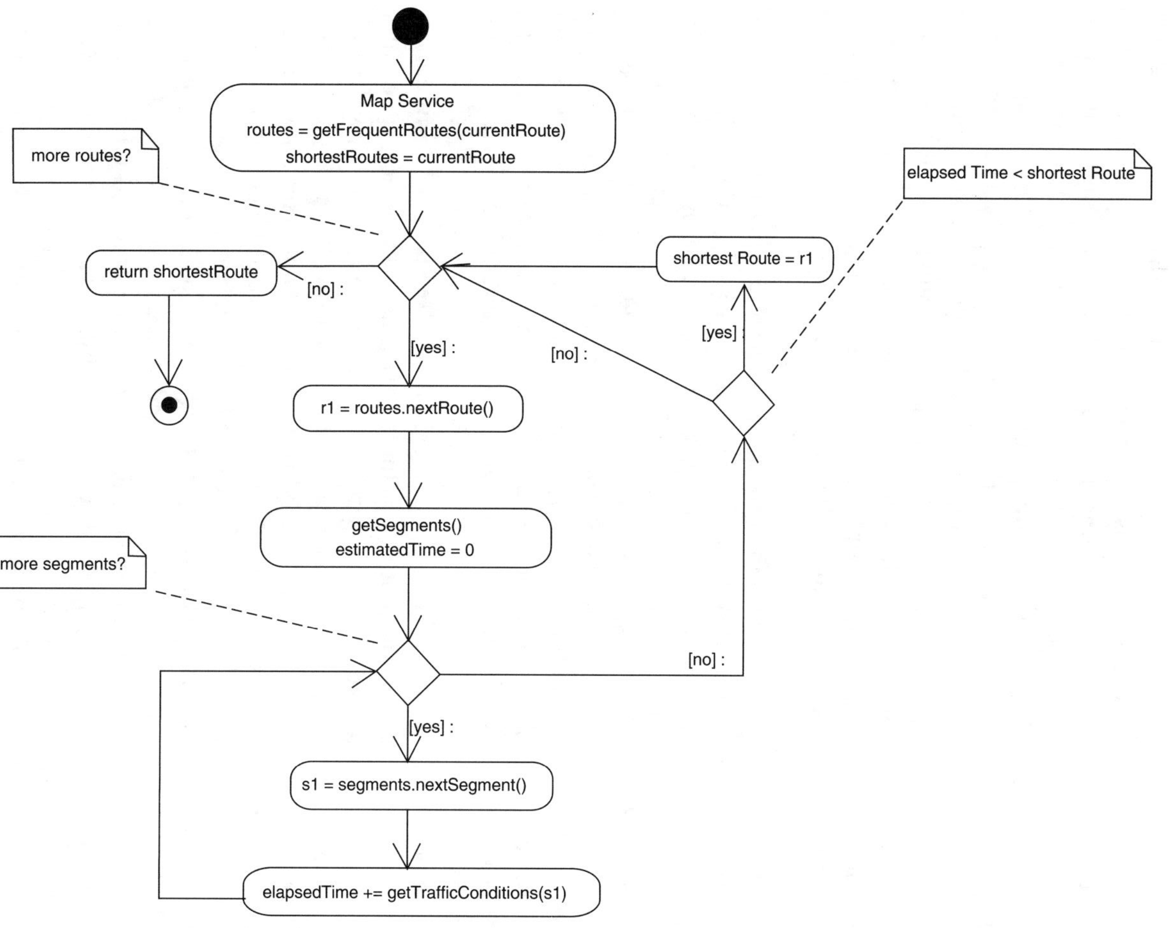

FIGURE 4.14. Activity Diagram for Finding the Fastest Route.

tools for encouraging software reuse as well, as they help to identify components that are useful for a variety of purposes.

Component diagrams are driven by interfaces, which can be thought of as faces that objects present to the outside world. Components can also make their interfaces available for use by other components. To accomplish this, the providing component publishes what is known as an export interface. Components that make use of the published interface use it as an import interface. Interfaces play an important role in encouraging component reuse, because a component implementing a given interface can be replaced by any other component that conforms to the same interface. A well-designed and maintained interface allows components to be used in a variety of systems. So, then, how do interfaces and component diagrams relate? A component diagram can be thought of as a way to make a component's interface information readily available to software developers. Additionally, because components conform to a specific set of interfaces, they can easily be replaced by other components conforming to the same set of interfaces. Designing your interfaces allows concurrent development to proceed on each side of its users.

A well-designed component structure makes it easy to replace outdated components with newer components that function the same as the original interfaces.

There are three general components that are represented by the component diagram: deployment components, work products, and execution components.

Deployment components are the final product of the development effort. They can be deployed and run. These include executables, Dynamic Linked Libraries (DLLs), and JavaBeans. Work products include the components that are used to create the deployment components. These include data files and source code. Execution components are components that are created by the running system.

Components are replaceable parts of a system that realize a set of interfaces. They model physical software entities including executables, libraries, tables, files, and documents and reside on nodes or computational resources. When we say that components are physical things, that can be a bit confusing, because most people tend to think of physical elements as being things like tables and other tangible things. In terms of a software system physical things are constructed not of wood or concrete, but of bits. An object, for example, is purely conceptual. It lives in memory and is simply a way of conceptualizing a system. A DLL, in contrast, is a relatively physical entity composed of bits and located, physically, on a storage device. Physical parts of a software system can either be executed themselves or participate in the system as it executes. These physical things are modeled as components.

Interfaces serve as a bridge between physical and conceptual software elements. They may, for example, by specified on a conceptual level and have realizing classes that are similarly conceptual. Those same interfaces, however, can also be realized by physical components. Most modern software languages and operating systems have direct support for the notion of components. In addition to source and executable code, other participants in an executing system, such as files and documents, can also be represented as components.

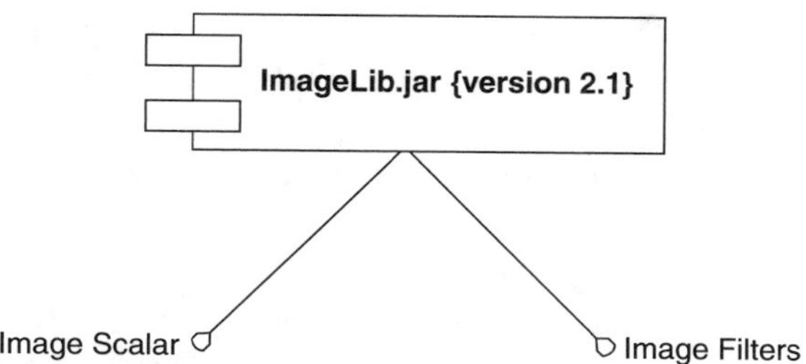

FIGURE 4.15. A Simple Component Diagram.

A component is required to be named so that it can be distinguished from other components (see Figure 4.15). Component names are typically either nouns or noun phrases and may provide file name extensions, such as .jar, or .dll. They can either be a simple name or a pathname. Because a component's name can be specified as a pathname, the name itself should not include colons except as required for the pathname to avoid confusion. Components can also provide compartments providing additional information about them and they may also specify tagged values, which are particularly useful for versioning information.

Often components will provide a compartment labeled "realizes," specifying the interfaces that particular component realizes. The similarities and differences among components and classes help to illuminate the role of components. Components and classes share many similarities. Both have names and are able to have relationships, including association, dependency, and generalization relationships. Additionally, they may be nested and may participate in interactions. Most importantly, both can realize interfaces.

Unlike classes, however, components typically specify only operations that are accessible through their interfaces. Classes are abstract and conceptual, as well, whereas components are physical and reside on physical nodes, as we described earlier. Components can be seen as implementing classes, that is, for representing them at a different, more concrete, level of abstraction. This can be modeled by a dashed line with an open arrowhead extending from a class to the component that implements it. When a component realizes an interface, that interface is an export interface of the component, and the component provides that interface as a service to other components that may use it. Components may have multiple export interfaces. When a component uses an interface, it is referred to as an import interface. Import interfaces are interfaces to which a component conforms and utilizes. Components may have multiple import interfaces. Additionally, components may have both multiple import interfaces and multiple export interfaces.

Component diagrams are most often used to model the software components that will comprise the system's deployment as well as the dependencies among components that relate to the compilation process. Additionally, they are frequently used to maintain version information about systems, both as they are developed and as they are updated subsequent to their initial deployment, as well as to visualize the impact of change on such systems. For large systems, component diagrams provide a useful means of showing how components are distributed across a system by showing on which nodes they are located.

Components rarely rely on one another directly. Rather, their tendency is to import interfaces that other components publish and to export interfaces that are used by other interfaces.

Some characteristics of component diagrams are listed in Table 4.10.

4.5.1 Applicable Stereotypes

There are five stereotypes that are commonly used with components. The executable stereotype specifies that the component is able to be executed. The library stereotype specifies that it is an object library (static or dynamic). The file stereotype specifies that the component represents a file composed of source code or data. The document stereotype indicates a file containing information other than source code or application data. The table stereotype indicates that the component represents a database table. Component-based systems have as one of their core principles the concept that they are composed of binary, replaceable components that, because they are each created to an interface-based specification, can be replaced easily as they become outdated. Because components that fulfill the same set of interfaces are easily interchanged, building systems in such a manner increases system longevity and facilitates software upgrades.

4.5.2 Deployment Diagrams

Deployment diagrams model a system's end points, or nodes. They typically model the physical aspects of a system. Nodes are computational resources with memory and a processor of some sort and are utilized by the system in some way while it is running. Nodes are used to model the hardware that a system runs on or interacts with, and they could indicate the type of operating system or database, a processor family, or the physical location of the components. Because components are actually source and executable code, they require hardware to execute, and that hardware is represented by its nodes.

When designing a system, it is important to consider not only how it fits together on a conceptual level but also how to model the physical aspects of a system to ensure that the system can be properly built, deployed, and executed. A node is modeled in the form of a cube, which has a name that can either be a simple name or a pathname. A node can contain stereotypes to qualify what type of node it is, as well as tagged values and additional compartments to provide more information as necessary. Additionally, nodes can be modeled as icons of the resource type they represent. For example, a node can be represented as a picture of a computer. Nodes, like components, can have association, generalization and dependency relationships, may be nested, can participate in interactions, and may have instances. Whereas components participate in the system's execution, nodes are the entities responsible for executing those components. Components can be deployed on any number of nodes. To indicate that a particular component is deployed an a particular node, you can provide a dependency relationship between them. A group of objects or components placed on a particular node for execution is known as a *distribution unit*.

Nodes may also specify attributes and operations. Common component attributes include the speed of its processor and the amount of memory that

Table 4.10. Artifacts of Component Diagrams

Element	Representation	Description
Component	Component1	A component is modeled as a rectangle that has two smaller rectangles protruding from its left-hand side. A component can represent source code or binary code, and it may have instances. Instances of components are ones that exist at run time. A component must have a name, which is followed by a colon (:) and then its type. Components may have aggregation relationships with other components, aggregates, and processes.
Dependency		Dependency is represented by a dashed line between two components, where the arrow points from the dependent component to the component it is dependent on. Dependency relationships illustrate the manner in which changes to a particular component affect changes in other components. There are a variety of dependency relationships (e.g., communication and compilation) that apply to component diagrams.
Interfaces	InterfaceName	An interface is specified on a component diagram as a small labeled circle attached to a component by a line.
Development Time Relationships		Development time relationships are useful in cases where a component is needed at development time but not at run time. Development time relationships are modeled as a dependency relationship, with dashed arrows. You can use stereotypes to further define the relationships.
Calls Relationships		Calls relationships are used to model calling dependencies among components and are illustrated as dashed arrows. For instance, the calls relationship is an appropriate means of expressing a case where one shared library utilizes the services of another.

component has, whereas a node's attributes generally include things such as restart and shutdown. The most common relationship to a node is the association relationship, which, in the case of nodes, represents a communication link of some sort, which can include a physical Ethernet connection or a nonphysical connection like an 802.11b wireless connection. As with all associations, associations among nodes can include roles, multiplicity, and constraints. You will typically model all of the significant components located on a particular node, although a single component may have duplicate entries in multiple nodes.

4.6 Summary

As we have seen in this chapter, UML gives us a complete tool for gathering requirements and representing software artifacts including those needed for design and implementation. Though, like any other tool, UML is not the perfect tool. The reason we will use UML in this text extensively is largely that it is a complete tool.

Keep in mind that our explanation of UML in this text has been very minimal. There are entire texts dedicated to discussing the basics of UML. Also, recall that our perspective of UML analysis has been a practical one: There is much more to UML, its semantics, and the mathematics-like mechanics that define it.

Today, mobile development is largely ad hoc with very little in the way of discipline. This is particularly the case because the design and development of a mobile application requires familiarity with a host of other areas addressed in this book, including wireless networking, location-based systems, and distributed application development. Because of this, UML offers us yet an added benefit: a language that software developers with experience in various domains can use to communicate.

In the remainder of this text, we will mostly focus on UML extensions that treat particular needs of mobile applications. However, keep in mind that basic UML, without any extensions, is still of primary importance. We simply will assume that the readers of this text are roughly familiar with the use and application of UML; therefore, when discussing UML without extensions, we will simply mention which type of diagram is relevant where.

SECTION 2

Device-Independent and Multichannel User Interface Development Using UML

CHAPTER 5

Generic User Interface Development

You can't pick up two melons with one hand.

Persian proverb

5.1 INTRODUCTION

We have now seen the basic tools we will use for the development process in creating mobile applications. The next step is to begin defining a methodology for building real applications and to show the implementation of the methodology in building these real applications.

Through the first four chapters, we discovered that, because of the condition of the mobile user and nature of the mobile application, the mobile application may interface with the user through a variety of devices and channels. In this chapter, we will take a closer look at the fundamentals of user interfaces to software applications, primarily mobile applications. We will focus on changing a paradigm shift in the application developer's thinking, moving him or her from thinking that an application will be used using a mouse, keyboard, and a monitor to thinking that an application may be used by a subset of any system input and output channel through which the user may receive stimuli from a system and respond to it. Finally, we will look at how to create user interfaces in layers so that we apply the principal of *separation of concerns* to orthogonal aspects of user interfaces. For demonstration purposes, we will use the XForms standard of W3C as an example for an XML-based tool designed to create the proper abstractions in user interface design.

There are a variety of standards and naming conventions for analyzing the problems of the user interface. Also, many aspects of user interface development such as issues related to human factors are not well defined. In this text, we will use terminologies outlined by ECMA (European Computer Manufacturer Association), W3C (World Wide Web Consortium), or similar noncommercial standards bodies. It is also important to note that user interface development for mobile applications is a new field; therefore, there will be occasions when these bodies have not decided on a standard way of addressing these problems. In such cases, we will build some logical vocabulary as built on top of the existing standards and as decided by the author of this book.

The first step in moving forward is to ask ourselves, "Why do we want to build generic user interfaces?" First, mobile applications are typically used by a wider array of operating environments and systems than a PC. Because there is such a wide array of end clients for mobile applications, we need to be able to adapt the application quickly, if not in real time, with very little or no additional development effort. Another byproduct of building generic user interfaces is elongating the effective life of the application. One of the biggest reasons that software has become "throwaway" in recent years has been the rapid evolution and changes in user interface technologies. It is obvious that the portion of the code concerned with presenting the user interface and taking input from the user has to be modified or rewritten whenever there are additional features in user interface devices or new user interfaces altogether. However, it is not necessary to rewrite or throw away the components that calculate the business logic or control the general interactions with the user. Our goal in this chapter will be to create the proper layers of abstraction in writing the user interface related code so that the commonalities of the various user interfaces are grouped into reusable components and the specific features of devices are encapsulated in isolated software components.

If you are familiar with some of the patterns used in user interface development, such as PAC and MVC, you will be wondering why there is no mention of those in this chapter. We will get there in Chapter 6 and look at these patterns while tying in the concepts introduced in this chapter. Let us begin by looking at some basic principles of user interfaces, what user interfaces are, their role in mobile applications, and the various aspects of the problem of designing user interfaces for mobile applications.

5.2 User Interface Development

A software application is started by a person, another software application, a hardware application, or a combination thereof. A demon program may invoke a server application at a particular time; this is an example of a software application being invoked by another software application. The operating system itself is an application that may be started by a hardware/software driven application, turning the computer on, providing power to the CPU, and allowing the initialization software permanently stored on the hardware to invoke an operating system. Excluding artificially intelligent systems, all software applications, at some point and perhaps through a long line of succession, are either started or scheduled to start by a person—a user.

The mechanism through which users access a software application is referred to as the *user interface*. Though today the user interface to a software application brings to mind a mouse, a keyboard, and a monitor, this is only a small subset of possible interfaces to computing systems. In fact, in the realm of mobile computing, the mouse, the keyboard, and the stationary monitor often do not fulfill the requirements. Yet, most of the software methodologies, techniques, and tools that we use today are intended for software that runs or is used by a PC. More importantly, the developers *think* and *design* with the PC framework embedded in their minds as the end user. The first task at hand is to make a complete paradigm shift away from this type of thinking and design methodology. Let us take a step back and look at the important aspects of user interface development.

First, there are the *human factors*. The way it is used has a great impact on the utilization of any computing system. Though defining human factors in one sentence is a difficult task, it can be defined as *the set of those concerns qualifying the interaction of the user with the software system*. Often, subsets of human factors considerations such as *usability* are referred to individually; however, human factors remains an encompassing term that refers to all those concerns that describe the quality of the interaction of a user with a system. Nearly all "touchy-feely" considerations of user interface design fall within the purview of human factors. We will take an in-depth look at human factors in mobile application design later in this chapter.

Although human factors considerations are of utmost importance, to deliver the most efficient mobile application, the application user interface must suit the condition of the user. For example, a voice user interface is better suited for an application designed for finding directions while driving than a graphical user interface because drivers cannot safely read or view the directions while driving though they can hear the directions safely. Therefore, mobile applications must be designed with *multiple channels* in mind: We will not limit ourselves to just voice or just graphical user interfaces. We will discuss mobile graphical user interfaces in Chapter 6 and mobile voice user interfaces in Chapter 7. We will call this *multichannel* user interface development and take a preliminary look at it later on in this chapter but cover the topic comprehensively in Chapter 8. In this chapter, we will lay down the taxonomy for decomposition of user interfaces so that we can build on them in the next three chapters. This taxonomy will be critical in understanding how to build generic interfaces that can be specialized to a wide range of devices using multiple user interface channels.

Let us start with the human factors aspects of mobile development.

5.2.1 Human Factors

Dix et al. define human factors, often referred to as ergonomics, as the study of the physical characteristics of the interaction: how the controls are designed, the physical environment in which the interaction takes place, and the layout and physical qualities of the screen [Dix et al. 1998]. This view is a bit biased toward GUIs. Later in the same text, the authors discuss other types of user interfaces. Regardless, their definition tells us that human factors is a very qualitative study.

For any typical application, we need to consider the following as the elements of human factors consideration:

1. the look and feel of the application and how the users "like" the user interface,
2. the ease of learning the interface well and becoming efficient at using the user interface, and
3. health issues in using the user interface.

This small list is a subset of many various issues to be considered for human factors as a summary of a study done by the Federal Aviation Administration (FAA) and the list of elements of human factors recognized by Dix et al. in the aforementioned reference. This is not a comprehensive list; we are only discussing a subset that applies to mobile application development later on.

You may ask yourself why is there an FAA study? The history of human factors started with aviation. Scientists and engineers tried to design airplane controls in a way that the pilots could navigate the airplane, using a large number and variety of instruments, for a long period of time. Since then, the field of aviation has made great contributions to user interface human factors design as innovation has been required to improve safety and performance for air traffic control systems, airplane navigation systems, and a variety of other complex systems used in aviation. In particular, an FAA study [FAA 1999] specifies the three keys to be technical usability, domain usability, and user acceptance.

Let us take a close look at these three key aspects. We will have the most focus on the first, the "user-friendliness" of the application in this text. This is one of the keys to what makes or breaks any application, particularly a mobile application. An application that is difficult to use is one that does not attract users. For this, not only do we need to make the application easy and efficient to navigate, but we need to consider things like color, noise, timing, esthetic quality, and a variety of other qualitative factors that make the user "like" the look-and-feel of the application. A user interface is well designed when the program behaves exactly how the user thought it would [Spolsky 2001]. So, another factor is to think of what a typical user considers desirable. Once again, this might include a variety of esthetics, timing, color, etc.

It is also important to keep in mind that most user interfaces are typically used many times, not just once. So, as the users interact with the user interface, there is an important learning process that must be taken into account. A user interface that may seem unintuitive or difficult to use the first time may prove to be an excellent interface after being used a few hundred times. This shows us that there is a cognitive element involved in interacting with user interfaces that not only is important in the greater picture of human-to-computer interface (HCI) but also is something that affects human factors. A background color that is very bright may seem nice the first time the device is used, but over time it may seem less and less desirable.

Finally, there is the health element. In fact, this is one of the prime areas of focus in the study of human factors; ergonomics and human factors are associated with things such as keyboard shape (so-called ergonomic keyboards), which help prevent the user from developing tendonitis. Health factors are very important and even particularly crucial in the case of mobile application development where the user's physical location is constantly changing. A typical example of a safety concern is using a mobile phone while driving, which, if not done with caution, can increase the risk of being involved in automobile accidents. There are numerous other health factors within the mobile domain; however, many of these issues are still being debated and studied as mobile applications are young relative to their stationary counterparts. We will mention these factors as appropriate throughout this text.

Covering the entire field of human factors is not something that we should attempt to do in this text, nor should we need to. But, before we understand the human factors of mobile applications, we need to take a brief look at human factors of stationary applications such as those designed for PCs.

5.2.2 Usability, Human Factors, and Other Considerations for Developing Stationary PC-Based User Interfaces

Since the 1980s, when the personal computer began to become a prevalent device, we have learned much about designing user interfaces for computing systems. Though some of what we have learned is applicable only to stationary applications, much of it can be applied to both stationary and mobile applications.

So, without attempting to go through a comprehensive study, let us list some issues that the software engineering industry, as a whole, deems to be important:

1. *Intuitiveness*: User interfaces should be intuitive. The first time a user uses an application, he or she should be able to navigate his or her way through without too much trouble, assuming a reasonable amount of familiarity with the application domain.
2. *Consistency*: A software application should present user interface components that are consistent with each other and consistent with their operating environments. For example, if one screen refers to the gender of a user by allowing the user to select between *man* and *woman*, other screens should not refer to gender in different terms such as *male* or *female*. Also, the user interface should be consistent with the user's operating environment. If the operating system is Windows, use Microsoft's conventions for the user interface of your application to stay consistent with the operating environment.
3. *Learnablility*: The user should be able to learn how to use the user interface within the first few times of using it and remember how to use it without having to refer to manuals. This goes hand in hand with the user interface being intuitive.
4. *Nonintrusively Helpful*: The user interface and the underlying application should provide help and hints. There can never be too much in the way of help and hints on a user interface. A key in implementing hints and help is to make them so that they do not hinder efficient use of the application. The little helper that pops up on the screen every few minutes without an explicit invocation of the user can be annoying and cut down on the efficient use of the user interface.

5. *Accommodating Expert Users*: A good user interface provides shortcuts for the expert users. Applications should be efficient and fast to use for expert users. As a user learns how to use the system better, he or she should be able to access the information and perform the tasks faster and faster.
6. *Trustable*: The user interface should be predictable, trustable, and easily understood. There should be a simple set of rules that are used in building the user interface that allow the user to be able to guess what the reaction of the user interface may be.
7. *Robustness* [Dix et al. 1998]: A good user interface should gracefully recover from user errors (e.g., display the proper dialogue boxes to guide the user when an error happens), should convey the relation to the application logic easily to the user (e.g., make sure that the user knows which data are changing, when transactions are committed, etc.), and should be fast enough and let the user know when there are long waits for responses.

Sometimes, as in many other engineering problems, satisfying these criteria presents us with some inherent conflicts. For example, performance of a user interface may have to do with the number of widgets and controls on it. By reducing the number of controls, we can improve performance, but the user interface may become less and less intuitive to use.

Nevertheless, simply keeping these principles in mind helps us tremendously in building a user interface. Also, remember that we are shooting to first build a generic user interface and then specialize it to the particular devices that may be used accessing it. So, we have an extra layer of indirection that will add complexity. Nevertheless, every layer has to be able to accommodate all of these principles and whatever other principles you have learned in designing good user interfaces for the Web or PCs.

5.2.3 Additional Consideration for Mobile Applications

Though mobile applications and devices have been around for years, the current and future generations of mobile applications and devices have some fundamental differences from their more mature siblings of the years past. Most mobile applications in the past were based on embedded software technologies. The devices were manufactured for mass use and the product manufacturing and delivery of the mobile application and the device that it ran on resembled the production of a refrigerator more than a typical stationary software application such as those used on PCs, Web appliances, or even mainframes. With this said, we know a bit more about human factors and usability aspects of developing mobile applications than some of their other aspects. During the past fifty years, we have seen how electronic calculators have been used, how mobile phones have become popular, and what makes some devices easy to use and other ones difficult. Based on this, we have understood the mobile problem better and begun to understand what human factor issues are particularly important for mobile applications. Yet, in the same way that building today's software applications is quite different from building a refrigerator, building an embedded system with custom devices is different from building a modern mobile application written in a variety of languages and deployable on a variety of devices. So, our knowledge of the mobile applications that deliver value through custom devices may not apply.

This is because mobile applications were really only a reality for those tasks that presented large economic benefits for an even larger customer base for a well-known problem domain. The devices used in grocery stores for keeping track of inventory are a great example. The problem of tracking groceries is well known: There are thousands of grocery stores, and there are clear ways of benefiting the business with custom devices. For such problem realms, custom devices will remain a possibility. But custom devices, as we discussed in Chapter 1, also present us with some problems. Custom devices require special training, are costly to manufacture, are even more costly to maintain, lend themselves to obsolescence easily if the business model changes even slightly, and require long development and testing cycles.

Our goal is to design mobile applications that are easily deployable, decoupled from the platforms to be deployed on, have short development cycles, cost less to develop and deploy, do not require the users to go through long training cycles, and are inexpensive to maintain and modify. These are the same reasons that have pushed PCs into a world in which the hardware and software are loosely coupled. The point is that when we introduce these new requirements, human factors and usability issues become more difficult to solve. So, we cannot simply take what we have learned from building customized inventory tracking devices used in grocery stores and apply them to the building of robust mobile applications.

First, we need to remember all those issues mentioned in Section 5.2.2. All of those principles that apply to developing a good interface for a stationary application apply to developing a good interface for a mobile application. Then, we need to consider additional considerations to take into account the "condition of the mobile user." The human factors we have to consider for mobile application development will obviously have to take into account that the mobile user is in a different environment than a stationary user. Let us enumerate again the requirements on the human factor aspects of mobile application design that are related to the condition of the user:

1. *Short Transaction Cycles*: Mobile users typically do not perform tasks that involve great amounts of data entry or long transaction cycles. Mobile users typically use the devices at their disposal to perform a few quick tasks.
2. *Expectations of Consumer Devices*: Mobile users have much higher expectations for consumer devices than for PCs. For example, users cannot handle waiting for their MP3 player, PDA, or cell phone to spend several minutes to "boot-up." Users expect to turn a device on, wait for a maximum of several seconds, and then begin to use the device.
3. *Lack of Focus*: Mobile users are not focused on the task of computing. Because the mobile user is frequently using the mobile application while moving (driving, walking, going from place to place, etc.), he or she has to do multiple things at the same time. This becomes a big consideration in the human factor aspects of the user interface design.

4. *Intermittent Network Connectivity*: Mobile devices have unreliable connections to the network, so the device may be disconnected from the network at any time.
5. *Multichannel User Interfaces*: As we will see later on in this chapter, mobile applications use a large variety of user interfaces to communicate with the user. This gives a mobile application more flexibility

From these requirements, we can conclude that the following are among the most important aspects of usability and human factors for mobile applications:

1. *System response time and system access time*: System performance and response time is a typical problem in computing, but long waits are absolutely unacceptable for mobile applications. Not only do long waits for system response detract the user from using a given feature, they may detract him or her from using the application or even the device altogether.
2. *Clean and efficient user interfaces*: Cluttered user interfaces are also unacceptable. The user interface of a mobile system should have only the bare minimum components to give the user the information he or she needs and no more. As already mentioned, not only is the user typically in a rush, but he or she also is not focused on the task of computing—not for long anyway. So, it is crucial that the maximum amount of information be conveyed through the fewest user interface components. An advertisement playing on the phone while you are trying to find some crucial piece of information through a voice user interface is unacceptable. Try to imagine the fury in a user who was just a few seconds away from hearing a phone number being sought through a voice-driven search system and was just disconnected because he or she passed through a tunnel while listening to an advertisement! If there is a large cost in performance to render colors to a PDA interface, color is best avoided. User interface designers can think of many other occasions when the performance and efficiency of the user interface is compromised in exchange for look-and-feel advantages in developing desktop or Web applications. This is not acceptable when developing mobile applications.
3. *Maintaining consistency across multiple user interfaces and multiple device types while accessing the system*: It is critical that the users have the same experience regardless of what type of user interface they use to access the system. This may require intelligent mapping of various look-and-feel features from one type of a user interface on a given device to another type of user interface on a different device. For example, in an HTML-based application we can convey a look-and-feel to the user by choosing a certain set of colors. The equivalent can be done using the voice inflection in voice user interfaces. There are two ways to address this issue of maintaining consistency: We can maintain consistency by outlining look-and-feel guidelines per the domain problem and the subdivisions of the domain problem or we can also create this consistency by creating guidelines for the various components of the user interface. Example 5.1 shows how we might have two such comparable guidelines for a loan origination application.

There is a really a bigger picture though. Consistency is maintained by various aspects of user interface context. Later in this chapter we will discuss context as an element of the taxonomy of user interfaces. Consistency should be informed within the different types of context.

4. *Accounting for the abilities and limitations of human sensory systems*: While designing single or multichannel user interfaces, it is critical to keep in mind the limitations of the human sensory system and the limitations of humans to react to given sensory. As the capabilities of devices improve and each device type is able to accommodate more channels with higher user interface performance, it will be crucial not to overload the user with information using any given user interface or any combination of user interfaces. For example, if an application is built to be used by a combination of voice and text user interfaces, hints should be provided for messages that are played by the voice user interface and relate to some counterpart on the GUI displaying the text. The user should not be expected to read and understand the text at the same time as he or she is listening and trying to understand the hint relating to the text. Also remember that the mobile user is typically not focused on the computing task. So, the mobile user is already missing some processing cycles (to use a computing metaphor) to process the data. Do not overburden the user with a user interface that expects quick responses from the user or is cluttered with output and prompts.
5. *Positional adaptability*: User interfaces to mobile applications may need to be modified depending on the location of the user and how the location of the user changes. For example, the fonts on a given user interface may need to be larger as the speed of the train increases (because speed and vibration are typically related in some directly proportional sense). As vibration increases, recognizing text becomes more and more difficult. So, to make this easier, we can increase the font size dynamically. Obviously, positional adaptability is something that is prevalent through the entire process of building a mobile application as the changing location of the mobile user, as we saw in Chapter 1, is one of the main dimensions of mobility. The dependency of the user interface on this positional change is not always obvious; therefore, sometimes, it is neglected.
6. *The ability to prioritize user interface elements*: The mobile application may be running on a device that is running out of battery energy, may be having a tough time connecting to the network or simply having an unusually low-bandwidth connection to the network, or experiencing one of the factors discussed in Chapter 1 that puts extreme stress on the device. In such situations, it is often helpful to know what elements of the user interface are absolutely necessary, what elements can be done without, and what elements are preferred. This issue should not be mixed with the issue of having a variety of user interfaces supporting the same application. Even after we create a mechanism by which the system can be accessed through multiple types of user interfaces, it may still be necessary to dynamically change the user interface at run time. For example, let us think about a WML application that may display maps. The user is lost and is trying to find directions to his or her destination. Although an advertisement may be acceptable at the bottom of the screen when the user has a

good network connection and plenty of battery left on his or her mobile phone, it is absolutely unacceptable if the mobile phone's battery is nearly drained or the network connection is unusually bad. Can you imagine how irate the user may become if the advertisement prevents him or her from getting the directions? Even if the user never finds this out, simply the fact that the advertisement may reduce the robustness of the application is not acceptable. At the same time, the advertisement provides the map service with some revenue. The solution in this case is to serve the advertisement if it does not cause a reduced level of delivered service to the user. But, if there is not much battery left or the network connection is poor, the advertisement should be removed. Though such logic really goes deeper into the application than just the user interface, the elements of the user interface should be prioritized so that the rendering engine can decide how to treat these elements. Also, the rendering engine should offer the functionality required to understand such priorities and use them to render a final user interface.

It is also possible that a combination of these guidelines be used. This is a more complicated problem because there may be some conflict between what user interface components may require as opposed to what the domain may require. In these cases, use of common sense prevails! First, see what the user wants; if that is still ambiguous, trust the domain before anything else. Remember that computing applications are built to serve some purpose. This purpose overrides any strictly technical preferences.

Example 5.1: User Interface Consistency Guidelines for a Mortgage Banking Application.

A) Guidelines by Domain:
   a. Color: Use white, black, scales of gray, and scales of blue only. These are the branding colors associated with ACME Mortgage corporation.
   b. VUI Prompts: All prompts relating to gathering information for the financial portions of the loan application should be recorded by a female voice talent. All prompts relating to gathering information for the personal sections of the loan applications should be recorded by a young male voice talent.

B) Guidelines by User Interface Components:
   a. Color: Use blue for all of the buttons. Use white for all of the backgrounds. Use black for all of the fonts. Use scales of gray for all other interface components.
   b. VUI prompts: All informative prompts must be recorded by a female voice talent. All warnings must be recorded by a male voice talent. When the user does not understand one prompt pronounced by a given voice artist twice, the voice talent should be dynamically changed to allow the user to understand the voice of another voice talent.

These are not the only user interface related issues of mobile applications. But, most of the other issues are tangled within the remainder of the application. For example, because of the unreliable connection to the network, the user may be disconnected at any time. So, it is important that the user interface always allow the user to get back to where he or she was in using the application before the disconnection occurred. If there is a multiple step process that the user is going through to accomplish the computing task, the user interface should always allow a way to get a quick summary of what has already been done. However, for the user interface to support such functionality, the application needs to have very advanced support for cross-device sessions. This, in and of itself, is a slice of functionality that is needed outside of the scope of user interface design.

We will discuss these issues as we get to them throughout our discussions. The list provided here can be used as a general guideline for things to remember when thinking about the usability and human factors of the user interfaces of a mobile application. Once again, all of those factors that apply to stationary applications must be kept in mind too.

Now, let us get back to the reason we started looking at how user interfaces work and look at the things we need to consider for building generic user interfaces.

5.3 Building Generic User Interfaces

As we discussed in the introductory part of this chapter, the reason for building a generic user interface for mobile systems is the wide variety of devices and user interfaces that an application might need to support. The idea here is to layer the different parts of the user interface, build a generic user interface, and then specialize it to a given device or type of user interface using a mechanism such as XSLT.

Before we go into this further, let us look at when we want to build generic interfaces and when we do not. Let us consider applications that can benefit from a layered user interface approach:

1. *Applications that change frequently*: Many applications change very frequently. Such constant changing of state may be caused by the business model that the application serves or a variety of other reasons. Some are of the school of thought that an application should stabilize as it matures. This is not necessarily true. The life of a software application is only meaningful as long as it is serving its economic or scientific reason for existence. Outside of this, a software application is meaningless. So, if an application is changing frequently because the customer requirements are constantly changing, we actually have a good situation. During the past ten years, application developers have become very good at separating concerns of business logic and presentation. We have also learned much about how to layer different parts of business logic so that as one part changes the other parts are not affected. However, whenever an application changes, the user interface needs to be modified too. And this is a problem with few good solutions.

2. *Applications that support a wide variety of devices*: We have talked about this several times now, so the reader should well know that mobile applications need to support a variety of device types. The advantage of building a generic interface to a system, and then specializing it, is that it minimizes the amount of code needed to perform the necessary tasks. And we all know that the less code we have, the better off we are. This is probably the most popular reason for building generic user interfaces.
3. *Applications that must have many loosely coupled parts*: One of the advantages of building a generic user interface to a system is that it enables loose coupling between the user interface components themselves and among the look-and-feel components, interaction logic, and application flow logic. This loose coupling is one of the principle features of various existing technologies such as XSL templates and CCS. Loose coupling also offers the advantage of being able to change one set of components without requiring changes to other components. Although this has been somewhat akin to "nirvana" in software, theory has not exactly delivered in practical implementations. Nevertheless, striving for loose coupling promises to at least lessen the amount of change required for one component when another component is changed.
4. *Applications that offer multiple user interfaces with a range of complexity*: A good reason to justify building systems with generic user interfaces is the requirement of supporting multiple user interfaces, each with some difference in the required feature sets. For example, on a PC-based GUI-only system, we may represent the directions to a destination with a map and some driving directions. We may provide the user with controls such as zooming. On contrast, with a WAP user interface that allows the reader to put in the information about the destination and hear the directions, we may want to offer directions that are read back to the user, through the telephony system, and have the functionality for the system pause while the user is driving to the destination. There are some commonalities between these two types of interfaces: They both offer a way for the user to give the system a start and an end point and request directions and they both give the user back some directions. However, one has to be able to display a map whereas the other has to be able to represent the directions serially (through an aural user interface) and wait for the user to be ready to hear each step. So, when implementing the generic user interface, we provide all of the possible functionality needed from the various user interfaces. In this way, we achieve several goals:
    a. We avoid building the logic for the user to interact with the system multiple times.
    b. We build a consistent way of accessing all functionality. Remember that maintaining consistency across multiple user interfaces for our system is a must. The first place to start to establish such consistency is with the way the back end expects the user interactions to behave. The API to the business logic is often biased toward one type of user interface over the others. In designing the back end of mobile systems, it is crucial to attempt to expose behavior of the system without any bias toward a user interface type.

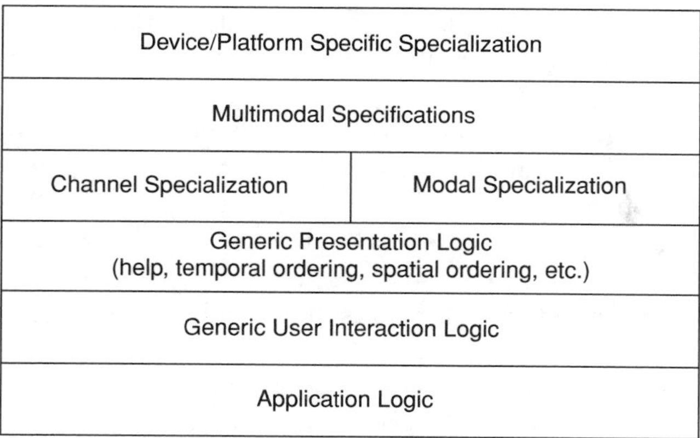

FIGURE 5.1. Layering User Interfaces.

c. If we decide to make the system statefull (so that the system remembers the things that the user does as he or she navigates through the system), we can easily maintain the state across different user interfaces. (We will look at exactly how to implement such functionality in Chapter 8.)
d. Changing the set of functionality supported by the various user interfaces becomes significantly easier. To support a piece of functionality supported by the generic user interface, all we need to do is to add the corresponding specialization features to the components that specialize the generic user interfaces.

It is also crucial to understand the antipattern [Brown et al. 1998]. You will be reminded of this time and time again in this text and elsewhere. There is no one solution to all problems or even all problems of the same type, in our case the mobile application development problem. Assess the needs of the application user, the available budget, and all other consideration before choosing an architectural solution to implement. It is very possible that your system may not require developing a generic user interface. Unusual performance requirements, the static nature of the application, the required implementation of a restricted set of devices, or a variety of other factors may justify sticking with the model of developing a monolithic user interface layer. Figure 5.1 shows one way of layering user interfaces on the top of a generic user interface layer.

Now, let us look at some of the factors involved in implementing a system that utilizes a generic user interface.

5.3.1 Binding and Specialization of Generic User Interfaces

It should be obvious that, at some point in the process of rendering a user interface, the generic interface has to be specialized to the specific intended user interface. The specialization process could include user settings, device settings, discovery of available channels, QOS of the network, and many other factors. In any case, a binding process has to take place between the components that produce the generic user interfaces and the components that specialize in the generic interfaces.

This binding can be done at run time for all user interfaces; alternatively, what binding is possible to do at compile time may be done then and the rest done at run time.

Run-time binding, for example, can be done by taking an instance of a generic user interface and then generalizing that instance, in its entirety, using the specialization components. This could be done through use of XSLT or similar transformation technologies but is not limited to such. Run-time binding, as you may guess, can be resource expensive.

There are a number of factors that must be considered when designing a system this way:

1. *Performance*: As a rule of thumb, layering software and performance are inversely proportional. The key here is to first evaluate the performance needs of the users and then to see what the cost of each additional layer is. The extreme case is when every microsecond counts. In these cases, a tightly coupled software system that takes advantage of every time-saving trick in the book may be the best choice. But, remember Moore's Law and recognize that hardware is always getting faster and cheaper. One or two percent performance improvement is negligible almost all the time. Run-time binding is at the other end of the spectrum. We can bind all the components and code together at run time. This gives us the most flexibility and the most elegant software design. But then, we always have to ask whether this prohibits proper performance when the number of users is at its peak.
2. *Development Process*: So, who develops the generic user interface and who develops the components that specialize it? The development processes for client–server and Web applications have had a few years to mature. So, today, a typical development team includes business analysts who gather the requirements, graphic and voice user interface designers who design the look-and-feel of the system, application developers who build the components that represent the business logic to be performed by the system, and database engineers who design the persistence layer. Obviously, there are many others with crucial roles in the delivery of a software product, but those roles lie outside of our current concern. Obviously, this model does not work for a system that needs to render multiple types of user interfaces. We will look at what sort of development team and process works for mobile applications in Chapters 15–18. The key for now is to understand the cost of changing the development process. For example, building consistency across multiple user interfaces requires proper documentation and communication among the developers who build the components to specialize the generic user interfaces.
3. *Where the Various Components Reside:* Probably the most important aspect of the design of a system that uses generic user interfaces is how the work is distributed among the servers, clients, or peers. Regardless of the type of architecture selected to implement distribution of the application, if the application is mobile, the chances are that it is distributed. In traditional Web development the server performed calculations, maintained state, stored data, and executed a variety of other tasks. Then, the server produced some markup language such as HTML,

perhaps with some mixture of a client-side scripting language in there (such as JavaScript), and shipped it to a client that basically just rendered this markup. There are techniques (e.g., by using hidden fields) that allow the client to hold pseudo-state.

An important factor to keep in mind while designing systems with generic user interfaces is the location where the specialization is done. In our case, do mobile devices specialize these generic interfaces themselves? Or does the server specialize them and send them to the client? Does the server maintain all states as the user navigates through the application (which is the model used with most Web applications)? Or should the mobile client be smarter, because network connectivity is not guaranteed, and hold some state in the container that specializes the user interface? There are no cookie-cutter answers to any of these questions. But, the questions must be asked and answered after careful consideration of system requirements. For binding the specialization components and the generic interface the question to answer is how the task is divided among the various components of the system.

So, our goal is going to be to build a generic user interface on top of an application and specialize it. We may render the final user interface centrally on some server or allow the mobile devices themselves to render them. We will look at how to do both of these later. To make some of these design decisions, we have to understand mobile user interfaces a bit more. To do this, let us take a step back and look at the components that make up a user interface.

To separate those elements of the user interface that can be made generic from those that are specific to various user interface types, we first have to outline what those elements are. So, let us look at the various things that make up a user interface and the way we interact with them.

5.3.2 The Elements of the User Interface

For us to understand how to layer the user interfaces for mobile applications, we need to understand some taxonomy (organized categorization and classification) of the components that make up the user interface and all of those elements, that we can qualify or quantify, and that describe the interactions of the user with the user interface.

User interfaces can be defined from several perspectives, none of which is inherently superior to the others. Some analyze user interfaces from a look-and-feel perspective, some look at them as a component in a communication system between humans and computers, and yet others look at the various functions that they (user interfaces) and their components perform. We will try to take a mixture of all of these approaches as applicable to developing mobile applications. First, let us look at channels: the different ways that humans and computers can connect.

Channels

In the generic context of communication systems, a channel *is the medium through which the sender and the receiver of a message communicate*. In this way, a user interface that uses multiple media such as sound, text, and video are often referred

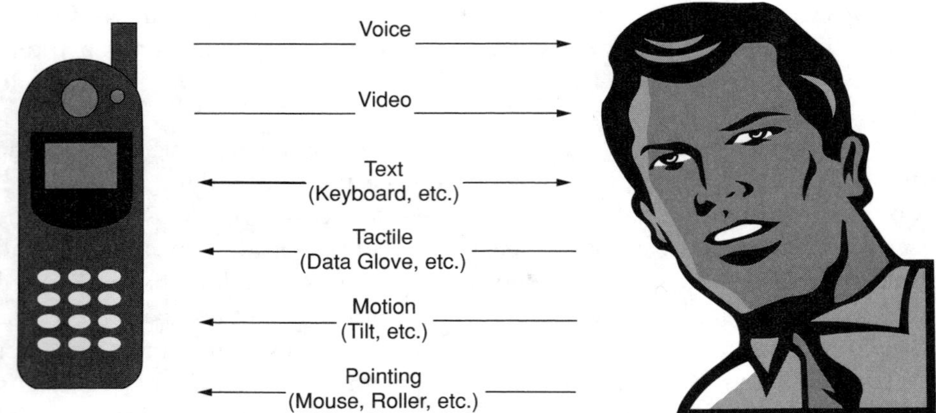

FIGURE 5.2. Channels: Tunnels of Communication between Humans and Computers.

to as *multichannel* interfaces as each type of medium requires its own channel. In the computing industry, this definition has also been extended to include presenting the same content, particularly text content, in multiple formats for multiple devices. Because various devices may render the same textual content in different ways, with a bit of a reach, we can say that each type of rendered text is part of the channel that sends messages from the system to the user. For example, the channel through which audio is communicated may be composed of a microphone and speakers. The channel through which text is communicated may include a keyboard, a mouse, and a monitor (see Figure 5.2). For our purposes, we will use the term multichannel to include both channels used by different senses and channels representing different types of interactions used by the same sense.

Though we will refer to channels as media that allow messages to be sent from the user to the system and from the system to the user, we can also define *input channels* and *output channels*. Input channels provide a mechanism for the user to send messages to the system. Output channels provide a mechanism for the system to send messages to the user. Once again, in the context of this book, we will refer to channels as mechanisms that can deliver messages from the user to the system and from the system to the user. Unless specifically specified, a channel, with our definition, is composed of one or many input channels and one or many output channels. ECMA defines input/output devices to be a physical mediator between the user and the system [ECMA TR-61 1992]. Though this ECMA document was intended to address visual user interfaces, this definition can also be applied to other user interface types such as voice.

Application development paradigms utilize a single type of channel for communicating with the user. For example, a call center application is built around a voice user interface and a voice channel. A Web application, in contrast, is built with a GUI in mind with a text channel. Some Web applications also provide other visual output channels, but most only support text for both input and output channels to the user. As we discussed earlier, the optimal mobile application uses the optimal user interface based on the condition of the user—location of the

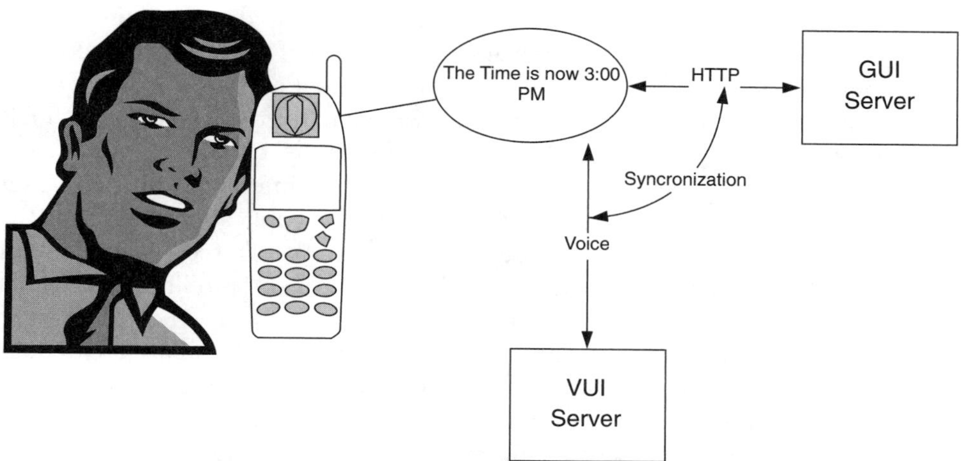

FIGURE 5.3. Multichannel Interface Systems.

user, the device the user may be using, the other tasks the user may be performing, and other mobile human factors with which we must concern ourselves. So, it is fair to assume that when developing effective mobile applications, we are almost always designing *multichannel user interfaces* (see Figure 5.3). We need to select the appropriate user interface based on the mobile condition of the user; therefore, selection and use of channels is a big part of designing a mobile application user interface.

This complicates the design of mobile applications by a factor of *n*, with *n* being the number of channels being used for a given application. Because the infrastructure supporting the rendition of each channel is probably vastly different and independent of all other channels—for example, a speaker is used to render voice whereas a monitor is used to render HTML Web pages and a small display is typically used to display WML pages—an entirely new set of concerns arises in creating a suitable solution. Namely, those concerns are as follows:

1. *Interchannel Synchronization*: The temporal aspects of the content being rendered by each channel, such as latency, will depend on the properties of the channel itself. However, we need to add additional control mechanisms to make sure that the content being rendered by each channel is synchronized with the others. For example, if there is audio content accompanying some text and video, a given sound clip must be played when the accompanying piece of text and video are being shown. These control mechanisms must be supported by the channel, the software protocols supporting the channels, and the applications using the channels. We will discuss this problem in more detail in Chapter 8. Meanwhile, for such synchronization to be possible, the generic user interface must be designed so that these temporal concerns are taken into account. So, whatever generic user interface we design either has to take into consideration these requirements or needs to allow other layers of software and components to implement such functionality without placing any restrictions on them.

2. *Customized Distribution*: The application must be able to distribute the content to be presented to the user through any combination of the channels supported by the devices required for the application. Treatment of the workflow is much the same: Workflow must be dynamically adapted to the user interface channels available and preferred by the user. For example, let us take an application that must be supported both through a voice user interface and a text user interface. If the user has set the device on mute, the application must have the ability to provide text input and output channels. Access to data and content may even be customized (or specialized) for each user's profile and personal preferences.
3. *Decoupling Different Layers of Presentation Logic*: There are many techniques intended to separate presentation and business logic, such as implementing the model-view-controller pattern [Gamma et al. 1995]. Even with frameworks using tag libraries such as Struts for Java developers, layer upon layer is added, causing exponential code base explosion as well as architecture complexity. Much of what we see today in the way of separation of presentation and business logic still leaves the separation of different types of presentation logic untreated. For example, validation of the user input to the system is intermingled with the logic for placement of elements on the screen in most user interfaces. Because of this, multichannel development is nearly completely disregarded in developing the user interface for typical software applications. Once again, because most applications are designed and developed with one particular user interface in mind, the design and implementation includes no decoupling between the various layers of the user interface that are inherently different and orthogonal in functionality. In this chapter we will look at some techniques that allow us to render generic user interfaces that can be handled, in a loosely coupled manner, by another layer of software that handles the decoupling of various layers of presentation logic.

All of these three fundamental differences between multichannel and single-channel user interface development must be implemented with the proper distributed computing model in mind for a particular application. Distribution of this added functionality among the various components of the systems, clients, servers, peers, etc. is a big part of designing multichannel user interfaces. We will look at synchronization issues with great detail in Chapter 11 and customized distribution of content and workflow spread throughout the next three chapters. Our focus in this chapter is on designing user interfaces that have abstracted various parts of presentation logic into highly decoupled layers. Now, let us look at different types of channels to get a better insight into what is possible so that we can factor commonalities between channels into layers of abstraction.

Channel Types

It is not possible to outline a comprehensive list of channel types, and devices that support them, that enable communication between machines and human beings. After all, there are new ones popping up every day, there are old ones that lend themselves to obsolescence, and there are channels that lend themselves only to a particular domain (for example, joysticks are typically only used for video games, simulation programs, or systems involving directing some sort of physical motion). These domain-specific channels are typically not used for a broad set of applications. Here we will only try to outline a subset of the most popular device types, each supporting a unique type of channel, being used in mobile systems today.

1. *Keyboards and Monitors* (*Text Entry and GUI Display*): Keyboards and monitors are perhaps the two most popular user interface mechanisms to any computing system. Keyboards are basically used to enter text that may be behavioral in nature (commands such as save, print, etc.) or data (such as typing in your user name and password). Keyboards remain the most popular mechanism to send messages to computing systems because they let us use a language, the primary form of communication between human beings, in its textual written form, to communicate with the system. Monitors provide a text channel. Monitors can also serve as an output channel for other visuals such as images and video. Though keyboards can be used to create images (e.g., by drawing widgets using the arrow keys), they are not very useful in creating visuals other than pure text. So a combination of keyboard and monitor makes an effective text-based channel. Typically the monitor's ability to provide other visual output channels are taken advantage of as well.
2. *Touch-Screens* (*Touch Entry and GUI Display*): Touch-screens have been around for a long time. In many environments such as manufacturing environments or mobile applications, a keyboard, a mouse, and other extraneous devices may not be suitable. They may be too cumbersome to use or be damaged too frequently because of dust, motion, or other environmental conditions. Touch-screens allow the user to touch pressure-sensitive screens to send messages to the system. They are particularly popular with kiosks. Touch-screens allow the monitor to be used as both an input and an output channel. However, they lend themselves more to command-type interactions (to be discussed in the next section) than text entry. Text entry is possible but fairly difficult.
3. *Stylus* (*Handwriting Recognition and Touch Entry*): The stylus is a penlike device used to write on a screen or press buttons on a screen. The stylus effectively functions as a keyboard and a mouse combined into one. Some devices such as the Palm even support some way of scribing text onto the screen of the device, thereby providing an arguably more user friendly input mechanism than the keyboard (but whether or not typing or writing is more efficient may be subjective to the user). The stylus is a very effective device for mobile environments. The stylus is light and enables multiple input channels to the same device. The stylus provides only an input channel. The output channel accompanying the stylus, once again, is typically some sort of a visual screen. The stylus can also be categorized as one of the many tools used to perform handwriting recognition. Other devices such as scanners can be used to allow handwriting as the input to the system.

4. *Telephone (Voice Recognition)*: The telephone is the most pervasive electronic communication device. Voice channels take advantage of our ability to be able to understand speech and hear sounds. Most of today's computer systems are driven either through a voice user interface or a GUI. The majority of voice user interfaces are call centers designed for some command and control interface for the telephone. The telephone provides a symmetric channel: input channel of voice and output channel of voice. The telephone provides one of the most ideal, if not the most ideal, user interface for the mobile user. Even if the user does not have his or her own device (mobile phone), it is almost always possible to find a pay phone somewhere nearby.
5. *Device Motion (Entry by Positioning)*: The position and orientation of the device itself can be used as an input mechanism. For example, to scroll down a page on the display of a device, the user can tilt the device slightly. The speed of scrolling may be dependent on the angle of the device and the speed at which it is rotated. The *Itsy*, a prototype device by Compaq Computer Co., is one of the first devices to take advantage of the motion and placement of the device itself as a user interface. Reading user input based on the physical condition of the device can be both a problem and a problem solver for mobile applications. While the mobile user is moving around, this motion can be used as an interface without user intervention; this provides for the ultimate convenience. At the same time, the user's motion may have a considerable amount of noise (movements that create errors and should not be taken into account by the device). Today, device motion and condition is more a research area than one used in commercial development. However, it holds promise as a user interface channel of choice by the mobile developers. Device motion is typically also only an input channel; ways to communicate messages to the user using the motion of the device itself have yet to be conceived.
6. *Dataglove (Entry through Touch)* [Dix et al. 1998]: As the name suggests, this is a glove that, when worn, can be used as a data entry device. This device is now used mostly in research environments, but it has made advances in performance and reliability during the past few years, making it more and more viable commercially. Typical use of this device is in virtual reality environments. Such environments try to use all the possible channels of input that are second nature to humans, thereby invoking the word "immersive" to describe the desired user interfaces.
7. *Printed Paper and Other Materials (Output Text and Graphics)*: In the early days of computing, paper was the main method of interfacing with computing systems. If I had a penny for every time I heard stories about how people carried stacks of cards to mainframes, I would be a millionaire! When scanners became commercially viable, many predicted the demise of paper. But, paper prevailed and its consumption has multiplied since the popularization of PCs and personal printers. Paper is easier on the eyes than a computer screen and provides us with a comforting way of reading data. Today, paper is used for both input and output: input in the form of scanning data into computers and output in the form of printing data for later use. Companies such as Xerox are also working on "electronic paper." Such devices may prove to be a breakthrough for mobile

computing as they will make it feasible for you to write things on the same device that stores the contents of several reference books that you may need. Imagine if you could get rid of all the sticky pads in your office, all of the books on your bookshelf, and all of the notebooks you write in. However, this "electronic paper" will probably never replace regular paper. Rather, it will become yet another complementary mechanism to paper.

As mentioned earlier, channels convey messages both ways from the user to the user interface and from the user interface to the user. Although a keyboard is used to enter data into a system, the keyboard itself is not used to send messages back to the user. The monitor is the device used to send messages back to the user. But, we defined channels as media that allow two-way communication: messages from a user to the system and messages from a system to the user. Therefore, the keyboard and monitor combine to make a channel. We call these types of channels *asymmetric channels*. Most user interface channels are asymmetric: Messages from the user are sent to the system using a different mechanism than the one that enables the system to receive messages from a user. Our eyes give us the largest amount of bandwidth, so the output of most systems—the way we receive messages from computing systems—are typically directed toward our visual senses using some sort of a screen.

Symmetric channels are seldom used in computing today. Symmetric channels allow the user to send messages into the system through the same mechanism as it receives messages from the system. An example of a symmetric channel is a system that moves the cursor on the screen to the place where the user's eyes are focused on. Voice-based systems typically offer the most popular form of symmetric channels, whether using PSTN (Publicly Switched Telephony Network) or packet switch networks. The same device is typically used for speaking and hearing.

The *temporal and spatial* properties of the channel are also very crucial. *The temporal properties of channels are those that define the limitations of the channel, on the messages being exchanged between the user and the system, with respect to time*. For example, a voice user interface that does not allow barge-in limits the messages to be sequential in time: The system sends a message to the user and the user has to wait for that message to arrive and finish playing before responding. Another spatial property of a voice channel may be the maximum number of words per minute per message. Temporal properties also apply to GUIs as the order, in time, in which various components appear and messages can be sent to the system determines much of the user interface functionality. Some channels allow free flow of information back and forth between the user and the system. For example, a PSTN channel established using a phone allows a user to talk with the system. While the system is reading some information back to the user, the user may "barge-in" and talk right over the information that is being put out by the system. All such factors are defined by the constraining factors of the user interface channel.

Spatial properties of channels are determined by the set of limitations that the channel places on the way different components are physically arranged on the user interface. For example, a particular GUI channel may allow overlay and transparency

SIDE DISCUSSION 5.1

Designing a GUI without Being Influenced by Back-end Implementations

One of the typical mistakes made today in designing software with GUIs or VUIs (Voice User Interfaces) is that user interfaces are designed with a high dependency on back-end transaction boundaries and data models. It is important to keep in mind, while designing any computing system, that if a system has a user interface, it is perhaps the single most important part of the system. Also, it is crucial to keep in mind that user interfaces should be more behavioral than data-oriented. Although data entry and retrieval are very important parts of the interactions between the user and the system, the bulk of the interactions between a user and a system are behavioral or "procedural." It is also typical that, as one moves from the front end of a system (the user interface) to the back end of a system (the database), one moves from a behavioral-driven perspective to a data-driven perspective. Though the two need to be married at some point, it is crucial that the user interface design not be tainted by the data-model design and the data-model not be tainted by the user interface.

of several different windows. In the case of mobile applications, the layout of the components on the user interface is highly dependent on the type of user interface channel as small devices typically have smaller user interfaces with less capabilities. A theoretical discussion of temporal and spatial properties of interactive user interfaces is not one that we can tackle in this text as our focus is on developing mobile applications. However, Shipman, Marshal, and Moran offer a brief and comprehensive look at spatial properties of user interfaces [Shipman, Marshal, and Moran 1995] and Kutar, Nehaniv, and Britton do the same for temporal properties of user interfaces [Kutar, Nehaniv, and Britton 2001]. As we introduce various concepts relating to building user interfaces for mobile applications, if you find yourself questioning some of the materials presented as facts in this text, you may want to refer to these two papers as well as other references listed.

Although the temporal and spatial properties of the channel itself are typically not a central consideration of the user interface or user interaction design, the limitations of the channel creates the constraining boundaries that determine the temporal and spatial properties of interactions, components, and other elements of user interfaces of computing systems. A key in developing mobile applications is to design them so that the functionality they offer is not tightly coupled to any particular user interface channel. This enables us to not only adapt to new user interface technologies as they become possible but also to easily build multichannel user interfaces that may take advantage of multiple types of channels simultaneously.

In the future, we will probably discover how to take advantage of some of our other senses in communicating with computers. For example, user interfaces that effectively take advantage of our sense of smell have not been designed yet. Neither do we use our sense of taste to communicate with computers. We may never have systems that use our taste or smell senses to communicate with computers. But, one thing is for certain: We will have user interfaces that we have yet to even think of and they will change computing, mobile or not, in a major way. So, once again, the reader should be reminded that the concepts that we emphasize in this chapter and the rest of this book are just that: concepts. Applying the concepts to new tools should prove to be trivial.

Interactions

We have looked at channels as the medium that deliver messages between the user and the computing system. These messages create dialogues [ECMA TR-61 1992], or interactions, between the user and the system. In this text, we will refer to a group of messages exchanged between the user and the system as *interactions* or *dialogues*. There are a large variety of interaction types. Once again, to understand the types of interactions between the system and the user, we need to decompose what an interaction is and understand the types of elements that make up the interactions.

Interactions, as mentioned, are composed of messages being passed back and forth between the user and the system. The messages being sent can take *atomic* or *composite* forms. Although these terms are typically used to describe data types in computing, the same concept may be applied to messages being exchanged between the user and the system. An atomic message is one that cannot be decomposed into parts that have meaning on their own. A composite message is a message made of two or more atomic messages, each having a complete meaning by themselves; yet, the meaning of a composite message may be greater than the sum of its parts. We interchangeably, when better suited for the context, refer to messages as interaction elements as they are the parts that make up interactions.

In the same way, interactions can be composite or atomic. An atomic interaction is made up of one message being sent from the user to the system, or from the system to the user, possibly accompanied by a response message from the respective counterpart. Also, atomic interactions may not be decomposed to other interactions that have meaning on their own. In a GUI environment, you can think of an atomic interaction as typing in "February 30" for the date field, thereby causing the system to pop up a window that says "This is an invalid date. Please enter another one." The single action done by the user—typing in the date—causes a single response from the system. Atomic interactions do not require that a response exists. For example, if the date is typed in as "February 28", and the system validates this date to be valid, the user may simply be allowed to continue on. *Composite interactions are those interactions that may be made up of two or more interactions that are meaningful on their own.* Let us look at an example.

Using a voice user interface, a user is prompted for his or her name by a prompt of "Please state your first name." The user's response is "Phillip." The prompt and the response to the prompt, together, comprise an atomic interaction. Neither the prompt nor the response to the prompt is meaningful on its own. However, if a user is prompted for his or her first name and last name by a prompt of "Please state your first and last name, for example Dave Seleno" and the response is "Phillip Lindsay," a composite interaction has taken place. This is because both the prompt

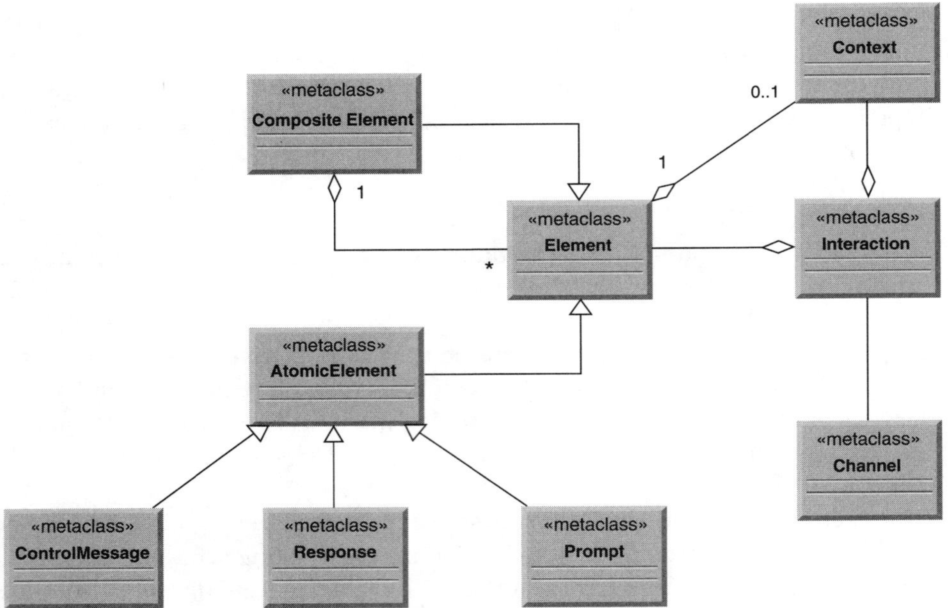

FIGURE 5.4. Atomic and Composite Interactions.

and the response to the prompt may be decomposed into other atomic or composite transactions. In this particular case, there could be two distinct interactions, one asking the user for his or her first name and the other asking the user for his or her last name.

In the context of this book, we will refer to interactions, or dialogues, as communication between the user and the system that involves one or more messages from both participants. In those cases where there is an interaction composed of only one atomic message, we will simply refer to the message. The UML class diagram in Figure 5.4 shows one possible meta-model to represent these relationships, mentioned here, among some of the elementary particles that make up user interfaces.

It is important to note that user interface interactions are not the same thing as back-end business logic transactions. A back-end process with transaction boundaries may specify that a user may not purchase an item without a valid credit card number. Transactions may be started, committed, rolled back, and ended. None of these concepts apply to interactions. Interactions merely define how the user communicates with the user interface of the computing system.

Although ECMA's taxonomy does not address the composite or atomic nature of messages and interactions, it has an orthogonal taxonomy of different types of dialogues by separating them into *menus, languages, direct manipulation*, and *form filling*. We will use this categorization as well. Higher level organization of the atomic messages can also help us in distinguishing the building blocks of user interface interactions. Let us look at these first.

Interaction Elements

The messages being exchanged between a user and the system during an interaction can be categorized by the type of task invoked by the recipient, the system or the person, when the recipient receives the message. In this text, we will recognize three types of interaction elements: control elements, prompts, and responses. Let us start with control elements.

Control Messages

Control messages control the flow of the application or cause the application to begin some process that has no user interface. Do not mistake these with so-called form controls. Control messages are messages sent from one actor to another (user to system in this case) whereas form controls are widgets on a given form. An example of a control message is clicking to close a window in a window-based GUI such as Microsoft Windows or X-Windows and causing the application to terminate. Another example of a control message is clicking the submit button on an HTML form to send all of the fields filled out by a user to an HTTP server. Both of these are examples of control of the application flow, the first terminating the application and the second moving the application to the next dialogue or interaction. Control messages can also cause a process that has no user interface byproducts, for example, pressing a button that starts a back-end batch job to process some data.

Control messages are often the starting point and ending point of an application user interface. *Workflow* is the automation of a business process, in whole or part, during which documents, information, or tasks are passed from one participant to another for action, according to a set of procedural rules [WFMC and Fisher 2000]. There is typically a direct linear relationship between the workflow of an application and control messages in an application: The control messages of the user interface typically are the markers between the different stages in the workflow. Workflow is typically extremely important to designing user interfaces, and although our focus in this text is not on workflow, it is important to know the close tie between user interfaces and workflow. Automation of business processes, managing documents, information, or tasks, as the WFMC guide specifies, is typically done through a user interface that dynamically adapts to the user's actions. Though all of the messages that the user sends to the application affect the workflow to some degree, control messages have the biggest effect.

Therefore, one of our challenges becomes creating efficient programmatic structures and algorithms that decrease the dependency of workflow on the specific type of device on which the application user interface is rendered. Because the lynchpins in the workflow are the control messages, the most important thing we need to keep in mind to design and implement generic user interfaces is to keep the flow of the application, controlled by these messages, independent of the specific user interfaces.

Control messages can also be thought of as markers between different states of the user interface. For example, the user may click on a button when finished filling out a block of widgets that allow data entry of the user's address. This may cause navigation to the next page (the next stage of workflow), jumping to another section of the page, or some other response by the system. Regardless of which happens, the control message sent by the user to indicate that he or she is finished filling out his or her address indicates the end of the address filling state and the beginning of whatever state follows.

Besides controlling the flow of an application, the users typically input some raw data for processing into the application. Prompts are the way the application tells the user when it is ready to receive this input and in what form it needs the data.

Prompts

Prompts are system requests for input by the user. We can also refer to the actual system query from the user as *a prompt*. Regardless of the input channel used to interact with the computing system, the computing system uses prompts to give the user some information about a piece of information it is looking for. In the last section, we mentioned an example of a simple prompt "What is your first name." Note that this prompt is valid regardless of the channel that it is being used through. Whether the system prompts a user who is on the phone to say his or her first name or a user who is using a PC monitor to interact with an application is prompted for a first name, the prompt asks for the same piece of information to continue the flow of the application: the user's first name.

Prompts, as with other pieces of information, may be designed generically and then transformed to the specific user interface channel. There may also be a dependency on the *context* of use of the prompt. We will introduce the concept of contexts later in this chapter. The context of a prompt is always known: The application developer always knows why the prompt is being presented to the user. Therefore, there is no such thing as an invalid prompt in the absence of programmatic bugs. However, prompts can be *ambiguous* depending on the context in which they are being used and the condition of the user. We will discuss ambiguity along with contexts.

A prompt is typically presented to look for a response from the user. Let us look at responses, another element in user interface interactions between users and computing systems.

Responses

There are two types of responses: system responses and user responses. The meaning of a *response* is simple to infer from the word used: It is the user input given to the system to satisfy what the prompt requests by the system. Whereas prompts are more deterministic by nature—we program them so we know how they are going to act, what they will look like, what they will sound like, etc.—responses are much less deterministic. For example, the user may not speak English at all and respond with simple silence to the "What is your name" prompt. The user may misunderstand the meaning of a given prompt or not understand it at all, causing a response that is not only incorrect but also irrelevant to whatever context within which the prompt may have been posed.

Interaction Types

We have already defined atomic and composite interactions. This categorization is based on the makeup of the interaction. But, we can categorize interactions in other ways too. We do this so that we may come up with some qualitative rules for the interactions allowed by the user interface of an application. Different types of interactions may be suitable for different applications. Although deciding what types of interactions best fit a particular user interface depends on the customer specifications and the user interface designers, our main goal here is to outline the different interaction types.

Commands

The simplest form of interacting with a system is through a predefined list of commands. The DOS or UNIX command lines are such examples. Though most systems provide some sort of help, the user must know what are possible commands and how they are used. Commands are applicable to various types of interfaces. A command can be specified by the number of times you press a button on a game pad, the way you move the gaming joystick, the text you type at a system prompt, or a "keyword" voice command given to a system. Command-based interactions are typically straightforward to implement. User interfaces that use command-based interactions normally perform well. Unfortunately, although command-based user interfaces work well for expert users, they are less ideal for novice or intermediate users. The user has to remember the commands and their use (in what sequence they can be used, what arguments they may take, etc.).

Command-based interactions are used less and less with stationary applications because sophisticated GUIs provide advanced features that obviate the need for users to know a list of commands. However, surprisingly, command-based interfaces are relatively useful for mobile applications. Advanced mobile users are trying to achieve their computing tasks fairly quickly without listening or looking at a list of options. Commands can also be abbreviated so that limited interfaces such as the number pad on a telephone can be used more efficiently. For the novice mobile user, though, command-based interactions are not very desirable. An ideal mobile user interface may give the user the option of selecting which to use: a user interface that uses command-based interactions heavily or one that does not.

Menus

Menus allow selection of one or more options presented by the user interface. Menus are similar to commands in that they allow a predefined and limited list of actions to be taken, but they are different in that they always present the user with possible choices. Menus are commonplace in GUIs, particularly in WIMP (Windows, Icons, Menus, and Pointers) environments, which rely on them as the basic way of interacting with the user. Menus are also popular with VUIs where the user is presented with a set of options to select from.

Menus are an advancement on command-only interactions, but they have their own set of limitations. Menus do not work well when there are many options to select from. The user typically does not want to deal with a menu that has 200 items under each main item or hear a list of 200 choices on the voice user interface. Of course, the way most developers try to alleviate this problem is by creating submenus that represent some treelike categorization of items. However, this gives rise to another set of problems. First, there may not be an obvious categorization of the options. In fact, most of the time, there are actually too many different ways of categorizing the same information. For example, if we want to present a menu-driven method of presenting all the operating system commands, we can divide them by whether they have I/O functionality or not (and then subcategorize from there) or by whether they perform local operations or network-based operations. The way the application may organize the menus and submenus could be obvious to one user whereas it could boggle the mind of another. Finally, if the menu/submenu nesting is too deep, the navigation sequence becomes very long. We have all had the nightmarish experience of dealing with VUIs that require listening to several different menus and punching in a dual tone multifrequencey (DTMF) number after each menu is presented only to find out that we end up at the wrong place and, frustrated, have to "zero-out" to an operator by pressing 0.

Menus are very useful in navigating through the application. Creating good menus and submenus requires a thorough understanding of the application domain. Also, it is crucial that menus across different user interfaces follow the same categorization scheme in presenting the user with the various options. Menus are particularly tricky when one is developing generic user interfaces. This is because, although specialization of a list of items to a particular user interface may render a good interface, specialization to another particular user interface may render an unusable interface. For example, a menu, several levels deep, that allows you to select a particular bank account in HTML may be too long with a voice user interface and too cumbersome through a WAP device. So, when we create user interface generic menus, we need to apply the following principles:

1. Provide several ways of categorizing the menu trees and allow the components that specialize the interface to select which one they need (at run time or compile time).
2. Make the menus as shallow as possible. Though too many submenus are not desirable, the alternative of having a long list may be worse for some user interfaces such as voice or small text displays on handheld devices. The users typically cannot remember a list longer than a few choices and the device may not have enough space or memory to render a long list of choices. However, if a component that specializes the generic interface wants to combine two different menus, it can do so. So, when it comes to mobile applications, break down the menus to submenus of a handful of items (five or less is always a good rule of thumb).
3. Do not overuse or abuse menus! Menus are not good tools for data entry. Provide the users with shortcuts to bypass menus. Tuck the seldom-used options in the menus in some submenu that is out of the way and does not hinder the efficient use of the user interface.

Forms

Forms are a popular medium of communication, not just in computing, but in all aspects of communication. When you apply for a job, you typically have to fill out a form. When applying for a visa to travel to a different country, you have to fill out a form. Forms are everywhere. They are perhaps the most popular method of gathering information from a user. And this is the concept that has given rise to forms on user interfaces.

Though the metaphor of form is most closely associated with a visual form, aural forms are possible as well. Forms simply consist of a group of prompts with required or optional responses. Other than navigation, the system does not do much with the elements of a form until the user is finished filling out the necessary information and then "submits" the form. Submission could be clicking on a button that says "submit" on a Web-based HTML form, pressing the # key on the mobile phone dial pad, or simply terminating the application. Forms are often made of prompt–response pairs. These prompt–response pairs are typically referred to as *form controls.*

Forms present the same complications as menus for mobile applications. Building forms generically, without any look-and-feel information, is a task that XForms standard by W3C tries to tackle. We will look at XForms later in this chapter. XForms specifies a standard way of representing forms in XML without bias to a particular user interface types, but it is the designer's task to figure out what form controls should be put on a particular form and how this form may be rendered with different user interfaces. Once again, for mobile applications, we should try to follow some guidelines:

1. Do not put too many controls on a given form. This makes the form confusing and unusable by some devices or channels.
2. Group the form controls together and identify the groups to the user. For example, when collecting the user information, a group of controls may collect financial information whereas others may collect educational information. Group each together.
3. Provide lots of help and hints if the user is ever confused.

Whereas menus are mostly used for navigation, forms are typically used for data collection. We can achieve both through *natural language*, which allows a mixture of commands and data in the same interaction message.

Natural Language

Natural language is a term most often used in dialogue design of VUIs. However, it applies equally across all different types of channels and modes of user interfaces to computing systems. A natural language-based interaction simply means that you tell the computer what you want it to do as if you were telling a live person. Imagine if you could just type "I want you to open my e-mail tool and delete all of the e-mails from Jos Bergmans" or say "I want to find what restaurant Jos recommended in Amsterdam. Could you search my e-mail and tell me what it was?" These are examples of natural language interactions with computing systems. As you may imagine, natural language-based interactions are extremely attractive, if we can implement them. However, implementing natural language-based user interfaces proves to be extremely difficult because of "ambiguity."

Ambiguity refers to lack of enough "context" (discussed later in this chapter) or information that helps the system understand the user or vice versa. Imagine, for example, that you are trying to design an application that provides the user with a natural language user interface for finding driving directions. The following could be a prompt and response sequence:

Prompt: Welcome. This system provides you with driving directions. Tell me what directions you want.
Response: I want to go home.

The response, obviously, is meaningful, but the system has no way of knowing where "home" is. If the application is designed to parse the text input by the user and match whatever comes after "to go" with some valid address, it would not be able to find an address that matches home. Now, let us assume that the user knows more about what he/she needs to provide the system:

Prompt: Welcome. This system provides you with driving directions. Please say the address of the destination.
Response: 2652 McGaw Avenue.

Once again, we have not provided the system with enough information because there is no information about the city, the zip code, or the country. Let us keep improving the prompt:

Prompt: Welcome. This system provides you with driving directions. Please say the address of the destination starting with the street address, then the city, and then the zip code.
Response: 2652 McGaw Avenue, Irvine, 92660.

Now, we are getting closer. If the system is well designed, it can actually accurately guess the location based on this response. The prompt can still be improved, but you get the point. Natural language responses are used more often in VUI-based systems because it is easier to separate the elements of the prompt and the response than in a GUI and it is no more difficult for the user to interact with such an interface. With a VUI, though, tremendous speed and efficiency is gained if we can implement natural language interactions with good accuracy and speed. We will look at these issues further in Chapter 7, where we look at VUIs in more depth.

Let us take a quick look at what we did to get a more accurate response from the user. First, we made sure that the user gives us an address and not some randomly named location. Then, we made sure that the user included the city and the zip code. We probably should have even asked for the country so that our application may be internationalized easily. Finally, we specified the temporal context (basically the order that the user should say things) of the expected response. Each step reduced "ambiguity" for the user: We narrowed down the things that the user could send to the system as a reasonable and acceptable response. We will discuss various ways of reducing ambiguity, but keep in mind that a good user interface minimizes the amount of ambiguity. This can be done through the use of various types of context, specific prompts, or other methods.

Reducing ambiguity is particularly important for mobile applications where the users' patience and attention span are less than for users of stationary applications. It is also important to reduce ambiguity in a way that can apply to a variety of user interfaces. Each specializing component can add its own set of clarifying content and behavior to the user interface to reduce ambiguity specific to that particular type of user interface.

For now, the important thing is that *any* user interface can use natural language interactions. Therefore, to build a generic user interface to the system, our implementation of a generic user interface needs to take into account natural language interactions. In cases that a given natural language-based interaction may be suitable for one user interface and not the others, the alternative must be provided so that the specialization components can select the most optimal choice.

Mixed Initiative

Mixed initiative, as in the case of natural language, is a terminology typically used in the design of voice user interfaces. However, it too is equally applicable to a variety of user interfaces. Natural language stipulates communication interfaces between humans and computers, and therefore user interface interactions, to be in a way most friendly to humans. Commands, menus, and forms, in contrast, are examples of discrete information units and messages that are more suitable for the way machines work. Mixed initiative is a marriage, or perhaps a compromise, between the two different models.

Whereas humans typically prefer natural language interfaces as they offer the "most natural" way of communicating, machines like commands and menus better. In fact, the most efficient approach is probably a mixture of both. There are many times when the user must be "directed" (thereby the term directed dialogue or directed interactions) in what response may be suitable. Look at our example of driving directions in the previous section. If one person tells another person "I want to go home," the response of the second person is probably going to be "where is home?" Eventually, an address will be required. So, the user interface is better designed if the user is directed to give the right answer to begin with. Menus and commands can help the user navigate to a point that a natural language response to a prompt can be limited by the machine and yet allows the user to efficiently communicate with the system.

We will look at mixed-initiative dialogues more carefully in Chapters 7 and 8. Now that we have gone over the basic channels and interactions, lets see how we can model them using UML. Just remember that UML is not a programming

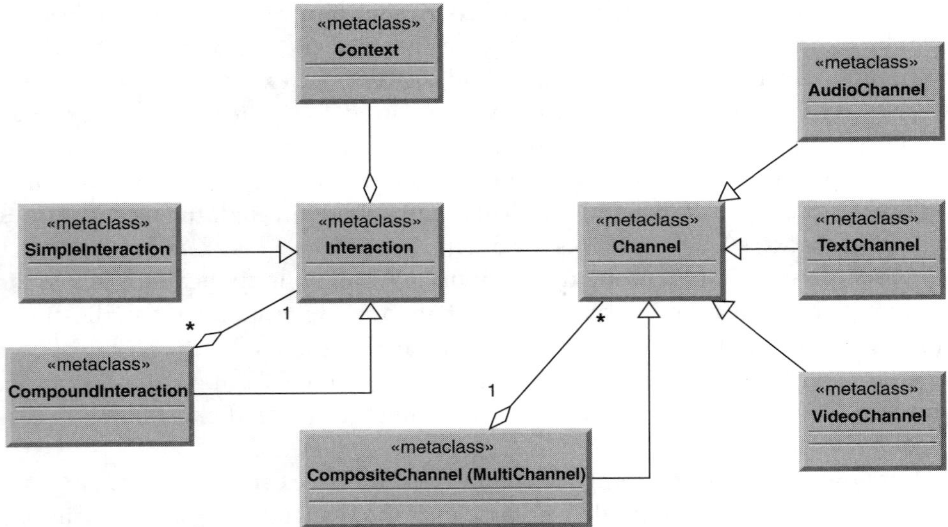

FIGURE 5.5. Metamodel of Interaction Taxonomy.

language. It is a modeling language designed to communicate designs and implementations and to help improve the design and implementation process.

Representing Interactions with UML

Because we will be using UML to communicate the design and functionality of the user interface, we need to know how interactions between the user and the system can be modeled in UML. In Chapter 4, we reviewed the basics of UML. Now we need to put those basics to work. First, let us use class diagrams to model everything that we have said about the things that make up interactions, the relationship between channels and interactions, and contexts. Note that the classes in our diagram are all metaclasses. This is because these are not actual classes that a developer would use in creating an application. Rather, they describe the model for the classes in an application. Such metamodels, as previously discussed in Chapter 4, can be used to determine the semantics of a framework that will allow us to implement the functionality that we need or to simply recognize whether a given framework can accommodate the functionality represented by this metamodel. Figure 5.5 shows the metamodel of some of the user interface components discussed to this point.

Class diagrams, though probably the most popular part of UML, do not really give us the functionality that we need to represent user interfaces. Class diagrams are perfect for representing metamodels as shown in Figure 5.5, the metamodels that are the classes for our objects, or class instances.

Use case diagrams can communicate the general use of the system, but they do not have the detail level needed to represent an interaction between the user and the system. Obviously, use case diagrams are still very much needed as any detailed requirement gathering process that utilizes UML involves creation of use case diagrams that map out the general functionality of the system. All of the other types of UML diagrams can be used for user interface development in one way or another. We will touch upon each one of them when appropriate in this chapter. But, the diagrams that seem to be perfect for representing interactions between the user and the system are, befittingly, the *interaction diagrams*.

An interaction diagram is a temporal representation of user interactions with the system: Individual interactions are represented sequentially in time. There are two forms of interaction diagrams as seen in Chapter 4: collaboration diagrams and sequence diagrams.

State and activity diagrams can also be used to represent generic user interfaces, but as they are largely State Machines, they apply to user interfaces that are state driven. We will consider their use later in this chapter. For now, let us stick with the interaction diagrams and start by looking at how to sequence diagrams to represent user interface dialogues.

Using Sequence Diagrams to Model User Interactions

Perhaps the most important thing to remember in using sequence diagrams to represent user interface dialogues is keeping the messages and stimuli to the most granular possible form so that they correspond to the atomic elements of dialogues. Let us look at our driving directions example once again.

The requirements are listed in Example 5.2.

Example 5.2: Requirements for Driving Directions Mutlichannel System.

1. To allow the user to get driving directions from the system using a PSTN phone call, browser-based HTML interface, and WAP interface.
2. To provide expedient ways of accessing driving directions, regardless of the user interface, for the expert user.
3. To provide help and hints for the novice user.

First, we need to decide what the objects of our sequence diagrams are. We will use an actor to represent the user and a generic object called "system" to represent the user interface of the system. Now, this is an overly simplified generalization of the system.

Next, we can derive some use cases from this. In a real project, we would do this with the potential customers. Example 5.3 gives one possible use case for the Example 5.2 requirements. (We will keep the use case very brief as it is not our focus for this example.)

Example 5.3: Driving Directions Use Cases.

Use Case 1: User calls into the system using a touch-tone phone. The system should present the user with a prompt that allows the user to specify the origin and then the destination. The system then reads the directions back to the user, allowing the user to pause the play back process intermittently.

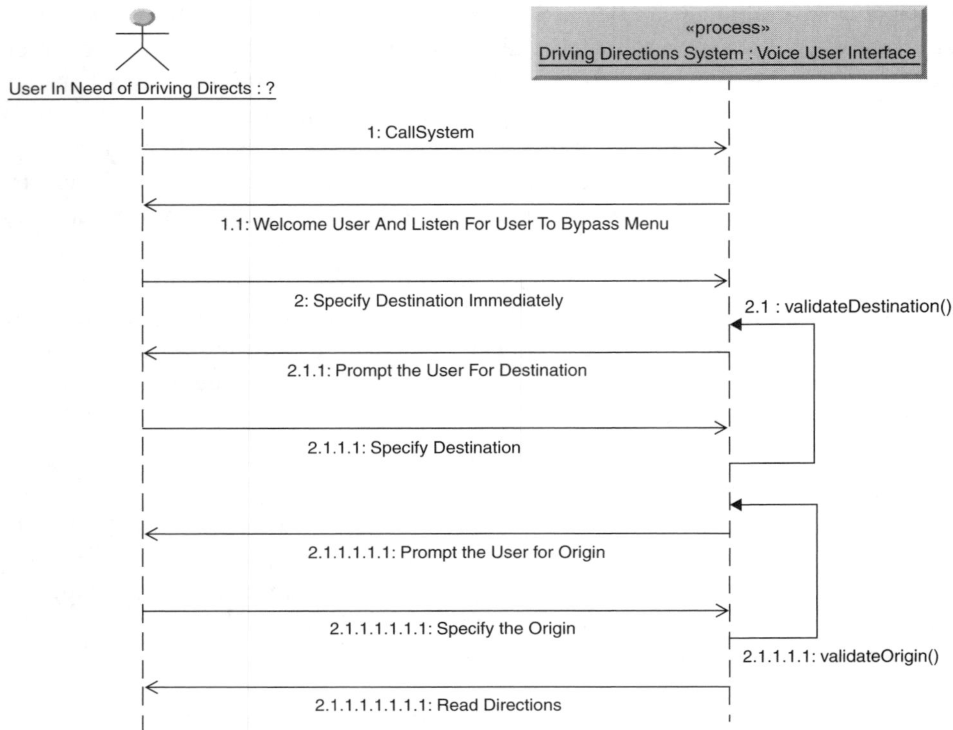

FIGURE 5.6. Sequence Diagram of Basic Interactions for Finding Driving Directions.

It is obvious that at some point we would have to further delve into the details of what "system" is; however, for now, our focus is to document and model the interactions between the user and the system.

Now, let us model the voice interactions in this use case with a sequence diagram.

Figure 5.6 shows the sequence diagram of the basic interactions that happen between the user and the system. You should note that this is a "starter" diagram. This diagram does not implement all the features offered by sequence diagrams to represent interactions, but it is a good point to start. Note the following about the diagram:

1. Sequence diagrams are typically used to indicate the interactions among the components or objects in an object-oriented system. The way we have used the sequence diagram here is perhaps a bit unorthodox. But, remember that UML is a tool and that we can use it in any way we want to improve our development process, provided we abide by the specifications of the standard. So, in this case, we have chosen an actor to represent the user of the system and a classifier to represent the system.
2. We have specified the system to be of the "type" voice user interface. Again, a type as we have used it does not particularly make much sense when thinking in terms of traditional uses of UML. However, we can communicate the semantics of what we want to get across without violating the specifications of the standard.

We could have similar sequence diagrams that represent the interactions of the user with the HTML user interface, Windows-based user interface, or others.
3. Sequence numbers label the interactions going back and forth between the user and the system. These can be of particular importance as they can represent the time sequence in which the interactions happen (temporal arrangement of the interactions).
4. Message 2 terminates with a half arrow. This means that the user can respond to the system asynchronously. The definition of an asynchronous message sent to a user interface varies depending on the type of user interface. In the case of a voice user interface, for example, we can say that asynchronous implies either "barge-in" capability or "universals" or both of them.
5. The destination and the origin are both validated. If either is not valid, the system goes back to the state of prompting the user for the appropriate information.
6. Not all of the messages displayed on the sequence diagram are atomic in nature. For example, interaction message 1.1 can be decomposed into other steps. It is possible to create another sequence diagram that further breaks down the interactions. In the case of 1.1 (Welcome User and Listen for User to Bypass Menu), the system may present the user the welcome message and continue on with an interruptible voice advertisement.
7. We could add notes to the diagram to represent the prompts that the user is presented with for more documentation.
8. Constraints, not shown graphically, could be placed on the user responses to specify the grammars used for recognizing user responses.

This example shows us that the sequence diagram is an effective tool for communicating requirements of a user interface at a high level. We will go further into specific use of sequence diagrams for VUIs in Chapter 7. The sequence diagram in Figure 5.6 specifically addressed VUIs. But, as we have been discussing, we want to build a generic user interface to the system and then specialize it. So, it is only logical to conclude that we want a sequence diagram that represents the user interactions with the system without bias to a particular user interface and then a set of diagrams that build on the generic sequence diagram to specialize this generic user interface. We will discuss the latter, diagrams that are used to specify specialization of the generic user interface, in Chapters 6–8 as we learn how to build graphical, voice, and multichannel mobile user interfaces. Now, let us focus on using UML to represent user interactions with the system in a generic manner without any bias to any particular user interface.

To build a generic interface that allows a user to retrieve driving directions, we recognize three types of dialogues that could take place:

1. *Form-Based Dialogue*: The user may fill out some prompts, presented through some user interface, that specify an origin and a destination. The system then presents the user with the driving directions using the addresses specified by the user (or a good guess that may be appropriate). This is how an HTML Web-based system that renders driving directions works.

2. *Natural Language Dialogue*: The user may give all of the information to the system in one or more natural language interactions. For example, the user may say or write "I need driving directions from home. I'll be going to Orange County Airport."
3. *Mixed-Initiative Dialogue*: The user may interact with the system using a mixture of natural language and form-based interactions. The interactions may be initiated by the user or the system (hence the name mixed initiative as discussed in this chapter). Such a dialogue could be:
   System: Welcome. Where is your destination?
   Response: Orange County Airport, Santa Ana, California.
   System: Where are you coming from?
   Response: Home.
   System: Ok, here are your directions. Please say "pause" if you want me to stop reading you the directions and wait. Say "continue" to start off where you said "pause."
   Let us assume that the system understands "Home" by the virtue of the user's registration process where a home address is provided. Based on this, the system can parse through the two messages sent to provide the user with the proper driving directions.

So, the generic user interface that we design may need to be based on either one of the three possible dialogues outlined here. For simplicity sake, let us take the form-based case. Regardless of the type of user interface, two things must be done in the case of the form-based user interface:

1. A set of prompts must be answered to provide the system with the proper information.
2. The system returns a response based on the prompts and allows the user to pause the response at different stages depending on the viewing mechanism.

Possible fields for item 1 are a destination address and an origin address. To maintain consistency throughout our system, we should probably communicate an address with the user the same way every time. So, it would make sense that we use the same sequence diagram to represent the interactions with an address user interface component as in Figure 5.7.

The diagram in Figure 5.7 can help us accomplish several different things:

1. *Maintaining Consistency*: Because we have outlined how a user will be interacting with the system to enter address information, in a form-based manner, we have created a mechanism to maintain consistency between various user interface implementations of an "address user interface component." For example, if a VUI component is built based on the sequence diagram in Figure 5.7, it will be consistent with an HTML frame that accomplishes the same thing.
2. *Encouraging Components*: By the virtue of representing the user interactions with the system in a generic way, we encourage stitching user interfaces together with components and reusing components. This has two benefits: First,

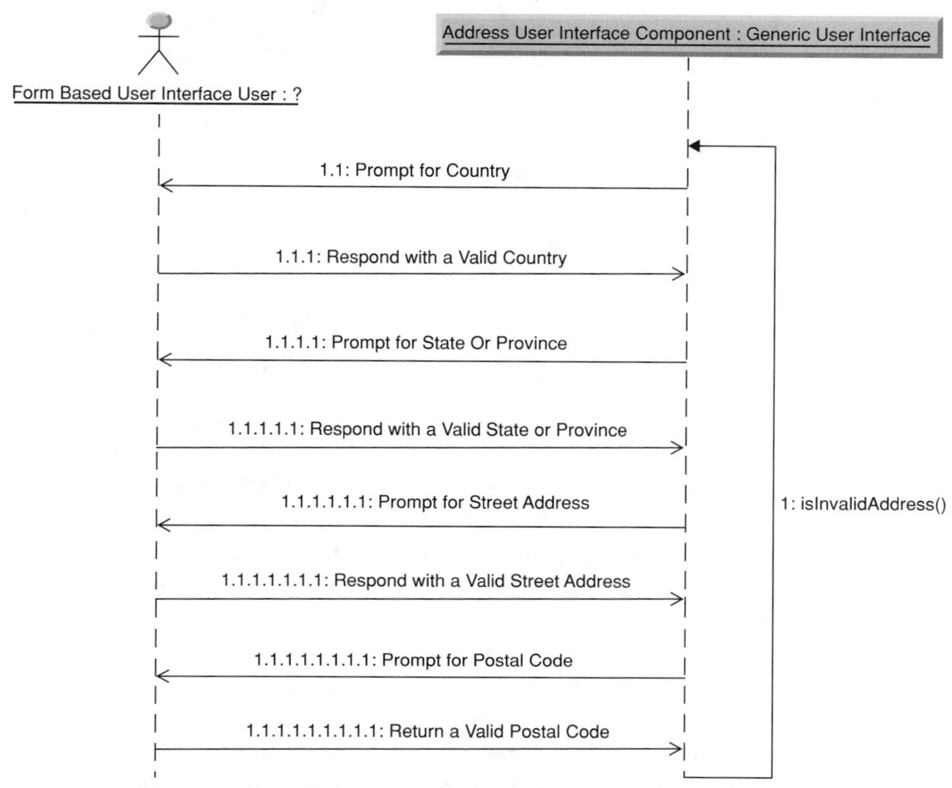

FIGURE 5.7. Representing User Interface Interactions in a User Interface Generic Manner with Sequence Diagrams.

we maintain consistency (as previously mentioned) throughout each type of user interface and across multiple types of interfaces. Second, we are able to reuse the components that specialize the generic user interface components. Figure 5.8 illustrates this. Let us say that we have another generic component that allows the user to fill in personal information such as name, age, etc. We will call this the user information component. Both the address component and the user information component can have accompanying specialization components that allow us to specialize each to a particular type of an interface (such as a voice or Web user interface as shown in 5.8). When we combine these two components to make a registration component, we will need to build more code to specialize this new composite component. But, we can leverage the components that allow us to specialize the elements of the composite components. Using a sequence diagram to represent the interactions with the components allows us to maintain component definitions consistently so that specialization of the generic interface components does not become prohibitively costly.

3. *Designing Documentation*: One of the biggest reasons to use UML is to maintain good documentation to communicate requirements among the managers, the user interface developers, and the application developers. A key purpose of a sequence diagram representing user interface interactions in a generic manner

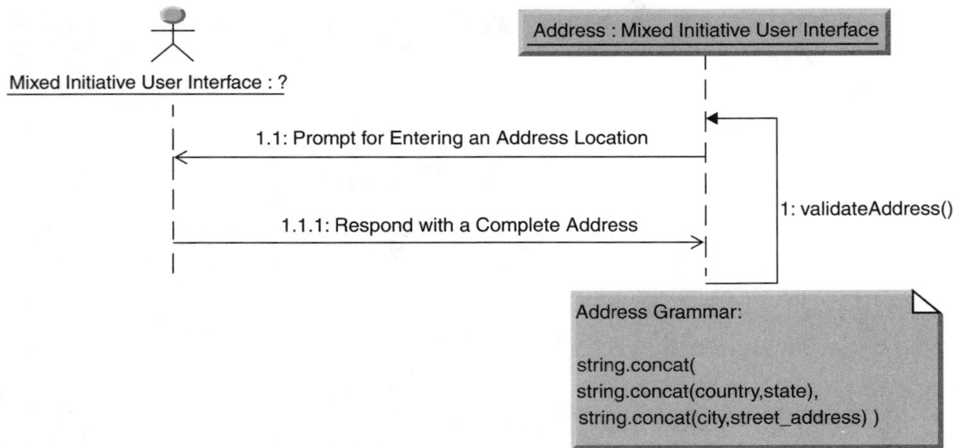

FIGURE 5.8. Using OCL to Model Grammars for Natural Language–Based Grammars.

is to dictate how the components that allow generic interface access to the system should be built and how they are to be used by the components that specialize them.

4. *Specifying Spatial and Temporal Behavior of Components*: Sequence diagrams can be used, as we have here, to specify where and when the user interface elements should be presented to the user. In our example, we have specified that querying the user for the country should come first. If order is implied by temporal (time-dependent) behavior of the component, such as in the voice user interface, this means that the user is prompted for country before being prompted for city. If order is implied by spatial (placement in three-dimensional space) behavior of the component, such as the case of an HTML user interface, this means that the form field asking the user for country appears before (to the left and higher up—in case of English) the form field for city.

In this way, with form-based user interface interactions and components, we can break down every interface to components and subcomponents and then represent the process of filling them out with sequence diagrams.

Although we can use sequence diagrams for natural language and mixed-initiative dialogues too, the problem becomes more complicated because we need to specify patterns of expected responses (grammars and constraints being two of the popular names used for these) from the user.

Natural Language Dialogues, Mixed-Initiative Dialogues, and Sequence Diagrams

Form-based dialogues lend themselves to a very straightforward implementation with UML sequence diagrams. Using the sequence diagrams for natural language and mixed-initiative interactions is a bit tricky. Not only are natural language and mixed-initiative interactions tough to handle inherently, but representing them in diagrams is difficult because there are too many different permutations of possible responses by the user.

To treat this, we can map grammars that define possible user responses to constraints and tagged values. As discussed in Chapter 4, constraints are treated as text in enclosed brackets ({}). OCL gives us a good way of representing constraints for objects. However, using constraints for specifying grammars is a different problem than representing grammars. It is also important to keep in mind that neither OCL nor grammars are designed to be used as programming languages that have features such as control flow.

Let us say that the system simply queries the user for a postal address. In this case, the system may expect a response that is similar to one of the following:

- 16825 Pacific Coast Highway, Huntington Beach, California
- 16825 Pacific Coast Highway
- 16825 Pacific Coast Highway, Huntington Beach
- Huntington Beach, California, 92626

There are obviously even more permutations that could include extraneous characters or words as well as different ordering of placement. Because both the ordering and composition of the elements of the grammar change the definition of the grammar, a grammar made of n elements has an n complexity level.

The user interface components, therefore, may have a difficult time interpreting the user's response as n increases. To keep n to a reasonable number so that a message can be interpreted within a reasonable amount of time, we need to specify two variables in our diagram: the constraints on the response that the user may give the system and the time that it may take to interpret the user's response. Keep in mind, also, that although purely natural language dialogues can be used for small atomic interactions such as obtaining a user's city and country, the number of permutations of the possible user responses prohibits us from building user interface systems that are purely based on natural languages. The problem with a pure natural language interface is not just the excessive processing time that it takes to interpret the message; it is also that the certainty of a correct interpretation decreases as the number of elements in the message increases. In other words, the more words that are in a sentence or phrase, the more complicated it is to understand that sentence or phrase and the more difficult it is to accurately interpret it.

So, practically speaking, although we can have small interactions that are fully based on natural language, complex interactions will have to be mixed initiative (a mixture of directed dialogue—interactions directed by the system—and natural language where the user sends a response back to the system in whatever format he or she wants).

Figure 5.8. shows the equivalent of our address example in a mixed-initiative dialogue using OCL. We have used the UML comments notation to represent the OCL graphically. The tool we are using (Object Domain), as well as most other UML tools, provides a mechanism for OCL entry.

Though we can map grammars to OCL and then use OCL in our UML diagrams, OCL was not designed for this purpose; therefore, it is not the best tool for this purpose. In general, the current UML specifications do not deal with natural language modeling issues.

There are other choices outside the UML specifications that can enhance our diagrams. There are an entire slew of proprietary specifications from a variety of voice system vendors for grammars. Most often, such proprietary standards are not interoperable and therefore tie the design model to a particular vender if used. However, W3C has defined its own set of standards for grammars. We will look at these in further detail in Chapter 8. We recommend using these standards, although, they too have a downfall: They are biased to VUIs. It is important to note that natural language and mixed-initiative interactions are not specific to VUIs. For example, a user could type "Find me a flight to go from Orange County, California, to Moses Lake, Washington, on Christmas Day" as well as say it. Unfortunately, most work currently being done on natural language and mixed-initiative interfaces focuses on VUIs as opposed to treating all interfaces in a generic manner.

W3C, too, does not seem to be immune from this. However, not only is W3C a vendor-neutral organization, but its bias is less toward VUIs than other alternatives. W3C's speech grammar specification, found at http://www.w3c.org/TR/speech-grammar, includes an XML-based standard with which to specify grammars. Figure 5.9 shows our sequence diagram using this standard to specify the grammar instead of OCL. We will discuss this further in Chapter 8.

In the Figure 5.9 example, we have only specified the grammar for an interaction that expects the city and state, but you get the idea. Even in our simple example, it becomes obvious that there is a significant amount of code in the UML diagram. As previously discussed, this is not a good idea. So, an optimal solution could be storing the grammars in text files accessible through URIs and referring to them in the sequence diagrams through the URIs.

This completes our look at representing user interactions with the system by using sequence diagrams. Sequence diagrams give us the most obvious alternative for modeling user interactions with a user interface. Particularly, we need to model these interactions first in a generic way (independent of the user interface type) as we have done in this chapter, and then specialize them to specific user interface types as we will see in the next three chapters.

To build user interfaces for mobile applications, we build generic interfaces and model them using UML, then we specialize them to specific interface types. Now, let us look at the glue that holds the user interface components together and tells the user what they mean: the context.

5.3.3 Context

The Webster dictionary defines context as 1) the parts of a discourse that surround a word or passage and can throw light on its meaning or 2) the interrelated conditions in which something exists or occurs. The word "context" is simply a loaded word. Any element of interactions between the computing system and the user has a meaning by itself, but possibly a bigger meaning by existing in a dialogue with other elements. As the definition of the word context implies, this bigger meaning comes from the relationship that exists between the different elements. So, within the realm of user interfaces, *we can define context as the sum of the relationships between the user interface components, the condition of the user, the primary intent of*

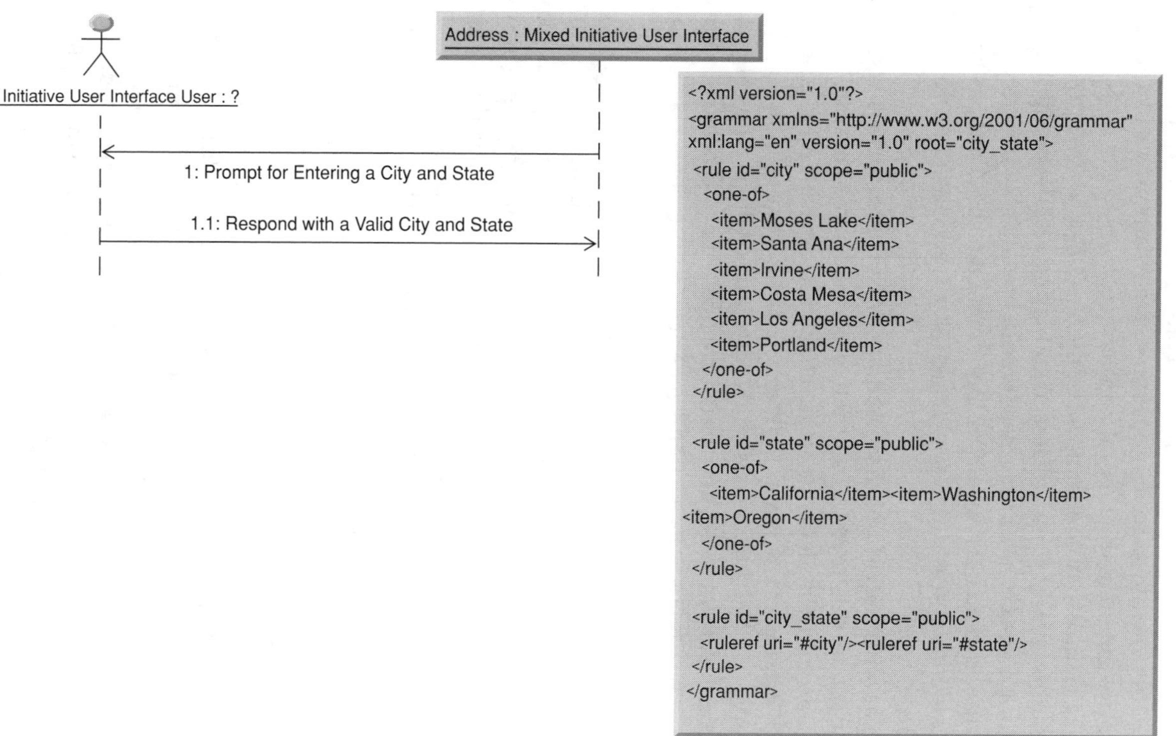
Mixed Initiative User Interface User : ?
Address : Mixed Initiative User Interface
1: Prompt for Entering a City and State
1.1: Respond with a Valid City and State
<?xml version="1.0"?>
<grammar xmlns="http://www.w3.org/2001/06/grammar" xml:lang="en" version="1.0" root="city_state">
<rule id="city" scope="public">
<one-of>
<item>Moses Lake</item>
<item>Santa Ana</item>
<item>Irvine</item>
<item>Costa Mesa</item>
<item>Los Angeles</item>
<item>Portland</item>
</one-of>
</rule>
<rule id="state" scope="public">
<one-of>
<item>California</item><item>Washington</item>
<item>Oregon</item>
</one-of>
</rule>
<rule id="city_state" scope="public">
<ruleref uri="#city"/><ruleref uri="#state"/>
</rule>
</grammar>

FIGURE 5.9. Using W3C's Grammars in UML to Specify Natural Language and Mixed-Initiative Interactions.

the system, and all of the other elements that allow users and computing systems to communicate.

A prompt, a response, or any other piece of information being communicated between the computing system may have a meaning on its own. However, the sum of the meanings of all such information is greater than the linear addition of such information. There is information hidden in relationships between these elements such as their placement and temporal appearance.

Contexts help the user understand what the system expects in response to various prompts more clearly. Contexts lessen ambiguity and the possibility of making errors. Without contexts, user interfaces would have to be extremely verbose and error handling and validation would be monumental tasks. Contexts complete the meaning of individual user interface elements and add meaning to groupings of such elements.

Contexts, as with previously discussed topics, have their own taxonomy. It is not in the scope of this text to comprehensively analyze context; such a study would protrude into the fields of artificial intelligence, linguistics, ergonomics, and others. Nevertheless, we will look at a few different axes for categorization of contexts. We will need to do this so that we know which types of contexts are specific to exact user interfaces and which are not. This will help us in abstracting context into different layers as we build generic user interfaces that are specialized to devices at run time.

Finally, though we will focus on the context of the more rudimentary elements of user interfaces such as the prompts, keep in mind that there may be relationships among the various groupings of elements. For example, a prompt, as part of one interaction, may have a relationship with an interaction preceding it. Contexts give us information, based on the relationships among the various elements of the user interface, that completes the picture and meaning of the user interface; there exist contexts among various parts of the user interface at different levels of granularity.

Taxonomy of Contexts by Domain

Both interactions and elements have contexts. Contexts can be *domain specific* or *domain independent*. We will simply define domain as a grouping of problems or a problem area. For example, we can discuss domains dealing with finances, engineering, or medicine, or the domains could be more fine-grained such as banking, electrical engineering, dermatology, or others. Applications are typically used by users who know of the domain of the problem being addressed by the application. For example, if the user opens a word processing application, the system already knows one thing about the type of interactions that will take place between the user and the system: They will all be within the *context* of word processing. Users open a word processor to type some text in it and not to create a three-dimensional image. Domain-specific contexts refer to the domain-based purpose fulfilled by an element within the application. For example, when a user goes to a Web-based business-to-business application, the definition of "buyer" and "seller" are meaningful within the context of business-to-business applications.

The overall context of the application as a unit, and therefore its user interface, is almost always domain dependent. There are very few computer applications that are not designed to solve very specific problems (these are either applications in the research areas surrounding artificial intelligence or applications being written by programmers of minimal intelligence). However, *a grouping of the user interface components of an application can have its own context*. For example, a grouping of five input fields of address, city, state, zip, and country has an address context. Although the input field of city (one type of GUI prompt) has a much broader meaning on its own, the context of filling address information eliminates much of the ambiguity of a prompt that just says city and expects a response from the user. Outside of the context, asking the user for a city would allow the user to enter the name of any valid city.

Any relationship between various elements of the user interface that is not implicitly or explicitly derived from the domain problem has a domain-independent context. Domain-independent contexts can be implied from the temporal, structural, functional, and artistic organization of the elements in the user interface. Whereas word processing tasks are the best known, they may be applied in any domain. Word processing task contexts such as spell-checking, deleting, and the many other tasks we know well can be used to create a legal document, an engineering document, or an essay. Regardless of the domain for which the application, or the specific functionality of the application, is being used, there is always some functional context associated with the task being performed that is independent of the domain-dependent tasks at hand. Database application, spreadsheets, word processors, and even computer-aided drawing programs can have spell-check functionality.

A topic we will not discuss much in this text book, but which is important to mobile computing, is the field of context-aware computing. In context-aware computing, the conditions under which the application is being used takes center stage. Though orthogonal to mobile computing, because of the great role that environmental conditions play in mobile computing, context-aware computing is of paramount important to us. There are also patterns and techniques that have evolved for context-aware computing uses in the mobile arena. Alatalo and Peraaho, for example, have suggested an approach for using contexts in specializing user interfaces [Alatalo and Peraaho 2001]. Before we proceed to look at some specific taxonomies of context, let us note some characteristics that Henricksen and colleagues point out when it comes to mobile systems [Henricksen et al. 2002]:

1. Context information exhibits a range of temporal characteristics.
2. Context information is imperfect.
3. Context has many alternative representations.
4. Context information is highly interrelated.

Before you think about using context-related information in your software application, you may want to think about creating a domain-dependent taxonomy of the various "context representations" or "elements of context." For example,

Munoz and colleagues do this for building a context-aware mobile communication system in a hospital and recognize the following elements [Munoz et al. 2003]:

1. *Location*: By our definition, this is really a dimension of mobility so this is not something that we would typically include in our context element list, but this is how Munoz and colleagues have taken into account location—as an element of context.
2. *Delivery timing*: This is an added time sensitivity to things happening in a hospital.
3. *Role reliance*: Individuals working in a hospital communicate and perform tasks based on roles (doctors, nurses, etc.).
4. *Artifact location and state*: This refers to the state, location, and availability of things that are used in a hospital. For example, if there are ten EKG machines and eleven people are under cardiac arrest, then the last one has to wait to get the first EKG machine that frees up.

In building software systems, it is important to separate all domain problems from those problems that are independent of the domain. So, while building generic user interfaces, it is important to be aware of this problem. Whatever mechanism is used to produce a generic user interface must enable the developer to encapsulate most of, or all, the domain-dependent context of the application into the generic user interface. After all, the domain of the application does not change regardless of how the user interface to the system is being rendered.

Extrinsic and Intrinsic Contexts

Contexts may be implied: We may understand the relationship between the elements of a user interface without the relationship being specified outside of the existence of the elements themselves; this is intrinsic context. Such contexts are very subjective to the perspective of the user. Intrinsic contexts are also often referred to as implicit contexts. Intrinsic contexts exist as a result of the existence of the elements whose relationship is explained by these contexts. Nothing in the user interface mentions them explicitly.

Contexts may need to be specified to convey the necessary information regarding the relationship between the elements. This may be done to remove the subjectivity in the interpretation of the relationship between the different elements of the user interface. It is also possible that a context cannot be inferred from the user interface. Andrew Page [Page 2000], a clinical neuropsychologist at University of Western Australia, defines extrinsic context to be synonymous with independent context, comprising both background (e.g., time/place where the word is read) and format (e.g., size/text font of the word) context; the defining feature is that extrinsic context is "*not* supposed to affect meaningful interpretation of target information." Likewise, he defines an intrinsic context as a kind of context that affects interpretation of target information. For example, seeing *bank* in the context of *river* will affect the semantic interpretation of *bank*.

Let us go back to our address example (see Figure 5.10). Note that the label stating "Billing Address" conveys an extrinsic context to the user: The user would

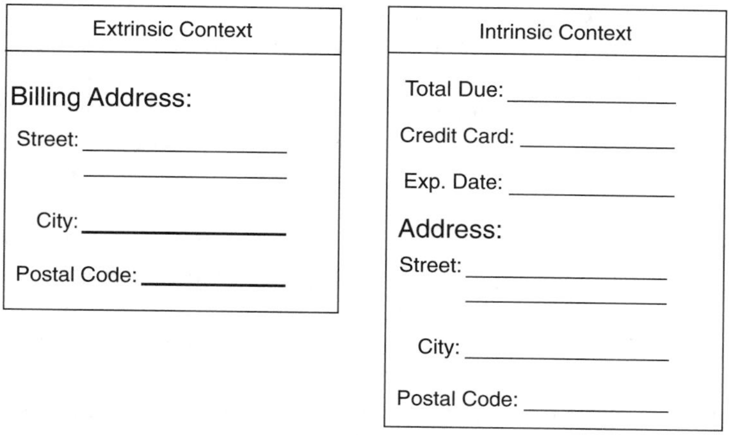

FIGURE 5.10. Extrinsic and Intrinsic Contexts.

not know what address to type into the fields otherwise. The name of the fields, how they are placed, and their order imply that the system is looking for a postal address; furthermore, the user knows, based on the implied context, that the city and country are the city and country of the address.

Taxonomy of Contexts by Structural Positioning

We have now seen that we can divide all contexts into domain-dependent and domain-independent contexts by whether or not they relate to the context of the application. Another way of categorizing the relationships among the various components of a user interface is by the relative physical positioning of the component, in other words "where" the component is placed in the application user interface.

Structural context is almost always information conveyed by relative placement rather than absolute placement. *Structural positioning of user interface elements is closely tied to localization and internationalization.* Some languages are written from left to right whereas others from right to left or top to bottom. This affects how the elements are positioned on a visual user interface. Also, some locales dictate a particular placement of a set of elements. Going back to our address example, in some countries, the address is written with the city and state first whereas in others the street address comes before the city and the state. The mere fact that an address is international may imply that the country, state or province, and city must come before the street address. The grouping of a street address with a city, state or province, and country name may imply an international mailing address context whereas the city name by itself does not have any particular meaning.

Maintaining consistency between the structural positioning of elements on various user interfaces used by a system is particularly important as it is a great part of the user experience and understanding of the system.

The physical positioning of user interface elements does not carry much meaning in nonvisual user interfaces. In VUIs, the placement of the element and its associated context is carried by its temporal position: when it appears with respect to the other elements as opposed to where.

Taxonomy of Contexts by Temporal Positioning

Interactions between a user interface and a person happen in some sort of a time sequence. Therefore, there is a relationship in relative positioning of interactions and their elements in time: when and in what order they take place. We call this time-dependent relationship between user interface components their *temporal context*.

It is extremely important that a generic user interface have complete and detailed information on the ordering of all of the elements of the user interface at the most granular level possible. This is because certain user interfaces, such as command-based VUIs, allow only one message to be passed from the system to the user or from the user to the system. Other user interfaces may use form-based strategies with which the user can send several messages to the system at the same time, but the size of the forms may vary depending on the specific type of user interface. Therefore, the implementation of any framework or design strategy must include some way of specifying the temporal positioning of every user interface component.

Temporal contexts are particularly important in removing ambiguity in nonvisual user interfaces. Depending on where a sentence, word, or phrase is said or heard, its definition is different. For example, if the user is prompted for a city after being asked for his or her current location, the user will probably assume that the city is the city of his or her current location. Conversely, if the user is prompted for a city after he or she was asked for billing address, the user will probably assume that it is the city of the billing address that the system is looking for.

Temporal context of a group of interface components can be intrinsic or extrinsic. If the order of every element (components, messages, interactions, etc.) is specified, and this is necessary for some types of user interfaces such as a VUI, the context is extrinsic. In other cases, particularly user interfaces that support visual forms, the temporal context of the components is implied from the structural order in which the components appear on the form.

Temporal and structural contexts of VUIs are often not orthogonal: They depend on one another, are inferred from each other, or are simply related. This is not quite the case with nonvisual user interfaces. The amount of information understandable by our visual senses (i.e., the bandwidth of incoming information) is exponentially higher than what our other senses can provide.

5.3.4 User Interface Components

Anyone who has developed a GUI for just about any personal computing platform, or any other platform for that matter, either uses a modern Integrated Development Environment (IDE) for development or has tried to use one. Most modern IDEs, regardless of the languages or platforms that they support, try to enable the GUI designer to "drag-and-drop" some widgets onto the screen and to wire them together to facilitate building a GUI. A big selling point for Microsoft's ActiveX components and JavaBeans, at least at their conception, was just this; they promised to allow you to not only program more intuitively with graphical tools but also to build the GUI much quicker using standard components that you could drag and drop.

The basic premise of most of these tools was to design some reusable components that modeled most typical user interactions with the system fairly accurately. These widgets could range from very simple to very complex. For example, some tools offer widgets that allow the user to draw forms, input fields, buttons, and other basic user interface tools, and bind them together, through mapping events or other methods, to create the skeleton of an interface component that facilitates one or more interactions with the user. Other tools allow yet more sophisticated and complex widgets such as calendar widgets, scrollable tables, and spreadsheets.

Both graphical and voice user interfaces, through such IDEs and other development tools, have developed some canonical ways of defining what components are. And though different vendors may use different terminologies for product differentiation purposes, within the GUI design world or the VUI design world, these components exhibit very similar behaviors and uses. These components have evolved to be generic templates for graphical or voice user interfaces that allow the developers to fill in some attributes and tie some things together to render a user interface. However, nearly all of these types of components and their supporting tools aimed to stencil templates for particular types of user interfaces and became very tightly coupled to the type of user interface they support. For example, a given tool may allow the developer to place an input field on the form, set its size and color, set its borders, set some constraints on what can be entered into the field, and then give the user another widget or keystroke to indicate when he or she is finished filling out the data.

Although these tools offered widgets tightly coupled to the type of user interface that they supported, one could say that whatever attributes and behaviors common between the different types of widgets for the different types of user interfaces can probably be abstracted out and related to generic user interfaces. And this is precisely what we shall do.

First, let us define what a generic user interface component may be. A generic user interface component may be defined as a user interface independent template for one or more interactions with the user. We have seen the elements of interactions. Components are the tools that provide the mechanism to allow the user to interact with the system. A component would obviously be useless if we cannot put it together with another component to make a more complex component. After all, that is why we break things into components: so that we can put the pieces together in different ways and make them useful again. But, we cannot simply put disparate components together and expect them to work. To put user interface components together, we need to provide "washers" that allow the components to fit together. These washers for our fittings are called *transitions* (see Figure 5.11).

We can define transitions as the *border* or the *thing that fills the boundaries* between the components. Transitions are meaningful whether they are talked about in the context of a VUI, a GUI, or any other type of user interface. When the eye scans a given area, it recognizes the boundaries between different objects and shapes. If there is no transition between two very distinct sounds (no transition between different aural components), the user's reaction is typically negative, causing any effective aural output to have smooth transitions between sounds and words.

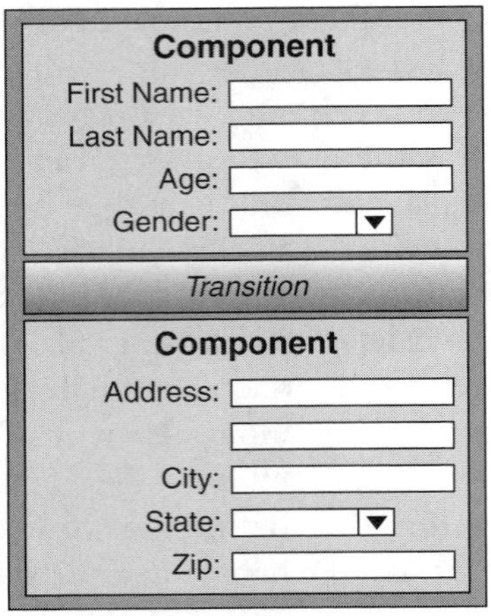

FIGURE 5.11. Components and Transitions.

When we talk about user interface components, we typically think about building components that are user interface specific such as user interface windows for visual components or voice dialogues for VUIs. However, to build mobile systems that can have any type of user interface, we need to build components that can interact with the user the same way regardless of the specific type of user interface. We can then specialize these components.

Generic User Interface Components

Now that we have introduced the generic components, how do we build them?

Note that building generic components is more of a design mentality than an application of some programming language. In fact, you can build generic user interface components with a variety of frameworks, tools, and programming languages. The simple key in building a series of generic components is to follow a few simple rules:

1. *Model only data exchanged between the user and the system that does not depend on the specific type of user interface.* For example, modeling an interaction that allows the user to change the color scheme of an application is a blatant violation of this: Color does not apply directly to VUIs. Leave any such interactions to the components that will specialize the generic interface components.
2. *Model everything at the most granular level possible.* Although you can group things naturally in one type of user interface, the grouping may not make any sense in another interface. So, leave it up to the specialization layer to decide how to group components together unless you lose some context by breaking apart the component. For example, if a component is used for registering a user into the system and it collects ten pieces of information, six of those may be superfluous to a VUI whereas a GUI will allow all of them to be rendered. Likewise, entering data on a small device with a constricted input device such as a cell phone is not practical, so only two of the ten fields may be required for registration when a cell phone is being used.

3. *Do not assume that everything is based on forms and menus.* Forms and menus work great for many applications, but mixed-initiative interactions are much better suited for many mobile applications. Understand the application domain and the user requirements before anything else (as in any other software endeavor). Then, build the right mixture of directed-dialogue and mixed-initiative interactions into the generic user interface components.
4. *Avoid making the transitions between smaller components that make up bigger ones specific to a type of user interface.* Often times, the way to build the smaller components in a generic way is obvious, but putting them together with the proper transitions is not. Transitions between components are typically specific to the particular type of user interface, so, if you see yourself implementing lots of transitions between generic components, you are probably doing something you should not be!

XML is an obvious base technology for the generic components, but it is not the only possible choice. It is possible, and even desirable, in some cases to design and implement generic components that expose non-XML textual or binary interfaces. But, in general, XML is a good choice for generic interfaces as it gives us a standard and structured mechanism to expose the interface to an otherwise non-human-readable system. Later in this chapter, we will look at W3C's XForms as the leading standard for building generic components to date.

Once we have these generic components, we need to specialize them.

Specializing Generic Components

Most developers who have worked with mobile applications think of specializing generic components in terms of using XML Style Sheets (XSL). However, this is a very narrow slice of specialization techniques. So, if you are thinking of generic components in terms of XML and specialization in terms of XSL, take a step back and look at the bigger picture. Specialization is not just transforming content. Specializing a generic interface may include modifications in the behavior of the interface and the workflow, adding device- or interface-specific features, removing features not supported by the intended user interface or device, synchronizing the interactions between the user and the computing system through different channels (such as simultaneous voice and text entry), and taking all of the other mobile dimensions into consideration. For example, the specialization component that creates the final interface for a mobile phone user should have the proper functionality to avoid display advertisements when the batteries on the user's device are running low, it should be able to synchronize the text and voice content being displayed to a user's mobile device on a packet switched network, etc.

Specializing generic components is not something that should be done from scratch every time a new component is developed. It is a complex problem that will be detailed during the next three chapters. As this book is being written, mobile UIMS (User Interface Management Systems) are evolving. To date, there is no proven predominant technology for creating generic components or specializing them. There are several standards, such as XForms, with reference implementations. Before looking at mobile UIMS, let us look at the typical classifications of

UIMS. This will help us better understand what they are all about. Then, we can see how mobile UIMS differ from their stationary counterparts.

5.3.5 Managing User Interface Components

As already mentioned, seldom do application developers write the entire application from scratch. In fact, the primary reason for writing frameworks and tools is to factor out the common functionalities that are needed across applications. There are probably more occasions to write things from scratch in mobile applications because of the resource-starved nature of these devices and the necessity of performance. Still, most of the time, it makes no sense to build everything from scratch, and frameworks and tools are handy. UIMS are used to manage user interface components. The primary goal of UIMS has always been to reduce the amount of effort required to create a new user interface [Olsen 1992]. X-Windows and other windowing systems are examples of UIMS where the developer, rather than developing everything from scratch, develops components that abide by the UIMS' APIs.

UIMS comprise a field of study in and of themselves, but it is useful for us to take a quick look at families of UIMS for conventional stationary applications and then mobile applications so that we understand how to build and deploy user interface components.

Conventional User Interface Management

There are three basic types of UIMS [Olsen 1992]:

1. *State Machine UIMS*: This is perhaps the most popular of all UIMS. State Machine UIMS are component management systems that manage the full life cycle of a user interface component. Components written for these UIMS specify their own possible states and events that may be emitted as they enter and exit these states. State Machine UIMSs also allow the developer to code a state chart that functions as the map for the UIMS' workflow engine that moves the components between the different states. State Machine UIMS start the user interface at some initial state and use the state chart to navigate the user through the various steps of interacting with the interface until an exit or final state is reached.
2. *Grammar UIMS*: These systems are designed for natural language interactions. Grammar UIMS rely on parsing the user input to understand the commands and the data sent by the user. Grammar UIMS are similar to State Machine UIMS in that they navigate the user through a set of interface interactions sequentially. Whereas the state chart (also referred to as the state table) is used to navigate the user in State Machine UIMS, the message and the commands that are interpreted from it are used to navigate the user in grammar UIMS.
3. *Event-based UIMS*: Event-based UIMS are typically used for GUIs. They allow every component to have some events that can be tied to other events handled by other components. In this way, messages are propagated through the user interface. The UIM starts with presenting the user with some initial interface;

every user interaction with the interface results in one or more events. Many GUIs today use event-based UIMS to handle user interactions.

Nearly all UIMS used for development of user interfaces for stationary systems today use one of these three different techniques. All UIMS use the ever-important inversion of control principle, which points out that while the user interface application is executing, it is the UIMS that is in control and not the authored user interface component. This is an important concept to remember as it carries an entire set of advantages and disadvantages with it. Although inversion of control makes for a more reliable code base, it prevents the developer from adding large features that are not supported by UIMS.

As you may guess, typical UIMS are designed for specific user interfaces. Interactive voice recognition (IVR) systems, for example, provide State Machine UIMS to render a voice user interface with VUI components. Because typical UIMS handle states, grammars, and events of specific types of user interfaces, they must be altered or enhanced to handle generic user interface components.

Managing Generic Components

Managing user interface components for a system that renders multiple types of user interfaces, particularly mobile systems, is a bit more complicated. Remember that the reason we want to build generic components first and specialize them is so that we can have a user interface that adapts itself to the user's condition: the device being used, the location of the user, the urgency of use, etc. Consequently, the system that manages our user interface components must have some additional features.

It is also crucial to understand that the UIMS can be the limiting factor in the interface architecture. Selection of the UIMS is a direct result of the user interface architecture. For a UIMS to be able to handle generic user interface components, it should allow the components to be written in a generic way with no bias to a particular type of user interface.

UIMS used in developing user interfaces for mobile systems must allow handling of generic user interface components. They, therefore, must have the following characteristics:

1. *They must allow the developers to specify some "importance" for the different interactions being exposed by each generic user interface component.* Not all of the interactions in a given user interface component are necessary to communicate with the user. Some are superfluous. For example, a generic user interface component designed to obtain user information for registration into the system may have an advertisement, some information to be obtained from the user essential to completion of the registration process such as the user's name, and some information that are not essential but can help in profiling the user such as the user's age. The UIMS must allow the component to specify some "importance" or "priority" level for every interaction so that specialization of the components can be done without explicit knowledge of implementation of the generic components themselves.

2. *They must allow the components to take advantage of context information shared among the various components*. This is often referred to as "context-aware computing." Though context-aware techniques are somewhat orthogonal to mobile computing and user interfaces, awareness of the context shared by several components can help in better specialization of the individual components as well as groups of components (composite components). Let us take, for example, a user interface for a loan origination system. Some possible user interface components could be the applicant's personal information, bank account information, or employment information. Each component may have an address subcomponent. Some user interface devices, such as PDAs, may not have enough room to display all of the components simultaneously. So, as the UIMS allows specialization of each component, and the composite of all of these components, it may need to display more verbose labels by reminding the user what each address refers to. The UIMS can do this through a predefined context that tells the UIMS how to modify the labels as it displays interactions belonging to the same generic user interface component in different sections.
3. *They should be able to specialize generic components to the types of user interface required with no additional necessary components*. Mobile UIMS must provide the facilities for adding specialization components and the facilities for determining, at run time or compile time, which specialization component should be applied for which channel and when.
4. *They need to support synchronization of interactions through multiple channels*. If a particular application has a multichannel interface, for example text and voice, the messages from the user interface to the user must be synchronized so that messages of one channel are not rendered before their matching messages on the other channel are. For example, we do not want the text to scroll by the eyes of a user while there is still audio playing about the text that has already gone by.

In addition, there is another set of desirable, although not required, features of mobile UIMS:

1. *They should allow the generic user interface components as well as the specialization components to provide features specific to mobile applications (dimensions of mobility)*. Mobile UIMS should support components that may need to behave differently based on location, available resources on the device, available power on the device, etc. Whereas hooks to some of these dimensions, such as location sensitivity, should be provided at the generic user interface layer, others, such as device screen size or availability of an aural interface, may be best fit for specialization components.
2. *They should allow for specialization of content in a distributed manner as may fit the particular application and as specified by the specialization components*. Sometimes specialization of the user interface should be done in a centralized manner; other times specialization at the node is best. Let us take our driving

directions example once more. A PDA may have enough processing power and memory to convert a generic component in XML to the desired interface format, say a Clipper application for the Palm. However, a mobile phone most likely does not have such resources. The UIMS, desirably a distributed UIMS, should provide the facilities for the specialization components, such as those that specialize the generic interface for a mobile phone and a PDA, to execute at the receiving node (on the PDA for this example) or at the sending node (on the server for this example).

3. *They should allow for internationalization and localization to be supported in a manner decoupled from the other specialization performed to render the final user interface.* Internationalization and localization are problems that can be well addressed by deploying the strategy of creating generic user interfaces. However, they should be done separate from specialization to channels and user interface types. This allows us to leverage internationalization and localization components across multiple user interface specialization components. It also has other obvious benefits such as maintaining consistency and reducing cost by not having to internationalize the same user interface components repeatedly.

There is currently no single user interface management system that supports all of the features that we have outlined here, but the standards that outline how the future mobile UIMS should support these features are either completed or on their way to completion. Later in this chapter, we will look at W3C's XForms, which is perhaps the most important standard for developing generic user interface components. During the remainder of this text, we will look at other standards such as SMIL for synchronization and VXML for specialization to VUIs. Because of the immaturity of mobile application development tools, we are focused on understanding the problem and the possible solution types rather than specific solutions. Nonetheless, UML promises to be the one tool likely to be supported by all development tools to facilitate the process of developing mobile applications. We looked at using UML to model interactions previously. Now, let us look at using UML to model the components themselves.

5.4 Using UML for Modeling Generic User Interface Components

We have already seen how to model interactions with UML. Now, we need to look at modeling the components themselves. Before doing this, remember that, although UML can be used for code generation, we do not advise building a software implementation strategy based on code generation with UML. As repeated throughout this text, UML is a modeling tool used for design and communicating designs. First-draft code generation is a possibility, but maintaining the application code through UML is ludicrous.

Let us start with showing a metamodel for contexts, components, and other elements that we have discussed so far.

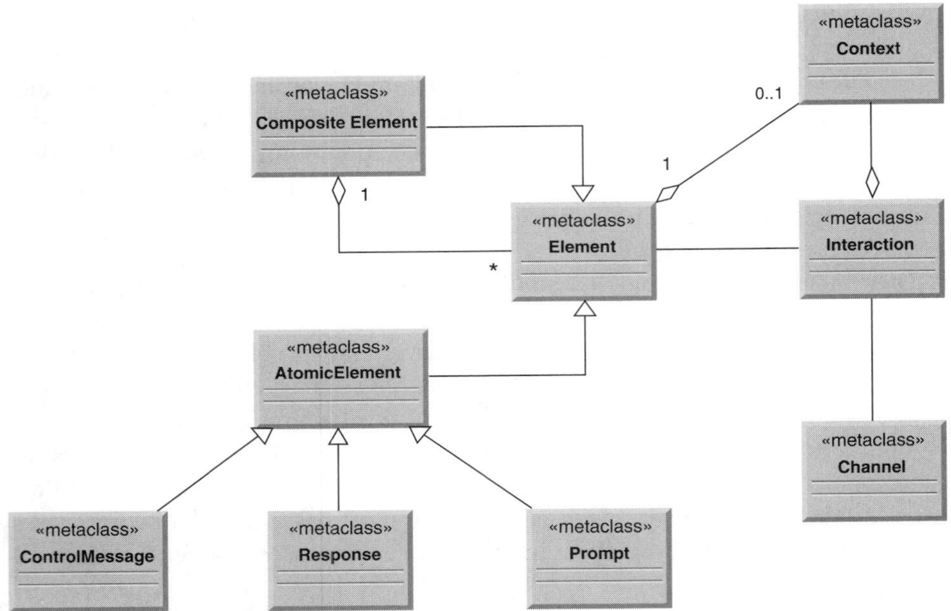

FIGURE 5.12. Basic Taxonomy of Elements of User Interface Components.

5.4.1 Modeling the Domain of Generic User Interface

Since the most pervasive use of UML is in modeling logical *domains*, it is only apt that we model the domain of generic user interfaces using UML. This will help us understand the problem of designing generic user interfaces better.

We looked at the metamodel class diagram representing interactions and subsequent diagrams that represent the actual interactions. Figure 5.12 shows the metamodel for user interface components (made up of elements such as prompts).

Next, we look at Figure 5.13. The GenericInterfaceComponent represents the type that our UIMS needs to be able to handle to render a user interface.

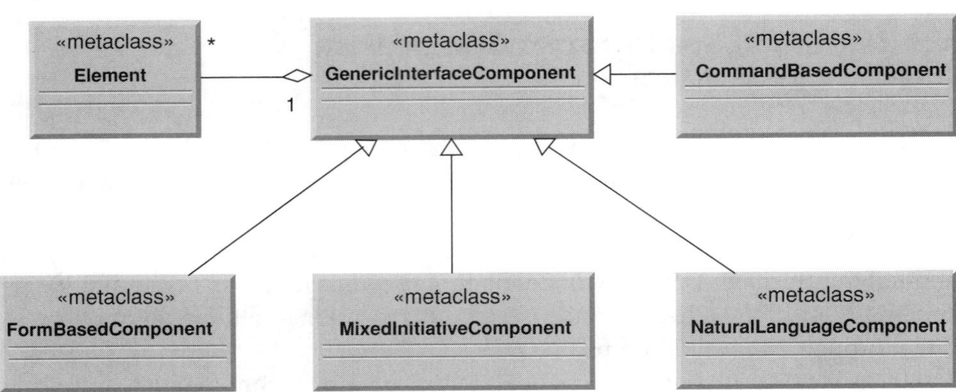

FIGURE 5.13. Types of Generic Components Modeled in UML.

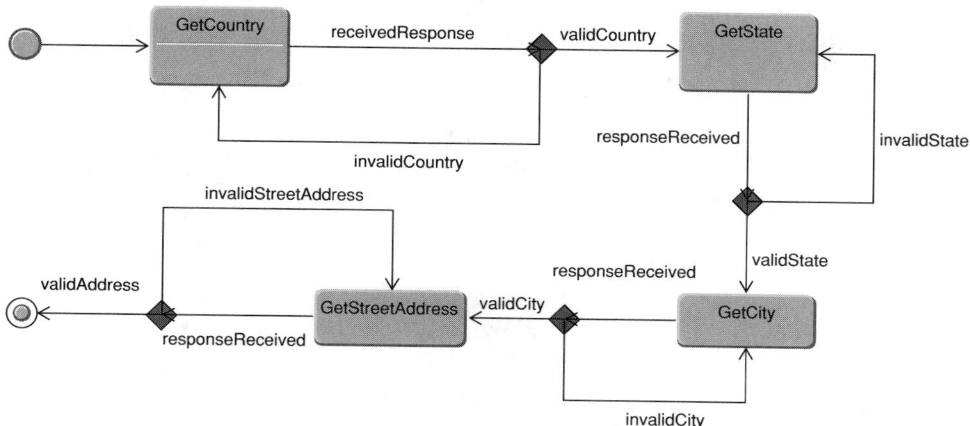

FIGURE 5.14. Representing the State of a Generic User Interface Component with UML State Diagrams.

For State Machine UIMS, state diagrams can represent the life cycle of the user interface component perfectly. This works particularly well for generic interface components as there is no need for interface-specific events such as button pushes. Figure 5.14 shows how we can model the life cycle of an address component. Obviously, this is a trivial example, but it shows how a user interface component can be handled by a State Machine UIMS.

Grammar UIMS rely on interpreting grammars. As discussed previously, UML does not deal with natural language issues such as grammar very well. So, the best we can do with grammar UIMS is to use sequence diagrams and refer to the grammars externally using W3C or other grammar standards.

Event-based UIMS are best modeled using the heart of UML: class diagrams. Class diagrams allow us to model classes and specify their behavior in terms of method calls. We can model events themselves, event sources, and event listeners with class classifiers (boxes with sharp corners) and the relationships they form.

Forms are another entity that can be easily modeled with class diagrams. Forms are essentially a collection of prompts to be filled with user responses. If the prompts are static (labels on forms typically do not change regardless of the instance of the form), we can use static variables with the proper stereotype (most probably a string type). If the prompts are dynamic, the dynamic nature of the prompt is somehow tied to either business logic or presentation logic, both of which can be modeled by other class classifiers. The instance data filled in by the user can be modeled using object diagrams. The type of such instance data can be specified in class diagrams. It is important not to mix the instance data filled in by a particular user with the data types or fields that can be filled in.

To specify spatial and temporal placement of various components, we can add attributes supported by the UIMS used to manage the generic components. The class diagram in Figure 5.15 shows how a loan origination form may be modeled by using address, user information, and loan form subforms. (Obviously, we have oversimplified the domain problem to demonstrate a solution briefly.)

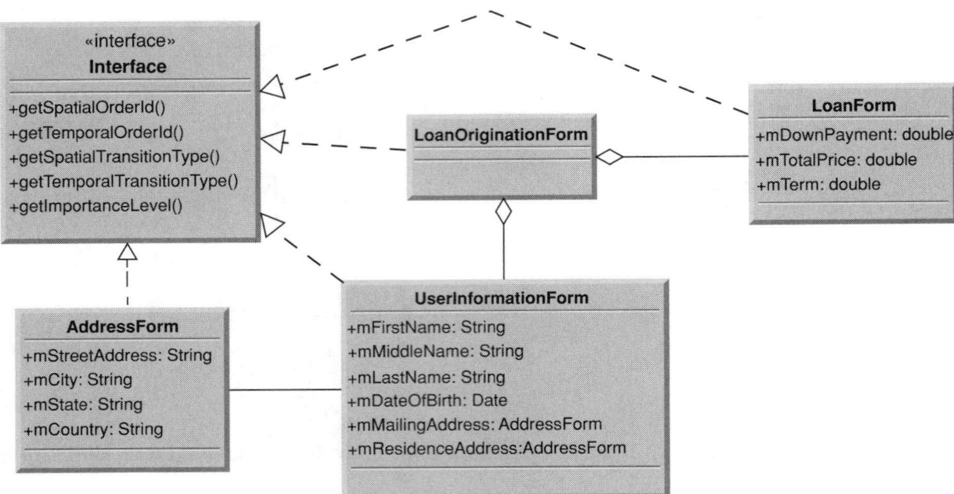

FIGURE 5.15. Using Class Diagrams to Represent Form-Based User Interfaces.

Now, let us say that our UIMS supports specialization of the components and that the method calls necessary to take advantage of specialization to a voice user interface and an HTML user interface are a spatial order ID (the visual order in which the various components are to appear), temporal order ID (the order in time in which the components are to appear), and transitions between the components (both in time and in positioning). The UIMS may require implementation of the behavior of each one of these behaviors or may leave them optional. Implementation of the behavior must be provided for the UIMS to be able to put the components together and make compound components.

As you can imagine, if our form components are being handled by a State Machine UIMS, we would have a full representation of the data and behavior of our forms with state diagrams of every class shown in Figure 5.15.

In this way, we can model the user interface components that model user interactions generically, without any bias toward a particular user interface type, in UML. This will allow us to maintain consistency and to communicate design across multiple user interface code bases. In the next few chapters, we will focus on using UML specifically for particular types of interfaces such as VUIs.

Now, let us look at XForms, one of the few standards available today that allows us to implement user interfaces generically and then specialize them.

5.5 XFORMS

XForms is a W3C standard designed to offer a Web-oriented solution set for creating generic user interfaces. We will use XForms as an example of a standard that attempts to separate concerns at the user interface layer the way we have talked about here. XForms attempts to separate the various user interface concerns in its component model. Before we begin deciphering the explanation of what XForms is, it is important to note that XForms is not the antipattern [Brown et al. 1998] (and, as mentioned earlier in this chapter, nothing is!). Neither is XForms the perfect solution. XForms is a standard created by W3C for the Web; keep in mind that not all systems are HTTP based and the Web is not the right solution for all systems. Increasingly, the distributed computing model is moving toward a peer-to-peer model. XForms was designed with a bias toward the world of HTTP and thin clients. XForms also does not address all of the concerns that we have focused on in this chapter.

Nevertheless, as previously discussed, the Web is the most pervasive network today. Therefore, it makes sense to discuss a framework that lends itself to the Web. Moreover, it is useful to select a standard that exists today and with tools available for development.

One can infer from the name that XForms is a technology that is based on the notion of forms—in particular Web forms. XForms is composed of four main loosely coupled sections: XForms Model, XForms Processing Model, XForms Submit-Protocol, and XForms User Interface. XForms ties into HTTP through its Submit Protocol, but each of its sections can be used independently. Therefore, we could use the XForms Model independently and with any protocol that we want. However, the ideas that have given birth to XForms initiated from the Web, thereby establishing it as a child of HTTP and HTML.

Also, at the time this book is being written, XForms standard is yet to be finalized or pervasive. However, it is already picking up considerable steam with major software vendors looking at supporting XForms processors in the next versions of their software.

Finally, it is important to keep in mind that we are only using XForms as an example of a technology that separates the concerns of the user interface. There are other technologies and more are sure to be created as an evolutionary part of computing. Nonetheless, the concepts discussed using XForms will apply equally to other technologies. Depending on the type of application needed, it is possible that a different standard is suitable. It is also possible to design your own context sensitive (domain specific or otherwise) application.

5.5.1 What Is It?

We will discuss HTTP and protocols in some detail in later chapters of this book. To understand XForms, however, we must take a quick look at HTTP, and the Web, as they are the parents to the ideas giving birth to XForms. The pervasiveness and success of HTTP can be largely attributed to its elegant simplicity: a single request initiated by a client to a server that is synchronically responded to, by the server, with a single response. When a client has to send several pieces of information to the server, the pieces of information can be collected by a FORM and submitted using the GET or POST commands. Therefore, the fundamental structure for the user to enter data into the system on the Web is the FORM. The FORM, however, was designed specifically for a system that uses HTML and HTML browsers. Though POST and GET are not dependent on HTML, there is tight coupling between the semantics of the HTML FORM itself and rendering of HTML content. As we mentioned in the beginning of this section, XForms achieves decoupling of presentation logic, protocol, and server-side information by dividing forms into four sections:

1. *XForms User Interfaces*: XForms User Interface defines a set of user interface elements for visual user interfaces, particularly for a browser environment as an HTTP client. It is important to note, however, that HTTP is not required for using XForms or any component thereof. HTTP is simply the most pervasive protocol and its companion of HTML was the first markup language to gain popularity. Therefore, HTTP is a natural default choice to be used with XForms or any of its components. Other markup types such as XHTML, WML, and VXML are produced through the binding process of XForms. With our earlier taxonomy of the user interface, XForms User Interfaces allows for structural typing of the interaction elements without creating dependencies on any particular type of user interface.
2. *XForms Model*: The XForms Model defines a form without any visual, or for that matter look-and-feel properties. Bound together with the XML User Interface or some other user interface model, it will allow a complete user interface. The binding process will be described later. Within the taxonomy that we laid out earlier, XForms Model defines the domain dependence of the interaction components. The XForms Model has several parts, which we will look at in further detail later. Two of them, XForms Instance Data and XForms Schema, are particularly prominent. XForms Instance Data is an instance of the data to be input to a form by a user. The XForms Schema, otherwise referred to as the XForms Model Schema to avoid confusion, is the schema for the instance data. An XForms Instance Data is to XForms Schema what an object is to a class in object-oriented programming. XForms Instance Data is important during state-full interactions between the user and the system. XForms Instance Data holds the temporal contexts of the application as the user navigates through it.
3. *XForms Processing Model*: To bring all of the separate parts of XForms together to make a sensible user interface, the XForms browser, or the application that uses the XForms output, needs to be able to bind these various parts together in a meaningful way. The instructions on how to bind the various parts together are called the XForms Processing Model. Processing of the various XML components in XForms is event based.
4. *XForms Submit Protocol*: XForms Submit Protocol is the mechanism provided to submit data from the clients to the server in much the same way as the HTTP-based submit works. It is not clear, at this time, whether the XForms Submit Protocol will be its own entity or if the W3C will simply use the XML Protocol standard currently being worked on to replace this. We will not deal much with the XForms Submit Protocol as understanding it is more pertinent to those who are writing the frameworks to support XForms functionality, whether as clients, servers, or peers.

In addition to these four main parts, there are some basic concepts necessary to understand XForms. First, XForms are form based. This means that it is assumed that every interaction with the user is composed of the user being presented with a form that conveys some messages to the user, responding to that form, and submitting the form to the system to continue. Though in most applications this paradigm will suffice, it may not be suitable for some applications. For example, some of what XForms offers is not very useful for an application whose primary purpose is browsing documents. However, when it comes to mobile application development, XForms Model and XForms User Interface are almost always pertinent because adapting to various user interfaces is one of the biggest challenges in mobile development.

To understand XForms and how to use it to build systems, the first step is to gain an understanding of how an XForms document can be handled and how it fits into the big picture of developing generic user interfaces. So, let us look at the XForms Processing Model, which specifies how the XForms browser (or XForms client) works.

5.5.2 XForms Processing Model

At its heart, XForms tries its best to be complementary and supplementary to the other XML technologies and specifications by W3C. The XForms committee has done a great job of avoiding the duplication of functionality offered by other XML-related specifications. The XForms Processing Model is really the specification that defines how a container should handle XForms documents. The "container" refers to the principle of inversion of control often discussed in this text. As we mentioned previously, the gist of this principle is that some container controls software components and their life cycle. Also note that the XForms container is a UIMS. It manages the XForms documents in a hybrid mode as both a State Machine UIMS and an event-based UIMS. In the case of the XForms container, often referred to as the XForms browser because of the evolutionary birth of XForms from the Web, the XForms documents are the components and the XForms container is the controller. Also, because instance data are separated from the template that describes them, one can think of the XForms container to be a type of State Machine or at least to have a State Machine internally. This helps in understanding how the different components of a document are processed. Figure 5.16 is a state diagram that shows how the container handles a given document.

One of the keys to understanding the XForms processing model described by Figure 5.16 is that all data, whether coming from the server or input to the system by the client, are treated the same. The *initialization* process can include information that comes from a previous XForm document, information stored by a server (permanently or temporarily), or information that is filled in based on some control action taken by the user (for example pressing a button or saying a keyword). Regardless, the initialization process produces the first version of the instance data for a given XForms document.

Once the document is initialized, the container allows the user to begin to interact with it. During these interactions, the state of the document may be changed. The state of the document is encapsulated in the instance data; therefore, the instance data change as the user interacts with the system. This is where it gets tricky. So, what happens if we have to intervene in the middle of the interactions and go back to the application server to get some data or perform some business logic?

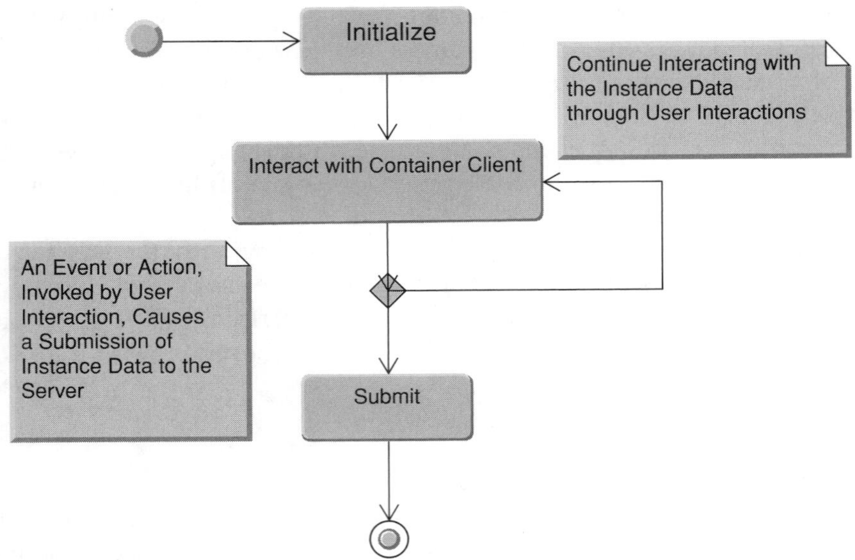

FIGURE 5.16. High-Level State Diagram of XForms Processing Model by an XForms Container.

Interacting with the server is not part of the XForm container job and is not taken into account when we talk about the XForms Processing Model. Indeed, this is one of the successes of the XForms technology. To go to the server, the container has to perform a *submit*. This is where the state of a given document ends. So, the XForms container initialized the document, collects information, and then submits the information.

XPath, XML Schema, and XML Events are prominent in the XForms specification. XPath is used, wherever possible, for connecting the various parts of XForms. XPath was covered in some detail in Chapter 3, but in case you do not recall, the primary task of XPath is to point to a segment of an XML document. Thus, the XForms Processing Model specifies that XPath is the way to point to the various elements in the same document. So, the instance data are bound to the other parts through XPath expressions, the binding expressions are bound to the other parts through XPath expressions, and so on.

As the user instance data are changed by user interactions or initialization, events can be produced. Events are also used to allow user interactions to indicate desired navigation through the user interface controls.

So, let us summarize how XForms container works:

1. XForms container initializes the XForms document by initializing the instance data.
2. The XForms container allows the client to interact with the form, thereby manipulating the instance data. The client could be a user if the XForms container is a browser viewable by the user or a client that serves its content to another client, which, in turn, interacts with the user. While these interactions are being done, the XForms container is responsible for monitoring various events that

happen based on the client input to the XForms container and modifying the instance data accordingly.

3. The XForms instance data are then submitted to the server once the user is finished interacting with the document and wants to send the data to some back-end process.

Now that we have looked at what the XForms container is supposed to do, let us jump forward to the XForms User Interface. This is probably the best way to see what the *effect* of using XForms is. And this effect is the most important thing about using XForms as far as mobile application development is concerned. Remember that the original reason we embarked on looking at XForms was that we can use it as a means to produce generic user interfaces consumable by another thin layer that can specialize this generic user interface to the specific needed user interfaces at run time.

5.5.3 XForms User Interface

The XForms User Interface outlines a set of interaction elements, called form controls, along with some processing instructions. The XForms User Interface defines various types of interaction elements (messages) from the user to the system as independent from specific user interfaces as possible. We will look at small code snippets on how to specify each of these controls to specific user interfaces at run time. Now, let us look at these controls.

XForm User Interfaces

XForms form controls are user interface prompt and control messages that ask the user for data input. These data, the response interaction elements, are later used to fill the instance data. Although each one of the form controls has its own set of optional and required attributes, every XForm control can have one of the following *optional* attributes:

Example 5.4: Usage of xml:lang Attribute.

Context Relevance:

```
<input ref="president" xml:lang="en">
    <caption>Managed Health Care</caption>
</input>
```

Translation:

```
<input xml:lang="en">
    <caption>First Name</caption>
</input>
<input xml:lang="fr">
    <caption>Prenom</caption>
</input>
```

1. *xml:lang*: This attribute allows the user interface to be internationalized. Internationalization using this attribute can be done by using the attribute to indicate the relevance of the control in the context of an interface dialogue within a particular language or to indicate what language the control is in. Let us go back to our address example for this. Example 5.4 shows two XForm code snippets that use a set of input controls. The first snippet shows a case where the user needs to be prompted for the insurance company that provides them with health care. This field may be applicable only to users speaking certain languages, for example English; countries other than the United States may have a social health care system. The second snippet shows translations of the same prompt: Namely, the user is being asked for their first name in two different languages.
2. *class*: This attribute refers to the style sheet class that may be applied to the XForm before intermediate or final rendition to the user. This class may be a textual CSS or an Aural Cascading Style Sheet (ACSS). Most developers familiar with Web development have seen CSS files, which can be used both on the client and the server, used with HTML. CSS is used to bundle look-and-feel properties such as font size so that changing such properties in a document is facilitated by simply changing the CSS. ACSS serves a similar task for VUIs. We will look into ACSS further in Chapter 7.
3. *navIndex*: This attribute allows us to specify the sequence in which the control may appear and can be any integer number from 0 to 32767. The explicit temporal and structural context of the interaction elements can be specified using this attribute. In other words, by specifying this attribute, we can tell the XForms client in what order the controls need to appear on a screen for a GUI or in what sequence they need to be conversed for a VUI. If this attribute is not specified, the XForms Processing Model outlines a default sequence in which the controls are rendered. We will discuss this later in detail.
4. *accessKey*: This attribute allows a shortcut key to be implemented to jump to a particular control. This attribute is equivalent to the Alt key pressed with some other key, such as the function keys, on a PC keyboard. This attribute lends itself to a platform-specific implementation, but it can be specified so that the XForms client provides the functionality to the user. For example, whereas the browser may translate a particular setting for this attribute to the F4 key on the keyboard for a user interface that uses the keyboard for input, it may allow the user to press the # button for a VUI that allows data entry through a phone pad or a so-called universal command spoken through a natural language command.

Example 5.5: Using XLink Expressions.

Translation:

```
<input xml:lang="en">
    <caption xlink:href="http://localhost/languagebundle.xml>
      First Name</caption>
</input>
```

In addition to these four attributes, which every control form element may have, other optional metadata may be provided for each form control through some optional XML elements. Let us go through these common elements.

1. *<caption>*: Caption can be thought of as the label for the control. This element can have all of the common attributes outlined previously (xml:lang, class, navIndex, and accessKey). Caption is typically used to give enough information to the user so that he or she knows how to fill the control with the proper response. When rendered, in a GUI, the caption may be the label for a text box and, in a VUI, it is the phrase uttered as a prompt before a user is expected to give a response. A quick reference to the W3C Schema [W3C XForms] tells us that there can only be one caption for every form control. If other text should be associated with the control, this has to be done through other optional elements, some of which can be repeated. Captions, as with most other features of XForms, can use XLink. This usage of XLink allows us to properly abstract out variations on a given form control. For example, we can simplify our previous code in Example 5.4 to the code snippet in Example 5.5.
2. *<hint>*: Like the <caption> element, the <hint> element serves to convey information useful for filling out the form control by the user. <hint> along with <help>, <extension>, and <alert> are the other elements that every form control can have and are grouped as the schema group optional UI Children (refer to the XForms Schema in [W3C XForms]). A form control can have none, one, or more groupings of these optional groups. Therefore, a given control can have no hint, just one hint, or several hints. The same apply to <help>, <extension>, and <alter>. Hints are particularly useful in directing the user further if the caption is not enough to disambiguate the expected response type. Hint, help, and alert all accommodate XLink expressions to refer to externally stored data. Again, this can be helpful for tasks such as internationalization, where there are several variations of the metadata or data associated with these elements, but the variations can be grouped in a sensible manner using content or context.
3. *<alert>*: Alerts are designed to notify the user of some error during the interactions with the forms. These errors may be related to the data entered by the user or the manner in which the user is trying to navigate through the application. Alerts may be interpreted into popup boxes by a GUI or an audio message in a VUI.
4. *<extension>*: The extension element allows us to extend controls with domain-dependent controls if need be. Whereas form controls, their attributes, and their elements are focused on creating a generic user interface independent of the domain model, it is possible to create user interface components that serve a particular domain. For example, if there is a particular XML format (defined by some XML Schema or DTD) that defines a governmental structure, it can be used for a user interface specific for displaying governmental structures. <extension> is particularly useful for RDF. RDF namespaces can be included within extensions.

Example 5.6: Using the Optional Attributes and Elements.

```
<input xml:lang="en" navIndex=1 accessKey="#" >
    <caption xlink:href="http://localhost/languagebundle.xml>
    Enter the name of your country's head of state
    </caption>
    <hint navIndex=1 xml:lang="en">
    Please enter the name of the head of the executive branch in
    your government. This may be a king, prime minister,
    president, or others.
    </hint>
    <hint navIndex=2 xml:lang="en">
    For example, this could be George Bush for US.
    </hint>
    <alert xlink:href="http://localhost/
      InCorrectHeadOfState.xml">
    IncorrectHeadOfState
    </alert>
</input>
<input ref="model_binding" id="device-tilt-measurement">
    <my_domain_model_name_space:government>
        <my_domain_model_name_space:president>
            President
        </my_domain_mode_name_space:president>
    </my_domain_mode_name_space:government>
</input>
```

One method to use resource bundles for these attributes and elements using XLink is to use the value of the element as the key in the XLink resource. A variety of mechanisms offered by W3C, such as XSL and RDF, can be used to bind this key to the XLink expression to retrieve the proper data at run time. This functionality could also be built into the XForms Processing Model implementation (the XForms clients). In Example 5.6, to lessen the amount of code, we have only used an external document for internationalization for the alert element. In the case of a real implementation, XLink expressions, and corresponding resources, would be used for all of the elements that may be rendered to the user at some point.

Now that we have looked at the common attributes and elements of form controls, let us see what the actual form controls are and how they are used.

User Interface Form Controls

The designers of XForms User Interface were admirably diligent in creating a standard that places very little bias, if any, on the end-user interface. The XForms User Interface currently comes closest to a neutral modeling of the user interface. The XForms specification says "form controls encapsulate high-level semantics without sacrificing the ability to deliver real implementations" [W3C XForms].

However, these form controls accomplish even more than that as their attributes and children elements allow some extensibility without violating the true form of their semantics. The prime example of this is the optional child element of <extension> mentioned in the previous section. These form controls are thought out based on the generic sense of some different ways a user can send messages to the system: a generic form of representing the responses to the prompts that the system sends to the user. The first of these form controls is the most basic one, the <input> control.

Example 5.7: Transforming the Input Element.

XForms:

```
<input ref="PresidentName" xml:lang="en" navIndex=1
  accessKey="#">
    <caption xlink:href="http://localhost/languagebundle.xml>
    Enter the name of your country's head of state
    </caption>
    <hint navIndex=1 xml:lang="en">
    Please enter the name of the head of the executive branch in
    your government.
    This may be a king, prime minister, president, or others.
    </hint>
</input>
```

VXML:

```
<field name="PresidentName">
    <prompt>
        Enter the name of your country's head of state
        <audio src="http://localhost/audio/headOfStatePrompt.
          wav"/>
    </prompt>
    <grammar src=http://localhost/grammars/PossibleHeadsOfState#
      PresidentName/>
<block>
```

1. *<input>*: The input tag allows us to get the most basic form of input from the user in the form of a simple unstructured response limited to atomic data types as defined per the Schema Data Types document of W3C [W3C Schema—2] except for the hex binary and base-64 encoded types. This means that the input from the user can take the form of a string, a number (integer, float, double, etc.), a Boolean, any date, or any URI. See Example 5.7. In this example, we show how the XForms input control is easily transformed into a VXML block. Obviously, transforming complex XForms pages is not this straightforward as there are interdependencies and complex contexts among the various form elements. Nevertheless, our example here shows that an XForms form control

is flexible regardless of the type of interface using it. However, the requirement of being able to put in just about any valid XML Schema data type can limit the type of user interfaces that can accommodate the <input> tag.

The data type of the <input> is specified through the *inputMode* attribute. Proper extensions have to be available, in the system rendering the final user interface, to provide for the proper input masks or formatting necessary to force the user to enter only the valid data type. For example, if the inputMode attribute is set to xsd:dateTime, then the final user interface, whatever it is, must provide the proper facilities to the user for input of a date and time.

2. *<secret>*: The <secret> form control is typically used for password or other information that should not be exposed to anyone seeing or hearing the user responding to the system. Though it is always possible for someone else to see the keystrokes of a user while the user is entering a password, or to hear the personal ID number as the user says it into a VUI, this tag specifies that the system should never echo back the user input, thereby providing some amount of security. This control can also imply use of other security measures such as voiceprint verification, fingerprint verification, or whatever security mechanism may be available for a given user interface. All the other issues we mentioned about the input element apply to the secret element. The principle difference is that <secret> implies requirement of some security. The implementation of such security is context dependent and may be specified by other parts of the XForms document such as actions, or by the extensions that are domain dependent.
3. *<selectOne>*: Besides entering simple input, another basic operation that is possible in nearly all user interfaces is to select one thing out of a list of things. An example is a simple menu. Menus can be used regardless of the interface channels: They can be read as a list for an aural interface or displayed as a select list, menu bar, or select box in a graphical interface. The <selectOne> form control can have some children elements, in addition to the common elements that we discussed earlier. See Example 5.8. Let us go through these elements.
   a. *<item>*: This is the simplest element that defines a selection in selectOne. Items are the menu items to be listed, one of which is to be selected. Each <item> in turn can have a caption element (<caption>), which is how it is labeled to be presented at the final user interface, and a value (<value>), which is the value stored in the instance data pointed to by the ref attribute of <selectOne>.
   b. *<itemset>*: The specification distinguishes <itemset> by its dynamic use. This can be deceiving: The specification is referred to dynamically in the sense that <itemset> allows the selection to be constructed, at run time, based on the instance data available in the XForms. This does not mean that we cannot produce dynamic results with <item> and <choices>. This could be done by holding the instance data in the object model that generates the XForms (for example, in Java, this would be the Servlet/JSP infrastructure when building Web applications). However, <itemset> offers a clear advantage over the other options for creation of a dynamic set of choices because we can separate the dynamic content by creating the instance data dynamically and letting

the XForms form controls remain static. The other advantage that this offers is that we can transform the XForms User Interface through one pass of XSL transforms instead of multiple passes. This improves the system by reducing code, reducing complexity, and improving performance.

To point to the particular instance data, the attribute nodeset is used. See Example 5.9 for how to use the itemset element to link to the instance data.

c. *<choices>*: This tag allows grouping of other choices, items, and itemsets. This tag is used when there are many choices and some logical grouping of these choices makes sense. In these cases, it is easier to group the items, itemsets, or choices (subchoices) together before presenting them to the user.

There are also additional attributes that can further define a <selectOne> element. Let us look at those quickly:

d. *selection*: The selection attribute of the <selectOne> tag specifies whether or not the user's selection is limited to the list of <item> elements. If this attribute is set to *open*, the user can enter whatever data, including the list of items. In real applications, this typically is transformed to the "other" selection at the final user interface upon which "other" may result in the system prompting the user for free-flow input. If the selection attribute is set to other, the processing model treats others as an <input>. The selection attribute can be either open or closed. By default, the selection attribute is set to closed. This implies that the user's selection is limited to the list of items.
e. *selectUI*: This attribute allows for five possible values (radio, checkbox, menu, listbox, or combo). This attribute is one of the rare instances where XForms specification seems to have gone astray in keeping user interface specific information out. We recommend against using this attribute because the possible value set for this attribute is biased toward a GUI controlled by a mouse and/or keyboard. For example, checkbox does not have any meaning in a VUI.
f. *ref*: This attribute points to the instance data that will hold whatever value the user chooses. As in other controls, ref is typically used as the "variable" that holds the value that the user chooses. (The term variable, though imprecise, helps in visualizing the functional mechanism.)

Now, let us look at an example of how we can use selectOne. Example 5.8 shows an example of how to create a generic interface that allows the user to select the name of a head of state.

Example 5.8: Using the <selectOne> Element.

```
<selectOne ref="domain:country">
    <item navIndex="1" accessKey="1">
        <caption>United States</caption>
```

```
        <value>US</value>
    </item>
    <item navIndex="2" accessKey="2">
        <caption>United Kingdom</caption>
        <value>UK</value>
    </item>
</selectOne>

<selectOne ref="domain:head-of-state">
    <choices navIndex="1">
        <caption>United States</caption>
        <item navIndex="1">
            <caption>Bill Clinton</caption>
            <value>Bill_Clinton</value>
        </item>
        <item navIndex="2">
            <caption>George Bush</caption>
            <value>George_Bush</value>
        </item>
    </choices>
    <choices navIndex="2">
        <caption>United Kingdom</caption>
        <item navIndex="1">
            <caption>Tony Blair</caption>
            <value>Tony_Blair</value>
        </item>
        <item navIndex="2">
            <caption>Margaret Thacher</caption>
            <value>Margaret_Thacher</value>
        </item>
    </choices>
</selectOne>
```

The document in Example 5.8 could have been generated dynamically or statically. If this content is to be generated dynamically, the entire document would have to be produced by some programmatic means of producing the document. Whether this is Java servlets, CGI, Microsoft ASP pages, PHP, or another mechanism does not matter. The entire document is produced dynamically.

Example 5.9: Using the <itemset> for Dynamic Data.

```
<xforms:model id="government">
    <instance>
        <domain:government>
```

```
            <domain:executive/>
            <domain:legislative/>
            <domain:judiciary/>
        </domain>
    </instance>
</xforms:model>

<xforms:model id="executive">
    <instance>
        <domain:executive>
            <domain:head-of-state country="US">
                <domain:name>George Bush</domain:name>
                <domain:value>George_Bush</domain:name>
            </domain:head-of-state>
            <domain:head-of-state country="UK">
                <domain:name>Tony Blair</domain:name>
                <domain:value>Tony_Blair</domain:value>
            </domain:head-of-state>
        </domain:executive>
    </instance>
</xforms>
<!------------------------------------------------------------------>
<xforms:selectOne model="government" ref="domain:executive/
  domain:head-of-state">
    <caption>Head Of State</caption>
    <itemset model="executive" nodeset="domain:executive/domain:
      head-of-state">
        </caption ref="domain:name"/>
        <value ref="@value"/>
    </itemset>
</xforms>
```

To avoid this, we can use the <itemset> tag instead as in Example 5.9. In this example, the XML segment above the comment line can be generated statically whereas the XML segment below the line can remain the same. The obvious advantage to this is separation of presentation logic that focuses on the method of presentation (the form control that is used to get the input from the user) from the dynamic generation of data. This gives us a huge advantage over the typical Web development model for dynamic generation of data. Whereas these models use tightly coupled patterns such as Model-View-Controller (MVC) design pattern to separate the concerns of presentation, data, and business logic, XForms gives us much better facilities than what is available today and this example obviates this.

In practice, the bottom part of Example 5.9 could be static, in its own XML file. The top part of the example, which holds the instance data, needs to be generated at run time. The implementing mechanism of the XForm processor, whether on the server side or on the client side, can first initialize the instance data, depending on the entry state of the application, then use XSLs (or some other mechanism) to put together the code in its entirety as shown, and finally provide the binding between the instance data and the user interface form controls. Further styling can then be done through CSS, ACSS, or XSL.

Though we have mentioned this in the past, once again it is important to remember that the modularity of XForms allows us to distribute various parts of this process to the client or the server side, depending on the requirements of the application and the available infrastructure.

Let us continue with our list of form controls.

4. *<output>*: This form control allows us to access instance data without providing any control or input mechanisms for the user. This element is most useful in producing instance data for returning some data to a user's request or in providing a way to create composites of the instance data for labels and other displayed portions of XForms. This element is typically used to describe text; therefore, if an aural user interface is to be used, it infers requiring a text-to-speech engine. This element, unfortunately, does not provide proper facilities to create a user interface–neutral method of putting together "resource-based" output interface elements. For example, you cannot create an output element that supports reading back to the user content comprising utterances of audio files as opposed to text to speech (at least this is what the current XForms Schema indicates). This may change in future versions of XForms.
5. *<range>*: The range form control gives us a way to specify an analog range between two different numbers. Although this control is typically translated to a range button for the GUIs, it can be used to specify limits around a given input to the user in both aural and GUIs. Example 5.10 shows the XML for a range control that allows the user to enter the points scored in a game. Range buttons can be specified to the particular user interface in three ways:
   a. *Server-side validation*: The user input may be validated on the server side. So, if the user puts in some information that does not fall within the minimum and maximum range specified, a trip to the server is necessary. This is probably not what the designers of XForms had in mind, though it does not mean that the XForms client cannot come back all the way to the server that serves up the XForm for the validation. In the case of a mobile application, it is very possible that this is necessary as most of the clients are resource-starved and cannot run scripting languages necessary to perform the validation. If the validation is done on the server side, the attributes do not impose any limitations. On the client side, in contrast, this validation may be difficult because, as the interval size gets smaller or the length between the start and end attribute becomes larger, more advanced mathematical computations are needed.

Example 5.10: Using the <range> to Limit User Input.

```
<xforms:range ref="team_one/score" start="0" end="7"
  stepSize="1">
    <caption>Please enter the first team's score</caption>
</xforms:range>
</xforms:range ref="team_two/score" start="0" end="7"
  stepSize="1">
    <caption>Please enter the second team's score</caption>
</xforms:range>
```

After a transformation and binding to the instance data, the equivalent VXML snippet could be:

```
<field name="team_one_score">
    <prompt>Please enter the first team's score</prompt>
    <grammar mode="voice" xml:lang="en"
        <rule id="scores" scope="public">
            <one-of>
                <item>one</item>
                <item>two</item>
                <item>three</item>
                <item>four</item>
                <item>five</item>
                <item>six</item>
                <item>seven</item>
            </one-of>
        </rule>
    </grammar>
</field>
```

b. *Client-side validation*: If the final user interface is rendered by a client that has the ability to run a scripting language such as ECMAScript (JavaScript), the validation can be done after the final user interface has been rendered. This means that the XForms form control maps into two different elements at the final destination: 1. the control that collects the information from the user and 2. the script that validates that information. Let us look at Example 5.10. In this case, our client is a VXML browser. The VXML can specify a new grammar for the possible scores, as shown in the example. The alternative is that, if there is a common grammar for numbers, we could use that grammar and then validate the user input after the number has been obtained from the user using ECMAScript along with our VXML. Client-side validation using a scripting language is less applicable to GUIs because the range control typically maps to a slider bar or a similar control that does not physically allow the user to input an incorrect piece of data.

c. *Validation through the control grammar*: Grammars are typically a term used in VUIs and seldom in GUIs. However, this terminology can be used on the client side as well because we can call the set of possible values allowed by a control its grammar. Therefore, in a list box that allows the user to select only from the values on the list, the grammar is the set of the list items. We can use the range and the interval to create a grammar for the control at the final user interface. Example 5.10 deploys this method. As you note, the transformation of the XForm range control generated a prompt with a custom grammar using the range and the interval specified by the range.

6. *<button>*: The button control allows the user to trigger an event without any textual input into a GUI. The button control is most applicable to GUIs. This control can be translated to a command in a VUI, but this transformation is not natural (as you will find out if you try to transform the button to one of the available commands in VXML). The XForms specifications says "the user agent must provide a means to generate an xforms:activate on the form control" [W3C XForms]. Because this button does not provide any bindings, the implementation of the XForms processor must allow an event to be created (specifically xforms:activate) when this button is "pushed."
7. *<textarea>*: The <input> form control typically places some limitations on the length of data to be entered by the user regardless of the user interface used. For example, in an aural user interface, this may be enforced by allowing the user to input a maximum of ten seconds of voice. In an HTML interface, this may be the number of characters allowed in the control. The <textarea> form control allows the user to input an unlimited amount of data (or at least not particularly limited because there may be limitations imposed by the supporting infrastructure such as possible amount of storage or maximum length of a maintainable open connection channel between the user and the system).
8. *<upload>*: The use of this element, at first, may seem very specific to the thin-client Web applications using HTML or similar markup languages. However, a closer look shows that this control could apply to a variety of user interfaces, supported by thin or thick clients. The upload element can be used to indicate the need to upload any type of media to the server. This element may be particularly useful for mobile applications. Imagine a mobile device that has a poor, an intermittent, or no connection to the network but has a reasonable amount of storage. Now, let us say the user needs to send an audio message to another user. The application can store the message, locally on the client or wherever the XForms processor is running. The entire concept of "upload" infers that some data were collected on the batch basis or that a data file simply exists: This is what is to be uploaded. Therefore, this form control can effectively only be used through user interfaces that support a data channel. Graphical user interfaces nearly always do. However, the same is not true of VUIs. Voice user interfaces that connect to the system with a PSTN do not support transfer of data and voice at the same time. So, for the user to upload a file, voice or otherwise, the mobile device must be able to provide a modem or a modem-like connection to upload the information. This works for most cell phones. But, the upload tag is not applicable to VUIs being accessed by a

regular telephone for there is no way for the end user to upload information. Now, there are those who argue that the XForm client can really be yet another server being connected to by a "dumb terminal" such as a regular phone.

It is true that in this case we could use the <upload> tag by the XForm client (which is really on the server side) to gather the information and then upload it to the server of the XForm client. This model, however, is not very interesting and does not seem to be in the spirit of what the <upload> tag was intended as. Developers should always keep in mind the cost of layers of indirection versus the benefits. If the final user interface generated by the XForms browser, or whatever the XForms client and the subsequent transformation process may involve, produces content that is served up to a "dumb terminal" type of client (one that cannot do much of anything but provide a simple display), a large part of the XForms value proposition is rendered useless. This is not to say that such use should be ruled out. Quite the contrary, as we mentioned previously, XForms has a very modular design and its various components can offer us great benefits individually. However, certain components or subcomponents (for example the upload tag and the accompanying functionality) may not lend themselves to appropriate use in particular systems and application architectures.

9. *<selectMany>*: This tag is much like its counterpart of <selectOne> previously discussed in this section. The final rendition of what is represented by this tag should allow the user to select multiple things, as its name implies, of a list of things. When using this form control, it is recommended that the <choices> tag be used to group families of options to simplify selecting multiple options, all of which may need to be selected, and all of which fall within that family of selections.
10. *<submit>*: This form control tells the user interface that the user is done filling out the form. A look at the XML Schema defining XForms shows that there may be multiple submissions in one XForms document. This allows better support for dynamic workflows that allow the user to use one "page" or section of the user interface to easily navigate to several other places while entering only the data required by the particular workflow the user wants. The <submit> control simply calls a submitInfo control pointed to by its submitInfo attribute.

Now that we have extensively looked at the various form controls provided by XForms, let us look at how these form controls are bound to the instance data on the form.

Binding the User Interface Elements to Instance Data

Example 5.11: Binding User Interface Components to Instance Data.

```
<xforms:model id="government">
    <xforms:instance xmlns=http://www.mysite.com/myModel.xml>
        <executiveBranch>
```

```
            <head-of-state>
               George Bush
            </head-of-state>
         </executiveBranch>
         <legislativeBranch>
         </legislativeBranch>
         <judicalBranch>
         </judicialBranch>
      </xforms:instance>
      <xforms:bind ref="government/executiveBranch/head-of-state"
        id="president"/>
   </xforms:model>
```

Binding with the ref attribute:

```
   <xforms:input ref="government/executiveBranch/head-of-state">
      <caption>Please enter the name of your country's head of
        state here.</caption>
   </xforms:input>
```

Binding with the bind attribute:

```
   <xforms:input bind="president">
      <caption>Please enter the name of your country's head of
        state here.</caption>
   </xforms:input>
```

Explicit binding:

```
   <xforms:input model="government" ref="government/
     executiveBranch/head-of-state">
      <caption>Please enter the name of your country's head of
        state here.</caption>
   </xforms:input>
```

As we saw in the examples in the previous sections, the form controls allow us to define the "static" portion of the user interface in a generic manner: They let us put some interaction elements on the user interface without any bias to a particular type of user interface (such as X-Windows or VUIs), without any bias toward a particular domain (such as financial industry, customer relationship management, etc.), and without any dependence on whether the data themselves are static or are being generated dynamically. This makes the process of binding these elements with the instance data, which holds the domain-dependent information, crucial. After all, it is this information that needs to be collected from the user.

All binding in XForms is really part of the XForms Model. However, here we will discuss it outside of the model because it is the user interface controls with which we are primarily concerned. The user interface controls can be bound to two types of nodes: model elements that exist on the same document accessed by referring to a single node ID (single node binding) and nodesets referred to by an XPath expression (Nodeset Binding). The type of binding is determined by which attribute is used.

To understand this, we need to look at some examples. First, let us take some instance data such as those in Example 5.11. Here, we use three distinct methods to bind the form controls to the instance data. Note that the <xforms:bind> tag allows us to create an "alias," namely "president," with which the desired instance data element can be bound at run time. This alias can later be dereferenced by using the *bind* attribute. We can also point explicitly to the instance model and then work our way down to the instance data element to be bound to the control using an XPath expression. Finally, we can use the *ref* attribute for dereferencing the instance element. We could also use the nodeset attribute for binding if there is a need to access the instance data element through an XPath expression and using the ref attribute does not suffice. This could be the case if the instance data are not all in one section of the document or in one document.

Hidden Form Controls

Hidden controls have been somewhat of a debated topic in XForms and other markup languages aimed at creating generic user interfaces. XForms treats hidden controls, or fields, as they are known in the HTML development world, very elegantly. Indeed, it is the instance data model that eliminates the need for hidden fields altogether.

Hidden controls in HTML, WML, and other similar markup languages are used to keep state around without having to maintain server-side state or to keep values that should not be seen by the user. The reason "hidden" fields are used is that there is typically no other mechanism to keep this information. In the case of XForms, however, because presentation and the data are separated, we do not need to worry about hidden fields. Remember that the form controls point to instance data. So, if there are instance data that are not used by form controls, we have the ability to keep whatever information is needed in those data.

We have now covered the basics of the form controls. The form controls are the touch points of the user or the client that might sit in front of the XForms container. To bring it all together, we will look at the events, constraints, and the other parts of XForms later. Let us now look at how XForms handles events.

5.5.4 Events in XForms

So far we have seen that the interactions are done through the form controls and that the form controls bind to the instance data. But how does the client to the XForms container tell the container to switch control to a particular control, that the client is done filling the form control, etc.? This is where the XForms events come in. The XForms event model is built based on the XML events, another W3C standard that we have looked at in Chapter 3.

Events are spoken of in many different contexts within XML; it is important to note that we are not talking about parsing events such as those that are created by SAX parsers. Our events are of two types: events caused by user interactions and events caused by the nature of the State Machine that is the XForms container.

The first group of events should be intuitive to the reader: Events are a typical method of handling user interactions with the user interface. Interaction events, as the W3C XForms specification document calls them, are those events that model the interaction of the user with the form controls. (The user actions may be going through an intermediate layer; nonetheless, as long as they cause one or more events to occur at the XForms container, they are considered interaction events.) Before we can understand XForms events, we need to quickly review what event-based messaging is.

Event-based messaging systems always have three basic components: the event listener, the event producer, and the event itself. (This is an object-oriented way of looking at messages, but then this is a text on developing mobile applications using UML so a certain amount of bias toward object-oriented systems should be implied.) Event producers are the components that create the events. In the GUI development world, a button can be an event producer. The event is the message that gets generated by the event producer. The event listener is the component that receives the produced event. An event producer can producer more than one type of event and there may be many different listeners for each event that is produced. "Event"-driven systems typically refer to synchronous operations whereas messaging typically refers to asynchronous operations. So, unless otherwise mentioned, when we say events, we mean synchronous events.

XForms form controls or the user interface components are not the only type of components that can use events. In fact, XForms Processing Model uses events to propagate notification of changes among the various components of XForms. For example, there are events that may cause changes in instance data or be produced as a result of changes in the instance data. In this way, events allow synchronous binding of the mutations that occur among the various parts of an XForms document at run time.

Let us start with the interaction events. We will keep the taxonomy identified by the W3C specification, which organizes events depending on the state of the XForms document during which they occur. However, we will also point out that the listener and producer of the event are critical to how we group various events.

Navigational Interaction Events

As in the case of form controls, the W3C XForms team has done their very best to keep the events generic and with no bias toward any particular type of user interface. But this has proved to be challenging as event models outside of GUI-based systems have not had many years to mature.

In traditional GUI programs, events that are used by GUI controls are prevalent. So, this is probably the most intuitive starting point. Let us start by going through the events associated with the form controls. Keep in mind that these events all take place during the interaction stage of the state diagram that represents the XForms processing model. The events we need to consider are as follows:

1. *<xforms:next>*: Do not confuse this with the NEXT button of your browser. The container provides the facilities for all form controls to have the ability to listen to this type of event. As we mentioned previously, one of the common attributes

in form controls is the *navIndex*. Regardless of what type of final user interface is being rendered, the user needs a way to move through choices, through a list, or through any other type of grouping of form controls. For example, in a GUI, the Tab key may be used to move through controls. Because the final user interface is not known, the only requirement in XForms is that the <xforms:next> event be issued. This event, in turn, tells the XForms container to move to the next form control.

2. *<xforms:previous>*: This event is the opposite of the <xforms:next> event—it tells the container to move the focus to the element that has the immediately lower navIndex. It is also important to notice that, in both previous and next events, if the navIndex is not supplied, the order of appearance of elements in the document is used to determine an implied navIndex. In other words, if element *a* appears before element *b*, and we assume that element a has a navIndex of *n*, element *b* has a navIndex of $n + 1$ (if navIndex is not specified explicitly). If none of the controls have explicitly specified their navIndex, the first control will implicitly have a navIndex of 0; the *n*th element will have a navIndex of $n - 1$. The effect of a navIndex of 0 is the same as no navIndex. In GUI environments, the previous and next events can be produced by a shortcut key whereas in VUI environments so-called universal commands can be used to produce such events. The listener of both previous and next is the container, which in turn shifts the focus from the current element to the previous or next element depending on which event is produced.
3. *<xforms:activate>*: The activate event is typically used for a button in a GUI or a navigational command in a VUI (and so the event producer of an activate event is typically a button or an analogous element in non-GUI environments). The event is used to put the focus on a particular form control after the event has been produced.
4. *<xforms:help>*: This event is produced by the XForms container client (which could be the user itself or another user agent that specializes the XForms User Interface to a particular type of user interface). The listener to this event is a form control whose help is to be displayed by the container or the client to the container (if the client is not the user).
5. *<xforms:hint>*: This control's behavior is identical to the <xforms:help> behavior except that the hint element of the form control is invoked instead of the help element.
6. *<xforms:focus>*: This event is typically produced by the XForms container client (which could be the user itself or another user agent that specializes the XForms User Interface to a particular type of user interface). The listener to this event is the container itself. When this event is issued, the container moves focus to the specified form control. In a GUI environment, for example, such an event could be issued by mouse movement and clicking. In a VUI environment, this could be done by a "universal" command or DTMF input. Another example may be the use of a hot key on a client such as a WAP client to gain the focus of a particular client.
7. *<xforms:blur>*: The behavior of this event is the opposite of that of the focus but its producer and listener are the same.

8. *<xforms:valueChanged>*: Form controls are bound to instance data. So, if the value being entered into the form control changes, then the instance data must be updated. However, this must be done only when the user is finished with updating the particular form control. This event is produced by the container when the user creates or changes the data in a form control and then indicates being finished by moving focus or clicking on submit.
9. *<xforms:valueChanging>*: This event is designed to notify the listener that a particular input to a particular form control is currently being modified. For example, if a user begins typing into an input box, this event is emitted. The event producer is the XForms container while, as in the case of valueChanged element, any control could be a listener.

These are all of the events that allow navigation through the form controls of a user interface. All of these are applicable across multiple types of user interfaces. There are yet more events. The remainder of events allow interactions with instance data, the XForms model, and other XForms User Interface elements. Are there other elements? Thus far, we only talked about the atomic element of XForms. Although we can make a generic user interface of only these elements, XForms provides us with some composite elements to give us more functionality. Let us look at these composite elements before we discuss the events that use them.

Composite XForms User Interface Elements

As we discussed previously in this chapter, composite elements of a user interface exist because a grouping of atomic elements can have its own behavior, additional attributes, and a contextual relationship with other composite and atomic components of a user interface. Having recognized this, the XForms standards group created a set of composite controls. Once again, this has been done in a manner that applies to a variety of user interfaces, keeping XForms a good option for creating generic user interfaces. Here are the composite elements as defined by XForms:

Example 5.12: Grouping Atomic Elements to Create Composite Elements in XForms.

```
<group ref="name">
    <caption>Full Name</caption>
    <input ref="firstName">
        <caption>First Name</caption>
    </input>
    <input ref="middleName">
        <caption>Middle Name</caption>
    </input>
    <input ref="lastName">
        <caption>Last Name</caption>
```

```
  </input>
  <selectOne ref="title">
    <choices>
      <item><caption>Dr.</caption><value>DR</value></item>
      <item><caption>Mr.</caption><value>MR</value></item>
      <item><caption>Mrs.</caption><value>MRS</value></item>
      <item><caption>Miss</caption><value>MISS</value></item>
    </choices>
  </selectOne>
</group>
```

1. *<group>*: The group element has a simple task implied by its name: It groups other group elements and/or atomic elements of XForms User Interface, the form controls that we reviewed in Section 5.5.3 (subsection on XForm User Interfaces). By allowing for the common attributes, this element allows us to creating large-grained components. The primary purpose of creating such user interface components may be to tell the final user interface to keep the integrity of the component together when specializing to a particular user interface (for example, not putting two given form controls on different pages if they belong to the same group, etc.), encapsulating some context that the contained elements may have when grouped, and putting the relationship between the contained elements inside the sandbox of the group element. Example 5.12 shows how the group element can be used. This element can also be used to bind a group of user interface controls to a structure of instance data.

Example 5.13: Using the Repeat Element for Collections.

```
<repeat nodeset="/invoice/item">
    <output ref="."/>
</repeat>
```

2. *<repeat>*: The repeat element gives us the ability to create lists of items for display purposes. Do not mistake this list with <selectOne> or <selectMany>. In the case of those elements, the user is selecting one or more items, depending on which control is used. This input then gets bound to some instance data. The repeat element displays all of the items on the list and each item may require some user input. It is provided as an iterating mechanism. For example, when creating a list of charges for an invoice, the size of the collection of the instance data may be variable. The other reason to use the repeat element is to avoid hard-coding enumerations. Example 5.13 shows how to display a collection of invoice items. Another advantage of using the repeat element is to take advantage of the separation of presentation and data for dynamic data. Although instance data might continue to change during the life of the XForms document in the XForms container (through user interactions), this form control can

SIDE DISCUSSION 5.2

P3P (Platform for Privacy Preferences) Project

P3P is another W3C standard. This standard specifies a mechanism for allowing Web pages or an XML document to contain information about the privacy implications of viewing them (whether the document is viewed by a user or a program).

update the rendering of the generic user interface to keep what appears to the container client updated with the instance data. There are two special events for the repeat element, *<scrollFirst>* and *<scrollLast>*. These two events are produced by a user interface action, such as pressing a button, and in turn causing the container to move to the beginning or end of the list, depending on which event is issued.

3. *<switch>*: The switch element allows limited logic based on the state of the instance data. The switch element allows the XForms user interface to represent a different user interface depending on the user's actions. The reader must be warned that this element can easily be misused and can easily introduce bugs into the application as, most of the time, not every state of the system is tested thoroughly during quality assurance. The switch element, just like the switch statement in programming languages such as Java, has cases. Each of these cases are specified using a *<case>* element. The case element, in turn, can have any of the atomic elements (form controls). It also has an attribute called *selected*, which can be set to *true* or *false*. This attribute is used by the XForms container to determine which case to display. The case with the selected attribute set to true is displayed. If there are multiple cases with the selected attribute set to true, the first is displayed and the container sets the selected attribute of the other cases to false. When the select attribute of a case is changed, an event is generated. This event is an <xforms:select> if the attribute is changed to true and is an <xforms:deselected> if the attribute is changed to false from true.

These three elements are the basic composite elements introduced by XForms. However, it is possible to create custom composite elements through adding desired context and relationship information to the transformation process while the XForms User Interface is being specialized to the user interface that the user is actually interacting with. All of the navigational interaction events that we looked at can be used with these composite elements just as we used them with the atomic elements. Because the composite elements are a grouping of other elements, the element with the lowest navIndex gets focus when the composite element has focus. When navigating through the composite elements, next, previous, and the other events are within the scope of the composite element.

Now, let us look at the remainder of the events. These events are related to the instance data or the state of the processing model.

Processing Model Events and Instance Events

Take, for example, a page that might request some information from your system stored in a cookie. Depending on your inclination on allowing others to see information stored in the cookies of your system, and depending on what the page is itself and who the owner of the page may be, you may or may not want to allow the page to retrieve some information. You can specify such settings in your viewing client permanently or put the settings in every time you view a page. P3P specifies a standard method by which resources and resource consumers on the Internet can tell each other what private information is allowed to be exchanged and what private information is needed or expected to be exchanged for a transaction. For more detail, refer to the W3C site (http://www.w3c.org/TR/P3P).

Let us return to Figure 5.16, which represents the state diagram of a document in the container. We went through some of the events that take place while the XForms document, living in the document container, is in the "Interact with Container Client" state. Now, let us take a look at the remainder of the events, starting with those that take place while the document is in the initialization stage.

The initialization state is focused mainly on the instance data. At this state, the instance data must be initialized. Initialization events are internal to the container, but we can use them to customize the initialization sequence of a given document (for example, what values are in the document and a chain of events that may be triggered based on the initial events that set up those values). So, let us start with the very first event:

1. <xforms:modelConstruct>: When this event happens, the container initializes the data based on some external source. If there is no external source, the initial data are simply left empty. The processing order of this event allows us to have some default values on the XForms document for the initial values and to override those default values using an external document. This event is internal to the XForms container.
2. <xforms:modelInitialize>: After the <xforms:modelConstruct> event starts the initialization state by finding the initial values, external or internal to the document, this event tells the container to check the validity of the data, to check some privacy rules using P3P (see Side Discussion 5.2), and to call the next event, <xforms:initializeDone>.
3. <xforms:initializeDone>, <xforms:UIInitialize>, and <xforms:form ControlInitialize>: The <xforms:initializeDone> element simply specifies that initialization of the instance data is finished and the UI can be initialized. <xforms:UIInitialize> tells the container to go through all of the form controls and issue an <xforms:formControlInitialize> for each one of them. This event basically forces an initial binding among the model, the instance data, and the form controls by the container. Although <xforms:modelConstruct> and <xforms:modelInitialize> initialize the model and the instance data, for these initial values to actually appear in controls, the controls have to be bound to the instance data and the model. This binding is done when the <xforms:formControlInitialize> event is issued.

That wraps up the events for the initialization state of the document. Keep in mind that if you are an XForms document author, you may never use some of the events, the features, or the functionality that we talked about in this chapter. For example, the <xforms:initializeDone> event would rarely be used by a developer who simply wants to use XForms as a means to develop a generic user interface for a mobile application. Many of the various features and functionalities of XForms that we discussed here are really just targeted for implementation by the developers of the XForms container (or the XForms browsers). Nonetheless, there are two benefits in a thorough examination of these features. The first is that we see the guts of how the container works. This helps us greatly in understanding why a particular bug happens and gives us a good intuition for how the document is processed by the container. Second, it is very possible that we want to implement an XForms container, a subset of an XForms container, or a client to an XForms container for a particular mobile platform. For example, we may want to create a system with user interfaces on PDAs, PCs, and WAP phones. Although we may use a set of XSLs to convert the XForms User Interface to WML for the WAP phones because writing an XForms container for a WAP phone is probably a bit too much, we may want to write an XForms container for the PDA and the PC. The container for the PDA may be a lighter version with fewer pieces of functionality implemented.

So, in this way, what we discussed in this chapter regarding XForms may apply to a particular application in bits and pieces. As we mention repeatedly throughout this text, this is the art and science of software engineering!

Now, let us move on the remainder of the events that affect the instance data and the model. Once the XForms document is initialized, it moves into the interaction state. In this state, the user interactions cause changes to the document, directly through interacting with the container or indirectly through interacting with a client to the container. So, instance data have to be manipulated. This is done by the following events:

1. *<xforms:insert>*: This event simply notifies the container that some data were inserted into the instance data from one of the form controls.
2. *<xforms:delete>*: This event notifies the container that an event from some form control caused some data to be deleted from the instance data.

And that is all there is to it! Instance data are really manipulated by the form controls and their events during the interaction state. That leaves us with a few events that handle the processing model and submission of the XForms document parameters:

1. *<xforms:refresh>*: This event causes the binding among the model, user interface controls, and instance data to be forced and, thereby, "refresh" what is on the user interface. Practically speaking, this event is useful when a control is in some strange state or if a form control was disabled and the user interface has not been updated. As in most cases, the idea of a "refresh" in a user interface is to obviate the need for the user interface developers to have to worry about all of the possible states of the container.

2. *<xforms:recalculate>*: This event allows a calculation of all of the XPath expressions in the XForms document. This event is particularly important if the value of an XPath expression is dynamically calculated based on some instance data. As the instance data change, for the value of the XPath expression to be correct, the expressions must be "recalculated."
3. *<xforms:reset>*: This event causes the container to return all of the instance data to its state immediately after the document initialization state. This event works much like the reset event does in HTML.
4. *<xforms:submit>*: This event indicates a user interaction with the system to show that he or she is finished interacting and wants to submit the data. The container then submits all of the instance data to some POST target. Though the XForms specification typically specifies things in terms of HTTP, remember that we can use other application layer protocols to interface with the XForms container (XForms document browser).

This wraps up our look at the XForms event model. The only remaining piece in processing a document is the container's treatment of constraints that may be placed upon the user's responses. These constraints can be used as validation.

The XForms Processing Model uses XML Schemas, which are discussed in Chapter 3 extensively. In fact, XForms uses the *XML Schemas' data types*. Although XML Schema data types are used, there are additional properties defining the metadata and behavior presented by an XForms Model document. These properties are called *model item properties*. Model item properties are either static or XPath expressions (also referred to as computed). We will refer to the collection of these properties, namely the XML Schema's data types and model item properties, as simply properties. Every item in an XForms Model document can have any of these properties.

There are eight model item properties:

1. *type*: XForms Model uses XML Schema data types to specify the type of the data element. The type of the data is important for both validation and binding. For example, if the type of data is a numeric type, characters outside of 0–9 and the decimal point must not be allowed.
2. *readOnly*: If true, this property indicates that the XForms control is not to be changed. By default the value of this property is false.
3. *relevant*: The instance data associated with some form controls may not need to be sent when a submit action takes place. If relevant is set to false, the instance data associated with the particular form control are not sent during submission.
4. *calculate*: This attribute can be any valid XPath expression that allows the value of the form control (instance data) to be computed dynamically based on some valid XPath expression.
5. *isValid*: This attribute allows us to put in custom validation logic for instance data filled into form controls. If isValid evaluates to false, the container does not allow the form to be submitted.

6. *maxOccurs*: For those elements that can be nested (e.g., selectOne), this attribute specifies the upper bound for how many times the elements may be repeated. By default, nesting is unbound.
7. *minOccurs*: For those elements that can be nested, this attribute specifies the minimum number of nestings that make the element meaningful. By default, this is zero.
8. *required*: A submit action cannot be taken until all of those form controls with this attribute set to true have instance data or an XPath expression pointing to valid data.

The XForms processing model also gives us binding for specializing the generic components that we build with XForms. However, the implementation of such binding is left to the implementer of the container. In other words, any mechanism can be used to convert XForms to VXML, XHTML, or whatever interface is desired.

This concludes our discussion of XForms. To understand XForms better, you may want to review the specification available at the W3C site. XForms is a very new standard, so it is sure to have minimal syntactical changes.

Let us look back at this chapter and see what we have learned about building user interfaces to mobile systems.

5.6 Putting It All to Work

In this chapter, we looked at the "how to" of designing and building a generic layer into the user interface components of a mobile application.

To date, UIMS that enable all the functionality we have mentioned here are few. Apache's Cocoon is one that implements such functionality using the centralized Web model. There are no released UIMS that implement such functionality in a distributed manner, over many peers and nodes; however, several are being finalized. The latest releases of J2ME and Qualcomm's BREW give the developers much of the aforementioned functionality needed to build generic user interfaces on the client, whereas IBM, HP, and Apache have software products that complement them on the server side.

We started the chapter by understanding what we need out of a mobile user interface and then followed by taking a step back and looking at what user interfaces are. Then, we looked at the atoms that make up user interfaces and saw how to model them, and groupings of them, by using UML. We did this so that we can provide consistency throughout the user interfaces and can design documentation that enforces good design practices as well as keeping the design decoupled from platform-specific implementations.

Finally, we selected XForms as an example of a standard technology to use to implement generic user interfaces. XForms is just about the only nonproprietary standard today, with widespread acceptance in the industry, that implements features needed by a generic user interface. The authors of XForms had much more in mind than just creating a standard that allows creation of generic user interfaces. If this was all they had in mind, the form controls and binding would have sufficed. Rather, they have created a framework where presentation logic can be distributed. The readings on W3C's Web site and other work considering various implementations of XForms and the use of XForms often refer to the concept of an "XForms browser."

In fact, a great deal of the beauty of XForms lies in the other W3C standards that give us the pieces we need to specialize XForms. W3C has engineered XForms and the other standards (XSLT, XPIPE, VXML, CC-XML, etc.) so that, together, a picture of the standards for implementation of a mobile UIMS is complete and coherent. We will look at these other standards and the other design concepts that will let us build mobile applications with multiple types of user interfaces for mobile systems during the next three chapters.

Chapter 6

Developing Mobile GUIs

The rose and the thorn, and sorrow and gladness are linked together.

Saadi

6.1 Introduction

In Chapter 5, we saw why and how to build generic user interfaces. The two types of interfaces that dominate computing today are Graphical User Interfaces (GUIs) and Voice User Interfaces (VUIs). So, when we specialize a generic user interface, we are typically specializing it to either a GUI (of which we will consider text-only user interfaces to be a subset) or a VUI. In this chapter, we will look at GUIs, in Chapter 7 we will look at VUIs, and in Chapter 8 we will see how to build multimodal user interfaces that use multiple channels to reach the user.

Let us remember our final goal: building mobile user interfaces. Mobile user interfaces inherently have different requirements than their stationary counterparts because of the dimensions of mobility and the mobile condition of the user. The dimensions of mobility affect design and implementation of user interfaces in two fundamental ways. The first is that the user interface has to accommodate functionality that relates to the dimensions of mobility. For example, user interfaces must be available on all of those devices through which the user of an application may access a system. Second, the dimensions of mobility create various concerns that require further separation of concerns when building user interfaces. Today's state-of-the-art techniques in model-view-controller (MVC) and presentation-abstraction-control are incomplete in treating these concerns so we will first examine them and then examine enhancements and alternatives to the existing techniques that allow us to design and implement with the proper separation of concerns for the new concerns introduced by the dimensions of mobility. We have already begun this process by looking at building generic user interfaces. Generic user interfaces simply model a user's interaction with the system (independent of the modality and the communication channels).

Because the process of building user interfaces for mobile applications is considerably more complex than their stationary counterparts, we will subsequently use UML as the tool that documents and drives the process of developing our user interfaces. We will note again that there are no specific methodologies recommended by OMG (the organization that maintains the UML standard) in regarding the use of UML to build user interfaces. Because there are no standards, we have selected some suggested techniques that fit our needs, namely development of user interfaces for mobile applications.

We will start by looking at the state-of-the-art in separation of concerns (user interface logic, business logic, publishing to multiple interfaces, delivery through multiple channels, etc.) when building user interfaces today.

6.1.1 Today's State of the Art: PAC, MVC, and Others

Before we lay out some options in building mobile user interfaces, let us look at our goal and the assumptions we make to narrow the solution set for the goal:

Our goal is to design and implement the user interfaces of our mobile applications so as to minimize the development effort and maximize the robustness of the user interfaces.

As you recall, we face multiple challenges in developing user interfaces for mobile applications. There are a multitude of devices and platforms used by the consumers (device proliferation), the user interface must be robust enough to allow the modalities that fit the condition of the mobile user at the time of using the system (support for a wide variety of user interfaces), and the user interface of one application may need to adapt itself to be used under a number of system conditions (low battery, poor QOS, and low device user interface capabilities). Because of the relative short lifetime of the mobile device acceptance in the marketplace and the large permutations of possible platforms (mobile operating system, hardware, network, deployment, etc.) we have to do our best to construct the device so that code is maintainable, extensible, and flexible. Whatever problems you may have faced in maintainability, extensibility, and flexibility of software for stationary applications are permutated by the dimensions of mobility.

Let us take a step back now. As we all know, software is somewhat like radioactive materials: It is always decaying. This decay is caused by the changing needs of the users of the system and the ever-evolving tools that serve those users. Given this decay, another genetic trait of software development is that there are always additional requirements and modifications during this decay process. So, once we have the first version of a piece of software, we must maintain it. Obviously, many of these additions and modifications are going to be additions and modifications to user interfaces or cause additions and modifications to user interfaces of the system. This problem is not unique to mobile applications. It is shared by all software applications. Although developing user interfaces for mobile applications is a problem compounded by the dimensions of mobility, developing the user interface to any software application is a fairly complex task. This complexity has given rise to several techniques that aim at easing the task of development of the user interface. Now, remember that by development we do not just mean the initial creation of the user interface, but the creation and maintenance of the user interface over the entire life cycle of the application.

The choice of the technique we use in developing the user interface depends on the core technologies used and the architecture of the system. For example, there are a series of techniques developed for building PC-based applications and other techniques developed for building Web-based applications. In the case of mobile applications, we face two general types of user interfaces: those that use the mobile device for rendering some or all of the user interface and those that use the end device merely as a communication channel to the user. An example of the first is a networked PDA application; an example of the second is a telephone used to communicate with a VUI at the other end of the phone call. All of the techniques that we will discuss in this text for building mobile user interfaces are primarily concerned with one aspect of software development: separation of concerns. These concerns include whatever we have experienced with developing user interfaces for stationary applications (separating business logic from presentation logic, separating validation from presentation logic, etc.) and are permutated by the dimensions of mobility. In this way, our goal will be to point out techniques that allow for separation of concerns, be it the typical concerns of developing any user interface or the concerns of mobile applications, to reduce the development effort in building user interfaces and creating the best experience for the end user. Unless you are building an embedded software application for only one type of device, you will find these techniques useful. But, be forewarned that none of these techniques are the antipattern (sometimes referred to as the silver-bullet or golden-hammer antipattern). The technique that you use must fit the problem that you are trying to solve and the needs of the problem are something that you as the engineer must assess.

There are a variety of software development techniques for developing the user interface to stationary applications, but we will focus on those techniques that have evolved from the study of object-oriented programming and design patterns. If your chosen language for building your mobile application is C++, Java, or another object-oriented programming language, these techniques will apply directly. However, even if you are using a language such as C (and the relevant tool sets), the concepts will still apply. You may need to apply some creativity (or read up on writing object-oriented applications with C) in adapting these techniques to the language of your choice.

Let us start with what is probably today's most popular technique for separation of concerns when it comes to building object-oriented user interfaces: the model-view-controller technique.

Model-View-Controller

Model-View-Controller (MVC) is an object-oriented design pattern for separation of concerns of applications with user input (see Figure 6.1). MVC is best defined by Buschmann, Meunier, Rohnert, Sommerlad, and Stal (also known as the "Gang of Five") in one of the staple texts of software application development called *Pattern Oriented Software Architecture: A System of Patterns*. MVC divides an interactive

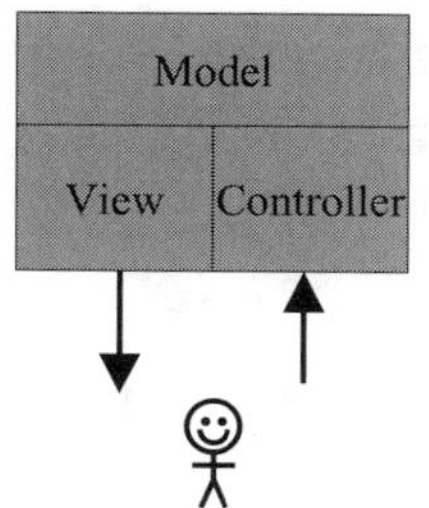

Figure 6.1. MVC Pattern.

application into three areas: processing, output, and input [Buschmann et al. 1996].

The model is the internal implementation of the application and does not encapsulate any data or have any behavior related to interactions with the user or the presentation of data to the user. The view encapsulates any output through the user interface to the user. What you can view on the screen or hear on the phone is rendered by the view. The controller processes the input of the user into the system. The text typed into the system, the mouse events, and the voice recorded by the system all come through the controller. The system may have one or more views and controllers. The controller allows the user to enter input. It then can modify the model. These modifications are reflected in the user interface through the view(s). MVC allows separation of three different concerns: receiving input from the user (controller), implementing components that model business logic and operations that build the core functionality of the application (model), and presenting information to the user (view).

MVC is widely implemented in stationary client applications and server-based (thin-client) Web-based applications. In such systems, there is typically only one type of view (HTML) and one type of controller (PCs and the relevant peripheries). Minor differences in things such as browser versions and monitor sizes are typically taken care of by work-arounds rather than by creating multiple views. When it comes to mobile application development, MVC has a couple of disadvantages. First, proliferation of views and controllers becomes unmanageable and very difficult to maintain as mobile applications have multiple user interfaces rendered through multiple channels and can receive input from numerous controllers. Second, the inherent asymmetry in treating the input and the output from the user to the model compounds the effect of this proliferation problem. For example, a system that offers a VUI and an HTML user interface for its users would need at least two separate controllers, one that can receives user input through a voice channel and another that receives input from the user through HTTP. Likewise, two different views would be needed, one that renders a GUI in HTML and another that renders an aural user interface through playback of audio. If we wanted access to the aural user interface through the PC as well as the telephony system, we would end up with two controllers and two views for the VUI. It is easy to see that the user interfaces and channels to be supported for a mobile application can become unmanageable. The maintenance of the controllers and views can become particularly unwieldy. The separateness of the views and controllers has

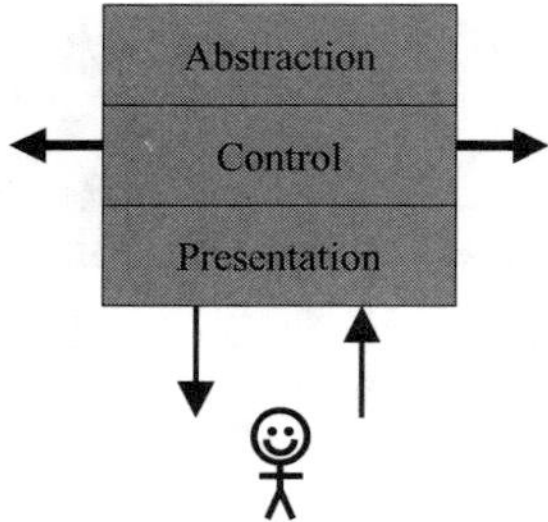

FIGURE 6.2. Presentation-Abstraction-Control.

another negative side effect: Maintaining consistency among the different views and controllers becomes cumbersome. For example, if a field has to be added to the HTML GUI, we must make sure that it is added in the same analogous point in the VUI, based on mapping the GUI interactions to the VUI interactions.

In addition to these problems, MVC does nothing to take into account the other dimensions of mobility. Namely, there is nothing that accommodates the adaptability of the controllers and views based on the dimensions of mobility such as location, QOS, device power supply, or device capabilities.

MVC still gives us some value in separating the three major concerns, but its tightly coupled and asymmetric nature, as well as its inability to treat multiple views and controller types elegantly, makes it less than ideal for user interfaces in mobile applications. Let us continue our search through existing techniques by looking at a similar design pattern, also exposed by the "Gang of Five" called PAC.

Presentation-Abstraction-Control

Presentation-Abstraction-Control (PAC) is an object-oriented design pattern that separates the concerns of a system by breaking it down into loosely coupled agents, each responsible for one task (see Figure 6.2). The Presentation-PAC architectural pattern defines a structure for interactive software systems in the form of a hierarchy of cooperating agents [Buschmann et al. 1996]. Every agent internally has components that serve one of three tasks: those components that abstract away the core functionality and data used by the agent (abstraction), those components that provide access to the agent (presentation), and those components that control the interactions between the abstraction and presentation layers (control). Note that the PAC pattern is similar to the MVC pattern in that it hides the internal implementation of the logical functions of the system from the user interface (i.e., the abstraction layer hides the business logic).

In PAC, the separation between the user interface and the functionality of the internals of the application is made by using the control component to pass messages back and forth between the two layers. Let us look at an example of how we can apply PAC in Figure 6.3.

Let us say we need to build a reusable user interface component that collects billing information from a user when he or she is purchasing something online using an HTML-based browser. This component is probably a panel that has some buttons, labels, and text fields. Internal to the system, this information may be

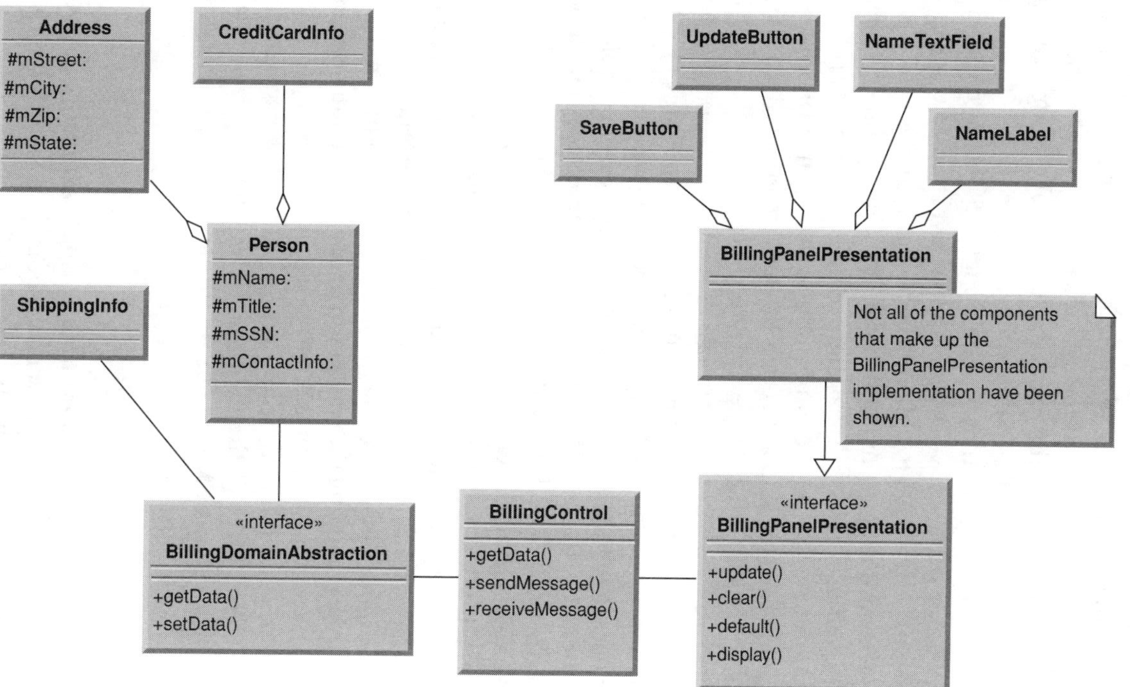

FIGURE 6.3. UML Class Diagram of a Sample PAC Implementation.

encapsulated in several different objects. We create an abstraction (whose interface is seen in the UML class diagram) to get the appropriate data out of the domain. The implementation of this abstraction may exist in the domain model or we may need to implement it (depending on whether the existence of the relevant information grouped as billing information is necessary or not). The abstraction provides the necessary behavior to exchange data with the BillingControl class. The implementation of the interface between these two components (the abstraction and control parts of PAC) is determined by what the controller needs from the abstraction. The presentation is the panel itself, probably dynamically generated using a scripting language such as JSP or ASP.

One key thing to note here is that the components of PAC are very decoupled. Although the example that we have shown is a low-level one, PAC scales very well. Various components can be tied together in a very decoupled way as it is very legal for controllers to communicate and collaborate with one another. Consequently, making complicated user interfaces based on simple components is more natural to PAC than it is to MVC because composition of the agents can be done without violating encapsulation. In fact, as defined by Buschmann et al. earlier, it is this treelike hierarchy of agents that define the PAC pattern.

In this way, we can imagine that because of its flexibility to composition and delegation and because of its decoupled nature, it is even possible to scale up PAC so that the various parts of PAC are completely separate processes. These properties are precisely what make PAC a good fit for mobile application development.

The PAC pattern fits the problem of mobile user interfaces much better than MVC. First, it provides us a well-defined place to hook in the various infrastructure pieces that take care of the dimensions of mobility and affect the user interface without exposing this functionality to the core logic of the application: the control component. This means that the control component can communicate with the location sensitivity system, the voice recognition engine, the speech synthesis engine, and all the other subsystems that we need to use to control and produce our user interface without violating the separation of concerns among the abstraction, shielding the business logic, and presentation.

PAC also provides one single layer for presentation, allowing us to encapsulate the channels and modalities of the presentation in the same layer. PAC gets us closer to what we need than MVC, but it still does not directly address all of our needs. We need to embellish on it to get an approach that will fit mobile applications well.

Transformation-Based Techniques for Mobile Applications

As we reviewed in Chapter 1, the first versions of mobile applications were essentially either custom embedded applications with custom architectures and designs or fully centralized applications with proprietary devices and networks as the end nodes. The first attempts at building mobile user interfaces has been to transfer today's HTML-driven Web model to handheld mobile devices. WAP's WML (which we will review in detail later in this chapter) and NTT Dococo I-Mode's cHTML are examples of subsets of HTML functionality. The goal of such markup languages is to take a subset of functionality of HTML. This has two benefits: 1. Only a subset is needed for devices with limited capabilities, bandwidth, power supply, etc. and 2. having a subset enables us to have a simpler and smaller browser that uses less of these scarce resources.

Because Web content is mostly in HTML, this means that HTML has to be transformed to the markup language supported by the target device. But because there are a variety of devices and slightly different implementations and variations of the markup languages, developers were left with a significant problem: how to automate the task of publishing to these various user interfaces. As we mentioned previously, one way is to continue using MVC and create multiple controllers and views. This is really not practical because as the number of controllers and views grows, maintenance becomes unmanageable. The PAC pattern gives us a better approach because there is only one presentation component that interacts with the user.

Developers began using two techniques to complement both PAC and MVC:

1. *Transcoding*: If the content is initially in HTML, we are dealing with a "view" of the existing system. Transcoding techniques focus on extracting the information out of this view to create an intermediate format that can in turn be used to produce other views. The process of creating this intermediate format is referred to as "transcoding." Prior to use in the moble context, the term transcoding typically meant conversion of one compressed format to another. And, as in the case of conversion of one compressed format to another, there is almost always some loss of data in conversion of HTML (or another markup language) into the intermediate format. The intermediate format is used like a generic user interface and then transformed to the various views using XSL or a similar technology.
2. *Transforming*: Although we can start with HTML (or some other presentational view of the system) and convert to other views of the system, this is a solution that should be done only as a last measure. The preferred situation is that all content is initially produced in XML that gives a presentation-neutral view of the system. This content can then be transformed to the appropriate views using XSL or similar technologies.

There are two main differences between transcoding and transforming. First, in transcoding, we are starting out with some final (specialized) content, not raw (generic) content. Second, transcoding is typically lossy and needs special instructions whereas transforming is not lossy and should not need special instructions (other than the transformation). Both transcoding and transforming are complementary to MVC and PAC. Figure 6.4 shows how the content produced by a system using PAC is transcoded and transformed to other forms of content for access by multiple user interfaces.

Note that transcoding and transforming the output of the system only solves the problem of publishing multiple types of output to the user. It does not deal with the fact that the input from the user may be coming from a variety of disparate channels such as HTTP, WAP, VoIP, or POTS. This problem has typically been solved by using a proxy that resides, on the server side, between the Web-based system that

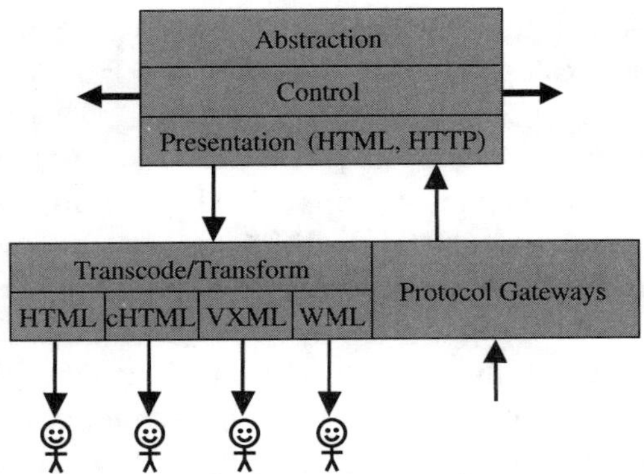

FIGURE 6.4. Using Transcoding/Transforming Techniques to Complement PAC in Producing User Interfaces for Mobile Applications.

supports HTTP and the infrastructure and communication protocol native to each type of mobile device. For example, in the case of WAP, WAP gateways act as a proxy and a protocol converter to convert all of the user input sent from the device to the WAP gateway in the native WAP protocol implementation to HTTP.

Figure 6.5 shows how generic XML content can be produced by the presentation layer and transformed using XSL (or any equivalent transformation technology can be used) to the final markup language to be used by the device. Once transcoding and transforming solutions were deployed, it became obvious that there needed to be a solution for an intermediate user interface format, one that treats the interactions of the user with the system in a generic way and independent of the properties of the specific devices. This, in turn has given rise to the genesis of several efforts including XForms, which we looked at in Chapter 5, and User Interface Markup Language (UIML).

We will look at UIML later in this chapter. At this point we should take a step back and note that UIML and XForms take fundamentally different approaches in allowing developers to create a generic user interface. As we saw in Chapter 5, XForms defines distinct and discrete controls and elements that define a language for building a generic user interface; XForms is an XML application. In contrast,

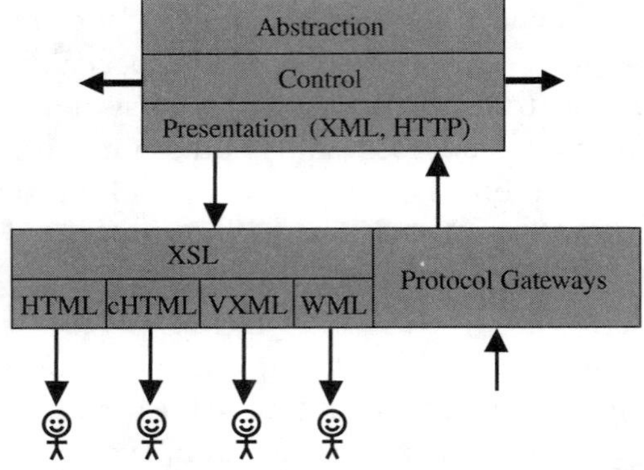

FIGURE 6.5. Using Transcoding/Transforming Techniques to Complement PAC in Producing User Interfaces for Mobile Applications.

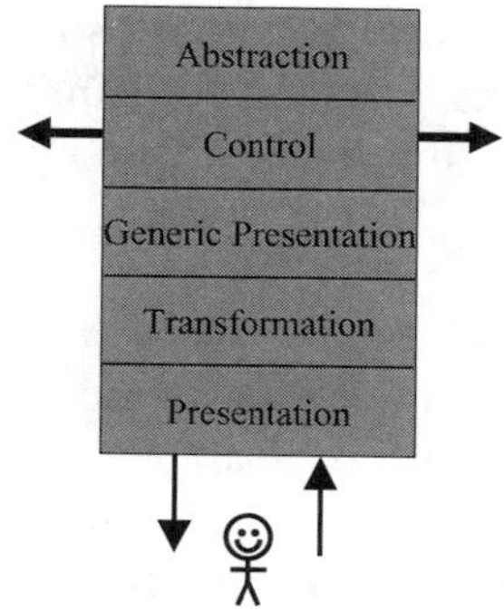

Figure 6.6. PAC-TG: A Variation on PAC for Mobile User Interfaces.

UIML is an XML-based vocabulary intended to define other XML-based applications that describe user interface interactions; UIML is not an XML application; rather, it is an XML vocabulary similar to XML Schema. UIML, in a way, is a meta-language intended to create other languages that are used to build user interfaces. Whereas UIML itself can be used to define XML applications to generate generic user interfaces such as XForms, it can also be used as a "metageneric" user interface in that it can be used by developers to define XML applications suitable for various types of user interfaces.

Note that all of the techniques discussed so far focus on selecting the right high-level approach in building our user interfaces. To build mobile user interfaces, we will combine the best of what these techniques have to offer.

6.1.2 PAC-TG

In this text, we will recognize PAC-TG, short for Transformation of Generic Presentation-Abstraction-Control, as a high-level design pattern for creating user interfaces to mobile applications. This pattern is not a new pattern (because patterns, by definition, are not invented but rather are recognized by prevalence of use and benefits). It is merely a specialization of the existing PAC pattern as recognized by Buschmann et al. Figure 6.6 shows how PAC-TG builds on PAC.

When we looked at the PAC pattern, we saw that it breaks down the task of creating a system or subsystem, in our case the user interface, into a series of agents. Each agent has three different components of abstraction which gave us an interface to the data and behavior model of the system; the presentation, which gave us the final mechanism to render the interface; and the controller, which controlled the interactions between the presentation and the abstraction.

We are going to specialize this pattern by making a restriction and an addition. First, we are going to restrict the presentation components to encapsulate information and behavior about interactions with the user that are independent of the final user interface viewed by the user. We discussed generic user interfaces in Chapter 5. Then, we are going to add transformation components that specialize the generic presentations. The generic presentation and transformation may be implemented in several different ways. We have already discussed some aspects of generic user interfaces and will discuss them further. We will also look at some implementation examples for the transformation.

Now, as we would with any other recognized software pattern, let us define the intent, motivation, known uses, business domains, problem forces, benefits, and liabilities. Then, we will delve into some sample implementations of PAC-TG.

Intent

The intent of PAC-TG is to combine PAC agents and transformation techniques to structure the production of multiple user interface types to a common application for various devices. Such subdivision separates the concerns of functional implementation of the application, interactions with the user through the user interface, and the variations in the user interface types presented to the user.

Motivation

PAC-TG is a modification on PAC that uses the treelike hierarchy of PAC, inversion of control, and the concept of specialization of generic user interfaces to various specialized user interfaces. Every PAC-TG agent is composed of at least five components, one component that provides an abstraction to the core functionality of the application (abstraction), one component that provides a generic user interface to be used by other components or systems (generic presentation), one or more components that transform the generic presentation to a specific presentation or presentations, one or more components that produce final user interfaces with which the users interact (presentation), and one component that facilitates messaging among all of the other components (control).

Known Uses

Commercial publishing frameworks and transcoding products include IBM's Transcoding Publisher, IBM VXML Portlets, and open-source projects such as Apache's Cocoon. (Cocoon components can be arranged both as an implementation of MVC or as an implementation of PAC depending on the usage as Cocoon as a component framework.) MATIS also uses a roughly equivalent pattern called PAC-Amodeus (see the last subsection in Section 6.1.2). Nunes' Wisdom architecture and methodology [Nunes 2001] also outlines use of this pattern without specific recognition of it.

Related Patterns

As we have mentioned, this is a variant on the PAC pattern. Various other low-level patterns such as the Visitor and Façade patterns can be used in the internal implementation of individual components of a given agent.

Business Domain

Development of applications that require more than one rendition of the same user interface or multiple types of user interfaces fall into the business domain.

Problem Forces

One of the problems to consider while implementing this pattern is that this is a high-level design pattern. The internal implementation of this design pattern can vary greatly. As we mentioned in the case of PAC, because of the loosely coupled nature of PAC-TG, agents and/or components can be run within separate processes. The method by which they communicate (protocol, etc.) is not restricted (i.e., they could be native protocols such as RMI and COM or open system protocols such as HTTP and CORBA).

Also, note that every agent (package of presentation, abstraction, control, and transformation components) maintains its own state. Because the user may give the system input while state information is being exchanged within the different agents, transactional integrity must be provided to make sure that illegal states are not possible.

Lastly, PAC-TG treats the concern of creating multiple user interfaces but does not treat the fact that these multiple user interfaces may be using multiple channels to reach the user (at the end device—for example, a VoIP voice channel as opposed to a regular POTS-based voice channel).

Benefits

We can outline the following benefits in using the PAC-TG pattern:

1. *Separation of concerns between the internal implementation of the business application and the implementation of the user interface.* This separation of concerns allows for possible reuse of components (though reuse takes more thought than merely utilizing design patterns), better scalability by distribution of the model and the interface concerns over different processes, and easier code maintenance during the application life cycle. This benefit is inherited from *PAC*.
2. *Separation of concerns between the device and interface-specific interactions of the user with the system and the different generic methods by which the user can affect the state and behavior of the system.* This separation allows us to develop reusable transformation components that transform a particular set of generic interactions to one or more specialized user interfaces. It also provides us with a tool to avoid very fast growth of the development effort to build n user interfaces for m types of device accessing a single application with which the interactions of various devices are fairly alike.

Liabilities

The first and biggest liability of PAC-TG is possible performance degradation because of the additional layers of abstraction (of course, this depends on the implementation). This is due to the higher number of objects instantiated and managed if implementation is object oriented. So creating each user interface in a custom way will invariably yield a user interface that requires less computing resources. This performance problem is more visible when all of the components of PAC-TG are being executed on the same process and the same physical device. To alleviate performance bottlenecks, distribution of the different components is recommended because the loosely coupled nature of PAC-TG allows this.

The second liability is that, as in the case of PAC, PAC-TG is a complex pattern to implement. Because of the various ways that it can be implemented, it typically requires considerable experience in recognizing the appropriate behavior of the interfaces and boundaries between the agents and between the components within the individual agents.

Examples

We can implement PAC-TG in three ways. In the first type, the control component may facilitate communication among all of the other layers. This is seen in Figure 6.7, where we have shown a Type 1 PAC-TG implementation for the billing panel that we discussed in the previous section.

This is the simplest implementation of PAC-TG. Note that we have shown the specific presentations in the model as multiple classes whose code is generated by the framework and not written by the developer. This is not the best implementation of PAC-TG as it creates a high level of coupling between the control component (called PACTGBillingControl in our example) and the specialized presentations of the user interface. The single control component in this implementation is responsible for communication among all of the other components.

Alternatively, we can break the control components into two separate control components: one that facilitates control and communication between the generic user interface and the abstraction of the system and the other that facilitates control and communication among the generic user interface, the transformation components, and the final user interfaces produced. Figure 6.8 shows how our Type 1 implementation shown in Figure 6.7 can be modified to do this.

The advantage in using Type 2 PAC-TG is that the type of behavior required to facilitate control and communication between the generic user interface and abstraction and those required to facilitate control and communication among the transformers, the generic user interface, and the specialized user interfaces are fundamentally different. So, by separating these tasks, we achieve a good separation of concerns.

We can make this yet more efficient by using Type 3 PAC-TG (Figure 6.9), where the control component is broken into two separate components as in Type 2, except that it communicates with the generic presentation layer instead of the control component that allows for communication between the abstraction and generic user interface. Once again, this provides us with a couple of significant improvements. First, there is less indirect communication. In Type 2, data going from the generic presentation to the specialized presentation layer have to go through at least two layers. In this model, we reduce that to one layer. This improves efficiency. Second, this setup is more in keeping with the spirit of the design pattern in enabling a high degree of decoupling so that each set of agents, containing abstraction, control, generic presentation, transformation, and specialized presentation components, can be run in a very decoupled manner (separate thread, separate process, or even possibly a separate operating environment altogether).

This brings us to the end of our discussions about separating the concern of creating a generic user interface and a specialized one. Our next task is to see this applied in building GUIs for mobile applications.

As we noted before, this pattern does not do anything to take into account the concerns of dimensions of mobility. Particularly, multichannel communication, location sensitivity, resource constraints of the device, and QOS conditions are

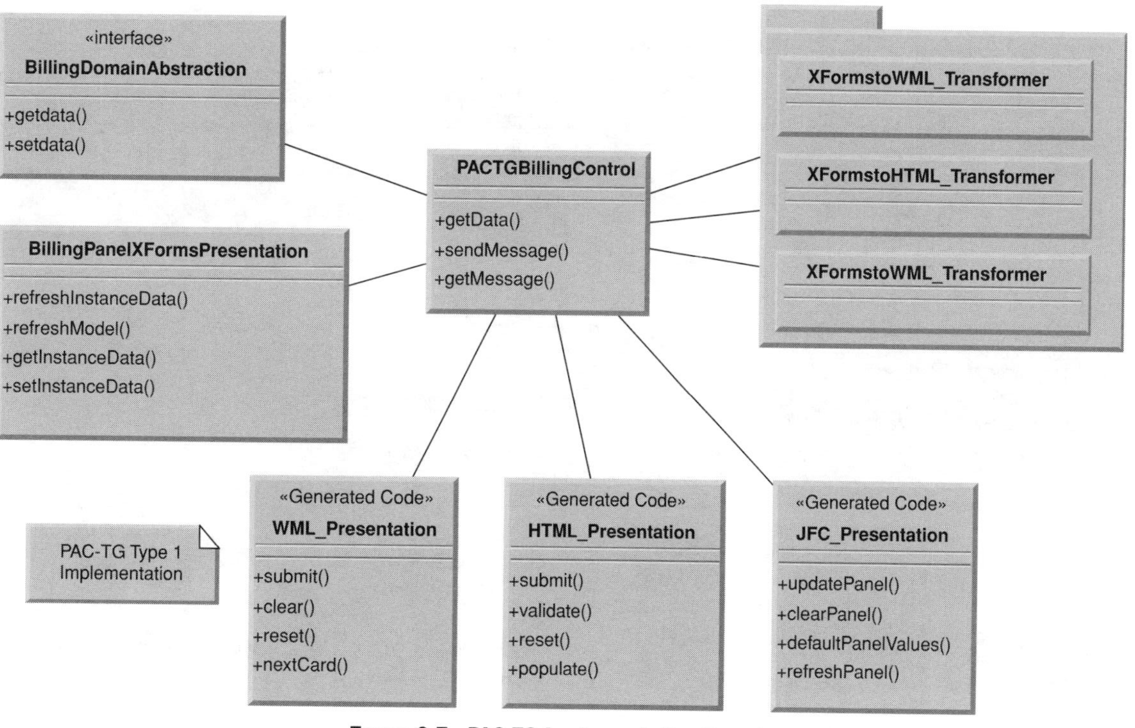

FIGURE 6.7. PAC-TG Implementation Type 1.

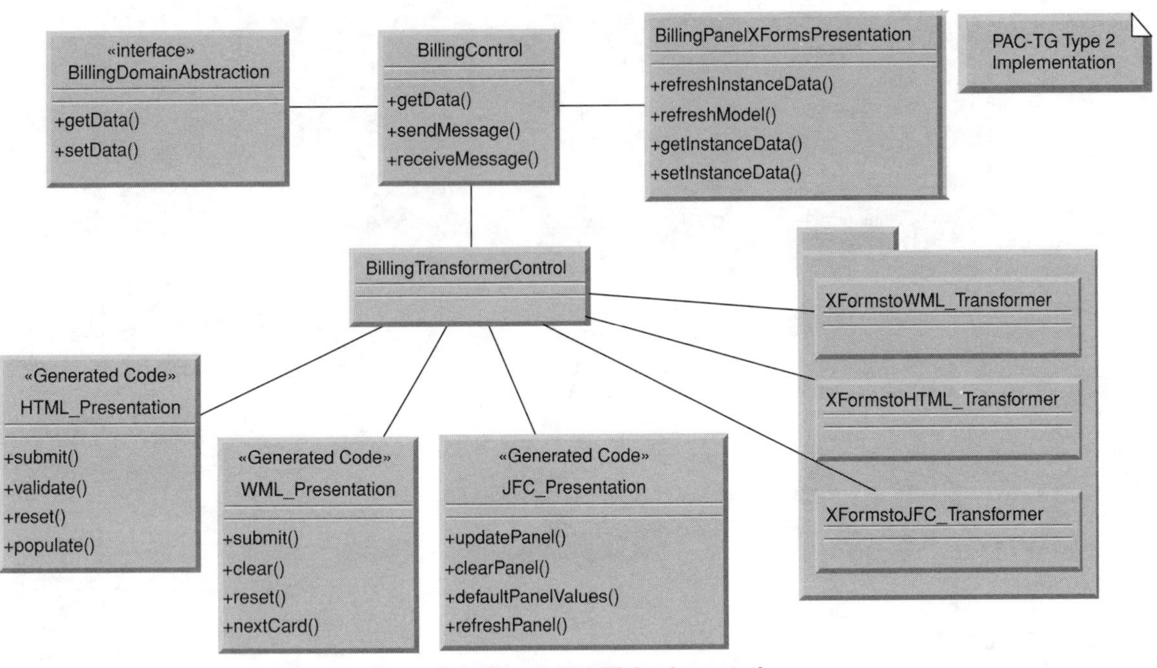

FIGURE 6.8. Type 2 PAC-TG Implementation.

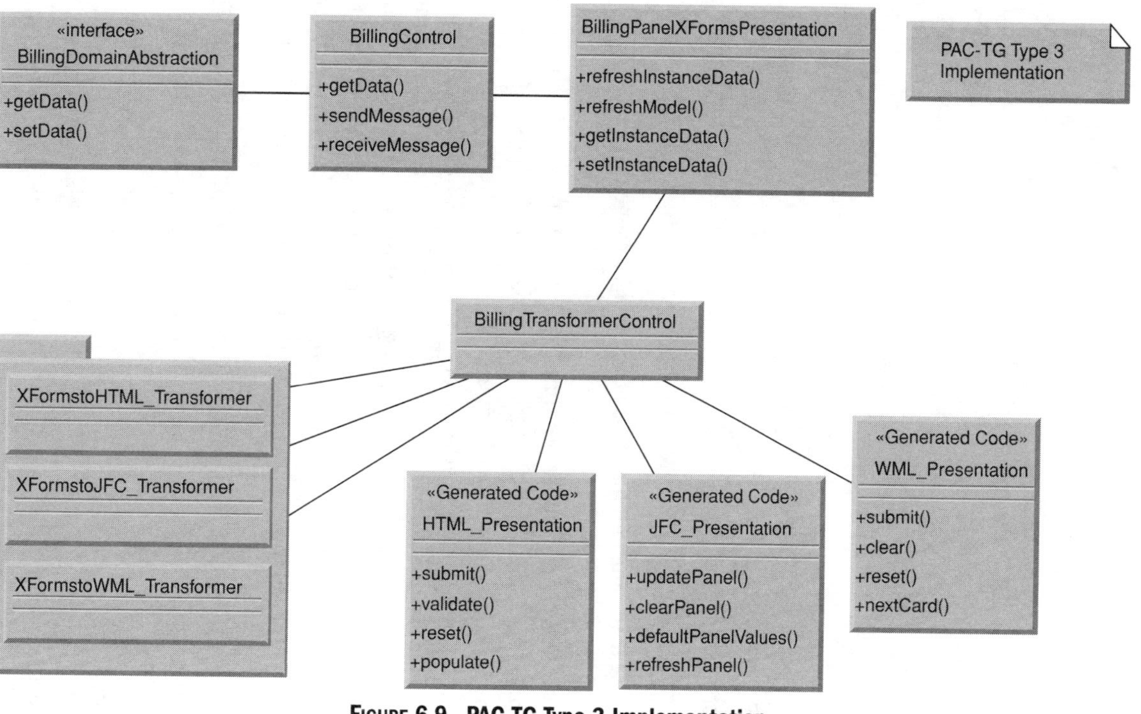

FIGURE 6.9. PAC-TG Type 3 Implementation.

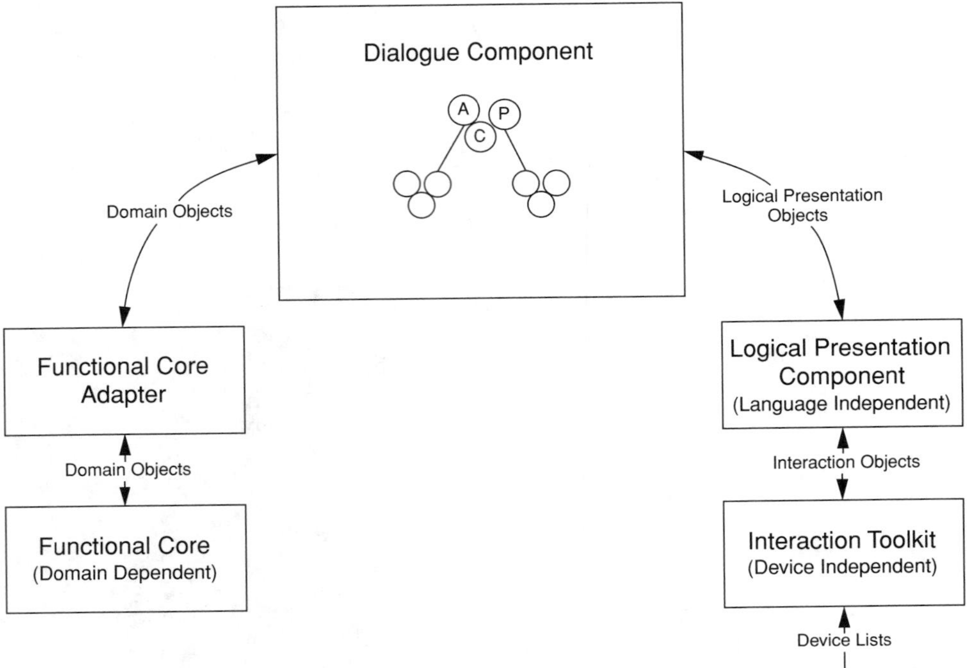

FIGURE 6.10. The PAC-Amodeus Functional Components [Coutaz 2002].

not taken into account. Remember that for a design pattern to be recognized, it must be applied and discovered rather than invented. Because mobile application development is a less mature software development field, there are no current patterns used among software developers to treat the dimensions of mobility.

It is, however, intuitive that we could extend PAC-TG to treat dimensions of mobility through creating additional types of control components that connect to tertiary components treating the various dimensions of mobility. We will leave this implementation to the reader of this text and hope that such patterns become recognized by the industry and are ripe for introduction in the next edition of this text.

Now, let us look at building some simple single-channel GUI applications for mobile applications.

PAC-Amodeus

Introduced by Coutaz [Coutaz 2002], PAC-Amodeus is very similar to PAC-TG, but it attacks the problem differently. The functional components of PAC-Amodeus are shown in Figure 6.10.

Of particular interest to us is the Interaction Toolkit Component, which provides device independence. This component represents a set of agents that provide functionality such as transformation needed for specialization of a generic user interface to the final user interface to be rendered for each particular device, modality, etc. The Dialogue Component encapsulates the functionality previously modeled by the PAC pattern and the Logical Presentation Component presents us with the

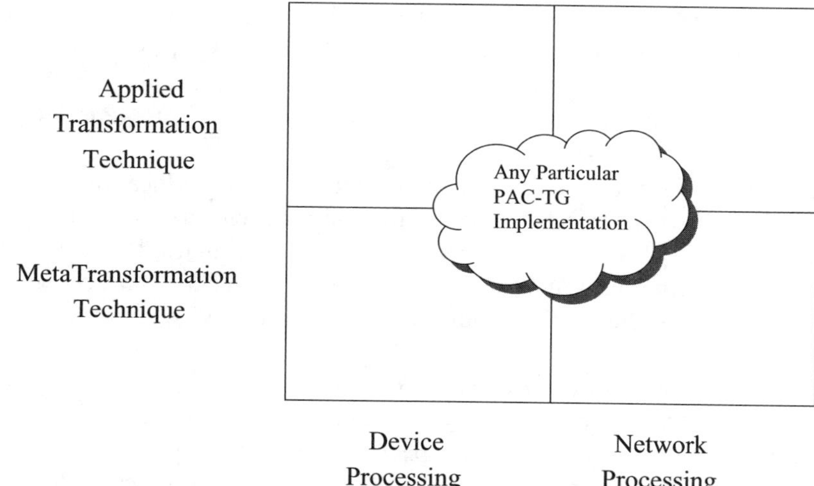

FIGURE 6.11. Division of PAC-TG Implementation Techniques.

generic user interface layer that provides a layer where the interactions of the user with the system are modeled in a user-interface-generic manner.

Essentially, PAC-Amodeus introduced by Coutaz covers PAC-TG at a high level and adds abstraction layers for the business logic (Functional Core Adaptor and Functional Core) that separate the access the Dialogue Component needs to the engine that models the logic from the access interface itself.

Coutaz than introduces MATIS (Multimodal Airline Travel Information System), which allows a user to retrieve information about flight schedules using speech, direct manipulation, keyboard, and mouse, or a combination of these techniques [Coutaz 2002]. MATIS is then used as an example of a PAC-Amodeus-based system. The referenced work by Coutaz is recommended reading to become more familiar with the details of this pattern.

6.1.3 Single Channel Specialization of Generic User Interfaces to Graphical User Interfaces

In this chapter, our focus is in understanding the implementation of GUIs for mobile applications. When dealing with GUI applications, we typically have a single channel of communication between the device and the network. We will consider multichannel user interfaces in Chapter 8. In the previous section we discussed PAC-TG as a design pattern that can help us produce multiple GUI-based user interfaces for a single functional core application. In this section, we will focus on the various implementation methods for the PAC-TG design pattern. The techniques used for such implementations fall somewhere on the plane graphed in Figure 6.11.

As shown in the picture, any PAC-TG implementation technique can distribute the processing between the end device used by the user as the interface to the system and the other processing units on the network (peers, servers, etc.). Also, every implementation technique may use a well-defined language and tool set for defining the generic user interfaces and transforming them (such as XForms for implementing a generically defined interface and XSL for transforming the XForms documents to specific markup languages). Alternatively, it may use a metalanguage and relevant tools such as UIML, which we will look at in this chapter as a tool to define metarules that can be used, at run time or batch time, to generate generic user interfaces and the relevant transformations.

We have already implemented XForms as a well-defined application of XML that allows us to create user interfaces whose interactions with users are independent of the device type. Using XSL is also a very popular method of transforming XML content to other markup languages such as WML, VXML, and HTML. Using XForms and XSL as the implementation tools for PAC-TG would put us on the top half of the plane of Figure 6.11.

If the core of the application (exposed to PAC-TG through the abstraction) resides on the network, then it only makes sense that the generic user interface is produced by the network (servers, peers, etc.). (Once again we refer to any processing being done on anything but the client as processing being done on the network because we are trying to treat the problem in an architecturally independent way.) If the core of the application (exposed to PAC-TG through the abstraction) resides on the end user device, then the production of the generic user interface and its transformation are both performed on the device itself. It is crucial that whatever tool is selected to create the generic user interface and perform the transformations is flexible enough to be used on the end device as well as on the servers and peers on the network. XForms and XSLT technologies, respectively for the production of the generic user interfaces and the transformations, provide us with such flexibility. We can have XForms browsers that reside on the device itself and transform the XForms controls and interactions to the appropriate user interface for the end device or we can have the transformation of the XForms document happen somewhere on the network and send simple markup languages such as WML, XHTML, HTML, or VXML to the browser. Note that this is as if PAC-TG is fully implemented outside of the end-user device (servers or other peers), we are practically looking at a model where either the device is a "dumb" client (such as a regular old telephone) or it has a browser such as a WML or HTML browser that simply converts the final markup language to the look-and-feel made available on the device.

Techniques that define the infrastructure for defining generic user interfaces and transformations thereof (metatransformation techniques) are only slightly different from their applied counterparts. This is because, by definition, generic user interfaces are about defining the metainteractions of the user with the system as opposed to the exact interactions. So, XForms and similar tools are in a way metatools. However, UIML and similar techniques can be used to also define tools such as XForms. There is a benefit and a loss in this case. Obviously, the metatool, something like UIML, is more flexible, but it is also more ambiguous and requires more decisions to be made by the designers of a particular application, more custom code, and, therefore, more complexity and less reliability in the final system. However, there is one very big advantage that a tool such as AUIML (Abstract User Interface Markup Language) provides that we have not mentioned:

SIDE DISCUSSION 6.1

The Common Thread in Generic User Interfaces

In a document aptly titled "Towards Convergence of WML, XHTML, and other W3C Technologies" by Dave Ragget and Ted Wugofski, they mention the common threads among the various tools to facilitate the creation of generic user interfaces and provide a transform mechanism [Ragett and Wugofski 2000]:

- extensible event handling mechanism,
- a means of providing default event handlers (templates) and overrides,
- a means of navigating to another dialogue or document in response to any event, and
- a means of managing state information in response to an event.

Keep these in mind when you look at the various tools that we introduce throughout this text. Note that the decoupled nature of PAC-TG allows for a particularly natural implementation of the last two (dialogue navigation and state management).

Metatools map well to UML. And because of this, they offer us the only possibility of defining a fully automated user interface generation system from UML to date.

We will look at UIML later in this chapter and subsequently see how it differs from XForms as a tool for generation of generic user interfaces.

Let us look next at how we can build a GUI for mobile applications.

6.1.4 GUI Specialization on the Server

To display a GUI to the user, we need to specialize the generic user interface to what the user eventually sees. The simplest way of doing this is to specialize the user interface on some server:

1. *Thin-Client Markup Language–Based Applications*: These are the run-of-the-mill WML, VXML, XHTML, HTML, or other types of markup languages that can be used in creating static documents or produced dynamically and then browsed on the client. WML is the most pervasive of these solutions for mobile environments to date. The generic user interface content may be transformed to the desired markup language using XSL or some other transformation mechanism.
2. *Mobile Agents*: We will take a closer look at mobile agents in Chapter 9. Although weak and strong mobility allow us to build applications that migrate to the device and do their work there (rendering of the user interface and interacting with the user), we can either use servers to select the right type of agent to be delivered to a device or we can have the server produce an agent and send it to the server in an automated fashion. An example of the first is a server that provides a provisioning system for J2ME midlets and BREW applications at the same time. The second is a bit far-fetched with the technologies that are available today; nevertheless, it is a possibility.

To specialize the content on the server, we can always build a custom application. Sometimes, this is needed because of special requirements of the application. However, when possible, it is typically "more economic to buy than to build." Using off-the-shelf applications for transcoding and transformation have the added benefit of providing tools as well as being used and tested by a large number of users, making them more resilient than custom software. Having said this, in this text we will look at two main tools for specialization of user interfaces on the server side: IBM's Transcoding Publisher and Apache's Cocoon. We will look at Cocoon in Chapter 8.

In this next section, we will look at some transcoding techniques and then look at how the IBM Transcoding Publisher allows us to specialize content on the server for various devices and user interfaces.

Transcoding Techniques

Transcoding is used when we do not have the raw content needed to transform (specialize) to the exact content that we need. So, we take some other content that has already been specialized (like HTML) and we transform it into the type of content desired (like WML). We can do this by directly turning the HTML to WML or by first turning the HTML into a raw format and then producing WML from that raw format. There are also binary formats such as images. In the case of binary formats, transcoding becomes a bit more difficult. There may not be a suitable raw format as there is in textual information. So, we can divide transcoding to three categories:

1. *Direct Transcoding of Textual Content*: This is when we convert one type of textual content to another type of textual content. Direct transcoding gives us good performance and as little loss of information as possible because the conversion is a custom conversion. However, because there are additional resulting formats needed, we may have to repeat the development process, thereby ending up with a lot of custom code and inconsistencies in how the content is transcoded from one type of content to several other types of content.
2. *Indirect Transcoding of Textual Content*: Often, we want to produce multiple types of content from one starting content set. If this is the case, this is best done with indirect transcoding: conversion to a raw intermediate format and subsequent transformation to the specialized formats. Because of the additional layer of abstraction, performance is less than that for direct transcoding and there is a higher possibility of loss of information. However, this method can drastically reduce development efforts. It may also be desired because it is easier to maintain consistency among the different user interfaces as a good portion of the transcoding process is the same for all interfaces (conversion of the content we start with to the raw content).
3. *Transcoding of Binary Content*: Conversion of binary information such as audio clips and images is almost always a custom conversion task. Very few formats provide us with enough information to map them to other formats and when they do, the mapping typically does not lend itself to conversion of the binary content to some intermediate format.

We can use the IBM Transcoding Publisher with all three of these transcoding methods. The IBM Transcoding Publisher ships with the following standard features:

1. *Request Viewer*: This is an administrative tool that allows the developer to set up the rules for selection and application of transcoding modules based on HTTP request headers and other properties.
2. *Snoop Tool*: This tool looks at the request headers, and as the request arrives, the transcoder is selected and then applied to the resource that was initially requested to produce the final content.
3. *XSL Trace*: This is an extremely useful tool if you use XSLT as the method of transforming your content. There are very few tools that allow you to step through XSL scripts: This one does. Furthermore, it is integrated with the rest of the IBM Transcoding Publisher, so it makes the development process simpler.
4. *Visual XML Transformation Tool*: This tool is another very useful one that allows creation of XSLs to convert one DTD to another DTD in a visual manner. The catch here is that there is always more than one XSL that maps one DTD to another DTD. This tool does not always produce the most canonical XSL depending on the usage. Also, so far, XML Schemas are not supported as an XML application definition language.

The IBM Transcoding Publisher is a very good tool if you are going to transcode content. There are two different types of transcoding modules that you can produce: XSL-based transcoding modules and Java-based modules called MEGlets. Here are some hints on how and when to use each type of transcoding module:

1. There are a series of XSLs and MEGlets that come with the IBM Transcoding Publisher. For example, WML and HDML are supported out of the box. Look at what is supported before you try to build your own transcoding module. If there is something that supports most of what you need, you can always extend the provided classes (because IBM Transcoding Publisher is based on Java and the interface is somewhat flexible for extensions).
2. Currently, there is no out-of-the-box support for XForms, UIML, or any other mechanism that allows us to build a generic user interface and then transform it. The Transcoding Publisher's out-of-the-box modules are really geared toward direct transcoding of the content. So, if you want to build your system with indirect transcoding, you will need to create your own transcoding module. You can do this by implementing interfaces provided in the SDK.
3. If you want to optimize performance, use MEGlets. You have much more freedom with the implementation of the parsing as all you need to do is to implement the interface that allows the Transcoding Publisher to discover the services required to serve as a MEGlet.
4. There are some binary transformations shipped with the Transcoding Publisher such as the one that converts some standard format images to WBMP for WAP.

If you want to transcode binary data not supported out of the box, you will need to build some MEGlets.

5. If the XSL transformation is beginning to become too complex, consider migrating to MEGlets. XSLs provide a higher degree of portability than Java as they can be processed by parsers of any language. However, they can get quite cryptic and unduly long if they are required to perform very complex tasks.

Now, let us take a step back and see what these so-called MEGlets are. Their components are as follows:

1. *Request Editors*: These classes are implemented to look at the incoming HTTP request and make some selection of where the request should go to get the content necessary for generating a response. Request editors can also modify the response itself and add additional information that can be used by the other components in the process.
2. *Monitors*: These components are rather passive, at least per the WBI documentation. (You can find the WBI documentation on IBM's developer Web site. The WBI framework is used in building the IBM Transcoder similar to the way Apache's Avalon is used in building Cocoon.) Monitors record information about the request and response for purposes such as logging and caching.
3. *Generators*: These components do what their name suggests. They generate data based on the request they receive from request editors. The produced documents may be static or dynamic.
4. *Document Editors*: These components allow us to modify the request content and the outgoing response content. For example, if some content is being posted through the HTTP POST method and we need to modify the content, this is the place to do it. Likewise, if we need to transform the outgoing document right before it goes out on its way to the browser, this is the place to do it.

The architecture supported by MEGlets is somewhere between PAC-TG and MVC implementation. The document editor essentially provides us with the implementation of a mechanism for transforming content. The generator provides a mechanism to produce the basic content. In this way, we have the tools we need that can be used to build generic presentation and transformation components. However, the initial request goes into a class that is different than the one from which the final response comes out. This asymmetry resembles MVC more than PAC-TG.

If you dig deep enough into the IBM Transcoding Publisher SDK, you will find a way to implement PAC-TG with Java, but this is really not how the tool is designed to be used. We will look at Cocoon in Chapter 8. It implements PAC-TG much closer to what we have described here. As we mentioned in Chapter 2, IBM's Transcoding Publisher is a suitable tool for developing thin-client interfaces for mobile applications because of its modularity, the tool set provided, and the tight integration with other products that we need for mobile application development in the IBM Everyplace Suite of products.

6.1.5 GUI Specialization on the Mobile Device

Despite the fact that most of the tools available today for mobile development push a thin-client architecture, a critical thing to keep in mind is that thin-client solutions are not the only solution for mobile applications. In fact, many have argued that thin clients are not suitable solutions for mobile applications at all because there are too many different types of clients, requiring too many browser implementations. The pervasiveness of the thin-client architecture has more to do with the pervasiveness of HTML and the wired Web as well as the familiarity of developers with producing applications for a thin-client environment.

As we mentioned previously, one of the advantages of the PAC-TG pattern is the very decoupled nature of the various components and the agent-based nature of the pattern. This means that we can implement the pattern so that abstraction, control, and generic presentations exist on the server and transformation and final presentation are done at the client.

Likewise, the advantage of XForms is the clear separation of concerns among the user interface model, specialization model, interaction model with the user interface, and the instance data that populates an instance of an XForms document.

At the time of authoring this text, the first XForms browsers that can operate on mobile devices are being released. One such product, produced by Handwise, a Finnish company, is called the Handwise XForms User Interface (Handwise XFUI). Handwise XFUI provides binding for two data channels, SMS and HTTP. Handwise XForms browser provides a GUI specialization of XForms for Symbian and Windows CE platforms. HTTP binding allows mobile devices on high-bandwidth connections (mobile wired devices or high-bandwidth wireless devices) to connect to the network through a persistent data channel. SMS binding is a particularly useful feature as most wireless mobile devices today do not provide high-bandwidth wireless connections but do provide SMS-based connectivity.

6.1.6 Distributed GUI Specialization

A third scenario to specializing the user interface on the client or on the server is to distribute the specialization. This distribution could be done in two ways:

1. *Distribution of Specialization by Tasks*: We define user interface tasks as does Nunes in his Wisdom architecture [Nunes 2001], which we will look at later in this chapter: A user interface task is a series of interactions with the user interface that accomplish a meaningful task. This may be answering a simple question in a text field, clicking a button, filling out all of the fields on one screen, or filling out multiple screenfuls worth of information. Depending on the available resources on the device, the type of information that needs to be displayed, and other application-dependent variables, we may decide to specialize one task or set of tasks on the server while specializing another task or set of tasks on the client. This, of course, requires a slightly more sophisticated client than just an XForms browser or anything like it because the browser would have to know when it is receiving XForms and when it is receiving some other markup language such as WML.

2. *Distribution of Generic Interface, Transformation, and Specialized Interface*: An alternative way of distributing rendition of the user interface is to produce a generic user interface with one process (possibly residing on one system), transform that interface with another process (possibly residing on another system), and present the final user interface for user interactions in yet another system.

Currently, XForms browsers offer the only way of distributing specialization of the user interface through distribution of the generic user interface, transformation, and specialization. This is possible when the server application produces an XForms document as the interface to the system (a generic user interface) and serves it to the XForms client, which then transforms XForms to the appropriate user interface and displays it to the user.

Otherwise, distributing the user interface is something that you have to implement on a custom basis today. If we wanted to achieve this through distribution of tasks, we may have a scenario where a thin client and a thick client are integrated on the device (something like a Java midlet and a WAP browser working together) or alternatively we might build our own client that functions as both a thick client-side application when it receives generic user interface content and a browser when it receives appropriate specialized content.

To build such custom applications that distribute the task of displaying a user interface, we would need to use some of the tools that we introduced in Chapter 2 such as WAP, XForms, and J2ME. Let us take a closer look at the capabilities of some of these tools and start building some simple GUI applications by using them.

6.2 A Deeper Look at WAP, J2ME, BREW, and Microsoft Platforms for Mobile GUIs

Currently, WAP, J2ME, BREW, and Windows CE each present a different approach to mobile application development as we reviewed in Chapter 2. Let us take a closer look at each one of these tools and how to build GUIs with them.

6.2.1 Wireless Application Protocol

Figure 6.12 shows the WAP stack. We gave an overview of WAP 2.0 in Chapter 2 when we reviewed various types of tools for developing mobile applications. In this section, we will take a closer look at the user interface—related issues of WAP 1.x and WAP 2.x and provide a bit more detail on the communication protocol and the markup language syntax.

There are many who think WAP was a first-generation technology and that it will fade in time, particularly given its initial flop in the marketplace. And there are those who think WAP will eventually thrive as it evolves and begins to fit the needs of the market place. We are not going to speculate on the fate of WAP, but one thing is clear: As a developer of mobile applications, you will need to know WAP. This is not only because most mobile applications deployed to date

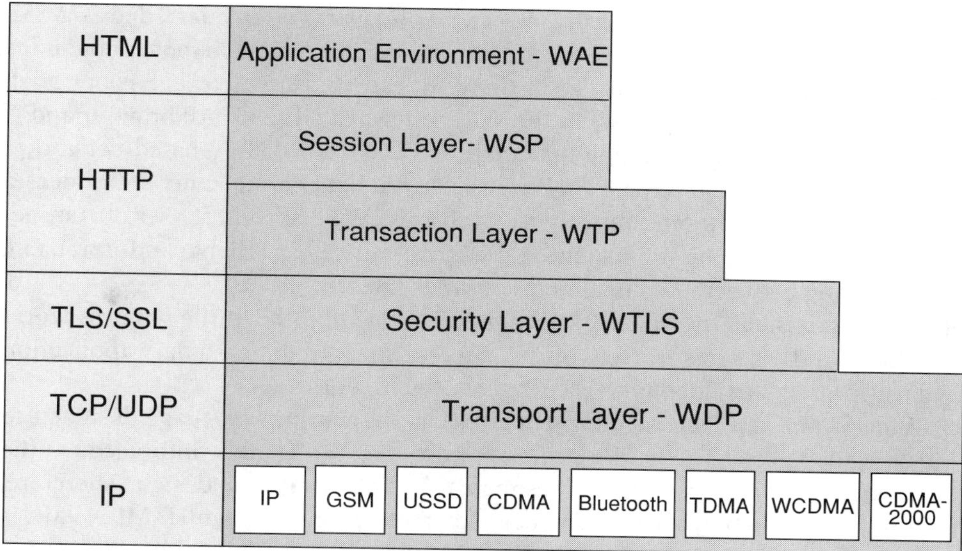

FIGURE 6.12. Wireless Access Protocol Stack.

(besides those deployed on proprietary infrastructures, embedded systems, and other specialized type applications) have been written in WAP. Specifically, most of these applications are WML applications deployed by Web developers. For this reason, we are going to take a survey of WAP 1.x and WAP 2.x. These two versions of WAP are significantly different, with WAP 1.x making up the majority of the deployments, and WAP 2.x just now beginning to be deployed.

WAP 1.x

The first version of WAP, namely WAP 1.0, 1.1, 1.2, and 1.3, introduced a series of innovations in creating a framework to produce thin client–based mobile applications. Perhaps the biggest feat of WAP 1.x was that it created an application layer communication protocol (the Wireless Application Protocol and hence the name WAP) on top of the large variety of lower layer wireless network protocols such as CDMA, TDMA, and GSM that was adopted by nearly all of the carriers internationally. WAP 1.x is the first application layer protocol that achieved this in the wireless arena. But, there is more to the WAP 1.x standard than the communication protocol. The WAP 1.x modules are as follows:

1. *Wireless Datagram Protocol* (*WDP*): This protocol layer is analogous (not equivalent) to TCP/IP on the wired Internet and is the lowest layer in the WAP protocol. WDP is constructed directly on top of the bearer protocol, which may be CDPD, CDMA, GSM, TDMA, SMS, or others. Both the WAP gateway and the WAP browser implement WDP the same way as Web servers and Web browsers, respectively, implement HTTP on the server and the client. WDP mostly provides an interface that should be implemented. The internal implementation of WDP may be UDP/IP, TCP/IP, or some other method.

2. *Wireless Transport Layer Security* (*WTLS*): This layer is often referred to as WSSL since SSL is the new name for the TLS, the security mechanism most popular for HTTP. WTLS is mapped to TLS at the WAP gateway. Use of WTLS is optional. WTLS is implemented between the WAP gateway and the WAP browser and is mapped to SSL when passing information to a TCP/IP-HTTP-based network.
3. *Wireless Transaction Layer* (*WTP*): Because wireless connectivity introduces a variety of intermittent connectivity problems, WTP specifies a set of transaction semantics to be implemented to provide so-called reliable and unreliable messaging between the client and the WAP gateway.
4. *Wireless Session Layer* (*WSP*): *WAP* positions WDP to be to the wireless world what TCP/IP is to the wired world; WSP is positioned to be a binary application layer protocol analogous to HTTP in the wired world.
5. *Wireless Markup Language* (*WML*): *WML* is the markup language designed to serve the special needs of mobile applications. WML takes into account the possible poor QOS and lack of resources on the device in its design. Therefore, it provides a better markup language for mobile devices than HTML. WML is part of the Wireless Application Environment (WAE). This is the application layer of WAP focused on providing the computer language–based tools to develop thin-client wireless applications.
6. *Wireless Markup Language Scripting* (*WMLScript*): WMLScript is based on ECMAScript, the standard created by ECMA and subsequently used to develop JavaScript and some other JavaScript-like scripting languages. WMLScript is designed to write client-side scripts that access WTA (Wireless Telephony Application) functionality, variable manipulation on the client side, and custom client-side functions such as dialogue boxes specified by the gateway. There are two important things to note about WMLScript: 1. The actual scripts to be called are stored in files separate from WML documents and 2. the definition of the calls made in the WMLScript must be present and authenticated on the WAP gateway. Once again, in the United States, developers have little access to WMLScript functions, whereas there is more openness in European networks.
7. *Wireless Telephony Application Interface* (*WTAI*): The first version of WAP was designed primarily for mobile phones. The WTAI provides access to the telephony features of the handset. It is a shame that there is very limited functionality in WTAI to implement interesting and useful features that use both the telephony and the data channels (voice and text user interfaces). Because telephony applications are by nature controlled by the network carriers, WTA servers can only run in a carrier's environment.

Note that one of the biggest differences between HTTP and WAP is the layer at which security is implemented. This gives rise to some complications though it is necessary because of the nature of wireless networks and wireless data.

Overall, you only need to know about WDP, WSP, WTP, and WTLS if you plan to implement your own WAP gateway or modify an existing open-source gateway. Currently, in the United States, operation of WAP is exclusively owned by the carriers and is not open to developers. Consequently, WAP development typically means developing WML pages whereas in Europe WAP deployment is somewhat more open. Because of this and the fact that our focus in this chapter is user interface development, we will focus on WML alone.

Basic WML 1.x

Perhaps the most important notion to understand about WML is the idea of cards. This is not something that exists in HTML and so is foreign to most first-time WAP developers who are used to developing Web applications using HTML. WML pages are divided into one or more cards. Because most WAP-enabled devices have small screens, displaying information requires multiple screens.

Using HTML, this is done through multiple round trips to the server to retrieve the subsequent pages one by one, or through URIs embedded within the same HTML (with all of the information shown on the same page and the URI mechanism used to reference anchors within the same page), or through the use of scripting languages such as JavaScript, which allow us to download all of the information to the HTML browser and dynamically change the user interface on the client side. None of these methods are appropriate for today's wireless environments. First of all, network traffic is precious because QOS is unreliable so we should do our best not to make round trips to the server for every user interaction. Second, there is not much CPU or memory on most devices targeted by WAP (cell phones, PDAs, etc.) which precludes the use of things like JavaScript on the client side (though as we will see, there is WMLScript). Finally, we cannot download the entire user interface in one shot and use the URI mechanism to navigate to anchors within the document because of the memory and CPU restrictions. (Loading a large document into a WML browser not only produces a poor user interface but is not even possible once the maximum size of the WML document for the WML browser is exceeded.)

WML cards allow us to load multiple user interfaces into the WAP device, interact with the user, collect some information from the user, and go back to the server in a single round trip. The concept of cards also allows us to render one card at a time, which helps in efficient use of resources on the device.

Let us turn now to WML 1.x syntax and follow that up with an example WML document. As we have mentioned, WML is an application of XML. Table 6.1 presents a list of the most important tags and their functionality in WML.

In addition to these tags used in WML, there is also WTAI-based URI references. Because, as we previously mentioned, WMLScript access and implementation is not pervasive, we can do a couple of simple things in WML to access the telephony agent. One of those is to dial a number. That is done by pointing an <anchor> or <go> to a WTAI-based URI (for example, wtai://wp/mc;7144546537).

Now, let us look at a sample WML document in Figure 6.13. Our example simply shows a page that overrides one of the event buttons (accept) and gets an input from the user. Note that this example shows a WML document that is either static or generated by some dynamic code. If we had utilized the PAC-TG pattern, we would have first created an equivalent XForms (or other equivalent generic user interface) document.

WML 1.x is being phased out in the future releases of WAP and replaced by XHTML. XHTML's modularization offers more flexibility in creating transformable

Table 6.1. WML 1.x Tag Description

Tag	Attributes	Description
<card>	id, title	Card is the container unit for one screen rendered on a WML browser. The id of a card within a WML document must be unique. A card is addressed through its id attribute. The title of the card is often rendered on top of the screen of the WML browser.
<p>	align, mode	All textual and graphical items to be displayed on the WML browser screen must be enclosed within <p> and </p>.The align attribute is used to specify the alignment of the displayable items. It can be set to right, left, or center. The mode attribute is used to specify whether word wrapping is used to wrap text that is longer than the width of the display. If this attribute is set to "nowrap" and the browser supports scrolling, the text is scrolled horizontally for viewing.
<b>		The text enclosed within the <b></b> tags are displayed bolded.
<i>		The text enclosed within the <i></i> tags are displayed italicized.
<u>		The text enclosed within the <u></u> tags are underlined.
<em>		The text enclosed within the <em></em> tags are somehow (based on the browser implementation) emphasized.
<strong>		The text enclosed within the <strong></strong> tags are made more notable in some browser-specific manner.
<big>		The text enclosed within the <big></big> tags is presented larger than other text. Implementation is browser specific.
<small>		The text enclosed within the <small></small> tags is displayed with text smaller than the normal text. Implementation is browser specific.
<a>	href	This tag enables creation of anchors on the WML page. Anchors are rendered in a browser-specific manner. Sometimes, they are rendered with the text enclosed in <a> and </a> as underlined and the left soft button reading "GO." Other times, it is translated by the browser to the a soft key or a menu option. (Soft keys are those keys that have variable meanings depending on the screen being navigated. For example, most mobile phones have two buttons immediately under the display, one to the left and

		the other to the right. These buttons are assigned variables values such as “options,” “ok,” “cancel,” etc. on the bottom of the display at the time of using the device. Hard keys, on the other hand, are keys that have at least 1 static value associated with them at all times. For example, the number keys on the mobile phone are hard keys.) Either way, it allows the user to use the keypad on the cell phone or PDA to navigate. Anchors are used to navigate to new cards in WML. If the new card is in a WML document different from the one currently loaded, then the new WML document is loaded; otherwise, the current WML document is kept and the card pointed to is displayed.
<anchor>		This tag is identical in functionality to the <a> tag in purpose. However, the implementation varies. The <anchor> tag must include the <go> tag to implement the actual action when the soft key or hard key are pushed.
<go>	href, method	This tag provides much the same functionality that the <a> tag does. However, this method can be used to send data back to the server using the POST or GET methods. If the method is set to “POST,” then the <postfield> elements encapsulated inside the <go></go> element are sent to the WAP gateway where they are converted to the HTTP format and sent to the Web server. If the GET method is used, then CGI-like name–value pair parameters are included in the URI.
 		This tag creates a carriage return or line feed (empty line).
<do>	type, label	This tag provides a way to catch events and perform some action. In other words, it allows us to override the functionality offered by various events thrown by the device and transferred to the browser. The action is enclosed within the <do></do> tags. The type attribute specifies what kind of event is created. The types of events are as follows: • *accept*: This event is emitted when the OK button, or the soft key equivalent thereof, is pressed. • *prev*: This event is emitted when the user navigates to the previous page. This may be done through the BACK button, if it exists, or through a soft key. • *help*: This event is emitted when the user presses the help button or the soft key equivalent thereof. • *reset*: This event is emitted when the reset button, if one exists on the keypad, is pressed. Not all WAP browsers implement this uniformly. Often, this event is not caught as the reset button causes the browser to exit altogether.

(continued)

Table 6.1 (continued)

Tag	Attributes	Description
		• *options*: This event is emitted when the options hard or soft button is pressed. The options soft key is often presented by the browser when more choices are offered than the particular phone is allowed to access (because some phones have more hard keys than others). • *unknown*: This event has custom implementation depending on the browser type. Consult the specific browser to see the implementation for the installed device. The action within the <do> tag is the <go> tag, enabling navigation to a particular card (within the same WML document or in a new document).
<select>	title	One of the most basic things to do in a GUI is to select one choice from several options. The <select> tag enables such selection. The title attribute should be set to the string that appears on the top of the browser. The select tag must be enclosed within the <p> tag. Though you can include other text within the same <p> tag, most browsers ignore any other text outside of the select tag or alternatively display an error.
<option>	onpick	The text to be displayed for the individual options for a selection list must be enclosed in the <option> and </option> tags. The onpick attribute specifies the card that is navigated to if the particular option is selected. The onpick attribute is not required by most browsers, though its absence effectively renders this control useless.
<onevent>	type	The <onevent> tag allows us to catch event smuch like the <do> tag. However, where the events of the <do> tag are associated with the device and propagated to the browser, the events caught by the <onevent> tag are specific to WML browsers and are not initiated by the device. The type attribute can be set to the following: • *oneventforward*: This event is emitted when a card is entered. So, if you want to execute something on the entry to the card (basically bound to navigation to another card, creating a timer task, doing a refresh, or executing WMLScript if it is supported on the device) this is the event to catch.

		• *oneventbackward*: If a card is navigated to through the back button or the <prev/> event, this eventbackward is thrown upon entry to the card and can be caught through this tag. • *onpick*: This event is thrown when an option in a select list is selected or deselected. As we mentioned, this is not a tag; it is an attribute of the option tag. • *ontimer*: This event is thrown when a timer expires. Timers are specified through the <timer> tag. The <onevent> tag must be used outside of the <p></p> tags since it is not something that is rendered or relates to the rendering of the card.
<timer>	value	This tag specifies that a timer should start when the card is navigated to. The value attribute is set to the amount of time that passes from the moment you navigate to the card to the moment when the timer expires. The value attribute is specified in tenths of seconds.
<setvar>	name, value	This tag is used to specify a variable and assign a value to it. Variables in WML are weakly typed (i.e., there are no type associations like integer, double, string, etc.). Basically, you can think of everything as strings. The name attribute is the name by which the variable can be referred to within the WML document by putting a $ in front of it. For example, a variable named X is defined by the setvar tag whose name attribute is set to X and is then referred to as $X. You can think of WML variables being referenced by value (with the browser simply replacing all occurrences of $X with the value stored in X when a pass through the card is made). The value attribute sets the value of the variable. The names of the variables in a WML document must be unique. If you want to update the value of the variable referenced in the document, you will need to enclose all occurrences of its references (in our example $X) within the refresh tags or simply reload the document.
<refresh>		This tag causes the browser to interpret the segment of code enclosed within the <refresh></refresh> tags.
<optgroup>		This tag is used to group a set of related options. Many WML browsers do not support this tag, so we discourage its use.

(*continued*)

TABLE 6.1 (continued)

Tag	Attributes	Description
<input>	name, format	This tag provides a text input prompt for the user to enter text-based information using the device (cell phone keypad, PDA, etc.). Multiple occurrences of this tag can be used within one set of <p></p> tags; however, most browsers render the resulting text box by itself. To create a label for the input tag, simply put the label text before the occurrence of the <input> tag to be labeled. The value entered by the user is stored in the variable named by whatever the name attribute is set to and can be referenced as other variables (by putting a $ before its name) like those defined by setvar. The name of the input tags in the same WML document must be unique and cannot conflict with other variables defined by the setvar tag. The format attribute allows us to specify an input mask (a format enforced by the input box) for the data entry. For example, an eight-digit date separated by dashes can be specified by format = "NN-NN-NNNN."
<postfield>	name, value	This tag is used to send name–value pairs to the server that resembles the HTTP POST method. Keep in mind that WML is the client to WAP and not HTTP. However, because the visibility of WAP is between the gateway of the device, and most WML content is created by Web servers that send the content to the WAP gateway, using an HTTP-like method seems natural. These name–value pairs are transported by WAP to the gateway where they are changed to the format specified by HTTP in the HTTP POST method.
<fieldset>	title	This element is used to pair input fields and select lists together, the primary purpose being clarity and good organization of the information on the interface. We do not recommend use of this tag as it is rarely implemented in the gateways and/or the browsers.
<table>	Columns	This tag lets you create tables. However, creating tables in a markup language that has been shrunk to provide a small set of functionality does not make much sense. This is probably why most WAP browsers do not implement this tag and therefore we discourage its use.
<tr>		This tag allows you to define a row in a table
<td>		This tag allows you to define a cell in a table row

```
<?xml version="1.0">
<!DOCTYPE wml PUBLIC "-//WAPFORUM/DTD WML 1.1//EN"
"http://www.wapforum.org/DTD/wml1.1.xml">

<wml>
    <head>
        <meta forua="true" http-equiv="Cache"Control"
          content="max-age=0"/>
    </head>
    <card id ="Hello">
        <do type="accept" label="NextPage">
            <go href="#World"/>
        </do>
        <p>
        This card is displayed first. Cards are navigated to
          in the order that they appear  in the WML document
          unless otherwise specified by the URI.
        </p>
    </card>
    <card id = "World">
        <p>
        This is the second page. What is your name?
            <input name="username"/>
        </p>
    </card>
</wml>
```

FIGURE 6.13. Sample WML Document.

content. This is an example where building WML interfaces on top of XForms interfaces (or some other generic user interface language) would benefit you greatly: Simply add the new transformations, and your system is ready for quality control (although you still need to go through the entire usability testing process as each type of user interface has its own usability requirements).

WMLScript

WMLScript is the ECMAScript implementation for WAP 1.x. The first important thing to know about WMLScript is that, like WML, it is compiled by the WAP gateway before it is sent to the device. Whereas the compiled WML format is WMLC, the compiled .wmls files are .wmlsc files. The problem with WMLScript is that a great number of operators do not offer any support for it and those that do, implement WMLScript with a considerable amount of inconsistency.

There are two types of WMLScript functions: standard functions and custom functions. Standard functions are those defined with the WAP specification. These should be provided in the WAP gateways that support them and you do not need

```
extern function helloWorld(fName, lName) {
    var fullName;
    fullName = fName + "" + lName;

    WMLBrowser.setVar("username", fullName);

    WMLBrowser.refresh();
}
```

WML file may be:

```
<?xml version ="1.0" ?>
<!DOCTYPE wml PUBLIC "-//WAPFORUM//DTD WML 1.1//EN"
"http://www.wapforum.org/DTD/wml_1.1.xml">

<wml>
    <card id="main" title="WMLScript Hello World">
        <setvar name="username" value="Susan Boettger"/>
        <p>Hello $(username). Click here to see your future
          name:
            <a href="calling.wmls#helloWorld("Susan",
              "B'Far")">
            </a>
        </p>
    </card>
</wml>
```

FIGURE 6.14. A Sample WMLScript Function.

to provide the source code. The custom functions are those that the developer authors.

For your WMLScript file to be compiled by the gateway and then provisioned to the device, it has to be authorized by the telecommunications carrier, and this is yet another barrier to real usage of WMLScript. At the time of authoring this text, this is possible in Europe and not the United States. In the United States, the operators' networks remain fairly closed to the developers. Nonetheless, let us take a look at a simple WMLScript so that you can get a feel for what it looks like. Figure 6.14 shows a sample WMLScript function. You can find a better specification of WMLScript through the Open Mobile Alliance (previously known as the WAP Forum).

It is important to note that perhaps the biggest feature of WMLScript is that it allows interactions with the WTAI agent on the handset, thereby making it a possible mechanism for creating a multichannel user interface (voice through the telephony channel and data through WAP). However, this is difficult to do because of the inconsistent support of WMLScript functionality among the carriers.

There is one interesting problem that we have not looked at: How does WMLScript map to a generic user interface? Let us note the following:

1. WMLScript, and for that matter all scripting languages for specialized user interfaces, can be excluded from the generic user interface altogether. There is an argument to be made that client-side behavior is specific to the type of interface used. This means that either we have custom scripts for every user interface or we must transform some generic user interface script to specialized user interface script. We leave this decision up to the implementer. However, you should know that mapping code from one scripting language to another scripting language is much more complex than mapping user interface widgets, structure, and instance data. Throughout the research that we did for this text, we did not find any research or development that presented a viable solution for mapping a generic user interface scripting language to a specialized one.
2. There is the matter of XForms events. Because WML does not have anything equivalent to XForms events, to support XForms events, we would have to translate them to WMLScript for WML or to transform the XForms so that those events are taken care of on the server side. If we decide to produce WML from XForms, and if there is a considerable amount of behavior in the XForms, we are better off translating XForms to server-side behavior such as Java Server Pages (JSP) or Microsoft's Active Server Pages (ASP). This is because such mapping is more reusable.

Regardless of how you decide to solve this problem, it is only relevant when dealing with a scripting language for a browser. We simply recommend that you do not abuse scripting languages provided along with markup languages (JavaScript, VBScript, ECMAScript derivatives, etc.). If you need a rich client, your solution is probably not one based on a browser and markup language. J2ME, BREW, Windows CE, and Symbian offer the capability to build applications that have rich user interfaces with complex behaviors.

WAP 2.x

WAP 2.x is a significantly different framework for developing wireless applications. We reviewed the basics of WAP 2.x in Chapter 2 along with the tools. Here, we will dig a little deeper into the GUI aspects of WAP 2.x. Namely, we will look at XHTML, which replaces WML in WAP 2.x, and MMS, which provides multimedia messaging.

XHTML

We have previously looked at various XML-based markup languages. Let us remember that XML itself is a subset of SGML and that HTML was designed based on SGML and not XML. So, HTML is not an application of XML because it is defined by SGML and some of what is used to define HTML falls outside of the subset of the SGML used to build XML. The design of XML as a markup language has brought about a set of tools and an industry-wide understanding of structuring content. Because HTML is not an XML application, the tools that are used to manipulate XML (such as parsers and development tools) cannot be used for HTML. This renders much of GUI content provided by the Web unusable in an automated fashion. At its core, XHTML aims at solving this problem. XHTML redefines the functionality and syntax of HTML so that it is an application of XML, thereby allowing us to use all of the tools and techniques that come with XML-based development.

One crucial feature of XHTML is its modularization. XHTML is broken into several different distinct modules. XHTML Basic can be augmented with any of the XHTML modules to add functionality. So, what XHTML Basic gives us is a subset of XHTML as the starting point for developing thin-client mobile user interfaces. Because, by its virtue of being an XML application, XHTML is extensible, we can add functionality to it by adding XHTML modules or by making custom extensions (though custom extensions are strongly discouraged for the reasons of portability). Let us present an overview of the syntax of XHTML and then we will look at XHTML Basic. XHTML 2.0 has the following modules:

1. *Text Module*: This module defines the tags that structure text in XHTML. Most of these tags allow for things like creating line breaks, defining headers, making divisions, and making other structural definitions for text as in HTML. However, there are some new tags such as the <cite> tag and the <acronym> tag (respectively marking a piece of text as a citation or an acronym) that try to define the semantic definition of text within a document (somewhat RDF-like).
2. *Hypertext Module*: This module has a single element of <a> inherited from HTML. This is the anchor element that allows navigation through the HTTP protocol and its URI mechanism.
3. *List Module*: This module defines tag elements that allow usage of various types of list constructs. List elements, ordered lists, unordered lists, and lists used for building navigational menus are defined in this module.
4. *Bidirectional Text Module*: This module has a single element, <bdo>. The purpose of this module, and its only element, is to specify the direction in which text must be displayed. Because some textual formats favor display of text in one direction or another, this element provides a way to specify the direction in which text, possibly of any language using UNICODE or other character sets, should be displayed.
5. *Client-Side Image Map Module*: This module is designed to specify image maps, a very popular technique in HTML for displaying complex or multisectioned images.
6. *Edit Module*: This module provides two elements, <ins> and <del>, respectively allowing for displaying modifications made to the document through insertion or deletion of portions of the XHTML document. This module's primary purpose is in providing a mechanism for viewing versioned edits in a single document.
7. *Link Module*: This module defines only one element, <link>, which is used to specify links to external documents. The difference between this element and the <a> element is that it is only used within the header (wrapped within the

<head> element) and that it is intended to be implicitly used by the XHTML browser instead of creating a user-driven navigation method like the anchor tag does. This element can be used for specifying things like style sheets that provide the formatting for a page.

8. *Metainformation Module*: This module defines only one element, <meta>, which like the <link> element can only be used within the header of the document.
9. *Object Module*: This module provides a mechanism for including external objects such as ActiveX objects or Java applets. This module provides two elements, <object> and <param>, the first of which is used to specify the object, its source, and other things that allow the XHTML browser to use the object and the second of which allows us to pass parameters to the object to initialize it.
10. *Presentation Module*: At version 2.0 of XHTML, this module has only three tags. <sup> and <sub> tags are used to specify superscripts and subscripts, respectively. The <hr> tag is used to specify insertion of a horizontal line. These tags are used inline with the content created based on the tags of the Text Module when the Presentation Module is included.
11. *Scripting Module*: This module specifies whether a piece of XHTML content has or does not have some script that is to be executed by the XHTML browser. The tags to specify this are <script> and <noscript>. The first tag is used much in the same way as it is used to specify scripts in HTML. The second tag is used to section off parts of XHTML that the XHTML browser should ignore for finding and executing any script.
12. *Server-Side Image Map Module*: Although images can be put together on the client side with the Client-Side Image Map, the same thing can be done on the server before serving the XHTML content up to the browser. This module provides the ability to specify how image maps are composed on the server side.
13. *Style-Sheet Module*: This module has one tag, <style>, that allows you to specify internal style sheets (used by the XHTML browser to add formatting to the XHTML document). This element must be used within the header content.
14. *Table Module*: This module provides tags that specify properties of tables within an XHTML document. An example of such a tag is <caption>, which specifies the caption that describes the table.
15. *Target Module*: The target of a link, an anchor, or a form can be an externally defined target specified by the attributes of this element.
16. *Structure Module*: This module defines the <header>, <body>, <html>, and <title> tags that allow us to specify, respectively, the following: headers, where the body of the XHTML document starts and where it ends, one or more chunks of one or more types of XHTML enclosed within the same document, and a title for the XHTML document.
17. *Forms Modules*: There are two forms modules. The first is the Basic Forms Module, which allows basic GET and POST methods of HTTP to be called from an XHTML document. The second is the Forms Module, which adds some cosmetic features such as buttons, options, and option groups within a form.

```
<?xml version="1.0"?>
<!DOCTYPE html PUBLIC "-//W3C//DTD XHTML 1.0
  Transitional//EN"
    "http://www.w3.org/TR/xhtml1/DTD/xhtml1-
      transitional.dtd">
<html xmlns="http://www.w3.org/1999/xhtml">
<head>
    <title>Hello World XHTML 2.0 Document</title>
    <meta name="author" content="Abdy B'Far"/>
    <meta name="keywords" content="semantic, mobile,
      webservices, XHTML 2.0 example"/>
    <meta name="description" content="Example of a
      basic XHTML document"/>
    <link rel='top' href='http://www.cienecs.com/'
      title='Home'/>
</head>
<body>
    <h id="documentTitle">w3future.com</h>
    <section id="pageHeader">
        <h href="http://www.w3.org/TR/xhtml-basic/">
          XHTML Basic</h>
        <blockquote cite='http://www.w3.org/TR/xhtml-
          basic/'>
            <p>Abstract</p>
            <p>
                The XHTML Basic document type includes the
                  minimal set of modules required to be an
                  XHTML host language document type, and
                  in addition it includes images, forms,
                  basic tables, and object support. It is
                  designed for Web clients that do not
                  support the full set of XHTML features:
                  for example, Web clients such as mobile
                  phones, PDAs, pagers, and settop boxes.
                  The document type is rich enough for
                  content authoring.
            </p>
        </blockquote>
    </section>
    <section id="mainSection">
        <h>This is a page in XHTML 2.0 format</h>
        <p>
```

FIGURE 6.15. Hello World XHTML 2.0 Document.

```
            Authoring GUI interfaces for mobile
              applications is somewhat more
              complicated than typical GUI development
              for stationary applications. Should this
              example have the words "Hello World"
              since it is a so-called Hello World
              example?
        </p>
    </section>
    <section id="pageFooter">
        <h>Current Time</h>
        <p>10/17/2002 </p>
        <p><a href="http://www.cienecs.com/examples/
          XHTML/">XHTML Tutorial</a></p>
    </section>
</body>
</html>
```

FIGURE 6.15 *(continued)*

There are a few other modules that are inherited from XHTML 1.1. As in the case of other tools and languages in this text, we introduced the bulk of what is relevant to mobile applications. An example of a simple XHTML 2.0 document can be seen in Figure 6.15. Note that the modularization of XHTML allows us to remove the parts that may not be applicable to some devices. For example, image maps on the client are an impractical proposition when it comes to WAP-based cellular phones.

XHTML has another very big advantage over HTML: Because it is an application of XML, and therefore well formed, it can be transcoded and transformed without any loss of information using existing technologies such as XSLs.

This brings us to developing user interfaces for mobile applications with XHTML. As we previously mentioned, XHTML is the user interface markup language for WAP 2.0. Let us see how the XHTML Basic and XHTML Mobile Profile are related to WML and how they enable us to develop thin-client mobile applications. Figure 6.16 shows a high-level organization of features for some of the markup languages that we're most concerned with, including XHTML and its mobile profile.

XHTML Mobile Profile

XHTML was still far too unwieldy for most small devices. Consequently, a subset of XHTML called XHTML Basic was selected by W3C to create a path as the markup language for resource-starved devices such as PDAs and mobile phones or those devices that simply do not have a full-blown XHTML browser running on a typical operating system designed for stationary PCs (such as electronic tablets, televisions, and Web appliances such as Web kiosks). At the same time

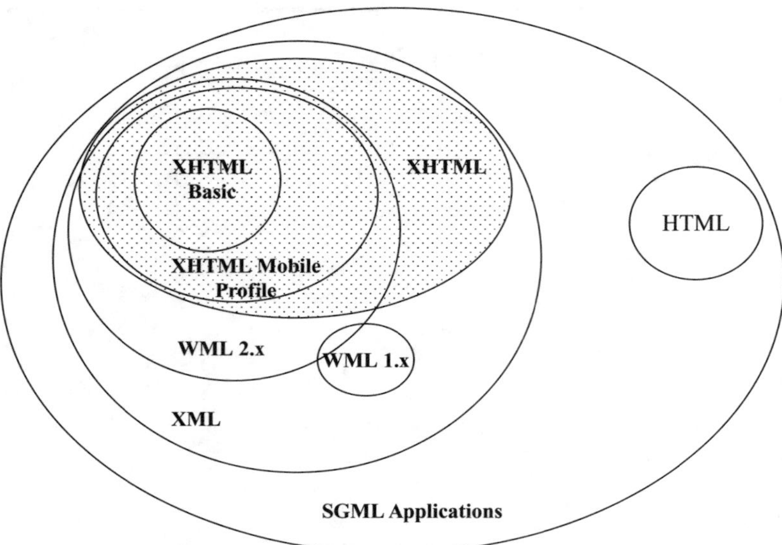

Figure 6.16. Taxonomy of Various Standard Markup Languages for Mobile Application Development.

that XHTML Basic was being put together, the WAP Forum was evolving WML 2.0 specifications. In an effort to consolidate these efforts, XHTML Mobile Profile extends the XHTML Basic to add some needed features.

Let us first see what is included in XHTML Basic and why:

1. The Scripting Module is not supported. There is no guarantee that the XHTML browser is running on a device capable of executing scripts.
2. The Basic Forms Module is supported to all the XHTML browsers to POST/GET content to the server.
3. The Basic Tables Module is supported.
4. The Frames and Client-Side Style-Sheet Modules are not supported. These operations tend to be too complicated for simple devices.

The Bidirectional Text Module is not supported because client-side rendering of complex output (such as multilingual content) is not necessarily possible on all devices.

XHTML Basic gives us the basic ability of rendering text on the client and sending parameters back to the server. As we mentioned, more advanced functionality can be included, if appropriate for the application and the devices for which the application is intended, by extending XHTML through including additional modules. Now let us look at the XHTML Mobile Profile syntax. Table 6.2 gives a subset of the XHTML tags used in the XHTML Mobile Profile.

Now, let us look at a simple XHTML page in Figure 6.17. In our example, we have used only modules that fall within XHTML Basic. This means that this page

Table 6.2. XHTML Mobile Profile Syntax

Tag	Application
<a>	The anchor tag is used to allow the user to navigate to other resources.
<abbr>	This tag specifies that the enclosed text is an abbreviation.
<acronym>	This tag specifies that the enclosed text is an acronym.
<address>	This tag may be used by the author of the document to provide contact information.
<big>	This tag specifies that the enclosed text should be displayed in a "big" font.
<base/>	This tag specifies a base URI for the relative URIs in the XHTML document and can only be used within the header.
<blockquote>	This tag specifies text that is enclosed within the quotation marks.
<body>	The body of the XHTML document must be enclosed within the <body> and </body> tags.
 	This tag forces a carriage return (line feed). Implementation is dependent on the specific user interface rendering the XHTML document.
<caption>	This tag is used in conjunction with a table and serves as a description for the table.
<cite>	This tag specifies if the text enclosed is a citation.
<code>	This tag specifies if the text enclosed is computer code.
<dl>	This tag defines definition lists. Definition lists are a list of name–value pairs of a term and the description of that term.
<dd>	This tag defines the description of the term within the definition list <dl> tag.
<dt>	This tag defines the name of the term within the definition list <dl> tag.
<dfn>	This tag allows you to define a term and a description (not part of a list, just an individual term and accompanying definition).
<div>	As in HTML, the <div> tag is used to provide an additional mechanism to add structure to the XHTML document by dividing it into sections.
<em>	This tag allows us to specify text that should be emphasized by the XHTML browser.

(continued)

Table 6.2 (continued)

Tag	Application
<fieldset>	This tag allows for grouping of controls within a form.
<form>	This tag defines the boundaries of a form in XHTML.
<h1>, <h2>, <h3>, <h4>, <h5>, <h6>	These tags allow you to specify the text enclosed within them to be of a particular hierarchy within the XHTML document. Each stands for a header level with <h1> being the highest level header and <h6> the lowest level header defined by XHTML.
<head>	The header of the document, including the <link>, <meta>, <base/>, and <style> tags is enclosed within this tag.
<hr>	This tag results a horizontal line in the XHTML document rendering.
<html>	The XHTML content of the document is enclosed within this tag. It is very important that the attributes of this tag specify the correct namespace and version of XHTML.
<i>	Text enclosed within this tag is italicized.
<img/>	This tag and its attributes are used to specify an image and the source from which it is loaded.
<input/>	This tag is used to specify an input field.
<kbd>	If some text is to be entered into the interface by the user, it is enclosed within this tag (for example, "please type <kbd>5<kbd/> for every choice").
<label>	This tag allows you to specify a label for a control such as the input or a form control.
<li>	This tag is used to specify a list item (as is in HTML).
<ul>	This tag is used to specify an unordered list (whose items are specified by using the <li> tag).
<ol>	This tag is used to specify an ordered list (whose items are specified by using the <li> tag).
<link/>	This tag is used within the header to specify links to other resources.
<meta/>	This tag is used to specify metainformation within the header.
<object>	This tag is used to include external objects such as Java applets and ActiveX objects within the XHTML document.

<param>	To pass parameters to the object specified by the <object> tag when it is instantiated and before it begins to execute, we can enclose the parameters in the <param> tag.
<opgroup>	This tag is used to specify a group of options. The options are specified using the <option> tag within this tag.
<option>	This tag specifies the options within an <opgroup>.
<p>	This tag is used to specify a paragraph of text. Display of spacing is up to the XHTML browser implementation on the device.
<pre>	White spaces are typically not preserved by the various XHTML tags. This element specifies that the white spaces enclosed within <pre> and </pre> be preserved as they may have semantic meaning.
<samp>	Text enclosed within this tag specifies sample code.
<select>	As in the case of HTML, this tag surrounds options from which the user must choose.
<small>	This element specifies that the text enclosed within it must be small (rendering is up to the XHTML browser).
<strong>	This element specifies that the text enclosed within it must be displayed strong (rendering is up to the XHTML browser).
<span>	As in HTML, this tag is used to unblock sections of the document. It is typically used for styling purposes.
<style>	This tag is used within the header and specifies style-sheet settings for the formatting of the XHTML document.
<table>	As in HTML, this tag is used to define a table.
<tr>	This tag is used to define a row within a table.
<td>	This tag is used to define a cell within a row.
<textarea>	This tag is used to define an area for entry of a large amount of text (as opposed to a single line of text or less typically entered through the input tag).
<th>	This is a special cell within a table. It is bolded and centered.
<var>	To specify a variable name in computer code, this tag is typically used within the <code> tag.

```
<?xml version="1.0"?>
<!DOCTYPE html PUBLIC "-//W3C/DTD XHTML Basic 1.0//EN"
  "xhtml-basic10.dtd">
<html xmlns="http://www.w3.org/1999/xhtml">
   <p>Welcome to Natasha's Home Page</p>
   <img src="natasah_welcome.gif" />
   <p>Natasha's Schedule This Week</p>
   <ul>
      <li>Monday – Dance – 6 PM</li>
      <li>Tuesday – Pick On Nikoo – All Night </li>
      <li>Wednesday – Soccer – 3 PM</li>
      <li>Thursday – Gymnastics – 6 PM</li>
      <li>Friday – Piano – 4 PM</li>
   </ul>
</html>
```

FIGURE 6.17. Simple XHTML Document.

will render without error in browsers that support XHTML Basic and XHTML Mobile Profile.

As you can see, XHTML Basic (and Mobile Profile) share more similarities with HTML than with WML (WAP 1.x). Gone is the concept of cards, mostly to simplify the language, and therefore the implementation of the browser. As in the case of WML, conversion of XForms to XHTML is probably a matter of authoring some XSLTs. Once again, you will have your choice of how to map XForms events over to XHTML.

MMS

MMS was introduced in Chapter 2 as part of WAP 2.x. MMS gives us a very unique mechanism to render graphics on the device. MMS does not really provide us with a framework to build a GUI. MMS is just about sending a message from one point to another. But because the message is a multimedia message, this makes it much richer than any other messaging technique. MMS requires an MMS client on the handset for sending and receiving MMS messages.

In this chapter, we are not concerned with addressing and delivery of MMS, although the presentation is of interest to us. The presentation of MMS provides us with a very rich method of presenting information to the user within the MMS client.

MMS message structure follows the MIME format used everywhere on the Internet. The specific MIME type is *application/vnd.wap.mms-message*. Every message is broken into headers and a body. In turn, the body is broken into the following parts:

1. *Presentation*: This is basically the metadata on how to render the remainder of the content in the body. Timing of audio playback and order of image rendering are examples of such instructions.
2. *Images*: This part encapsulates the single image, multiple images, or frames of a moving video.
3. Text: This part has basic text.
4. *Audio*: This part encapsulates any audio to be played back.

By default, the presentation part of the message content should use SMIL, which we will look at in Chapter 8. Building an MMS client involves writing a client that can communicate through the WAP protocol (WSP).

Finally, if you are planning to build a mobile client that supports full multimedia capabilities, there is probably great benefit in using the MMS presentation model (the content format) as it is well thought out and exchangeable with other devices that support MMS.

Mobile SVG

Scalable Vector Graphics (SVG), a standard by W3C, is an XML-based language designed to represent two-dimensional graphics using a vector-based representation. SVG documents can be written to represent static or dynamic graphics.

Of particular interest to us is the Mobile SVG Profile, SVG Basic, and SVG Tiny, each specifying a grammar for representing two-dimensional graphics on mobile (or other resource-starved) devices. Because SVG provides a way to specify shapes rather than draw out a graphic pixel by pixel, it provides for a more efficient way of specifying graphics. The drawback is that creating DOM objects in memory is expensive.

As in the case of other markup languages, we can produce SVG on the server and send it to the mobile device where it is to be rendered. So, SVG is typically used in a thin-client environment when dealing with networked mobile applications. The think client is either a dedicated SVG viewer or a browser that is SVG-enabled (e.g., Microsoft's Internet Explorer). So, when you are building your mobile application, you need to SVG-enable it using some component, build the SVG-enabling components yourself, or use a preexisting browser on the mobile device that is SVG-enabled as the application environment.

SVG is currently at its version 1.1. SVG, like XHTML and some of the other W3C standards that we have discussed, is modularized. The two profiles (collections of modules) that we are most interested in are SVGT (SVG Tiny Profile) and SVGB (SVG Basic Profile). SVGT is intended for those devices that are extremely resource-constrained such as cell phones whereas SVGB offers more functionality and is more intended for slightly more powerful devices such as PDAs. More advanced graphics features such as opacity, gradient color ranges, and patterns are not included in SVGT. Both are complementary to XHTML Mobile Profile though their use means that the client (thick client or browser running on the mobile device) must support the features.

Various subsets of SVG have a lot going for them: SVG is XML based, can be used along with other standards such as XSLT and SMIL, and is compatible with legacy technologies such as HTML.

Building GUI Palm Applications

The Palm OS is currently one of the most popular operating systems for handheld devices. At this time, Palm OS only supports an IP-based data channel for network connectivity and a GUI. Though some Palm-based PDAs can function as mobile phones as well, the operating system does not expose much, at this time, in the way of controlling the telephony channel for customized purposes.

There are two ways to build a GUI Palm:

1. You can write a client-side application for the Palm. There are several different choices here. You will get the best performance out of a C-based application using the Palm SDK. To do this, you need to download the Palm SDK and use a C/C++ development environment. You can always use free tools such as Gnu's compilers, but you will find it much easier to develop with a more advanced tool such as MetroWerk Code Warrior. You can also write Java programs that run with acceptable performance on the Palm platform. There are various Java Virtual Machines (JVMs) for the Palm like IBM's J9. At the time of authoring this text, the J2ME PDA Profile is being worked on with Palm as the reference implementation platform. There are also some variations for the Basic programming language. Devices that have Palm OS typically have enough resources to support a fair amount of functionality on the client side, but you will still need to be very conscious of the device's limited resources.
2. You can write a Palm Query Application (PQA). PQAs are written using HTML and reside on the Palm device. There is another piece to this puzzle called Web Clippings. Web Clippings are also written in HTML. The idea is to put static HTML into the PQAs so that the content is not downloaded every time the page is requested. Web Clippings provide the Web content that changes. PQAs are compiled using PQA Builder, a tool downloadable from the Palm. Figure 6.18 shows a trivial sample of a PQA application before we compile it. Compilation instructions are included within the meta tags in the header. There are only three meta tags: PalmComputingPlatform, which indicates whether the page was designed for the Palm platform or not, HistoryListText, which specifies what should be displayed in the Palm history list, and PalmLauncherRevision, which specifies the version of the PQA but is strictly for documentation purposes (i.e., there is no provisioning functionality built into the Palm OS based on this tag). If you want to build a PQA, look further into the allowed tags and the subset of HTML supported on the Palm GUI platform.

Building GUI Symbian Applications

Symbian is perhaps the most popular operating system for PDA and mobile cellular devices in Europe. Like Palm, it provides an open-platform C/C++-based API. There is also a high degree of support for Java on Symbian as well as some Basic and Visual Basic applications. (Once again, we discourage the user from writing

```
<html>
    <head>
        <title>Hello World!</title>
        <meta name="PalmComputingPlatform" content=
          "true">
    </head>
    <body>
        Hello World!
    </body>
</html>
```

FIGURE 6.18. Sample PQA Application Before It Is Built.

serious mobile applications with Visual Basic or like tools as they do not provide for enough optimization capabilities for most resource-starved devices.)

The big advantage that Symbian offers over Palm and Windows CE is its superior support of communication protocols. The Symbian APIs provide seamless integration with SMS and IP-based communications as well as RS-232 communications for testing (serial port). Let us take a quick look at building a Hello World program for Symbian so that we can get a feel for what it would be like to program in Symbian. We will use the C++ API, though there is a both a full-blown JVM and a Personal Java implementation available for Symbian. Every application for Symbian has at least four components:

1. *View*: This is basically the layout of the user interface. The buttons, input boxes, text, etc. are all put onto this component.
2. *Application UI*: This class handles all of the events emitted by the various components of the interface and what happens when those events are emitted. Whereas the View defines the layout, the Application UI defines the behavior of the user interface. The Application UI must extend the class CEikAppUI, which delivers some standard behaviors.
3. *Application Shell*: This is what wraps around the entire application. This class must extend CEikApplication.
4. *Document*: Though this component is not used in all applications, one must exist for all applications. The Document is applicable only to those applications that have some persistence or have the concept of a real document (such as word processing, spread sheets, etc.). To create a Document, the developer must extend the CEikDocument class.

As you can see, authoring even a simple C++ application for Symbian takes quite an effort. But then, this is typical of any C/C++ application development environment. Java presents us with the option of a simple development path in exchange for loss of performance. As we mentioned earlier, Java on Symbian means Personal

```
package com.symbian.devnet.quartz.qjava;

import com.symbian.devnet.quartz.awt.*;
import java.awt.*;
import java.awt.event.*;

public class QJava extends QFrame implements
  ActionListener
{
    static MenuItem mHelloWorld = new MenuItem("Hello
      World");
    public QJava(int i)
    {
        // Default constructor takes in an integer to
        // create a number of "cards." Similar to WML card
        // concept.
        super(i);

        Panel pt = getCardAt(0);
        pt.setLayout(new BorderLayout());

        appMenu.add(mHelloWorld);
        mnuExit.addActionListener(this);

        setVisible(true);
    }

    public void actionPerformed(ActionEvent anEvent)
    {
        if (anEvent.getSource().equals(mHelloWorld))
        {shutDown();}
    }
    // Test Method
    public static void main(String[] args) {
    // Delay for the emulator to start before starting
    // the application
        if (args.length > 0) {
            String s = args[args.length-1];
            if (s.equals("sleep")) {
                try
                {Thread.sleep(50000);}
                catch (InterruptedException e)
                {}
            }
        }
```

FIGURE 6.19. Rudimentary Symbian Application with Java.

```
            QJava myQuartz = new QJava(2);
            GridPanel myPanel = new GridPanel();
            Checkbox myCheck = new Checkbox("Test!");
            TextArea myTextArea = new TextArea(6,24);
            Choice myChoice = new Choice();
            myPanel.add(myTextArea,0,1);
            myPanel.add(myCheck,0,2);
            myChoice.addItem("Good Bye");
            myChoice.addItem("Hello World");
            myPanel.add(myChoice,0,2);
            qTest.setCardAt(myPanel,0);
            myQuartz.displayCardAt(0);
        }
    }
```

FIGURE 6.19 ***(continued)***

Java: This is a custom virtual machine for the platform with the APIs that make sense for the platform.

When writing applications for Symbian, we typically deal with a DRFD (Device Family Reference Design). There is a DFRD for every device type, because what Symbian does on a very small device is much different than what it does on a powerful PDA. Symbian's approach is much like J2ME. In other words, DRFDs are similar to the J2ME profiles.

A simple class written for the Crysal DFRD is shown in Figure 6.19. You can see that programming a user interface with Java on Symbian is very similar to programming Java on any other platform. This is the benefit you gain in programming mobile applications in Java for the price of performance and a bit less flexibility. We have now discussed the basics of the most popular tools in building GUI interfaces for mobile applications. As promised, let us go back and look at UIML as an alternative to XForms for building generic user interfaces.

Building Mobile GUIs with Microsoft Platforms

Like Palm and Symbian operating systems, we can either produce markup languages to be displayed at the device using a browser or produce a custom application to run on the device to display a custom GUI. There are currently a variety of versions of Microsoft Windows CE that run on a variety of devices. It is important to note that all of these versions are very different operating systems as they have been tuned to run on different devices.

Most of the upper end devices offering Windows CE operating system, such as the Compaq IPQA, offer either a full-blown HTML browser or a WML browser. Sometimes, a subset of HTML is used. In essence, building thin-client mobile applications for Windows CE is no different than building the same thing for Palm, WAP browsers, or Symbian. Microsoft offers ASP as the server-side language (which can be a little different depending on which version of Microsoft platform you are using—.NET or older versions) and C#, C++, and Visual Basic to build components used by ASP pages.

When it comes to building applications for the Windows CE platform, development is done in C/C++/C#, compilation is done on a PC, and the application is uploaded to the device. So far, the Microsoft platform does not offer a provisioning system (some way of deploying and distributing the application to the intended targets, remotely or locally) for mobile applications such as that of BREW and the forthcoming versions of J2ME.

The one unique thing that the .NET platform offers is the better ability of the more powerful Windows CE devices to integrate the use of Web services. Process of creation and deployment of Web service–based applications on Windows CE devices is simplified greatly with the Microsoft development tools. Also, there are numerous commercial user interface components optimized for each Windows CE version available for developers.

6.2.1 J2ME GUIs

We mentioned in Chapter 2 that functionality such as GUI specifications are part of the J2ME profile specifications and not the core J2ME implementation. Currently, the MIDP 2.0 profile has yet to be implemented by any device manufacturers. MIDP 2.0 offers more in the way of GUI functionality than does MIDP 1.0. There are also other profiles such as the PDA Profile that provide different APIs to build GUIs on various J2ME platforms and implementations. Nevertheless, because the idea of J2ME is to cut out superfluous functionality from the typical Java platform functionality, the profiles always have less than you would want as a developer. So, you always have to build more custom code than desired, but this is so that the basic platform can be kept to a bare minimum.

To see how J2ME profiles treat the GUI problem, let us just quickly look at the MIDP 1.0 treatment of building GUIs. MIDP 1.0 provides basic components that need to be extended to be meaningful such as *Canvas*, entire functional components such as *List* that do not need any further embellishment to be useful as a complete user interface, and components that are essentially GUI containers and need to be embellished with further placement of components within them such as *Form*.

Figure 6.20 shows an example of J2ME MIDP 1.0 code to create a simple GUI application. Refer to Chapter 2 to see the basic differences in J2ME and the process of developing J2ME applications with J2SE and the process of developing J2SE applications. Also note that a real-world J2ME application would probably look more functional than the purist object-oriented view we have shown in our example for the sake of efficiency. This is just an example and we will leave the implementation details of your application to you.

Now that we have looked at these different tools a bit more in depth, let us look at UIML as a comparable technology to UIML.

User Interface Markup Language

Throughout this text, we have chosen to use XForms for our examples in building generic user interfaces. We have done this for a variety of reasons, among the most

```
import java.util.Enumeration;
import java.microedition.lcdui.*;

public class VoteList() {
    private DomainVotes          mVotes;
    private List                 mVotesList;
    private Display              mDisplay;
    public HelloWorld(Display aDisplay) {
        mDisplay = aDisplay;
        mVotesList = new List("Vote:",Choice.EXCLUSIVE);
        visit(mVotes);
    }
    public void visit(DomainVotes aVotes) {
        Enumeration e = aVotes.getVoteEnumeration();
        while (e.hasMoreElements()) {
            mVotesList.append((String) e.nextElement();
        }
    }
    public void getSelectedVote() {
        mVotes.getSelectedVote(mVotesList.
          getSelectedIndex());
    }
    public void setDomainVotes(DomainVotes aVotes)
      {mDomainVotes = aVotes;}
}
```

FIGURE 6.20. Sample Class for a Simple GUI for MIDP 1.0.

important of which are that XForms is a W3C standard and that it is a well-defined application of XML with some momentum in being adopted by the open-source community and by commercial browser makers. However, AUIML presents us with a viable alternative to XForms. We will look at it in this section.

We should also note that there are two markup languages very closely named: AUIML, which is the Abstract User Interface Markup Language, and UIML, which is the User Interface Markup Language. AUIML is also known as DIML. AUIML was started by IBM; this effort is one of the roots of what has eventually given rise to XForms. UIML is an open but proprietary (controlled by Harmonia Inc.) standard that addresses the same problem. UIML is different from XForms in that UIML defines a metalanguage in which to define languages such as XForms. We already discussed the comparison of the approaches between a generic user interface language such as XForms and a user interface metalanguage such as UIML in a subsection of Section 6.1.1. (Transformation-Based Techniques for Mobile Applications).

To give you a better feel of how UIML is implemented, let us go through some of the syntax and look at what the designers had in mind when creating it. UIML

SIDE DISCUSSION 6.2

Comparing XForms and UIML

UIML specifications recommend that the mappings specified at http://www.uiml.org/toolkits be used. However, this is somewhat against the concept of defining a metalanguage to build generic user interfaces. The idea behind any metalanguage, for example the metamodel introduced by UML, is to provide a customized extensibility mechanism. So, instead of describing specific solutions, it describes the way to come up with a solution. Using the same set of mappings over and over for the same metalanguage eliminates the need for having a metalanguage.

This inconsistency is one of the reasons we selected XForms over UIML for our examples. Nevertheless, the concept behind UIML, a metalanguage for describing user interfaces instead of a language for generic user interfaces, remains very valid.

breaks down the task of describing a user interface into describing four aspects of user interfaces:

1. *Headers*: The headers in a UIML document are enclosed within <head> </head> tags. Headers provide a way to describe the document using XML tags. They also give us a way to provide extra information to the UIML parser or browser not enclosed within the remainder of the document.
2. *Interface*: All those tags needed to describe a given type of a user interface itself are enclosed within <interface></interface> tags. We will look at these elements a bit later.
3. *Peers*: Peer elements, defined by <peer></peer> tags, are used to map structure and behavior of UIML to other user interface markup languages. For example, if we wanted to define the mapping of UIML to VXML, this would be done inside the <peer></peer> tags.
4. *Presentation*: This element encloses the legal vocabulary for describing the user interface (mostly done in the interface section of the UIML document) enclosed in <presentation></presentation> tags.

The basic structure of a UIML document is described in Figure 6.21. UIML is implemented using XML, so let us review the XML tags as we have been doing for other XML-based technologies. These are listed in Table 6.3.

First, nearly all elements in a UIML document have the attribute of *id*. The id attribute must be unique within the document. The interface elements have the attribute *class*. This is based on the W3C CSS class that allows addressing of elements by type so that styling can be applied to a class of elements.

Many UIML elements have the attribute *source*. This attribute is always set to a Web style URI. There are two uses of this attribute within the various UIML elements. When it points to a UIML document, it is used as an "include" mechanism and the external UIML document is included within the document that points to it at the point of occurrence of the element with the source attribute. If the URI points to a non-UIML document, the target is used by the UIML parser in a parser-specific manner (by including it in the specialized user interface instance,

```
<?xml version="1.0" ?>
<!DOCTYPE uiml PUBLIC "-//UIT//DTD UIML 2.0 Draft//EN"
  UIML2_0f.dtd">

<uiml>
    <head>...</head>
    <interface>...</interface>
    <peers></peers>
    <template></template>
</uiml>
```

FIGURE 6.21. Basic Structure of a UIML Document.

by ignoring it if the file type is not understood, etc.). The way the external source is treated may be specified further by specifying a *how* attribute when available.

6.2.2 From Generic UIs to Specialized Graphical User Interfaces

So what does this all mean? How do we use it all to build GUIs for our mobile applications?

The tools that we have looked at let us build applications on mobile devices that render user interfaces or build markup language–based documents that are rendered by a browser on the mobile device. Alternatively, the mobile device may have an application that consumes a markup language such as XForms and produces a user interface.

In the previous chapters, we looked at building generic user interfaces and specializing them. Then, we introduced specific development techniques including design patterns that help us implement user interfaces in a manner that minimizes the development effort and maximizes the flexibility of the application to changes during the software life cycle. We had already looked at high-level architectures in Chapter 1.

From there, it is up to the software engineer to understand the requirements of the application and to select the right architecture, implementation techniques, and implementation tools to build the application. As for any software problem, there is no "golden hammer" solution to building GUIs for mobile applications. The left-hand side of the equation is a problem represented by the requirements of the customer and the right-hand side is a solution, selected by the engineer(s), that fit the problem. Obviously, the design and implementation of the GUI are not the only considerations in selecting the tools and techniques to build the application. There may be many other considerations, such as availability of specific functionalities on the tools (such as GPS for location services), time constraints that may affect development techniques chosen, and budgetary constraints that might affect the choice of development tools. Our goal here has been to introduce the tools that you need to build your mobile application in an educated manner.

Of course, while we are building the GUI to our mobile application, we need to use a tool that guides us during the development process. Note that the tool

Table 6.3. Description of Some of the UIML Tags

Tag	Attributes	Description
<meta>	name, description	This tag is used within the <head></head> tags and encapsulates metadata to be used by the document parser or the reader of the document. The name and description attributes provide a name–value pair mechanism for specifying the metadata.
<structure>	id, resource, how, export	This tag is used within the <interface> tag and specifies the structure of the particular user interface instance (screen, dialogue, etc.). This is where we specify the mode and channel-dependent structure of a particular type of user interface.
<part>	id, class	This tag is used within the structure tag and allows us to define specific types of user interface elements such as buttons, combo boxes, and others.
<style>	id, source, how, export	This tag is used within the <interface> tag and specifies the specific formatting of various user interface components defined in the rest of the document. The user interface components formatted through the style section of the <interface> are addressed through the <property> element.
<property>	name, source, how, export, part-name, part-class, event-name, event-class	Properties are various styling descriptions of user interface elements relevant to those particular elements. For example, we can create a property whose name attribute is set to "color" and describes the color of a user interface component that is visual. Most of the time, you can think of properties like adjectives that describe the interface components. Another example of a property is a font. Those user interface components (defined in the structure section by parts) to which the concept of font is relevant (anything that has text or is text) could have a font property.
<call>		One of the big differences between XForms and UIML resides in this tag. Whereas XForms uses XEvents as the mechanism to handle client-side events, UIML allows defining an interface to call external functions without any awareness of the implementation of this function (implementation dependence is on the UIML parser/browser).

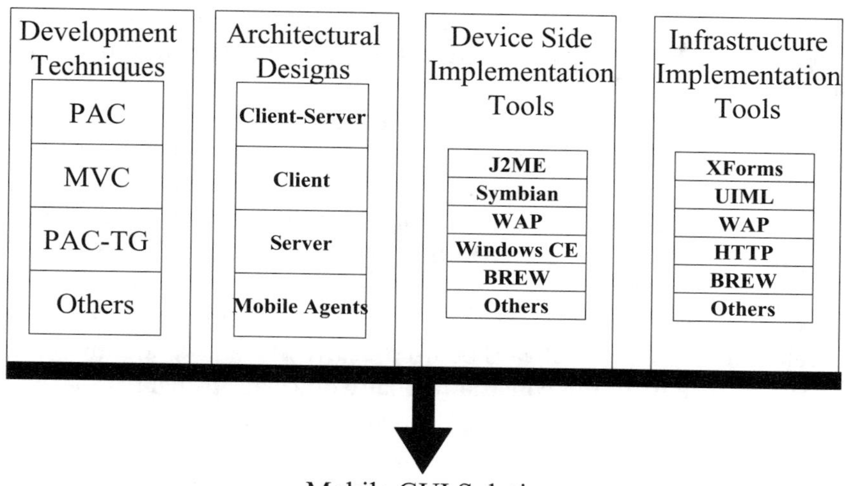

FIGURE 6.22. Arriving at a Mobile GUI Solution for Your Mobile Application.

alone will not be enough and that we will need a process that uses the tool. For example, many organizations use the Rational Unified Process for development of complex stationary applications. We are not going to outline such a process here; rather, we are going to give you the tools you need to complement whatever process you select to take into account the dimensions of mobility. UML has been the tool that we have uniformly used throughout this text to do this and we will continue to look at UML as the tool to guide us through the development process and to bind the various pieces of the development process together. Figure 6.22 shows the typical component strategy in designing Mobile Applications that have significant user interfaces.

Modeling GUIs with UML

Since its inception, UML has been mostly used in modeling business processes, domain models that represent business logic, and other types of object models internal to the operations of the system. Although use cases are widely used to specify user requirements, screen mockups are the tool of choice for most projects. This is because most software development projects aim at building an application for a specific user interface type, mostly a GUI. Note that at the time of authoring this text, UML 2.0 has not yet been released. There are distinct differences between UML 1.4 and UML 2.0. The early drafts are available and, unfortunately, the modifications and additions to UML 2.0 do not seem to address the dimensions of mobility as we are concerned with them. Nevertheless, keep in mind that some of the basic definitions of various diagrams may be different with UML 2.0. This book has been authored based on UML 1.4; however, there are no barriers to applying the extensions that we introduce here to UML 2.0.

Only recently has there been a concerted effort in using UML to model GUIs and the users' interactions with GUIs. The motivation of this effort has been mainly in creating a seamless software development process around UML. Although we are interested in this aspect as well, our motivation in using UML to model user interfaces and the users' interactions with user interfaces is in creating a uniform method of documenting UI architecture, design, and implementation that is independent of the type of GUI used and the type of channel(s) through which the GUI is displayed to the user.

Although there are no recommended ways of using UML for user interfaces by OMG, the organization that controls the evolution of UML, there have been a variety of papers published on this topic suggesting many different ways to use UML for user interfaces. In this section, we will take a survey of the various methods suggested to date and relate them to our problem, namely, developing GUIs for mobile applications.

UML may be used in many different ways to facilitate the process of user interface development. OCL can always be used nearly like a programming language to allow us to specify all the constraints that would encapsulate all of the information needed about a user interface. However, by the time we do this, we end up having implemented the user interface in another programming language: OCL. So, we will use OCL very judiciously. We will mainly try to use UML diagrams to represent user interfaces and the user's interactions with them. In this light, let us begin with UML Activity Diagrams.

6.2.3 Using UML Activity Diagrams for GUI Development

As you may recall from Chapter 4, activity diagrams are a type of state diagram with some subtle differences with UML state diagrams such as the fact that end points are not required. Activity diagrams are primarily used in modeling process flows. And, the way we will use them to model GUIs is to model the activities that take place between the user and the user interface.

Lieberman [Lieberman 2001] recognizes some stereotypes for extending UML activity diagrams in modeling user interfaces: *page*, *frame*, *exception*, *presentation*, and *connector*.

The *connector* stereotype is used for the purpose of nesting activity diagrams so that user interactions with the GUI or the interactions between the different GUI components can be reused the same way that we may reuse GUI components themselves. The other advantage of nesting activities is that it allows us to "drill-down" into the details instead of being inundated with the details of many different activities or, alternatively, not representing enough detail in the activity diagrams representing the various user interface interactions. This stereotype can be particularly useful in designing mobile GUIs because some interactions may be applicable to some GUIs and not others (based on device, available channels, etc.).

Page and *frame* stereotypes borrow their definitions from HTML pages and frames. A page represents a displayable unit that occupies the entire display; a frame can be any part of that display, outlined in a logical manner. It must be noted that Lieberman's analysis is primarily done for representing complex GUIs such as Web pages. We are not guaranteed what type of functionality is supported by the various mobile devices and how complicated the GUI may be. So, although the concept of page is always applicable, we are not guaranteed that the concept of a frame is applicable to a particular user interface or not.

The *presentation* stereotype is a stereotype on an action (as are the other stereotypes we have mentioned here) and indicates interface interactions between the user and the system.

The *exception* stereotype is designed to represent an "exceptional" condition. This could be a user error (perhaps the result of rejected validation) or simply an event that does not fit within the predictable workflow. The exception stereotype fits well within the context of our discussion since, regardless of the type of interface we are dealing with, validation may be a requirement and various unforeseen events may occur (such as connection timeouts, etc.).

Lieberman also color codes the various states with which each of these stereotypes are associated. Use the reference paper if you wish to use color coding in UML diagrams for better clarification. Here, we will not be using color coding, simply the stereotype tags indicated by <<exception>>, <<page>>, <<frame>>, and <<connector>>.

Let us look at a simple example where the user's address is collected in Figure 6.23.

The obvious problem with our diagram is that it does not really show the fact that the user could enter the requested data in any possible order. To do this, we could use forks and joins: We use the fork to show the various possible routes the user may take and then use the join to bring these routes back together where the next action is the same for multiple permutations. If you want to express that the user can enter the data in any order then you could use a fork and a corresponding join, but then we cannot show, in one diagram, that either case could be true. We could indeed draw all of the possible state transitions from the beginning and create an initial state that would simply represent the user viewing the screen. However, as you can imagine, representing a large system with many workflows would lead to an activity proliferation problem. This would detract from the usefulness of using UML to begin with. Nevertheless, as long as we are not concerned about the asynchronous nature of some interactions between the user and the user interface, we are able to model the interface using the activity diagram in a very reasonable way.

Now, let us make our interactions a bit more sophisticated and include some validation messages when the user enters wrong information into the system. We will do this only for the first frame of the activity diagram of Figure 6.23. This is shown in Figure 6.24. Note that this time we use an escalating prompt that only takes two user errors and then exits the component. Though in real life, we may not do this for collecting a user's address, this is a good example of how exceptions stereotypes are used.

In our example, we use a transition called "Token_Filled," which simply indicates that the user has indicated, in some way by clicking, tabbing, etc., that he or she is finished with giving input to the giving component. Also, note that we have used a frame to model an individual field. This may seem like overkill for a Web page or thick-client application on a PC, but it is semantically correct as defined by Lieberman. The reason for doing this is that we do not know how many components may fit on a particular display page at a time. Some displays may allow for all of the components to be displayed on the same page (for example, HTML

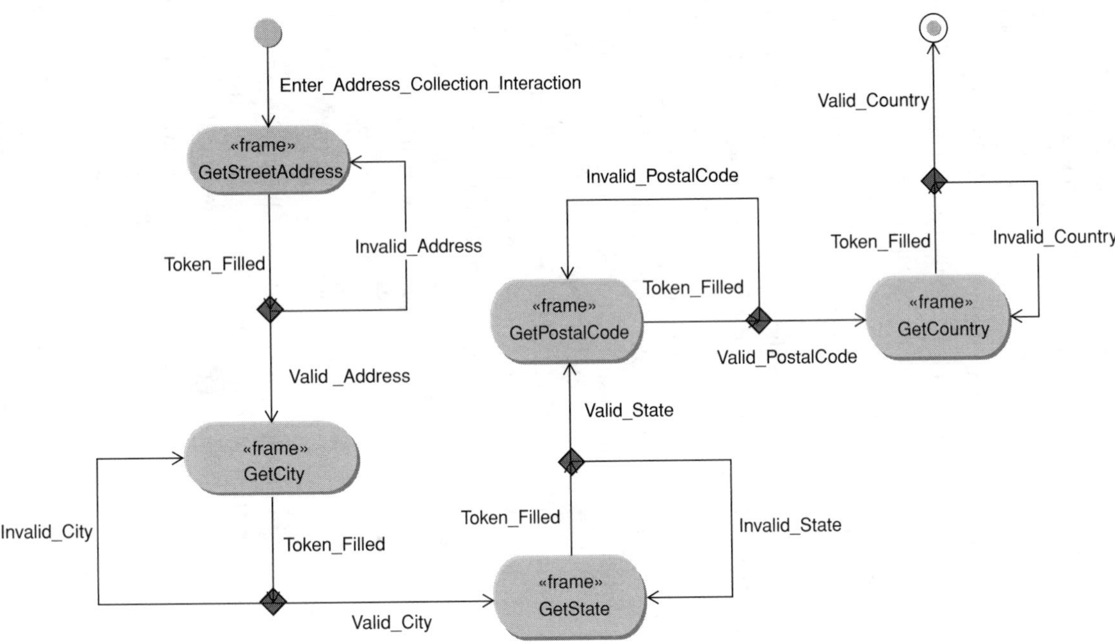

FIGURE 6.23. Using an Activity Diagram to Represent a GUI Component to Collect Address Information.

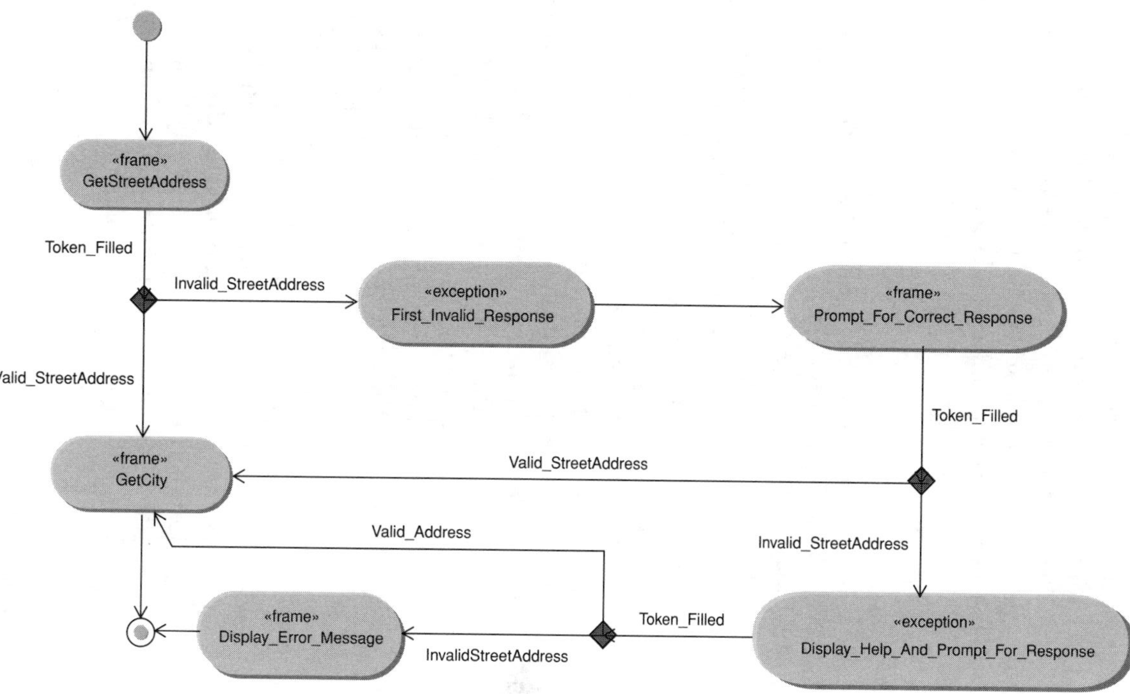

FIGURE 6.24. Using Exception Stereotypes for Modeling User Interface Validation with Activity Diagrams.

browsers), whereas other components will require one page per component (for example, WML 1.1).

Now, let us use the page stereotype by including the address component, whose interactions with the user was modeled in Figure 6.23, in a component that takes a user's name, address, and phone number.

In his doctoral thesis, Nunes [Nunes 2001] takes the approach of using activity diagrams one step further and recognizes the development of user interfaces with respect to the entire development process and developing what he calls the "Wisdom approach." The Wisdom approach, per Nunes' prescription, has merit in any type of software development, but let us see how it applies to the development of mobile applications, generic user interfaces, and specialization of those generic user interfaces.

The Wisdom Approach

Nunes [Nunes 2001] is one of the first and few who have recognized the importance of two things in developing user interfaces. First, user interfaces should be developed with more abstractions such as when building generic user interfaces and then specializing them. Second, UML and its extension mechanisms can be used to facilitate the process of developing user interfaces (and further that this results indirectly in better integration of the user interface development process with the other parts of the development process). As we did earlier, Nunes recognized PAC and MVC as the state-of-the-art architectural design patterns for building layered user interfaces and points out their shortcomings.

Although Nunes outlined an entire software user interface–focused design methodology, in this text, we do not outline a software methodology framework explicitly. However, we do implicitly outline a software methodology focused on developing mobile applications. The two are inherently orthogonal. However, Nunes' Wisdom model architecture and Wisdom notation, respectively dealing with UML extensions for the user interface and the corresponding notational augmentations to UML, are directly relevant to our topic. So, let us review the Wisdom model architecture and the Wisdom notation. If you are interested in learning more about the Wisdom methodology of software development and applying it to your software projects, we recommend Nunes thesis, which clearly outlines the process. We will borrow from Nunes' methodology to outline a rough draft for the process of developing mobile applications in Chapter 15. But, as we will note then, mobile application development is far too young at this point to start relying on a particular software development methodology. Software development methodologies are evolutionary and come from years of learning from mistakes.

The Wisdom Model Architecture

Like Lieberman, Nunes recognizes the advantages of activity diagrams in representing the user interface. But, in his Wisdom model architecture, he recommends the following implementation models:

1. *User Role Model*: This model is easily represented by the typical use case diagrams and focuses on the responsibilities of actors and the high-level

interactions of actors with each other and with the use cases. Note that the use case diagrams of the user role model must focus on the interaction of the user with the system; therefore, they should be heavily biased toward how an end user sees the system as opposed to the internal implementation of the system.

2. *Domain Model and Use Case Diagrams for the Domain Model*: The domain model is one of the first things that UML users learn and perhaps presents the most prevalent use of UML in software implementation. Domain models in the Wisdom methodology are represented with class diagrams as they are in all other UML-based methodologies. Nunes also suggests the use of use case diagrams to specify the interactions between the different users and the system as represented by the various internal components of the system. The difference between these use case diagrams and the ones in the user role model is their perspective is from the internal implementation of the application. Therefore, the sum of the diagrams in the domain model focus on aspects like which use has access to what component, what classes make up that particular component, and the details of how the internal classes are related to each other.
3. *Analysis Model and Interaction Model*: Whereas the analysis model focuses on the interactions between the internal components of the system and the activities that take place while the system is operating, the interaction model focuses on how the user interacts with different parts of the system. It is important to note that although there may be a one-to-one or other type of mapping between the internal components and the external user interface segments, this is not necessary. This is essentially the difference between the two models. Both focus on the flow and interaction of components, but one deals with the flow and interaction of user interface components with the user (interaction model) and the other with the interactions and workflows among the different components internally (analysis model). Nunes introduced some UML extensions for the interaction model that will be extremely handy to us. Remember that one of our biggest hurdles lies in using UML to represent generic and specific interactions between the user and the system.
4. *Design Model and Dialogue Model*: The dialogue model focuses on the different interactions with the system with respect to time. As we discussed in Chapter 5, dialogues are made of atomic interactions between the user and the system. The dialogue model gives us a method to represent these atomic interactions. Wisdom introduces some UML extensions for dialogue models. The design model represents the same atomic interactions, but this time among the components of the system. The design model relies heavily on UML state diagrams.
5. *Presentation Model*: This model helps us represent the final user interface presented to the user. In our case, these final interfaces can be text based, graphical, voice driven, based on motion, etc. There are extensions introduced here as well. As one may expect, the presentation model is well linked to the dialogue model and this will help us describe the specialization of generic interfaces into specific user interfaces.

6. *Implementation Model*: What Nunes calls the implementation model is really not a model; it is the actual implementation of the system. The reason it exists is to provide a link between the other models and real code. Tools that support round-trip engineering use the same approach by having some implementation model that abstracts the model away from the code (which could be automatically generated).

These various "models" can be thought of as different views of the same model. However, depending on the view with which you look at the system, the actual model of the system may be different. In other words, how one models the internals of a system depends on the perspective with which one has looked at the system.

This gives us a general feel for how the Wisdom architectural model differs from the other typical UML-based models in using the diagrams throughout the development process. What we are really interested in are the extensions that Wisdom provides us. These extensions have a great value in and of themselves without the methodology and the architecture: They help us recognize what categories of stereotypes are needed to model user interface components. In this way, Wisdom UML extensions are valuable regardless of the overall software methodology used in the project.

Let us dive right into these extensions and see what value they may offer us in developing mobile applications.

The Wisdom UML Extensions

Nunes had a great approach in the way he designed his UML extensions in the Wisdom model. He used stereotypes to define the extensions and then augmented them with graphical widgets that accompany these stereotypes. Using stereotypes alone has value in recognizing a taxonomy of types of things in a particular domain. However, the real value of stereotypes are much more readily apparent when they are accompanied by new graphical widgets that allow software developers, user interface developers, and business analysts, all equally, to view the base functionality of the system and the user interface.

The three "inventors" of UML [Jacobson, Booch, and Raumbaugh 1999] break down the problem of modeling into modeling *behavior, information*, and *interface* (where the term *interface* is not about the interface of a class but about the interface to the system—the human-to-machine barrier). Wisdom breaks down the problem further. First, it breaks down the problem of user interface–based modeling to the analysis model and the interaction model, with the analysis model focusing on the internals of the system and the interaction model focusing on the user interface interactions of the system. The analysis model then has the same dimensions that Jacobson, Booch, and Raumbaugh recognized for modeling: behavior, interaction, and interface. The interaction model still has information as one of its dimensions, but it introduces the new concepts of *dialogue* and *presentation*. We have already talked about dialogue in Chapter 5. The concept of dialogue in Wisdom is the same one that we introduced: a series of interactions that take place between two parties (in our specific case the user and the system). Presentation represents the look-and-feel or the sound-and-feel of the user interface. The interaction model

TABLE 6.4. Basic Iconic Representation of Model Types

Analysis Model (Representing the System Internals)			Interaction Model (Representing the User Interface)		
Behavior	Interface	Information	Dialogue	Information	Presentation
◌	⊢○	Ω	⊛	⊢○	⊘

is not related to the internal implementation of a system but rather is a perspective of an outside observer over the way a system interacts with a human actor. Table 6.4 shows the widgets that we use to represent these concepts.

We can use these iconic representations of the model types in use case diagrams for modeling the interaction of actors with a given type of model or for modeling the interactions of the internals of a system.

It is notable at this point to mention that Nunes' Wisdom methodology does not use all of the available UML diagrams. Unlike Wisdom, we do not prohibit you from using any of the techniques and diagrams available in UML regardless of how advanced they may be. The key is to have enough tools to correctly communicate the requirements and design of a mobile application.

Let us outline the specific extensions to the entities of each diagram type and the corresponding widgets under the Wisdom methodology in Table 6.5.

Now, let us look at why we need to distinguish each of these stereotypes:

1. *Essential Use Cases*: Essential use cases are technology free and do not contain any unnecessary restrictions or limiting assumptions regarding a specific implementation detail reduced to its minimal form of expression [Nunes 2001]. In other words, essential use cases exist to describe a grouping of a set of interactions that take place between the user and the system and are essential to describe the purpose of the system.
2. *Human Actors*: This is an explicit abstraction of the person who actually interacts with the system. The benefit of this abstraction is mainly in its ability to group a set of roles that are meaningful only to the system into a bucket that can represent an actual person. For example, someone named Phil may have the duties of janitorial engineering as well as release engineering on an MS Windows platform. Phil would be a human actor and each of his duties would be roles.
3. *System Actors*: This represents a grouping of all the roles that a system can play when users use it. For example, a given system could be responsible for keeping a history on the location of users as well as integrating with external GPS systems to get the location of the user to begin with. Each of these is a system role, whereas the system that actually accomplishes them is a system actor.

TABLE 6.5. Wisdom UML Extensions for Building User Interface–Driven Modeling

Diagram Type	Stereotype	Iconic Presentation
Use Case Diagrams	<<essential use-case>>	
	<<human actor>>	
	<<system actor>>	
Class Diagrams	<<Task>>	
	<<Interaction Space>>	
	<<Boundary>>	
	<<Control>>	
	<<Entity>>	

4. *Tasks*: Task classes are used to model the structure of the dialogue between the user and the system in terms of meaningful and complete sets of actions required to achieve a goal [Nunes 2001]. Think of tasks as large-grained workflows that have a beginning and an end that comprise a meaningful start and stop to a business action. For example, making a deposit to your bank account can be considered a task.
5. *Interaction Space*: This stereotype roughly models the concept of an input and an output channel from the user to the system. We have touched upon this concept previously. It is a core concept for developing applications that use multiple channels (such as audio telephony, text screens, graphics screens, etc.) because distinguishing between the types of channels is crucial to the design of such applications.
6. *Boundaries*: In heterogeneous environments where multiple systems are communicating, it is important to model the "boundary" lines between those systems. These systems may be abstract (all of the systems could be running under the same process, same thread, etc.) or they could be actual distinct processes and threads. Boundaries are MMI lines.
7. *Controls*: These type of classes represent all logic that is not business logic. In other words, they represent all logic relating to the handling of other classes

and objects. For example, if a class is designed to control the life cycle of other classes, then it is a control class.

8. *Entities*: Entity classes represent the business logic that represents the real-life problem being solved. For example, a class that reads and writes the user's personal information is an entity. This class might use another class that merely encapsulates the data structure that represents a user's personal information, in which case that class would be an entity as well. Note that the class that reads and writes the user's personal information to a file is not a control class because the manner of persistence (reading and writing to a file) is application specific and not a generic problem of handling any other classes.

Now that we have looked at the new UML extensions in Wisdom, let us look at some additional extensions to associations provided in Wisdom that allow the new entity extensions we just discussed to communicate with one another or other entities in a UML model. These are shown in Table 6.6.

As you may recall, we discussed dialogues in some detail in Chapter 5. Representing dialogues has traditionally been one of the most difficult parts of modeling user interfaces. UML 1.4 by itself certainly does not address the problem of modeling the user interface. Nunes' approach is to use the ConcurTaskTrees (CTT) as the foundation for building extensions that represent dialogues properly.

Once again, as you may recall, in Chapter 5 we defined dialogues as being composites of one or more interactions between the user and the system. These interactions take place in some sequence and this sequence is part of what defines the temporal context of the dialogue and the temporal context of the interactions making up the dialogue. This temporal context is what Nunes borrows from CTT. Therefore, the following atomic interactions may take place:

1. The interactions can start at any time and end at any time independent of one another and be represented as T1 | | | T2.
2. The user may choose any interaction, but once one is chosen, no other interactions can be performed until this interaction is finished; this may be represented by T1 |[]| T2.
3. The interactions may start and end at any time, but they have some sort of interdependency (they pass messages to one another, etc.) so that they must be synchronized in some manner. This may be represented by T1 | [] | T2.
4. The termination of one interaction (T2) may cause the termination of one (T1) or more interactions in the dialogue; this may be represented by T1[>T2.
5. The activation of one interaction (T2) may cause the activation of one (T1) or more interactions in the dialogue; this may be represented by T1>>T2.
6. Iteration and finite iteration allow you to indicate an unlimited or limited repetition of a task until it is signaled to stop. They are respectively indicated by T* and T1(*n*).

Optional tasks are indicated by [T] and model tasks whose completion does not affect the workflow and continuation of normal interaction with the system.

Table 6.6. Breakdown of Additional Models Introduced by Nunes' Wisdom

Interaction Model	Communicate (Association between an actor and a use case or between boundaries, controls, and entities)	This association is intended to represent passing of messages between an actor and a use case or between boundaries, controls, and entities. It is important to note that this stereotype indicates passing of messages in a very generic way without describing the method used for passing the messages (publish–subscribe, point-to-point, etc.)
	Subscribe (Association between two classes representing internal implementation of the system, between boundaries and entities, between controls and entities, or among entities)	This association type also indicates passing of messages, but unlike the communicate association, it indicates a specific type of messaging, namely publish–subscribe. There are two cases: 1. one of the classes is the publisher and the other the subscriber and 2. an entity is the publisher and the boundary, control, or another entity is the subscriber.
	Specializes (Associations between human actors or essential use cases)	This association simply denotes that the human actor or essential use case specializes (inherits in this case because implementations for use cases or actors do not make much sense) the properties of another human actor or use case.
	Includes (Associations between human actors or essential use cases)	This association is just like the specializes association, except that it denotes an aggregation relationship (a human actor can have another human actor or an essential use case can have another essential use case). In the case of the human actor, the purpose is to be able to represent a group of one or more actors or to describe a new actor using the properties encapsulated by others. This relationship must be used carefully. Remember that the premise of the existence of the human actor is to get as close to a real human as possible (thereby better specifying the needs of the user in relation with the user interface).

Dialogue Model	Refine task (Association between two tasks)	This stereotype is used when one task represents a higher level of detail than the other task. The parent task (the one with less detail) is the source.
	Infopass (Association between two tasks)	This stereotype is used when two tasks are exchanging information through messaging or some other mechanism.
	Seq (Association between two tasks)	This task indicates that a given task "sequentially" follows another task. In other words, it starts when the task that it depends on ends.
	Seqi (Association between two tasks)	This task indicates that one task can start another task by signaling it in some way. Note that this is similar to the seq stereotype except that the seq stereotype indicates a clear temporal relationship in one task ending to start the other. In this case, there is no assumption made on what particular event causes the start of the second, simply that the task that it depends on tells it to start.
	Deact (Association between two tasks)	This stereotype models a relationship between two tasks, one of which can signal the other to end.
Presentation Model	Navigate (Association between two interactions)	Navigate models the "transition" from one interaction to another as defined in Chapter 5. In cases when the transition is temporally or spatially sequential (e.g., a voice interaction that follows another voice interaction through a transition), this association is unidirectional. In cases when it is not (e.g., when there are multiple input boxes on the same form that can be navigated to in any order), this association is bidirectional.
	Contains (Association between two interactions)	If one interaction includes another interaction, they are related through a contains association. As discussed in Chapter 5, the contains stereotype allows for modeling of composite interactions. Because there is a strict parent and child relationship in the case of contains, this relationship is always unidirectional.

(continued)

TABLE 6.6 (*continued*)

Input element (Stereotype on an attribute—a class)	As we mentioned in Chapter 5, every type of user interface has a variety of mechanisms to receive input from the user. The <<input element>> stereotype allows us to model the mechanism for receiving input from the user in a generic way (further specification can be done by setting attributes on the instance class, relationship between classes, etc.). Examples could a be a VUI prompt and the following silence that is awaiting a recording or the input box that is proceeded by a label.
Output element (Stereotype on an attribute—a class)	Like the input element stereotype, the <<output element>> stereotype allows us to model output of information to the user. In a VUI, this could be some audio play back to the user; in a GUI, this may be graphic, text, or video presented to the user.
Action (Basic component of activity diagrams)	Whereas methods (or operations) indicate behavior in object-oriented programming, the <<action>> stereotype allows us to model something that the user does. It is recommended that this stereotype be used at a high level instead of accounting for every mouse movement and letter typed. For example, an action stereotype could be used when a user is done filling a form and clicks on the submit button.

These symbols are used more like cardinality than an OCL, on top of the Wisdom UML diagrams, to give enough refinement to the relationship between tasks so that it is not necessary to make any assumptions regarding the presentation logic. It should be noted that look-and-feel is not something that we can, nor intend to, model using Nunes' methodology or any other UML-based tool. What we have introduced here, in leveraging works from Lieberman and Nunes, is principally to help us develop UML diagrams for GUIs so that we can get a handle on the user interface, the interactions of the user with the user interface, and various other aspects of the mobile human-to-computer interaction concerning our mobile applications without being tied to a particular platform or a particular implementation.

Thus far, Nunes offers the most comprehensive approach to modeling user interfaces with UML. It is possible that future versions of UML mandate Wisdom or some other extension to better model user interfaces and use interactions with user interfaces.

6.2.4 UML Extensions for Mobile Applications

Our goal in this text is to first understand how to build mobile applications and then to use UML to facilitate that building process. There are proven methods of using UML that apply equally to stationary applications as well as mobile applications. But there are those aspects of mobile applications that are not accommodated by the vanilla implementation of UML and require us to use the extension mechanism. In the previous two sections, we discussed useful extensions for representing the user interfaces in UML. We recommend the use of Nunes' Wisdom extensions when developing mobile applications and their user interfaces. Now, hold this thought.

We briefly talked about mobile agents in Chapter 1 and later, in Chapter 9, we will look at extensions that model mobile agents. We will see how mobile agents differ from client–server applications and how to represent their unique properties by using UML. These extensions, added together with extensions to model user interfaces, particularly Wisdom extensions, will take us most of the way there to representing mobile applications with UML. But, there are some holes. Namely, there is nothing that distinguishes a mobile user from a stationary user, nothing that distinguishes mobile use cases from stationary use cases, and nothing that allows us to represent dimensions of mobility and the mobile condition of the user. Specifically, we need both a semantic and an iconic representation of these things so that we have a well-defined and meaningful semantic and visual representation of the application we intend to build and how it is going to be used. Therefore, let us introduce the stereotypes in Table 6.6.

The extensions listed in Table 6.7 focus on the use case model and representing the user interactions with the system. We introduced a couple of stereotypes relating to location sensitivity that we will discuss again in Chapter 12. We discussed these because they extend existing definitions from Wisdom.

Table 6.7. Additional Mobile Application Development UML Extensions

Stereotype	Description	Icon
<<Mobile Actor>>	This stereotype extends Wisdom's <<Human Actor>> to be used in use case diagrams and is intended to indicate a human actor who is definitely mobile at the time of interacting with a particular use case or interacting with another actor. (The arrow notation is borrowed from the mobile agent UML extensions we will look at in Chapter 9.) This stereotype is strictly introduced to indicate the condition of the user at the time of using the application. It does not indicate whether the application itself is one that is designed or implemented as a mobile application or not. If it is not, then whether the user is mobile or stationary at the time of interacting with the application, Wisdom's <<Human Actor>> stereotype should be used.	
<<Stationary Actor>>	This stereotype extends Wisdom's <<Human Actor>> to be used in use case diagrams and is intended to indicate a human actor who is definitely stationary at the time of interacting with a particular use case or interacting with another actor. This stereotype does not indicate that the application itself is designed as a stationary application. The application may be mobile, but a particular use case may only be relevant when the user is stationary. If the application is not mobile, then whether the user is mobile or stationary at the time of interacting with the application, Wisdom's <<Human Actor>> stereotype should be used.	
<<Mobile Use Case>>	This stereotype extends UML's use case stereotype. It is used to indicate that a use case is a mobile use case (further discussed in Chapter 15). By a mobile use case, we mean that the implementation of the use case involves usage or consideration of the dimensions of mobility.	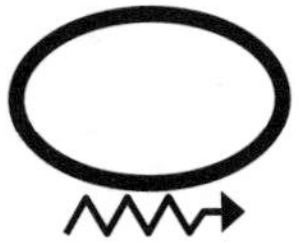

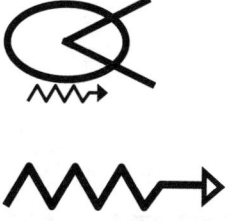

<<Essential Mobile Use Case>>	This stereotype extends Wisdom's <<Essential Use Case>>. It is to be used to indicate that the particular use case is a mobile use case and that it is necessary to describe the functionality of a mobile application. This stereotype is to be used in Wisdom interaction models (user interface–oriented extension to the use case diagrams).	
<<Mobile Communicate>>	This stereotype extends Wisdom's <<communicate>> stereotype in the interaction model. It indicates communication between any actor and any use case while that actor is mobile. Note that this symbol is *not* to be used to indicate communication between the internal classes of a mobile application as it would cause confusion with extensions already defined for mobile agents (to be discussed in Chapter 9). As you recall in the definition of the interaction model, the focus is on the user interface interactions.	
<<Single-Channel Communicate>>	This stereotype extends <<Mobile Communicate>>. This stereotype is to be used when communication between the actors and use cases is done through only one communication channel. We defined channels in Chapter 5. Specification of the channel can be done through text added to the symbol.	
<<Multi-Channel Communicate>>	This stereotype extends <<Mobile Communicate>>. This stereotype is used between actors and use cases or actors and other actors in interaction model diagrams. It indicates that the communication with a specific use case is done through two or more channels. OCL may be used to specify whether messages may be passed synchronously or asynchronously through every channel. Specific channels may be specified through text added to the symbol.	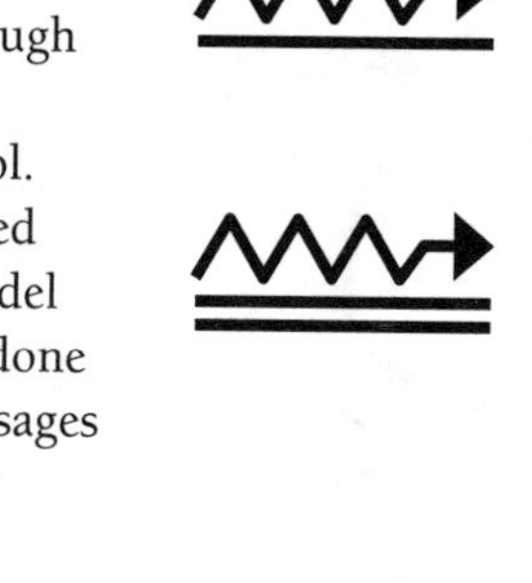
<<Location Based Control>>	This stereotype extends the <<Control>> stereotype of Wisdom. As you recall, the <<Control>> stereotype was put on a class that provides coordination among other classes, objects, and components (Wisdom analysis model). A location-based control is a special type of control that uses location information to perform one or more of its tasks.	

(*continued*)

Table 6.7 *(continued)*

Stereotype	Description	Icon
<<Location Based Boundary>>	This stereotype extends the <<Boundary>> stereotype of Wisdom. As you recall, boundaries are used to indicate the interface lines between subsystems and components that make up the application. Location-based boundaries are used to specify the boundaries between the core functionality of the application and the system(s) or subsystem(s) whose sole functionality is to provide GIS (Geographical Information Systems) information. We will look at <<Location Based Boundary>> and <<Location Based Control>> further in Chapter 12.	LBS
<<Mobile Task>>	This stereotype extends Wisdom's <<Task>> stereotype. This stereotype defines a complete set of interactions between the mobile user and the system to achieve something meaningful in terms of the business process.	

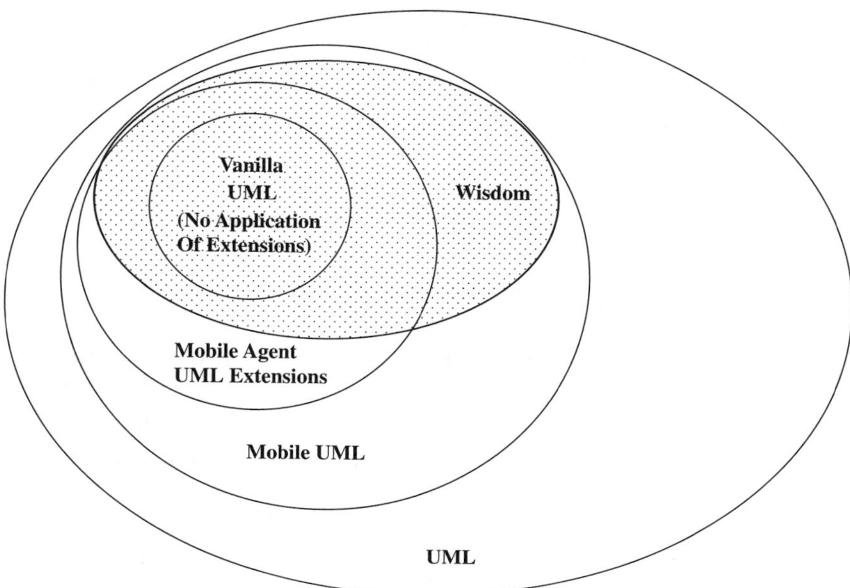

FIGURE 6.25. Mobile UML: Building a Collective Set of UML Extensions for Mobile Application Development.

Although we focus on using UML for user interface development in this chapter, we will see other extensions in future chapters. In fact, throughout this text, you will see both the application of the UML standard without any extensions or profiles and incrementally introduced extensions that better refine how we will use UML. We have not specified any "UML Profiles" that collect a certain set of the extensions we have introduced. We leave this up to the reader. Figure 6.25 shows the taxonomy of what we will collectively refer to as "Mobile UML," simply meaning a collection of methodologies that we will use to build mobile applications using UML and its extensions. The diagram refers to UML, as an OMG standard and as of version 1.4, without any extensions and profiles, as "Vanilla UML."

At this point, you must be waiting for an example of how this is all used. But you will have to wait till the last chapter of this book. There we use a real project to go through the step-by-step use of UML extensions that we introduce here and the implementation code that goes along with it.

Optimization of Mobile GUIs

We have now looked at different techniques and tools for building mobile GUIs. One of the things we have not discussed yet is how to design efficient user interfaces. As we have said repeatedly in this text, mobile applications typically require support for more than just one interface. Every interface type and every device has a different set of properties: the data entry method, the screen size, etc. Therefore, every interface type and device has a unique set of requirements for optimization. Obviously, we cannot outline the "best practices" of the user interface for every type of mobile device and every type of interface. Besides, even if we did, it would nearly immediately be obsolete as we see new types of interfaces and devices entering the marketplace every day.

Nevertheless, we can approach the problem with one of our favorite words in this text: "meta." We can outline a set of instructions that specify a "metasolution"—a set of instructions that may be applied to different types of user interfaces for purposes of optimization from the usability standpoint. We first need some metrics that allow us to define what optimization of the user interface means when it comes to mobile applications. So, let us map the dimensions of mobility and the mobile condition of the user:

1. *Lack of Focus*: We mentioned that the user is not focused on the task of computing. This means that the mobile user may be driving, walking, or doing a variety of other things while using the application. So, we need to minimize the number of interactions the user has with the application without reducing functionality.
2. *Limited Power Supply*: Most of the time, battery life is precious. If the device provides information regarding battery life, then we can use it to dynamically decide if things like advertisements should be displayed or not. If the device does not provide such information or we cannot obtain it for our application for some other reason, then we need to assume the worst-case scenario and make sure all unnecessary evils are nonexistent. The more superfluous materials are included on the user interface, the longer it takes the user to digest the information on the screen and the more power is consumed in rendering.
3. *Device Proliferation*: As we have seen earlier, there are numerous existing devices and interfaces, and new mobile devices and interfaces are continually being introduced to the marketplace. When optimizing our user interfaces, we have to keep them consistent for maintaining a consistent user experience regardless of the device used. It is also often desirable (though not always possible) to automate the process of publishing to multiple user interfaces: Whatever optimization we do must be accounted for in the publishing mechanism.
4. *Limited Input Mechanisms*: Most mobile devices are limited in the input mechanism that they offer because they are designed to be portable and accessible on the move. We need to optimize our user interface to require the minimum amount of information to be input to the system with the minimum amount of difficulty.

Let us now turn to some optimization techniques. Note that by introducing these techniques, we are trying to make a science out of an art; do not assume that what we introduce here is all-inclusive. Optimizing usability and designing user interfaces are still much more of an art learned through years of experience; nevertheless, we will attempt to quantify and qualify some techniques to optimize user interfaces for mobile applications.

Optimizing GUIs through "Path of Least Resistance"

One of the most obvious things we can do to improve the usage of a user interface is to minimize the number of interactions the user has with the system. In this text, we refer to this *as user interface optimization through path of least resistance* with the idea being that we are trying to minimize the resistance of the user interface to what the user wants to use the computing system for. The question is how to quantify the interactions of the user with the system. Discussing this in detail for all types of user interfaces is outside of the scope of this text; as always, we focus on those things that concern mobile applications most. The goal of the discussion is twofold.

First, we want to outline techniques that help us optimize our user interfaces during the design and testing phases. We need techniques used during the design phase to select the best user interface. If we somehow do not select the best interface or miss some optimizations, this should be caught during the quality assurance and testing process. Second, if we want to use automation in generating the user interfaces to different devices, these techniques should be integrated into the implementation of the run-time engine of the user interface publishing mechanism (though this automation may not be possible or desirable depending on the project). Because of the art (as opposed to science) involved, the techniques we introduce here are merely to be used at the discretion of the developers. In addition, one would apply the typical user interface usability techniques outlined by Nielson [Nielson 1994] and others.

Let us see what it is that we need to quantify and then see how we can measure each:

1. *Data Output to the User for Each Individual Interaction*: The more data the user has to receive through as output from the system (read on the screen, hear through the speakers, etc.) to accomplish the necessary task, the higher the impedance is between the user and the user interface.
2. *Date Input by the User for Each Individual Interaction*: The more data the user has to input into the system (type on the keyboard, push on the phone keypad, stab on the screen with the stylus, etc.) to accomplish the necessary task, the higher the impedance is between the user and the user interface.
3. *Navigation from One Interaction to the Next throughout the Application*: The higher the number of controls and screens are, and the more complex the navigational model among those controls and screens are, the higher the impedance is between the user and the user interface.

We will start with Fitts' Law, developed in 1954 by Paul Fitts and based on Shannon's theorem, and one the most basic principles in information theory:

$$\text{Capacity} = \text{bandwidth}^* \log_2(SNR + 1),$$

Where SNR is the signal to noise ratio (signal divided by noise). In the context of user interfaces, Fitts applied Shannon's theorem so that capacity represented the effectiveness of the information exchange between the user and the system. Fitts defined two quantities, the Index of Performance (IP) quantifying the ability of a human and his or her mechanical reflexes and skills and the Index of Difficulty (ID) quantifying the difficulty of dealing with something that required mechanical reflexes and skills.

Fitts' law then states that for visual interactions

$$ID = \log_2(2A/W),$$

where A is the distance from the starting point to the center of the target and W is the width of the target. You can think of A as the distance that one may have to move a mouse pointer to get it to the center of the control and W as the width of a control such as a button. We will not go through the proof here, but this makes intuitive sense: The smaller the control, the more difficult it is to deal with it; the farther we have to move the mouse pointer to reach the control, the more difficult it is.

Fitts then measures the performance of the person interacting with the system based on the amount of time spent to interact with a particular task. In other words, he states that

$$MT = ID/IP,$$

where MT is the so-called Movement Time. We can also conclude from this that to minimize Movement Time, we need to minimize ID and maximize IP. We do not have much control over the user's efficiency in using the application other than making it easier to learn. But, we can reduce the Index of Difficulty.

There is also variety among the types of applications, which means that the graph of Movement Time may be shifted up or down by some constant. Taking this into account and substituting for the Index of Difficulty, we get

$$MT = a + b \log_2(2A/W),$$

where $b = 1/IP$.

So, our goal will be to provide the ideal values for $2A/W$. In other words, make it so that the user has to do the least amount of work and be as inaccurate as possible and yet get the job done. Unfortunately, the problem is a bit more complex than that. Making controls bigger means that we can have less of them per screen and this in turn means that we have to navigate through a number of screens, making it much more difficult. So, we need to apply this principle not just over a single screen but to the collection of all interactions over the entire user interface of the system. This is where Andrew Sears' work on Layout Appropriateness comes in.

Sears' Layout Appropriateness looks into this issue. The cost of a layout is computed by assigning a cost to each sequence of actions and weighting those costs by how frequently each sequence is used [Sears 1992]:

$$\text{cost} = \sum_{\text{All Transitions}} [\text{Frequency of the Transition}^* \text{ Cost of the Transition}].$$

The Layout Appropriateness is then computed as

$$LA = 100^* \left(\frac{\text{Cost of the } LA \text{ Optimal Layout}}{\text{Cost of the Proposed Layout}} \right)$$

But, what is a transition? In Chapter 5, we defined transitions as the boundaries between different user interface components. These boundaries can be spatial or temporal. In other words, we may be talking about transitioning from one screen to the next where the transition is a temporal (time-dependent) one or we may be talking about the transition between two panels appearing on the same screen where the transition is a spatial one.

The cost of the transition depends on the type of user interface with which we are dealing and the specific project. If we are using this methodology to create a tool that produces user interfaces, then the tool must provide the proper configurations that allow us to add new devices and user interface types and specify the cost, or weight, of each transition.

Now, there is one piece left to our puzzle. We need to account for the cost of individual interactions that involve things like typing as opposed to moving something across the screen with a mouse. We can use Fitts' Law for things like moving a mouse, but what do we do for things like the difficulty of key presses on a mobile phone keypad?

We can accommodate this by taking every type of entry, assigning it a "weight" that is relevant to the difficulty of its use, and then attempt to minimize the sum of all entry values. Although we can assign a value using Fitts' Law to some of these, others are more difficult. Let us take for example the Palm shorthand technique called Graffiti as an example of this. In such cases, you will need to decide the weight based on a user survey or usability tests designed to measure the difficulty of entry of each symbol and subsequently measure the difficulty of entry of the symbols by a given input method (such as the Graffiti) compared to another method (such as a phone keypad). Obviously, the weight of every action changes depending on the type of user interface. For example, entering data into a keypad is much more difficult than entering data using a keyboard. So, the application of these equations for evaluation and comparisons of several versions of a user interface should be done with consideration to the specific user interface for which they are being implemented.

We can continue to leverage the Sears approach in adding the "impedance" or the "cost" of each control in a linear manner to get the cost of a given screen. Then add in the cost of navigating between those screens and you have the final cost of the user interface.

Let us apply all of this theory and look at a quick example based on a WAP application that uses a phone keypad.

Finding the Path of Least Resistance for a WAP Application

Most WAP applications are accessed through a mobile phone. Mobile phones have at least one method of data entry: a telephone keypad that has ten digits of 0–9, each mapped to a standard set of letters. Although some phones provide additional software that facilitates faster typing of content (such as predictive software and others), we will assume that the only thing available on the target device for data entry is the standard phone keypad with the standard mapping to the English alphabet (or use the appropriate mapping for other languages where they apply). There are also some standard auxiliary buttons for Yes/No answers or scrolling. Then, we are concerned with a set of input actions. Let us call these input actions

$\{P_1, P_2, P_3, \ldots, P_n\}$. Let us define the following:

1. P_1: *Single Scroll Action*. We will assign a weight, W_1, to every single scroll action, defined by one press of the scrolling button on the keypad.
2. P_2: *Multiple Scroll Action*. We will assign a weight, W_2, to every multiple scroll action. For the sake of simplifying our model, we will assume that pushing the scroll button twice is equally as difficult as three times and so on (though this assumption may not be correct).
3. P_3 *and* P_4: *Repeating Keys*. Certain text, such as letters "s" and "k," require multiple pushes from the same button. This is cumbersome because you must be speedy in pushing the same button multiple times to get the desired letter (e.g., three quick pushes on the number 5 produce the letter "l"). We will assign a weight of W_3 any time a multiple push character is required and a multiplier of W_4 as a coefficient for the number of times that button must be pushed (twice, three times, and so on).
4. P_5: *Alpha Entry*. Depending on the device, certain characters such as "(" or "$" might require navigation to a different screen. Most of the time, this is indicated by a prompt allowing the user to navigate to an area marked "ALPHA." Such characters cause extra confusion and force the user to do extra navigation. We will assign a weight of W_5 to any character that requires navigation to another screen.
5. P_6: *Forward Navigation Button*. It is possible to use various buttons (such as the left-top button on Nokia phones used as OK) for navigation. Various devices map the available keys to different navigation rules. We will assign W_6 to use any device-specific navigation.

We can recognize other variables if we further specify the device family, but, for the sake of simplifying our example, let us stay with these six variables. So, any set of WML 1.x screens on this particular device family can be described by a cost, defined by Sears in the previous section as

$$\text{cost of interactions per screen} = \sum_{i=1}^{6} n_i W_i,$$

where n is the number of times a recognized input type is pressed (we defined the set of $\{P_1, P_2, P_3, \ldots, P_n\}$ by looking at the keypad) and W_i is the weight that we assigned for how difficult it may be to activate the input type (in our case how difficult it is to push the button).

Now we can apply this to optimize the user interface of a real-life application:

1. We may have two or more sets of possibilities for our screen layouts. Each set of screen layouts will have a cost of interaction per screen and a cost of navigation between the screens. We can compute these costs, add them up to come up with a total cost of interaction for a set of screens, and see which set of screen layouts give us the minimum cost.
2. We may have the choice of using other input types such as a stylus for Graffiti input, tilt-based scrolling such as that used in the Compaq Itsy, or voice user

interfaces. We can create a weighting system for each type of interface and compute a total cost of interactions for the user interface implemented in each individual interface type. So, we would have a cost of interactions for using only the keypad, using only the stylus, using only the voice user interface, and so on.

If we have a multimodal and multichannel interface (which we will look at in Chapter 8), we can have sets of user interface implementations that use multiple channels, modes, input mechanisms, and so on. In this scenario, we have to assign the weights to the individual input mechanisms based on looking at all of them in a single set as opposed to weighting them separately in their own buckets. In other words, we have to compare the difficulty of pressing a particular button to the difficulty of saying something or to the difficulty of writing the same thing with a stylus on a Graffiti pad. Obviously, this is not only difficult, but it requires gathering empirical data from a set of sample users.

This method of calculating the cost of interaction between a user and the mobile user interface can be invaluable for finding the best user interface to present to the user in an objective way. As we mentioned repeatedly, the weights of individual interactions can be determined with empirical experimentation. We could always make an educated guess on these weights, but the results will not be as useful nor as reliable.

Application of Direct Combination to Mobile GUIs

As you may recall, in Chapter 5, we discussed putting together simple user interface components to build more complex components. This technique can prove particularly useful as user interface types proliferate. Even if we have nirvana and all commercial and academic entities agree on one language, such as XForms, for building user interfaces, we still will have a large variety of devices with each displaying the user interface in a different way. So, how do we compose more complex interfaces from simpler parts?

Commercial technologies such as IBM Portlets have tried to tackle this issue, but existing solutions are simple and not context sensitive. Basically, nearly all solutions that allow the system to build a complex GUI based on smaller components are concerned with only the spatial context of the components and whatever metadata the developer may assign the individual component to give it additional context. Though this approach is valid, it is very rudimentary and difficult to fit into a multichannel and multimodal world such as that of mobile applications. We do not claim to have a solution to present to you in this text. When we build composite user interface components from smaller ones, besides needing to make sure that all the components "fit" onto the composite component, and besides needing to make sure the smaller components fit together and within the bigger component contextually, we need to ensure that whatever it is that we have come up with is the best possible solution or at least one of the better possible solutions. In other words, we need to do some optimization in composing a larger component from the smaller ones. Without touching this subject, we would have neglected an important topic in developing mobile GUIs and so we will present you with a summary of the work of Holland and colleagues, an approach that looks at the optimization of mobile HCI.

Holland and Oppenheim [Holland and Oppenheim 1999] first introduced Direct Combination, building on Direct Manipulation, introduced by Smith, Kimball, Verplank, and Harslem at Xerox in the early 1980s [Smith et al. 1982]. Direct Manipulation basically states that GUI components should be built to allow the user to reversibly, incrementally, simply, and through physical actions manipulate metaphors that allow interactions with the user interface. A menu is a good example of this. The user can click on a choice that takes him or her to another place, perform a task, return, and click on another menu choice. Direct Manipulation deals with the user's interactions with individual user interface metaphors. Direct Combination is a way of extending Direct Manipulation by focusing systematically not on single interaction objects but on pairs of interaction objects and the essential requirement for Direct Combination is that for every pair of interaction objects in the system, there should be at least one or more operators defined and available to the user [Holland and Oppenheim 1999]. Direct Combination looks at the user's interaction with things like dragging and dropping where there is more than one GUI widget involved in the interaction. One of our goals for producing better composite user interface components is that the user should be able to interact with the composite component, which is really a collection of simpler components plus added context, in an optimal way.

Therefore, the relevance here to Direct Combination is that by keeping in mind a set of principles, we optimize the interactions of the user with the composite component and thereby optimize the composite component itself (because optimization is really a matter of improving the interactions between the user and the user interface). The major driving forces of Direct Combination as applied to mobile GUIs, as stated in Holland et al.'s paper [Holland, Morse, and Gedenryd 2002] are as follows:

1. Every object of interest, both virtual and in the environment should be
   a. visible (or perceptible) and
   b. capable of a range of useful interactions with any other object of interest.
2. The available interactions between pairs of objects should be
   a. diverse and
   b. tailored to each pair (or *n*-tuple) of object types.
3. Direct Combination interactions must be implemented in such a way that they are immediately available but do not impede access to preexisting interaction styles.

The first two are recognized as *principles of visibility and n-fold interaction.* The third is recognized as the *principle of subsumption.* Now, let us interpret this to real-life mobile GUI design situations.

The principle of subsumption is probably the most obvious: We do not want to put simple components together that will hinder one another's operation. Most of the time, this is not allowed by the language that we use. For example, we cannot put select widgets and input widgets together on the same WML card: The card will not compile to WMLC (you will get an error in the WAP browser or the emulator will tell you that you have an error on your card). However, this is not always the case. For example, we may put a select box and an input box together on the same canvas in J2ME. And there is nothing that says this is necessarily problematic. But, if we are publishing multiple user interfaces, we may get inconsistencies across different interfaces if two or more components can live in a composite in one specialized interface although they combine just fine in another specialized user interface.

The principle of visibility and *n*-fold interaction tells us that when we put a bunch of user interface components together, they should all be visible and that they should be able to interact with one another, directly or indirectly through the container. The cases when this applies are a bit more obvious: We do not want to have one component hide another component, include components that do not have the proper interfaces exposed to interact with the container or other components, or put components together that are all essentially the same (for if that were the case, then they should have been the same user interface component to begin with).

Both these principles are key to designing your transformations to specialize a generic user interface to specific types of interfaces. If you want to keep your user interfaces consistent (which you should), creating transformations is not as easy as you may think.

6.3 Summary

We started this chapter by looking at some techniques in turning a generic user interface into a specific type of GUI for a mobile application. From Chapter 5, we knew that we could use XForms to represent the interactions of a user with a computing system in a generic way and why it is important to do this for mobile applications. Here, we delved into techniques that help us in converting this generic user interface to specific GUIs that can be displayed to the user. We did not touch upon the subject of channels. For everything we did here, we assumed that there was an available data channel, such as TCP/IP or WAP, that is well known to us. We also looked at various design patterns, specifically MVC, PAC, and variations on PAC, that can be used for building user interfaces to mobile applications.

We then looked at the user interface capabilities of our development tools a little closer and then went on to studying what types of interfaces they can allow us to implement. There, we changed gears and looked at how to use UML to drive the process of user interface development for mobile applications and help us in designing and documenting the user interface. We will look at a case study that uses the various extensions we introduced here in Chapter 19. We recommend you look at that example to get a better feel for using these extensions to build a real system.

Finally, we looked at some optimization techniques. Because of the large variety of interfaces, input mechanisms, and other factors, we may be faced with choices to make during the design and implementation of a mobile GUI. Though our discussion here was short, these optimization techniques are quite useful whether you are building tools for mobile GUIs or simply implementing mobile GUIs.

Note that there are still many issues related to mobile GUIs that we have not covered in appropriate depth. For example, we have not addressed how to design the GUI best for a distracted user who may push the wrong button frequently or how to modify the user interface, dynamically and over time, as the battery is depleted. There are a variety of these types of issues, mostly revolving around usability, that we will leave out of this text merely to control the scope.

Our dealing with mobile GUIs does not end here. Visual interfaces are one modality among several. And, we have yet to discuss multichannel GUIs. We will leave these subjects to Chapter 8, once we have become familiarized with VUIs in Chapter 7.

CHAPTER 7

VUIs and Mobile Applications

> It is forbidden to kill; therefore all murderers are punished unless they kill in large numbers and to the sound of trumpets.
>
> Voltaire

7.1 INTRODUCTION

As their name indicates, voice user interfaces (VUIs) are interfaces that allow users to interact with computing systems through use of voice. Although our voice can be used in different ways, VUIs typically refer to communication through the use of language. This narrows down the problem at hand as communication through VUIs is a subset of communicating through aural user interfaces. It is possible to communicate with computers through sounds other than pronounced words and sentences. Different sounds can be used to communicate information through their frequency, amplitude, duration, and other properties that make them unique. However, language is how we naturally communicate, be it through voice or text; therefore, when referring to VUIs, we refer to communicating with machines using pronounced language.

It is also true that most of us have had very frustrating experiences trying to bypass the voice recognition system and reach an operator. However, this is not an indicator of the lack of value of voice recognition systems. In fact, most systems that lead users to be frustrated are those that have not been well designed or those that require a high degree of cognition by the computing system: something that computing systems do not do well yet. As we have already seen, the user interface problem is one of the biggest problems in mobile computing. To reiterate, the mobile user cannot carry a sizable keyboard and mouse, nor is the user always physically stable enough to be able to rely on text entry. Whereas there are a variety of ways to communicate with computing systems, one of the most natural is voice. And, when it comes to mobile applications, the clear advantage it offers is that human beings can talk while they are moving around much more easily than they can type, write, or use any other means of communicating with computers that requires our visual sensory systems. So, although today's VUIs and the foundation technologies on which they depend are very rudimentary, they still offer a very effective way to solve many of the mobile user interface problems.

There are three basic technologies at the heart of systems that interact with users through the use of voice, namely *voice recognition, voice transcription*, and *speech synthesis* (a subset of which is referred to as *text-to-speech*). So, the first task at hand is to introduce these foundation technologies. Of course, when it comes to various voice-based interface technologies, more than just the voice interactions is involved; there is understanding the meaning of what is said by the user (typically covered in the field of cognitive computing and artificial intelligence), there are various aspects of linguistics in both understanding the spoken words and producing spoken words from text, and there are various other broad topics to be considered. For the most part, we will not go into any of these topics as they divert from our main purpose, which is to see how to build mobile applications.

Voice transcription and voice recognition systems are used to treat user input. Although both of these systems are often referred to as voice recognition systems, within this text, for the purpose of clarity and brevity, we will refer to free-flow conversion of speech to text, whether speaker dependent or speaker independent, as voice transcription. We will call those systems that are able to understand speech that fits predefined patterns and grammars in a speaker-independent manner voice recognition systems. Voice transcription systems are also often referred to as speech dictation systems; voice recognition systems are referred to as command-and-control voice recognition systems.

Speech-synthesis systems produce speech from binary or textual data. Although the industry uses the terms "text-to-speech" and "speech synthesis" interchangeably, it is important to understand that text-to-speech systems are a subset of speech-synthesis systems. Speech-synthesis systems can take a variety of data types as their input whereas text-to-speech systems only take text, formatted or not, as their input. Text-to-speech systems do just what their name says: They turn text into speech. There are different types of text-to-speech technologies that we will look at later in this chapter. The problem of text-to-speech, in general, is an easier technical one to solve than those for voice recognition or voice transcription. The reason is somewhat obvious: Computers are years, perhaps centuries, away from having cognitive abilities like humans. We will mainly look at text-to-speech systems, but, when reading this text, you should understand that speech-synthesis systems that do not take text as input can typically replace text-to-speech systems in your architecture in a modular manner.

In this chapter, we will start out by looking at what speech is and what qualities differentiate speech from other types of sounds. Then, we will move on to look at the various infrastructure technologies available to build VUIs for applications, mobile or otherwise. Finally, we will delve into the heart of the matter and see how to build a real VUI for mobile systems, how to model voice-based interactions using UML, and how to fine-tune the VUI after deployment.

If you are already familiar with VUIs, you may want to skip Sections 7.2 and 7.3 as they are introductory. If you would like to learn more about VUIs, there are a number of good textbooks that discuss VUIs in much greater detail than what we discuss here. We are concerned with VUIs only because of the value they offer mobile computing applications, but they can be used for stationary software applications as well. Refer to the references at the end of this chapter for some suggested texts. Now, let us take a closer look at what speech is and some of the basic technologies we use to communicate with computing systems through speech.

7.2 Qualities of Speech

The qualities of speech are those things that differentiate speech from other types of aural input. To build good VUIs, a general understanding of the physical qualities of speech not only give us a better high-level insight into the operation of voice recognition engines but also leads us toward building better VUIs. So, let us take a survey of what these qualities of speech are.

7.2.1 Amplitude

Speech, as in any other type of aural input, has a loudness level. The loudness of a sound is based on the amplitude of the sound wave that makes the sound. The amplitude of speech is important in that input devices are designed to receive sounds within certain amplitude thresholds. If the sound is too loud, it causes distortion in conversion of the sound, in our case the speech, into an electrical signal that can then be digitized. Though most distortion can be filtered, distortion always introduces some additional errors into the final processed data left over after speech is completely scrubbed into a digital signal. Likewise, if the amplitude of the signal is too low, there is not enough signal strength to convert the speech into a meaningful digital signal. So, to accomplish voice recognition or transcription of a speech signal successfully and within some predictable error rate, the amplitude of the speech signal must fall within some upper and lower bounds.

There is also the matter of signal-to-noise-ratio, or SNR for short. If the amplitude of the signal is high enough but there is significant noise, caused by sound sources in the background, by the process of digitizing, or by the communication channel that delivers the final signal to the voice recognition and/or transcription system, the digitized speech signal may not have enough meaningful information for processing. Making out the content of a speech signal also strongly depends on whether the SNR is above a minimum threshold. This threshold depends on the specific task at hand (whether we are recognizing or transcribing speech, what the size of the allowable grammar may be, etc.).

Of course, voice recognition and transcription systems have to deal with much more than just the amplitude thresholds of a speech signal and the SNR. A given user's speech amplitude rarely ever stays the same during an interaction with a

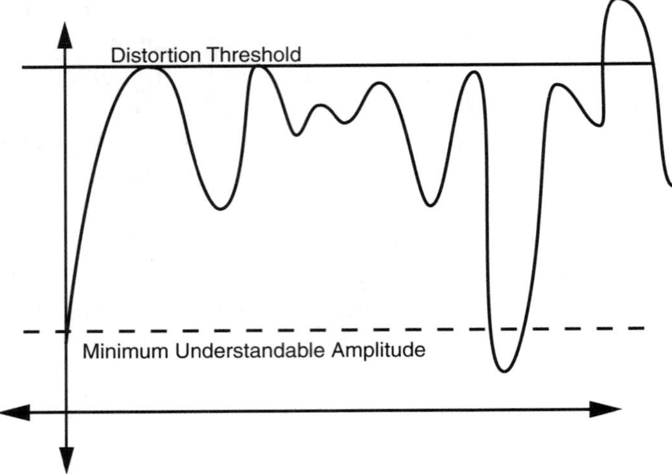

FIGURE 7.1. Amplitude of the Speech and Relevant Thresholds.

computer system (see Figure 7.1) because speech amplitude is one of the ways humans express emotions. Computer systems that deal with interpreting a user's speech must be able to mark the beginning and end of speech segments, using speech amplitude, and the various properties of speech amplitude, among other qualities of speech. There are other qualities of amplitude that are used by computer systems that interpret voice. The important thing to remember is that signal amplitude is one of the most crucial parts of getting recognizable speech into a computer system.

7.2.2 Frequencies and Pitch

Another quality of speech is the set of frequencies that make up the sounds that in turn make speech. Along with the amplitude of our voice, the combination of these frequencies is what makes up the different pitches and sounds that we use to make speech. Devices that capture speech typically act as band-pass filters, cutting out the lowest and highest of the frequencies that make up speech. Today's voice transcription systems are user dependent and rely on a training process that familiarizes them with the pitch and tone of a specific user's spoken words. Therefore, when using most voice transcription systems, changes in the frequency and pitch will cause errors. Voice recognition systems tend to be user independent so they rely less heavily on the frequencies of the spoken words. However, even voice recognition systems have some boundaries with acceptable pitches and frequencies as they are statistically optimized and tuned to yield the best recognition results for the average listeners.

Frequencies and pitch are not just important in the speech input to the system; they are also critical in the output side when the user receives aural messages from the system. For example, a female voice can be more soothing to a male user by the virtue of the frequencies and pitch that make a female voice different from that of a male voice. Frequencies and pitches provide a great tool in creating the right type of "hear-and-feel" to the listener.

7.2.3 Meaning and Context

Sounds make up words, words make phrases and sentences, and a combination of spoken sounds, words, phrases, and sentences make up spoken language. Individual sounds can have meaning (such as "hmmm..." expressing a thinking pause). Words, phrases, and sentences, each and on their own can have meaning too. However, the meaning of different combinations of sounds, words, phrases, and sentences in spoken language depends largely on the context in which the spoken language is used. Although the phrase, "Isn't the sky blue!" can be broken down into the three keywords of "sky," "isn't," and "blue," it is not possible to derive the facetious meaning of the answer to a question that must certainly have a positive response, such as "Are software engineers typically poor communicators?" In the context of the phrase being the answer to an obvious question, "Isn't the sky blue!" means "Yes," but this not the meaning of any of the words, nor is it the literal meaning of the sentence. Idioms and metaphors are examples of spoken language segments that have meaning based on other contexts in addition to the meaning of the words that make them up. Remember that we talked about context and that user interface components have various types of context in Chapter 5.

Homophones and words that sound similar make context that much more important in voice recognition. For example, consider the two words "blue" and "blew." The pronunciations of the words are exactly the same. So, how does a voice recognition engine know which was said?

As we will see later, we limit the choice of possible words by grammars in voice recognition systems. Grammars, then, in a way limit the contexts in which a VUI can be used. Using a context-dependent way of limiting the possible interactions between the user and the system is the only way that speaker-independent speech recognition can be achieved with today's technologies. When building GUIs, the words are already known because of their textual existence: There is no "guessing game" in interpreting what has been said. This is not the case for VUIs as the biggest part of the problem is to recognize what has been said, and context is crucial in helping achieve recognition.

7.2.4 Utterance

Utterance is simply a "chunk" of speech marked by a beginning and an end. An utterance may be a sentence marker or an incidental sound such as "hmmm"; it may be a single word, a combination of words in a phrase or a sentence, or even a combination of sentences. The biggest significance of utterance is that it has well-defined start and end points. Utterances are most relevant to voice recognition and voice transcription systems as they represent the individual units that these systems convert to text. The size of the utterance is important as the larger it is, the more difficult it is to transcribe or recognize.

When dealing with mobile applications, utterances are typically shorter. As we previously mentioned, mobile users are not focused on the task of computing; therefore, we need to tell the user as much information as possible in as clear and concise of a manner as possible. User utterances to be interpreted by the system are also typically shorter as users tend to be more abrupt and to the point when interfacing with a mobile application.

7.2.5 Language

Language is a way of combining audible sounds, signs, and gestures to allow people to communicate. When dealing with VUIs, we are concerned with spoken language, which is the subset of the aural things that can represent a language. Interpreting this spoken language is the final goal of both voice recognition and voice transcription systems. Pronouncing written language is the goal of text-to-speech systems. Because of context of usage, spoken language can be very complicated as the sum of its parts can have a larger set of meanings than the sum of the meaning of the individual parts.

7.2.6 Speaker Dependence

All those qualities of speech that we have discussed—the amplitude, frequencies, and context—are unique for every single user. This makes a person's voice much like a person's fingerprint: inherently unique. This uniqueness, however, presents us with a new problem in that VUIs must be designed with the ability to understand more than just one user and be able to give input back to the user with a flexible persona that takes advantage of the qualities of speech. A VUI may be speaker dependent or speaker independent. Although most systems strive to be speaker independent, today's voice transcription systems are nearly all speaker dependent as speaker-independent transcription of voice remains somewhat of an unsolved technical problem. Voice transcription systems typically require training by the specific user who will use the system so that the system gets familiarized with the qualities of the particular user's voice. In contrast, most of today's voice recognition systems are able to perform speaker-independent recognition. We will discuss the differences between voice recognition and voice transcription systems a bit later on.

Sometimes, however, VUIs are purposefully designed to be speaker dependent. As we mentioned, the voice is just like a fingerprint; it is unique to the speaker. Therefore, speaker dependence can be used as a very reliable security mechanism to authenticate a user.

Generally, speaker independence is something desired when building voice recognition–based user interfaces. Making the interface truly speaker independent, however, is a bit more difficult than simply using a recognition engine that provides speaker-independent facilities. Voice recognition engines that provide such functionality take care of the speaker-independence when it comes to the basic qualities of speech, but they do not treat building bigger components in a speaker-independent manner; this is something that is left up to the VUI developers.

7.2.7 Internationalization, Languages, and Dialects

Voice input to computer systems is only meaningful within the context of a given language. Without knowing the language, computers cannot recognize what is said, because, in the end, it is the meaning of the language that is used to perform actions. Translation of user interfaces is really a two-dimensional problem: First there is the literal translation of the individual interactions and then there is the contextual translation. In other words, when translating a user interface from one language to another, not only do the individual interactions between the user and the system have to be translated, but also the appropriateness of the way each interaction is designed must be reconsidered.

7.2.8 Locale

In the same way as language, though not as palpable, the location of the user is important in understanding the user's speech. People living in different locales, in the same country or territory speaking the same language, may use language in different ways. For example, a user in Huntington Beach, California, may say "that is tubular" meaning that there is a great wave to surf on or that something pleasant happened. The same thing in Boston, Massachusetts, may only have one meaning: that something has a cylindrical shape. Once again, grammars, which we will talk about later, take into account the difference in what may be said in different locales. Locale is not only important in defining the meaning of speech; it is also an important factor that other qualities of speech depend on. For example, in locations where the humidity in the air is greater, the signal received by the voice transcription or voice recognition engine may end up being slightly different than in a location with very low humidity. In this particular case, different algorithms may be required for conversion of speech to a signal that is subsequently recognized as speech.

7.2.9 Other Qualities

There are a variety of other qualities that make a speech signal and understanding it into a unique problem. Speech can be spoken among multiple parties. The user's gender, mood, and a variety of other physical and psychological factors make up other factors that create differentiations among the voice of various users or in the voice of the same user at different times.

Understanding the general principles of what make up speech is important, but we do not have to worry about the implementation details of infrastructure software such as voice recognitions systems. To build VUIs, we will be employing off-the-shelf software such as voice transcription and voice recognition systems that implement algorithms to understand or synthesize speech.

Let us start by looking at voice transcription systems, the Holy Grail of speech technologies today.

7.3 Voice Transcription

Courtroom clerks and secretaries have transcribed voice recording as well as real-time voice from third-party speakers for years. Transcription of speech is something that our brains do very well very fast. So, it is something that we generally take for granted. However, speaker-independent automated transcription of voice remains one of the Holy Grails at the edge of computing technology today. The main problem is that people basically pronounce things differently. Basic differences may be locale related: where they are born, where they learn to speak, where they live, etc. But things get much more complicated. Education level, speech impediments, mood, context of conversation, and other factor all make speech recognition between a computer and a live person a problem whose challenges rely more within the realm of artificial intelligence and cognition then they do in simple analysis of waveforms and the sound produced in speech.

There are automated voice transcriptions today, but they are speaker dependent. This means that the voice transcription system has to learn the speech patterns of the user through a training process. This training process can be long, taking several hours, before enabling the system to recognize the user's voice reasonably well. Even then, voice transcription systems fall short in delivery: They typically have a limit on how well they transcribe the user's voice without errors regardless of the amount of training; they do not deal very well with homophones (words that have different meanings but similar pronunciations); they do not deal with incorrect grammars very well (which is acceptable especially in natural user interfaces); multiple-user systems require that one user at a time uses the system and switching between users is either explicit (you have to execute a series of commands that tells the system a new user will start speaking) or is done through automated speaker recognition (using various complex digital signal processing algorithms to determine who the user is) and is extremely CPU intensive.

The first step in making voice transcription a reality has already been taken: You can purchase a piece of software, install it on your PC, train it, and then try to dictate a word processing document. However, you will often have to correct it and pay close attention to mistaken homophones or unrecognized words. You will also have to be careful not to say anything that you do not want transcribed (so you cannot begin dictating and talk to someone on the phone at the same time). Most people find that simply typing the document is simpler. Today's voice transcription technologies still do have economically viable reasons for existing in assisting the handicapped and other special circumstances.

We are more than a few years away from dependable and reliable technology that transcribes a person's voice with reasonable accuracy without knowing much about the user's speech patterns and even farther from a system that allows multiple users to interact with it simultaneously by voice transcription.

Using voice transcription for mobile applications is an interesting proposition. When it comes to the mobile user, the primary method of accessing a VUI is telephony. Moreover, most mobile users are connected through some sort of wireless device. Today's voice transcription systems are not well suited to be used with the noise levels that typically surround the mobile user. Another problem lies in the fact that voice transcription systems are very resource intensive (in terms of both CPU and memory) and mobile devices are resource-starved, a fact that has prevented their implementation on today's mobile devices. However, mobile devices are becoming more and more powerful and some or all of the transcription can be done in a centralized manner. The noise problem is bigger, but its solution is not too far down the road. The value of speaker-dependent transcription with mobile applications remains somewhat of a question under research. Will users want to train the system? Can users afford the errors made by the transcription system? Can we build a centralized scalable system able to transcribe voice for many users? For a plethora of reasons, grammar-based voice recognition is typically a better solution for mobile applications until such time when voice transcription systems and the statistical modeling techniques on which they rely improve by orders of magnitude.

Although voice transcription allows for natural interactions, voice recognition gives us a more realistic way of recognizing what the user's speech means with technologies that are available today in a user-independent manner. We can build voice recognition systems so that interacting with them feels relatively natural, but we can never achieve a free-flow natural language conversation with computers based on voice recognition systems. This does not lessen their value though. Let us now look at voice recognition systems and their use in building mobile applications.

7.4 VOICE RECOGNITION

Unlike voice transcription, voice recognition has not been so illusive in achieving. *Voice recognition allows the recognition of a word, a phrase, a sentence, or multiple sentences pronounced by voice against a finite set possible matches.* In other words, the computing system tries to match something said by the user to a given set of possibilities that it already understands. For example, telephone companies have used this technology for years in their directory systems asking the user to "Please say one to reach Bob and two to reach Phil." If the user says "three," the system cannot find a match and tells the user "That's not a valid option; please say one to reach Bob and two to reach Phil." Though the term *voice recognition* is often used as an encompassing definition of voice transcription and voice recognition, in this text, we will use it to recognize the so-called command-and-control type of recognition. Some major distinctions between voice transcription and voice recognition, as defined in this text, are the following:

1. Voice recognition systems rely on predefined interactions with the user. These interactions can be composed of predefined words, phrases, or sentences. The interactions can also be composites of predefined words, phrases, or sentences. *Grammars* are how these words, phrases, sentences, or their composites are predefined.
2. Voice recognition systems attempt to map these predefined words, phrases, sentences, or composites to something that is understandable by the computing system.
3. Voice recognition systems are typically used for "command and control" of a computing system as opposed to dictating text. Though it is possible to create dictation systems using voice recognition systems, it is awkward to do so. Besides, voice recognition, by definition, is limited to a finite vocabulary that constrains not just possible words, but the possible combination of words into phrases and sentences. Therefore, an exploding vocabulary set typically makes voice recognition systems inadequate for transcription tasks.
4. Performance of voice recognition systems is inversely related, typically exponentially, to the size of the grammar vocabulary for a given transaction. This is

System: "Welcome home Bob. Would you like me to turn on the lights for you?"
Bob: "I don't know."
System: "I'm sorry Bob. Please say Yes or No. If you want me to stop, say Quiet."
Bob: "Yes."
System: "Which lights would you like me to turn on. Bathroom, bedroom, your office, kitchen, or living room?"
Bob: "Bathroom."

FIGURE 7.2. Directed Dialogue.

not necessarily true of voice transcription systems as their performance is much less dependent on the specifics of a particular user interaction.

5. Voice recognition systems are typically speaker independent. Whereas most voice transcription systems are tuned to a given user's voice and enunciation patterns, voice transcription systems are designed to be independent of the user's voice.

Because the strength of voice recognition systems is in command and control, it is most valuable when building navigation controls in VUIs. The weakness of voice recognition is in accepting the free flow of speech from the user. Functionality offered by today's voice recognition systems could be in one of several of the following forms:

1. *Directed Dialogue*: As the term suggests, this is the case when every response by the user is preceded by a list of acceptable responses as well as an explanation of them. An example of such a dialogue is shown in Figure 7.2. As you see in this example, the dialogue is directed by the system. The analog of this type of dialog in the GUI world would be an interface entirely comprised of list boxes that are bound to predetermined selections.
2. *Natural Language*: The ultimate goal of voice recognition is to be able to have the computing system understand the commands that you give it even if things are paraphrased or are put into the wrong order. Figure 7.3 is an example of a natural language interaction, taking place between a user and the computing system. As you can see in this example, although the system can only understand sentences and words that concern turning on and off lights or adjusting the temperature in the house, the user is able to put those words and sentences in any order desired. This is where nearly all of today's voice recognition products are striving to be. Most offer some natural language capabilities, but none provide a truly smooth experience as in the case of our example. This is mainly because of two reasons. First, there are thousands of possible combinations of words that can indicate the desired meaning by the user in a natural language dialogue—merely recognizing these possible combinations is something fairly difficult. Second, performance degrades as the number of combinations increase; therefore, thousands of combinations may not be acceptable performance-wise. The

System: "Welcome home Bob. How was your day? Can I help you tonight?"
Bob: "Yeah. Turn on the lights in the garage, will you?"
System: "Lights are already on in the garage Bob. Is there anything else I can do for you?"
Bob: "Can you warm up the dinner please?"
System: "I'm sorry Bob, I only understand tasks related to lighting and temperature. You'll have to upgrade me to help you with the other household controls?"
Bob: "Ok, well, turn on the lights in the kitchen and go into quiet mode."
System: "Thank you Bob. Lights are now on in the kitchen. Just say 'Genie' if you need me."

FIGURE 7.3. Natural Language.

best way to get some natural language capabilities is to design the dialogs as a mixture of natural language and directed-dialog interactions (often referred to as mixed-mode or mixed-initiative).

3. *Mixed-Mode Dialogues*: Mixed-mode dialogs are often referred to as mixed-initiative or natural language as well (though this second is a bit of a misnomer as mixed-mode dialogues are not as flexible as natural language dialogues). Mixed-mode dialogues allow natural language interactions while directing the user so as to contain the possible responses to a given question to a minimum. Figure 7.4 shows an example of a mixed-mode dialog between our fictitious system and Bob. Note that although the system drives the conversation taking place with the user and tries to limit the expected responses from the user, it understands the user's natural language response.

Much of the design of a VUI involves selecting initial dialogs that allow the user to conveniently interact with the system and iterate to final dialogs that minimize the unexpected answers and recognition failures that may result in user frustration. Before we look at the process of designing a VUI, let us look at its components. Then, we will put these components together to create the full picture. We will

System: "Welcome home Bob. How was your day? Can I turn on any lights or adjust the temperature for you tonight?"
Bob: "Yeah. Could you turn on the lights please?"
System: "Where would you like to turn on the lights Bob? Your bedroom, the bathroom, the kitchen, or the garage?"
Bob: "My Bedroom and the bathroom lights please?"
System: "Ok Bob. Those lights are now on."
Bob: "Great. You can go into quiet mode now."

FIGURE 7.4. Mixed-Initiative Dialogs.

System: "Welcome home Bob. Would you like me to turn on the lights for you?"
Acceptable Responses: Quiet, Stop, Yes, No.
System: "Which lights would you like me to turn on. Bathroom, bedroom, your office, kitchen, or living room?"
Acceptable Responses: Bathroom, Living Room, Bed Room, Garage.
System: "Would you like to change the temperature?"
Acceptable Responses: Quiet, Stop, Yes, No.
System: "What would you like the new temperature to be adjusted to?"
Acceptable Responses: Seventy, Seventy-One, Seventy-Two, Seventy-Three, Seventy-Four, Seventy-Five, Seventy-Six, Seventy-Seven, Seventy-Eight, Seventy-Nine.

FIGURE 7.5. Decomposition of the User Responses to Create Grammars for Figure 7.2.

start with grammars, the tool used to define the vocabulary set that constrains the understandable responses from the user.

7.4.1 Grammars

To constrain the possible responses by a user, we need a linguistic method of specifying the constraints to the computing system. This is done through grammars. *Grammars specify the constraints of the expected utterance, whether initiated by the user or given to the system as a response to a directed dialogue.* Grammars can be quite complex or very simple. For example, a particular grammar may specify that the user can say one of two things: yes or no. Another grammar may specify how a user can order food from a menu in natural language. *Utterances* are the sounds, words, phrases, or sentences that the user may say. Of course, to specify grammars, there are a variety of scriptlike languages. We will look at these a bit later. For now, let us focus on how we may come up with a particular grammar.

Let us use our previous examples of Figures 7.2–7.4. The first, Figure 7.2, is a short directed-dialogue taking place between the user and the system. Our home automation system may turn on by sensing the opening of a door and kicking off the dialogue. From there, the system asks the user (Bob) what he would like to do. The system asks the user if he wants to turn on any of the lights or change the temperature. So, the expected response is going to address one or both of these. Anything that does not include either of these is going to return a no-match condition that tells us we should instruct the system to ask the question again to get an expected response. The first step, then, is to go through a set of possible dialogues between the user and the system. This is equivalent to creating user interface mockups for the GUI developers. The difference is that it is much more difficult to constrain the user responses. Figure 7.5. shows the decomposition of the possible answers that are allowed by the system in the directed-dialogue interaction set of Figure 7.2. Whereas in the directed dialogue case we are facing only a few possibilities for responses the user can give, the possibilities begin to grow by factorials as we allow the user to respond with phrases and sentences

System: "Welcome home Bob. How was your day? Can I turn on any lights or adjust the temperature for you tonight?"
Acceptable User Responses:
1. "Yeah. Could you turn on the lights please?"
2. "Hmm . . . Please turn on the lights."
3. "Please turn on the lights."
4. "Lights on."
5. "Lights."
6. "Turn on the lights."
7. "Flip on the lights."

System: "Where would you like to turn on the lights Bob? Your bedroom, the bathroom, the kitchen, or the garage?"
Acceptable User Responses:
1. "Hmm ... Bedroom and bathroom."
2. "Bedroom."
3. "Bathroom."
4. "Living room and bedroom."
5. "Bedroom, living room, and bathroom."
6. "Living room."
7. "Only the living room please."
8. "Quiet."
9. "Stop."
10. "Shut up."

FIGURE 7.6. Decomposition of the User Responses to Create Grammars for Figure 7.3.

as in the example in Figure 7.6 (the decomposition of possible responses to Figure 7.3).

This returns us to the types of dialogues that we discussed: directed dialogue, mixed-initiative, and natural language. Grammars for directed-dialogue interactions are typically well defined and limited to a small vocabulary set. Therefore, the recognition engine can do a faster and better job of recognizing the command. However, creating grammars for complete natural language interactions is nearly, if not completely, impossible as the number of different responses grows very fast. Mixed-initiative interactions lie somewhere in the middle. Designing the grammars for mixed-initiative interactions, then, becomes part art and part science.

A good strategy to take in designing mixed-initiative dialogues is to start with directed dialogues and to iteratively make them more and more "natural." This iterative approach allows the VUI designer to make the qualitative decisions that balance the two diametrically opposed factors: guiding the user to limit his or her responses to make the technical problem a solvable one and making the VUI "natural" enough. We will look more closely at the process of designing voice interactions for voice recognition systems later.

Now that we have learned about the basics of grammars, we need to look at how they are represented programmatically.

Representing Grammars Programmatically

Traditionally, IVR (Interactive Voice Response) systems have been fairly proprietary. Therefore, each system has traditionally had its own programming interface, including its own language for defining grammars. However, recently, there has been much movement in standardizing the syntax by which grammars are defined. There are many obvious reasons for this along the same line as standardizing the syntax of programming languages.

Most of today's popular voice recognition systems support one of a few standard grammar syntax types. The standard grammar can then be compiled, much like an application written in a high-level programming language is compiled into assembly, to something understandable by the particular voice recognition engine deployed. There are two basic types of grammars, *rule grammars* and *dictation grammars*. In this text, we will deal strictly with rule grammars. Dictation grammars impose fewer restrictions on what can be said, making them closer to providing the ideal of free-form speech input [Apaydin 2002]. Dictation grammars are typically refined at run time using some statistical model. The details of how different types of grammars work are not something we are concerned with here as this is specific to the implementation of the voice recognition engine. Rule grammars are those grammars that let us define a set of rules that in turn define a limited set of responses from the user. These grammars are implemented successfully today and with little or no user dependence. These are the types of grammars that most voice recognition systems use.

Building VUIs requires knowing one or more of the most prevalent grammar languages. Let us survey some of these.

JSGF

As we have seen throughout this text, when there is a need of a standard syntax, there is typically a solution offered by the Java platform. The need for a standard syntax for grammars is no different: *JSGF*, *Java Speech Grammar Format*, is one of the more popular grammar formats supported by voice recognition platforms today. It should be noted that although JSGF uses similar syntax to Java, it can be used by non-Java-based systems. In fact, in those cases where the grammar is to be compiled dynamically at run time, it may be a wise decision to have native code perform the compilation to improve performance. JSGF is a rule grammar.

JSGF is designed to syntactically define the possible components of an *utterance* (*any block of speech that can be marked by a starting and an ending point*). Now, let us get started in understanding how to create JSGF grammars and then we will learn to use them.

Naming

As in the case of a programming language, rule grammars are written in a human-readable format in text and saved into files. There are a set of rules to be followed for the naming of these files and the grammars that go into them based on how grammars are going to be used and their contents. These naming conventions tend to be specific to the grammar language.

Example 7.1: Simple JSGF Grammar.

```
#JSGF V1.0;

grammar com.cienecs.yes_no;

// Body
public <YES_NO> = (Yes | No) *;
```

In the case of JSGF, the conventions of the Java programming language are used to build the name of the grammars. Specifically, there are two concepts: package names and grammar names. Package names are a dot-separated string representing the directory structure in which the grammar file exists. Each grammar file represents a single grammar only. Example 7. 1 shows a very simple JSGF grammar. The grammar file has one or more header lines at the top. The first line of the header must be a directive that specifies the version, character encoding, and locale of the grammar. The format for this line is as follows"

```
# JSGF version char-encoding locale
```

Specifying the version is necessary for the obvious reason of compatibility among different versions of the syntax if and when the grammar language is changed for different versions. Character encoding and locale go hand-in-hand. As in the case of Java programming language, locale and character encoding provide us with a method of providing multiple grammars for one or more locales (geographical locations with a particular set of characteristics) that may require one or more character sets for one or more languages spoken in those locales. This directive makes it possible to determine which grammars should be chosen when the voice recognition system first starts up or, in the case of more robust systems, dynamically at run time.

The second line of our header in Example 7.1 shows the name of the grammar. Every JSGF grammar can be referred to by two names: a *full grammar name* or a *simple grammar name*. The simple grammar name is just the name of the grammar, in the case of our example, it is *yes_no*. The full grammar name includes the package name, in our case *com.cienecs*. Packaging is used primarily for organizing the grammars and name resolutions. Let us say, for example, that we want to have two different sets of grammars, one for more formal direct dialogue interactions with the user and the other for more informal mixed-initiative interactions. They could both be named yes_no, but packaged differently, for example, *com.cienecs.formal.yes_no* and *com.cienecs.informal.yes_no*. Then, the package can be selected based on some configuration settings or other rules and the proper grammar can be used. For those familiar with the Java programming language, the full grammar name is similar to the fully qualified name of a class and the simple grammar name is similar to the name of the class by itself.

The last line of our simple example shows a rule. Every grammar is made up of one or more rules. Every rule has a name and a scope. Only those grammars that are public are exposed to the other grammars and can be used through composition. In JSGF, the rule begins with a scooping keyword (such as public in our example) and is followed by the name of the grammar enclosed in <>. Rule names can be anything but <NULL> or <VOID>. <NULL> defines a rule that is automatically matched, that is, matched without the user speaking any word; <VOID> defines a rule that can never be spoken. Inserting <VOID> into a sequence automatically makes that sequence unspeakable [JSGF 2002]. <NULL> and <VOID> are used mostly for development purposes or for situations where the grammar is dynamically (at run time or startup time) recompiled based on a set of application-dependent rules.

The remainder of the last statement in our example is how the rule is defined. We will look at the syntax for building the rules in the next section.

Rules and Tokens

Tokens, also sometimes referred to as slots, are the placeholder for what the user may say. In a purely directed-dialogue situation, tokens are typically just various individual words that the user may say. As the interaction becomes more natural, these tokens can be used to represent incidentals, markers, words, phrases, or sentences.

An individual token is only one word, but incidental, or marker, multiple tokens can be put together to make a sentence. Example 7.2 shows how we put together the words "could" and "be" to get "could be," one possible answer to the system when the user wants to give an uncertain yes answer. Tokens are separated by spaces. The other characters seen in the rule allow combining the tokens. Table 7.1 outlines what each one of these symbols mean as well as some keywords in the JSGF syntax.

Example 7.2: Simple JSGF Grammar.

```
#JSGF V1.0;

grammar com.cienecs.yes_no_maybe;

// Body
public <YES_NO> = (Yes | No) *;
public <MAYBE>=(Possibly | Maybe | Could be | It's Probably) *;
```

This wraps up the summary of the most important syntactical points in JSGF. Next, we look at modularization of grammars into cleanly separated components that we can put together to build VUIs.

Nesting

Building a VUI of any significance requires a large set of interactions with the user. In a way, the number of permutations of dialogues with the user is directly proportional to the number of grammars. So, when building a VUI, modularization of grammars is something fairly critical. Modularization of grammars not only allows us to break up large unmanageable grammar files into smaller manageable ones but also allows an easier and methodical tuning of the individual grammars for a better VUI.

Table 7.1. Symbols Used in Building Grammar Rules

Symbol	Definition
<>	As we mentioned previously, the greater and less than signs are used to enclose the name of the grammar.
“”	Quotation marks are used to encapsulate written words that are to be said in a single word utterance. For example, the word “Los Angeles” should be enclosed in quotation marks to clarify the fact that it is one word and to provide a mechanism to distinguish it from individual pronunciations of Los and Angeles.
\	The back slash is used as an escape character for other symbols. For example, if you want a quotation mark (") to be part of the grammar, then it must be included as \" When dealing with symbols, however, this type of usage is discouraged. Most recognizers deal better with “ampersand” than “\&.” Besides, seldom does a good VUI need to use symbols because symbols are more relevant to written language than they are to spoken language. There are, however, exceptions, such as possessives in the English language. Depending on the voice recognition engine, “Bob's” or “Bob\'s” may be acceptable.
;	The definition of every rule must be terminated with a semicolon. Many programming languages such as Java follow this convention.
//	Two forward slashes are used to include a single comment line. They must be placed in the beginning of the comment and can be placed inline after the code.
/	Whether dealing with a directed-dialogue or a more natural user interface, there may be several different choices for the same thing. For example, a rule call YES may have “yeah,” “yes,” or “yep” as possible answers. The probability of some answers being given by the user is more than the probabilities for others. This may be application or context dependent. We may not know the various probabilities until we have deployed and tuned the system (which will be discussed later during the chapter) or we may know the probabilities fairly accurately based on the application. Regardless, there may be probabilities associated with each possible answer. This probability is referred to as a “weight.” For our example, we could have a 10% chance of the user saying “yep,” a 60% chance of the user saying “yes,” and a 28% chance of the user saying “yeah” (with the remainder due to errors or other ways of saying “yes” not accommodated by the particular grammar).

(*continued*)

Table 7.1 (continued)

<table>
<tr><th>Symbol</th><th>Definition</th></tr>
<tr><td></td><td>The forward slash (/) is used to enclose a wait associated with a token in a rule. Therefore, our rule YES would be

public <YES> = (/10/ yep | /60/ yes | /28/ yeah);

In JSGF, all of the weights must be positive floating-point numbers or zero and at least one of them must not be zero. There are no other restrictions on the total amount of the weights dictated by JSGF; however, there may be restrictions imposed by the voice recognition system. Not abiding by those restrictions should simply render the weights useless as opposed to causing a compilation error. As a rule of thumb, it is a good idea, for the reasons of readability of code, to stay with the same numbering system throughout all of the grammars for a given system (so, if you use the weights to represent a percent-based probability, then the weights of a given rule should add up to be 100 or less).</td></tr>
<tr><td>()</td><td>Parentheses are used to group subsections of rules and to set precedence for resolution of tokens. For example, in

public <YES_NO> = (Yes | Yep | Yeah) (Please)

the user will be expected to give two answers. The first word will be recognized to match Yes, Yep, or Yeah. The second word will be recognized to match Please. Parentheses may not be left empty.</td></tr>
<tr><td>[]</td><td>Brackets are used to enclose optional tokens. They are particularly useful for incidentals and markers used in speech. Let us look at an example:

public <NATURAL_YES_NO> = [Please | hmmm | well] (Yes | Yep | Yeah) [Please | Thank You]

Optional grouping functionality represented by the brackets in JSGF gives us a very important tool to begin developing a more natural interface. As you can see in this quick example, the user may say a variety of things such as

Hmmm, Yes Please.
Yes Please.
Yes Thank You.
Hmmm, Yep.

or a variety of other combinations and return a proper recognition. As in the case of parentheses, brackets may not be left empty.</td></tr>
</table>

<table>
<tr><th>Symbol</th><th>Definition</th></tr>
<tr><td>*</td><td>The Kleene star (*) is used to indicate that a given token can happen zero or more times. For example, a user may say

Yes, Yes, Yes

This could be accommodated by the following grammar:

public <YES> = (Yes | Yeap | Yeah) *;

The Kleene star is one of the three unary operators (operators that work on one token or one group of tokens).</td></tr>
<tr><td>+</td><td>Another unary operator is the plus sign. It indicates that a token may occur one or more times. The only difference between this operator and the Kleene star is that the token has to occur at least once.</td></tr>
<tr><td>{}</td><td>Curly brackets are used to indicate the third and last type of unary operator in JSGF, namely tags. Tags are used as a mechanism for application-specific values. Their primary purpose is to return a value when a token is satisfied. For example, if we have a rule

public <YES> = (Yes {YES} | Yep {YES})*;

the value returned to the application is "YES" whether the user says "Yes" or "Yep." Tags are associated with the tokens that they follow immediately.</td></tr>
<tr><td>=</td><td>The equal sign is used to separate the name of a rule from its definition.</td></tr>
<tr><td>public</td><td>The public keyword is used to specify that a rule can be referred to externally by other rules. If a rule is not preceded by the public keyword, it is not exposed to other grammars, in the same package or other packages, that may want to use it.</td></tr>
<tr><td>/* comment */</td><td>As in the Java programming language, /* and */ are used to enclose single or multiple lines of comments in the grammar.</td></tr>
<tr><td>grammar</td><td>The grammar keyword precedes the simple or fully qualified name of the grammar. It is recommended that a packaging scheme is always used for grammars to promote reusability of the grammars.</td></tr>
<tr><td>import</td><td>The import keyword allows importing all of the rules of one grammar into another grammar. Use of "import" enables composition of grammars. We will look at nesting rules and grammars in the next section.</td></tr>
</table>

(continued)

Table 7.1 (continued)

Symbol	Definition
@	The @ symbol is used to create Java-Doc (documentation enclosed inside the code as a part of a documentation standard for Java programming language) style documentation for your grammars. Namely, it may be followed by the keywords *author*, which defines the author of the grammar; *version*, which defines the version of the grammar; *example*, which can allow the developer to include sample rules; and *see*, which points to the other grammars that have some relationship to the particular grammar at hand.

We have already looked at the "import" statement, which allows us to import one grammar definition set into another grammar definition set, thereby using rules from one in the other. JSGF also provides a syntactical naming convention to refer to rules from within other rules. Namely, we can refer to a rule, by reference, through usage of the rule name enclosed in <>:

```
public <YES> = (yes | yep | yeah)+;
public <INCIDENTAL>= (please | "thank you" | sure);
public <NATRUAL_YES> = <INCIDENTAL>* <YES>+ <INCIDENTAL>*;
```

In the first two rules, we define a set of words that can be used to respond as YES and another set of rules for the incidental words used to express politeness. Because the rules to express politeness may be used in a variety of contexts, it may be that we want to put them in a separate grammar file and include them, through the use of the import statement, in other grammar files. So, without having to redefine the politeness incidentals, we have defined a rule that defines them, then referred to it in our new rule NATURAL_INCIDENTALS. Example 7.3 puts some of the tools in JSGF to work to produce a grammar that uses other grammars.

Example 7.3: Building Modular Grammars.

```
# JSGF V1.0 ISO8859-1 en;

grammar com.cienecs.examples.voice.home_automation;
import <com.cienecs.examples.voice.basic.YES >;
import <com.cienecs.examples.voice.incidentals.politeness>;

/**
  * @author   Reza B'Far
  * @see      com.cienecs.examples.voice.basic.YES
  */

public <LIGHTS_ON>=<YES>* <POLITENESS_INCIDENTALS>* turn*
  lights on
```

Example 7.4: Building Recursive Grammars in JSGF.

```
# JSGF V1.0 ISO8859-1 en;

grammar com.cienecs.examples.voice.home_automation;
import <com.cienecs.examples.voice.basic.ON >;
import <com.cienecs.examples.voice.incidentals.politeness>;

/**
  * @author   Reza B'Far
  * @see      com.cienecs.examples.voice.basic.ON
  */

public <LIGHTS > = on* <POLITENESS_INCIDENTALS>* off*
  lights on;
public <LIGHTS_RECURSE> = <LIGHTS_RECURSE>* (on | off)*
  <LIGHTS_RECURSE>*;
public <LIGHTS_ON> = <ON> | <LIGHTS_NEST_RECURSE>;
public <LIGHTS_ NEST_RECURSE> = another thing <LIGHTS_ON>;
```

The last significant form of nesting is *recursion*. Using recursion in grammars is not for the faint of heart. It can cause bugs and slow down performance if not used properly. However, it can be a powerful tool in building complex grammars. It is also important to note that recursion is not a feature supported by all voice recognition engines.

There are two types of recursion in JSGF, *right recursion* and *nested right recursion*. Let us say that you want to turn a light on and off *n* times in one interaction with the system. This would mean that an utterance could be something like "on please, off, on." Now, if *n* is a constant, say three, we can write a grammar such as that in rule LIGHTS of Example 7.4. But, if *n* is a variable, we need to use recursion. This is demonstrated by the rule LIGHTS_RECURSE. This is an example of the right recursion in a grammar.

In the same example, LIGHTS_ON and LIGHTS_NEST_RECURSE show an example of nested right recursion in which LIGHTS_ON refers to LIGHTS_NEST_RECURSE and LIGHTS_NEST_RECURSE refers back to LIGHTS_ON. Use of nested right recursion is strongly discouraged except for those cases when it is absolutely necessary to simplify overly complicated grammars.

This wraps up our discussion of JSGF. Obviously, this is not a comprehensive discussion of JSGF; Sun Microsystems provides extensive documentation freely available to developers if you are looking at a voice recognition system that uses JSGF.

W3C Speech Grammar Specification

W3C, whose standards we have discussed several times previously in this text, has started a speech recognition grammar standard based on JSGF, but more platform-independent in nature. This standard is simply called the W3C Speech Grammar Specification. Because it has been based on JSGF, we will simply point out the differences between the W3C Speech Grammar Specification and JSGF:

1. W3C Speech Grammar Specification provides two formats: Automated BNF (Backus-Naur Form) Syntax (ABNF) and XML based. The two formats can be linearly mapped and transformed. Obviously, the XML format is more verbose as it has a series of tags surrounding the grammar syntax elements; however, there is an advantage to this method: The grammar can be parsed by any XML parser. Although the ABNF syntax is the one that is nearly syntactically identical to JSGF, the XML format is, in spirit, the same. The following tags are used to wrap the elements of concern to us:
   a. <ruleref>: This is the tag that specifies a rule. You can think of this as the equivalent to a rule name tag.
   b. <token>: This tag is used to identify a token to be recognized.
   c. <item>: Items wrap tokens and their attributes (such as their weight attribute).
   d. <one-of>: This element wraps around several items and it has the same effect as the or gate (|) in ABNF syntax.
   e. <grammar>: This tag specifies the version of the grammar and the language of the grammar, points to the schema to validate the grammar, and finally adds a mode attribute (see item 3).
2. Referencing rules, created by a naming and packaging mechanism similar to that of Java, are also provided as a URI-based mechanism in W3C Speech Grammars:
   a. The dollar sign ($) is used in the ABNF format to refer to rules: $rulename. A tag called ruleref is used to refer to rules in the XML format: <ruleref uri="grammarname#rulename">.
   b. An additional special rule called GARBAGE is provided (remember that the two special rules in JSGF were NULL and VOID). Garbage provides a token that matches any utterance until that utterance is ended and the next one is started. The next token is used for the next utterance.
3. Whether the user is giving the system input through voice or some other audio input such as DTMF tones is left outside of JSGF. The W3C Grammar Specification pulls this in and provides a mechanism to specify whether the input is voice or DTMF. (In this way, if there are other possible audio inputs to a voice recognition system in the future, extension is done by a simple change of the XML Schema to accept additional alternatives for the attribute). This is done through a mode command in the ABNF format (e.g., mode voice;) and a mode attribute for the <grammar> tag in the XML format.
4. W3C grammars also allow specification of lexical pronunciations of tokens in the rules of the grammars. These lexical pronunciations can be fed into a voice recognition system to extend its recognizable vocabulary set. Documents that hold lexical pronunciation information are referred to through the URI mechanism. In the ABNF format, they are represented as a single line: lexicon http://grammars.cienecs.com/examples/yeap.lex; In the XML format, they are represented as an example element: <lexicon uri=http://grammars.cienecs.com/examples/yeap.lex>

5. As may be expected, the W3C Grammar Specification also adds metadata capabilities to the starting base of JSGF. This is done so that we can find out information about the grammar files without having to look at the lexical content of those files. There are two types of metadata in W3C grammars. The first is a metatag equivalent to the http-equiv tag. This tag is basically used to add metadata in name–value pair format to the grammar document. Because the format is unstructured (simple name–value pairs), it can be represented in either the ABNF or XML formats. Name–value pairs can be an inefficient method of storing metadata because metadata may have structure and complexity beyond simple name–value pairs. It is also possible to add XML metadata to W3C grammars; however, this is only possible in the XML representation of the grammar
6. Comments in the ABNF format are identical to those in JSGF. In the XML format, XML-style comments, enclosed between <!-- and --> are used.

There is extensive documentation on the Web, particularly on the W3C site, on W3C grammars. Though JSGF is more prevalent across most voice recognition platforms, W3C will grow as it is a bit more comprehensive and very similar, in syntax, to JSGF.

Though there are a variety of syntaxes for representing grammars, they are not much different than JSGF and W3C grammars. There are a couple of common problems with grammars when developing VUIs of any significant size:

1. Porting VUIs from one platform to another is often problematic because of lack of documentation and modeling for the grammars. Porting grammars from one platform to another often means reverse engineering every grammar, sometimes prohibiting migration from one voice recognition platform to another.
2. Grammars can grow in complexity exponentially as they are nested, reused, and changed over the life cycle of the VUI development project or during the maintenance of the system.

These two problems, particularly the second, give rise to an entirely new set of problems. One of the most time-consuming processes in designing VUIs is the tuning process; the complexity of grammars or porting them between platforms can render the tuning process indefinitely long. UML was not designed to represent grammars, but we are going to try to use it to address some of these problems because it gives us a series of graphical tools to tie grammars with the other parts of the system.

Representing VUI Grammars in UML

Though grammars are not objects, they are often organized as classes are organized in OOP languages. So, let us compare grammars and classes:

1. Grammars in JSGF and W3C grammars have rules with well-defined scopes and can be nested. These two properties enable grammars to display the same type of behavior as aggregation and composition in OOP.

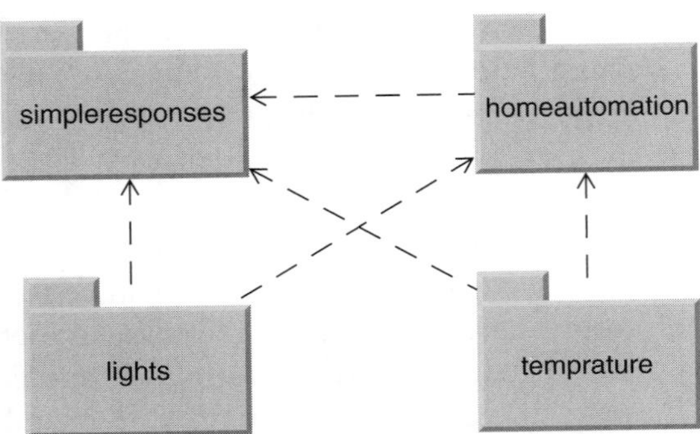

FIGURE 7.7. Representing Grammar Packages in UML.

2. To keep grammar files under control, making them into logical groups is recommended. These logical groupings resemble name spaces (also known as packages) in object-oriented languages.
3. A grammar has one or more rules. These rules encapsulate data as well as logic. However, the invocation of the logic is not done through delegation of method calls. In this way, grammars differ from classes. Grammars are typically compiled into something understandable by the voice recognition program. They are then used, at startup time or run time, by the voice recognition engine.
4. As we noted, grammar rules can have weights associated with the tokens that make up the rules. Classes do not have anything that compares to this, though it is possible to create name–value pairs that model these weights in UML.

Because of the structure of grammars, we can represent them with class diagrams. Let us walk through an example.

Example 7.5: A Simple Grammar Representing "Yes," "No," and "Maybe."

```
# JSGF V1.0 ISO8859-1 en;

grammar com.cienecs.examples.homeautomation.yes_no_maybe;
import <com.cienecs.examples.simpleresponses.YES >;
import <com.cienecs.examples.simpleresponses.NO>;
import <com.cienecs.examples.simpleresponses.MAYBE>;

public <YES_NO_MAYBE> = (<YES>* | <NO>* | <MAYBE>*);
```

Example 7.5 outlines a JSGF grammar representing the answer to a simple question such as "Would you like to eat dinner now?" There are three options: Yes, No, and Maybe. As we saw earlier, there are multiple ways of saying Yes and this is defined in the grammar com.cienecs.YES; there are multiple ways of saying No and this is defined in the grammar com.cienecs.NO; and so on. First, we see that this grammar is in a particular package and uses grammars in other packages. The diagram in Figure 7.7 shows how we may model the relationship among the packages to which the individual grammars belong.

Then, we need to show the relationship between the grammars inside the packages, in our case the individual grammars YES, NO, MAYBE, and YES_NO_MAYBE.

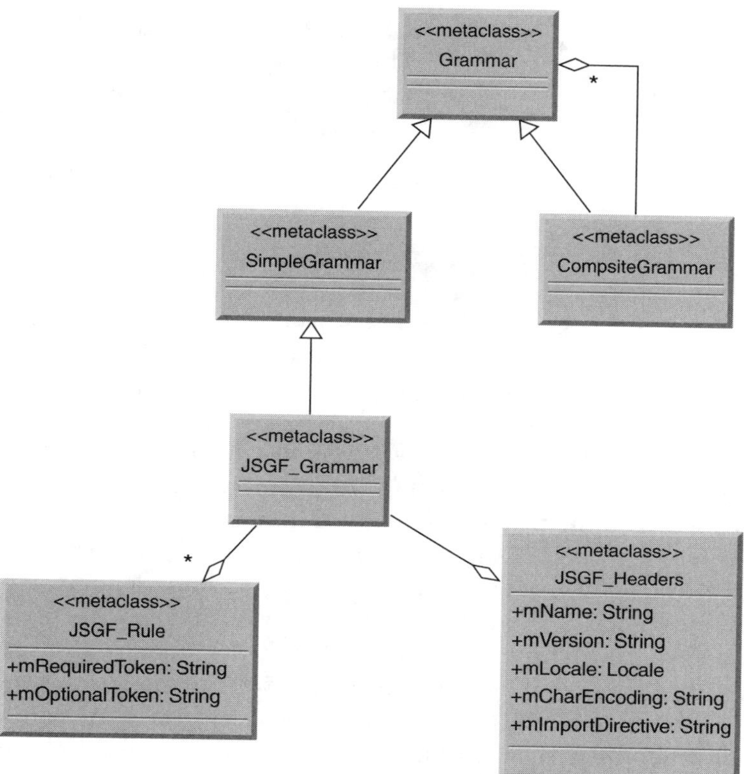

FIGURE 7.8. Suggested Metamodel for JSGF.

But before we move on, we need to think about representing the structure of grammars in UML. We can do this in a few different ways. Let us look at some of the possible alternatives:

1. *Metamodeling*: We can define our own metamodel with our own metaclasses. Unfortunately, to date, there are no standard efforts to create a metamodel that represents grammars, particularly those used in VUIs, in UML. Figure 7.8 shows a simple metamodel that we propose for modeling JSGF. This metamodel is not canonical; nor is it part of any standards effort. The UML extension mechanism is flexible enough to allow defining the metamodel for the grammar in a way that fits the needs of a project and the interpretation of the implementers of the project. Metamodels give us a clean and layered way of representing grammars; unfortunately, lack of efforts in standardization may cause problems. In our example, we have simply used a class diagram representing the metaclasses for JSGF grammars. The graphical widgets of your choice may be added for additional graphical support in modeling grammars though it is probably not necessary.
2. *OCL*: OCL may be used to define custom constraints on attributes and behavior of objects and their defining classes. The use of OCL in representing grammars has the advantage of representing the grammar independent of implementation syntax such as JSGF. However, OCL itself is a textual, not a graphical, language.

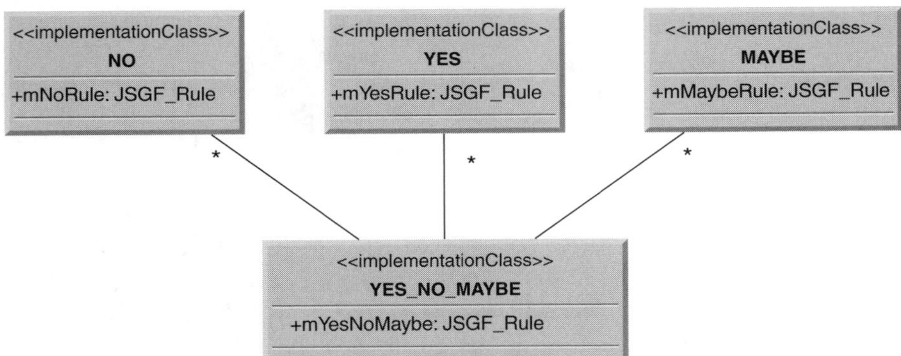

FIGURE 7.9. Using UML Class Diagrams to Model Grammars.

Therefore, it does not do much in the way of reducing complexity; in fact, if anything, using OCL to represent VUI grammars probably adds complexity. OCL is not something that we recommend in representing VUI grammars.

3. *Class Diagrams*: Figure 7.8 shows a metamodel-level class diagram of what JSGF grammars are, but we can represent grammars without defining a metamodel layer. The advantage here is that nothing is created, at the metamodel layer, that is not standard. The disadvantage is that there is no separation of concerns between the definition of JSGF and an instance of a JSGF grammar (because we cannot really use objects to represent an instance of JSGF grammars as we may use them in representing an instance of a class as grammars are classes and not inherently time dependent).

Figure 7.9 shows an instance of the metamodel of Figure 7.8 for the YES_NO_MAYBE grammar we outlined in Example 7.5. Note that we have used association links as opposed to aggregation links. Because grammars are really not instantiated the same way as classes are to create objects, using aggregation to model relationships between various grammars may imply too much. Therefore, we use associations, which give us a looser definition of dependency between different classes. In our case, of course, we do not have classes, but grammars. Associations are also a better method of modeling relationships between grammars as grammars use the rules defined in other grammars as opposed to using other grammars in their entirety.

Also, note that the multiplicity (Kleene star) is used to indicate that grammar YES_NO_MAYBE can use each one of the subgrammars multiple times.

It is also possible to define grammars without an underlying metamodel by simple use of classes, defining all of the things that make up a grammar (tokens, rules, headers, etc.) as data members of the classes. Such use is still useful although not as semantically correct when looking at UML and where the meta-metamodel, the metamodel, and the model layers exits. By representing grammars at the model layer, we would ignore the difference in the "type" of things that grammars are from all other things that UML may be used for. Although semantically incorrect, remember that the more important goals of using UML in building mobile applications are to maintain consistency, to provide a platform-independent way of representing application logic and structure, and to create a uniform way of documenting. It is important to maintain the semantics of UML so that we are not creating our own modeling language; nevertheless, we must balance this with practical application of UML as a tool to enhance the development process and not another layer of complexity. Therefore, any of the suggested methods can be used to represent grammars in UML based on the specific application. UML tool makers may even decide to provide their own widgets corresponding to a particular metamodel (which would be very helpful in providing a unique way of visually representing grammars). Meanwhile, this is too much work for an end user (mobile application developer) who may choose to represent grammars with no metamodel in simple class diagrams.

Grammars for Mobile Applications

As we have defined in this section, grammars help us to decompose the elements of one or more utterances and to recognize the contextual meaning of the utterances and/or the parts of the utterances. We also mentioned that the interactions of a user with a VUI may be different between mobile and stationary users. So, this brings us to try to see if there are differences between grammars of mobile applications and their stationary counterparts. Of course, the answer is yes. Let us see what those differences are by enumerating those dimensions of mobility that have an effect on grammars:

1. *Localization*: As we have seen, both JSGF and W3C grammars allow for specification of some locale-based information. This is particularly crucial in the case of mobile applications. For example, an application may use Euro's as the monetary unit in one region while offering Pounds in another region. As the user may move from one location to another, the application should provide the appropriate grammar for the user to perform a transaction. The location information can be provided by the mobile device or the user may need to provide the information; regardless, the applications may need to provide the functionality. Therefore, providing the grammars for the appropriate locale is a necessity for VUIs designed for mobile applications and not a nicety as in the case of their stationary counterparts. Tuning the grammars is also a locale-dependent process as users have different accents in different locales or use slightly different dialects of the language (for example, there are subtle, but apparent differences in the accents and use of the English language between southeastern and southwestern states in the United States).
2. *Higher Use of Discourse Markers and Incidentals*: The mobile user is not focused on the task of computing. Therefore, he or she is much more apt to use unnecessary words. For example, the mobile user may be a passenger in a car who is carrying out a conversation with someone else in the car as well as using the VUI. Because of this lack of focus, the user is more apt to use words such as "hmmm," "shoot," "well," "wait," "ok," etc.
3. *Effects of QOS*: There are two side effects on the VUI when the QOS of the connectivity of a mobile user is low. First, if the mobile user is connected to the network through a wireless connection, the quality of signal may go down

to a point where the SNR is not acceptable for recognition. In such cases, it is recommended that the VUI be designed to slowly move away from a natural language–based VUI to a DTMF-based VUI. Machine-generated tones are much easier to recognize and have much less stringent SNR requirements. In other cases, the user may be losing signal intermittently altogether. Mobile VUIs should be designed to detect this and to dynamically adjust themselves to present more concise prompts while presenting the user with more clear options. This implies that the size of the grammars should decrease as does the QOS. Although many of today's voice recognition engines are designed to take into account noise levels for wireless connections, it is important for the VUI designers to understand that a mobile application delivering a piece of functionality and accessible through a VUI may have a different set of grammars than a stationary application delivering the same set of functionality.

VUIs are affected in more ways than just this by the mobile condition of the user and the dimensions of mobility but at higher granularity levels than the grammars and rules that make them up. We will look at these effects next.

Now that we have a basic understanding of how to build grammars in JSGF or W3C grammars for a basic VUI interaction, we next need to look at a method to build scripts that enable a voice recognition system to perform a series of interactions with the user.

7.4.2 Building VUI Interactions

Grammars help us break down a given response by the user, but a VUI is created by putting a series of prompts presented based on the responses given one after the other. So, the next thing we will look at is how to build VUIs by using some of the more popular languages and techniques used in the industry today. To understand the motivations behind some of the design principles used in the various languages that we will look at, let us first look at some basic properties of VUIs.

VUIs are inherently state driven. As we discussed in Chapter 5, State Machines are one of the most popular mechanisms for implementing user interfaces in general, but they fit VUIs particularly well. This is because a VUI consists of a serial set of interactions with the user where the user is presented with a series of questions or requests and gives the system a series of responses. These responses are the triggers that change the state of the user interface. Because of this, IVR systems, the first generation of computer systems that allowed users to interact with the system through voice, have typically had development environments that basically provide a mechanism for the interface developer to construct a state chart of the user interface.

Although State Machine UIMs are the choice for those VUIs, using strictly directed-dialogue, grammar-based UIMs prove useful for those VUIs that involve more natural interactions with the user. As you may recall from Chapter 5, grammar-based UIMs are used to represent interactions that involve parsing of some response to match a given set of grammar rules. Earlier in this chapter, we also mentioned that a complete, user-independent, natural language–based

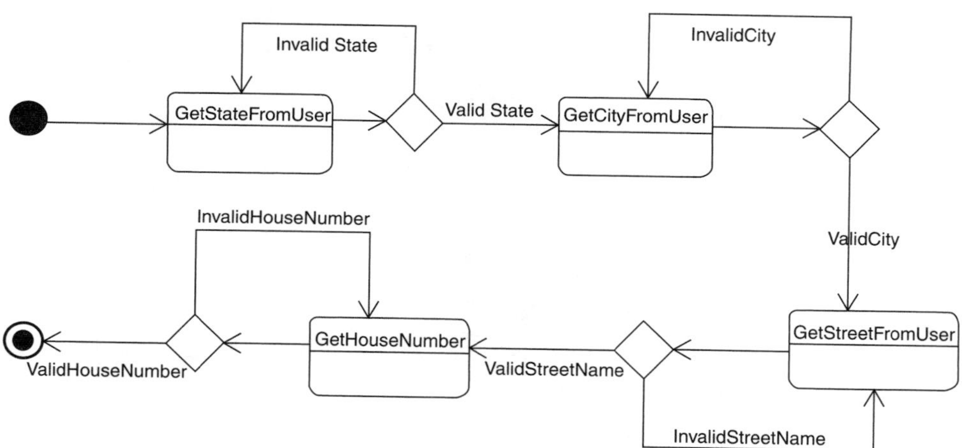

FIGURE 7.10. UML State Diagram for Obtaining a User's Address.

user interface is not possible with today's voice recognition and/or transcription technologies. So, we can draw the following conclusions regarding VUI UIMS:

1. Grammar-based UIM's are architecturally well suited for building very natural VUIs. If the underlying infrastructure of such a system relies on voice recognition, grammars are required to limit the vocabulary used in the interactions. For automated voice transcription, when and if it becomes a reality, grammars will help in defining what may be a valid or an invalid input to the system by the user.
2. As we mentioned previously, full-fledged natural language–based VUIs are not a commercial reality today. At the opposite end of the spectrum are the directed dialogue–based systems. In a purely directed dialogue–based environment, State Machine UIMs make the most sense. These systems are available today; in fact, the great majority of IVR systems are based on such systems. Figure 7.10 shows a simple state chart that may be used by a State Machine UIM for obtaining a user's address.
3. Building mixed-initiative VUIs requires using an overall architecture that most resembles the State Machine UIMs of directed-dialogue systems but includes implementation of grammar-based components that operate on the individual natural-language interactions between the user and the system. Whereas navigating between large-grained interactions is handled by a State Machine UIM, the individual small-grained interactions are handled by grammars that are processed by grammar-based components that analyze how many tokens in a given rule are filled by a given user response and then ask the user to fill the unfulfilled tokens. Figure 7.11 shows a state chart used to obtain a user's contact information, one of which is the user's address (in a natural language–based interaction as opposed to a directed-dialogue interaction).

Now, before we get started on a real example of how to build a VUI, let us look at some tools and languages that allow us to build them.

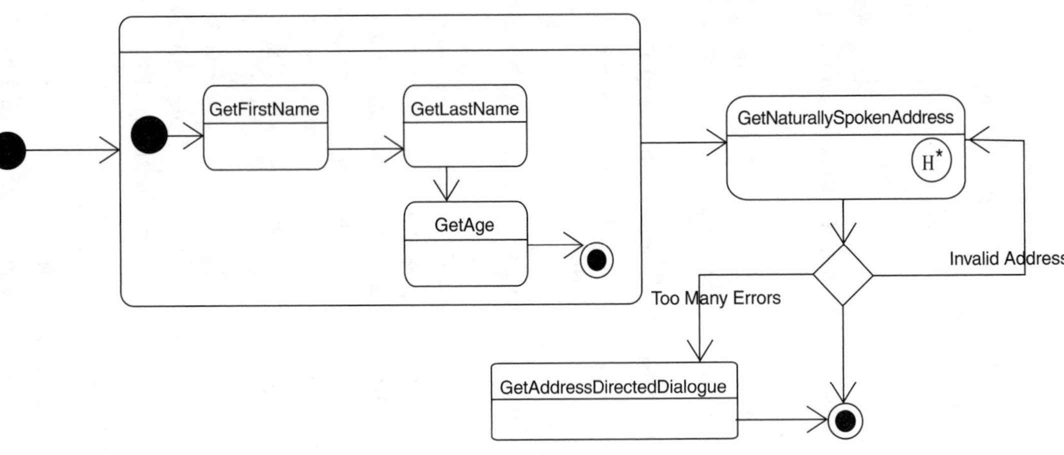

FIGURE 7.11. UML State Diagram for Obtaining a User's Personal Information.

Custom Application		Custom Application		Custom Application		Custom Application	
Third-Party IDEs and Development Environment (BeVocal, TellMe, Voice Genesis, etc.)							
Java	C++	Java	C++	Java	C++	Java	C++
Nuance		IBM		SpeechWorks		Others	

FIGURE 7.12. Building VUIs Directly on Vendor-Based Voice Recognition Systems.

Languages for Building a VUI

Figure 7.12 shows tools and languages that can be used on some of the more popular speech recognition and synthesis platforms to build a VUI. Figure 7.13 shows the same thing but eliminates the use of middle-man service providers such as BeVocal or TellMe. So far, we have seen that we recognize user utterances based on grammars and that a state-driven UIM is the basic infrastructure that will control our VUI components. There are two basic approaches to building VUIs:

1. *Build applications that interact with the voice recognition system directly*: We can build the VUI to model the State Machine or build our own State Machine infrastructure. Either way, we would have to use some API to directly communicate with the voice channel to obtain the voice data and some other API to communicate with the voice recognition system to hand it the voice input (in real time or batched) as well as specifying the grammar for the voice input.
2. *Leverage existing frameworks on top of voice recognition systems*: Software refactoring techniques show us that we need to factor out the commonalities that various problems share and build tools that allow us to avoid solving the same problems and implementing the same solutions repeatedly. The case is no different for building VUIs than for any other piece of software. There are a variety

Custom Application		Custom Application		Custom Application		Custom Application	
Java	C++	Java	C++	Java	C++	Java	C++
Nuance		IBM		SpeechWorks		Others	

FIGURE 7.13. Building VUIs Using Vendor-Provided APIs.

of tools and frameworks that allow us to expedite building VUIs. They include the following:

a. *IDEs*: IDEs are used in nearly all disciplines of software. They facilitate faster development by automating some development tasks, providing textual and graphical interfaces for faster development, and assisting in the development process (development, debugging, unit testing, etc.). Most vendors of voice recognition systems such as Nuance, IBM, and Speech Works provide IDEs that accompany their voice recognition systems. IDEs that accompany voice recognition systems, however, are typically tightly coupled to the vendor's voice recognition system, providing an environment that is specific to the voice recognition platform. There are also third-party vendors such as TellMe, BeVocal, and others who provide vendor-neutral IDEs. VUI IDEs that offer a GUI typically offer some way of diagramming state diagrams that basically outline the behavior of a State Machine UIM for the particular VUI. An example of this is Nuance's V-Builder, which allows design and implementation of VUIs in a graphical environment that supports state chart notation as specified by Nuance. One of our goals in this text, however, is to push the developer to use UML and its accompanying notation. Because of this, we will model the states of user interface components with UML state diagrams instead of using proprietary notations and tools.
b. *High-Level APIs Using Standard Programming Languages*: The internals of voice recognition systems are typically written in C or assembly because of the high performance requirements. If the internals were to be exposed through an API, the job of developing a VUI would be very difficult as it would require a deep understanding of the operation of voice recognition engines. Besides, vendors are not too keen on exposing too much of the internal APIs as they deem it to be a source of possible leak of the intellectual property used in building the voice recognition implementation. So, most vendors, provide high-level APIs in standard application development languages such as C, C++, and Java that allows straightforward and easy access to the functions of voice recognition systems. For example, Nuance provides Java Speech Objects as well as a C++ API to the Nuance voice recognition engine. Nonetheless, invariably, the vendors produce different interfaces for their APIs partly because the implementations of the voice recognition engines are different and partly because it provides them a way to differentiate their products from competitors. However, this is not a good thing for the consumer, the developer.

   Using proprietary vendor APIs leads to building nonportable VUIs, reducing the choice of changing voice recognition engines during the life of the application, thereby possibly limiting the quality of delivery of a solution to the end consumer. There are efforts to eliminate this problem through specifying APIs and allowing vendors to implement the APIs. The most successful of these efforts to date has been the Java Speech APIs. Much like the other standard Java APIs, a group of industry experts and vendors gathered and decided on the interface of the APIs that a vendor must implement to provide a Java Speech API interface.

c. *Integration with Various Telephony Hardware*: One of the routine tasks that has to be done upon every interaction with the user is to capture the voice and send it to the voice recognition system. We may also have to get the speech produced by the text-to-speech engine and play it over whatever audio channel is provided to interact with the user. So, integration with the audio channel providers becomes crucial. Audio channels may be telephony systems (POTS, cellular telephony, etc.) accessed by phones, microphones, or other hardware. Most voice recognition and text-to-speech systems today provide this integration with the popular hardware platforms. This has two advantages. First, the performance of the integration between the voice recognition or text-to-speech platforms is tuned by their vendors on the various hardware platforms. Second, and more importantly, the application developer does not have to be concerned with dealing with the audio channel and the related hardware (such as the telephony channel and the hardware to support it).

   Integration with telephony hardware or other audio channels such as sound cards affects the APIs accessed by the VUI application that interfaces with the user. Support for the appropriate hardware must be checked prior to the start of development. Depending on the audio channel hardware and types of channels supported by the combination of the voice platform and the hardware that it is to run on, the development cycle may be affected as well because frequent unit testing often requires use of sound cards as opposed to a telephony channel.

d. *Voice Browsers*: After the success of the Web, the idea of a thin client proliferated into various software development fields, one being VUI development. Voice browsers allow the interpretation of a markup language that outlines voice output to the user as well as accepting voice input for recognition. VXML is the most popular of these markup languages and the only standard markup language (ratified by W3C and implemented by vendors of most voice recognition platforms). There are other proprietary markup languages such as SALT sponsored by Microsoft. The downside of a proprietary markup language such as SALT is loss of portability across voice platforms. VXML and SALT are competing technologies. Whereas VXML fits within the bigger picture of the markup languages designed by the W3C, design and implementation of SALT has been driven primarily by Microsoft and with the specific purpose of offering VUIs to Microsoft-specific infrastructure. When it comes to our examples, we will use VXML. We recommend that you do so too for implementation of your VUIs.

Now, we will try to build some simple user interfaces using each one of these techniques.

Speech and Call Control with High-Level APIs

Figure 7.14 expands on Figures 7.12 and 7.13: it shows how we can layer VUI applications if we use XML as the binding between our custom application and the voice platforms. As we previously discussed, one approach to building VUI

Custom Application	Custom Application	Custom Application	Custom Application
Browser (VXML, CCML, and other ML Support)	Browser (VXML, CCML, and other ML Support)	Browser (VXML, CCML, and other ML Support)	Browser (VXML, CCML, and other ML Support)
Java | C++	Java | C++	Java | C++	Java C++ | Other
Nuance	IBM	SpeechWorks	Others
TTS | VR | CC	TTS | VR | CC	TTS | VR | CC	TTS | VR | CC

FIGURE 7.14. Building VUIs Using an Integrated Environment of TTS, Voice Recognition, and Telephony Platforms.

applications is to use high-level APIs that allow access to the voice infrastructure: voice recognition system, speech-synthesis system, audio channels, and all of the other basic necessary technologies to create voice interactions with the user.

These APIs are either specified by a standards body and implemented by the vendors or specified and provided by the vendors themselves.

When building a VUI, there are currently two practical approaches. The first is to use the high-level speech and call control APIs provided by the vendors. The second is to use markup languages and build so-called voice browsers using the first tool: the high-level speech and call control APIs.

Vendor-Based APIs

Vendor-based APIs are the first set of APIs through which VUI developers were able to access the functionality of speech-synthesis engines and voice recognition systems. These APIs are typically provided in C, C++, or Java programming languages and allow access to the speech recognition engine, speech-synthesis engine, and an underlying telephony platform if one is applicable (where the audio channel can be a microphone or something else).

An example of such an API is the Nuance Speech Object APIs. Nuance Speech Objects provide object-oriented APIs on top of the Nuance C/C++ APIs that provide access to the Nuance voice recognition system.

The speech object APIs provide a framework to build a VUI as components in a State Machine–based UIM. Specifically, the APIs provide classes such as SODialog, SORecord, and others that are to be extended (through inheritance). To provide the proper behavior in the user interface, a specified set of methods must be overridden; a behavior is specialized through overriding of the behavior.

Vendor-provided APIs provide a very rich set of APIs that allow full access to the underlying infrastructure and do much of the work that needs to be done to build a VUI for the application developer. For example, Nuance Speech Objects include implementations of classes that provide intelligent processing of input from the user that is expected to be a date, a number, a choice in a menu, or a telephone number.

Vendor-provided APIs also typically offer little degradation in performance (as a result of the added abstraction layer) as they are tightly coupled with the underlying implementation of the speech platform. Unfortunately, another one of the advantages of vendor-provided APIs—the fact that they are able to provide an API that takes full advantage of all of the features provided by the underlying platform—is also their biggest disadvantage. If you use a vendor-provided API to build your VUI application, you will most probably need to completely rewrite your VUI application if you decide to change infrastructure vendors (for speech-synthesis engine, speech recognition engine, etc.). Let us look at the Java Speech APIs, another offering by the Java platform that aims at making the vendors abide by a canonical set of APIs so as to provide the application developers and customers with more flexibility on their choice of voice platform.

Java Speech APIs

As in the case of other APIs, the Java platform offers a canonical API, agreed upon by the various vendors of speech-related software. JSAPI, or Java Speech APIs, is this canonical API. Although this API is no different than any other API, considering it has two benefits. First, because it has been agreed on by more than one commercial entity, there is less bias in it toward any particular platform implementation. Second, it gives us a good high-level view of what any API may implement in providing access to the underlying technologies for a VUI.

There are three main packages in JSAPI:

1. *javax.speech*: This package provides the infrastructure to connect to the voice channels for input and output and to manage dictionary vocabularies dynamically. It also provides the interfaces that are later used by the other two packages in JSAPI.
2. *javax.speech.synthesis*: As its name may suggest, this package provides an API suitable for providing an interface to speech-synthesis systems. This package provides the utilities to adjust the different values for the quality of speech provided by the speech-synthesis engine for tighter control of the synthesis. It also provides JSML hooks into the system so that the synthesis can be done based on JSML.
3. *javax.speech.recognition*: This package provides the interfaces for managing grammars, rules, recognition results, and the settings of the recognition engine. As may be suspected, it takes advantage of JSGF,

Today, several of the major vendors of speech synthesis and speech recognition software, such as IBM and Lernout & Hauspie, provide JSAPI implementations for their systems.

Perhaps the biggest advantage that JSAPI provides over proprietary vendor APIs is portability. And, portability is so very important when dealing with voice systems in a mobile environment. Currently, the various products available in the marketplace outperform one another depending on the usage. Some voice recognition platforms do a better job than others when recognizing speech input with noise caused by bad wireless QOS. Others do better when recognizing speech input with environmental noise. There are many other variables like this that make the choice of infrastructure platform very much dependent on the business requirements of the application. Therefore, portability is absolutely crucial when dealing with voice applications. JSAPI provides such portability.

It is also important to note that in its 1.0 incarnation, JSAPI was primarily designed to be used as a server-side product (J2SE and J2EE platforms discussed in Chapter 2). JSAPI 2.0, in the process of ratification at the time of authoring this text, is intended to address J2ME. This means that the API will be designed in a modular manner with some modules available for J2ME, J2SE, and J2EE, and other modules available only for the J2SE and J2EE platforms. This also is a sign of more and more of the VUI processing moving to the edge of the network (in our case, the mobile device).

The example in Figure 7.15 provides a sample VUI component authored using JSAPI. Once again, as with Nuance Java Speech Objects, it is very evident that the component is authored as a component using a framework that runs based on a State Machine.

JSAPI provides a speech recognition and synthesis API to access the underlying infrastructure. And though it provides a mechanism to get a handle on the underlying speech channels so that the voice can be acquired for recognition or played back after synthesis, it does not provide a way to manipulate specific types of voice channels such as telephony channels.

Obviously, the most popular method of accessing a VUI is through telephony. Once again, there are a variety of telephony APIs typically referred to as TAPIs. Because we have used various Java-based standards for our examples so far, we will continue in this manner with JTAPI, the part of the Java platform that addresses telephony control. But before we start, keep in mind that when it comes to choosing a telephony platform, it is crucial that some sort of standard API support is available for it. There are telephony vendors whose products are not well supported or who do not provide standard compliant APIs. Telephony equipment and systems are commodities that may need to be changed. It is crucial that the VUI application does not prohibit this by being tightly coupled to a platform without support for standard APIs.

JTAPI

JTAPI version 1.3 takes a comprehensive approach to addressing APIs for telephony call control. Four major categories of problems in call control are treated: basic call control problems, problems associated with mobile telephony systems, problems associated with the various types of media used by the telephony systems, and problems associated with various types of telephony channels (Voice over IP [VoIP], POTS, etc.). As we have done before, let us go through

```
import javax.speech.*;
import javax.speech.recognition.*;

public class Address extends ResultAdapter {
    public static Recognizer mRecognizer = null;
    private String[] mGrammarFileNames = null;
    private RuleGrammar mGrammar = null;

    public void resultAccepted(ResultEvent e) {
        Result myResults = (Result) (e.getSource());
        ResultToken myTokens[] = myResults.getBestTokens();
        /*
         * Do whatever needs to be done with the recognition
           results here
         * (for example, the content may be posted to some
           HTTP Listener).
         */
         mRecognizer.deallocate();
    }

    // This method initializes the handle to the recognition
    // engine as well as the grammars
    public void init() {
        try {
                if (mRecognizer == null) {
                    mRecognizer = Central.createRecognizer(
                        new EngineModeDesc(Locale.ENGLISH));
                }
                mRecognizer.allocate();
                FileReader myGrammarFileReader = new
                  FileReader(mGrammarFileNames);
        } catch (Exception e) {
            e.printStackTrace();
        }
    }

    public void initGrammars() {//load the grammars here}

    // Unit Testing
    public static void main(String[] args) {
        try {
                Address myAddress = new Address();
                myAddress.init();
                mRecognizer.addResultListener(myAddress);
                mRecognizer.commitChanges();
                mRecognizer.requestFocus();
                mRecognizer.resume();
        } catch (Exception e) {
            e.printStackTrace();
        }
    }
}
```

FIGURE 7.15. Sample JSAPI Class.

the JTAPI packages and see the general intent of the classes provided in each packages:

1. *javax.telephony*: This package defines the interfaces for all basic telephony control such as the definition of a source and destination telephony address (a phone number with POTS, an IP address with VoIP, etc.), interfaces for the basic events, and others. All the other packages are included inside this package as extensions.
2. *javax.telephony.callcenter*: Call centers have long been a staple of telephony system applications. Routing, predictive calling, associating data from a call with an application, and call distribution are examples of typical call center functionality. A great deal of functionality offered within this package is typically used for telemarketing applications or customer relationship management (CRM) applications.
3. *javax.telephony.callcontrol*: Call control is one of the most basic functionalities required for handling telephony channels. Examples are conferencing two or more calls and transferring calls.
4. *javax.telephony.capabilities*: This package allows for dynamic discovery of what is possible and what is not possible with the telephony platform and the underlying APIs. It is important to remember that reliability and stability are much more important in VUIs where the user's tolerance and patience are much lower. This package is mostly designed to provide queries that enable the programmer to make sure run-time exceptions are avoided at all costs.
5. *javax.telephony.events*: State Machine UIMs change states of components based on a variety of events. This package defines the interfaces to the basic events in JSAPI. The other individual extensions also include their own events that extend the events in this package to provide more specific functionality.
6. *javax.telephony.mobile*: This package deals specifically with the issues of the telephony channel in mobile networks. Mobile telephony networks such as cellular networks typically have very different underlying infrastructure than typical telephony networks. For example, cellular users can roam to an area where their own network provider does not provide coverage but where another provider that supports a protocol understood by their phone (such as CDMA) does. We will look at this extension in more depth shortly.
7. *javax.telephony.media*: The input and output to the telephony channel may be of a variety of formats. This package provides the basic interfaces for specifying what sort of input to expect (DTMF, voice, etc.), what events to generate depending on the type of media received, and handling of media that is to be streamed over the audio channel back to the user.
8. *javax.telephony.privatedata*: This package is provided to allow the JTAPI application to take advantage of platform-specific functionality (provided by the TAPI layer). Use of this package is discouraged unless absolutely necessary as it can prevent portability of JTAPI applications across different voice infrastructures (because using this package basically circumvents JTAPI).
9. *javax.telephony.phone*: Some telephony infrastructures provide for information about the end telephony device. This information could include the setting on

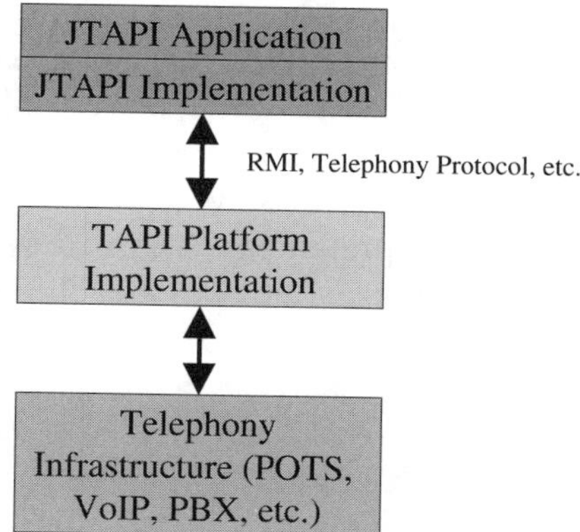

FIGURE 7.16. Typical JTAPI Application Architecture.

the ringer (whether it is set on a high, medium, or low volume), whether there is a graphical display available, and other similar information. Such information can be particularly useful in the case of mobile devices and integration with a multimodal application that provides the user with multiple user interfaces. Keep in mind that currently most of the wired telephony infrastructure does not provide much in the way of advanced functionality in a consistent manner if at all.

JTAPI applications are designed as clients to the server provided by the telephony infrastructure. As you can see in Figure 7.16, the application sits on top of the JTAPI implementation. The JTAPI implementation is the set of classes and accompanying native code that maps the native telephony APIs to JTAPI. The JTAPI Application and JTAPI Implementation in the diagram must reside on the same system whereas the TAPI implementation can be on the same or different system. The communication protocol between the JTAPI implementation and the TAPI implementation depends on the JTAPI implementation.

JTAPI's Mobile Package

We saw in the last section that one of the extensions in JTAPI 1.3 addresses mobile telephony. Let us take a closer look at the interfaces provided in this API as it can give us an insight into the differences between cellular telephony infrastructure versus the wired telephony infrastructure:

1. *MobileAddress*: Whereas wired phones are often associated with a geographical location (home, office, etc.), mobile phone numbers are typically associated with a device. This association of the end address with the device as opposed to an end location is a fundamental difference between the wired and wireless telephony infrastructure. Sometimes mobile phones have SIM cards (such as GSM chips) that can be moved from phone to phone to carry the addressing identity with them. This dynamic nature of addressing mobile phones is addressed by using this interface.

2. *MobileNetwork*: Wired phone calls have static network end points associated with the provider to which the wired phone is connected to. Mobile phones are not the same. Mobile phones are carried from place to place and can connect to a variety of networks. Therefore, knowing the information about the network to which the device is connected can be a very important piece of information.
3. *MobileProvider*: The provider represents the software system that is either part of the TAPI implementation or communicates with the TAPI implementation to provide the TAPI functionality on the given network and/or hardware platform.
4. *MobileRadio*: This interface provides the QOS information about the connectivity of the device to the network. For example, we can query the signal strength or whether the device is available.
5. *MobileTerminal*: This interface represents the end-point telephony terminal (the phone). This end point can be a variety of devices such as a mobile phone, a PDA, etc. This interface is mostly used for two purposes: to uniquely identify the device and to provide DTMD generation information about the device. (Tones are typically not generated at the device in cellular networks; they are generated by the network by proxy.)
6. *NetworkSelection*: Although the device is connected to the network, it can be connected through a variety of systems. For example, in GPRS networks, the phone can be connected through a regular TDMA connection or through a GPRS connection. This interface allows for selection and/or discovery of the connectivity method.

Today, the landscape of wireless telephony is rapidly changing. In addition to this, there is the chance that ad hoc (such as WIFI, etc.) networking technologies can be used to place and receive calls. Therefore, the mobile part of JTAPI is sure to be changing and expanding to provide for the proper interfaces to take advantage of new features in the wireless networks.

Using UML in Building VUIs with High-Level Speech APIs

As we saw in Chapter 6, Nunes' Wisdom UML extensions give us a great utility in extending generic user interfaces. In this chapter, we looked at a metamodel for VUI grammars. Now, let us continue with applying the principles we already learned about Nunes' and other methods of extending user interfaces.

1. We can use the *Wisdom UML extensions* for modeling the use cases. Just like GUIs, VUIs are composed of interactions and dialogues. So, these high-level extensions should work just as well for a VUI.
2. We mentioned that the UIM of choice for VUIs is one based on State Machines. This would lead us to conclude that *state diagrams* are a good tool to model the internals of a VUI. To model the grammars, we can refer back to the metamodel that we previously discussed.
3. We can continue to use *activity diagrams* to show the detailed interactions of a user with the system.

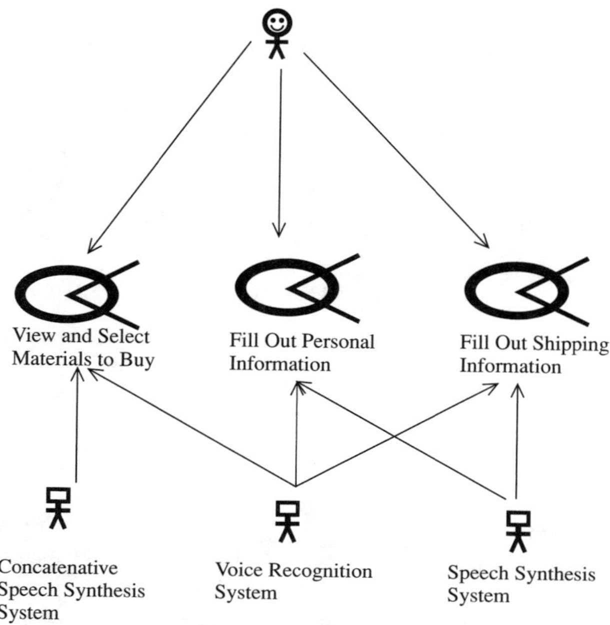

FIGURE 7.17. Wisdom UML Use Case Diagram for a Point-of-Purchase VUI.

4. Because VUI interactions are almost always temporally sequential, we can use the CTT extensions, as does Wisdom, to specify the interdependencies of interactions and tasks.
5. Because of the very sequential nature of voice interactions, sequence diagrams may be very useful as well. Sequence diagrams are easy to create and interpret when there are few permutations of the order in which the interactions can take place.

Now, let us take an example and see how these principles apply in practice. We will start with something simple. Let us assume that we need to build a VUI that takes the user's personal information when the user is purchasing something by using a VUI.

Figure 7.17 shows a very simplified overview of the functionality that the system may offer. First, we have a human actor who is interacting with the user interface of the system. Then, we have the system actors: the speech recognition system and two different speech-synthesis systems, one for producing concatenated speech and the other for machine-generated speech. Note that the voice user interacts with all three essential use cases. The voice recognition is the same because it has to recognize whatever the user gives the system as input. Although the speech synthesis for the prompts in interacting with the user in two use cases are done with machine-generated speech synthesis, the prices and names of products are prerecorded and another speech-synthesis system with better concatenation abilities is used there. This diagram gives us a good example of how we need to augment our use cases for representing the user's interactions with the system at

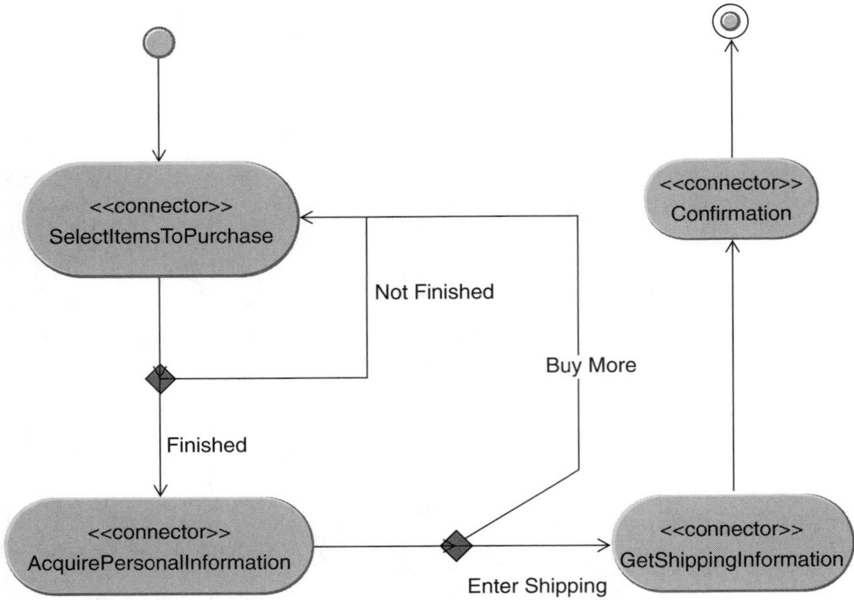

FIGURE 7.18. High-Level Activity Diagram with Lieberman Stereotypes for User-Based Actions.

a high level. Keep in mind that we still need the typical use cases that we would otherwise gather. There is a slight chance that there may be a one-to-one mapping between the "essential use cases" and the system use cases. However, remember that the essential use cases present the interactions of the user with sections of the user interface from the user's perspective. Typical UML use cases represent the chunks of functionality as seen from the business logic perspective. In the case of our example in Figure 7.17, the breakdown of typical use cases may be Registration, Billing Information, Authentication, Authorization, Material Search, Shopping Cart Management, Shipping, and Confirmation.

Next, we need to represent the details of the interactions between the user and the system. For this, let us use an activity diagram. For our example, we will only look at the essential use case of filling out personal information.

Figures 7.18–7.20 show activity diagrams representing the voice interactions necessary to gather the user's personal information given that the personal information is a collection of a small set of billing information, name, and address. Here, we are going to borrow a page from Lieberman [Lieberman 2001] whose work we looked at in Chapter 6. If you remember, Lieberman defined stereotypes of <<exception>>, <<frame>>, <<connector>>, <<presentation>>, and <<page>>. We will use the <<exception>> stereotype to identify recognition errors, <<connector>> stereotype to drill down from a large dialogue to subdialogues, and <<frame>> to indicate a grouping of voice interactions. Because <<frame>> and <<page>> were stereotypes designed based on GUI concepts, one may have chosen <<page>> instead. We chose frame in this case as it is semantically more representative of a grouping of atomic elements that allow user interface interactions rather than specification of a physical space. Note that although

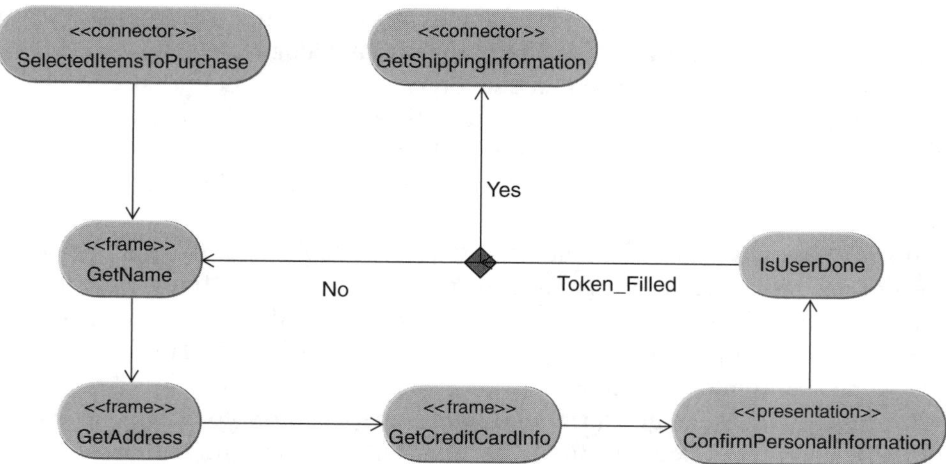

FIGURE 7.19. Using Lieberman's UML Extensions for State Diagrams in VUIs.

Nunes lays down a high-level foundation of extensions for user interfaces, Lieberman gives us specific treatment of the actions within an activity diagram.

When using activity diagrams for representing VUIs, we will almost never use join states (forks) to represent the user interface itself. This is because although a user interface action may give rise to multiple concurrent system actions, the user is never presented with two things concurrently (e.g., prompted for two inputs concurrently). The only time when a join state (fork) makes senses within the context of describing the presentation of a VUI is when modeling barge-in (as seen in the subsection on voice browsers later on in this section). Barge-in allows the user to cut-off an aural output being played back by the system with his/her own input to the system.

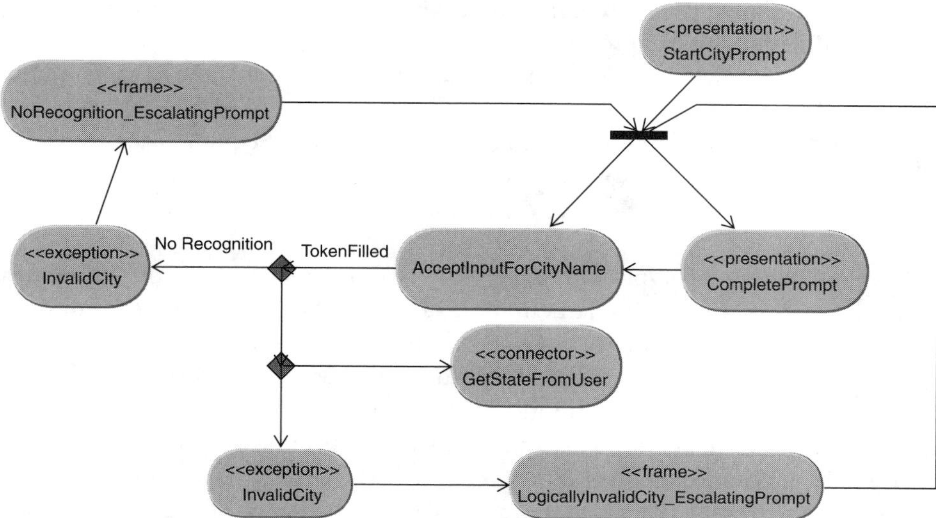

FIGURE 7.20. Activity Diagram Representing part of GetAddress frame in Figure 7.19.

Also, note that the highest level of granularity with activity diagrams is nearly equivalent to the detailed description of the actual dialogues.

This all leads us to see some new stereotypes that we can define specifically for representing VUIs with UML. (These stereotypes apply to classes used to model the internal operation of a VUI; however, the state of an instance of the class can be used to represent the user interface in state diagrams.) These stereotypes are listed in Table 7.2.

Figure 7.21 shows a metamodel class diagram of Table 7.2. Now, let us look at the internal implementation of a subdialogue (represented by a frame stereotype in our examples) that gets the user's address and utilizes the stereotypes that were defined in Figure 7.22. Figure 7.23 shows the usage of UML class diagrams for modeling VUI implementations.

Because there is currently no industry wide acceptance on iconic representations of these stereotypes, we will simply use the stereotype tags on the classes of the particular types. Note that the metaclasses that we have defined relate to the implementation of a VUI rather than the interactions with the user interface.

We can do one of three things to model the interactions of the user. First, we can use a state diagram to show the state of a subdialogue as in Figure 7.22. However, these stereotypes model the structure and behavior of the components that cause the reactions to the users responses to the interface. Our second choice is to use sequence diagrams to model the VUIs. This can be very effective because of the heavily temporal nature of VUIs. Although sequence diagrams do not give us the most desirable tool for GUIs (they are very temporal as the messages are ordered in time as one moves down the diagram), they can do a great job of modeling interactions with a VUI system. To do this, we need to create some message stereotypes. These stereotypes will be similar to the stereotypes that we have already defined for the GUI components. Finally, we can use state diagrams to model the state of the interactions themselves in a given dialogue between the user and the system.

Table 7.3. shows the stereotypes that we define to help us with meaningful sequence diagrams that represent VUIs.

Figure 7.24 shows us an example of how we can use a sequence diagram to model VUI interactions.

Note that we only represented two of the interactions. Sequence diagrams with accompanying notes can provide considerable detail for describing VUIs.

Now, let us summarize how we can model a VUI with UML:

1. We can create stereotypes of typical VUI components to represent the building blocks of the internal implementation of a VUI. We did this with building a metamodel with some of the more common types of behaviors and data bundled in classes used to build VUIs. You can add your own stereotype as you discover commonly used classes in building VUIs. Then, based on these stereotypes, you can build class diagrams that represent the internal implementation of subdialogues and dialogues.
2. We can create state diagrams that represent the behavior of a dialogue or subdialogue based on the events that trigger a move from one state to another in the dialogue or subdialogue.

Table 7.2. Using Stereotypes to Represent Different Types of Atomic Voice Interactions with a User

Stereotype	Definition and Purpose
Escalating Prompt <<escalating_prompt>> Stereotype on Class Inherits from Wisdom's <<input element>>	This stereotype represents an aural input whose prompt changes, if it is given incorrect or unrecognizable input, in an escalating manner.
Record <<record>> Stereotype on Class Inherits from Wisdom's <<input element>>	This stereotype indicates free input of speech. If the speech given to the system is not to be recognized, but merely recorded for playback or some other reason, we use this stereotype.
Natural Input Prompt <<natural_prompt>> Stereotype on Class Inherits from Wisdom's <<input element>>	It is important to distinguish between those inputs that expect natural responses from the user as opposed to those that expect a command. As we have seen in this chapter, we cannot achieve true natural language HCIs. In our case, we are defining a <<natural_prompt>> stereotyped input as any input that is expecting more than one token to be filled by the user's input.
Confirm <<confirm>> Stereotype on Class Inherits from Wisdom's <<input element>>	Some user input is always repeated back to the user to make sure that it was understood properly. This may be done through a speech-synthesis engine or by other techniques. The <<confirm>> stereotype is used to model such aural inputs.
Voice Print <<voice_print>> Stereotype on Class	A user's voice may be recorded solely for the purpose of authentication. Voice clips can be used just like fingerprints to uniquely identify a given person and whether the voice is coming from a live person or if it is a recording. This stereotype helps us model an input from the user that is to be used for this purpose.
Speakable <<speakable>> Stereotype on Class Inherits from Wisdom's <<ouput element>>	For a speech-synthesis engine to produce voice from text, the text information must be pronounceable. Some text is not speakable. For example, if the synthesizer is set to synthesize words in English and there is a text segment in Farsi, the speech-synthesis engine is unable to produce meaningful speech. To avoid such errors, we want to "mark" the objects that are pronounceable versus those that are not. The speakable stereotype allows us to do this.

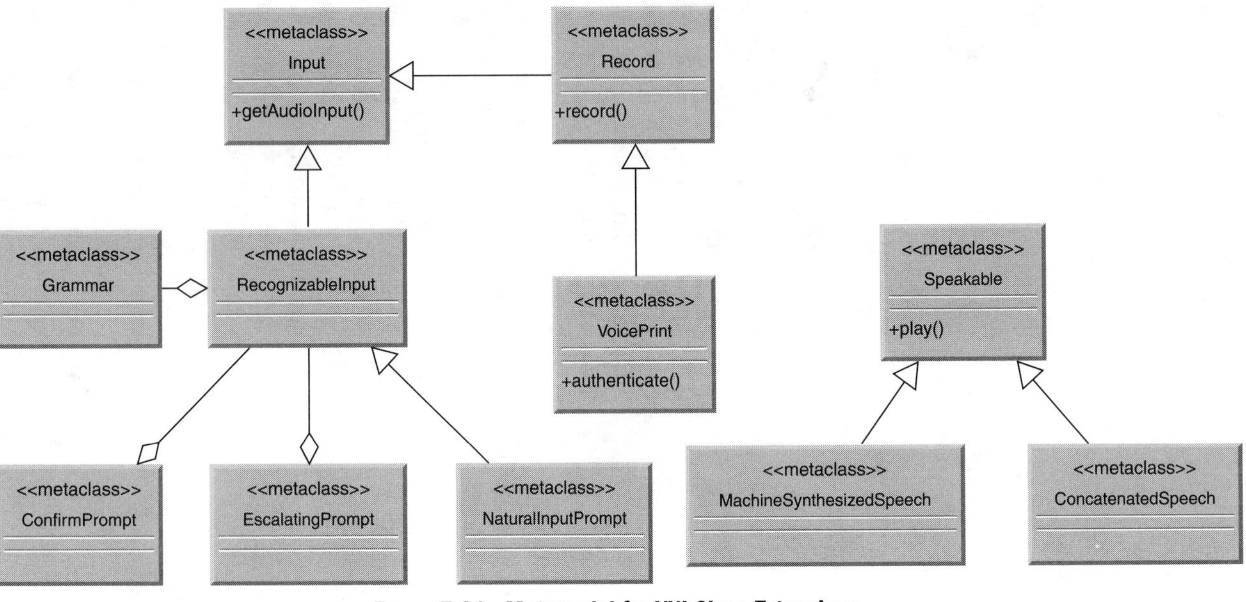

FIGURE 7.21. Metamodel for VUI Class Extensions.

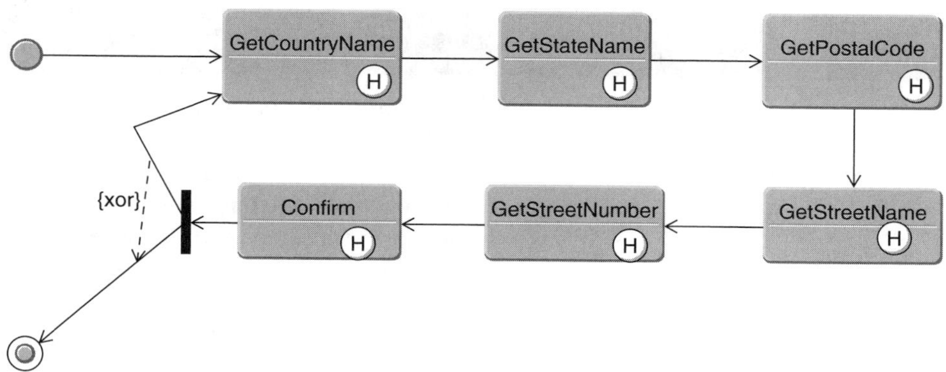

FIGURE 7.22. Using State Diagrams for Dialogues and Subdialogues.

3. We can use activity diagrams to show the activities that take place when the user interacts with the system.
4. We can use Nunes' Wisdom extensions to create use case diagrams that give us a greater amount of detail for the VUI and are centered on the user interface.
5. We can use sequence diagrams to show voice interactions in their temporal order.

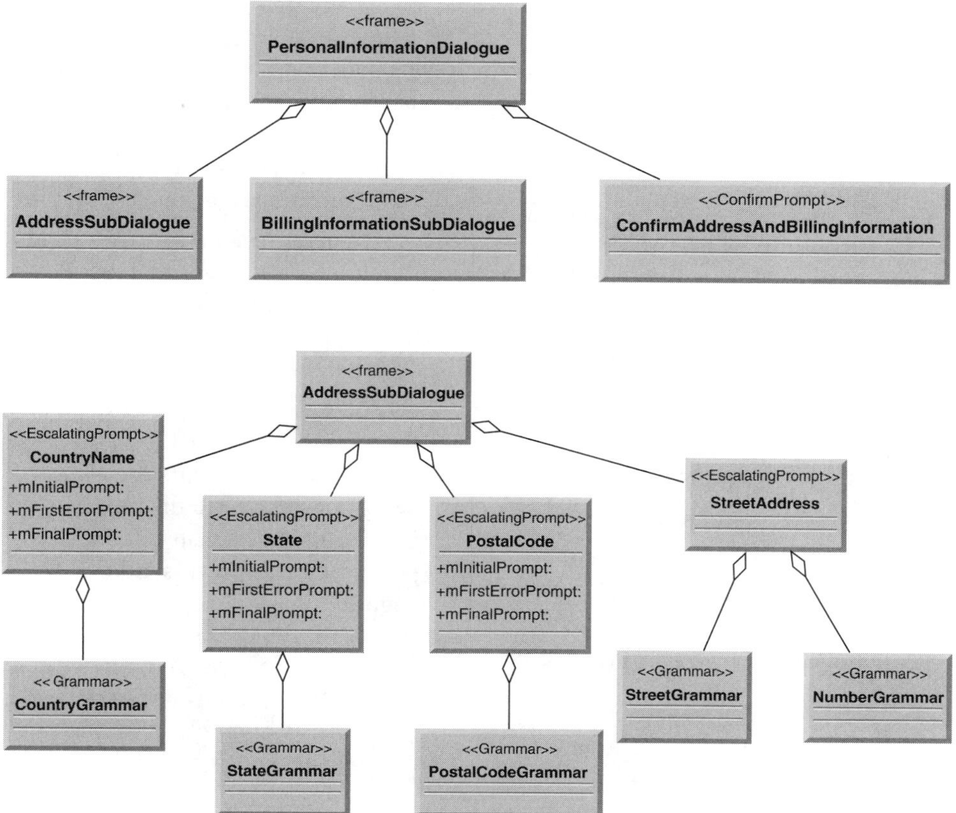

FIGURE 7.23. Using Class Diagrams and VUI Stereotypes to Model VUI Implementation.

TABLE 7.3. Specializing Sequence Diagram Messages for Modeling VUI Interactions

Stereotype	Definition and Purpose
Escalating Message <<EscalatingMessage>> Stereotype on Association Inherits from UML Message Stereotype	This stereotype represents a message or messages generated by the system in an escalating manner (if the response the user gives is incorrect or unrecognizable, the prompt that requests the information changes every subsequent time). This is a unidirectional association from the system to the actor.
Natural Response <<NaturalInput>> Stereotype on Association Inherits from UML Message Stereotype	A user's response to the system may contain more than one token along with markers and other utterances that are unimportant for recognition. In such a case we will refer to the response as a "NaturalResponse" (though as we have mentioned repeatedly throughout this text there is no such thing as true natural dialogues with today's technologies). This is a unidirectional message from the actor to the system since we assume that the user understands whatever the system aural output is.
Confirm Request Message <<ConfirmationRequest Message>> Stereotype on Association Inherits from UML Message Stereotype	This stereotype is a message sent from the system to the user that plays back what the system recognizes to be the user input and requests the user for a "Yes" or "No" type response as a confirmation. This is a unidirectional message.
Concatenated Speech <<ConcatenatedSpeech>> Stereotype on Association Inherits from UML Message Stereotype	This stereotype represents some speech being played back to the user that consists of concatenated audio produced by a speech-synthesis engine.
Machine Synthesized Speech <<MachineSpeech>> Stereotype on Association Inherits from UML Message Stereotype	This stereotype allows us to model some speech being played back to the user that consists of purely machine-generated speech from text.

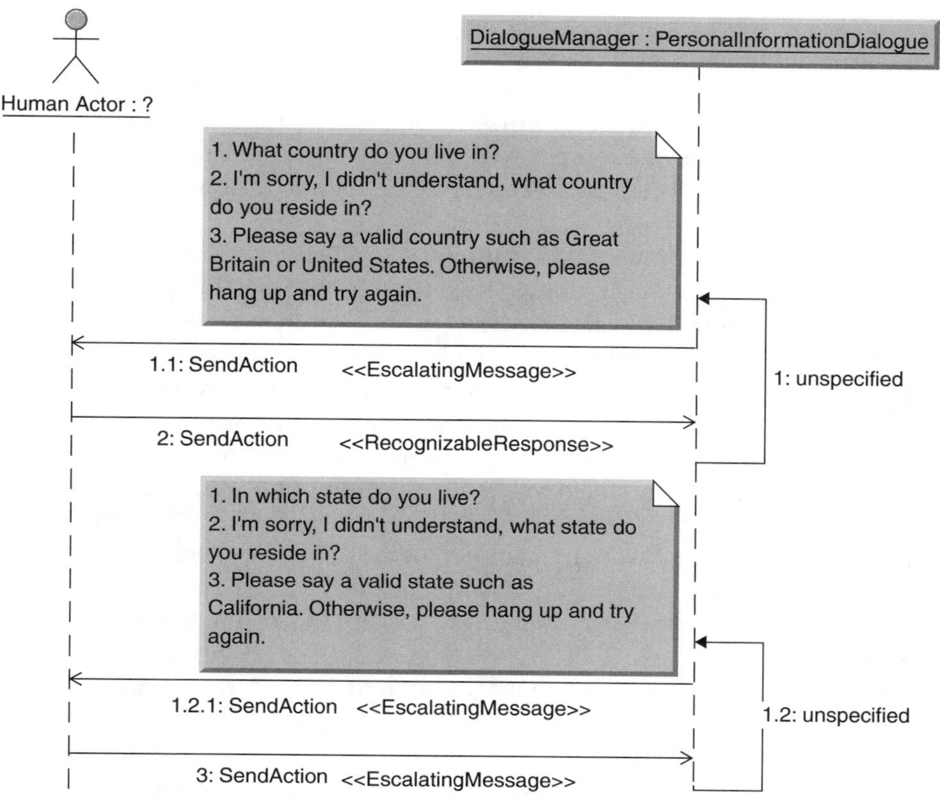

FIGURE 7.24. Using Sequence Diagrams to Model VUI Interactions.

We will leave the discussion of specializing a UML model that represents a generic user interface to a specific user interface (such as a VUI) to the next chapter because specialization of interfaces is mainly to provide a maintainable mechanism for multiple user interfaces to the same system. If the VUI is the only way we access a system, then we need not worry about specializing the interface and the associated problems.

The number of diagrams you use to model your VUI depends on the size of the project and your requirements. Generally, the larger the project gets, the more diagrams are needed so that every detail is documented, nothing slips through, and the complex web of user interactions with the system can be deciphered visually using the UML diagrams. However, if you are just building a prototype, then you do not need much other than some basic activity diagrams and perhaps some class diagrams (only if it makes sense for the language and API in which you have chosen to author your VUI).

We now know how to build basic VUI applications based on voice recognition and voice transcription using vendor-provided APIs or standard APIs such as JSAPI. We also know how to model these applications using UML. Now, let us look at how various Web technologies have contributed to VUI design to give birth to a new way of implanting VUIs with so-called voice browsers.

Voice Browsers

The success of the Web in creating a flexible and distributed system for accessing visual content has driven the VUI development community to make an attempt at emulating the architecture. Voice browsers are the child of such efforts. Perhaps the most important distinction between the voice browsers and HTML browsers is that voice browsers are still a server-side technology because a phone is typically unable to execute programs.

Whereas voice browsers emulate, the model of HTML browsers is in consuming a markup language and their ability to execute ECMAScript. Voice browsers are built to communicate with voice recognition and speech-synthesis systems. They are also typically built to communicate with telephony systems. A voice browser is essentially a VUI application built to communicate with voice recognition, speech synthesis, and telephony vendors from one or more vendors.

Like the Web browsers, voice browsers maintain the concept of a *session*. Whereas a session is maintained by the cooperation of the Web browser and the Web server through the use of cookies or URL rewriting for the Web browsers, the voice browsers do all the work in maintaining the session because their clients are not smart enough nor is the communication channel to their clients sophisticated enough (typically a telephony channel) in assisting to maintain the notion of a session.

There are several markup languages designed for consumption by voice browsers. VXML (pronounced Voice XML) is the most popular as well as the industry de facto. CCML (Call Center Markup Language) and SSML (Speech Synthesis Markup Language) complement VXML in providing markup languages for call control and speech synthesis, respectively. Microsoft's SALT is a markup language designed to work with the Microsoft platform and voice browsers. Our consistent bias will be to stick with technologies recommended by nonproprietary standards bodies such as the W3C. Therefore, we will look at VXML, CCSML, and SSML for short case studies on how voice browsing technologies work. If you are interested in building a VUI application based on a proprietary technology such as SALT, you will still be able to apply the principles and concepts introduced here. Let us get started with VXML.

VXML

VXML has its roots in efforts by Motorola, AT&T, and a group of other companies. The goal was to create a model similar to the thin-client GUI Web browsers such as Mosaic, Netscape Navigator, or MS Internet Explorer. As various markup language were suggested by different groups, it became apparent that a standard language was needed and this is when various commercial entities, under the direction of W3C, began to develop VXML. VXML version 2.0 is the latest ratified version of VXML. Before we go into the syntactical aspects of VXML, let us take a step back and see what VXML is and what it is not:

1. *VXML is normally not consumable by the end telephony device.* Perhaps the biggest misconception about VXML is that, like HTML, it is consumed by a browser that runs on a device that is in control of the user. VUIs are accessed through an audio

channel, typically telephony. A traditional phone typically has no processing power at all. Even if one could write a browser to parse VXML on a mobile phone or any other phone with processing power, it is not conceivable that a voice recognition engine could be run on the same device. As we mentioned in the previous section, the term *voice browser* comes from the architectural similarities rather than the implementation or usage similarities between VXML and HTML.

2. *SALT and VXML are not equivalent in functionality, architecture, or any other aspects.* SALT and VXML are largely competing technologies. VXML has been designed to fulfill the voice recognition piece of the puzzle in a larger architectural design along with a series of other standards such as CCML, SSML, SMIL, and others. SALT provides a cross section of the functionality offered by these various standards. If you are only building a voice application, SALT may be worth looking at depending on your platform preferences; however, SALT does not fit the bigger picture of building multichannel user interfaces.
3. *Whether VXML can be used on a project depends on whether the voice recognition platform offers a VXML-compliant browse.* VXML simply offers us an easier method of specifying the states and navigation methods between the different states of a VUI. We still need the voice recognition engine and an API to access its functionality. The voice browser is just an application, implemented by a third party or the voice recognition system vendor, built on top of the voice recognition engine and its APIs that allows for building VUIs using a high-level markup language, in this case VXML.
4. *VXML can be static or dynamically generated.* Just like HTML, we can have static VXML documents, generate the VXML in batches, or we can generate the documents at run time based on a set of rules. One of the values that VXML offers is that we can leverage existing Web-based technologies such as Microsoft's Advanced Server Pages (ASP) or Java's JSPs and J2EE framework in generating VXML. Alternatively, for mobile systems, we can simply specialize the generic user interface, in XForms or something else, using existing transformation technologies.

VXML has the following set of goals:

1. To provide a simple mechanism to build VUIs.
2. To separate the concerns of business logic from the concerns of building VUIs.
3. To provide a language that is portable across multiple voice recognition platforms.
4. To enable one VXML document to hold multiple voice interactions. This lessens the number of interactions between the application running on the voice platform and applications, databases, or other interfaces providing the business logic necessary to generate the VXML document.
5. To offer a small but sufficient set of features for basic telephony call control and text-to-speech interactions. Although the functionality through VXML for these functions are sufficient for smaller efforts, it is recommended that more comprehensive efforts, particularly for mobile applications, defer telephony control to CCPP and text-to-speech generation to SSML.

TABLE 7.4. VXML Syntax Tags

Tag Name	Attributes	Definition
<vxml>	xml:lang, xml:base, version, xmlns,	This is the root tag of VXML documents. As in the case of other XML-based syntaxes, the version attribute is used to specify which version of VXML is used for the particular document. Likewise, the xmlns attribute specifies the namespace, the current version of which points to http://www.w3.org/2001/vxml by default. The attribute xml:base is used to define a base URI for all of the relative URIs in the document. So, for example, if xml:base="http://www.cienecs.com/examples" then the URI "/voice/test/a.wav" points to "http://www.cienecs.com/examples/voice/test/a.wav." As with other XML-based languages, the xml:lang attribute is used for dealing with multiple languages.
<property>	name, value	Sometimes it is necessary to insert some platform-specific parameters into the VXML document because voice browsers are dependent on the voice recognition platform on top of which they run. In such occasions, the <property> element is used to specify these name–value pairs. It is strongly recommended that this tag be inserted into the document in a dynamic and configurable manner to maintain the portability of the VXML documents.
<block>		This element surrounds other elements that either play back some sound to the user or perform some control structures. As we mentioned in the introduction to this section, VXML does provide control structures. It is crucial not to overuse these control structures to build business logic programming. Otherwise, there is no separation of concerns, business logic bleeds into the user interface, and maintaining any specific user interface, let alone maintaining consistency among the user interfaces, is difficult. For example, the submit element must be enclosed within <block></block> because it is a control structure.

<meta>	name, http-equiv, content	We can associate two types of metadata with the document. The first type is a name–value pair that may be consumable by the voice browser. For these types, we use the attributes name to specify the name of the property to be specified and content to specify the value assigned to the property. We can also include some HTTP headers in the document because VXML is specifically designed to be suitable for transport via HTTP. For these properties, we specify the http-equiv attribute as the name of the property and content as the value of the property. Alternatively, the contents enclosed within the <meta> and </meta> tags can be RDF content. As discussed in Chapter 3, RDF is a great way to make documents accessible and to create a widely interoperable environment. Therefore, if possible, it is recommended that this method be used instead of the simple name–value pairs.
<var>	name, expr	This tag allows for specification of a variable in the document's scope. The name attribute is used to specify the name of the variable; it must be unique to the document (after the first usage, they will all refer to the same variable). The expr attribute is used to assign a value to the variable. Variables in VXML are variants (weakly typed); therefore, they can take on any static value as well as pointing to the result of any ECMAScript. All of the following definitions are valid: <var name="BirthDay" expr="MyScript.getBirthDate()"/> <var name="Age" expr="31"/> <var name="firstName" expr="Reza"/>
<assign>	name, expr	With this element, we can assign a value (in expr) to an existing variable pointed to by the name attribute.
<script>	src, charset, fetchhint, fetchtimeout, maxage, maxstale	To use ECMAScript, which is executed by the voice browser ("client side"), the script must be included in the VXML document. At the same time, the script must be separated from the rest of the document content. ECMAScript snippets are to be encapsulated within <script></script> tags.

(continued)

Table 7.4 (continued)

Tag Name	Attributes	Definition
		Just like grammars, ECMAScript can be specified inline or externally. If the script is external to the VXML document, the src attribute is used to point to the URI where the script exists. Otherwise, the script is encapsulated within [!CDATA[and]] tags (which are, in turn, inside the <script> tags. The charset attribute is used to specify the character set used for ECMAPScript authoring (internal and external). fetchhint, fetchtimeout, maxage, maxstale are used to set the timeouts for retrieving external resources as well as expiring and refreshing those resources. For ECMAScripts, these settings apply to external ECMAScript settings.
<form>	id, scope	See Figure 7.25. VXML documents are made of dialogues. VXML forms are one way of specifying dialogues. Conceptually, VXML forms are very similar to HTML forms: They present the user with a series of prompts and collect the information requested by those prompts. The id of every form must be unique to allow proper referencing through the standard URI mechanism. As we saw in the discussion of grammars, grammars and their rules have scope. The scope attribute of the form element specifies the scope of all of the grammars within the form, determining whether they are accessible outside of the form or not. The state diagram in Figure 7.25 shows how a form is handled. The form is the basic unit handled by the voice browser State Machine UIM. Navigation within the same form or from one form to another form is, then, determined by the state of the form. The state of the form is based on the prompts that it plays, the responses it receives, and the matches made after the voice recognition system compares the received responses to the corresponding grammars. Forms contain control items and input items.

<field>	name, expr, cond, type, slot, modal	This element allows us to play a prompt to the user and receive an unconstrained response. The name attribute allows us to specify a name, unique within the document, that enables access to the field. The expr attribute lets us set an initial value to the field result and the cond attribute allows us to specify a condition that is true or false. The cond attribute is true by default. The cond attribute is the piece of this element that allows us to see whether a condition has been met or not and to build the state of the form based on that condition (move on to the next field or next form or perform whatever navigation step may be required). Within forms, you may find a variety of elements that allow playback of audio to the user, capture of audio from the user, testing the content received from the user, and finally submitting the results to a URI. As we saw with grammars, every grammar returns a value when one of the tokens is satisfied. These values are often referred to as *slots*. Because every grammar within the field may have more than one token, there may be more than just one slot filled. The slot attribute of the field element tells the voice browser which slot value is to be used to fill the value of the field element. The modal attribute can be set to true or false. If it is set to false, all grammars in scope of the document are used for making a match and filling the slot. If it is set to true, only the grammar specified explicitly in the same field or through the type attribute is used. This is important for two reasons. First, the number of active grammars in a voice recognition system is inversely proportional to the performance of the system. In other words, the more grammars are active, the slower the system gets. Second, although certain words may be allowable in some parts of the form (for some fields, etc.), they may not be allowable in other parts.

(*continued*)

Table 7.4 (continued)

Tag Name	Attributes	Definition
<prompt>	bargein, bargeintype, cond, count, timeout, xml:lang	This element is used within other elements and its main purpose is to play audio to the user. As we previously mentioned, SSML, which we will look at in a later section, is a better fit for producing synthesized speech. And the designers of VXML recognized this. So, there are two ways to produce speech in VXML. First, we can put the text to be synthesized by the text-to-speech engine within the <prompt> and </prompt> tags. This defers the conversion of text to speech to the implementation of the voice browser and how it communicates with the speech-synthesis engine. For example, a prompt could be <prompt>Hello World<prompt> The alternative is to enclose SSML syntax within the <prompt> and </prompt> tags. In this case, we include all of the SSML tags except for the root tag of <speak>. So, a particular prompt could be <prompt> <paragraph> <sentence>Hello World</sentence> <audio src="GoodBye.wav">Good Bye</audio> </paragraph> </prompt> The bargein attribute can be set to true or false, allowing the user to speak at any time during the prompt if it is set to true and forcing the user to wait through the entire prompt if it is set to false. It should be noted that this attribute is honored only if the underlying voice recognition system and hardware support bargein.

		The bargeintype attribute can be either "hotword" or "speech" and is only relevant if the bargein attribute is set to true. If the bargeintype is set to hotword, the prompt is not interrupted until the user says a keyword. For example, our keyword may be "Genie," in which case the prompt would not be interrupted unless the user says the word "Genie" somewhere in his or her speech. If the bargeintype is set to "Speech," the prompt is interrupted with any speech, regardless of the content. Any utterance said after speech is interrupted constitutes speech to be used as an utterance to be recognized so that a slot is filled for the field. The cond attribute allows us to dynamically select whether we want a particular prompt played or not. The cond attribute can operate on constants, ECMAScripts in the document, and variables declared and defined in the VXML document.
<grammar>	mode, xml:lang, version, root, src, type	There are two types of grammars in VXML documents: inline grammars and external grammars. Inline grammars use the W3C grammars. VXML browsers are guaranteed to support the XML syntax for W3C grammars. However, implementation of the ABNF syntax is optional. When the mode attribute is specified, it is implicit that the content inside of the <grammar></grammar> tags is W3C grammar syntax for an inline grammar. There are two valid modes, "voice" and "dtmf," referring to the type of input that the grammar is used against to do the appropriate matches. (Obviously dtmf output requires a different type of grammar than voice because dtmf input is limited to input of positive integer numbers.) However, it is possible for the parent element (like field) to have two grammars, one with a dtmf mode and the other with a voice mode. For external grammars, the src attribute points to a valid URI from where the grammar can be. Likewise, the type attribute is set to indicate the type of grammar pointed to by the src attributed.

(continued)

TABLE 7.4 (continued)

Tag Name	Attributes	Definition
<link>	next, expr, event, eventexpr, message, messageexpr, dtmf, fetchaudio, fetchhint, fetchtimeout, maxage, maxstale	The link element allows us to navigate among VXML documents or among the dialogues of the same document. Alternatively, the link element allows us to throw an event that can then be handled by the voice browser, ECMAScript, or another document. If the link is to navigate to a static URI, the *next* attribute is to be used. (This static URI may point to a dynamic document; for example, http://www.cienecs.com/test.jsp is a URI that does not change but returns dynamic content.) If the link is to navigate to a URI that is an evaluated ECMAScript, the URI must be pointed to using the expr attribute. Alternatively, if the link causes an event that is static per instance of the document, it is specified using the event attribute, and if it is determined with ECMAScript, then it is pointed to using the eventexpr expression. A message (which can be used to warn the user, etc.) can be associated with the thrown event. Once again, if the message is static per instance of the VXML document, the message attribute is used, and if the message is determined using ECMAScript, the messageexpr attribute is used. fetchhint, fetchtimeout, maxage, and maxstale all apply as previously discussed.
<menu>	id, scope, dtmf, accept	Nearly all user interface types have one or more constructs that allow users to select from a list of choices. <menu> lets us build a list of choices to be selected by the user. The individual choices are specified using the <choice> tag. The id attribute is a unique identifier that allows the menu to be navigated through the use of events and links. The dtmf attribute is used to assign automatic dtmf numbers to the choices. The numbers 1–9 are assigned sequentially to the first nine choices. If a menu has more than nine choices, those choices past nine are not assigned a dtmf shortcut. However, having more than nine choices in a VUI is not recommended because users have a tough time remembering long lists that are read to them sequentially.

<choice>	dtmf, accept, next, expr, event, eventexpr, message, messageexpr, fetchaudio, fetchint, fetchtimeout, maxage, maxstate	One or multiple choice elements are used inside the menu element to specify the exact choices offered by the menu. The behavior of the attributes dtmf, next, expr, event, eventexpr, message, messageexpr, fetchaudio, fetchhint, fetchtimeout, maxage, and maxstate are identical to the behavior of a link. Basically, when a choice is selected, it is treated as a link to some point. The accept attribute is provided to optionally override the menu accept attribute for a specific choice. Every choice can have its own grammar by including a grammar element. Also, although the menu specifies a prompt, each choice can add its own additional prompts through the use of prompt elements. Therefore, the grammars for each choice can be inline or external and prompts can be specified in SSML, use concatenated audio, or leave it up to the VXML browser to apply a default behavior to how the text is converted to speech.
<subdialog>	name, src	If you remember our discussion of components and composite components in Chapter 5, you will have an easy time understanding what subdialogs are. Subdialogs are the individual VUI interactions that make up sets of interactions with the user. For example, gathering a user's address through a VUI takes getting the street address, city, state or province, and country. Gathering each piece of information may be done in a subdialog. Breaking larger dialogues into smaller ones allows us to have reusable dialogue components (what we call subdialogs in VXML). Consider, for example, the address case. We may want to get the city in which the user was born as well. When this is required, we can simply recall the city subdialog. To reference subdialogs, they are assigned a name that has to be unique per VXML document. Alternatively, if the subdialog being accessed is in a different VXML document, the src attribute is provided to point to the URI of that document.

(continued)

Table 7.4 (continued)

Tag Name	Attributes	Definition
<object>	name, classid, data, expr, codebase, codetype, type, archive, fetchhint, fetchtimeout, maxage, maxstale	This tag is the only tag whose use may prohibit portability of a given VXML document. The object tag is specifically designed to allow access to platform-specific functionality, which inherently leads to portability problems. The name attribute of this tag provides a unique name by which the object can be accessed throughout the VXML document. The classid attribute includes the platform-specific string that is used to invoke a component specific to the platform. For example, the classid may equal "com.cienecs.com.TestClass," referring to a class provided in the Java API to a system. The external component to be accessed may be accessed through a URI pointed to by the data attribute and the parameters to be passed to the component before it is invoked are put into <param></param> tags that have name–value pairs encapsulated in their attributes of name and expr (which can be dynamically resolved through the invocation of an ECMAScript method).
<if>	cond	The <if> tag is one of the three conditional structures in VXML; the other two are <elseif> and <else>. The cond attribute can be any valid ECMAScript or a method that evaluates an inline or external ECMAScript call. If the condition is true, then the code within <if> and </if> is executed. Otherwise, the code within the <else></else> is executed if one exists. The else and elseif tags are used only inside <if></if>.
<else>		See <if>.
<elseif>	cond	The elseif is just like the if, except that it is performed when a previous if condition evaluates to false. If cond returns true, the code within <elseif> and </else> tags are executed.
<event>		There are numerous telephony or other events that can be created in VXML. This tag is used to THROW an event (create an event and notify listeners). For details on all of the available events with this event, please refer to the VXML specification document at W3C.

<catch>	event, cond, count	Events are thrown to be caught so that some sequence of things can begin. The catch tag allows us to catch different types of events. The event attribute must be set to the name of the event thrown. It is important to keep in mind that VXML events, unlike events in most programming languages, are caught by name instead of type. In other words, if we have two different help events named "help1" and "help2," we cannot really catch all help events. Rather, we catch the "help1" event by setting the event attribute of the catch element to "help1" and we catch "help2" event by setting the event attribute of the catch element to "help2." Once the event is caught, the control logic within the <catch> and </catch> tags are executed, except when the cond expression evaluates to a false. As before, cond can be set to static values or dynamic values computed by ECMAScript. How many times an event is invoked may make a difference in what we do. For example, let us assume we have some validation that causes an error event to be thrown called "error1." The first time the event is thrown, we may simply want to replay the same prompt, whereas the second time around we may want to play a different prompt with more explanation of what is expected of the user. <error>, <noinput>, <nomatch>, and <help> are some shortcuts for common events of, respectively, an error, no input from the user, no match found against the grammar, or help requested by the user. Because they are simply shorthand representation of an <event> tag with the event attribute set to the respective name, they can take on the other two attributes of cond and count.
<record>	name, expr, modal, cond, beep, maxtime, finalsilence, dtmfterm, type	This construct allows us to record audio input from the user and submit it if desired. The audio being recorded starts at the end of the last prompt played and after the execution of the <record> tag and continues until a DTMF tone is received (when user pushes a button on their phone if that is the device being used), there is silence that passes the specified timeout, or the length of the recording exceeds some predefined length.

(continued)

Table 7.4 (continued)

Tag Name	Attributes	Definition
		The attribute name is used to point to the stored audio recording. (The storage is done under the covers by the VXML browser; depending on the platform implementation the audio content may be stored in a file system, database, or whatever mechanism is used by the platform.) If cond does not resolve to true, the audio is never recorded. The type attribute specifies the format of the recording (RAW mono with μ-law companding, RAW mono with a-law companding, etc.).
<transfer>	name, expr, cond, dest, destexpr, bridge, connectiontimeout, maxtime, aai, aaiexpr, transferaudio,	This tag allows us to switch sender audio channels (redirect the user to a different phone number, etc.) or switch to a different voice application. Like many other elements, the <transfer> element is identified by a unique string in the name attribute. The transfer will happen only if the cond expression evaluates to true. If the destination of the transfer is a constant, it is specified through the dest attribute; if it is dynamic (determined by ECMAScript), it is specified through the destexpr attribute. It should be noted that this element mostly lends itself to use with various telephony applications as opposed to VUIs accessed by microphones or other devices. How the actual transfer happens is platform dependent. However, voice browsers should have implementation of "bridged" or "blind" transfers. Blind transfers are somewhat like call forwarding. We simply forward the caller to another destination. Bridged transfers connect to the destination and then bring the caller into the same connection, creating something that is similar to a three-way call if we think of the caller, the current application, and the bridged applications each as a participant in the call. If the attributed bridge is set to true, the transfer is bridged. Otherwise, the transfer is blind. Some of the other attributes of the transfer element are really designed assuming that the destination of the transfer is possibly another voice browser or an application smart enough to know that it can receive transferred calls from a voice browser.

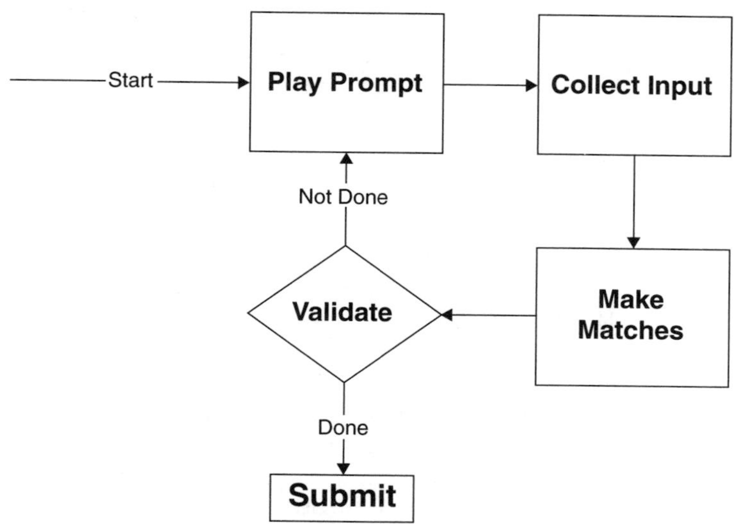

FIGURE 7.25. UML State Diagram of Voice Browser Handling of Forms.

VXML provides both a markup language syntax as well as support for ECMAScript (the parent to JavaScript and Jscript) for implementation of "client-side" logic. We will first look at the VXML syntax and then look at the different ways we can add dynamic behavior to the generation of VXML and handling of VXML on the voice browser using ECMAScript. VXML is a fairly large language so we will not be treating it in its entirety here. We will show enough so that the reader may understand the basics and then move on to use VXML in building VUIs and multichannel user interfaces for mobile applications.

Table 7.4 shows a basic syntactical review of VXML. Now that we have reviewed the basic syntax of VXML, let us look at a sample VXML document in Figure 7.26.

UML and VXML

We have already seen how to use UML to represent VUIs, the interactions of a user with VUIs, and the internal implementation of VUIs using UML. VXML is a tool that we use to build VUIs. So, all of what we have talked about generically about UML and VUIs apply to VXML. In other words, we can utilize the methods mentioned in the section entitled Speech and Call Control with High-Level APIs for modeling VXML documents and VUIs built of multiple VXML documents. Now, let us see how we can utilize UML specifically to represent VUIs built with VXML.

As we mentioned in Chapter 5, there are various reasons to design and implement mobile user interfaces as components. In the case of VXML, there are two ways of doing this: We can create VXML components that leverage subdialogues or we can create VXML dynamically using a server-side scripting language such as ASP or JSP.

UML can help us create models that make reusability of these components simpler because managing a large number of VXML components can make using them prohibitive. We can use UML class diagrams to represent the relationships

```
<?xml version="1.0"?>
<vxml version="1.0" >
   <form id="hello">
      <field name="country">
         <prompt>In Which Country Do You Live?</prompt>
      </field>
      <field name="Country">
         <prompt>Please enter your credit card
           number.</prompt>
      </field>

      <filled>
         <!-- The Country Name is Sent to the Server -->
         <result name="United States">
            <prompt>Please say the name of the city in
              which you live</prompt>
            <filled><result name="Huntington Beach">
               <prompt>Greatest Town in the US!</prompt>
            </result></filled>
         </result>
      </filled>
   </form>
</vxml>
```

FIGURE 7.26. Basic VXML Example Obtaining Country and City.

among multiple VXML documents from an internal representation perspective. From the user-interface perspective, we can use Wisdom extensions of task and presentation models to represent the navigation between VXML documents and the relationship among VXML documents. Figure 7.27 shows the shopping dialogue that we discussed earlier in this chapter using Nunes' Wisdom extensions. Wisdom task and presentation models are particularly helpful at a high level.

We can use the Wisdom presentation model in a similar way. Remember that these tools simply augment the ones that we have already outlined to model VUIs. VXML is just a tool to build VUIs based on a browsing technology.

Now, let us see if and how we can use a tool for building generic user interfaces such as XForms with VXML to produce a VUI from a generic user interface.

From XForms to VXML

One of our goals throughout this text is to build user interfaces in a consistent manner and in a way that suits mobile applications. As we reviewed in Chapter 5, mobile applications often refer to many different user interfaces. So, we showed that one way of reducing the complexity of the development problem as well as solving other problems such as maintaining consistency among different user interfaces is to create a generic user interface that models the interactions of the

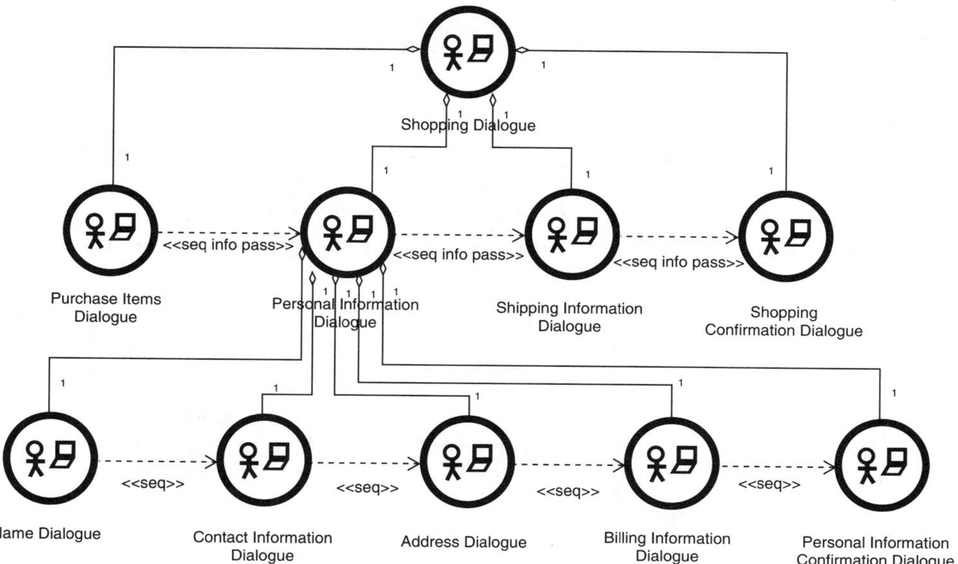

FIGURE 7.27. Using the Wisdom Task Model to Represent VXML Dialogue Structures.

user with the interface and then specialize this interface for the specific interfaces that are needed.

We should try to use the same approach for voice. As we have reviewed, VXML is a markup language and it is fully plausible that we should be able to convert XForms to VXML using XS's or some other type of transformation technology.

The catch is that both XForms and VXML are designed to be "statefull." By this, we mean that an XForms browser is designed to do some of the exact same things as a voice browser is designed to do: It is designed to hold a document that is very much form based and can take input from the user, it can have validation logic, and it can have multiple states. The XForms container basically operates on the state of the XForms documents like a State Machine.

So, let us see what our choices are in producing VXML from a generic user interface:

1. *We can use XForms to represent generic user interfaces in a stateless manner*. In this case, we would almost be using XForms as the markup language for a stateless Web service that has some generic information about the user interface. In this way, the voice browser would maintain state, while periodically requesting a new document from a source that returns an XForms document to be transformed by a proxy or by the voice browser itself.
2. *We can divide the state information between XForms and VXML in a manner that the state of the generic interactions between the user and the system (such as validation of the data that are returned by the user) are kept in the XForms browser and the state of the information specific to the VUI (such as audio-channel information and grammars) are kept in the VXML brower*. This is probably the most elegant technical solution, but it is relatively difficult and time consuming to implement.

The key here is to first organize the state information specific to the VUI and then to cleanly separate it from the state information that would need to be kept track of in any type of user interface.

3. *The VXML browser can be "XForms enabled."* One easy way to solve the problem is to make the VXML browsers understand XSL and XForms so that they can take an XForms document, transform it to the appropriate VXML document using style sheets, and then start it up. However, we are not aware of any current commercial or open-source efforts to support XForms on any VXML browsers.
4. *Create an XForms browser that is VXML enabled.* XForms browsers are designed to treat XForms, whose main purpose is to deal with a generic markup language. To support VXML, the XForms browsers would have to include SSML and CCML implementations to deal with speech synthesis and call control in addition to having some modular way of connecting to various voice recognition systems.
5. *Transform the XForms documents to small enough VXML documents so that the VXML document does not use any state informtion.* Although this approach circumvents one of the main design goals of VXML, namely lowering the traffic between the VXML browser and other applications to improve performance, it can be implemented with reasonable simplicity without any demands on the feature set supported by XForms browsers or VXML browers outside of what they support today.

By now, you probably see that the central impedance mismatch for using VXML with XForms is that they are both designed to be *stateful*. Keeping two stateful browsers synchronized creates a tremendous amount of network traffic and presents an undue processing burden on both browsers so it is not an option. Which one of the choices you select as the solution to your requirements depends on the details of your problem.

To date, there is no published canonical XForms to VXML mapping in XSL or any other language. However, Table 7.5 shows a rough mapping of some of the XForms and VXML constructs.

There are some things that do not map between the XForms and VXML:

1. *VXML <grammar> tags*: The concept of grammars is used to limit the possible things a user can say to the system. This is really not a problem that we face with graphical or textual user interfaces as there is no natural language to be parsed and there is no voice to be recognized.
2. *XForms <secret> tags*: There is no way to mask voice input from the user. Voice verification may be used for authentication instead of username and password.
3. *Binding to user interface components*: VXML provides no separation between the instance, the model, and processing of the document. The VXML browser processes a particular instance of the VXML document.
4. *Generic channel control*: This is by design, but it makes the mapping between XForms and VXML a difficult one if channel control is required from the document.

TABLE 7.5. VXML and XForms Construct Mapping

XForms Construct	VXML Construct
<selectOne> tag allows us to specify multiple options and select one option.	<menu> tag allows us to specify multiple options and select one option.
<item> tag is for specifying the individual choices inside the <selectOne> tag.	<choice> tag allows us to specify the individual options from which one is to be selected when contained within the <menu> tags.
<selectMany> tag allows us to select multiple items at the same time.	There is no good equivalent in VUIs to this type of functionality. However, we can get similar behavior out of the <menu> and <choice> combinations if the grammar specified for a given <choice> contains multiple tokens and the returning value from the choice includes multiple values within it.
<input> tag allows us to get input from the user.	Depending on the usage, the <input> tag may map to one of the following: 1. the <record> tag, which simply records the contents of the audio interactions taking place between the user and the system, or 2. the <field> tag, which allows us to specify a prompt and then return a slot filled against a specified grammar.
<range> tag allows us to specify a range between two numbers.	The functionality of the XForms <range> tag can be emulated by restricting the grammar of the field tag to include the upper and lower range numbers as well as all of the acceptable numbers in between based on the specified interval (for example, if the finest interval is 0.01, the min is 0, and the max is 0.5, the grammar would have to include all proper tokens for the set {0,0.01,0.02,...,0.50}).
<button> event allows us to trigger an event without any input.	There is no good equivalent to buttons in a VUI. However, we can simulate a similar behavior in a VUI with <link>, <event>, or <goto> depending on the exact desired behavior while the form is initialized, while it is being filled, or after it is finished being filled.

(continued)

Table 7.5 (*continued*)

XForms Construct	VXML Construct
<upload> allows us to upload data.	The only meaningful information that can be uploaded to a system using the lowest common denominator voice channel (such as POTS telephony) is audio content. This audio content can be recorded and submitted through the <record> tag.
<submit> allows us to send information to the server.	<submit> allows us to send information to the server.

(Although we try to stay away from recommending code generation solutions, particularly for the user interface, that rely on UML, generating a first cut of the VXML documents from the collective set of UML diagrams described in the following may be a worthwhile effort. This does not mean that maintaining your VXML code in UML is practical, but you can at least get the first version generated and then go from there.)

In conclusion, there is no industry-recognized canonical method of mapping XForms to VXML. However, this is not to say that we cannot map XForms to VXML. We can certainly do this fairly well at build time (before run time) using XSLs or some other transformation mechanism or use another one of the methods mentioned here. Nonetheless, the mapping is not exactly straightforward. Now, let us see how we can use VXML for building mobile applications.

Using VXML for Mobile Applications

Though there is a great deal of effort today to implement embedded voice recognition systems onto mobile devices, resource-starved devices do not lend themselves to voice browsing technologies. So, when it comes to using VXML for mobile applications, we are primarily referring to the server-side interpretation of the VXML document.

VXML can be produced from existing GUIs using transcoding mechanisms that convert another user interface markup language to VXML, using XSLs or other technologies. In theory, the primary advantage of using VXML in this manner is to reduce the necessary development, create consistency among different interfaces, and to reduce the cost of changes and maintenance during the lifetime of an application. In practice, things do not quite work that way because of a number of factors. Some of these are as follows:

1. There is a large performance cost in using VXML on the server side. Consequently, many commercial applications that have moved from the traditional IVR model of building on top of vendor-specific APIs suffer some performance loss. This problem can typically be easily solved by increasing CPU and memory. Because CPU and memory are now mostly inexpensive commodities, the

problem is not significant. Nevertheless, it is important to be aware of the performance loss when moving from a legacy VUI to a VXML-based VUI.

2. Because VXML has been designed as a browser that utilizes ECMAScript to reduce traffic with the other applications, it is stateful. And because it is stateful, the task of transforming a generic interface to VXML can be a fairly complicated one.
3. Generating VXML with typical server-side technologies such as JSP or ASP has the drawback of increasing network traffic although it has the advantage of allowing us to apply the same techniques used for generating HTML-based Web pages to generate VXML pages.
4. Automated conversion mechanisms that consume HTML or XHTML to produce VXML are typically flawed. Whereas the same technologies do a fair job with text and GUIs, VUIs are much more sensitive to errors. One wrong or poorly designed interaction with the user will turn the user off from using the system. The key with VUIs is that the user interface must be as close to perfect as possible. Users are simply not as patient with VUIs as they are with GUIs.

In the context of mobile application development, VUIs are usually meaningful as a way for the mobile user to access the system through a wired or wireless telephony channel (cell phones or land lines). When dealing with wirelessly connected users, there is a decreased SNR. This in turn causes the recognition times to increase and the successful recognitions to decrease. So, we need the best possible VUI we can design.

Using VXML for mobile applications should be done only after careful consideration of requirements. Whereas architecturally it provides a plethora of benefits, its weak point corresponds to one of the GUI Web technologies' strong points: scalability and performance. Where VXML can meet the requirements of your project performance-wise, it is clearly the best choice among the available technologies today. It provides a platform-independent infrastructure built the same way as many GUI Web-based applications are with HTML; therefore, it lets us use proved technologies to provide VUI access to existing systems.

We have now reviewed the basic VXML syntax and its applications to the mobile environment. Let us see how we can integrate VXML into CCML, a markup language designed to deal with the telephony call control aspects of VUIs.

CCML

The Call Control Markup Language, CCML (also referred to as CCXML) is the W3C standard that complements VXML and SSML in controlling telephony channels, the primary channel utilized by VUIs. Although CCML is designed to be well integrated with VXML, it is a separate language. VXML allows us to interact with one user and handle events thrown during interactions with that user through one audio channel. However, there is no mechanism provided for switching back and forth between audio channels, transferring audio channels, or taking any other action that involves multiple channels. CCML is designed to do this. Obviously, because a VXML document has no hooks into any other channels but the one that it operates on, CCML must have hooks into XML documents to provide an integration point. And it does. It is important to understand that the CCML container becomes the first point of entry for the incoming calls so it has control over the dialogue browsers. The CCXML browser does most of its communication with the dialogue browsers through an event model. As we will see in the syntax review of CCXML, the events in CCXML have been designed to be very close to those of VXML to avoid an impedance mismatch in the event models.

One last thing to keep in mind is that CCML containers are State Machines. This is very evident in the design of the language, which is based on the CCML document, the various states that it may be in, how it handles events, and how it controls the state of dialogue browsers by the events that it emits and receives.

Table 7.6 presents a subset of the VXML syntax.

We have not covered the entire syntax or the concepts behind CCML, but remember that our focus here is on the general concepts. Refer to the specifications at W3C for details. Now, let us look at integration of CCML and VXML.

As we mentioned earlier, either the voice browser understands CCML or the voice browser understanding VXML can communicate with an application that understands CCML. It is important to keep in mind that the implementation details of the interactions between the CCML browser and the VXML browser, if not handled by the same voice browser, are platform dependent. Figure 7.28 shows a CCML document that accepts a call and then points it to a dialogue browser that obtains a user's address.

Note that our example is very simple. There is a single active state called "active." There are three different events that can be emitted at this state, each leading to a different transition. If there is an incoming call event, a call id is created and assigned to the call (we have called this the "waiting" state). Once this is done, an event should be thrown that tells the system the call is connected (connection.CONNECTION_CONNECTED). We have called this transition "to_vxml." It is the transition that tells the infrastructure to bind a VXML document instance to the call addressed by the callid. When the dialogue in the VXML is finished, a dialog.exit event should be thrown that causes the transition "existing" to be performed. This in turn exits the CCML application.

Obviously, this is an overly simplistic example. The functionality encapsulated in most telephony-controlled VUIs would require multiple CCML documents, each much longer in length than the one we looked at in this example. This example, however, shows us the basics of how to bind to VXML dialogue browsers and make two simple telephony-related calls.

You can see by looking at our simple example that CCML is very much based on a State Machine UIM. Also, CCML documents can be very long and convoluted, making them a perfect candidate for modeling with UML state diagrams to achieve simplification and better documentation.

CCML and UML

As we saw in the previous section, CCML is built on three major concepts: states, events, and transitions. These are the same concepts that are involved in any State Machine–driven system. Let us now use UML state diagrams to model the CCML document in Figure 7.28. This is shown in Figure 7.29.

Table 7.6. CCXML Syntax Tags

Tag Name	Attributes	Definition
<ccxml>	version	This is the root of CCXML documents. As in the case of most XML-based languages, version is used for matching the document to the proper schema or DTD as improvements are made to ccxml and new versions are ratified.
<if>	cond	<if>, <elseif>, and <else> are the basic conditional control structure tags in VXML. If the cond attribute, which can be a static value or ECMAScript, resolves to true, the statements within the <if> and </if> statements are executed. The <elseif> statement is the same, but it is preceded by an <if> statement, which must resolve to false whereas the cond attribute of the <elseif> resolves to true. The else statement is executed if the cond attribute of the preceding <if> resolves to false.
<elseif>	cond	See <if>.
<else>		See <if>.
<dialogstart>	callid, src, type, namelist, dialogid	This is the tag that allows us to bind a dialogue document (for example a VXML document) with a call. The src attribute points to the dialogue document whereas the callid attribute can be a static value or a dynamic value calculated by ECMAScript to point to a particular call instance (instance of an audio channel). The source of the dialogue document can be of any format understandable by the voice browser. The type attribute is used to specify the MIME type of the document. For example, for VXML, the type attribute is application/xml+vxml. The namelist attribute allows us to pass some parameters via name–value pairs in the URL. Its content is the comma-delimited name of parameters to be passed through the URL. The dialogid attribute lets us keep a hook into the dialogue while it is still going on. It plays the role of a session id that lets us access it later on if needed.

(continued)

TABLE 7.6 (continued)

Tag Name	Attributes	Definition
<dialogterminate>	dialogid, immediate	This element lets us terminate an existing dialogue. The dialogid attribute is established via the <dialogstart> element, which establishes the dialogue. The immediate attribute may be set to true or false and its meaning is somewhat platform dependent. The idea of this attribute is to specify whether the call should be terminated regardless of the application state or whether some cleanup tasks, be they interactive tasks with the user or just application maintenance type tasks, should be performed.
<event>	name, dialogid, callid	As we mentioned previously, the CCML container is designed to communicate with the dialogue document browsers through events. The name attribute specifies a name for the event by which it can be caught. The dialogid attribute let us us send the event to the right dialog. Remember that dialogid's are assigned through the dialogstart. callid attribute specifies the id of the call whose audio channel is being used by the dialogue browser. There are a variety of call control–based events. To find an enumeration of those events, refer to the CCML specification [CCML 2002].
<var>	name, expr	<var> element does the exact same thing as the VXML <var> element.
<assign>	name, expr	<assign> element does the exact same thing as the VXML <assign> element.
<script>	src	This element can wrap around inline ECMAScript or alternatively point to an external URI, which returns ECMAScript through the src attribute.
<eventhandler>	id, statevariable	This element is a container for one or more transition elements. The id attribute lets us address the eventhandler. The statevariable acts like a contained data member that maintains the state of an eventhandler.
<transition>	name, state, event, cond	The transition element models the transition between different states in a State Machine. The name of the transition allows us to address it.

		The state attribute points to the state at which the CCML must be in for this transition to apply. The cond attribute is a static value or a dynamic value evaluated based on ECMAScript. If the cond attribute does not resolve to true, the transition does not happen. If the cond attribute resolves to true, an event of the type pointed to by the attribute event is created. CCML recognizes a wide variety of telephony events that are independent of the network type (VoIP, POTS, etc.), the carrier network (commercial providers such as AT&T in the United States and Vodafone in Europe), and call control application vendors (PBX vendors, switch vendors, etc.). These events include events that relate to establishing a call and terminating a call. For a list of these events, please refer to the CCML specification at the W3C site [CCML 2002].
<send>	event, target, name, delay, namelist	This tag lets us emit events to other processes, including dialogues and other CCML applications. If a set of properties are to be sent to the target, their names are to be listed in the namelist attribute. The type of event is specified by the event attribute and the specific process to receive the process is specified through the target attribute.
<move>	endpoint, event, sessionid	This element (end point) causes an event to be returned when the CCXML application reaches its end point. This element is most useful in allowing a target CCXML document to return control to the parent document that invoked it.
<accept>	callid	This element allows an incoming call to be accepted. Because the call must be addressable throughout the CCML application, a unique id must be assigned to it through the callid attribute.
<redirect>	callid, reason, dest	One of the most basic operations in telephony is routing calls. The <redirect> element allows us to send a call that has been accepted or created, addressed through the assigned callid, to a destination addressed through the attribute dest. The attribute reason allows us to specify a reason for the redirect of the call, through the reason attribute. This attribute can be used to give feedback to the user or used for passing values among the CCML application(s) in play.

(continued)

Table 7.6 (continued)

Tag Name	Attributes	Definition
<reject>	callid, reason	Occasionally, we may want to reject an incoming call. Although using both callid and reason attributes are optional, we can use them to associate an id number and a reason for rejection in case keeping track of the rejected call is of some significance.
<createcall>	dest, name	This tag is used when we need to initiate an outbound call. As you may note, there is no callid attribute associated with this element. This is because the call is created asynchronously, and the processing of the CCML document is continued once this call begins to process. When and if the call is successful, an event is created and this event is how we get a handle to the call. So, every createcall element must have an associated transition element (discussed previously) that specifies what happens after the call is received.
<createconference>	id	This element creates a placeholder for a conference call and assigns it an id. The conference call can then be joined through the <join> element.
<destroyconference>	id	This element destroys an existing conference call, causing all existing participating calls into the conference to be disconnected.
<join>	id1, id2, duplex	The join element is used to join two existing calls together (which in effect creates a conference call of two participants, but without a conference object and the subsequent handling functionality that it offers), to join an existing conference into an existing call, or to join an existing call into an existing conference. The duplex tag may be set to "full" or "half" depending on who should be able to hear what.

		If the duplex level is set to "full," then all participants can hear all the other participants. If the duplex level is set to "half," then the participant marked by id1 (an existing call or an existing conference) can hear the participant marked by id2, but the participant marked by id2 cannot hear the participant marked by id1. This functionality is particularly useful when an application has to handle conferencing as well as voice Webcasts (where one participant does all the talking and the other users are listening for most of the call, but the participants can interactively join in during the question and answer part of the voice Webcast).
<unjoin>	id1, id2	We can unjoin a caller from a conference call using this element. One of the attributes must be assigned to the id of the call to be removed from the conference and the other to the id of the conference.
		If both attributes point to joined or bridged calls without a conference, the calls are unbridged.
<disconnect>	callid, reason	This element allows us to disconnect an existing call addressed by the callid attribute. It may be desired to keep track of the information about the call after it has been disconnected, so this information remains addressable through the callid. The reason attribute can be used to specify a reason for the disconnect as a string.

```
<?xml version="1.0" encoding="UTF-8"?>
<ccxml version="1.0">
   <var name="incoming_callid" expr="'incoming'" />
   <var name="mState" expr="'active'" />
   <eventhandler statevariable="mState">
      <transition state="waiting" event="connection.
        CONNECTION_ALERTING" name="evt">
          <assign name="incoming_callid"
            expr="evt.callid" />
          <accept callid="incoming_callid" />
      </transition>
      <transition state="to_vxml" event="connection.
        CONNECTION_CONNECTED" name="evt">
          <dialogstart callid="incoming_callid"
            src="'address.vxml'" />
          <assign name="mState"
            expr="'AddressDialog_State'" />
      </transition>
      <transition name="exiting" state="'active'"
        event="dialog.exit" name="evt">
          <exit />
      </transition>
   </eventhandler>
</ccxml>
```

FIGURE 7.28 Using CCML to Control VXML Applications.

Note that this diagram represents the CCML document exactly. If we were to represent the states of the CCML document, we may want to incorporate the states of the CCML container as well. This would mean that each transition would lead into a different state because the CCML browser would be at a different state. In

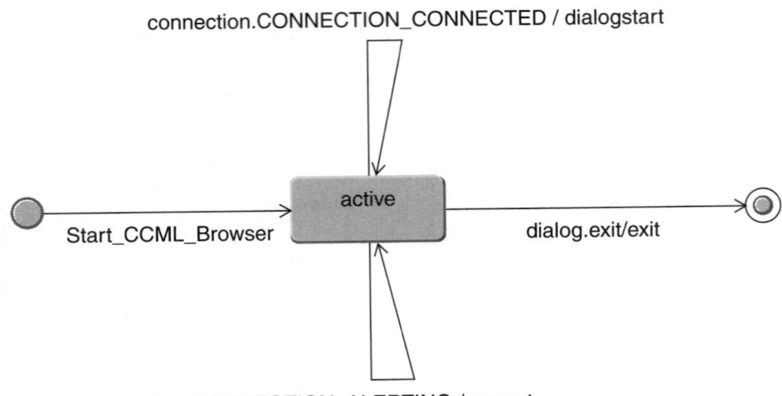

FIGURE 7.29 Using UML State Diagrams to Model CCML Documents.

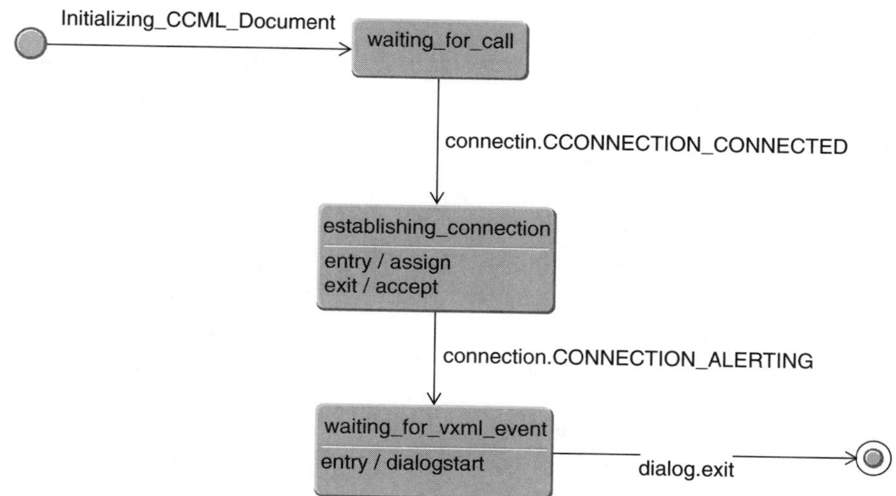

FIGURE 7.30 UML State Diagram Representing the State of the CCML Document Container.

our example, there would be three states, waiting for a call, waiting for the VXML browser to return an exit event, and finally exiting. See Figure 7.30.

Which way you select to represent your CCML documents in UML depends on your usage. If you are using UML to generate CCML code, then you probably want the first representation (plus whatever OCL code, stereotypes, and tags you want to add to get the right representation of CCML) as there is a more straightforward mapping between the definition of widgets to CCML elements and attributes. If you are trying to model the entire system in a uniform manner, then you are probably better off using an approach more similar to the second representation that includes the state of the CCML browser. This representation would be less specific to CCML.

As in the case of VXML, we can use the Wisdom task and presentation models to, respectively, represent the internal implementation of the relationship among multiple CCML documents and represent a high-level interaction of the user with the system interface (in this case the telephony navigation).

From a Generic User Interface to CCML

Generic user interfaces do not encapsulate any knowledge of the channel through which they are displayed to the user; CCML is designed primarily for handling telephony channels. Therefore, CCML is somewhat orthogonal to user interface design.

This is not to say that we can neglect handling of channels in a user-specific manner. The experts have recognized the need for handling all types of different communication channels, but the channels themselves are very different in nature. We are, however, fortunate that the handling of channels (audio, visual, and the various technologies such as VoIP, HTTP, etc. that provide transport infrastructures) is not a problem to be solved at the application layer. Infrastructures such as those designed to handle SMIL, and all of the channels that are supported by it, help us handle different types of channels and bind them to the appropriate user interface. We will take a closer look at this in Chapter 8.

XHTML Voice Profile

As we saw in Chapter 6, XHTML is the next generation of the hypertext markup language. Creation of different extensions to XHTML through an organized set of modules is the way it has been designed to deal with different document types. XHTML allows for the integration of voice interactions into XHTML documents that represent GUI interactions. Moreover, as we previously discussed, XHTML is a "specialized" markup language, meaning that we can create XHTML from XForms using one of many specialization techniques discussed in this text.

In a sense, XHTML wraps around VXML and other voice standards of W3C to provide a markup language for multimodal access to the system. It accomplishes this by modularization of VXML into XHTML. This allows VXML snippets to be called by events within the rest of the XHTML document.

There is one big difference between an XHTML document utilizing the XHTML Voice profile and the other type of markup languages we have discussed for building VUIs: It assumes a multichannel browser. In other words, the same browser environment that understands the textual syntax of XHTML and renders a GUI is also interpreting the VXML and controlling the audio channel. This means that we have one of three situations:

1. An XHTML document may be browsed by a text browser or a voice browser and the sections that are not understood by each browser are simply ignored.
2. An XHTML document may be browsed by a browser that is able to handle both audio and visual channels.
3. An XHTML document may go through an intermediary or proxy to provide understandable content to the end client.

The third case makes little sense because there is no reason to build a generic interface, specialize it to XHTML, and then take it apart again before delivering it to the client. We could go straight from XForms or some other markup language designed to represent user interfaces and accompanying interactions in a generic manner to the final interface without using XHTML.

So, either the XHTML browser is able to handle both audio and text or it is going to ignore the type of interactions it does not understand. Remember that XHTML browsers are running on the end-client device. For example, we could serve up an XHTML page that displays "Hello World" on a Palm device. The markup language is interpreted by a browser running on the Palm device. This, in turn, means that XHTML Voice profile makes sense only if we assume that the end-user device is going to be able to have a browser that can deal with both audio and text. Most mobile devices are not advanced enough today to accomplish such a task. This means that the XHTML Voice profile may not be the best choice for mobile devices. There may soon, however, be XHTML browsers on PCs for handling both audio and text channels, thereby making laptops or other similar powerful mobile devices possible candidates for using the XHTML Voice profile.

Now that we have looked at a few different standards and technologies for designing VUIs, let us look at how we build VUIs for mobile applications.

7.4.3 Designing Voice Recognition–Based VUIs for Mobile Applications

We have seen the general components that go into building a VUI, looked at different types of architectures within which VUIs are built, examined some tools such as JSAPI and VXML used to implement such interfaces, and seen how we can use UML to model VUIs in general and use UML with VXML or other tools. As with many other topics discussed in this text, there are many good texts out there for VUI design. Although we took a quick survey of building VUIs, our focus is on building mobile user interfaces that use voice interactions as a way to present the mobile user with a better way of communicating with the system. We will now quickly survey some of the most important principles in designing VUIs and then move on to discuss how the dimensions of mobility add to the typical concerns of designing VUIs. Our focus here will be user-independent-based VUIs. It is important to remind you that, to date, these systems are essentially based on command-and-control voice recognition rather than voice transcription. The single most important aspect of building VUIs is to understand the user who is interacting with the system. Consider this throughout all of the stages of a VUI and for each and all of the concerns that we distinguish here.

A common mistake that the typical reader of this text may make is to design a VUI as if the interactions are based on written sentences rather than spoken language. This is where we will start.

Design for Speaking, Not Writing

Speaking and writing are inherently different. Besides idioms used to communicate when speaking, most people use slightly different vocabulary sets to write than they do to speak. Whereas incorrect grammar is intolerable for writing, it is quite acceptable when speaking. In fact, idiomatic dialogues may be considered preferable in certain circumstances based on the user and the application. Incidentals such as "Hmmm," "Okay," "Oops," or "By the way" can give the dialogue taking place between the user and the system a more natural feel. Such incidentals can even be introduced into the dialogue randomly so that the user does not begin to recognize a pattern of how they are used.

Whether the recognition is strictly directed dialogue or a more natural dialogue, the prompts or other voice output from the system can integrate incidentals to make the dialogue much more natural. There are other ways of making the discourse more natural. The choice of words, phrases, and sentences to be used in creating the grammars for the user input as well as those words, phrases, and sentences used for system output should suit the application and the profile of the user of the application. For example, a banking application should use very clear instructions, make no or little use of incidentals and idioms, and employ a voice talent that conveys the serious nature of the application. However, an application that tells you the results of the games your favorite sports teams were involved in may be less formal when using idioms that suit conversations focusing on sports, and add in incidentals that present happiness or sadness depending on whether your teams won or lost.

Understanding the User

As we previously mentioned, the single most important factor in designing VUIs is to know the user. The information about the user can be divided into three categories:

1. *Information Collected During the Session.* As the user interacts with the system we can collect a "history" or a list of the things that are done during a given session. Session boundaries are typically dependent on the communication channel used for the VUI. For example, the session boundaries of a phone call begin with the user dialing a phone number and end with the user hanging up. During the session, information can be collected based on the responses given to help us prompt the user with better prompts or give the user better responses. For example, a particular user may intuitively prefer directed dialogue over natural language interactions. This may be concluded if he or she is able to navigate and interact with the system more quickly when using a directed-dialogue interaction as opposed to a mixed-initiative dialogue. In such a case, as the session progresses, we may have the logic in the system to present more directed-dialogue interactions to the user. Example 7.6 shows such a case. In this example, either the prompts are not clear enough or the user does not recognize the fact that to check the score of a game, he or she has to first say the name of the league and then the name of the team. The user is given the chance to interact through mixed-initiative dialogues, but once he or she does not provide the system with an easily understandable response, the system goes into a directed-dialogue mode for the remainder of the session. Also note that, as in the case of any typical application, some settings can be remembered from previous interactions with the user. In this example, the user has set some profile information that specifies his or her favorite sports teams.
2. *Application-Dependent (Domain-Dependent) Assumptions about the User*. Making assumptions about the user is not only acceptable but may even be necessary to build a good VUI. If the user is using a complex accounting application, it is fine to assume that he or she has a fair amount of knowledge in accounting. This can tell us much about the profile of the user. To limit the grammar of the dialogues between a user and a system, we can make assumptions about the user that increases the usability of the application by orders of magnitude to the majority of the users (although it may make it more cumbersome for a small subset of the user base).
3. *Specifics of the Mobile State of the User*. It is important to understand the specifics of the mobile state of the user and to design the user interface appropriately. In other words, a good mobile user interface is dynamic enough to adjust itself to the condition of the mobile user. For example, if the user is driving in a convertible and communicating with the system through a mobile phone, it may be appropriate to switch to a female voice with a higher pitch so that the user has an easier time making out the words. Every VUI interaction for a mobile system should be designed with the mobile condition of the user (Chapter 1) in mind.

Example 7.6: Sample of a Directed-Dialogue Interaction.

System: Would you like to hear the scores? Please say the name of the league first and then the name of the team.
User: Sure, how did the Bronco's do?
System: I'm sorry, I didn't get that. Which league did you want to check, NHL, NBA, or NFL.
User: NFL.
System: Did you want to check the Denver Bronco's Score?
User: Yes.
System: Denver beat New England 24–16 today. Would you like to continue?
User: What happened in the Laker game?
System: I'm sorry, I didn't get that. Would you like to check an NHL game, NFL game, or NBA game?
User: NBA.
System: Which team would you like, the Los Angeles Lakers or the Los Angeles Clippers? If you'd like another team, please say the name of the team.
User: Lakers.
System: The Lakers didn't have a game today. Would you like the most recent score?
User: No, thanks. Quit.
System: Thank you for using the SportsAreLife Portal. Good bye.

Using Pronouns and Other Markers

Mobile users are not focused and usually rushed so we need to keep interactions concise. However, they also need a little more time to understand prompts and other aural output as they are typically doing multiple things at the same time. So, as a general rule of thumb, when building mobile VUIs, keep the content of the prompts short and to the point, but use markers and pronounce frequently. For example, instead of prompting the user "Please say the five digit postal code of your address now," we should prompt the user as "Ok, what is your zip code?" Such prompts also tend to be more informal. In the context of mobile applications, using pronouns and markers to make the user interface more friendly takes precedence to abiding to a consistent look and feel (as, for example, with formal communications in a banking application).

Consistency

It may seem too obvious too mention, but in the case of VUIs, as in any other type of user interface, consistency is crucial. Maintaining consistency is important at three levels:

1. *Interface Details*: Keeping the same voice talent, identity, vocabulary sets, and other details used in communicating to the user is crucial. For example, if one part of the application uses incidentals, markers, and pronouns to deliver a more natural interface and another part does not, the user will "feel" as if he or she

is communicating with two different systems, thereby creating a discontinuity in the user's experience.

2. *Interface Metadesign Decisions*: When designing a VUI, there are some principles that drive the design strategies. Although these principles may vary by application, they should stay the same for a given application. For example, we may decide to use escalating error correction for an application. If so, than the entire application should use escalating error corrections as opposed to other options. Whereas maintaining consistency in the details of the interface (the first principle) helps deliver a consistent "look, hear, and feel" to the user, maintaining consistent metadesign decisions helps us deliver cognitive consistency while the user is interacting with the system.
3. *Analogous Components of Other User Interface Types*: Often times, the VUI is not the only interface to the application. As a part of designing a good multichannel user interface, the VUI components should be consistent with their counterparts in GUIs. For example, let us take an application that provides cooking recipes and is available for access through both a Web and a VUI. In the Web version, there may be a wizard available that the user utilizes to navigate through the steps of cooking on his or her own time. The same analogous functionality must be available through voice, say, for example, a voice wizard where the VUI asks the user whether the user wants more time, wants to move on to the next step, or wants to hang-up (if accessing voice through telephony) and call back again to follow up with the next steps.

Confirming User Input

As you noted in the previous sections, we already introduced a stereotype called "confirm" to specify the VUI components that confirm the user's input. Confirming the user and allowing the user to correct the input is crucial for mobile users. The mobile user is not focused and is much more error prone in responses given to the system. You can confirm things in steps (e.g., confirm the address before moving on to the next subdialogue) or confirm everything at the end. A well-designed VUI finds a balance between these two. If the confirmation is too long (contains a lot of information), the user just gets confused (because the user of a VUI does not have the luxury of a GUI user to scan the graphics and text on the screen multiple times and any order desired). Too many confirmations begin to annoy the user. So, the key is to find just the right balance.

Correcting User Input

When the user makes an error, the system should correct him or her. This is obvious. What is somewhat of an art is how to correct the user. There are several possibilities:

1. *Escalating Corrections*: Repeating the same error message often simply leads to user frustration. So, a good way of handling errors is to start with concise correction messages and get more and more descriptive as the same mistake is repeated. This type of interaction can occur so frequently that we created a stereotype to represent it.

2. *Transferring to a Live Person*: Numerous VUIs support larger back-end transactions. An example of this is a hotel reservation system. For such cases, it is prudent to have a small team at a call center to help out those users who get frustrated by the system's inability to recognize their input.
3. *Start Natural and Move to Directed-Dialogue*: If mixed-initiative or natural language interactions are used to build the user interface, errors could be caused by a limited grammar set, performance limitations, or poor design. As we discussed earlier, the more natural the interaction with the user, the larger the grammar set, and subsequently, the larger the chance for misunderstanding possible responses. So, if the system does not get an understandable response in the mixed-initiative mode of interaction, design it so that it gradually moves to a more directed dialogue. Example 7.7 displays an example of such a case. Note one more thing: Once we have gone into a directed-dialogue mode, we stay there. Whether the system is designed to escalate to a directed-dialogue mode and stay there or whether it is designed to go back to a more natural discourse once the context of the interaction with the user is changed is up to the designer. This decision should be made based on the context of the interaction with the user.

Example 7.7: Correcting the User by Moving from Mixed-Initiative to Directed Dialogue.

System: Would you like to adjust the temperature or the lights?
User: This room is very dry. Please increase the humidity.
System: I'm sorry, I didn't understand that. Could you repeat?
User: It's dry in here. Increase humidity.
System: I'm sorry. I can only change the temperature or the lighting levels. What would you like to do: adjust the temperature or turn on the lights?
User: It's too dry in here.
System: Please say one of the following: lights or temperature.
User: Temperature.
System: Would you like it higher or lower?
User: Lower.

In addition to these, correcting the mobile user may need to differ from correcting users of other applications. Because the mobile environment introduces considerable noise, whether because of a low-quality wireless connection or because of the noise of various activities going on in the background, correction of the user must incorporate the dimensions of mobility. Namely, we need to consider the following:

1. If the background noise is too high, inform the user so that he or she may change the environmental conditions to eliminate the background noise, thereby improving the accuracy and consistency of recognition. Recognition results may be low because of background noise. However, the user may be oblivious to this. A feature desired for voice recognition systems being deployed in mobile environments is an interface that allows the application to determine the amount

of background noise and enables it to distinguish the background noise from white noise caused by low QOS. In this way, if the voice recognition system fails in recognizing the user input, the noise can be examined; subsequently, if the background noise level is too high, the user can be presented with a prompt such as "I'm sorry, I can't recognize what you are saying because there is too much background noise. Could you go somewhere quieter or say that louder." It should be noted that the user saying something louder does not guarantee better recognition as the audio interface (microphone, phone, etc.) has some saturation limit beyond which raising the voice actually causes further degradation of the quality of the received signal. This is just an example of a prompt. Depending on the application and the context of the interaction with the user, a more meaningful prompt can be presented. For example, if a mobile application is targeted for construction field workers, the standard background noise can be recognized by the appropriate filters and corresponding message can be presented as "Sounds like there is some hammering going on in the background; could you please go somewhere with less noise."

2. If there is white noise, or other types of noise, caused by low QOS of a wirelessly connected user, let users know that their connection is of low quality. In such cases, it is best to let the mobile user know that the problem with the interface is in the connection. Once again, by changing location or some other action, users can improve the quality of the connection. Also, the reality of applications is that the end goal is to deliver a service to a customer and to keep that customer happy. It is critical that, if there are problems outside of the application itself, with the device, the connectivity to the network, or others, the user is informed. This helps manage the user's frustrations as well as pointing them to the right source to correct the application problems. A simple message such as "You are not receiving enough bandwidth in this area. Please contact your carrier." can go a long way in reducing the frustration of a user with an application.
3. Verify location information and present the proper error information. Knowing where the user is gives us a great deal of information and can often be used in presenting more meaningful error-correction prompts. Example 7.8 shows how a system can use such information to limit the grammar and give the user more meaningful error prompts. Note that by knowing that the mobile device to be contacted was within the vicinity of the user, the system helped the user. Also note that this particular "correction" was a contextual correction as opposed to a recognition correction. Regardless of the type of correction, the same strategy may be used by using the location information to guide the user to give us the proper response.

Example 7.8: Using the User's Location to Improve Correction Prompts.

Let us assume that we know that the user is at home. In this scenario, we assume that the system is the user's (Bob's) cell phone communicating with a centralized voice recognition system.
Phil: Call my daughter Maria.

System: Phil, Maria's cell phone is currently located within one-hundred meters of your location. Do you want me to call her somewhere else?
Phil: Yeah, call her at her friend's house.
System: I'm sorry Phil, I didn't understand that. If you have an alternate number for Maria, could you say it. Otherwise, please say the name of the person whose number you'd like to call.
Phil: Call my wife.
System: Calling your wife now.

4. Take advantage of the multichannel user interface when possible. Many mobile applications use multichannel user interface, with voice being one of the channels of communication with the user. If your correction through the VUI fails consistently, it may be suitable to switch to a GUI or, at least, to prompt the user if he or she wants to use a GUI. For example, if recognition errors are increasing because of excess background noise, the user can be directed to use a GUI. Once the noise level is reduced, the VUI can come back on.

Clarity

We have mentioned brevity and clarity many times already. We reemphasize that giving mobile users clear and concise directions to request their input is crucial. Also, we once again emphasize the fact that the mobile user is typically doing something other than interacting with the computing system that is more important to him or her (which is probably why the user is mobile to start with). So, mobile users have little tolerance for listening to long aural output from the system. Design your prompts to be to the point, clear, and concise. Yet, make sure that you do not sacrifice a "friendly" tone.

Persona

When designing and implementing a VUI, put yourself in the user's place. The user is communicating with the system through voice. The perception of the user is similar to communicating with the system because of these voice-based interactions. So, to make the user feel more comfortable and to make the system easier to use, create a "persona" for the system. The persona of a VUI is the same as the look-and-feel of a GUI. It is the perfect vehicle for conveying the corporate look-and-feel, friendliness, and all those other things that may be desired to be communicated to the user. The persona of a system delivers a consistent VUI that can make the user feel more like he or she is communicating with a person rather than a computer. And this is one of the most important goals in designing a VUI.

Tuning a VUI

The process of testing and refining a VUI is a bit differernt from that for a GUI. In fact, we may want to remove some of the methodologies used in refining VUIs and apply them to GUIs. There are some common problems that need to be solved. One is that a VUI is designed with a set of assumptions about the typical user, some of which may end up being untrue. We may also get unexpected responses that cause no recognition because the grammars would not account for them. In addition, environmental conditions such as background noise may be different than planned for.

We cannot take a comprehensive look at testing and tuning a VUI in this text. Our goal is merely an introductory one. However, here are some typical steps to take while tuning:

1. After you are done designing and implementing, test the system with ten to twenty randomly sampled users in sample environmental conditions. Use the recognition errors and any pointers that these users may have for an initial round of tuning. Do this first round of tuning without any telephony. This way, you can separate the problems associated with the handling of the voice channel from the problems associated with the voice interactions themselves.
2. Repeat step 1, but this time have the users use telephones. Repeat the tuning process again.
3. Now, take the same users and have them test the system under mobile conditions through wireless telephony. Repeat tuning again.
4. Now, select another set of randomly sampled users and go through the steps again.

Your system and budget may not allow for ten to twenty sample users. However, the project may be large enough to allow for more users. Use your judgement and the project size to adjust the sampling size, but stick with the process. Also remember that if the sampling size gets too small (less than five to seven users), you may end up going in circles and never actually tuning the system because the input from those users may not be representative of the median user of the system. The problem of tuning is inherently a statistical problem. So, apply the principles accordingly.

7.5 Text-to-Speech Technologies: Converting Written Language to Spoken Language

So far, in this chapter, we have discussed mostly how to deal with aural input generated by the user to be processed by the system. VUIs are at their most natural when both input and output of the system are spoken words. This is where the text-to-speech technologies come into play. *Text-to-speech applications are those applications that change written language into spoken language*. There are two main categories of software programs that convert written language into spoken language: those that produce spoken language by concatenation of words spoken by live human beings and those that attempt to produce speech without help from prerecorded words. Let us look at the two.

7.5.1 Speech Synthesis by Concatenation

Today's best VUIs concatenate prerecorded utterances to make up synthesized speech. This is typically referred to as *speech synthesis by concatenation*. Good speech-synthesis engines are able to meld the ends and beginnings of utterances together. Also, the size of the bank of prerecorded utterances makes a large difference in the quality of speech produced: The more prerecorded utterances there are, the better quality of speech is produced. For example, different pronunciations of the word "that" could be prerecorded so that the speech-synthesis engine can decide the usage of the right pronunciation depending on the structure of the sentence and the possible meaning of the word within the context of the phrase, sentence, or paragraph.

7.5.2 Pure Speech Synthesis

The sound most echoed in people's mind when hearing fully machine-generated speech is similar to that of the synthesized voice of the famous physicist Stephen Hawking. With today's technology, this is not far from what purely machine-generated speech sounds like. What we refer to as "pure" or "fully machine-generated" speech synthesis in this text simply refers to speech synthesis that does not utilize concatenation of prerecorded voice segments. This type of speech synthesis typically costs less because there is no need for the voice talent or the licensing fees that go along with the voice talent. However, the quality of the final delivered product is considerably lower than speech synthesis by concatenation. Though today's speech-synthesis engines are getting better and better at synthesizing speech in this way, they are still several years away from delivering solutions that rival speech synthesis by concatenation.

7.5.3 Speech-Synthesis Languages and Tools

The same categories that we used in the taxonomy of tool types for voice recognition apply to speech-synthesis tools. As we previously saw, JSAPI already has a section of its APIs dedicated to speech synthesis. Let us look at SSML, the W3C standard for writing text-to-speech applications using XML.

SSML

SSML is another piece of the puzzle in building VUIs based on voice browser technologies. SSML gives us the ability to interface with speech-synthesis engines provided by various vendors in a uniform way to facilitate portability. SSML is another one of the W3C standards and is based on JSML, the JSpeech (Java Speech) Synthesis Markup Language. SSML is a bit more comprehensive in terms of the problems that it tries to tackle as well as being less coupled to Java as a platform (and therefore being platform neutral).

SSML is designed with the following basic principles in mind:

1. *SSML is an XML-based lnguage.* Not only is this valuable in terms of providing a standard textual parsing mechanism, but it uses the capability of XML to present structured data to mimic the structure in written language (words, sentences, paragraphs, etc.).
2. *Text normalization is provided.* Text normalization is the ability to tell the system to pronounce 40# as "forty pounds" and not "forty number sign." Text normalization is implemented through the use of XML tags.

3. *SSML supports pronunciation specification using phonemes*. Phonemes are those strange-looking characters used in the dictionary to show how something is pronounced. A phoneme is a basic unit of sound in language [SSML 2002].
4. *It has the ability to specify some of the qualities of speech*. The SSML specification refers to the ability of changing the pitch, timing, speaking rate, and a variety of other features that make machine-generated pronunciations more humanlike, such as *prosody*. SSML was designed with the goal of providing the facilities to specify such qualities of speech.
5. *It has the ability to integrate audio into the generated output*. Many platforms have special functionality in producing more humanlike speech. SSML provides a hook for such functionality so that if some of the audio is produced by functionality outside of SSML it can be integrated. This requirement also provides for implementation of concatenative speech synthesis (to be discussed later in this chapter).
6. *It can apply styling in a modular manner*. With Web-based GUIs, we have the ability to apply CSS to modularize the formatting and look-and-feel. One of the considerations in design of SSML was the ability to apply ACSS (which we will look at in the next section) to modularize the "sound-and-feel" of the speech being generated by the speech-synthesis system. An example may be generating speech with a British accent for users of a given system in England as opposed to generating speech with an American accent for users of a given system in the United States.

Now, let us jump into the SSML syntax.

SSML Syntax

As we mentioned, SSML is an XML-based syntax. Table 7.7 outlines the SSML tags.

Now, let us look at a sample SSML document that reads some directions to the user in Figure 7.31.

Note that we have wrapped various fragments of text within the <sentence> </sentence> tags. This is not necessary but may help in enabling some speech-synthesis systems to apply the right prosody. SSML is a new standard. Although it is not pervasively implemented among the text-to-speech vendors, more and more vendors are moving toward offering it as a standard interface to their systems.

SSML allows us to define speech content to be played back to the user; in a way, it is like HTML or other markup languages used for text and graphical content. As in the case of those markup languages, we can separate the concerns of formatting and content by creating style sheets. This is the purpose of ACSS, the Aural Cascading Style Sheets.

Cascading Style Sheets for Aural Interfaces

The idea of cascading style sheets began in abstracting the look-and-feel of Web pages away from their content. This helped with reducing development time as well as maintaining consistency across many documents. In the late 1990s, the W3C began an effort to create Aural Cascading Style Sheets to implement an

Table 7.7. SSML Syntax Tags

Tag Name	Attributes	Definition
<speak>	xml:lang, version, xmlns	This is the root attribute of any SSML document. It specifies that anything enclosed with the tags is to be converted to speech by the speech-synthesis engine. The language attribute (xml:ns) allows for internationalization and dealing with multiple languages. The version attribute exists to specify the version of the SSML XML Schema used for validating the document. The xmlns attribute points to the document specifying the schema specified through any valid URI (e.g., http://www.w3.org/2001/10/synthesis).
<paragraph>	xml:lang	This tag mimics the definition of a paragraph. Though the language can be specified per paragraph and sentence, it is not a feature required of the speech-synthesis platforms and, therefore, not recommended when portability is an issue.
<sentence>	xml:lang	Similar to the <paragraph> tag, this tag defines the boundaries on textual structure, in this case sentences.
<say-as>	type	This attributes allows us to specify a pronunciation format by the type attribute. These "types" of pronunciations can be limited to those specified by SSML or can be custom types. For portability, we recommend that their use be limited to those types specified by the SSML Schema. The following types are specified for <say-as> by SSML: 1. *acronym*—The text enclosed by <say-as> and </say-as> is to be treated as an acronym and pronounced by its full pronunciation. For example, if the text enclosed is SSML, it is to be pronounced as "Speech Synthesis Markup Language." 2. *spell-out*—The text enclosed by <say-as> and </say-as> tags is to be pronounced as a series of letters. This tag is really the opposite of the acronym tag. This tag is used if we want the acronym (or other text) pronounced by the letters that make it up. For example, if the text enclosed is SSML, it is to be pronounced as "S-S-M-L."

(continued)

Table 7.7 (continued)

Tag Name	Attributes	Definition
		3. *number:ordinal*—This implies that the text enclosed within the <say-as> and </say-as> tags is a number and is to be pronounced as an "ordinal." Ordinal pronunciations are pronunciations such as "fifteenth" or "forty-second." 4. *number:cardinal*—This implies that the text enclosed within the <say-as> and </say-as> tags is to be pronounced as a "cardinal." Examples of cardinal pronunciations are "twenty-seven" or "nine." 5. *number:digit* —If the number enclosed within the <say-as> and </say-as> tags are to be pronounced as the individual digits that make them up, use this type. Examples may be "five five five one two one two" if the text enclosed is 555–1212. 6. *date:[specified format]*—Pronunciation of dates may be specified in a variety of ways, depending on whether the day, month, year, or any combination thereof is to be used in the pronunciation. The [specified format] can be replaced by 'm' for month, 'd' for day, or 'y' for year. For example, if we want to produce the pronunciation "March 12, 1972" we specify the format as date:mdy. Any permutation of the three is an acceptable date format. 7. *time:[specified format]*—Like dates, we may specify formatting for time using the keys 'h' for hour, 'm' for minutes, and 's' for seconds. However, unlike date, the 'h' must always be specified and 'm' must be specified if 's' is specified. In other words, time must be pronounced in decreasing units with the larger units always pronounced first. We may, for example, have time:hm but not time:ms nor time:mh. 8. *duration:[specified format]*—The same units as time specifications are used and although the order of larger to smaller must be preserved like time, it is not required to have the larger units. For example, time:hm and time:ms are both valid wheras time:mh is not. The pronunciation of duration and time are different in that durations are pronounced with time unit delimiters such as "one hour, twenty minutes, and thirty seconds" whereas times are pronounced with duration unit delimiters such as "two thirty-five fifty-five seconds pm."

		9. *currency*—If the text enclosed within the <say-as> and </say-as> tags refers to a monetary quantity, for example $25.67, it is to be pronounced as such (twenty-five dollars and sixty-seven cents). 10. *net:[Specified Type of Internet Address]*—The text enclosed within the <say-as> and </say-as> tags is to be pronounced as an Internet address. Currently support for two types are provided ([Specified Type of Internet Address]): net:email and net:uri. 11. *name*—This type exists strictly to assist the speech-synthesis engine in putting the right pronunciation rules on proper names such as names of companies, persons, etc. 12. *telephone*—special formatting may be provided for pronouncing phone numbers. Setting the type attribute to telephone instructs the speech-synthesis engine to apply the special formatting to the text enclosed within the <say-as> </say-as> tags. 13. *measure*—Special formatting may be provided for pronouncing measurements such as weights, lengths, and others. Applying this type causes the activation of those special formats. For example, we may want "54 m" pronounced as "fifty-four meters."
<phoneme>	ph, alphabet	This element provides a way to tell the speech-synthesis engine to pronounce a particular piece of text in a specific way. Whereas the pronunciation is included in the ph attribute, the text to be pronounced is enclosed within the <phoneme></phoneme> tags, and the alphabet attribute indicates what character standard is used to specify the phoneme. The International Phonetic Standard (IPA) is the alphabet set used by default, but whatever the desired alphabet is may be specified. Because IPA characters are cryptic, the W3C is working toward coming up with an easily understandable alphabet for representing the pronunciation of phonemes.

(*continued*)

Table 7.7 (continued)

Tag Name	Attributes	Definition
<sub>	alias	The text enclosed within the tags contains the written text to be displayed and the alias attribute of the tag contains the text for the pronunciation of the text. As we will see later, it is crucial not to overuse or misuse this tag as we will be generating VUIs based on a specialization of a generic user interface. As you noted in Chapter 6, we did the same with graphical and textual user interfaces. Generating VUIs from a textual or GUI that has already been specialized is typically an architectural mistake unless there are some extraordinary circumstances.
<voice>	xml:lang, gender, age, variant, name	This element is used to specify change in the "sound-and-feel" of the speech generated by the speech-synthesis engine. This tag is very useful in delivering the sound that a given user might prefer based on his or her profile. The xml:lang element, as before, specifies the language to be used; be very careful in the usage of this attribute as its implementation is optional and you are never guaranteed of the granularity of internationalization implementation by the speech-synthesis engine that you are using. Let us go through the other attributes: 1. *gender*: The values that can be assigned to this attribute are male, female, and neutral. As its name suggests, the gender attribute allows us to specify whether the generated speech sounds like a male, sounds like a female, or is neutral. This attribute is useful when dealing with a diverse user base as users typically feel more comfortable and at ease communicating with a female voice whereas male voices communicate sternness and clarity in applications that may suit such needs. 2. *age*: Like gender, whether dealing with concatenated speech or generated speech, the produced voice can have qualities similar to that of a person of a particular age. This attribute helps specify, as an integer number, the age of a hypothetical person to whose voice would be closest to the produced speech.

		3. *variant*: If there are several variations of each of the other attributes (gender, age, etc.) made available by the speech-synthesis engine, the variant attribute allows us to specify which one to use. For example, if there are two possible variations of a thirty-five-year-old female voice made available, we can first select variant 1 and, if the user has a tough time understanding her, switch to variant 2. The variant attribute must be an integer. 4. *name*: More sophisticated user interfaces create entire personas to emulate real human beings. The name attribute provides a hook into such personas. Each persona can have a particular type of prosody, as well as other qualities, associated with its voice.
<emphasis>	level	Just as in GUIs, there are segments of the information communicated to the user that may be more important than others. In SSML, these sections can be included within the <emphasis></emphasis> tags. The level attribute allows us to specify how emphasized a section of content becomes when converted to speech. The level attribute can be set to *strong*, *moderate*, *reduced*, and *none*. The first three are handled by the speech-synthesis engine, preferably in a language-dependent manner, to emphasize or deemphasize particular segments of speech. Setting the level attribute to "none" allows one to remove emphasis from a small section of text that is a segment of a bigger text portion that is to be emphasized. In other words, "none" works like negative logic.
<break>	size, time	This tag specifies pauses in speech that can be considered roughly equivalent to physical spacing (spaces, tabs, carriage returns, etc.) in graphical return interfaces. The size attribute allows us to specify a relative length (restricted to *none*, *small*, *medium*, and *large*); the time attribute allows us to specify an exact period of time in seconds or milliseconds (such as time = "2s" or time = "40ms").
<prosody>	pitch, contour, range, rate, duration, volume	This element can wrap around the other elements (but not the root element of speech) to specify fine-tuned attributes of the sound-and feel of the speech synthesized. The attributes that allow us to control prosody are as follows:

(*continued*)

Table 7.7 (continued)

Tag Name	Attributes	Definition
		1. *contour*: Contour, also known as the pitch contour, specifies how the pitch changes over a particular speech segment. In a way, if pitch is graphed vs. time, contour is the first derivative of the curve. Contour is specified as sets of (*interval, target*), where interval is specified as a percentage of the duration (between 0 and 100%) and target is the absolute or relative value of the pitch increase or decrease. 2. *pitch*: Pitch may be specified in hertz or as a relative value to be assigned *low, medium, high*, or *default*. It may also be specified as a percentage of the range accommodated by the speech-synthesis engine. 3. *range*: The range of allowable pitches can be specified in hertz or in a relative manner using *medium, high, low*, or *default*. This range is subsequently used by other relative measurements for the other attributes referring to the pitch. 3. *rate*: This attribute determines how many words per minute are pronounced by the speech-synthesis engine. To specify a relative rate, *slow, fast, medium*, and *default* can be used. 5. *duration*: The duration, in seconds or milliseconds, is how long the text enclosed within the <prosody></prosody> tags takes to pronounce. 6. *volume*: The volume of the speech to be generated within the tags can be specified in a relative manner (*default, silent, soft, medium*, and *loud*) or as a floating-point number from 0.00 to 100.00.
<audio>	src	This element is provided to allow us to create speech output by concatenation of prerecorded audio. The src attribute is used to point to the source of audio (e.g., src="helloworld.wav"); the content within the <audio></audio> tags is replaced by the contents of the audio file when speech is synthesized.
<mark>	name	This tag is used to create markers within the SSML document. These markers can be used by the speech-synthesis engine or by the application. For example, if we want a particular section repeated, a marker can be used to mark segments where the repetition sequence may begin.

```
<?xml version="1.0" encoding="ISO-8859-1"?>
<speak version="1.0" xml:lang="en-US" xmlns="http://www.w3.
  org/2001/10/synthesis">
    <paragraph>
    <voice gender="female" age="35">
        <say-as type="name"> Cienecs, Inc. </say-as>
        <sentence>is located at </sentence>
        <say-as type="address">1906 Pine Street, Huntington
          Beach, California 92648</say-as>
        <sentence>To arrive at </sentence>
        <say-as type="name"> Cienecs </say-as>
        <sentence>from Huntington Beach, please follow these
          directions:</sentence>
        <!---The actual directions would be here -->
        <sentence>The duration of your trip will be
          approximately</sentence>
        <say-as type="hms">2:25:34</say-as>
        <sentence>If you have any questions regarding the
          services offered by</sentence>
        <say-as type="name">Cinenecs, Inc.</say-as>
        <sentence>please e-mail us at</sentence>
        <say-as type="net:email">rbfar@cienecs.com</say-as>
        </voice>
    </paragraph>
</speak>
```

FIGURE 7.31. SSML Document for Pronouncing Simple Directions.

analogous technology for speech-based content. However, as W3C moved toward standards that treated multiple user interfaces and channels, it became obvious that ACSS needed to be integrated into a bigger picture of styling that treated both aural and visual contents. Therefore, ACSS has been integrated into the Cascading Style Sheets 2 (CSS 2).

Before we go any further, it should be noted that because SSML is an XML-based technology, we can use XSLs for styling. The trade-off between using XSLs for formatting of aural content instead of CSS 2 is that XSL implementation is more complex. Most voice browser vendors elect to implement CSS and not XSL. If XSLs are to be used for formatting, the application developer must build the proper layering mechanism using some XSL transformation engine such as Xalan. Just like GUI browsers, VUI browsers typically do not implement XSLs as a formatting mechanism for the client side (though in the case of aural user interfaces, the client side typically means applications that run on servers). So, if we decided to use XSLs, we would need to feed a finalized SSML to the voice browser. In other words, whereas most voice browsers will probably know how to bind CSS 2 and SSML documents together to produce a resulting SSML document, they do not know how to use XSL to do this. Of course, to build a complex multimodal application, we should avoid the antipattern of trying to use the same tool for all problems and use both CSS and XSL to produce the final document in an appropriate manner. We will discuss this further in Chapter 8.

CSS syntax is simple. Things called "Properties" are specified and can be applied to elements within the document to which the CSS is being applied. This is accomplished through things called Rules. Rules are specified as follows:

```
PropertyName {Value, Initial, Applies to, Inherited,
  Percentages, Media}
```

PropertyName is a *selector*. Selectors are the method by which the browser knows what elements to apply the rule to. Selectors can be specific types or expressed as an expression that defines a regular-expression-type syntax for finding what elements to apply the rule to. The other parameters are used to specify a value for the various attributes of a selected element.

We will not go through the syntax of CSS 2 or ACSS here as it is readily available on the W3C site and because there are no complex concepts introduced that we have not already covered. However, it is good to look at the taxonomy that the ACSS specify. Namely, the selectors can be one of the following:

1. *Volume*: This allows us to adjust the volume of aural output from the system to the user.
2. *Speak*: This is the text to be converted to voice through Text-To-Speech (TTS).
3. *Pause-Before*: This allows us to pause before rendering an aural element.
4. *Pause-After*: This allows us to pause after rendering an aural element.
5. *Pause*: This allows us to pause a specified amount of time.
6. *Cue-Before*: This allows us to play back an auditory icon before an aural element.
7. *Cue-After*: This allows us to play back an auditory icon after an aural element.
8. *Play-During*: This allows us to play background audio while an element is playing.
9. *Speech-Rate*: This element exists to specify how many words per minute are pronounced.
10. *Voice-Family*: Think of this attribute as your "aural font." This attribute is only applicable if multiple voices are provided by the underlying voice platform (such as male, female, young, old, etc.).
11. *Pitch*: This allows us to specify the average pitch of the aural element. This is applicable when dealing with pure machine-generated speech synthesis or filtered concatenated synthesis.
12. *Pitch-Range*: As we mentioned when discussing the qualities of speech, human speech has an upper bound and a lower bound frequency for speech. Pitch-Range is used to specify these boundaries.
13. *Stress*: This allows us to stress different aural elements (or words if TTS is used) while outputting voice to the user.
14. *Richness*: This allows us to specify how "rich" the voice is. This is not the volume of the voice. Rather, it depends on the number of frequencies projected by the voice (thereby called richness).
15. *Speak-Punctuation*: This allows us to specify whether a punctuation mark is pronounced by its name (such as the ";", which is pronounced semicolon)

```
<smil xmlns="http://www.w3.org/2001/SMIL20/Language">
   <body>
      <par>
         <ref src="GetAddress.html" begin="0s" />
         <ref src="address.ssml" begin="1s"/>
      </par>
   </body>
</smil>
```

FIGURE 7.32. SMIL Document Using the SSML Document in Figure 7.31.

or whether it is used to determine accents of other words throughout the playback.

16. *Speak-Numeral*: This allows us to specify the pronunciation of numbers.

CSS 2 Aural Style Sheets are not very pervasive among the voice browsers; however, there is some current effort to provide for CSS 2 Aural Style Sheets (or equivalent styling technologies for VUI markup languages) in voice browsers.

Interoperability with SMIL and CCML

You may have already wondered how one integrates the content coming from a text-to-speech synthesis engine with other content and input from the user. One of the tools in integrating the various types of markup content offered by W3C is SMIL. We will discuss SMIL in detail in Chapter 8, but for now let us introduce a quick example of what a SMIL document may look like. The document in Figure 7.32 provides us with driving directions.

We are not going to discuss the SMIL syntax at this point, but it should be clear that integrating an SSML document into an SMIL document is fairly simple.

When it comes to integration with CCML, SSML should be used within VXML. So, we integrate SSML into CCML using the SSML document as a part of a VXML document whose dialogue browser can communicate with our CCML container.

7.5.4 Voice Portlets

If you recall, we discussed the idea of user interface components in Chapter 5. Portlets are simply independent user interface components that can be used to create portals. Portals have been a concept promulgated by the Internet and Web sites such as Yahoo! and others that provide a one-stop shop for information. As the Internet evolved, these Web sites began allowing users to customize their user interface to access the site through putting together components that provided independent pieces of information. These components became popular and are now referred to as portlets. As you may imagine, this concept is one that was conceived within the confines of GUIs.

Nonetheless, we can apply the same concepts to VUIs. A voice portlet is simply an independent dialogue, encapsulating a set of voice interactions, that can be put together with other voice portlets to create a voice portal. The key in designing and implementing voice portlets is the same as for their GUI counterparts:

1. A voice portlet must be designed to avoid dependencies on voice interactions not encapsulated in its implementation.
2. A voice portlet must be designed to implicitly create dependencies on it by other voice portlets or any voice interaction outside of the voice portlet.
3. A voice portlet must be designed to allow for easy integration with other portlets to produce a voice portal.

The first thing we need for creating voice portlets is a platform-neutral framework tool such as JSAPI or VXML. Also, because portlets have traditionally been defined as components that are made using markup languages, we narrow our choice down to VXML.

We do not recommend that as a developer you develop your own voice portal framework. Most major vendors of voice recognition and speech-synthesis products provide a framework to build basic portal functionality. For example, Nuance"s product is Voyager. Voyager provides a framework for building portal modules such as news, weather, etc. Voyager and its competitive products are shipped with a prebuilt set of voice portlets that provide some basic functionality (such as driving directions).

7.6 Summary

Before moving on to the next chapter where we learn how to mix modes, channels, and interfaces to build dynamic mobile applications, let us review what we learned in this chapter and see how we can apply it to build real mobile applications.

We started the chapter by learning about the basics of VUIs, the core technologies required to build a VUI, and the taxonomy of the tools available to build VUIs. Next, we looked at JSAPI and VXML, respectively a Java API and an XML application for creating VUIs, as examples of the existing tools. We also saw that most of today's VUIs are primarily designed for telephony systems and, therefore, looked at CCML and JTAPI as two methods of building VUI application that involve call control. We then saw how we could use UML to model voice applications.

Later in the chapter we took a step back and looked at some principles that we should apply in building good VUIs. We recommend that the reader study designing VUIs in more detail if they are to be used for a mobile application. Our attempt here was to take a quick survey of the technologies and tools used and to learn how to build a simple VUI. The best mobile applications are typically mutichannel and multimodal, allowing the users to access the system through any channel desired and in any chosen media format. VUIs are only one piece of the puzzle.

Now that we have learned about mobile VUIs and GUIs, let us move on to discuss mobile multichannel and multimodal user interfaces.

CHAPTER 8

Multichannel and Multimodal User Interfaces

Seek first God's Kingdom, that is, become like the lilies and the birds, become perfectly silent. Then shall the rest be added to you.

Søren Kierkegaard

8.1 INTRODUCTION

We have thus far discussed user interfaces in some detail. We have seen that, depending on the function of the mobile application, we may want to interact with the user through audio, a traditional GUI, or a combination thereof. We have also seen that, because of the wide variety of capabilities among mobile devices and the proliferation of the platforms, there are a great number of user interfaces that we may have to implement for a given application. Although we have looked at mobile GUIs and then VUIs individually, we have not looked at the discipline of building applications that may use more than one channel of communication with the network or interact with the user through more than one mode of their user interface. This is what we will be discussing in this chapter.

First, let us define what multichannel and multimodal mean for these two terms have been incorrectly used widely in the literature on mobile computing. To start, remember that multimodal and multichannel are not the same thing. Multichannel may have two different meanings. First, it can be used to imply a user interface that establishes more than one communication channel to the user. For example, a user interface may present an audio and a video channel to the user. It can also be used to refer to the number of different types of channels that a networked mobile application uses to reach other nodes on the network: If there is more than one channel—for example, a PSTN channel and a TCP/IP channel—the application is a multichannel application.

Multimodality refers to the number of ways a user interface for an application may be presented. Hence, an application that only has a GUI but makes this GUI available to Palm devices as well as Windows-based desktops is a multimodal application. Multimodality is a superset of the first definition of multichannel we discussed (where multichannel refers to the number of channels of communication between the computing apparatus and the user).

Within the context of this text, we will use the term "multichannel" to refer to the number of channels established between a networked mobile application and the other participants in the network. We will use the term "multimodal" to refer to applications with user interfaces that have multiple methods of presenting the output to the user and receiving input from the user.

Next, we need to define what "modalities" or "modes" are in and of themselves. Obviously, there are many ways to define them, but we will choose the definition used by UTMS [UTMS P1104 2002], which defines five main modes based on the human senses (audio, vision, touch, smell, and taste). To date, the three major modes that are important in communicating with computing devices are audio, vision, and touch. Within the context of this text, we will define modalities or modes to be the unique variations of these three communication methods as implemented by the computing system. For example, a monitor provides a visual modality whereas a three-dimensional hologram provides a different visual modality. Likewise, DTMF input to a phone provides one form of audio-based modality whereas voice recognition offers another modality.

It is equally as important to distinguish between multimedia and multimodal. Multimedia refers to the content presented to a user; it is purely a term applicable to the output channel of the user interface.

Our focus in this chapter will be to first see the problem set associated with building multimodal and multichannel applications and then move on to some techniques and tools that help us deliver solutions to these problems. In the process, we also hope that the examples will show the reader why we want to introduce multimodality and multichannel properties to mobile applications. We will discuss multimodal architectures, tools for multimodal user interface development, the relevance of multimodality to mobile application development, and how we can use UML to help us develop multimodal applications.

Before we delve into the design concerns of multimodal and multichannel applications, let us look at the mobile user's "user experience." Improving the user experience is largely the intent of multimodality.

8.1.1 Multimodality, the User Experience, and Usage Context

Why do we need multimodal applications? The answer is simple: to make the application more convenient to use given the condition of the mobile user and the dimensions of mobility. By default, all human communication behavior is multimodal; people are known to gesture even during telephone conversations, despite the fact that they know that the other interlocutor cannot see these gestures [UTMS

P1104 2002]. Obviously, one of our goals in building any type of user interface, not just mobile ones, is to get as close to the natural state of human-to-human communication for human-to-computer interactions. Such considerations are what form the user experience.

But what are the critical factors that affect the user experience of the mobile user?

The answer to this question brings us to fields that are orthogonal to mobile computing; nevertheless, they play an important role in building well-designed and well-implemented mobile applications. In addition to the mobile condition of the user and the dimensions of mobility we have discussed repeatedly in this text, *contextual* and *environmental* factors are two factors that spur the use of multiple types of channels in communicating with the user, thereby making multimodal development that much more important.

1. *Context-Aware Computing*: We have talked about the mobile condition of the user, which describes those added dimensions that affect the user's state of being while interacting with the mobile application. However, there also the context in which the user is using any computing application, be it mobile or not. This context adds meaning to when, where, and how the user interacts with the computing application and gives a different meaning to the individual interactions. Much of the context is defined by the domain: What is the problem that the application is trying to solve (commerce, navigation, game, etc.)? Users typically think of context-aware applications as "smarter" (if they are well designed). What this translates to is a better usage experience by the user.
2. *Environmental Factors*: We know that our target users are mobile. We also understand that the dimensions of mobility distinguish the design and implementation of mobile applications from their stationary counterparts. Environmental conditions can further complicate the problem. For example, an application that is to be used in a rugged environment with low visibility may have additional requirements when it comes to the user interface.

To evaluate the user's experience with a mobile application, we suggest utilizing techniques that analyze the user's response iteratively throughout the development process. Consolvo and Walker outline such a technique in their Experience Sampling Method (ESM), which is borrowed from the field of psychology alerts [Consolvo and Walker 2003]. Essentially, participants fill out several brief questionnaires every day by responding to a questionnaire. In their study, Consolvo and Walker define a technique by which to acquire information about the experience of the mobile user instead of defining what and how to acquire from the user. In other words, they define a "metatechnique" for gathering information from the users. This is very valuable because it can be applied to any mobile application regardless of the context and the environment. Other variables such as the domain of the application, the context of its usage, and the environment of its usage can then be used to further refine the information-gathering process and to define the actual questions that the users are asked.

To apply this technique to mobile applications, Consolvo and Walker introduce the concepts of *alerting, delivering*, and *capturing*. Delivery and capturing refer to how the questionnaire is presented to the user and how the answers are collected; alerting provides a method for seeing user responses to what we have referred to as an active interaction in this text. Consolvo and Walker use PDAs to collect their data from the user in their study. Because the user is mobile, he or she uses the PDA to answer the questionnaire whether prompted by an alert or otherwise. The great advantage that this technique offers, for mobile applications, is that the user's experience can be captured at the moment when he or she is mobile and interacting with the mobile application.

So, how does all of this help us? To build good mobile applications, we need to build as good of a user interface as we possibly can. Remember, once again, the condition of the mobile user (the lack of focus, etc.). However, simply building a multimodal interface does not mean that we are building a good interface. In fact, introducing multimodality can decrease the efficiency and worsen the usage experience of an application, particularly if not done prudently. To know how and when to use multimodality (for example, which interactions are better presented in audio than visually), we need to understand more than the domain. We need to understand the context in which the mobile application is used by a mobile user and the various environments in which it may be used. ESM as specified by Consolvo and Walker give us a scientifically valid way of collecting data that leads to the right decisions. ESM is an ecologically valid user study technique that provides the opportunity for collecting quantitative and qualitative data [Consolvo and Walker]. (Ecologically valid means that the technique is verified to be valid in the environment in which it is being used.) In this way, we can collect information from the user, while the user is mobile, on whether we are effectively using a multimodal user interface to interact with him or her.

There continue to be more techniques that help in defining discrete methods of quantifying user's experience and thereby optimizing that experience, especially in mobile computing. What we have mentioned here is simply an example. Whereas there are many ways to improve the user's experience with multimodality, it is equally as important to know when not to use a particular modality. For example, Dahl [Dahl 2003] identifies privacy, fear of disturbing others, costs, and accuracy as some of the hurdles in using speech for multimodal applications. So, for example, if the user is to enter a password into the system (privacy) we do not want him or her to have to say this password in an environment where the password may be heard. Conversely, voice may be used as a voiceprint to identify the user. So when it comes to mutimodality, usability becomes a twofold study: First, we have to see the usability aspects of every individual modality being used in a set of interactions and then we have to look at the interplay of these modalities as one contiguous stream of information being exchanged between the user and the system.

Our ability as application developers to deliver a very friendly user interface to the end user is constricted by the limitations of our tools for development and the underlying infrastructure for which we develop our mobile application. So, next we will look at this infrastructure.

8.1.2 Multimodality, Multichannel Communication with the Network, and Network Infrastructures

Once we get past deciding how and when to use multimodality to build our application (at least the first phase of it as this should ideally be an iterative process), we need to implement it! This is where we start hitting some roadblocks. As we have seen, most mobile devices are resource-starved. This means that there is typically some bottleneck in network communication, CPU, permanent storage, memory, or some other capability of the device. Implementing multimodality-related features, not unlike any other feature that we may wish to build into the mobile application, requires CPU, storage space, memory, and other resources. So, multimodality is not always desirable or possible based on the amount of resources on the device. For example, communicating with the user with an audio and a visual channel may make the application exceed the amount of memory available on the device or drain the power too quickly.

Once we get past the device, if it is capable of rendering a multimodal user interface that we desire for our particular application, we need to see whether the underlying network supports all the communication channels we need for the various modes. Fortunately, here, we typically only have to worry about three different types of channels: data, audio, and video. Unfortunately, there are variants of each channel as standardization has not limited them to a manageable number.

For data, the world is a bit clearer: TCP/IP is dominant. But TCP/IP's dominance is primarily because of its dominance in wired networks not because it is specially well suited for wireless networks. With mobile IP (IPv6), which we will look at later in this text, we find a more suitable data channel for wirelessly connected mobile devices. PDAs have traditionally been limited to a data channel. Cell phones, however, have most recently offered data through WAP along with the mainstay of providing voice access.

With GSM and any cellular system prior to GSM, there is only one channel to the mobile device. This channel may be used to provide voice or data, but not both at the same time. In this sense, we can write a multimodal application for these networks that provides access to one channel at a time but not both simultaneously. There is no provisions for video as the limited bandwidth precludes having a meaningful video feed. Moreover, the switchover between voice and data is typically very clunky because the handshake between the network and the device to establish a voice or a data connection takes a finite amount of time, making it difficult to produce a seamless application.

General Packet Radio Service (GPRS) is the first type of network that enables multiple channels to exist simultaneously. The two predominant network technologies are TDMA and CDMA. Currently, on the CDMA side, the BREW development platform provides an integrated, but closed, programming environment for third-party developers. BREW offers the infrastructure and bandwidth for multiple channels. Several companies have already begun to implement VoIP on top of the TCP/IP connection provided in BREW. VoIP allows us to use the same type of channel, namely an IP-based channel, to transmit both voice and data. CDMA2000 and WCDMA will provide enough bandwidth to make it possible to address the problem of streaming video over the long-range wireless connection, but these networks have not yet been deployed in any significant capacity.

Furthermore, WLANs (wireless LANs) such as WIFI (wireless fidelity, further described in later chapters) and Bluetooth are becoming more and more pervasive, thereby offering high-bandwidth access to the network through IP-based technologies. Although it will be a long time until long-range wireless technologies will offer comparable bandwidth to WLANs, WLANs can be used today as a method of connectivity that provides enough bandwidth for not only voice and data but also for real-time video streaming.

Let us not forget about the device. More and more, PDAs and phones are converging into one device. A good example is the Handspring Treo. With a telephony channel and a data channel available, the only barrier to writing multimodal applications that offer voice and data access simultaneously remains the underlying network and a mobile device operating system that can handle these multiple channels.

In the very near future, perhaps by the time you are reading this text, most mobile platforms and networks will offer data and voice channels that may be accessed simultaneously. To author applications that have no limitations on the user interface you can use and the kind of data that can be presented or collected from the user, improvements must be made in QOS and bandwidths of the long-range wireless networks. Additionally, devices will need to become more powerful.

In this chapter we will disregard such infrastructure limitations that apply to the process of developing a mobile application, but keep in mind that what you can do is limited by the infrastructure on top of which you are authoring your application. We will address most concerns at a high level so that you can take these notions and concepts and apply them to whatever infrastructure is available at the time of developing your application. One of the most important taxonomies that allow us to organize ideas about multimodality are the types of multimodal content and interactions. This is what we will look at next.

8.1.3 Types of Multimodality

We discussed taxonomy of user interfaces, user interface components, and mobile application development concerns in Chapter 5. We then defined multimodality and looked at developing graphical and aural user interfaces. Now, let us further define some abstractions and taxonomies that help us in handling the problem of multimodality.

As we defined in Chapter 5, user interfaces establish channels of communication to the user. There are input and output channels depending on whether the channel can present information to the user, obtain information from the user, or do both. Multimodality, then, is the use of two or more channels. What we define is as Wahlster [Wahlster 2003] defines the notion of symmetric and asymmetric multimodality. Symmetric multimodality means that all input modes (speech, gesture, facial expression, etc.) are also available for output, and vice versa; a dialogue system with symmetric multimodality must understand and represent not only the user's multimodal input but also its own multimodal output. Furthermore, we borrow from our discussion of natural language, mixed-initiative, and directed dialogue in VUI development and extend it to development of multimodal applications. Multimodal user interfaces are a superset of VUIs; therefore, they may be able to communicate with the user in any of these modes (see Chapters 5 and 7 for an in-depth discussion of natural language, mixed-mode, and directed-dialogue interactions with the user).

The goal of most user interface research efforts today is to move user interfaces toward a more natural and symmetric multimodal environment. However, the limited capabilities of mobile devices, limitations of the existing wireless networks, and other factors discussed in this text make it very difficult if not impossible to build natural and symmetric multimodal user interfaces. It is even very difficult to build just a symmetric multimodal (directed-dialogue interactions) or a natural asymmetric interface. Building symmetric multimodality is difficult because most user interface channel types have been designed to do either input or output but not both (voice being an exception). For example, whereas the monitor is used to display visual information, the keyboard and the mouse are used to enter information into the system. This comprises an asymmetric channel.

A touch-screen comprises a symmetric channel. Obviously, at some point in the internal implementation of the interface channel, be it hardware or software, things are not symmetric: The mechanism used to light up the pixels on the screen is different than the mechanism that collects the user's touch on the screen. Also, we could say that touch-screens are not symmetric because the tactile sense is also used (in addition to the visual output and the need for visual inspection of the screen to enter input). However, we are only concerned with symmetry at the layer where the user interacts with the system. In this case, this is the display. And, hopefully, this is also shown as a symmetrical software interface (API, etc.) to the user interface channel.

We can also recognize the type of multimodality applicable by recognizing the type of input. The input side of the equation is typically much more complex in any interface system, particularly a multimodal system, whereas the variables in producing the proper multimodal output are more well known and more easily controllable. So, the complexity of a multimodal user interface depends largely on the number and type of input channels. Niklfeld, Finan, and Pucher recognize the following by leveraging work from the W3C [Niklfeld, Finan, and Pucher]:

1. *Sequential multimodal* input is the simplest type, where at each step of the interaction, either one or the other input modality is active, but never more than one simultaneously.
2. *Uncoordinated, simultaneous multimodal* input allows concurrent activation of more than one modality. However, should the user provide input on more than one modality, this information is not integrated but will be processed in isolation, in random order.
3. *Coordinated, simultaneous multimodal* input fully exploits multimodality, providing for the integration of complementary input signals from different modalities into a joint event, based on timestamping.

Most of what is available today supports only the first type of multimodality outlined here, namely sequential multimodality. Most mobile devices (PDAs, WAP phones, etc.) run simple operating systems that are single threaded (or single process) and are only able to present one mode at a time to the user. Once the devices, operating systems, and networks support, respectively, modalities, multiple processes, and channels of communication, we need a tool to write applications that allow us to specify the coordination (temporal, spatial, etc.) of the various modalities. We will be discussing SMIL later in this chapter as such a tool.

Another rather obvious method by which we can create a type of system for multimodality is to recognize the various groupings of the individual modalities that make up a particular implementation of a multimodal interface. For example, we can say that voice and text combine to make one modality or that voice in a GUI can combine to make another modality (in fact, this is how W3C's XHTML + Voice (X + V) standard defines multimodality). This way of typing multimodality is obvious and somewhat insignificant as new types of multimodality surface everyday owing to continuing advances and innovations in creating new devices and dependent user-interface types, which in turn give rise to new modalities.

Oviatt [Oviatt, Jacko, and Sears 2002] provides us with additional taxonomy of input modes by distinguishing active from passive input modes. Active input modes are ones that are deployed by the user intentionally as an explicit command to the computer system (e.g., speech); passive input modes refer to naturally occurring user behavior or actions that are recognized by a computer (e.g., facial expressions and manual gestures).

The final taxonomy of multimodality may be based on the type of interactions between the user and the user interface. Bernsen [Bernsen 2002] introduces a taxonomy of interaction types for multimodal user interfaces based on the characteristics of interactions through individual modalities and a collection of modalities. This taxonomy is multidimensional. First, he defines *atomic* and *composite* modalities. As the names imply, atomic modalities are those modalities that cannot be decomposed into a combination of other modalities without losing their meaning. Composite modalities can be defined completely by the nature of the atomic modalities that make them up. The other dimensions are linguistic/nonlinguistic, analog/nonanalog, arbitrary/nonarbitrary, and static/dynamic. *Linguistic representations* are based on existing syntactic–semantic–pragmatic systems of meaning; linguistic representations such as speech and text can somehow represent anything, and one might therefore wonder why we need any other kind of modality for representing information [Bernsen 2002]. Basically, Bernsen is referring to the use of natural language versus mixed-initiative versus directed-dialogue forms of communicating with the system. It is obvious that using natural language is the ideal solution, but because of technology limitations, we have to use other forms, some of which may fall within the nonlinguistic category. The distinction between *nonarbitrary* and *arbitrary* representations marks the difference between representations that, to perform the representational function, rely on already existing systems of meaning and representations that do not [Bernsen 2002]. Clearly, the user interface functions better when it is built on nonarbitrary representations, at least as defined by a typical user. For example, if the typical user expects to both hear and see a confirmation message at the end of some financial transaction with the user interface, and this is how we design our user interface, then we are abiding by nonarbitrary representation. *Analog* representations are also often referred to as iconic representations. Although all of this may seem overly theoretical, it provides us with a general framework for thinking about the different types of things that make up multimodal interactions with the user interface.

8.1.4 Usability-Centered Usage of Multimodality

As with any technology, engineering technique, algorithm, methodology, architecture, or any tool in our toolsmith bag of software engineering, it is important that we do not use multimodality for the sake of using multimodality or for the sake of making a "cool" application. The point of building multimodal user interfaces is to improve the usability of an application.

However, multimodal user interfaces are a relatively new technology. Understanding usability issues is something that comes about after years of maturity and deployment experience for a particular technology. Because of this it is neither possible nor in the scope of this text to outline all possible uses of multimodality. In this section, we will simply outline the following examples of good uses for multimodality:

1. Most of the readers of this text should be familiar with usage of DTMF to disambiguate unrecognizable speech input. Multimodality can serve as a general disambiguation mechanism for those systems whose primary interface is through voice but that also allow for other types of data entry. A voice recognition system augmented with DTMF is an example of this. Another example could be a VUI accessed through a cell phone that allows for disambiguation through a text-based user interface (WAP, J2ME, etc.). In a study that includes surveys of the users' various responses to multimodality as the disambiguation mechanism for a VUI, Oviatt [Oviatt 2002] shows that this strategy can be quite effective. Furthermore, this same study generalizes more to say that multimodal architectures can stabilize error-prone recognition technologies, such as speech input, to yield substantial improvements in robustness. In other words, not only can this technique be specifically used in the case of VUIs, but we can use multimodality as a general way of helping the user and the system lower the number of mistakes in the communication.
2. Not only does multimodality offer a set of user interface–based solutions to the problems introduced by the dimensions of mobility and the mobile condition of the user but it also enables us to build user interfaces that are inherently more adaptive to a wider audience, members of which have varying expectations and preferences when dealing with computing systems. A flexible multimodal interface offers users the freedom to use a combination of modalities, or to switch to a better-suited modality, depending on the specifics of their abilities and preferences, the task at hand, or the usage conditions [Oviatt 2000].
3. Multimodal user interfaces are extremely useful when dealing with disabled, novice, or young users who either are unable to or do not have the knowledge

to operate a GUI. Multimodality is more natural to humans; therefore, they present a way of communicating with a human that reduces the possibility of input error.

4. Simultaneous multimodality (to be defined later) provides a higher bandwidth from the user to the computing system: There are more channels to input information into the system so we can do it faster. In some cases, we can also use simultaneous multimodality for output to the user, though there are limitations imposed by the human brain's ability to process multiple inputs. Cheyer and Julia, for example, show us how to use multimodality in combining aural and visual input and output for using maps [Cheyer and Julia 1995].

Multimodality lends itself particularly well to providing avenues to create solutions that deal with the mobile condition of the user. This is why it is particularly important to us. In conjunction with the aforementioned taxonomy, Pinhanez and colleagues recognize six different dimensions in which a visible display can be measured; [Pinhanez et al. 2003]:

1. *Maximum Width*: We can think of this as the maximum amount of information we can put into one temporal frame. For example, in the aural world, this could be words per minute.
2. *Portability*: This aspect measures the convenience of use of user interface (e.g., the weight of the device based on its screen size, keyboard, etc.).
3. *Ubiquity*: How available is the user interface? Does one have to have a very expensive device to access the system or is it accessible through just about any device, even the plain old telephone?
4. *Saliency*: This has to do with the condition of the mobile user that we mentioned in Chapter 1. Saliency indicates how well the application can interact with the user considering that the user is not focused on the task of computing.
5. *Simultaneity*: This is not the same as simultaneous multimodality. Simultaneity refers to how many different users can be accessing the application simultaneously, collaboratively, or individually. For example, many users can hear from a speaker phone or see a presentation on a projector screen whereas fewer can hear from a headset (just one) or see a presentation on a laptop screen (just a few).
6. *Privacy*: This quality determines how much control we have over making various pieces of user information private.

These dimensions can be extended to other modalities.

8.2 Modeling Multichannel and Multimodal Applications with UML

As has been our convention in this text, we will now look at modeling multimodal user interfaces with UML. The value of doing so is, once again, to provide a consistent technique to design and document our system. There are, of course, many aspects to multimodal user interfaces. These various aspects include the multimedia content, the handling and management of the content, synchronization of the various types of content, and specifying various ways to create composites of single-mode content. Because each of these domains constitutes a different problem set, we need different UML extensions to represent each specific domain. As we have done with other extensions in this text, we will be leveraging works by various academics and commercial organizations.

We have already looked at Nunes' UML extensions, which we have used as our main guiding light in modeling user interface extensions to UML. We recommend continuing usage of these extensions to represent user interfaces and their interactions with the user. Whereas we can use Nunes' Wisdom extensions to represent many aspects of multimodality, as is popular in UML, we can introduce other diagrams to show some of the same properties (and some additional properties) of multimodal systems.

Mandel, Koch, and Maier attack a portion of our problem in their paper "Extending UML to Model Hypermedia and Distributed Systems" [Mandel, Koch, and Maier 1999]. They begin with modeling distribution of an application based on the client–server architecture and creating a UML class diagram, relying on the YAON (yet another object notation) approach to distribution of applications. This is outside of the scope of our discussion. Next, they treat the so-called hypermedia system, which is defined to be a system that supports text, images, sounds, video, and hypertext and is specific to the Web. UML is extended with navigational modeling features (i.e., a graphic notation added to UML) to describe which objects are going to be visited (and how) and in which contexts; in addition, an abstract user interface is given [Mandel, Koch, and Maier 1999]. Here, they leverage the OOHDM (Object-Oriented Hypermedia Design Method).

Mandel, Koch, and Maier use *abstract data views* to basically represent the two-dimensional spatial layout of a GUI. This is essentially a functional mockup of the user interface for GUIs. Next, they introduce *configuration diagrams*; these diagrams can be quite useful in representing properties of multimodal user interfaces. They have the following characteristics:

1. They show the composite structure and composite behavior of the user interface as well as showing the inputs and outputs into a user interface.
2. They also show, at a very high granularity level, the relationship between user interface components and non-user-interface components in the system.
3. They are describable, with UML metamodeling, as a real UML extension.

Figure 8.1 shows a configuration diagram for a basic two-mode user interface that uses voice and keyboard/monitor system for its inputs and outputs. The big advantage here is that we can model relationships between large-grained user interface components and large-grained back-end components. Some of these components may be those that perform business logic, but others may be components needed to provide the necessary functionality for a certain type of modality. For example, we can model transcoding components or voice recognition components.

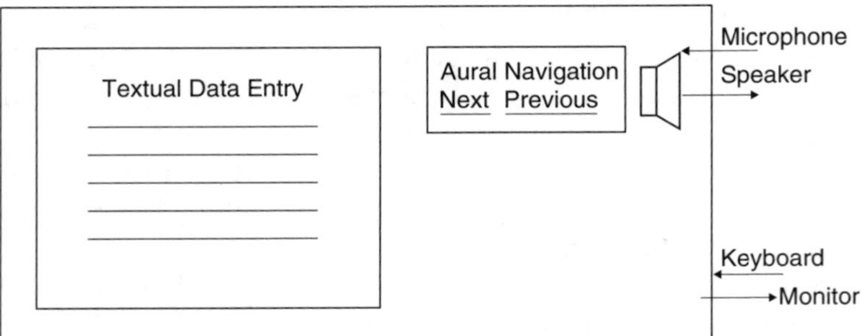

FIGURE 8.1.

Next, Mandel and colleagues introduce an improved version of ADVcharts to provide a visual schema for the specification of the dynamic aspects of the user interface [Mandel, Koch, and Maier 1999]. Normal ADVcharts provide functionality similar to mockups but also include information such as that of state diagrams. So, in a way, they allow us to model the state of the user interface as the user interacts with it. The morphed version of ADVcharts by Mandel and colleagues adds some abstractions to provide for representation of multimedia content as shown in Table 8.1.

Note that to use these abstractions in UML, we need to express them with a metamodel. Mandel et al. do not specify a metamodel for these abstractions; however, we have outlined all of the properties and constraints that would define the classifiers that, in turn, define the appropriate stereotypes.

There are two other abstractions that we do not need: applications and system events. Depending on what type of UML diagram we use, these abstractions exist in one form or another. The important thing to note here is that Mandel et al. have defined these abstractions with some bias toward the WWW as the central content repository. This assumption is not necessarily a bad one since the Web is indeed the largest repository of textual and visual content today so that it is not a far-reaching interpolation to assume that it will be the largest repository of multimodal content as well. However, the content in the mobile system that you deploy may or may not be founded on Web-based technologies; so, keep this assumption in mind. Also, note that one of the biggest reasons that we selected this particular approach to extending UML for multimedia content is that Mandel et al. rely on proven taxonomies of multimodal content as opposed to creating their own, thereby risking simply making errors in their taxonomy or creating impedance mismatch with other existing taxonomies.

Works by Hausmann, Sauer, Heckel, and Engles use UML and its extensions to model multimedia content (which is typically synonymous to multimodal content). These extensions are called the Object-Oriented Modeling of Multimedia Applications (OMMMA). There are three basic stereotypes in OMMMA as shown in Table 8.2.

As you may note, the OMMMA model is somewhat biased toward the MVC design pattern. However, as we mentioned in previous chapters, MVC and PAC are closely related and the same principles introduced by Sauer can be applied to

TABLE 8.1. Hypermedia Extensions for ADVcharts by Mandel, Koch, and Maier

Abstraction Name	Description	Iconic Representation
User Input	This abstraction is created to show the data items that the user gives the system. You can think of these as form fields. Though, per Mandel et al.'s specifications, these are data items that are requested from the user and there is nothing that keeps us from using this abstraction for natural-language or mixed-initiative input modeling.	InputName FieldName1 FieldName2
Anchors	Anchors are the starting points of the navigation [Mandel, Koch, and Maier 1999]. You can think of them as the initial state of a UML state diagram or a UML sequence diagram. This is largely a concept from the design and implementation of HTTP and HTML. Anchors are a navigational tool in HTML	AnchorName
Collections	This abstraction is basically created to indicate that some composition of the other abstractions is itself a valid abstraction; for example, a viewable table may be recognized as a collection.	Collection Name *Object 1 *Object 2
Sound	This abstraction provides a method to represent sound being played back to the user. It is thus an abstraction for an audio output channel. There are two forms of specialized sound abstractions, a sound that starts once the container that holds it is navigated to (for example, the Web page that is to present the audio) and a repeating sound (for example, a background music audio that plays at some specified interval). The first is indicated with a triangle inside the sound icon and the second has a loop above it.	

Table 8.2. Basic OMMMA Stereotypes

Stereotype	Description
Presentation	This stereotype represents the encapsulation of the job of those objects that are responsible for rendering the content, through the relevant channels, to the user. These objects are responsible for determining things like the position of a certain icon on the screen, when a sound should be heard, and other temporal and spatial properties of the user interface.
Media	This stereotype represents an encapsulation of the content. For example, we could have an Audio class (which could be further specialized) or a VisualText class. We can model the commonalities and differences among various media content types using inheritance, aggregation, and more complex design patterns.
Application	This stereotype represents the abstraction of the link between the business logic components and the rest of the system. Application objects can be seen roughly as the equivalent of the model portion of MVC (discussed in earlier chapters).

PAC as well as to MVC (with little modifications in the definition of the stereotypes so that they fit the PAC design pattern a little better). An important point is that OMMMA models multimedia content and not multimodality as a whole. So, it is much better suited for representing and modeling the behavior of the system output while presenting the content and the nature of the content itself than it is to representing user input to the system through various modalities.

Temporal relationships between elements of media presentations are the key characteristics of multimedia applications; the behavioral model of an interactive multimedia application has to account for both the timed and synchronized rendering of predefined scenes and the alteration of the course of presentation caused by user interaction [Hausmann, Heckel, and Sauer 2002]. So, based on the nature of the multimedia content and the defined UML stereotypes, *multimedia sequence diagrams* are introduced.

As we saw in previous chapters, sequence diagrams are the best tool in UML to show temporal interactions among the various components and objects in the system. This is precisely why the sequence diagrams are extended. Hausmann, Heckel, and Sauer first introduce a collection of theorems and then lay out a method by which to specify what they refer to as *dynamic metamodeling*, where they specify rules instead of static relationships in their metamodels. (The details of these techniques lie outside the scope of our discussion.) Then, they use this technique to extend sequence diagrams for representing the properties of multimedia content. For their icons and detailed stereotypes, they use stereotypes very similar to those of Mandel, Koch, and Maier. Specifically, they too use the trapezoid-like shape (the symbol typically used to indicate a speaker on audio-enabled devices) to indicate

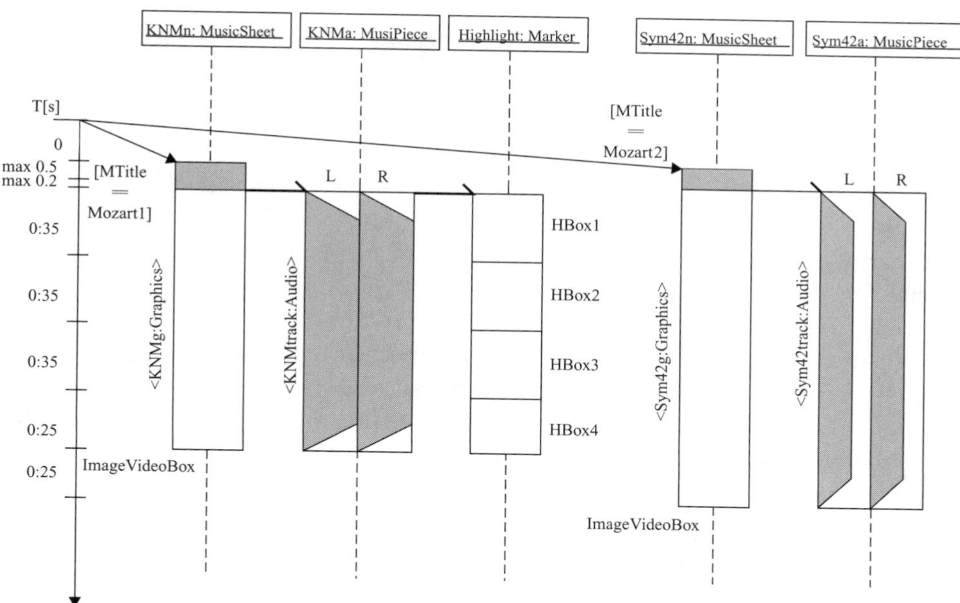

FIGURE 8.2. Example of an OMMMA Sequence Diagram [Sauer and Engles].

audio media. Sauer and Engles have also added markers and a *Y* axis on the side of the sequence diagram to more exactly indicate the time constraints on presenting the various types of media [Sauer and Engles 1999].

Figure 8.2 shows an example of an OMMMA sequence diagram.

This brings us to the end of our discussion of UML extensions that address multimodality. It is important to keep in mind that UML, even without these extensions, is of great value when developing multimodal applications. Let us see how and why.

8.2.1 Using Basic UML Diagrams to Describe Multimodal Applications

Since Chapter 5, we have introduced a series of UML extensions that will allow you to use UML to facilitate developing your mobile applications. Keep in mind that even using UML without any extensions specifically designed for mobility is still very useful in mobile application development. Many mobile application problems are identical to those for stationary applications and those types of problems can be modeled with UML without the need for extensions. For example, we can continue to use class diagrams to represent the internal implementation of our application, interaction diagrams to represent the interactions among the various components and objects in the system, and component diagrams to show the large-grained distribution of responsibility among the components that make up our mobile application.

You should be reminded that we do not form UML profiles on purpose. Based on our discussion in Chapter 4, all of the extensions that we introduce are meant to address some specific problem with mobile computing. It is also not the place of this text to decide how a profile is defined. Though many professionals and academics have created very relevant and useful extensions to UML for addressing problems associated with mobility and mobile applications, there is no standard aggregate of these extensions in the form of profiles. Indeed, it is not the place of this text to specify such profiles. Therefore, there are two options, collect the set of extensions that your project needs and use those. Alternatively, profiles will organically form over time. Extending the functionality of the better UML tools in the marketplace, such as has been done with Object Domain's UML tool, is fairly trivial. So, selecting and implementing the extensions for your project will be well worth it.

Of particular importance are the interaction diagrams. Multimodality complicates the representation of user interactions with the system. In fact, this is where the bulk of complexity is introduced to the modeling and requirements gathering process. This is where interaction diagrams (sequence and collaboration diagrams) become crucial. Sequence diagrams, particularly, provide us with the appropriate tools to model the temporal properties of the interface and the timing relationships among the various channels.

Along the same line of thought, note that we introduce the following series of extensions in this text that can enhance the modeling of multimodal user interfaces:

1. In Chapter 10, we introduce Use Case Maps (UCMs). These can be used to model the multichannel infrastructure that allows multimodality (channels being defined as the various ways the device can connect to the network). UCMs are very similar to activity diagrams, but they are more useful in modeling channels and the temporal behavior of the channels.
2. In Chapter 6, we introduced Nune's Wisdom extensions; these lie at the heart of our approach in using UML to model user interfaces.

In typical stationary applications, the majority of the complexity of the application resides in implementing some business logic. However, this is not the case in most mobile applications. The complexity of design and implementation of most mobile applications involves dealing with the dimensions of mobility. (This is not to say that the business logic complexity is reduced; it is simply that the complexity of dealing with the dimensions of mobility is of higher order qualitatively and quantitatively.) When dealing with mobile applications, the user interface implementation, and particularly multimodality, is one of the most complex aspects of design and implementation. Therefore, not only do we need UML extensions, but we also need a new way to use UML, a new UML process. The typical UML-based development processes do not take into account the special needs of mobile applications (the dimensions of mobility). Therefore, they tend to neglect to address the complexities of multimodal user interfaces. For mobile applications, it is typically beneficial to choose a development process that is biased toward addressing the complexities of the user interface, such as that of Nunes' Wisdom or UWE (UML Extensions for Web Applications) [Hennicker and Koch 2001]. The UWE builds on the Wisdom approach, and though it is biased toward Web development (which is not inherently multimodal), it offers some valuable lessons on a development process that is very much biased toward solving the complexities of the user interface.

Finally, there is something to be said about UML not being sufficient, in its current form, to represent multimodality altogether because UML itself is a visual only and that visual representation of aural, tactile, or other physical input/output techniques into computing systems contains an inherent loss of information. This is in addition to the inherent lossiness of any model: There is a loss of information in representing something without a full replication of all of its being. Of course, the solutions to this are not within the reality of application development tools within the near future.

8.3 Multimodal Content

One of the current points of contention in standards for multimodal user interfaces surrounds the creation and storage of multimodal content. SMIL gives us a standard for synchronizing different types of single-mode and single-channel content; it is a fairly well established standard. However, there are competing standards that address the composition of various media-specific content and other competing standards to describe user interactions with the system through multiple channels.

There are two approaches here. Some build on existing standards by mixing and matching the appropriate standards. For example Flach and Courvoisier [Flach and Courvoisier 2001] create a content repository by using tools for administering and analyzing the given information sources using RDF and use XSLT to specify various ways to combine them. Similarly, W3C's X + V working group combines XHTML and VXML to create dual-channel multimodality with providing XHTML that can be rendered by browsers and VXML that allows us to outline voice interactions.

Others make the argument that the existing standards were not designed for dealing with multimodal user interfaces or multimodal content and that new techniques are needed. These folks have spurred on various efforts, standard or proprietary, such as SmarkKom's M3L language.

The advantage of the latter approach is obvious in that it allows us to address problems specific to multimodal content canonically. However, there are several disadvantages too. First, creating a new syntax based on a multimodal way of thinking invariably means that we have to do a lot of work to convert or integrate existing content and user interfaces into the new syntactical paradigm. This mapping is certainly not going to be a linear and easily recognized deterministic mapping so it will take a considerable amount of programmatic or manual work to convert existing content to the desired content. There is also the problem that the existing standards have been well thought out and have matured; the same certainly could not be said of any emerging standard on multimodality.

Various solutions falling into one category or another spark "religious" debates on what is the best technology or whether we are creating a high-level architecture or selecting the syntax of the stored content. So, instead of focusing on which technology is better, we will outline the requirements that tools and technologies built for multimodal content must support.

Bunt and Romary [Bunt and Romary 2002] give this topic—the requirements for tools and technologies for multimodal content—a complete and proper treatment. Namely, Bunt and Romary specify that any tool that we select to represent multimodality architecturally and syntactically must be expressively and semantically adequate. The former means that the tool (syntax, architecture, etc.) should be able to represent the properties and features of multimodal content appropriately. Semantic adequacy means that the representation structures should themselves have a formal semantics; that is, their definition should provide a rigorous basis for reasoning (whether deductive, statistical, in the form of plan operators, or otherwise) [Bunt and Romary 2002]. After specifying these two general guidelines, Bunt and Romary give us three more properties that this tool (or collection of tools) should posses:

1. *Incrementality*: It should provide a mechanism for creating composite multimodal content from atomic elements that may be single mode or multimodal. Because we want to provide the maximum amount of freedom to the systems that process the multimodal content, the tools should be able to represent the content so that we can represent any of the multiple modes.
2. *Uniformity*: Though there are different types of input and output (e.g., text and voice) and different types of input and output channels (e.g., keyboards and speakers), the tools that represent multimodal content should represent these different types of input and output in the same manner.
3. *Underspecification and Partiality*: This basically refers to the concept that we have called a "generic user interface" in this text. What is recommended is that the tool allows us to specify as little as possible in the way of the semantic meaning of the information and also provide for a way to disambiguate the user's input.

All of this may seem overly theoretical, but indeed, we need this level of discipline. Multimodality is a complex problem as it is a composition of two or more sets of problems associated with two or more modes of presentation. In a way, what Bunt and Romary are specifying as the properties of the tools used for authoring and presenting mutlimodal content are some of the properties of linearly deterministic and causal control systems. They are specifying that the tools should allow us to create multimodal content so that we can take content apart, put the pieces back together, decompose various pieces, and enable the individual pieces to be used. The tool should be able to represent the compositional nature of the content, to do this generically, to allow specialization, and to do this while preserving the integrity of the single modal content so that if one or more of the channels are not presentable, we do not run into a problem. As a side note, if you think back to Chapter 5 where we had an in-depth discussion of XForms, you can see that XForms meet all of the qualifications specified here as a tool for multimodal content.

By contrast, the W3C X + V effort essentially combines VXML and XHTML for multimodality. The advantage to this approach is that it is practical. Both VXML and XHTML are proven technologies that have been around for a while; they are fairly mature. The disadvantages are many. First, this solution is very biased to the thin-client, browser-based architecture. Although this model works great for basic Web content, it is not very versatile. Second, VXML and XHTML taxonomies were developed separately and therefore show some obvious inherent differences that cause problems when you are trying to fuse them together in your multimodal application (whether the framework does this or your application does it, there is an impedance mismatch in the way things are defined). VXML is the browser-based solution for a dialogue manager–based UIM (which is grammar based) whereas XHTML is designed for browsers (typically State Machine or event based). Meanwhile, X + V gives us a good path for implementing a server-side-only solution using technologies that are currently fully mature and commercially available.

8.3.1 X + V

X + V stands for XHTML and VXML. X + V is an interim technology: Its use will be limited and only relevant to the duration of migration of content from XHTML/HTML and VXML content to truly multimodal content represented in a markup language designed with the needs of multimodality.

The benefits of X + V are that both technologies are rather proved and that implementation of a multimodal interface can be done with relative speed. The problems with X + V are multifold. First, it assumes that we can tie together VXML, a language designed for representing VUIs, and XHTML, the younger but more mature sibling of HTML designed for visual user interfaces, and come up with a multimodal interface. Obviously this is a flawed assumption as it neglects the contextual and semantic information shared among various modalities in interacting with the user. Second, it forces a thin-client/browsing model that is not easily implemented or intuitive. Most VXML implementations are designed for server-side interpretations whereas XHTML implementationss are designed for interpretation on the client side. Besides, as we have seen throughout this text, the thin-client model should not be used for every application. In many instances, it is not suitable.

8.3.2 M3L

The M3L, yet another acronym for the Multimodal Markup Language, has been created for SmartKom. SmartKom is a multimodal dialogue system that combines speech, gesture, and facial expressions for input and output; it provides anthropomorphic and effective user interface through its personification of an interface agent [Wahlster et al. 1998].

In addition to SmartKom, there is some limited commercial support for M3L such as the KMMP platform provided by Kirusa, a multimodal platform company in the United States. M3L tackles more than just our problem of multimodal user interfaces for mobile computing. It addresses some issues specific to using gestures (like pointing, smiling, etc.) as input and output channels and outlines a syntax

```
....
<intentionLattice>
   <hypothesisSequence>
   ....
   </hypothesisSequence>

</intentionLattice>
....
<presentationTask>
   <presentationGoal>
   <presentationContent>
      <abstractPresentationContent>
      </abstractPresentationContent>
      <panelElement>
      </panelElement>

   </presentationContent>
   </presentationGoal>
</presentationTask>
<gestureAnalysis>
   .....
   <type>tarrying</type>
   <referencedObjects>
   ....
   </referencedObjects>
</gestureAnalysis>
```

FIGURE 8.3. Sections of an M3L Document.

for representing them along with the textual and aural modalities that we typically discuss when talking about multimodal user interfaces. M3L's syntax is fairly large so we refer you to the SmartKom Web site (http://www.smartkom.org) for further research on this topic. M3L builds on top of RDF and XML. Figure 8.3 shows a code sample of what some sections of an M3L document may look like.

M3L makes a great attempt at not only representing the various aspects of multimodality but also at representing the semantics of multimodal user interfaces. M3L does address the temporal behavior of multimodal content and multimodal interactions, which is the largest part of the problem in specifying multimodality syntactically.

8.3.3 MML

There are now many different markup languages presented by different entities called Multimodal Markup Language with various acronyms; we have already looked at M3L. As far as we are concerned, MML is the Multimodal Markup Language as introduced by Rossler, Sienel, Wajda, Hoffmann, and Kostrzewa [Rossler et al.]. In somewhat of a similar approach to X + V, MML combines HTML and

Table 8.3. MML Tags

Tag Name	Description
modalityOut	This tag shows the modality of the element and its treatment for output presentation by various channels.
modalityIn	This tag encapsulates the information needed for processing of various types of input coming in from the different channels.
production	This tag is specific to speech synthesis (TTS). It encapsulates the information needed to produce the appropriate quality of speech (see Chapter 7) such as pitch, rate, etc.
Timing	This tag allows us to specify the temporal sequence of how various information such as text and audio are rendered (output).
BargeIn	This tag lets us specify if the user should be able to interrupt the presentation of multimodal information. (On a visual screen, this could be pressing the stop button on a browser whereas it is a simple interruption of audio played by the system through audio input in a VUI.)
initiative	This tag lets us specify if our dialogue is in mixed-initiative or directed mode.

VXML as a recognition of their pervasiveness. But it also tries to fill in the fundamental holes in addressing the issues with multimodality in providing some tags that provide metainformation about modalities and their fusion. These additional tags are listed in Table 8.3.

At present, MML is not very well formed nor is there much published information about it. Consequently, it is more of an academic study. The interesting thing about it (and the reason we are mentioning it here) is the approach: Take existing markup languages and fill in the gaps with metatags. Note also that these few metatags enable specification of how natural the communication between the user and the user interface is through each modality (natural, mixed initiative, and directed dialogue) and inherently specify a dialogue-based approach to the UIM.

8.3.4 EMMA

Extensible Multimodal Annotation Markup Language (EMMA) is a standard being worked on by W3C, in the draft stage at the time of authoring this text, that addresses Web access through multimodal user interfaces. The conceptual design of EMMA takes after some of the other W3C user interface standards such as VXML, XHTML, and XForms. First, EMMA is naturally XML based. Next, EMMA defines *metadata*, which encapsulates information about the document, a *data model*, which defines what type of data can be instantiated, by the browser of the document, and *instance data*, which encapsulates things like the actual data, text, and pointers to files to be presented. This separation is a very good thing. As in the case of XForms, the structure of what should be presented and the actual instance data are bound at run time so it is up to the user agent to decide how to manifest modalities. This allows us to have user agents that have different capability levels without the necessity of additional instructions. Obviously this is a problem in the mobile world because of platform proliferation.

The creators of EMMA have also recognized something else that is crucial to multimodal interfaces: the semantic and contextual meaning of things. In the current draft of EMMA, it is proposed that RDF be used for representation of semantic and contextual data about multimodal content. In addition, EMMA is designed to fit into "fusion" or "integration" of modalities, subjects we will look at later in this chapter. Table 8.4 lists at a subset of general syntax tags that make up an EMMA document.

EMMA takes us a significant step forward in defining a sufficient syntax for specifying multimodal interactions, but it has some way to go to be perfect. For example, the version whose draft specifications are published at the time of authoring this text specify no method of outlining an interpretation that relies on two or more modalities simultaneously. An example of this could be a user touching a touch-screen pad and saying "delete this one." To interpret the action, we need to know what "this one" means, but this means that we have to know what else the user is doing at the same time. Though we can use some elements such as one-of, sequence, and group to bundle interpretations, the syntax falls short in allowing us to specify coordinated and simultaneous multimodality.

8.3.5 MPML

Multimodal Presentation Markup Language (MPML), designed by a team at Ishizuka Laboratories in Japan, is a well-defined XML-based language that allows for the specification of dialogue-based interactions for a multimodal user interface. At present, MPML is at version 3.0. This version has well-defined tags that identify the temporal properties of multimodal content to be played back as well as some semantic and contextual information about the user and the multimodal content. Table 8.5 shows a summary of the tags that define MPML 3.0.

Note that there is no "action" tag. Rather, actions are a category of tags that are atomic and cause some sort of an action by the system. Included are WAIT, EXECUTE, EMOTION, CONSULT, PAUSE, PLAY, SPEAK, and THINK. For a better understanding of the MPML syntax, we refer you to the references used here as well as the University of Tokyo Computer Science Department Web site (http://www.is.s.u-tokyo.ac.jp).

MPML's big advantage over the other languages that we have mentioned here is its maturity. It also pays special attention to the contextual information surrounding the dialogue-based interactions between the user and the system. Most notably, it treats multimodal interactions in terms of scenes of interactions between the user and the system that have emotional, contextual, and temporal properties. However, MPML also has some significant downfalls.

First, there is no organized metamodel or principles (at least that are mentioned through the public materials released on MPML 3.0) in the design of the language. Second, there is not enough separation of concerns between those of generic user interface design and those of multimodal user interface design. It is important to

Table 8.4. Some EMMA Tags

Tag	Description
<emma:emma> attributes: version (required), xmlns:emma (required), xmlns:rdf (required); other namespaces can be optionally added as attributes if they are used within the document	Note that we have explicitly specified the namespace, which is EMMA. This tag encapsulates the section of the XML document described by EMMA. Because EMMA is defined in XML and can be described by an XML schema, we can have an EMMA document on its own or we can have a section of a document defined by EMMA tags and other section(s) described by some other syntax described by another valid XML namespace/language.
<emma:interpretation> attributes: id	This tag encapsulates the handling of a single modality dealt with through some XML-based syntax. Basically, this tag wraps around a grammar that defines what values are expected from the atomic dialogue taking place between the user and the user interface through a specific modality. This element has one attribute, id, whose uniqueness is enforced for a valid EMMA document.
<emma:one-of> attribute: id	This element encapsulates one or more interpretation elements and specifies that an atomic dialogue between a user and the user interface can have only one interpretation out of the possible options. Like the interpretation element, this element has an id attribute whose uniqueness must be enforced. This tag and the sequence and group tags described in the following are referred to as "interpretation containers" because they wrap around one or more interpretations. They can also be nested; in other words, interpretation containers can include other interpretation containers.
<emma:model>	This is an optional element that may be used to provide constraints on the model (structure and content of the instance data). Note that the definitions of structure, model, and instance data in EMMA are very similar to those of XForms. This tag can be used within the interpretation tag, any groupings of interpretation tags such as one-of, or within a semantic definition of the document encapsulated within an RDF segment in the EMMA

(continued)

Table 8.4 (continued)

Tag	Description
	document. This attribute points to a valid URI, which in turn has the rules used by the document browser to enforce the constraints.
<emma:sequence>	This tag includes other interpretations or interpretation containers that should be processed in a sequential manner (timewise).
<emma:group>	This tag wraps around multiple interpretation tags. It allows us to group a set of grammars.
<emma:tokens>	This tag allows us to specify the input tokens related to any input to the system through any single modality or a group of modalities. These tokens are very similar to the tokens that we defined in Chapter 7 for VUIs. Again, because the approach is dialogue and grammar driven, a grammar is specified to be matched with any input given by the user. The tokens are those variables of interest that we are trying to fill. They may be obtained through directed-dialogue, mixed-initiative, or natural language interactions with the user.
<emma:process>	This tag specifies how the interpretation was generated and points to a URI. The process of obtaining the interpretation depends on the modality and channel of the input. For example, a process may point to a URI where the speech-recognition process is defined by a grammar, a speech-recognition engine, and the other components necessary to interpret user input. This tag can be included within the RDF section of an EMMA document or inline with the individual interpretations. When used inline, it becomes an attribute of the interpretation element. There are two advantages in putting the process information in the RDF section of the document. First, by using RDF to point to the process, EMMA remains decoupled from the specific processes. Second, RDF allows for a semantically organized way of linking the EMMA document to the processes by which the interpretation of the user input is done.

<emma:no-input>	Once again, this is a page taken out of VUI design. Because the user may not answer to a question during a directed dialogue or a mixed-initiative interaction or the answer may not be "recognizable" (owing to problems with the input channel such as a faulty touch-screen or too much background noise for voice input), this tag allows us to specify what to do when there is no input. Once again, we can use this tag inline while specifying interpretations as an attribute of the interpretation tag or in the RDF section of the EMMA document.
<emma: uninterpreted>	This tag is identical to the no-input tag in definition and application except for one thing: Whereas no-input means that the system received nothing that it recognized as input, uninterpreted means that the system received something that it recognized as input but that it could not interpret this input. Let us use *graffiti* (also called "ink") input to the system. The graffiti pad may be designed to ignore all marks that are made at a very high speed and regard them as a shaky hand. So, if you draw a line very quickly across the pad, the system will see this as no input. However, if the system requests that the user input his or her full name and the user enters a signature instead, the system cannot interpret the input because the graffiti input is not given in a recognizable format. This second case is the uninterpreted case.

Table 8.5. MPML Tags

Tags	Description
<MPML>	This tag is the root document tag for an MPML document.
<HEAD>	This tag takes after the header tag in HTML: It allows the developer to specify data about the document. The tags META, TITLE, AGENT, and SPOT may be included within the HEAD tag. The tags META, AGENT, and SPOT may be repeated multiple times. The tag TITLE is optional and can only exist one time for a valid MPML document.
<META> attributes: id, name, description, content, charset, http-equiv, scheme, lang, dir	This tag allows us to specify metadata about the document. As can be seen from the attributes, it is very similar to the HTML meta tag and is designed to specify information such as the author of the document, the character set used in the document, and other standard XML attributes.
<TITLE>	This tag can only exist once, within the <HEAD></HEAD> tags. It is roughly equivalent to the HTML<TITLE> tag in its functionality and has no attributes.
<AGENT> attributes: id, name, description, system, character, sport, location, x,y, voice, agreeableness, activity	This element allows us to specify system or user agents. For example, we can define an autonomous component that processes the user's speech input as the "Voice Recognition Agent."
<SCENE> attributes: id, name, description, agents	This tag defines a scene; a scene is used to structure the presentation (as in a theater) and decides which agents are visible [Sylvain 2001]. Scenes are broken down into a set of sequential actions, a set of parallel actions, moods, actions, and pages. Scenes can also be nested.
<SEQ> attributes: id, name, description, agents	This tag provides a method by which to group a set of actions together that should be executed sequentially, based on the order of their appearance within the tag. A sequence of actions is identified by a unique id, can have a name and a description, and can be assigned a processing agent. Sequences can nest other sequences, scenes, parallel actions, moods, pages, and other actions.

<PAR> attributes: id, name, description	This tag and the SEQ are inspired by SMIL. This tag provides a method by which we can specify concurrent execution of a set of actions. It is important to keep in mind that we can only guarantee the concurrent start of the actions. The end of the action depends on the duration of the media as it is being processed by the agent.
<MOOD> attributes: id, name, description, assign	This tag defines the mood of the agents; with no mood tag, the agents have neutral mood [Sylvain 2001]. The "mood" of the agent can be used during the generation of output to the user (background colors, tone of synthesized voice, etc.) and in the interpretation of the incoming input. The assign attribute is used to set the mood of a specific agent.
<EMOTION>	If the system is able to determine the emotional state of the user (through measuring the user's input styles such as his/her voice, speed of entry through a keyboard, etc.), it may be useful to specify reactions, by the agent, to each one of these emotions.
<EXECUTE> attributes: id, name, description, target	This tag is designed to provide a hook into executing JavaScript. The target tag is set to the name of the JavaScript function to be executed.
<WAIT> attributes: id, name, description, target	This tag simply causes a wait time until some JavaScript variable, specified by the target attribute of this tag.
<CONSULT>	This tag provides for conditional logic. The implementation is similar to a switch statement in Java. A variable is specified to be tested and the test cases are specified. When the variable (defined by JavaScript) satisfies some specified value, then we can perform some logic.
<TEST>	This tag is used (similar to the case statement in Java) within the CONSULT tag to specify the individual test cases within the CONSULT tag (which as we mentioned works like a switch statement). We can specify a sequence of actions to be performed, within this tag, through the use of the SEQ tag.

(*continued*)

Table 8.5 (continued)

Tags	Description
<PAUSE> attributes: id, name, description, pause	This tag simply causes an unconditional pause specified in milliseconds (through the pause attribute).
<MOVE> attributes: id, name, description, spot, agent	This tag is somewhat specific to usage in visual user interfaces (GUIs, text-based interfaces, etc.) and specifies the area of the screen to be processed by the agent.
<PLAY> attributes: id, name, description, agent, act	This tag allows us to kick off the playback of some prerecorded media such as audio, animation, etc. The act attribute allows us to specify a mood for the playback that can be used by the agent to apply to the media being played back.
<THINK> attributes: id, name, description, agent.	This tag is somewhat of an anomaly and is used to represent the system or the user "thinking." The implementation of this tag may be a bubble-up "think" in a GUI or a distinct voice for a thought background.
<SPEAK> attributes: id, name, description, agent.	This tag allows us to specify when the agent should "speak"; this may mean speech synthesis, playback of prerecorded audio, etc. This tag can include emotions, breaks, and text. The text included may be used by the speech-synthesis engine to produce audio, the emotions can be used to change the quality (tone, pitch, etc.) of the voice, and the breaks allow us to divide speech segments.
<NB> attributes: id, name, description, agent	This tag allows us to create logical breaks within the contents of other elements. For example, this could be a new paragraph in a textual interpretation or a change of inflection at the end of the sentence and a pause for an aural user interface.
<TXT> id, name, description, agent	Used within other tags, this tag allows us to specify text that is used by the other tags (such as the SPEAK tag).
<ASK>	This tag allows us to prompt the user that we need some sort of input.
<CHOICE>	This tag allows us to specify single or multiple choices to be selected by the user.

note that what we learned in Chapter 5 in designing generic interfaces is orthogonal to concerns of multimodality. What we ideally need is a language that provides for a specialization mechanism that takes generic content and specializes and also provides a mechanism for specifying the treatment of individual modalities and the fusion/fission of those modalities.

8.3.6 MMIL

The Multimodal Interface Language (MMIL), proposed by Kumar and Romary, focuses on specifying an interface among the various components of a multimodal architecture, specifically one that leverages multimodal integration and dialogue-based user interactions (both of which will be discussed later in this chapter). MMIL contains both generic descriptors related to dialogue management, comprising general interaction concepts used within the system, and domain-specific descriptors related to the multimedia application dealt with in the project [Kumar and Romary 2003]. It should be noted that the authors of MMIL designed MMIL to serve a general purpose; however, the process of developing MMIL primarily involved designing exchange formats among modules in the MIMM project, which is an application of a multimodal interface to a jukebox (a project whose intention is primarily research oriented in delivering a better understanding of multimodal user interfaces through the building of a real-life application). Of course, like other multimodal languages that we have introduced, MMIL is XML based also.

To define an interface language among various components of a multimodal user interface we first have to assume some standard roles for each one of these components. These roles then tell us what function each component performs; this leaves us to derive the appropriate interface standards among the various components. To do this Kumar and Romary recognized six types of so-called information streams: *word and phoneme lattice*, *dependency representation forest*, *dependency representation*, *word/phoneme sequence*, *visual-haptic semantic representation*, and *graphic-haptic layout*. This taxonomy identifies, respectively, speech or speechlike input that can be broken into distinguishable parts with start and end points (with lattice referring to all of the connected starting and end points); the lattice and semantic information regarding interdependencies among the members of the lattice; dependencies to other modalities such as visual and haptic input; the synthesis of visual, aural, and haptic output; spatial placement of visual-haptic components; and GUI output to the user.

Based on what you have seen so far, you must have realized that MMIL is very well thought out. Another place where this foresight is shown is in the specification of a metamodel, represented in UML, for the domain (multimodality and the components of a multimodal architecture) before the syntax was created. Figure 8.4 shows this metamodel. Based on this metamodel an XML-based syntax is created with the structural tags listed in Table 8.6.

Kumar and Romary aptly recognize the fact that how we specify this element and the other elements in the event element largely depends on how we define the modalities within our system and design our architecture to allow us to build the components to provide the functionality for these modalities. So, although they introduce some possible tags, they also recognize that further formal specification

TABLE 8.6. MMIL Metamodel Structural Tags

Tag	Description
<mmilComponent> attributes: id	This element corresponds to the MMIL level class in Figure 8.4. It wraps around the other elements that specify the details of the component interface. As can be seen in the diagram, an MMIL level can have events and participants. Participants are defined as the users who interact with the system and events are input and output into the user interface. The id attribute must have a unique value that identifies this element uniquely. This same attribute is used throughout the main structure of an MMIL document (four tags) for unique identification.
<event>	Events are characterized temporally. Events can have other events or time levels (represented by the tempSpan tag) because the specification of the user input and output in MMIL revolves around the temporal nature of the input and output.
<participant>	This tag allows us to include information about the user.
<tempSpan>	This element represents the time level. The startPoint attribute specifies when the event begins, the duration specifies how long it lasts, and the end point specifies when it stops (only one of duration or end point must be specified).

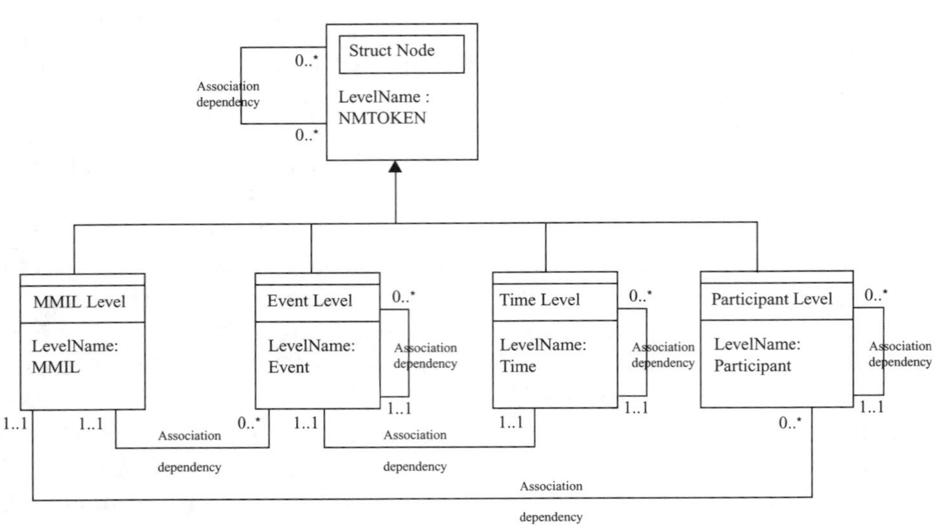

FIGURE 8.4. UML Diagram of the MMIL Metamodel [Kumar and Romary].

Table 8.7. Additional Tags for Outlining Specific Modalities

Tag	Description
<evtType>	This is an element included within the event tag that allows us to specify the type of modality as applicable to our architecture. For example, we can specify "speak" as the value of the event type or "telephonySpeech" to be the value of our event type. The former allows us to specify an event type for all incoming speech whereas the latter allows us to specify an event type that applies only to speech received through telephony.
<dialogueAct>	As its name indicates, this tag allows us to specify what type of action was taken by the participant or the system. An example of a value could be "request" where the user is asking the system for something.
<addressee> attribute: target	This tag is used to specify who the user is addressing. This could be useful, for example, if the user is speaking to someone else at the same time as using a telephone to speak to the system.
<speaker> attribute: target	This attribute allows us to specify how this event applies to the various incoming input. For example, we may have multiple users using the system at the same time. The target attribute, like the addressee, allows us to point to a specific participant.
<relation> attributes: type, source, target	This tag allows us to relate the various events together by specifying a temporal relationship among them. When events are nested within events, the type attribute specifies if an event is the starting or the ending event, the source attribute specifies what the parent event is, and the target attribute specifies the child event.

of the language takes agreement between the standard bodies and the development community. Let us look at some tags that they specify (see Table 8.7).

Once again, please keep in mind that this second set of tags is just a sample that can be built on top of the metamodel based on the architecture and definitions of the domain.

Kumar and Romary do so many things just right! Before they set out to build a language to represent multimodality, they created a framework of rules. They also recognized the importance of specifying interfaces for interoperable components that handle various parts of a multimodal system. Unfortunately, MMIL's only small downfall is that it is extremely biased toward dealing with multimodality in terms and notions of handling speech. The model used to identify the component types neglects to recognize the importance of other forms of input such as graffiti. MMIL seems to be the most well-thought-out representation of multimodality out of all the tools and languages mentioned and researched here. MMIL is expressive, semantically adequate, incremental, extensible, uniform, open, and underspecified. We see the same approach in MMIL's design in these principles as well as its metamodel as seen in HTTP in REST.

Nevertheless, it still has a long way to go before becoming something sufficient for representing features of multimodality without bias toward any particular type of user interface.

8.3.7 InkML

InkML (Ink Markup Language) is an effort by the W3C multimodal interaction working group to create a markup language for supporting text entry through a digital pad and a styluslike device. The idea of InkML is to allow us to create graphical and text-based user interfaces that can be used just like pen and paper. Although InkML is not specifically designed for multimodality, it is a significant markup language for developing multimodal user interfaces.

As Larson [Larson 2003] points out, InkML is a great complement to VXML: Noisy environments, areas that require privacy, and meetings are some of the examples where a pen-based user interface offers a good alternative to voice. Like VXML, XHTML, and various other markup languages designed to represent different modalities, InkML can be included within a multimodal markup language that allows usage of other markup languages (a document that points to multiple namespaces and validates against a schema or DTD that allows inclusion of other markup languages). At present, InkML is in draft stages; we refer you to the W3C site for syntactical specifics on this language.

8.3.8 CUIML

CUIML, the Cooperative User Interfaces Markup Language, is developed by Sandor and Reicher as an extension to UIML, which we previously discussed in Chapter 5 and 6. The interesting thing about CUIML is that it ties in the concept of generic user interfaces with the concept of multimodal user interfaces. As we have mentioned previously in this chapter, these two concepts are orthogonal. Whereas generic user interfaces allow us to outline content and interactions in a generic matter and then specialize them, multimodal user interfaces are about the way the various modalities combine and interact together to deliver meaning and functionality to the user. Because CUIML's syntax is based on UIML, we will defer a detailed discussion of the syntax to Chapters 5 and 6, as well as the reference paper. Figure 8.5 shows the general approach in the design of CUIML; namely, CUIML relies on extension of the MVC design pattern. To achieve faster response times, changes to the View should be done by the Manipulator instead of rendering new CUIML descriptions according to the View. Views described by markup languages can be accessed by the DOM [Sandor and Reicher 2001].

The work of Sandor and Reicher on CUIML is important not because they introduced yet another markup language, but because they introduce a useful design pattern that allows us to tie in a layered approach in specialization of

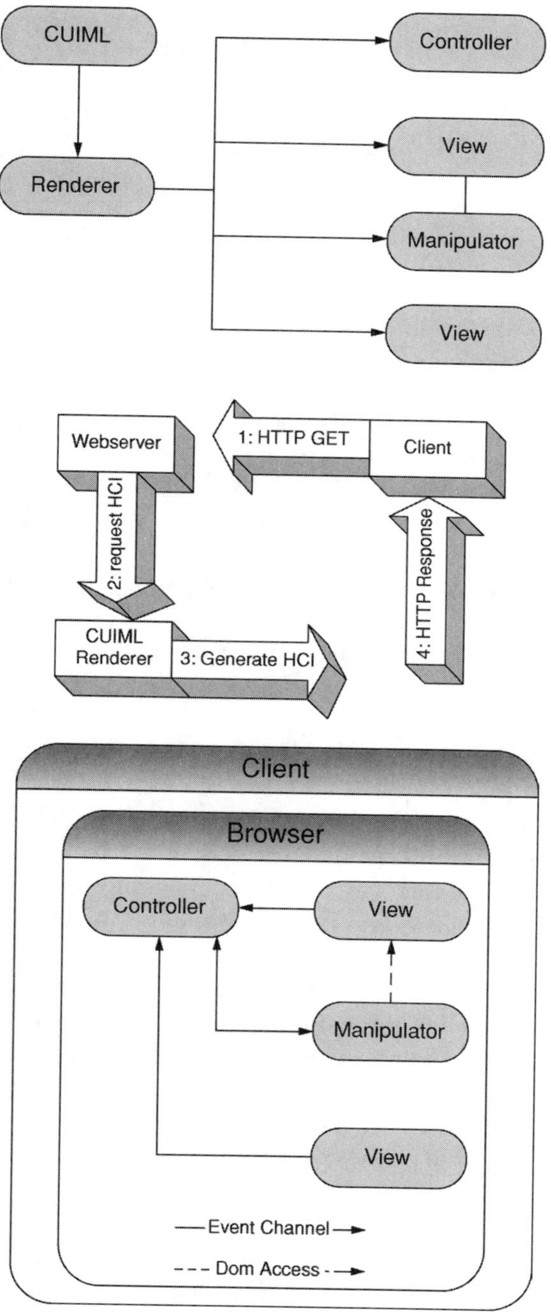

FIGURE 8.5. Design and Usage of CUIML [Sandor and Reicher 2001].

user interfaces to building multimodal interfaces. Their design pattern outlines a technique for specializing generic user interfaces into multimodal interfaces. Furthermore, they build on an existing technology for generic user interfaces, namely UIML, and extend a proved design pattern to address possible performance

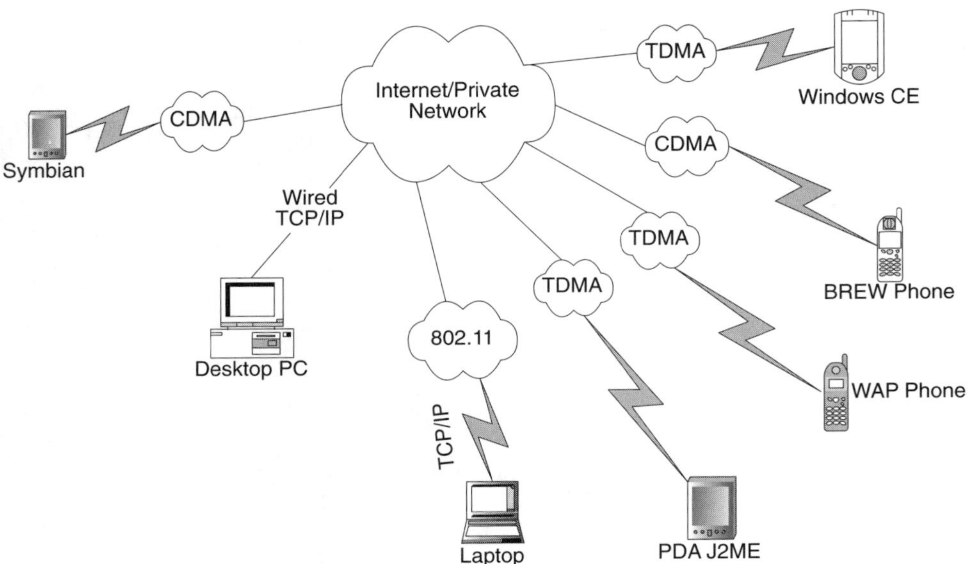

FIGURE 8.6. Channels, Modalities, Devices, and Content Delivery to the Mobile Device.

problems in temporal synchronization of various modalities in a multimodal user interface.

8.3.9 Delivering Multimodality through Use of Markup Languages

So far, we have looked at a variety of markup languages that allow us to represent multimodal content. Some even make an attempt at representing the behavioral nature of multimodality. But how do we use this multimodal content to delivery multimodality? Figure 8.6 shows some examples of different devices using different channels to communicate with one another. Content-based markup languages have historically been processed by some form of browser. Because the most popular of the early markup languages is HTML, most markup languages are inspired by some sort of client–server frame of mind that assumes there is a browser that executes the instructions in the document after the document is downloaded. So, where is our browser? Or do we have a browser at all?

As we mentioned in the previous sections, X + V and similar efforts look at the world in this way: They try to fit everything into the browser-based thin-client model. However, many modern markup languages have evolved to be more than their parents (e.g., HTML). A markup language such as MMIL or others can be parsed into a DOM that drives a programmatic model. This lets us think of the document as the initial state of a State Machine along with the instructions that tell us how to transition from one state to another based on external events. In fact, this is precisely the fundamental thought behind what XForms, MMIL, and others base the separation of instance data, structure, and events on. So, what does all of this mean in the real world?

The markup language has to be interpreted at some point to cause some action. This means that some program, residing on the mobile device or some other part of the network that it is connected to (e.g., servers) needs to interpret the document. Where this interpretation is done depends on two factors: the implementation of the communication channels (voice, text, video, etc.) and the architecture selected for the application. The implementation of the communication channel itself depends on two factors: 1. what the platform offers (the combination of the device, operating system, development environment; for example, J2ME running on a Symbian operating system on a Nokia device) and 2. what the network allows us to do, with each specific carrier offering its own implementation of each channel (video, audio, data, etc.) on its network infrastructure.

As application developers, we do not have much say in what the networks or platform manufacturers do. However, we should be familiar with the offerings of each platform. In this way, let us review platform offerings in the way of multimodality:

1. *Java*: Currently, Java remains the most pervasive client-side application development platform for mobile applications (not counting markup languages such as WML because the capabilities of a markup language are inherently considerably less than a programming language). Furthermore, it also offers the most contiguous development environment with significant standardization on various APIs that are important to multimodality, such as dealing with various types of media (Java Media Framework), distributed application development (servlets, RMI [Java Remote Method Invocation], etc.), and a variety of other technologies that are crucial to developing multimodal applications. As we saw in previous chapters, Java on a mobile device may mean either J2SE or J2ME. Whereas the former allows for implementation of multimodality, it is designed for devices that have a significant amount of resources (processing power, storage, etc.). Currently, most mobile devices that can host J2SE are very expensive. Unfortunately, J2ME, which is the part of Java designed for less powerful devices, does not explicitly provide support for multimodality on mobile devices (we are referring to the CLDC and MIDP 2.0 here). However, pieces of the puzzle are offered. Although MIDP 2.0 provides a basic framework for network connectivity, MMAP (Mobile Media Specifications) provides a framework for dealing with multimodal content, and several other APIs deal with other aspects of mobile applications, there are no standard APIs for coordinating different modalities, synchronizing various communication channels, or handling multiple communication channels simultaneously (if made available by the operating system, device, and network). Therefore, Java still has some significant milestones to achieve for delivering a platform for multimodal user interfaces on mobile devices.
2. *BREW*: Of all the tools that we have discussed, BREW and Symbian provide the most true support for multimodality. The main reason for this is that BREW 2.0 provides a TCP/IP-based connection that takes advantage of the robustness of CDMA networks. Specifically, it is possible to stream any data over a TCP connection. The reliability of the connection is another issue. QOS and bandwidth of most CDMA networks are still not at levels that enable us to stream media with high-bandwidth requirements reliably (keep in mind that bandwidth and QOS,

though related, are not the same thing). However, with WCDMA, CDMA2000, and the various other advanced CDMA networks (to be discussed more closely later in this text), BREW provides a robust platform for developing multimodal applications. Though there is currently no true multithreading support for delivery of coordinated simultaneous multimodality, there is no virtual machine in BREW and the application is written in the C language so there is plenty of room for performance optimization. The higher bandwidth delivered by CDMA networks coupled with the robust programming environment allow us to build coordinated multimodality (not simultaneous coordinated multimodality) with BREW.

3. *Microsoft*: Like the Java platform, Microsoft has a variety of solutions for the mobile market. Included are the so-called Stinger platform and Windows CE. These platforms range from the very proprietary smart phones to the more open Windows CE running on PDAs such as the Compaq Pocket PC. The only way of implementing multimodality, at present, with the Microsoft platform on a mobile device is on the higher end hybrid phone–PDA devices running Windows CE. Such devices provide a telephony API as well as a data call API. Even in those cases, there is no support for simultaneous coordinated multimodality because multithreading models (thus far) are cooperative. The data channels provided are not as robust as those provided by BREW and the APIs are not as open or prolific as J2ME CLDC and supporting APIs.
4. *Symbian*: As we mentioned previously, Symbian and BREW are currently the two most advanced and prevalent mobile development platforms for multimodality. Like BREW, Symbian offers an advanced communication API. Whereas BREW's APIs are implemented and optimized for communication over a CDMA network, Symbian's communication APIs are designed and optimized for GPRS and similar standards that sit on top of slightly lower layer base communication protocols of CDMA and TDMA. Symbian devices also benefit in being able to use GSM. Symbian is unique in that it offers an extensive set of Java-based functionality with Personal Java in addition to the native C/C++-based API. In this way, it is far more robust than the other platforms. Currently, there is support for JavaPhone 1.0, the Java Telephony API, and Java APIs for a variety of communication protocols such as UDP, SMS, serial port, and infrared. In this way, Symbian offers a very robust framework for developing multimodal applications.
5. *WAP*: The collection of the WTAI agent providing telephony access on mobile devices and WML allows WAP developers to have multiple modes, but it does not guarantee coordination nor does it provide simultaneous access to channels. WAP 1.x was the first platform to deliver multimodality in that it enabled developers to access the telephony agent on the phone to make phone calls. The implementation of most of the WTAI functionality was very poor in the initial releases of WAP so it inhibited developers greatly. However, things have improved with WAP 2.x browser releases. WAP provides a multimodal solution that recognizes the pervasiveness of the phone channel (e.g., PSTN) as the primary means of delivering voice to the user. By providing access to the telephony channel, the user can interact with the text-based browser, select an

option that causes an outbound phone call, and, upon termination of the phone call, return to the browser. The unfortunate part is that the user cannot use the browser while the phone call is in session. Hence, not only does WAP fail to deliver coordinated or simultaneous coordinated multimodality, but there are some latencies in switching modalities from the textual mode to the voice mode and back.

What we just looked at were the software platforms, but what about the devices? There are typically three key device categories when it comes to multimodality: legacy, transitory, and next generation.

1. *Legacy*: Most mobile devices built before year 2000 have very little or no support for multimodality. Such legacy mobile devices are very limited in their processing power and functionality and are built on operating systems and hardware that is outdated and is unable to take full advantage of modern wireless networks.
2. *Transitory*: These are devices such as WAP phones and some PDAs that allow minimal amount of control over the various channels and modalities. For example, in WAP 1.x, we can make an outbound phone call and establish a voice channel, but there is no concept of simultaneous multimodality. Most of these devices have been distributed in the marketplace after year 2000. The limitations on these devices are due to the resources on the device as well as the communications protocols for which they are designed to communicate (WAP, TDMA, etc.).
3. *Next Generation*: These devices are built on a hardware architecture that is designed to deliver coordinated and simultaneous access to multiple channels. The fact is that if the hardware platform does not support a feature, the software sitting on top of it cannot build on the nonexisting feature! This is the case with many of the devices today. New devices supporting key hardware technologies such as the Intel PCA architecture, ARM/StrongARM technologies, and other hardware architectures specifically designed for mobile devices will allow the application developers to design applications that support simultaneous multimodality. The newer and more advanced mobile operating systems such as Symbian OS 7 and Palm OS 5 will play a major role in this as well. Because most application developers will be writing their applications on top of some mobile operating system, it is crucial that the operating system provide asynchronous I/O and other required mechanisms for providing simultaneous and coordinated multimodality (if supported by the hardware).

The user interface is ultimately rendered at the mobile device itself. Consequently, the mobile device and its network connectivity are typically the two factors that become the biggest barriers in implementing any potential multimodal functionality.

8.3.10 Delivering Video to Mobile Devices

Streaming video is a higher level of multimodality than integrated pictures: It is a sequence of pictures accompanied with a particular timing (typically uniform throughout the sequence) and possibly accompanied, and synchronized, with some audio. As we have discussed several times throughout this text, mobile devices are limited in their capabilities because of their small size. Furthermore, within the near future of release of this text, long-range wireless networks will not be able to deliver ample bandwidth for a free-flow usage of video streaming. So, to deliver video to the mobile device, we need to use creative techniques to compress the data to get it to the mobile device and then replay it based on the available display capabilities of the mobile device.

There are two points of concern with video content: its format and the method by which it is delivered to the mobile device. Most preexisting digital video content on the Internet, and elsewhere, is exchanged in the formats specified by the Moving Pictures Expert Group (MPEG). To date, there is no prevailing streaming format and the market is dominated by formats from Real Networks, Microsoft, MMS vendors such as Nokia and Ericsson, and a series of other proprietary solutions.

We have discussed MMS first when we looked at WAP in Chapter 2 and then when we looked at visual user interfaces in Chapter 6. MMS is interesting because it provides an application layer channel for multimedia content. Though this does not mean that MMS makes multimodality possible, it does mean that it facilitates the task of the developers. Having said this, let us enumerate some of the major characteristics of the MMS architecture:

1. *MMS Context*: The context is the collection of information shared between two points during an MMS session that is required for the two to send and receive MMS messages.
2. *Virtual Manufacturing Device (VMD)*: The VMD is the MMS object that has at least one network-visible address [Falk and Robbins 1997].
3. *CRUD Operations*: There are a set of operations (Create, Get, Set, and Delete) that respectively allow for the so-called CRUD (create, read, update, and delete) operations on MMS objects.
4. *Events*: Events are used by the carrier network to determine the state and handling of messages. There are three types of event-based objects: Event Condition, Event Action, and Event Enrollment.
5. *Semaphore*: This is the same concept as a UNIX semaphore. Semaphores are basically values that can be read and changed by various processes to coordinate activities, such as resource use, among them.
6. *File*: MMS provides a mechanism for transferring a complete file.

There is much more to the MMS architecture components, but the aforementioned are the main components. The MMS server is part of the WAP infrastructure in the back end. The MMS client resides on the mobile device. The WAP 2.x infrastructure supporting MMS acts as a proxy between the MMS peers as MMS is intended to act as a peer-to-peer system (though a message has to go through considerable handling in the network infrastructure). Developing an MMS infrastructure is a fairly complex task so it is not something that the software application developer can do on his or her own. The best thing about MMS is that the infrastructure is there and all that the developer needs to do is create an application that can interface with the MMS infrastructure. This may include servers that provide the appropriate content and a client running on the mobile device (J2ME, BREW, etc.).

MMS content is largely based on a subset of SMIL. Typically, devices can record data (through a phone camera and the phone speaker for example) and send it to some network node through a standard or proprietary mechanism. Alternatively, the content may be recorded. Either way, the content must be translated to something consumable by an MMS-enabled client, which means something that can understand SMIL. Formats for audio include audio/x-amr, audio/x-wav, and others. Formats for graphics include JPEG, Progressive JPEG, WBMP, and others. Binding is done at the MMS client using the SMIL document.

MMS provides two things that are useful for multimodal user interface: 1. an infrastructure that supports multimodal content and 2. a standard for multimodal messaging. Nonetheless, it is crucial to keep in mind that MMS is asynchronous. This means that you cannot design a multimodal user interface using MMS. However, you can use the MMS messaging format to send your content back and forth and the MMS support on your device to get the input from the user (video and audio).

Returning to our discussion of the video content type, we may be delivering video that has been prerecorded or stream video in real time. The task becomes significantly easier when dealing with prerecorded video, audio, or any other type of content. The requirements for the QOS are considerably higher for streaming real-time content than they are for preexisting content. We also have to build special features into the application such as buffering and skipping if we are considering a real-time solution. Though this is a piece of the mobile application to be "bought" rather than "built," there are always the development costs of integration and the resources that are taken up by the modules that must implement these special features for streaming. So, streaming is inherently more difficult, and therefore more costly, than replay of batch video. Another problem that should not go unnoticed is that video typically increases power consumption by orders of magnitude. First there is the fact that it typically must be decompressed (because compression is required to use the bandwidth more efficiently) and then displayed, which takes turning many pixels on and off or changing the colors (leading to more power consumption than just leaving the same picture up on the screen).

Current technologies transmit video at about 4 to 7 frames per second; however, efforts such as those at the University of California at San Diego are on their way to increase this to at least 15 frames per second (of good quality video) [Paulson 2003]. In this section, we will look at pictograms, MMS, and Enhanced Messaging Services (EMS) as existing technologies for doing this. Currently, MMS is the only standard designed that addresses specific issues with the delivery of video to a mobile device with a weak connection to the network.

Whereas most video content may exist in MPEG format, or at least be convertible to an MPEG format, the carriers, the networks that they deploy, and many mobile devices that are distributed to the consumers support other proprietary or open formats specially designed with additional compression or accountability for QOS problems. Additional software techniques and architectural solutions have been designed to combat these problems. For example, Yu and colleagues [Yu et al. 2003] outline a technique by which compression and decompression of video may be done in stages. This is particularly useful in mobile computing as we can distribute the compression and decompression across the various components of the system (the servers, the mobile device, proxies, etc.) to accommodate all of the required platforms. The technique developed by Microsoft researches [Yu et al.] and similar techniques are useful because they layer the video content and the processing of it (compression, etc.) so that, depending on the type of device used, we may need to use one, two, three, or *n* layers of processing corresponding with the capabilities of the device and the wireless connection with which it reaches the rest of the network. This technique is useful even if we stay with MPEG: We can determine the number of colors and the resolution of the image at run time while serving a content to a particular device.

This gives us the perfect segue way to the processing of dynamic and static content through multiple stages (as in the case of layered processing of video). Throughout this text, we have referred to Cocoon, an Apache project, as a tool that can help us with various aspects of mobile application development. One of those tasks that it allows us to do conveniently is to create a "pipelining" process through which we break down the processing of content into sequential stages.

8.3.11 Cocoon

We have mentioned Cocoon, in passing, or as an example of a server-side framework used for user-interface-independent development. In this section, we will delve more into how Cocoon works and write some simple applications for it. Before we go any further, let us look at a brief history of Cocoon.

Cocoon was started as a simple Java servlet, in 1999, that allowed XSL transformations and some minor additions for creation of rules for when and how to perform these transformations. Stafano Mazzochio was the original author of Cocoon, an Apache project. Today, there are dozens of contributors in the core team including several renowned software engineers. Since its inception, Cocoon has grown by leaps and bounds and has become one of the most popular frameworks for building server-side applications that require publishing to a variety of user interfaces. Cocoon is at its 2.x version at the time this text is being written.

Brett Mclaughlin, now one of the contributors to the Cocoon project, in his book *Java and XML*, gives a very good introduction to Cocoon 1.x [McLaughlin 2000]. For those users interested in using the 1.x version of Cocoon, in addition to the documentation at the Apache Web site, this is perhaps the best reference available. However, Cocoon 2.0 was radically redesigned as there were some scaling issues with large documents for Cocoon version 1.x. Version 1.x of Cocoon operated on XML documents exclusively with a DOM that was loaded into memory. Although this is not problematic for small documents (and, in fact, could have some performance advantages because disk I/O can be slow), it introduced problems with larger documents. The Cocoon 2.x design also lends itself to better separation of various interface concerns, which, as previously seen, is one of the main concerns of mobile application development. Historically, the features of Cocoon 1.x were the first of their kind but it was not until version 2.x that Cocoon became a commercial-grade product with improved architecture. We recommend the *Cocoon Developer's Handbook* by Moczar and Aston [Moczar and Aston 2002] for learning Cocoon 2.x.

Here are some recommendations in working with Cocoon before you start using it:

1. Read the log files when you run into problems. The error pages that you will get back will often be difficult to understand and cryptic. This is understandable, and even somewhat unavoidable, as there are many layers of processing. By the time an error is actually displayed, its real cause may be buried deep inside Cocoon. Nonetheless, the log files are an excellent source of finding the root of the problem. There are several log files.
2. If you are used to using IDEs to develop, you will need to brush up on your manual coding skills and begin to be more thorough. None of the popular IDEs support Cocoon's XSPs at this time. The byproduct of this is that writing XSP pages is similar to writing JSPs several years ago when there were no tools for rapid JSP development. Most of today's Java-based IDEs allow for color coding of JSPs just as they do for regular Java. Some, such as JBuilder, can even compile these JSPs. You will not have such luck with XSPs unless you are out to write your own compiler or retrofit the various compilation components that come with Cocoon into an IDE. (If you try to do that, you either have too much time or are too advanced to be reading this part of the textbook!)
3. Cocoon is an open-source project. If you find a bug, report it. Most open-source projects use their users as their quality assurance team, so it is the responsibility of the users to inform the developers of problems or bugs.
4. Use the latest release version of Cocoon that you can use. Although there are beta versions available too, we do not recommend using beta versions of any open-source project for learning purposes. Once you have become more familiar with Cocoon, then you can venture into the beta versions.

With this said, keep in mind that since the inception of Cocoon, many commercial products have started copying some of the concepts and delivering commercial-grade software. Product selection for your project is up to you. We have simply chosen Cocoon because it is open source, it was the first of its kind, and it includes all the necessary concepts we want to convey to the reader.

In Chapter 2, we took a good look at the Cocoon 2.x architecture and its usage in creating user interfaces for multiple devices as a publishing framework. Now, we are going to see how Cocoon helps us in creating multimodal user interfaces.

Cocoon and Multimodality

The most important feature that Cocoon offers the mobile developer is a clean architecture for creation and specialization of generic user interfaces. When it comes to multimodality, Cocoon is useful because of the following:

1. It provides a well-designed infrastructure for building a fusion/fission engine. We will look at various architectures for multimodal systems in Section 8.4. You

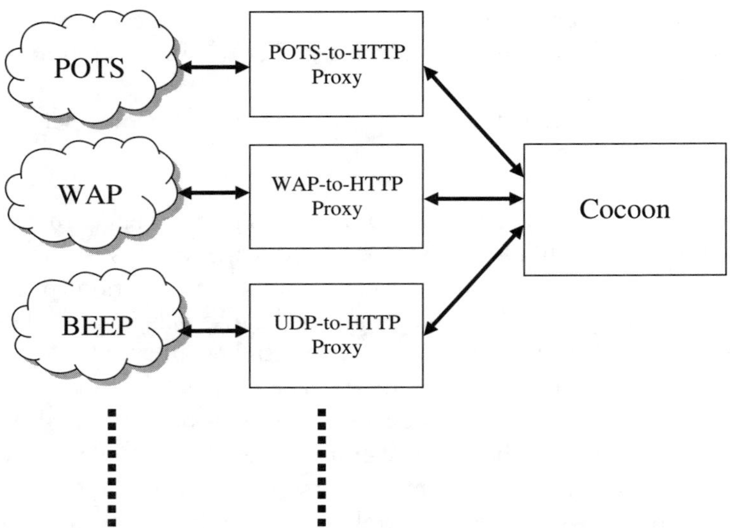

FIGURE 8.7. Extending Cocoon to Provide Non-HTTP Communication Channels.

will see that the core of the frameworks that enable us to deliver multimodality is an engine that allows binding of the various content in different modalities delivered through a variety of channels as well as temporal coordination of actions between the different channels. Cocoon does not provide a complete fusion/fission engine. However, it does provide us with the component framework to make it into one. It provides a mechanism for pipelined XML transformations, content aggregation, and publishing the content. Unfortunately, Cocoon is intended mainly for various Web-based technologies. So, this means that Cocoon provides only a single input channel: HTTP. Fortunately, there is a way to get around this as you can build proxies that treat individual channels as separate processes and in turn communicate with Cocoon. Figure 8.7 shows how this may be possible.

2. Cocoon provides a good framework to tie together two orthogonal user interface concepts for mobile applications, namely generic user interfaces and multimodality, in a cohesive manner and within the same application framework.

Now, let us look at the mechanisms that Cocoon provides for fusion/fission of multimodal content:

1. Cocoon transformers can be used as a mechanism to aggregate content intended for multiple channels (as a fuser). This aggregation can be done using CInclude, Xinclude, or Pipelining [Moczar and Aston 2002]. Both CInclude and XInclude allow inclusion of external content specified by URIs. XInclude is a W3C standard and CInclude is a Cocoon tool. Each has its advantages. Obviously, we recommend the usage of standards (XInclude in this case). You can also use Cocoon pipelines to get the same effect.
2. Matchers and selectors can be used for fission. Although, as we can see in Figure 8.7, not all of the delivery channels for the various modalities will

be HTTP (matchers and selectors being largely designed to take advantage of HTTP-based features), the proxies can translate channel-specific features (specific to POTS, BEEP, etc.) to HTTP headers, URI parameters, or some other value that can be used by Cocoon to pick the appropriate processing pipeline.

3. DELI (DElivery Context LIbrary), contributed to the Cocoon project by HP labs, provides support for CC/PP and UAProf within Cocoon. This means that we can use DELI to detect the multichannel capabilities of a device and select the appropriate pipeline, using the respectively appropriate channels and modalities. DELI was originally created to address WAP-based devices. However, there is nothing to keep us from using it, and extending it, to interface with other devices using other channels.
4. There is a particular Cocoon transformer that is of special interest to us: the I18ntransformer. This transformer, along with the rest of the Cocoon infrastructure, provides a clear way of separating the concerns of multimodality from those of internationalization.

This brings us to the end of our discussion on Cocoon. We refer you to the references we have mentioned here if you are interested in implementing a project based on Cocoon. Next, we will look at the SMIL and the problem of temporal synchronization that lies at the heart of the multimodality problem.

8.3.12 The Synchronization Problem

Perhaps the most important difference in the design of single modality and multimodal user interfaces is the temporal coordination between the channels. Let us say, for example, that we intend to use a telephony channel for sending audio back and forth between two nodes and a TCP/IP-based channel for graphical data. There is a particular sequence in which the graphical information must be displayed while audio is being heard. Because we are dealing with two different channels, the content coming out of those channels must be synchronized first on the server side and then on the client side. Even if we are dealing with simple TCP/IP sockets, the sockets could be established between one mobile device and multiple network points. Each network point may have certain QOS qualities that may cause the temporal behavior of the abstract channels to be different. The problem only gets more complicated with a more in-depth look.

There are various design patterns that have been well explored in the development of stationary applications. Some are based on the concept of synchronization and the techniques to implement synchronization between different channels. One high-level pattern recognized by Fujino [Fujino 2002] encompasses many of these patterns. The pattern is simply referred to as the *temporal representation*. Fujino recognizes the common theme that runs through all of the patterns that deal with the temporal nature of changes in state.

So, the forces of all patterns that deal with temporal representation focus on solving the ever-changing state of the software (if we are dealing with object-oriented systems, these are objects). The rate of change of the state of various internal components are not necessarily uniform and it is not only possible, but probable, that the state of something is “forgotten” at some point (some component is out of synchronization with others). In our world of multimodal interfaces for mobile applications, this means that, in addition to all of that which we have discussed, we need to understand that the timing and latency properties of the individual channels may vary from one another and that we need to deal with possible problems in timing, latency, and reliability of the data delivery by each one of the channels in a way that does not affect the processing of the other channels. We will look at the two concepts of fusion and fission later (analogous to their use in physics) that focus on putting together multiple things and then taking them apart. These are two things that multimodal tools, frameworks, and architectures must enable us to do to deliver multimodality: to fuse things based on their temporal properties and to take them apart for use in a temporally appropriate manner. For example, Flippo and colleagues have created a framework that defines a fusion manager where direct manipulation and conversational interaction run in parallel and may influence each other [Flippo et al. 2003]. We will look at other work later in the multimodal architecture section.

For these various patterns and architectures to work and be effective, we need a linguistic tool to specify the temporal nature of the multimodal content and the multimodal interactions between the user and the system. This is where SMIL comes in.

SMIL

SMIL, developed by the W3C, is perhaps the most important standard of concern when it comes to the delivery of multimodal content to the mobile device. SMIL defines an XML-based language for specifying multimedia content and multimodal interactions. To date, the latest version of SMIL stands at 2.0. SMIL 2.0 differs slightly from SMIL 1.0: Although supporting all SMIL 1.0 documents through deprecation, SMIL 2.0 is designed to be processed using the DOM because managing the temporal nature of multimodal interactions and multimedia content are closer to navigating through various states of a user interface rather than parsing through an XML document and emitting events based on the content (SAX model).

SMIL follows the same convention as the most recent W3C standards such as XHTML in providing modularization. SMIL is broken down into a set of modules to provide flexibility and extensibility; depending on the functionality offered by each module and the intended usage, the developers can mix and match modules somewhat freely. In this section, we will look at SMIL as it may apply to mobile applications. SMIL is a very large specification and deals with many different aspects of multimedia content and interactions. For a complete understanding of SMIL we refer you to the SMIL specifications at the W3C Web site [SMIL 2.0]. A collection of modules is referred to as a *profile* (the same terminology is used in W3C standards that use modularization). Table 8.8 shows the required modules for the *host language conformant* profiles and *integration conformant profiles*.

Each module may be validated independently through a DTD provided publicly by the W3C. For example, the DTD for the animation module may be found at http://www.w3.org/2001/SMIL20/SMIL-anim.mod.

TABLE 8.8. Satisfying Host and Integration Conformance in SMIL

Profile/Module	Host Language Conformant	Integration Conformant
Structure	Required	
BasicContentControl	Required	Required
BasicLayout	Required	
BasicLinking	Required	
BasicMedia	Required	Required
BasicTimeContainers	Required	Required
MinMaxTiming	Required	Required
RepeatTiming	Required	Required
SkipContentControl	Required	
SyncbaseTiming	Required	Required
BasicInLineTiming		Required

Host conformance basically means that the document root namespace is SMIL. In other words, the main purpose of a document that is host conformant is to describe multimodal interactions and multimedia content. However, SMIL modules can be used by other W3C XML base standards. If a document does so, for it to be integration conformant, it needs to include support for the modules specified under the collection of integration-conformant profile. The root element of a host-conformant document is <smil>. The SyncbaseTiming module may be excluded from either profile for mobile devices that are resource-starved.

Table 8.9 lists a small set of the tags provided by the SMIL standard.

The core of SMIL is provided through two sets of elements: those elements that provide information regarding the timing of things (grouped in a collection called TIMING-ELMS) and those elements that provide information (grouped in a collection called MEDIA-ELMS).

SMIL and Mobile Applications

SMIL provides a standard taxonomy and language for representing the temporal behavior of multimodality. However, because of the breadth of issues that it tackles, it can be too heavy to interpret for resource-starved mobile devices. Therefore, a subset of SMIL may be useful. This is the SMIL Basic profile. The SMIL Basic profile is the foundation for MMS specified in WAP 2.x. As its name suggests, SMIL Basic is a subset of SMIL that provides only the absolutely essential functionality offered by SMIL.

When it comes to processing an SMIL document, we are processing it on a device that either has the necessary resources to deal with a document based on the complete specification (such as servers, PCs, laptops, etc.) or one that does not (such as most cellular phones, PDAs, etc.). In the first case, we simply need an SMIL browser; the second case is more complex. Figure 8.8 shows an example architecture.

TABLE 8.9. Summary of Some of the SMIL Tags

Element	Description
<par>	The par tag (which stands for parallel) allows us to specify a set of elements that should be presented simultaneously. Simultaneity is defined by the start time of the presentation of the elements.
<seq>	This tag allows us to specify a set of elements that should be presented sequentially. This tag and the <par> tag are the two main tools in specifying the temporal relationships among the various media in SMIL.
<switch>	This element allows the developers to specify different sets of scenarios for presenting multimedia content or the multimodal interactions with the user based on evaluation of one or more attributes. It should be noted that this tag should not be misused for placing business logic into the SMIL document or snippet. This tag is intended strictly for presentation logic. So, just like JavaScript with HTML or VXML, be weary of misusing logical tags provided by SMIL. In the case of mobile applications, because most end devices are resource-starved, we want to preprocess as much of the logic on other devices on the network (servers, PCs, etc.) as possible. For example, one use for the switch statement may be to display a different size graphic on the device depending on the screen size. However, we may be able to perform this on the server side if the device is getting the SMIL document from the server. In many cases where the device is resource-starved this is preferable. Even in those cases where the device is not resource-starved, it is a bit risky to use this statement (unless absolutely necessary) because different applications (SMIL-enabled browsers and other applications that consume SMIL) will have small differences in their interpretation of the document.
<head>	This tag is used consistently as in the case of the other W3C standards to specify the document header. It holds information about the document (metainformation) itself. This can include metainformation, information about the layout of document, or information about customized extensions included within the document.
<body>	This tag wraps around the other tags that specify the temporal behavior of the content and interactions that define the multimodality properties of the user interface. Both this tag and the head tag belong to the structure module; therefore, their use implies support for the structure module.
<layout>	This is the element that is used within the <head> tag to specify the layout of the document. This tag provides roughly analogous functionality to SMIL to what CSS offers for XHTML and HTML.

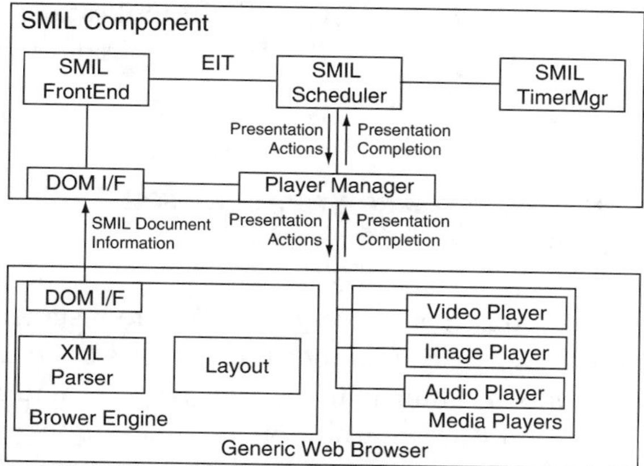

FIGURE 8.8. Example Architecture for Processing SMIL Documents on a Mobile Device [Hieda et al. 2003].

When processing an SMIL document on a resource-starved mobile device, most of the time we will opt to use the SMIL Basic profile. Because there may be other tasks that need to be performed on the mobile device at the same time, the processor of the SMIL Basic profile is probably a component in a bigger application. This is why Hieda et al. outline a technique for integrating a processor of the SMIL Basic profile into an application, referring to the general technique as SMIL Component (which is probably not a good name because the word component is one of the most overused words in the computer science vernacular). SMIL Component is composed so that it can be attached to a generic Web browser preinstalled in mobile terminals and does not have the generic browser functionality such as a parser and a layout manager [Hieda et al. 2003]. The basic idea is that we should be able to integrate SMIL capabilities into a variety of mobile applications

```
<smil>
   <body>
      <par begin="1s">
         <audio id="splash" begin="0s" dur="7s"
           src="splash.wav"/>
         <img begin="1s" end="splash.end-2s" fill="freeze"
           src="splash.gif"/>
      </par>
      <seq>
         <video id="splash_vid" end="5s" src="splash.mpg"/>
         <text dur="3s" repeatCount="1" max="5s"
           src="splash.wml"/>
      </seq>
   </body>
</smil>
```

FIGURE 8.9. SMIL Basic Profile Sample Code.

running on a resource-starved mobile device. These applications may be browsers or other types of applications. Figure 8.9 shows a simple SMIL basic profile document.

8.4 Software and System Architectures for Delivering Multimodality

Multimodal systems are constructed very differently from standard GUIs, largely because of the nature of human communication; whereas input to GUIs is atomic, certain machine perceptions of human input such as speech and gestures is uncertain, so any recognition-based system's interpretations are probabilistic [Oviatt and Cohen 2000]. Though multimodality has its advantages, not just for the user but also for the user interface developer who can use multimodality to reduce interface ambiguity and increase friendliness, it also has the disadvantage of exponentially increased complexity. In this section, we will review some of the general architectural solutions for building multimodal systems. Note that the architectures that we introduce are not mutually exclusive, nor are they necessarily competing architectures. Although they solve some common problems, each also addresses a unique set of problems.

First, let's go through a survey of the various high level architectures prevalent in creating multimodal systems.

1. *Multimodal Integrator*: Recognized by Oviatt [Oviatt OHSU 2002], this architecture relies on the processing on the input and output from the individual channels individually and then integrating the processed results in a multimodal integrator. This multimodal integrator (a software component that could be its own system or a subsystem of another system) encapsulates the logic for interpreting and integrating the various input and output being directed from and into the multiple channels. This architecture has some very significant advantages. First, we do not have to reinvent existing software components designed, implemented, tested, and proved for processing of the input and output to the individual channels. Second, most of the logic to handle multimodality is concentrated in one software component, thereby adhering to the separation of concerns that we have mentioned so many times throughout this text. Finally, it is an extensible and flexible architecture. We can add new input and output channels to the software that have minimal effect on the existing components; likewise, we can change the functionality of the existing software components written to handle individual channels while avoiding cascading modifications with the other components. Figure 8.10 shows a block diagram that depicts an architecture that relies on the multimodal integrator to coordinate tasks of multimodality. This pattern is also recognized by Corradini and Cohen [Corradini and Cohen 2002]. Oviatt, Cohen, and Corradini also refer to the multimodal integrator component as the *fusion agent* where the single-channel handling of the input and output is handled by other agents such as a *speech agent*. There are a few things that we should note about this architecture:

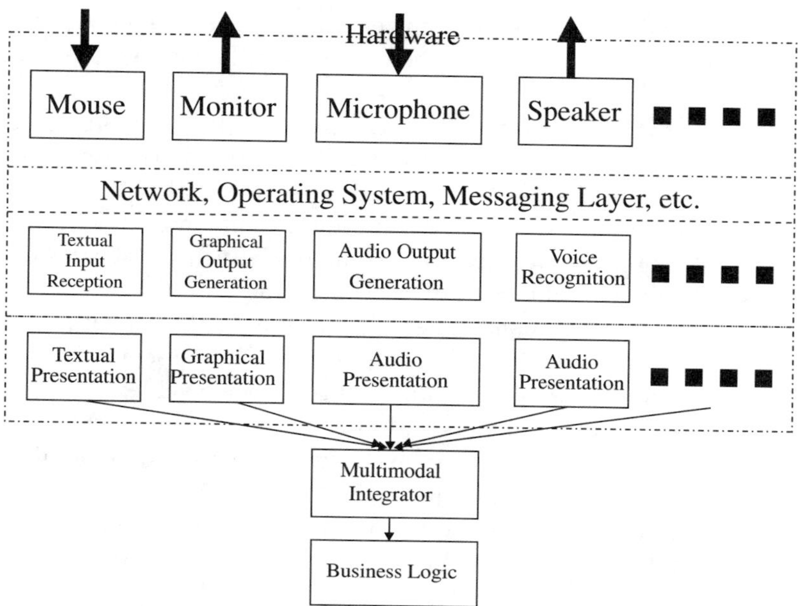

FIGURE 8.10. Multimodal Integration (Fusion Agent) Multimodal Architecture.

a. There may be several variants of this architecture as the number of layers that come before the multimodal integrator (fusion agent) is not dictated by this architecture. We may be integrating the raw data coming from each channel (bits, bytes, text, or whatever the raw data interface may be) or we may be integrating the meanings of this input and output. In either case, the task of the multimodal integrator is largely to coordinate the activities and content involved in single-mode rendition into a multimodal system.
b. This architecture is orthogonal but related to PAC and PAC-TG as introduced in previous chapters. Although we can still have generic content that is being specialized for each modality, the specialization may be done inside or outside of the fusion agent. The act of "fusing" or "integrating" has more to do with integrating the input/output of each channel, or integration thereof, rather then the specialization of the content going into and coming out of each channel.
c. A list of various more granular software patterns such as the broker, the mediator, or collaboration may be used in the internal implementation of the larger grained components in the diagram in Figure 8.10. Note that this diagram and the idea behind it represent a high-level pattern. There are variations on this architecture. The act of "integration" or "fusion" can be done in multiple stages during the processing (or pipelining) of the content through each modality and channel. In other words, we can have multiple types and instances of the multimodal integrator coordinate the efforts among the interpreters, recognizers, and generators. The terms "early fusion" and "late fusion" are often used in the literature as reference to some of the variations on this architecture.

d. Oviatt and colleagues also recognizes, in a separate paper [Oviatt, Jacko, and Sears 2002], that there are the following different levels of "fusion" or "integration":
   i. *Frame-based fusion* is where we may use structural properties, such as the visual boundaries (thereby the usage of the term frame-based), associated with the various inputs being fused
   ii. *Semantic fusion* is where we obtain the semantic meaning of the various parts being integrated and have some predefined set of rules that allow us to integrate them based on their meaning
   iii. *Unification-based fusion* is where the meaning of the parts is programmatically driven from some set of rules (similar to the semantic fusion).
   iv. *Feature-level fusion* is a method for fusing low-level feature information from parallel input signals within a multimodal architecture; this has been applied to processing closely synchronized input such as speech and lip movement [Oviatt, Jacko, and Sears 2002].

   Note that the usage of one of these techniques does not prohibit the others. In fact, any combination of them may be used in building the integration/fusion logic.

2. *Generic Multimedia Multimodal Dialog Architecture* (MMDA): Recognized by Djenidi, Ramdane-Cherif, Tadj, and Levy [Djenidi et al. 2002], a basic MMDA allows the user to decide which modality or combination of modalities is better suited to the particular task and environment. MMDA leverages various software agents that cooperate to get the task of "fusion" done. Recall that mobile agents are autonomous and asynchronous and can move around among various hosts. The agents of the MMDA architecture are autonomous and asynchronous but it is not necessary that they be mobile among different hosts. The focus of MMDA is to provide a "dynamic" architecture where the agents can reconfigure themselves and the way they communicate in different circumstances. This architecture builds on variations of the first architecture that we introduced, namely early and late fusion.

   The problem with MMDA is that today's base technologies (operating system, programming languages, etc.) do not lend themselves well to dynamically configurable software components. Much of what MMDA proposes is very difficult to actually implement with today's technologies for commercial environments.

3. *Multimodal Integrator and Multimodal Dialogue Manager*: This architecture is a further refinement of the multimodal integrator architecture but is worthy of mention on its own for two reasons. First, it recognizes some further separation of concerns among the integration or fusion process, the disambiguation process, and the management of the interactions with the user in specific scenarios. Second, it recognizes that a viable way to handle the interactions with the user in a multimodal is through the concept of dialogues. We looked at dialogues in Chapter 7 while discussing VUIs. In the case of multimodality, the concept of a dialogue allows us to encapsulate interactions with the user based on their content and general behavior as opposed to properties specific to a given channel. In other words, we specify what needs to be presented to the user instead of

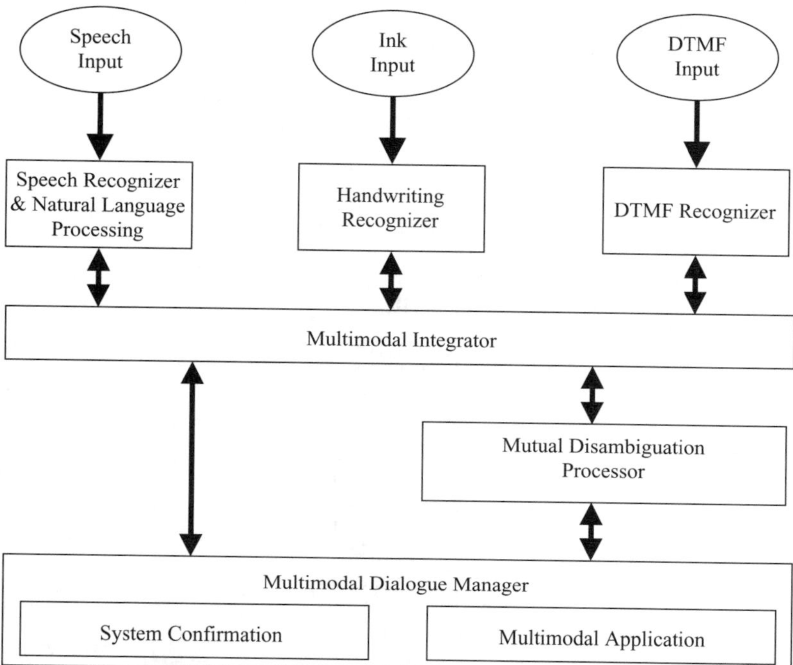

FIGURE 8.11. Multimodal Integrator and Dialogue Manager Architecture [Trabelsi et al.].

how and we do it in a scripted and sequential manner. Trabelsi et al. [Trabelsi et al. 2002] recognize an application of this architecture for using voice and text (through handwriting) for mobile devices; this is shown in Figure 8.11.

4. *Sharma's Dialogue Management for Multimodality:* Sharma and his colleagues at Pennsylvania State University have created an interesting architecture for managing multimodal dialogues. This architecture, seen in Figure 8.12, has a large focus on solving VUI problems, but it is interesting in that the treatment of the VUI problem is extensible and adaptable to other user interface modalities and channels. The crowning achievement of this architecture is that it focuses on creating a grammar-based user interface controller (as discussed in Chapter 5) that can handle multimodality. Sharma and colleagues build a crisis management system based on this architecture and, along the way, also mix in the idea of our multimodal integrator. However, whereas the centerpiece of the previous architectures we have discussed in this section have been the multimodal integrator and its fusing capabilities, here the centerpiece is the dialogue manager and everything else is a subsystem built around the dialogue management tasks. This architecture, appropriately so, aims to solve the input problem with multimodal user interfaces. As we have mentioned previously in this chapter, the variables for the output are more deterministic and, as application developers, we have more control over them. Another notable aspect of Sharma's techniques is that he and his colleagues set out to solve an application problem, namely, to build a multimodal crisis management

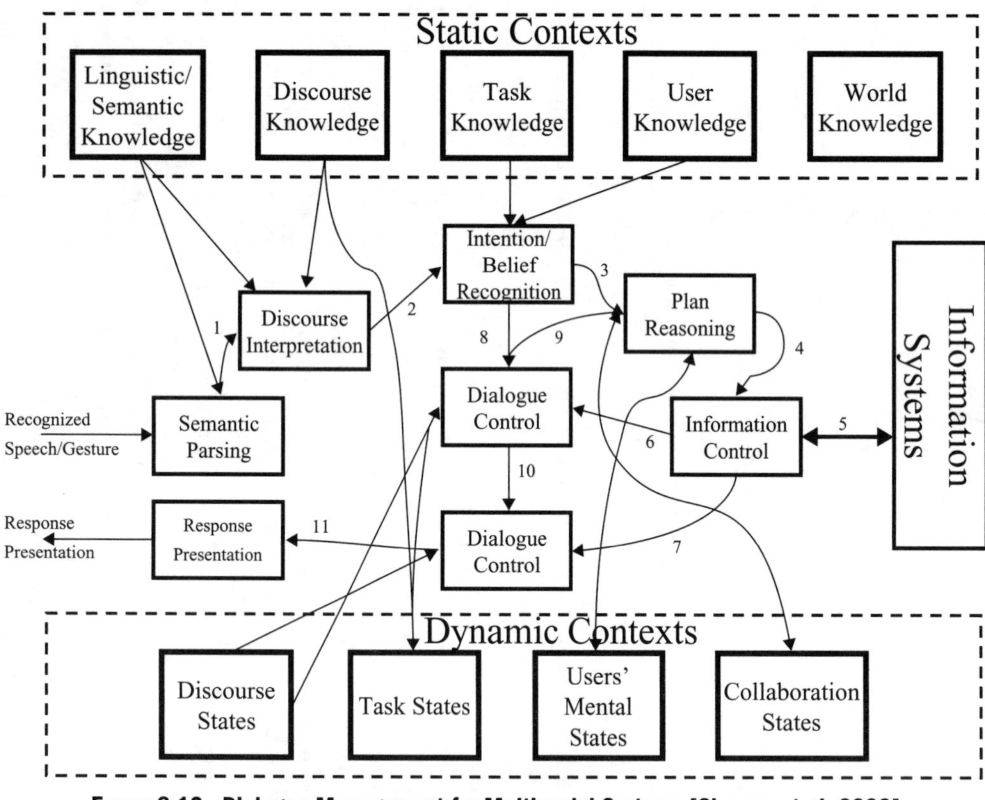

FIGURE 8.12. **Dialogue Management for Multimodal Systems [Sharma et al. 2003].**

framework, rather than to build a framework that generically serves many purposes. The advantage to this approach is that the architecture is put through the rigors and questions of at least one real-world problem and solution implementation (in this case multimodal crisis management system) and thereby is more refined.

5. *DFKI Multimodal Architecture*: The German Research Center for Artificial Intelligence (DFKI) has made great strides in developing new techniques for multimodality. These efforts revolve around the SmartKOM project, which we have mentioned throughout this chapter. (Recall that M3L was created for use in SmartKOM.) This architecture, which is referred to as the MULTIPLATFORM TestBed (a somewhat confusing name because the term multiplatform is extremely overused in software), is used for a variety of projects by DFKI, one of which is the SmartKOM project. Remember that we discussed M3L as one of the more significant languages for expressing multimodal interactions previously: This is the language designed for SmartKOM and is part of the MULIPLATFORM TestBed. This architecture focuses on seven principles and recognizes seven respective components as follows:
   a. *Recognizer*: Recognizers are modality-specific components that process input data on the signal level. Examples include speech recognition, determination of prosodic information, or gesture recognition [Herzog et al. 2003].
   b. *Analyzer*: This component interprets the semantic meaning of the input produced by the recognizer.
   c. *Modeler*: The modeler basically holds the "model" (logic, business rules, or the things that the software system needs to understand and that are discretely defined for it). The model, for example, could be home–automation interactions.
   d. *Generator*: Generators are knowledge-based components that determine and control the reactions of the dialogue system through the transformation of representation structures [Herzog et al. 2003].
   e. *Synthesizer*: An example of a synthesizer is a speech-synthesis engine or a Braille-creation engine (creating Braille from textual input). Synthesizers produce specific types of content.
   f. *Device*: This is the abstraction of the input and output hardware used to get the input from the user and send the output back to the user. Software may accompany this hardware to produce input that is consumable by the recognizers and consume output that is producible by the synthesizers.
   g. *Service*: These modules allow us to connect our multimodal application to some external service provided by a well-encapsulated piece of functionality. Basically, these are adaptors or connectors that hold the complexity introduced by the integration of all of the different pieces.

   For a deeper understanding of this architecture, we refer you to the reference [Herzog et al. 2003]. Once more, you can see that this architecture has much in common with the others in requiring the semantic interpretation of the input in a manner that is more complex than simply interpreting the input from the individual modalities.

Coutaz and colleagues correctly recognize that the taxonomy of the multimodal architectures are two dimensional: They may be classified by how they achieve fusion/fission and by the degree of parallelism (simultaneous multimodality) that they offer [Coutaz et al. 2003]. Likewise, there are two approaches, recognized by Minh, to creating a language tool to outline application-specific multimodal behavior User Action Notations (UAN) and LOTOS (Language of Temporal Ordering Specification) [Minh 1997]. UAN refers to a language tool that allows us to specify the interactions of the user with the interface. LOTOS refers to a language tool (such as SMIL) that allows us to specify the temporal behavior of the interface while the user interacts with it.

We can think of these architectures as high-level system patterns for multimodal application development. Most notable of these patterns is the first one: the multimodal integrator. The idea of fusing or integrating separately processed semantic meaning of the input and output from various communication channels with the user is the theme that seems to reoccur throughout the patterns that we have outlined here. Keep in mind that these architectures can internally use PAC, MVC, or the variations thereof for each component or as the basis of implementation of the core functional pieces such as the integrator (fuser). These architectures can also be coupled with techniques such as transcoding and transforming, which we looked at in Chapters 5 through 8.

Because the field of mobile development and the orthogonal but related field of multimodal user interfaces are both rather young disciplines in computing, there will be frequent innovations and new architectures. The best thing to do then is to understand what properties these architectures must have to qualify as finalists in any evaluation process. These properties are as follows:

1. *Coordinated Decoupling of the Modalities*: To reduce complexity, we want to separate the various concerns in any piece of software and isolate them into encapsulated components. Doing this can be tricky. Particularly, in the case of multimodal user interfaces, we need to be able to separate the concerns of treating the individual channels and modalities to components that are decoupled from one another. Yet, we must be able to coordinate the behavior of these components across modalities and channels (e.g., the timing of rendering various parts of the output content). A multimodal user interface architecture must be able to decouple the various components and yet provide some mechanism for coordinating the interactions among the various modalities and channels.
2. *Localization and Internationalization*: At least when we use multimodal user interfaces for mobile systems, we need to ensure that the architecture allows for clean and proper implementation of localization and internationalization. Users of future mobile services are likely to consider their mobile terminal as a universal access device for all the services they subscribe to and they will expect these services to "behave" in the same manner, irrespective of the place where they happen to be at a given point in time [UTMS P1104 2002]. Whatever architecture we select must either provide for, or have the capability to be extended to treat, the problems associated with internationalization and

localization. These problems include the usage of various languages, currencies, and other variables related to the specific domain of the application.

3. *Validation*: The validation of user input becomes a very difficult problem in multimodal applications because the input from each individual channel, in and of itself, may be invalid whereas the fused inputs from all modes may be valid. The architecture that we choose must be able to accommodate the implementation of a multimodal validation strategy through which we can validate user's input to the system as a whole.
4. *Extensibility for Future Modalities and Channels*: Whatever architecture we use to implement multimodality in our application, it should be able to be extended to support modalities and channels not well defined or required at the time of the implementation of the architecture. In other words, if there is some new device recording the user's eye movement that replaces the mouse, we should not have to reengineer the system. We should be able to simply snap in the new system with the software components required for the appropriate support in the architecture. This is obviously much easier said than done, but then, that is the purpose of having an architecture.
5. *Cross-Modal Disambiguation:* One of the biggest utilities of multimodality in mobile applications, as we have mentioned, is to provide a better disambiguation mechanism. Multimodal architectures chosen for mobile applications should implement an extensible mechanism that implements, or allows for the implementation of, disambiguation of the user's input in a cross-modal way. In other words, if the user's hand is shaking too much while he or she is writing, we can ask user "Did you mean to write 'that shake's great' or 'the shark's jaws'?" Another example may be disambiguation of user's voice input through DTMF or by text input into a device.
6. *Semantic Treatment of Multimodal Input and Content*: As we mentioned in the introduction of this chapter, two factors that are very critical in the case of developing multimodal user interfaces, especially for mobile applications, are contextual and environmental factors. To deal with either one, we need to be able to deal with the semantics of information and not just raw data. In other words, we need mechanisms that deal with the meanings of things. Our architecture needs to be able to handle the fact that spoken words and written text have different meanings depending on the environment and contextual surroundings. This is not something that every multimodal architecture will have, but it is a definite plus. Processing of semantic information is one of the hotly researched areas of computing that is orthogonal to our discussion here, but its current state and evolution has a large impact on multimodal user interfaces and their applications within mobile applications.

As in the case of any user interface management system, there are different approaches to designing multimodal applications. These approaches are similar to the UIMS of the GUI world: grammar based, event based, and State-Machine based. Dialogue management, whose trails are seen in most of the architectures we have presented here, seems to fit the multimodal world well. Implementations are probably the best indicator of this. For example, HP's Mavrick project builds around DialogML and WML to create a grammar-based multimodal user interface infrastructure [Hickey W3C].

To build a system like the ones whose architectures we have been discussing, we need some tools: programming or scripting language, development environment, devices that can connect to our system, viable host environments, etc. All of the major entities in the world of operating systems such as Microsoft, Apple, Palm, Linux, and others are busily adding capabilities to support multimodality in one way or the other. Unfortunately, not all of these entities have chosen standard paths (to benefit their bottom line and at the detriment of the consumer's good in the long haul). So, what we have tried to do here is to introduce architectures and the guiding principles behind the design and implementation of the tools. It is certain that in a year or two after you read this text, the tools will not be the same, but, using the principles that we have mentioned here, you will be able to select the appropriate language tools and apply them to the architecture of your selection.

At present, we would approach the problem as follows:

1. There are given standards that have been established, such as SMIL, and are prevalent in the marketplace. Do not divert from these unless your application absolutely requires you to. Standards do not just offer benefits because they are open and create easy integration among disparate systems. Standards are typically very well thought out by industry experts. So, if you are using a standard, you are leveraging the expertise of people who really understand the domain well.
2. Determine the available and required channels of communication to your multimodal application both from the user's perspective (input and output devices) and from the system's perspective (PSTN, TCP/IP, etc.).
3. Lay out your architecture based on the project requirements. We recommend selecting one of the high-level architectures that we have outlined here.
4. Select a language tool and start coding!

8.5 Internationalization and Localization

We have discussed internationalization and localization when dealing with various aspects of mobile applications earlier in this text. Internationalization and localization of multimodal applications introduces the following entirely new set of problems:

1. *Managing the Content and the Channels*: In a world of single modalities, all we need is to manage one type of content for one type of channel. The $n \times m$ content to channel matrix means that we have to know what content is available in what language and localization rule sets for which channel.
2. *Synchronization*: The rules for synchronizing change too! Because the length of the content in one language or localization set may be shorter or longer than

the other and the synchronization points may be different, our system must be smart enough to provide the infrastructure for specifying the appropriate synchronization rules for our $n \times m$ content to channel matrix.

3. *Decoupling the Concerns in Localization and Internationalization:* There are multiple problems here: languages, translations, different currencies, different rules of doing business, preferences of the users depending on where they are from and where they live, and all the other more atomic concerns that we grossly define as internationalization and localization. Separating these concerns allows us to build a more extensible and flexible software system and to possibly reduce the development time by reducing the focus on certain concerns that may not be of much interest when delivering the functionality to the end customer. For example, as the Euroscom report recognizes, localization can be restricted to the presentation layer, where linguistic representation of the information can be generated and subsequently rendered on the screen [EURESCOM P1104 2002]. Though this is a very gross approximation, there may be a circumstance where providing a multilingual multimodal application suffices and localization is of less interest. You can extrapolate this sort of thinking to breaking down the granular components that make up localization and internationalization.

We recommend using a framework or a tool such as Cocoon to solve the internationalization and localization problem. This problem has a tendency to spread its claws throughout the software, causing it to mix with unrelated concerns.

8.6 The Evolving Definition of Multimodality

Today, a multimodal application typically refers to an application that uses visual and aural user input similar to those of telephones and PCs. This definition, however, will be evolving during the coming years. First, there are various types of sensors being introduced to the marketplace to accept various types of input from the user. Examples of these are sensors that track eye movement, handwriting recognition, and other types of sensors to more naturally receive input from the user. There is also on-going research on receiving user input without a user's active participation. For example, a user's location (or that of the user's device) or geospatial orientation can be used as an input. Compaq's Itsy, which we have mentioned several times in this text, is an example of a device that uses the physical positioning of the device for user input (tilting, for example, is used for scrolling). Some other modes of input on the horizon are gesture recognition; data gloves that enable various types of input from hands, fingers, and even the rotation of wrists and arms; and body suits that can use things like body position and temperature as input.

The number of input and output channels are expected to increase considerably as user interface research aims for creating more natural and efficient user interfaces. So, as you may have noted by reading this chapter, we can not define multimodality in terms of some static number or types of channels and content types. Therefore, creating multimodal applications becomes more about coming up with flexible and extensible design structures that do not limit the definition of multimodality.

This ever-changing nature of multimodality reinforces the design principles that we have been stressing, the most important of which is to create a generic user interface that is then specialized to the specific modalities and bound to the specific channels.

SECTION 3

Additional Dimensions of Mobile Application Development

CHAPTER 9

Mobile Agent and Peer-to-Peer Architectures for Mobile Applications

To the "Drive" and No. 7

9.1 INTRODUCTION

In Chapter 16, we briefly look at five different architecture types: fully centralized, client–server and its variations of *N*-tier, mobile agents, and peer-to-peer. You may want to refer to this chapter intermittently or read it first. In this chapter, we will focus on the latter two, namely mobile agents and peer-to-peer systems, as relating to mobile application development.

We focus on these systems for two reasons. First, the application of mobile agents and peer-to-peer architectures in the mobile application realm is not well documented because both are fairly recent concepts. Second, both mobile agents and peer-to-peer architectures promise to play an integral role in mobile application development as it matures. We have already discussed the properties of these two architectures that make them more desirable for mobile application development. Furthermore, we have surveyed both of these technologies. Now, you may wonder why we are making an association between the peer-to-peer and mobile agent architectures. We can find the answer in looking at some of the properties of the two architectures and their contrasts with the client–server model.

Peer-to-peer and mobile applications are similar in the following ways:

1. *Unlike the centralized and client–server architectures, there is no necessity for a centralized server.* There is no inherent difference between the system-level

participants of peer-to-peer and mobile agent architectures, respectively peers and hosts, within the confines of the respective architecture, as there is between the client and the server in the client–server environment.

2. *The participants of the system can be interconnected to each other in any manner.* Both peer-to-peer architectures and mobile agent architectures allow for self-organizing and ad hoc networks.

This is not to say that mobile agents and peer-to-peer application infrastructures are synonymous or the same. Quite the contrary, they are two completely different paradigms. However, their requirements and properties are not mutually exclusive. For example, whereas mobility of code and data is at the heart of mobile agent architectures, peer-to-peer architectures do not impose any such requirements. However, the peer-to-peer infrastructure can also provide a substrate for deployment of a mobile agent framework.

In this chapter, our focus will be on mobile agent technologies. You will want to keep in mind that agent technologies are not as mature as client–server technologies within the context of reading this chapter.

Peer-to-peer architectures are of extreme importance in mobile computing, but the fundamentals of their design and usage is closer to client–server computing than to that of mobile agents. For this reason, our discussion of peer-to-peer computing and mobility will be brief. To better understand the similarities and the use of peer-to-peer and mobile agent architectures, we need to take a closer look at each one. Let us quickly review what we discussed in Chapter 1 and then go on to look at mobile agents in more detail.

9.1.1 Basics of Agent Technologies

As we mentioned previously, mobile agents require mobility of code and data. When the agent moves from one host to another, it needs to preserve its data and, in case of strong mobility, execution state. Mobility of the data is something that should be somewhat familiar to most developers who have used client–server architectures. The data held by one or more objects that make up an agent can be persisted or streamed and moved from one host to another. In practice this may be as simple as writing the data to a file, binary or otherwise. Once the data are moved, it should go through a *binding* process to the agent at the destination. The mobility of the code and its state of execution, however, are a bit more complex.

According to Fugetta, Picco, and Vigna [Fuggetta et al. 1998], there are two types of code mobility: *strong mobility and weak mobility*. In strong mobility, the execution state of the agent returns to the point at which it stopped before migrating to the new host. Weakly mobile agent systems cannot do this; all they can do is to migrate the code and initialize the code with the data. In the context of this book, unless mentioned otherwise, when we say a mobile agent, we are referring to strong mobility. Fugetta et al. go on to recognize three types of participants in mobile agent systems: *components, interactions*, and *sites*. Huang [Huang 2000] divides the participants into *mobile agents, clients that launch the agents*, and *agent hosts*. These divisions exist throughout the various research and implementations of mobile agents. Essentially, though, both groups recognize that there is a component that moves around the mobile agent infrastructure. We will refer to this component as the *mobile agent*. Fugetta's sites are approximately Huang's agent hosts; we will refer to an instance of either as a *host*. As defined previously, hosts are the places where agents can operate. We will refer to the interactions between the mobile agents as *collaborations* and the interactions between the hosts and the mobile agents as *interactions*. It is also important to note that both words, collaboration and interaction, are also used in UML; the definition of collaboration and interaction with the world of mobile agents is unrelated to the definition and usage of the same words in UML. Ideally, there are no direct interactions among the hosts themselves. However, in practicality, most implementations of mobile agent systems are hybrid and allow for client-server-type interactions among the hosts.

Fuggetta et al.'s paper on code mobility [Fuggetta et al. 1998] gives us one of the best short references for understanding the theoretical nature of mobile agents. The theoretical coverage we have given mobile agents so far should suffice for building mobile applications.

Now, to understand how mobile agents work, we need to look at the basic services that the mobile agent platform must offer to handle agents. We can do this by starting at the host. The sequence of events that take place, on the host, are as follows:

1. The agent program arrives at this host. If the host is capable of multiprocessing, and if the agent platform supports processing of multiple hosts at the same time, the agent starts a new process for the new agent that has just arrived. Otherwise, the host suspends or stops the operation of the current agent and starts up the new agent.
2. The host facilitates rebinding of code, data, and state. The agent then continues at the next instruction. As we mentioned previously, there are two parts to the state, the state of the data and the execution state.
3. When the agent is either done or needs to migrate to another host, it finishes executing the current instruction.
4. Then, the host collects the agent code, data, and state and puts them into a message in a host-independent format.
5. The message can be shipped to an exact destination or it can be sent to a post office that holds the logic for determining the destination host and shipping the message to the destination host.
6. The destination host receives the message and continues with Step 1.

This series of events can be further refined if the mobile agent platform is object oriented. If the code is a collection of classes, it can be cached. So, if the classes at the source and destination hosts are identical, the classes do not need to be shipped as a part of the message. This can be thought of as a caching mechanism. The instance data of the classes comprise the state of the agent and the next method of the driver class is the execution state. Note that we do not represent these sequences of events with UML diagrams at this point because vanilla UML diagrams (with no extensions) do not suffice in correctly representing the complexity of mobile agents in a brief manner. (We could do this with several state diagrams; however, state diagrams are typically not useful for seeing the interactions among the various components of a system). Consequently, we will add some UML extensions later on and represent mobile agent systems using UML diagrams.

It is important to note that the agent itself is the mechanism that decides when it is time to move. The agent is autonomous and controls its own life cycle so it decides when it starts, stops, moves, hibernates, or undergoes any other type of state change.

Those readers familiar with client–server technologies that control the life cycle of components, such as J2EE, may wonder what the difference is between the functionality offered by an application server that manages the life cycle of objects and that of mobile agents. The key here is that the host is not a container that manages the life cycle of the agent. Rather, the host provides the agent with the execution thread and machine resources it needs to do what it needs to accomplish. Also, such technologies use mechanisms based on RPC or ROI (Remote Object Invocation) to exchange information.

Bauer notes that, compared to objects, agents are active because they can take the initiative and have control over whether and how they process external requests [Bauer 2001]. Moreover, agents act not only in isolation but in cooperation or coordination with other agents. This has a twofold meaning for us: First, it clarifies the difference between objects and agents and second it verifies that UML, with no extensions, does not suffice to represent agents and their interactions. (When we say "with no extensions," as previously mentioned in this text, we mean use including only the basic types and classifiers as defined by the UML specification, without the introduction of profiles or modifications to a metamodel for accommodating some domain of problems.)

Also, as you read through this chapter, it may be helpful to think of agents as larger grained components than objects. (Once again, note that although there may be a linear mapping between software components and UML components, within the context of our discussion, we are not necessarily referring to a UML component, but rather the loosely, and frequently, used term of "software component.") Though mobile agents are typically implemented using object-oriented languages, and an agent *can* be comprised of a single object (an instance of a single class), mobile agent behavior and useful properties are observed at a higher level of granularity.

Before we delve further into details and implementations of mobile agents and infrastructures that support mobile agents, let us look at hybrids of mobile agents and client–servers that offer an alternative to both mobile agent and client–server architectures.

9.1.2 Hybrids of Mobile Agents and Client–Server

Although mobile agents have many advantages over their client–server counterparts, there are times when the client–server architecture is superior. For example, in a pure mobile agent environment, if two agents need to exchange a small piece of information, either both or one of the two have to migrate so that they are on the same host. This may be effective when there are many different exchanges, between the agents, that must be completed, but it is superfluous if the interactions are limited.

For this and similar reasons, hybrids of the mobile agent and client–server architecture, where the mobile agents can assume the role of a client or a server in the client–server model, can prove to be more effective than either the mobile agent or the client–server architectures. In a hybrid of mobile agent and client–server architectures, the autonomous agents decide, based on the interaction that they need to initiate, on what mechanism to use to interact with other agents on the system. The agent itself can decide whether it is more efficient, or suitable, within the context of the transaction that needs to be initiated to use RPC, ROI, or similar client–server mechanisms, or if it needs to be at the same host as the agent with which it must interact.

Client–agent server gives us the best of both client–server and mobile agent architectures: When the network conditions are suitable for client–server communication, the agents can collaborate and assume the roles of clients and servers. When the network cannot provide the continuous bandwidth needed but bursts of connectivity are available, or when the application needs to have a response time that is closer to real time, we can have the agents migrate for communication purposes. The important thing to remember is that a variation on the client–server architecture uses mobile agent technology. In the client–agent server model, the clients communicate with an agent on the host, which acts like a server in the client–server environment. The agent then does whatever it needs to do within the network-based mobile-agent region or agency.

We will not discuss the client–agent server much because we assume that you understand the basics of client–server communication and we intend to cover details of mobile agents in this chapter. When agents assume the roles of clients and servers, they can communicate as if they were pieces of a system based on the client–server architecture. You should be able to deduce the properties of such systems based on your knowledge of client–server technologies and our discussion of mobile agents.

9.1.3 Separation of Concerns in Mobile Agents

When writing code for mobile agents, we can apply separation of concerns much as we did in the *N*-tier architectures to separate typical concerns such as those of the user interface, persistence, communications, business logic, and others.

Recall that in the three-tier architecture, persistence, user interface, and business logic were three of the main concerns. The same can be said in the case of mobile agents. To separate these concerns, it is prescribed that a different agent or group of agents be responsible for each one of the three. In this manner, a driver agent that understands the general goal of the application can collaborate with a persistence agent or agents to retrieve the data, a business logic agent or agents to compute whatever computational logic may be involved, and a user interface agent that has the proper services for rendering the functionality of the application, on the particular host, to the user. Note that the driver agent may collaborate with the other agents, based on the available resources on the host and application requirements, on the migration and life-cycle patterns of the agents. For example, if the device does not have enough memory to load all of the agents at the same time, they may be loaded sequentially, yet autonomously, and the driver agent may collaborate with the other agents to handle the necessary data and parameters among the different agents as they migrate in and out of the host.

A great example of separation of concerns with mobile agent architectures is given by SARA [Yang et al. 2000]. The SARA (Synthetic Aperture Radar Atlas) digital library is an image archive system that has grown complex beyond the ability of typical client–server computing models for scaling. Though in the case of SARA, the mobile agents are used to comprise a stationary software application (with the primary use of mobile agents in SARA being to take advantage of scaling advantages of mobile agents), the architecture of the implementation outlined in the aforementioned paper shows a marvelous separation of concerns within the mobile agent architecture. For example, local retrieval agents can translate a query task and retrieve information from a local archive, which could be a database system or a file system [Yang et al. 2000]. SARA also has user agents that render a generic interface to the system called *user presentation agents* and agents that specialize the user interface for final rendition called *user interface agents*. Separation of concerns within the structure of the agents is crucial for the following reasons:

1. Without enough separation between orthogonal tasks, agents may become bloated. In this case, mobile agents become unsuitable for mobile application development and begin to lose their flexibility and ability to solve scaling problems.
2. If the services to be offered by the agents are not carefully grouped into the right agent(s), collaboration among the agents either emulates client–server communication (in which case the desirable properties of mobile agent systems are lost) or the agents have to migrate too frequently.

For example, let us say that we want to use mobile agents for making airplane ticket reservations. The user may want a smart application that searches for the right price and then contacts the user before the chance of purchasing the ticket is lost. One way of making the application would be to create one large monolithic agent that does everything from searching for the data, to finding where the user may be, and finally to presenting the data to the user. This would not be a good way of using mobile agents. The application would be difficult to modify, it would take a large amount of burst bandwidth as it travels the network, and it would not make use of any other existing agent(s) in the system. Essentially, this would be equivalent to authoring a monolithic server program. The second option would be to create several agents that do not encapsulate orthogonal tasks: One agent may search to find the right data and store it temporarily and another agent that finds the user and presents it to him or her. Though this is an improvement over the monolithic agent, it still does not take full advantage of the mobile agent paradigm. Multiple, unrelated services are offered by the same agent and there is no clarity on how the agents should migrate and collaborate.

The most effective way of designing the agents would be to have clear separation between the tasks that each accomplishes. The first simple pass at such design may include the following:

1. agent(s) responsible for user interface rendering on a variety of specific environments,
2. agent(s) responsible for providing a generic user interface to all agents except for those responsible for rendering of specific environments,
3. agent(s) responsible for comparing the qualifications of the different tickets based on the user specifications,
4. agent(s) responsible for connecting to a variety of data sources that have information about airplane tickets, and
5. agent(s) that customize the overall application to how the user wants it to run.

Obviously, it is possible to come up with a finer grained division of responsibilities among the agents. The granularity of the tasks assigned to the mobile agents must be balanced with the following:

1. *Migration latency*: If there are too many agents, each doing some very small task, they constantly have to migrate back and forth between different hosts.
2. *Collaboration latency*: If there are too many agents, each doing some very small task, they have to continually pass information back and forth, reducing the autonomous nature of mobile agents and creating large latencies while the information is being passed back and forth.

Also, note that by separating the concerns among the different agents, we can promote reuse of agents. For reuse, agents can be thought of as any other type of software component: Reuse is only possible if the component is not too large, not too small, and shaped just the right way with the right semantics and services.

It is also possible to come up with an altogether different scheme for separating the concerns among the different agents. For the sake of simplicity, we have separated the concerns in a way familiar to most client–server developers: persistence, user interface, and business logic. Tasks can be divided in many different ways. As with many other aspects of software design, perfecting this design methodology becomes somewhat of an art and requires some experimentation on the part of the software designer. However, this example should demonstrate that application of separation of concerns is critical, not only for reuse (as is true for all software) but also for optimizing the performance of the mobile agent system.

Finally, refer back to Chapter 6 to see our discussion on the PAC pattern. Remember that the PAC pattern is a collection of so-called agents comprised of presentation, abstraction, and control components. It is plausible that, in implementing a mobile agent–based application, there could be a $1 - N$ mapping between PAC agents to mobile agents. The cooperation between PAC agents is easily implemented in the collaborative environment of mobile agents.

We will not delve too much into the topic of internal implementation of mobile agents for this broad topic lies outside of the scope of this text. Refer to the references if you are interested in a better understanding of implementation of mobile agent infrastructure and implementing mobile agents. Our goal here is to use mobile agents for mobile application development and this is what we will look at next.

9.2 Mobile Agents for Mobile Computing

As we mentioned in Chapter 1, the key distinguishing factors of mobile agents are the following:

1. *Code and state are mobile.* For a software program to be a mobile agent, it has to have both mobile code and data properties. This means that it should be able to move from one instance of the mobile agent environment (a platform that supports the particular mobile agent framework) to another instance without losing the state at which it was before moving. Moreover, it has to be able to return to the exact state at which it was before moving to the destination once it arrives there.
2. *Mobile agents are autonomous and asynchronous.* They control their own life cycles and there is no required timing synchronization between the activities of two or more agents.

In this text, we will refer to a computing unit that can allow execution of a mobile agent as a *host*. A host may be a device with some hard-wired software, a device with an operating system, a device with an operating system and a virtual machine, or a variety of other combinations of software on a device. Regardless of what comprises the host, it, in its entirety, includes the framework that allows the mobile agents to move around and operate. Hosts are also referred to as *agencies*. We will refer to the act of two or more agents communicating to achieve some task as *collaboration*.

There are also other properties that mobile agents can exhibit such as *intelligence* and *recursion*. Intelligence is the ability of the agent to learn from the information it gets and make decisions (e.g., to decide where to move next); recursion is the ability of the agent to create child agents for subtasks if necessary [Huang 2000]. Note that intelligence and recursion are not required for classifying an infrastructure as one that uses mobile agents.

Now, let us see why mobile agents are particularly suitable for mobile application development. The following are the primary reasons:

1. *Because of their autonomous nature, mobile agents are inherently active.* They do not have to be invoked by some external means to start up, do work, communicate, or emit some event.
2. *Mobile agents use less of the network bandwidth in comparison to RPC or ROI mechanisms of client–server architectures.* In client–server architectures, two disparate applications send data back and forth using RPC. Every transaction includes at least one call from the client to the server. In mobile agent architectures, the code and its instance (the data) move from one host to another host. Once they

arrive at the destination host, they perform some task autonomously without having to communicate with other hosts on the network. This does not mean that mobile agents never communicate with other hosts on the network, just that because of their autonomous nature, they do not have to use the network for every transaction

3. *Mobile agents can display better response times owing to reduced effect of network latency on the application.* Once an agent arrives at the destination, it can respond faster, uninhibited by network latency.
4. *Mobile agents are inherently heterogeneous.* Mobile agent architectures typically assume that not all hosts are the same. In dealing with this heterogeneity of hosts, they solve a big portion of the problems posed by having a variety of devices and platforms that mobile applications must support.
5. *Mobile agents are autonomous and asynchronous and so can deal with intermittent network connectivity gracefully.* A mobile agent application can continue normal operation even with no network connectivity. This is not true of the thin-client model or many other implementations of the client–server architectures.
6. *Mobile agents can adapt extremely well.* Mobile agents are autonomous and so can adapt to their execution environment. This is particularly critical in adapting to the device capabilities, be they user-interface-related capabilities or others. A working user application may be composed of multiple mobile agents. Each can determine its own life cycle and execution state depending on the available resources on the device.

By now you should know that mobile applications and mobile agents are completely different things. However, because of their nature, mobile agent frameworks make themselves suitable for mobile application development. Namely, there are three things that make mobile agents somewhat of a "killer platform" for mobile applications:

1. Mobile devices are often connected to the network through a wireless connection. The nature of wireless networks is very ad hoc. Whether the network is a cellular network or another type of ad hoc network such as 802.11a and 802.11b, the device may come in an out of connectivity with the network, and thereby in and out of connectivity with other devices. Whereas the agent may reside on the device, it is also very natural for a mobile agent to "follow" around a particular device, when and if the device cannot serve as a host, to the nearest connectivity station, based on the location of the network to which the device connects, and serve as a proxy for the device.
2. Because of the QOS problems associated with mobile computing, mobile agents provide one way of having the application continually service the user even while the device is disconnected from the network.
3. Mobile agents can run on any host, whether a mobile device or a powerful server, allowing us to distribute computing tasks in a way that best fits the requirements of the application. In other words, we can decide what gets done where based on the dimensions of mobility and the mobile condition of the user (and thereby the user's mobile device).

Nevertheless, strong mobility is something that is not implemented by most pervasive commercial products. BREW comes closest to allowing us to implement strong mobility. Unfortunately, BREW's mobile agent capabilities are restricted by Qualcomm's closed provisioning system, so there is not much that the developer can take advantage of as far as the mobile agent features of the BREW platform is concerned. It should be noted that strong mobility is not natively supported by the BREW platform; however, because the programming language is C/C++ based, we can play tricks to mimic strong mobility (particularly, making use of the execution state). As we have mentioned, weak mobility is offered by J2ME, .NET framework, BREW, and other products. Most of the work done today to implement mobile agents on mobile devices is being done on J2ME because it is the most pervasive and open platform. We will look at some of these efforts later in this chapter.

One may wonder why mobile agent platforms are not more prevalent. There are three primary reasons for this:

1. Developing software for mobile agent systems is considerably more complex and presents developers with many more issues to consider than their client–server counterparts.
2. Different vendors implement mobile agent platforms quite differently. OMG tries to address this second issue with a standard named MASIF. We will discuss the issues of mobile agent systems and MASIF later in this chapter.
3. Security tends to be a complicated issue when dealing with most mobile agent platforms and implementations.

Now, let us dig a little more into the nitty-gritty of mobile agent systems and how they work before relating them to mobile application development. Keep in mind that mobile agent usage for mobile applications is very much an area that is still undergoing research and development. Before delving into specific implementations of mobile agents (frameworks, languages, etc.), let us look at how we represent mobile agents with UML.

9.2.1 RoadBlocks in Pervasive Usage of Mobile Agents for Mobile Computing

The main roadblocks in using mobile agents more pervasively are twofold:

1. It is a very difficult task to create a host environment that allows agents to roam freely from one host to another on hardware platforms that differ greatly in their resources and availability in performing computing tasks.
2. Some security problems remain unsolved.

We will look at the security problem in the next section, but let us look at why it is so hard to create an agent environment, particularly one that fits the needs of mobile applications.

As we have mentioned, the dimensions of mobility dictate that there are a wide variety of devices, some specialized for certain tasks, with very little available resources. We can have very lightweight hosts that do not provide too many services and can thereby reside on any of the platforms that we specify for a given mobile application. The less functionality the host environment offers, the more the mobile agent needs to be able to do. This means that the minimum amount of code required for the agent itself grows.

So, if we author a set of classes that make up an agent, we need to either select a minimum set of functionality that works on all devices or author multiple applications for different hosts. In the first case, a move will include saving the state of data and execution of an agent, destructing the agent, selecting the right equivalent set of classes that make up the agent in the target host, recreating the agent on the target platform, and restoring the data and execution state on the target platform. The "substitution" of agents based on the platform somewhat, but not completely, violates the mobile agent paradigm. Nonetheless, this is the only practical way that we can implement mobile agents in an environment where there is a great amount of disparity between the weakest of the hosts involved and the most powerful.

So, "how strong" of a mobile agent platform do we need? What does this mean in terms of the distribution of functionality, and therefore device resources, between the agents and the platform? The logic for the application and the agent behavior of the application must reside somewhere. And many mobile devices are simply not powerful enough for this approach. There are two realistic solution to this: Either we implement weak mobility because strong mobility is considerably more complex or we have to standardize on mobile devices that have mobile agent platforms built into them because the devices themselves, in their hardware, can support a standard mobile agent framework.

J2ME takes the first approach. J2ME implements only weak mobility. With the right provisioning platform on the more powerful hosts (servers), we can select the right implementation of the same agent and provision it to the right client, then restore the state of the data. We will look at some sample implementations of mobile agent applications with J2ME.

Qualcomm's BREW takes the second approach. Qualcomm's BREW takes advantage of the powerful DSP capabilities built into CDMA phones and provides a provisioning framework.

Alternatively, we will look at LEAP and Grasshopper, both commercial efforts by, respectively, multiple commercial entities and IKV++, to develop a mobile agent platform that can support mobile applications. Both these platforms build on top of J2ME partly because of the openness of J2ME and partly because of its pervasiveness.

Before we see these concrete examples, we will discuss two issues. First, we will look at some specific security problems and then we will look at some standardization efforts for mobile agent platforms and the features that they offer.

Security Issues with Mobile Agents

As we have mentioned repeatedly, the biggest problems with implementation of mobile agents lie in the security arena. Let us look at some of the specific security problems associated with mobile agents:

1. Host environment platforms such as Java that provide a virtual machine do not provide a mechanism for limiting the amount of resources that an agent can

take on the host (from the virtual machine). Therefore, it is easy for a malignant agent to bring down the host by simple overuse of resources.

2. Because mobile agents are autonomous, they control initiation of communication with other agents and environments outside of the host. Therefore, there is method by which the host can impose any restrictions on when and how the agent establishes such communication without breaking the agent paradigm.
3. Mobile agent platforms are inherently heterogeneous. So, not only must the interfaces for the security mechanism be standardized but so must the required and optional security implementations. This will be difficult to enforce in real life because the implementation is typically the closed part of a software system and the interface is the open part. However, the actual implementation of security features become important here.

Mobile agents used within a mobile application are also faced with the other typical security problems that plague any mobile application. We will discuss those in Chapter 14.

9.2.2 MASIF

As we previously discussed, one of the key features of mobile agents is that they can work in a heterogeneous environment. With a variety of manufacturers producing different platforms for mobile agent systems, OMG has created a standard for interoperability among the different mobile agent platforms called MASIF (Mobile Agent System Interoperability Facility). The problem is more difficult than just creating a standard set of canonical APIs as in the case of some of the other standards that we have used in this text.

MASIF addresses the following:

1. *Management of Agents*: Although the host implementations may be different, they should create, move, clone, and provide all of the other services that hosts provide in a mobile agent framework the same way.
2. *Transfer of Agents*: For an agent to move from one environment to another (host and region), the mobile agent platforms have to treat the move operation between hosts and regions in the same way.
3. *Naming*: For different regions and hosts to address the agents, there has to be a uniform way of naming agents, hosts, and regions. Names for agent and agent systems (hosts, regions, etc.) are standardized in MASIF.
4. *Agent System Types*: As we will see in the case of LEAP and JADE, we are not guaranteed that all of the hosts in a mobile agent system are of the same type (capabilities, functionality offered, etc.). So, every host and region must have some type information associated with it. MASIF specifies the standards for this typing system so that the hosts and regions of various mobile agent platforms can recognize the capabilities of one another. Such recognition is used for things such as allowing an agent to move, security, etc.
5. *Location Syntax*: For regions and hosts to interoperate, they need to be able to find each other and identify each other's abilities. MASIF provides this naming and finding mechanism.

The MASIF specification recognizes the basic ideas that we have already learned: agents, the state of the data encapsulated in the agent, and the state of execution of the agent. It also recognized the following:

1. *Stationary Agent*: This is an agent that can run only where it is created.
2. *Agent Authority*: An agent's authority identifies the person or organization for whom the agent acts [MASIF 1997].
3. *Agent System Type*: This is a way to specify some of the implementation of the mobile agent and, therefore, specify its ability to run particular types of agents. For example, Aglets are a type of agent system built on top of the Java Virtual Machine and the Java programming language.
4. *Agent Location*: This is a way to specify where a particular agent is located. This means specification of the host and the region in which the agent exists. MASIF refers to the key combination of host and the region to which the host belongs as a *place*.
5. *Agent Name*: Every agent must have a unique name with respect to its authority. In other words, whatever it is that invokes that agent (person, organization, or a proxy for one of those two) should be able to call the agent with a unique name within the boundaries where it can call it. (Boundaries may be a host, a region, etc.)
6. *Agent System*: This is an abstraction to identify the collection of platforms that a host runs on and the host that allows the agent to exist. The agent system is the thing that allows a mobile agent to exist.
7. *Interconnections*: Communication within all of the participants in a mobile agent infrastructure is regulated through a mobile agent *communication infrastructure* (CI). There are two types of CIs: those between agent systems and those between regions. You can think of the CIs at the system level as network layer communication infrastructure and those at the region level as application-layer communication infrastructure.
8. *Code Base*: This simply refers to the collection of classes required to instantiate a mobile agent.
9. *Serialization/Deserialization*: For an agent to move, we have to stop it, save its state (data and execution), then instantiate its code base at the target location, restore its state (data and execution), and finally tell it to resume operation. The process of saving the information following stoppage of the agent is called *serialization*. The process of instantiating the new agent and restoring the state from the saved blob (file, memory location, etc.) to the agent before it resumes operation at the new location is called *deserialization*.

MASIF also introduces some other terminology for more refined recognition of components and the interactions among the components in a mobile agent system. We refer you to the MASIF specification [MASIF 1997] and OMG's Web site for further exploration.

There is one more important thing that MASIF addresses and that is security. As we previously mentioned, the biggest problem with mobile agent implementations tends to be security. Because the agent host and regions should be able to authenticate agents and assure that the authenticated agent acts in a secure way, MASIF recognizes the security problems associated with mobile agents and their existence in a heterogeneous environment and specifies a level of security implementation that all MASIF-compliant mobile agent platforms must support.

Among the security issues that MASIF recognizes with mobile agents and their supporting frameworks are the following:

1. *DOS Attacks*: DOS (Denial of Service) attacks should be familiar to anyone who has developed Web-based applications. There are several ways that DOS attacks happen. Some DOS attacks happen at the network layer by unrecognizable incoming packets. Others happen at the application layer such as sending the same request over and over again. DOS attacks vary in form and complexity depending on the infrastructure that they attack. DOS attacks to mobile agent frameworks may take advantage of the CI among the agents and/or the CI between hosts and regions.
2. *Authorization Failure*: The type of operation that a human or system actor can invoke in a mobile agent depends on the authority of the human or system actor. Authorization failures happen when a human or system actor who is not supposed to have access to a particular operation is able to perform that operation. The same is true if the state of the mobile agent or some piece of information in the system is changed or destroyed without authorization.
3. *Eavesdropping*: Communication among the different components of a mobile agent system is to be secure. This communication can be monitored by different techniques, thereby breaking the security.
4. *Authentication*: If an agent uses some mechanism such as spoofing, masquerading, or replay to pose as a valid agent, it can break the authentication system.

To combat these types of threats, MASIF specifies the following security measures:

1. *Network-Level Security*: At the network level, MASIF requires confidentiality, integrity, authentication, and replay detection. These are standard measures meant to, respectively, make sure that, at the network level, the information is not recorded, modified, coming from a nonsecure source, or being played back from a recorded transaction from a valid source.
2. *Mutual Authentication of Agent Systems*: Network applications that are based on mobile agents are composed of multiple types and instances of hosts, regions, and agents. These hosts, regions, and agents must be able to authenticate one another when communicating with each other. For example, if a region requests the code base for an agent from another region, it needs to be authenticated before its request is fulfilled.
3. *Agent Authentication and Delegation*: For agents to be able to move from host to host, they need to carry around their credentials for repeated authentication by subsequent hosts. This can be done by including the authentication information with the agent itself or by transferring the credentials separately (with the second being preferred as it is more secure and protects better against stolen identity).

4. *Agent and Agent System Security Policies*: An agent should know how to limit access to itself and protect itself from unauthenticated or unauthorized third parties invoking its behaviors. Agents and agent systems must include and enforce an ACL (Access Control List).
5. *Authentication of Clients for Remote Agent Creation*: The systems that interact with mobile agent systems may be based on nonmobile agent technologies or may not be compliant with MASIF. In these cases, there should be a mechanism for authentication of such systems before any interactions are initiated.
6. *Agent System Access to Authentication Results and Credentials*: When an agent receives communication from a host or another agent, it should verify the credential of the initiator of the communication.

The syntax of the rules enforced by MASIF is very much like that in CORBA. For those of you unfamiliar with distributed-object APIs, we recommend that you look into OMG's CORBA or Microsoft's DCOM as examples of APIs to distributed-object systems. You can find these APIs, respectively, at OMG and Microsoft Developer Network Web sites. Note that though agents are a higher level abstraction concept, they rely on objects, and because they move around, they are distributed. Therefore, mobile agent platforms have much in common with distributed-object platforms and technologies.

What we have reviewed here should give you a good feel for what the interoperability issues in mobile agents are and how MASIF addresses them. Besides OMG, FIPA is the other significant organization that addresses standardization for mobile agents. We will look at FIPA and its standards in the next section.

9.2.3 FIPA

The Foundation for Intelligent Physical Agents (FIPA) is an organization that focuses on standardization of agent-based systems and their interactions. FIPA's membership includes commercial and academic participation. To date, FIPA has published standards that cover architectural concerns of mobile agent systems, communications among the various components of mobile agent systems, management of agents, and implementation of agents themselves. By all counts, FIPA's treatment of the mobile agent problem is more comprehensive than OMG's MASIF (which focuses on the interoperability issues only). Here is an overview of the FIPA specifications:

1. *Abstract Architecture Specification*: This is the highest level of all FIPA specifications for mobile agents, systems that allow for creation of mobile agents, interactions and communications among the components of mobile agent systems, and applicability issues related to mobile agents (such as that of applying mobile agents to mobile application development). If you are going to build a mobile agent system, this specification document is a must read [FIPA Arch 2001].
2. *Agent Management Specification*: The primary purpose of hosts, regions, and whatever infrastructure is provided by a mobile agent platform is to allow mobile agents to do what they need to do. However, as we have mentioned,

because of the heterogeneous nature of mobile agent platforms (the fact that we are not guaranteed that all mobile agent hosts and regions are of the same type and/or same implementation), mobile agents must be guaranteed some minimal amount of services. The agent management specification outlines the functionality that must be supported for managing the mobile agent framework and the interfaces for this functionality. Among these are the specifications for directory facilitator, agent management system, and message transport service. The directory facilitator encapsulates the set of functionalities required to provide a directory of agents by the environment (host, region, etc.). The agent management system encapsulates the set of functionalities required to create and destroy agents as well as monitoring their move from one host to another. The message transport service specifies communication among agents. There are other parts of the FIPA specification that expound on some of these individual issues in more detail. These include the following:

a. *Messaging Interoperability Service Specification*: This part of the specification addresses communication among agents in detail.
b. *Agent Configuration Management Specification*: This part of the specification outlines the configuration management issues for agent systems and their components.
c. *Agent Message Transport Envelope Representation in Bit-Efficient Encoding Specification*: This part of specification details an efficient way of representing messages that are sent back and forth between agents.
d. *Agent Message Transport Envelope Representation in XML Specification*: Like its binary counterpart, it specifies the format for the messages to be exchanged among agents, except that this format is specified in XML.
e. *Agent Management Support for Mobility Specification*: This part of the specification focuses on the management of agent systems that are deployed on mobile devices or that interact with mobile devices.
f. *Agent Message Transport Protocol for HTTP Specification*: As HTTP is currently the most pervasive application-layer communication protocol (and this is not likely to change for a long time after this text is written), FIPA has specified how to use the HTTP protocol to transport MTP (Message Transport Protocol) messages among the agents. This is important for our purposes of using mobile agents to build mobile applications as most mobile devices and mobile operating environments have some sort of support for HTTP.
g. *Agent Message Transport Protocol for IIOP Specification*: IIOP is an object-oriented communication protocol. This specification describes how to use IIOP to transfer MTPs (analogs to using HTTP to transport MTPs).

3. *Nomadic Application Support Specification*: This section of the FIPA specification is particularly designed to address "nomadic" environments. Nomadic environments are those where either some part of the system or the user is mobile. This specification addresses QOS issues, negotiation of transport protocols for the messages exchanged among the different components of a mobile agent system, and most importantly extensive adaptability to mobile devices. This part of the FIPA specification hits the nail right on the head! The dimensions of mobility, with the exception of location-based services, are treated in this part

of the specification, albeit at a high level. There are the following additional parts of the FIPA specification that address the dimensions of mobility in more depth:

a. *Quality of Service Ontology Specification*: This part of the specification deals specifically with QOS issues in the mobile agent infrastructure.
b. *Device Ontology Specification*: As we have previously mentioned, one of the problems of mobile computing is to understand the capabilities of the devices that are used by the mobile user. Unfortunately, the ontology specified by FIPA is not based on RDF and XML. Therefore, there is a mismatch between the implementation, even if we use functionality specified in CC/PP and UAProf.

4. *ACL Specifications*: Messages passed back and forth between agents must have a particular format. This format is specified through the FIPA specifications. The following properties are specified:
   a. *Communicative Act Library Specification*: ACL stands for Communicative Act Library. This part of the FIPA specification outlines the basics and semantics of the ACL syntax. Atomic interactions among agents are outlined, described, and defined in a well-defined structural manner.
   b. *ACL Message Structure Specification*: This specification outlines the structure of parameters to be included in an ACL message. The actual format (text, binary, etc.) is specified according to the serialization type (XML, simple strings, etc.). This part of the specification simply outlines what parameters must be included for a message to qualify as an ACL message and the structure of those messages, in whatever serialization format they may be.
   c. *ACL Message Representation in XML Specification*: This specification simply outlines a DTD for representing ACL messages in XML.
   d. *ACL Message Representation in String Specification*: This specification simply outlines how to serialize an ACL message into a character-based string.
   e. *ACL Message Representation in Bit-Efficient Encoding Specification*: This specification outlines a binary format for serializing ACL messages.
   f. *Agent Message Transport Service Specification*: This specification outlines a reference model for the Message Transport Service (MTS) and the functionality that such a service must implement to be able to transport ACL messages among agents.
   g. *Propose, Subscribe, Recruiting, Brokering, Contract Net, Query, Request, Interaction Protocol Specifications*: These specifications collectively outline the Agent Interaction Protocol (AIP). AIP is an interaction protocol for mobile agents and their infrastructure. This part of the specification leverages works done by James Odell and others in development of AUML (which we will look at in the next section). Namely, it ties in AIP to ACL and specifies the parameters to be inserted into an ACL message for AIP-based interactions. The AIP interactions are described by the AIP diagrams, which we will see in the next section.

Note that FIPA specifications do not outline the various parts of the specification in the taxonomy that we have introduced here. The taxonomy we have chosen here is based on our need for the treatment of mobile agents as applied to mobile application development as well as the introductory basis that we have built, thus far, regarding mobile agents.

The FIPA standard is extremely well thought out and gives the dimensions of mobility a first-class treatment. If you are looking at choosing a mobile agent platform, we strongly urge you to make sure that it is FIPA compliant. If you are looking into building your own mobile agent platform, there is no better place to start than the FIPA specifications, not just because you will need to build a framework that is FIPA compliant for interoperability reasons, but also because the specifications bring out all of the challenges in building in mobile agent platform.

We are now finished looking at the basic concepts of mobile agent development, the relationship between mobile agents and mobile applications, and the standards that not only specify interoperability interfaces but also specify the most important features and implementation details about those features.

Before jumping into building mobile applications based on mobile agents, we will look at how to model mobile agents in UML so that we can continue to use UML as the primary tool for development.

9.3 UML Extensions for Mobile Agents

As in the rest of this text, we are going to discuss how to use UML to model mobile agents for our mobile applications. When it comes to UML extensions or profiles for mobile agents, there are currently no standards ratified by OMG or any other significant standards body. What we will present here is a collection of disparate but significant efforts by academic and commercial institutions in modeling mobile agents with UML. We will pick and choose what best applies to mobile application development. First we will discuss AUML. There are two categories of extensions specified by AUML: 1. UML extensions to the classifiers representing structural components of a mobile agent system such as the agents themselves, hosts, and regions and 2. UML extensions to support the various interactions among these structural components.

Then, we will look at some other efforts, primarily by Rausch and Sihling [Rausch et al.], to extend UML for mobile agents. We will conclude by selecting a subset of the union of these extensions as the set of extensions that we will use for mobile agents in mobile application development.

Let us start with AUML because it is the most organized effort in introducing UML extensions for mobile agents.

9.3.1 AUML

AUML, or Agent UML, is an effort stemming from work by James Odell, H. Van Dyke Parunak, and Bernhard Bauer during the late 1990s and early 2000s to introduce a set of UML extensions for proper representation of mobile agents and their interactions with UML. To date, AUML is the only organized body that has made such an effort though there is a tremendous amount of independent work done by academic and commercial institutions that we will summarize in the next section.

At the time of authoring this text, there is no official specification for AUML. It remains a working document to which the aforementioned contributors along with other individuals make contributions. This working document is composed of a series of papers written by the major contributors. We will review the summary of these papers.

As we mentioned, there are two types of UML extensions for mobile agents: those that extend structural components of UML and those that support the interactions among the extended components. Bauer [Bauer, Odell, and Muller 2001] contends that, for extensions describing the communication among structural components of a mobile agent system, we first need to define the types of communication that takes place among such components. There is where Bauer starts and introduces *agent interaction protocol diagrams* to satisfy the need for diagrams that represent interactions among agents properly. AIP diagrams look like sequence diagrams. They simply have some added iconic semantics to support the UML extensions based on stereotypes and utilize OCL for further specification of constraints.

In addition to these diagrams, we can use collaboration diagrams to model communication of messages among different agents. Because agents and their roles can be modeled using object notation, this comes naturally to collaboration diagrams.

State diagrams can be used to model the states of an agent as it is created, moves from host to host, assumes different roles, performs different operations, and finally dies when it is finished. We can use state diagrams to model mobile agent life cycles without any extensions.

AUML Agent Interaction Protocol Diagrams

As we mentioned, AIP diagrams are a new type of diagram, introduced by Bauer, Odell, and Muller [Bauer, Odell, and Muller 2001] to model interactions among different components of a mobile agent system. In essence, protocol diagrams combine the functionality of sequence diagrams and activity diagrams to allow us to represent interactions among agents (which map to object instances) in time. As Bauer and colleagues define protocol diagrams, they are used to modeling interactions through any AIP. Therefore, protocol diagrams can represent agent interactions without implementation dependencies because UML is not language dependent. Table 9.1 shows the UML extensions that make up protocol diagrams. In addition to these extensions, protocol diagrams use lifelines. Lifelines are the dotted vertical lines that are used in sequence diagrams to indicate how long an agent lives. The only distinction is that an agent can change roles during its life. Therefore, the extensions of XOR, AND, and OR introduced in Table 9.1 allow us to place markers on the lifeline that indicate the dependency of the future role and interactions of one agent based on the message received from another agent/actor.

The papers that make up the current working document of AUML also specify other extensions that provide more detail in AIP diagrams. We refer you to the references cited in this text to find a fit in including more detailed descriptions of your mobile agent–based system. Not among these extensions, though, are stereotypes of associations that indicate moves, clones, and the building blocks of a mobile agent system (hosts, regions, etc.).

Table 9.1. UML Extensions for AUML Protocol Diagrams

Extension	Description	Iconic Representation
Agent Role	This extension is used to specify the type of role that the agent is taking on at a given time. This is not a stereotype or extension of an existing type in UML. Rather, it is used to determine the "role" that a given agent plays during a particular set of interactions. Agent roles are indicated in the same way as roles are represented in sequence diagrams. Specifically, they are indicated, inside a square box and at the top of the protocol diagram, as follows: Agent Name/Role:Class	Not applicable
XOR Connector	This connector, along with the OR and AND connectors, is used in two ways. It may be placed to fork or merge messages going into or coming out of an agent. This is done because the role of the agent may vary depending on the incoming message. Messages end at a role of an agent. When the XOR connector is used on the lifeline, it may indicate that only one of two or more rules can be assumed at the same time.	x
OR Connector	Like the XOR connector, this connector can be used either on a lifeline or between messages. If this connector is used to fork two or more messages, one or more of the messages may exist depending on the condition (because forked messages are not mutually exclusive as in the case of the XOR connector). When the OR connector is used on a lifeline it is there to indicate that the agent can assume either one of the roles at the time of receiving a specific message or set of messages.	
AND Connector	Like the XOR connector, this connector can be used either on a lifeline or between messages. When the AND connector is used on a lifeline, it is there to indicate that the agent can assume both of the roles at the time of receiving a specific message or set of messages. Note that an agent can assume multiple roles at the same time.	

The problem with AUML is that it adds a great deal of complexity in its extensions. Although treatment of roles is needed in mobile agent modeling, logical operators of XOR, AND, and OR make any sort of significant AIP diagram fairly complex to read and understand. AIP diagrams tend to display the state of the agents both through time and through agent role (which itself is a function of the location of the agent, the interactions of the agent with other agents, etc.).

Also, current efforts in the AUML working document still do not address modeling some of the properties of mobile agent frameworks. For example, there is no clear iconic method of representing an agent moving from one host to another. However, there are other efforts to provide UML extensions for such a need. We will look at these in the next section. We will use a mixture of AUML and other extensions in Section 9.3.3 for some examples of modeling mobile agents as applied to mobile application development.

9.3.2 UML Extensions for Mobile Agents

Besides AUML, there are several significant works done by variety of academic and commercial groups to extend UML to model mobile agents and their behavior using UML. These works rely on the UML extension mechanism. In this section, we will take pieces of these works and form a set of UML extensions that allows us to model mobile agents with UML. There are two reasons that we do not stay with AUML as the one and only method to represent mobile agents in UML: 1. AUML is still not an official specification supported by OMG and 2. AUML does not provide some of the metamodel pieces that we need to allow us to model mobile agents in a mobile application environment. The majority of what we will be discussing in this section is based on the work of Andreas Rausch and Marc Sihling, who are frequently referenced throughout this section.

In the previous sections, we have defined the major concepts of mobile agents. Now, let us see what Rausch and colleagues [Rausch, Sihling, and Wen 1998] add as UML extensions to help us represent mobile agents with UML. Table 9.2 lists these extensions.

Before we can put these extensions to use, let us create a small union of them with AUML to create a set of extensions for mobile agents used for mobile application development.

9.3.3 Mobile Agent UML Extensions for Mobile Applications

Rausch et al.'s extensions are particularly useful because we can represent the structure and the actions taken by mobile agents easily with the existing type of UML diagrams. To these, we will add the AUML AIP diagrams. This is what we will utilize as our extensions to model mobile agents used in a mobile application infrastructure.

Now, let us put this to quick use. Let us start with a use case diagram that shows the use case outlined in Figure 9.1. Agent B is always looking for the right restaurant and Agent A is always keeping track of the user. Agent B and Agent A can communicate. Figure 9.1. shows a UML use case diagram that represents our use case. We learned this back in Chapter 6.

Table 9.2. Rausch's Iconic UML Extensions to Represent Mobile Agents in UML

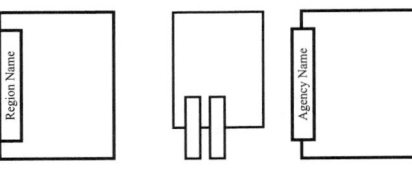

Stereotype	Description	Icon
<<mobile agent>> Class, Object, Sequence, and Collaboration Diagrams	This is the most basic concept of mobile agent–based systems. This stereotype indicates a class (which may be a wrapper around other classes, packages, etc.) that encapsulates strong or weak mobility as we have defined previously. Remember that mobile agents are autonomous and asynchronous. Because this stereotype extends the UML class, then it is represented by the same symbol (optional stereotype text on the class icon) and can be used in diagrams that can include classes. Another very important note is that this is *not an instance*; this stereotype is used to model the code that results in an instance agent.	<<mobile agent>>
<<region>> Sequence, Collaboration, and Activity Diagrams	A region represents a grouping of two or more hosts. Regions typically have a registry that keeps track of what agent is on which host and the ability of a particular host to serve as a host for a particular agent (because different hosts in a region need not have the same capabilities). This stereotype may be applied to a class or a package.	Region Name
<<agent system>> Deployment and Component Diagrams	This stereotype extends the UML component stereotype and is represented by the same symbol. The agent system is used to represent the host environment in a component diagram.	
<<agency>> Class, Object, Sequence, Collaboration, and Activity Diagrams	This stereotype represents the concept of a *host* (synonymous to agency in mobile agents). It represents an environment that support the features needed for at least *weak mobility*. This stereotype extends a UML class or package.	Agency Name

<<move>> Sequence, Collaboration, State, and Activity Diagrams	Mobile agents move from host to host. When an agent moves from one host to another, it is deconstructed, transported, and reconstructed. The transition between the agent before it is being deconstructed and the agent after it is reconstructed is indicated using this stereotype. In this case, it indicates a *dependency* (in those diagrams where dependency is relevant) between agents (really, instances of the same agent in time). This stereotype is also used to indicate the *action* (in those diagrams where action is relevant) of moving from one host to another host. Note that this stereotype inherently indicates *strong mobility*. In other words, the state of execution is preserved from the time when the move starts to the time when the move ends and it is resumed thereafter on the host to which the mobile agent has moved.	
<<clone>> Sequence, Collaboration, State, and Activity Diagrams	Mobile agents have the ability to clone themselves if they are to be defined as mobile agents. This is true for both weak and strong mobility. This stereotype allows us to indicate whether one agent is the clone of another agent (in this case it extends the UML dependency). Alternatively, it can be used to represent the action of cloning in diagrams that represent activities and states (in this case it extends the UML action). In the case of weak mobility, the clone is a copy of the source agent, but it starts at zero execution state. In the case of strong mobility, the state of the cloned agent begins at the time when the cloning process started on the source agent.	

(continued)

TABLE 9.2 (continued)

Stereotype	Description	Icon
<<remote execution>> Sequence, Collaboration, State, and Activity Diagrams	This stereotype is used to indicate a move from one host to another host, by an agent, where the state of execution of the agent is not preserved. Therefore, this stereotype indicates *weak mobility*. Once the agent arrives at the destination host, it starts executing at some static starting state. Keep in mind that strong mobility is a superset of weak mobility; therefore, a system that is able to support strong mobility could still have some agents that move in a weakly mobile manner (what Rausch calls "remote execution").	
<<role change>> Sequence, Collaboration, State, and Activity Diagrams	Agents can exhibit a different set of functionality depending on the logic that can be specified in the mobile agent itself, region registry information, or the host to which they migrate. We call the set of functionality that a mobile agent exhibits and performs its "role." If the role of a mobile agent changes owing to a move or some other event, we indicate it using this stereotype. This stereotype extends the UML dependency stereotype as it is between the mobile agent and itself at two different points in time.	

Let's assume that we have a series of mobile agents that follow the user around, based on the user's location, to provide some services for the user. A real example of such could be agents that are traveling on a collection of small wireless networks (WIFI, etc.) forming a so-called hot-spot. Let's say that there are two types of agents: those that can reside anywhere on the network including the mobile device, the servers, personal computers, etc. and those that can reside only on stationary systems (PC's, servers, etc.). We need to model the following. The job of Agent B is to allow the user to enter some preferences that allows it to search for the local restaurants of a particular type. The job of Agent A is to follow the user around and notify the user, based on his location, if he/she is near one of the restaurants.

The use cases are:

1. Editing Search Preferences: For the sake of the example, let's say that we only want to allow the user to edit their preferences on their PC or PDA. They can't do it on devices with less capabilities (cell phones, etc.).
2. Editing Contact Information: This enables the user to enter his/her contact information, register devices, and any preferences on when he/she doesn't want to be reached or when he/she doesn't have any of his/her devices along.
3. Notification: The user should be notified of the restaurant within 5 minutes walking distance or 0.25 Kilometers, which ever is longer (because a direct line from the user's location to the location of the restaurant may be much shorter than walking streets that are the only route and not a direct route).

There may be other use cases, but let's assume that these are our essential use cases. (See Chapter 6 for the definition.)

FIGURE 9.1. Use Case of a Mobile Agent in Mobile Computing.

The use case diagram does not use any of our new extensions. This brings out something very important: Implementation of a system of mobile agents is not related to use cases. The user never sees, hears, or knows about the type of implementation. So, all those diagrams that are used to model use cases or user interfaces remain the same whether we are building a client–server mobile application or a mobile application based on mobile agent technologies. Note also that we are using Wisdom-style use case diagrams to focus on the interaction of the user with the system for the essential tasks. We will use other diagrams to show the internal implementation.

Let us assume that we have a series of mobile agents that follow the user around, based on the user's location, to provide some services for the user. A real example of such could be agents that are traveling on a collection of small wireless networks (WIFI, etc.) forming a so-called hot spot. Let us say that there are two types of agents: those that can reside anywhere on the network including the mobile device, the servers, PCs, etc. and those that can reside only on stationary systems (PCs, servers, etc.). We need to model the following: The job of Agent B is to allow

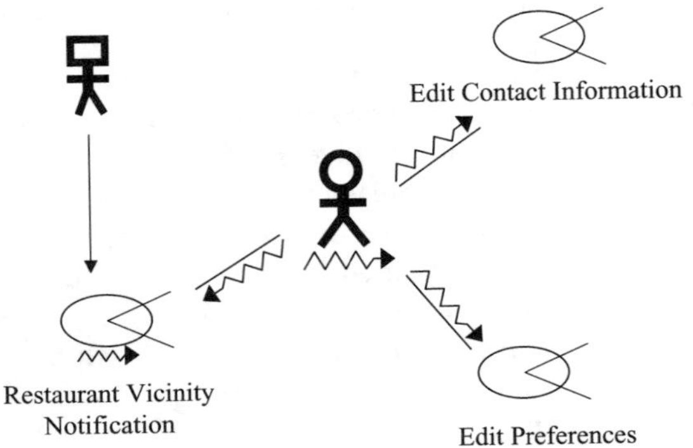

FIGURE 9.2. Mobile Use Cases for Example in Figure 9.1.

the user to enter some preferences that allow him or her to search for the local restaurants of a particular type. The job of Agent A is to follow the user around and notify the user, based on the user's location, if he or she is near one of the restaurants.

The use cases are as follows:

1. *Editing Search Preferences*: For the sake of the example, let us say that we only want to allow the users to edit their preferences on their PC or PDA. They cannot do it on devices with less capabilities (cell phones, etc.).
2. *Editing Contact Information*: This enables the user to enter his or her contact information, register devices, and set any preferences on when he or she does not want to be reached or does not have any devices within reach.
3. *Notification*: The user should be notified of the restaurant within five minutes walking distance or 0.25 kilometers, whichever is longer (because a direct line from the user's location to the location of the restaurant may be much shorter than walking streets that are the only route and not a direct route).

There may be other use cases, but let us assume that these are our essential ones.

Next, we need to show the internal implementation of how things are going to work. We need to show the following:

1. Agent A and Agent B communicate.
2. Agent A can migrate among all of the different hosts that participate in our system.
3. Agent B can migrate to most of the different hosts that participate in our system (all but the least powerful devices).
4. Agent A gathers information from a GPS system that is on the device.
5. Agent B communicates with a database that holds restaurants and their locations.

Next, we need to model the implementation that will provide the functionality. Figure 9.2 shows how some basic mobile use cases can be modeled using the extensions that we have learned so far. Let us use a collaboration diagram first.

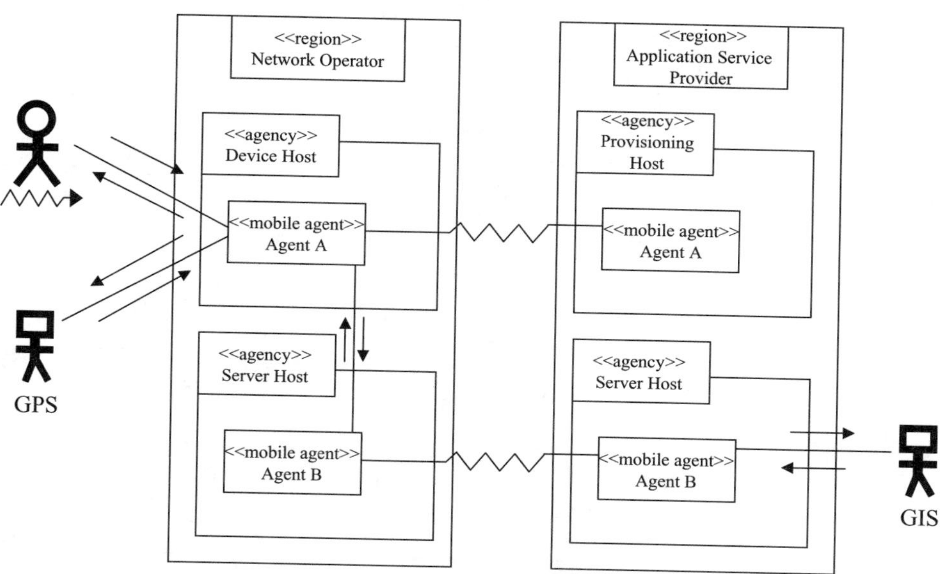

FIGURE 9.3. Collaboration Diagram for Example in Figure 9.1.

Figure 9.3 shows a collaboration diagram that shows how the two agents and the infrastructure work together to provide the necessary functionality to the end user.

As you can see, Figure 9.3 shows the two separate regions. The Application Service Provider Region is simply the region that encapsulates the hosts of the provider of the application. The network operator has its own region to enforce its own security, billing, user registry, and other concerns that are typical for network operators when dealing with their users. Agent A has to communicate with a system actor and a mobile human actor (defined in Chapter 6) as well as with Mobile Agent B. Mobile Agent B must be able to communicate with a GIS (Geographic Information System) system actor as well as with Mobile Agent A. We have not modeled the collaboration with databases and other applications that may hold the information about restaurants. It will be a good exercise for the user to add these to the diagrams.

Next, to show the temporal series of events, we are going to build a sequence diagram in Figure 9.4. Note the following things on this figure:

1. Communication between the user and the agent on the handset is asynchronous because the agent notifies the user in an active manner, based on the user settings and the response time of the system components.
2. We have used regions and agencies to show boundaries that are not part of standard sequence diagrams. We specified these extensions in the last section. They are very useful in allowing us to see how messages are passed back and forth among regions, agencies, and agents. The separation among these three layers is crucial. We may decide to include the sequence of messages and actions between agents in one sequence diagram, use another diagram that shows agencies only, use yet another diagram that shows agencies and agents, or produce any other combination of these three depending on the needs of the mobile

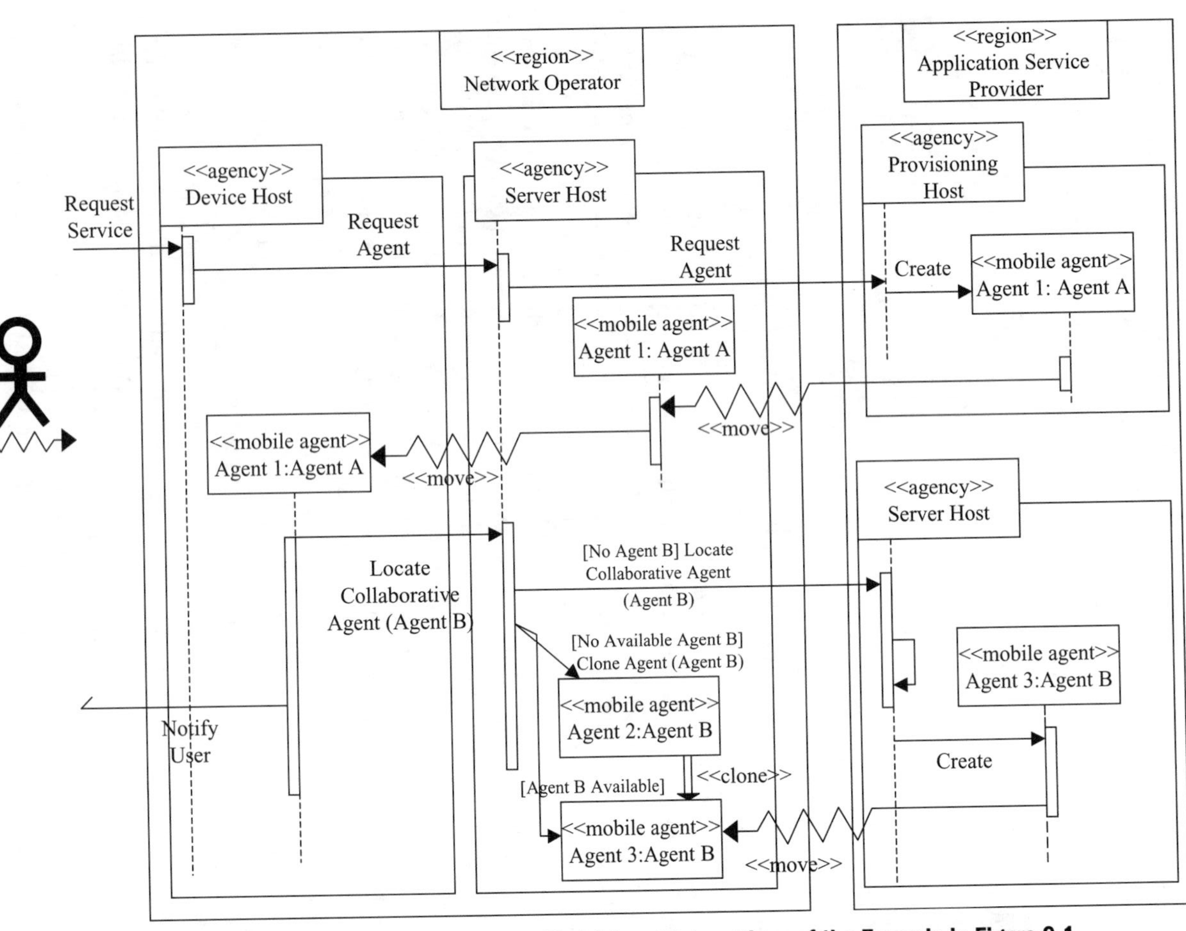

FIGURE 9.4. Using Sequence Diagrams to the Model Agent Interactions of the Example in Figure 9.1.

application and the complexity of the implementation. Typically, there are two reasons for showing regions and agencies (hosts). The first is if there are a variety of different types of hosts in the system. Remember that although agents can migrate from host to host, it is not a requirement that agents be able to migrate to all of the hosts nor is it a requirement that the implementation of the host on the various platforms be identical. Second, we may want to show regions because the security issues are typically resolved at the region level. The registry of viable agents for the hosts in the region as well as authentication and authorization of the interactions among the users and the agents and within the agents themselves is implemented within the region. So, showing the regions and hosts on the sequence diagram can clarify logical boundaries that are very useful.

3. Our example here is somewhat trivial. Nonetheless, it shows you the usage of the basic stereotypes that we introduced and indicates how to put them together to build a sequence diagram. There is a diminishing return on increasing the level of detail in most UML diagrams (Although some make the argument that the graphical artifacts of UML are only the surface, the counterargument that this surface is the most valuable part of UML in practice nearly always holds true.) Assess the requirements of the project and how UML is being used before deciding what you are going to model with UML and at what level of detail you are going to do it.
4. Our sequence diagram documents a very important design and implementation detail: Agent A and Agent B types communicate through an RPC-like mechanism. We could require that Agent A moves to the same host or region as Agent B and then communicate with Agent B. This may be advantageous. Remember that a move operation uses considerable burst bandwidth because the entire agent has to move from one host to another. A move to communicate with another host makes sense if there are numerous interactions going on between the two agents and if the agents are in physically disparate locations. Typically, there is some sort of mapping between regions and physical locations of the platform. Therefore, migration from one host to another host, or from one region to another region, may make sense if it saves communication bandwidth, if the network provides high-burst bandwidth and low continuous QOS, and if the application requirements allow it. It is important to note that being a mobile agent does not require that communication be done only within the same region or the same host.

Next, let us look at an AUML AIP diagram in Figure 9.5. Because our agents do not change roles, this diagram looks similar in nature to the sequence diagram that we already introduced. We can, however, treat whether the agent notifies the user as a role. This is because if the agent notifies the user, then it has to render an interface; otherwise, it is just running in the background. This brings us to another conclusion: AIP diagrams are most useful when dealing with applications that include mobile agents that can play multiple roles. Sequence, state, and collaboration diagrams deliver more value in cases where the agents do not change roles much.

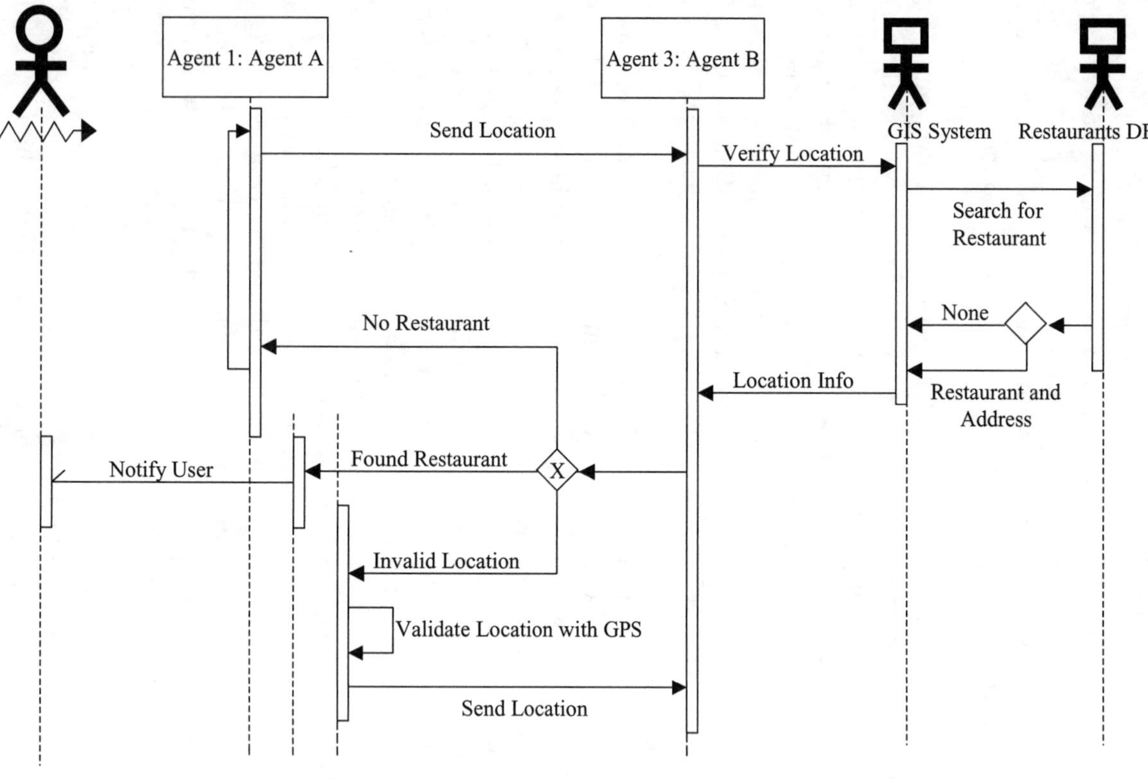

FIGURE 9.5. Using AIP Diagrams to Model Agent Interactions.

This brings us to the end of our discussion on using UML for modeling mobile agents. UML and the extensions that we have introduced here offer a tremendous amount of value in building agent systems. Mobile agent–based systems tend to be more complicated than client–server systems. UML helps us reduce the complexity of dealing with the problems by allowing us to create visual models and break down large interaction sets by representing them with several such diagrams. Now, let us get to the core reason why we are looking at mobile agents and learn how to build mobile applications with mobile agents.

9.4 Applications of Mobile Agents to Mobile Applications and Implementation Tools

The example in Figure 9.4 in the previous section demonstrates the two types of uses that mobile agents may have in a mobile application environment:

1. *Pervasive Usage*: Mobile agents can run on mobile devices to provide application-layer functionality to the user. When mobile agents are used pervasively throughout the mobile application infrastructure, they can move among hosts with a wide range of capabilities.
2. *Limited Usage*: Mobile agents can run on the network that supports the mobile devices but not on the device itself. In these cases mobile agents run on servers, PCs, and other stationary computing devices with enough necessary computing power to support the mobile agent framework as well as the mobile agents. However, the mobile agent framework, in this case, may be too large to be run on the devices. The agents are used to provide data and functionality to an application on the device, which, in turn, delivers application-layer functionality to the user. Such limited usage of mobile agents is typically implemented in a hybrid environment with client–agent server architecture. Mobile agents, in this case, really make up the fabric of a middle-ware system that supports mobile applications rather than make up the actual mobile applications.

To build these mobile agent applications, we need mobile agent platforms. It is much easier to build a mobile agent platform to use mobile agents in a limited way, as a middle-ware, to support mobile applications than it is to build a mobile agent platform that allows mobile agents to freely move among mobile devices and the underlying supporting network made of the stationary systems. Also, weak mobility is simpler to implement than strong mobility, particularly when dealing with pervasive usage of mobile agents in building our mobile applications. So, it is obvious that we need to take a detailed look at the tools that let us build mobile agent–based applications.

As we have mentioned before, because Java is, at least in theory, a "write-once-run-anywhere" platform, it provides today's most basic base platform for building mobile agent frameworks. It is important to note that, by itself, Java and its existing supporting APIs in J2SE, J2ME, and J2EE are insufficient to build the mobile agents used pervasively throughout the mobile application infrastructure. However, there are several mobile agent platforms built on top of Java and its supporting APIs such as JADE and LEAP, which we will look at later in this section.

Of course, Java is not the only alternative as a platform. Besides mobile agent platforms built on C and C++, there are many agent platforms that use scripting languages such as TCL. The concepts that go into building the mobile agents themselves are no different for a mobile agent platform based on Java than those based on C, C++, or some other programming language. The major difference lies in the fact that C and C++ code (as well as most other languages) are typically fairly platform dependent, as we discussed in Chapter 1. The implementation of the platform is typically more difficult in C and C++ because the mobile agent platform would have to bridge the gap between all the underlying hardware and operating system platforms that the hosts can run on. The same is true for scripting languages such as TCL but for a different reason. Although implementing programs in a scripting languages does not change from platform to platform, something has to implement the scripting language itself (compilation, interpretation, etc.). This extra functionality of compilation and/or interpretation adds to the complexity of the mobile agent platform implementation So, such scripting languages are not necessarily a suitable technology for resource-constrained devices.

Once we have looked at a few examples of tools to build mobile agents, we will look at the various usages of mobile agents for dealing with dimensions of mobility and how they can solve the challenges we face in building mobile applications. So, let us start with Java, the mobile agent platforms built on Java, and some examples of how to build mobile agents for such platforms.

9.4.1 Java and Mobile Agents

Java, developed by Sun Microsystems, offers the facilities to build systems with weak mobility. The Java Virtual Machine (JVM) abstracts the hardware and operating system platform from the application developer, thereby providing a homogeneous development environment on an otherwise heterogeneous background. Java provides a complete *mobile code platform* if the platform is able to support the full JVM. Regardless of the host, as long as it supports the virtual machine, it can load classes and other supported resources. The JVM loads classes from files of byte code (platform-independent, compiled Java code) as needed. Once the class has been loaded, it is always returned to its initial state. The serialization mechanism of Java allows us to restore data to the initial state of the class, but there is no mechanism to return to some previous execution state.

Java can provide support for a system with strong mobility *if and only if* every host uses only one process with one thread for one agent at a time. Java does not offer thread-level control; therefore, with the current implementation of the virtual machine (JDK 1.4) in a multithreaded environment controlled by the virtual machine, it is impossible to capture and return the state of execution of any thread without some degree of uncertainty.

There are also applets, Aglets, and MIDlets. These are collections of classes that make up an application. The supporting framework for each supports mobility to a degree. Let us take a closer look at them.

Applets, Aglets, and MIDlets

Java was originally conceived as a portable language for client-side programming more so than the server side. Java has found its success in large, scalable server-side programs that could be ported among platforms, depending on the usage, without much in the way of modifications; nevertheless, Java applets were the instrument that gave Java its first claim to fame.

Applets are complete applications that can be loaded by Web browsers and run on the same computer using the virtual machine that is installed on that computer. Web browsers are not required to know how to run applets. In fact, though applets have a formal specification published by Sun Microsystems, they are a de facto standard (a standard that develops slowly by becoming pervasive as opposed to a standard that is formed by a committee and formally accepted) for platform-independent applications on the Web. Applets implement mobile code within the browser that implements their usage. An applet is written by extending a base class provided in Java. Applets require a full-blown JVM (J2SE JVM). Applets implement code mobility for all those environments that can run the JVM and a Web browser powerful enough to take advantage of the JVM features. Applets run within the browser security "sandbox." In other words, they only have access to what the browser allows access to. You can think of the host for the applet as a combination of the JVM and the browser. So, compared to other types of mobile agents, applets are fairly secure.

Aglets are an implementation of weak mobility in using Java. Aglets are a newer incarnation of mobility using Java; they are not pervasive throughout the development community. Nevertheless, they are worth looking at as one of the few available mobile agent mechanisms today.

MIDlets, which we briefly discussed in Chapter 2, implement weak mobility for the J2ME environment. As we have learned, J2ME targets resource-starved devices that cannot run the full JVM or the full set of supporting APIs in J2SE. The code base for MIDlets is not portable between J2ME to J2SE. Neither is the code base for applets (which run using the full-blown JVM) portable to J2ME. This is the gap that exists in the Java platform to implement agent mobility pervasively throughout our mobile application and, thereby, gives rise to the need to build additional software on top of the Java platform to provide such functionality.

Now, let us look at applets, Aglets, and MIDlets in more detail.

Applets

Applets are a great example of mobile code but do not display any state mobility properties. Therefore, applets are not mobile agents. An applet is a Java program downloaded by a browser as a part of an HTML page directive. This Java program is then executed by the virtual machine present on the machine that hosts the browser. Every time an applet moves, it returns to its initial state.

The only significant difference in the code for an applet and a typical Java program is that the driver class has to extend the class applet and the main method is replaced by an initial method. Figure 9.6 shows sample code for the skeleton of a "Hello World" applet.

```
Public class HelloWorldApplet extends Applet
{
    public void init() {
        drawHelloWorld();
    }
    public void drawHelloWorld() {
        ....
        ....
    }
}
```

FIGURE 9.6. Skeleton of an Applet.

Applets cannot be made to implement mobile agent capabilities because the security model requires the following:

1. An applet can only communicate with the host that it came from. This is the server from which it was originally downloaded.
2. An applet cannot run a local executable on the host. This prohibits an applet from cloning itself or creating another applet.

This does not mean that mobile code is not useful for mobile computing. Quite the contrary, the applet model can be utilized quite effectively because one of the biggest problems that we face in designing mobile applications is lack of volatile and nonvolatile storage resources. It is much more practical to load the application on demand and run it rather than to permanently store it. Nevertheless, the applet model by itself is limiting. Applets require the full J2SE virtual machine, which is too resource-starved for most mobile devices. J2ME's MIDlets, discussed later in this chapter and previously in Chapter 2, borrow much from applets and do not require the full-blown J2SE virtual machine.

Aglets

If you look at the Webster dictionary, aglets are defined as those plastic things at the end of shoelaces! Now, Aglets are also the name of mobile agents written for a mobile agent specification created by the IBM research group in Japan. Aglets, like applets, are a model for mobile code. However, they also implement weak mobility, meaning that they can carry their state from one host to another.

Aglets use the Java serialization mechanism to store their own state before migration. After migration, they use the serialization mechanism once more to restore their state. Serialization is possible when one of the two interfaces, *externalizable* or *serializable*, are implemented by a Java class. When a Java object is serialized, its state from the heap is written into a byte stream. This byte stream may be a file, a database, or some other persistence mechanism. The byte stream, in its completeness, can then be used to reconstruct the same object. Because serialization does not allow us to capture any information about the object or the application in the stack, the state of execution is lost. This prohibits implementing strong mobility. Also, when the agent (the Aglet) needs to migrate, it must first be warned. This is because there is no telling whether all of the objects in the Aglet have placed all of the information critical to a meaningful restoration of state in the heap.

Now, let us briefly look at some implementation details about Aglets.

The Aglet Architecture

As previously discussed, mobile agents are asynchronous and autonomous. This makes the life cycles of mobile agents of utmost importance. Because Aglets are collections of Java objects, this translates to the life cycle of a collection of Java objects:

1. *Creation*: Aglets are created by the Aglet host. This host can later be accessed by the Aglet as the *Aglet context*.
2. *Dispatch*: This is the term used for migration. An Aglet is said to be dispatched when it migrates from one host to another.
3. *Deactivated*: In this state, the Aglet is persisted and not running.
4. *Activated*: An Aglet is said to be activated when its state is restored and it is given the necessary resources to begin running autonomously.
5. *Disposed*: Disposing an Aglet deletes its state. This is the end of the life cycle of an Aglet. By definition, the end of the life cycle of a mobile agent may cause the deletion of the mobile code as well. In the case of Aglets, this is typically not necessary because Java classes may be cached for later usage.

Although these states are required in presenting mobile agent behavior, Aglets can also display the following additional behavior that may be desirable:

1. *Cloning*: An Aglet can copy itself to a new agent. This agent is then autonomous and not dependent on the Aglet that created it.
2. *Retraction*: An Aglet can be recalled to the host it came from.
3. *Messaging*: Aglets can communicate synchronously or asynchronously with one another.

It is important to note that cloning, retraction, and messaging are necessary for Aglets: They are part of the specification. However, they are extraneous to mobile agent systems.

Aglets are transferred from one host to another using Aglet Transfer Protocol (ATP). ATP allows usage of a framework different from the Aglet framework to handle the Aglets and then allows for various hosts to interoperate to enable the migration of agents. Unfortunately, Aglets do not support MASIF. This is a significant downfall as ATP is not a widely accepted protocol by the other agent platforms we will look at later. FIPA and OMG are the key organizations whose standards are of importance when evaluating mobile agent platforms. Now, let us see how we can write an Aglet.

Hello World Aglet

Let us go back to our infamous "Hello World" sample program. As one would guess, the most basic Aglet would simply need to know of its own life cycle and be able to communicate with the host. As can be seen in Figure 9.7, we extend the Aglet class and override the methods that make up the standard interface of an Aglet. This standard interface is what is used by the host to start up an agent after its move and to destroy an agent when it is finished or ready to move.

The Aglet Tools

To develop an Aglet, you'll need to install the Aglet Software Development Kit (ASDK). The Aglet specifications and API can be found at http://www.trl.ibm.com/aglets. The specifications and API outline the requirements of the host as well as the mobile agents.

The Aglet API is built on the top of JDK 1.1, therefore, it is not typically suitable for mobile devices. Most mobile devices do not have enough resources to run the full J2SE suite let alone a framework written on the top of it. One of the current short comings of Aglets is that they do not run on J2ME. The Aglet framework is simply too heavy for J2ME.

J2ME and MIDlets

In Chapter 2, we discussed the functionality offered by J2ME. Here, we will look at J2ME and how it can provide a mobile agent platform. As we discussed previously, Java itself provides the facilities needed to build a mobile application infrastructure that supports weak mobility. However, the JVM (the virtual machine for the J2SE) is too big for most mobile devices today. Even as devices get better and faster, there is always going to be a resource starvation problem on some devices. For this reason, there is J2ME and its virtual machines, the KVM and the CVM. The KVM and CVM are both smaller than the JVM. The KVM implements less functionality, but it is much more compact. For a detailed discussion of J2ME refer back to Chapter 2. The point is that J2ME provides a mobile code environment for mobile devices, even the most resource deprived of them. However, J2ME, like J2SE, does not provide a mobile agent platform because it does not provide for continuation of execution state. As we mentioned in Chapter 2, there are two possible base-line configurations for J2ME: CLDC and CDC. To date, only CLDC has had real implementations. CDC remains in the specification phase to be implemented in the near future.

The most significant feature eliminated from CLDC, when it comes to mobile agents is serialization. This means that CLDC does not support weak or strong mobile agents by itself. MIDP (functionality added on top of CLDC for Mobile Information Profile) has support for so-called MIDlets. MIDlets can be made to support weak mobility. MIDlets are complete applications and can control their own life cycles. The initial state of a MIDlet can be set as a resource file that can contain the value of the various members of the classes; however, this means that some sort of serialization mechanism must be implemented manually for the mobile agent, in this case the MIDlet, to read the values from the resource file.

```
import java.io.*;
import java.net.*;
import java.util.*;
import java.awt.*;
import com.ibm.aglet.*;
import com.ibm.aglet.util.*;
import com.ibm.aglet.event.*;

Public class HelloWorldAglet extends Aglet
{
    private String mHello;

    //This is the execution method.
    //Put whatever the Aglet needs to do during its
    //life cycle here.
    public void run(){
        System.out.println(mHello);
    }

    //This method is called when the Aglet is first
    //created by the host.
    public void onCreation(Object o) {
        mHello = "Hello World Was Created At" +
          System.currentTimeMillis();
    }

    //This method is called when the Aglet is told it
    //needs to die.
    public onDisposing() {
        System.out.println("Disposing of Hello World
          Agent At" + System.currentTimeMillis();
    }

    //This method is called when a message is sent to
    //the Aglet.
    public boolean handleMessage(Message m) {
        mHello = mHello + "Message Arrived At" + System.
          currentTimeMillis();
        return true;
    }
}
```

FIGURE 9.7. Hello World Aglet.

J2ME, as with the other editions of Java, cannot support strong mobility. One look at the MIDP and CLDC specifications shows you that the designers really had many of the features and properties of a mobile agent system in mind. However, it seems that because of security concerns and lack of consensus among the handset manufacturers, they were unable to arrive at a true mobile agent platform. We already looked at a Hello World MIDlet in Section 2.4.1 so we will not discuss them all over again.

The JADE–LEAP platform builds on top of J2ME and J2SE to provide a true mobile agent platform that allows agents to move among mobile devices and the mobile network with much more flexibility than what is provided in the vanilla J2ME.

JADE and LEAP

Let us start with JADE, the Java Agent Development Framework. JADE version 2.6, which is the latest version so far, is a mobile agent framework, completely developed in J2SE version 1.2. JADE has been integrated into LEAP, the Lightweight Extensible Agent Platform, to produce an agent framework that uses J2ME and J2SE with the goal of creating a mobile agent framework that can serve mobile and stationary applications at the same time. Both JADE and LEAP are aimed at building a FIPA-compliant agent framework. FIPA, along with OMG, are the leading standardization bodies when it comes to mobile agent APIs and specifications. Whereas OMG has specified the interoperability issues, FIPA is focused on addressing the infrastructure problems of building a mobile agent platform. FIPA is the leading organization in the LEAP project (which now includes JADE as a part of it), but there is also participation from W3C, giving the project additional standardization and acceptance support. LEAP is administered under the GNU Lesser General Public License so it is an open source and free piece of software.

Figure 9.8 shows how LEAP breaks down the different host types for different families of hardware platforms. You can download LEAP at http://leap.crm-paris.com and JADE at http://jade.cselt.it. Once you download JADE and LEAP, you will need to install JDK 1.2 or JDK 1.3 to run the JADE environment. Whereas the agents supported by JADE–LEAP can reside on hosts of a mobile device, development and deployment is a task left for the J2SE on PCs and servers.

Every host implementation of the JADE–LEAP host is accompanied by a GUI tool that allows for administration of the settings that enable mobile agents to migrate on and off the host. Obviously, because of the different host implementations and the different device capabilities for which the hosts are implemented, the configuration and administration of the hosts will differ. However, the mobile agent paradigm is preserved by providing the same application-layer APIs to the agents regardless of the hardware platform and host implementation. This does not mean that the same agent can run on any of the hosts, but this is not a requirement of mobile agent frameworks either. The requirement is that the mobile agents can migrate from one host to some other host in an autonomous and asynchronous manner. This requirement is satisfied by the JADE–LEAP framework. Note that there are three types of hosts. There is the *light container*, which is the lightweight implementation of the container providing the minimal set of

Agent X | Agent Y | Agent Z | Agent A | Agent B

Homogeneous JADE-LEAP API's

JADE-LEAP Light Container (J2ME Host)	JADE-LEAP Container (J2SE Host)	JADE-LEAP Container PJava Host	JADE-LEAP Main Container (J2SE Host)
J2ME	J2SE	Personal Java	J2SE
PDAs, Cell Phones, etc.	PC's, Servers, Powerful PDAs	PDAs, Appliances, etc.	Servers

FIGURE 9.8. JADE–LEAP Host Implementation Paradigm.

functionality for the host to allow agents to migrate on and off the device and execute their tasks. This container is designed primarily for the resource-starved devices. Then, there is the regular container, referred to simply as the *container*. This is a slightly heavier implementation sitting on top of J2SE and Personal Java. Then there is the *main container*, which provides communication compatibility with other mobile agent platforms and facilitates communication within a network of LEAP hosts. The main container is unique and acts as a front end for the platform; it maintains platform-wide information and provides platform-wide services [Bergenti and Poggi 2001]. Matching this with the theory that we learned earlier about mobile agents, the main container provides the *registry* and *region* functionality. Because each type of host is implemented on a different platform, and because each platform has its own set of communication protocols, LEAP provides a mapping between the communication protocols. This integration is made possible through what LEAP documentation refers to as ITP, Internal Transport Protocol. Underneath this, the implementation may be TCP/IP, IIOP, or Java RMI. Obviously, RMI and IIOP are too resource intensive and require a lot of code for the light container, so TCP/IP is the prevalent implementation for communications among light containers, containers, and main containers (the variety of hosts that make up the list of hosts in a LEAP network).

An important aspect of LEAP is that it connects the hosts in a peer-to-peer manner. Every host is connected to the network through a socket and can send and receive messages to an IP address with a port. This allows LEAP hosts to provide for an infrastructure that supports active behavior for the mobile agents (i.e., they can push information out to other agents instead of just listening for requests and responding to the request).

Let us look at the some of the JADE–LEAP Java source implementations in Table 9.3 This will give us an insight into what type of functionality the host

TABLE 9.3. Overview of the Some Important Packages in JADE–LEAP

Package	Description
jade.imtp.leap	This package provides the basic interfaces for building agents and internal communication of the hosts. It includes the following: 1. serialization classes (which are required to provide the basic agent capabilities of constructing agents, moving them, and reconstructing them), 2. skeleton classes for the containers, and 3. skeleton classes for the internal communication classes.
jade.util.leap	This package builds on the existing J2ME utilities (because they are very limited) to provide iterators, linked lists, hash maps, sorted sets, and comparators. Obviously, the implementation of these classes provides minimal functionality compared to their J2SE counterparts. Nonetheless, for those who have programmed using J2ME, it is obvious that these classes need to exist to provide the minimal functionality that a host would need to contain agents, keep track of them, and keep track of minimal information on them.
jadelang.sl	This package holds classes processed by JavaCC. You will need to download and install JavaCC if you want to modify any of the functionality here. (We do not recommend modifying the functionality of this or any other packages that ship with JADE–LEAP. This is a complex framework and modification is not for the faint of heart. The fact that it is open source does not mean you have any obligation to modify it and use it.) The source for this package exists in semantic language (SL) along with the rest of the source code when you download the package. SL0 is Semantic Language version 0. Depending on when you download the LEAP–JADE packages, you will probably find a different version of the parser. SL is similar to RDF in its purpose. For a review of RDF, refer to Chapter 3.
jade.lang.acl	This package is similar to jade.lang.sl in that it is compiled using JavaCC except that it supports ACL. The Agent Communication Language (ACL) is the FIPA standard language for creating messages exchanged between agents. SL code can be included in an ACL message.

Package	Description
jade.imtp.leap.JICP (J2SE implementation)	This package holds the implementation of the JADE–LEAP API implementation specified in other packages. Depending on the ANT (an Apache Build tool for Java code) parameters that you set when building JADE–LEAP, you will compile a particular version of the host (or you can build so that you compile multiple versions at the same time).
jade.imtp.leap.JICP (J2ME implementation)	This package holds the implementation of the JADE–LEAP API implementation specified in other packages. Depending on the ANT parameters that you set when building JADE–LEAP, you will compile a particular version of the host (or you can build so that you compile multiple versions at the same time).
jade.imtp.leap.JICP (shared classes among all of the container implementations)	This package holds the classes that encapsulate running and communication of the container at a higher layer, abstracted from the platform implementation (J2ME, J2SE, etc.).

platform offers and how we can write agents for it. Then, we will return to look at the big picture again.

Now, let us consider a real example. Let us say that we want to implement Agent A in the example of Figure 9.1. In this case, we need the agent to be able to migrate to the J2ME host as well as to the J2SE and Personal Java hosts. To separate our concerns properly, let us list the different types of things we need to implement:

1. a user interface for every platform,
2. some way for Agent A to communicate with Agent B,
3. the logic that enables Agent A to know when to notify the user, and
4. an interface between Agent A the GPS system on the device.

We can approach this problem in two different ways. We can either implement the PAC-TG pattern for the user interface separation of concerns or select a simpler solution and build different GUIs for each supported platform. Deciding between these two methods would come down to the resources available on the device and the number of devices we need to support. If we need to support numerous devices, then it might be advantages to use the PAC-TG pattern, with the transformations taking place on the server side to generate specialized user interface code for J2ME, J2SE, and Personal Java. Alternatively, we could have the J2ME agent actually implement PAC-TG in itself. However, this is probably too code- and resource-intensive for a J2ME application. Yet another option would be to write XForms-to-J2ME and XForms-to-J2SE transformations, build only an XForms interface

```
package com.cienecs.mobile.agent.examples;

import jade.core.*;
import jade.lang.acl.*;
import com.somegpsapi.*;
import jade.core.behaviours.*;

public class RestaurantFinderAgent extends Agent {
    private GPS_API_Stub      mLocationFinder;
    private GUI_Class         mGUI;
    private AID               mDestinationHost;

    public void setup() {
        //First, set up the destination host that the
        //agent is being started on.
        try {mDestinationHost = new AID((String)
          getArguments()[0], AID.ISLOCALNAME);
        } catch (Exception e) {System.out.println("Setup
          Failed. Destination Host Not Found.");}

        //Then, set up the GUI that fits the host. This
        //is not the most elegant way to implement
        //discovery of the right host. We can use things
        //like CC/PP and UAProf for a more elegant
        //implementation. Start with the lowest common
        //denominator and work up to the most
        //complex one.
        try {mGUI = (SpecializedInterface)
            Class.forName("com.cienecs.mobile.agent.examples.
              AgentAMIDP");
        } catch (Exception e1) {
            System.out.println(e1.toString());
            try {mGUI = (SpecializedInterface)
                Class.forName("com.cienecs.mobile.agent.
                  examples.AgentAPDAP);
            } catch (Exception e2) {
                System.out.println(e2.toString());
                try {mGUI = (SpecializedInterface)
                    Class.forName("com.cienecs.mobile.
                      agentexamples.AgentJ2SE");
                } catch (Exception e3) {System.out.println
                  (e3.toString());}
            }
        }
```

FIGURE 9.9. Agent Wrapper Class.

```
        // Set up Location Capabilities
        mLocationFinder = GPS_API_Stub.getInstance();

        //Add the ability to communicate with Agent B and
        //notifying the user.
        mGUI.initialize(this);
        addBehaviour(new Notification(this));
    }

    void sendLocationtoAgentB(Agent anAgentB) {
        ACLMessage mMessage = new ACLMessage(ACLMessage.
          INFORM);
        msg.addReceiver(anAgentB);
        send(mMessage);
    }
}
```

FIGURE 9.9 ***(continued)***

for all of the agents, and leave the creation of the user interface to the agent at run time.

We will take the easier route and simply look at implementing the different user interfaces manually. Because the JADE–LEAP mobile agent platform limits the user interface types to J2ME, J2SE, and Personal Java, we are not concerned with an overwhelming number of interfaces to implement. First, we need a wrapper that instantiates the right classes for the right platform. You can see this in Figure 9.9.

The LEAP project provides a well-thought-out network connectivity solution. The smallest of the mobile devices that LEAP provides a host for, cellular phones, can connect to the network using SMS or TCP/IP over GSM. For PDAs, connectivity is available through SMS, 802.11, and TCP/IP over GSM. Personal computers, servers, and other more powerful stationary or mobile hosts that use the J2SE implementation connect to the network using TCP/IP.

The JADE-LEAP platform gives us a FIPA-compliant mobile agent platform with hosts that can run on most of the devices for our mobile applications and, therefore, allows pervasive usage of mobile agents throughout the mobile agent–based system. Grasshopper is a mobile agent platform that currently provides hosts only for more powerful systems such as PCs and servers. It can be used to provide agents that support mobile applications. Let us take a closer look at Grasshopper.

Grasshopper

To date, IKV++ Berlin's Grasshopper is the only MASIF-compliant mobile agent platform. Grasshopper can run on any operating system supported by the full J2SE JVM including Windows CE. Unfortunately, Grasshopper is not supported

```
package com.cienecs.examples.agents

import de.ikv.grasshopper.agent.*;
import de.ikv.grasshopper.agency.*;
import com.cienecs.gps.locationfinder.*;

public class HelloWorldAgent extends MobileAgent {
    private int mState;
    private Location mCurrentLocation;

    public void live() {
        switch(mState) {
            case 0: {
                while (mState == 0) {
                    try {
                        Location myLocation = LocationHandler.
                          getInstance().getCurrentLocation();
                        System.out.println("Hello World. My
                          Location is:" + myLocation.
                          toString());
                        mCurrentLocation = myLocation;
                    }catch (LocationException e) {
                        e.printStackTrace();
                        mState = 2;
                    }
                }
                break;
            }
            case 1: {
                mState = 0;
                System.out.println("Hello World. Current
                  Location is:" + mCurrentLocation.toString());
                break;
            }
            default: {
                System.out.println("Invalid State or Could Not
                  Obtain Location Information");
                break;
            }
        }
        System.out.println("Agent is finished. It is going to
          be destroyed now.");
    }

    // This method is called before the agent is destroyed.
    public void beforeRemove() {
```

FIGURE 9.10. Trivial Mobile Agent for Grasshopper Platform.

```
            PersistenceHandler myPersistenceHandler =
              PersistenceHandler.getInstance();
            myPersistenceHandler.saveAndAssociateWithAgent
              (mCurrentLocation, this);
        }

        /** This method allows the host to pass in
          additional parameters possibly provided by the
          user, host specific, location specific, etc. **/
        public void init(Object[] args) {
            mState = 0;
            mCurrentLocation = (Location) args[0];
        }
    }
```

FIGURE 9.10 ***(continued)***

on J2ME CLDC devices at this time. Grasshopper's Distributed Agent Environment (DAE) encapsulates familiar concepts that we have already discussed: hosts, regions, agencies, and agents. To create mobile agents using Grasshopper, you will need to download the DAE and install it. You will be writing your agents in Java. Communications among the different components of the mobile agent system in Grasshopper are done using CORBA, IIOP, RMI, or TCP sockets. In a way, Grasshopper is more of a client–agent server environment as its design and implementation take into account synchronous and asynchronous communication between components and allow agents to assume roles of clients and servers. In addition to this, Grasshopper also provides a multicast communication mechanism that allows one component of the mobile agent system (agent, host, etc.) to send one message to multiple destinations in one transaction. This can be a particularly handy feature. For example, it can be used to clone one agent multiple times with one transaction.

Grasshopper offers several methods of securing communications including symmetric and asymmetric encryption algorithm implementations, SSL, and others. Compared to most other mobile agent implementations available to date, it offers the best-thought-out security measures, thereby addressing one of the biggest concerns with mobile agent–based systems.

Unfortunately, Grasshopper 2.2.4, which is currently the latest version, does not support HTTP. Though HTTP is not the ideal protocol for stateful communication such as those that may be required by mobile agents and their supporting infrastructure, because of its pervasiveness and because of the existence of security barriers that block everything but HTTP traffic to certain networks, it can be handy to have an HTTP-based implementation available. For an overview of the Grasshopper architecture, visit the Grasshopper Web site [IKV 2001].

Let us get write a simple agent for Grasshopper. Figure 9.10 shows the trivial "Hello World" agent for the Grasshopper platform.

In our simple example, the agent prints out its current location to whatever console it has a handle to (most probably the console of the host system that in which it resides at the time of calling this method). If there is a problem initializing the agent or when the source of location information (GPS unit or else) no longer returns a valid location, the agent stops.

As you can see, Grasshopper agents, like the other types of agents that we have looked at, extend a class. To add the functionality necessary for the agent to operate, you simply override the implementation of the methods that you need.

Currently, Grasshopper offers the most complete MASIF-compliant implementation of an agent-based platform. It offers an ideal platform for mobile agents to operate as the supporting infrastructure to mobile applications. As we mentioned before, however, there is no implementation of a Grasshopper host for PDAs, cell phones, or resource-starved mobile devices. Nor are there any implementations of the communication mechanism of Grasshopper based on UDP/IP or similar protocols that lend themselves to use in an environment where the connection to the network is unreliable. We do need to remember, though, that mobile computing includes usage of laptops that are intermittently connected to the network or connected to the network through 802.11a or similar networks that provide high-bandwidth wireless access. The spectrum of mobile devices is somewhat discontinuous at this time, ranging between PDAs and mobile devices. However, this will change in the near future, with a variety of devices that can access "hot-spot" wireless networks, thereby providing access to devices with more features and more power than a PDA as well as being smaller than the smallest laptops on the market today. This means that the role of more sophisticated mobile agent platforms such as Grasshopper can become more and more prominent in mobile computing.

Now that we have looked at several mobile agent platforms based on Java technologies, let us look at JINI, which is a Java technology often used by many mobile agent platforms. This section is mostly pertinent to those interested in building a mobile agent platform for mobile computing rather than to the users of such platforms. A good mobile agent platform should hide the internal implementation tools.

JINI for Mobile Agents

As we mentioned in Chapter 2 when we looked at the tools for mobile application development, JINI provides a mechanism by which services are offered and clients can access these services. In a way, JINI provides a flexible-application-layer, ad hoc grouping mechanism that allows grouping of services and the usage of those services. JINI addresses ownership of services, distribution of services, issues caused by network unreliability such as fail-over, and leasing of services to clients who want to use those services. In this context, JINI can be very useful for implementing the security infrastructure for a mobile agent platform. Remember that agents need to be granted rights to execute various sets of actions on the host, including the basic actions of migration and cloning.

The first problem with mobile agent systems is that they employ active objects and therefore have automatic access to the resources of the machines to which their agents travel. A solution to this problem would be to move the agents from one machine to another as passive objects, but move them to a JINI service that would then oversee granting—at the appropriate time and priority—a thread of control to that agent [Waldo 2001].

Unfortunately, once again, JINI implementations exist only for J2SE at this time. This rules out systems such as JADE–LEAP that provide a mobile agent platform that may be used pervasively throughout the mobile application framework. The only work-around is to create a gateway or adaptor to replicate the functionality that JINI offers to the lower end hosts, but this is effectively creating an entirely new set of security and transfer problems.

JINI can be effectively used for distribution and movement of objects, under the covers, by the mobile agent platforms that target the higher end hosts.

Mobile Agent Platforms for Microsoft's .NET

Although Microsoft platforms have offered a variety of distributed computing functionality, up to the release of the .NET framework, there was no consideration paid to code mobility in the Microsoft platform. As we have seen, code mobility is the first step for agent mobility. The .NET platform, for the first time, offers academics and commercial vendors the opportunity to build mobile agent platforms for the Microsoft platform. Microsoft's .NET CLR (Common Language Runtime) allows for different (though prespecified) versions of libraries to be loaded into the same execution space, but it leaves prevention of potential calamitous interaction of those versions up to the component developer (e.g., if both versions create and use the same temporary file, no protection is offered) [Cook 2001]. Overall, the Microsoft .NET framework provides much of the same functionality as the Java Virtual Machine does when it comes to building a mobile agent framework.

As of yet, there are no mobile agent frameworks that offer weak or strong mobility for the .NET framework. However, this is certain to change. What is not certain is the penetration levels of the .NET CLR into the mobile device market. Because most mobile devices are manufactured by handset manufacturers that provide their own operating systems (such as Nokia, Motorola, Palm, Handspring, etc.), there are compatibility issues between a mobile agent framework built on the .NET CLR (which is designed to run on the variations of Microsoft Windows operating system) and other systems.

9.5 Solving Mobile Application Development Problems with Mobile Agents

As we mentioned previously, mobile agents have some properties that allow them to solve the problems associated with mobile applications well. In Chapter 1, we defined the dimensions of mobility and the condition of the mobile user: those things that are unique to mobile applications as opposed to their stationary counterparts. Now, let us see how mobile agents are able to address the dimensions of mobility better than other approaches to distributed computing systems.

9.5.1 Mobile Agents and Context

We talked about context and its implications for the user interface in Chapter 5. Context-aware computing is an entire field in itself and encompasses various aspects of dependency of computing operations in the context of the actions they perform and the context of the conditions under which computing is performed. In fact, much of the research done for mobile agents is driven by intelligent systems and context-aware computing. This is outside of the scope of our discussion. However, the context of the mobile condition of the user and the usage of the mobile application is something of particular interest to us.

For example, we may use the context of the usage to select the user interface components to be stitched together at run time to render a user interface. The mobile context is something that a mobile agent is very well suited to "understand" and "process." By this, we mean that mobile agents are uniquely positioned to acquire the necessary information about the context of the usage of the mobile application (because they rely less on network connectivity, etc.) and that they can process this information in a more efficient way than the available alternatives.

The final point of all of this is that context-aware mobile applications are best accommodated by mobile agents because mobile agents offer a higher system availability rate than their counterparts (client–server and centralized) and have a more immediate and accurate information set that describes the context of computing.

9.5.2 Mobile Agents and Location Sensitivity

Whether we use mobile agents in a supporting role for mobile applications or use them to build the mobile applications themselves, mobile agents have inherent properties that make them desirable for computational tasks related to the location of the user and or the device. Namely, mobile agents migrate and their migration is associated with hosts. Hosts are some application running on some machine somewhere. And, there is typically a one-to-one association between hosts and hardware. This means that when agents migrate from one host to the next, they are probably changing their physical location.

Particularly, if the mobile agent platform can run on the mobile device (such as JADE–LEAP), the location information can be obtained from the device. The location information, obtained through triangulation or a GPS unit on the device, can be used by the agent. Conversely, mobile agents that run only on the supporting network can obtain the location of the device through triangulation or the device program may serve as a peer or client to the agent and send the location obtained through the GPS unit on the device.

We will discuss the various methods of obtaining location information in later chapters. The important thing to note here is that mobile agents present a more natural framework for acquiring and processing location information because there is some linear mapping between the concept of hosts and physical location of the user, the device the user is using, or the network node that the device accesses.

Mobile agents have lifecycles while they exist on a host; however, information also has a useful life (distributed data requires synchronization, done by agents or traditional techniques). The calculation of these lifecycles combined as relating to implementing application functionality is extremely complex. Murphy [Murphy 2000] takes a close look at this and other concerns that arise when using mobile agents to integrate location information into your mobile application.

9.5.3 Using Agents to Build User Interfaces

We have seen, throughout this text, that user interface problems of mobile applications are orders of magnitude more difficult to deal with than their stationary counterparts. In Chapters 5–8, we discussed creating generic user interfaces and specializing them. Let us tie that discussion into mobile agents. We can use mobile agents to create mobile user interfaces in the following two ways:

1. We can create series of agents that are solely responsible for specializing the generic user interface for which another set of agents may be responsible. In this manner, the agents that specialize the interface may migrate to the device and communicate with the agents that produce the generic user interface. This model is more of a hybrid (client–agent server) because the agent specializing the user interface on the device basically is a client to the agent that generates the generic user interface. The advantage of using agents here is that the agent that migrates to the client can take advantage of the mobile context, location sensitivity, and all of the other pieces of dimensions of mobility that are more accessible on the device as opposed to the network.
2. We can create a series of agents that represent the entire application or whole parts of the entire application. Let us take for example the restaurant finder application that we discussed previously. This mobile agent may be part of a bigger "travel agent" that helps the user with finding not just restaurants, but also hotels, gas stations, public transport, museums, and other travel-related information. Each atomic functional part of the application can be an agent. In this case, we can have a collection of mobile agents performing as one seamless application, one finding the nearest restaurant, another finding the nearest hotel, and so on. The advantage to this approach is that the entire user interface problem can be encapsulated into one agent without much traffic going back and forth to the network. Conversely, the disadvantage is that separation of concerns inside a mobile agent that is going to run on a resource-starved device is going to be resource prohibitive. In other words, it does not make any sense to create a large degree of separation between the different parts of a given agent if the code base that makes up the agent is fairly small. Much of the separation of concerns in such a situation can be provided by the host API that allows the agent to perform certain tasks. For example, the restaurant agent may be less than 100 lines of code in totality. Breaking it up into user interface component, logic component, communication component, and control component may not have enough benefit to justify the cost. There is another disadvantage to this as pointed out by Yim and colleagues [Yim et al. 2001]: As the number of agents increases, it cannot be avoided that more dependencies among agents will exist;

> agents communicate with other agents in keeping independence; finally, the concept of software architecture, which software systems consist of components and connectors, supports the design to minimize the interconnection among agents. So, functional separation of concerns should be accompanied by meaningful usage of the concept of "roles," where one agent can have multiple roles. The grouping of roles into agents may be based on a variety of factors such as the code base used to perform each function and the interconnectivity of the various tasks to be performed when an agent assumes a particular role.

Dimitri [Dimitri 2002] presents a comprehensive study of both of these cases, how to implement each, and, furthermore, the costs and benefits of each on various platforms.

The Mobile Agent to User Interaction (MAUI) project presents us with yet a third way of thinking, designing, and implementing user interfaces to mobile agents [MAUI 2000]. In MAUI, Mihailescu, Gamage, and Kendall define a taxonomy of three types of interactions that a user may have with a mobile agent: *Initial interactions* are the set of interactions between the user and the system that eventually cause the creation or invocation of the mobile agent; *in-progress interactions* are those interactions taking place while the mobile agent is doing work; and *completion interactions* are the set of interactions that take place to inform the user of some results before finishing. Likewise, as we have seen with mobile agents, these mobile agents can be running on the local device, in our case the mobile device, or be somewhere else on the network and produce a user interface for the local device (generating HTML, WML, etc.).

Therefore, MAUI creates a taxonomy of tasks to render user interfaces based on the types of interactions. For example, we may have an agent that is invoked from a markup-based user interface such as WML, then migrates to the device, begins interacting with the user so that the in-progress interactions are encapsulated in an interface rendered by the agent on the device, and renders the completion interactions to multiple user interfaces, one of which may be the device the user is using at the time. This is a very novel and valid approach.

The approach you choose in building the user interfaces to your mobile agents has a symbiotic relationship with the mobile agent platform you choose and the tasks that your agents are to accomplish. So, you should gather accurate requirements on what your system is supposed to accomplish and the plausible mobile agent platforms that you can use to build your system, then weigh the various design strategies for building the user interfaces to these agents.

9.5.4 Mobile Agents and QOS

Mobile agents and QOS have a symbiotic relationship. Mobile agents can be used to provide information regarding QOS within the underlying communication network. However, as we have mentioned repeatedly, one of the problems that mobile agents solved for mobile computing is dealing with lack of reliable continuous bandwidth.

Mobiware, created at University of Columbia, is an example of a mobile agent middleware that provides specific API calls for the agent interfaces for allowing you to specify different behaviors based on the QOS. Mobiware will measure QOS and supply the hooks to enable the application to react and adjust [Afnan 2002] according to the QOS levels.

Also, because of the collaborative nature of mobile agents, they can become very handy in forming ad hoc networks that provide services to mobile devices. If the wireless networking infrastructure that provides communication to the mobile application is based on an ad hoc networking technology (WIFI, 802.11a, etc.), the application-layer services offered can be offered in an equally ad hoc manner. In other words, we can offer a set of application-layer services to the device that joins an ad hoc network upon joining the network. Mobile agents can be used to move through networks, as proxies or device-independent agents that offer various services, to provide services throughout a mobile application.

9.5.5 Mobile Agents as Proxies

One usage of mobile agents in mobile applications is as so-called proxy agents. Agents can be proxies for mobile devices or proxy for an application that resides on the mobile device (mobile code or otherwise) but does not comply with the rest of the mobile agent framework.

In the first case, we can have an agent that follows around a device. Whenever the device connects to the network, the agent migrates to the "closest" node to the device (closeness being defined in various terms based on the mobile agent platform) and performs some tasks on behalf of the device. The device may not have any capabilities in running an application (such as a regular old phone), it may be able to run some minimal applications that use the mobile agent on the network as a server, or it may be able to support a host environment for mobile agents, in which case the mobile agent on the device may migrate to the network to communicate with the proxy or may use RPC-like mechanisms to communicate with the agent on the network.

This approach does introduce some scalability concerns. CPU cycles, memory, and bandwidth for supporting every existing device in a networked application that engages any substantial number of users and mobile devices can grow polynomially versus the number of users as each user may have multiple devices, roaming from one network to another, using a combination of devices, and performing fairly complex tasks or tasks that require a significant amount of communication between the proxy agent and the supporting systems.

9.5.6 Mobile Agents and Performance-Related Problems Associated with Mobile Computing

One of the biggest problems to be experienced, by existing Web-based and non-Web-based systems that will attempt to serve mobile computing environments, will be performance-related issues. Remember that the tolerance of the mobile user for long waits is much less than that of the stationary user and that numerous computing cycles have to be spent to just deal with the problems associated with the mobile condition of the user and the dimensions of mobility. So, we have several different types of scalability problems: Not only do we have to build systems that perform and scale well as they grow, but we also have higher performance expectations for a mobile application than its stationary counterpart. Simply measuring the performance of mobile agent–based systems is quite complex because of all of the factors involved. Let us review some performance and scalability issues with mobile agents used in mobile computing:

1. In one way, mobile agents can help reduce the scalability problem by massively distributing computing tasks. They allow the resources of the collection of hardware systems that make up a system (mobile devices, servers, etc.) to be utilized more effectively because we can make them migrate to the host with the most available resources (CPU, memory, etc.)
2. The acts of migration, cloning, and other properties and structures that must be supported by the mobile agent framework have a high overhead. Simply utilizing a mobile agent framework has a high price that is only justifiable if there are ample computing resources (CPU, memory, etc.) on the hosts and the number of hosts justifies usage of mobile agents. This means that we probably would opt not to use a mobile agent system if there are only two hosts involved at all times.
3. Performance of a mobile agent system depends on the properties of the underlying communications network. However, this relationship is neither straightforward nor linear. The dependency of the mobile agent system on the network is a function of available continuous bandwidth, available burst bandwidth, and the reliability level of the network. The actual function is defined by the implementation of the mobile agent framework.
4. Performance of the mobile agent system depends on the range of hardware platforms to be supported. The higher this range is, the lower the performance; the lower the range is, the higher the performance. This is because more optimization of the agents is possible with fewer supported platforms.

In addition, there are various research and development efforts in defining techniques that identify ways of measuring performance and scalability issues involved in mobile agent platforms. The AMASE project [AMASE 1999] is among those. This project attempts to define metrics on the practicality of porting a host to a small device, the resource cost of the participation of such a device on the network (the cost of proxies and other special measures that may need to be taken to accommodate the resource-starved devices), storage requirements on the device to allow for installation of the host and operation of the agents, latencies in loading and unloading the agents, service lookup latencies, migration latencies, and a variety of other metrics that allow for measuring the performance of a mobile agent–based system.

9.5.7 Mobile Agents and Device Adaptation

When mobile devices are able to serve as the host platform for mobile agents, or run some third-party software that is able to serve as the host platform, the mobile agent has the perfect opportunity to be able to adapt the mobile application (whether the mobile agent is the entire mobile application or whether there are other parts to the mobile application) to its environment. Let us look at a couple of possible cases.

If a mobile application is implemented as a mobile agent and is responsible for the rendering of a user interface, it can discover the user interface capabilities of the device and immediately adapt the application to those capabilities that suit the device. Elsewhere, if the agent is designed to somehow utilize the device location, it can discover the mechanism for obtaining the location information, be it GPS, triangulation, or some other method, when it moves onto the device. The alternative to these two cases is if we represent the capabilities of the device with CC/PP, UAProf, or some other mechanism, is to use RPC-based communication to communicate the capabilities of the device back and forth among the device, the nodes that it communicates with on the network, and the provisioning server responsible for sending it the right version of the application based on its capabilities. This has the following benefits:

1. The usage of mobile agents and their properties to adapt the state and behavior of the application (which could be the mobile agent itself or otherwise) to the device reduces the complexity of the entire system. The complexity of provisioning is reduced, the complexity of the repository of the devices and their capabilities are reduced, and the number of transactions among the different components of the system is reduced.
2. The network traffic between the device and the network is reduced, thereby saving precious bandwidth, which is most probably provided using an intermittent wireless connection to the network.

We have now seen how mobile agents can help us with problems of mobile computing. Let us look at techniques that we can use to build agents.

9.6 Techniques for Agent-Based Software

We have talked a lot about the basics of mobile agents, looked at some mobile agent platforms that can come in handy in developing mobile applications, seen some samples of how to write basic agents, learned how to use UML to model the behavior of mobile agents, and briefly reviewed some possible benefits of using mobile agents to build mobile applications. But, thus far, we have laid out no basic plan of attack or strategy on how to do this. The fact is that there are very few techniques such as design patterns and architectural patterns for mobile application development because the field is much younger than that of centralized and client–server computing. And using mobile agents for mobile computing efforts is an even younger field of endeavor. Nevertheless, there are some significant research efforts that suggest some generic techniques in building agent-based software with applications to mobile computing.

The first and simplest question to be answered is whether we should use mobile agents for our mobile application at all. Besides the factors that we have mentioned previously (such as QOS concerns) Grassi et al. [Grassi et al. 2002] define an analogy that should be considered when looking at mobile agent solutions for mobile application problems. First, let us break down the problem into functional chunks that communicate with one another (such functionality chunks may have an *n* to 1 mapping to mobile agents). Now, let us assume that these functional chunks are people. A key question to ask is whether the people in the system can collaborate more efficiently through writing letters or whether the collaboration is more efficient if they visit each other and talk. This analogy is overly simple and is meant to be applied to mobile code rather than mobile agents. However, we can apply it to mobile agents and it is indeed powerful for both mobile agents and mobile code. This is a simple litmus test that can show us the type of interactions, and therefore implied QOS concerns and other factors, required to deliver a successful application. Once you get past the simple litmus test of whether or not to use mobile agents to solve the problem, then we need to address "how" we implement the agents.

Yim et al. [Yim et al. 2001] outline a development methodology that leverages UML-based methodologies and existing design patterns; unfortunately, it does not use any of the various UML extensions, and the ideas behind those extensions, that we have introduced in this text. Yim et al. point out the following principles in designing mobile agent systems:

1. Multiagent structure consists of agents having roles of components and connectors.
2. An agent is a primitive building block for the design of multiagent systems.
3. Architecture-centric design favors pattern-based mechanism over inheritance.

We have looked at the idea of roles several times throughout this chapter. The second principle basically points out that when we are designing the agent-based application, we should not be concerned with the internal implementation of the agent. Rather, the agent should be represented by some abstract or wrapper class that completely models the external interface and usage of the agent. Then, Yim points out the fact that usage of aggregation and composition is preferred over inheritance when dealing with agents (in fact, many argue this is true in general for object-oriented programs). Whereas composition versus inheritance has fueled many heated discussions throughout the object-oriented design community, using inheritance becomes less attractive when dealing with agents as it adds rigidity to large-grained component structures where each component (agent) may encapsulate many complex behaviors and states and assume roles that depend on communications with other agents. Yim introduces some UML extensions to model various types of component-wise substitution that display this preference of substitution over specialization of agents and components of agent-based systems.

Although there is no prevailing consensus on what modeling tool should be used in design and development of mobile agents, nearly all research and development done in the mobile agent arena points out the absolute need for modeling structures and interactions of agents because of their complexity. Obviously, we recommend the usage of UML and the extensions that we have introduced in this chapter to accommodate this design.

There is also the matter of code generation. Although we have repeatedly questioned the over usage of code generation for user interface parts of mobile systems, it is very plausible that, other than the user interface code, everything else may have to be generated. In fact, code generation may be particularly attractive in the case of mobile agents because of the degree of complexity involved in implementation of even those agents that perform moderately complicated tasks. There are currently several tools in the marketplace that generate code based on UML diagrams but none that provide any support for mobile agents and associated behaviors. Whatever code-generation tools that arise in this area must be able to support FIPA and OMG standards that specify functionality and interoperability standards for mobile agents and their supporting infrastructure.

If you are interested in implementing your own code-generation technology for mobile agents, Sparkman et al. [Sparkman et al. 2001] present some techniques that can be a good starting point.

To date, techniques for design, development, and implementation of mobile agent systems for mobile applications remain in an adolescence stage. Design and architectural patterns for mobile agents should become pertinent in time as they are developed, utilized, and evolved.

Before we end this chapter, let us take a quick look at peer-to-peer application infrastructures and how they are leveraged for mobile application development.

9.7 Peer-to-Peer Applications for Mobile Computing

We gave a brief introduction of peer-to-peer concepts in Chapter 1. To remind the reader, one can think of a peer-to-peer network of networks as networks of decentralized systems (devices, applications, etc.) where the systems communicate and collaborate as equal members. Note that in client–server computing, the server provides services and the client requests services. So, in peer-to-peer, any peer can serve both as a client and a server. Of course, there are numerous such collaborations based on the peer-to-peer infrastructure, the range of capabilities of the participating systems, and a host of other factors. Nevertheless, we can use this gross generalization to see the relationship between peer-to-peer computing and mobile computing. The important thing to note here is that peers communicate with RPC-like mechanisms; unlike for mobile agents, there is no migration of applications required in peer-to-peer computing.

9.7.1 The Basics

There are three styles of peer-to-peer communication: one-to-one, one-to-many, and many-to-many. As may be implied from their names, they indicate the accessibility of the participating peers in the network. In the mobile computing case, two PDAs can communicate directly through the infrared port or a TCP connection (one-to-one), one PDA can communicate with another PDA and a PC (one-to-many), or we can have many PDAs and PCs communicating (many-to-many).

Peer-to-peer networks have a variety of desirable properties for mobile applications. These include the following:

1. They provide better fault tolerance through introducing more fail-over points.
2. They lower the latencies by allowing for peers to provide services to one another.
3. As we will see in later chapters, peer-to-peer networks offer some unique properties that can be useful in providing location-based services.
4. They provide an excellent platform for building mobile agent frameworks. Because peer-to-peer networks typically provide a standard communication protocol for the peers as well as a predefined set of functionality for the applications using such protocols, much of the specification for what hosts are responsible for is addressed within the peer-to-peer architecture.
5. They provide a natural provisioning mechanism for delivery of mobile code to the mobile device even if the mobile code is not being used as a mobile agent or within a mobile agent framework.
6. They provide high scalability and availability for data replication. Peer-to-peer replication is particularly well suited for maintaining replicated data in a mobile environment [Reiher et al. 1996]. Imagine if you have several devices, each getting wireless connectivity through a different network. If these devices are joined in a peer-to-peer network, they can collaborate in providing each other with synchronization and replication of data more effectively than a client–server scheme where the server may be unavailable or out of date because of network QOS problems on one or some of the sources that modify data.

Of course, these are not the only benefits of peer-to-peer mobile computing, just a few important ones.

One way to establish a peer-to-peer network with mobile devices is to put a Web server on every peer. This has given rise to a multitude of efforts to create so-called micro Web servers: Web servers for very small devices with some minimal HTTP server functionality. These micro Web servers exist for a variety of mobile operating systems including Windows CE, Symbian, and Palm.

Like mobile agents, the biggest downfall of peer-to-peer-based systems is security. The lack of a centralized server introduces possible holes in the security scheme. However, these problems are dealt with in a fairly easy manner by moving to a hybrid model where there are one or more servers that act as a registry and provide security functionality to the rest of the peers.

9.7.2 JXTA

JXTA stands for "juxtapose"; it is the peer-to-peer networking protocol supported by the Java platform. JXTA allows peers to discover each other, self-organize into groups, communicate, monitor other peers, and discover network resources.

The JXTA protocol's reference implementation is open source and it only defines a set of interfaces. JXTA is language independent, so peers can be authored in any language and not just Java.

JXTA creates a taxonomy of the components and services for peer-to-peer computing that include the following:

1. *Peers and the services that they offer*: JXTA defines a minimal interface for an application to qualify as a peer and provides the interfaces for introducing its services. JXTA components are addressed through a URN-based format like urn:jxta:uuid-22222AAAA444444444AAAA or a URI-based format like jxta://mypeer/pipeId. It is important to note that there is no centralized server keeping track of security or naming.
2. *Advertisement and discovery*: JXTA allows for publishing and discovery of services. It is important to note that the actual behavior to be invoked may be done through a Web service protocol such as SOAP or other communication protocols such as RMI depending on the type of available network infrastructure and security concerns. JXTA defines an XML DTD for creating XML documents that "advertise" the resources engaged in the JXTA-based peer-to-peer network. Peers are advertised by a peer id, a group id, a name, a description, and parameters that identify public end points and the services offered by the peer. Channels are advertised by a name, an id, and a type and can be unicast (one-to-one), secure unicast (secure one-to-one), or one-to-many.
3. *Exchange of messages among peers*: Messages are propagated by embedding the propagation information into the message itself. *Rendezvous peers* provide the propagation of messages within groups. For a peer to send a message, it must obtain a lease from a rendezvous peer.
4. *Pipes*: These are basically communication channels among the peers. They are unidirectional and asynchronous, thereby allowing the maximum amount of flexibility in messaging peers. Pipes are established between end points. We can establish a single pipe between an initiating end point and another end point or many pipes between the initiating end point and many other end points. The former provides the ability to do multicast-like messaging. SSL is supported for secure communication
5. *End points*: The end point is a concept used for routing of messages. This is because a message may take several hops before actually arriving at the destination.
6. *Groups*: These are logical assemblies of endpoints to provide proper routing functionality, security, and other functionality useful when dealing with large numbers of peers.

One of the most important things about JXTA is that it offers binding to TCP, BEEP, HTTP, and TLS (SSL) whereas most Web-service-based peer-to-peer technologies offer only binding to HTTP. BEEP is of particular interest as it has properties that can be quite useful. Another notable point is that the JXTA specification is actually fairly small, so its implementation on mobile devices is not prohibitive because of its size. Because JXTA assumes a great deal of XML-based communication, though, the XML parsing presents some technical difficulties in the more resource-starved devices. There is an implementation of the JXTA framework for J2ME called JXME. You can download the source code for this project at http://jxme.jxta.org.

There are also a variety of commercial vendors that provide JXTA-compliant peer-to-peer platforms (e.g., Endeavors Technologies, maker of the MAGI platform).

9.8 What Lies Ahead

Mobile agents have been around for several years now but they have not yet found their niche. Although the architecture is more complex than client–server computing, it does not offer much that client–server computing does not already accomplish with stationary applications running on wired and fairly reliable networks.

As mobile computing begins to flourish, mobile agent technology will begin to get the opportunity to achieve more widespread usage. For the first time, there is something that mobile agents can do better than client–server computing systems: They can provide the mobile user improved service in a network with poor continuous QOS. There are always those who contend that network QOS will not be a problem as networks improve. However, this is somewhat of a shallow perspective as mobile computing inherently produces QOS problems regardless of the viability and performance of the underlying wireless networks because physical obstacles such as a mountain or a concrete wall will always block a large portion of the signal, leaving the possibility of a poor QOS in connectivity to the network.

Implementations of mobile agents for mobile computing such as the LEAP project are very recent at the time of authoring this text. The question, and the opportunity, for the mobile agent enthusiasts will be whether these experimental implementations will deliver improved service to the user without posing new computing problems or making the mobile application implementations overly complex.

With current implementations of mobile agent platforms such as those that we have reviewed in this text, and those implementations planned for the near future based on current design ideas of mobile agents, it is possible to make a gross generalization: Choosing mobile agents for mobile applications makes sense if we have the necessary CPU and memory on the device to support a mobile agent platform and if the mobile agent platform is robust enough to support a variety of devices and agents that can move among hosts on very different types of devices and yet retain meaningful functionality. And, of course, there is always the ability of whether or not we can run a mobile agent platform on all of the devices required by a certain application: Some mobile devices provide more facilities to enable operation of a mobile agent platform (Palm, Windows CE, Symbian, etc.). Others, such as simple mobile phones that run very rudimentary operating systems, do not.

CHAPTER 10

Wireless Connectivity and Mobile Applications

The transparency of thought in existence is inwardness.

Søren Kierkegaard

10.1 INTRODUCTION

One of the first topics that we discussed in this text was the definition of mobility and how it differs from wireless connectivity. By definition wireless connectivity between a mobile device and another device requires a physical layer of networking technology. To cover all of the subjects that will allow one to comprehensively understand wireless connectivity and its currently existing permutations is impossible, not just in this text, but even in a dedicated text. One may require an entire library to gather all of the various topics on wireless connectivity and related inventions. So, the first thing that we might do is to reduce the scope of what wireless connectivity may mean in our discussion of mobile computing.

In this chapter, we will first look at a basic introduction to wireless communication that will include examples of techniques and technologies from the various abstraction layers in wireless communications.

We can qualify two types of connectivity to the network: *strong* and *weak*. We use the concept of strong and weak connections in various places in this text. Essentially, a weak connection refers to lower QOS than strong connectivity but higher than disconnection. This way of distinguishing weak and strong connections is fairly subjective and relative to the application. Unfortunately, because of the changing landscape of communications and computing, we cannot quantify the QOS properties of strong and weak connectivity. At present, connectivity to a wireless network through WIFI may be considered strong connectivity whereas connectivity through WAP 1.x may be considered weak connectivity. It is important to keep in mind that most mobile devices are not always strongly connected to the network because of their mobile nature regardless of the networking technology. The primary reason for making the distinction between weak and strong connectivity is to imply the importance of a mobile device being able to operate without network access; applications that are designed to be weakly connected to the network must place a greater importance on disconnected operation than those strongly connected. Although some networking technologies provide better connectivity under a certain set of physical circumstances (e.g., within a given radius of a transmitter), physical location and the surrounding environment make it so that the best case scenario is connectivity ranging from weak connectivity to strong connectivity and the worst case scenario is connectivity ranging from disconnection to weak connectivity.

Our focus in this text is on the design and implementation of mobile applications; therefore, the nature of the connectivity is what is most important to us: This factor is what we need to account for in our application. We will survey various wireless technologies so that you understand the ramifications of using a particular wireless technology for your application. We do not intend to address design and implementations of wireless technologies as, in and of themselves, they are orthogonal to design and implementation of a mobile application.

The other side of the equation comprises the requirements for our mobile applications that drive the required bandwidth. Figure 10.1 shows the type of functionality that a mobile application may offer and the rough bandwidth requirements associated with such functionality. Note that although we can use a variety of techniques to make things like video conferencing possible in lower bandwidth ranges, these techniques always come at a high resource cost on the device (because of compression using CPU, memory, etc. on the device) or cause significant loss of quality.

We will look at technologies that offer various ranges of bandwidth and the delivery of such bandwidth to the mobile device. Furthermore, we will look at the properties of these technologies and the type of required infrastructure for offering such connectivity.

We can create a variety of taxonomies of wireless networking technologies based on various criteria. In this introductory section, we will look at modulation techniques and transmission techniques as the two main methods for distinguishing the various types of wireless technology solutions.

10.1.1 Modulation Techniques

One method of categorizing the various wireless communication techniques is by using the modulation technique(s) that each may use. Electromagnetic waves are analog in nature—they are continuous. Therefore, they are digitally modulated so that we can encapsulate the digital data used by the computing devices in them.

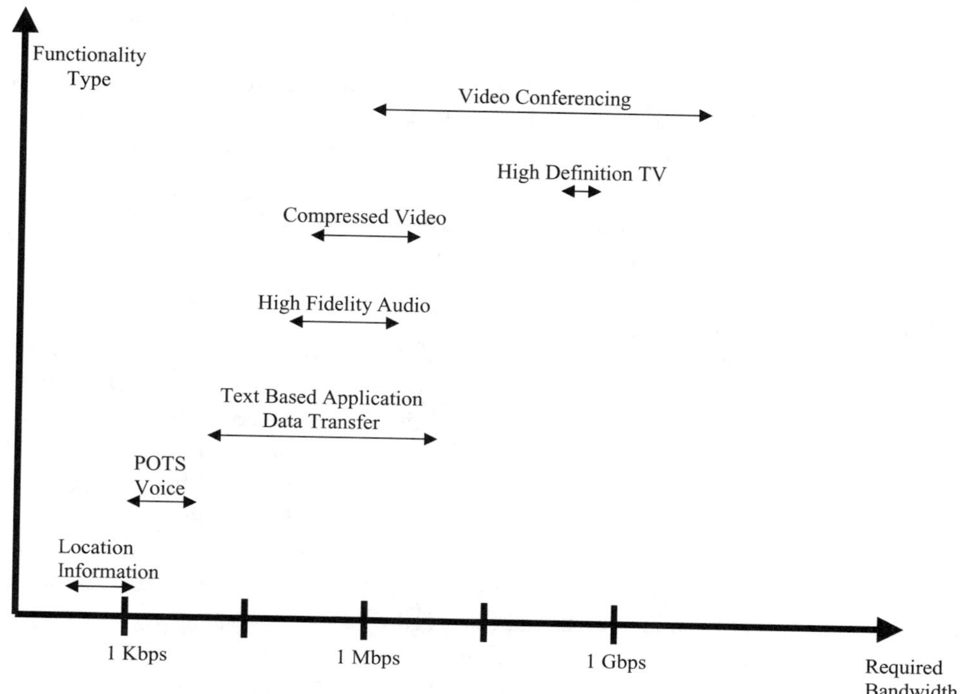

FIGURE 10.1. Spectrum of Functionality and Corresponding Required Bandwidth.

These modulation techniques each have their advantages and disadvantages, ranging from simple ones that provide minimal bandwidth efficiency and compression to complex ones that provide greater bandwidth efficiency and compression. For example, we can modulate electromagnetic waves by their amplitude: The amplitude of the wave may be used to contain the basic information needed to transmit. This type of modulation is called *amplitude modulation* (AM). If you have used a radio before, this is where the name of the AM channel on your radio comes from. Likewise, if we use the frequency of the signal to contain information, we call the modulation technique *frequency modulation* (FM), and hence the name of the FM channel on the radio. Some other modulation techniques are Minimum Shift Key (MSK), Gaussian Minimum Shift Key (GMSK), and a variety of Phase Shift Key (PSK) techniques. There are many textbooks, such as that authored by Lathi [Lathi 1989], in the field of communications engineering that discuss these digital communication techniques. This is not our concern in this text. However, these modulation techniques and their different properties are one of the main differentiators between the commercially available wireless communication systems such as CDMA, TDMA, CDPD for cellular wireless communication or IEEE 802.11 and other medium-ranged wireless communication systems.

What makes a basic awareness of these modulation techniques important is that the properties of each type of high-level wireless networking technology such as CDMA and TDMA stems from the basic properties of the modulation technique used. These properties include the *spectral efficiency* and *power efficiency* of the modulation technique, *complexity of modulating* in real time, *effectiveness of the modulation* technique within a given spectral frequency range, and *resiliency to interference*. Modulation techniques make up a large portion of the genetics of a wireless communication technique. Just like fiber optics inherently have a better capability for carrying data than a twisted pair of wires, some modulation techniques provide a better and more efficient transmission medium than others.

Next, we will look at a taxonomy of wireless communication systems based on the system of transmission and reception nodes.

10.1.2 Transmission Techniques

How we transmit and receive signals in a wireless network largely depends on the size and the environmental conditions of the coverage area in mind. Of course, the frequency range of the signal being transmitted is dictated both by these conditions and the necessary amount of bandwidth. The more bandwidth we need, the higher in the spectrum we should go: This helps us minimize the relative band of frequency that we are using. It should be noted that when making a graph that represents a large portion of the spectrum, we typically use a logarithmic scale. This is because the relative range occupied by a band is more relevant than the absolute range. It should also be noted that regardless of the type of wireless technology that we use, a rule of thumb is that the amount of bandwidth delivered to the receiving device from the transmitter decreases as the movement (speed) of the receiver increases. This relationship may be linear, exponential, or nonlinear in nature. In any case, the speed of the intended user is something that must be taken into consideration while bench-marking any wireless technology.

We can roughly divide today's commercially available wireless technologies into three categories by the nature of their transmission and reception of signal:

1. *Satellite-Based Wireless Communication*: Systems such as Iridium use a cluster of satellites to provide global wireless connectivity. The advantage of such systems is that coverage is available almost everywhere, whether in the Sahara Desert or in Beverly Hills. The two main disadvantages of satellite-based systems are their cost and the limitations on the bandwidth. Satellites are expensive to send into orbit, to maintain, to operate, and to replace. This cost, of course, is transferred to the end user. Also, at present, the bandwidth available through satellite communication is considerably less than that available with other methods. This is because all of the users are using the same frequency range and, because the coverage is global, we cannot reuse the channel(s) in different geographical locations. There are three types of satellite-based wireless communication systems: Low Earth Orbit (LEO), Medium Earth Orbit (MEO), and Geosynchronous Earth Orbit (GEO).
2. *Cellular Wireless Communication*: The major concept behind cellular communication is to divide and concur. An area is broken down into many cells (see Figure 10.2). Each cell can communicate with its neighboring cells. Cellular communication dominates today's deployments of long-range wireless communication systems. The cells "hand off" the connected devices based on the location of the connected device and the distribution of the load across the

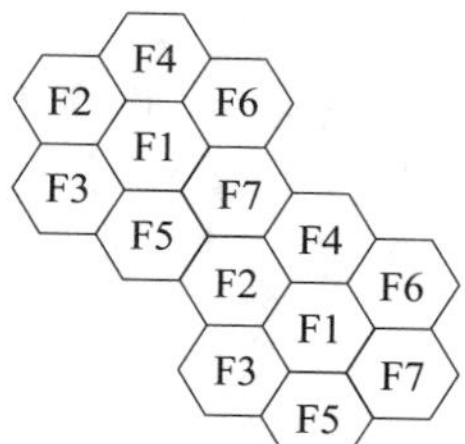

FIGURE 10.2. Covering a Geographical Area with a Cellular Network.

cellular network. Also, the cellular structure of such wireless communication systems allows us to implement other features such as location detection using triangulation (which we will discuss later in this text). In addition to cellular technologies, there are *microcellular* wireless technologies. Microcells are popular in Japan in highly populated areas. Microcells make sense where the density of use is extreme. They have several advantages over typical cellular systems: switches are less expensive, base stations are smaller, antennas are smaller, hand-off capability is better, and they can offer higher bandwidths [Katz 1995]. The distinction between microcellular and cellular technologies is slowly fading. Microcells typically cover a 100-meter range, about the same range as some WLANs. So, in effect, WLANs become a competitor to microcells; frankly, they are a better alternative as they offer IP-based networking. Also, although the individual microcell stations costs less, the maintenance of hundreds of base stations is very labor intensive. These labor costs, in time, make microcells as expensive or more expensive than alternative cellular technologies.

3. *Short-Range Transmission*: These technologies include anything from IrDA using infrared range frequencies to the 802.11 standard. The idea here is that the standard is specifying transmission of a signal, between two peers or in a radio-broadcast manner, in a small geographic area. Just like radio towers, we can have wireless transmission nodes that cover a radial area to provide service to all devices within the circle of coverage. Bluetooth, 802.11 standards, and a series of other WLAN (wireless local area network) and WPAN (wireless personal area network) standards fall within this category. Then we can cluster the small coverage areas together to cover a larger area. Though this technique, at first glance, may seem similar to cellular transmission, there are very distinct differences. For example, there is typically no coordinated cooperation among the transmitters, in this model, to provide handoffs (though 802.11 standards are now actually adding this). Rather, larger networks are built with the smaller networks based on concepts such as scatternets, which we will discuss later in this chapter. Also, the area of coverage of each node is considerably smaller than that of a typical cell in a cellular telephony system. There is a wide range of base technologies used to build short-range wireless communication systems. We will discuss a fair sampling of these technologies.

Obviously, there are other types of wireless technologies. However, for the purposes of our discussion about mobile application development (software), we will stick with these three types of networks as they comprise what we are most concerned with. Before delving into a discussion of the individual networking technologies though, let us discuss the concept of QOS, which we introduced to be a dimension of mobility in Chapter 1. The ideas surrounding the QOS of connectivity provided by the network affect the design and implementation of mobile applications immensely.

10.2 Quality of Service

As we have mentioned throughout this text, the QOS in connecting to an underlying network, particularly through a wireless connection, is one of the dimensions of mobility: things that make mobile applications fundamentally different from their stationary counterparts. But how is it that QOS affects our mobile application design and what measures do we need to take into account in the design and implementation of our mobile application to compensate for these effects? The answer to this question will be the topic of the discussion in this section. To start, let us look at some main points:

1. *Failure and Recovery Mechanism*: Because variable QOS means that the reliability and robustness of the communication between the device and the world surrounding it are variable, then we need to be able to recover from failures when they occur. Although the wireless networking infrastructures take into account these failures, the mobile application itself also must know how to treat failures and/or failure and recovery messages bubbled up from the network layer.
2. *Variable Bandwidth*: Although we may lose connection altogether, more frequently, we will see variable bandwidth in a wireless network. A mobile application must take into account this variable bandwidth and further be able to optimize the use of available bandwidth.
3. *Computing Distribution*: Networks of mobile devices are inherently distributed. How the various tasks of computing are divided throughout the different devices and what is communicated among the different participants in the network should take into account QOS. Take for example a mobile application that has an adaptable user interface. For the more powerful mobile devices and with poor network connectivity, the application may decide to download the specialization components to receive the minimal information needed to render a user interface when the QOS conditions are particularly poor. Likewise, if we have built our mobile application on top of a mobile agent framework, the mobile agents' migration patterns may directly depend on the amount of bandwidth available.
4. *Discovery Mechanism*: Every wireless technology provides a mechanism by which the mobile device intending to connect to the network discovers the network and transmits to it (or vice versa). In any case, there has to exist a discovery mechanism by which the sender and receiver of the signal find each other and then transmit and receive. One of the keys we have to consider in building our mobile application is whether this discovery mechanism is always on or whether it is variable depending on QOS conditions.

5. *Variable Latency*: Because there is probably some higher level protocol such as TCP/IP that delivers digitized data on top of lower level communication protocols used by the wireless network such as CDMA, the latency in the arrival of the chunks of data (packets in the case of TCP/IP) is unpredictable. Based on the usage of the network, the bandwidth available to the device at its geographical location, and a series of other factors, latency is variable. The mobile application designer must be aware of this fact.
6. *Performance Feedback*: A distributed application that uses a wireless network to transfer information among its pieces can itself change the QOS of the network. For example, if we put too much communication load in one part of the network, we may actually worsen data loss and latency problems. The behavior of a distributed mobile application running on a wireless network, then, directly affects the condition of the network as does the condition of the network affect the performance of the application.

The solution to each of these problems largely depends on the architecture we decide to choose for implementing our system. For example, failure may be detected by a mobile agent and be communicated to our mobile application based on a client–server architecture, which has recovery built into it. The point is that we have to think about QOS as we design and implement the application. Another example of a solution to these problems can be seen in the WAP gateway model, where the gateway is responsible for addressing much of the QOS problems.

To understand QOS, we need to define it a bit more. For this, we need to create a model of all of those variables that are the properties of QOS. In other words, QOS is an aggregate of a bunch of different properties in the network and we need to determine what these properties are. The right question to ask is probably what type of properties define QOS because the actual breakdown of the properties can be somewhat subjective and depend on the model we use to represent the properties of the wireless network itself (see Section 10.3.3).

The first place we can look to is the UMTS specifications and documents where special attention has been paid to QOS.

UMTS breaks down QOS into five classes as follows:

1. *Traffic*: QOS is measured, at the most rudimentary level, by the fundamental characteristics of handling of traffic such as packet loss. So, the analysis of traffic gives us the most basic qualification of QOS.
2. *Conversational*: When two entities, a sender and a receiver, are exchanging information through a channel, there are further requirements such as timing. For example, for voice and video, we have to guarantee a degree of certainty in the temporal behavior of the packets in addition to the integrity of the data.
3. *Streaming*: Multimedia streams have yet more stringent requirements on the temporal behavior of the data channel. So, there are additional properties of the channel that help us in qualifying the QOS.
4. *Interactive*: HTTP transactions like those that run the WWW dominate many of the network-based transactions. These types of transactions and their stateless request–response nature are unique. The requirements are less stringent then

the conversational interactions between two nodes. UMTS recognizes these types of exchanges between two nodes as interactive and recognizes the fact that the QOS that concerns them must be qualified uniquely.

5. *Background*: Whereas conversational, streaming, and interactive exchanges between two nodes all have temporal requirements, there are transactions that do not require specific timing. These exchanges are typically background transactions in the mobile world. They have much less stringent requirements on the QOS because we can have indefinite retries to accomplish the necessary tasks.

Furthermore, ITU-T X.641 defines a taxonomy for the network and the elements that make up the definition of QOS. Although there are other standards and frameworks that attempt to do the same, we will use the ITU-T QOS model. In the next section, we will look at this model translated to UML diagrams and extensions as represented by Asensio, Villagra, Vergara, and Berrocal [Asensio et al. 2001].

10.2.1 Modeling QOS with UML

Because QOS can have a great effect on the desired behavior of the mobile application, it is very helpful if we can model it in UML. In this way, not only can we properly model and document the structure and behavior of the systems that provide network connectivity and hence exhibit QOS properties, but we also can tie QOS-related behavior and data to the rest of our mobile application.

There are two scenarios in which UML is useful for us:

1. When the infrastructure that provides the application-layer, communication layer, and the supporting protocols are object oriented. In this case, we can model the interface (to such an application-layer communication protocol) with UML and follow this by representing the QOS qualities of such a network with UML. An example would be if we have a Java RMI implementation on top of a TDMA network. For this type of a situation, we will leverage the work by Asensio, Villagra, Vergara, and Berrocal [Asensio et al. 2001] that introduces UML extensions to represent QOS properties.
2. When we use UML to model the QOS properties of the network while treating the network as one subsystem. We can model the behavior of the networking system and its QOS properties using state diagrams, component diagrams, and other artifacts that focus on representing the behavior of the system as observed externally. Also, we can use interaction diagrams, collaboration diagrams, and sequence diagrams to show any significant interaction taking place between the mobile application and the underlying wireless networking infrastructure and its QOS properties or behaviors.

Asensio and his colleagues attack the problem by creating two UML profiles based on the ITU-T QOS taxonomy. Keep in mind that these two profiles attempt to describe problems, and solutions to problems, of QOS at the application level. Also, note that a good portion of these solutions (class diagrams, etc.) are only valid when we can apply an object-oriented model to the solution because UML is designed primarily to represent design and implementation of object-oriented

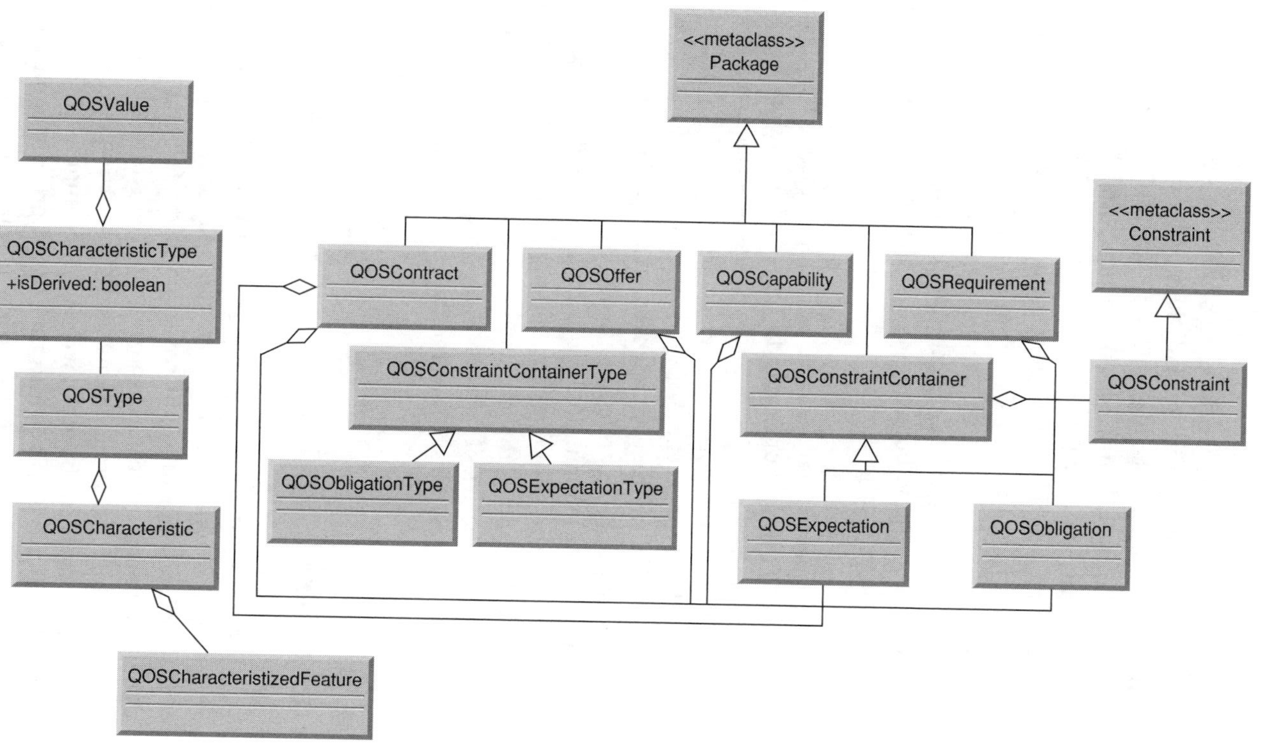

FIGURE 10.3. Basic UML Metamodel of UML-Q.

systems (though it can be used to represent other types of systems). The solution is offered by creating the following two UML profiles, which essentially provide new UML metamodels to extend the UML [Asensio et al.]:

1. UML-Q allows us to specify QOS requirements and properties (at design time) such as how long it should take to obtain the results of the invocation of a method of a particular object of an application. UML-Q metamodel focuses on the types of QOS information that can be described by UML, how such information can be represented with UML classifiers, and how these classifiers can be related and combined. The UML-Q metamodel is created mainly by using OCL to define these notions. Figure 10.3 shows a basic representation of UML-Q with a class diagram.
2. UML-M focuses on specifying that QOS requirements are satisfied at run time. Monitoring QOS properties and behaviors is half the problem because we need a way to measure these properties and then communicate these measurements.

Like the other UML extensions that we have introduced in this text, many tools such as Object Domain's UML tool or Borland's TogetherJ will allow you to implement your own extensions by creating custom widgets described by meta-models (preferred), using OCL, or using both together.

Let us refocus. All of this discussion of QOS, its properties, and its modeling has but one intention: to define the dependencies of mobile applications on QOS of the network (most probably a wireless network), to properly treat the various conditions of QOS in the implementation of our mobile application, and to create clean decoupling between the core of the mobile application and the parts that treat QOS issues using the models that we have introduced or similar models.

Next, we will survey the basics of wireless technologies that comprise the underlying networks providing wireless voice and data services to most of the devices currently on the market.

10.3 Survey of Wireless Networking Technologies

As promised, we will now survey various wireless networking technologies used for mobile computing. We will break these technologies into three categories, by the geographical distances that they can cover: short range, medium range, and long range. When comparing these categories, you will find that the coverage area of wireless technologies is typically inversely proportional to the maximum amount of bandwidth provided. In other words, long-range wireless networking technologies typically offer less bandwidth than the short-range ones. One of the reasons for this is that the longer the range of the wireless networking technique, the larger the coverage area is and hence the higher the number of probable connected devices there are. Another reason is that maintaining a good SNR at higher frequencies requires more transmission power. Also, our survey is not comprehensive and is very much susceptible to obsolescence as it revolves more around specific technologies than design concepts. We will not discuss medium-range wireless technologies in this section. What we refer to as medium-range wireless is covered by wireless metropolitan area networks. The IEEE 802.16 standard, which addresses these groups of networks, is being worked on at the time of authoring this. We will start by looking at a few short-range wireless technologies and work our way into the longer range ones.

10.3.1 Short-Range Wireless

How we define short range is very subjective. Within the context of this text, we will define short-range wireless networking technologies as all of those with a range equal to or less than the range specified by IEEE 802.11 and 802.15 specifications. These will include WLANs and WPANs. These two standards are a subset of the IEEE 802 project, which includes a large spectrum of networking standards in the local area network and metropolitan area network domains such as Ethernet, Token Ring, and others.

Short-range wireless technologies are a rapidly developing field. Leeper recognizes the reasons for this growth as the following [Leeper 2001]:

1. There is a growing demand for wireless data capability in portable devices at higher bandwidth and with lower cost and power consumption than that envisioned for third-generation cellular devices.
2. There is a crowding in the radio spectra that regulatory authorities segment and license in traditional ways.
3. There is tremendous growth of high-speed wired access to the Internet in enterprises, homes, and public spaces.
4. Both the cost and power consumption for signal processing of semiconductors are shrinking.

Short-range wireless networks, connected to one another to cover wide area network (WAN)-size areas, are sometimes referred to as "hot spots." WIFI, or Wireless Fidelity, is a term used to refer to the various short-range wireless networking technologies specified by IEEE 802.11; it does not refer to all short-range wireless technologies.

With the exception of Bluetooth, current state-of-the-art short-range wireless specifications address only data, typically in the format of TCP/IP or some other IP-based technology. Though we can always use voice-over IP or alternative solutions for transmission of voice over a data channel, one of the areas in need of more research and development is support for voice in short-range wireless networks.

We will start this section by looking at Bluetooth and then look at the IEEE 802.11 standard. There are other important technologies, but our intention is to look at the most prevalent and these are the two key players.

Bluetooth

Bluetooth is a short-range wireless networking technology designed to provide an infrastructure for application-layer ad hoc networking. In the case of Bluetooth, short-range is defined as approximately 10 meters (approximately 33 feet). Bluetooth is specifically designed to take into account the requirements of both voice and data transmission, so it is very well suited for short-range multichannel communication. Finally, the other very important part of the Bluetooth [Bluetooth] specification is that it is designed to enable ad hoc networking. In other words, various Bluetooth-enabled devices can connect to one another in an ad hoc manner. In this section, we are aiming only to give a short introduction to Bluetooth. Our purpose is to provide enough information so that you can recognize how Bluetooth and the functionality that it offers may be relevant to your project.

The Bluetooth specification was designed by the Bluetooth SIG (Special Interest Group) as a joint effort among several different commercial entities including Ericsson, Nokia, IBM, Intel, and Toshiba corporations. With its origins deeply embedded in the Scandinavian countries, Bluetooth gets its name from King Harald Blatand (which means Bluetooth in English and refers to his dark complexion), the king of Denmark more than 1,000 years ago. Historically, the Bluetooth SIG was first officially formed in 1998 and intended to solve several problems including specifying an air interface, an application-layer protocol stack, and an interoperability specification. Since then, the SIG has reorganized several times and is composed of several different working groups. Today, Bluetooth is also supported by the IEEE. Specifically, it is covered under the IEEE 802.15 specification, where the concepts of WPANs is covered. The key idea of these personal area networks (PANs) is to allow connectivity among a set of devices located within the radius of a user's "personal operating space" while keeping the implementation cost and power usage to a minimum.

Although 802.15 is a superset of Bluetooth specifications, and although these efforts began separately, they have now merged and the Bluetooth specification is now part of the IEEE 802.15. Currently, IEEE 802.15 is broken into six different task groups, the first of which focuses on Bluetooth. The specifications of the first task group is also referred to by IEEE 802.15.1.

Let us look at the specification of the physical communication among Bluetooth-enabled devices. Bluetooth operates on the 2.56-GHz ISM band and uses Frequency Hop Spread Spectrum (FHSS) and GFSK modulation. Bluetooth receivers must be sensitive to signals as low as –70 dBm. Bluetooth devices are sometimes referred to as "rude radios" because they do not check to see if someone else is using the spectrum in that range. A Bluetooth radio simply broadcasts its messages radially 1,600 times per second. Frequency hopping occurs among seventy-nine channels (the number of channels into which the Bluetooth specification breaks its available spectrum).

The smallest PAN in Bluetooth is also referred to as a Piconet. A Piconet allows up to eight devices to be connected to one another (seven slaves and one master). The slaves use the master's clock to correctly perform hopping among different frequencies (FHSS). Scatternets are collections of up to ten Piconets. Amplifiers can be used to extend the reach of Bluetooth to as far as 100 meters (approximately 330 feet). Bluetooth signals are transmitted radially in all directions (also called omnidirectional); it does not require line-of-sight positioning of two peer units connecting to one another. Figure 10.4 shows the formation of a Bluetooth Scatternet.

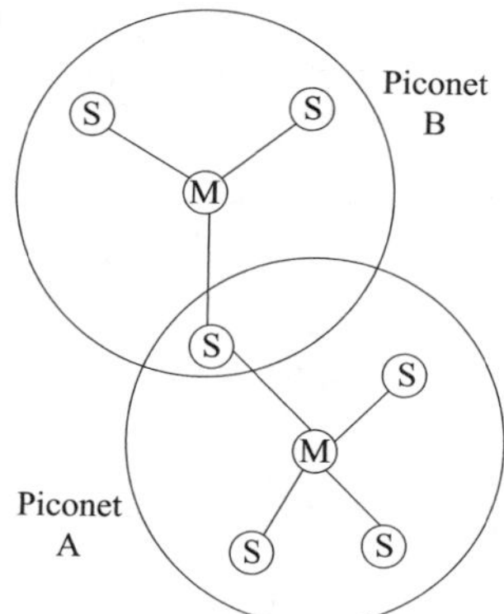

FIGURE 10.4. Formation of a Scatternet with Multiple Piconets.

The conceptual architecture of Bluetooth (see Figure 10.5) can be broken into the following eight parts [Bannon et al. 2002]:

1. *Bluetooth Baseband, LMP (Link Management Program), Radio*: This is basically the implementation specification for the hardware and the physical communication layer. This portion is implemented by the device manufacturers.
2. *HCI*: In this text, we have typically referred to HCI as a human-to-computer interface. Within the discussion of Bluetooth architecture, HCI refers to the abstraction between the hardware and the software layer. Basically, the HCI functionality is provided through device drivers. HCI within Bluetooth is really a HAL (Hardware Abstraction Layer).
3. *L2CAP* (*Logical Link Control and Adaptation Protocol*): This layer sits directly on top of the hardware abstraction layer. L2CAP is an adaptation layer for hiding the baseband protocols from higher layer transport protocols and applications [Bisdikian 1999].
4. *SDP*: Service Discovery Protocol (SDP) is a protocol that allows Bluetooth devices to discover the services that other Bluetooth devices are willing to share [Scott 2001]. SDP provides the basic functionality of discovery for ad hoc networking techniques implemented at the application layer.
5. *Serial Port Layer*: This layer provides RS232 [RS232 2003] emulation on the top of the physical layer implemented above.

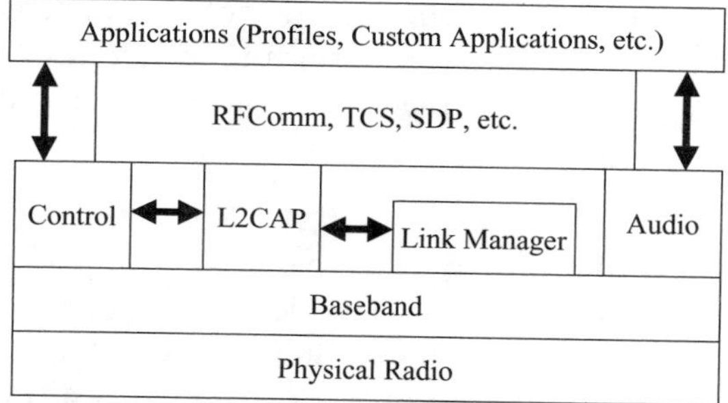

FIGURE 10.5. The Conceptual Architecture Model of Bluetooth.

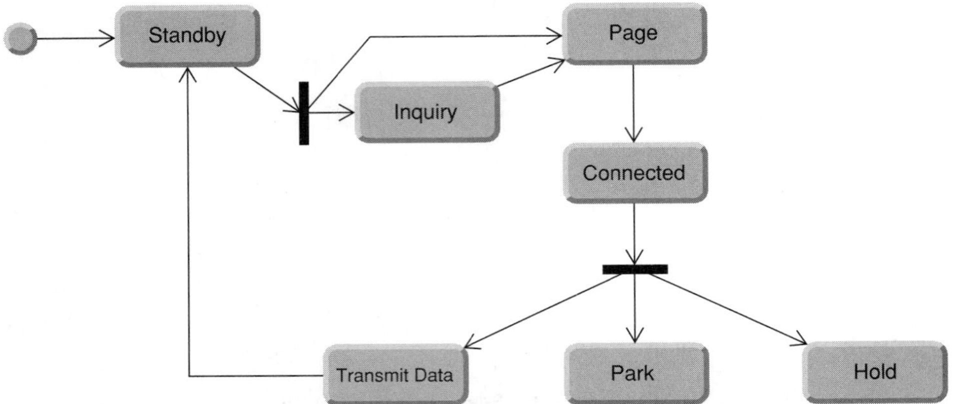

FIGURE 10.6. States of a Bluetooth Device.

6. *Network Layer*: This part of the stack provides data and voice channels. It is particularly important as this is the first part of the protocol that separates data access from voice access. PPP emulation as well as AT (Attention) commands (modems) are available.
7. *Internet Layer*: This part of the stack adds TCP/IP functionality. Because most networks today are based on TCP/IP, this is another crucial functionality as it allows Bluetooth to be fundamentally interoperable with other networking technologies that use TCP/IP.
8. *Application Layer*: This part of the stack simply specifies where the application using Bluetooth resides. This is our mobile application.

Once a Bluetooth-enabled device is turned on, it goes through a set of states, represented in Figure 10.6, to connect to a Piconet. These states are as follows:

1. *Standby*: The device is waiting to join a Piconet. This is the first phase of the discovery stage.
2. *Inquire*: The device broadcasts a signal and listens for responses to discover a radio to connect to. This is the second phase of discovery.
3. *Page*: Once a valid master is discovered, a page is sent to specify the master–slave relationship in the Piconet.
4. *Connected*: This is the state in which the device is connected to a Piconet and transacting with the other slaves or master in the Piconet.
5. *Park/Hold*: This is equivalent to the "power-save" mode in which the device is conserving as much power as possible.

This last state of Park/Hold brings us to the fact that Bluetooth gives a suitable treatment to the power constraints of mobile devices, one of the dimensions of mobility typically neglected with most mobile and wireless technologies. While in the standby mode, Bluetooth requires less than 0.3 mA, in the voice mode it requires from 8 to 30 mA, and in the data mode it requires an average of 5 mA with a peak of 30 mA and a low of 0.3 mA. In the Park/Hold mode, Bluetooth only requires 60 μA.

Bluetooth also gives full treatment to the problem of data synchronization, which is a result of intermittent connectivity to the network. We discuss this aspect of Bluetooth further in the next chapter, which focuses on topics related to data synchronization and replication. In fact, synchronization is one of the *profiles* of Bluetooth: the *synchronization profile*. Bluetooth profiles address certain usage domains of Bluetooth. For example, another profile is the *generic access profile*, which addresses the problem of interoperability with other networking technologies. Additionally, there is the *ultimate headset profile*, which specifies connectivity among various usages of Bluetooth-enabled wireless headsets for usage with computers or phones for audio. This profile is minimal and specifies call transfer and volume control. Some other profiles worth mentioning are the *dialup networking profile*, *cordless telephony profile*, *file transfer profile*, *LAN access profile*, and *fax profile*.

Depending on the mobile device, the operating system on the device, and how Bluetooth is used, the chunks of software are provided by different parties ranging from the device manufacturers, to third parties, to the carriers. Most of the functionality, though, is typically implemented by the device manufacturers. Typically, an independent software developer does not have much in the way of access to the device for adding functionality—we use what we can to build our application. It is important to note though that because some of the functionality we have mentioned is optional, some devices will provide implementation for part of the functionality whereas others will not. The important thing here is that, if you take advantage of Bluetooth's networking capabilities in your application and if you use any of the profiles, either make the application smart enough to gracefully discover what is offered by the device and what is not (RDF, CC/PP, UAProf, or some other mechanism) and/or understand the subset of Bluetooth-enabled devices on which your mobile application will be deployed and the functionality that they offer.

Though Bluetooth itself is not a LAN technology, we can build LANs based on Bluetooth. An example of this is an effort by the Siemens Research Group called *blu21*. The blu21 LAN access solution comprises access points and access server software; the access points are directly connected to the Ethernet; Bluetooth-enabled terminals are used to communicate with the access points [Goose et al. 2002]. In addition to addressing basic LAN functionality, this project also addresses user interface issues. As a side note, whereas blu21 is an interesting project that delivers a good architecture for networking Bluetooth devices together in a LAN, it is probably a bad idea to have inserted user interface issues into the scope of this particular project as it confuses the issues of user interface and networking. Nevertheless, blue21 represents a good example of how higher level networking functionality can be built on the basic, and very flexible, networking functionality offered by Bluetooth.

This brings us to the end of our discussion on Bluetooth 1.0. Bluetooth 2.0 is mostly new profiles and improvements to be made to the existing functionality of Bluetooth (faster data rates, more reliability, etc.) with no major changes to the base functionality. Bluetooth 2.0 will also be tackling the problem of possible

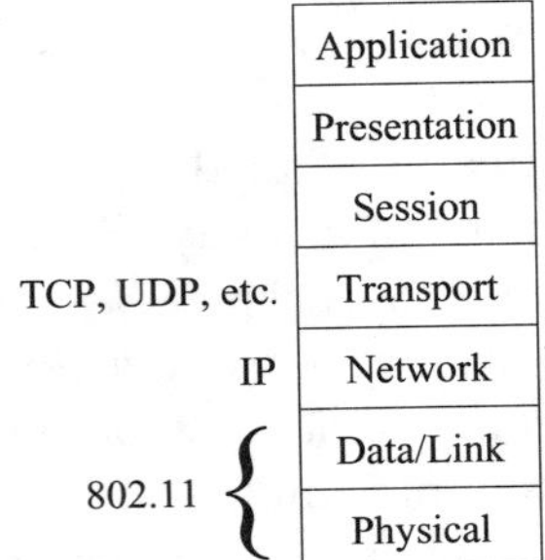

FIGURE 10.7. 802.11 Standard Coverage.

conflicts with other short-range wireless networking technologies that may operate in the same frequency range (which are currently unregulated by the FCC in the United States). Among the profiles with dedicated working groups in Bluetooth 2.0 will be working groups that address telematics (wireless communication, mobile devices, and locations services integrated into vehicles), multimedia-based communications between the network and the device, and closer integration of location information services into Bluetooth.

Bluetooth is the only short-range wireless networking technology to be used, in the real world, for mobile commerce (m-commerce) applications such as vending machines. Other uses of Bluetooth networking include mobile medical devices that collect biometrics and real-time data, home networking equipment, replacement of wired PC peripherals (such as a wired mouse with a wireless one) and synchronization with PDAs, and limited usage in short-range voice devices such as cordless phones. Bluetooth promises to be one of the most prominent short-range wireless technologies for years to come.

The 802.11 Standard

Figure 10.7 shows where the 802.11 standards sit on a stack relative to other layers of a communication system. There are currently a number of 802.11 standards available ranging from 802.11a to 802.11g. The IEEE 802.11 standard addresses WLANs. Because we are already familiar with Bluetooth and WPANs, let us begin defining WLANs by contrasting them to WPANs. First, as opposed to WPANs, which are designed for personal devices, WLANs can be used by either personal devices or by other devices that may be connected more conveniently through a wireless connection, mobile or stationary. WPANs such as Bluetooth are designed to get rid of wires in the work space of a single person. The range of coverage of WLANs is considerably larger spanning an entire building or even multiple buildings depending on the size of the building and the specific WLAN technology used. Also, as we have seen, there are limits to the number of participants in the Piconets and Scatternets of Bluetooth. WLANs are designed for both stationary and mobile systems whereas WPANs are designed primarily for very mobile systems. These limitations mainly exist because of the ad hoc application-layer networking behavior displayed by these systems and the fact that the participants in such networks are very mobile; WLANs do not exhibit these properties.

The 802.11 standard, like the wired Ethernet standard, is based on a bus topology. The difference is that the physical medium for the bus, in the wired world, consists of wires and a hub (or router). In the wireless world, there is still a hub or a router (typically referred to as a Wireless Access Point or WAP—not to be confused with the Wireless Access Protocol whose acronym is also WAP) that manages the traffic coming in and going out of the network but the bus is the space through which the waves propagate. Currently, there are three 802.11-based standards, namely 802.11a, 802.11b, and 802.11g, whose implementations are available commercially in the form of hubs and network cards. Let us review the different subgroups that exist within the 802.11 standards group:

1. 802.11a operates in the 5-GHz range and provides data rates between 6 Mbps (megabits per second) and 54 Mbps. Ironically, because 802.11a became commercially available after 802.11b, it is less prevalent.
2. The 802.11b standard uses the same frequency range as Bluetooth at 2.4 GHz. 802.11b divides the assigned band into fourteen 22-MHz channels that are assigned to access points. It provides data transmission rates of 5.5 Mbps to 11 Mbps.
3. The 802.11c working group is the group that produced the standard for how wireless access points used in the other 802.11x standards must operate.
4. Because the 5-GHz frequency range is regulated differently in various parts of the world, the 802.11d working group's job is to define and solve interoperability issues.
5. The 802.11e standard, in progress at the time of authoring this text, will address multimedia transmission over wireless connections. This is an area largely neglected by the other 802.11x standards because higher QOS requirements of video and audio and other concerns are not properly addressed.
6. The 802.11f protocol specification addresses the roaming need for transmission for a user from one access point to another and ensures the continuity of transmission; it would ultimately provide an inter–access point protocol [Vichr 2002].
7. 802.11g provides data rates of 20 Mbps on the same frequency range as 802.11b (2.4 GHz). Most 802.11g equipment is being manufactured to be backward compatible with 802.11b.
8. 802.11h is an extension of 802.11a to satisfy regulations in Europe for the spectrum band of 5 GHz by providing dynamic channel selection (DCS) and transmit power control (TPC) [Vichr 2002].

In an environment with several access points, the node searching for an access point chooses the access point based on signal strength and error rates.

IrDA

Infrared Data Associations (IrDA) is a short-range wireless technology that has been used for several years to provide PAN-like functionality. The major difference in the physical implementation between IrDA and Bluetooth is that it requires a clear line of sight with no physical obstacles in between the sending and receiving parties. Of course, IrDA also lacks all of the provisions for mobile computing made in the Bluetooth specification. Nevertheless, IrOBEX (Infrared Object Exchange) and IrMC (Infrared Mobile Connectivity), respectively the object exchange and synchronization mechanisms developed by IrDA, are actually used by Bluetooth as they hold years of proven service in consumer applications such as synchronization between handheld devices and PCs.

IrDA delivers transmission rates of 2,400 to 115,200 bps depending on the emitter, receiver, and the length and condition of space in between them. IrDA requires a clear line of sight between the transmitter and the receiver. The maximum reach of IrDA is specified to be 1 meter, though a subset of IrDA, low-power IrDA, has been defined for distances of 10 cm or less. Line of sight is approximated by a 30-degree window evenly distributed around a straight line between the transmitter and receiver (though the closer to 0 degrees, the closer we can get to the maximum range as transmission is radial). Data are transmitted asynchronously in the serial port format. Additional modulation techniques have been used to increase the data rate to 4 Mbps with CR-32 correction.

In addition to specifying the physical layer protocol, IrDA defines higher layer protocols. Because it was the first to establish such protocols, some of these are now being used by other short-range wireless protocols such as Bluetooth. They include IrDA Transport Protocol (Tiny TP), IrDA Object Exchange Protocol (IrOBEX), IrDA Infrared Link Access Protocol (IrLAP), IrDA Infrared Link Management Protocol (IrLMP), and IrDA Infrared Transfer Picture (IrTran).

IrDA is frequently used in synchronizing PDAs with PCs, PDAs with other PDAs, or other mobile devices and applications that can easily have line of sight. IrDA is typically used as a means of very occasional commands (such as in TV remote controls) or synchronization. It is not designed as a means for continuous transmission between two mobile devices because mobility breaks line of sight. During the transmission, the transmitter and the receiver have to be roughly stationary to provide the requirement of line of sight.

This brings us to the end of our discussion on short-range wireless networks. Next, we will look at long-range communication technologies.

10.3.2 Long-Range Wireless Communication

As in the case of short-range wireless communication, defining long-range wireless communication systems is difficult and subjective. For the purpose of our discussions in this text, we will define long-range wireless communication systems to be any wireless system that provides geographical coverage that exceed that of WLANs. This translates to a wide-ranging spectrum: anything from satellite communication to cellular telephony networks to clusters of WLANs that make up WANs or larger coverage areas. For the purpose of this section, let us eliminate satellite communication and wireless WANs that are made of clusters of WLANs (also referred to as hot spots). Our focus will be on cellular telephony technology that provides both voice and data transmission.

Most deployments of cellular wireless data networks today are either *packet switched* or *circuit switched*. Circuit-switched networks can deliver data rates ranging between 9.6 and 14.4 Kbps (this is the average legacy network installed in the

United States and Europe). They use a single voice channel for transmission of data for every connected mobile device. Circuit-switched networks are continuously connected to a single routing connection. This design came about because they have mainly been designed to provide a voice channel and this is a good way to treat voice, which tends to be a continuous stream.

In contrast, packet-switched networks send and receive bursts of data to and from the network. Each burst contains a sequence number, allowing creation of the blocks of data once all data are sent [Stemberger 2002]. The fact that the bandwidth is not completely occupied by one device at all times allows packet-switched networks to use the available bandwidth more efficiently (despite there being some small inherent inefficiency in the packetizing things such as header packets, etc.).

GSM, which we will look at in this section, is a standard for circuit-switched networks. Of course, various compression and modulation techniques can be used to increase the data transmission rate, but the rate of transmission at the physical layer is limited by the frequency range of transmission, the bandwidth allocated for the channel, and the switching technology used.

CDPD

Cellular Digital Packet Data (CDPD) was first created by McCaw Cellular and IBM. CDPD uses GMSK modulation. It provides a data network layer on top of analog cellular telephony systems using 30-kHz channels at the 800-MHz frequency range and provides up to 19.2 kbps of digital bandwidth on an IP-based infrastructure. CDPD is actually fairly impressive in that it offers a considerable amount of bandwidth and IP support on top of *analog* cellular telephony. Note the following:

1. *Mobile End Station* (*M-ES*): In our case, this is basically the mobile device that is connected to the system through a wireless connection (PDAs, cell phones, laptops, etc.).
2. *Mobile Data Intermediate Systems* (*MD-IS*): The MD-IS provides mobile routing using the Mobile Network Location Protocol (MNLP). This subsystem is responsible for locating the end stations (where the wireless devices are connected to the network) and routes the data to the proper network node.
3. *Fixed End Systems* (*F-ES*): This subsystem typically includes accounting, connects to billing systems, authenticates the end systems upon connection, authorizes them to use the appropriate functionality offered by the network provider, and manages the routing of data among the fixed points in the network infrastructure.
4. *Mobile Data Base Station* (*MD-BS*): The MD-BS stations are located at the same place as the cellular voice equipment and provide allocation of frequencies and modulation on top of the analog voice signal provided by the analog voice equipment. They also provide the ability to hop among different frequencies as requested by the analog telephony equipment.

Today, CDPD is primarily deployed on top of TDMA, pairing two analog or digital TDMA voice frequency channels for one CDPD channel at the physical layer. Note that CDPD is a network layer protocol. Its two main competitors are proprietary protocols that are built on top of CDMA, TDMA, and other basic networking technologies that specify physical layer protocols and Mobile IP. CDPD and GSM do not really compete because CDPD only addresses data; GSM addresses a much larger superset of concerns including voice. Whereas Mobile IP promises to be more prevalent than CDPD deployments in the future, there are quite a few legacy TDMA-based CDPD networks still in existence. We will discuss Mobile IP in more detail later in the chapter. The CDPD system component deployment is very similar to what you will see with Mobile IP; both have a home agent system and an attachment agent system. Mobile IP and CDPD differ mainly in the messages being passed back and forth among these system components, the content they encapsulate, and the higher level protocols used to specify the arrangement of the messages in a meaningful transaction among the system components.

Next, we will look at TDMA, a lower layer protocol on top of which many CDPD deployments are built.

TDMA

TDMA, or Time Division Multiple Access, basically multiplexes the usage of a given frequency channel to multiple users by time. In other words, in a given span of time interval Δt, if there are n devices connected, each device is allotted an equal time interval of $\Delta t/n$ or a weighted time interval of $w\,\Delta t/n$.

Commercially speaking, TDMA and CDMA are the two major competitor's in the cellular telephony market today.

CDMA and Its Variations

Code-Division Multiple Access (CDMA) technology, developed by Qualcomm, uniquely encodes every data session (every connection to a mobile client), allowing the now famous analogy of "multiple conversations at the same time but in different languages" as multiple mobile devices are transmitting at the same time and on the same frequencies. CDMA is a competing technology to GSM. Because Qualcomm owns most of the patents on CDMA-related base technologies, typically an implementation of a part of CDMA means paying some royalty fees to Qualcomm. Although some consider CDMA to be a technically superior technology to TDMA, on which most current GSM-based systems are built, this sole ownership of CDMA, along with the ever-improving TDMA standards, has made it difficult for many carriers and device manufacturers to decide on which technology to use.

As its name implies, instead of using different frequency channels or time-based phase shifting, CDMA differentiates the connected users by coding the messages exchanged with each mobile device uniquely. This means that, ideally, all other conversations seem like simple noise to the two parties involved in one CDMA-based conversation. There are two types of basic CDMA technologies: those that use frequency hopping (FHSS) modulation and those that use direct sequence spread spectrum (DSSS) modulation. For this reason, devices that use CDMA typically have to have much more computing power than that needed for the other protocols and modulation techniques that we will talk about: Much of this computing power is spent coding and decoding messages. We will forego the details of FHSS and DSSS modulation techniques and their ramifications as they divert from our focus. Because of its design, CDMA lends itself very well to digital data–based messages. Critics of CDMA initially claimed that it would fail in the delivery of high-quality scalable voice solutions, but pervasive voice usage in the United States has dispelled this notion.

There are now variants on CDMA. These variants include Wideband CDMA (WCDMA). Voice, images, data, and video are first converted to a narrow-band digital radio signal; the signal is assigned a marker (spreading code) to distinguish it from the signal of other users; WCDMA uses variable rate techniques in digital processing and it can achieve multi-rate transmissions [Ericsson 2002]. Because WCDMA is designed to be used as a base technology for third-generation (3G) devices, 3G specifications address interoperability issues between GSM and WCDMA.

Another variation on CDMA is CDMA2000. CDMA2000 offers a CDMA migration path, beginning with CDMA2000 1X, at a maximum sub-3G data rate of 153.6 Kbps [Garber 2002]. The next step is the CDMA2000 1xEV-DV, which provides data rates of up to 614 Kbps and subsequently to CDMA2000 3x, providing a 3G-compliant data rate of 2.05 Mbps. The main difference between WCDMA and CDMA2000 is that WCDMA supports asynchronous base stations whereas CDMA2000 relies on synchronized base stations [Bahl 2002]. This means that CDMA2000 requires some external timing mechanism whose time is synchronized for all of the base stations. In this way, adjacent cells can use the same frequency ranges but use a different phase shifting to distinguish themselves (the signals being communicated to and from each cell).

Use of CDMA and its variations is growing because of their high bandwidths. In addition to Qualcomm, there are third-party licensees who manufacture CDMA handsets and other CDMA-based equipment. On a tangent note, BREW, a mobile application development platform that we discussed in earlier chapters, is available only for CDMA networks and takes particular advantage of CDMA, its variants, and the features that they offer.

Finally, there is a variation of CDMA called TD-SCDMA that is currently in experimental deployment in some East Asian countries.

Other Long-Range Base Technologies

Although CDMA and TDMA currently comprise the bulk of long-range cellular network deployments and continue to see increased usage, there are other technologies on the horizon. These technologies, as any technology should be, are driven by new requirements. Fourth-generation (4G) networks must not only offer more bandwidth and higher degrees of reliability from the network, but they also must have additional features, the most important of which is interoperability with short-range networks. For example, Orthogonal Frequency Division Multiplexing (OFDM) is beginning to gain attention in research circles as the tool to deliver large amounts of data. For example, IEEE 802.11a and 802.11g WLAN standards offer theoretical maximum speeds of 54 Mbps, with real-world data ranges of up to 22 Mbps; service providers are looking at OFDM for their broadband mobile services including those used in cellular phones and PDAs (long range and short range) to solve these problems [Vaughan-Nichols 2002]. OFDM utilizes techniques that are typically used in digital signal processing (such as fast Fourier transforms) to provide yet more efficient modulation of the signal for delivery of the data. Of course, there remain some problems with such technologies as OFDM. For example, OFDM in particular requires more power usage in the transmitter and receiver than the comparable technologies such as TDMA and CDMA. There are also several variations of OFDM; which will become prevalent in building 4G networks is still a open question.

OFDM is obviously not the only contender for the future and there is no crystal ball to tell us which technology will succeed and which will fail. There are two important aspects to this that the mobile application developer should constantly be aware of while designing and developing:

1. Avoid tight coupling between your application and the underlying network infrastructure. Network infrastructures and the services that they deliver change rapidly. A robust application is easily adapted to new wireless technologies.
2. Continue to be aware of the technology being deployed on the network(s) with which your application will interact and make sure that there are no inherent requirements in your application that cannot be delivered by the underlying network. Furthermore, while designing and implementing your mobile application (prior to the first deployment), remember that you are designing and implementing for an infrastructure that may be significantly different from what you test in the unit-test environment. Make sure that you are properly diligent in your research to find out the network conditions at the time of first deployment and from that point onward.

Next, we will look at standards, including 3GPP, that specify further usage of TDMA and CDMA technologies, specify additional functionality built on top of the two, specify interoperability requirements, and aggregate various higher level functionality (such as billing, location sensitivity, etc.) that helps in successful deployments. These standards are particularly important to the mobile application developer as they provide the interface point of the mobile application with the underlying wireless communication network and the capabilities of the wireless communication network that can be used by the mobile application.

3GPP

The Third-Generation Partnership Project Agreement, or 3GPP, is simply the umbrella organization that maintains the specifications for GSM, GPRS, EDGE, and WCDMA. So, 3GPP is an organization and not a technology. Its headquarters are based in Sophia Antipolis, the Silicon Valley of France. To date, perhaps the most significant of these overseeing functions has been the move from GSM to 3G beginning with deployment of GSM in the early 1990s and progressing to 3G migration in the early 2000s. We will spend much of the following sections discussing technologies that fall under 3GPP recommendations and specifications.

1G, 2G, 2.5G, 3G, and 4G

The "G" in these acronyms simply refers to the word "generation" of cellular transmission technologies. These generations are not defined by time periods, rather by types of technology. First-generation technologies, which we call 1G here (a term that is rarely used), refer to analog cellular telephony technologies such as Advanced Mobile Phone Service (AMPS) and Frequency Division Multiple Access (FDMA). These technologies were first introduced in the early 1980s by AT&T in the United States and primarily intended for telephony voice. In the late 1980s, the second generation of cellular telephony technologies broke into the scene in Europe. At present, these technologies are frequently referred to as 2G and comprise the bulk of deployments of voice and data services in Europe and the United States. They include, but are not limited to, the three most popular base technologies of TDMA, GSM, and CDMA. TDMA and GSM are somewhat open standards wheras CDMA is solely owned by Qualcomm.

The name 2.5G has been given to those transitional technologies that will provide higher data rate services than 2G technologies but are not quite as able as 3G technologies. These technologies also provide a crucial migration path for the telecommunication companies. These technologies include General Packet Radio Services (GPRS), which is a GSM extension that transmits data in short packets at a rate of up to 100 Kbps and High-Speed Circuit-Switched Data (HSCSD), another GSM extension that allows operation of GSM channels up to 57.6 Kbps.

Third-generation (3G) technologies are intended to transmit data to fast-moving mobile users (e.g., in cars) at 144 Kbps and slow-moving mobile users (e.g., walking users) at 384 Kbps. It aims to deliver up to 2 Mbps connectivity between stationary fixed-location nodes. At this time, there are different implementations of 3G technologies depending on the geographic location. Although Europe is forging ahead with Universal Mobile Telecommunications System (UMTS) standards, the picture is more murky in the United States with Qualcomm owning CDMA and related 3G technologies and CDMA, TDMA, and GSM being comparably pervasive in the network infrastructure deployments. Included in 3G deployments will be WCDMA, TD-CDMA, CDMA2000, and other technologies. Most importantly, 3G will provide a network infrastructure that gives us an IP-based communication system, thereby providing interoperability with existing data network infrastructure as well as making it easy for software developers to deal with building software systems. A true 3G system must be IPv6 compatible.

Fourth-generation (4G) technologies are yet to be deployed and are in research stages at the time of authoring this text. With 4G, users will have access to different services, increased coverage, and convenience of a single device; one bill with reduced total access cost; and more reliable wireless access even with the failure or loss of one or more networks [Varshney and Jain 2001]. 4G services will deliver some type of IP-based technology for data access and may offer bit rates of around 50 Mbps. The remaining issues under research and development of 4G networks focus on value-added services such as native accommodation for multimode and multichannel interactions with the network, providing QOS information to all of the participants in a particular network, tight integration of short-range and long-range wireless technologies, and interoperability among networks operated by different carriers or providers based on fundamentally different technologies. Additionally, 4G networks will offer fast handoff between different cells as well as better and faster security.

UMTS

UMTS promises to deliver data ranges of up to 2 Mbps. This is an enormously higher bandwidth than all other specifications available to date. Enhancements to UMTS will provide even higher data rates. However, the first networks to become UMTS compliant will only support approximately 200 Kbps by year 2006 during which time the mainstays of high-rate data delivery will remain GSM-based technologies such as GPRS and EDGE.

UMTS builds on WCDMA and TDMA networks to specify higher level services, particularly support for multimodal and multichannel interactions as well as support for location information. UMTS is mainly designed as an evolutionary step to GSM. Like 3GPP, UMTS is more of a collection of specifications than a single one. The UMTS Forum acts as the organizational arm. Unlike 3GPP, which tends to lean more toward addressing technical concerns, UMTS tends to publish documents that are more business related and focus on the sales and marketing aspects of wireless technologies. In fact, the technical aspects of UMTS is all covered under the various 3GPP specifications [UMTS 2002].

GSM

The hallmark of GSM (Global System for Mobile) is the SIM card, which enables users to switch phones without having to change their electronic identity or to switch their electronic identity without changing phones. Obviously, this is a trivial byproduct of one of the most important standards in mobile computing and wireless communications. GSM provides an internationally accepted standard for encoding and transmitting voice on mobile telephony networks. The GSM specification has been largely created for TDMA-based networks.

The GSM specification is very comprehensive. It covers not only base voice and data-related services but also services related to location information, billing, provisioning, distribution of devices, and QOS as well as value-added applications delivered by network providers and device manufacturers. However, if you are authoring an application for a mobile device with heavy data use, you are probably looking for a GSM add-on such as GPRS and EDGE to deliver the higher data rates.

GPRS

GPRS is a GSM upgrade that provides packet data and rates up to approximately 170 Kbps. GPRS modulation is based on Gaussian Minimum-Shift Keying (GMSK) modulation. It is very important, though, to understand that this is the maximum bandwidth delivered. Most of the time, depending on the QOS of the location of the device and many other factors, users get only a fraction of this bandwidth. Figure 10.8 shows the general system architecture that the careers must deploy to provide GPRS service. Note that as a software application developer, unless your application runs as a part of the telecommunication infrastructure, you simply see

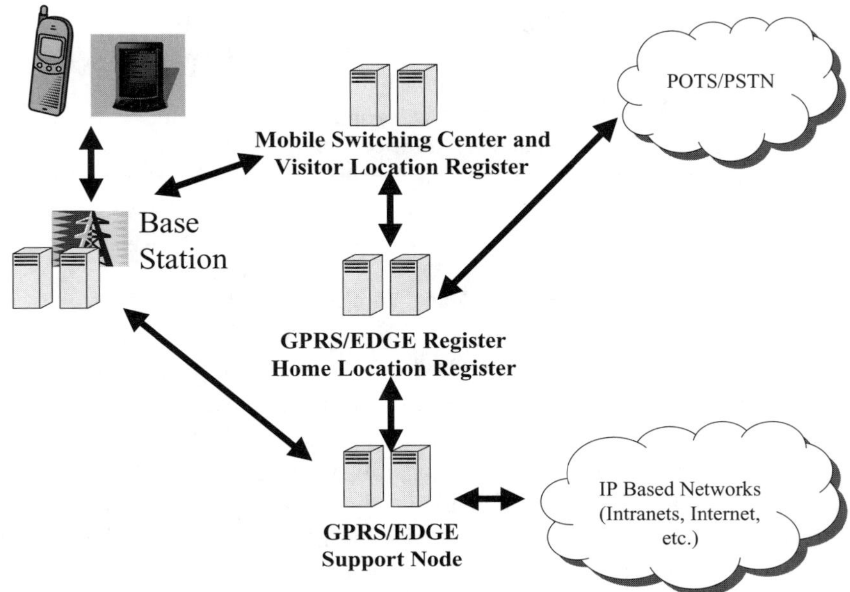

FIGURE 10.8. EDGE and GPRS System Architecture.

an IP-based access to the system. This is true for nearly all the technologies that we discuss in this section including EDGE. GPRS and EDGE are both technologies that bridge the gap on our way to 3G technologies that provide multichannel, multimedia connections to the network at high bandwidths with very good QOS capabilities.

Because GPRS is an add-on to GSM, a GSM-enabled mobile device does not necessarily support GPRS. To use GPRS and EDGE, the device must be specifically enabled for the appropriate technology, the carrier must be able to support the service, and the carrier must enable the device account to use the service. Also, in the case of both GPRS and EDGE, it is possible to saturate the base station node, particularly because these technologies are typically deployed on TDMA.

EDGE

EDGE, yet another GSM upgrade, is designed to provide data rates up to 384 Kbps and was initially developed by Ericsson and scheduled for commercial use in 2002 using 3G transmission technology but working in the GSM frequency range [Garber 2002]. EDGE deployment will primarily be in the United States as it is best suited for the infrastructure there.

EDGE can achieve this higher rate by introducing 8PSK modulation technique (which breaks the 360 degrees of a sinusoidal wave into eight phase shift keying). At this point you may be wondering why we do not simply increase the order of the phase shift keying. There are many reasons for this, the biggest of which is the increase of errors and hence the necessity of introducing more and more elaborate correction techniques. So, although the promised bit rate of 384 Kbps may be delivered under ideal conditions, because of the higher chance for errors, the minimum bandwidth delivered may be much lower than this. EDGE may be implemented

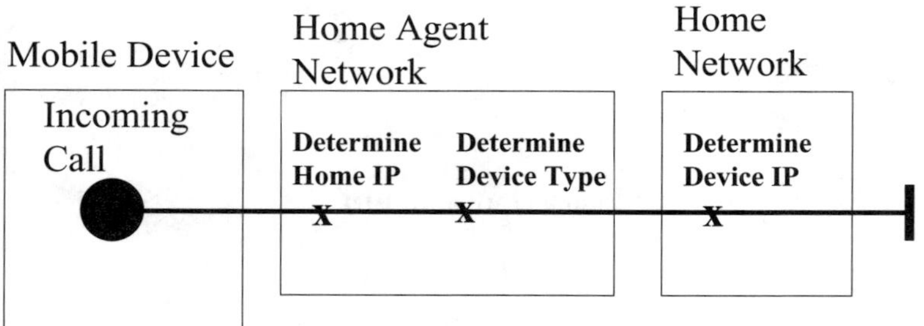

FIGURE 10.9. Using UCMs to Model Wireless Network Interactions.

on both packet radio and circuit-switched networks. EDGE and GPRS essentially require the same type of system architecture from the telecommunication careers as seen in Figure 10.8.

This brings us to the end of our discussion on long-range wireless networks. As you must have noted, our focus was mainly on cellular telephony technology and the various modulation techniques, at a high level, that allow for delivery of data and voice to the mobile device.

The various networking technologies that we have looked at are typically commercially bundled with some additional services, both to provide additional revenue streams for the carriers and to make them more useful to the end users and the application developers. As an application developer, to use such functionality, we need to first have a high-level of understanding of the type of services offered and then we need to build an interface with these services. As previously mentioned, the goal is to create a clean interface between our application and these services. To do this, we need to understand the model of services offered by various wireless networking services. We have already used UML to represent such a model for QOS as a dimension of mobility and an aspect of wireless communication.

10.3.3 Modeling Wireless Network Communications with UML

Previously in this chapter, we discussed the merits and methods of modeling QOS properties of a wireless network with UML. In the bigger picture, it is also useful to model the other aspects of wireless network communications with UML. First, we can use the existing artifacts of UML diagrams to represent collaboration among the various components of a wireless network (collaboration diagrams), temporally organized interactions among these components given specific circumstances (sequence diagrams), discrete software components with well-defined functionalities (component diagrams), and the overall division of the delivered functionality (use case diagrams). In general, UML 1.3 and above, without any extensions, allows us to model network communications, wired or wireless, fairly well. However, there is always room for improvement. In this section, we will look at some proposed extensions that will allow us to more efficiently model certain properties of wireless networks. This is not to say that all, or any of, these extensions hold a magic key to making the modeling process more efficient; rather, you can use any of these extensions, at your discretion and based on the nature of your project, to enhance your UML-based documentation. Also, there is a close relationship between synchronization and wireless network access (because one of the reasons to have synchronization is intermittent connectivity); refer to Chapter 11 to see how we model data replication and synchronization with UML. The same is true with location information, which can be obtained from the network and its topology; this is discussed in Chapter 12.

Let us start with extensions to use case diagrams, the starting point of any UML-based technique.

Use Case Maps

Proposed by Amyot and Andradel, the visual notation *Use Case Maps* (UCMs) aim to capture operational requirements of communicating and distributed systems [Amyot and Andradel 2001]. UCMs are not proposed as a UML extension by Amyot and Andradel though they can be represented, as we propose here, and modeled as a UML extension. In other words, the artifacts that have been introduced to build UCM diagrams can be described by stereotypes, constraints, and tags.

Because of their causal and temporal nature, UCMs can be thought of as something in between UML sequence and use case diagrams. UCMs use behavior as a concrete, first-class architectural concept. They describe scenarios in terms of causal relationships between responsibilities [Amyot and Andradel 2001]. They are useful in representing wireless communications because the nature of communication systems is temporal and causal and because, as proposed by Amyot and Andradel, a reference model for wireless communication is provided where roles of some typical components in a wireless communication system are predefined. Amyot and Andradel first define a few simple artifacts for their UCMs and then recognize some entities and create stereotypes based on the functionalities that these entities perform in a wireless network. They make use of the following functions:

1. authentication control function,
2. call control function,
3. location registration functions,
4. mobile station access control function,
5. radio access control function,
6. radio control function,
7. radio terminal function,
8. service control function,
9. service creation entity function,
10. service data function,
11. service management function,
12. service switching function,
13. service management access function, and
14. specialized resource function.

For the description of each of these, refer to the paper by Amyot and Andradel referenced here; these are mainly concepts of component-based services for wireless telecommunication systems. The artifacts are simple and are listed in Table 10.1.

Table 10.1. Use Case Map Artifacts

Start Point	Represented by a full circle, this artifact indicates the start of a temporal process.	●
Causal Path	These are simple lines that attach the other artifacts to one another. They imply a causal temporal behavior.	—
Responsibility	Responsibilities are indicated by an X that crosses the causal paths. Responsibilities are roughly large-grained functionality provided by the system.	X
Components	Components provide a way to map the responsibilities to systems and subsystems that actually perform those responsibilities. They are indicated with boxes that surround the included responsibilities. Note that UML already defines components; however, they have to be redefined within the framework of the UCMs.	□
End Point	As every process has a start, it must also have an end. The end point, indicated by a straight vertical line that ends the last causal path, represents this ending.	|

Figure 10.9 shows a simple example of an incoming call using these artifacts.

In UML terms, UCMs fill the gap between requirements described as (natural language) use cases and detailed behavior based on components and messages (e.g., sequence, collaboration, and state diagrams) [Miga et al. 2002]. UCM diagrams are simple and similar to the other diagrams that we have learned. For the mobile application developer, they are most handy when he or she has to model the functionality offered by a wireless network system or needs to create interfaces that rely on such functionality. Next, we will look at UML.

How to Model Network Services

One of the most important things in understanding the services offered by any wireless network is the "service model" offered by the network. Whereas some networks only offer rudimentary communication services to deliver packets of data back and forth, other networks have special considerations for more advanced features such as billing, QOS, and other functionality. Unfortunately, one of the great unresolved fundamental problems of software engineering is that the model with which we represent a system is very much dependent upon our perspective and that the behavior of two systems built to solve the same problem represented by two different domain models vary.

This means that the model with which we decide to represent a system is of paramount importance. For this reason, there are many organizations tackling the standardization of domain problem. Although there are still some variations because there are competing standard bodies in many of these domains, the success and survival of standards is often proven in an organic manner and by the simple passage of time.

Traditionally, ITU's (International Telecommunications Union) Specification and Description Language (SDL) is the tool of choice for the engineers within the telecommunications community. However, unlike UML, SDL is not very pervasive among software developers. Selic and Raumbaugh (two of the forefathers of OOP and UML) have defined a mapping from SDL to UML by creating a UML profile that defines stereotypes, constraints, and tagged values to extend existing UML artifacts [Selic and Raumbaugh]. These extensions also leverage the rational real-time (often referred to as RRT) extensions to UML designed to treat problems specific to real-time computing. For details of this mapping, we refer you to the aforementioned reference; indeed, if you are a mobile application developer within the telecommunications community or one who has to communicate with colleague members of the telecommunications community, we strongly recommend that you read this document. A digest of this paper can be presented as follows [Selic and Raumbaugh]:

1. UML RTT capsules, represented by the <<capsule>> stereotype can be mapped, by further specialization, to SDL's system, block, service, and process.
2. Ports, stereotyped by <<port>>, and attributes of capsules that allow representation of communication among capsules, can be mapped to SDL's gates.
3. Because UML state machines are more general than SDL state machines, they can be used to model the semantics of SDL state machines.
4. There is a one-to-one mapping between SDL and UML signals.
5. An SDL variable can be represented by a UML RTT capsule attribute.
6. SDL inputs are translated into UML transition triggers.

These are only a small subset of what Selic and Raumbaugh have specified as the mappings from SDL to UML and the UMLRTT extension. For those readers familiar with both SDL and UML, this should give you a taste of the mapping. Once again, for more details see the reference paper mentioned. Because SDL was designed specifically for the telecommunications industry, this mapping allows us to use UML for design or representation of the operation of wireless systems. However, we have yet to see what a typical domain model of a wireless communication system may look like.

In the case of modeling wireless network behaviors, like many other domain problems, there are competing organizations. For the purposes of this text, we will look at the model defined by the EUROSCOM P809-GI project. EUROSCOM is a community of European telecommunications carriers that includes British Telecom, Deutsche Telekom AG, Telefonica, and FINNET Group. One of the reasons we select the EUROSCOM model is that project P809-GI uses UML and object-oriented concepts in modeling the domain of services offered by a wireless network.

P809-GI focuses on the problem of interacting with intelligent networks that provide a variety of advanced services such as multimedia content to users, other terminals, nonintelligent systems, and other intelligent systems. Though these

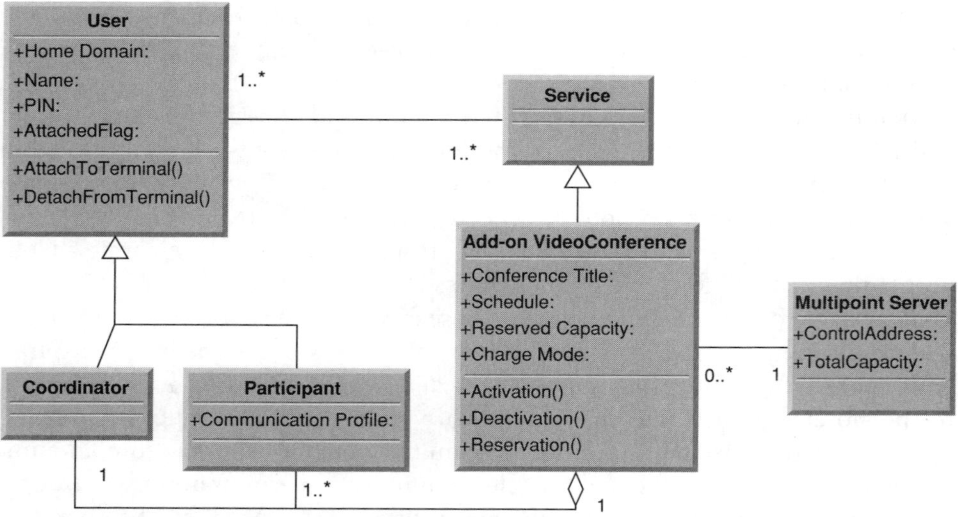

FIGURE 10.10. Add-on Video Conference Service Classes [P809-GI 1999].

definitions are not limited to wireless connectivity, the focus is on wireless systems. Now, let us look at some of the models outlined by this project:

1. Figure 10.10 shows the basic model for a video conference. Once again, the model is simple: A video conference may have many participants but only one coordinator.
2. Figure 10.11 shows the general participants in a mobile interaction. This model is rather basic. There is a user, a terminal (the mobile device that the user is

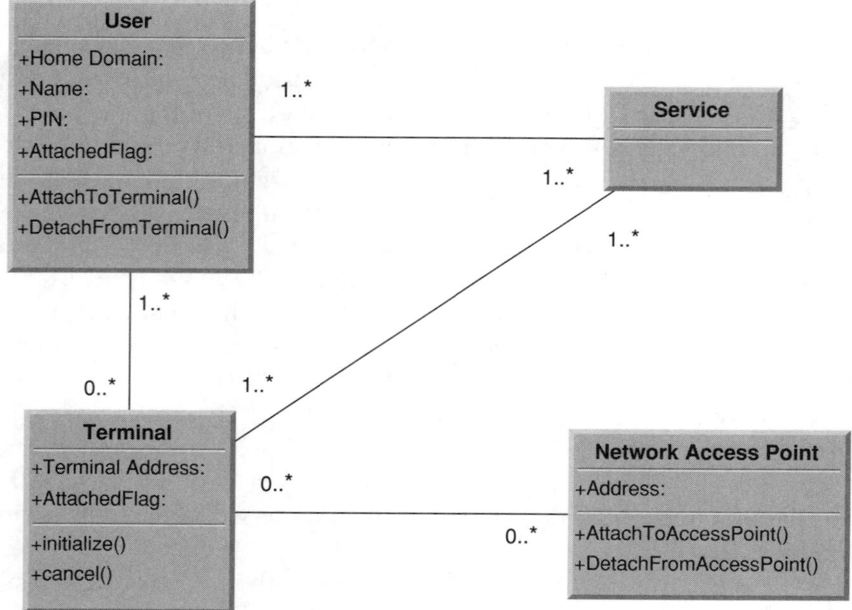

FIGURE 10.11. Mobility Classes and Relationships [P809-GI].

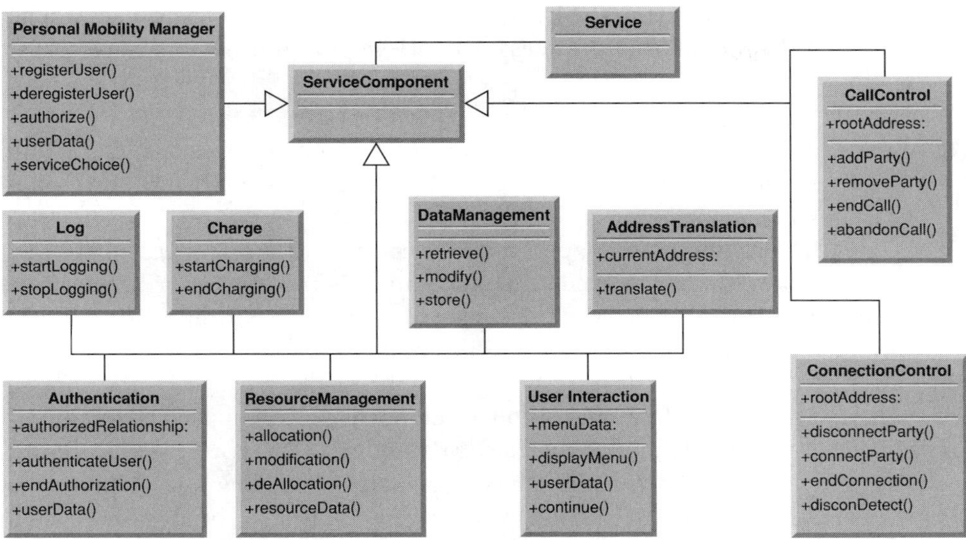

FIGURE 10.12. Service-Independent Classes [P809-GI].

using), and an access point to which the mobile device connects to utilize the underlying wireless network.

3. Figure 10.12 shows those basic data elements and structures that are independent of the individual value-added services in a wireless network but that are used by all various services on the network. As you can see, this part of the model tackles more problems but still does it in a very generic manner. It demonstrates the requirement for any mobile system connected to the network through a wireless connection to have an authorization and authentication mechanism, proper logging, management of network and device resources, persistence data store management, and address translation for interoperability. We also see the basic concepts of controlling the channels to the network in ConnectionControl and CallControl classes. Furthermore, there is one aspect of wireless networks and mobility that we do not look at in this text: billing. Billing is not a dimension of mobility, but its role in mobile applications is very unique and different from that in stationary applications. Because most mobile applications are connected to the network through a wireless network, the network infrastructure and the application are responsible for tracking network usage. Billing is one of the most complicated deployment problems as telecommunications carriers have complex schemes for bandwidth and service usage.

Besides defining these models, the EUROSCOM Project 809-GI continues to create more refined definitions of the recognized entities. As generic as these definitions and the model itself is, other entities have defined these same models in a different manner. Also, inheritance is, at least semantically, overused in the P809-GI model. An experienced object-oriented programmer knows that overusing inheritance leads to an inflexible model that cannot be easily extended. For this reason, we recognize the models that we have introduced here as more useful because of the proper distinctions of the entities rather than the way the relationships among the entities are represented in the UML model. As a mobile application developer, you may find the model of the wireless network important to you because of the following:

1. You need to understand the service model of the network to write simulation or unit-test programs that emulate the environment in which your mobile application will exist.
2. A core part of your mobile application uses the various services offered by wireless networks and you need to create clean APIs and interfaces that separate the concerns of the adapters that couple you to the network infrastructure(s) from the core functionality of the mobile application.

You will find that, as a mobile application developer, you will not need too many advanced development techniques such as UML modeling for representing network behavior. Most of this work is done by the creators of the lower layer protocols and the base services that they offer. However, you will need to be able to use such functionality and model the behavior of your application, which potentially can be centered around the functionality of the wireless network, with precision and quality.

Unfortunately, thus far, carriers and equipment manufacturers involved in the creation and deployment of wireless networks have not been willing to agree upon some universal model for various aspects of providing wireless networking services that can be represented in UML. This is largely because carriers and manufacturers differentiate themselves by using different models for providing wireless networking services.

10.4 Mobile IP

IP addresses, with IP-based deployments dominated by TCP/IP, have traditionally been associated with stationary computing systems that are located in the same location for long periods of time. This is the foundation for much of the routing techniques used for TCP/IP-based networks. The biggest problems in using TCP/IP and the accompanying technologies in mobile computing are related to routing. Whereas applications in TCP/IP use the IP address and a port to identify an end point, end points in the mobile world are not static: A mobile device may connect to one network, be assigned an IP address, move to another network, be assigned another IP address, and so on all in a very short period of time and while the same application needs to continue to operate properly. This problem is the primary reason for the existence of Mobile IP.

Although the term Mobile IP is used by a variety of specifications and technologies, we will be using it as specified by the Internet Engineering Task Force (IETF). Keep in mind that Mobile IP is being designed to be in line with mobility solutions offered based on IPv6, but because most of the infrastructure of the Internet only supports IPv4 at this time, backward compatibility to IPv4 is a requirement. The two biggest improvements in the Mobile IP implementation of IPv6 over IPv4 are that security is integrated into the design of the protocol and that handovers among different subnets are possible without having packet loss. At present, MIPv6 (Mobile IP for IPv6) has not been finalized by the IETF. Although Internet service providers are currently balking at adopting MIPv6, many big companies support the technology and say it eventually will become widespread [Vaughan-Nichols 2003].

Mobile IP requires maintenance of two IP addresses for each end point. One address is used to locate the end point and the other is used to uniquely identify it. So, one IP address is used to locate the home network of the mobile device. Once the datagram arrives at the home network, it is routed to the "care-of-address," which is the address of the end-point device. In this way, the home network can change the "care-of-address" once the datagram arrives. Now, let us review some of the basic functionality requirements for Mobile IP nodes:

1. A Mobile IP node should be able to communicate with other nodes after changing its link-layer point of attachment to the Internet, yet without changing its IP address [Campbell 2001].
2. Mobile nodes should be interoperable with other IP-based nodes.
3. Because this usage of two IP addresses for each node leaves the protocol vulnerable to new types of security attacks, all messages must be authenticated before routing.
4. Assignment of IP addresses should have no other constraints.

Whereas the *mobile host* is defined as a host on the network similar to a normal IP host there are some new concepts introduced in Mobile IP as follows (see Figure 10.13):

1. *Home Agent*: The home agent receives and routes the datagram based on the home network IP address. The home agent is the first contact point of a datagram that exists outside of a subnet but is addressed to that subnet. The home agent is always the same regardless of the location of the device. Instead, it is tied to the specific device.
2. *Foreign Agent*: This is the agent that the mobile device connects to. Because the mobile device roams around among different subnets, the foreign agent varies based on the location of the device.
3. *Mobile Node*: This is the mobile device connected to the network through some sort of connectivity, most probably wireless.

There are also some basic processes that go on in the routing of messages with Mobile IP:

1. *Agent Advertisement*: Both home agents and foreign agents send out periodic advertisement so that they may be properly discovered. The mobile node is listening for these advertisements.

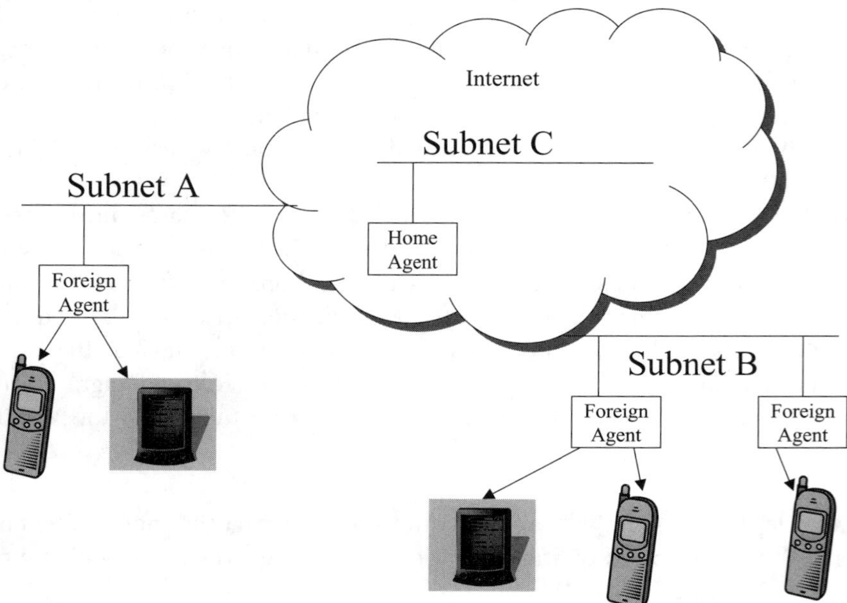

FIGURE 10.13. Mobile IP System Components.

2. *Registration*: Once a mobile node has discovered a home agent and/or a foreign agent, it registers with them for a limited period of time. Registration always expires after some time and must be renewed.
3. *Advertisement*: The home agent advertises the public IP address of the mobile node so that other routing points in the network can route the datagrams properly.

The biggest concerns with Mobile IP are its ability to deliver reasonable QOS and provide appropriate security.

Of course, we cannot have a discussion of IP without one of TCP. The combination of these two comprises the foundation of the Internet. One of the biggest efforts in the telecommunications community has been to build an effective TCP/IP implementation on top of the networks that we have discussed in this section. Unfortunately, TCP does not lend itself to wireless networking naturally. Wireless networks connect and disconnect frequently and intermittently and the connect/disconnect cost in TCP/IP is considerable. Things like handoffs between relays, which are very natural to the basis of wireless networks, cause problems in TCP/IP implementations. Also, TCP assumes that packet loss is caused by either network congestion or reordering of packets—an assumption that is not true in the case of wireless networks.

Two solutions have been suggested. Some systems simply use a different protocol such as UDP (User Datagram Protocol). Unfortunately, this too has its drawbacks. First, wired networks perform much better with TCP so this causes an inherent impedance mismatch. Second, UDP tends to be a less efficient and slower protocol for long-lived sessions, and most transactions between users and the mobile application involve more than one or two simple transaction and require some state to be kept. This is not impossible in UDP, merely not as natural to UDP as it is to TCP. Other solutions have focused on creating variations on TCP such as Multimode TCP. A mode is a subset of the entire TCP state [Zhang 2001].

To date, there is no clear canonical solution for wireless networking that is similar to TCP/IP. The best we have done is simply port TCP/IP to run on wireless networks. And this simply is not a very good solution because of the fundamental differences in wireless and wired networking.

10.5 SMS

SMS is the delivery of alphanumeric messages to mobile phones over wireless networks [Malhotra 2002]. SMS is not inherently a wireless communication technology. It is a value-added service designed to run on long-range wireless networks. Nonetheless, we have left its discussion to this section of the book because it only lives within wireless networks and, to many 1G and 2G data networks, it is the only or the most important form of data communication. SMS messages can be sent from a mobile device or from an SMSC (Short Messaging Service Center), routed by an SMSC, and arrive at a suitable destination as an SMS message, an e-mail, or some other form of electronic message. Two things make SMS fundamentally different from the other data access technologies: It can be delivered whether or not there is an ongoing voice call and it is an asynchronous messaging system that allows for flexibility in the temporal behavior of the network and related delivery attributes.

SMS was first deployed in Europe in the early 1990s and became prevalent in the mid 1990s. In the United States, it was not until the very late 1990s that SMS was available and usage grew slowly but steadily from thereon. To date, SMS is by far the most successful data application used on wireless networks.

SMS does not require usage of one type of wireless network over the other; it can be implemented over whatever network is available. However, to date, it is primarily implemented on TDMA and CDMA networks and will be supported by the 3G variants of those networks or more modern networks. Figure 10.14 shows the basic architecture of a telecommunication infrastructure that can deliver SMS messages.

One important thing to note is that SMSCs all implement Signaling System 7 (SS7) connectivity. This is crucial for delivery of messages among disparate networks and is a big part of what the implementation of an SMSC gateway includes.

Most carriers, for security reasons, do not offer third-party connectivity to their SMSC or any connected part of the infrastructure of an SMS system. Unfortunately, this means that the only way for a programmer to write an SMS application is to interface with the carrier's SMTP servers that are then connected to the SMSC. Carriers either create an alias at some domain (user@carrierdomain.com) or the phone number is used (7145555555@carrierdomain.com). In other words, creating an SMS message, as far as we are concerned, is the same as creating an e-mail. Whereas the length of the message is supposed to be 160 characters, depending

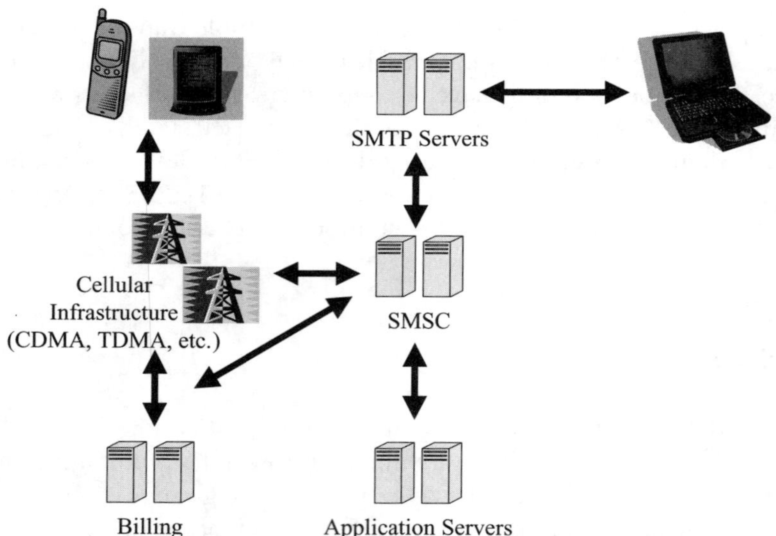

FIGURE 10.14. Basic System Diagram for an SMS-Enabled System.

on the network, you will see a maximum of anywhere from 100 to 280 characters for an SMS message.

Of course, we only have to do this if the device we are using is not SMS enabled. With SMS-enabled devices (typically mobile phones and PDAs), you simply compose your short message and address it to the phone number of the recipient and off it goes.

There is one other way to send SMS messages: You can use a mobile phone, or another SMS-enabled device, as a proxy into the carrier's network. Here are the steps to do this:

1. Connect your mobile phone, PDA, or whatever SMS-enabled device you have to your PC with an RS232 cable, USB cable, or whatever connector is provided.
2. Install that phone as a modem to the PC.
3. You can now send an SMS message using the SMS-enabled device as a modem by sending an "AT" command. This message would be formatted as follows:
   a. AT+CMGS="17144546537" ➔ Enter key
   b. Enter the text message ➔ Ctrl-z
   c. AT OK AT+CMGF=1 OK AT+CMGS="17144546537",129 >Hello+ CMGS:3 OK

SMS will eventually be replaced with the more advanced EMS and MMS, which we have discussed previously in this text.

One interesting thing about SMS is that, because of its pervasiveness, it is occasionally used as a text-based application-layer transport protocol. In other words, we can build a mobile application that resides on the device, in one of the environments we have looked at such as J2ME and Windows CE, and use SMS to send and receive messages from some other node on the network. The SMS messages could, for example, hold SOAP envelopes. Though most typical

SOAP envelopes would be too large to put into one SMS message, we can split the messages in several different SMS messages.

10.6 What Now?

We have certainly not covered all of the various areas of wireless networking that relate to mobile application development. Our attempt has been to give an introduction to some of the most pervasive technologies to give us a good understanding of the limitations and capabilities of the infrastructure that our mobile applications will be using for communication. The core services of the more advanced data networks such as various 802.11 networks and 3GPP-based networks may evolve along a number of different paths. The governing rules for determining this evolution will be largely driven to an equilibrium point where the wireless carriers can make money and expand their markets, the device manufacturers can continue to introduce more and more advanced devices, the third-party application developers will find a way to introduce applications quickly to a mobile software marketplace suffocated by the carriers, and the consumers will continue discovering new value in mobile applications that they can use through their wireless connection to the network.

Wireless networks will be changing fast. The key for the mobile application developer is to keep up with these changes and to design applications that resist becoming obsolete by these changes.

CHAPTER 11

Synchronization and Replication of Mobile Data

Doubt is the key to knowledge.

Persian proverb

11.1 INTRODUCTION

The word *replicate* means "to produce a copy of itself" and originates from the Latin word *replicates*. The word *synchronize* is defined by the Webster dictionary to mean "to represent or arrange (events) to indicate coincidence or coexistence." Synchronization and replication are two essential operations in distributed computing. Although synchronization can mean a variety of things, replication is typically used in reference to data. Like the literal definitions of synchronization and replication in the English language, their definitions within the field of computing are different but related. In this chapter, we will limit our discussion of synchronization and replication to *data synchronization* and *data replication*. As you may have already noted, we used the term synchronization, in Chapter 8, when synchronizing contents and actions transmitted across multiple communication channels. We are discussing synchronization in the context of data replication in this chapter.

Data replication, in its broadest sense, simply refers to copying data from one or more data storage locations to one or more other data storage locations. Note that these locations are virtual locations and not physical locations—it is not required for the virtual locations to be at different physical locations. The taxonomy of the types of replication technologies depends on the domain problem as well as the infrastructure on which replication is being performed. However, we can break nearly all data replication into two groups: *complete replication* and *partial replication*. When we replicate data completely among two or more nodes, all of the data are copied. Partial replicas allow us to set up behavioral rules that allow us to specify a subset of the data to be copied among two or more nodes participating in the replication process.

Data synchronization, in its broadest sense, assures that there are no *conflicts* or *discrepancies* among two or more instances of the same data. The problem with this definition is that conflicts and discrepancies are domain dependent. In other words, whether two or more data sources are synchronized depends on the definition of "conflicts and discrepancies" within the data domain. Whereas in most domains this means that the different instances of the same data must be *identical* (hence the relationship with replication), this is not necessarily the case. Hansmann defines data synchronization, as applied to mobile applications, by stating that "Data synchronization allows a consistent local 'copy' of various kinds of data, from a central corporate datastore or a service provider datastore on the user's device" [Hansmann 2002]. This definition is correct but does not encompass all aspects of data synchronization needed by mobile applications. Like replication, we may synchronize data only partially. Partial replication or synchronization may be based on a set of domain dependent rules, the infrastructure performing the synchronization, or even temporal properties of the data and the act of synchronization itself.

When it comes to mobile computing, there is an obvious use for data replication and synchronization: Allow the user to access an application and data when the end-user device is disconnected from the network. But there is a deeper relationship here. There is a graduated, inversely proportional, relationship between QOS of the network connectivity provided to the device and how replication and synchronization are to be used. For example, when the user is often completely disconnected from the network, we may need a complete replica and frequent synchronizations to keep the data updated for those times when the user is disconnected from the network. In contrast, if the network connection is typically very reliable but slow and the device is resource-starved, then we may use partial replicas to improve performance almost like a caching mechanism. We will not intend to quantify the relationships among QOS, replication, and synchronization in mobile environments with any degree of exactness, but we will go through some general concepts and the mechanics of implementing these general concepts that will give the reader a qualitative feeling for these relationships.

We will also discuss some basic concepts in data replication and synchronization, see the relevance of replication and synchronization in mobile applications, look at how we can represent replication and synchronization actions with UML, and look at SyncML as a syntactical tool that we can use for implementing replication and synchronization solutions.

Before we delve into implementations of how we can replicate data onto our mobile device and synchronize the data from there on, let us first take a more diligent look at the various types of data replication and synchronization and the relationship of synchronization to the dimensions of mobility.

11.2 Taxonomy of Replication and Synchronization

So far, we have learned about complete and partial replications. Now we introduce the concept of *master* and *replica* in any replication process. We are always replicating from a source to a destination: The source is typically called the *master* and the destination is typically called the *replica*. The replica, then, may be a complete or a partial replica of the master. In a system with many devices (PCs, mobile devices, etc.) connected together through a network, it is conceivable (actually typical) that a data source may need to play the part of a master or a replica and that the way the devices connect to each other depends on the network topology and the application that they sit on top of and the application-layer communication protocols provided for the devices to communicate with one another.

A quick review of basic networking theory tells us that the network-based topology can be a *star*, *a ring*, *a bus*, *peer to peer*, or any variation and combination of those four. Although all of these network-layer protocols *can* provide for the data platform that performs the replication and synchronization, some lend themselves in a more effective way to particular types of data replication. This is somewhat obvious, but let us review it quickly:

1. *One-to-Many Replication*: In this case, there is one central host that creates complete or partial replicas and with which all of the nodes synchronize partially or completely. At the network layer, star, bus, and peer-to-peer networks allow this to be done efficiently whereas the application-layer communication architecture can be centralized, client–server, or peer to peer. An example of this may be a set of configurations that is hosted centrally and is to be replicated to many node devices. After the initial replication, this information may need to be synchronized periodically.
2. *One-to-One Replication*: In this case, there are only two participants. There is one master and one replica. Though, as we mentioned before, the roles of master and replica are typically static to the life cycle of the application, sometimes the replication tool allows for reversal of the roles. An example of this in the realm of mobile computing is when a user creates a complete or partial replica of his or her contacts on a PDA device and synchronizes the contents of the data from that point on. Many software packages that provide for such replication also allow the user to connect his or her device to a different device and serve as the master to create a replica of itself.
3. *Many-to-Many Replication*: In this case, there are many masters and replicas in the replication and synchronization scheme. Any one of the instances of the storage systems that can assume the role of a master can replicate a new replica. From that point on, replicas, whether partial or complete, can synchronize with masters or among themselves.

Another angle with which we can build a taxonomy of replication and synchronization technologies is through the structure of the data being replicated and synchronized. We can grossly generalize persistence mechanisms for mobile devices to three categories:

1. *Proprietary (Binary) Storage*: Most of the lower end devices have limited storage and this storage is typically built on a proprietary technology (which could be standards based but is definitely hardware driven) that optimizes the storage technique for the minimal amount of storage available on the device.
2. *Flat Files*: Storage may be done using text or binary flat files. This is becoming more and more prevalent in the lower end devices as the definition of lower end is moving up (devices are becoming more powerful and thus offer more persistence storage). Flat files do not offer any special searching and indexing features; therefore, they are only practical for information with simple structure.
3. *Database Files*: Although databases offer us more advanced functionality such as searching and indexing, having even a small subset of basic database functionalities is fairly resource intensive but also very useful for higher end mobile devices. Products such as PointBase and other microdatabases are designed to run on PDAs. Such microdatabases provide some minimal set of functionality of a relational, object-oriented database. Some of these microdatabases are interoperable (replication, synchronization, etc.) with their larger siblings running on more powerful nodes of the network (servers, PCs, etc.).

Mixing these two taxonomies gives us a mixture of storage types at various nodes or allows networks of interconnected mobile devices and mobile applications that can connect together in a variety of different ways.

This means that one important task becomes the interoperability of the various storage systems on various devices within a particular application network. In other words, we may have a PDA that can have a microdatabase with a small set of functionality that distinguishes it from file systems, a mobile phone that has the simplest of persistence forms implemented in a proprietary way with a proprietary API, and servers that host database systems that are fully SQL compliant. Obviously, there is a large impedance mismatch among the abilities of these different storage forms. This impedance mismatch is indeed one of the biggest drivers in the birth of various standards, such as SyncML, that try to address the problem of standardizing data synchronization schemes, in a flexible and extensible manner, across many different platforms. The problem of replication is a bit easier, since, prior to the start of replication, there is no replica, thereby leaving all of the logic with the master, which can create a replica that includes a replica with some subset of functionality and data of itself but never exceeding the functionality and data that it (the master) possesses.

There is yet another axis that we can introduce in breaking down types of replication and synchronization. Replication and synchronization can be done *manually* or *automatically*. This means that we can only replicate and synchronize data when the user explicitly requests it (the manual method), we can replicate and synchronize data automatically without any user involvement or notification of the user, or we can have schemes that sit somewhere in between allowing the user to set some settings and then perform the act of replication and synchronization in a manual or automatic way.

Lee [Lee 2000] makes yet another distinction between types of synchronization and replication, particularly when used in mobile environments. Namely, he defines the terms *strongly connected* and *weakly connected*. The former implies that the connection among all nodes of the network is robust, highly available, and offers a sufficient amount of bandwidth without the possibility of bottlenecks for replication and synchronization. The latter is defined as an intermittent connection with unreliable amount of network bandwidth: the type of connection that most mobile devices provide (typically a wireless connection). Note that strong and weak connectivity do not have anything to do with the strong and weak mobility mentioned in Chapter 9 within the context of mobile agents.

Finally, we can type data replication and synchronization techniques by the likelihood of conflicts. *Pessimistic* replication and synchronization techniques assume that conflicts are likely whereas *optimistic* replication and synchronization techniques assume that conflicts are unlikely. Obviously "likely" and "unlikely" are relative to the data storage systems, network availability, and the application logic. Pessimistic approaches typically force locking on certain portions of data (files in file-based storage systems, rows in databases, etc.) whereas optimistic approaches present the possibility of more frequent data conflicts. There is also the matter of whether we can automate the resolution of data conflicts. Depending on the type of application and the data that it stores, some or all data conflicts can be resolved without the involvement of the user; however, it is very possible that some human intervention is needed to resolve some data conflicts. Sometimes, it is also beneficial to store various versions of the data. In fact, versioning is built into the more sophisticated storage systems. However, keep in mind that keeping multiple versions of the same data on a mobile device is very expensive. So, if we want to do this, do it on the network (PCs, servers, etc.).

It is also important to keep in mind that replication and synchronization are transactional. In other words, there is an atomic nature to the smallest messages being sent back and forth between the different nodes of the network during synchronization and replication. If only half of a single transactional message is received and the rest is lost because of a broken connection, timeouts, etc. the entire message must be retransmitted.

Finally, replication and synchronization are typically *stateful*. This means that there is typically more than one single atomic transaction during a synchronization session and that it is useful to maintain information about these various atomic transactions as they are executed and completed. In fact, in the case of one-to-many, many-to-many, or many-to-one replication, this statefulness is necessary to ensure that data conflicts do not cause data corruption if multiple nodes are synchronizing during the same time period.

Now, let us take a look at some additional considerations when designing and implementing mobile systems that use data replication and synchronization.

11.3 Data Replication and Synchronization for Mobile Applications

First, we need data replication and synchronization for mobile devices because we assume that most mobile devices are sometimes disconnected from a network and operating in isolation. This means that they need to access local data so that the device operator can continue to use the applications on the device. The amount of data to be stored varies based on the device capabilities, the application types, and the user preferences. Typically, the sequence of events taking place are as follows:

1. *Initial Replication*: Some data are replicated from the master to the replica. Normally, the master is a PC, server, or some other device that hosts some data and the replica is the mobile device, but this does not have to be the case. The mobile device can act as a master and create replicas on other devices.
2. *Local Data Modification*: This stage entails all of the user or machine interactions that modify the data for one node. Usage of the data while the device is weakly connected or disconnected may result in the data in other nodes becoming partially or completely obsolete (or in conflict if the same data are modified at some other node with different information).
3. *Synchronization*: This stage entails exchange of synchronization messages that update the obsolete data and either resolve the conflicts in an automated fashion or present the user with the necessary information to resolve the conflicts manually.

After the initial replication, steps 2 and 3 can be repeated as many times as desired.

Now, let us look at some considerations on how frequently we may want to synchronize after the initial replication:

1. If the mobile device operating system allows for multithreading or multiprocessing, then consider running the replication and synchronization threads in the background. Users typically accept having to wait for their data to be synchronized, but they want to be able to continue using the device for other purposes.
2. If there are many different mobile clients modifying the same data, then try to make the synchronizations as frequent as possible while preventing "hoarding" conditions when synchronization is taking up a considerable amount of the continuous bandwidth and other resources of the device for a long period of time. The higher the number of nodes that can modify the data to be synchronized, the higher the probability of synchronization conflict becomes. One of the most important things to do is to try to avoid possible synchronization conflicts.
3. We should make sure that the infrastructure used in synchronization minimizes the amount of data shipped back and forth across the wire. Most modern databases and other storage mechanisms that support synchronization keep

track of changes and optimize synchronization based on which pieces of data have been changed on the two nodes being synchronized because those two nodes were last synchronized together. There are other methods of optimizing the synchronization process as well. For example, Lee [Lee 2000] suggests the concept of *compact operations* instead of *value shipping*. In this case, before the changes are transmitted, they are analyzed. If it is possible to transmit the command that tells the other node to make the necessary changes to reflect the changes, this is done. In other words, instead of shipping the individual values to be synchronized, it is possible to recognize operations that both nodes involved in the synchronization process are aware of. Synchronization through transmission of these operations can prove to be much more efficient though it means that the synchronization mechanism becomes very tightly coupled with the application implementation.

4. Trickling reintegration is a term introduced by the Cods project of the Carnegie Mellon Computer Science Department for a project whose focus is in addressing replication and synchronization issues of weakly connected devices [Mummert 1996]. The central idea is to use whatever bandwidth is available in the most efficient way. Trickling reintegration stipulates the following:
   a. We should try to use whatever bandwidth is available in the most efficient way for replication and synchronization.
   b. The size and shape of the replication and synchronization transactions must be designed with weak connectivity in mind if the connection to the network is weak.
   c. Providing temporally dependent partial replicas is often needed in mobile systems.
   d. We should keep in mind usability issues while implementing trickling reintegration.

   This technique can well lead to initial unnecessary hoarding of the resources and then to complete saturation of the available resources on the device.

With this in mind, we should be looking for tools that provide trickling reintegration based on similar techniques for replication and synchronization of data to and from mobile devices. Such techniques maximize the usage of weak network connectivity.

Let us keep in mind the obvious: Data replication and synchronization is most applicable to mobile computing when we are dealing with devices that can store more than trivial amounts of data. Two-way synchronization is only meaningful in cases where the mobile device has an acceptable input HCI so that modifying the data through the mobile device is realistic. One-way synchronization does not have such a requirement as the mobile device could merely be updated by some network-based mechanism (servers, PC, etc.) that does have an acceptable input HCI mechanism.

Now, let us look at some of the issues involved with data replication and synchronization in mobile applications.

11.3.1 Scalability Issues Involved with Synchronization and Replication in Mobile Application Infrastructures

As we eluded to earlier, whatever type of replication and synchronization is required for an application may dictate the functionality needed from the networking and communication infrastructures. For example, if we have one centralized datastore of which all of the devices have complete or partial replicas of and with which all of the devices must be synchronized, then a star communication topology provides us with the most efficient infrastructure for the one-to-many replication and synchronization. However, the problem is that the networking and communication infrastructure typically comes before the synchronization problems and there are other considerations that often take precedence in the networking and communication infrastructure. Therefore, our task when designing mobile applications that use replication and synchronization is typically to create the canonical design for a given networking and communication infrastructure without demanding much in the way of changes to it.

We also previously mentioned that there exists a relationship between QOS and replication/synchronization of data on mobile devices. This relationship is symbiotic and not easily quantifiable. Namely, as the QOS drops off, we may want to do more frequent synchronizations; however, numerous synchronizations may hoard the available bandwidth and cause secondary problems such as bandwidth starvation to the mobile device. So, frequently the design decisions with which the mobile developer is faced includes how much of the data should be synchronized and within what periodicity this synchronization should take place. At the same time, an elaborate synchronization scheme may require more computing cycles on the client side. We have to be aware of the techniques we used so that we do not increase the requirements on the device while trying to deal with the network connectivity restrictions.

Multidevice synchronization is more difficult, because maintaining the consistency of several devices might require many individual synchronizations between pairs of devices [Agarwal, Starobinski, and Trachtenberg 2000]. This presents us with somewhat of a scalability nightmare. The problem is then twofold: First, the more devices that are connected to our datastore as replicas, the more replication and synchronization interactions we need. At the same time, we have to make sure that the system performs well, the number of conflicts is kept to the absolute minimum, and the burden on the resource-starved devices is also kept to a minimum.

So, let us summarize the scalability-related variables that we have to take into account when designing a scaleable mobile data replication and synchronization solution:

1. *Transaction Boundaries*: Transactions should be sized to take maximum advantage of the available bandwidth and, yet, not cause hoarding in the case of failures.
2. *Chunking*: The data encapsulated in the transactions must be of a size whose integrity can be consistently guaranteed for delivery between replication and

synchronization nodes. Otherwise, replication and synchronization will be far too slow because of the numerous retries.

3. *Number of Nodes to Be Synchronized*: It is somewhat obvious that the higher the number of nodes to be synchronized, the more difficult the scalability problem becomes. What is less obvious is that some network and data synchronization topologies handle this better depending on the nature of synchronization. In other words, the star topology is not always the optimal topology (we are talking about the application layer here and not the lower layers such as the physical layer). Take, for example, a software provisioning system that provides the latest version of an application to hundreds of thousands of mobile devices. Such a system may use a replication and synchronization scheme to update the mobile devices with the latest versions of a software application that executes on the device and the local data files that go along with that (mobile) application. In this case, it may be efficient and sufficient to centralize provisioning. Now, think about a mobile application that we want to distribute to the market in a viral manner. In such a case, we may want every mobile device to be able to contact any other mobile device directly (e.g., like the Palm platform allows thorugh the IR port or like Bluetooth-enabled devices allow) and download the application or synchronize the latest data files that go along with the application. In this case, we would need an ad hoc networking infrastructure and the data replication and synchronization infrastructure that allows many-to-many replications.

Of course, in addition to these considerations, we need to apply everything else that has been learned from the "Internet experience" as well as building scalable and robust mobile application infrastructures. Yet, there are certainly some unique considerations when it comes to building scaleable applications that require data replication and synchronization.

11.3.2 Approaches to Solving the Mobile Synchronization and Replication Problem

In this text, we have discussed architecture often. One of our main goals has been to lay out design strategies without getting bogged down in the implementation details involved with specific platforms. Regardless of what platform and protocol we use for performing data replication and synchronization, the mobile device is either synchronizing directly with another device or going through a proxy for this.

In essence, there are two scenarios for mobile devices and mobile applications. Either the device is able to connect to a peer device, through some ad hoc networking technology or some other means, and begin a one-to-one replication process, or the device is able to connect to a network with some centralized control (servers, etc.). In the latter case, although the server may host the data itself, it may also act as a proxy for some other device that holds the datastore with which the replication and synchronization is to be performed. Whereas some mobile application systems may require one or the other, other systems may require both.

Nearly all mobile devices that are based on open-systems technologies allow for some one-to-one synchronization of data with some other device. The usage of the proxy-based model where the mobile device interacts with some intermediary first is required for a few different reasons. First, the two different datastores to be synchronized may be stored on platforms that cannot communicate with one another readily. Second, data replication and synchronization may require robust functionality such as conflict resolution that cannot be implemented on resource-starved devices; the intermediary can offer us a place to do this computing. Finally, the different mobile devices may have better and more reliable connectivity to the intermediary than to each other; for example, we can synchronize the PIM (Personal Information Management) datastores of two different mobile devices in very disparate physical locations through a server on a communication network that both devices have access to at all times. Each of these datastores may be on the mobile device itself or stored on some proxy somewhere.

Now, let us take a quick look at how the most popular mobile platforms handle data replication and synchronization.

11.3.3 Synchronization on the Most Popular Mobile Platforms

In this text, we have looked at Java, Palm, BREW, Symbian, and Windows CE as examples of mobile device platforms. Let us look at how each provides for a synchronization mechanism. Because J2ME is the most pervasive of mobile device platforms, we will discuss it in a bit more detail later in this chapter. For now, let us consider the other platforms:

1. The Palm platform, which also has very good support for Java applications (thereby allowing for Java applications to use Java-based replication and synchronization techniques), also offers the so-called HotSync synchronization protocol. HotSync is primarily designed for the Palm-based PDAs to synchronize their data with data on a PC through any physical interface allowed by the particular device. There are two types of HotSync synchronizations: Slow Sync and Fast Sync. Slow Sync is really more like a replication (where a complete set of data is copied). It is designed for when a Palm device first connects to a new PC, in which case data are copied back and forth rather than compared and synchronized. Fast Sync is a real synchronization process in which only records modified since the last synchronization or the initial replication are compared. Like a real synchronization process, Fast Sync includes conflict resolution.
2. Microsoft offer s a variety of techniques to synchronize and replicate data between Windows CE devices and PCs. The primary mechanism for synchronization of applications on the Windows CE platform is the ActiveSync API. ActiveSync is fairly robust in allowing Windows CE devices to synchronize with other Windows platforms (Windows NT, 2000, XP, etc.). There is also the programmatic model in which a subset of Microsoft's data objects are available for the Windows CE platform (.NET platform) and programmatic interface is provided for synchronization and replication. Of course, the Microsoft PIM products such as Outlook have their own internal databases that are different

SIDE DISCUSSION 11.1

SyncML Leveraged by Wireless Protocols

Some wireless protocols such as Bluetooth include some specification of synchronization functionality. Although all specifications are converging at SyncML, SyncML does not address some issues specific to each particular communication technology. Therefore, it is foreseeable that many of the existing and upcoming wireless standards will continue to specify at least some amount of synchronization functionality. This does not imply in any way that there is overlap with Sync.

The Bluetooth synchronization profile, for example, offers two modes: a general synchronization mode in which the client and server are connected and can synchronize and an initialization synchronization mode in which the server is in a mode to be discovered or synchronized with but the interaction between the client and server does not include everything needed for a two-way synchronization. These modes are more a byproduct of the nature of a Bluetooth ad hoc network than anything related to synchronization itself. There is a detailed discussion of the Bluetooth synchronization profile in Section 11.4.2.

than what is offered to the programmers. Therefore, replication and synchronization is bit different with those products.

3. Whereas BREW offers a very rich programmatic interface, a built-in provisioning system, and persistence on the device, there is no built-in data replication or synchronization with BREW at this time. You will have to build your own synchronization or replication mechanism or find a third-party vendor that provides one (remember that BREW is a C/C++ platform).
4. When it comes to Symbian, the choices are many. Symbian offers a very rich C/C++ platform and there are several open-source and commercial tools that allow synchronization of data between a Symbian device and other devices. There is a close affinity between Symbian synchronization and SyncML, which we will look at later in this chapter. Nearly all products that address the synchronization issue on the Symbian platform support SyncML.

For two datastores to replicate and synchronize data, they need to "speak the same language." In other words, we need a protocol for communicating synchronization messages. A data synchronization protocol defines the workflow for communication during a data synchronization session when the mobile device is connected to the network [SyncML White Paper]. There are many standard and proprietary data synchronization protocols for mobile and stationary datastores. To date, there is only one standard accepted by the majority of mobile platforms for data replication and synchronization: SyncML. Let us see what SyncML is all about and how we can use it to build mobile applications with data on the device.

11.4 SyncML

As we saw earlier in this text, XML makes the ideal format for content when it comes to mobile computing. It gives us the required structure, the existence of a framework to represent metadata, and it is widely accepted, thereby helping us with device proliferation issues. The Synchronization Markup Language (SyncML) is an XML-based standard for data synchronization between two nodes. The SyncML Initiative was established in February 2000 by Ericsson, IBM, Lotus, Motorola, Nokia, Palm Inc., Psion, and Starfish Software [Leufven 2001]. Its primary purpose is to specify a protocol for synchronization of data between mobile devices and the network. SyncML addresses two problems: The *Sync Protocol* specifies how different synchronization methods are to be implemented with SyncML and the *SyncML Representation* specifies how the results of synchronization operations are represented. SyncML is a protocol primarily designed for client–server interactions though it can also be used in a peer-to-peer environment or a mobile agent environment where the peers or agent can assume the roles of clients and servers and communicate through an RPC-like communication protocol.

From the commercial perspective, most mobile middle-ware and most mobile devices that have a medium to high amount of storage resources (more than 256 kB of storage) support a SyncML interface for synchronization of data. Examples of such are DB2, Oracle, and Sybase products for both servers and hand-held devices. As we will see later, many handset manufactures, such as those that are partners in Bluetooth, also support SyncML on top of whatever device-specific replication and synchronization mechanism may be available on those devices.

SyncML defines a SyncML client and a server. The client can send messages to the server along with payloads and receive messages from the server. The server can do the same but also needs to do some operations related to data analysis (possible existence of conflicts, stale data, etc.) and conflict resolution. It is important to note that SyncML is *not* an application-layer communication protocol. SyncML can be bound to application-layer communication protocols such as HTTP. SyncML has primarily been designed with three transport protocols in mind: OBEX, HTTP, and WSP (WAP). We have already looked at HTTP and WSP in some detail. OBEX is a transport protocol well suited for short-range ad hoc wireless networking such as Bluetooth. At this point, it is important to note that there is a close relationship between SyncML and the Bluetooth synchronization profile.

The Bluetooth synchronization profile is a critical part of the Bluetooth standard that allows PDAs and other mobile devices supporting Bluetooth to synchronize with other Bluetooth-enabled devices such as PCs, USB Bluetooth adapters, etc. to synchronize data such as contacts in a PIM.

SyncML provides the following synchronization types:

1. Refresh synchronization from client: In this case, the client updates its information with the latest information on the server. The client does no writing of data back to the server.
2. Two-way synchronization: In this case, the client and server synchronize a partial or complete set of data on the client. Because the server is to resolve the conflicts, the client sends its data to the server first. See Figure 11.1.
3. Slow sync: The “slow” in Slow Synchronization should really be termed as “thorough” because slow synchronization means that all data are compared between the client and the server, field by field. This type of synchronization is rarely

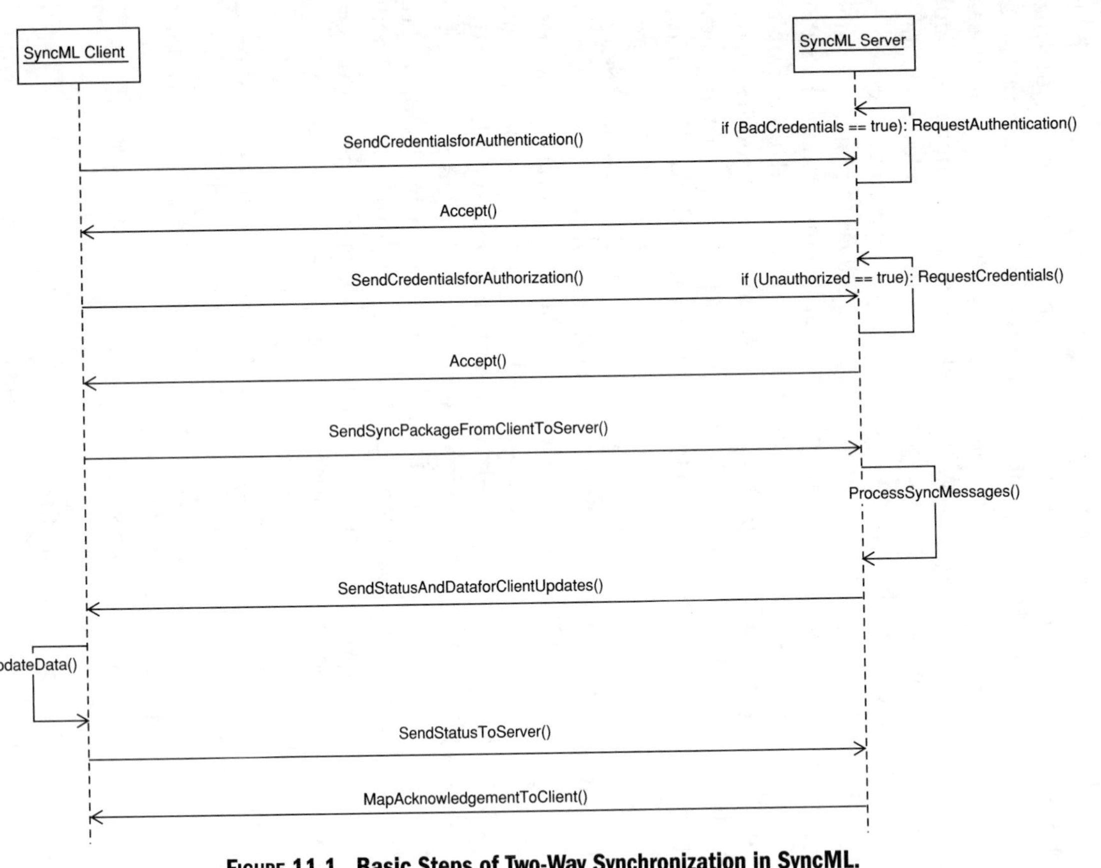

FIGURE 11.1. Basic Steps of Two-Way Synchronization in SyncML.

required, but it is necessary occasionally to recover from data corruptions or other problems.

4. One-way synchronization from client: This is a sync type in which the client sends its modifications to the server but the server does not send its modifications back to the client [SyncML Specification 1.1].
5. One-way synchronization from server: Many times the data on the client are read only or, alternatively, modifications to data are only persistent if they are made at the server. In such conditions, a one-way synchronization from the server, where only the server sends the data modified since the last modification to the client, is desired.
6. Refresh synchronization from client: There are situations in which the data sent by the client always completely replaces the data on the server without any synchronization. For example, the server may merely be a backup system for the client, or the server may hold data updated by several clients and the latest set of updates received from a client always overwrite all other changes. SyncML calls these types of synchronization refresh synchronization from client because the data on the server are refreshed without any analysis for conflicts.
7. Server-alerted synchronization: If some vital data on the server change and the client needs to know about this, it may be desirable for the server to notify the client so that the client can start to synchronize. In these situations, a server alerted synchronization is desirable.

Before we move on to look at the SyncML syntax, let us look at some terms and their definitions as defined by SyncML:

1. *Datastore*: In this text, we use the terms "data store" and "datastore" interchangeably. Datastores, as defined in this text and in SyncML, are simply a generic way to refer to some data storage mechanism, be it a database, a file system, or some other mechanism, that provides persistent storage of data.
2. *Device Info*: Because SyncML is designed with mobile applications in mind, and because the datastore on one device may need to synchronize with many different datastores on many different devices, the capabilities of the device determine the appropriate operations during synchronization. Device info is metadata about the devices involved in synchronization. It encapsulates the capabilities of the device related to data replication and synchronization.
3. *Meta Info*: Besides the information about the device, there is information about the specific synchronization to take place, about the specific datastores involved in a particular synchronization action and about the data to be exchanged in a specific synchronization action. Such information is really metadata about the synchronization commands and the data to be synchronized. Such information can include the average data chunks, the number of commands to be executed, etc.
4. *Message*: The term message is simply used to describe an envelope of information exchanged between a SyncML client and a SyncML server. Messages contain a header and a body. The body encapsulates the commands.

```
<SyncHdr>
    <VerDTD>1.0</VerDTD>
    <VerProto>SyncML/1.0</VerProto>
    <SessionID>session01</SessionID>
.....
</SyncHdr>
```

FIGURE 11.2. Sample SyncML Header Element.

5. *Command*: Commands are CRUD (Create, Read, Update, Delete) and similar operations that encapsulate the information about the actual data to be changed or they request some programmatic behavior to be invoked on the other node (e.g., the server can send the client an alert).
6. *Status Code*: SyncML specifies a series of status codes used in messages exchanged between the SyncML client and SyncML server that indicate the results of commands, for example the type of conflict between two data elements.

There are three main DTDs to SyncML: the main SyncML DTD, the Meta Info DTD, and the Device Info DTD. It is important to note that because SyncML documents may be encapsulated within other XML documents, SyncML messages must be well formed, but they do not have to be valid XML. This is because there can only be one instance of the DOCTYPE and XML version tags

```
<?xml version="1.0" encoding="UTF-8"?>
<!DOCTYPE application PUBLIC....>
```

per XML document. These tags are replaced by <VerDTD></VerDTD>, which wrap around the version number of the XML document on which the SyncML chunk is based, and <VerProto></VerProto> tags, which wrap around the version of SyncML used. Both of these tags are part of the SyncML header enclosed in <SyncHdr>. Therefore, we can have something like the code in Figure 11.2.

This brings us to the fact the SyncML XML document is broken down into a header and a body. The header, as you may expect, holds some metadata about the SyncML document. The next section is the SyncML body, which can include a variety of elements that specify commands for synchronization of data. These commands are as follows:

1. *<Sync>*: This command wraps around the other synchronization commands that outline a set of actions for data synchronization of two data collections. Anything unrelated to adding, deleting, or updating of records in one of the two data stores is not included.
2. *<Add>*: This command allows the server or the client to request a new record to be added. This command can only be specified within the <Sync> command.

3. *<Delete>*: This command allows the server or the client to specify that a data element or a collection of data elements must be deleted. This command allows for specification of whether the data to be deleted should be archived or not. If the data are archived, the term *soft-delete* is used. If they are not, the term *hard-delete* is used. This command can only be specified within the <Sync> command.
4. *<Update>*: This command allows the server or the client to specify that a data element or a collection of data elements should update existing data with new information. This command can only be specified within the <Sync> command. Note that an update means a complete replacement of the data element. The data element's segments (if such segments exist and can be programmatically recognized) are ignored.
5. *<Get>*: This command is used to request metainformation about an element. It is important to note that this command is not requesting the element or collection of elements that include the data values themselves. Rather, this command is a request for metainformation about the data that can be used for many reasons including determining what the next set of transactions should be, etc. Because this command does not include the actual data values, then it is not to be included within the <Sync> element.
6. *<Put>*: Like the <Get> command, this command must be used outside of the <Sync> command.
7. *<Alert>*: This command allows the initiator of a synchronization transaction to notify the recipient.
8. *<Atomic>*: This tag specifies transaction boundaries in SyncML. In other words, all of the commands inside this tag have to be successfully performed for the results to be committed to the corresponding data stores. Because of the transactional nature of the commands inside this tag, the order of the commands is also important: There may be interdependencies among the commands that are executed.
9. *<Copy>*: With this command the sender of the command asks the recipient to copy a data element or a collection of data elements.
10. *<Exec>*: Either the client or the server can ask the other to execute some executable program through this command. This command is subject to security restrictions.
11. *<Map>*: With this command the sender of the command asks the recipient to update the identifier mapping between the two elements or two data collections.
12. *<Results>*: This element wraps around the results of a <Get> or a <Search> command. The content returned is in *response* to a <Get> or <Search> request.
13. *<Search>*: Either the client or the server can ask the other to execute a query on its datastore and return the results with this command.
14. *<Status>*: Like <Results>, this element indicates the status of an operation requested by the client. This element is returned in response to a client request.

```
<SyncHdr>
    <DevInfo>
        <SwV>0.80</SwV>
        <HwV>1.0</HwV>
        ....
    </DevInfo>
    <MetaInf>
        <FreeMem>6400</FreeMem>
        <MaxMsgSize>1024</MaxMsgSize>
        ....
    </MetaInf>
....
</SyncHdr>
```

FIGURE 11.3. Sample Meta and Device Info SyncML Documents.

As we mentioned before, other DTDs define Meta Info for the synchronization session and the capabilities of the device that is the client during the synchronization process. Once again, because we want the ability to include SyncML information within other XML documents, Meta Info and Device Info SyncML documents are well formed but do not have to be valid XML documents on their own. Figure 11.3 shows samples of these documents.

It should be noted that the Device Info document is not just for describing the client, in our case the mobile device. It can be used by all of the nodes in a system supporting data replication and synchronization including servers, PCs, and other participants.

Here are some other notable features offered by SyncML:

1. *Chunking*: The SyncML specification calls this “Large Object Handling.” Specific attention has been paid to the fact that, because of the weak connectivity nature of most wireless connections and because of the limited resources on devices, the amount of data transferred in one message may be limited. For this reason, there is the <MoreData/> tag, which effectively provides a mechanism by which we can chunk the data.
2. *Security*: Obviously, one of the biggest concerns when dealing with data synchronization is security. Both parties have to assure that the other party is properly authenticated and authorized to avoid malignant behavior such as spoofing (a term to be explained in Chapter 14). To achieve this, first, we have to have the concept of a session. As we have seen already, stateful transactions are supported by SyncML as this is a necessary part of data replication and synchronization even without security concerns. The rest of the authentication process nearly mimics the HTTP authentication mechanism. Even the status codes are similar. It is important to remember that, though we may bind to a different transport protocol than HTTP, these status codes will remain the same. This is a very

good thing because we need to implement authentication and authorization independent of the transport layer binding. Notable in the authentication process is that security is broken down into authentication and authorization (as is customary with security). Figure 11.4 shows the basic authentication process. Note that the server may return a 200, in which case it is necessary for the client to reauthenticate, by sending the credentials to the server, along with every subsequent message.

3. *Initialization*: Before a SyncML client and server engage in a synchronization, an initialization process has to take place. Note that this is not same as an alert sent by the server to the client. Rather, the initialization process encapsulates authentication and exchange of device capabilities. In other words, the server first authenticates the client and then the two exchange what they can and cannot do so that the synchronization commands are executed with the capabilities of the two nodes in mind. The initialization information is encapsulated in the SyncHdr element. We noted before that the DTD for the metainformation and the device capabilities are separate from the SyncML body DTD, but this does not mean that separate documents are used. The metainformation and the device capabilities are placed in the header through the use of XML namespaces.
4. *Errors*: Synchronization and other errors are well defined in SyncML. Whereas some implementation of the SyncML server behavior is optional, you can count on some basic messages that will notify you of basic errors such as incomplete SyncML documents, data conflicts, etc.
5. *Alert Codes*: There are a set of well-defined alert codes through which the server can alert the client in an efficient manner.
6. *WBXML*: We previously mentioned the usage of WBXML (Chapter 3) as a content format for the data being shipped back and forth with SyncML. There has been special consideration given to WBXML because it is a more compact format for XML-based data.

We have made considerable generalization and summarization in our discussion of SyncML for the sake of brevity. Note that our main purpose here is to see the basic functionality encapsulated in SyncML so that you can effectively use it in your mobile applications. In most cases, the base operating system platform will either offer a SyncML implementation or you will be able to easily find an example of a commercial or open-source implementation of a programmatic interface for SyncML implementation on the device and servers. An example of such is Sync4J, which we will look at next.

11.4.1 Sync4J

Sync4J is a complete open-source implementation of SyncML with the Java programming language. Currently, Sync4J is only available for the full-blown JVM (J2SE and J2EE); therefore, it is primarily intended for the higher end devices that can run the full-blown JVM. There are two parts to the Sync4J project: the client and the server. At present, Sync4J uses basic XML parsing APIs such as SAX and DOM to parse SyncML documents.

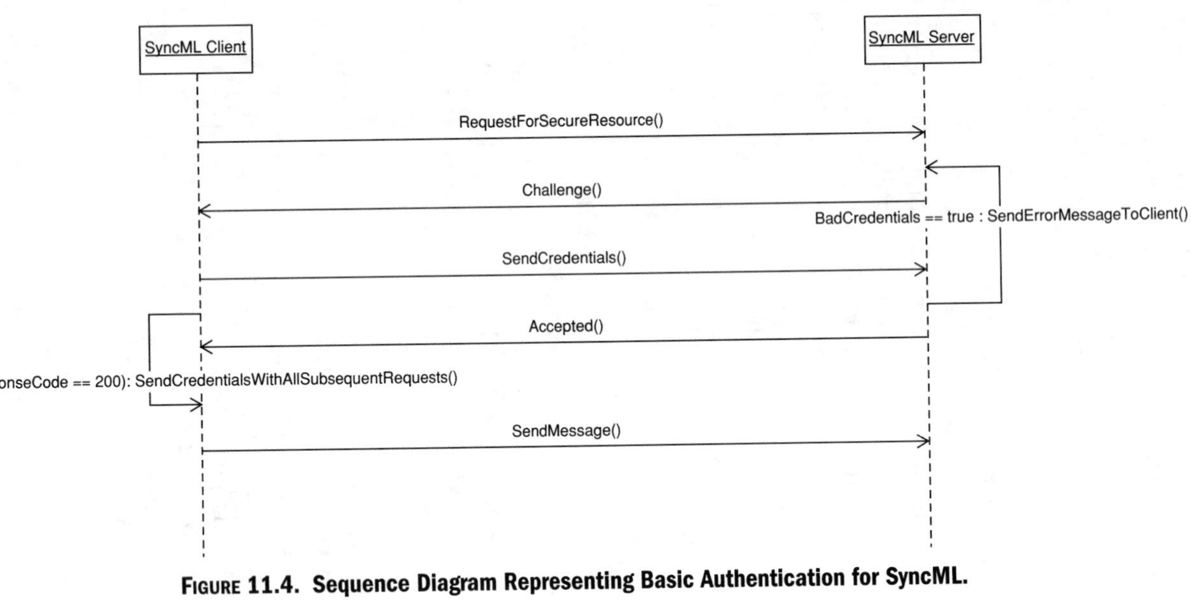

FIGURE 11.4. Sequence Diagram Representing Basic Authentication for SyncML.

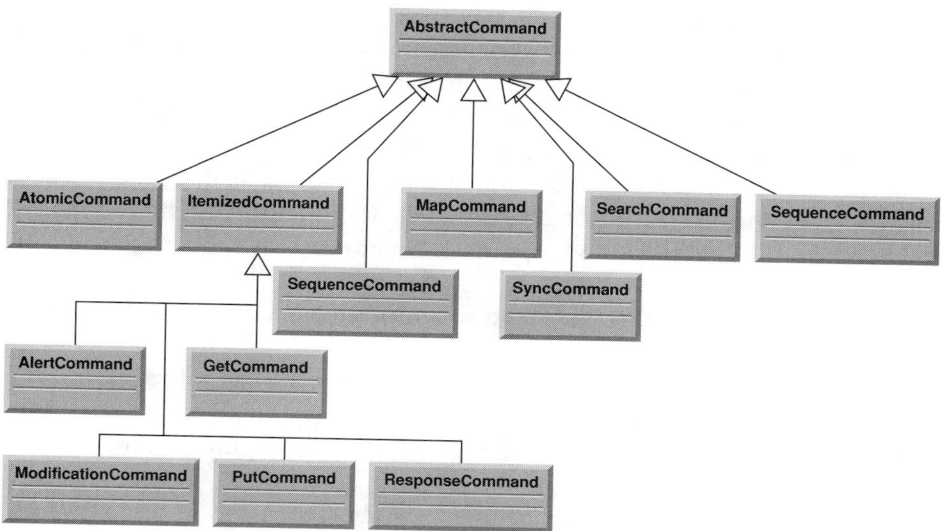

FIGURE 11.5. Class Diagram of Sync4J Implementation of SyncML Commands.

The single biggest value of Sync4J is that it completely hides the complexity of SyncML, which as we have seen is a fairly complex and comprehensive specification, from the Java developer while exposing a natural Java-based API. Figure 11.5 shows the UML class diagram that depicts some of the internal implementation of Sync4J, particularly the mapping of the SyncML body to classes exposed through the Sync4J APIs.

At the time of authoring this text, there is no standard implementation of SyncML, nor a useful subset thereof, for the J2ME CLDC/MIDP platform. However, implementing the crucial CRUD commands is not too big of a task. Depending on what type of J2ME device you have, you may find a different persistence mechanism and therefore have different abilities and application requirements for implementation of data replication and synchronization.

11.4.2 Bluetooth Synchronization Profile

As we mentioned in Side Discussion 11.1, Bluetooth has a synchronization profile. We looked at Bluetooth as a short-range wireless ad hoc networking communication channel in Chapter 10. The Bluetooth synchronization profile enables us to use Bluetooth as a tool to perform data synchronization and replication between the Bluetooth-enabled mobile device and another Bluetooth-enabled mobile device, a Bluetooth-enabled PC, or some other converter such as a Bluetooth-to-USB converter that eventually connects to a data store.

The Bluetooth synchronization profile allows for client-initiated, server-initiated, or automatic synchronizations. It should be obvious that data synchronization through Bluetooth falls under the one-to-one synchronization model because the two devices form an ad hoc network after which they exchange data. This means that once the two devices are connected together through the ad hoc Bluetooth network, we can sit at the PC and press a button on an application that initiates synchronization, we can push a button on the PDA that performs the synchronization, or, alternatively, we can schedule a synchronization on time intervals, connection intervals, or based on some other event on which either the server or the client initiate synchronization automatically.

Bluetooth synchronization is mainly intended to support at least one of the basic PIM features of a phonebook in vCard format, a calendar in vCalendar format, a simple message in vMessage format, or a note in the vNote format. Because the application-layer transport protocol for Bluetooth is OBEX, then data synchronization is performed on top of OBEX in one of the following ways:

1. Either the client or the server sends a connect message to the other party to initiate synchronization.
2. Either the client or the server sends a put message to send information to the other party during synchronization that includes synchronization information.
3. Either the client or the server sends a get message to get information from the other party during synchronization.
4. Either the client or the server can send an abort message to discontinue all transactions.
5. Either client or the server can signal the end of the synchronization sequence by sending a disconnect message.

You may wonder at this point whether you will have to write a lot of code, or get a library, that implements the OBEX calls if you want to synchronize with a Bluetooth device. The fact is that there is a close relationship between the Bluetooth creators and SyncML creators. So, most devices that support Bluetooth have an implementation of SyncML on top of the Bluetooth synchronization profile (which in turn uses OBEX). Consequently, you probably will never have to worry about implementing the Bluetooth synchronization profile, but you may need to understand the SyncML binding with OBEX for your implementation.

11.5 WebDAV

WebDAV (Web-based Distributed Authoring and Versioning) is a set of HTTP extensions that allows us to modify and update a set of files in a collaborative environment. WebDAV was conceived at the University California at Irvine and has since gained a great amount of adoption throughout various open-source and commercial products, the most famous of which is the Microsoft Windows Web Folders. There are also products such as Endeavor Technologies' MAGI, which provide a comprehensive and ubiquitous collaborative work environment that is based on WebDAV. Many WebDAV-based products such as MAGI support mobile platforms such as Windows CE and the Palm operating system. It is important to note though that because the concept of a file is important to WebDAV, the mobile device and platform for which you are considering using WebDAV should at least be able to support basic files. In addition, for two-way communication, you will need to be able to run an HTTP server and an HTTP client on the device. For one-way communication, you can get away with having only one of the two.

WebDAV provides functionality for locking and unlocking files remotely and performing basic file-based operations such as moving, copying, removing, adding, and querying the system for a list of files. Although WebDAV does not provide data synchronization and replication, it does provide a mechanism to modify and update a set of files by multiple users. Therefore, it provides a basic infrastructure on top of which replication and synchronization may be built. The difference between the functionality provided by WebDAV and typical database replication and synchronization type functionality is twofold: No conflict resolution is provided and granularity is at the file level.

WebDAV is extremely well thought out. First, it is built on the top of the RESTful HTTP (see Chapters 1 and 16). Second, it uses XML as the underlying messaging format. WebDAV is a true HTTP extension that does not violate any principles of HTTP design (as do many of the various Web services available). Finally, WebDAV is small, thereby making its implementation light and possible on mobile devices.

WebDAV can be quite useful in substituting for data replication and synchronization in the following mobile environments:

1. If the data are only being modified at one node and then replicated to other nodes, we can use WebDAV to replace the replication mechanism by simply copying the files.
2. If the record granularity is equal to file granularity (every record is its own file), we can use WebDAV. This happens rarely, but it does happen.

WebDAV does not offer us a data replication and synchronization mechanism; however, it offers us two possibilities: building a real data replication and synchronization on top of it or using it to substitute the simplest of replication and synchronization mechanisms, thus giving us a lightweight elegant solution to providing HTTP-based access to files.

11.6 Mobile Agents, Replication, and Synchronization

One of the biggest promises of mobile agents for mobile computing is their ability to operate equally well whether or not the mobile device is connected to the network. In this way, mobile agents can be very helpful in replicating and synchronizing data. Here are the scenarios with which mobile agents can assist us in replicating and synchronizing mobile data:

1. Mobile agent A running on a mobile device constituting host C can be invoked, begin running, scan the local datastore, and recognize the stale data based on some set of rules. Conversely, it may migrate to a host B, where it analyzes the data on the datastore residing on host B and recognizes the stale data. Subsequently, it migrates back to the host from which it came from, host C, and performs the data replication and synchronization. The mobile agent can carry the actual data back to host C, can carry metadata (meta info in SyncML terminology) about the synchronization to take place, or communicate with

some other mobile agent D, which resides on host C, or is aware of the data replication and synchronization to take place on host C.

2. Mobile agent A can act as a proxy for other mobile agents or systems that provide synchronization or replication and cannot communicate directly because of impedance mismatch in various parts of the system, anywhere from the underlying communication networks, to the replication and synchronization protocols, to the datastores themselves. In this scenario, mobile agent A can migrate to the different hosts while carrying the actual data to be synchronized or carrying metadata about the data to be synchronized and perform data replication and synchronization iteratively or completely.

As we mentioned in Chapter 9, mobile agents present us with a very promising technology to solve many of the different mobile application problems. However, like some of the other areas that we have already seen, the usage of mobile agents to perform data replication and synchronization is an area mostly in the research stages at the time of authoring this text. It is important for you to keep in mind the possibility of using mobile agents for data replication and synchronization as these technologies are being developed at a rapid pace.

Let us end this chapter by a quick look at how we can use UML to represent data replication and synchronization.

11.7 Using UML to Represent Data Replication and Synchronization Schemes

As with everything else that we have covered in this text, once again, we would like to continue to use UML diagrams to represent design and implementation of our system. Reading any UML book or the UML specifications, you will run into the word "synchronized" or "synchronous" many times. However, most of the time, this is a reference to a synchronized object (an object that can be accessed by one thread at a time) or a synchronous transaction (where the current thread must finish executing the specific synchronous transactions before any other transactions are executed).

To represent data synchronization in UML, we do not really need any extensions. The subject of object-to-relational mapping and representing data stores (specifically databases) in UML is a topic that has attracted the most number of proposed UML extensions. Our topic is somewhat orthogonal to this because we are discussing replication and synchronization of those datastores and not the representation of them or the mapping between their internal implementation and object-oriented programs. Usage of UML to represent synchronization while using any such extensions will depend on what the specific extensions are. Because there is a broad range of disagreements on the topic of object-to-relational mapping and representation of datastores with UML, we will leave such extensions out of our topic of discussion.

However, this does not mean that we cannot use UML to represent synchronization. In fact, UML's sequence diagrams offer us a perfect tool to represent sequential interactions between clients and servers—the model that most synchronization technologies utilize. The temporal nature of data replication and synchronization, and the fact that it happens between multiple datastore entities, make it ideal to represent with a sequence diagram at a high level.

Collaboration diagrams can prove useful as well as synchronization is about direct or indirect collaboration of two datastores in a client–server environment. If we are using mobile agent technologies to synchronize data, then we may want to use state diagrams to show the various states that the agent goes through or utilize the extensions that we introduced earlier in Chapter 9 for representing the behavior of the agent.

The point here is that we have already introduced all of those tools that we need to represent data replication and synchronization in UML outside of the hotly debated topic of data modeling with UML. As with the other uses of UML, it is the job of the designer to recognize the appropriate use of UML diagrams for representing data replication and synchronization in his or her mobile application.

CHAPTER 12

Mobility and Location-Based Services

> If the rich could hire someone else to die for them, the poor would make a wonderful living.
>
> Jewish proverb

12.1 INTRODUCTION

Location, location, location. The changing location of the user and the device used by the user make mobile applications fundamentally different from their stationary counterparts. Yet, most software developers, even those who have some experience with mobile applications, have little experience and understanding in how location-based information is gathered and distributed and how this information may be utilized by mobile applications. Although we will not be able to cover all aspects of location-based information in mobile applications, we will try to tackle the basic problems in this chapter.

If you have looked into developing mobile applications, you have certainly heard of "location-based services." The UTMS Forum defines location-based services as follows:

> Business and consumer 3G services that enable users or machines to find other people, vehicles, resources, services, or machines. They also enable others to find users as well as enabling users to identify their own location via terminal or vehicle identification.

This definition is somewhat narrow as it limits location-based services to 3G services. There are many location-based services that do not have any relationship with 3G services. So, location-based services are those things that provide the mobile device, the mobile application, and the mobile user with location information about themselves or other devices, applications, and users.

In this chapter, we will first look at different ways of obtaining the user's location information and how location information, including maps and other artifacts thereof, has historically been treated. Next, we will look at some sample mobile applications that take advantage of location information. Because the field of location information is still in its infancy, most developers are not even familiar with the myriad ways that location information may be used. This will help us set up some context for showing how to use location information to build mobile applications. Finally, we will see how we can use UML to model the changing location of the user and the mobile device so that we can create more meaningful models of our applications before setting off to implement them.

Let us get started.

12.2 Data Acquisition of Location Information

To use location information in our application, we first have to have a way to get it. As we mentioned in Chapter 1, there are three major techniques for locating things: triangulation, proximity, and scene analysis. Figure 12.1 shows how GPS systems use triangulation. As a quick review, *triangulation* relies on age-old geometric methods that allow calculation of the location of a point that lies in the middle of three other points whose exact locations are known. If the distance to each one of the three points is known, we can use geometric techniques to calculate the exact location of the unknown point. *Proximity*-based methods measure the relative position of the unknown point to some known point. *Scene analysis* relies on image processing and topographical techniques to calculate the location of the unknown point based on a view of the unknown point from a known point.

For the purposes of mobile computing, scene analysis is the least important and the one that we will not discuss much here. There are two categories of systems to acquire location information of a device: those that are based on the GPS and those that are not. Triangulation and proximity are both used in GPS and non-GPS-based systems. Of course, there are additional techniques that combine other techniques that may fall within one or both of these categories. Among the second category are methods that use properties of wireless networks such as cellular networks or short-range WLANs. Location information acquired by either method has some margin of error. There are also some methods, within the latter group, that do not give us an absolute location; rather, they provide information about location relative to some other known location. The various methods and their relationships are depicted in Figure 12.2.

Finding the location information is not where things end. Once the location of a device, and thereby a user, is determined, we may need to update this information with some frequency. We may want to permanently store this information or compare it with some database of location information. How we obtain the location

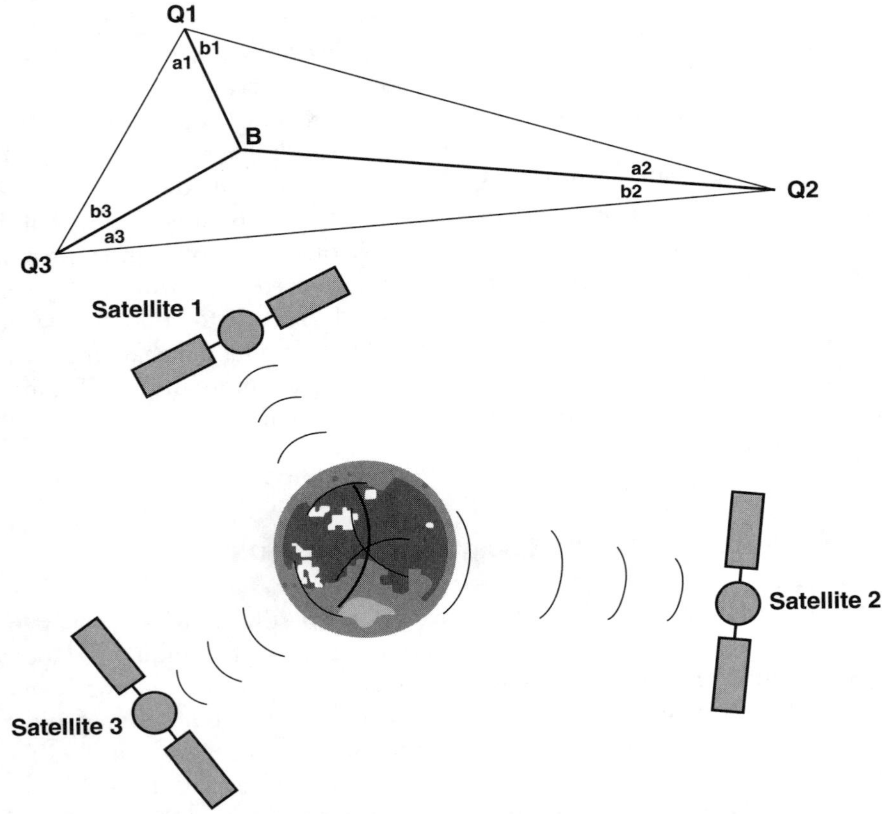

FIGURE 12.1. GPS: A System of Satellites Providing Location Information.

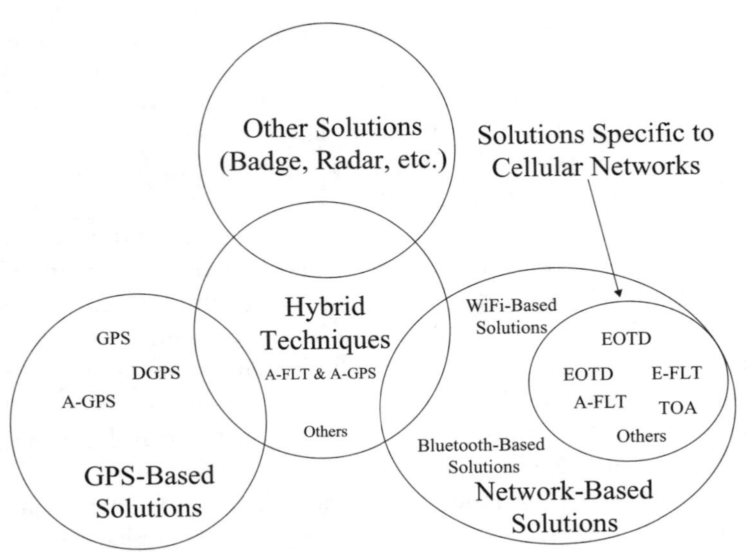

FIGURE 12.2. Taxonomy of Today's Popular Location Acquisition Techniques.

information also makes a difference in how difficult it may be to use the information in our application.

Now, let us look at GPS, the most established method of obtaining location information electronically.

12.2.1 GPS-Based Solutions

In Chapter 1, we briefly talked about the GPS. A system of satellites is positioned around the earth, with each broadcasting a signal that can be used, by a GPS-enabled device, to determine its location. GPS devices typically use the signal coming from three or four different satellites. Sometimes, the device itself does the triangulation and sometimes it sends the information back to the network where the calculation is done. The accuracy of the position determined by using GPS is anywhere from 5 to 40 meters. Of course, a GPS uses a signal broadcast by a set of satellites, the GPS-enabled device must have an electronically unobstructed path to the satellites. This could mean a lot of things! Basically, the SNR drops off because the sky may not be clear, the device may be used in a building where the physical structure reduces the SNR, or because of other factors.

The major advantage of GPS is that it is a simple solution. There are currently single-chip solutions that include an entire GPS system. Such chips will undoubtedly get smaller as the technology improves. Also, using GPS allows us to calculate a latitude and a longitude as opposed to a relative location. Such absolute location (well, not quite absolute according to Einstein, but absolute enough for our purposes) has many inherent computing advantages.

A-GPS, or Assisted GPS, uses network receivers that are positioned in intervals of 200 to 400 kilometers. The wireless network can then provide location information as well in case there is a problem with receiving enough signal at a particular location from the GPS satellites. By providing the location information through the wireless network, A-GPS provides a more reliable location information service to the device. It also reduces the TTFF (Time-to-First-Fix), which can be in excess of 20 seconds.

Differential GPS, or DGPS, is similar to A-GPS in that the location information from GPS is improved by the network. DGPS increases the location accuracy of conventional GPS, but it does not increase the sensitivity of GPS receivers; A-GPS improves the performance of conventional GPS receivers in low-SNR conditions and can be combined with DGPS to increase the geolocation accuracy as well [Djuknic and Richton 2002].

The military had used GPS for years for acquiring accurate location information prior to year 2000 while GPS access was provided, but the U.S. government had intentionally degraded the GPS signal to provide less accurate information to non-military devices. This is called "selective availability." However, this degradation was removed in year 2000 and GPS with the highest accuracy possible can now be used in commercial applications.

GPS System of Satellites

The GPS system consists of a constellation of twenty-four satellites, orbiting the earth every twelve hours, in groups of four following six separate orbits. These satellites transmit two signals, one at 1575.42 MHz and the other at 1227.60 MHz. Commercial GPS devices use the signal broadcast on 1575.42 MHz. The signal being broadcast from the satellite includes a timestamp and the identity of the satellite that allows the GPS device to calculate distance to the satellite based on the when the signal is received. This of course relies heavily on exact correctness of the internal clock of the GPS device. Whatever inaccuracy inherent in the device clock (and most clocks are not perfectly in sync with the satellite clocks) is reflected in the calculated location. The GPS device then uses triangulation of its distance to three or more satellites to calculate its location.

GPS Receivers

There are several types of GPS receivers: *sequential receivers*, *continuous receivers*, and *multiplex receivers*. Sequential receivers receive a maximum of two signals at a time, looking for the signals coming from the different satellites in a sequential manner. These receivers have the slowest TTFF, typically between 20 and 45 seconds. Continuous receivers can receive signals from all of the satellites at the same time (more than three at a time because three is the minimum number of satellites needed to do triangulation). Continuous receiving gives us the best performance, offering at least four receiving channels that can be operated simultaneously. Multiplex receivers cannot track as many satellites as continuous receivers simultaneously; however, they can multiplex between the available channels and track more satellites than the sequential receivers, thereby yielding performance that lies somewhere in between the sequential and continuous receivers.

Single-chip GPS solutions are being deployed in small mobile devices such as mobile phones and PDAs. We will look at some of these devices later in this text. For the purposes of mobile computing applications, we are most interested in GPS receivers that can integrate and attach to mobile devices or those that can be used in building mobile devices. The scenario of the user carrying two separate devices, a GPS device and a mobile computing device such as a PDA or mobile phone, is not a likely one for our purposes.

12.2.2 Non-GPS Location Solutions

There are a variety of schemes and methods designed to discover the location of things without the usage of GPS. These methods range anywhere from radar systems to badge-based systems. We will only look at those systems that we surmise to be of most significance to mobile applications. Most of these positioning systems use the properties of the wireless network for locating the device that is using the wireless network. Whereas GPS is the most robust method of obtaining location information to date, there are some clear advantages in not using GPS-based systems. First, the availability of GPS signals is not guaranteed. As we previously mentioned, these signals were intentionally degraded until very recently and there is nothing that guarantees they will not be degraded again, for security or other reasons. Also, a GPS signal can be unreliable when inside buildings, when underground, in bad weather, or under any other circumstance that reduces SNR. Like their GPS-based location solutions, some non-GPS location solutions obtain the raw information on the device, send it to the network for calculation of the actual location, and get back the actual location if needed. Other solutions put all of this computing on the device. This depends on the technique used to obtain the location and the computing capabilities of the device. Among the subcategories of non-GPS-based solutions are *network-based* solutions, which use the properties of an underlying wireless network, *MS-assisted network-based* (where MS stands for Mobile Station) solutions, which require the nonactive participation of the mobile device (often referred to as mobile station within the wireless networking community), and *MS-based network-assisted* solutions, which require the active participation of the mobile device in determining the location.

Cell Identification Solutions

Cell ID–based solutions are probably the most rudimentary way of obtaining the location of a device that uses a cellular wireless network. The location of a device that uses a cellular network as a method of wireless connectivity can be approximated by the absolute location of the cellular node to which it is connected. This can be enhanced with Timing Advanced (TA) measurement. TA is the measured time between the start of a radio frame and a data burst [Andersson 2002]. The accuracy of this technique depends largely on the type of cellular network (how wide of a range each cell covers, how reliable the handoff process may be, etc.). Typically, with networks in Europe and the United States, the best-case accuracy here is about 500 meters. The position of the device is calculated by the network and transmitted to the device if the information is required by the device (i.e., the application that is running on the device).

Time-of-Arrival Solutions

One way of determining distance is to measure the time difference between when a signal is transmitted and when it is received. This distance can then be used to calculate a rough geographical position, based on the location of either the source or the destination of the signal. Time-of-Arrival (TOA) solutions calculate the distance of a mobile device from a cell node based on the time it takes for a signal coming from the mobile device to the network cell node. As the cell node can also obtain the direction from which the signal is coming, it can calculate a distance and direction for the position of the mobile device, thereby calculating the position of the mobile device based on the position of the cell node that receives the signal. (This depends on the specific cellular technology; some cellular systems do not provide accurate directional information.) The accuracy of this method depends largely on the type of cellular network; the margin of error can be as low as 100 meters. Figure 12.3 shows the effect of the cell size and structure on the accuracy of location: the smaller the cell sizes, the more accurate the location information.

Obviously, this method of obtaining the location information is specific to mobile applications and devices that connect to the network with a wireless cellular network such as TDMA, CDMA, CDPD, or others. TOA techniques provide an absolute location based on the relative location of the mobile user to the cell node whose absolute position is known. TOA has some advantages over cell ID–based techniques in offering somewhat more accurate location information for those cell

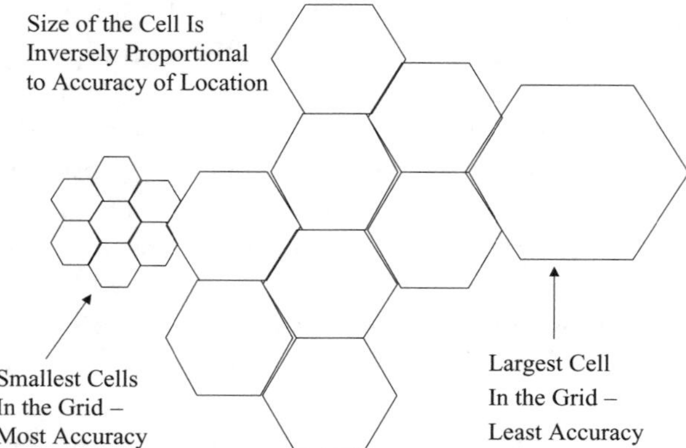

FIGURE 12.3. Effect of the Cell Size on Accuracy of the Location Information Provided by Network-Based Methods for Cellular Networks.

networks that have larger cells. Also, TOA techniques are more easily implemented in legacy wireless networks, though upgrades are still very expensive.

Enhanced Observed Time Difference

The Enhanced Observed Time Difference (E-TOD) method is similar to the TOA method in that the time it takes for the signal to travel is used to calculate distance. However, this time, it is the time that it takes the signal to reach the mobile device from the source of the signal. GPS is typically used to provide an absolute position for the source, which is sent to the device. The device, then, uses its relative position to the source and the absolute position of the source to calculate its absolute position. The accuracy of this method is roughly 125 meters. The important distinction here is that the work is being done on the device itself. Theoretically, this method is really a hybrid of GPS and non-GPS-based techniques because GPS is typically used at the base stations to obtain absolute locations. E-TOD is an MS-assisted network-based solution. Of course, base stations typically do not move, so, practically speaking, it is not a hybrid method.

Other Network-Based Techniques

There are a variety of other techniques that provide more accurate location information, adding features to the basic techniques that we have mentioned. Others take advantage of properties of specific networks. Forward Link Trilateration (FLT) is a pure network-based solution that uses a single cellular network base station. There are two techniques that build on FLT: Advanced Forward Link Trilateration (A-FLT) and Enhanced Forward Link Trilateration (E-FLT). A-FLT uses the mobile device to improve coverage and accuracy (MS-assisted network based). E-FLT uses network properties unique to CDMA networks. Performance is enhanced by complementary methods, including pattern matching of RF (radio frequency) characteristics, statistical modeling, round-trip delay measurements, and AOA (angle of arrival) [Djuknic and Richton 2002].

Wireless LAN-Based Solutions

Short-range wireless networks such as WIFI and Bluetooth have properties that can be used to determine the location of various nodes. First, the signal quality degrades quadratically proportional to distance (or with an even steeper falloff as there would be additional degradation owing to noise). In the case of WLANs, this degradation is fairly significant (which is why they are suitable for local and not wide area networking). Larger networks can be composed of WLANs whose coverages are next to each other, or even have some overlap, so that the mobile device can move through several networks without losing connectivity for a significant amount of time (or not at all as operating systems and wireless networking equipment improve in quality).

Simply connecting to a particular WLAN tells us that the connected device is within the range of the WLAN's coverage. If the WLAN's transmitting location (wireless hub, router, etc.) is known, then we can use it as an approximate location for the mobile device. In so-called hot spots we can easily track the motion of the user as he or she moves from one WLAN to the neighboring one. Furthermore, by adding some software, we can cut down the margin of error by using the signal attenuation. This, however, is an unreliable method of improving our location information because some physical obstacles reduce SNR more than others. Alternatively, if there is significant overlap among the different WLANs, we can use triangulation to get a more accurate fix on the connected device.

There are also some unique problems associated with location sensitivity and WLANs. If you consider a hot spot covered by many different WLAN segments, with some crossing coverage boundaries into the coverage areas of others, the implementation of the ad hoc networking technique has a substantial effect on the accuracy of the fix on the connected device. This is mainly because, for load balancing or other purposes, a given device may not be connected to the nearest available WLAN; likewise, because of the topology of the WLANs, one or more of the WLANs may be "hidden" when a given user is in a particular location.

Despite these challenges, WLANs offer an excellent method for getting approximate locations of a user in enclosed spaces such as shopping malls.

The relationship between WLANs and location sensitivity is symbiotic: WLANs can use location information to perform their primary task of routing data as well. Particularly, location information can be used in mobile ad hoc networks, known as MANETs. MANETs are not exclusive to short-range wireless networks, but they tend to be more popular in this arena because long-range technologies such as TDMA and CDMA require stationary cell sites. The location of the various participants in the ad hoc network can be provided through the use of GPS or other related systems that do not rely on the network topology (as this would create a circular dependency between location of the participants of the network and how they form the network). From a graph viewpoint, routing in a MANET is like finding a path—typically the shortest—from a source to a destination in a graph [Tseng et al. 2001]. There are several network routing protocols currently being worked on to use location information as either the base routing protocol or a method to enhance the short-range wireless network. Location-Aided Routing

[Ko and Vaidya 1998], Geographic Distance Routing [Lin and Stojmenovic 1999], and Geogrid [Liao et al. 2000] are among them. A key feature of these protocols is the use of location information to reduce traffic during the discovery process and to reduce the number of hops required to reach a destination.

We have now looked at a variety of methods to obtain the location of a mobile device. Before we move on to see how we can use this information, let us look at GIS systems, a piece of the puzzle required to use location information whether the system is mobile or stationary.

12.3 GIS

A geographic information system or GIS is a configuration of computer hardware and software specifically designed for the acquisition, maintenance, and use of cartographic data [Tomlinson 1990]. The usages of GIS for stationary applications are numerous. They are used in a variety of applications from providing real-estate solutions to assisting firefighters. These systems are specially designed to store geographic data such as maps, aerial photos, and surveys; provide flexible querying mechanisms for retrieving such information and reporting on the stored data; and provide advanced features such as transformations, modeling, and performing statistical analyses on the stored data. In many ways, GIS systems are similar to databases, but they are designed specially to input, store, and retrieve geographic data in a way natural to the domain of study of the surface of the earth.

So, GIS systems encompass the integration of databases, computer cartography, location sensing, and computer-aided design (CAD) systems. In this text and within the domain of mobile application development, we will refer to all such functionality as the GIS system except for that which handles the actual acquiring and providing of the location of a mobile device using GPS, network-based methods, or any other technique. We refer to the latter as the "location-based service" or the "location sensitivity" system. The reason for making this distinction is to simply keep things clear. Within the framework of developing mobile applications, we are much more concerned with acquisition and usage of the location information than with cross-referencing it and usage of maps and other tools. This is not to belittle the importance of such tools; merely, we do not discuss those parts of GIS systems because they have been used for stationary applications and have matured; there are many sources to learn about them and use them for your mobile applications (see, for example, works by C. Dana Tomlinson [Tomlinson 1990], Jeffrey Star, and John Estes [Star and Estes 1990]).

GIS applications are used by civil engineers, geologists, structural engineers, military intelligence, and a host of others. When it comes to mobile applications and location-based services, their biggest use is in cross-reference systems to retrieve information such as maps, surveys, directions, and other things that relate to one or more sets of location coordinates. So, a typical problem for you as a mobile application developer may be to obtain the location of a user using location-sensitivity technology (GPS, non-GPS, etc.) and then use that information to pull a map from a GIS system to show the user where he or she is. In fact, this is a great part of the functionality that many of the automotive navigation systems (telematics) to date offer.

Based on this definition and the respective role of GIS in designing and implementing location-sensitive mobile applications, first we need to have a basic understanding of how GIS systems work, then we need to see some examples of how they can be useful in mobile applications, and, finally, we need to see how we can create well-designed interfaces between our mobile applications and GIS systems.

12.3.1 The Internals of GIS Systems

Let us start by looking at what sort of data GIS systems store. GIS systems can store data much like Computer Aided Drawing and Drafting (CADD) or CAD systems do: using elementary geometry. In other words, they can store information about points, which may be locations, or store various shapes such as lines, polygons, curves, and others, which can be represented using various coordinate systems (Cartesian, cylindrical, spherical, etc.) and can be vector based or raster based. In addition to these types of information, GIS systems can also store symbolic information such as floor plans, roads, city maps, infrastructure plans (water lines, etc.), and other types of categorized spatial information. GIS systems can also hold graphic maps, which may be simple bitmaps with no associated metadata or complex and composed of semantically meaningful metadata accompanied by layered graphics.

In addition to storing data, GIS systems can process data. Most GIS systems have at least some advanced image-processing capabilities that allow meaningful processing of maps, they provide statistical analysis tools for analyzing the stored data, they allow correlating and layering of different types of spatial information about the same location (e.g., layering the water lines on top of the terrain), and they enable other types of operations to be performed on the stored information. Most recent GIS systems provide pattern recognition algorithms that allow the clients to analyze the stored information for recurring patterns. We will discuss issues of security and privacy in Section 12.8.

Finally, GIS systems provide multiple methods of retrieving the stored or processed location information. This is going to be the part that most mobile applications use. GIS systems allow us to pull the map for a given area, acquire information about the number of floors of a particular building that the user may be in, and find out the elevation of the natural terrain at a given latitude and longitude.

GIS systems are increasingly designed and implemented with object-oriented languages as geographic information lends itself to object orientation very naturally. Because of this, the programmatic access to most GIS systems has moved toward an object-oriented API.

GIS systems typically have to be run on higher end hardware that provides fast processing of images and good floating-point arithmetic.

Among the most popular commercial GIS systems are ArcGIS, a product of ESRI, GeoMedia, a product of Intergraph, and MapInfo, a product of MapInfo Corporation.

12.3.2 Using GIS for Mobile Applications

Simply locating a device or a user is useful. This is done through the location-sensing technologies that we surveyed earlier in this chapter. However, the usefulness of just knowing this location is miniscule compared to all of the relevant information that we can gather regarding that location. For example, let us say we know that a given user is standing at the corner of a street. We can provide some basic services based on knowing just the location. Using a GIS system, however, we can find out directions to the destination and pull up a map that he or she can view. We can tell the user whether he or she is near a favorite place (restaurant, friend's house, or whatever may have been entered into that user's profile that may be cross-referenced for distance and directions through the GIS system). GIS systems have been used, along with mobile devices, to track endangered species to determine migration patterns and other information crucial to avoiding their extinction.

And this is just the beginning.

Historical information of the movement of a mobile user comprises some of the most useful information we can have. Using a GIS system, we can recognize patterns in those movements. For example, we can tell the user which way is statistically the fastest way to get home based on his or her travel patterns and which restaurants he or she visits more frequently. We can also use historical location information of a group of users to determine behavioral patterns about that particular group. Correlations of such patterns and geographical patterns, in turn, can yield extremely useful information.

12.3.3 Building Interfaces between Mobile Applications and GIS Systems

Most legacy GIS systems offer proprietary APIs, each with some bias toward the domain(s) of the customers that a given product catered to. However, in recent years, there has been a move to standardize the interface to GIS systems. As in the case of most other systems, you can build your own (which we definitely recommend against), buy, or subscribe. GIS systems are far too complex to build. Even if you have a small subset of a GIS system, do not attempt to build it. There are a variety of service-based GIS systems, the simplest of which start with the likes of MapQuest, that can offer you a Web service–based interface. For larger organizations that want to own their own GIS-related data, purchasing a GIS system may be an option; nevertheless, most GIS systems are very expensive and buying one falls outside of the buying power of most medium-sized companies.

The interface that you build to access information on a GIS system is either from an application running on the device or from an application running on the network. There is typically no need to build this interface directly to an application running on the device: GIS systems are typically used to reference information that is first acquired by the location-sensitivity technology, on the device or otherwise. We recommend, that if your architecture and requirements allow, you hide the interface to the GIS system from the mobile device even in the case where there is a mobile application running on the mobile device. Regardless, network connectivity is needed because GIS systems are foreign to the core mobile applications;

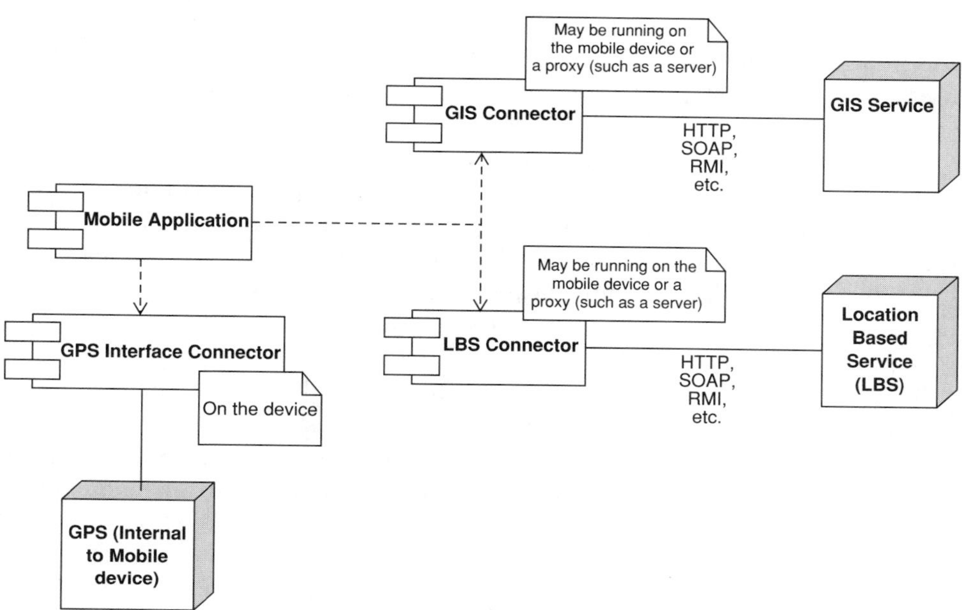

FIGURE 12.4. Typical Mobile Application Architecture for Communicating with a GIS System.

therefore, the mobile application may as well rely on a the network-based portion of application to do the interfacing with the external GIS system.

A typical mobile application architecture for communicating with a GIS system is shown in Figure 12.4. The protocols used to interface with GIS systems depend on the implementation of the GIS system and on how the various concepts related to location and changing of location are modeled. The actual specific protocols, obviously, are not as important as the governing principles that drive the design and implementation of these protocols. APIs to commercial applications such as GIS systems will come and go as the commercial products, themselves, are born, evolve, and eventually die off. However, if you design your mobile application properly, it can interface with foreign mobile systems with minimal coupling to any specific GIS system. To do this, we need to get a better understanding of the driving forces of design and implementations behind location APIs, the most important of which is how spatial information is modeled.

12.4 LOCATION INFORMATION MODELING

Now that we have seen some methods for obtaining the location information as well as systems that allow us to cross-reference useful information such as maps using the location information, let us explore some of the programmatic techniques for representing location information. Although we will look at modeling location information with UML later on in this chapter, we need to consider expressing location information in a more rudimentary level. Namely, we need some way of organizing location information so that it can be stored and made accessible to various computer systems, so that various computer systems can exchange this information among themselves and, for our specific purposes, so that we can use location information in an architecturally clean manner for usage in mobile applications.

Obviously, this has been something to which the academic and commercial communities have given considerable thought. In this text, we will present some of the standards that represent the more promising solutions for this problem (although, obviously, there is a great deal of subjectivity here). These standards are important because they not only create means for interoperability but, more importantly, reveal various approaches to representing data and behavior of location information.

The efforts to come up with such standards can be divided into two branches: standardization of modeling of the location data and standardization of ways to interface with various location information systems. Of course, some standards try to address both concerns. Also, it is important to note that the taxonomy of how each standard chooses to treat location is largely based on the domain whose problems it attempts to address.

Some of the organizations taking up the task of standardization are the IETF, the W3C, and the Open Mobile Alliance (OMA). (OMA and Location Interoperability Forum efforts are done collaboratively.)

To represent location-based data, we will look at the Geographic Markup Language (GML) developed by the Open GIS Consortium (OGC). We will look at NVML as a tool to represent navigational information. We will also look at IETF's SLoP (Spatial Location Protocol) as a protocol that allows simple text-based transactions for location information (a standard that is more on the behavioral side). On the behavioral side, we will look at a variety of Java APIs, some designed for mobile applications and others designed for the servers that support the network. We have selected Java out of all of the other programming languages for mobile because, it is currently the only one that has given any special treatment to issues concerning location sensitivity. Finally, we will look at some of the standards involved in the wireless world, such as those of OMA and 3GPP, that give some treatment to issues of location sensitivity. There is of course the "markup language du jour." Nonetheless, we have selected a subset of those markup languages that we feel deliver true open standardization and a somewhat canonical and nonbiased representation of location information. Let us start with GML.

12.4.1 GML

Before getting into the details of GML, let us look at the benefits and purpose of this markup language in representing location information:

1. Because GML is XML based, and because its schema allows us to specify the types of positioning and navigational data, it is easily possible to use XML-based technologies to get a view of the location information that fits the needs of the application.
2. GML implementations use SVG (see Chapter 6). This allows us to render maps, animated directions, and other graphical renderings of location information in

a more robust way than just displaying single bitmap graphics, which are not very efficiently used to produce animated graphics, for zooming in and out, or for a variety of other features.

3. GML's XML Schema is really the representation of the location model created by the OGC. In this sense, GML is more than a mere XML Schema; it is the reference implementation for OGC's location model.
4. GML allows for both absolute and relative representations of location. This is done by allowing a client system, requesting from a server system that provides location-based services, to request a Spatial Reference System (SRS).
5. GML provides support for XLink and XPointer. XLink and XPointer allow us to link documents together and reduce complexity of single XML documents by distributing them over multiple documents (while gaining other benefits such as reuse through modularization).
6. XSLT—the transformation technology that can be handy in many usages of XML including producing XML-based mobile user interfaces—can be used to transform GML to other types of XML or vice versa.
7. Many legacy GIS and CADD systems are moving toward supporting GML as the standard interface for external access. This puts a lot of weight in GML's corner as integration is one of the biggest problems facing the mobile developer.

The GML Specifications [GML Specifications 2002] also point to the concept of separation of content (geodata) from presentation (graphics and maps). This is a different separation of concerns between content and presentation than the one that we have looked at earlier in this text (Chapters 5–8). Namely, this separation specifically concerns geographical data. Topology and spatial properties of topology can be represented using graphical representations such as pictures and three-dimensional models. Meanwhile, these properties can also be described with metadata that describe the attributes of the topology and space.

Now, let us move on to the implementation details of GML. The OGC has been very clever: They used UML pervasively throughout the specification document to ease the process of understanding the taxonomy they have chosen for modeling location information. This can be seen in Figure 12.5.

Whereas the class diagram model represents the high-level model of taxonomy of entities that define location information as defined in GML, this is more like a metamodel from a UML perspective. Every individual class in Figure 12.5 is described in the GML specifications by its own class diagram that presents more details of the implementation of how location is represented; we will not look at those models as they are outside of the scope of our discussion. What is important to note is the extremely well-thought-out representation of the GML model in UML class diagrams and that, by usage of inheritance, the designers of GML have provided a mechanism for a hierarchical mechanism of defining and refining location information.

The UML class diagrams are also related to the XML Schema that defines a GML document. Namespaces are defined by placing an underscore before the class name of the diagram in Figure 12.5. So, for example, the namespace of Coverage class is *gml:_coverage*.

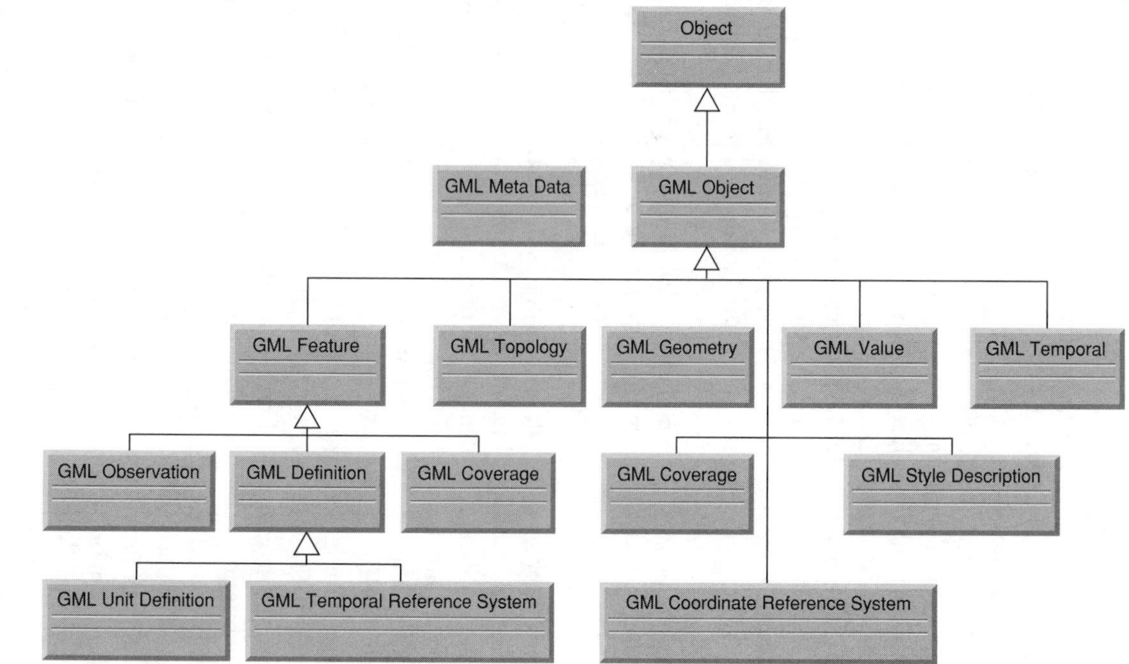

FIGURE 12.5. High-Level Semantic Definition of Location Information as Defined by GML Specifications and Represented with UML Class Diagrams [GML 3.0].

We will leave the complete description of the GML syntax to the GML Specifications by the OGC. Here we will merely list some notable features:

1. The highest level class defined in the diagram of Figure 12.5, "Object," can have the four attributes of *name, type, abstract*, and *substitutionGroup*. The name attribute allows us to give the element a lexical name; this name should represent the meaning of the element. The abstract attribute conveys the same concept as abstract classes in OOP: whether or not this element is actually the representation of a real thing (in which case this attribute is false) or whether it is created as an abstraction that helps us model ideas and things that are actually tangible (in which case this attribute is true). Note that because these attributes are attributes of the root object, they are inherited throughout all elements (except GML Meta Data, which does not inherit from Object).
2. XLink values can be used to specify attributes by reference. This is done through the URI mechanism and standard XLink expressions with an href.
3. A GML Feature is a meaningful object in the selected domain of discourse such as a Road, River, Person, Vehicle, or Administrative Boundary [GML 3.0]. As can be seen in the UML model, Feature is further refined to Observations, Definitions, and Coverages. However, if there is a symbolic, relative, or absolute object or location that you cannot find under the derived classes to fit your domain, you can always extend the gml:AbstractFeatureType. The basic concept of location is defined in the Feature schema (gml:_feature namespace). The details of how a location is then defined can be found in this part of the GML specification.
4. A GML Geometry defines meaningful boundaries that are location-independent. Geometries include points, lines, closed curves, surfaces, solids, composites of any of those, and any other things that are geometrically describable. This is probably the largest and most important part of the GML Specification. It encapsulates the heart of how the shapes of things are categorized and dissected.
5. The Coordinate Reference System defines the coordinate system used in the document to describe geometries, features, and everything else. Without a coordinate system, mathematical measurements are meaningless. If only one coordinate system is specified, then the application becomes rigid. This part of GML gives the application developers the flexibility to deal with multiple coordinate systems depending on the problem domain and the external applications that need to be integrated.
6. The Topology constructs define the topological properties of the geography that is being described by the GML document. The constructs of topology allow characterization of the spatial relationship among objects using simple combinatorial or algebraic algorithms [GML 3.0]. Topological properties can be unintuitive to understand: They describe those things that do not change as the geography and shape of the thing whose location we are describing may change. In practical terms, what this part of GML allows us to do is to define things like the space shared between two different spatial areas defined by two different spatial boundaries.

7. The Temporal construct allows us to describe the properties of the location that may change over a period of time. This part of GML first defines how temporal characteristics are measured through describing basic temporal types and then relates those characteristics to the spatial properties associated with other GML objects.
8. Temporal Reference System and Unit Definitions define measurement systems for temporal and spatial properties. The allows us to define a reference system that can be used to describe temporal properties in relative terms and defines unit measurements that give meaning to various measurements of objects defined in GML.

There is much more to GML than what we have described here. The specification document for version 3.0 is more than 500 pages! GML gives a truly proper treatment to defining an extensible, flexible, and scaleable mechanism for representing information related to absolute, relative, or symbolic measurements of spatial properties and locations. Nevertheless, you should remember that GML is one of many standards in the marketplace. Which standard becomes the prevalent one will be an evolutionary process.

Later in this chapter we will look at possibilities of generating GML with UML. Whereas GML is a markup language designed to represent a model of location information, there are also XML languages that are designed around models of tertiary domains that use location information. An example of such is NVML, which focuses on representing navigational information.

12.4.2 NVML

One of the most applicable areas of location information in mobile applications involves helping users with navigational problems such as driving directions. Though navigation itself is a small subset of the location-based functionality that can be presented by a mobile application, it is an excellent example of a well-defined model of usage of location information to produce useful applications. In this section, we will look at the Navigation Markup Language (NVML). Although, in and of itself, NVML is just another XML-based standard, it gives us a good demonstration of how we may use a tertiary location-based standard.

NVML is a submission to W3C by Fujitsu, but it is not yet a standard. The following are some major features of NVML:

1. NVML provides a model for geographic navigation with route assistance and point guidance. Route assistance provides step-by-step help along the travel path; point guidance provides information about things around a geographic point.
2. NVML has features that facilitate its integration into a multimodal and multichannel user interface.
3. Because NVML is an XML-based technology, we can take advantage of all those things that XML-based technologies can take advantage of: transformations, integration with Web services, etc.

4. An NVML document is made of two major parts: a header enclosed within <head></head> tags and a body enclosed within <body></body> tags. The header element encapsulates other elements that hold information about the entire document, such as the title of the document, and some textual, graphical, or aural (in the form of text to be consumed by a speech-synthesis engine) information about the document. Interestingly enough, neither the <head> nor the <body> tags have any attributes.
5. The body element is broken down into two main elements: navigation, enclosed within <navi></navi> tags, and guide, enclosed within <guide></guide> tags. The navigation element holds information about the starting and ending points of the route, information about the route such as the distance and duration, and other related information. The guide element holds information about the surroundings of a geographic point.

NVML's usefulness and elegance is in its simplicity. But this simplicity is also its downfall because, unfortunately, NVML does not integrate with GML or any other markup language that approaches the definition of location modeling in a comprehensive way. Although extending NVML is possible because it is an XML-based technology, it is not recommended.

Nonetheless, NVML is still a very useful markup language if your mobile application needs to convey directions to the user. At a higher level, our short analysis of NVML is important in one way: Its implementation model is not as crucial to our location-based mobile application as GML was. Fundamentally, this is because NVML is a higher level application of XML to location information and it treats a more narrow band of problems. The moral of the story is that a solution such as NVML is great if your application only needs to treat a narrow problem set. However, if you have to treat a large set of location-related problems, then you should make sure that the foundation—built on the location model—is sound and robust. In our case, if we needed directions to be available based on relative, absolute, and symbolic location information, NVML would not be a canonical solution. We would look for something that has a solid foundation such as GML or another extensible and comprehensive location model.

12.4.3 MPP

The Mobile Positioning Protocol (MPP) is a protocol to be used to request and receive location information. At present, MPP remains a technology proprietary to the wireless giant Ericsson. However, this protocol is under serious consideration for adoption as the positioning protocol of choice by ETSI (European Telecommunications Standards Institute). Such standardization would bolster the case of MPP for industry-wide standardization for most mobile applications to use as the protocol of choice for communicating location information. MPP is based on HTTP. Therefore, it is a stateless, request-response-based protocol. Meanwhile, it is possible to request the position of multiple mobile nodes in one request and get multiple results back in one response.

Figure 12.6 shows the general architecture for implementing mobile positioning using MPP. Note that those mobile devices that are GPS enabled can acquire

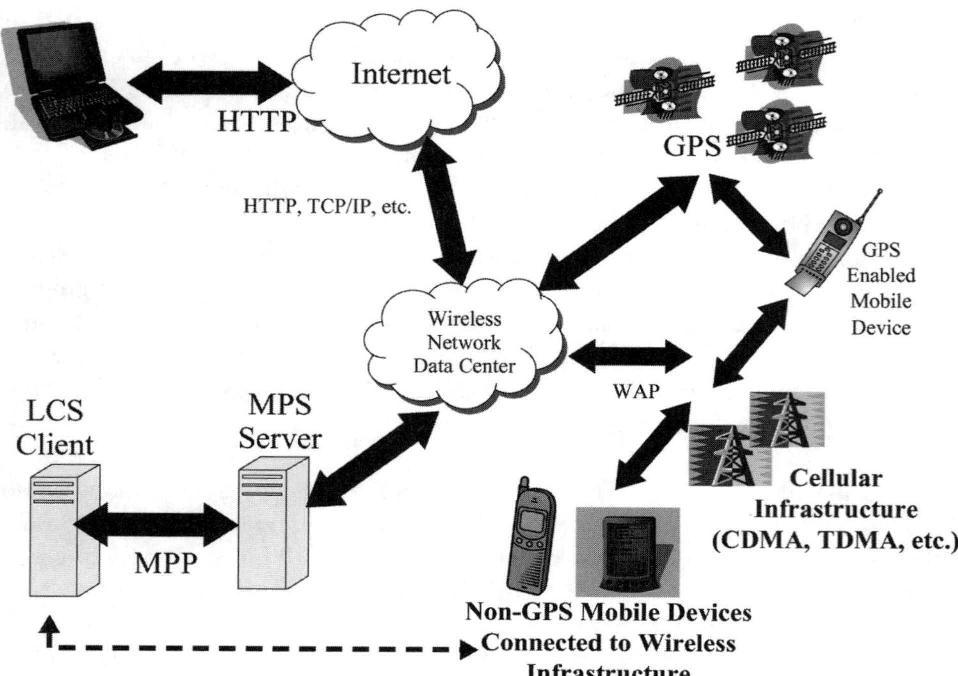

FIGURE 12.6. Using MPP and Supporting Architecture to Provide Location Information to Mobile Applications.

location information directly from the GPS system. Those devices that are not GPS enabled have a virtual connection to the MPP client, which then provides the location information. This information is most likely provided through the same network that provides data and voice connectivity to the mobile device. Therefore, the connection to the MPP client is a virtual one. Of course, we can have an MPP client on the device itself or implemented as a proxy on the network.

As we previously mentioned, MPP is request response based. The URI mechanism of HTTP is used to request the position of a mobile device. Parameters can be passed in the request, in the typical HTTP GET fashion with name value pairs appended to the end of the URI. MPP also supports TLS (in the form of HTTPS) for sending the request in a secure way. The request URI must include the following parameters:

1. USERNAME: The value of this parameter must be the user name used for the positioning of the device to be located.
2. PASSWORD: The value of this parameter must be the password used for the positioning of the device to be located.
3. POSITION_ITEM: This must be set to the MSISDN of the mobile device. The MSISDN provides a unique identifier for the mobile device shared by the network and accessible by the device and the supporting network infrastructure. The ID is different depending on the communication protocol between the

devices and the network. For example, in the case of WAP, this ID is in the HTTP headers (x-sub-no).

4. POSITION_TIME: In the current implementation of MPP, this parameter may only be set to the current time, implying that the current location of the mobile device is requested.

The newest versions of Ericsson's MPP are moving toward encapsulating all of the request content in an XML document and using the HTTP POST method to send this content to the location server. We will avoid reviewing the syntax in great detail as it is in somewhat of a state of flux.

Ericsson provides a development tool kit that includes an emulator for developing location-based applications. This tool kit is only applicable to developing location-based applications that operate exclusively on the server side. In other words, currently, the tool kit does not offer APIs for any particular device, or platforms designed for mobile devices such as J2ME, to access location information. Rather, location information is obtained through the MPP on the server side. This information can then be made available to a J2ME application on the client or used to create a thin-client user interface for the client as previously discussed.

The response is an XML document that contains the request ID along with the absolute position of the mobile device and the description of the network properties at the time the location information was gathered of the cell node(s) responsible for gathering it (e.g., the radius of the coverage arc, the angle of incidence, etc.)

One notable terminology you will encounter is the Mobile Positioning Center. This is basically the logical grouping of all the software and hardware required in the data center that make up a positioning server available with the MPP proposal.

The current version of the MPP server implementation by Ericsson provides a software development kit. This development kit can be used to communicate with the MPP server. There are handlers and utilities that simplify sending a request and parsing the contents of a response. In this way, a dynamic mobile application that uses basic Web technologies to access the MPP server can be designed by writing some server-side code. MPP promises to be one of the core pieces of technology standards for accessing mobile positioning information in the future.

The Java API provided by Ericsson is too heavy for mobile devices, so this is a case where the acquisition and processing of the location information will need to be done on the server side (or, if a mobile agent platform is used, by a mobile agent residing on the server-side host). We will look at JSR-179, which provides a J2ME-based API for access by resource-starved devices running J2ME. At this time, the tool of choice for open platforms to access location-based information provided by the network is Java.

12.4.4 SLP and SLoP

One of the important standards in acquiring, processing, and using location information in mobile applications promises to be IETF's SLoP. SLoP allows us to represent the coordinates of a single point. At the same time, the OGC is working on a similar, and somewhat complementary standard, called SLP, standing once again for Spatial Location Protocol. The difference, in general, seems to be that SLP defines a more detailed ontology of location types whereas SLoP sticks with defining general location information that can be leveraged on a per-application basis to build application-specific ontology definitions of location types. Whereas SLP gives us a more defined model, SLoP offers a smaller and more flexible definition of location information. SLP, for example, creates definitions for addresses, roads, etc. SLoP focuses on defining a flexible framework for absolute and relative locations of things.

12.4.5 Location Interoperability Forum

The Location Interoperability Forum (LIF) is a commercial consortium established in September of 2000 whose goal is to promote (not to create) interoperability standards for location services used by mobile devices and users. This means that LIF works with other standards bodies to align their efforts to avoid redundancy and conflict among the standards and to call attention to any shortfalls that a given standard may have. These standards cover four general areas:

1. MMI (Machine-to-Machine Interface) Content: These are the standards governing the interface to location-based services and the methods by which mobile applications communicate with location-based services.
2. Location Content: As we have seen with GML, one of the biggest technical problems is the uniform and canonical representation of the location data provided by the location service. LIF attempts to standardize this content.
3. Roaming and Billing: One of the biggest problems in wireless telecommunications, and for that matter all of telecommunications, is billing. LIF's charter includes standardizing the interfaces for billing among disparate systems, controlled by disparate commercial entities, some providing location information and others consuming location information.
4. Privacy and Security: As we will see at the end of this chapter, security is of utmost concern when it comes to location information. The location of a user, the patterns of where he or she travels, and any other related information are some of the most private information about a person. It is of utmost importance that such information remain privy only to those parties authorized by the user during and after the information exchange.

The Mobile Location Protocol (MLP) is one of the first standards constituted by LIF. It defines an MMI interface for location-based services to communicate with location-based consuming applications and has been adopted by 3GPP (3GPP is discussed in Chapter 11). MLP is an application-level protocol for querying the position of mobile stations independent of underlying network technology [LIF Specifications 2000]. Version 3.0 of MLP specifies a service-layer protocol that can be piggybacked on top of any application-layer transport protocol such as HTTP or SOAP. In other words, MLP only specifies the content and context of content exchanged between a location-based service provider and a client using the Web-service communication model. The basic services specified by MLP are as follows:

1. *Standard Location Immediate Service (SLI)*: Through this service, a client can request be to sent obtain location information about a single location and is guaranteed to have its request fulfilled by a response within a predefined time period.
2. *Emergency Location Immediate Service (ELI)*: This service is used to obtain the location information for the user of a mobile device who has initiated an emergency call. Like SLI, the response to a request sent to this service must be fulfilled within a predefined time period.
3. *Standard Location Reporting Service (SLRS)*: This is a service that is used when a mobile subscriber wants an LCS client to receive the MS (mobile device) location [LIF Specifications 2000]. This service is an active transaction.
4. *Triggered Location Reporting Service (TLRS)*: This service provides a way to set up an automatic update of the location information for a particular device based on some time frequency accomplished through polling.

As of MLP Version 3.0, there are six separate DTDs, each describing the content of some part of the required data exchanged between systems regarding the location of a mobile user. We will not go through every DTD, but here is a summary of the structure of the DTDs that make up the location definition as defined by MLP:

1. *Element Layer Definitions*: This DTD defines how a mobile device is identified, the current location and speed of the mobile device, metadata on the collection method and accuracy of the location information, any contextual information that may be relevant in obtaining the location information such as the identification of the requester and the service responding to the requester, properties of the network used to acquire location information, and the error margin.
2. *Service Layer Definitions*: Each message may have two main parts: a context or header part and a body part [LIF Specifications 2000]. The header, as in the case of an HTTP request header, includes information about the client making the request.

These DTDs have been tied together, and wrapped into a group, with an extension mechanism using a parameter *%extension.param*. This mechanism allows the extension of the individual DTDs or the sum of the collection of DTDs as a single extensible mechanism.

This brings us to the end of our discussion on protocols and specific technologies that provide location acquisition or access to systems that provide location acquisition. Our intent here was to impart a feel for what APIs and protocols in the realm of location-based services accomplish and how they accomplish it. There is a very large set of standards, APIs, and protocols. Some are complementary and others are competitive. The choice of the specific protocol, APIs, and tools that you use to build your location-sensitive mobile application must depend on the requirements as well as the availability of technologies.

Now, let us look at how we use location information in building a mobile application.

SIDE DISCUSSION 12.1

The Killer Mobile or Location-Based Application

Some have argued that there are no "killer applications" for mobile computing or location-based systems. The fallacy of such an argument is that today's stationary killer applications are merely a collection of smaller useful applications that have grown together to form a larger killer application. For example, the word processor is the collection of spell-check, thesaurus, text-entry, text formatting, document template creation, and other functionalities that existed alone at some point in the past.

The killer mobile or location-based applications will themselves evolve over time as various smaller applications gravitate together in an organic manner to form larger applications. Like most great advances in technology and science, killer applications are only born after years of hard work, persistence, and evolution accompanied by some degree of ingenuity.

12.5 Location-Based Services Applied

As in the case of the other dimensions of mobility, very few developers have a good intuition and sense for usage of location information in a mobile application. There are some obvious uses that come to mind, among which are navigation applications, emergency road-side assistance, and active notification of the user when he or she is located in a particular place. However, location information can be used in many other ingenious ways to enhance mobile applications whose primary purpose is not sensing the location or mobile applications but to combine location information with other dimensions of mobility or business logic to create new usages of computing power or improve efficiency in processes.

In this segment, we will go through few novel experiments and ideas that are the results of research done by academic and commercial institutions to create unique applications that utilize location information. Here are some examples:

1. Created at the University of Glasgow's Department of Computing Science, the Lab Support System is a Web-based application, deployed on static workstations and wireless-enabled palmtop computers, that supports student–tutor interaction in computer laboratories, particularly the process of students asking for help and tutors delivering it [Crease, Gray, and Cargill 2001]. Whereas the students are at the same stations during most of the lab time, the tutors move around. They are requested based on the progress of the students in the lab. There are a variety of topic types and, depending on the information exchanged between the tutor and the student, the information may be broadcast to the entire lab (of course, every lab station has a computer). For more details reference the cited paper. This project is an excellent example of how an otherwise stationary application can first be made mobile by giving the tutors mobile devices and then further augmented by location information to make helping the students more efficient.

2. Another project, at University of California at San Diego, utilizes the user's location information to facilitate interactions in an academic community such as a college campus. By using the context of location, time, and one's stated colleagues, a display in the form of a map or labeled list helps a participant see opportunities that are within reach and act upon them by physically moving to them or clicking on their links to learn more [Griswold et al. 2001].
3. There are a variety of mobile research efforts that involve tracking the user, with some sort of a mobile device that may be wearable, through various locations. At a rudimentary level, this information can be used for emergency situations such as a user having a seizure or a heart attack. However, it can also be used for nonemergency situations. There may be a correlation between the user's location and environmental conditions that affect short-term or long-term health. Such correlations may only be discoverable through a long-term tracking process. There may be other environmental correlations with medical conditions that may be revealed by the analysis of location information of a group of individuals instead of a single person. Applications of mobile computing and location information in the medical field are countless. Locating patients during crisis time, hospital resources, and monitoring patient habits are some examples.
4. If a mobile agent framework is used to build the mobile application or to support it, location information exists symbiotically with the system providing the location information. Agents can move from one host to another based on location information (e.g., based on the user's location, a restaurant finder agent may migrate from the network to the device to present the menu of a specific restaurant). Likewise, the agents can direct the user to go to a specific location based on the information provided by the location system (e.g., tell the user to go one block north, two blocks east to find a great three-star restaurant).
5. Goßmann and Specht show how location information is used to augment the LISTEN project, which provides users with intuitive access to personalized and situated audio information spaces while they naturally explore everyday environments [Goßmann and Specht 2001]. In this project, the user's location information is used to improve the user's experience by guiding him or her through audio zones that are defined by location parameters. In this case, we can see the beginnings of usage of location-based awareness and mobile computing in creating a virtual reality environment, enhancing the user's interface experience to the computing system, or creating other immersive applications.

There are numerous other examples. Here, we have only tried to give the reader a taste of what is possible. It is noteworthy that a couple of our examples were related to college campuses. This is not only because of the obvious (academic research is done by people on university campuses who try to leverage technology in examples useful to the immediate environment) but also because of the less than obvious: The people on a campus are typically very mobile and that daily experience with physical mobility creates an environment where necessity becomes the mother of invention.

Usefulness of location information and mobile applications typically go hand in hand. If an application is mobile, then the chances are that it needs, or can be

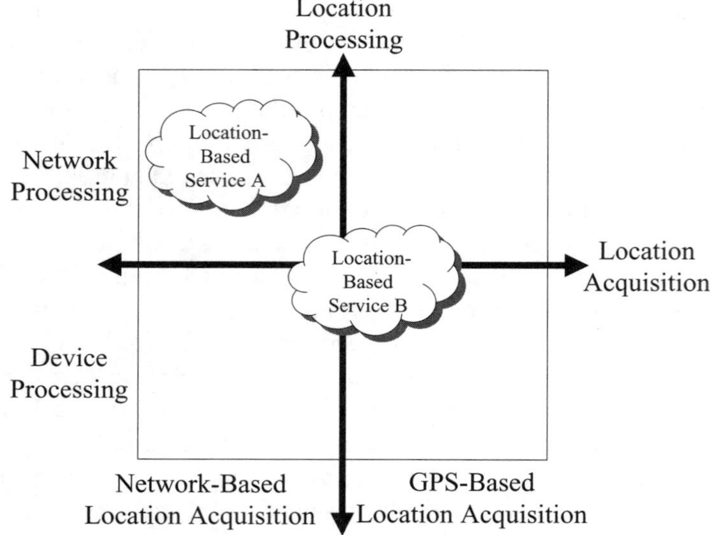

FIGURE 12.7. Taxonomy of Functional Delivery of Location-Based Services to Mobile Applications.

improved by having, location information. If the location of the user is changing frequently, then the chances are that a mobile application is a good fit.

Now, let us work our way to building a mobile application that takes advantage of location information, starting with the high-level analysis.

12.5.1 System Architecture for Offering Location Services

Whenever an application developer or a team of developers sets off to build a distributed application, one of the most critical things to do is to have a system-level picture of "what the world should look like" if the application is successfully designed and implemented. This has been one of the reasons we have touched upon architectural concerns for mobile applications throughout this text.

What the system architecture of your location-based mobile application looks like depends mostly on two things: the location acquisition mechanism and the usage of the location information. We have already looked at several location acquisition techniques and have seen that these techniques can be categorized along two axes: GPS or non-GPS based on one axis and on-device or in-network processing of the information on the other (Figure 12.7). In Figure 12.7, Location-Based Service A uses the network infrastructure for obtaining the location information and does all the processing of the location information, to present programmatically useful location information, in the network; an example of this could be a location-based service that uses MPP infrastructure with network-based TAO. Conversely, Location-Based Service B uses the network infrastructure and GPS to acquire location information. A client application may be involved in doing some of the processing of the location information. An example of this would be a system that uses GPS location accessed through a J2ME application on the client augmented by some network location-based technology. The processing of

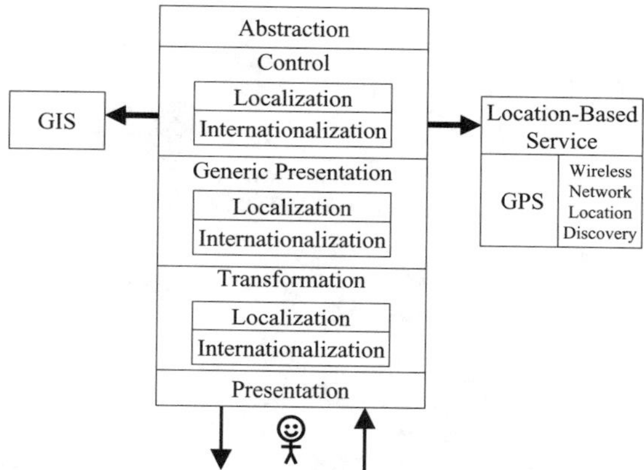

FIGURE 12.8. Layering a Mobile Application for Offering Location-Based Services.

the data may be distributed between the J2ME application running on the GPS-enabled mobile device and the network.

Based on this architecture, the mobile application must interface with systems that provide network-based location services, GPS, systems that process location information, or a combination thereof. Furthermore, the location information can be used as a cross-reference key for other information to be pulled from a GIS system or other systems that hold location information. Figure 12.8 shows how we can extend our previous layered model to include location-based functionality. Note that because localization and internationalization can affect the logic of the application, the control of the application, generic interactions of the user with the system, and the transformation of the generic presentation to a specialized presentation, Control, Generic Presentation, and Transformation layers must all have localization and internationalization logic. The location information, itself, is obtained from the location-based service whereas any cross-referenced information is obtained from a GIS system. Here, we did not make the separation between any internationalization and localization logic at the abstraction layer and the so-called business logic of the application. Making such a distinction is optional as, most probably, separation of concerns and its implementation in the abstraction layer are domain dependent. The application described in Figure 12.8 could be a mobile application whose parts are running on a mobile device, one that runs completely on the network and provides a thin-client user interface to the mobile device, or one whose parts are distributed between running on the network servers and the mobile device (GIS is almost certainly not implemented on the mobile device).

There may also be other systems and subsystems that offer functionality such as navigation, location-based billing, travel services, and emergency assistance services that depend on information obtained from the location-based service. Such systems and subsystems would typically interface with the control and abstraction components and do not have a direct effect on the presentation-related components.

So, a system-level architecture may look something like that of Figure 12.9. You should now have a good high-level view of some of the alternative designs for integrating location information to your mobile application infrastructure. Next,

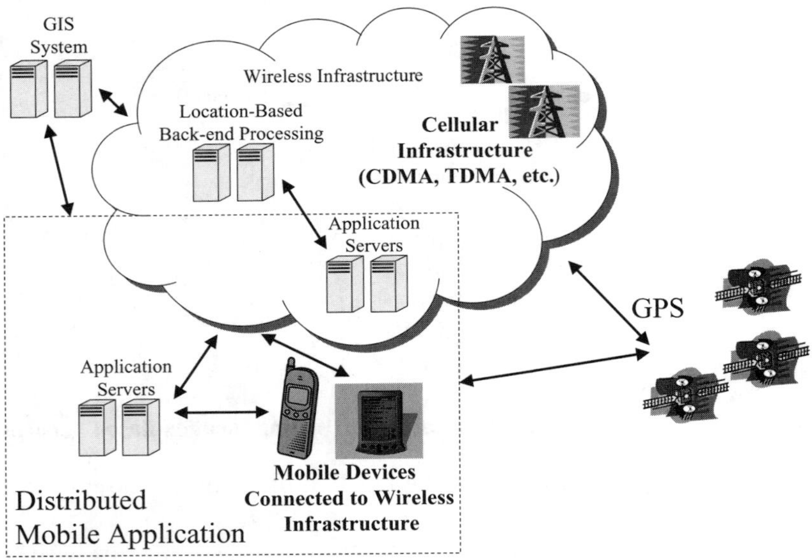

FIGURE 12.9. High-Level View of Mobile Applications Supporting Location-Based Functionality.

we are going to dig a bit deeper and look at the architecture, implementation, and interface of the location-based systems to gain better insight into how to utilize them. Then we will look at implementation details of accessing systems that offer location-based services.

12.6 UTILIZING LOCATION-BASED SERVICES WITH MOBILE APPLICATIONS

We have seen that location is a dimension of mobility, looked at a variety of methods to obtain location information, and have overviewed some programmatic tools such as GML and MPP that help us in building mobile applications that take advantage of location sensitivity.

Our first task is to set forth a set of design and architectural principles to do this. As location sensitivity and mobile applications are very young areas of software development, it is difficult to model such designs and principles after real-life successes. What we will present here utilizes largely research work done commercially and academically. As with all research, you will need to make adjustments suitable to your application of these technologies.

Jonathan Agre [Agre et al. 2001] and colleagues at Fujitsu Laboratories present a taxonomy of accessing the subsystem providing the location-based information. First, they define a logical abstraction for the software subsystem that provides the location information, calling this a Location Service Module or LSM. The LSM is composed of a Location Dependent Layer (LDL), basically representing the abstraction of the actual method used to retrieve the location information, and the Location Adaptation Layer (LAL), which is used to convert the information retrieved to a format easily usable by applications that need this information.

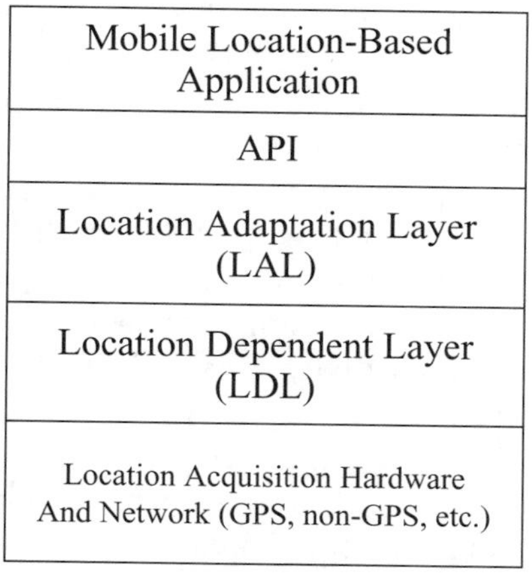

Mobile Location-Based Application
API
Location Adaptation Layer (LAL)
Location Dependent Layer (LDL)
Location Acquisition Hardware And Network (GPS, non-GPS, etc.)

FIGURE 12.10. Software Abstraction Layers for Developing Mobile Applications That Use Location Information.

Figure 12.10 shows this type of abstraction as applied to mobile applications and their usage of location-based information.

Agre and colleagues define a minimal subset of a functional interfaces that must be supported, by the API layer, to provide a behavioral interface to the location sensitivity system [Agre et al. 2001]. Their interface provides the following:

1. an absolute position—for example, a method called GetPositionAbsolute(),
2. a relative position—for example, a method called GetPositionRelative(),
3. a symbolic position (rooms, roads, etc.)—for example, a method called GetPositionSymbolic(),
4. a flexible mechanism to set the point whose location is used to measure relative positions—for example, a method called SetRelativeCoordinates(Coordinates someCoordinates),
5. a flexible mechanism to input customizable information into the location-sensing subsystem to build a symbolic coordinate system—for example, SetSymbolicInformation(InformationSet someSymbolicReferenceSystem), and
6. an optional support for orientation of the device—for example, information regarding which way the device points may be used to render a map in the proper direction such as GetOrientation().

Next, naturally, one may want to know how to design and implement a real application using location-based information. Though there will soon, perhaps by the time you read this text, be many different products and tools that allow software developers to take advantage of location information, at present, the number of tools are limited. In practical terms, we can build a mobile application that takes advantage of location information under three conditions: when the device has some sort of access to an implementation of MPP (through WAP or otherwise), then the device has a GPS unit with the appropriate integrated software development tools, or when the device is enabled with short-range wireless networking access such as WIFI or Bluetooth. A fourth solution is proprietary and specific to Qualcomm's BREW infrastructure on CDMA. We will stick with the first three solutions.

J2ME and MPP provide solutions at the LAL. In other words, the network may or may not support MPP; if it does, then you can write an application that uses the MPP to communicate with a service that already provides neatly packaged location information. The same is true for J2ME with JSR-179. The method of retrieving the location information is abstracted away. There are currently several standards being worked on for short-range wireless networks (typically ad hoc), such as WIFI-based location sensitivity APIs at the LAL.

Another approach is presented by Hightower and colleagues [Hightower et al. 2002].

As you may recall, in Chapter 9, we also eluded to a symbiotic relationship between mobile agents and location sensitivity. Because mobile agents can move from one host to another, they can facilitate processing of location information by first migrating based on the location of the user, the mobile device, or the network and then obtaining the location information closer to the "edge" of the network where the application is actually being used, thereby allowing for better performance properties.

Let us first assume the most universal case where the location information is provided by a GPS.

12.6.1 Accessing a GPS Device Programmatically

The National Marine Electronics Association (NMEA) published a standard method of communicating with GPS devices, by establishing a superset standard for MMI for marine devices. Most GPS devices today are accessible through this standard. This interface is a character-based standard that specifies a message header, latitude (north–south), longitude (east–west), and altitude (in meters above sea level). The information is extracted as multiple "sentences" (with a sentence often used to refer to a character-based string). The keyword in the beginning of the sentence specifies the format and meaning of the data included in the sentence. A particular sentence may be the following:

```
$GPGGA,111323,4356.323,N,32310.047,W,2,04,6,111,M,12,M,,*44
```

Before the advent of the World Wide Web, a hybrid device that included a GPS component could typically access the GPS subsystem through a serial (RS232) interface. Since the advent of the Internet, some GPS devices also provide an HTTP interface.

If you have a stand-alone GPS device with a serial port, you can connect it to your PC and programmatically access it through the serial port; you could do the same if you have a hybrid device (a device that has a GPS unit on it but whose functionality is not limited to providing location information—such as GPS-enabled PDA, etc.). Some GPS-enabled mobile devices may provide programmatic access integrated with custom C/C++ APIs for the platform.

In some cases, as the case of J2ME, there are evolving standards for further definition of a programmatic interface to GPS devices. We will look at JSR-179, which deals with accessing location information on the device, in the next section. Also, as there is a move toward converting all forms of content to XML, standards bodies are moving toward representing the location information in XML as in the case of GML. This has one disadvantage: XML parsing can be resource intensive for a resource-starved device. This is somewhat offset by the fact that, because of the importance of XML, even the most starved devices now have some way of parsing XML.

Although we can use a variety of client-side applications that we have talked about in this text such as BREW, J2ME, and others, we will use J2ME as our reference model in the next sections. There is a direct mapping for most concepts that we will discuss.

12.6.2 Location-Based J2ME Application

J2ME can be used in two ways to get the location information. First, it can get the location information of the device from the network. Alternatively, if there GPS is available on the mobile device or there is a GPS attachment, and if either provides some programmatic access, we can use J2ME to get GPS-based location information. Figure 12.11 shows an example of a simple class that allows access to a GPS-enabled J2ME device that provides access to its functionality through either an RS-232 interface or an HTTP interface.

Note that we have only extracted information regarding the longitude, latitude, altitude, and the time at which the location information was obtained. As we have noted, there is much more that an LAL interface, which J2ME is, can do for us. For this reason, Java Community Process in JSR-179 is developing a location API for J2ME.

JSR-179

J2ME is evolving to offering a full treatment of various dimensions of mobility on resource-starved mobile devices. Although there is as yet no part of J2ME implemented on available platforms that support obtaining or processing of location information, things are in the works through the Java Community Process. Namely, JSR-179, principally let by Nokia, is in the public review process. In this section, we will review JSR-179 as a possible up–and-coming solution to acquiring and processing location information on mobile devices.

The location model defined by JSR-179 is a small one. We have created a UML class diagram of the JSR-179 classes in Figure 12.12.

Note that there are two main concepts: landmarks and locations. Also, note that the classes are all in a javax.microedition.location package and that all classes but the interfaces extend java.lang.Object or java.lang.Exception.

The location model supported by JSR-179 currently implements the following features:

1. It supports the concept of an address, typically associated with a human-made defined system of countries, states, counties, cities, streets, etc. The necessary attributes of an address are implemented in AddressInfo. This object encapsulates the necessary data, but not much in the way of behavior.

```
public class locator {
    private String mSerialDestination="comm.:2;
      baudrate=2400;bitsper char=8"
    private String mHttpDestination = "http://gps/GPS.html";
    private String mLongitude;
    private String mLatitude;
    private String mAltitude;
    private long mTime;
    private int mConnectionMethod;

    public locator(int aConnectionMethod) {
        mConnectionMethod = aConnectionMethod;
    }

    public void refresh() {
        InputConnection mySerialInput;
        InputStream myInputStream;
        switch(mConnectionMethod) {
            case 1: {
                InputConnection mySerialInput =
                  (InputConnection) Connector.open(
                  mSerialDestination);
                myInputStream = mySerialInput.
                  openInputStream();
                break;
            }
            default: {
                HttpConnection myHttpInput = (HttpConnection)
                  Connector.open(mHttpDestination);
                myInputStream = myHttpInput.openInputStream();
                break;
            }
        }
        parseInput(myInputStream);
    }

    public void parseInput(InputStream anInputStream) {
        // Implement the parsing of the NMEA String here . . .
    }

    public String getLongitude() {return mLongitude;}
    public String getAltitude() {return mAltitude;}
    public String getLatitude() {return mLatitude;}
    public long getRefreshTime() {return mTime;}
}
```

FIGURE 12.11. Accessing GPS Data with J2ME.

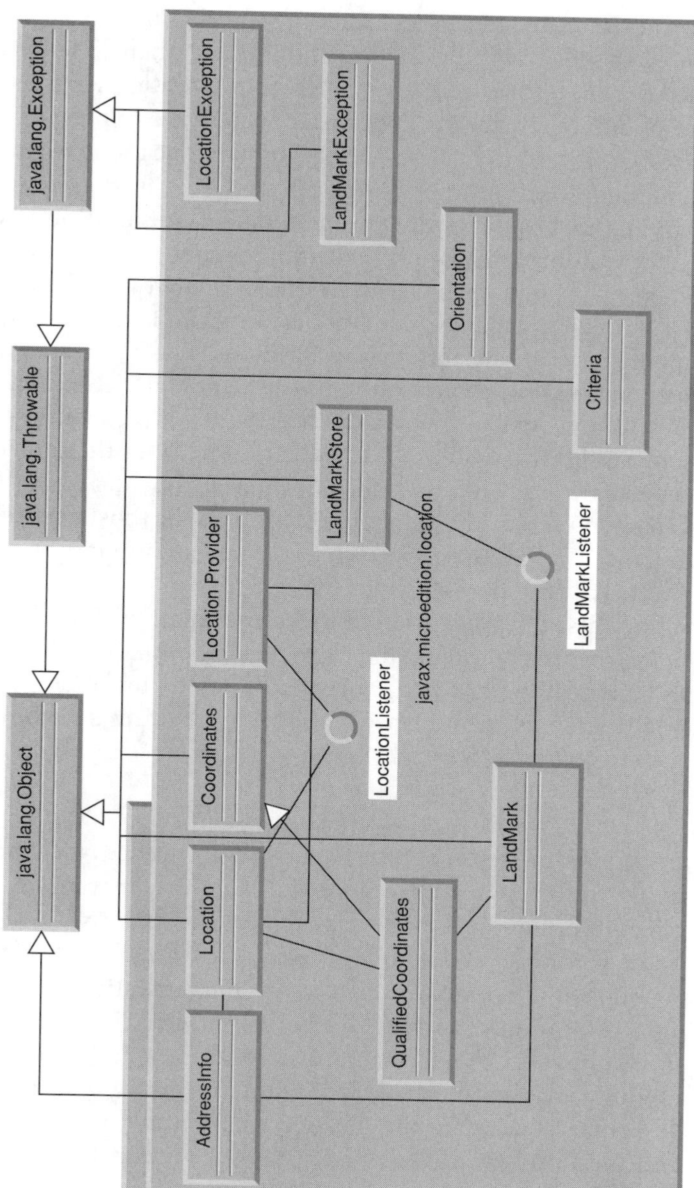

FIGURE 12.12. UML Class Diagram of JSR-179.

2. The Coordinate class encapsulates the necessary data for a WGS84-based location, which is a geographical location specified by a longitude, latitude, and altitude. The supported behavior allows for calculation of bearings between two points, locations between two points, and conversion of formats.
3. The LocationProvider class gives us a singleton to the implementation, on the device, of the location-based service. This class relies on the Criteria class to determine how the location information should be gathered. This is because devices may offer more than one way of obtaining location information with a various set of options including cost, speed, where the information is being requested, etc. All of the other classes that begin with Location provide a mechanism for handling Location information encapsulated in the Location class. The Location class encapsulates the coordinate-based specification of a location as well as how the information was obtained, the margin of error, when it was obtained, where the thing whose location was measured is heading, and how frequently measurements may be taken. Location class is the mechanism that provides support for absolute and relative locations.
4. Symbolic locations are supported through the LandMark class. Though this support is not full or flexible, we are talking about J2ME, which is designed for resource-starved devices after all. LandMarkStore does the same thing for LandMark as LocationProvider does for Location: It provides a singleton with which one can obtain actual LandMark information. Like those classes that start with Location, those classes that start with LandMark are supporting classes that allow the LandMark provider to give us LandMarks.
5. The Orientation class allows us to determine the orientation of the device whose location is being reported. Orientation, as defined by JSR-179, is bearing, pitch, and roll. This information can be extremely important in future devices that may depend on orientation as an information input mechanism such as Compaq's Itsy.

By the time this text is published, JSR-179 should be ratified and implementations by cell phone and PDA manufacturers will be on their way. At such time, and when location information is made available by the carriers, it will facilitate implementation of location-based mobile applications on mobile devices.

We have now looked at two disparate areas of implementing a mobile application that supports location sensitivity. We have seen a quick summary of using GPS-based information. Using GPS directly is an example of a case where we obtain just the raw information and have to do the processing within the mobile application. Obviously, processing the location information is something that a well-thought-out location model does better, so we have looked at JSR-179 as an example of an API that gives us an interface to processed location information on the device for accessing location information based on a location model. Next, we will take a high-level look at the relationships among the context of usage of an application, location information, and the user interface to a mobile application.

12.6.3 Mobile Applications, Location, Context, and User Interfaces

In Chapters 5–8, we looked at the various concerns of mobile user interfaces. Recall that some of the problems of mobile user interfaces are that mobile devices are limited in the graphical user interfaces that they offer. There are other concerns with voice user interfaces such as ambiguity of prompts to get the correct response from the user, creating natural interfaces, and others. One of the conclusions we drew then was that we need to do whatever we possibly can to make the user interface convenient and easy to use. We also noted that the more contextual information we are able to leverage into building our application, the more user friendly we can make the user interface and the rest of the application.

Location information gives us one of the best sources for context. Where the user is, how he or she came to be there, where he or she is going, things that are in the user's vicinity, and the entire set of variables that are location dependent give us context for improving our application as a whole and the user interface in particular. Furthermore, time and location are the two best triggers for active transactions. Before we go on to show the different ways we can improve the contextual information of our application with location information, notice that there is always a certain amount of ambiguity in the location information too. This ambiguity is associated with the margin of error in acquisition of the location information and with the user's motion through the coverage area of whatever the location-sensing technology may be.

Moreover, the type of location information that is useful in determining better context for the usage of an application depends on the type of application. Some applications require very exact location information with frequent updates whereas others need occasional updates and can afford more error without loss of contextual information.

Because of the complexity of dealing with contextual location information, we need something that resolves the complexity of location information and its relationship with the context of the application usage. Rather than a location model, what is needed is a comprehensive object model that captures properties that describe the object within the context of the space in which it exists [Burnett, Prekop, and Rainsford 2001]. Of course, there have been a variety of models suggested, each with some bias toward solving the problems of a particular domain, much in the same way that XML standards and programming APIs for location information have evolved. A domain-independent model to location information used by mobile applications may not even be a feasible one. Nevertheless, we will present pieces of the models suggested by various studies and projects in this section. Embellishing on the work by Burnett, Prekop, and Rainsford [Burnett, Prekop, and Rainsford 2001], we represent a piece of the puzzle in Figure 12.13. Here a class diagram is used to model some basic location-related pieces of the location-aware context-sensitive mobile application.

Note that this is just the start of a simplified model of an object that shows the relationships among the entities involved in locating something and then using it. The model can be further augmented in a domain-specific manner. In our

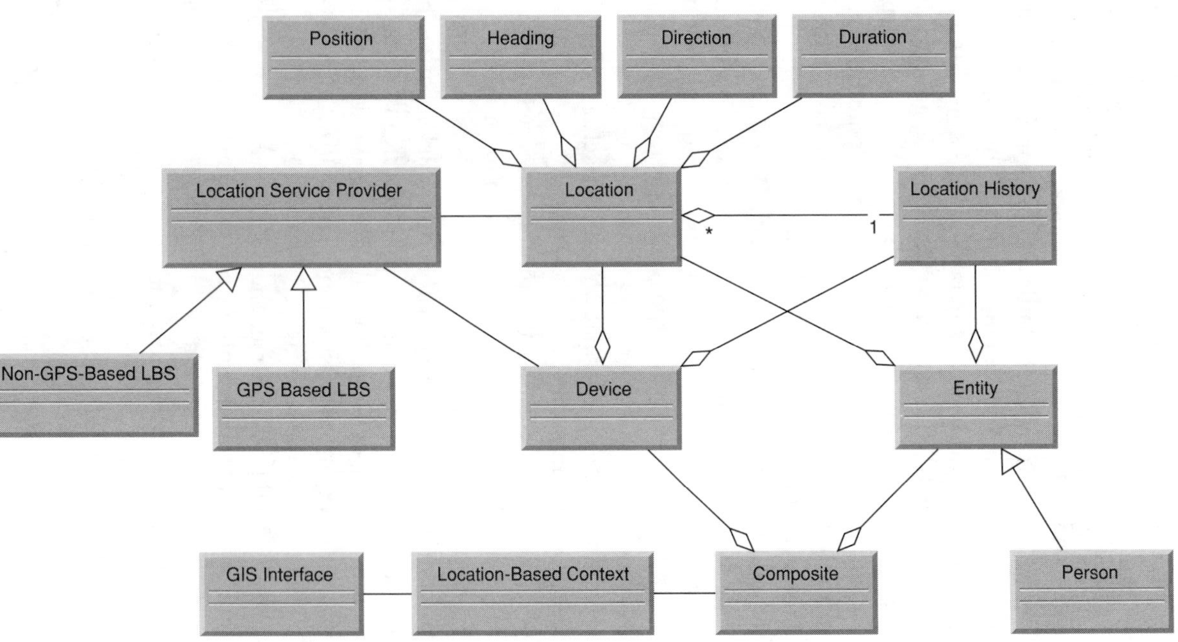

Figure 12.13. Rudimentary Representation of Location-Based Context.

model, we have also leveraged work by Schleider, Vogele, and Werner, who look at the spatial relevance of chunks of application functionality. Each spatial region determines a subpattern: the sequence of elementary motions that occur within a region; this hierarchical structure is called a *partitioned motioned pattern* [Schlieder et al. 2001]. Finally, keep in mind that location-based context is *not* orthogonal to the location-based model we use. The way we model location depends on the context of usage of location information and how useful location information is; how we use it depends on the location-based model that we choose.

Depending on the type of location-based information available, the mobile application can be designed to adjust its behavior to fit the mobile condition of the user. Namely, the location of the user and the changes in the location of the user give us a big chunk of information about his or her mobile condition. The work done by Shlieder, Vogele, and Werner clearly demonstrates this as applied to an application in a museum. Once they define the concept of "spatiothematic regions," in which there is a theme associated with some region defined by specific physical boundaries (such as rooms, wings, exhibits, etc.), they continue on to relate these spatiothematic regions to appropriateness of application functionality, thereby first creating a framework for representing location-based context and then demonstrating how to use this location-based context to improve the functionality of an application.

This approach is extremely useful in design and implementation of mobile user interfaces in two ways. First, as we have mentioned, we can adapt the functionality offered by the application to suit the condition of the user based on his or her location. Second, we can adapt the user interface, not the core functionality, offered by the application to suit the location and motion of the user.

12.7 Representing Location with UML

As with the other aspects of mobility and the various solution techniques that we have looked at in this text, it is desirable to model location information and the change in location information in UML. In the case of representing location, UML, with no additional extensions, actually is fairly sufficient in providing most of what we need.

However, there is nothing in UML that provides a good representation for motion. We already saw this in the case of mobile agents. So, in this section, we will first take a quick look at how we can use standard UML tools to model location information and the behavioral aspects of location-based models. Then, we will present a few stereotyped extensions that allow for better representation of the mobile user and the mobile applications.

One important thing to remember here is that there are two levels of modeling that are of concern when it comes to location-based systems. First, we have to select some general method for modeling the location information and interacting with the location information to describe this information. For example, GML defines a model for geographic information. So do some of the other standards defined by ISO, the OGC, LIF, and other standards bodies. Although we have reviewed some of these standards and have gotten a bird's-eye view of the models they define for location information, the discussion of that arena lies outside of the scope of a discussion on mobile computing. Second, there is another type of modeling that concerns mobile computing more; this modeling is done with UML or a similar tool that lets us define location information, interactions with systems that provide location information, and data or behavior information concerning mobility that is a function of a variable location. UML is our obvious choice because it has allowed us to model the other dimensions of mobility and aspects of mobile computing discussed in this text.

With this in mind, let us see how we can use various UML diagrams to help us model location information and location mobility. We will start with class diagrams.

12.7.1 Using Class Diagrams to Represent Location Information

As we mentioned previously, there are symbolic locations, relative locations, and absolute locations. Relative and absolute locations specify some location that may be specified in a Cartesian coordinate system with a single point, though there may be inaccuracies involved, and other coordinate systems used to represent the actual value. In both cases, we are either specifying the distance to something else whose location is known or specifying a latitude, longitude, and altitude that tell us the exact location. Symbolic locations are largely domain dependent—how we define a symbolic location is based on how we use it. For example, a symbolic location may be a room number; this room number is meaningful within the context of a building and usage of rooms as a measure of location by the domain. The domain in this case may be a medical application that tells a nurse which room to visit next based on the current condition of patients.

Based on this, symbolic locations can be modeled within the constructs used by the actual application. In this way, our example of the hospital and nurse is almost identical to the infamous "elevator" example that many OOP courses use to introduce objects to novice computer scientists. There is almost a one-to-one mapping between symbolic location models and a UML class diagram. In other words, we can model atomic abstractions in our location model with object-oriented classes and, subsequently, show the relationships among these atomic abstractions, represented by classes, in a UML class diagram.

Representing absolute and relative locations depends on how we define them. We will look at work done by Gronmo, Solheim, and Skogan that focuses on generation of various representations of absolute and relative locations by using UML.

12.7.2 Using UML for Modeling Relative and Absolute Geographical Locations

In this chapter, we have already seen that representing a geographical position, whether it is absolute or relative, can be done in many different ways. In Norway, a small country that does much more than its fair share of research and development in mobile computing, a group of researchers with SNITEF Telecom and Informatics have suggested that code generation can be one way of resolving the impedance

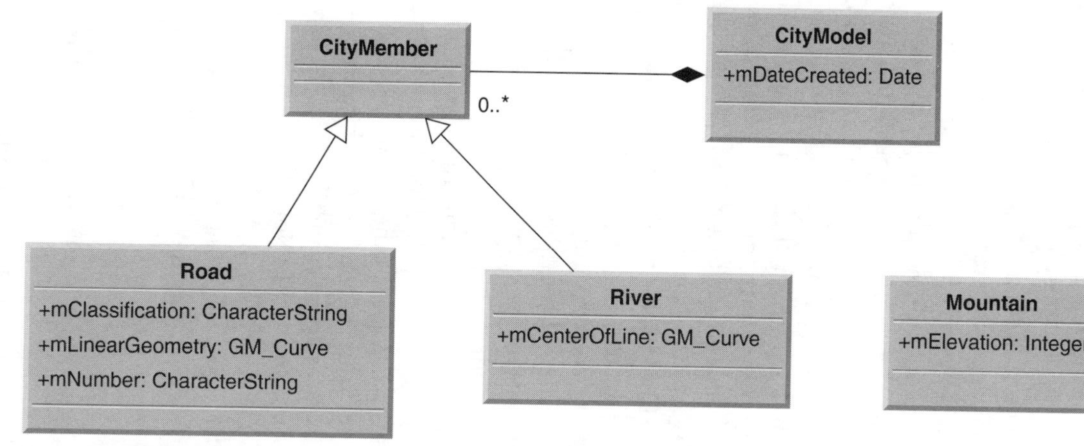

FIGURE 12.14. Example of Using UML Class Diagrams to Represent Symbolic Models of Location Representation [Berre 2001].

mismatch among the different models of location and changing of location. Earlier in this text, we have noted that code generation with UML is not a golden hammer that can be used for any project and any time; in fact, we have generally discouraged extensive use of code generation because UML was not designed to have the level of detail that a programming language does and putting that type of detail into a model is just as, or more, laborious than creating the code to begin with. This is not to say that things are stagnant. With UML 2.0 and later versions, the designers of UML are equipping UML with features that get it closer and closer to a tool suitable for code generation.

Furthermore, if UML is used in modeling something that is fairly dynamic, a dynamic business domain or many different business domains, there is potentially more complexity introduced by the nuances of modifying the generated code, modifying the model, and keeping all modifications in sync. The domain of location information, however, is an area where code generation with UML can be very useful. There is another point to make: Diagrammatic environments are simply not that good for expressing lots of details. Even though you can combine OCL with your diagrams, then it is still more difficult to combine diagrams and OCLs than to just read code! Also, the top programming languages such as C++, Java, and C# are practically the same syntactically so it is not that hard reading Java code if you only know C++.

First, the inherent domain of location information and location mobility does not change much. Locations are described by a set of spatial and physical attributes. In the case of absolute and relative geographic locations, despite the fact that we can describe them with a variety of coordinate systems, the domains remain very static. The definitions of points, shapes, and geographic terrain are described by a finite and small number of models. Even in the case of symbolic locations, there are a finite and small number of permutations that are used to describe locations: architectural models (buildings, rooms, etc.), boundary-based models (countries, states, counties, cities, etc.), and some others. Gronmo, Solheim, and Skogan of SINTEF [Gronmo, Solheim, and Skogan 2002] agree that representing location and aspects of mobility that concern location in UML is beneficial. Their efforts focus in generating GML based on UML. Note that the actual model that generates the code is not significant. Rather, the study focuses on whether it is possible to generate GML based on UML and what the advantages and disadvantages of such an effort might be. Their work [Gronomo, Solheim, and Skogan 2002] can then be summarized as follows:

1. It is possible to model location information, particularly represented in GML, in UML.
2. It is best to avoid multiple inheritance. Of course, this is something that every good object-oriented programmer knows; multiple inheritance is a very rarely used properly and, even when used properly, it is likely to cause the object model to be overly rigid as an application matures. In this case, it is particularly important because multiple inheritance cannot be implemented with XML (the document format on which most location information standards are based) and

some programming languages such as Java. The goal of using UML to model location information is to introduce flexibility.

3. OCL or stereotypes may be used to define the differences among various static models of location information and mobility.
4. Gronomo, Solheim, and Skogan also specify a mapping of the XML Schema to UML classes. This mapping has been done with two things in mind: 1. the needs and definition of a location-based system and 2. the location model defined in the GML Schema.

When we looked at GML, we also saw that the GML specification has been written so that the location model is actually represented in UML. Not only is this further affirmation of UML class diagrams being a suitable tool for representing location models, but it also makes a great starting point for any mapping that one might want to do between UML and GML at a detailed level.

We have now discussed relative, absolute, and symbolic location modeling techniques and their representations using UML artifacts. There is yet another category of modeling techniques—hybrid location modeling techniques—that combine two or more of the aforementioned techniques (relative, absolute, and symbolic modeling). Domitcheva [Domnitcheva 2002] addresses the relationships between these modeling techniques. For example, a particular location model could use both symbolic and absolute location models, specifying which room in a building as well as exact coordinates of a device. The combination of the two may be much more useful than either one for particular types of applications.

Figure 12.14 shows how class diagrams can be used to represent various symbolic location models. UML class diagrams can also be used in these cases where the goal is to show the relationships among the parts that make such hybrid models.

12.7.3 Modeling Motion in UML

To date, we have not found any published works that enable us to represent a mobile user or a mobile system. Therefore, we leverage previously introduced works in Chapters 9 and 6, where works by Nunes (Wisdom UML extensions) and others were leveraged to create new stereotypes for mobile agents and user interfaces. We propose the extensions in Table 12.1. We have introduced some of these extensions previously when dealing with modeling mobile user interfaces. Under the context of location sensitivity, we can use some of the same stereotypes and add new ones.

Once again, we have leveraged Nunes' Wisdom work greatly, first recognizing how we can create new stereotypes to facilitate reading use case diagrams that involve location information and then creating widgets that properly represent them.

This brings us to the end of our discussion of modeling location-based services and location sensitivity aspect of mobile computing with UML. We used class diagrams to represent location models and augmented use case diagrams to represent high-level specification of a system that involves mobile components.

Now, let us take a quick look at security and privacy aspects of location-based services before ending this chapter.

Table 12.1. UML Extensions to Model Location and Motion in Mobile Applications

Stereotype	Description	Icon
<<Mobile Actor>>	This stereotype extends Wisdom's <<Human Actor>> to be used in use case diagrams and sequence diagrams. It is intended to indicate a human actor who is definitely mobile at the time of interacting with a particular use case or interacting with another actor. (The arrow notation is borrowed from the mobile agent UML extensions we looked at in Chapter 9.) This stereotype is strictly introduced to indicate the condition of the user at the time of using the application. It does not indicate whether the application itself is one that is designed or implemented as a mobile application. If the question is the mobility of the user interacting with the application, Wisdom's <<Human Actor>> stereotype should be used.	
<<Mobile System Actor>>	This stereotype extends Wisdom's <<System Actor>> to be used in use case diagrams and sequence diagrams. It is used to indicate that a particular system is mobile. For example, a mobile phone is a mobile system actor. Any applications that run on a mobile system, by definition, are mobile applications.	
<<Stationary Actor>>	This stereotype extends Wisdom's <<Human Actor>> to be used in use case diagrams and is intended to indicate a human actor who is definitely stationary at the time of interacting with a particular use case or interacting with another actor. This stereotype does not indicate that the application is itself designed as a stationary application. The application may be mobile, but a particular use case may only be relevant when the user is stationary. If it is not, whether the user is mobile or stationary at the time of interacting with the application, Wisdom's <<Human Actor>> stereotype should be used.	

Stereotype	Description	Symbol
<<Mobile Use Case>>	This stereotype extends UML's use case stereotype. It is used to indicate that the use case is a mobile use case. By a mobile use case, we mean that the implementation of the use case involves usage or consideration of the dimensions of mobility.	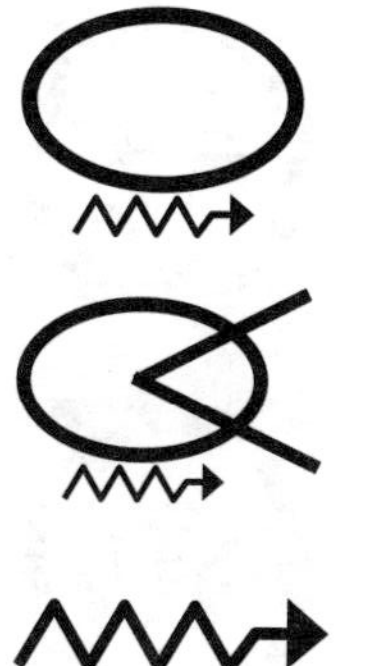
<<Essential Mobile Use Case>>	This stereotype extends Wisdom's <<Essential Use Case>>. It is to be used to indicate that the particular use case is a mobile use case and that it is necessary to describe the functionality of a mobile application. This stereotype is to be used in Wisdom interaction models (the user interface—oriented extension to the use case diagrams).	
<<Mobile Communicate>>	This stereotype extends Wisdom's <<communicate>> stereotype in the interaction model. It indicates communication between any actor and any use case while that actor is mobile. Note that this symbol is not to be used to indicate communication among the internal classes of a mobile application as it would cause confusion with extensions already defined for mobile agents (discussed Chapter 9). As you recall in the definition of the interaction model, the focus is on the user interface interactions.	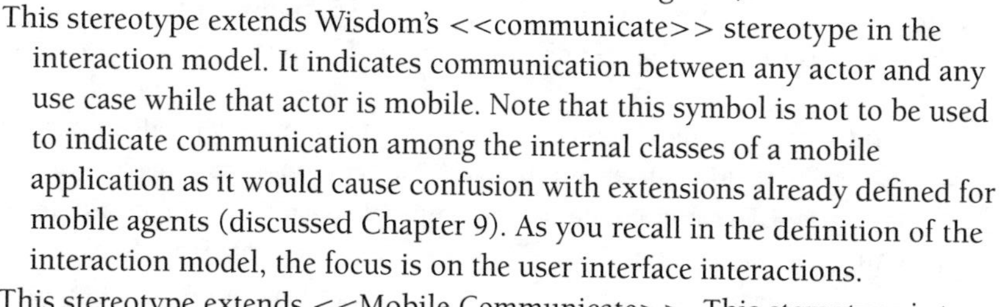
<<Single-Channel Communicate>>	This stereotype extends <<Mobile Communicate>>. This stereotype is to be used when communication between the actors and use cases are done through only one communication channel. We defined channels in Chapter 5. Specification of the channel can be done through text added to the symbol.	
<<Multi-Channel Communicate>>	This stereotype extends <<Mobile Communicate>>. This stereotype is used between actors and use cases or actors and other actors in interaction model diagrams. It indicates that the communication with a specific use case is done through two or more channels. OCL may be used to specify whether messages may be passed synchronously or asynchronously through every channel. Specific channels may be specified through text added to the symbol.	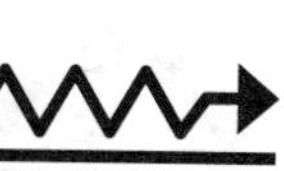

(*continued*)

Table 12.1 (continued)

Stereotype	Description	Icon
<<GIS Control>>	This stereotype extends the <<Control>> stereotype of Wisdom. As you recall, the <<Control>> stereotype was put on a class that provides coordination among other classes, objects, and components (Wisdom analysis model). A GIS-based control is a special type of control that uses GIS information to perform one or more of its tasks.	GIS
<<Location-Based Control>>	This stereotype extends the <<Control>> stereotype of Wisdom. As you recall, the <<Control>> stereotype was put on a class that provides coordination amongst other classes, objects, and components (Wisdom Analysis Model). A location-based control is a special type of control that uses location information to perform one or more of its tasks.	LBS
<<GIS Boundary>>	This stereotype extends the <<Boundary>> stereotype of Wisdom. As you recall, boundaries are used to indicate the interface lines between subsystems and components that make up the application. This stereotype is used to specify a boundary between a GIS system and the rest of the mobile application.	GIS
<<Location-Based Boundary>>	This stereotype extends the <<Boundary>> stereotype of Wisdom. As you recall, boundaries are used to indicate the interface lines between subsystems and components that make up the application. Location-based boundaries are used to specify the boundaries between the core functionality of the application and the system(s) or subsystem(s) whose sole functionality is to provide GIS information.	LBS
<<Mobile Task>>	This stereotype extends Wisdom's <<Task>> stereotype. This stereotype defines a complete set of interactions between the mobile user and the system to achieve something meaningful in terms of the business process.	

12.8 Security and Privacy of Location Information

Security and privacy are of utmost importance to location-based services. Without providing proper security and privacy, few users are willing to use a system that can reveal their current location or history of locations to third parties. Examples of problems that may arise if proper security is not implemented for location services are unwanted marketing, invasion of privacy by governmental or commercial entities, and identity theft or other criminal activities. There are several aspects to security and privacy of location information, The most important are the following:

1. *Access Security*: There must be a proper authentication and authorization mechanism in place for those systems that access the location of a given device. Any system that can obtain location information must in turn provide secure access to any related data through proper authentication and authorization.
2. *Data Security*: Any system used to cross-reference any information that identifies the user associated with a device through profiles, billing, etc. must be completely secured. The content that specifies the location of the device must be transmitted through a secure mechanism (e.g., encryption).
3. *User Control*: The user must have control in specifying whether the location of his or her device is shared with any secondary systems within or outside of the primary wireless network.

Some of the key features of a system that offers location-based service and the clients to such a system must be the following:

1. The system must allow the users to configure policies regarding where and when their location information may be obtained and/or shared.
2. The system must allow the users to specify with whom their location information may be shared.
3. The system must automatically remove all historical data about a user's location unless otherwise allowed by the user.
4. The location-based service must not expose specific information to its client systems on why the location of a particular user may not be available. For example, the client system must not be able to request whether the user has specified to be unavailable to that particular client or during a particular time window.
5. The error margin in the exact location of the user must not be provided unless specified by the user.
6. The client system must specify a reason for which the location is obtained. Only trusted systems should be able to obtain location information.

All other features typical to a secure computing interface such as authentication, authorization, and encryption must be made available by the location-based service to its clients. Of course, what we have outlined here is only a small, but important, subset of features needed for truly secure acquisition and exchange of location information. In Europe and the United States there are existing and evolving legislation to assure the privacy rights of the users.

Then there is the matter of privacy. There are many instances when a user will allow his or her location to be known, but only within a certain range of accuracy and with anonymity. In this context, we describe two metrics that Beresford and Stajano have developed for measuring location privacy, one based on anonymity sets and the other based on entropy [Beresford and Stajano 2003]. The two hypothesize that although location information may be exposed, the number of nodes that can link a given location to an actual identity associated with the thing whose location was measured make up the anonymity set. It should seem obvious that the bigger the anonymity set size is, the more private the interactions of the thing with the outside world become. Likewise, the more things inside the set move around and the more the locations that we are measuring move around (entropy), the more privacy the thing whose location is being measured at some fixed time(s) has. This work is significant as a start in allowing us to quantify just how private the location information associated with something or someone may be. This quantification of privacy may eventually be used, directly or indirectly, as a user-adjustable threshold.

The security and privacy of the location of devices that are open to the network is one of the ongoing areas of research, development, and legislation brought about by consumer concerns. Whereas location data about a particular user or aggregates of users can be extremely helpful in many applications, the user must always have the control over whether or not such information is obtained and with whom and which subsystems it may be shared.

12.9 Localization and Internationalization

Internationalization and localization standards for mobile applications are typically much more stringent than their stationary counterparts. Namely, because the users of mobile applications are moving, they are passing through different locales. An application whose business rules may change (e.g., the tax rate may be different between adjacent locale boundaries such as states or provinces) can benefit greatly from knowing where the user is or where the user is heading—information that may be provided by a location-based service. Likewise, because the spoken language, the written language, units of measurement, business rules, and a variety of other things may change when the mobile user crosses the boundaries of one country into another, location information can be of great help in determining the location. The key here is that internationalization and localization can benefit from location-based information in that determining the location of the user and the subsequently reliant application rules can be automated. However, location-based systems do not really rely on internationalization and localization techniques; the location model as well as the implementation of the location-based system typically does not depend on the location being measured. The association between location and locale information may need to be personalized. For example, a bilingual user who speaks both English and German may travel from the United States to Germany with a GSM phone and want to see the appropriate interface depending on the location. In contrast, an American user who does not speak German may go to Germany and may want to continue viewing the system in English though there may be some incorrect data (e.g., prices may have a dollar sign instead of a Euro sign).

Therefore, location information facilitates easier, better, and more automated localization and internationalization of other aspects of the mobile application such as the user interface. Also, based on the network infrastructure, the implementation of the location-based systems may vary. Nonetheless, inherently, neither the implementation of location-based system, nor the interface to it, requires localization and internationalization.

12.10 Latest Developments in Location-Based Efforts

At the time of authoring this text, location-based services are one of the fastest growing areas of computing. The most recent efforts focus on making location information pervasive throughout all computing systems while allowing mobile computing devices and systems to take advantage of this information. A prime example is the SRI International's Digital Earth project. The goal of the Digital Earth project was to develop infrastructure for an open, distributed, multiresolution, three-dimensional representation of the earth, into which massive quantities of georeferenced information can be embedded [Brecht et al. 2002].

Digital Earth has been designed to be able to provide geographic representations of locations in three modes: *text based*, *map based*, and *TerraVision based*. The text-based format is for the simplest of devices, within which the resource-starved low-end mobile devices such as some mobile phones may fall. The map-based representation allows viewing of locations with PCs, high-end mobile devices capable of rendering graphics well, and other devices with sophisticated two-dimensional GUIs. TerraVision is a distributed, interactive terrain visualization system developed by SRI International [Brecht et al.]. It allows three-dimensional viewing of geographical locations, using GeoVRML, a set of extensions for VRML. It is important to note that this project takes into account human-made structures as well as the natural terrain of earth. Consequently, buildings and other types of human-made structures are modeled and updated periodically.

Along with this, the Digital Earth project leverages DNS (Domain Name Server) and HTTP, two of the base technologies for the Internet, to build a fault-tolerant, scalable, and secure system for providing location information. SRI has recently proposed a new DNS extension of .geo, to ICANN, to be used for retrieval of location information using the Digital Earth project.

There is one more crucial thing about the Digital Earth project. The GeoWeb is fully described in RDF. This is a very significant achievement because it allows the integration of geographical information with other semantic information available on the Web. This in turn gets us one step closer to producing a better environmental context for applications by integrating the semantic meaning of the geographical information with semantic meanings of all of the other information and behavior involved in the application.

There are also remaining challenges. As Jensen recognizes [Jensen 2002], current GIS systems and supporting applications do not posses the necessary robustness and scalability criteria to hold detailed data about movement of mobile things, whether these are users or things that make up the topography of the geography, as rapidly as needed. We still need further standardization in the modeling of spatial information, and we need to create standards accepted by governmental, academic, and commercial entities that implement solutions for accessing location and mobility information.

Location sensitivity is one of the dimensions of mobility that offers the most promise for new ideas in automating tasks to make mobile computing valuable. Usage of location information is certain to become more prevalent in mobile computing.

CHAPTER 13

Active Transactions

People demand freedom of speech as a compensation for the freedom of thought which they seldom use!

Søren Kierkegaard

13.1 INTRODUCTION

We have used the term *active transactions* in this text only for the lack of a better term that encapsulates the *active participation of a computing system in interacting with the user*. What we refer to as active transactions in this text includes all those behaviors exhibited by the system that are started autonomously by the application without the immediate and synchronous invocation of the software by the user. A subset of active transactions is often referred to as *push-based technologies*. Although the term "push" is better used in defining the implementation of the application, one part of the application could "poll" or "pull" and still exhibit active participation in interacting with the user.

What is important to note right away is that active transactions are not limited to push. Let us look at some examples of what we may mean by active transactions:

- An active mobile application that collects end-of-day field results can scan through the records of a salesperson's visits and if he or she has failed to fill out a time sheet with the appropriate visits, the application locates the salesperson by contacting him or her at all pertinent contact points. For example, the application may call the salesperson on the phone and ask him or her to say how many hours were worked and where the work was performed. The salesperson may have simply forgotten to log his or her hours; this process would not only contact the salesperson but also give the salesperson the opportunity to provide the required information during the same session. Conversely, if the salesperson is purposely avoiding logging in his or her hours or picks up the phone but does not respond, the system may send a report to the supervisor indicating the time the user was contacted, whether the user answered the phone call, etc.

- An active mobile application can monitor various air-travel fares while looking for a particular route and time to be available at a certain rate. The application notifies the user as soon as there is an available ticket that meets the criteria. Furthermore, by continuing the interaction initiated by the mobile application, the application may allow the user to proceed to purchase the ticket.

Obviously, this type of active behavior is not required of a mobile application. However, it enhances the value of mobile applications greatly; remember that one of the conditions of the mobile user is that he or she is not focused on the task of computing. Therefore, the application must take greater initiative in initiating interactions with the user to make itself worthwhile. Regardless of the implementation techniques used in providing active behavior, one or more of the following is always exhibited by active mobile applications:

1. The components of the system must have the ability to be *persistently, identifiably*, and *reliably* connected to the network.
2. There must be an *identifiable presence* of the user or the mobile device used by the user. For the system to begin one or more interactions with the user, it has to be able to identify the user and the specific device being used by the user at the time the first interaction is to be initiated by the system. Presence is a concept that is necessary for instant messaging, but it is also a desired attribute for many active interactions with the user. Knowing whether a user is present and whether he or she wants to be allowed to be contacted can be very helpful if not essential to commencing an active interaction with the user.
3. *Intelligent agentlike behavior* is often exhibited by active mobile applications. For example, many times the reason for an application being active is that the user wants to set it off searching for something and come back and notify him or her with the results when found.

These three properties can be seen in other computing applications such as messaging (asynchronous or instant) and agent applications (i.e., not mobile agents but rather agents that do work on behalf of users). Messaging and intelligent agents share many attributes with effective mobile applications, and a well-built mobile application borrows from years of experience in those fields. Note that we exclude single-event notifications such as an alarm clock going off. Though these types of notifications are absolutely crucial in mobile applications, they are not "transactions" per se. In other words, there is no "transacting" taking place between the user and the machine. The machine simply notifies the user of something and then goes away. Such notifications are indeed active but do not have transactional or interactive properties.

Our focus in this chapter will be on those technologies that enable this desired active behavior by our mobile applications and on seeing how best to integrate this behavior into our mobile applications. We have already covered some of the basic technologies involved such as SMS. In a way, SMS is the most rudimentary type pf enabling technology for active transactions: a simple message initiated by the system that requires no reply from the user. SMS is typically used as a messaging system between two users but it can be used to send messages to the user that are generated by the system.

However, SMS does not allow the user to enter into a transactional interaction with the system. So, it is not the complete solution that we need. As of yet, there are no deployments of such a complete solution that allows a fully active behavior by the mobile application to be implemented. But this will change in the near future. Examples that we will look at will be WAP 2.0, Mobile IP, and SIP.

Finally, before delving into a detailed discussion of various technologies, it should be noted that everything we discuss here is at the session layer and up on the OSI (Open Systems Interconnection) model. Most of the functionality of push-based technologies, or any other type of technology that can initiate an interaction with the user, is implemented at the application layer (the highest layer of the OSI model) with some implementation seeping into the presentation layer and session layer (gateways such as those seen in the case of the WAP 2.0 Push Proxy Gateway). There is no fundamental difference between active and passive interactions between two computing systems at the transport layer or lower down: Packets are packets, regardless of the direction of travel.

Let us begin our discussion with an overall look at the wireless infrastructure that offers the skeleton for the system to send the initial message out to the user and allow the user to follow with subsequent messages from thereon.

13.2 Active Computing and Wireless Infrastructure

For the system to actively initiate interactions with the user, we can have one of the two following conditions:

1. Some condition, observable by the mobile device or the application running on it, occurs and there is a mobile application running on the mobile device that can recognize this condition. This application can then decide to initiate a series of interactions with the user. For example, this may be a simple reminder of an appointment that allows the user to push a snooze or a cancel button. The information for the appointment may reside in the PIM (mobile application on the device) that notifies the user.
2. The condition that is to trigger the initiation of the interaction with the user, part of the application that interacts with the user, or all of the application that interacts with the user is somewhere else than the mobile device on the network. This means that the act of initiating an interaction with the user includes some network traffic. This is a more complicated model because it requires some way of connecting to a device, recognizing the presence state (whether the user has the device on, wants to be contacted, etc.), and finally pushing the initial message out over the network.

For the first case, in which all of the application and the data it needs are on the mobile device, active behavior of the mobile application can be implemented in several different ways:

1. The underlying API on top of which the mobile application is being written (device operating system, device drivers, etc.) may offer events that are thrown when certain events (timers, ad hoc network handshakes, etc.) occur. These events may then "wake up" the mobile application (or a part of the mobile application or some tertiary application that in turn signals the mobile application) and start it on a path to eventually interact with the user.
2. Some sort of polling, either inside the mobile application or through an external agent on the mobile device, may be monitoring various states of the physical device. In other words, the mobile application, directly or indirectly, may be polling the device for states that will trigger some event in the application.
3. The first two cases here assumed that the trigger lies within some event in the device. The trigger could also be a logical event (e.g., it could notify the user when he or she is more than 60% over scheduled in his or her calendar). In this case, the application typically polls the data that it has access to or the application framework does the polling and bubbles up, through the API, an event to the mobile application.

Any one of these three cases are basically dictated by the type of device and the available operating system and application development framework that make up the mobile platform (e.g., J2ME on Nokia phones). The reason for recognizing these different approaches is that each dictates a different implementation strategy. Strategies and design patterns for event models and polling are common to stationary applications. We will leave the reader to research such strategies and patterns in textbooks regarding multithreading, software design patterns, and push–pull implementation.

The more complicated case is when network-based transactions are required to establish an active interaction with the user. And as we have stressed, there are both wired and wireless mobile applications. For the wired case, we go back to the paradigms developed for distributed computing techniques for stationary systems such as Java's RMI or IIOP where, once the mobile application establishes the connection with the network through a wired network, things work much the same way as the stationary applications when it comes to initiating active interactions with the mobile application at the node.

In the wireless case, we have to have wireless infrastructures that support a mechanism by which we can notify the mobile device. Before looking at how the wireless infrastructure may provide a substrate for active transactions, let us define some terms that we have already seen a few times in this chapter: push and pull. The terms push and pull have been used differently within various disciplines of computer science such as network management, communication, content management, and others. For our purposes, communication, most likely in the form of messaging in an MMI, is the domain within which to define these terms.

First let us look at a pull. The HTTP request–response mechanism is a good example of a pull mechanism. In a pull mechanism, one party sends a message to the other party and blocks (a term used to indicate synchronous waiting) until the other party returns a response. In this way, pull is synchronous. Typical usage of the pull model in building an active interaction with a mobile device would be a case where the mobile device (or the application running on it) submits a request to a server and blocks until the response is sent back, then proceeds to interact with the user based on the returned results. The initial request may be invoked by a timer, a background thread polling a local event, or some other event. Conversely, if we have a listener (microserver, etc.) running on the mobile device, some other node on the network can send it a request and wait for a response. The initial request may start a chain of actions that lead to an active interaction with the user. The response back to the initiator node may be a simple acknowledgement of the receipt of the message or it may hold data regarding the state of the device, the subsequent interactions of the user with the application, etc.

Like pull, push is used in many different contexts to mean different things. Push is defined, by Openwave's WAP 2.0 Technology Overview, to be "the delivery of content to the mobile device without previous user interaction" [Openwave 2002]. However, this is probably not enough of a specific definition because we can deliver content to the mobile device with pull without previous user interaction. The additional factor that makes push unique is that it is *asynchronous* in nature. In other words, when node A pushes something to node B, it does not block and wait for something to come back, though something may eventually come back. Whatever message is sent back is sent asynchronously and without timing guarantees. Of course, specific implementations can add in application-type timeouts, but these timeouts should be configurable as they are not part of the semantics of defining push. Push has gained a bad reputation based on the failure of some Internet companies such as PointCast whose claim to fame was going to be based on a proprietary network that pushed content to the user's desktop. Other companies have used push exclusively as the primary mechanism for updating and provisioning software. Within the context of this text, because we are referring to push in the realm of communication, specifically mobile communications, *we define push as delivery of application layer messages, without invocation of the message from the recipient, and in an asynchronous manner*. This definition is why SMS makes the simplest form of a push: It is a text message sent to a mobile device without a synchronous wait for a reliability reply (or any other type of reply for that matter), though the SMSCs can send a message to the initiator of the message if there is a problem with the delivery of the message to its destination.

It is very preferable for wireless infrastructures to support some sort of a push in the application-layer infrastructure so that messages of an asynchronous nature may be sent to a device destination by an initiator. Otherwise, the only other way of delivering an active interaction with the user is to have a client-side piece of software running on the mobile device; this application should then serve as a listening server or a polling client. Neither of these situations is ideal, as we have seen, devices are resource-starved. Even as these devices become more and more powerful, the asynchronous nature of a push makes it desirable in providing active interactions because the unreliable device connectivity resulting from the mobile nature of mobile devices makes implementation of synchronous interactions between clients and servers difficult. The mobile device is not always on, nor is it always connected. Moreover, the QOS or available resources may not be desirable to accept a message. In such situations, asynchronous delivery of messages to the device makes much more sense. Note also that whatever mechanism is deployed should minimize power usage.

Both push and pull can be performed in either an aperiodic or a periodic fashion; aperiodic delivery is event driven—a data request (for pull) or transmission (for push) is triggered by an event such as a user action (for pull) or data update (for push) [Franklin and Zdonik 1998]. Also, we can unicast, multicast, or broadcast push. In other words, we can send the same initial message to one destination, several specific destinations, or all destinations present in a network. Various wireless network infrastructures provide different levels of support for the permutations of destination addressing (unicast, multicast, and broadcast) and periodicity of the message arrangements.

We will look at WAP 1.2 and 2.0 Push in the next section. At present, WAP Push is the most widely implemented push mechanism in the wireless world.

13.2.1 WAP Push

We discussed WAP in the earlier chapters of this text. WAP creates a very well defined infrastructure for pushing information to WAP-enabled mobile devices. WAP Push was first made available in WAP 1.2, which saw very little deployment and is being superseded by WAP 2.0.

The WAP 1.2 Push architecture relies on a *Push Proxy Gateway*, commonly referred to as a PPG, and a Push Initiator, PI. The PI contacts the PPG through PAP. PAP is a high-level application-layer protocol that can be piggybacked on top of HTTP, SMTP, or other like protocols. The interactions coming from and going to the PI in PAP are translated to the Push OTA (over-the-air) protocol of WAP by the PPG, which allows the PPG to reach the WAP client. Note that the PPG is a WAP gateway with additional functionality for implementing push.

The PPG also takes care of addressing translation. To begin the push process to a WAP client, we need to be able to address that client. This addressing can be done by uniquely identifying a device (device address) or uniquely defining the user of the device. Whereas addressing the device is straightforward, addressing the user is a bit more complex as the user may be using one of many devices and which device is used by the user is unknown to the network. Device addressing is done by using IPv4/6 or Mobile Subscriber ISDN Number (MSISDN). IPv4 is the prevalent addressing scheme for IP-based networks (addresses in the form of xxx.xxx.xxx.xxx, where x is a numeric value), IPv6 is the standard for which most Mobile IP–based standards are designed to be integrated with, and MSISDN is an addressing scheme that is somewhat specific to the type of underlying network. MSISDN will probably give way to Mobile IP–based addressing and IPv6, but do not expect this to happen very soon. The MSISDN install base is very large globally and includes a variety of telephony systems. It will be challenging to migrate even a significant portion of the infrastructure and devices to supporting IPv6.

Whereas a device can have one of these three specific types of addresses, the PPG takes care of user-based addressing. The PPG can hold the logic, or can be connected to an application server that holds the logic, for the link between a specific device and a specific user at a given time.

Because we have already looked at the different types of underlying networks, the two things worth further discussion here are PAP and WAP OTA. How do messages get pushed to the PPG and then pushed, by the PPG, to the WAP client?

PAP's payload is XML and it is defined with a DTD in WAP 1.2, though it will eventually be defined by a schema. PAP specifies two types of operations: those that are required to implement WAP 1.2 and those that are optional. The required operations are the following:

1. *Submission*: This includes the initial message sent from the PI to the PPG and a response from the PPG to the PI. The content of the message sent by the PI to the PPG is a MIME document that may be made of multiple segments. If the message gets to the PPG in good order, then the PPG must send back an acknowledgment of the good receipt to the PI.
2. *Bad Message Response*: If the PPG has a problem with receiving a message from the PI or if the message is corrupted, it sends back a Bad Message Response to the PI.
3. *Result Notification*: Simply making sure that the message is delivered to the PPG by the PI is not good enough. We need to know if the end client received the message. However, the end client and the PPG communicate through a fundamentally different infrastructure than the PI and the PPG. The PI and the PPG typically communicate through a much more reliable network whereas the connection between the PPG and the end client is much more unstable.

The optional operations of PAP are the following:

1. *Push Cancellation*: This operation is like the "unsend" that every e-mail user wishes, at one time or the other, he or she had. As there is a finite amount of time spanned between the time when the message is first generated by the PI and sent to the PPG and the time when the message is sent, through the Push OTA and by the PPG, to the end device, the PI may decide to cancel the sending of the message. This could be caused logically (based on application logic) if the response received from the PPG is not the desired response (e.g., a bad push submission is received or no response is received).
2. *Status Query*: Once the PI sends a message to the PPG, then it should have a way to know the status of the delivery of the message to the end client. This mechanism is provided by the Status Query operation. This status could be used by some external application, used as a means to time out and call a cancellation, or used by one of many other application-based operations that depend on the specific usage of the pushed message.
3. *Client Capabilities Query*: Because any type of content can be pushed out to the client, then the PI and/or the back-end applications using the PI should know what types of content the end client can handle and what other general

capabilities it has. This operation allows the PI to query the PPG for the capabilities of the client. In the case of more sophisticated clients, the PPG may then query the device and proxy the response back to the PI. However, most of the time, the PPG knows the type of the connected device and its capabilities and simply responds to the PI based on this known information.

4. *Quality of Service*: As we saw in previous chapters, one of the dimensions of mobility is the QOS of the connectivity of the device to the network. PAP allows, optionally, for specifying the delivery of messages to the end client based on the available QOS. For example, we do not want to push advertisements to a user who is currently experiencing bad QOS conditions and take up the little bandwidth that he or she has available.
5. *Delivery Timing*: Once again, optionally, PAP allows us to specify when a message should be delivered to the target and then request a notification when the message is received by the end user.

There can be three entity types in a multipart PAP message as specified in the WAP 1.2 Specification: a *Control Entity*, which has information about the delivery of messages throughout the WAP-based infrastructure such as addressing; a *Content Entity*, which can hold any valid XML or MIME type that either the PPG or the end-client understand; and a *Capabilities Entity*, which is used to communicate the capabilities of a device. (Incidentally, it is a mystery why CC/PP and UAProf have not been used for this latter purpose in PAP.)

As far as the mobile application developer is concerned, the PI is the integration point for the back end of the mobile application. Rarely do carriers expose the PPGs to third parties; therefore, a WAP Push to the mobile application developer means interfacing with an existing PI or creating an application that acts as a PI and communicates with the PPG. If you are dealing with a third party vendor's software whose tools are installed within the carrier's telecommunications infrastructure (such as Nokia or Phone.com's WAP infrastructure software), you may also be able to get your hands on some tools that provide custom interfaces to these servers. By now, you may be asking yourself how the device is notified by the PPG.

A WAP 1.2–enabled device must first support the Push OTA protocol as specified by the WAP Forum. In addition, it also has to have a Session Initiation Application (SIA). The SIA application is alive while the device is on and is listening for messages being sent to it. Once it receives a message, it passes it on to the WAP-enabled application (WAP browser, etc.), which is also referred to as the application dispatcher.

As you will see later in this chapter, PAP is very similar, in design and intent, to SIP (Session Initiation Protocol). Although PAP and SIP were designed for entirely different purposes, it is interesting to see how they have both evolved from HTTP and how similar they are in some of their basic operations. This leads us to recognize the inherent similarities in the requirements for a system that supports push such as PAP and a system that supports instant messaging such as SIP.

Architecturally, there is not much difference between WAP 1.2 and WAP 2.0 Push. But there are some differences at the implementation level. For example, as the content compilation and encoding scheme moves from WML, WMLC, and WBXML in WAP 1.x to XHTML in WAP 2.0, the content handled by a WAP 2.0 Push proxy may be different from that handled by a WAP 1.2 Push proxy. Of course, a WAP 2.0 Push proxy should be able to handle the older content types (being backward compatible), but, in real-life, this may prove to be somewhat unreliable as WAP deployments are often pieced together (at least in the United States) and are made of a various servers by different vendors, not all of which may provide the same amount of backward compatibility. So, though in theory backward compatibility should always be there, it is sometimes not seen in the real deployments of WAP 2.0 infrastructure because of such differences as the content type.

Although WAP 2.0 can use a Mobile IP–like addressing scheme, its core infrastructure is not based on Mobile IP. Future versions of WAP will continue to move toward a completely IP-based network, perhaps Mobile IP.

13.2.2 Mobile IP and Push

The goal of IP mobility support is to provide the means by which applications on distinct computers are able to communicate when one or both computers have changed their physical network location; Mobile IP tries to provide such support with a solution at the network layer [Singh et al. 1999]. Mobile IP is significant to active interactions with the mobile device because it offers the only IP-based solution, to date, to providing a persistent connection between the device and the network regardless of the type of connectivity.

It is easy to fall into the trap of assuming that the mobile device may be connected only through long-range wireless networking technology, or conversely, only through short-range wireless networking technology. This situation is becoming more and more not the case! As device manufacturers are realizing, the type of wireless connectivity to the network desired may be different depending on the location. As an example, a particular user may always have GSM connectivity on his or her PDA, but when the user crosses into a short-range wireless hot spot (Bluetooth or WIFI), it may be desirable to switch to the connectivity mechanism through the hot spot and, as the user exits the hot spot, it may again be desirable to switch to GSM for an uninterrupted usage experience by the user.

The implementation of Mobile IP across the different types of wireless networks (short range and long range, including technologies such as GSM as well as WIFI) not only allows seamless roaming among different networks but also guarantees us a reliable and clean fabric on which to build mobile applications. Mobile IP would allow us to start an active set of interactions with the user in one network and end it in another network without violating the transactional integrity of the session.

13.2.3 Session Initiation Protocol

SIP is an IETF standard for communications between users and is addressed by the 3GPP Specifications. The strongest supporter and implementer of SIP today is Microsoft and its most pervasive usage is in instant messaging applications, mobile or not. SIP addresses how to establish a session between peers, how to maintain

```
INVITE sip:user@cienecs.com SIP/2.0
From: Susan Boettger<sip:susan@pianoedge.com>
Subject: Piano Lessons
To: Laurna Griffits <sip:laurna@pianoedge.com>
Via: SIP/2.0/UDP someserver.someisp.com
Call-ID: 15555555.1.1@1.1.1.1
Content-type: application/sdp
CSeq: 1 INVITE
Content-Length:

v=0
o=A1 53655765 2353687637 IN IP4 1.1.1.2
c=IN IP4 1.1.1.1
t=0 0
m=audio 7865 RTP/AVP 0
```

FIGURE 13.1. Sample SIP Code.

this session, and how to exchange data during a established session. Like HTTP, SIP is an application-layer protocol built for IP-based networks.

A sample SIP code is shown in Figure 13.1.

SIP defines transactional boundaries for its messages: Each complete message passed from one node to the other is called a *transaction*. All transactions are independent and are identified by a sequence number. SIP defines the following roles for the components involved in a SIP-based transaction:

1. *User Agent Client*: This is also referred to as UAC and is equivalent to the client in the HTTP world. In our case, this is the mobile device. Note that defining a client and a server makes SIP a client–server protocol.
2. *User Agent Server*: This is also referred to as UAS and is the server listening for client requests.
3. *Proxy Server*: Once again, just like HTTP proxies, SIP proxies sit between a client and a server, passing the requests through the network. They can also create multiple requests from a single request.
4. *Redirect Server*: These servers simply redirect requests to other servers.
5. *Registrar*: This is a concept unique to SIP; it allows the users to register with a centralized mechanism so that this centralized mechanism can provide presence information.

Either the proxy or the registrar system(s) can be responsible for maintaining the presence state of the connected devices. Alternatively, another system can be used to maintain the presence information. Whatever system is used to do this is referred to as the *presence agent*. This presence is addressed in a single user and multidevice manner. In other words, it is able to maintain the presence information about a user who may be connected through multiple devices at the same time or different times. This functionality is crucial in being able to deliver a robust active mobile application because a mobile user may be changing what device he or she is using rapidly and unpredictably. The presence agent is also responsible for authenticating the user. Unfortunately, the SIP specification does not address authorization, but it is assumed that authorization is application specific.

Seeing all of the similarities of SIP with HTTP, you should not be surprised that SIP also defines a set of methods. These methods are as follows:

1. INVITE: This method invites another registered user to a session.
2. OPTIONS: This method queries another user about the capabilities of the device and platform being used. Note that this is only a query about the capability of the other user; no invitation is made to participate in a session.
3. BYE: This method ends a current session in progress with another user.
4. ACK: Much like the ACK used in TCP, it is used to acknowledge the receipt of a message.
5. CANCEL: This message stops a search.
6. SUBSCRIBE: This method allows a subscriber (which could be an end system or a proxy) to be notified of the presence state of a user (or his or her device).
7. NOTIFY: This is the message sent to a subscriber about the presence information to which he or she has subscribed.
8. MESSAGE: This is basically a single text-based message sent from one participant to another.

Once again, just like HTTP, there is a header and a body. Many of the headers, as you will see, are borrowed from HTTP. SIP also uses the concept of URIs extensively. As you can see at this point, SIP is really just a modified version of HTTP that fits instant messaging better than HTTP does. Overall, this is probably a much better idea than simply using HTTP for instant messaging (which is still being tried, demonstrating that the antipattern mentality lives on!). So, why not just use HTTP? Not only does SIP address the question of presence, but it also makes special considerations for voice-based interactions. This is particularly important in the multichannel and multimodal mobile world.

There is something else that is important. SIP and similar technologies are really somewhat competitive with push-based technologies. Although the implementation of the technologies are vastly different, they enable essentially the same functionality: allowing software systems to exhibit active behavior. Of course, SIP and SIP-like technologies were primarily designed for instant messaging, but the functionality that is delivered is well suited for active interactions between the user and a computer system. Besides, instant messaging and active interactions share many properties; the main difference between them is that, in instant messaging, the messages are being sent back and forth between live users and, in active interactions, some software agent is producing at least some of the messages.

13.3 Practical Considerations of Building Active Systems

By now, you know that it is important to consider various ways of actively keeping the user of your mobile application involved. There are some practical considerations, when implementing active behavior for the different parts of your system, that you should keep in mind. These are as follows:

1. You must assure that your user has the ability to protect his or her privacy in any sort of an active interaction. If the user does not want to be contacted by the application and/or is not bound by his or her employer or another organization to participate in some interaction with your application, allow the user to personalize it so. Personalization and active behavior of an application go hand in hand. The problem that active interactions solve stem from the condition of the mobile user: a fundamental lack of focus on the task of computing. Make sure your application does not "annoy" the user (e.g., avoid things such as unwanted advertisements pushed to the mobile device).
2. We have talked about push and pull in this chapter. Surely we want to pick the best way to implement the solution, but we often do not have enough control over the infrastructure that we are going to use. More often than not, we are given an infrastructure and have to implement the application on top of it. The point is to make the user experience as good as possible. The value of any software application is not in its artistic architectural beauty but rather in the value it delivers to solving some problem. So, implement the active behavior in the best possible manner.
3. Some implementations of push take up enormous amounts of bandwidth because they keep the data channel between the mobile device and the network fairly busy. Make sure that, if you are going to use some push-based technology as the underlying implementation of the active behavior in your system, it does not suck up a great deal of the valuable wireless bandwidth to the mobile device.
4. Mobile agent–based systems, discussed in some detail in Chapter 9, inherently implement active behavior. There is no need for a "push" in such systems because they can simply migrate to the host where the active behavior must be displayed. This is a great advantage of mobile agent systems. Combined with some intelligence (sometimes referred to as *intelligent agents*) that implement some work that the end user may otherwise have to do, mobile agents give us much of the infrastructure we need to build active behavior into our mobile application.
5. Because the wired Internet is based on TCP/IP, UDP is often neglected as an option. As UDP does not guarantee the reliable delivery of datagrams, it is by nature asynchronous—it does not block waiting for some response. In this way, UDP can be extremely useful in building systems that exhibit active behavior. It can be used in broadcasts and multicasts. It can also be used as a mechanism to "wake up" some application on the mobile device that begins interacting with the user. That initial atomic interaction and its trigger are the keys for the mobile application to exhibit active behavior at the application layer, and UDP is ideally suited for addressing this problem.

Chapter 14

Mobile Security

Everything that man does in his symbolic world is an attempt to deny and overcome his grotesque fate.

Ernst Becker

14.1 Introduction

Security is always one of the biggest concerns when designing any application, but particularly distributed applications. Distributed applications operate over networks, involve multiple users, and have many other properties that make them more vulnerable to security breaches. Though there are stand-alone mobile applications, as we have discussed earlier in this text, most mobile applications, at their core, are distributed applications. Unfortunately, to date, there remain many unsolved problems with security concerns of mobile applications.

Our goal in this chapter will be to first introduce a taxonomy of mobile application security problems, look at a few general approaches in solving these problems, and finally review those problems that remain unsolved. Security also tends to be a system-wide problem, not just an application problem, whether dealing with mobile or stationary applications. So, we are not out to show you sample code, standards, or specific techniques; such discussions are completely beyond the scope of our discussion. Our main purpose is to take a step back and look at the big picture of mobile application design and see where security concerns may be. Security is intimately bound to the design of the platform for which the mobile application is being built. Dealing with such concerns can be trivial as all we need to do is to understand the security infrastructure of the mobile platform and implement the appropriate APIs in our applications (e.g., what WAP may let us do with WTLS or how we can author secure applications on the Palm platform).

However, most mobile application or mobile platforms do not exist in isolation. Therefore, the bigger picture is that most mobile applications are really distributed applications being used by mobile users on mobile devices. And this is where security gets tricky. In this chapter, we will concentrate on the big picture that lets us see as many holes as possible. The solutions may be dependent on the mobile infrastructure on which you must deploy your application or the mobile application itself.

Just like all of the other topics in this text, our interest is not in reviewing solutions and problems specific to some specific technology or review APIs. We consistently believe, in approaching the various problems associated with mobile application development, that focusing on specific implementations is not the right approach because mobile technologies are changing far too quickly. So, let us start with a general taxonomy of the type of security problems that we may approach during the life cycle of our application.

14.1.1 Taxonomy of Mobile Security Problems

We need security for two reasons: 1. to keep out those malicious parties who are trying to get access to things that they are not allowed to access and 2. to ensure that information and system access are not inadvertently given to parties not actively seeking a system breach. So, the goal is to keep data and system access from being exposed to parties who should not access them, whether or not those parties are actively seeking a breach. Such a breach can happen at different points: hardware, software, and communication channels. Because of this, we can use the OSI model and its taxonomy to group the various types of security concerns for mobile applications. We will start from the top and work our way down:

1. *Application Layer Security*: This the most important layer for securing our mobile application. As software application developers, practically speaking, we have the most control at this layer. Assuming that all other layers below this one are not secure, we can still build a secure application if we exercise due caution at this layer. This does not mean that this is the best course of action to take, but as this is the layer over which we as software application developers have the most control, we need to pay the most attention to it. In the case of standalone applications, the OSI model does not have much meaning as it is primarily used to represent networked applications. Nevertheless, we can think of a standalone application to exist entirely at this level: We have complete control over whatever security features we need to implement. The operating system may provide features that make things easier. For example, for a simple Palm application that uses no networking, the security concerns may entail encrypting all of the data and using sufficient usernames and passwords for authentication and authorization in the application. At this same layer, the application layer, a networked application that uses HTTP for communication on the same platform (Palm OS) may additionally include usage of encrypted communication using techniques such as DS3 or a similar technology as well as authentication for whatever other computing system is communicating with our application.

2. *Presentation Layer and Session Layer Security*: SSL (Secured Socket Layer) is probably the most important technology of interest here. Though there are other possible techniques that use public and private keys for secure transfer of data, SSL is by far the most popular and the one for which nearly all platforms provide support. If you remember, when we looked at WAP, the security mechanism of WTLS provides the SSL implementation for the WAP protocol. Implementing SSL (by which we mean actually writing the SSL specification as a library for your operating system or trying to implement it on an end-to-end system such as WAP) is not something that we will worry about in this text as it is outside of the scope of the typical work that an application developer has to do; it is nothing trivial! What is interesting to note is that the size of the public and private keys may be smaller than desired because of the resource limitations on mobile devices. Keep in mind that the effort to break a security key by brute force is, in the case of the best encryption algorithms, exponentially relative to the size of the public and private keys. Here we encounter a problem that is not solved in a simple manner: If the device does not have enough resources, it is tough to justify spending whatever it has on encryption and decryption. There has been discussion among mobile device vendors in providing hardware-based solutions for SSL to provide a more efficient method for secure communications.
3. *Transport Layer and Network Layer Security (IPSec)*: These layers are, respectively, the home of TCP and IP (as well as other equivalent protocols). Whereas SSL assures that all communications are secure, IPSec assures that the nodes that are communicating are not malicious and masquerading as nodes that they are not. IPSec also provides more low-level encryption and allows us to do "IP Tunneling." IPSec is particularly important in the infrastructure that supports the mobile application. As Mobile IP technologies mature, IPSec will become more and more relevant to the actual mobile device. Because of the lack of deployment prevalence, there are no solid security solutions introduced specific to the needs of Mobile IP (but, as discussed in Chapter 10, there are home agents and foreign agents and this architecture brings additional considerations not properly addressed by IPSec). There are some suggested solutions. For instance, Fasbender, Kesdogan, and Kubits [Fasbender et al.] propose a nondisclosure method that first recognizes the differences between a system based on Mobile IP deployment and a regular IP-based system and then tries to address these new requirements (see the reference for further details). However, these various techniques have yet to be employed in real deployments and stand the test of time and the patience of hackers.
4. *Data Link Layer Security*: This is where things like MAC (Medium Access Control) addresses belong. It is tough to cause a security breach through the data link layer because it is typically hardware implemented. Hardware is also, of course, susceptible to security problems, but hardware vendors typically test much more rigorously than software vendors (as the costs of mistakes are much higher) and it is much more difficult to get significant malicious programs such as viruses onto the hardware to begin with.
5. *Physical Layer Security*: Perhaps the biggest differences between security implementations of mobile systems and stationary systems are a byproduct of the

fact that mobile systems are typically connected to the network through a wireless connection. Wired systems, whether fiber-optic cables, coaxial cable, or twisted-pair wires, limit access to the bits and bytes traveling across the communication channels that they provide inside their physical medium. However, bits and bytes are all over the space between two wireless nodes waiting to be read as there is no limiting "conduit" in the case of wireless communication. Not only that, but intrusion detection is enormously more difficult in wireless systems where signal attenuations, phase shifts, and other phenomena are part of the physical condition of the network and cannot be used reliably to indicate security breaches.

Considering this taxonomy of security issues based on the OSI model, the dimensions of mobility, and the mobile condition of the mobile user leads us to the following security issues that are unique from any of those concerns experienced by stationary applications:

1. secure authentication and authorization of nodes,
2. secure communications between the authenticated and authorized nodes of the network over a wireless connection (at various OSI layers using the correspondingly appropriate techniques such as SSL at the presentation/session layers),
3. secure deployment of an application on the target device,
4. secure storage and retrieval of information on the mobile device,
5. securing information collected or provided by the mobile application infrastructure (e.g., location information),
6. securing any conversion of content required for supporting multimodal applications,
7. securing synchronization and exchange of information among different channels in a multichannel communication environment,
8. defending against the fraudulent usage of the wireless service, and
9. defending against various Denial of Service attacks that may interrupt service to the network users (mobile application users in our case) or make other security breaches possible.

In addition to these concerns, once again, we bring up the dimensions of mobility. As we have repeatedly mentioned in this text, the dimensions of mobility are the fundamental bases for those difference we see between mobile applications and stationary applications. Security is a part of most stationary and mobile applications. So, we can go back to the dimensions of mobility to see the differences in requirements, design, and implementations of security between mobile and stationary applications. In other words, wee need to consider the following:

1. How do security concerns change when the location of the device and application are changing, when the application is using location information in its internal logic, when there exists some LBS infrastructure, and when the location information must be provided not only securely but also privately?

2. Is security compromised by the QOS? For example, some systems do not appropriately secure dropped packets. Although this level of security may not be important for a given system, we still need to be aware of it. Also, we noted that QOS is a dimension of mobility largely because of the intermittent connectivity of the mobile user but also because the connectivity may be provided through a wireless network. As most wireless networks for consumer mobile devices are cell based, we need to be worried about an entire arena of security problems that occur because of the cell-based architecture such as security at handover points. It is also important to keep in mind that we have to provide offline-security. The user may need to use the application while it is not connected to the network, so we may be required to implement different security mechanisms including implementing authentication and authorization on the device and on the network.
3. Security is almost always dependent on device capabilities as it takes device resources to encrypt/decrypt data. For example, the size of the encryption key may need to be smaller for some devices than others as they may not have the processing power to encrypt and decrypt the data in a timely manner.
4. The power supply is only important in security if the device has different modes of operation depending on the available amount of power. Obviously, not every application or transaction within the same application requires the same amount of security. The key is to make sure that the security of those transactions that must be secure is never compromised regardless of the device mode of operation.
5. Various user interfaces require different types of security. For those developers who have developed GUI-based applications, the biggest difference is in understanding the very different security techniques used in VUIs. For example, it may be fine to display some secure and private information to the user on the GUI application as he or she may be able to hide it from the surroundings, but the same is not true in the case of a VUI; we do not want to play a text-to-speech clip of the user's bank account balance or, at the very least, we want to give the user the choice to hear or view his or her balance. Voice itself can also be used to test liveliness as well as authentication. These features are very critical. Although there is no way to tell who is typing information on a mobile device (unless the device has a fingerprint reader or some other biometric interface, which is very unlikely), there are proven technologies that not only allow us to recognize a user but also allow us to make sure that the user is live at the time of the recognition and the audio being received by the system is not a recording. Examples of such technologies are included in products offered by Nuance, IBM, and Speech Works. Another critical issue is to provide proper security for intermodal and interchannel communications. As we saw in Chapters 5–8, the modes and channels involved in a multimodal user interface are not independent. There are interactions that may be linked to one of many different aspects such as temporal synchronization between different channels or multimodal sessions that involve some user interface logic to render various components through the appropriate channel and mode. Many security issues are compounded by the multichannel and multimodal nature of interactions in mobile applications.

6. As we have noted, because mobile devices are smaller and cheaper than PCs, they have proliferated greatly. There are more different types of devices in the mobile market; their life cycle is shorter than the life cycle of PCs for many reasons, among which is the much lower cost to manufacture them. The problem of device proliferation, coupled with the distributed nature of mobile applications, magnifies the scalability problem of implementing security. Each user may have many different mobile devices. For example, a typical user may have a mobile device in his or her automobile (telematic device), a cell phone, a PDA, a laptop, and possibly a tablet PC, each of which may connect to the network thorough a distinct channel or set of channels and have its own set of security needs and requirements.
7. Actively interacting with the user presents us with more privacy problems then security problems. Whereas we can use the user's response to the initial transaction for authorization, we must be able to authenticate the user prior to sending out that initial message. Sending the initial interaction or pushed message to the wrong user in itself is a security flaw.
8. In addition to the dimensions of mobility outlined in Chapter 1 (whose effect on security has been discussed in points 1 through 7), the mobile condition of the user introduces the following new concerns:
   a. Mobile devices are more susceptible to theft and loss. It is much more difficult to misplace your PC than it is your phone. The physical size of the device has much to do with this. The smaller things become, the easier it is to lose them. Though location-based technologies can help us in finding the device, device security and important information may be compromised by the time the device is found or recovered.
   b. With mobile users, there is a range of environments to consider in a security policy; with or without a VPN (Virtual Private Network), users may connect to the network directly, through a corporate Internet service provider, or through their own Internet servive provider, thereby using a variety of different security guidelines established by different organizations [Clarkin 2003]. These differences may cause security breaches because something that is secure in one network may not be secure in another.
   c. As we noted, the life cycle of mobile devices tends to be shorter than their stationary counterparts, the average being somewhere between eighteen and twenty-four months. Rapid development of mobile technology to meet higher user expectations has led to security being seen as too much work in a compressed timeline [Claessens et al. 2003].
   d. Many mobile devices use SIM cards. Securing the configuration and reconfiguration of these SIM cards in itself is a security issue. Although this is largely out of the hands of a mobile developer who is developing third-party software for mobile devices, it is crucial to have a system for detecting when the configurations on the SIM card change, thereby leading to a change of behavior or intention on the part of the device.

Having discussed all of these various concerns and how we can categorize them for mobile applications, we must take a further step, before all others, in designing a secure system: *We must determine the threat levels*. This is perhaps the single most neglected step in most systems. One of the antipatterns that we have mentioned has been that, once a solution works, we have a tendency to use that solution for all sorts of problems, whether or not the solution is a good fit. This is often the case for system-wide or application-layer security implementations. Without the proper threat recognition in which the various levels of threat, sources of threat, and the cost of security are addressed, trying to solve the security problems of a system, whether mobile or not, becomes a haphazard series of jumps between isolated symptoms instead of a systematic solution to the roots of security problems. In the case of mobile applications, what you need to keep in mind while determining the threat levels are the following:

1. Mobile applications are a superset of their stationary counterpart. Therefore, you must take into account all of those concerns of stationary applications.
2. Consider the new security concerns introduced by the various dimensions of mobility and the very distributed nature of mobile applications.
3. Consider the appropriateness of the level of security concern for each part of the mobile application. It is easy to overestimate or underestimate the level of security required for a particular transaction. The requirements-gathering process is critical here. Also, different parts of the application may require different security levels.

Finally, determining the threat level alone will not answer the questions that management will ask. Management is always looking for a return on investment in any project and implementing security is no different. In fact, security tends to be an area that is often not properly assessed. Some numbers that can help here have been published by Stanford and MIT's Sloan School of Management. They have defined a Risk on Security Investment (ROSI) that, based on the empirical evidence they have gathered, is at 21% at the design stage, 15% at the implementation stage, and 12% at the testing stage. This further verifies our approach that security is largely an architectural and a system-wide problem that must be solved at design time [Intel 2003]. We will not go into the details of the justifications of these numbers; refer to the papers referenced here for those justifications.

Although in this chapter we will concentrate on the security provided by wireless technologies that give the mobile application connectivity to the network, somewhere along the line we will also look at security issues of things that are very unique to mobile applications such as security within ad hoc networking technologies and mobile agent security.

Currently (and likely to be the case for the near future), security is implemented in a very proprietary manner by many wireless networks that provide network connectivity for mobile applications. This is particularly true in the long-range wireless technologies, where it makes sense for the large telecommunication companies to implement proprietary technologies closely tied to their infrastructure assets (such as CDMA equipment). However, there are also standards that give security a full and open treatment such as WAP, Bluetooth, and 802.11 standards (though, as we will see, 802.11 security features have been much maligned).

In this next section, we will look at the specific concerns associated with some of the wireless technologies we have discussed earlier in Chapter 10.

14.2 Security in Wireless Networks

Before reading this section, make sure that you have read Chapter 10 because we will make references to concepts and technologies initially introduced in that chapter.

A general problem with wireless communication is that the data can simply be plucked right out of the air! Because the medium of communication is space itself, the data being communicated is more accessible. With wired communications, there is a communication conduit that must be tapped (twisted-pair wires, coaxial cable, fiber optics, etc.). This is not the case in wireless communication. There are no conduits nor physical barriers: The bits and bytes are everywhere out in space to be picked up by all listeners, legitimate or otherwise.

In Chapter 10, we looked at various wireless technologies that are most relevant to mobile computing. Particularly of interest are Bluetooth and WIFI in the short-range family and CDMA-based and GSM/3GPP/TDMA technologies in the long-range family. We will look at the various security aspects of these technologies individually in this section.

Generally speaking, we are not only concerned with securely establishing communication channels and securing the transmission over the channel, but there is a concern typically foreign to stationary devices and networks: fraudulent usage of bandwidth. Because of the physical barrier that exists with the wired infrastructure in wired communications, stealing network bandwidth typically costs more than it is worth. This is not so in the case of wireless communications because there are no physical barriers.

There are numerous problems at the bottom layers of the OSI model that hardware manufacturers must deal with. For example, maintaining the ability to decrypt data packets in the presence of packet loss is very difficult [Aziz and Diffie 1993]. This is especially true when we also do not want the dropped packets themselves to become a tool for a security breach. Fortunately, most if not all of these problems are the concerns of hardware manufacturers and typically do not even concern those writing operating systems for mobile devices.

14.2.1 Bluetooth Security

One of the short-range wireless networking technologies that we discussed in Chapter 10 was Bluetooth. Every Bluetooth device in a Piconet generates a secret key when the user enters a personal identification number (PIN). Devices authenticate each other in multiple steps as follows:

1. The claimant (the device trying to be authenticated) sends a message based on a 48-bit address to the verifier (the device challenging the authentication).
2. The verifier sends back a 128-bit random number as a challenge.
3. The claimant then creates a signed response based on using a Secure Hash Function (specifically SRES). This function is, in turn, based on the secret key

of the device, the random number sent during the challenge, and the 48-bit address and sends the message back to the verifier.

4. The verifier generates its own SRES and compares the SRES received from the claimant to the one that it generated.
5. The claimant also creates its own 96-bit cipher to encrypt the messages once authenticated.

A Bluetooth deployment can operate in three different security modes. First, we can have no security, which means any Bluetooth-enabled device can join the network without requiring authentication. Second, we can enable service-level security, which basically means turning on security at the data link layer and monitoring access to various services. In this method, we have authenticated and authorized nodes accessing services in each other and the communication between them is confidential. Finally, in the third method, link-layer security is enforced by having each node authenticate the other node that it connects to (two-way authentication) and then encrypt all of the messages back and forth based on a key that only the two nodes involved in the communication share. The general problem with ad hoc PANs such as Bluetooth is that once the security of one node is compromised, it spreads throughout the system; it is tough to track down where the breach started.

The basic assumption of Bluetooth and similar PANs is that the user is in control of the network and participates in the process of distributing the secrets that are to be shared among the nodes [Candolin 2000]. This should be somewhat obvious based on the definition of PANs, but it tends to get lost in the fact that Bluetooth is being used to form larger networks that are more like LANs. Bluetooth provided adequate security for what it is meant to do: replace wires!

14.2.2 802.11 Security

The other set of short-range wireless technologies that we discussed were 802.11-based technologies. The first version of the security mechanism in 802.11 is called Wired Equivalent Protocol (WEP). 802.11 requires the maintenance of an ACL of MAC addresses. The access point is always considered to be secure and maintains this list of MAC addresses. So, the end points have to authenticate with the access point. This is done by a 40-bit shared-key RC4 (Rivest Cipher four, designed by Ron Rivest of RSA) for exchanging the data and an encryption challenge issued by the access point followed by response encrypted by the end station. There is also the temporal key integrity protocol (TKIP), which is a patch for 802.11 implementations designed to correct vulnerabilities in the wired equivalent privacy protocol, particularly the reuse of encryption keys [Varshney 2003]. TKIP is also to be addressed under the yet to be released (at the time of authoring this text) 802.11i standard.

This security scheme has been highly scrutinized because the birth of 802.11. In fact, security varies in the different flavors of 802.11. The criticisms of 802.11, particularly 802.11b, have been that eavesdropping is possible (though not easy) and that the dropped packets are not properly encrypted. Typical security threats to 802.11 come at the physical layer. Active attacks include simple transmission at the 2.4-GHz frequency range that can cause denial of service as well as a host of other problems. Passive attacks can include masquerading a malignant client as a valid participant in the network and causing problems by flooding the access point with bad transmission or using other techniques. Another type of attack may include sniffing packets in the air, modifying them, and retransmitting them either to reveal information that will open other security holes or to send bad data so that the messages are altered even though parties remain authenticated and authorized. Finally, RC4 key generation implementations in the first versions of 802.11 devices were "weak" and left a security hole by producing keys that could be discovered in a matter of hours.

When an 802.11 network is deployed, we can set it to authenticate the users that try to join with a one-stage challenge–response called Open System Authentication or with a two-stage challenge–response called Shared-Key Authentication. The Open System Authentication model is the default setting on most 802.11 equipment (routers, etc.) and basically allows anyone to join the network. This is actually one of the most significant ways in which an 802.11 network is exposed! Many home users and even some commercial users of 802.11 equipment buy the equipment and install it without understanding the security implementations.

We can also set the 802.11 equipment to operate in a Shared-Key Authentication mode, which basically means enabling encryption of transmissions between the joining node and the network. Joining the network is only possible if the node trying to join has knowledge of the "secret key" (a password) based on which cryptographic keys are generated. Some of the common complaints about this have been the following:

1. RC4 key scheduling is weak. It is not impossible to break RC4 keys.
2. The client does not authenticate the access point. This is a big problem! This means that a malicious party masquerading as the access point has a good chance of hijacking unsuspecting nodes.
3. The user does not participate in the authentication process. Many have suggested that every session should have its own "secret key" to enable user participation.
4. Denial of Service attacks are fairly easy to stage as you can keep the access point busy by continually trying to authenticate with it.
5. There is nothing currently built into the 802.11 standard that addresses anomalies or intrusions. For instance, data can be extracted out of the air and analyzed so that the encryption keys may be discovered. It is hard to tell if a full-proof technology for intrusion and anomaly detection will exist for wireless transmissions but being aware of this vulnerability is important. A suggested solution here is to have an external system monitor the over-the-air transmissions external from the 802.11 network itself to assure that there are no malicious parties.
6. Because 802.11 deploys one-way authentication, it is vulnerable to man-in-the-middle attacks.

One of the common mistakes in deploying 802.11x-based networks, or any other type of short-range wireless network in the same frequency range, is relying on the coverage range as a security mechanism. The "Pringles can" trick (where the aluminum-coated cylindrical can of Pringles potato chips is used to form an antenna) or other types of antennas can catch signals considerably beyond the maximum range specified.

Another big way that network security may become compromised in 802.11x networks is with the theft or loss of the device. Because each device that connects to a WAP-enabled 802.11 network has a key, security is compromised by loss or theft of the device. As with any other point of breach, this can cause further security breaches in the system.

Of course, one suggested solution to all of these problems has been to strengthen the application-layer security (firewalls, antivirus software, etc.). Nonetheless, 802.11 technologies have some significant security holes. Perhaps the single best solution to making 802.11 networks secure is to use all of the measures that are available to us at the same time: LEAP, TKIP, TLS/SSL, and whatever else may be offered by the vendors. Most of the time, even in wired systems, either we cannot make a system 100% full-proof secure or the cost of doing so is much higher than the cost of data loss and security breach. In the end, success derives from the value delivered to the customers. So, the best solution is to make it as difficult as possible for malicious parties to breach the security of the system. Of course, an inefficient alternative to all of this is to use a VPN that encrypts all transmissions. This is a bit redundant and inefficient because of multiple encryptions performed by different layers of hardware and software.

14.2.3 Security in Long-Range Wireless Networking Technologies

We discussed long-range wireless network technologies and standards such as CDMA, TDMA, GSM, and 3GPP in considerable detail previously in this text. As previously discussed, we are most interested in various cellular-based long-range technologies. Each one of the technologies and standards that we discussed in Chapter 10 addresses security concerns in its own way. Some standards build on other standards while adding their own security mechanisms on top of the security mechanism offered by the underlying technologies. Of particular interest in the real world are two categories of cellular technologies: those tied to the CDMA family of technologies and those tied to the GSM family of technologies (remember that most GSM deployments are currently on TDMA-based networks).

One of the first and most prevalent security problem with 1G and 2G networks has been the fraudulent usage of the network, also known as "bandwidth theft." These thefts include simple techniques such as stealing identification codes of vulnerable devices and masquerading as those devices and more sophisticated attacks such as redirection attacks, in which a device is redirected to contact a false base station, thereby giving it the authentications signals it needs to contact a valid base station, authenticate, and authorize. Subsequently, the false base station uses the authenticated session for fraudulent network usage or may cause other security breaches such as stealing and modifying the communications emanating from or going to the wireless node. To prevent fraudulent use of wireless service, the GSM network authenticates the identity of a user through a challenge–response mechanism, in which the user proves its identity by providing a response to a time-variant challenge raised by the network [Zhang 2002]. Keep in mind that 3GPP addresses both CDMA- and TDMA-based networks. 3GPP expands on the 3G security by adding features to prevent false base stations from hijack devices, increasing the length of the encryption keys for stronger security, adding inter-network security for secure communication among different networks, and moving security from the base station (where servers are a bit more susceptible to attacks) to switches [3GPP 2000].

Most 3G cellular telephony networks have some sort of Anomaly Detection System (ADS) or an Intrusion Detection System (IDS). As networks evolve, those who have deployed IDSs are moving toward ADSs. This is because although an IDS can detect only intrusions, an ADS can also detect other types of anomalies that could possible be security breaches. In a way, we can think of ADS as a superset of IDS in functionality. ADSs have a couple of major advantages compared to other intrusion detection approaches [Buschkes et al.]:

1. They do not require any prior knowledge of the target system.
2. They provide a way to detect unknown attacks.

The downside is that there is much more data to analyze in an ADS, so there is a scalability problem. Also, because the definition of an "anomaly" is difficult to define based on the distributed nature of cellular networks and the mobile devices connected to them, the privacy of a user's data may be compromised in search for a security breach.

For long-range wireless connectivity, most of the time the mobile developer is building on top of a higher level protocol such as TCP/IP or even WAP and HTTP. For example, WAP security includes an implementation of TLS/SSL. WAP provides a handshake process that uses UDP datagrams. After that, it uses TLS on top of whatever the WDP implementation may be (again, typically UDP or TCP). WTLS certificates are smaller in size; the WAP gateway does the job of being the intermediary between WTLS and HTTPS implementations on the Internet. As devices are becoming more powerful and WAP is evolving, there is a move toward implementing TLS/SSL throughout all layers.

Like WAP, BREW offers its own security mechanism. As we saw previously, BREW provides a TCP/IP connection mechanism. Because BREW communication is built for CDMA networks with little backward compatibility to1G and 2G networks, and because SSL implementation for HTTP is made available for the BREW platform, BREW provides a security mechanism very similar to that provided on the wired Web. Also, as CDMA is inherently based on code-division multiplexing, there is a certain amount of low-layer fundamental security within it.

Long-range wireless systems (cellular systems being the most prevalent) are much more mature and secure than their short-range partners principally because they have had more time to evolve and there is a great amount of financial motivation on the part of the carriers to make them secure to avoid revenue loss. If you are building a mobile application based on GSM, GPRS, CDMA, or any of the other 3G and 4G technologies that we discussed earlier, you are probably envious of the amount of bandwidth available for developing for wireless LANs and PANs.

However, you do have one advantage: Your security concerns are diminutive compared to those of WLANs. The flip side of the coin is that carriers have a tendency to take away features (often for financial reasons) and use security as an excuse. For example, security might be used as an excuse to stop users from pointing to a preferred WAP gateway.

14.3 Security and Ad Hoc Networking Technologies

Unlike stationary computing systems where a device is bound to be connected to the same network for an elongated period of time, mobile devices come in and out of networks frequently. This has been part of the rise in ad hoc networking technologies implemented at different layers of the OSI model that we looked at previously. MANETs (mobile ad hoc networks) introduce an entirely new set of concerns in security. Let us see how some of the previously discussed concerns change when dealing with MANETs:

1. Because most MANETs allow more information exchange with an unknown network (e.g., unknown IP address) and because the communicating nodes of a network are constantly changing, *masquerading* is a larger threat in MANETs than other comparable environments. Extra caution must be taken in authentication of a participating node before any data are exchanged.
2. *Eavesdropping* is always a threat and even more so in wireless environments, but this probably increases even more with ad hoc networks because every participating node is always revealing just a little more information than it would if it were not a participant in an ad hoc network.
3. Depending on the type of MANET, *DOS attacks* may become very easy. The most rudimentary attack may be simply disguising as a different node every single time and going through the discovery process. Though without the proper credentials no access is granted, the system may be flooded with network traffic and one or more nodes may be stressed while participating in the discovery process an endless number of times.
4. The possibility of attacks from previously authenticated nodes is substantially increased in MANETs. Although prior, during, and shortly after authentication, a node may not be acting malicious or become infected with a malicious program such as a worm or virus, it may become malicious or become infected after it has been authenticated because it may be participating in other MANETs.

Ad hoc and peer-to-peer systems have an entire slew of security concerns of their own that lie outside the scope of this text. Keep in mind that all of these problems are typically at the application layer unless the peering or ad hoc connectivity features are being provided by the wireless networking infrastructure. If so, you need to make sure that you understand the features of the underlying infrastructure and the settings that will allow your particular application to operate securely within the boundary of the threat-level assessment and return on security investment.

14.4 Location Information, Security, and Privacy

One of the biggest hurdles in making location information available to mobile applications has been security and privacy concerns. In a world where users find more and more information collected about them every day, it is very important to make sure that they retain the right to block the mobile application from discovering their location. Furthermore, we must ensure that whatever location information is exchanged remains completely safe within the system. From this perspective, the availability of location information opens a whole new can of worms when it comes to security. At the same time, location information can be used to strengthen whatever security mechanism is in place.

Specifically, we can use location information to keep malicious parties from spoofing and making DOS attacks. If a given device is introducing itself with one identity and the location information about the device indicates some conflict with this identity, we know that there is a significant possibility that this device poses a security threat to our system. Also, if one node tries to initiate DOS attacks on a MANET or similar type of a network where the discovery mechanism of the network can be used to attack it, location information may be used to "block out" nodes that may be exhibiting such behavior because identifying them any other way may not be possible (for if they are masquerading, then we cannot use their identity to block them out).

We strongly recommend that all information regarding location information, whether relative or absolute, be encrypted when transmitting at the application layer. In addition, it is also recommended that all networked mobile applications use SSL or a similar technology for transmitting the location information at the presentation and session layers. Although this may seem overkill, we simply recommend it to keep the data secure if the system is compromised either at the application layer or at the presentation and session layers.

We know by now that most of our concerns lie within the application layer where we have the most amount of control So, how is security different here for location-based services and applications that use those services? Leonhardt and Magee [Leonhardt and Magee 1997] recognize two different methods of solving the problem within distributed applications: label-based and matrix-based protection. The label-based model, also referred to as the Mandatory Access Control, specifies a read and write level for a resource that a user is trying to access. The matrix-based access control list basically extends the traditional one-dimensional ACL security model where each security right is mapped to a specific location, be it relative or absolute, depending on the implementation of the application. Matrix-based access control offers a flexibility and expressiveness far superior to label-based access control [Leonhardt and Magee 1997].

14.5 Security: The Unsolved Problem for Mobile Agents

In Chapter 9, we talked about mobile agents in detail. We also mentioned that the central reason that is keeping mobile agents from being more widely deployed is security. The various security problems with mobile agents stems from the fact that they are autonomous; this autonomy makes it difficult if not impossible to identify mobile agents with complete certainty (an authentication problem) and keep them from doing something they should not be doing (an authorization problem). The security threats of mobile agents can be classified into four broad categories: agent to agent, agent to platform, platform to agent, and other to agent [Jansen et al. 1999].

At the same time, because of their autonomy, mobile agents can come in handy in building security software such as an antivirus and intrusion detection software. Jansen and colleagues, for example, show how to build an intrusion detection system. In fact, in the mobile environment where there is a proliferation of devices, mobile agents can present an ideal way of detecting intrusion as they provide a scalable solution to a distributed security problem (both because they can run on multiple platforms where the mobile agent host is available and because the workload is distributed among many nodes at run time). In fact, Jensen and colleagues specifically recognized several technologies of interest to us as areas where either we need to consider the security aspects of mobile agents or mobile agents may be a suitable solution for our system:

- wearable computing, in which the mobile computing device may be worn,
- pico-cellular wireless systems, in which the network is made of many very small cells,
- ad hoc networks, in which autonomous systems are used for networks in an ad hoc manner (as previously discussed),
- and other mobile devices in general where mobile agents may make sense.

Also, active networks are another novel approach to network architecture. In such networks the switches of the network perform customized computations on the messages flowing through them; active networks make use of intelligent packets that are no longer just data bits but contain mobile code that allows for the active participation in routing, fault-tolerance, and QOS decisions [Jansen et al. 1999]. Hence, mobile agents can be a suitable solution for addressing the various security concerns within active networks.

14.6 Distinguishing Privacy and Security

The mobile application developer faces two distinct challenges: delivering a secure application and delivering a private application. Privacy means very different things in different countries and is subject to country-specific sets of laws. For our purposes, we define security within the confines of laws and regulations in United States, Australia, and Europe, which tend to be somewhat similar compared to the rest of the world. Candolin defines privacy within the realm of wirelessly connected systems to be of four components [Candolin 2002]:

1. *Data Privacy*: The contents of the transaction should be protected from disclosure to an unauthorized party.

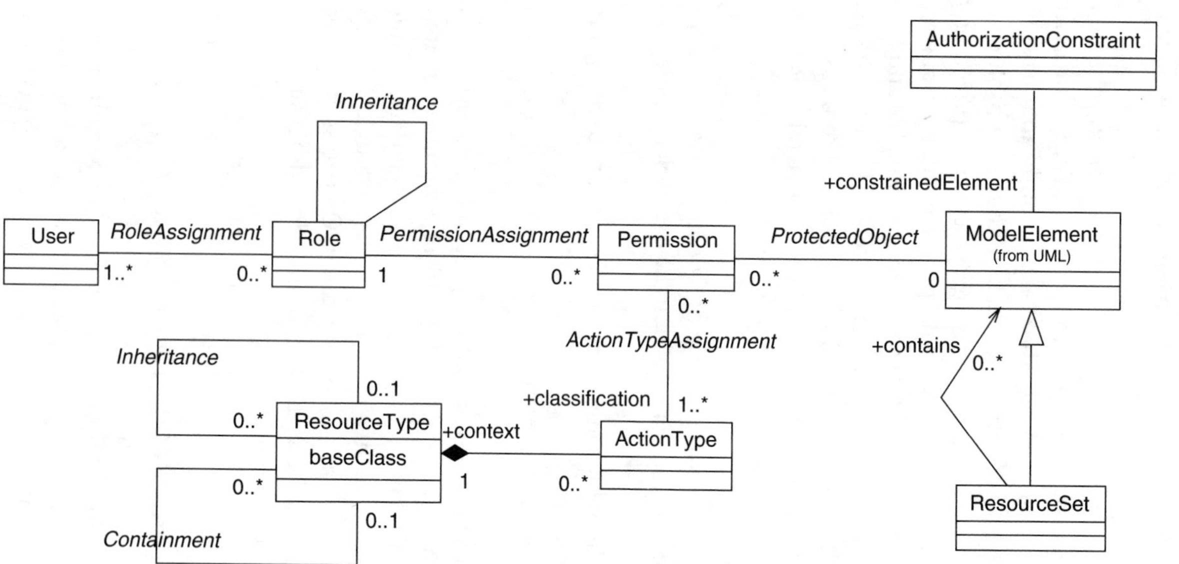

FIGURE 14.1. SecureUML Metamodel [Lodderstedt et al. 2002].

2. *Source and Destination Privacy*: The parties involved in the transaction should not be revealed to an unauthorized party.
3. *Location Privacy*: The location of the parties making the transaction, whether physical (geographical) or logical (with respect to the network), should not be disclosed to an unauthorized party.
4. *Time Privacy*: The exact time when a transaction occurs should not be disclosed to an unauthorized party.

The definition by Candolin is meant to address wirelessly connected mobile applications, but it is indeed sufficient for all mobile applications as the wirelessly connected mobile applications face a superset of challenges of wired mobile applications to provide proper security and privacy.

Obviously, the first step in providing privacy is achieving security. So, in a way, although security and privacy are two completely different things, security is a precondition to privacy.

14.7 Modeling Security with UML

As we mentioned previously, security is largely a design-time problem. So, in the manner that we have selected in this text, let us try to use UML to document this design-time concern and its effect on the implementation of the system.

We have already seen that UML component diagrams allow us to show high-level system diagrams, interaction diagrams provide a way for showing how various systems may interact securely, and class diagrams are ideal for the internal implementation of our application. We can still apply all of these diagrams to show the high-level design and behavior of secure applications. SecureUML, as proposed by Lodderstedt and colleagues, is a methodology, with UML extensions, to integrate information relevant to access control into application models defined with UML [Lodderstedt et al. 2002]. The SecureUML metamodel can be seen in Figure 14.1. The focus of SecureUML is to define a metamodel that can be used to define a framework within UML with which to model various security processes such as authentication and authorization.

As conceived by its authors, SecureUML is mainly used for stationary server-side applications. Nonetheless, there is nothing in the metamodel that would keep us from applying it to mobile applications. Along with the other extensions that we have introduced, particularly those that address location mobility, SecureUML allows us to create diagrams that represent the three basic principles of security: determining *who* has what *roles* and what roles and users in those roles should be able to access *which* resources.

SECTION 4

Putting the Project Together

CHAPTER 15

The Mobile Development Process

Yazdi Koja Tashreef Darad? (Where has the one from Yazd descended upon?)
M. Ali Karimzadeh (my grandfather)

15.1 INTRODUCTION

Thus far, in the first three sections of this text, we have focused on recognizing the new problems facing mobile application developers, tools to solve those problems, and how to use those tools to solve each specific problem.

Let us now look at the macro view of developing mobile applications. When we develop a stationary application, we gather requirements, lay out an architecture and design, select some tools to help us implement the application, develop the application, test, and deliver. Although this is a gross oversimplification of the application development process, it lays out the rough steps of developing stationary applications. There are development methodologies that go into each of these steps in a detailed manner and lay out a methodical approach to tackle them.

The question to ask now that we know how to deal with the detailed problems of mobile application development is whether these methodologies can be used as is or whether they must be modified to develop mobile applications.

15.2 BACK TO THE DIMENSIONS OF MOBILITY

If there is one thing you should know by now, it is that the dimensions of mobility are what make mobile applications different from their stationary counterparts.

The dimensions of mobility and the mobile condition of the user, cumulatively, are what make the process of developing mobile applications different from the process of developing stationary applications.

Today, there are plenty of software development methodologies that claim to solve everything but world hunger! And most software development processes claim that they can be applied in just about any environment and for developing any type of application. Obviously, this is a gross case of the "golden-hammer" syndrome we have so often talked about in this text. We will not outline another golden-hammer methodology in this text. Rather, we will outline one suggested method of how to build mobile applications based on the dimensions of mobility, the mobile condition of the user, and UML as a central tool for the development process. Keep in mind that our method is nothing more than a set of suggestions to point out a road map to building mobile applications. It is not exclusionary of your application of any other methodologies to your software development process as long as you are able to discern the important principles that we are trying to integrate into the development methodology.

We have used UML to facilitate development of pieces of the application throughout this text. There are a variety of methodologies that use UML as the centerpiece of development and build a methodology around it; these include the Rational Unified Process (RUP) and Model Driven Architecture (MDA). Let us start by looking at the Wisdom methodology, a development methodology centered not only on UML but also in the user interface, suggested by Nunes [Nunes 2001], whose worked we looked at in Chapter 6.

15.3 Applying the Wisdom Methodology to Mobile Development

As you may recall, we used Nunes' work [Nunes 2001] to establish a foundation for one of our suggested methods of using UML diagrams to represent user interfaces. Nunes also outlines a development process to better accommodate the development of user interfaces. This is not exactly what we need, but it gives us a piece of the puzzle to come up with an approximate model for the process of developing mobile applications because some of the biggest problems of mobile computing concern the user interface.

What is it that makes Wisdom a good pointing start? First, it uses UML. Second, it focuses on better integration of developing user interfaces into the development process. This is essential for mobile application development because although we used activity diagrams to model fairly detailed views of the users' interactions with the user interface, the Wisdom methodology suggests that we accompany use cases with UML activity diagrams as well. These sets of diagrams focus on the large-grained processes involving the user interfaces. Nunes defines these large-grained processes as *Wisdom essential task flows represented by Wisdom essential use cases*. Nunes states "The critical difference between the Wisdom use case modeling approach and the conventional use case approach is related to the fact that top level tasks, required by the users to accomplish actual work, drive development not the inherent internal functionality" [Nunes 2001]. The premise is that use case diagrams are far too high level to convey enough information to gather the requirements and convey them to the user interface developers in a meaningful way. More importantly, typical use case diagrams are not user interface–centric. What Nunes' extensions offer us are additional diagrams that allow us to represent the use cases from the perspective of the user interface interactions and components. This is particularly helpful because of the *n*th degree of complexity with which the typical complexity of an application is multiplied for supporting *n* different user interfaces. This is not to say that we do not need use case diagrams but rather that they must be augmented by activity diagrams that describe the user interface interactions provided by the user interface of each use case. So, to establish a UML-based methodology for developing mobile applications, we will take the lessons from typical UML-based development methodologies, add in the Wisdom extensions, and introduce some new ideas to cover the remaining issues to treat the dimensions of mobility and the mobile condition of the user.

15.4 UML-Based Development Cycle for Mobile Applications

Taking all of what we have learned throughout this text on solving the individual problems involved with developing mobile applications, we need a straightforward, lightweight, and UML-based outline of the development process. In this text, we are not intending to create development processes like the Rational Unified Process. We are simply going to outline some of the steps that must be part of any development process that intends to address the problem of developing mobile applications.

Along the way, our goal will be to fill any holes that are introduced by the fact that existing methodologies such as RUP and others fail to address the dimensions of mobility.

We will start at the beginning with UML use cases. Use cases are a tool that can be used by not just engineers (actually, preferably not engineers because most engineers do not do a very good job of understanding the users' requirements), but also business analysts, project managers, and others involved in interfacing with the customer and delivering the desired application.

At present, and for the next several years, the biggest difference in dealing with customers of mobile applications as opposed to their stationary counterparts will be their ignorance of what mobile applications are and how they can get the most value out of a mobile application. Because of this, the major component we will need to integrate into the development process involves educating the customer and the users of the system of what they can do, what they cannot do, and the ramifications of the decisions they make. Let us see how we adapt the requirements-gathering process to mobile application development.

15.4.1 Mobile Use Cases

Mobile applications are a superset of their stationary counterparts. So, by nature, the first step of creating mobile use cases is to gather whatever use cases may be required by the customer and then introduce additional use cases as necessary. If you are building a mobile application, the chances are that the customer already expects you to provide a PC-based interface, such as a Web-based interface, to the system. Let us take a sample application that delivers driving directions to the users. The use cases could be those defined as follows:

Use Case 1: User uses home as the source address, enters a destination, and requests directions.
Use Case 2: User enters source address, destination address, and requests directions.
Use Case 3: User enters source address, destination address, and requests a map.
Use Case 4: User requests the "time-in-transport" (the time it takes to go from the source to the destination or from the current location to the destination if already in transport).
Use Case 5: User asks the system for some means of transportation between the source and the destination.

At this point, we still do not really know anything about the mobile users of the system or care about the ramifications of the application being usable by mobile users.

Now, let us assume that the customer (user) is asking for the ability to be able to have the directions heard while driving. However, the customer may have ignored all the other values that a mobile directions application can offer. Let us see what else we may be able to offer the user:

1. We may be able to sense the location of the user, or at least the user's approximate location, thereby avoiding the data entry for the user's current address.
2. We can have the user put in the starting and ending addresses prior to the beginning of the drive on his or her PC and send the directions to his or her phone.
3. The directions can be sent to the user at a specified time, when the user is at a specified location, based on some other rules set by the user's personal preferences, or by the explicit request of the user (such as dialing up to receive the directions).
4. The user may want to receive the directions through the voice channel and the address via text.
5. When the quality of the user's connection (QOS) is too low or erratic, the directions should be sent to the user as a text message in one complete message instead of multiple messages.

We will assume that the infrastructure for the mobile application provides us with all reasonable functionality (such as providing the location information, QOS information, etc.). Although at the time of authoring this text, this is not necessarily true, wireless infrastructure and devices are evolving rapidly and will likely be offering such functionality by the time you read this.

The key is to inform your customers of all those things that they may be able to do, and conversely, what they may not be able to do. Among the things we want the customer to ponder are the following:

1. Does the customer understand the value of VUIs? Do they know that voice transcription is not yet a reality with existing technologies? Under what conditions (e.g., a noisy room) will the VUI be used?
2. Has the customer considered all of the scenarios under which the system may be used by a mobile user (connected, disconnected, connected but running out of battery, etc.)?
3. What are the exact target devices? Which channels fit which devices?
4. Are all devices equally as likely to be used? Do different classifications of users use different families of devices? Under what conditions may each device or device family be used?
5. Are there any scenarios for notifications and active transactions that the customer has not considered?

We also need to consider factors such as the available budget and requirements for scalability, reliability, and fault tolerance of the system. These factors must be addressed whether the application is a mobile or stationary one. Once again, remember that the concerns of a mobile application are a superset of the concerns of a stationary application.

Considering all of what we have mentioned, we should now revisit the use cases with the customer and come up with whatever additional use cases may be required. It may be that the customer had a full understanding of mobile applications and had a very specific task in mind for the application. Or, perhaps the user interfaces devised as a result of the aforementioned points lead to additional use cases or modification of some of the existing use cases. Once we have reviewed all of the possible functionality available (within reasonable limits on budget, time, etc.) for the mobile application, and come up with a revised use cases based on these reviews, we are left with what we will call the *mobile use cases*. Obviously, we can model and document these mobile use cases with the techniques previously outlined in this text. Once again, these use cases should be a superset of the stationary use cases, though the user may decide to eliminate some of the typical use cases after considering the mobile condition of the user, the dimensions of mobility, and the additional functionality available given the infrastructure and devices used for mobile applications.

Now we have a set of use cases that must be implemented by a development team with members who have a variety of skills. Also, as in just about every development methodology today interim deliverables and milestones are a must, we must also prioritize which use cases should be delivered first so that we may iterate to a final application with customer input in the process.

The *mobile use case evaluation matrix*, shown in Table 15.1, provides us with a tool to manage some of these issues. On the left side of the matrix, we have specified the various functional pieces that give mobile applications added value:

1. Mobile applications can be used by mobile users (who may be connected to the network through a wireless connection).

TABLE 15.1. Mobile Use Case Evaluation Matrix

Relevance Index Table	Use Case 1	Use Case 2	Use Case 3	Use Case 4	Use Case *N*
Aural User Interface					
Location-Based Functionality					
Active Functionality					
Wireless Access					
Multichannel Access					
Disconnected Usage					

2. Mobile applications may need to use a variety of user interfaces depending on what devices are available and what interfaces are convenient (VUIs and multichannel user interfaces).
3. Knowing the location of the user may be of value (location sensitivity).
4. It is important to deliver information and functionality to the user actively without the user's invocation of the application (active transactions).

The six items that make up the rows of the matrix provide a taxonomy of functionality, mobile condition of the user, and dimensions of mobility of the application to help us categorize and prioritize our use cases. The columns headings are the mobile use cases that we have gathered. The empty squares in the matrix are to be filled with a number between 0 and 1 (or alternatively 0% to 100%) called mobile evaluation indices. We can have multiple instances of this matrix, each helping us with a different set of problems as follows:

1. *User Usage Evaluation Matrix*: Because of the large variety of functionality that a mobile application may deliver to the end users, we need to understand how important each use case is to the users. We can recognize *user usage* as a metric that is simply determined by polling a sample of the users (or asking the customer for this information) on the predicted usage of each use case. What every polled user needs to provide us with is whether or not they will use the use case and how often they will use it if at all. The number indicates the fraction of the users using the functionality of the use case (functionality is specified by the row and use case is specified by the column). It is critical that we do not mix the different groups of users who may be using different use cases altogether. Let us take for example a field automation application in which the mobile application facilitates the work of delivery personnel in the

field as well as the sales force. In this case, the project may consist of two sets of use cases, use cases that provide functionality for the sales personnel and another set that provides functionality for the delivery personnel.

Polling the delivery personnel on whether they use a use case involving the sales force is probably going to lead to an index of 0 or close to 0. Each instance of the user usage mobile use case evaluation matrix should have use cases that are used by the same group of user to yield meaningful data. Table 15.2 shows an example of the user usage mobile use case matrix for our driving-directions example. The user (corresponding to the Wisdom human actor) is the end user. Alternative users may be the operator contacted by the user (if the user becomes frustrated with the system) or a specialization of the end user such as "the lost end user" or "the geographically challenged end user."

Let us go through what the matrix in Table 15.2 reflects. Of the ten surveyed users,

six would sometimes or always use a VUI to get directions;
six would sometimes or always use a VUI to make an association between a contact person in their PIM and the driving directions;
zero would want to retrieve map-related information by aural description of area from the system;
five would sometimes or always use a VUI to retrieve the time-in-transport;
eight would sometimes or always use a VUI to find transport (such as a taxi, bus route and times, etc.) to go from the source to the destination;
seven would sometimes or always depend on the location-sensitivity system built into their devices for discovery of their current location compared to manually specifying it;
all would depend on the system to make an association between the destination, once they have reached it, and a contact person in their PIM;
three would sometimes or always want the system to retrieve the map for their current location discovered automatically by the system;
five would sometimes or always want updates on the time of arrival based on the current location;
three would sometimes or always would want to find the most convenient transport method based on their current location (e.g., which is closer, the bus station or the subway station?);
ten would sometimes or always retrieve their directions by using a wireless device;
four would use a wireless device to make associations between the directions and a contact person in their PIM;
six would sometimes or always use a wireless device to find out their time of arrival;
eight would use a wireless device to find transportation to go from the source to the destination;
four would ask for the directions through one channel (voice or text) and receive it through another channel (voice, text, or animated video directions);
seven would find the directions through an aural interface but make the association between the directions and the contact person through the text user interface;

TABLE 15.2. End-User Mobile Evaluation Use Case Matrix

Relevance Index Table	Retrieving Directions from Home to Address	Associating Directions with Contact Person	Retrieve Map of Area	Get Time-In-Transport from Source to Destination	Find Transport from Source to Destination
Aural User Interface	0.6	0.6	0	0.5	0.8
Location Based Functionality	0.7	1.0	0.3	0.5	0.9
Active Functionality	0.8	0.8	0.3	0.1	0.3
Wireless Access	1.0	1.0	0.4	0.6	0.8
Multichannel Access	0.4	0.4	0.7	0.4	0.3
Disconnected Usage	1.0	1.0	1.0	0.1	0.1

three would find directions through one channel (voice or text) and ask for transport through another channel (voice or text);
all would, sometimes or always, want the directions stored in their device in case they are disconnected;
all would, sometimes or always, want to store the map in their devices for disconnected access;
one would, sometimes or always, want to retrieve a time-in-transport table into his or her device to access it in case he or she is disconnected;
one would, sometimes or always, want to put in a request for finding transport while disconnected and be notified of the information whenever the device is able to connect to the network.

Note that an argument could be made that each one of the cells in the matrix represents a different use case. Our choice to represent the use cases in this manner comes from the fact that we have recognized mobile applications as a superset of stationary applications and that our end goal is to recognize the effects of the dimensions of mobility and the differences between the stationary and mobile version of an application.

2. *Infrastructure Integration*: One of the most complex tasks in developing mobile applications is to integrate the different infrastructure technologies such as the wireless communications platform, the mobile devices, the voice recognition platform, the speech synthesis platform, and others into the core application. Consequently, we need to prioritize the treatment of every infrastructure. In our case, being customer driven as we are, we accomplish this task by instances of the mobile use case evaluation matrix for each infrastructure piece. In this case, our indices are specified somewhat subjectively because there is no way to know the exact relevance of a use case to the infrastructure until what sits in the middle—namely the application we are trying to build—is actually built. So, these indices are largely "guesstimates." Nevertheless, these guesstimates can show the predicted amount of integration with different infrastructure pieces. Let us take the same set of use cases as the last example and create an infrastructure mobile evaluation use case matrix for integration with a location sensitivity infrastructure in Table 15.3.

For this example, we will assume that location information is provided through GPS. Note that infrastructure components are often orthogonal to some dimensions of mobility or the functionality to satisfy solving the problems associated with those dimensions of mobility. Table 15.3 was based on the following observations on the boundary points of the location system (GPS in this case) with the use case and the mobile functionality:

1. The VUIs for retrieving directions do not interface with the GPS system.
2. The VUI for describing the map to the user may interact, in the background, with the GPS system. Because a map is not something that can be rendered through a VUI, the VUI may use the user's current location and location history

Table 15.3. Location Sensitivity Infrastructure Mobile Evaluation Use Case Matrix

Relevance Index Table	Retrieving Directions from Home to Address	Associating Directions with Contact Person	Retrieve Map of Area	Get Time-In-Transport from Source to Destination	Find Transport from Source to Destination
Aural User Interface	0	0	1.0	1.0	0
Location-Based Functionality	1.0	1.0	1.0	1.0	1.0
Active Functionality	1.0	1.0	1.0	1.0	1.0
Wireless Access	1.0	1.0	1.0	1.0	1.0
Multichannel Access	0	0	1.0	1.0	1.0
Disconnected Usage	0	0	1.0	1.0	0

to iteratively go back to the GPS system and the other subsystems that can provide a textual description of the surroundings of the user, the destination, and the source. This information can then be used to describe the equivalent of a map to the user.

3. Time-to-transport of the user describes how long the user will be in transport to his or her destination. This information will depend on the current location of the user.
4. All location-based services use the location information directly so there is obvious dependence there.
5. The system can be personalized to send out the directions actively when the user is in a particular location, so the active transactions involving directions can be dependent upon the location information provided by the GPS.
6. The map, or the aural equivalent of the map, may be sent to the user based on the user's current location.
7. The user may require that the remaining transport time be sent to him or her actively (e.g., messages sent at some particular interval) based on the location information.
8. Wireless access to the system may be changed depending on the network. Though this technology is not provided in most devices today, we are assuming that our use cases dictate the device switching between networks depending on the location (which may have some benefits on the billing side). This may be made possible with devices that can have multiple SIM cards.
9. When the user is disconnected from the network, he or she cannot request directions or try to find transportation information (assuming that this information is far too large for the device to store and must be retrieved from the network). Therefore, there is no dependency between these use cases and location information.
10. Providing a local map based on current location may still be available based solely on location information because a limited number of maps can be stored on the device. Also, time-to-arrival can be computed on the device while disconnected based on the current location and a destination that may have been cached.

Keep in mind that this is only an example. Use of information location to switch between wireless networks, for example, is an esoteric requirement that is not achievable by most of the devices in the marketplace today. Also note that this matrix does not dictate or describe design or implementation. It simply shows the amount of direct or indirect interactions between the subsystem and the cross-section of the use case and mobile functionality. Use of various UML diagrams, including those recommended by Nunes in his Wisdom extensions, may be a good idea for a graphical representation. Our goal here is to simply use numbers to quantify the relationship between the requirements and various aspects of the design and implementation of the mobile application.

In this example, we did not delve far enough into the requirements and the high-level design of the system to see the amount of integration between the cross-section of each use case and mobile functionality with the external subsystem (location information based on GPS). Therefore, our indices are binary. A more accurate representation could be obtained (on an analog scale from 0 to 1) if the relative weights of the integration at the boundary points were used. Once again, this would be a guesstimate and the only reason to use these guesstimates would be to first quantify the integration points with the infrastructure and to thenprioritize design and implementation tasks.

3. *Application Distribution:* As we have seen throughout this text, mobile applications can be implemented in a variety of ways using a variety of architectures ranging from fully centralized to fully distributed. The architecture, design, and implementation of any computing system must be driven by the user requirements; however, it is easy to select a design a system based on the initial set of requirements that does not lend itself to accommodating additional user requirements during the development process or post delivery of the project. To avoid this problem, we can use instances of the mobile use case matrix whose indices indicate the *estimated relative amount of computing tasks performed on a particular system*. For example, we may have an instance of the mobile use case matrix for WAP phones, called a *WAP client mobile use case matrix*, whose indices indicate the relevance of each mobile functionality category (such as aural user interface) of the use cases for WAP clients. Another example could be an instance of the mobile use case matrix for an application server that contains our server-side application, called an *application server use case matrix*. Table 15.4 shows the J2ME client mobile use case matrix. Let us go through how we have arrived at these indices:
   a. Currently, J2ME clients are too limited to make an attempt at implementing voice recognition or any other part of the VUI.
   b. It is possible that the device vendor provides a J2ME extension for accessing the location information provided by GPS. For our hypothetical application, the information about the current location of the user may be obtained by the J2ME client and sent to the server for retrieval of directions or other information. As the actual information about directions is retrieved by the server, we are estimating 50% of the task of finding directions to be on the server and the other 50% to be on the client. These are not necessarily representative of the "amount of code" or "number of lines." Rather, they are estimates of the portion of total tasks achieved by the client and the server.
   c. Our hypothetical J2ME client may be fully able to calculate the time-in-transport by using a small amount of cached information, GPS information, and some simple logic.
   d. Our hypothetical J2ME client may be able cache a short list of transportation modes based on the GPS location. If others are needed, it can get them off of the server.
   e. The current J2ME MIDP 2.0 profile only offers some minimal access to the device speaker and no access to the telephony channel on the device. Therefore, we are estimating that 50% or less of the functionality needed to deliver a multimodal and multichannel application can be put into the J2ME client.

Table 15.4. J2ME Client Mobile Use Case Evaluation Matrix

Relevance Index Table	Retrieving Directions from Home to Address	Associating Directions with Contact Person	Retrieve Map of Area	Get Time-In-Transport from Source to Destination	Find Transport from Source to Destination
Aural User Interface	0	0	0	0	0
Location-Based Functionality	0.5	0.5	0.5	1.0	0.8
Active Functionality	1.0	1.0	1.0	1.0	1.0
Wireless Access	0	0	0	0	0
Multichannel Access	0.5	0.5	0.5	0.5	0.5
Disconnected Usage	1.0	1.0	1.0	1.0	1.0

f. J2ME does not provide a wireless communication protocol. There is a generic connection framework that maps to the networking capabilities provided by the device maker and the carrier to which this API maps. Therefore, J2ME and wireless networking are orthogonal.

g. When disconnected from the network, the J2ME client can provide minimal functionality, cached information, or simply messages that let the user know the network is not available.

The information on any instances of the mobile use case matrices must be updated in an iterative manner throughout the development process because we are bound to discover more and more about the requirements of the system as we begin to design and implement the system.

Getting back to our examples, we may draw the following conclusions from our mobile use case matrices:

1. Our application requires more than just a thin client to satisfy the users. We need an application to run on the mobile device for those times when the user is not connected to the network.
2. If some or all of the devices that will be part of this system do not provide an API to the GPS system on the client, the server-side application will need to communicate with the GPS directly, through the wireless infrastructure, or through some other means. (Note that we are assuming that a GPS subsystem is available on all of the devices that are to be the end-user devices in this system.)
3. We will need to integrate the system with a messaging system (such as SMS, MMS, etc.) that allows for actively pushing messages to the client.

Obviously, we could make various other conclusions as well. For example, we could multiply the indices in the end-user mobile evaluation matrix with the corresponding matrices in the other two diagrams to determine the priority of tasks in delivering the location-sensitivity integration compared to integration with other subsystems or to determine the priority of tasks in delivering the J2ME client compared to the other clients or components in the system.

From these conclusions, you can see that the mobile use case matrices are not the end, but rather the means, to understand the customer requirements better.

15.4.2 Mobile Development Process

In the previous section, we looked at a simple matrix as a way to augment the process of gathering use cases. But what happens after we gather use cases? We could probably write another entire book on what follows the requirements-gathering process. However, that is not in the scope of our discussion. So, what we will do is take a step back and look at the big picture and see how it changes when dealing with mobile applications. Whatever the development methodology adapted by the readers' organization may be, it is adaptable by integrating some principles. We will point out the principles and leave the integration up to you.

Today, there are a variety of UML and non-UML-based development processes such as Ken Beckett's Extreme Programming or Rational Software's RUP. At a high

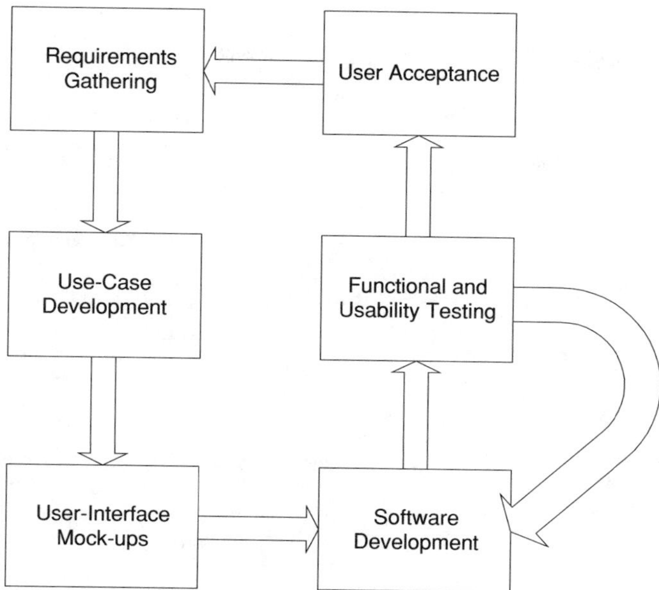

FIGURE 15.1. High-Level Software Development Cycle.

level, all development processes follow the same processes and flow shown in Figure 15.1.

Conversely, Figure 15.2 shows this high-level process as modified for mobile application development. The overall differences can be enumerated as follows:

1. There are proven methodologies for developing VUIs that are very different from GUI development methodologies. VUIs have much more stringent usability requirements as we discussed in Chapter 6. The development process is affected by this.
2. As we discussed in Chapters 5–7, building multichannel user interfaces requires additional layers of abstraction. The implementations of these additional abstraction layers requires modifications to our existing process.
3. We have bundled the integration of location-based infrastructure as well as wireless infrastructure into the development box. At this point, there have been no studies, research projects, or implementations that have been able to properly recognize the effects of location sensitivity and wireless connectivity on the application architecture at the application layer (discounting the well-known effects that wireless connectivity has at the layers that sit under the actual application we are authoring). As such abstractions become clear, they must be integrated properly into the development process as has been the case for the effects of VUIs and multichannel user interface development shown in Figure 15.2.

Throughout this text, we have solely focused on the steps that follow the development of mobile use cases and end at quality assurance. Most of what we have

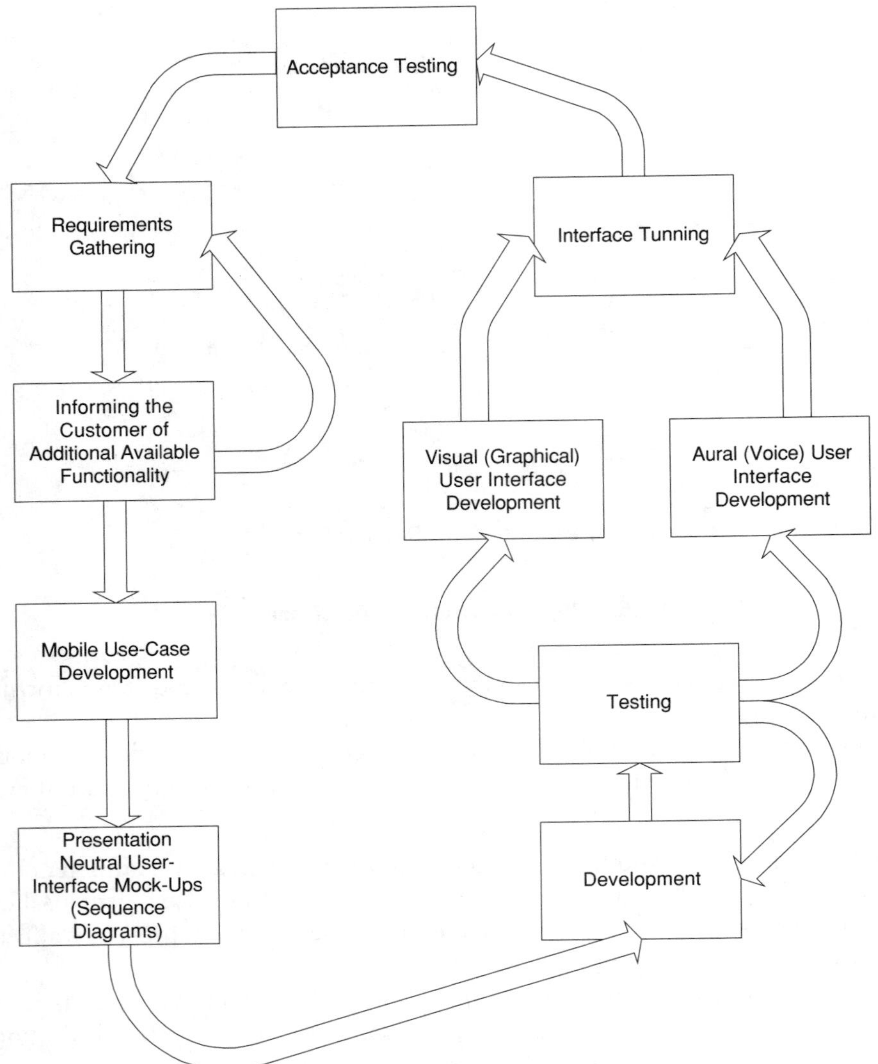

FIGURE 15.2. High-Level Software Development Cycle for Mobile Application Development.

talked about has focused on the box called Development in our diagram. Let us review the steps that follow the determination of mobile use cases:

1. Create the relevant and appropriate instances of mobile use case matrices by polling the users and/or estimating.
2. Create a series of UML diagrams that convey the external functionality of the user interface as well as the internal functionality of the system. The UML diagrams that focus on the user interface are abstracted so that we can build user interfaces in a layered manner, specializing generic user interfaces to specific user interfaces. The following iterative approach that separates the concerns of the system is recommended when developing the UML diagrams:

   a. First, develop your use case diagrams and the Wisdom extensions of the UML diagrams.
   b. Develop UML diagrams that represent the various aspects of the user interface by using the techniques we have introduced here. Divide the GUI and VUI diagrams into two different groups.
   c. Develop user interface diagrams that involve multichannel and multimodal access to the system.
   d. Develop use case diagrams that separate the mobile users from the stationary users and the mobile systems from the stationary systems.
   e. Develop UML diagrams that represent any mobile agents in the system.
   f. Develop UML diagrams that relate to the internal implementation of the system for the various components (clients, servers, peers, etc.).
3. Choose an architectural approach and lay out high-level designs of how the system should implement the expected functionality and meet the customer requirements.
4. Build the generic user interfaces based on the UML diagrams that convey the requirements as well as high-level architectural implementations.
5. Consider building user interface mockups. If support for a large number of user interfaces is required, break them down into families and use a set of mock-ups to represent the average look-and-feel or persona of a given family. If there are a large number of families to be supported, simply mock up enough to first get meaningful feedback from the customer and second communicate the user interface requirements properly to the development team.
6. Build the internals of the application that delivers the business logic functionality to the end user. This includes integration with the mobile infrastructure such as device specific functionality, location information, wireless network connectivity, and others.
7. Perform unit tests, white-box tests, and black-box tests on the internals of the application delivered from step 3.
8. Build the mechanism by which the generic user interfaces are to be specialized.
9. Perform unit tests, white-box tests, and black-box tests on the user interfaces that allow access to the system. Regressive black-box testing is of crucial importance here.
10. Borrow a page from voice user development and tune the user interface iteratively.
11. Go through the customer acceptance process in which the customer sees the delivered slice of functionality or the entire product, accepts the product, or gives us additional requirements and modifications to the existing requirements that send us back to the first step.

Remember that you can never have too much information about the requirements. Misunderstanding the requirements is one of the typical pitfalls of software development, but it is definitely the biggest pitfall of projects that involve technologies with which the customers are not familiar. Also, remember that UML, the UML extensions that we have introduced, and any other techniques such as the mobile use case matrix are simply tools. Software development tools are to be used at the discretion of the engineers and based on the size, budget, time frame, and specific business requirements of the project.

15.5 Summary

In this chapter we brought together the various pieces of modeling and high-level development strategies discussed throughout this text to outline an overall plan of attack in developing mobile applications. Obviously, any development methodology, or component thereof, is only as valuable as the collective improvements in the efficiency of the development process and the quality of the final product. Once again, what we have outlined here is not necessarily a methodology, but rather the features that any development methodology addressing the problems of mobile application development must address. Augment what we have introduced here with the experience that you gain as you develop mobile applications.

In the remaining chapters, we will look at selecting the right infrastructure pieces for your mobile application, some of the typical hurdles in developing mobile applications, and the process of testing mobile applications.

CHAPTER 16

Architecture, Design, and Technology Selection for Mobile Applications

We're gonna be rich!
Jos Bergmans (in 1999 while holding shares of AdForce, in which he would not be vested until after the company's demise during the post-Internet boom)

16.1 INTRODUCTION

Much of what we have discussed in this text has been focused on design problems and high-level approaches to building mobile applications. We have intentionally stayed away from a more syntactical-driven approach because languages and tools are evolving rapidly in the space of mobile applications. We have looked at a variety of design patterns and architectural solutions that address the problems associated with mobile applications. In this chapter, we are going to take a step back, look at some very high-level architectures, and discuss how we should use them in building our mobile applications.

In an abstract manner, a software system is to the domain problem it solves what the solution may be to a math problem. Through the years, mathematicians have refined "canonical" solutions to a wide variety of mathematical problems. "Canonical," as defined by the Webster dictionary, is an adjective for something "conforming to a general rule or acceptable procedure." Much of the purpose of various fields of engineering is to define these canonical "best practices and ways" of doing things for given problems. A large part of the field of software engineering involves defining canonical solutions for developing software applications so that every problem in building a software application does not have to be solved from scratch.

To define these general rules and acceptable procedures, the software engineering discipline has borrowed concepts and terminologies from more established engineering disciplines such as structural engineering. In a physical sense, building software, at design stages, resembles building physical structures. First, the builder assesses the requirements of the inhabitants of the structure. Then a high-level overall plan or design that meets those needs is put together. Finally, the plan is implemented by carving out pieces of work and then building the structure. Structural engineers and builders refer to the high-level overall plan as *architecture*. "Architecture," as defined by the Webster dictionary, is "the art or science of building; specifically: the art or practice of designing and building structures and especially habitable ones." Webster also defines architecture as "a method or style of building." Through years of designing buildings, builders of structures discovered that one way to improve the design and creation process is to come up with typical ways of putting the structural pieces together and then use these methodologies to design a high-level plan of the structure, namely the architecture. So, the architecture of a building is largely the implementation of these canonical methods that allow engineers to create standard pieces to be used in structures (reuse), refine the patterns of doing things in an evolutionary manner (tried-and-true), and describe, compare, and contrast the structures. Architecture helped engineers in building complex physical structures to identify types of structures, divide the complicated problem of building them into pieces, and apply their bag of best ways and practices to create an overall scheme that ties together the pieces. Finally, the IEEE 1471 defines architecture to be "the fundamental organization of a system embodied in its components, their relationships to each other and to the environment, and the principles guiding its design and evolution" [IEEE 2000].

Much of the nature of software is similar to complex physical structures. Just as perceiving the overall and high-level plan of a building is one of the most difficult and most important tasks an architect or structural engineer has, putting together a high-level organization of software components in an architecture can be a daunting task for a software engineer. "Software systems have no tangible representation which allows us to directly perceive the realization of the large scale abstractions which were used in the design. This makes it difficult to identify them unambiguously and communicate them to others" [Baragry and Reed 1998]. So, software architectures play the same role for software engineers that building architectures do for builders; they allow software engineers to get a high-level view of the computing systems and to divide and concur complex problems. Also, they allow us to categorize computing systems by their architectures. So, as a summary of the various perspectives of architecture that we have discussed here, we will define software architecture to be *a particularly high-level abstraction of the system and how its components fit together*.

Designing the architecture of a software system should be the step immediately following the requirements-gathering process. It is crucial that the system is designed before the tools of implementation are selected. One of the most prevalent mistakes in designing software systems in general, and mobile software systems in specific, is that architecture is done as an afterthought to a group of products and frameworks selected. For example, many engineers design systems using only a given manufacturer's platform (such as Microsoft Windows). This means that they are limiting the architecture of the system, the feature set of the final system, and the fulfillment of the requirements of the customer to what the platform dictates. Platforms and tools should be selected based on the architecture of the system and the architecture of the system should be based on the required functionality dictated by the user and available budget. Fielding [Fielding 2000] has a comprehensive study of software architecture and its components. It can serve as a definitive reference survey of application architectures. Our focus will be on architectures of mobile computing systems. Now, let us take a look at a few of the most popular network-based application architectures that have emerged as the prevalent mobile architectures.

16.1.1 Mobile Computing Architectures

Because access must be granted to the same application ubiquitously through any device and interface means that mobile applications are inherently distributed network-based systems. Therefore mobile architectures are inherently network-based computing architectures. To understand mobile application architectures, we will first survey today's prevalent network-based architectures.

The primary distinction between network-based architectures and software architectures in general is that communication among components, in network-based architectures, is restricted to message passing [Andrews 1991, Fielding 2000], or the equivalent of message passing if a more efficient mechanism can be selected at run time based on the location of components [Fielding 2000, Tanenbaum and van Renesse 1985]. Therefore, we can say that network-based architectures are a subset of distributed computing architectures.

Our discussion is limited to issues concerning the design and implementation of mobile applications; consequently, we are concerned with the application layer. We will limit our discussion to software architectures at the application layer and avoid discussions of network topologies, hardware, and other layers of computing systems that reside at layers beneath the application layer. Then, we will look at the effects of the mobile condition and the dimensions of mobility on the architecture of a computing system.

The first network-based systems used a central computer to do all of the complicated computing work such as calculations and data storage. All of the other computers in the network were simple terminals used to interface with this central computer. Such systems have been called a variety of names, the most popular of which are *fully centralized* systems or *mainframe* systems.

16.1.2 Fully Centralized Application Architectures

Centralized application architectures (see Figure 16.1) offer the first type of distributed computing architectures. Perhaps the best way to think of the centralized architectures is in terms of the mainframe. For this reason, fully centralized architectures are often referred to as mainframe architectures. In a centralized

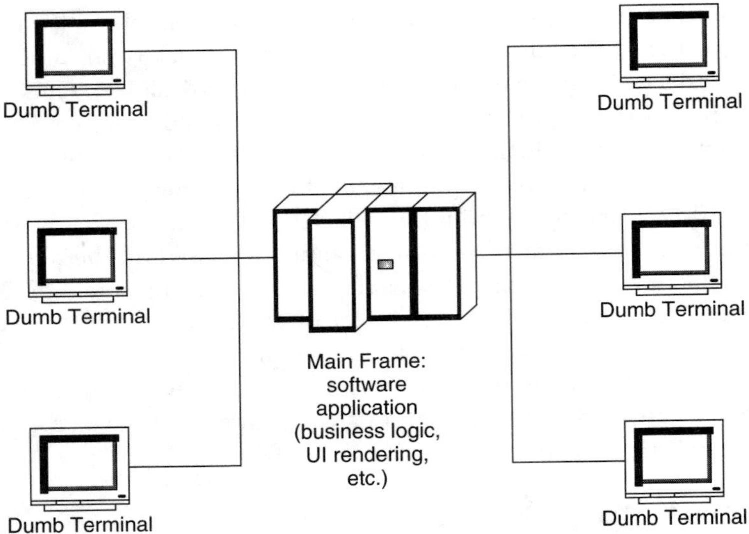

FIGURE 16.1. Centralized Application Architectures.

architecture, all of the intelligence of the computing system resides within a central host [Sadoski 1997]. At the edge of the network, remote terminals provide nothing more than a dumb interface to the central host. Mainframe architectures are often accessed by a variety of systems such as PCs and other systems; nevertheless, they are fully centralized as no part of the task that they fulfill can be distributed to the systems that access them. Every computing function including data storage, logical computations, and rendering of the user interface is done on the central server. Typically, the terminals at the edge of the network are used simply to display the prepared content to be displayed at the central server. The systems that access them are there for one reason: to allow the user to interface with them.

Fully centralized systems were the first and the oldest type of network computing systems. Many systems such as automated teller machines (ATM), grocery store cash registers, air-traffic control terminals, and other mission-critical-type systems remain centralized to this day. Mainframe architectures tend to be extremely reliable because all of the software resides on the central host. This eliminates the possibility of having software glitches ("bugs"), many of which can occur at the interfaces of software components interdispersed across multiple systems. It also reduces the complexity of software design as the networking and the application development process are both affected by the distribution of computing in a minimal manner.

With all of the benefits of mainframe computing, there are several major drawbacks with fully centralized computing. First, to access the central host, network connectivity to the central host is a requirement; this means that network connectivity is always required no matter how trivial the computing task. Also, as the central host should be able to handle large amounts of traffic, make numerous calculations, and store vast amounts of data (after all, the central host is basically all there is to this type of computing system), it is typically very expensive.

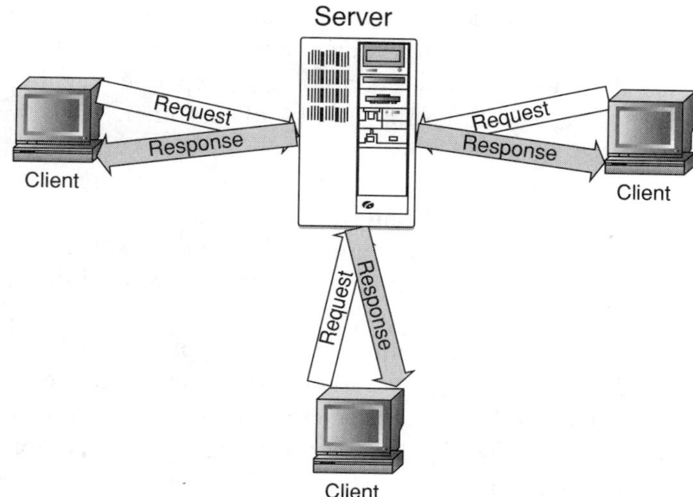

FIGURE 16.2. Client–Server Architectures.

Fail-over and backup costs are also very high as the entire system fails if any single part of it fails. Most of the time the only reliable fail-over mechanism is a full duplicate of the central host that is continually updated and ready to come online in case of a failure. Fully centralized systems are also very inflexible. Any type of customization to the application has scalability and maintenance ramifications because the entire application is in one place as one piece of software.

Many of today's existing mobile computing systems are fully centralized systems. For example, many grocery stores use hand-held mobile scanners to keep track of inventory connected to a central host. However, centralized mobile applications are very costly and typically very inflexible. Most of these types of applications can only be implemented when the financial benefits of using the system exceed the total cost of devices, the centralized hardware, and the software. The devices are often designed with very specific needs and requirements and, as those needs and requirements change, they are rendered obsolete. The application cannot readily be modified and modification may involve recall of the end-user devices or hardware modifications.

In the late 1970s and early 1980s, software engineers began to modularize applications and realize that, by breaking applications up into pieces, they could reduce the cost and complexity of modifying applications. With the advent of modern operating systems such as UNIX and databases, it became clear that applications could be made more flexible by being pieced. At the same time, the PC was becoming pervasive, and it became obvious that pushing some of the computing to the nodes on the network would make the systems much more flexible. Out of this arose the client–server architecture.

16.1.3 Client–Server Architectures

Client–server architectures (see Figure 16.2) were the first network-based computing architectures to become commercially viable and prevalent. Distributed computing architectures had always existed, but most commercial systems that allowed network computing were based on a centralized model. In a client–server model, there are two distinct programs residing on separate machines [Mohseni 1996]. One program is said to be the "client" of the other. The other program is said to "serve" the client and, therefore, is the "server." In an abstract sense, there is one server for one or more clients. Client–server architectures provided a feasible means of distributing applications and computing in a network.

The distribution of various components of data and logic between the server and the client was not very well defined in the first versions of the client–server architecture.

The major feat of the client–server model was an application of one of the basic principles in software engineering—separation of concerns—to create distributed applications. In other words, the client–server architecture stipulated that the client can do more than just being a hardware interface with no computing power. The change in the role of the client was a significant evolutionary step over the fully centralized architecture. The benefits were numerous. For example, most information about the abilities of the client to interface with the user of the system is available at the client itself. So, it knows best how to render a user interface. Consequently, it quickly became popular to move the user interface concerns to the client. Another example of the benefits is the handling of server downtime. In the fully centralized model, in the event of any problem in the network or the server, nothing works. In a client–server system, the client can give the user a message that tells the user why the server is not accessible (e.g., the server is not responding or cannot be found). During such a time, there may be cached information at the client for temporary use.

Over time, in an evolutionary manner, variations of the client–server architecture have arisen. These variations are created by the breakdown of the types of responsibilities assigned to the client and the server. For example, some variations of the client–server architecture push all of the storage responsibilities to the server. This allows more efficient usage of storage devices and prohibits creation of complex software that replicates and synchronizes the data among the clients.

Modern databases were one of the first real commercial examples of the server in the client–server architecture and have done much in popularizing the client–server architecture. The primary task of databases, as servers, is to store data, but they can also hold business logic. This logic can be implicit in the form of the structure and content of the data or explicit in the form of stored procedures and queries. Usage of databases through some connectivity protocol is a very good example of client–server computing. Typically, a database program runs on one computer and is accessed through some database connectivity protocol such as ODBC (Open Database Connectivity) or JDBC (Java Database Connectivity) by the clients. The clients may use the server to store data and retrieve data using stored procedures or other mechanisms.

A comprehensive of origins and properties of client–server computing systems can be found in works by Fielding [Fielding 2000] and Orfali and Harkey [Orfali and Harkey 1997]. Client–server systems are one of the predominant network-based computing architectures today. As the client–server model evolved, software

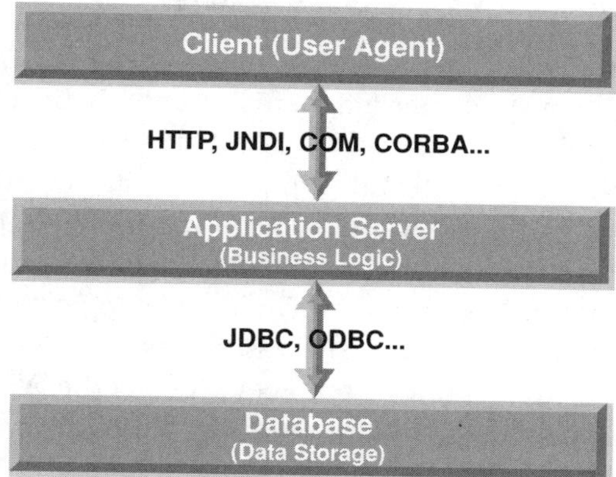

FIGURE 16.3. A 3-Tier Architecture.

engineers began to recognize that this network-based computing architecture could to be better defined by further separation of concerns to better distinguish the roles of the server and the client. *N*-tier architectures are the result of this further evolution in client–server architectures.

16.1.4 *N*-Tier Architectures

Databases were one of the first types of servers in the client–server model. As the client–server architectures evolved, it became obvious that there still needed to be further separation of concerns among tasks. For examples, server applications were often being written as monolithic applications that held data, business logic, and user interface information. Clients, as well, were being written with no predefined communication semantics with the servers, with no standard way to deal with user interface issues, and with other issues left unaddressed. This made client–server applications difficult to maintain, trouble-shoot, and improve.

It was clear that some distinct tasks, whether at the client or the server, needed to be decoupled. Some tasks needed to be centralized and others needed to be at the clients. *N*-tier architectures try to further apply the principle of separation of concerns to the client–server model by separating the concerns into a set of *n* layers. *N*-tier architectures began with the 2-tier architecture. The client was the application and the database was the server. In the 2-tier model, the client application was typically responsible for performing business logic calculations, the rendering of the user interface, and whatever additional computational tasks needed to be done to complete the application functionality. In the context of this text, we will refer to the logical computations that the application makes to model the tasks of some domain as business logic. For example, in a mortgage banking application, calculation of the interest rates may be part of the business logic.

Because the 2-tier architecture did not scale well for complicated server applications, 3-tier architectures were devised (see Figure 16.3). The 3-tier architecture separated the concern of business logic computations from the rest of the application. The database did the storage of the data and the "application server" took care of the computation of the business logic that needed to be accessed by the clients. Hence, in the 3-tier architecture, the application server is the client to the database server and the user interface application, or whatever renders the user interface components, is the client to the application server. This chaining of components in a client-to-server manner is essentially the evolutionary step in the *N*-tier architectures over the simple 2-tier client–server models.

These 3-tier application architectures had numerous benefits, including better scalability and reliability properties. They achieved this by separating three concerns: storage of data in the database, business logic in the application server, and rendering the user interface in the client. Today, a large portion of the infrastructure of the WWW, arguably the most successful model of distributed computing, is based on 2-tier and 3-tier architectures. Let us look at the WWW and how *N*-tier architectures have symbiotically flourished along with it.

N-Tier Architectures and the World Wide Web

The Web is essentially a client–server system where the clients and servers communicate through HTTP (Hyper-Text Transfer Protocol). The clients are browsers that interpret user interface instructions in HTML (Hyper-Text Markup Language) and other client-side scripting languages such as JavaScript for rendering a graphical user interface. The servers are so-called Web servers that serve the requests of the clients coming in through HTTP with responses that contain HTML. Though there are other types of content that can be served by the Web server, the most popular is HTML. The format of content is often referred to as the MIME (Multimedia Internet Mail Extensions) type of the content. Regardless of the format of the content, content can be grouped into two families: *static* and *dynamic*.

Static Web content is the content that does not change at the time of the request from the client or because of the request from the client. Examples of static Web content are static HTML files, static pictures in JPEG and other formats, and static video clips in MPEG and other formats. Static content can be dynamically generated in a batch mode. Even at that state, we call them static pages because, as far as the server is concerned, the page is a static resource that may be retrieved through access to the file system. Web servers such as the Apache Web server [Apache 2000] implement the specifications of the HTTP as a server and serve static content to the clients. The 2-tier model worked perfectly fine for the static content.

Dynamic content is generated at run time and is based on information specific to the instance of the client, the request, or the session. A good example of dynamic content is a personalized Web portal. The pages are tailored to the needs of the user and every time the same user goes back to the portal, the arrangement of the information is tailored to his or her specifications. Most of the e-commerce industry on the Web is based on the creation of dynamic content with request- and session-based functionality such as shopping carts that are filled and emptied by the client's requests. CGI (Common Gateway Interface) programs were the first tools to create dynamic content. CGI programs used the URL (Universal Resource Locator) and the GET/POST mechanisms of the Web to specify a command to a server application along with some parameters passed to this command. The CGI program, in turn, dynamically creates content based on the command and the parameters passed to it. The Web server then serves this content to the client. This mechanism remains a popular method of creating dynamic content.

However, retrieval of data and logical computations were tightly coupled. This created monolithic server applications that had some of the same problems as the mainframes; namely, scaling was expensive and only possible through additional hardware, adding functionality to monolithic applications was difficult, and fault tolerance of any component of the system was only possible by replicating the entire system. As mentioned previously, *application servers* attempted to solve this problem by separating the concerns of data storage and business logic. Therefore, most of today's scalable and reliable Web applications with a large amount of dynamic content are based on *N*-tier architectural models.

Today's most popular *N*-tier systems are or the 3-tier type simply because the Web is the most pervasive network. HTTP and the Web dictate a thin client. This means that the primary purpose of the client nodes on the Web is presentation. Clients on the Web are the browsers and they provide a user interface to the user. On the Web, the browsers are clients to the Web servers, the Web servers are clients to the application servers, and the application servers are clients to database servers.

So, for most typical Web systems, the concerns are storage, business logic, and presentation of data to the client. This yields $n = 3$ for the *N*-tier architecture. The important thing to note about *N*-tier architectures is that they favor centralization over decentralization. Because the clients of *N*-tier systems, such as Web browsers, can communicate with each other, doing logical operations or storing data at the client either is very cumbersome or creates big problems. The strength of *N*-tier architectures lies in their ability to separate concerns at a central node in the network, thereby allowing for scalability and reliability. It is also important to note that *N*-tier architectures are an evolution of client–server architectures: The layering is done at the server and there is no change in the construct of the client.

N > 3 for Mobile Applications

The first generation of mobile applications quickly exposed a weakness of the 3-tier variation of the *N*-tier architecture: Every device type needed a different type of content and the application server began to be responsible for both business and presentation logic. The first-generation Internet-enabled mobile systems had many of the properties of the mobile systems that we have talked about: The user interfaces varied, the QOS was unreliable, etc. This was not what the 3-tier systems of the Web were designed for. Already, HTML had been a marvel that was beginning to be stretched to its limitations by developers trying to create rich graphical user interfaces with a markup language whose original purpose was simple presentation of information. Now, with the mobile systems, it was obvious that HTML just would not do. WAP and i-mode (NTT Docomo) tried to address this issue by creating new markup languages. And this, once again, quickly exposed another problem: Having to present to *m* types of browsers now meant having to produce *m* types of content. This was unacceptable.

The 3-tier systems of the Web were designed to produce one type of user interface for one group of browsers. As long as the browser could understand HTML

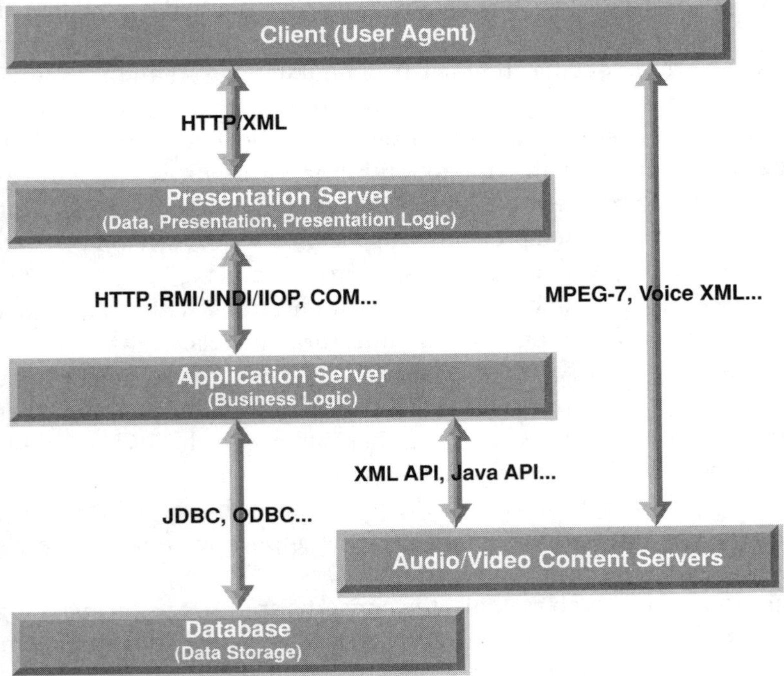

FIGURE 16.4. ***N*-Tier Architecture ($N = 4$).**

and JavaScript, the user interface was fairly easy to render. As the Web evolved, the Web browsers also began to use a variety of plug-ins, such as Macromedia Flash, that would prohibit use of content in a resource-starved mobile environment.

The first solution to this problem was to detect the type of the client and to serve the appropriate content to the client. For the Web, this could be done through querying the request for the browser type and serving the content type that the browser could understand. This solution, however, does not address the fact that there are different branches of content to be served for the different devices and that the behavior of the application may need to be fundamentally different depending on the condition of the mobile user. Presentation servers such as the Apache's Cocoon and IBM's Wireless Transcoding Publisher solved this problem by separating this concern into another tier. We will look more closely at presentations servers in the next chapter.

The majority of mobile commercial solutions in the market today focus on data-driven mobile solutions with *N*-tier architectures. A simple version of such *N*-tier architecture ($N = 4$) may be seen in Figure 16.4. The "wireless Web" is a problem that has been tackled by numerous vendors, each with its own version of the presentation server, promising to "wireless-enable" the Web (an unsuitable terminology because wireless connectivity and mobility are not the same thing as we discussed earlier in this chapter). Presentation servers have allowed the *N*-tier architecture to evolve further to address the diversification of devices. Nevertheless, *N*-tier architectures remain in the client–server family. The clients still cannot communicate with each other directly. We will discuss two architectures in this text that are a fundamental departure from client–server architectures: peer-to-peer architectures and mobile agent architectures.

16.1.5 Peer-to-Peer Architectures

N-tier client–server architectures, with all of their benefits, do not address several dimensions of mobility. *N*-tier architectures, for example, require that the user be connected to the network because the servers are somewhere else on the network. If one client has the data that another client needs, there is no way for them to discover each other and exchange the information. The great failure of centralized and client–server models lies in their inability to recognize, let alone exploit, the growing power and information resources at the edges of the network [Bolcer and Oreizy 2000]. For example, in a client–server and centralized application model, the server typically cannot initiate interactions with the client. Neither can clients store and interchange information without going through the server.

Peer-to-peer (P2P) application architectures allow any participant of the network to communicate with any and all of the other participants provided those participants adhere to the rules of the network-based application architecture. In P2P application architectures, all the participants, naturally referred to as *peers*, are autonomous and equal participants. P2P architectures can operate between two participants or among many participants.[PEQ1] It is important to note that, in such an architecture, it is not a requirement that all nodes have the ability to connect to each other (as seen in Figure 16.5). It is particularly important to note that this is not a requirement in mobile environments, where the ability of a device to connect to other device may depend on a variety of variables such as security, device capabilities, and network services. Nevertheless, from the figure, the difference in the topology between P2P and client–server systems should be quite clear. If every given node can reach many of the nodes, but not all of the nodes, we still have a P2P architecture.

P2P application infrastructures satisfy the problems presented by the dimensions of mobility much better than do client–server and centralized architectures. P2P architectures do not require connectivity to a server or centralized host; therefore, if a network participant, or peer, needs a piece of information, there may be a variety of other peers that can satisfy its need. Although connectivity to one or more may not be available, the probability of finding a peer with the required resources is much higher than for the client–server or centralized cases. Because P2P architectures rely on the computing power available at the edge of the network (closer to the place where the actual user of the system is) they can deal better with specialization of content to the required user interface.

We have already looked at P2P in Chapter 9 where we discussed mobile agents. Let us look at them next.

16.1.6 Mobile Agent Architectures

We dedicated Chapter 9 entirely to discussions that revolve around mobile agents, but, if you are reading this chapter out of order or if you skipped Chapter 9, we will give you a quick digest of mobile agents here.

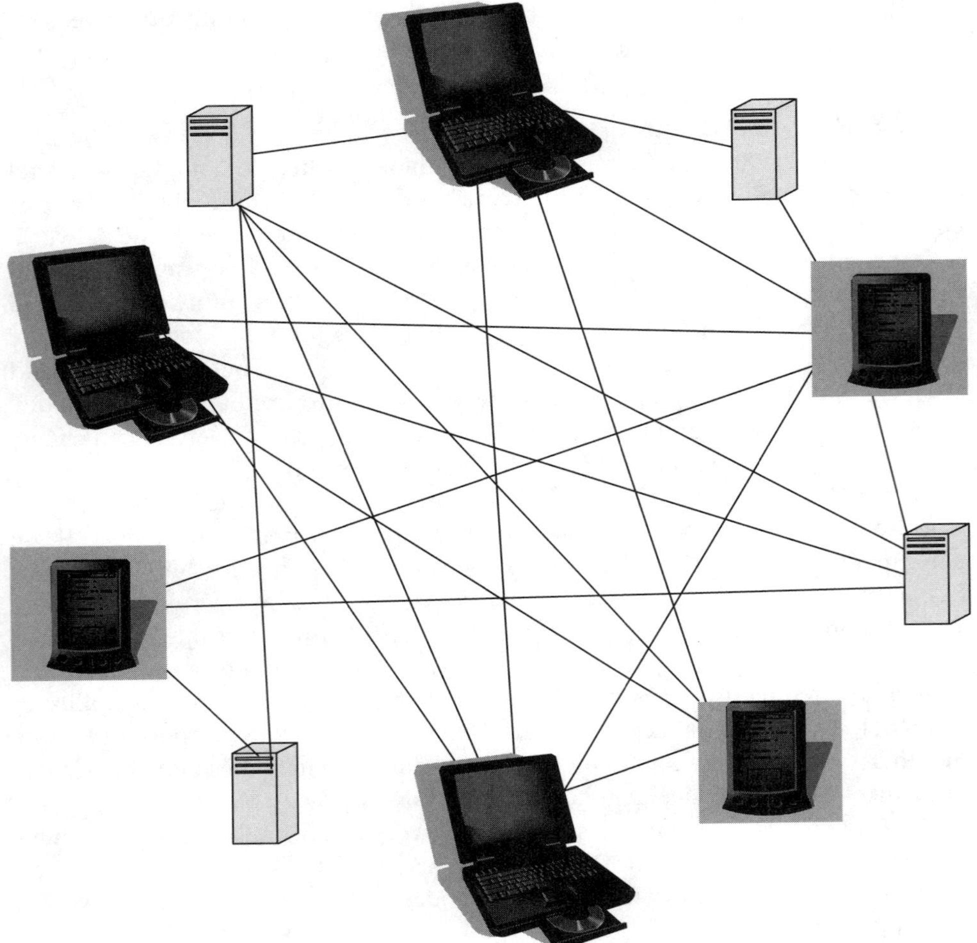

FIGURE 16.5. Peer-to-Peer Architectures.

Mobile agent–based software systems are a drastic departure from centralized, client–server, and *N*-tier systems. Mobile agents have the following properties:

1. They are programs that encapsulate data and code, which may be dispatched from a client computer and transported to a remote server for execution [Chess 1993].
2. They execute asynchronously and autonomously [Yang et al. 2000].

The term *mobile agent* has no relation to the mobile user, the mobile device, or any of the other aspects of mobility that we have discussed so far. Rather, mobile agents are software components that can move from server to server in the network while keeping the state of the application intact. Mobile agents manage their own life cycles based on the logic programmed into them.

Because of their autonomy and their ability to move from one environment to another, mobile agents seem particularly promising for building mobile applications.

Imagine having an application environment that can load one application, perform what needs to be done without having to communicate with other devices, and, once finished, unload itself from the device and, if necessary, store data on some other device such as a server. You have just imagined mobile agents. With the exception of real-time distributed computing, there is nothing that mobile agents can do that the aforementioned architectures cannot do. However, mobile agents offer some very significant advantages that happen to be aligned with the dimensions of mobility.

Mobile agents are autonomous: They can manage their own life cycles. This means that we do not have to store many applications on a device or manage loading and unloading the applications manually. Therefore, usage of CPU and memory resources are optimized and simplified. Also, because the management of code and state is something that the application or the application framework handles, mobile agents are much better at adapting to whatever user interface may be needed on a device, at a given time, at a given place. For example, a mobile agent application can load the interface code for a voice user interface or the text user interface depending on the user's preference or device support. Most importantly, mobile agents do not have to access the network every time some computing task must be done. They can be used as stand-alone applications for the most part. This reduces latency in systems that are massively distributed such as mobile systems.

Nevertheless, mobile agents, as with any other computing system, have their downfalls too. Mobile agents are much more complex than the previously mentioned application models. Also, the minimum resource requirement of mobile agents can be slightly higher than that of clients of the client–server architecture. Security is also a big concern in mobile agents.

If mobile agents (sometimes referred to as mobile code) seem a bit too complicated to fathom, do not be weary. Mobile agents are not a very prevalent computing paradigm today, although they promise to be much more prevalent in the future.

Throughout this text, client–server, P2P, and mobile agent architectures are the three that we will consider for designing and implementing mobile applications. These three are the most relevant to creating mobile applications using technology that exists today. Now that we have looked at the prevalent software architectures of today, let us look at a road map of the four sections of this book on how we will look at designing and implementing mobile applications.

16.2 Practical Concerns with Architectures

Vendor neutrality is one of the points that we have stressed throughout this text. The argument may be made that vendor neutrality is not important. For example, building applications that run only on the Microsoft platform is as valid as any other approach. This may be true for disposable software for well-known domains: those applications that have a short lifetime and are written for an environment where the problem is very well known. The problem is that software engineers are typically faced with the task of building systems where the problem is not very well known (or where the requirements are hazy at best). Also, software applications typically live much longer than their original authors have ever thought, particularly if they hold any significant amount of business logic (because they can be hard to understand and document) and writing vendor-neutral software is particularly important in a young discipline such as mobile application development. Mobile software vendors change, and along with their changes they create new platforms and new tools; the worst thing you can do is to rely on a vendor whose customer base may be very diverse (thereby being pulled in many directions) and has only its own bottom line in mind.

The practice of building software architectures on vendor specifications must stop. As a discipline, we must start relying on bodies such as W3C, ACM (Association of Computer Machinery), IEEE, IETF, and other organizations to set forth standards that serve the interest of the consumer and the industry as opposed to individual vendors. As you may have noted, this was a practice that we tried to adopt throughout this text. Vendor products should compete based on their implementations and feature robustness as opposed to tying down customers and the development community.

16.3 Architectural Patterns for Mobile Applications

Architectures are inherently evolutionary. Therefore, like fine wine, architectures and architectural patterns that have been correctly recognized mature well. The architecture of a given structure may be conceived by putting together two or more such mature architectural patterns. Although mobile application development is a very young discipline, there are some architectural patterns that have surfaced as applicable. We have looked at some of these patterns within the context of the relevant dimension of mobility in this text. Namely, we have looked at the following:

1. *Fusion and integration within multimodality*: The applicability of this architectural pattern was in fusing various modalities to create a multimodal user interface. We looked at this in Chapter 8.
2. *PAC and its variants*: The applicability of this architectural pattern was in creating separation of concernsamong the various aspects of user interface. We looked at this in Chapters 5–8.
3. *MVC and its variants*: Like PAC, the applicability of this architectural pattern was in separating the concerns of the user interface from the rest of the application. We looked at this in Chapters 6–8.

Another crucial architectural pattern that is a must read for anyone dealing with distributed computing (because most mobile computing is distributed) is Roy Fielding's REST [Fielding 2000]. We consider REST not only an architectural pattern, but an architectural principle that may apply to a variety of distributed systems that involve multiple pieces communicating with one another. We strongly recommend reading the reference on this topic.

We did talk about use of voice, location information, and mobile agents. Mobile computing has only recently begun to take advantage of these technologies to offer new and useful features; consequently, we have not recognized any architectural patterns within these areas as far as mobile development is concerned. These areas are evolving rapidly. There is no doubt that such architectural patterns will emerge within the near future.

16.4 SUMMARY

Software architecture is probably just as much of an art as it is a science. So, we cannot "teach" the reader, nor can any other author(s) claim that they can "teach" their readers, the art of creating good architectures. As in building physical architectures for creating buildings and monuments, it requires years of practice, design, testing, experienced failures, and experimentation to make an engineer a good architect. However, even the best architects are often not aware of at least some architectural patterns in software development. For this reason, software architecture is also not an individual art, rather a team art, where the best architectures are created by exchange of ideas within the software community.

All we have done in this chapter is to introduce some already well-known architectures and discuss a few architectural patterns previously discussed in this text within the discipline of mobile application development. To become a good software architect, you will need to experiment, exchange ideas with other engineers, continually read on new findings by academics and practitioners, and seek the weaknesses of whatever architectures you or your colleagues develop or find (the antipatterns).

CHAPTER 17

Mobile Application Development Hurdles

> Whatever one man is capable of conceiving, other men will be able to achieve.
>
> Jules Verne

17.1 Introduction

Much of the research done in software engineering is dedicated to solving practical problems that come up when building software applications. Techniques such as Extreme Programming and RUP are two such techniques and methodologies, addressing some of the issues associated with the process of building software applications.

The dimensions of mobility, as we have seen, add to the complexity of developing mobile applications. In this way, an entirely new set of hurdles and problems are introduced. In this chapter, we will briefly look at a few of these problems. Some of these problems will be addressable by the tools that we have introduced previously in this text; others will not.

Some of the basic hurdles are caused by the fact that most developers either have experience building call centers and other types of voice systems using the telephony channel or they build PC applications with GUIs. So, we will start by looking at hurdles associated with building a VUI for those developers who come from a server-side or GUI-based development background.

17.2 Voice User Interface Hurdles

The first question that will come to your mind will be related to the infrastructure. This will be a hurdle in real deployments. Whether to have your own voice infrastructure (telephony systems if you need to support telephony, voice recognition servers, etc.) will largely depend on two factors: which is the financially viable solution and which is the best decision for the core business.

First, let us assume that you have to own the development platform (which is typically the case because frequent unit testing is either not possible or difficult if you do not own the development environment). This means that you have a voice recognition engine, speech-to-text engine, and/or speech-synthesis engine on your environment (whether it was a free development license or whether you had to pay for it). Unit testing is typically made possible by using the speakers on your development platform (Linux, MS Windows, etc.) to emulate the telephony channel.

VSPs (Voice Service Providers) offer infrastructures on which you can deploy your voice application for testing and production. You can buy the software (e.g., Nuance or Speechworks) and the hardware (e.g., Dialogic) from the vendors and create your own deployment environments. Pricing is typically the major factor here, but keep in mind that it is not the only factor. VSPs are typically very restrictive on what you can do on their systems if they host the system and support the system. You always have the most amount of control if you own both the hardware and the software.

The flip side of the coin is that deploying on a VSP sometimes actually forces the development team to follow better software engineering (specifically release engineering) practices and create a cleaner development and deployment process.

17.3 Hurdles with Multimodal Applications

Some of the basic hurdles are caused by the fact that most devices, at present, do not offer the hardware capabilities to have true simultaneous multimodality. This form of multimodality tends to be the most useful form. Also, most devices that connect to a network wirelessly today are not capable of offering two or more separate connections with reliable QOS. Only recently have operating systems such as Symbian OS and Palm OS 5.0 begun to provide the basic capabilities for offering simultaneous multimodality on the handset such as multithreading. However, such features are at the top of the list for the operating system and device manufacturers as they add features to their products. Though multimodality does not, in and of itself, give birth to killer applications, it has the ability to make applications much more user friendly and thus improve their commercial value.

The other problem with multimodality lies on the server side, where synchronization of many different products, such as some of those introduced in this text (speech recognition, transcoding publishers, etc.), creates latencies among the different modalities. These problems can indeed be solved with today's technologies, but not in an elegant manner. The solutions typically give rise to other problems in integrating third-party systems or scaling the server-side software properly.

17.4 Problems with Building Location-Based Applications

Integrating location information into an application may possibly be the most exciting possibility for mobile applications. Location information offers a whole new realm of applications. The biggest single problem with location information is not in the technology, but in the use of it: privacy. Whereas knowing the location of the mobile user can be very handy in offering very useful services, it can also violate basic privacy rights of a user. So, the users are often faced with a choice whether to "opt-in" or "opt-out"; participating in the program means signing a form that basically gives up a great deal of privacy, but not signing results in a lack of access to the desired services.

Currently, there are no technologies that allow for "opting-in" or "opting-out" of sharing one's location on a granular interactive basis. In other words, there is no *easy* way for the user to specify when, where, and how his or her location should be known and when, where, and how his or her location should not be known.

The second and third biggest problems with today's location systems are price and power use. Good GPS-based systems are still fairly expensive and if you want to add GIS information to that to get value-added services such as finding restaurants, etc. you are looking at subscription fees. Also, most location devices are a considerable drain on the batteries, though this is an area of focus in the location industry and should be addressed within the near future.

17.5 Power Use

We trust that the clever reader of the book has noticed how we neglected addressing issues of power use. The problem seems to be that operating system vendors and hardware manufacturers have largely dropped the ball on providing enough software control for the third-party developers, through APIs or otherwise, to monitor and control the power use on devices. This leaves the developers somewhat helpless. For example, we cannot disable certain functionality in the application based on the amount of power left. At the time of authoring this text, the developers can only affect power use by optimizing the operation of the application. This remains a hurdle in writing better, smarter, and more user-friendly mobile applications.

17.6 Summary

Throughout this text, we have pointed out various hurdles in building commercially successful mobile applications. There are many that we have not mentioned here. It almost seems as if mentioning the hurdles will detract the enthused novice readers from trying to build mobile applications. However, in the hurdles that we have mentioned and the ones that we have not, you can also seek commercial opportunity. There is no doubt in anyone's mind that mobile applications will someday be as commercially successful as foreseen during the late 1990s. However, the slowdown in the commercial success has been largely due to these hurdles and poor execution on the part of developers who have ignored the dimensions of mobility and simply built PC applications that fit on mobile devices. The investors and entrepreneurs are just as much to blame in their hasty approaches to create "killer" applications while not understanding that every killer application (such as spreadsheets and word processors) evolved through many years and came from other applications (such as text editors and spell-checkers) whose commercial success were doubted at first.

Chapter 18

Testing Mobile Applications

Common sense is the collection of prejudices acquired by age eighteen.

Albert Einstein

All sects are different, because they come from men; morality is everywhere the same, because it comes from God!

Voltaire

18.1 Introduction

Proper testing and quality control of software has been said to be one of the most neglected areas of software development. Whereas this streamlining of testing and quality control can reduce the budget and the time frame for delivery of projects, the quality of the delivered product is ultimately sacrificed. Although lack of testing and quality control can be the cause of failure, or at least customer dissatisfaction, of many software products, it has been tolerated in the world of PC applications. This is mostly from the tolerance that the users have to buggy software with stability and functionality issues. However, this tolerance does not exist in the world of mobile application development. Mobile devices are always looked upon, even if they are not, as embedded devices. To the users, there is no difference between a way a PDA, a cell phone, and a VCR should operate: The user interface must be simple and there is zero tolerance for problems relating to security, stability, performance, and all of those other things that these same users have built an immunity toward during the usage of PCs.

The best tool to meet these higher user expectations is to implement proper quality control and testing procedures to eliminate problems before an application ends up in the hands of the costumers. To do this, we first restate one of the major axioms in this text: *Mobile applications are a superset of their stationary counterparts.* Therefore, all the best techniques to be deployed in quality control and testing of stationary software applications are a subset of the best techniques to be deployed in quality control and testing of mobile applications. Because a plethora of materials exist in the commercial and academic community regarding the testing of stationary applications, we will leave it up to the reader to explore such sources. In this text, our major concern is first to look at any additional measures that we must take to ensure the quality of a mobile application and second to analyze the effect of the dimensions of mobility in our testing procedures and techniques. Once again, we use the dimensions of mobility as the starting point for the differences between mobile applications and their stationary counterparts and build from there.

Perhaps the most important difference between testing mobile applications and stationary applications is that *testing for mobile applications begins prior to development*. Moreover, it lasts all the way through the development cycle. Let us see why and how.

As we have seen, mobile applications may be deployed on a variety of devices, connect to the network in a variety of ways, offer several different input and output mechanisms, use the user's location and movement patterns, and display fundamentally different behavior than their stationary counterparts. Because of these factors, the quality of a mobile application largely depends on the infrastructure on which it is deployed. Although there is an analogous infrastructure for stationary applications if they operate in a network environment, this infrastructure typically does not vary much from one stationary application to the next and is based on stable and proven technologies that are more than a decade old. The same is not true of the infrastructure on which mobile applications are built. Much of the technology used to build these infrastructures is based on very new technologies and there is a considerable variation in the infrastructure used for development and deployment from one mobile application to the next (differences in the carriers, location-service providers, user interfaces required, etc.). Therefore, the first step in putting together a successful mobile application is to test the infrastructure on top of which the application is to be deployed.

18.1.1 Testing the Mobile Infrastructure

As we have recognized throughout this text, there are some core pieces of technology that a mobile application may use to provide the necessary functionality to the end user. In fact, in a way, most mobile applications involve some degree of integration with external applications. Although these external services and applications are also involved in the development of many stationary software systems, the way mobile applications use them typically differ from that of stationary applications. This is because, as we have mentioned, mobile applications fundamentally differ from their stationary counterparts by the dimensions of mobility. So, the services and external applications that provide the unique infrastructure of the mobile application are those that provide functionality related to the dimensions of mobility. Namely, we are concerned with hardware and software infrastructure providing the following:

1. location-based information about the mobile device,
2. wireless network connectivity,

3. voice recognition and speech synthesis,
4. multichannel connectivity to the network (base network that provides voice, data, and video to the device),
5. synchronization of data between the mobile device and the network,
6. power consumption and available power on the device,
7. capabilities of the device (input and output mechanisms, memory, CPU, storage, etc.),
8. QOS of network connectivity,
9. active transactions (push and similar functionality), and
10. data synchronization.

Because, typically, a mobile application does not use all of these pieces, and every mobile application uses these pieces in a unique way, then our first task in the development cycle is to perform proper testing on these infrastructure pieces to assure that they can deliver sufficient functionality and meet the performance requirements of our mobile application. The process of testing each one of these infrastructure pieces must include, but is not limited to, the following:

1. We must assure that the infrastructure piece individually, and the required infrastructure pieces together in concert, can deliver the proper functionality required of an application. For example, we do not want to discover that the wireless connectivity does not provide enough reliability to obtain location information or that one or more of the devices slated to be used by the application have problems supporting a VUI if the requirements of the project include location-based information as well as accessing the system through a VUI.
2. While developing a mobile application, developers typically use emulators. Emulators have two main benefits. First, deploying the application on the device may be cumbersome and time consuming; emulators lessen the development and quality control time by providing a starting point for unit testing as well as quality control. Note that all different tests must eventually be performed on all of the actual devices; however, emulators help us eliminate all those bugs that we can catch without going through the sometimes long and arduous process of deploying the application. Second, because many mobile devices operate with less exception-handling capabilities than PCs, some software bugs can lock up the device or even cause hardware problems. Though these problems are typically undoable, this can be cumbersome and time consuming. Before we start developing, we must map out any differences between the emulator of a device and the actual device. These differences will provide a metric, primarily for the developers, on how reliable the emulator is while development and unit testing are done iteratively. These differences also provide a starting point for unit testing the application on the actual device as well as a starting point, for the quality control team members, to look for bugs. So, prior to development, you must select your emulators and test (or obtain the information in some other way) the emulators themselves to see how true they are to the devices that they emulate. Of course, emulators are not just used for devices. They are also used to emulate network conditions, location services, and the other

external systems that are crucial to the dimensions of mobility. Apply the same treatment to all emulators: Know what emulators you are going to use for which piece of the infrastructure and how accurate the emulator is before you begin developing.

3. We must assure that the scalability requirements of the mobile application can be met. Remember that each user may have multiple devices and that features such as cross-device sessions are desirable. The combination of such features, the higher performance and reliability expectations on the part of the user, and possible impedance points in an environment where there is a large set of possible MMI points make scalability a larger issue than normal, especially for those mobile applications that rely largely on a server-side infrastructure. Although it is often not possible to have exact metrics and measurements on the scalability and reliability robustness of an infrastructure, typically an acceptable guesstimate can be made.
4. We must assure that the customer's expectations of the usability limitations of the application are going to be based on reality and not a guesstimate by the customer or the development team. In other words, before you begin developing, create some user interface mock-ups that demonstrate the types of user interface limitations that the user will face when using the application. For example, if you are going to build an application that collects large pieces of information from the users through a VUI and then displays some text through a visual display, you might want to create a "Hello World"-like example that demonstrates the sequence and types of inputs and outputs that the real users will deal with. This will give the customer a sense of whether the user interface is intuitive or whether the engineers have gone bonkers with offering too many functionalities. There are many other added benefits from doing this. A large portion of customers, as discussed in Chapter 15, have experience with stationary applications but do not really understand the possibilities of a mobile application. For this reason, it is important to properly demonstrate and communicate a fair representation of features such as the user interface implementation to the users. Note that this is different from the typical user interface mock-ups used during the first stages of user interface development. The goal here is to test whether there is a gap in understanding of usability issues between the development team and the users.

Once again, remember that the process of testing a mobile application begins before its development does. Once we start developing, we want to develop the application in a manner that does not hamper unit testing or white-box testing efforts. The first step for this is to have well-thought-out coding standards.

18.1.2 Coding Standards

Coding standards have long been a major part of software development. Coding standards give us myriad benefits, including better readability and reusability of code as well as usage of automated tools to help us throughout the development process. Once again, a comprehensive discussion of coding standards is outside of the scope of this text. However, there are some considerations, when it comes to coding standards, specific to mobile applications. Namely, there may be a variety of syntaxes involved in the development of one mobile application as different devices, or device families, may require different languages; some may offer J2ME support whereas others are BREW devices, etc. Not only should we maintain fairly strict coding standards per programming language but we should also try to maintain a high degree of consistency across the different programming languages and tools used in the project. Particularly, if we are using two tools, such as Java and C++, that lend themselves to similar coding standards, it is important to keep those coding standards as similar as possible. Whereas developers can be individually religious on where they use a carriage return or a curly bracket, these personal preferences must not hamper readability, reusability, and testing efforts. Because it is typical for mobile applications to have many different devices and language tools involved in their development, it is impractical to have a dedicated person in the quality control group assigned to a given part of the application using a specific language. The quality control team, as with all of the other teams in the development process, is restricted by some budget, and quality assurance (QA) engineers must often float among different modules, multiplexing a variety of tasks. If we do not maintain good coding standards across the different parts of the mobile application, we risk the chance of having very slow unit testing and white-box testing phases.

Fortunately, UML, which is the central tool used for development in this text, is an excellent tool to maintain consistency across different implementations. Detailed UML diagrams of implementation can assist in readability, maintainability, reusability, unit testing, and white-box testing of code by serving as documentation and clarification to the code.

In addition to coding standards that address cosmetic issues, we can also use coding standards to specify a limited and generic set of coding techniques to be used or to be avoided. For example, if we know that a programming language on a given device family shows bad performance when doing string comparisons, we may recommend that character-based comparison techniques be used for that language and on that given device family. Therefore, when it comes to mobile applications, coding standards can serve a bigger purpose in communicating appropriate programming techniques for a given project.

18.1.3 Unit Testing

Unit testing involves testing the smallest possible unit of an application [Budrovich 2001]. To produce any reliable software application, we absolutely need to integrate unit testing into the development process; however, the granularity of the units is a topic of much argument in the development community. Whereas some developers believe in testing the absolute smallest possible units such as data structures and individual classes, other developers believe in testing *functional* units that may be made of several smaller units. This is not to say that testing functional modules and unit testing are the same thing. Module testing typically refers to testing modules that have an encapsulated piece of functionality that makes sense from the end-user perspective. For example, we may want to test the module that obtains the user's personal profile information. In contrast, from the developer's perspective, we can recognize units that are aggregates of only a few other atomic units (units that cannot be broken down into other meaningful units such as classes and data structures) and have functionally significant importance. For example, testing a class that defines a name called Name, has no methods, and has three different strings representing first name, last name, and middle name is somewhat of a waste of time. However, testing a class called Person that includes some behavior and aggregates Name as well as other classes such as those encapsulating the age, title, and other personal information about the person makes more sense. In object-oriented environments, a good rule of thumb is to unit test all those classes that have significant usage by the application (in our case, Name does not have significant usage outside of a Person).

When it comes to mobile applications, we leave the choice of how unit testing is actually done to the developer's judgment, while noting that it is crucial that the defined units are not too big (for otherwise unit testing begins to lose its value) and not too small (in which case unit testing can begin to slow down the development process unnecessarily).

Unit testing is probably the most neglected type of testing in typical software development practice and is perhaps the most efficient way of catching and fixing software bugs. Unit testing is typically done by the developer(s) of the module being unit tested. For mobile applications, we can use a variety of tools for unit testing:

1. For visual interfaces on mobile devices, there are fairly good emulators that accompany the SDK for most devices.
2. Most voice recognition and speech-synthesis engines provide a development version of the software that can be locally installed on the development platform (Windows-Intel-based PCs, Unix machines, etc.) with the telephony channel redirected to the microphone input.
3. GPS emulators can be used to provide emulation of location-based information.
4. We can use the typical unit testing tools used for stationary applications. These tools are typically language specific. For example, JUnit is an open-source project that allows unit testing of Java programs. There are similar tools for C, C++, and other languages.

Once the developer is satisfied with the quality of code and the functionality of a functionally meaningful chunk of program from the user's perspective (we will call this *module* for the lack of a better word), it is time to get the QA engineers involved. The process typically begins with *black-box testing*.

18.1.4 Black-Box Testing

Black-box testing, sometimes also referred to as functional testing, is done when the module is treated as a black box, we give it some input, and make sure that it produces the right output. In other words, black-box testing assures that the module meets the functional specifications.

Black-box testing of mobile applications must be done with real devices, on the real network, and with the real infrastructure in place. No more usage of emulators is allowed. To perform black-box testing, we need a test plan made up of a road map for testing along with specific test cases that specify what is to be tested. The results of these tests are then recorded for later analysis by the QA and development teams. These test cases must be used for proper regressive testing as more test cases are added at a later time.

For mobile applications, a particular emphasis must be put on testing the functionality that directly demonstrates the relevance of dimensions of mobility: location sensitivity, multichannel user interfaces, etc. Whereas tools can be used for performing black-box tests for those parts of the mobile application that reside on the server side, there are not many testing tools available that run on mobile devices. This is partly because mobile devices are resource-starved and running a testing environment is sometimes difficult if not impossible and partly because mobile applications are fairly young and there are few well-known testing techniques developed for them.

Black-box testing is an area where there is not much dispute over the techniques or the importance of performing such tests. Black-box tests are typically the core of testing done on any software system. Once we are done with black-box testing, it is time to start *white-box testing*.

18.1.5 White-Box Testing

Once again, as its name implies, white-box testing includes performing a variety of tests on the system while looking at the exposed internals of the software. The purpose of white-box testing is to find hidden problems that may not be exposed by black-box testing test cases, to find violations of coding standards, and to expose other problems that only reveal themselves by looking at the execution of the code. This is somewhat similar to "stepping through the code," a technique that many developers use to debug and unit test their programs. The major differences here are that there are a variety of tools for white-box testing and that white-box testing must be performed by the QA team and not the development team.

Once again, as in the case of unit testing, there is much argument over how to do white-box testing, the granularity level at which white-box testing should be done, and the involvement of the development team in the white-box testing process. White-box testing can prove to be difficult and time consuming in the case of mobile applications because of the complexity of the infrastructure and the variation in the code base. The amount of white-box testing done and the distribution of the tasks between the QA and development team depends on the organizational strategy selected by the development team and is orthogonal to development of mobile applications.

There is one place where white-box testing can prove to be invaluable in mobile development and that is in the user interface development. This is the case if a layered approach such as building a generic user interface is used. In this case, if there is a bug in the generic user interface, it is more easily discovered with a white-box test. Fixing such a problem will avoid further bug documentation and reporting of the specialized user interfaces.

18.1.6 Regression Testing

Regression testing is absolutely crucial to assure that new bugs are not introduced into modules that have already been tested and approved. It is done by rerunning all the tests regressively, as various modules are tested and integrated, additional modules are added, and modules are changed. Once again, regression tests must be done on the real environment and infrastructure as opposed to using emulators. Whereas regression testing is typically highly automated for stationary applications, this is tough to do with mobile applications because the computing environment is very distributed, with mobile devices doing some of the computing and the network the rest. Once again, automation of testing on mobile devices often proves to be very difficult because most of them are resource-starved, they run a lot of embedded software, and manufacturers like to upgrade models frequently.

Regression tests must be done at least at the end of each integration cycle—integration happens at the end of each incremental release as the various components are gathered and integrated to make a cohesive application.

Black-box testing, white-box testing, and regression testing are all testing procedures that have proved effective for testing stationary applications. However, each of these testing procedures are greatly affected by the nature of mobile applications and the users of mobile applications. Let us start looking at the additional measures that we need to take for testing mobile applications in greater detail.

18.1.7 Problems Specific to Mobile Applications

The two biggest areas of difference in testing mobile applications and stationary applications lie in usability testing and infrastructure testing. We have already touched upon testing the mobile infrastructure and will look at the usability issues later in this chapter. However, there are other issues too.

First, the device manufacturers, compared to the makers of PCs and servers, have a much higher relevance to the development process. Because mobile devices are typically more commoditized than their stationary counterparts, device manufacturer's rely on changing and improving the devices as a source of revenue stream. This means that devices are changing frequently and the application must constantly be tested on new platforms. Although the same is somewhat true for PCs and servers, the frequency of change in the world of mobile devices is higher by orders of magnitude, and, therefore, so is the effect on the testing process. A widely deployed mobile application that can run on a set of devices requires constant testing on the newest version of the device.

Second, unlike most of stationary networking technologies, which are based on TCP/IP and are fairly open, wireless networks are based on a variety of proprietary and standard protocols and are not nearly as open. This closed environment is partly due to security issues and partly due to the carrier's business models, which typically rely on value-added services. These value-added services are implemented on top of the basic network infrastructure; therefore, to monitor the applications, the carriers keep access to their network and devices fairly closed. This puts us in for another loop in the testing process: We must test the mobile application on whatever networks it is to be deployed on and keep track of any changes to these networks so that proper regression testing can be performed. There are some problems here that might require special consideration during the black-box, white-box, and regression testing stages of a given mobile application:

1. Some quality of service conditions are not repeatable on some networks. It is important not only to perform the test on reasonably wide coverage areas but also to perform the test several times, sometimes with random frequency and sometimes depending on physical conditions such as the weather, to assure of the proper testing results under as many testing conditions as possible.
2. Traffic conditions and patterns can be very difficult to replicate. There may be underlying causes for patterns of usage and connectivity not well known during the unit test, white-box test, black-box test, and stress-testing (testing the application beyond the load that it is meant to take under normal operating conditions) stages.
3. "Certifying" your application with the carrier is something that you might want to consider. "Certification" is a term often used in the software industry to indicate a superficial understanding of a product without thorough theoretical knowledge of concepts that go into it! Vendors use it as a mechanism to produce an outsourced workforce who sells their product as well as implementing it because of a vested interest in the time spent in certification. Nevertheless, certifying your application with the carrier may be something that is worthwhile because 1. all the wireless carriers have an enormous amount of power as they own the infrastructure and 2. certification typically includes thorough testing of the mobile application on the carrier's infrastructure. This testing is normally helped through by the carrier (at some cost, which is typically minimal) and this is somewhat invaluable as there are nuances to the carrier's network about which the carrier knows best.

Though not all mobile applications are wireless, many mobile applications are indeed wireless. And, in the wireless world, the carriers are gods. There are not many of them in any given geographic area; they deal in a market with high barrier to entry and little threat of competition from small entities, and, therefore, can impose their will on the manufacturers and users (within some given price restriction).

Besides the economic power of device manufacturers and carriers, there are indirect effects that they exert that must be taken into account in the testing process. These include the following:

1. Device manufacturers often provide modular power sources (batteries, adapters, etc.) that can be used interchangeably with a variety of devices. The power supply demands of the device must be taken into consideration during testing. For example, some batteries provide a better sustained source of power and others provide better bursts of power. A mobile application that runs on the mobile device has a direct affect on the usage of power on the device. Therefore, the performance, reliability, and stability of an application may depend on the power supply provided with the device. For this reason, it is crucial that devices be tested with the various possible power supplies and that the results be provided to the end users directly (by informing them of things like how long a type of

battery on a type of device will last while running a specific mobile application) or indirectly (by recommending a set of power supply sources to be used or not used with a particular device under specific performance needs).

2. Form factor is of great importance. Although the device manufacturers decide the form factor, they occasionally just design devices with bad form factors or sometimes have to compromise the form factor to appeal to a broad market of users. Form factor is not something that the software development team can affect, but usability testing aspects of the form factor are extremely important as the form factor of a device may render the mobile application useless. For example, if the way you scroll on a particular device is too cumbersome, then either the device should not be supported (if there is as choice of many devices to support the application) or scrolling should be eliminated from the application. Remember one thing: It is better not to support a device than it is to support it ineptly. The unhappy users make their feelings known to all users and after a while your application will get a bad reputation.

Before either testing or development, there is the process of requirements gathering. We looked at the overall software development process for mobile applications closely in Chapter 15. But now, let us look at the requirements-gathering process and its relationship with testing more closely.

18.2 Validating the Mobile Use Cases before Development

As you recall, we mentioned in Chapter 15 that one of the biggest differences between the customers of mobile applications and customers of stationary applications is that, because of the lower amount of exposure, customers do not understand what they can and cannot do or what they should or should not do with mobile applications. (Some would say the same about stationary applications, but because PCs and applications that run on them have become so prevalent, customers certainly have a better idea of what stationary applications can do.) In a sense, the testing process begins immediately after the requirements-gathering process: The requirements should be carefully analyzed, the documentation of the requirements, whether in use cases or some other form, must be tested by an objective third party who was not involved in the requirements-gathering process (QA engineers), and this verification process must be repeated regressively throughout the project as requirements come in.

The dimensions of mobility are those things that make mobile applications inherently different from their stationary counterparts. So, let us see their effect on testing procedures.

18.3 The Effect of the Dimensions of Mobility on Software Testing

In this section, we will look at how the dimensions of mobility affect testing procedures. We have already discussed certain aspects such as limited power supply and QOS. We will now touch upon those areas of the dimensions of mobility and mobile condition of the user that we have yet to discuss or those that deserve further discussion when it comes to testing.

18.3.1 Testing Mobile User Interfaces

We dedicated three chapters of this text to user interface concerns of mobile applications. This is because the multichannel, multimodal, and device-proliferated nature of mobile applications complicate the development of mobile applications by orders of magnitude. This complexity extends into the testing process. Whereas functional testing and usability testing are the two areas of concern for stationary applications, special considerations must be taken into account for multichannel and multimodal applications. In addition to this, testing the usability of a mobile application tends to be more complicated than its stationary counterpart.

18.3.2 Testing Multichannel User Interfaces

Most test plans for user interface testing of stationary applications include testing one interface through one channel. Obviously, this is not the case for mobile applications.

We touched upon various types of ways we can quantify measuring effectiveness of GUIs, including techniques such as direct combination, in Chapter 6. It is important to educate the QA engineers who are testing the mobile user interfaces in such techniques so that they may devise the appropriate test plan for assuring that such optimizations are taken into account.

The testing efforts for the different channels and modes of presenting an application must not be disjointed. In other words, we should either have the same people do the testing for the VUI as those who do the GUI testing or have them work together closely. It is crucial to maintain consistency among the different modes and channels of the user interface and the only way to maintain this is to have a cohesive quality assurance effort that keeps the developers in check.

Quality assurance for stationary applications, particularly for Web applications or desktop applications, are mature areas with specific target clients. Web applications are always rendered on a browser and, like desktop applications, are displayed completely on a GUI (though sound can accompany the application). There are practices that have been perfected for testing such applications. The QA team should be retrained to forget about most of these practices because they assume a certain set of input/output devices and a stationary user. Not only have similar techniques not evolved, but such evolution may not happen for a long time. This is because the mobile device industry is in a high state of flux and many evolutionary steps are being taken, rapidly, in improving and changing mobile devices. Whereas these techniques are evolving, it is important to first determine the metrics for testing a mobile application before actually starting to perform the tests. In other words, for a given mobile application user interface, we need to determine the relevant tests and then design the test cases.

These principles must be applied to the different stages and types of testing (black-box testing, white-box testing, etc.). The multimodal and multichannel nature of mobile applications present us with yet another layer of complexity in usability, white-box, black-box, and regression testing.

18.3.3 Usability Testing

There are an enormous amount of usability-related issues with today's mobile applications. Unfortunately, most of these issues exist because of bad design and insufficient quality assurance. For example, Landay, Mathews, and Waterson [2002] have outlined the following for the users of mobile devices that provide GUI access to Web content:

1. difficulty with scrolling,
2. frequent errors because of connectivity problems,
3. confusing wording of the prompts to get the proper response from the user,
4. long download times, and
5. difficulty with the input mechanisms.

There are many more that have not been outlined here—and that is just for the mobile devices that provide GUI access to Web content. When one adds VUIs and all of the other possible complexities of mobile applications, the usability issues grow exponentially. In this section, we will simply list as many different aspects of usability that are unique to, or at least occur more in, mobile application development as possible.

Perhaps the biggest of the usability issues surrounding mobile applications involves the mobile condition of the user:

1. As verified by Jameson [Jameson 2002], the mobile user is not focused on the task of computing. There are a variety of acoustic and visual distractions as well as time pressure and the mere fact of physical mobility (walking, driving, riding, etc.) that distract from the primary task of computing. This noise has several effects. First, it is a variable that must be taken into account directly when designing VUIs or multimodal user interfaces that use voice for recognition and synthesis purposes. Second, it must be taken into account as a distraction to even purely nonaural user interfaces. When testing mobile applications, the user interface must be tested under real acoustic noise conditions.
2. Previous theory and experimental results suggest that certain features of the user's motor behavior (e.g., tapping especially hard on the touch-screen, or tapping on the wrong icon) ought to occur more frequently under conditions of cognitive load and/or time pressure [Lindmark 2000]. Such behavior must be simulated when testing mobile applications.
3. Varying lighting conditions are another set of environmental variables that must be taken into account when dealing with mobile applications that utilize visual user interfaces. In such cases, proper testing should be done under all "real-life" lighting conditions for all of the use cases.
4. User tolerance for errors is much lower when using mobile applications than stationary applications. There is a variety of reasons involved here. The mobile user does not have as much time and cognitive attention to use a mobile

application because of his or her mobile condition, but there is, once again, some economic realities as well. Mobile devices are less expensive and mobile applications are less costly than their stationary counterparts. The lower price commands a lower customer loyalty: If it does not work, the user will get rid of it and pick up a new device, subscribe to a new network, or use a different application. Besides, as we have previously mentioned, mobile devices are treated more like a VCR than a PC: The user expectations are completely different. Crashes and long waits are absolutely unacceptable, however infrequently they may be.

The first implementation and distribution of WAP applications is a prime example of pure usability testing causing the initial failure in acceptance of a technology. Although WAP itself provides a robust platform, the applications that were built using WAP were HTML applications migrated to WML: the best way to guarantee failure of a mobile application. Users were expected to use the cumbersome keypads to enter significant amounts of data to navigate long trees. This is not to say that they did not do it. SMS has succeeded despite the cumbersome data entry mechanisms. However, transferring Web applications with complex work flows and navigation trees to WML in the restricted user interface caused the failure of a great number of mobile applications and ruined the reputation of WAP and nearly all mobile applications altogether.

Many WAP applications were designed with little or no input from usability testers. Do not be surprised if the entire user interface to a stationary application must be rethought before implementing a mobile interface. Remember that mobile applications are a superset of stationary applications, but this does not mean that the user wants to get everything out of a mobile application that he or she wants out of the equivalent stationary application.

18.4 Stress Testing and Scalability Issues

We noted earlier that the load on a mobile application can be very heavy. There are simple reasons for this—such as the fact that the total number of end-user mobile devices (PDAs, cell phones, GPS systems, etc.) in the world exceeds the total number of desktops used by the users—and more complex reasons—such as the fact that many active transaction solutions are implemented through polling as opposed to true push solutions.

Though most stress test scenarios do not do the real stress scenarios justice, we have to make our best attempt at simulating the stress conditions. For the server-side portion of our mobile application, we can use tools that simulate connected users. For the portion of the application that executes on the mobile device, we are probably faced with some custom development. For example, if the mobile platform allows a background process, we need to test our mobile application as some other background process is consuming a great portion of the resources on the device. It is also important to see how the application, on both servers and the mobile device, reacts when the various parts of the system fail (the server operating system crashes, the network connectivity goes down, the device hangs, etc.). Once again, because of the higher expectations of the mobile user, we need to make sure that the application recovers, in a very graceful manner, from any failures and hangs.

18.5 Testing Location-Based Functionality

If your mobile application uses location-sensitivity technology, then you need to know the accuracy and margin of error for the application and communicate it, accurately, to the user of the application. Remember that reliability is crucial in a mobile application: Incorrect data will alienate the users quickly. When testing location sensitive mobile applications, we must perform the following:

1. Test the application for every applied internationalized and localized version of the application. In other words, unit, functional (black box and white box), and regression testing must be done on the software for every localized and internationalized operational permutation (languages, character sets, etc.).
2. Test the reliability of the infrastructure providing GIS and location-sensitivity information as well as the coupling between the mobile application and this infrastructure.
3. Test the reliability of the location information provided by the location-sensitivity system and assure that the margins of error are acceptable by the location-based logic in the application (white-box test) and by the end user (black-box test and regressions).

This brings us to the end of our discussion on testing mobile applications. We have not treated the testing process of mobile applications with the breadth that it deserves in this text because of scope reasons. We recommend that the reader look into additional sources, such as the references used here, for more information on testing mobile applications. Keep in mind that the importance of testing increases proportionally with the size and budget of the project.

CHAPTER 19

A Case Study

The people in your life are like pillars on your porch. Sometimes they hold you up; sometimes they can lean on you. Sometimes it is just enough to know they are standing by.

19.1 INTRODUCTION

Because of the depth of the design discussions in this text, we have had little chance of discussing coherent examples of mobile applications as applied to the various techniques introduced. The goal of this chapter will be to create a large fictitious project, based on a real project, define requirements for it, and then build the application using the techniques introduced. Obviously, we will not be able to use all of the techniques that we have discussed; there are far too many in this text. Nonetheless, we will aim at discussing as many as possible in reasonable detail.

The example we will be introducing will be in the field of automation. Namely, we will be creating an application to help an electrical repair crew with a variety of tasks in the field. We will start by working on the requirements, then create an architecture that satisfies the requirements, follow it up with a detailed level design, and work our way into implementation.

19.2 REQUIREMENTS DRIVING THE ARCHITECTURE

First, let us understand the basic needs of the customer for which we are building an application. The reader should know that this example is based on the needs of a real company, the Noor Electrical and Engineering Company, located in Costa Mesa, California.

The customer is an electrical field-service company that provides electricians for commercial, industrial, and residential customers. There are two types of jobs:

short-term trouble-shooting and long-term on-site jobs. Trouble-shooting tasks are initiated by a customer calling the company's call center. The jobs are logged into a system at the call center by a phone assistant. The phone assistant filters the calls that are not relevant from those who are from existing or potential customers. The foreperson is then given the qualified call and proceeds to enter the task into a scheduling system.

Before getting the specific use cases from the customer, during an initial meeting, the customer expresses that the following high-level functionalities are required:

1. To provide one integrated application and user interface to deliver all of the necessary functionality (not several different applications that need to be accessed individually).
2. To provide voice access to those tasks where the field technician's hands are occupied by doing some manual task.
3. To provide alerts to the field technicians for cancellation of jobs if they either have not departed to go to the job site or are en route to the job site.
4. To provide real-time travel routes as tasks change throughout the day so as to minimize the time spent in transport (en route from one location to another) by the technicians.
5. To provide all of the functionality of the application on as many devices as possible so that the company is not required to buy new hand-held devices (a desirable feature, but not a requirement).

Typically, customers present the project manager with an entire slew of features that they want when the project manager starts to identify the exact requirements of the project. A good project manager manages to narrow down the feature set into small slices that are separate releases. The incremental release approach often works best for projects where the customers are not technical so that the customer can be involved in the development process as much as possible. This lessens the chance of miscommunication and misconceptions that lead to creation of an application that is significantly different from that required by the customer. (Although there are always some differences between what a software development team interprets of the requirements and what the customer has in mind, the key is to keep these differences to a minimum.) With this in mind, we will utilize use cases to represent the exact features desired from phase 1 of this project. First, here are the verbal descriptions of the use cases:

Use Case 1: Field technician retrieving the schedule for the day on the hand-held device.

Use Case 2: Foreperson sending out an alert to the field technician closest to a particular job site (typically, because of an event that took place unknown to the field technician).

Use Case 3: Field technician retrieving where to go next (map, driving directions, tasks to perform, etc.). There may be also cases where the schedule has changed because of a cancellation.

TABLE 19.1. Mobile Use Case Evaluation Matrix

Relevance Index Table	Use Case 1	Use Case 2	Use Case 3	Use Case 4	Use Case 5	Use Case 6	Use Case 7	Use Case 8
Aural User Interface	0.55	0.50	0.45	0.80	0.80	0.50	0.00	0.45
Location-Based Functionality	0.00	1.00	0.80	0.20	1.00	0.10	0.25	0.00
Active Functionality	0.50	1.00	0.80	1.00	0.80	1.00	0.00	0.00
Wireless Access	1.00	1.00	1.00	1.00	1.00	1.00	1.0	1.00
Multichannel Access	0.20	0.50	0.50	0.90	0.80	0.50	0.00	0.22
Disconnected Usage	1.00	0.00	1.00	1.00	0.20	0.00	0.25	0.50

Use Case 4: Field technician logging the number of hours and the materials spent at the job site.
Use Case 5: Field technician finding the closest materials depot for pickup of a part not in the field unit truck.
Use Case 6: Call center assistant canceling an appointment and alerting the field technician.
Use Case 7: Field technician requesting the schematics of a particular electrical part (such as a power transformer) to view on the device.
Use Case 8: Field technician accessing an electrical knowledge base for a question on an electrical part.

Now, let us see how we came up with our mobile use case evaluation matrix (Table 19.1). There were eleven field technicians, one foreperson, and one call center person. The actors in each use case were all queried about their use of the application and what would be most useful. Table 19.2 shows the answers to a couple of these use cases. These answers were then translated to the numbers seen in Table 19.1.

Note that our example is very crude. There is an entire psychological aspect of how the questions are designed so that the answers reflect the intent of the questioned personnel as accurately as possible. The importance of these types of questionnaires must also be stressed to the participants in the study (the customer). Participants have a tendency to go through these questionnaires quickly and use only a certain set of numbers (for example, use 0, 5, or 10 for all answers).

One of the things that the matrix does is to force us to come up with questions that reveal possible usage of mobile functionality that had never occurred to the customer. For example, the customer may think of an alert as only a text message; however, an alert could also be an automated outbound phone call.

The customer expresses that every field technician currently has a mobile phone with which they are willing to purchase one more device under $300 for every field technician if that device satisfies all the needs of the application. The customer has no server-side hardware infrastructure and wishes to host the software and hardware off-site. After some research, looking at the need for local storage on the

TABLE 19.2. Questionnaire Created for Mobile Use Case Evaluation Matrix

Question	Actor(s)	Answers	Average Score
On a scale of 0 to 10, how important would it be to be able to hear your daily schedule instead of getting a print-out or seeing it on the screen of a PDA or phone?	Field Technician	4 of 11 answered 5 4 of 11 answered 6 1 of 11 answered 0 1 of 11 answered 9 1 of 11 answered 7	5.45 (Use Case 1—Aural User Interface)
On a scale of 0 to 10, how important is it to have access to your schedule throughout the day even when the PDA or cell phone has no connection?	Field Technician	11 of 11 answered 10	10 (Use Case 2—Disconnected Usage)
On a scale of 0 to 10, how important is it to find a technician close to the job site in case of a variety of situations (emergency, no one on that site, etc.)?	Foreperson	1 of 1 answered 10	10 (Use Case 2—Location-Based Functionality)

device (being that some of the functionality has to be accessed in a disconnected mode per use case evaluation matrix) and the availability of location information, we select an unnamed device based on the Palm OS 5.0 that can run a J2ME KVM, is light enough to carry as a cell phone, has cell phone capabilities, and also has Bluetooth connectivity for short-range wireless networking. The device operates on a GPRS/TDMA network (a selection partly influenced by the customer having a contract with a wireless provider whose network is based on GPRS/TDMA).

Before we proceed any further, note that, even in a case where there is not much in the way of infrastructure for a mobile application, there are existing boundaries that impose some decisions. In this case, the customer already owned some cell phones and had a contract with a wireless provider. Also note that many of the technical decisions may be imposed by the financial restrictions at hand, whether the total budget of the project or some restrictions that the customer imposes, budgetary or otherwise, on subsections of the project.

Based on the information we have so far, the first thing we do is to create some mobile use case diagrams based on the Wisdom extensions we introduced previously. It is very important to recognize that although our starting point was UML 1.4, we added many things to represent those properties of mobile applications that UML 1.4 did not properly represent. So, the diagrams here are not really compliant with UML 1.4. They are a superset of what UML 1.4 gives us.

First, we look at Figure 19.1, which shows us the basic actors communicating with three of the basic use cases. If you do not remember what some of the symbols that we introduced with our extensions mean, please refer back to the previous chapters, particularly Chapter 6.

Based on the use cases and our evaluation of the relevance of the various dimensions of mobility, we now need to think about a basic architecture for the application.

The budget of this project is very small; therefore, we will stay away from any experimental technologies and go with the proved client–server architecture. Essentially, we will design a system comprised of a Java application running on the Palm OS 5.0 – based device with a PointBase (a commercial product that offers databases for small devices) database that stores some local information. For the aural access to the system (the VUI), we have both a client piece and a server piece. In the case of the PDA, the voice is recorded on the device and sent to the server through a GPRS connection. When a PDA is not available, the user's will be calling in and accessing the VUI through telephony.

When it comes to the user interface, we decided to take an open-source XForms browser, modify it, and make it into the shell for the user interface of the PDA. The actual XForms documents are cached on the PDA and stored centrally on the server. Figure 19.2 shows the very high level components in action.

Note that we intend to design and implement the server-side application so that there may be differing number of instances of each. Also, note that we may have not represented all of the possible components such as routers, front-end load-balancing servers (e.g., instances of Apache), or other supporting subsystems. We

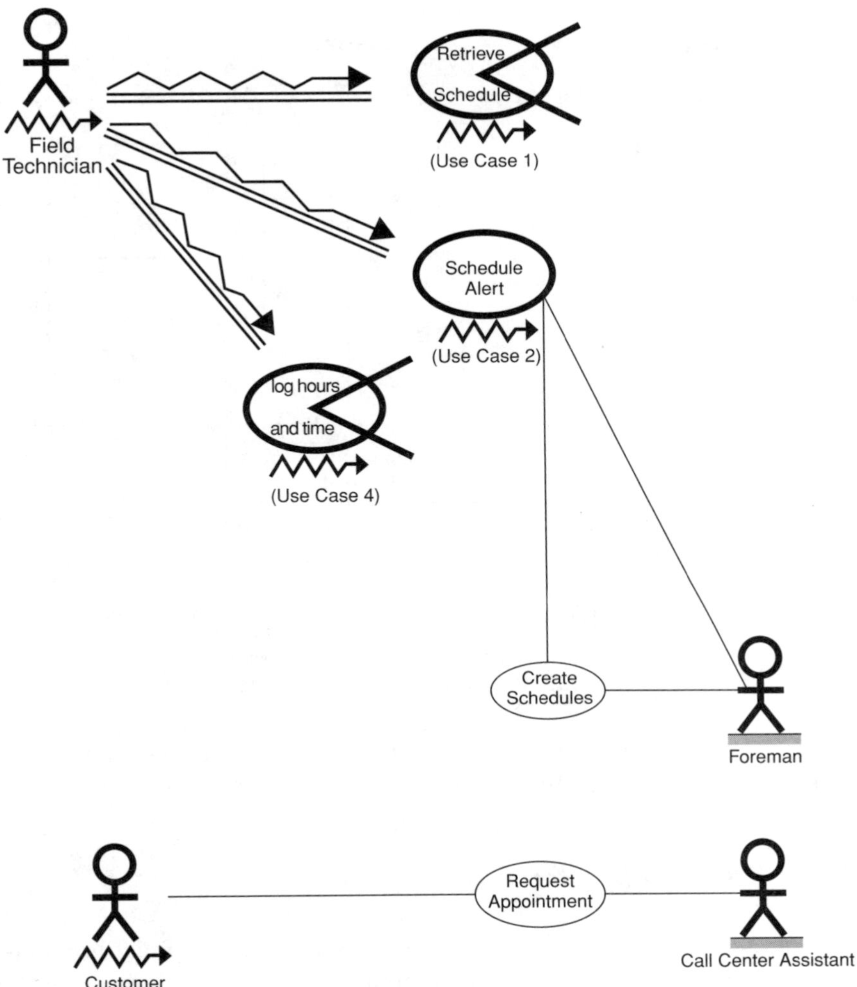

FIGURE 19.1. Mobile Use Cases for Use Cases 1, 2, and 4.

have shown the basic features of the system. Next, we look into the individual systems.

As we have discussed in the previous chapters, the telephony system, the voice recognition system, the database, and the GIS system are server-side components that we buy. This may be a purchase through an application service provider or the purchase of the actual software and the infrastructure necessary to operate the software. In our instance, the operation is far too small to own and maintain the hardware. Therefore, we choose a VSP who gives us machines running Linux with Intel Dialogic equipment for the incoming calls. We then use Nuance software hosted at the VSP's site to do the recognition as well. We have an application service provider provide both the machines and the database for our application. The GIS system is provided by a Web service interface through yet another application

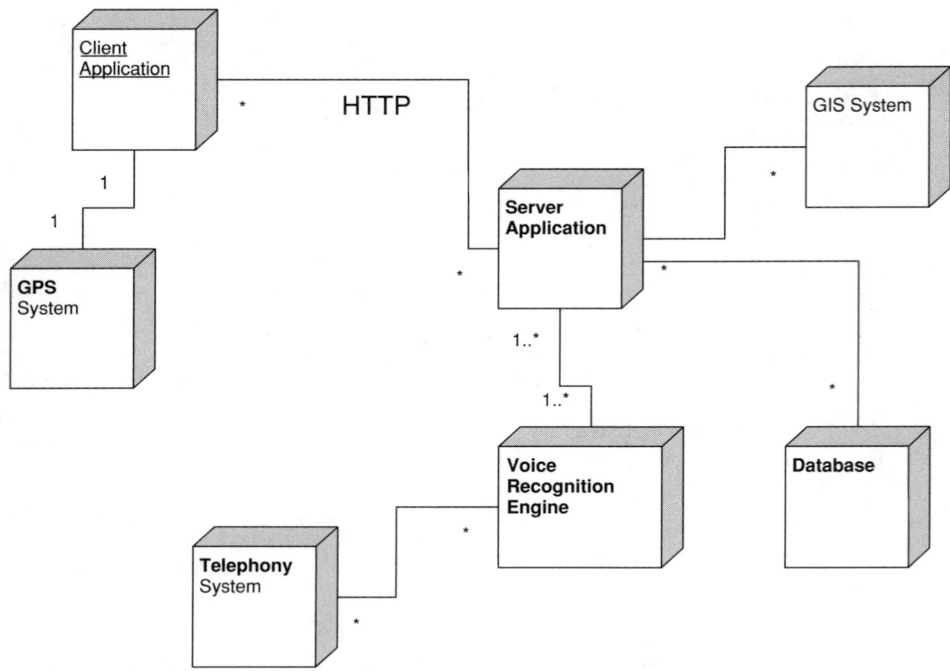

FIGURE 19.2. Case Study Deployment Diagram.

service provider. Now, let us discuss the detailed design and selection of specific implementation tools and technologies.

19.3 THE DETAILED DESIGN

The bulk of the development effort will be in two parts: developing the client-side application for the Palm OS 5.0 – based mobile device and developing the server-side application. Let us start with the client side. We know that we have to store some information on the client and that this information has to be queried in a variety of ways when the device is disconnected. We also know that much of the functionality of the application depends on the awareness of the location of the mobile device, both by the PDA itself and the server. Based on this and the user interface decisions that we mentioned in the last section, we come up with a basic component diagram of Figure 19.3. Figure 19.4 shows the basic components on the server.

The GPS unit comes with its own APIs; we have to write some code to make that interface adapt with the functionality that our application needs. Namely, our application needs to periodically send its location back to the server so that the foreperson is always aware of, at least, the approximate location of any given field technician.

Next, because we decided to first record the voice interactions, then send them to the server, and get back an audio recording in response, we need an audio

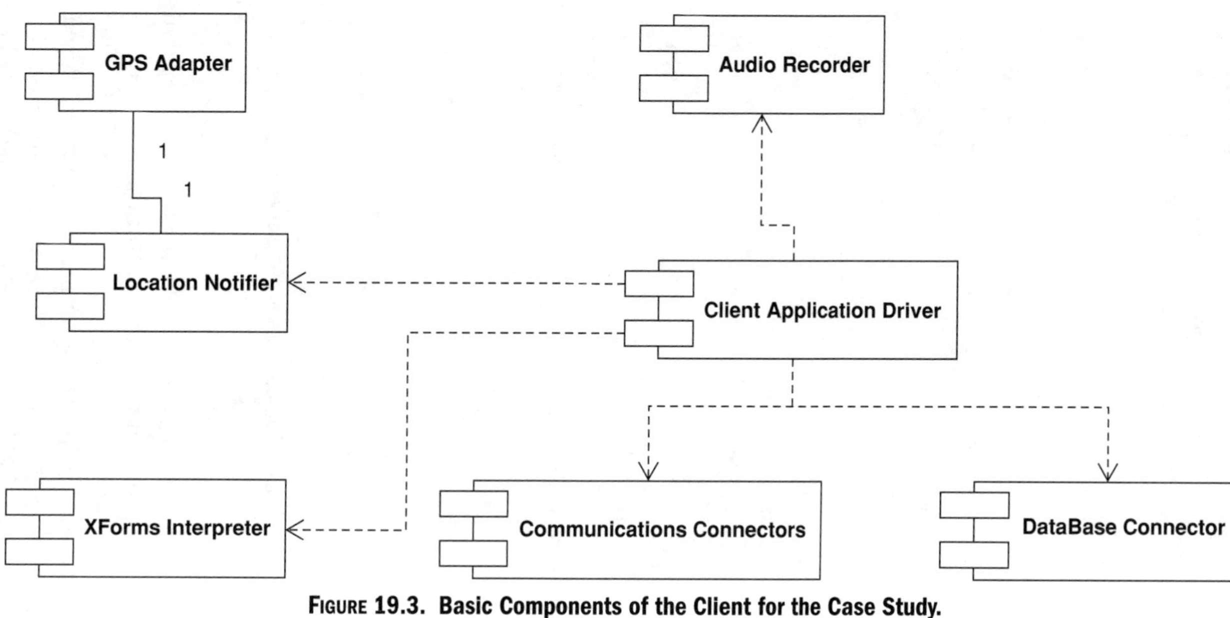

FIGURE 19.3. Basic Components of the Client for the Case Study.

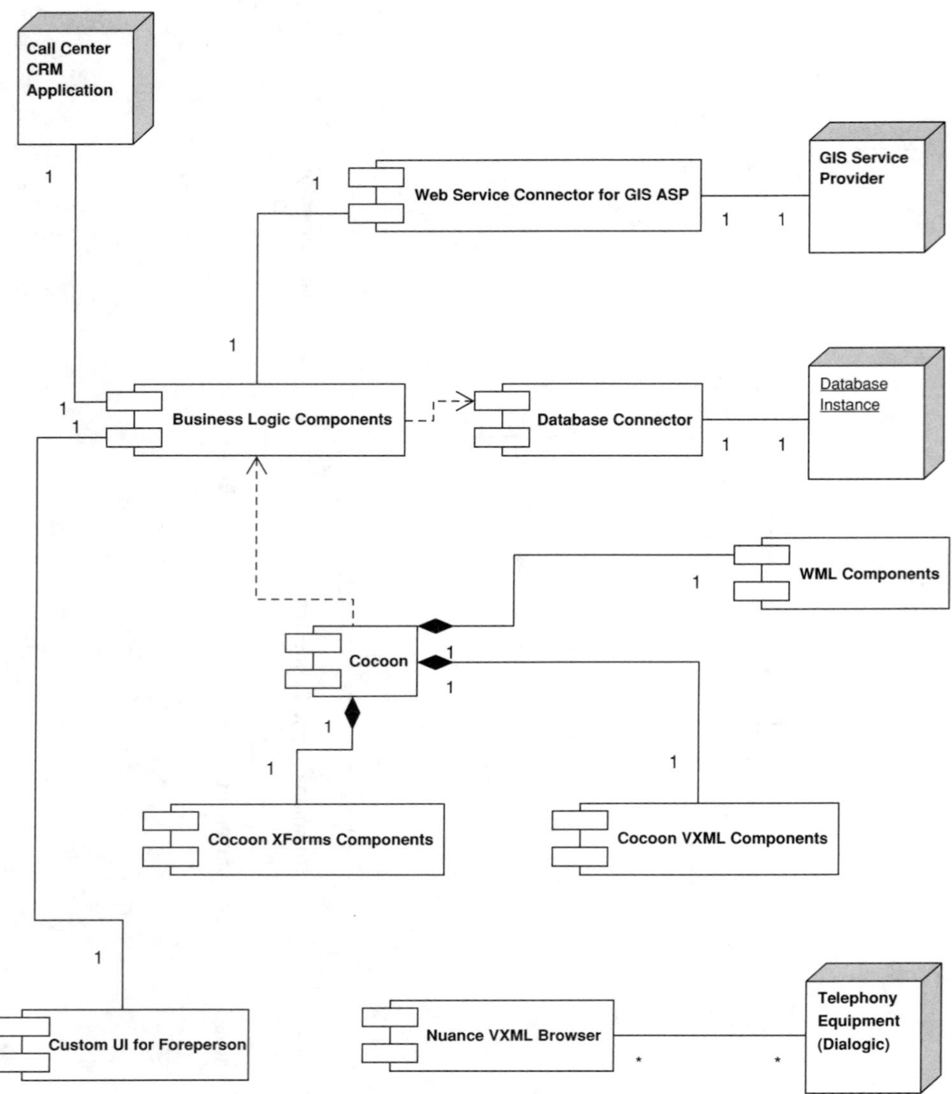

FIGURE 19.4. Basic Components of the Server for the Case Study.

recorder and player adapter that takes advantage of the capabilities offered on the device and lets us programmatically control those features through the user interface.

Next, we need to take care of the disconnected operation. Based on the amount of persistent memory available on the device, the PointBase database lets us create a basic schema and some queries to get our data out of the local database. We can use this database to record user's interactions when he or she cannot connect to the network or, conversely, use some cached information without going back to the server.

Note that we selected Apache's Cocoon as part of the engine for the system. First, we are going to build a set of core components that represent the base functionality of the application: things like what a time sheet is, the interface to the inventory database, when alerts should be sent out, etc. Certain parts of the application must then be accessed through a user interface on the mobile device. These parts of the application may be accessed through a telephone call that connects the user to a VUI, a graphical interface provided by the PDA (thick-client application written in J2ME that we already designed), or the WML browser on the existing cell phones. We use Cocoon to transform the basic user interface written in XForms to these various user interfaces.

19.4 THE IMPLEMENTATION

A discussion of the implementation of the entire application is beyond the scope of this textbook. So, we will only take a couple of use cases and bring them all the way to the final implementation. Let us start with the fourth use case, where the user has to fill out his or her time sheet. We need to recognize the major interactions between the user and the system so that we can design our XForms interactions properly. This is the perfect place to bring in some more of the user interface – based extensions offered by Wisdom extensions that focus on the interactions of the user with the system. As you remember, XForms allows us to model the user interactions with a user interface without specifying the details of a particular type of user interface. Specifically, the dialogue/task diagrams of the Wisdom interaction model will fit this best.

Figure 19.5 shows the dialogue model specifying the tasks for one of the use cases. Note that the amount of detail could be much greater. For the case study, we created such high-level diagrams for every use case. We use the term CRUD prevalently to indicated Create, Read, Delete, and Update. Because the technician does not have the right to create appointments, you can see that there is no task for creating appointments. However, there are tasks for updating (logging the appointment details after the appointment is completed).

We followed that up by creating some presentation diagrams like that shown in Figure 19.6. These also fall under the interaction diagram category under Nunes' Wisdom methodology.

Once again, you should note that Figure 19.6 could be much more complicated to explain all of the details of the user interactions. Note, however, the great value of Figures 19.5 and 19.6: We can practically design the basics of our XForms-based interface on the basis of these two diagrams structurally and behaviorally. Our tasks correspond, either in a one-to-one cardinality or a one-to-many cardinality, to XForms document that represent the interaction of the user with the system in a generic manner as discussed in Chapter 5. For example, Figure 19.7 shows a snippet from an XForms document that represents the interaction required for the on-site cancellation. Note that we are just showing two segments of the XForms document. The developer may choose to modularize the XForms

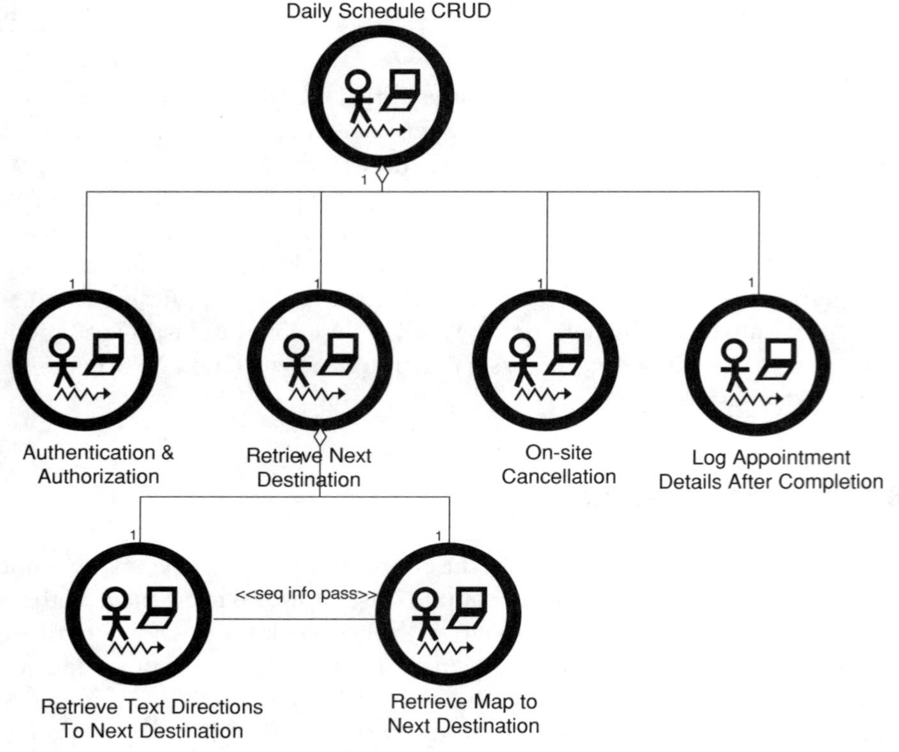

FIGURE 19.5. Dialogue Model of the Basic Tasks for Use Case 1.

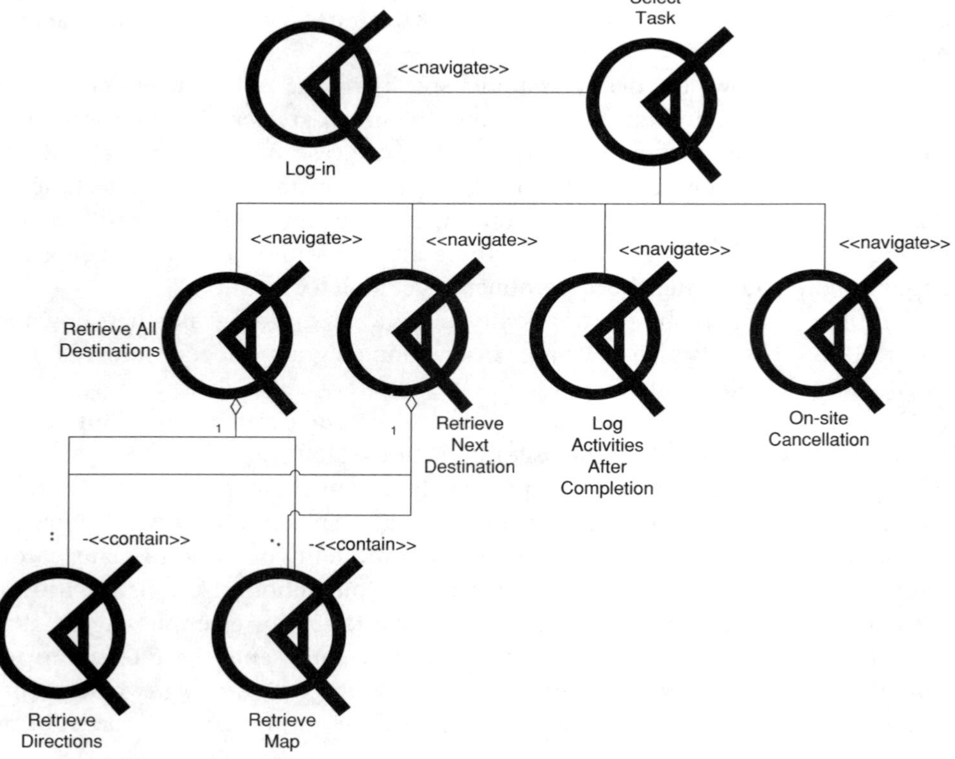

FIGURE 19.6. Presentation Diagram of Part of Use Case 1 for the Case Study.

```
...
<input ref="JobName" xml:lang="en" navIndex=1 accessKey="#">
    <caption
xlink:href="http://localhost/languagebundle.xml>
    Please Say The Job Name.
    </caption>
    <hint navIndex="1" xml:lang="en">
    The Job Name is the company name for commercial and
      industrial projects. It is the home owner's first name
      and then last name for residential projects.
    </hint>
</input>
...
<!-- There is some code between these two segments that we
  are not showing to keep the example readable. -->
...
<selectOne ref="domain:Cancellation">
    <item navIndex="2" accessKey="1">
        <caption>Cancel Job at Customer Request</caption>
        <value>Cancel</value>
    </item>
    <item navIndex="3" accessKey="2">
        <caption>Delay Job at Customer Request</caption>
        <value>Delay</value>
    </item>
    <item navIndex="4" accessKey="2">
        <caption>Customer Not Present</caption>
        <value>Absent</value>
    </item>
</selectOne>
...
```

FIGURE 19.7. Snippet from the XForms Document for the User Interface of Use Case 1.

documents to as granular as needed. There is no science to this; this is typical of modularization in software. The canonical modularization is typically domain dependent (if such a thing as a canonical modularization exists, which is debatable in itself).

Once we have the XForms documents, we have a generic user interface that can be specialized for the mobile device running the J2ME application, for a server-side VUI, or for a WAP browser by specializing to WML. Obviously, we could easily extend this system to support other types of user interfaces.

We use PAC-TG on the server side for the implementation of the various components. We initially try to write an XForms interpreter with J2ME for the device that has been selected. However, it becomes clear that doing everything at run time makes the application very slow owing to the limitations of the device and J2ME itself. So, we add a minor but notable tweak: We use our specialization framework of Cocoon, write a component to generate an intermediate format that is easier to consume by a J2ME client, and then write the J2ME client to consume that format instead of the XForms documents themselves. What is then published, by Cocoon, for usage by J2ME on the client side is optimized for J2ME so that we do not have to do a great amount of run-time parsing of XForms. In this manner, we still have the benefit of using XForms to model the user interactions in a generic way, specializing these interactions in a uniform manner to different types of user interfaces.

19.5 Summary

In this chapter, we tried to tie in a bit of every concept introduced in this book. Obviously, we were not able to integrate everything we learned because real projects do not require every tool in the shop. For example, because of the small size of this project, we never considered mobile agents. Mobile agents are still a very young technology; therefore, the development and deployment of a mobile application with mobile agents involves at least some research. Although this may be justifiable, given the benefits mentioned in Chapter 9, in the larger projects, for smaller projects with smaller budgets, it is not a good fit. We also left out the cycle of mobile application development that we previously discussed and the integration of quality control and testing.

Overall, you were able to see how we started with requirements, assessed those requirements, started creating various UML diagrams, and then continued on with writing actual code. If we were to implement the real project, we may end up with twenty to thirty different diagrams, several XForms documents, and several transformation components (in this case probably written using XSPs and XSLs for Cocoon).

This brings us to the end of our text. It has been a long journey! At times, you may have thought that we were jumping around frequently and introducing lots of new ideas. This was unavoidable because of the multidimensional nature of mobile application development in a complete manner. If you take away one thing from this book, it should be that developing mobile applications is fundamentally different from developing applications for the Web or for the PC desktop, or from developing any other type of applications. Developers with experience in distributed application development will have the least amount of difficulty getting used to mobile development.

References

[3GPP 2000] *3rd Generation Partnership Project: Technical Specification Group SA WG3; A Guide to 3rd Generation Security*, 3G TR 33.900, 3GPP TSG, 2000.

[ACSS 1998] *W3C CSS 2 Aural Style Sheets Specification*. 1999, available at http://www.w3.org/TR/1998/REC-CSS2–19980512/aural.html.

[Afnan 2002] *Mobile Code for Mobile Devices: Migration for Improved Application Performance*. O. Afnan, Carleton University, Ottawa, Canada, 2002.

[Agarwal, Starobinski, and Trachtenberg 2000] *On the Scalability of Data Synchronization Protocols for PDA's and Mobile Devices*. S. Agarwal, D. Starobinski, and A. Trachtenberg, Boston University, 2000.

[Agre et al. 2001] *A Layered Architecture for Location-Based Services in Wireless Ad Hoc Networks*. J. Agre, A. Akinyemi, L. Ji, R. Masuka, and P. Thakkar, IEEE Press, November 2001 available at http://www.flacp.fujitsulabs.com/~rmasuoka/papers/200203-LocationProtocol7.doc.

[Alatalo and Peraaho 2001] *Designing Mobile-Aware Adaptive Hypermedia*. T. Alatalo and J. Peraaho, University of Oulu, Finland, OWLA project, 2001, available at http://owla.oulu.fi.

[AMASE 1999] *AMASE Bench Marking Report*. L. Sacks, T. Michalareas, and W. S. Lee, University College London, 1992, available at http://www.ee.ucl.ac.uk/~pants/projects/amase/.

[Amyot and Andradel 2001] *Description of Wireless Intelligent Network Services with Use Case Maps*. D. Amyot and R. Andradel, University of Ottawa, 2001.

[Andersson 2002] *Mobile Positioning—Where You Want to Be!* C. Andersson, Wireless Developer Network, 2002, available at http://www.wirelessdevnet.com/channels/lbs/features/mobilepositioning.html.

[Apache 2000] Apache Software Foundation, available at http://www.apache.org.

[Apache XML 2002] Cocoon Web site at Apache Foundation, http://xml.apache.org/cocoon.

[Apaydin 2002] *Networked Humanoid Animation Driven by Human Voice Using Extensible 3D, H-ANIM, and Java Speech Open Standards*. O. Apaydin, Thesis, United States

Navy Post Graduate School, Monterey, CA, 2002, available at http://www.movesinstitute.org/Theses/ApaydinThesis.pdf.

[Appleby et al. 2000] *An Introduction to IBM WebSphere Everyplace Suite Version 1.1*. J. R. Rodriguez, R. Appleby, B. Bisgaard, H. Wang, A. McGory, A. Mryhij, A. Patton, and M. Omarjee, IBM Corporation, International Technical Support Organization, Research Triangle Park, N.C.

[Arbaugh 2003] Firewalls: An Outdated Defense. W. A. Arbaugh, *IEEE Computer Magazine*, Vol. 36, No. 6, June 2003, 112–113.

[Asensio et al. 2001] *UML Profiles for the Specification and Instrumentation of QOS Management Information in Distributed Object-Based Applications*. J. I. Asensio, V. A. Villagra, J. E. Lopez de Vergara, J. J. Berrocal, Technical University of Madrid, Spain, 2001.

[Aziz and Diffie 1993] *Privacy and Authentication for Wireless Local Area Networks*. A. Aziz and W. Diffie, Sun Microsystems, 1993.

[Bahl 2002] *An Overview of Cell Search in WCDMA*. S. K. Bahl, University of Maryland, 2002.

[Balani 2002] *Build Java Apps, Like an EPOC-based Phone, for the Symbian OS*. N. Balani, IBM Developer Works, available at http://developer.ibm.com.

[Bannon et al. 2002] *Extraction of Axis OpenBT Bluetooth Stack*. R. Bannon, A. Chin, F. Kassam, and A. Roszko, University of Waterloo, CS 798 Software Architecture Course Notes, 2002.

[Baragry and Reed 1998] “Why Is It So Hard to Define Software Architecture?” J. Baragry and C. Reed, *IEEE Conference Proceedings, Asia Pacific Software Engineering Conference*, IEEE, 1998.

[Bauer 2001] “UML Class Diagrams: Revisited in the Context of Agent-Based Systems.” B. Bauer in *Proceedings of Agent-Oriented Software Engineering*, Springer-Verlag, Heidelberg, Germany, 2001, 101–118.

[Bauer, Odell, and Muller 2001] *Agent UML: A Formalism for Specifying Multiagent Interaction Agent-Oriented Software Engineering*. P. Ciancarini and M. Wooldridge, eds., Springer-Verlag, pp. 91–103, 2001.

[Baumeister, Koch, and Mandel 1999] *Towards a UML Extension for Hypermedia Design*. H. Baumeister, N. Koch, and L. Mandel, Institut für Informatik Ludwig-Maximilians-Universität München and Forschungsinstitut für Angewandte Software Technologie (FAST e. V.), 1999.

[Beresford and Stajano 2003] *Location Privacy in Pervasive Computing*. A. R. Beresford and F. Stajano, *IEEE Pervasive Computing Magazine*, Vol. 2, No. 1, March 2003, 46–55.

[Bergenti and Poggi 2001] *LEAP: A FIPA Platform for Handheld and Mobile Devices*. F. Bergenti and A. Poggi, 2001, available at http://leap.crm-paris.com/public/docs/ATAL2001.pdf.

[Bernsen 2002] *Multimodality in Language and Speech Systems—From Theory to Design Support Tool*. N. O. Bernsen, Kluwer Academic Publishers, 2002.

[Berre 2001] *The Model-Driven Approach to Geographic Information System Standardization—Lessons Learned*, A. J. Berre, SINTEF, Oslo, Norway, Distributed Information Systems, 2001, available at http://www.omg.org/news/meetings/workshops/presentations/uml2001_presentations/08-3_Berre-Case_Study_GIS_Final.pdf.

[B’Far 2000] “Next Generation of Internet: The 4th-Tier Is Born.” R. B’Far, *IEEE Tools 2000 Conference Proceeding*, IEEE, 2000.

[Bisdikian 1999] "L2CAP—Logical Link Control." C. Bisdikian in *Bluetooth Developer's Conference Proceedings*, 1999.

[Bluetooth] Bluetooth Specifications, available at http://www.bluetooth.org.

[Bolcer 2000] "Magi: An Architecture for Mobile and Disconnected Work Flow." G. A. Bolcer, Endeavor's Technology, *IEEE Internet Computing*, May–June 2000.

[Bolcer and Oreizy 2000] *Introducing Peer-to-Peer*. G. Bolcer and P. Oreizy, White paper, Endeavors Technology, 2000.

[Booch et al. 1999] *UML for XML Schema Mapping Specification*. G. Booch, M. Christerson, M. Fuchs, and J. Koistinen. Rational Rose Corporation and CommerceOne Inc., 1999.

[Bozinovska and Gusev] *Push Technology*. N. Bozinovska and M. Gusev, Institute of Informatics, Faculty of Natural Sciences and Mathematics, SS Cyril and Maethodius University, Macedonia.

[Brannan 2003] *How to Build an XMLForm Wizard*. H. Brannan, Apache Software Foundation, 2002–2003.

[Bray and Brickley 2001] *What Is RDF*? T. Bray and D. Brickley, XML.com, available at http://www.xml.com/pub/a/2001/01/24/rdf.html.

[Brecht et al. 2002] *SRI's Digital Earth Project*. Y. Leclerc, M. Reddy, M. Eriksen, J. Brecht, and D. Colleen, Stanford Research Institute, 2002.

[Broadbent and Marti 2002] "Location Aware Mobile Interactive Guides: Usability Issues." J. Broadbent and P. Marti, CB&J and University of Siena. *Proceedings of the Fourth International Conference on Hypermedia and Interactivity in Museums (ICHIM97)*, 1997.

[Brown and Singh 1996] *M-UDP: UDP for Mobile Cellular Networks*. K. Brown and S. Singh, University of South Carolina, 1996.

[Brown et al. 1998] *AntiPatterns: Refactoring Software, Architectures, and Projects in Crisis*. W. H. Brown, R. C. Malveau, H. W. McCormick III, and T. J Mowbray, Wiley, 1998.

[Budrovich 2001] "Techniques for Preventing Wireless System Software Errors." V. Budrovich, *Proceedings of Wireless One, SIGS 101 Conference*, 2001.

[Bunt and Romary 2002] *Towards Multimodal Content Representation*. H. Bunt and L. Romary, Computation Linguistics and AI, Tilsburg University, Netherlands, and University de Nancy, France, 2002.

[Burnett, Prekop, and Rainsford 2001] *Intimate Location Modeling for Context Aware Computing*. M. Burnett, P. Prekop, and C. Rainsford, Department of Defense, Fern Hill Park, Australia, 2001.

[Buschke et al. 1998] *How to Increase Security in Mobile Networks by Anomaly Detection*. R. Buschke, D. Kesdogan, and P. Reichl, *Informatik* 4, 1998.

[Buschmann et al. 1996] *Pattern Oriented Software Architecture: A System of Patterns*. F. Buschmann, R. Meunier, H. Rohnert, P. Sommerlad, and M. Stal, Wiley, 1996.

[Campbell 2001] Wireless and Mobile Networking Course Notes, E6951, Mobile IP. A. T. Campbell, Columbia University, 2001.

[Candolin 2000] *Security Issues for Wearable Computing and Bluetooth Technology*. C. Candolin, Helsinki University of Technology, 2000.

[Candolin 2002] *Transaction Privacy in Wireless Networks*. C. Candolin, Helsinki University of Technology, 2002.

[CC/PP P3P W3C 2001] *CC/PP Implementer's Guide: Privacy and Protocols*. H. Ohto, L. Suryanarayana, and J. Hjelm, W3C Working Draft, December 20, 2001.

[CC/PP W3C Specification] *Composite Capability/Preferences Profiles (CC/PP): Structure and Vocabularies*, W3C Working Draft 15 March 2001, available at http://www.w3.org/TR/2001/WD-CCPP-struct-vocab-20010315.

[CCML 2002] *Voice Browser Call Control*. R. J. Auburn, 2002, available at http://www.w3.org/TR/ccxml/.

[Chess 1993] "Itinerant Agents for Mobile Computing." D. Chess, B. Grosof, C. Harrison, D. Levine, C. Parris, and G. Tsudik, *Journal of Personal Communication*, Vol. 2, No. 5, October 1993, 139–151.

[Cheyer and Julia 1995] *Multimodal Maps: An Agent-Based Approach*. A. Cheyer and L. Julia, SRI International, June 9, 1995.

[Claessens et al. 2003]. "Pioneering Advanced Mobile Privacy and Security." J. Claessens, A. Fuchsberger, C. Gunther, S. Holtmanns, G. Horn, K. Howker, R. J. Hulsebosch, C. Mitchell, K. Paterson, B. Preneel, D. Schellekens, and M. Schuba, *Security for Mobility*, IEEE Communications Series, Vol. 51, IEEE Press, 2003, 383–432.

[Clarkin 2003] "10 Tips for Mobile Security." M. Clarkin, *Communication News*, January 2003, available at http://www.comnews.com/stories/articles/co/03wireless.html.

[Cocoon 2002] *Introducing Cocoon 2.0*. S. Mazzocchi, February 2002, available at http://www.xml.com/pub/a/2002/02/13/cocoon2.html.

[Consolvo and Walker 2003] "Using the Experience Sampling Method to Evaluate Ubicomp Applications." S. Consolvo and M. Walker in *IEEE Pervasive Computing*, Vol. 2, No. 2, April–June 2003. 24–30.

[Cook 2001] *Software Engineering Concerns for Mobile Agent Systems*. J. Cook, New Mexico State University, 2001.

[Corradini and Cohen 2002] *Multimodal Speech-Gesture Interface for Handfree Painting on a Virtual Paper Using Partial Recurrent Neural Networks as Gesture Recognizer*. A. Corradini and P. R. Cohen, Oregon Graduate Institute for Science and Technology, 2002.

[Coutaz 2002] *Software Architecture Modeling for User Interfaces*. J. Coutaz, Laboratoire CLIPS (IMAG), 2002.

[Coutaz et al. 2003] *Towards Automatic Evaluation of Multimodal User Interfaces*. J. Coutaz, D. Salber, and S. Balbo, ISOLDE Publications, *Knowledge Based Systems*, Vol. 6, No. 4, 2003.

[Cranefield 2001] *UML and the Semantic Web*. S. Cranefield, Department of Information Science, University of Otago, New Zealand, 2001.

[Cranefield et al. 1999] "UML as an Ontology Modeling Language." S. Cranefield and M. Purvis in *Proceedings of the Workshop on Intelligent Information Integration, 16th International Joint Conference on Artificial Intelligence 1999*, ACM, 1999, 41–42.

[Crease, Gray, and Cargill 2001] *Using Location Information in an Undergraduate Computing Science Laboratory Support System*. M. Crease, P. Gray, and J. Cargill, University of Glasgow, 2001.

[Dahl 2003] "The Role of Speech in Mutilmodal Applications." D. Dahl in *Speech Technology Magazine*, May/June 2003.

[Davis and Prashar 2002] *Latency Performance of SOAP Implementations.* D. Davis and M. Prashar, IEEE Cluster Computing and the GRID, IEEE, Compaq Corporation, and Department of Computer Science at Rutgers University, 2002.

[DCM 2001] *A Complete Solution for Remote Synchronization*, Version 1.0. DCM Technologies LTD, August 6, 2001.

[Development tools for Mobile and Embedded Applications 2002] Microsoft Corporation, 2002, available at http://msdn.microsoft.com; C. Muench.

[Dewan 2002] *Replication for Mobile Computing.* P. Dewan, University of North Carolina, 2002.

[Dimitri 2002] *Mobile Platforms for Mobile Agents.* V. Dimitri, University of Brussels at Vrije, 2002.

[Dix et al. 1998] *Human-Computer Interaction*, A. J. Dix, J. E. Finlay, G. D. Abowd, and R. Beale, Prentice Hall Europe, 1998.

[Djenidi et al. 2002] *Dynamic Based Agent Reconfiguration of Multimedia Multimodal Architecture.* H. Djenidi, A. Ramdane-Cherif, Pr. C. Tadj, and Pr. N. Levy, Electrical Engineering Department, Ecole de Technologie Superieure, 2002.

[Djuknic and Richton 2002] *Geolocation and Assisted-GPS*, G. M. Djuknic and R. E. Richton., Bell Laboratories, Lucent Technologies, 2002.

[Domnitcheva 2002] *Location Modeling: State of the Art Challenges.* S. Domnitcheva, Distributed Systems Group, Swiss Federal Institute of Technology, 2002.

[Dru and Saada 2000] *Location-Based Mobile Services: The Essentials.* M.-A. Dru and S. Saada, 2000, available at http://atr.alcatel.de/hefte/01i_1/gb/pdf_gb/14drugb.pdf.

[Dubinko 2002] *Interactive Web Services with XForms*, M. Dubinko, January 2002, available at http://www.xml.com/pub/a/2001/09/26/xforms.html.

[ECMA TR-61 1992] *User Interface Taxonomy Report.* European Computer Manufacturer Association, 1992.

[EMMA W3C 2003] *EMMA: Extensible Multimodal Annotation Markup Language.* R. Pieraccini, W. Chou, D. A. Dahl, and D. Raggett, W3C Working Draft, August 11, 2003.

[Ericsson 2002] *Wideband Code-Division Multiple-Access.* Ericsson, 2002, available at http://www.ericsson.com/technology/WCDMA.shtml.

[Eronen 2000] *JINI–A Technology for Interconnecting Heterogeneous Devices.* L. Eronen, Department of Computer Science, University of Helsinki, available at http://www.cs.helsinki.fi/u/campa/teaching/laur-final.pdf.

[EURESCOM P1104 2002] *Multimodal Multilingual Information Services for Small Mobile Terminals.* L. Boves and E. den Os, eds., Project P1104, EURESCOM, 2002.

[FAA 1999] *A Human Factors Process Survey of the Ground Delay Program—Enhancements.* Federal Aviation Administration and Crown Consulting, Document No. G004-001-002, 1999.

[Falk and Robbins 1997] *An Explanation of the Architecture of the MMS Standard.* H. Falk and J. Robbins, 1997, available at http://www.sisconet.com/downloads/mmsarch.pdf.

[Fasbender et al. 1996] "Analysis of Security and Privacy in Mobile IP." A. Fasbender, D. Kesdogan, and O. Kubitz, Lehrstuhl fur Informatik 4, *Proceedings of 4th International Conference on Telecommunication Systems, Modeling and Analysis*, 1996.

[Fielding 2000] *Architectural Styles and the Design of Network-Based Software Architectures.* Roy Thomas Fielding, Dissertation, University of California at Irvine, 2000.

[FIPA Arch 2001] *FIPA Abstract Architecture Specification*, 2001, available at http://www.fipa.org/specs/fipa00001.

[Flach and Courvoisier 2001] "XML-based Multimedia Content Management for Wireless-Oriented Applications." G. Flach and T. Courvoisier in *CG Topics Magazine*, 2001, available at http://www.inigraphics.net/press/topics/2001/issue2/2_01010.pdf.

[Flippo et al. 2003] *A Multimodal Framework: Rapid Development of Multiodal Systems.* F. Flippo, A. Krebs, and I. Marsic, Rutgers University, 2003, available at http://www.caip.rutgers.edu/disciple/publications/icmi2003.pdf.

[Foley and Van Dam 1983] *Fundamentals of Interactive Computer Graphics.* J. D. Foley and A. Van Dam, Addison-Wesley, 1983.

[Fowler and Scott 1999] *UML Distilled*, 2nd ed. M. Fowler and K. Scott, Addison-Wesley, 1999.

[Franklin and Zdonik 1998] *Data in Your Face: Push Technologies in Perspective.* M. Franklin and S. Zdonick, ACM Publications, 1998.

[Fuggetta et al. 1998] "Understanding Code Mobility." A. Fuggetta, G. P. Picco, and G. Vigna, in *IEEE Transactions on Software Engineering*, Vol. 24, No. 5, 1998, 342–361.

[Fujino 2002] *Patterns for Analogous Representation.* T. Fujino, InArcadia, Ltd., Tokyo, Japan, PLOP, 2002.

[Gamma et al. 1995] *Design Patterns.* E. Gamma, R. Helm, R. Johnson, and J. Vlissides, Addison-Wesley, p. 4, 1995.

[Gamma et al. 1999] *Design Patterns, Elements of Reusable Object-Oriented Software.* E. Gamma, R. Helm, R. Johnson, and J. Vlissides, Addison-Wesley, 1999.

[Garber 2002] "Will 3G Really Be the Next Big Wireless Technology?" L. Garber in *IEEE Computer Magazine*, Vol. 35, No. 1, January 2002, 26–32.

[Gervais and Muscutariu 2000] *Towards an ADL for Designing Agent-Based Systems.* M.-P. Gervais and F. Muscutariu, LIP6 and University of Paris X, 2000.

[GML 3.0] *Open GIS Geography Markup Language (GML) Implementation Specification.* S. Cox, P. Daisey, R. Lake, C. Portele, and A. Whiteside, January 2003.

[GML Specifications 2002] *The OpenGIS Geography Markup Language (GML) Specifications*, 2002, available at http://www.opengis.org/pressrm/summaries/20011127.TS.GML.pdf.

[Goβmann and Specht 2001] *Location Models for Augmented Environments.* J. Goβmann and M. Specht, Hyperinteraction with Physical Spaces (HIPS) as supported by EU LTR project in ESPRIT, 2001.

[Goose et al. 2002] "Toward Improving the Mobile Experience with Proxy Transcoding and Virtual Composite Devices for a Scalable Bluetooth LAN Access Solution." S. Goose, G. Schneider, R. Tanikella, H. Mollenhauer, P. Menard, Y. Le Floc'h, and P. Pillan, in *IEEE Proceedings of the Third International Conference on Mobile Data Management* (MDM.02), IEEE Publications, 2002, 169–170.

[Gorin et al. 2002] "Automated Natural Spoken Dialogue." A. L. Gorin, A. Abella, T. Alonso, G. Riccardi, J. H. Wright, in *IEEE Computer Magazine*, Vol. 35, No. 4, April 2002, 51–56.

[Graham 2002] "Using UML to Drive Java Can Alleviate Chaos." B. Graham in *EE Times*, Rose Real-Time Technical Marketing, Rational Software Ltd., Kanata, Ontario, April 1, 2002, available at http://www.33times.com/story/OEG20020329S0025.

[Grasshopper 2001] *Grasshopper, The First Reference Implementation of the OMG MASIF*. S. Covaci, German National Research Center for Information Technology, Research Institute for Open Communication Systems, Intelligent Mobile Agent Center for Competence, 2001, available at http://www.fokus.gmd.de/ima.

[Grassi et al. 2002] *Performance Validation of Mobile Software Architectures*. V. Grassi, V. Cortellessa, and R. Mirandola, Rome University and L'Aquila University, Italy, 2002.

[Griss and Pour 2001] "Accelerating Development with Agent Components." M. L. Griss and G. Pour. *IEEE Computer Magazine*, Vol. 34, No. 5, May 2001.

[Griswold et al. 2001] *Using Mobile Technology to Create Opportunistic Interactions on a University*. W. G. Griswold, R. Boyer, S. W. Brown, T. M. Truong, E. Bhasker, G. R. Jay, and R. B. Shapiro, University of California at San Diego, 2001.

[Gronmo, Solheim, and Skogan 2002] "Experiences of UML-to-GML Encoding." R. Gronmo, I. Solheim, and D. Skogan, *SINTEF Telecom and Informatics. 5th Agile Conference on Geographic Information Science*, April 2002.

[Hager 2002] *Mobile Adhoc Network Security*. C. T. Hager, Virginia Polytechnic Institute, 2002.

[Hansmann 2002] *SyncML: Synchronizing Your Mobile Data*. U. Hansmann, Prentice-Hall, 2002.

[Hardison 1998] "Spoken Word Identification by Native and Nonnative Speakers of English: Effects of Training, Modality, Context and Phonetic Environment." D. M. Hardison in *Proceedings of the 5th International Conference on Spoken Language Processing*, Causal Productions PTY Ltd., Sydney, Australia, 1998.

[Hashman and Knudsen 2001] *The Application of JINI Technology to Enhance the Delivery of Mobile Services*. S. Hashman and S. Knudsen, PSINaptic, December 2001.

[Hausmann et al.] *Towards Dynamic Meta Modeling of UML Extensions: An Extensible Semantics for UML Sequence Diagrams*. J. H. Hausmann, R. Heckel, and S. Sauer 2001, available at http://www.upb.de/cs/ag-engels/Papers/2001/HausmannHCC01.pdf

[Hausmann, Heckel, and Sauer 2002] *Dynamic Meta Modeling with Time: Specifying the Semantics of Multimedia Sequence Diagrams*. J. H. Hausmann, R. Heckel, and S. Sauer, Department of Computer Science, University of Paderborn, Germany, 2002.

[Hauswirth and Jazayeri 1999] *A Component and Communication Model for Push Systems*. M. Hauswirth and M. Jazayeri, Technical University of Vienna, Distributed Systems Group, available at http://www.infosys.tuiwien.ac.at.

[Hennicker and Koch 2001] *Modeling the User Interface of Web Applications with UML*. R. Hennicker and N. Koch, Institute of Computer Science at Ludwig-Maximilian-University of Munich and F.A.S.T. Applied Software Technology GmbH, 2001.

[Henricksen et al. 2002] "Pervasive 2002." K. Henricksen, J. Indulska, and A. Rakotonirainy, in *Modeling Context Information in Pervasive Computing Systems*, Springer-Verlag, 2002, pp. 167–180.

[Herzog et al. 2003] "MULTIPLATFORM Testbed: An Integration Platform for Multimodal Dialog Systems." G. Herzog, H. Kirchmann, S. Mertn, A. Ndiaye, and P. Poller,

German Research Center for Artificial Intelligence, *HLT-NAACL 2003 Workshop: Software Engineering and Architecture of Language Technology Systems*, Pate 75–82, May–June 2003.

[Hickey W3C] Position Paper for W3C/WAP Workshop on the Multimodal Web. M. Hickey, Hewlett-Packard, 2000.

[Hieda et al. 2003] "Design of SMIL Browser Functionality in Mobile Terminals." S. Hieda, Y. Saida, H. Chishima, N. Sato, and Y. Nakamoto, in *Proceedings of the Sixth IEEE International Symposium on Object-Oriented Real-Time Distributed Computing*, IEEE Publications, 2003, 143–145.

[Hightower and Borrielo 2001] "Location Systems for Ubiquitous Computing." J. Hightower and G. Borriello, *IEEE Computer*, Vol. 34, No. 8, August 2001, 57–66.

[Hightower et al. 2002] "The Location Stack: A Layered Model for Location in Ubiquitous Computing." J. Hightower, B. Brumitt, and G. Boriello, *Proceedings of the Fourth IEEE Workshop on Mobile Computing Systems and Applications* (WMCSA), IEEE Computer Society, 2002.

[Holland and Oppenheim 1999] "Direct Combination." S. Holland and D. Oppenheim in *ACM CHI 99 Proceedings*, ACM, 1999, 262–269.

[Holland, Morse, and Gedenryd 2002] "Direct Combination: A New User Interaction Principle for Mobile and Ubiquitous HCI." S. Holland, D. R. Morse, and H. Gedenryd in *Human Computer Interaction with Mobile Devices, 4th International Symposium, Mobile HCI 2002 Proceedings*, Springer-Verlag, 2002.

[Huang 2000] *Communication Infrastructures and Protocols for Mobile Agents*, F. Y. Huang, December 2000, available at http://www.cs.queensu.ca/home/huang/cisc837/cisc837paper.html.

[IEEE 2000] *IEEE Standard 1471–2000*. IEEE Standards Office, Piscataway, NJ, 2000, available at http://standards.ieee.org.

[IKV 2001] *Grasshopper Basics and Concepts*, Release 2.2, available at http://www.grasshopper.de.

[Indal 2002] *Development of Mobile Agents in J2ME or Similar Technologies*. E. Indal, Hovedoppagave, Department of Mathematics and Information Technology at University of Norway, 2002.

[Intel 2003] *Mobile Systems and Security. Technologies for Safe, Anywhere/Anytime Computing*. White paper, Intel Corporation, 2003, available at http://whitepapers.zdnet.co.uk/0,39025945,60063878p-39000516q,00.htm.

[Introduction to eVC++] Microsoft Corporation, 2002, available at http://msdn.microsoft.com.

[Jacobsen and John 2000] *Two Case Studies in Using Cognitive Walkthrough for Interface Evaluation*. N. E. Jacobsen and B. E. John, 2002, available at http://reports_archive.adm.cs.cmu.edu/anon/2000/cmv_cs_132.pdf.

[Jacobson, Booch, and Raumbaugh 1999] *The Unified Software Development Process*. I. Jacobson, G. Booch, and J. Raumbaugh, Addison-Wesley, 1999.

[Jameson 2002] "Usability Issues and Methods for Mobile Multimodal Systems." A. Jameson, German Research Center for Artificial Intelligence and International University in Germany, *Proceedings of the ISCA Tutorial and Research Workshop on Multi-Modal Dialogue in Mobile Environments*, SIG Media, 2002.

[Jansen et al. 1999] *Applying Mobile Agents to Intrusion Detection and Response.* W. Jansen, P. Mell, T. Karygiannis, and D. Marks, National Institute of Standards and Technology (United States Government). 1999.

[Jensen 2002] *Research Challenges in Location-Enabled M-Services.* C. S. Jensen, Aalborg University, Denmark, 2002, available at http://www.cs.auc.dk/~csj.

[JSGF 2002] *Java Speech Grammar Format Specifications.* Sun Microsystems, available at http://java.sun.com/products/java-media/speech/forDevelopers/JSGF/JSGF.html.

[JTAPI 1999] Java Telephony API documentation, Sun Microsystems, 1999, available at http://java.sun.com/products/jtapi/index.html.

[Katz 1995] *Adaptation and Mobility in Wireless Information Systems.* R. H. Katz, University of California Berkeley, 1995.

[Kleinrock 1996] *Nomadicity: Anytime, Anywhere in a Disconnected World.* L. Kleinrock, J. C. Baltzer AG, Science Publishers, Mobile Networks and Applications, pp. 351–357, 1996.

[Knudsen 2002] *Parsing XML in J2ME: XML in MIDP Environment.* J. Knudsen, March 7, 2002, available at http://wireless.java.sun.com/midp/articles/parsingxml.

[Ko and Vaidya 1998] *Location-Aided Routing (LAR) in Mobile Ad Hoc Networks.* N. Ko and Y.-B. Vaidya, IEEE Press, 1998.

[Korkea-aho and Tang 2001] *Experiences of Expressing Location Information for Applications in the Internet.* M. Korkea-aho and H. Tang, Nokia Research Center, Finland, 2001.

[Kumar and Romary 2003] *A Comprehensive Framework for Multimodal Meaning Representation.* A. Kumar and L. Romary, Laboratoire Loria, B.P. 239, 2003.

[Kunins 2001] *VoiceXML: Strategies and Techniques for Effective Voice Application Development with VoiceXML 2.0.* C. Sharma and J. Kunins, Wiley, 2001.

[Kutar, Nehaniv, and Britton 2001] *NGT: Natural Specification of Temporal Properties of Interactive Systems with Multiple Time Granularities.* M. Kutar, C. Nehaniv, and C. Britton, University of Hertfordshire, U.K., 2001.

[Landay, Mathews, and Waterson 2002] *In the Lab and Out in the Wild: Remote Web Usability Testing for Mobile Devices.* S. Waterson, J. A. Landay, and T. Mathews, 2002.

[Lang 1997] *Java Aglet Application Programming Interface (J-AAPI).* D. Lang, IBM Research group in Japan, 1997, available at http://www.trl.ibm.com/aglets/JAAPI-whitepaper.html.

[Lanowitz 2002] "Testing Is a Mobile Application Imperative." T. Lanowitz, *Gartner Group Note Number COM-14-1970*, February 11, 2002, available at http://gartner2002hec.ca/research/104400/104433/104433.html.

[Larson 2003] "Technology Trends: InkML and Speech." J. Larson in *Speech Technology Magazine*, October 2003.

[Lathi 1989] *Modern Signal and Analog Communication Systems.* B. P. Lathi, Holt, Rinehart, and Winston, 1989.

[Laukkanen 2002] *Java on Handheld Devices–Comparing J2ME CDC to Java 1.1.* M. Laukkanen, Department of Computer Science, University of Helsinki, available at http://www.cs.helsinki.fi/u/campa/teaching/j2me/papars/cdc.pdf.

[Lawton 2001] "New Technologies Place Video in Your Hands." G. Lawton in *IEEE Computer Magazine*, Vol. 34, No. 4, April 2001, 14–17.

[Lee 2000] *Operation-Based Update Propagation in Mobile File Systems*. Y.-W. Lee, The Chinese University of Hong Kong, January 2000.

[Leeper 2001] "A Long-Term View of Short-Range Wireless." D. G. Leeper in *IEEE Computer Magazine*, Vol. 34, No. 6, June 2001, 39–44.

[Leonhardt and Magee 1997] *Security Considerations for a Distributed Location Service*. U. Leonhardt and J. Magee, Imperial College, London, England, 1997.

[Leufven 2001] *Synchronization in a Wireless World*. U. Leufven, Royal Institute of Technology and Microsoft Mobile Internet Laboratories, June 2001.

[Liao et al. 2000] "Geogrid: A Geocasting Protocol for Mobile Ad Hoc Networks Based on GRID." W.-H. Liao, Y.-C. Tseng, K.-L. Lo, and J.-P. Sheu, *Internet Technology*, Vol. 1, No. 2, 2000.

[Lieberman 2001] *UML Activity Diagrams: Detailing User Interface Navigation*. B. Lieberman, The Rational Edge, Rational Software, October 2001, available at http://www.therationaledge.com/content/oct_01/t_activityDiagrams_bl.html.

[LIF Specifications 2000] *Location Interoperability Forum Mobile Location Protocol TS 101 Specification*. Version 3.0, June 2002.

[Lin and Stojmenovic 1999] "Gedir: Loop-Free Location Based Routing in Wireless Networks." X. Lin and I. Stojmenovic, *Proceedings of Conference on Parallel and Distributed Computing and Systems*, IEEE Press, November 3–6, 1999, 1023–1032.

[Lindmark 2000] *Interpreting Symptoms of Cognitive Load and Time Pressure in Manual Input*. K. Lindmark, Master's thesis, Department of Computer Science, Saarland University, 2000.

[Lodderstedt et al. 2002] *SecureUML: A UML-Based Modeling Language for Model-Driven Security?* T. Lodderstedt, D. Basin, and J. Doser, University of Freiburg, Germany.

[Maes 2002] *A VoiceXML Framework for Reusable Dialog Components*, S. H. Maes, IBM T. J. Watson Research Center, Yorktown Heights, N.Y., 2002.

[Malhotra 2002] *Introduction to SMS*. V. Malhotra, IBM Developer Works, 2002, available at http://www.ibm.com/developerworks.

[Mandel, Koch, and Maier 1999] "Extending UML to Model Hypermedia and Distributed Systems." L. Mandel, N. Koch, and C. Maier, in *Bayerische Forschungsstiftung*, February 1999, available at http://projekte.fast.de/projekte/forsoft/intoohdm/index.html.

[Mantyla 2002] *User Experience Research*. M. Mantyla, Helsinki Institute for Information Technology, 2002.

[Martin-Flatin 1999] *Push vs. Pull in Web-Based Network Management*. J.-P. Martin-Flatin, Swiss Federal Institute of Technology, Lausanne, 1999.

[MASIF 1997] *Mobile Agent System Interoperability Facilities Specification*. GMD FOKUS, IBM Corporation, with cooperation from Crystliz, Inc., General Magic, Inc., and the Open group, 1997.

[MAUI 2000] *Mobile Agent to User Interaction (MAUI)*. P. Mihailescu, C. Gamage, and E. A. Kendall, Monash University, Australia, 2000.

[McClure, Scambray, and Kurtz 1999] *Hacking Exposed: Network Security Secrets and Solutions, McGraw-Hill Osborne Media*, 1999.

[McLaughlin 2000] *Java and XML*. B. Mclaughlin, O'Reily & Associates, 2000.

[Melnik and Decker 2000] *A Layered Approach to Information Modeling and Interoperability on the Web.* S. Melnik and S. Decker, Stanford University, available at http://www-db.stanford.edu/~melnik/pub/sw00/sw00.pdf.

[Meyers 1993] *Why Are Human-Computer Interfaces Difficult to Design and Implement?* B. A. Meyers, Carnegie Mellon University, July 1993.

[Miga et al. 2002] *Deriving Message Sequence Charts from Use Case Maps Scenario Specifications.* A. Miga, D. Amyot, F. Bordeleau, D. Cameron, and M. Woodside, Carlton University at Ottawa, Canada, 2002.

[Minh 1997] *Multimodal User Interface Research (MUIR), Modal, Specification and Design.* C. Minh, Master's Thesis, Department of Computer Science and Technology, Peking University, June 20, 1997.

[Moczar and Aston 2002] *Cocoon Developer's Handbook.* L. Moczar and J. Aston, Sams Publishing, 2002.

[Mohseni 1996] *Web Database Primer Plus.* P. Mohseni, WAIT Group Press, 1996.

[Mummert 1996] *Exploiting Weak Connectivity in a Distributed File System.* Lily B. Mummert, CMU-CS-96–195, December 1996.

[Munoz et al. 2003] "Context-Aware Mobile Communication in Hospitals." M. A. Munoz, M. Rodriguez, J. Favela, A. I. Marinez-Garcia, and V. Gonzalez, in *IEEE Computer Magazine*, September 2003.

[Murphy 2000] *Enabling the Rapid Development of Dependable Applications in the Mobile Environment.* A. L. Murphy, Washington University Server Institute of Technology, 2000.

[NCC 2002] *Wireless—A New Challenge in Software Testing.* National Computing Centre, available at http://www.ncc.co.uk/ncc/myitadviser/archive/issue9/technology.cfm.

[Nettech 1999] *Beginner's Guide to Implementing a Successful Wireless Solution.* Nettech Systems, Inc., 1999, available at http://www.nettechRF.com.

[Nielson 1994] *Usability Engineering.* J. Nielson, Morgan Kaufmann, 1994.

[Niklfeld, Finan, and Pucher 2001] *Component-Based Multimodal Dialog Interfaces for Mobile Knowledge Creation.* G. Niklfeld, R. Finan, and M. Pucher, Telecommunication Research Center, Vienna and Mobilkom, Austria, 2001.

[Nunes 2001] *Object Modeling for User-Centered Development and User Interface Design: The Wisdom Approach.* D. N. J. Nunes, University of Maderia, Funchal, Portugal, April 2001.

[OASIS tML 2001] *tML Guidelines for Mapping UML Notation to XML Schemas and Vice Versa.* OASIS Committee T1–Telecommunications working group T1M1 in conjunction with Sprint Corp., available at http://www.oasis-open.org.

[Olsen 1992] *User Interface Management Systems: Models and Algorithms.* D. R. Olsen Jr., Morgan Kaufmann Publishers, San Mateo, Ca., 1992.

[Openwave 2002] *WAP Push Technology Overview.* Openwave Systems Inc., May 2002, available at http://demo.openwave.com/pdf/wappush_tech_overview.pdf.

[Openwave 2002] *WAP Push Technology Overview.* Openwave Systems, Redwood City, CA, available at http://www.openwave.com.

[Orfali and Harkey 1997] *Client/Server Programming with Java and CORBA*. R. Orfali and D. Harkey, John Wiley & Sons, 1997.

[Oshima, Karjoth, and Onon 1998] *Aglet Specification 1.1 Draft*. M. Oshima, G. Karjoth, and K. Onon, IBM Research Group in Japan, 1998, available at http://www.trl.ibm.com/aglets/spec11.html.

[Oviatt 2000] *Designing Robust Multimodal Systems for Diverse Users and Environments*. S. Oviatt, Computer Science Department, Oregon Graduate Institute of Science and Technology, 2000.

[Oviatt 2002] *Taming Recognition Errors with a Multimodal Interface*. S. Oviatt, National Science Foundation, Special Extension for Creativity, 2002.

[Oviatt and Cohen 2000] *Multimodal Interfaces That Process What Comes Naturally*. S. Oviatt and P. Cohen, Center for Human Communication, Department of Computer Science, Oregon Graduate Institute of Science and Technology, 2000.

[Oviatt OHSU 2002] *Multimodal Interfaces for Future Geographical Information Systems*. NRC Committee on Beyond Mapping: The Challenge of New Technologies in the Geographic Information Sciences, August 2002.

[Oviatt, Jacko, and Sears 2002] *Handbook of Human-Computer Interaction—Multimodal Interfaces*. S. Oviatt, Center for Human-Computer Communication, Computer Science Department of Oregon Graduate Institute of Science and Technology 2002.

[Owen 2002] *When Data Sync Breaks*. J. Owen, White Paper, XcelleNet, Inc., 2002.

[P809-GI 1999] *Mobility in the Broadband Environment Based on IN Evolution*. P809-GI project of EUROSCOM, Network Architectures for Broadband Mobility, Vol. 1, Architecture for the Benchmark Services, 1999.

[Page 2000] *Neuropsychology of Memory*. A. Page, University of Western Australia, available at http://www.psy.uwa.edu.au/user/andrew/.

[Paulson 2003] "New Techniques for Speeding Wireless Streaming Video." L. D. Paulson in *IEEE Computer Magazine*, Vol. 36, No. 5, May 2003, 21.

[Pinhanez et al. 2003] "Fostering a Symbiotic Handheld Environment." C. Pinhanez, M. Raghunath, and C. Narayanasuwami, in *IEEE Computer Magazine*, Vol. 36, No. 9, September 2003, 56–65.

[Pohl, Kobsa, and Kutter 1995] *User Model Acquisition Heuristics Based on Dialogue Acts*. W. Pohl, A. Kobsa, and O. Kutter, Working Group Knowledge-Based Information Systems, University of Konstanz, 1995.

[Raggat and Wugofski 2000] *Towards Convergence of WML, XHTML and Other W3C Technologies*. World Wide Web Consortium, available at http://www.w3.org/ 2000/09/Papers/Wugofski.html.

[Rausch et al. 2001] *Extensions of the Unified Modeling Language for Mobile Agents*. C. Klein, A. Rausch, M. Sihling, and Z. Wen, Siemens ICN, Munich, Germany, Institut fur Informatic, Technische Universitat Munchen, Munich, Germany, 2001.

[Rausch, Sihling, and Wen 1998] *Extensions of the UML around Language Concepts for Mobility*. A. Rausch, M. Sihling, and Z. Wen, 1998, available at http://www4.in.tum.de/~rausch/publications/2001/MobileUML.pdf.

[Reiher et al. 1996] *Peer-to-Peer Reconciliation Based Replication for Mobile Computers*. P. Reiher, J. Popek, M. Gunter, J. Salomone, and D. Ratner, University of California, Los Angeles, 1996.

[RFC822] RFC 822, available at http://www.faqs.org/rfcs/rfc822.html.

[Rodriquez et al. 2000] *An Introduction to IBM WebSphere Everyplace Suite Version 1.1*. J. Rodriguez, R. Appleby, B. Bisgaard, H. Wang, A. McGrory, A. Mryhig, A. Patton, and M. Omarjee, IBM RedBooks, 2000.

[Rossler et al. 2001] *Multimodal Interaction for Mobile Environment*. H. Rossler, J. Sienel, W. Wajda, J. Hoffmann, and M. Kostrzewa, Private Network Department, Alcatel SEL AG Research and Innovation, Germany, 2001.

[RS232 2003] *RS232 Quick Reference*, available at http://www.rs485.com/rs485spec.html.

[Ruuskanen 2000] *JAVACARD*. J.-P. Ruuskanen, Department of Computer Science, University of Helsinki, Finland, available at http://www.cs.helsinki.fi/u/campa/teaching/ruuskanen-final.pdf.

[Sadoski 1997] *Client–Server Software Architectures–An Overview*. D. Sadoski, Carnegie Mellon University, 1997, available at http://www.sei.cmu.edu/str/descriptions/clientserver_body.html.

[Saeyor et al. 2003] *Multimodal Presentation Markup Language on Mobile Phones*. S. Saeyor, K. Uchiyama, and M. Ishizuka, 2003.

[Sandor and Reicher 2001] *CUIML: A Language for Generating Multimodal Human-Computer Interfaces*. C. Sandor and T. Reicher, 2001, available at http://wwwbruegge.in.tum.de/publications/includes/pub/sandor2001cuiml/sandor2001cuiml.pdf.

[Sauer and Engles 1999] *OMMMA: An Object-Oriented Approach for Modeling Multimedia Information Systems*. S. Sauer and G. Engels, University of Paderborn, Germany Information Systems Group, 1999.

[Schlieder et al. 2001] *Location Modeling for Intentional Behavior in Spatial Partonomies*. C. Schlieder, T. Vogele, and A. Werner, Bremen University, 2001.

[Scott 2001] *Service Discovery Protocol (SDP)*. M. Scott, 2001, available at http://www.dcs.ed.ac.uk/home/slipc/protocols/sdp.html.

[Sears 1992] *Layout Appropriateness: A Metric for Evaluating User Interface Widget Layout*. A. Sears, Human–Computer Interaction Laboratory & Computer Science Department, University of Maryland, December 8, 1992.

[Selic and Raumbaugh 2003] *Mapping SDL to UML*. B. Selic and J. Raumbaugh, Rational White Papers, May 8, 2003, available at http://www.rational.com/media/whitepapers/sdl2umlv13.pdf.

[Sharma et al. 2003] "Speech-Gesture Driven Multimodal Interfaces for Crisis Management." R. Sharma, M. Yeasin, N. Krahnstoever, I. Raushert, G. Cai, I. Brewer, A. S. MacEachren, and K. Sengupta, in *Proceedings of IEEE Special Issue on Multimodal Human-Computer Interface 2003*, 2003.

[Shipman, Marshal, and Moran 1995] "Finding and Using Implicit Structure in Human-Organized Spatial Layouts of Information." F. M. Shipman III, C. C. Marshall, T. P. Moran, *CHI '95 Proceedings*, ACM, 1995.

[Singh et al. 1999] *RAT: A Quick (And Dirty?) Push for Mobility Support*. R. Singh, Y. C. Tay, W. T. Teo, and S. W. Yeow, IEEE Publications, 1999.

[Sissonen 2002] *Wireless Applications Evaluation and Development Process: Case-Paper Industry Logistics*. A. Sissonen, Lappeenranta University of Technology, February 1, 2002.

[SMIL 2.0] *Synchronized Multimedia Integration Language*, J. Ayars, D. Bulterman, A. Cohen, K. Day, E. Hodge, P. Hoschka, E. Hyche, M. Jourdan, M. Kim, K. Kvbota, R. Lanphier, T. Michel. D. Newman, J. Ossenbruggen, B. Saccocio, P. Schmitz, W. Tenkate, 20001, available at http://www.w3.org/TR/2001/REC-smil20–20010807/smil20.html.

[Smith et. al. 1982] "Designing the Star User Interface." D. C. S. Smith, C. Irby, R. Kimball, B. Verplank, and E. Harlem, *Byte*, Vol. 7, No. 4, April 1982, pp. 242–282.

[Sparkman et al. 2001] *Automated Derivation of Complex Agent Architectures from Analysis Specification*. C. H. Sparkman, S. A. DeLoach, and A. L. Self, 2nd International Workshop on Agent-Oriented Software Engineering (AOSE-2001), Montreal, Canada, May 29, 2001.

[Spolsky 2001] *User Interface Design For Programmers*. J. Spolsky, 2001, available at http://www.joelonsoftware.com.

[Spyrou, et al.] *Wireless Computational Models: Mobile Agents to Rescue*. C. G. Spyrou, P. Pitoura, and E. Evirpidou.

[SSML 2002] 2002, available at http://www.w3.org/TR/speech-synthesis/

[Star and Estes 1990] *Geographic Information Systems: An Introduction*. J. Star and J. Estes,. Prentice-Hall, Englewood Cliffs, NJ, 1990.

[Stemberger 2002] *Is Buetooth WI-FI*? S. Stemberger, IBM Developer Works, 2002, available at http://www-106.ibm.com/developerworks/library/wi-net.html.

[Sun Micro J2ME Spec 2000] *Introduction to Java 2 Micro Edition and KVM*. Sun Microsystems, May 19, 2000.

[Sylvain 2001] *MPML 3.0 Specifications*. D. Sylvain, Master's Student, Internal Report, Ishizuka Laboratory, June 15, 2001.

[SyncML Specification 1.1] *SyncML Sync Protocol*, Version 1.1. Available at http://www.syncml.org/docs/syncml_sync_protocol_v11_20020215.pdf.

[SyncML White Paper 2003] *Building an Industry-Wide Mobile Data Synchronization Protocol*. SyncML White Paper, 2003, available at http://www.syncml.org.

[Tanenbaum and van Renesse 1985] "Distributed Operating Systems." A. S. Tanenbaum and R. van Renesse, *ACM Computing Surveys*, December 1985, 419–470.

[Tomlin 1990] *Geographic Information Systems and Cartographic Modeling*. C. D. Tomlin, Prentice Hall College Division, 1990.

[Trabelsi et al. 2002] *Multimodal Integration of Voice and Ink for Pervasive Computing*. S. Trabelsi, S.-H. Cha, D. Desai, and C. Tappert, CSIS Pace University, 2002.

[Trantor 2002] *kXML and kAWT*. Andreas Bettsteller, http://www.trantor.de.

[Tseng et al. 2001] "Location Awareness in Ad Hoc Wireless Mobile Networks." Y.-C. Tseng, S.-L. Wu, W.-H. Liao, and C.-M. Chao, *IEEE Computer Magazine*, Vol. 34, No. 6, June 2001, 45–52.

[Tuning 2000] *How Do You Test an Interface How Do You Test an Interface You Can't See?* Nuance Communications, 2000, available at http://hci.stanford.edu/cs377/nardi-schiano/NLeD.talk.pdf.

[UMTS 2002] *UMTS White Paper 1*. 2002, available at http://www.umts-forum.org/servlet/dycon/ztumts/umts/Live/en/umts/MultiMedia_PDFs_UMTSF-White-Paper-1.pdf.

[UTMS P1104 2002] *Multimodal Multilingual Information Services for Small Mobile Terminals*. L. Boves and E. den Os, eds., Eurescom UTMS, 2002.

[Varshney 2003] "The Status and Future of 802.11-Based WLAN's." U. Varshney, *IEEE Computer Magazine*, June 2003.

[Varshney and Jain 2001] *Issues in Emerging 4G Wireless Networks*. U. Varshney and R. Jain, Georgia State University, 2001.

[Vaughan-Nichols 2002] "OFDM: Back to the Wireless Future." S. J. Vaughan-Nichols in *IEEE Computer Magazine*, December 2002.

[Vaughan-Nichols 2003] "Mobile IPv6 and the Future of Wireless Internet Access." S. J. Vaughan-Nichols in *IEEE Computer Magazine*, February 2003.

[Venners 1997] "The Architecture of Aglets." B. Venners, *Java World*, April 1997, available at http://www.javaworld.com/javaworld/jw-04–1997/jw-04-hood_p.html.

[Vichr 2002] *The ABC's of 802.11*. R. Vichr, IBM Developer Works, 2002, available at http://www.ibm.com/developerworks.

[VXML 2002] *Speech Synthesis Markup Language*. D. C. Burnett, Nuance, M R. Walker, Intel, and A. Hunt, SpeechWorks International, World Wide Web Consortium, 2002, available at http://www.w3.org/TR/speech-synthesis/.

[W3C Schema—2] *W3C XML Schema Part 2—Data Types*, Revision 2, January of 2001, available at http://www.w3.org/TR/xmlschema-2.

[W3C Semantic Web] Semantic Web documentation on World Wide Web Consortium Web site, 2002, available at http://www.w3.org/2001/sw.

[W3C Speech Grammar 2002] *W3C Speech Grammar Specifications*. A. Hunt and S. McGlashan of W3C, 2002, available at http://www.w3.org/TR /2001/WD-speech-grammar-20010103/.

[W3C XForms] *W3C XForms Specifications Working Draft 18*, January 2002, available at http://www.w3.org/TR/2002/WD-xforms-20020118.

[W3C XML Pipeline] *XML Pipeline Definition Language Version 1.0*. N. Walsh and E. Maler, Sun Microsystems, W3C Note, February 28, 2002.

[Wahlster 2003] *SmarkKom: Symmetric Multimodality in an Adaptive and Reusable Dialogue Shell*. W. Wahlster, German Research Center for Artificial Intelligence (DFKI), 2003.

[Wahlster et al. 1998] *SmartKom: Towards Multimodal Dialogues with Anthropomorphic Interface Agents*. W. Wahlster, N. Riethinger, and A. Blocher, German Research Center for Artificial Intelligence 1998.

[Waldo 2001] "Mobile Code, Distributed Computing, and Agents." J. Waldo, in *IEEE Intelligent Systems*, March/April 2001.

[WAP 2.0] *Wireless Application Protocol WAP 2.0 Technical White Paper*, WAP Forum, available at http://www.wapforum.org/what/WAPWhite_Paper1.pdf.

[WAP Architecture 2001] *Wireless Application Protocol Architecture Specification WAP-210-WAPArch-20010712*, Wireless Application Protocol Forum, July 2001, available at http://www1.wapforum.org/tech/documents/WAP-210-WAPArch-20010712-a.pdf.

[WAP MMS Encapsulation 2002] *Wireless Application Protocol MMS Encapsulation Protocol.* Wireless Application Protocol Forum, Ltd. WAP-209-MMS Encapsulation-20020105-a, Version 05-Jan-2002.

[WAP Professional 2000] *WAP Professional 2000.* C. Arehart, N. Chidambaram, S. Guruprasad, A. Homer, R. Howelll, S. Kasippilai, R. Machin, T. Myers, A. Nakhimovsky, L. Passani, C. Pedley, R. Taylor, and M. Toschi. WROX Press Ltd., Acocks Green, UK, 2000.

[WAP UAPROF] *Wireless Application Protocol WAP-248-UAPROF-2001 1020-a*, Wireless Application Protocol Forum, available at http://www.wapforum.org\.

[Welch 2000] *A Survey of Power Management Techniques in Mobile Computing Operating Systems.* G. F. Welch, University of North Carolina at Chapel Hill, 2000.

[WFMC and Fisher 2000] *The Work Flow Handbook 2001*, Work Flow Management Coalition, October 2000.

[Yang et al. 2000] *Mobile Agent on the SARA Digital Library.* Y. Yang, O. F. Rana, D. W. Walker, and C. Georgousopoulos, and R. Williams, 2000, available at http://cacr.library.caltech.edu/archive/0000019/01/cacr.186.pdf.

[Yim et al. 2001] *Architecture-Centric Object-Oriented Design Method for Multi-Agent Systems.* H. Yim, K. Cho, J. Kim, and S. Park, KAIST (Korea Advanced Institute of Science and Technology), Korea, 2001.

[Yu et al. 2003] *Scalable Portriat Video for Mobile Video Conferencing.* J. Keman Yu, T. He, Y. Lin, and S. Li, Microsoft Research Asia, 2003.

[Zhang 2001] *Mobile Computing and Wireless Networks.* Y. Zhang, 2001, available at http://www.cs.utexas.edu/users/ygz/395T-01S.

[Zhang 2002] *Provably-Secure Enhancements on 3GPP Authentication and Key Agreement Protocol.* M. Zhang, Verizon Laboratories, Waltham, MA, 2002.

Index

D

E

L

M

N

X